P9-DZN-988

LAW AND MINIMUM WORLD PUBLIC ORDER

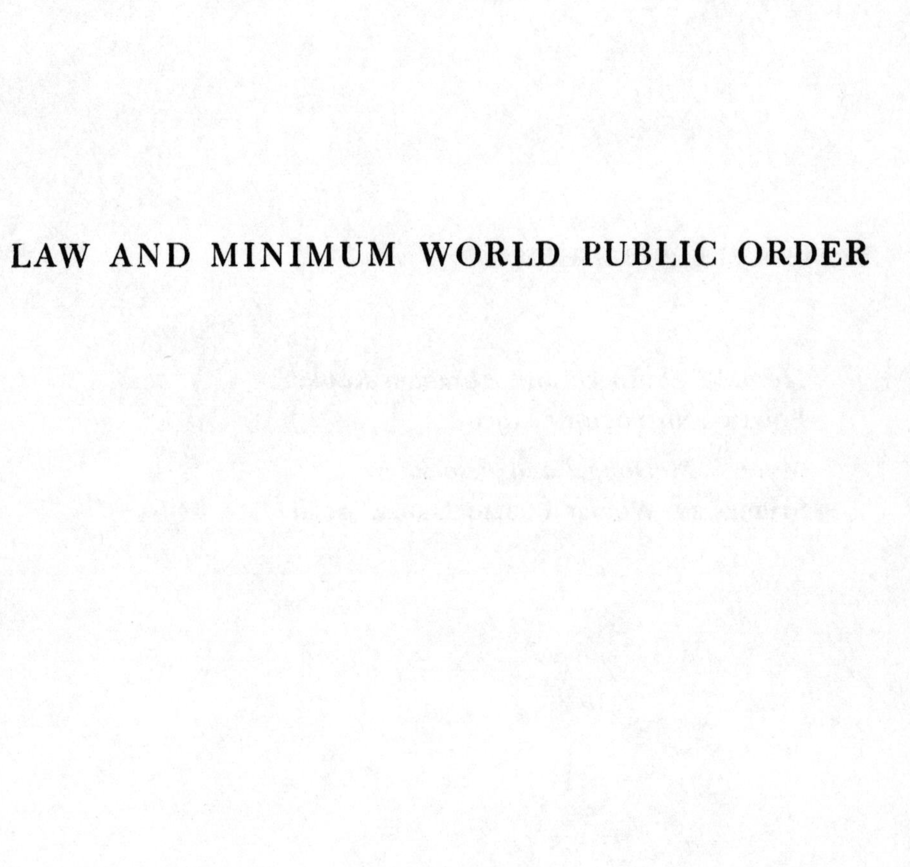

PREVIOUSLY PUBLISHED

Harold D. Lasswell and Abraham Kaplan
POWER AND SOCIETY. 1950

Myres S. McDougal and Associates
STUDIES IN WORLD PUBLIC ORDER. 1960

LAW AND MINIMUM WORLD PUBLIC ORDER

The Legal Regulation of International Coercion

by Myres S. McDougal and Florentino P. Feliciano

NEW HAVEN AND LONDON

YALE UNIVERSITY PRESS

Second printing, July 1967.

Set in Baskerville type
and printed in the United States of America by
The Murray Printing Co.,
Forge Village, Mass.

Library of Congress catalog card number: 61-14435

TO
JOSEPHINE MYRA
REGINA STELLA
JOHN LEE

PREFACE

INTERNATIONAL LAW may be most realistically observed, and fruitfully conceived, as a process of authoritative decision transcending state lines by which the peoples of the world seek to clarify and implement their common interests in both minimum order, in the sense of the prevention of unauthorized coercion, and optimum order, in the sense of the promotion of the greater production and wider distribution of all values. This book, written from the observational standpoint of responsible citizens of the larger community of mankind addressing themselves to other such citizens, is designed as a contribution to the clarification of the common interests of all peoples in the establishment and maintenance of minimum order.

The broad outlines of how we conceive our subject are developed in Chapter 1 and each subsequent chapter deals with one or more important particular problems.

In Chapter 1 we recommend comprehensive orientation in the factual processes of coercion which cross state lines, attempt an economic categorization of the major recurring types of controversies which raise common issues in policy or are affected by common conditioning factors, and indicate the more important features of the process of authoritative decision by which the general community seeks to regulate and control the processes of coercion. Brief preliminary clarification is offered, also, of the principle of minimum order and of the requirements of the basic community policy of the minimum destruction of values in relation to each of the other major types of problems.

In Chapter 2 we seek to demonstrate that traditional discussions of the many different problems commonly subsumed under headings like "The Initiation of War" and "The Commencement of War" in fact pose a falsely unitary problem, and that the reference to "time" in such discussions relates not to a special, particular type of controversy, but rather to arguments or justifications about many different types of controversies, involving many different policies.

In Chapter 3 we consider the most difficult problem of all, that of facilitating appropriate interpretations of the distinction—indispensable to any system of minimum order and now incorporated in varying terms in the United Nations Charter—between impermissible and permissible coercion. Rejecting the defeatist view that nothing of consequence can be said in aid of particular interpretations and applications of this distinction, we propose principles of interpretation, of both content and procedure, relating comprehensively to the whole process of coercion and its context, and suggest a general mode of analysis by which responsible decision-makers may rationally discipline their examination of relevant factors and policies. It is our conviction, which we seek to support by detailed illustration, that such decision-makers can, by explicit, systematic, and contextual examination of processes of coercion and by the careful relation of the major features of such processes to impacts upon human dignity values, interpret and apply the basic distinction between impermissible and permissible coercion in particular instances in ways designed to enhance not only minimum order, but perhaps even an optimum order of human dignity.

Chapter 4 turns to the problem of sanctions—that is, of securing the effective implementation of clarified policies of minimum order. This problem is conceived as encompassing not only the invention and evaluation of institutional practices, authority structures and procedures, appropriate to many varying contexts, but also, even more fundamentally, the creation and fostering of the necessary predispositions in effective decision-makers to put such practices into operation. In contrast with the common notion of sanctions as particular or isolated forms of strategy, invoked in episodic reaction to occasional violation, we outline and recommend a more comprehensive conception which embraces most of the constitutive process of authoritative decision in the world arena. Certain more specific goals of sanctions strategy—prevention, deterrence, restoration, rehabilitation, and reconstruction—are identified, and a number of principles of content and procedure are suggested as illustrative of the possibilities of improvement in the management of sanctions strategies. Some of the major defects in contemporary sanctioning practice, and various proposals designed to remove or alleviate these defects, are noted. Concluding appeal is made for the employment of new alternatives in communication and collaboration for the creation of more appropriate sanctioning perspectives.

Chapter 5 is addressed to claims relating to participation and nonparticipation ("neutrality") in processes of coercion, and considers claims relating both to the assumption of responsibility for the restoration and maintenance of minimum order and to specific belligerent-nonparticipant confrontations during processes of coercion. It is observed that the whole structure of nineteenth-century doctrine about neutrality depended upon the premise of a sovereign right of states to make war and, hence, that the acceptance of the principle of minimum order as fundamental community prescription, as in the United Nations Charter, must work a revolutionary change in traditional perspectives of authority. The goals of contemporary prescription are described as including both the establishment of common responsibility adequate to secure minimum order against disruption and the mitigation of the destruction of values which inevitably attends the breakdown of public order. A brief review is offered of principal past efforts to secure a wide assumption of shared responsibility for the maintenance of minimum order and of the more important trends in decision about the particular interactions of belligerents and nonparticipants. Policies recommended include not only the widest possible assumption of responsibility by the members of the general community for the maintenance of minimum order, but also discrimination in various ways in favor of the forces of the active sanctioners and against the offending belligerent.

Chapter 6 explores general community regulation of "combat situations," that is, of situations in which contending belligerents mutually apply violence at peak intensities by the overt and destructive use of the military instrument. Claims to the prescription and application of authority with respect to such situations are categorized as relating both to the lawfulness of particular detailed practices of violence and to the efficacy of certain particular defenses commonly raised by individuals charged with violations of the law of war. The first type of claim extends to every important feature of contexts of combat, embracing specific claims with respect to such features as permissible combatants, permissible areas of operation, permissible objects of attack and intensities of destruction, and permissible instruments and means of attack (including nuclear, chemical, biological). The second type of claim emphasizes the relevance of such specific defenses as military necessity, reprisal, superior orders or act of subordinates, and action in official capacity. The whole process of community response to these claims is observed as a continuous effort by the established decision-makers to adjust and accommodate the familiar principles of military necessity and minimum destruction of values to the requirements of common interest in particular combat situations in particular contexts. The case is urged that it is perhaps not impossible even under contemporary conditions to clarify in more detail a common interest in both these complementary goal principles for important types of problems which may still be expected to recur.

Chapter 7 sharpens the focus of attention upon combat situations to specific contexts of "belligerent occupation," by which reference is made to situations following an invasion of enemy territory in which a considerable measure of effective control has been established over such territory, though complete and final victory is not yet achieved. The most important feature of such contexts is that the expectations of the inhabitants of the area, and of other participants in general community processes, as to whose authority will ultimately prevail in the occupied territory remain largely fluid and indeterminate. The major types of claims to authority, made at different times to different established decision-makers, relate to the establishment and operation of governmental processes in the occupied territory, to the control and policing of the inhabitants of the territory, and to the control and exploitation of material resources or wealth processes. In the resolution of controversies embodying such claims, the established decision-makers of the general community are observed to project policies, beyond the as always inescapable balancing of military necessity and minimum destruction, designed to secure a modest protection for the reasonable expectations of the inhabitants of the area, and of others who deal with them, which are based upon the transiently effective, if ultimately precarious, authority of the military occupant.

In our initial planning of this book we had projected further chapters on the control of enemy persons and property within a belligerent state, captured enemy personnel, and the termination of coercion. It is still our hope that these may some day be added.

The reader who is professional in this field may note that our documentation, though considerable, is not exhaustive. In accord with our major emphasis upon the clarification of basic policy issues, we have sought only an illustrative, representative documentation. More complete references may easily be found in such standard treatises as Oppenheim, *International Law* (7th ed. Lauterpacht, 1952), and Stone, *Legal Controls of International Conflict* (2nd printing, rev. with supplement 1953–1958, 1959).

The basic framework of inquiry which we employ in this book is spelled out in somewhat greater detail in the opening chapters of McDougal and Associates, *Studies in World Public Order* (1960) and in Lasswell and Kaplan, *Power and Society* (1950). Still other statements and applications of the general framework will shortly be made in *The Public Order of the Oceans: A Contemporary International Law of the Sea,* with William T. Burke, and *Law and Public Order in Space,* with Harold D. Lasswell and Ivan A. Vlasic.

The mere fact that we have written this particular book indicates, as Professor Lasswell comments in his Introduction, that we are not without hope that mankind may still be able, avoiding both self-destruction and the universal establishment of totalitarian orders, to make some further movement toward a minimum order of human dignity. We are quite aware, however, that this hope can be realistic only in the degree that responsible citizens in every area of the globe, or of the now emerging earth-space arena, come to share it and act upon it to the utmost of talent, skill, and opportunity.

The special indebtednesses we happily acknowledge extend, appropriately, from New Haven to Manila.

At the New Haven end of our enterprise, our principal intellectual debt is to Harold D. Lasswell, not only for his Introduction and direct assistance in the drafting of principles of sanctions strategy, but also for wise counsel and encouragement throughout our study. H. Peter Stern assisted, first as our student, in formulating the broad outlines of our inquiry and, later, as vice-president of the Ogden Foundation, in a different, though no less indispensable, way. William T. Burke and Ivan A. Vlasic read, and ably disputed, most of the text at different stages of its drafting. Oscar Schachter, as seminar associate, debated many of the more important policy issues with us. Leon Lipson and Joseph W. Bishop offered critical comments upon two of the chapters. Eugene V. Rostow was unsparing in the multiple kinds of encouragement and aid that good law school deans alone can give. Many of our students, too many for appropriate mention, made important contributions to the clarification of specific points. Harry Bitner and his library staff members, especially Pauline Wildman, James Golden, John Gummere, and B. T. Davis were efficient, accommodating, and patient. Dorothy Egan and her secretarial staff, especially Isabel Malone, Sylvia Land, and Isabel Poludnewycz, never quailed under what might have appeared an intolerable burden. Franklin J. Okin effectively performed various dreary tasks in the final preparation of the manuscript and of the indexes. John Lee McDougal assisted in many important ways throughout our enterprise. The patience of Virginia Feliciano and Frances McDougal was relatively indestructible.

In Manila, we would thank Mr. Justice Pedro Tuason, retired member of the Supreme Court of the Philippines and former Secretary of Justice, Mr. Justice Jesus G. Barrera, also of the Supreme Court of the Philippines and former Undersecretary and later Secretary of Justice, and Hon. Alejo Mabanag, Secretary of Justice—all three for making it possible for Mr. Feliciano to go on extended leave from the Department of Justice, Government of the Republic of the Philippines. Similarly we would thank President Vicente G. Sinco, University of the Philippines, and Dean Vicente Abad Santos, College of Law, University of the Philippines, for their friendly encouragement and for granting extended leave from teaching duties. Mr. Catalino T. Macaraig, Jr., in unremitting friendship, acted in Mr. Feliciano's stead at the Department of Justice during the period of his leave.

The American Society of International Law and the *Yale Law Journal* have very graciously consented to the reproduction of materials, Chapter 2 and Chapters 1 and 3 respectively, which were originally published under their auspices.

Our very genuine appreciation for generous financial assistance is expressed both to the officers of Yale University and to four foundations: the Ford Foundation, the Ralph E. Ogden Foundation, the Stimson Fund of Yale, and the Wenner-Gren Foundation for Anthropological Research.

The officers of the Yale University Press have been consistently helpful and tolerant, and we would especially thank Marian Ash, our editor, for the understanding, skill, and patience which she has brought to a difficult task.

Myres S. McDougal
Florentino P. Feliciano

New Haven
Manila
March 30, 1961

CONTENTS

INTRODUCTION: UNIVERSALITY VERSUS PAROCHIALISM

by Harold D. Lasswell

This is not to be an Introduction in the conventional sense of certifying to a prospective audience that something of great worth from unknown authors is now available to them. The book by Messrs. McDougal and Feliciano is of enormous importance and of commanding professional merit. But this is taken for granted by anyone conversant with creative scholarship in the field of jurisprudence and international law. My comments are intended to put certain aspects of the present publication in the perspective within which the authors work, but which they have not had an opportunity to elaborate within the limits of a specialized treatise. I write as a colleague in the task of remolding jurisprudence into a major instrument of science and policy.

The perspective of the present study and its family of interrelated publications [1] is most succinctly characterized as value-oriented jurisprudence. More precisely, the distinctive orientation is the jurisprudence of human dignity. The value goal is universal in scope, and evaluates the institutions of any time and place according to the criterion of general, not narrow, participation in the shaping and sharing of the values yielded by man's life in society. Within the reference frame provided by this objective it is incumbent upon the scholar or the decision-maker to locate himself in the moving context of past, present, and future events. Within the estimated opportu-

1. The broad outlines of the perspective are indicated in McDougal and Lasswell, "The Identification and Appraisal of Diverse Systems of Public Order," 53 *A.J.I.L.* 1 (1959) and Lasswell and Kaplan, *Power and Society* (1950). Illustrative studies are collected in McDougal and Associates, *Studies in World Public Order* (1960), with further citations at p. 1024.

nities and limitations of the future, the challenge is for the discovery of policy alternatives which, when put to the test, foster the eventual emergence of a public order of free men.

A few short years ago the idea of a world under one roof seemed Utopian. Neither the France of Napoleon nor the Germany of Wilhelm II or Adolf Hitler had been able to overcome the hostile coalitions whereby the diversity of the world arena protected itself from the predominance of a single member. Given the scientific and technological juggernaut of today the position of the authors of this book is impressively sound: build at least minimum public order now. Build mainly by consent and avoid the fratricidal destructiveness of general war. For the political elite of every member state this advice means that the goal of minimum security cannot be achieved without running risks to personal, party, and state interests. Hence a cost, a potential sacrifice, is implied. This is the nub of the problem.

Messrs. McDougal and Feliciano do not confuse the role they play with the role of final decision-makers. They are explicitly cognizant of the fact that they occupy an observational vantage point. True, what is said in a treatise of this kind flows into the stream of knowledge, prediction, and proposal reaching the decision-makers of many nations and associations. In the end, however, the decision-makers are the ones who must expect to be better off—in terms of all their values—by following the lines of policy put forward in this book than by continuing to rely upon the strategies that keep mankind at the brink.

The attention which the authors devote to an enormous mass of technical detail could suggest, however inaccurately, that they entertain over-sanguine views of the future, and that they give insufficient weight to the predispositions of mankind that must be overcome by enlightened public men. It may be helpful, therefore, to provide a few reminders of the dimensions of the task of instituting world order, stressing factors well understood by the authors, though necessarily mentioned in summary fashion.

The true magnitude of the issues that confound mankind comes most emphatically into view when we recall the great landmarks in the relation of men to their social, biological, and physical environment since *homo sapiens* first appeared. Identifiable human types are now estimated to be approximately five hundred thousand years old. Since man's brain capacity has remained notably constant during all these years it is evident that the most significant changes have been in the patterns of culture. These are the practices by which valued outcomes are sought by strategies that cope with other human beings and with the physical environment.

It is generally agreed that the domestication of animals and the invention of agriculture were among the early though unrecorded steps by which human beings learned to create and transmit to successor generations an environment of cumulative complexity. But the most explosive potentialities were not released until a few thousand years ago when cities were concurrently invented in a few great river valleys, notably the Nile, the Tigris-Euphrates, and the Indus. With the appearance of city culture came the territorial state in place of kinship aggregates, and the growth of literacy, a complex division of labor, rising productivity, taxation, legislation, bureaucracy, and many other interconnected developments of the utmost importance to modern civilization.

So far as the pattern of coercion is concerned the sequence we have sketched is crucial for the understanding of the present state of world affairs. The point is expressed in Gordon Childe's remark that for about ninety-five per cent of his existence man has lived a precivilized life.[2] More specifically this means that human beings lived in folk societies, whether nomadic or sedentary. In these societies *homo sapiens* learned how to live with others and acquired through long apprenticeship the syndrome of parochialism.

Part of this syndrome is composed of expectations regarding the intentions and capabilities of strangers. The basic expectations are that strangers are malevolent and in all probability strong, and that they are likely to resort to violent coercive measures. Another fundamental perspective comprising the syndrome is the demand upon the self to fight if necessary to defend and extend the value position of the tribe. The ego of the individual is absorbed in overwhelming identification of the self with the folk society. In the tens of thousands of years of man's early existence the social discipline of the parochial syndrome enabled him to emerge successfully in combat with near-human and proto-human bands and tribes.

Today it is clear that the syndrome of parochialism has been continued into a world environment in which it has become species-destroying, not species-protecting. Yet the fundamental features of

2. In 1 Singer, Holmyard and Hall, *A History of Technology* 42 (1954).

the world are legacies of the syndrome from the past, and are in turn perpetuated by the net advantages that effective decision-makers throughout the world community expect to obtain by keeping it alive. The fact is that if the active members of the world's political elite—in Washington, Moscow, Peiping, London, or elsewhere—ever expect to be better off by at least a minimum system of world public order, the world will have it at once.

It is enlightening to explore the factors that keep alive a frame of mind whose consequences so flagrantly contradict man's stake in survival. In some ways the most illuminating way to proceed is by considering the position of a Secretary of State or head of State in a popular government who is sincerely devoted to the ideal of human dignity. Such a man desires to initiate measures looking to effective reduction of arms. At the same time he is committed to the obligation of sustaining the freedom of his nation and its allies from external control, especially when the most formidable opposing powers are in fact totalitarian, regardless of their public rhetoric. It will be obvious to the Secretary, if he is at all experienced in world affairs, that unilateral reduction of arms does not necessarily initiate a chain reaction of arms reduction. It may, on the contrary, precipitate aggressive policies intended to take advantage of the alleged "weakening" or "softening" of his nation. In addition to these considerations the Secretary will recognize that if he appears to be "selling the nation short" he will find himself under attack not only by members of the party opposition at home, but by factions and individuals within his own party upon whose support he must rely. Given the constraints of the situation in which the Secretary operates at home and abroad, the conscientious public figure may consider resigning from office. Everyone recognizes, of course, that it is easier to become resigned *to* office. The man of integrity may satisfy a scrupulous conscience by reflecting upon the fact that, retired from the fray, his opportunities to work an effective change in institutions of public order will be sharply curtailed.

The situation of the conscientious statesman inside a totalitarian regime is even more circumscribed on matters related to minimum world order than his opposite number within a popularly governed state. It may be asked whether we can, with any plausibility whatever, imagine a "conscientious" friend of peace in a top spot within a totalitarian set-up. We think so. It is to be recalled that the doctrines of any political system are open to changes of many kinds, particularly in the intensity with which they are held and the specific interpretations to which they give rise. Considering the sobering realities of the world picture, it is well within the range of possibility that totalitarian leaders will come to believe—in the privacy of their ruminations—that the common peace is to be preferred to common disaster, and that the conditions of at least minimum public order can be achieved at bearable cost. More tangibly this implies that mutual "concessions" could be made in negotiation which would significantly diminish the crisis without seriously endangering the internal or external position of the negotiating elites.

Granted that a conscientious leader *can* exist within a totalitarian hierarchy, what can he do? His room for manoeuvre is drastically limited. How can he initiate or accept proposals likely to be perceived by many if not most of his rivals, allies, and dependents as "betrayals" of the totalitarian dream?

Observe in all this that the leaders are trapped within the context that continues to give vitality to the syndrome of parochialism. Hence it is not inapposite to underline the melancholy fact that the arena of world politics has always been divided, and that the expectation of violence has fed upon self-confirmation, and upon the civic and legal imperatives to sacrifice all, if necessary, in loyalty to a less than universal social group.

In the light of these antecedents of the global situation it is eminently rational to hold less than a sanguine view of the future. However, it is not rational to say that world division will inevitably persist or that world conquest is the only hope of world order. We are not confronted by a crisis of such subtlety that it cannot in principle be comprehended by the common man. And if expectation systems change, interpretations of goal change; with these revisions, basic strategies can be modified.

Under the impact of crisis, scholars and politicians have repeatedly declared that the principal opportunity for relief, hence responsibility for action, rests with the active politicians. At the same time it is acknowledged that the realities of the political process are such that decision-making elites are remarkably impotent as well as undermotivated for the job.

A further proposition is that no panacea exists. By itself no magic reiteration of worthy purpose can elicit the flood of motivations which are indispensable to the mastery of such opportunities as present themselves in the daily conduct of world affairs.

What, then, is to be said? So far as the basic requirements of the situation are concerned, there is little if anything to be added to what has for many centuries been the counsel of highminded men who have transcended the syndromes of parochialism into which they were born and succeeded in making articulate a message of love for life—all life—reaching to the furthest limits of at least the human species. Many philosophers, religious leaders, and poets have approximated in themselves the perspectives appropriate to a citizen of the commonwealth of man. To choose a sample statement, almost at random, consider Martin Buber's remark that "The antithesis of constraint is not freedom but unitedness." [3] This proposition puts the emphasis upon the affirmative aspect of ending coercion. From your perspective or mine the creative opportunity is to achieve a self-system larger than the primary ego; larger than the ego components of family, friends, profession, or nation; and inclusive of mankind. A self-system of this kind does not abolish the primary ego nor deny loyalty to intermediate groupings. Rather, it provides a frame of survival and fulfillment for articulating the demands and expectations appropriate to any component of human society. In our terminology voluntary self-commitment is an act of freedom; in this sense Buber should read: "The antithesis of constraint is unitedness voluntarily attained."

But in the world community of our day, whatever the limitations, there are scholarly advisors of active decision-makers cognizant of the great traditions of international law and jurisprudence. As part of the social process, the world of scholarship has no possibility of orbiting as aloof Cyclopean eyes. Legal scholars, especially, are capable of perceiving the realities of the situation, and of sharing an enlightened map of the globe with others, not excluding the decision-makers themselves.

Most senior members of the power elites of the contemporary world received their political orientation and training in the pre-atomic and pre-astronautic age. In view of the recent gigantic expansion of the sciences it is almost correct to add that they date from a proto-scientific epoch, and that the components of the elite who

3. In the phrasing of Herbert Read in 1 Gutkind, *Creative Mobilization* xvi (1943).

enjoy the closest contact with reality are members of the mid-elite. While it is true that no audience should be neglected, relative emphases are admissible means of economizing scarce resources. In this sense a wise strategy of communication seeks to reach the mid-elite, since it is from among those who occupy junior positions that top elite members are most likely to be drawn.

The cruciality of the mid-elite for more distant years does not imply that the mid-elites are irrelevant today. The senior elite undergoes chronic attrition. More than that, the policies of elite individuals and factions within the senior elite are affected by the currents present among the mid-elite as these currents are perceived by seniors. Hence we assert that changes in outlook occurring at mid-levels can affect policy now, even when allowance is made for the fact that inner changes "down the line" are typically concealed behind façades of superficial conformity which seniors do not fully penetrate.

The rise of realism in perceiving the world is counteracted by many factors whose total impact is to strengthen rather than weaken the parochial syndrome. We have in mind the expanding population characteristic of the world as a whole and especially of certain countries. As the population of a country expands, more individuals *may* come into contact with foreign nationals. However, the percentage of the population that spends some time living abroad for purposes of politics, jobs, trade, study, religion, and tourism does not necessarily go up. This is notably true of large nations, especially those whose elites are afraid that foreign contact will undermine the effective bases of their authority. Visitors and residents from abroad may be excluded; or if permitted, made subject to formal and informal restrictions upon freedom of communication with the local population. Fellow nationals who go abroad are viewed as possible agents of contamination, which is a source of weakness in political infighting. The conclusion is that expanding interdependence within a divided world arena does not necessarily undermine parochialism. On the contrary both direct and reported contacts with contrasting ways of life enhance preoccupation with the self. Over longer intervals the "self-reference effect" may lead to the remodelling of personality and culture by the incorporation of traits of the "other." But this does not necessarily lead to identification with *all* the world. Through any period the process is more likely to supplement the perceived limitations of the initial self by aligning an enlarged image against "others" within the world arena. In a divided world the apparent gains of belonging to a large though not a universal identity have seemed greater than an identification with an ineffectual "all." Hence identifications are more readily redefined *within* the whole—thus saving the syndrome of parochialism—than by alignment with an imperfectly organized "whole." Obviously no one can wisely underestimate the strength of "egopetal" [4] culture systems or the strength of the sense of obligation to sacrifice if necessary for the exclusive interests of national units.

The authors of the present treatise are fully alert to the fundamental features of the world social process. As men of compassion they are capable of empathy with harassed men and women who complain with Orwell:

> "I wasn't born for an age like this;
> Was Smith? Was Jones? Were you?" [5]

Yet their posture is affirmative. Leaders of thought have had much to do with molding and remolding the past, and the authors propose to work with those who are willing to strive to remake the world arena of the future. They recognize the role that scholars, and particularly legal scholars, can play in perceiving the realities of the inclusive interests of mankind, and showing how the traditional instruments of legal order can be flexibly adapted to the urgencies of the age. Messrs. McDougal and Feliciano have placed a formidable set of professional tools at the disposal of all who are willing to take every opportunity to consolidate at least a minimum degree of universal public order, and to proceed by enlarging the practice of consent and reducing the occasion for coercive imposition.

4. An expression of Lawrence Durrell in, for example, *Collected Poems* 63 (1960).

5. George Orwell, *Such, Such Were the Joys* 9 (1953).

LAW AND MINIMUM WORLD PUBLIC ORDER

1. THE PROCESSES OF COERCION AND DECISION: GENERAL COMMUNITY POLICIES

The importance today to every human being of community control of international coercion needs no pedant's footnotes to bestow upon it a sense of reality. The increasingly rapid multiplication and diffusion of weapons capable of shattering the globe, the most recent successful orbiting of artificial satellites and launching of guided and ballistic missiles of intercontinental reach,[1] the continued, if decelerated, hostile polarization of power in the world arena, the ever more precarious equilibrium between the polar opponents, the high and still rising levels in tension and expectations of comprehensive violence—all these and many other aspects of the contemporary world arena magnify with chilling insistence, even for the willful blind, the urgent need for rational inquiry into the potentialities and limitations of our inherited principles and procedures for controlling violence between peoples and for the invention and establishment of more effective alternatives in principles and procedures.[2] This urgent

1. On the implications of artificial satellites and missiles for international security see Berkner, "Earth Satellites and Foreign Policy," 36 *Foreign Aff.* 221 (1958); Davidon, "The Modern Roman Circus," 13 *Bull. Atomic Scientists* 331 (1957); Rabinowitch, "After Missiles and Satellites, What?" 13 id. at 346. Preliminary inquiry into certain anticipated problems of community control is made in McDougal and Lipson, "Perspectives for a Law of Outer Space," 52 *A.J.I.L.* 407–31 (1958).

2. This need has not gone unacknowledged in the more recent literature. See, e.g., Stone, *Legal Controls of International Conflict* xxxi–lv (1954) (hereinafter cited as Stone, *Legal Controls*); De Luna, "Fundamentación del Derecho Internacional," 60 *Revista de Derecho Internacional* 210 (Cuba, 1952); Downey,

---

Designed from the beginning as an introduction to this book, this chapter was previously published in 67 *Yale L. J.* 771–845 (1958) under the title "International Coercion and World Public Order: The General Principles of the Law of War." Minor revisions have been made in text and annotation. Reprinted with permission.

need—not far removed, if at all, from that of simple survival—when considered in relation to the rising demands of people all over the world, whatever the perspectives of their rulers, for the securing of all their values by peaceful procedures, free from coercion and violence, confronts students of international law with unparalleled challenge and opportunity.

To meet this challenge legal scholars, unfortunately still much too often, speak from one or the other of two contrasting attitudes, both destructive in high degree of efforts to clarify principles and procedures appropriate to a world public order honoring human dignity. The first of these attitudes, expressed in the accents of ultra-sophistication and disenchantment, affirms that man's destructive impulses and instruments of violence have escaped all bounds and that little or nothing can be done by law either to control international coercion or to minimize the destruction of values once violence erupts. The contrasting attitude, manifested in continuing high deference to certain inherited terms of art, affirms an excess of faith in technical concepts and rules, divorced from contexts and procedures, as determinants of decision and exhibits much too little concern for the clarification of policies in detailed contexts and for the search for new principles and procedures. It will require but brief illustration to indicate the inadequacies of each of these attitudes and to emphasize the need for an alternative approach.

The first attitude, that of cynical disenchantment with law, may be illustrated by reference to certain writers who take what they describe as a "realistic" attitude toward the possibilities of legal regulation of coercion and violence among states. Emphasizing the "unlimited forces" that total war unleashes and pointing to the fearful potentialities of modern weapons, Judge de Visscher insists that "in its essence the problem of control [of such weapons] is wholly political" and adds:

"Revision of the Rules of Warfare," 43 *Proc. Am. Soc. I. L.* 102 (1949); Kunz, "The Laws of War," 50 *A.J.I.L.* 313 (1956); Kunz, "The Chaotic Status of the Laws of War and the Urgent Necessity for Their Revision," 45 id. at 37 (1951); Lauterpacht, "The Problem of the Revision of the Laws of War," 29 *Brit. Y.B.I.L.* 360 (1952); Phillips, "Air Warfare and Law," 21 *Geo. Wash. L. Rev.* 311, 395, 415 (1953). See also Pound, "Potentials for World Stability in the Field of Law," in *Prospects for World Stability* 5 (Proc. Inst. World Affairs, 26th Sess., 1949).

> The new weapons of mass destruction have revolutionized all the data of war, and it is above all for this reason that the jurists will be well advised to waste no further time in what some of them still persist in calling the "restatement" of the laws of war. To try to adapt these laws to the new conditions is not only labor absolutely lost; it is an enterprise that in certain of its aspects may be dangerous, as was demonstrated by the indefinite extension given in the second world war to the notion of the military objective. There is better work to be done today than picking up the fragments of an obsolete body of rules.[3]

The attitude here exhibited may be only a particular piece of the contemporary disillusionment which characteristically minimizes the actual and potential function of law in the world power process, exaggerates the role of naked power, and deprecates continuing concern with legal principles and procedures as legalism—as an "intoxication with moral abstractions" and as one of the "great sources of weakness and failure" in foreign policy.[4] Even so distinguished a

3. De Visscher, *Theory and Reality in Public International Law* 293 (Corbett, trans., 1957). For comparable pessimism expressed after World War I see "The League of Nations and the Laws of War," 1 *Brit. Y.B.I.L.* 109 (1920–21).

4. See Morgenthau, *In Defense of the National Interest* 4, 101 (1951); cf. Kennan, *American Diplomacy, 1900–1950,* 95 (1951): "I see the most serious fault of our past policy formulation to lie in something that I might call the legalistic-moralistic approach to international problems. This approach was like a red skein through our foreign policy of the last fifty years. It has in it something of the old emphasis on arbitration treaties, something of the Hague Conferences and schemes for universal disarmament, something of the more ambitious American concepts of the role of international law, something of the League of Nations and the United Nations, something of the Kellogg Pact, something of the idea of a universal 'Article 51' pact, something of the belief in World Law and World Government. . . . It is the belief that it should be possible to suppress the chaotic and dangerous aspirations of governments in the international field by the acceptance of some system of legal rules and restraints."

For criticism of Professors Morgenthau and Kennan's position see McDougal, "Law and Power," 46 *A.J.I.L.* 102 (1952). See also Corbett, *Morals, Law and Power in International Relations* 2–16 (1956); Oliver, "Reflections on Two Recent Developments Affecting the Function of Law in the International Community," 30 *Texas L. Rev.* 815 (1952).

For comparable underestimations of the function of legal principles and rules see Schwarzenberger, *Power Politics* 203 (2d rev. ed., 1951): "In a society in which

humanitarian as Dr. Fenwick has given candid expression to such attitudes:

> The laws of war belong to a past age and except for a few minor matters of no consequence, it is futile to attempt to revive them. . . . Let's face the facts. War has got beyond the control of law, other than the elementary law of humanity, if that can be discovered among the ruins of devastated cities.[5]
>
> Gone, and it is to be hoped, gone forever is the naive belief that it is possible to draft new laws of war for new wars . . .[6]

The most obvious inadequacy in this attitude is that, because of its comprehensive deprecation of the role of authority, it offers no real alternative to naked force in an era in which the unrestrained exercise of such force against peoples threatens the very continuance of the human species. It is, of course, possible that the future may, as the world explodes in the holocaust of unlimited nuclear war, prove these writers to have been correct. Such pyrrhic vindication will, however, appeal to few, and for the scholar who cherishes both human life and human dignity, such a possibility can scarcely be permitted to deter renewed efforts to clarify the principles and procedures of a world public order in which human life and dignity may be made more secure. Fortunately, history does disclose a few examples of eras in which appropriate organizing principles and procedures were achieved, in contexts of sustaining effective power, for the restraint of generalized violence and for the minimization, in at least modest degree, of barbarism in conflict.[7] There has yet to be demonstrated any inner necessity in either human nature or the nature of human society that makes it inherently impossible for men

---

power is the overriding consideration, it is the primary function of laws to assist in maintaining the supremacy of force and the hierarchies established on the basis of power and to lend to such system the respectability and sanctity of law. In a variety of ways, international law serves these purposes." For brief comment see McDougal, "Dr. Schwarzenberger's Power Politics," 47 *A.J.I.L.* 115 (1953).

5. 43 *Proc. Am. Soc. I. L.* 110 (1949) (Fenwick).

6. Fenwick, "The Progress of International Law," 79 *Hague Recueil* 5, 63 (1951).

7. Europe during the greater part of the nineteenth century is the most frequently cited example, as to which see 1 Wright, *A Study of War* 361–2, 639, 653–5 (1942).

to discover and employ policies and institutions for harnessing the new instruments of destruction to the purposes of order rather than to their final mutual obliteration.[8]

The second attitude, that of overoptimistic faith in the efficacy of technical legal concepts and rules, is exemplified in the continued emphasis, evident in much of the contemporary literature of the law of war, on normative-ambiguous[9] definitions and formulations and in the common underlying assumption that certain predetermined "legal consequences" attach to and automatically follow—independently of policy objectives, factual conditions, and value consequences

8. See May, *A Social Psychology of War and Peace* cc. 1, 2, 9 (1943), whose main thesis is that "war and peace are basically and fundamentally the products of the types of social conditioning that have occurred in the large masses of people of the leading nations of the world" (id. at vii). Pear, "The Psychological Study of Tensions and Conflict," in *The Nature of Conflict* 118, 131 (1957), points out that the view which posits an "innate, independent, instinctual disposition of man" toward aggression is not supported by more recent studies on psychology, social psychology and comparative ethnology. 2 Wright, *A Study of War* 1224 (1942): "The attitude conducive to peace is neither that popularly attributed to the ostrich, which denies the possibility of war, nor that of the cynic, who considers war inevitable, but that of the rational man who appraises the opinions and conditions tending to war and the direction of human effort which at a given point in history might prevent it." Cf. *Tensions That Cause Wars* 17 (Cantril, ed., 1950): "To the best of our knowledge, there is no evidence to indicate that wars are necessary and inevitable consequences of 'human nature' as such." See also Klineberg, *Tensions Affecting International Understanding* c. 5 (1950); *Human Nature and Enduring Peace* cc. 2–4, 26 (Murphy, ed., 1945); Wright, *Problems of Stability and Progress in International Relations* 129, 146–7 (1954); Almond, "Anthropology, Political Behaviour, and International Relations," 2 *World Politics* 277 (1950); Cook, "Democratic Psychology and a Democratic World Order," 1 id. at 553 (1949); De Luna, "Es la guerra inevitable?" 8 *Revista Espanola de Derecho Internacional* 11 (1955); Malinowski, "War—Past, Present, and Future," in *War as a Social Institution* 21–31 (Clarkson and Cochran, ed., 1941); Pear, "Peace, War and Culture Patterns," in *Psychological Factors of War and Peace* 21–45 (Pear, ed., 1950).

9. A statement is "normative-ambiguous" when its terms make indiscriminate reference to the events to which decision-makers respond, to the policies which are assumed to guide and justify decision and to the decisions ("legal consequences") themselves. Such statements commonly attempt in a single reference to describe past decisions, to predict future decisions, and to state what future decisions ought to be. Further exposition of normative-ambiguity may be found in Lasswell and McDougal, "Legal Education and Public Policy: Professional Training in the Public Interest," 52 *Yale L. J.* 203–95 (1943).

as perceived by determinate decision-makers—from such definitions and formulations. This overemphasis on formal concepts and rules begins with the customary definition of war as a "legal state" or "condition" and extends through all ancillary concepts. The conception of war offered by Professor Hyde is representative: "War may in a broad sense be fairly described as a condition of armed hostility between States. . . . A state of war is a legal condition of affairs dealt with as such, and so described both by participants and non-participants. It may exist prior to the use of force." [10] The formulation by Lord McNair is even more explicit illustration:

> An important point . . . which, I think any good definition must bring out, is that war is a state or condition of affairs, not a mere series of acts of force. It is a state of affairs to which International Law attaches certain far-reaching consequences, and it is by reason of those consequences that it is necessary, as a matter of practice rather than of speculation, to define the state of affairs giving rise to them. . . . Moreover, Peace and War are mutually exclusive; there is no half-way house. . . . There are many measures of redress falling short of war, but the state of the relations between the State by whom and the State against whom such measures are taken continues to be peace until by one or both of them it is converted into war.[11]

More recently, Professor Tucker has written: "War—or the resort to armed force—is an action constituting a legal status defined by law. This status consists in bringing into operation certain rights and duties as between the belligerent states." [12]

The primary difficulty with all these definitions,[13] and the comparable expressions of subsidiary concepts,[14] consists in the fact that

10. 3 Hyde, *International Law* 1686 (2d rev. ed., 1945).

11. McNair, "The Legal Meaning of War, and the Relation of War to Reprisals," 11 *Tr. Grotius Soc.* 29, 33 (1926).

12. Tucker, *The Law of War and Neutrality at Sea* 9 (1957).

13. See the definitions collected in Eagleton, "The Attempt to Define War," 291 *Int. Conciliation* 237, 258 (1933); Green, "Armed Conflict, War, and Self-Defense," 6 *Archiv des Völkerrechts* 387 (1957); McNair, note 11 supra at 31–2; Ronan, "English and American Courts and the Definition of War," 31 *A.J.I.L.* 642 (1937).

14. On "neutrality" see, e.g., Orvik, *The Decline of Neutrality 1914–1941* 11 (1953): "Neutrality signifies primarily a nation's status of non-participation in

they not only attempt to refer at once to both "facts" and asserted "legal consequences," to both the time-space events of coercion and the responses of authoritative decision-makers to such events, but also purport to break each of the two distinguishable processes of factual coercion and of legal decision into the illusorily simple and dichotomous categories of "war" and "peace."

This conception of sharp discrimination between the "state of war" and the "state of peace," each with its distinctive and mutually exclusive sets of world prescriptions, is as ancient as Cicero's *inter bellum et pacem nihil est medium,* upon which Grotius relied.[15] It is, however, no new thought that this dichotomy is hardly a faithful reflection of the fluid and complex process of coercion in the contemporary world arena or of the equally complex process of legal authority. By resting on such an oversimplification, the legal scholar frequently compounds many particular confusions: he does violence to the great variety and differing intensities of the events in the coercion process,[16] obscures the creative role of the authoritative

---

hostilities when other countries are at war. Yet in international law a neutral state also undertakes certain duties and claims certain rights." See also Tucker, note 12 supra at 196.

15. 2 Grotius, *De Jure Belli Ac Pacis* 832 (Kelsey, trans., 1925). For more recent formulations of this dichotomy see Lord Macnaghten, in *Janson v. Dreifontein Consol. Mines, Ltd.,* [1902] A.C. 484, 497–8; Stowell, *International Law* 491 (1931); 2 Twiss, *The Law of Nations* 49 (2d rev. ed., 1875).

16. Osgood, *Limited War: The Challenge to American Strategy* 20 (1957), offers lucid exposition of this point: "[I]t would be a mistake to regard war as a single, simple, uniform entity or as an independent thing in itself, to which one applies a wholly different set of rules and considerations than properly apply to other forms of international conflict. It is more realistic in the light of the complex and multifarious nature of international conflict to regard war as the upper extremity of a whole scale of international conflict of ascending intensity and scope. All along this scale one may think of sovereign nations asserting their wills in conflict with other nations by a variety of military and nonmilitary means of coercion, but no definition can determine precisely at what point in the scale conflict becomes 'war.' In this sense, war is a matter of degree, which itself contains different degrees of intensity and scope." See Hartmann, *The Relations of Nations* 41–2 (1957); Strausz-Hupé and Possony, *International Relations* 41–5 (2d ed., 1954); Wright, *A Study of War* 10–12 (1942). Description of processes of conflict between social units or systems in terms of continua between polar extremes is almost commonplace in contemporary sociology. See, e.g., Bernard, "The Sociological Study of Conflict," in *The Nature of Conflict* 33, 44–5 (1957).

decision-maker in responding to such events, removes from the focus of his attention many important variables which in fact affect decision, and confuses the fundamental policies, differing as the events of coercion differ, for the securing of which the public order of the world community establishes and maintains authoritative decision-makers.

Some recognition that the classical twofold categorization of the process of coercion has but minimal correspondence to contemporary realities in the interactions of states is apparent in the work of a number of modern scholars. This recognition is perhaps most explicit in Professor Jessup's recent recommendation that a new "legal state of intermediacy," a "third status" intermediate between war and peace, be recognized and elaborated in international law as a means of bridging the gap between traditional concept and contemporary practice and of avoiding confusion in policy.[17] The set of events which Professor Jessup would designate as "intermediacy" would be characterized by a "basic condition of hostility and strain" or "tension" between the opposing participants, by issues of "so fundamental and deep-rooted a character that no solution of a single tangible issue could terminate [the hostility]" and by "reluctance" of both sides "to resort to war." [18] Professor Jessup did not detail the legal consequences of intermediacy but did suggest that, in the third state, conduct "which would not be peaceful and yet would be short of . . . 'total war' " would be permissible.[19]

The proposal of Professor Jessup is not without precedent. A decade earlier, Dr. Schwarzenberger called attention to the fact that the "doctrine of the alternative character of war and peace" minimized or ignored the "reality of state practice." [20] States, he pointed out, have frequently applied against each other more or less limited amounts of coercion, military and nonmilitary, while continuing to

17. Jessup, "Should International Law Recognize an Intermediate Status Between Peace and War?" 48 *A.J.I.L.* 98 (1954); Jessup, "Intermediacy," 23 *Nordisk Tidsskrift for International Ret* 16 (1953).

18. Id. at 18–19.

19. Id. at 24.

20. Schwarzenberger, "Jus Pacis Ac Belli?" 37 *A.J.I.L.* 460 (1943); cf. Stone, *Legal Controls*, xxxiv, xxxvi–xxxvii, who speaks of a condition of " 'neither peace nor war' which dominates our actual world" and of the " 'normality' of this condition of 'no peace-no war.' " See also Schwarzenberger, "The Fundamental Principles of International Law," 87 *Hague Recueil* 195, 327–8 (1955).

maintain "peaceful relations" and denying that a "state of war" existed. Such noncomprehensive uses of force, commonly denominated "measures short of war," are incompatible, Dr. Schwarzenberger urged, with the states of both peace and war and have "created rules pertaining neither to those of peace or war, but constituting a *status mixtus*." [21] Thus he would, like Professor Jessup, recognize three instead of two "states of typical legal relations between states": a "state of peace" where states are limited in their mutual contentions to the use of economic and political power, a "*status mixtus*" where these forms of power are supplemented by the use of military power, and a "state of war" where states use "all available forms of power." [22]

A major purpose of this essay is to suggest that the events of interstate coercion and the flow of decisions about coercion are even more

21. Schwarzenberger, "Jus Pacis Ac Belli?" 37 *A.J.I.L.* 460, 474 (1943). "Forcible measures short of war" have always been a source of annoyance to those concerned with tidy categorizations. For earlier suggestions about a "state of reprisals" intermediate between peace and war, see Grob, *The Relativity of War and Peace* 124–40 (1949); Hindmarsh, *Force in Peace* 91 (1933). Expressions such as "quasi-war," "imperfect war," "partial war" and "partial hostilities" reflect the same difficulties of classification; they are roughly equivalent to "state of reprisals." See 7 Moore, *A Digest of International Law* §§ 1101–2 (1906); 3 Wharton, *Digest of International Law* § 333 (2d ed., 1887).

22. Schwarzenberger, "Jus Pacis Ac Belli?" 37 *A.J.I.L.* 460, 474 (1943). Cf. Kotzsch, *The Concept of War in Contemporary History and International Law* 241 (1956), who apparently regards recognition of a "legal state of intermediacy" as undesirable on the ground that "legal thinking would degenerate into political arbitrariness without the confining walls of the firmly established distinction between war and peace." More accurately, "legal thinking" based on the distinction has been used to support political arbitrariness. See the statement of a North Korean representative at the Korean armistice talks at Panmunjom in connection with the North Korean proposal that the Soviet Union be included in the Neutral Nations Supervisory Commission: "Is your [the United Nations] side now in a state of war with the Soviet Union? If not, how can your side deny that the Soviet Union is a neutral nation apart from the two belligerents?" Quoted in Jessup, "Should International Law Recognize an Intermediate Status between Peace and War?" 48 *A.J.I.L.* 98–9 (1954). See also Joy, *How Communists Negotiate* 90–101 (1955). Some difficulties relating to the ancillary concept of neutrality are noted in Fraga Iribarne, "Guerra y Paz: Nuevas Problemas del Concepto de Neutralidad," in *Estudios de Derecho Internacional: Homenaje al Professor Camilo Barcia Trelles* 339 (Universidad de Santiago de Compostela, 1958).

complex than the modern literature has so far explicitly recognized, and that a method of analysis more comprehensive and flexible than either dichotomy or trichotomy seems necessary if clarity in fundamental conceptions and rationality in decision-making are to be promoted. It would seem open to doubt whether a trichotomy which makes simultaneous and undifferentiated reference both to facts of the greatest variety and to responses which various decision-makers for varied purposes make to varying constellations of such facts is any more apt than a dichotomy of similar reference to lead to consequential insight and policy clarification.

An adequate theory for the analysis of practices and decisions must start with manageable conceptions of, and a careful distinguishing between, the factual process of international coercion and the process of authoritative decision by which the public order of the world community endeavors to regulate such process of coercion. Each of those two distinguishable processes has its own participants—seeking different objectives, acting by different methods, and being affected by differing conditions. Appropriate analysis of the process of coercion may make possible intellectual isolation of the major recurring types of problems which raise common identifiable issues of policy and which involve common patterns of conditioning factors. Such analysis may also make it possible to avoid the preoccupation with exercises in derivation and legal syntactics in which scholars have unfortunately often engaged with minimum reference to the actualities of coercion and violence among states. An appropriate analysis of the process of authoritative decision may permit, with respect to recurring problems, the more careful observation and comparison through time of past trends in decisions, identification of the more important factors which have influenced and shaped decision, delineation and appraisal of the policies which have been sought in decisions, and projection of future probabilities of decision. And, finally, from such analysis may emerge alternatives in the formulation and application of policy [23] better designed to promote a world public

23. Some amplification of these intellectual tasks which the authors regard as indispensable to policy-oriented inquiry may be found in Lasswell, "The Political Science of Science," 50 *Am. Pol. Sci. Rev.* 961, 977–8 (1956); Lasswell and McDougal, "Legal Education and Public Policy: Professional Training in the Public Interest," 52 *Yale L. J.* 203 (1943); McDougal, "El derecho internacional como ciencia política," 3 *Revista de Derecho y Ciencias Sociales* 142, 149–50

order embodying the values commonly characterized as those of human dignity in a society of freedom and abundance.[24]

THE PROCESS OF COERCION

The factual process of coercion [25] across state boundaries may be usefully described, in broadest generalization, in terms of certain participants applying to each other coercion of alternately accelerating and decelerating intensity, for a whole spectrum of objectives,

(1956–57); McDougal, "Law as a Process of Decision: A Policy-Oriented Approach to Legal Study," 1 *Natural Law Forum* 53, 58–9 (1956); McDougal, "International Law, Power and Policy: A Contemporary Conception," 82 *Hague Recueil* 137, 140–1 (1953).

24. For indication, in some detail, of the reference assigned to such values see Lasswell and McDougal, "The Jurisprudence of a Free Society: Studies in Law, Science and Policy," Pt. III, pp. 1–39 (mimeographed materials, Yale Law School, 1954); Bebr, "International Protection of Human Rights and Freedoms," 29 *Phil. L. J.* 307, 314–28 (1954); Lasswell, "Democratic Character," in *The Political Writings of Harold D. Lasswell* 465 (1951); Lasswell and McDougal, "Legal Education and Public Policy: Professional Training in the Public Interest," 52 *Yale L. J.* 203 (1943); McDougal, "International Law, Power and Policy: A Contemporary Conception," 82 *Hague Recueil* 137, 188–91 (1953); McDougal and Leighton, "The Rights of Man and the World Community: Constitutional Illusions versus Rational Action," 14 *Law and Contemp. Prob.* 490 (1949).

25. We think of "process" as a complex of interacting variable factors moving through time; its principal connotation is that of continual change in relationships over a time period. The importance of presentation and analysis in terms of process has been well stated in Millikan, "Inquiry and Policy: The Relation of Knowledge to Action," in *The Human Meaning of the Social Sciences* 158, 174 (Lerner, ed., 1959): "[F]rom a policy point of view the most important characteristic of our times is that societies are changing in almost all their fundamental dimensions at a rate unprecedented in history. All our most crucial international policy problems require an appraisal not of states of affairs but of patterns of evolution. Economic development, newly emergent nationalism, trends in the character of Communist society, the political implications of changing weapons technology—these are all questions which cannot even be posed in other than dynamic terms. If the social scientist is to help the policy maker deal with these situations at all, he must find ways of introducing process explicitly into both his analytical frameworks and his empirical observations."

See also Easton, *The Political System* 172–5 (1953); Snyder, Bruck, and Sapin, *Decision-Making as an Approach to the Study of International Politics* 54 (1954). "Coercion" is used to refer to a high degree of constraint exercised by means of any or all of the various instruments of policy (see text at note 73 infra)

by methods which include the employment of all available instruments of policy, and under all the continually changing conditions of a world arena.[26] In the course of this seamless process of action and reaction, and as an integral part of it, participants also continuously assert against each other many varying claims respecting the lawfulness or unlawfulness of the various coercive practices employed by and against them, invoking in support of their respective claims both world prescriptions and world public opinion.

Participants

The historic participants in this process are customarily and summarily described as the attacking and target states and their respective allies.[27] For purposes of precision in description, however, as well as for the application of certain sanctioning procedures such as those providing for criminal liability, one must frequently go behind the institutional abstraction "state" and refer to the effective decision-

---

and with respect to all values. Other terms used below are "force" and "violence." Unless otherwise indicated, the reference of "force" is to the infliction of severe deprivations of the value well-being through uses of the military instrument. "Violence" is used to refer to the most intense attacks on well-being by means of military weapons. In this connection, see Lasswell and Kaplan, *Power and Society* 76, 90, 97–102 (1950).

26. For fuller description of these categorizations see McDougal, "International Law, Power and Policy: A Contemporary Conception," 82 *Hague Recueil* 137, 165–79 (1953). Cf. the categories which Talcott Parsons regards as necessary for the "minimum differentiation of structural elements" in an "action frame of reference": "ends, means, conditions and norms," Parsons, *The Structure of Social Action* 732 (1937), and those employed to describe processes of conflict by Professor Wright, "International Conflict and the United Nations," 10 *World Politics* 24 (1957). See also Wright, *The Study of International Relations* 531–67 (1955); Wright, "The Value for Conflict Resolution of a General Discipline of International Relations," 1 *J. Conflict Resolution* 3 (1957). For a brief survey of contemporary efforts to describe, in mathematical terms, social systems in processes of conflict and war see Bernard (note 16 supra), at 63–73. See also the notational matrix scheme adopted in Strausz-Hupé and Possony, *International Relations* 45–9 (2d ed., 1954).

27. For a typology, grounded on system analysis, of states as national actors in the international system see Kaplan, *System and Process in International Politics* 54–6 (1957). See also Wright, "International Conflict and the United Nations," 10 *World Politics* 24, 34–7 (1957); Wright, "Design for a Research Project on International Conflicts and the Factors Causing Their Aggravation or Amelioration," 10 *Western Pol. Q.* 263, 267–9 (1957).

makers, the officials or representatives—political, military, or otherwise—and members of the participating states.[28] Recently the officials of international governmental organizations have become formal and effective participants in this same process. The officials of third states, while seeking to avoid direct roles in the process of coercion, commonly take active part in the assertion of claims and counterclaims about the lawfulness or unlawfulness of various exercises of coercion; to this extent, they too should be listed as participants.

Nor does this list exhaust the groups and entities who in varying measure effectively participate in the world power process and hence in the process of coercion. A fuller listing would include those whom Dr. Schwarzenberger called "the minor members of the international cast": [29] transnational political parties, pressure groups, private associations, and the individual person.[30] Since the inception of the

28. See Snyder, Bruck and Sapin (note 25 supra), at 35–54, for a suggested framework for studies of states as decision-making units in the international arena. See also Snyder and Furniss, *American Foreign Policy: Formulation, Principles, and Programs* 89–134 (1954); Easton, "An Approach to the Analysis of Political Systems," 9 *World Politics* 383 (1957).

The concept of the elite, or top effective decision-makers, is of obvious relevance in the determination of individual criminal responsibility under international law. The tribunal in "The High Command Trial," 12 *Law Reports of Trials of War Criminals* 69–70 (1949), said: "It is not a person's rank or status, but his power to shape or influence the policy of his state, which is the relevant issue for determining his criminality under the charge of Crimes against Peace. . . . Those who commit the crime are those who participate at the policy making level in planning, preparing, or in initiating war. After war is initiated, and is being waged, the policy question then involved becomes one of extending, continuing or discontinuing the war. The crime at this stage likewise must be committed at the policy making level." See also "The Krupp Trial," 10 id. at 127–8 (1949); "I. G. Farben Trial," 10 id. at 37–8; *The Charter and Judgment of the Nuremberg Tribunal—History and Analysis* 58–61 (U.N. Doc. No. A/CN. 4/5) (1949) (memorandum submitted by the Secretary-General). Recent elite studies include: De Sola Pool, *Satellite Generals: A Study of Military Elites in the Soviet Sphere* (1955); Lasswell, Lerner and Rothwell, *The Comparative Study of Elites* (1952); Lerner, *The Nazi Elite* (1951); Mills, *The Power Elite* (1956); North, *Kuomintang and Chinese Communist Elites* (1952); Schueller, *The Politburo* (1951).

29. Schwarzenberger, *Power Politics* 126–46 (2d rev. ed., 1951).

30. See McDougal, "International Law, Power and Policy: A Contemporary Conception," 82 *Hague Recueil* 173, 174, 237–56 (1953). These groups and entities, as well as states and international organizations, are of course but specialized roles which the individual human being creates for himself in satisfying, or

modern state system, however, states have been, and in all probability will remain in the calculable future, the major and most significant participants in the international coercion process; they are ordinarily possessed of the greatest organized bases of power. Thus states and organizations of states must remain as the principal focus of inquiry. The other participant groups and entities frequently either act through the state or function as instrumentalities of state policy.

Objectives

The objectives of states participating in this process of coercion may, like those of any actor in any system of action, be most broadly characterized in terms of a maximization postulate: any particular participant acts to maximize certain or all of its values in relation to the other participants in the world arena.[31] Such objectives embrace, in most general statement, all the characteristic value demands of nation-states, including the demand to protect and expand their own bases of power and other values and to weaken or disintegrate the bases and values of those defined as enemies or potential enemies.[32] On another level of abstraction, the objectives of any participant may be generalized as a demand that the enemy accept certain terms with respect to specified policies and accordingly alter its previous behavior [33]—for instance, withdrawal or abstention from

---

attempting to satisfy, his value demands. For comprehensive study of the extent to which the individual, through such groups and entities, effectively participates in the world power process, see Jeffries, "The Individual and International Law" (unpublished thesis in Yale Law Library, 1954).

31. See Lasswell and Kaplan, *Power and Society* 69–70 (1950).

32. See, generally, Kaplan, note 27 supra at 149–65; Hartmann, *The Relations of Nations* 68–82 (1957); Morgenthau, *Politics Among Nations* 35–79 (2d rev. ed., 1954); Schwarzenberger, *Power Politics* 126–46 (2d rev. ed., 1951); Spykman, *America's Strategy in World Politics* 17–19 (1942); Strausz-Hupé and Possony, *International Relations* 1–21 (2d ed., 1954); Jessup, "Ends and Means of American Foreign Policy," in *International Stability and Progress* 11–21 (1957); Nitze, "Aims and Methods of United States Foreign Policy," 13 *Bull. Atomic Scientists* 292 (1957).

33. "The object on the part of each belligerent is to break down the resistance of the other to the terms which he requires for peace." 2 Westlake, *International Law* 53 (1907).

a hostile policy or projected policy, or affirmative adoption of some policy demanded by the acting participant.[34]

A typology of the more particular demands of contending participants might perhaps be constructed on the basis of a number of possible criteria, such as the dominant value or values sought, the position assigned to particular demands in an order of priority established for the allocation of means, and the time dimension of objectives as "long term" or "short term." [35] Such a typology, while useful in other contexts, does not seem to be the most relevant for the purpose of clarifying the fundamental legal policies here at stake. What is necessary is a mode of characterizing the specific objectives of participants which relates them more precisely to variables which do and should affect the prescription and application of authority—a set of categories which may and should be relevant in the making of community decisions about the permissible or nonpermissible character of the coercion exercised to secure such objectives. A few tentative categorizations may be suggested.

CONSEQUENTIALITY

At least three dimensions of consequentiality are relevant: the importance and number of values affected, the extent to which such values are affected, and the number of participants whose values are so affected. A participant may demand from another many values or only one or a few and may seek to affect such values drastically and substantially or only to a modest degree. A participant's objectives may relate to and affect the power and other values of only one nation-state or a number of nation-states. They may even include a demand for a monopoly of power or other values from the rest of the world community. The demands of participants may thus be of almost infinite variety in degree of consequentiality; in terms of polar

34. The descriptive categories "absention," "withdrawal," "cooperation," "modification" and "reconstruction" are suggested by Lasswell, "Political Factors in the Formulation of National Strategy," 6 *Naval War College Rev.* 19, 34–5 (1954). They are intended to describe the responses sought by strategists in nation-states. For elaboration and illustration of this mode of categorizing objectives, see McDougal and Lasswell, "World Community and Law: A Contemporary International Law," c. 3 (mimeographed materials, Yale Law School, 1955).

35. Snyder, Bruck, and Sapin, note 25 supra at 60.

opposites, the possible range is from the most limited to the most comprehensive. More concretely, the spectrum of particular demands asserted through coercion may range from such limited ones as the payment of a debt owed by the target state or its nationals [36] or the temporary passage of troops through its territory,[37] through the relinquishment of the target state's control over a specific portion of its territory [38] or acceptance of certain limitations on its freedom of decision-making,[39] to the complete absorption of the target state,[40]

36. The blockade of Venezuela by British, German and Italian warships in 1902–1903, for example, was imposed as a result of the failure of the Venezuelan Government to pay certain claims of nationals of the blockading powers. See Venezuelan Preferential case, 1 Scott, *Hague Court Reports* 55 (1916); 6 Moore, *A Digest of International Law* § 967, at 586–94 (1906).

37. In 1914, in its ultimatum to the Belgian Government, Germany demanded permission for German troops to march through Belgian territory, promising in return that "when peace was concluded . . . Belgium and all its possessions should be protected to the fullest extent, that its territory should be evacuated, and that if Belgium would preserve an attitude of friendly neutrality towards Germany, the German government would engage to pay cash for all supplies needed by the German troops and would indemnify her for all damage caused." 2 Garner, *International Law and the World War* 188 (1920).

38. The Soviet-Finnish war in 1939 was preceded by a demand of the Soviet Government for a thirty-year "lease" of certain islands in the Gulf of Finland and the cession of certain areas at the head of the Gulf, the islands and areas totaling 2,761 sq. kms., in exchange for Soviet territory on the Finnish border with an area of 5,529 sq. kms. These demands were apparently prompted by Soviet concern over the security of Leningrad. See *The Finnish Blue Book: The Development of Finnish-Soviet Relations during the Autumn of 1939 Including the Official Documents and the Peace Treaty of March 12, 1940*, 13–19 (1940).

39. The Anglo-Soviet intervention in Iran in 1941 compelled the Shah's government to accept, among other things, the stationing of Allied forces in Iranian territory for the duration of the war and Allied control over means of communication and transportation in Iran, and to undertake "not to adopt in [its] relations with foreign countries an attitude . . . inconsistent with the alliance" forced on it by Britain and the Soviet Union. The Iranian Government continued to exist and its functions, except in the particulars specified in the treaty of alliance, were not displaced. The text of the treaty is found in 6 *Dept. State Bull.* 249–52 (1942). See, generally, Kirk, *The Middle East in the War: Survey of International Affairs 1939–1946*, 129–41 (1952); Lenczowski, *Russia and the West in Iran, 1918–1948: A Study in Big-Power Rivalry* 167–92 (1949).

40. The seizure and incorporation of Austria by Nazi Germany in 1938 is illustrative. For a brief recounting of the events leading up to the annexation of Austria, see "Judgment of the International Military Tribunal at Nuremberg," in *Nazi Conspiracy and Aggression* 17–24 (1947).

the annihilation of its people,[41] and the establishment of a universal empire.[42]

INCLUSIVENESS OR EXCLUSIVENESS

The reference of the categorization suggested here is both to the degree of participation admitted in the sharing of the values demanded and to the degree of comprehensiveness of the identification system, the definition or interpretation of "self," in the name of which value demands are made.[43] The demands of a participant may be exclusive and made on its own behalf purely and simply; the "self" system may be restrictively defined to include only the demanding participant's "primary self." Demands may, on the other hand, be more inclusive and be asserted on behalf of a greater or lesser number of other participants—even on behalf of "humanity" in general or the entire world community; other participants are, for the time being at least, made components of the expanded structure of the claimant's "self." Whether the value demands pressed by any participant in any particular instances of coercion are in fact, and not merely in the propagandist's word, inclusive and the extent to which they are so, are, of course, matters for empirical investigation. History exhibits no dearth of examples of states seeking exclusive values by coercion; wars of conquest and self-aggrandizement—in our own century the Abyssinian adventure of Fascist Italy,[44]

41. This is exemplified by the Nazi German policies toward the civilian population in Poland and the Soviet Union. The International Military Tribunal at Nuremberg found that "the evidence shows that at any rate in the east, the mass murders and cruelties were not committed solely for the purpose of stamping out opposition or resistance to the German occupying forces. In Poland and the Soviet Union these crimes were part of a plan to get rid of whole native populations by expulsion and annihilation, in order that their territory could be used for colonization by Germans" (id. at 66–7).

42. Among those who have attempted, after Rome, to re-establish a universal empire are the Hohenstaufen, the Hapsburgs, Louis XIV, Napoleon, the Kaiser, Mussolini, and Hitler. 2 Wright, *A Study of War* 966 (1942).

43. On identification or "self" systems, see Lasswell and Kaplan, *Power and Society* 11–13, 30–1 (1950).

44. See 2 *Survey of International Affairs 1935: Abyssinia and Italy* (Royal Institute of Int. Affairs, 1936). The Committee of Six created by the Council of the League of Nations found that the "Italian Government . . . resorted to war in disregard of its covenants under Article 12 of the Covenant of the League of Nations" (*League of Nations, Off. J.*, 16th Yr., 1223–5, 1935).

Japan's wars in Manchuria,[45] China, and southeast Asia,[46] and Nazi Germany's wars in Europe [47]—are only the most obvious ones. Perhaps the clearest recent instance of relatively inclusive demands asserted forcefully is the United Nations' enforcement action in Korea. Comparable instances may be found in the last century in the collective action of the great powers in Europe to restore the balance of power that Napoleonic France had disturbed,[48] and in the "humanitarian interventions" designed to compel the Ottoman Sublime Porte to stop the persecution and massacre of its Christian subjects.[49]

EXTENSION OR CONSERVATION

A participant exercising coercion may be acting either to conserve and defend values already enjoyed or to attack and acquire values held by another.[50] Of course, in concrete situations of interstate

45. See, generally, *Survey of International Affairs 1931*, 430–505 (Royal Institute of Int. Affairs, 1932); *Survey of International Affairs 1932*, 432–67, 515–86 (Royal Institute of Int. Affairs, 1933); *Survey of International Affairs 1933*, 478–518 (Royal Institute of Int. Affairs, 1934). See also the Lytton Report which found that there was "no question of Chinese responsibility" for "events since September 18, 1931." This Report was adopted by the Assembly of the League of Nations on Feb. 24, 1933. See "League of Nations Assembly Report on the Sino-Japanese Dispute," 27 *A.J.I.L. Supp.* 119, 147 (1933).

46. See, generally, 1 *Survey of International Affairs 1937*, 154–305 (Royal Institute of Int. Affairs, 1938); "The Far East 1942–1946," *Survey of International Affairs 1939–1946*, 4–97 (Royal Institute of Int. Affairs, 1955); Jones, *Japan's New Order in East Asia: Its Rise and Fall 1937–45* (1954); Horwitz, "The Tokyo Trial," 465 *Int. Conciliation* 475 (1950).

47. See "Judgment of the International Military Tribunal at Nuremberg," in *Nazi Conspiracy and Aggression* 4–46 (1945).

48. See Morgenthau, *Politics Among Nations* 170–1 (2d rev. ed., 1954). 2 Wright, *A Study of War* 749 (1942), emphasizes the relatively inclusive character of balance of power policies. Cf. Lawrence, *Principles of International Law* 130–1 (7th ed., Winfield, 1928).

49. See Stowell, *Intervention in International Law* 63–6 (1921). See also Hodges, *The Doctrine of Intervention* 87–96 (1915); 1 Oppenheim, *International Law* 312–13 (8th ed., Lauterpacht, 1955) (hereinafter cited as Oppenheim-Lauterpacht); Thomas and Thomas, *Non-Intervention* 372–4 (1956). Garcia-Arias, "La intervención internacional por causa de humanidad," in *Foundamental [sic] Problems of International Law: Festschrift für Jean Spiropoulos* 163 (1957), stresses the inclusive nature of the purposes embodied in "humanitarian intervention."

50. Cf. the threefold categorization adopted in Haas and Whiting, *Dynamics*

coercion, it may be unusually hard to identify and distinguish demands of defense or "self-preservation" from demands of attack or "self-extension"; vehemently proclaimed objectives of "self-preservation" may in fact disguise the most ambitious projects of "self-extension"; and the characterization of demands in these terms is largely a function of the observer's definition of the material time sequence within which initiation and response are to be distinguished from each other. But difficult as it may be to draw a sharp line in theoretical construction between conservation and extension, and as susceptible to extravagant interpretation by partisan claimants as the distinction may be, the distinction which the world public order has long emphasized in past prescriptive formulation is important and will probably wisely continue to be emphasized until the world community is much more effectively organized.

RELATION TO THE PUBLIC ORDER OF THE ORGANIZED COMMUNITY

A participant may be observed to be exercising coercion in support of officials or organs of international governmental organizations or against them. Categorization of participants' objectives in these terms of course assumes that, in the particular instance of coercion considered, the decision-making process in such organization was successfully activated and has resulted in a decision, whether a formal

---

of International Relations 59–69 (1956): "self-preservation," "self-extension," and "self-abnegation"—a classification derived from Wolfers, "The Pole of Power and the Pole of Indifference," 4 *World Politics* 39, 50–63 (1951–1952). See also Morgenthau, *Politics Among Nations* 35–79 (2d rev. ed., 1954): "policy of the status quo," "imperialism," and "policy of prestige"; he concedes that the third is rarely sought for its own sake and is much more frequently pursued in support of either the first or the second type of policy.

Characterization of objectives of contending participants in terms of extension or conservation of values is in line with contemporary sociological conceptualizations of conflict which regard mutually exclusive or incompatible values as inevitable characteristics of conflict. Incompatibility of values is conceived of as arising from "position scarcity" and "resource scarcity." See Bernard, note 16 supra at 38, 41–2; Bernard, "Parties and Issues in Conflict," 1 *J. Conflict Resolution* 111, 113 (1957); Mack and Snyder, "The Analysis of Social Conflict: Toward an Overview and Synthesis," 1 id. at 212, 218–19. "Position scarcity" and "resource scarcity" seem especially observable in the earth arena where the entire land surface of the globe, except the Arctic and the Antarctic areas, have been so allocated among territorially based polities that terrestrial extension of one polity must always be at the expense of another.

"decision" or a "recommendation," with reference to which the objectives of specific participants may be examined for conformity or contrariety. So far as a participant other than those originally involved in the situation of coercion is concerned, conformity or contrariety to the decision would refer essentially to whether the new participant sided with the party determined, in the community decision, to be exercising lawful defense or "police action" or with the party identified as having impermissibly resorted to coercion. The action of the People's Republic of China, for instance, in joining the forces of the North Korean authorities against the Republic of Korea and other members of the United Nations, was an obvious contravention of the decision of the Security Council embodied in its resolution of June 27, 1950, urging assistance to the Republic of Korea.[51] In such cases, to inquire into the concordance of a participant's objectives with the world public order is implicitly to refer to that participant's identification structure.

Conditions

The conditions under which participants resort to and exercise coercion include all the variable and interacting component factors of a global power process in a world arena.[52] Such variables—or, more precisely, the participants' "images" or estimations of them[53]—affect and influence both the expectations of the participants as to whether, in any given configuration of events, they can more economically secure their objectives and value goals by coercion than by persuasion, and their expectations of the level and techniques of coercion required. A few of the more important variables on which an inquirer should focus will be suggested.

51. In Resolution 498(V), Feb. 1, 1951, the General Assembly found "that the Central People's Government of the People's Republic of China, by giving direct aid and assistance to those who were already committing aggression in Korea and by engaging in hostilities against United Nations forces there has itself engaged in aggression in Korea." *Y.B. of the United Nations 1951*, 224–5.

52. See Wright, "Design for a Research Project on International Conflicts and the Factors Causing Their Aggravation or Amelioration," 10 *Western Pol. Q.* 263, 269–70 (1957); Levi, "On the Causes of War and Conditions of Peace," 4 *J. Conflict Resolution* 411 (1960). Relevant broad perspectives are offered in Roberts, "The Nature of Contemporary Conflict," 2 *World Polity* 9 (1960).

53. Cf. Snyder, Bruck, and Sapin, *Decision-Making as an Approach to the Study of International Politics* 38 (1954).

The contemporary structure of the world arena—including the number, power, and posture of the participants—is clearly of prime importance. Until a few years ago it was customary to present a picture of a world moving rapidly toward the pattern of bipolarity, of power being more and more rigidly structured around the hostile poles of two giant or "superpowers." [54] In power and influence, all other nation-states were regarded as marginal or submarginal in relation to either of the two superpowers, and as orienting or tending to orient themselves firmly in policy and action toward one or the other pole of power. Recently, some observers have been able to speak of a "reversal," certainly at least a deceleration, of the trend toward bipolarism.[55] Amorphous, fluctuating, and unorganized groupings of "uncommitted" states have appeared which, by resisting pressures toward definite alignment and becoming objects of competitive attention and blandishment on the part of major powers, mutually inhibited by approximately equivalent nuclear capabilities, have acquired some mobility and freedom of action.[56] Whether, or to what

54. See, e.g., Goodrich and Simons, *The United Nations and the Maintenance of International Peace and Security* 23–44 (1955); Lasswell, *World Politics Faces Economics* 15 (1945); Morgenthau, *Politics Among Nations* 322–40 (2d rev. ed., 1954); Schwarzenberger, *Power Politics* 122–5 (2d rev. ed., 1951); Snyder and Furniss, *American Foreign Policy: Formulation, Principles and Programs* 579 (1954); Wright, *Problems of Stability and Progress in International Relations* 76, 115, 235, 268 (1954); Buehrig, "The United States, the United Nations and Bipolar Politics," 4 *Int. Orgànization* 573 (1950); De Luna, "Fundamentación del derecho internacional," 60 *Revista de Derecho Internacional* 210, 230–4 (Cuba, 1952); Fox, "The United Nations in the Era of Total Diplomacy," 5 *Int. Organization* 265 (1951); Lasswell, "The Prospects of Cooperation in a Bipolar World," 15 *U. Chi. L. Rev.* 877 (1948); Lasswell, "The Interrelations of World Organization and Society," 55 *Yale L. J.* 889 (1946); Schwarzenberger, "The Impact of the East-West Rift on International Law," 36 *Tr. Grotius Soc.* 229, 231–2 (1950).

55. Haas and Whiting (note 50 supra), at 530; Reitzel, Kaplan, and Coblenz, *United States Foreign Policy 1945–1955,* 317–18, 324, 425–6, 453–4, 457, 462 (1956). See also Lippmann, "Breakup of the Two-Power World," in *Foundations of National Power* 777 (2d ed., Sprout and Sprout, 1951); Morgenthau, "Neutrality and Neutralism," 11 *Y.B. of World Affairs* 47, 67 (1957).

56. Ibid. Recent comprehensive studies of the "uncommitted" states—most of which are also embraced in the terms "underdeveloped" and "modernizing"—include: *The Politics of the Developing Areas* (Almond and Coleman, 1960), and Emerson, *From Empire to Nation: The Rise to Self-Assertion of Asian and African Peoples* (1960). Efforts to organize the Arab world have included, and

extent, a countertrend toward diversification of the pattern of polarity has actually emerged is still hidden from sight. The basic fact remains, however, that the two major powers continue to confront and engage each other in hostile opposition, each seeking to match and balance every increment of power achieved by the other. The arena of interaction is still a military one: high levels of tension and insecurity and expectations both of catastrophic and of limited violence continue to prevail and deeply affect the perspectives and policies of all participants.[57]

The posture of each participant vis-à-vis every other participant is influenced, if not determined, by the relative inclusiveness or exclusiveness of their identifications—their definition and redefinition of each other as, in varying degree, an ally or an enemy or an "uncommitted." And the expectations of each as to the continuing relative fighting capabilities—described in terms of the combat "force-in-being," economic capacity, administrative competence, motivation for war and defense, and recuperative abilities [58]—of itself, of

---

indeed previously centered on, the establishment of the Arab League. See Ismail, "Regionalism in the Middle East: the Arab League" (unpublished thesis in Yale Law Library, 1955). See also Dib, *The Arab Bloc in the United Nations* cc. 4, 5 (1956). On the Afro-Asian bloc, particularly on the 1955 Bandung Conference, see Kahin, *The Asian-African Conference, Bandung, Indonesia, April 1955* (1956); Parkinson, "Bandung and the Underdeveloped Countries," 10 *Y.B. of World Affairs* 65 (1956).

57. "Precisely because national communities expect further international violence, they seem to have resigned themselves to the recurrence of war. . . . Thus the expectation of future violence is part and parcel of political consciousness. As long as this fatalistic mode of thought continues, no demonstration of interdependence can be expected to change national loyalties to devotion to a global system of values. Anticipation of violence seems to breed continued acceptance of national values and interests and not a desire to transcend them." Haas and Whiting, note 50 supra, at 18–19. See also *World Tension—The Psychopathology of International Relations* (Kisker, ed., 1951); Lasswell, *World Politics and Personal Insecurity* 52–74 (1935); Allport, "The Role of Expectancy," in *Tensions That Cause Wars* 43–78 (Cantril, ed., 1950). As to the possibilities of control of expectations of violence, see Lasswell, " 'Inevitable War': A Problem in the Control of Long-Range Expectations," 2 *World Politics* 1 (1949).

58. See Knorr, *The War Potential of Nations* (1956); Strausz-Hupé and Possony, *International Relations* 157–74 (2d ed., 1954); Knorr, "Military Potential in the Nuclear Age," in *Military Policy and National Security* 137–61 (Kaufmann, ed., 1956); Knorr, "The Concept of Economic Potential for War," 10 *World Politics* 49 (1957).

its allies, of its enemies and potential enemies, and of international policing agencies, are written large in its formulation and execution of strategy. The range or inclusiveness of a participant's identifications profoundly influence its decisions not only about resort to coercion but also about the conduct of coercion. Where a participant defines its opponent as an absolute enemy, one belonging to a different mankind whose gods are utterly false and as such completely excluded from its identification system, violence pitiless in its savagery may be expected unless reprisals are feared. An eminent publicist, who anticipated an insight furnished by contemporary studies on the sociology of war, wrote: "It is almost a truism to say that the mitigation of war must depend on the parties to it feeling that they belong to a larger whole than their respective tribes or states, a whole in which the enemy too is comprised, so that duties arising out of that larger citizenship are owed even to him." [59]

The expectations of participants as to the state of technology and techniques of coercion and violence available to themselves, their enemies, and their potential enemies obviously weigh heavily in their estimation of the probable costs of resorting or responding to coercion. The contemporary technology of military violence has yielded basic-energy weapons and delivery systems that perhaps have raised the possible costs of coercion to the annihilation of entire nations and the conversion of large portions of their territories into uninhabitable wastelands. Such may be the result of the type and degree of destruction those weapon systems have made possible,[60] the general

59. Westlake, *Collected Papers on Public International Law* 274 (Oppenheim, ed., 1914). See also Morgenthau, *Politics Among Nations* 219 (2d rev. ed., 1954); Renn, *Warfare: The Relation of War to Society* 20–1 (1939); Speier, *Social Order and the Risks of War* c. 18 (1952).

60. In an exercise conducted by the Federal Civil Defense Administration in which 250 "dirty" nuclear or thermonuclear weapons representing 2,500 megatons, with damage zones ranging from 3 to 5 miles, were "dropped" on cities, industrial targets, and airfields throughout the United States, "under a rather typical meteorological situation," the following estimations of effects on the population (based on 1950 population figures) were made:

	Dead	*Injured*	*Uninjured*
1st day	36,000,000	57,000,000	58,000,000
7th day	51,000,000	42,000,000	58,000,000
14th day	61,000,000	31,000,000	58,000,000
60th day	72,000,000	21,000,000	58,000,000

vulnerability to their use, the attractive possibilities they seem to offer of swiftly overwhelming the enemy's will or ability to resist by shattering bombardment of industrial and population centers, and the expressed willingness of the powers possessing them to carry out such massive nuclear bombardment.[61] Modern weapons, particularly those capable of massive destruction, underscore the enormous power differential between the major states which possess them and the smaller ones which do not; [62] the distribution of these weapons at once reflects and reinforces the structuring of power in the international arena. Future developments in weaponry, presaged by artificial satellites and rocket missiles, do not seem likely to eliminate that differential.[63] On the other hand, should the possession of "space-

---

See *Hearings before the Special Subcommittee on Radiation of the Joint Committee on Atomic Energy,* 85th Cong., 1st Sess., Pt. 1, at 92–6, 117–18 (1957); id. Pt. II, at 1539, 1549–63.

On the radiological effects on individuals of nuclear explosions see Brues, "Somatic Effects of Radiation," 14 *Bull. Atomic Scientists* 12 (1958); Libby, "Distribution and Effects of Fall-Out," 14 id. at 27; Neuman, "The Somatic Effects of Fission Products," 14 id. at 15; Rotblat, "Nuclear Weapons in War," 14 id. at 57.

On the genetic damage caused by atomic radiation see *Hearings,* supra, Pt. II, at 1564–87, 1827–52; Crow, "Genetic Effects of Radiation," 14 *Bull. Atomic Scientists* 19 (1958); Muller, "How Radiation Changes the Genetic Constitution," 11 id. at 329 (1955). See, further, "Report of the United Nations Scientific Committee on the Effects of Atomic Radiation," U.N. Gen. Ass., *Off. Rec.,* 13th Sess., Supp. No. 17 (A/3838) (1958).

61. See, e.g., the British White Paper on Defense, Feb. 13, 1958, where the British Government declared that in case the Western Powers are attacked by the Soviet Union, "even with conventional forces only," they would retaliate with strategic nuclear bombardment. *N.Y. Times,* Feb. 14, 1958, p. 1, cols. 2–3. See also the note sent by the Soviet Union to West Germany warning the latter that it would be a "veritable cemetery" in war if it uses nuclear arms or permits such arms to be stationed in its territory (id. April 28, 1957, p. 1, col. 5, p. 27, cols. 1–2).

62. Wright, *Problems of Stability and Progress in International Relations* 74, 312–13 (1954); Wright, "Modern Technology and the World Order," in *Technology and International Relations* 186 (Ogburn, ed., 1949). Surveys of the state of modern military weapon systems and techniques may be found in Bush, *Modern Arms and Free Men* 12–47 (1949); Baldwin, "The New Face of War," 12 *Bull. Atomic Scientists* 153 (1956); Sternberg, *The Military and Industrial Revolution of Our Time* (1959).

63. A recent possibility is that of employing techniques of weather control and modification as a weapon. H. T. Orville, Chairman, Advisory Committee on Weather Control, is reported to have said that weather control could have

weapons" become more widely diffused, even the ascertainment of the identity of the initiator of an attack may become extremely difficult for the target-state.[64]

Improvements in the means of applying coercion have not, of course, been limited to the field of military weapons. Refinements in the techniques of economic pressure, and of propaganda and subversion, as well as relative capability and vulnerability in respect of their use, form part of the complex of factors conditioning participants' expectations of the value costs of exercising coercion.

Attention may also be appropriately focussed on the major trends observable in the world social process which affect, and are themselves affected by, the pursuit by nation-states of power and other values through coercion.[65] Among the more obvious of these trends is the increase in frequency and intensity of contact and interaction among peoples made possible by the modern inventions in communication and transportation, which have drastically shrunk physical, economic, and strategic distances between states and fostered the rapid diffusion and unification of material culture.[66] This trend has

---

results more disastrous than atomic discoveries. *N. Y. Times,* Jan. 28, 1958, p. 19, cols. 5–6. Dr. H. G. Houghton of the Massachusetts Institute of Technology has stated that "international control of weather modification will be as essential to the safety of the world as control of nuclear energy is now." Houghton, "Other Aspects of Weather Modification: Present Position and Future Possibilities of Weather Control," in 2 *U.S. Advisory Comm. on Weather Control, Final Report* 286, 288 (1957).

64. Such a situation would present obvious difficulties in the determination of responsibility for aggression. The Indian representative to the Sixth Committee pointed out that "one of the key questions which arose in any attempt to define aggression was to find out who had attacked first. In an atomic war, quick action gave a decisive advantage and it had become extremely difficult, if not impossible, to determine who had made the first move. New developments in science had a tendency to alter old established notions, and had raised new problems of great complexity." U.N. Doc. No. A/C.6/SR.520, at 13 (1957).

65. See Stone, "International Law and Contemporary Social Trends: Some Reflections," 29 *Rocky Mt. L. Rev.* 149 (1957). Davis, "Identification of Fundamental Social Changes Which Condition Inter-Nation Relations" (International Relations Conference, Northwestern University, April, 1959, mimeographed) deals with changes and trends observable within and among nations. Deutsch, "Toward an Inventory of Basic Trends and Patterns in Comparative and International Politics," 54 *Am. Pol. Sci. Rev.* 34 (1960) offers one way of specifying and quantifying component variables.

66. E.g. Mende, *World Power in the Balance,* c. 2 (1953); Mitrany, *Progress of International Government* 101, 115 (1933); Staley, *World Economy in Transi-*

in turn contributed to and probably accelerated the rising unity of demand among peoples everywhere for wider participation in the production and sharing of all values and for opportunity so to participate free from coercion and apprehensions of coercion.[67] A somewhat parallel trend is manifested in the growing interdependence of the same peoples in the attainment of their demanded values.[68] The fact of interdependence is exhibited in every value-institutional process: power interacts with power throughout the world arena, with wealth, enlightenment, respect and every other value; wealth interacts with wealth, power and all other values, and so on.[69] The patterns and degrees of interdependence in the international system, and the resulting aggravated sensitivity of the entire structure of that system,[70] must affect the estimates by participants of the probable value costs of coercion and violence.

---

tion 3–20 (1939); Woytinsky and Woytinsky, *World Commerce and Governments* c. 7 (1955); 1 Wright, *A Study of War* 204–8 (1942); 2 id. at 1241–6; Angell, "International Communication and the World Society," in *The World Community* 145 (Wright, ed., 1948); Brown, "Science, Technology and International Relations," in *The Changing Environment of International Relations* 19 (1956); Hart, "Technology and the Growth of Political Areas," in *Technology and International Relations* 28 (Ogburn, ed., 1949); Leigh, "The Mass-Communications Inventions and International Relations," in id. at 126; Ogburn, "Aviation and International Relations," in id. at 86; Wright, "Modern Technology and the World Order," in id. at 174.

67. See, e.g., Wright, *Contemporary International Law: A Balance Sheet* 6 (1955); 1 Wright, *A Study of War* 170–81 (1942); Kirk, "Mass Aspirations and International Relations," in *The Changing Environment of International Relations* 1 (1956); Berle, "The Peace of Peoples," 77 *Hague Recueil* 1 (1950); Lasswell, "The Interrelations of World Organization and Society," 55 *Yale L. J.* 889, 903–8 (1946).

68. See Eagleton, *International Government* 7–12 (3d ed., 1957); Eagleton, *The Forces That Shape Our Future* 9–29 (1945); Haas and Whiting, *Dynamics of International Relations* 1–10 (1956); Kalijarvi, *Modern World Politics* c. 8 (3d ed., 1953); Levi, *Fundamentals of World Organization* c. 3 (1950); Muir, *The Interdependent World and Its Problems* (1933); Commission To Study the Organization of Peace, "Fourth Report," 396 *Int. Conciliation* 97–101 (1944); Cole, "International Economic Interdependence," 369 id. at 240 (1941).

69. For detailed exposition, see McDougal and Lasswell, "World Community and Law: A Contemporary International Law," c. 9 (mimeographed materials, Yale Law School, 1955).

70. "[T]he interdependence of all its parts makes the modern order much more sensitive than a simpler form of economic organization. Indeed, the more

Increased interaction, expanding uniformity of material culture, rising common demands, and interdependence might be supposed to be leading eventually toward a world of greater integration, freedom, peace, and abundance. The fact is, however, that there are at least equally conspicuous trends—stimulated by chronic tensions, insecurity, and expectations of violence—of ever greater centralization and concentration of power within the state apparatus, of increasingly comprehensive governmentalization and regimentation, of intensifying politicization of all internal value processes.[71] These trends, which vitally affect many of the detailed policies of the law of war, may, by hardening national frontiers into walls of insulation and thereby establishing conditions which have been described as the "nationalization of truth" and the "breakdown of human communication," [72] effectively counter and nullify the forces moving toward integration and cooperation. The problem of regulating international coercion and violence may well be, in its most fundamental aspect, one of controlling, decelerating, and reversing these fractionalizing trends.

Methods

The methods by which participants engage each other in coercion to effect the realization of their objectives include all the contemporary instruments of policy, employed in varying combination and sequence and with constantly changing—not simply dichotomous—degrees of intensity. These instruments or types of strategy may be

---

minutely the individual parts of a large mechanism fit into one another, and the more closely the single elements are bound up together, the more serious are the repercussions of even the slightest disturbance. . . . [I]n the world economy of the present day overproduction in one market becomes the misfortune of other markets. The political insanity of one country determines the fate of others . . . since the interdependence of the modern social organism transmits the effects of every maladjustment with increased intensity." Mannheim, *Man and Society in an Age of Reconstruction* 50 (1950).

71. See Lasswell, *The World Revolution of Our Time* 36–9 (1951); Lasswell, *The Analysis of Political Behavior* 146–57 (1948); Wright, *Problems of Stability and Progress in International Relations* 150, 273–4, 300–1 (1954). See also Ayala, "Liberty, Security and Modern Technology," 2 *Int. Soc. Sci. Bull.* 326 (1950).

72. Stone, *Legal Controls* xli–xliii; Stone, "Of Sociological Inquiries Concerning International Law," in *Foundamental* [sic] *Problems of International Law: Festschrift für Jean Spiropoulos* 411, 414, 418–19 (1957); Stone, "International Law and International Society," 30 *Canadian Bar Rev.* 164, 170–1 (1952).

conveniently categorized according to the distinctive means employed (negotiation, words, goods, or arms) and the distinctive effects sought (the unity or disunity of elites or of masses, abundance or scarcity, protection or destruction).[73] The resulting categories permit distinction between the diplomatic, the ideological, the economic, and the military instruments. Each of these instruments may obviously be used either singly or in combination with any or all of the others to achieve the desired level of coercion.

The diplomatic instrument has traditionally been concerned with the characteristic channels and rituals of inter-elite or inter-official communications and negotiations.[74] The coercive impact of a use of diplomacy may be the direct result of the content of the communication conveyed: the communication may contain a threat of grievous deprivations, exemplified by Nazi Germany's threat in 1939 to destroy Prague by bombardment from the air unless President Hacha accepted immediate German occupation of the Czech state.[75] It may, on the other hand, be the net effect of complex diplomatic strategy designed to isolate or encircle the target-state by securing from third states either agreements to support the initiator-state [76] or by inducing them to withdraw or withhold support from the target.[77]

73. McDougal and Lasswell, "World Community and Law: A Contemporary International Law," c. 9 (mimeographed materials, Yale Law School, 1955).

74. See, generally, *The Diplomats 1919–1939* (Craig and Gilbert, ed., 1953); Haas and Whiting, note 68 supra c. 7; Mowat, *Diplomacy and Peace* (1935); Nicolson, *The Evolution of Diplomatic Method* (1954); Nicolson, *Diplomacy* (2d ed., 1950); Satow, *A Guide to Diplomatic Practice* (4th ed., 1957); Strausz-Hupé and Possony, *International Relations* c. 10 (2d ed., 1954); Wellesley, *Diplomacy in Fetters* (1944). On communist techniques of diplomacy, see *Negotiating with the Russians* (Dennett and Johnson ed., 1951); Joy, *How Communists Negotiate* (1955); and Vatcher, *Panmunjom: The Story of the Korean Military Armistice Negotiations* (1958).

75. 3 *Survey of International Affairs 1938*, 266–9 (Royal Institute of Int. Affairs, 1953), contains an account of Hacha's interview with Hitler.

76. E.g. the efforts of the French Ambassador to Moscow in 1936–1938 to secure a tight military alliance between France and the Soviet Union to contain Nazi Germany. *The Diplomats 1919–1939* c. 18 (Craig and Gilbert, ed., 1953).

77. The efforts of Premier Bulganin to weaken the NATO alliance by sending diplomatic notes to each of the members containing pointed reminders of their vulnerability to nuclear retaliatory blows, which efforts apparently stimulated a "neutralist trend" among some members, afford recent illustration. *N. Y. Times*, Dec. 15, 1957, p. 34, cols. 1–2; id. Dec. 18, 1957, p. 1, col. 7.

Some measure of coercion may perhaps be achieved by the denial or withdrawal of access to internal arenas of authority through the refusal of recognition or the suspension or termination of diplomatic relations. Here, however, the coercion effectively exerted on the target-state may be so slight as to be largely "symbolic" and nominal.

The use of the ideological instrument commonly involves the selective manipulation and circulation of symbols, verbal or nonverbal, calculated to alter the patterns of identifications, demands, and expectations of mass audiences in the target-state and thereby to induce or stimulate politically significant attitudes and behavior favorable to the initiator-state.[78] It includes, in combination with other instruments, all the techniques of propaganda, infiltration, subversion, and *coup d'état* which have been refined and developed to such high efficiency as to have given rise to repeated proposals to condemn their use for certain objectives as a distinct form or mode of aggression.[79] The particular shape of ideological strategy will of course depend on the definition of the target as ally, enemy, or "uncommitted." Specific strategies may include the creation and fomentation of attitudes oriented toward abstention or withdrawal from a hostile

78. See Murty, "The International Regulation of the Ideological Instrument of Coercion" (unpublished thesis in Yale Law Library, 1957); Haas and Whiting, note 68 supra c. 9; Lasswell, *Propaganda Technique in the World War* (1927); *Propaganda in War and Crisis* (Lerner, ed., 1951); Lerner, *Sykewar: Psychological Warfare against Germany D-Day to V-E Day* (1949); Linebarger, *Psychological Warfare* (2d ed., 1954); Dovring, *Road of Propaganda: The Semantics of Biased Communication* (1959); Speier, *Social Order and the Risks of War* cc. 26, 27, 29, 32 (1952); Strausz-Hupé and Possony, *International Relations* cc. 17–19 (2d ed., 1954); Ferreus, "The Menace of Communist Psychological Warfare," 1 *Orbis* 97 (1957); Lasswell, "Propaganda," 12 *Encyc. Soc. Sci.* 521 (1934); Speier, "International Political Communication: Elite v. Mass," 4 *World Politics* 305 (1952).

79. See, e.g., the draft definition of aggression by the Soviet Union submitted to the 1956 Special Committee on the Question of Defining Aggression, U.N. Doc. No. A/AC. 77/L.13, Annex II, at 1–3 (1957) (distinguishing between "indirect" and "ideological aggression"); the definition drafted by China, id. Annex I, at 8–9; the definition submitted by Bolivia to the 1953 Special Committee, id. Annex I, at 10; the definition proposed by the Philippines to Committee III of the Third Commission of the 1945 San Francisco Conference, Secretary-General, "Question of Defining Aggression," U.N. Doc. No. A/2211, par. 115 (1952); and Arts. 2(5), (6), "Draft Code of Offenses against the Peace and Security of Mankind," International Law Comn., 3d Sess., Report, U.N. Gen. Ass., *Off. Rec.*, 6th Sess., Supp. No. 9, par. 9 (A/1858) (1951).

policy or toward cooperation with or incorporation in the initiator state. They may also include the incitation of the audience to the violent reconstruction of the elite structure or the decision-making process in the target-state.[80] The highly emotionalized appeals for the overthrow and assassination of the King of Jordan which the Egyptian radio and press directed to the Jordanian people are among the more recent instances of such a strategy.[81] So-called "propaganda of the deed" may range from an offer and shipment of relief goods in case of disaster to the carefully timed announcement or demonstration of new weapons.[82]

The employment of economics as an instrument of coercive policy may, in broad statement, be described as the management of access to a flow of goods, services, and money, as well as to markets, with the end of denying the target-state such access while maintaining it for oneself. All the familiar methods of economic warfare developed in the last two world wars may be included, such as the blocking or freezing of the target's assets; the imposition of import and export embargoes, total or selective; blacklisting of foreign firms and individuals who deal with the target-state; drying up of foreign supplies by preclusive buying; control of re-exportation from a nonparticipant's territory; and control of shipping through selective admission to credit, insurance, stores, fuel, port and repair facilities.[83] These by no means exhaust the available economic techniques of exercising coercion. The monetary system of the target-state may be substan-

80. See Murty, note 78 supra cc. 2, 7.

81. See *N. Y. Times,* Nov. 9, 1957, p. 1, col. 4. The Egyptian appeals gave rise to demonstrations in Damascus, Syria, by Palestine refugees calling for the death of the King of Jordan (id. Nov. 12, 1957, p. 1, col. 6).

82. See Brodie, "Military Demonstration and Disclosure of New Weapons," 5 *World Politics* 281 (1953).

83. Detailed accounts of these techniques may be found in Bailey, *The Policy of the United States towards Neutrals, 1917–1918* (1942); Basch, *The New Economic Warfare* (1941); Einzig, *Economic Warfare 1939–1940* (1941); Gordon and Dangerfield, *The Hidden Weapon: The Story of Economic Warfare* (1947); Jack, *Studies in Economic Warfare* (1941); Medlicott, *The Economic Blockade,* Vol. 1 (1952), Vol. 2 (1959); Ritchie, *The Navicert System during the World War* (1938); Siney, *The Allied Blockade of Germany 1914–1916* (1957); Wu, *Economic Warfare* (1952); Medlicott, "Economic Warfare," in *The War and the Neutrals, Survey of International Affairs 1939–1946,* 1–104 (Royal Institute of Int. Affairs, 1956). Welton, *The Third World War: Trade and Industry—The New Battleground* (1959).

tially impaired by skillful manipulation of foreign exchange markets, withdrawal or refusal of credits, dumping of large quantities of currency to compel the target-state to pay in gold; by psychological methods calculated to cast doubt on the target-state's ability or willingness to pay; and by simple counterfeiting of its currency.[84] Other techniques include the creation of artificial scarcity and high prices and the retarding of technological development through cartelization schemes and the control of patents,[85] the refusal to grant loans or to pay for previous loans, and, of course, the taking, expropriation, or confiscation of enterprises and property of nationals of the target country. In the last category, a fairly recent striking example is the taking over or "supervision" of banks, factories, plantations, commercial establishments, and other properties of Dutch nationals by the government of Indonesia,[86] in apparent retaliation for the refusal of the Netherlands to transfer sovereignty over West New Guinea. One other variety of economic strategy that deserves particular mention is the granting or witholding of "foreign aid." Foreign aid programs may be provided with mechanisms of donor control: the initial grant of money, goods, technical assistance, or military arms, and the subsequent continuation of the flow, may be made contingent upon the accommodation or coordination of the recipient's policies with those of the donor.[87] Foreign aid and foreign investment may perhaps also

84. Strausz-Hupé and Possony, *International Relations* 509–16 (2d ed., 1954).

85. Wu, *Economic Warfare* 146–84 (1952).

86. *N. Y. Times,* Dec. 10, 1957, p. 1, col. 3.

87. See Haas and Whiting, *Dynamics of International Relations* 233–42 (1956). See also the Mutual Defense Assistance Control Act, 65 Stat. 644 (1951), 22 U.S.C. § 1611 (1952), which declares it to be the "policy of the United States that no military, economic, or financial assistance shall be supplied to any nation unless it applies an embargo on such shipments [of strategic materials] to any nation or combination of nations threatening the security of the United States, including the Union of Soviet Socialist Republics and all countries under its domination." The act requires the termination of all military, economic, or financial assistance to any nation that "knowingly permits" such shipment; however, the President may direct the continuation of aid, if the shipments are not of "arms, ammunition, implements of war, and atomic energy materials" and if he determines that "cessation of aid would clearly be detrimental to the security of the United States." Once terminated, aid can be resumed "only upon determination of the President that adequate measures have been taken by the nation concerned." No case has occurred where a recipient of United States aid intentionally exported arms, ammunitions, or atomic materials to the Soviet Bloc.

be managed to effect the penetration and reorientation and conceivably the eventual capture of the economic and political structure of the recipient.[88]

While substantial degrees of coercion may be achieved by the skilled utilization of the diplomatic, ideological, and economic instruments, the attainment of the maximum intensity of coercion normally requires the supplementation of such instruments with military force. Contemporary military weapons and weapon systems are unique in at least two aspects. They present a wide spectrum of degrees of destructive capability: in terms of the number of men one man can kill by a single operation, the range is from one-to-one weapons such as bayonets and pistols, to weapons of theoretically unlimited capability such as thermonuclear explosives and biological weapons.[89] The other aspect relates to the high degree of mechanization and automatism of modern weapons, presently exemplified par excellence in the long-range ballistic missile, and to the tendencies toward the "depersonalization" of the process of violence and the "dehumanizing" of armies that flow from the interposition of space and mechanical-automatic devices between the attacker and his target.[90] Both the vast destructiveness and the depersonalization of

---

The Strategic Trade Control System 1948–1956, 12 (Ninth Report to Congress on Operations under the Mutual Defense Assistance Control Act of 1951, 1957).

On the difficulties of insulating foreign aid programs from the rest of the foreign policy of the donor or grantor country, see Schelling, "American Aid and Economic Development: Some Critical Issues," in *International Stability and Progress* 121 (1957). On the objectives of United States foreign aid programs see *U.S. Foreign Aid* 11–56 (McClellan, ed., 1957). Perhaps the best recent treatment is Liska, *The New Statecraft: Foreign Aid in American Foreign Policy* (1960).

It hardly needs to be added that provision for donor or grantor control does not pre-empt the character of the objectives sought by the donor or grantor, which may be entirely legitimate legally and morally.

88. Cf. Strausz-Hupé and Possony, *International Relations* 516–19 (2d ed., 1954). See also Knorr, *Ruble Diplomacy: Challenge to American Foreign Aid* (Center of International Studies, Memorandum No. 10, 1956); Parkinson, "Soviet Aid to Under-developed Countries," 11 *Y.B. of World Affairs* 184 (1957); Berliner, *Soviet Economic Aid: The New Aid and Trade Policy in Underdeveloped Countries* (1958).

89. Cf. Morgenthau, *Politics Among Nations* 351–2 (2d rev. ed., 1954).

90. Stone, *Legal Controls* 339; cf. Nef, *War and Human Progress* 371–4 (1950); Liddell Hart, *The Revolution in Warfare* 32–7 (1947). "The multiplica-

the process of military violence may be expected to affect significantly many of the fundamental policies of the law of war. For instance, the further diminution of face-to-face confrontation between contending troops may result in the reduction of the "principle of chivalry" to vestigial import for all save the historian of the law of war.[91]

From the foregoing brief and impressionistic references to the categories of means of policy, it should be evident that many varying intensities of coercion may be obtained, and that various types and degrees of destruction will result, from differing uses of different instruments or combinations of instruments. The possible range is from the mildest to the most intense coercion, from minor damage to the prestige of the opponent state, for instance, to its permanent physical liquidation. The intensity of the coercion which a participant applies and the level of destruction that it seeks or secures bear a close relation to the nature and scope of the objectives it sets for itself. The relationship is approximately one of direct proportionality: the more comprehensive and ambitious the objective is, the higher tend to be both the degree of intensity of coercion which must be applied and the level of destruction effected to achieve such objective, for the greater will be the target's resistance.[92] Participants

---

tion of machinery has sterilized the romance of war, by diminishing the value of human qualities. Courage and skill are of little avail against a superiority of machinery" (id. at 117). The process of depersonalization of the means of war started with the discovery of gunpowder which marked the beginning of "the technological epoch of war, the hidden impulse of which is the elimination of the human element both physically and morally, intellect alone remaining." Fuller, *Armament and History* 77 (1945).

91. Cf. Stone, *Legal Controls* 337.

92. This is one of the principal lessons to be derived from Clausewitz's thinking, which stressed that the political objective must dominate and delimit both the immediate military aim and the military effort. Clausewitz wrote: "The smaller the sacrifice we demand from our adversary, the slighter we may expect his efforts to be to refuse it to us. The slighter, however, his effort, the smaller need our own be. Furthermore, the less important our political object, the less will be the value we attach to it and the readier we shall be to abandon it. For this reason also our efforts will be the lighter. Thus the political object as the original motive of the war will be the standard alike for the aim to be attained by military action and for the efforts required for this purpose." Clausewitz, *On War* 9 (Jolles, trans., 1943).

Cf. Maurice, *British Strategy: A Study of the Application of the Principles of War* 73 (1929): "War being a political act, the political object must govern the

ordinarily tend to apply a degree of coercion and quantum of destruction roughly proportionate to the scope of their objective and the value they assign to it. The obvious implication for legal policy would seem to be that limitation of the degree of coercion and destruction depends in great measure upon limitation of objectives.[93]

Apart from the corporal dissolution sought by Rome and inflicted by Scipio on Carthage, it is difficult to point to historical examples of totally unlimited belligerent objectives and applications of the absolute maximum of destruction. Some instances may be noted, however, where the objectives of participants and the degree of destruction they applied approached the upper extremes of theoretical ranges of comprehensiveness and intensity: the wars of Genghis Khan, the religious wars of the sixteenth and seventeenth centuries, the French Revolutionary and Napoleonic wars, and the two world wars furnish ready examples. Where the objective is more modestly defined and valued and where violent destruction is not specified as an end in itself, the coercive use of instruments of policy is commonly designed not to destroy the enemy but rather to modify the expectations entertained by the effective decision-makers in the enemy state and to create new expectations of net advantage in adopting the policies demanded by the acting participant.[94] Prominent among the

---

other objects of war. The political object may be such as to require the complete conquest of the enemy; or it may be obtained if the enemy is compelled to sue for peace on terms satisfactory to the Government; or the object may be to induce other powers to join as allies; or it may be to cause the enemy to abandon the purpose for which he went to war. Each of these objects influences variously the amount of force required to gain the object and the method of employing that force." Maurice offers historical examples of the operation of this principle, id. at 73–6. See also Corbett, *Some Principles of Maritime Strategy* cc. 3, 4 (1919); Liddell Hart, *Strategy* cc. 21–2, especially at 369–70 (1954); Nickerson, *Can We Limit War?* 32–3 (1934).

This lesson from Clausewitz on the predominance of the political objective has not been lost on Soviet political and military strategists. See Garthoff, *Soviet Military Doctrine* 12–13 (1953).

93. "The decisive limitation upon war is the limitation of the objectives of war." Osgood, *Limited War: The Challenge to American Strategy* 4 (1957). See also Furniss, *American Military Policy* 114, 127–30 (1957); Kissinger, *Nuclear Weapons and Foreign Policy* 87, 140–1 (1957); Kaufmann, "Limited Warfare," in *Military Policy and National Security* 102, 126–7 (Kaufmann, ed., 1956); Brodie, "More about Limited War," 10 *World Politics* 112 (1957).

94. The Spanish-American War of 1898 and the Russo-Japanese War of 1904–

motivations of participants is, of course, a desire not to provoke retaliatory destruction which necessarily raises the costs of achieving an objective. Coercion and destruction in excess of the amount necessary to reconstruct the expectation structure of the enemy elite represent inefficient and wasted expenditures of force and constitute an invitation to costly retaliation. Underlying the processes of coercion is a fundamental principle of economy. Concise exposition of this principle is offered by Professor Osgood:

> It [the principle of economy of force] prescribes that in the use of armed force as an instrument of national policy no greater force should be employed than is necessary to achieve the objectives toward which it is directed; or, stated in another way, the dimensions of military force should be proportionate to the value of the objectives at stake.[95]

1905 have been suggested as examples of the limitation of war by restriction of political objectives. Nickerson, *Can We Limit War?* 32 (1934). The Korean war of 1950 is another, more recent, illustration.

95. Osgood, note 93 supra at 18. Cf. the particularized application of "economy of force," as a principle of military strategy and tactics in Garthoff, *Soviet Military Doctrine* c. 7 (1953); Maurice, note 92 supra c. 6; Brown, "The Principles of War," 75 *U.S. Naval Institute Proc.* 621, 630–1 (1949); Preston, Wise and Werner, *Men in Arms: A History of Warfare and its Interrelationships with Western Society,* "Introduction" (1956).

The specific limitations imposed upon conduct by application of a principle of economy in force must vary with both purpose and the segment of time into which purpose is projected. Force that is unnecessary for a limited objective may be necessary for a more comprehensive objective, and force that is economic in the short run may be most uneconomic in the long run.

The objection is sometimes made that a formulation in terms of economy in force lacks realism because it assumes that men act only from rational and conscious expectations and do not err. The usefulness of a principle of economy in force is not, however, dependent upon any such assumption. It may be agreed that men act from unconscious as well as conscious motivation, that they often err, and indeed that all events are subject to an unknown degree of chance variation. The only assumption necessary to the usefulness of a formulation in terms of economy in force is the assumption that men may, by modification of their conscious attitudes, in some measure anticipate through time the probable effects of alternative courses of action and thus either maximize their gains or minimize their losses. See Bross, *Design for Decision* (1953); Knight, *Risk, Uncertainty and Profit* (1921); Sprout and Sprout, *Man-Milieu Relationship Hypotheses in the Context of International Politics* (1956).

The usefulness of formulations in terms of economy in force extends to vari-

To the student of history, the coincidence of "economy of force" as an underlying principle of the rational application of coercion with "military necessity" as a basic principle of the law of war will be apparent.[95A]

Claims

It is, of course, the claims and counterclaims the contending participants make against each other about the lawfulness or unlawfulness of their various coercive practices which are of most immediate and detailed concern to an inquiry into law. For it is these opposing claims as to the requirements of authority which, in many differing

---

ous intellectual tasks. Past applications of coercion may be described in terms of the actors' objectives and calculations of proportionality, and comparison may be made of effects achieved. The hypothesis of economy in action for the maximization of gains and minimization of losses may also be applied to processes of coercion, as of persuasion, to stimulate comprehensive and detailed inquiry about variables in context which do in fact affect choices. Formulations in terms of economy in force, specifically related to community perspectives both of purpose and proportionality, may, further, be projected into the future as appropriate criteria for authoritative decision. Whatever successes the law of war has in the past achieved, and there have been some, are testimony to the efficacy of this effort.

It is sometimes suggested that men shape the proportion of their violence not so much from perspectives of economy, or of humanitarianism, as from fear of reprisals. The short answer is that minimizing risks of reprisal is precisely an aspect of economy in force. An application of force that results in the applier's sustaining retaliatory destruction can scarcely be described as economic. In terms of effects upon the humanitarian goals we recommend, moreover, it does not matter too much whether decision to limit destruction is based upon calculation of long-term self-interest, whether for preserving potential assets or minimizing risks of retaliation, or upon humanitarianism for fellow man. The contemporary world arena is so tight that none of the scorpions is likely to forget the danger from the others or entirely to ignore a practical humanitarianism which includes the self. To have the prescription and application of law dependent upon a nice interrelation of reciprocities and potential retaliations is no new-found invention. Malinowski, *Crime and Custom in Savage Society* (1926). The fact that the same participants in the world arena who on some occasions are belligerents are on other occasions authoritative decision-makers merely facilitates the transformation of the principle by which self-interest is calculated into the community expectations about common interest which are called international law.

95A. Perceptive comment on this point is made in O'Brien, "Legitimate Military Necessity in Nuclear War," 2 *World Polity* 35, 55–7 (1960).

particular contexts, constitute the specific controversies to which authoritative decision-makers must respond in search of resolution. A categorization of such claims must therefore be achieved which will enable an inquirer to identify both uniquely applicable policies and uniquely determining conditioning or explanatory factors in the recurring types of controversy. For tentative working purposes, the following sevenfold set of broad groupings, which move from the initiation through the management to the termination of coercion, is suggested. The focus is primarily upon the military instrument, and claims are paired in terms of assertion and opposition.

INITIATION OF COERCION

In this type of problem [96] the primary claim is that, in order to achieve objectives, coercion of high intensity, which ordinarily means the destructive use of the military instrument, may lawfully be initiated. Frequently, it may be more accurate to speak of a claim lawfully to intensify drastically the degree of coercion already being applied by and between the claimant and the target. The opposing claim is that such anterior coercion or intensification is not lawful and that unlawful violence gives a right to respond in self-defense with counterviolence.

PARTICIPATION IN COERCION

Here, two types of problems are posed by two distinguishable sets of opposing claims. In the first set, one claim is that states other than the initiator and the target, as members of international governmental organizations, are required to, or may lawfully, participate in community action organized to repress coercion and violence designated as unlawful. This is opposed by the claim that nonparticipation in community intervention, "neutrality," is permissible. In the second set, the claim that third states which escape involvement refrain from participation in augmenting the bases of the enemy's war-making power is paired against the claim that participants refrain from interfering with the nationals, resources, and operations of non-participants.

96. Our reference here is to the fact of resort to coercion. In Ch. 2, we seek to show that there is really no separate general legal policy problem of initiation or commencement of war as that problem has been commonly conceived and dealt with by commentators in the past. In Ch. 3, we deal comprehensively with the problems of resort to coercion.

MANAGEMENT OF COMBAT SITUATIONS

The problems here are created by the opposing claims of the contending belligerents about the detailed modalities of the violence by which they seek forcibly to deprive each other, by capture or destruction, of bases of power and to secure compliance with terms. In more detail, the claim is to apply a certain quantum of violence through the employment of certain combatants and certain weapons in certain areas of operation against certain objects of attack. The countering claim is that such violence is unnecessary, disproportionate, or pointless, and therefore inhuman and unlawful, or in corresponding detail that certain persons are illegitimate combatants, that certain weapons are not permissible, that combat operations may not be conducted in certain areas, and that certain objects are legally immune from attack and capture or destruction.

CAPTURED ENEMY TERRITORY

The set of contraposed claims here consists, on the one hand, of the claim to control and utilize enemy territory, captured through successful combat, as well as the peoples and resources there situated, and thereby to sustain and augment the captor's own means of carrying on combat in other still unoccupied areas; on the other hand is the claim that the loyalties, human dignity, private property, relationships, and fundamental institutions of peoples in the captured territory be respected and maintained.

CAPTURED ENEMY PERSONNEL

The captor state's claim is to control and utilize captured enemy personnel so as to secure their continued neutralization as elements of enemy power and to promote the captor's own war effort. The claim in opposition is for maintenance and protection of the lives, well-being, and loyalties of such personnel.

MANAGEMENT OF NONCOMBAT SITUATIONS

The principal claim of participants is so to define, control, and utilize "enemy" persons and property in their respective territory as to maximize their own capabilities for exercising violence and to ensure against secret utilization by the enemy. The broad negating claim is that the loyalties, property, and other human rights of the "enemy" persons in a belligerent's control be recognized and respected.

TERMINATION OF COERCION

On this concluding type of problem, the major contraposed claims include, on one side, claims that the process of coercion has been authoritatively terminated and the contending participants disengaged, that captured bases of power, personnel, and resources must be restored, and that relations between participants be "normalized" by resumption of the process of persuasion and friendly intercourse. The claims on the other side may be generally to continue coercive practices, in varying degrees of deceleration, to retain control over captured enemy personnel, resources, and other fruits of coercion, to establish controls on the defeated participant, and to recoup the costs of coercion. The duration of the termination phase or the rate of deceleration of coercion, and the precise claims and counterclaims asserted in such phase, may be deeply affected not only by the nature of the objectives which the successful participants sought but also by their expectations as to the emerging configurations of power in the world arena. The years since 1945 have amply shown that the termination phase may coincide with the initial stages of a new cycle of coercion during which may take place a reinterpretation of identifications and objectives by the successful participants and a realignment and regrouping that may cut across the lines drawn in the preceding process.

THE PROCESS OF DECISION

The process of legal decision through which the world public order seeks to subject coercion to community controls may, like the factual process of coercion, be perhaps most conveniently and comprehensively described in terms of certain established decision-makers, seeking certain common objectives, under all the varying conditions of the world arena, by the employment of certain methods or procedures in the prescription and application of authoritative community policy.

Decision-Makers

The authoritative decision-makers established by the public order of the world community for resolving controversies about international coercion are substantially the same as those established for other—"peacetime"—problems. Reflecting the decentralized structure of decision-making in the international community, they include not only the officials of international governmental organizations and judges of international courts and military and arbitration tribunals but also the officials of nation-states, whether participant or non-participant in the coercion process. Such authorized nation-state officials who respond to claims to exercise coercion may of course be the same officials who, at other times and in another capacity, assert claims to apply coercion; they may alternately be claimants making claims on their own behalf and decision-makers assessing the claims of others. This dualism in role and function,[97] in a decentralized and primitively organized arena, permits reciprocity to operate as a sanctioning procedure and promotes recognition of the common interest in self-restraint. Conspicuous among decision-makers is, of course, the military commander who must on occasion, and at least in the first instance, pass upon the lawfulness both of his own proposed measures and of measures being taken against him.[98]

97. See Georges Scelle's conception of the dual capacity—*dédoublement fonctionnel*—of officials of states: as organs of their respective national communities and as organs of the international community. Scelle, "Le Phénomène juridique du dédoublement fonctionnel," in *Rechtsfragen der Internationalen Organisation: Festschrift für Hans Wehberg* 324 (1956). Cf. Kelsen's notion that "states as acting persons are organs of international law, or of the community constituted by it," a notion tied up with the "dynamic decentralization of the universal legal order," i.e. the fact that "general international law does not establish any special organs working according to the principle of the division of labor" but instead "leaves it to the parties to a controversy to ascertain whether one of them is responsible for a delict, as the other claims, and to decide upon, and execute, the sanction." Kelsen, *General Theory of Law and State* 327, 351 (1945). See also Kelsen, *Collective Security under International Law* 12, 38 (1957); Kelsen, *Principles of International Law* 21, 25 (1952); Gross, "States as Organs of International Law and the Problem of Autointerpretation," in *Law and Politics in the World Community* 59, 67, 70–4 (Lipsky, ed., 1953).

98. See, e.g., Department of the Army, *The Law of Land Warfare* par. 497(d) (FM 27–10, 1956), which requires commanding officers to assume responsibility for retaliative measures "when an unscrupulous enemy leaves no other recourse against the repetition of unlawful acts." The decision of the commander to resort to reprisals "may subsequently be found to have been wholly unjustified," in which case the responsible officer subjects himself to "punishment for a violation of the law of war." A similar provision is found in Department of the Navy, *The Law of Naval Warfare* par. 301(a) (1955); see Tucker, *The Law of War and Neutrality at Sea* 372–3 (1957).

Objectives

The policy objectives sought by such authoritative decision-makers in the resolution of conflicting claims respecting coercion are many and complex and of varying levels of generality. On one level of abstraction and realism certain fundamental objectives may be noted. First is the prevention of alterations in the existing distribution of values among the nation-states by processes of unilateral and unauthorized coercion and the promotion of value changes and adjustments by processes of persuasion or by community-sanctioned coercion. Contemporary expression and reiteration of these most fundamental policy purposes [99] are found in the constitutional documents of international governmental organizations—which commonly set forth both prohibitions of resort to force or the threat of force and commitments to settle disputes by pacific means [100]—in the decisions

99. Earlier expression is to be found in the League of Nations Covenant, Arts. 10, 12, 13, 15, and in the Pact of Paris. In the Pact of Paris, the parties stated that they were "convinced that all changes in their relations with one another should be sought only by pacific means and be the result of a peaceful and orderly process." In "The High Command Trial," 12 *Law Reports of Trials of War Criminals* 1, 70 (1949), the tribunal articulated the fundamental policy embodied in the Pact of Paris: "The nations that entered into the Kellogg-Briand Pact considered it imperative that existing international relationships should not be changed by force. In the preamble they state that they are 'persuaded that the time has come when . . . all changes in their relationships with one another should be sought only by pacific means.' This is a declaration that from that time forward each of the signatory nations should be deemed to possess and to have the right to exercise all the privileges and powers of a sovereign nation within the limitations of International Law, free from all interferences by force on the part of any nation. As a corollary to this, the changing or attempting to change the international relationships by force of arms is an act of aggression and if aggression results in war, the war is an aggressive war."

100. See U.N. Charter, Art. 2, pars. 3, 4; id. Arts. 33, 37; Organization of American States Charter, Arts. 5(e), 5(g), 15, 16, 18, 22 (text in Subcommittee on Disarmament, Senate Committee on Foreign Relations, *Disarmament and Security: A Collection of Documents 1919–1955*, 84th Cong., 2d Sess., 160–2 (1956). See also the Inter-American Treaty of Reciprocal Assistance, Arts. 1, 2 (1947) (text in id. at 650); American Treaty on Pacific Settlement, Art. 1 (1948) (text in id. at 654); North Atlantic Treaty, Art. 1 (1949) (text in id at 530); Southeast Asia Collective Defense Treaty, Art. 1 (1954) (text in id. at 612); Arab League Pact, Art. 5 (1945) (text in id. at 618); Warsaw Treaty of Friendship, Cooperation and Mutual Assistance, Art. 1 (1955) (text in id. at 551).

The most explicit expression of the broad policy objectives is, of course, to

of the war crimes tribunals, and in the affirmation by the United Nations of the "Nuremberg Principles." [101]

A second major objective is the reduction to the minimum, when the procedures of persuasion break down and violence is in fact resorted to, of unnecessary destruction of values. This overriding policy has in the past consisted mainly of securing as much humanitarianism as is realistically possible in the mutual application of violence; [102] it may in the future come to consist, in barest minimum, of the preservation of the earth as a habitable abode for man and the continuation of human social processes as we know them now. This basic common policy pervades all the detailed prescriptions of the *jus in bello* which seek to define, with varying degrees of specificity, the permissible maximum of violence and destruction in particular types of situations. It finds its most explicit and recent embodiment in the

---

be found in the preamble and statement of purposes of the United Nations Charter.

101. U.N. Gen. Ass., Res. No. 95(I), Gen. Ass., *Off. Rec.,* 1st Sess., Plenary 55 (1946). See also the "Essentials of Peace" Resolution, U.N. Gen. Ass., Res. No. 290(IV), Gen. Ass., *Off. Rec.,* 4th Sess., Plenary 261 (1949).

102. In the preamble of Hague Convention No. IV of 1907, "Respecting the Laws and Customs of War on Land," the parties declared that they were "animated by the desire to serve, even in this extreme case [of an appeal to arms], the interests of humanity and the ever progressive needs of civilization," and that the provisions of the annexed regulations were "inspired by the desire to diminish the evils of war, so far as military requirements permit." The texts of the Convention and Regulations are reprinted in Department of the Army, *Treaties Governing Land Warfare* 5–17 (Pamphlet 27-1, 1956).

In Department of the Army, *The Law of Land Warfare* par. 2 (FM 27-10, 1956), the purposes of the law of war are expressed as: "(a) Protecting both combatants and noncombatants from unnecessary suffering; (b) Safeguarding certain fundamental human rights of persons who fall into the hands of the enemy . . . (c) Facilitating the restoration of peace." These same purposes are put in slightly different phraseology in Department of the Navy, *The Law of Naval Warfare* par. 200 (1955); see Tucker, note 98 supra at 363. The modest character of this policy objective is underscored by Professor Winfield: "War is . . . essentially a brutal and inhuman affair, however we view it. The remark is trite enough, but it must be emphasized in order to understand that the Laws of War can at best do no more than modify the brutality and inhumanity of it; they cannot eliminate those characteristics." Winfield, *The Foundations and the Future of International Law* 59 (1941). See also 2 Westlake, *International Law* 3 (1907).

conventions for the protection of war victims which in effect are human rights conventions for contexts of violence.[103]

The regulation of the conduct of coercion and violence in such manner as to permit and facilitate the restoration of the processes of persuasion is a third objective.[104] There is more than sarcasm in a comment of Mr. Dooley upon the Second Hague Conference of 1907: "This made th' way clear f'r th' discussion iv th' larger question iv how future wars shud be conducted in th' best inthrests iv peace." [105] Underlying the formulation of detailed rules on the permissible limits of violence are at least two assumptions, one of which is that unrestrained, gratuitous destruction of values so tends permanently to acerbate and embitter the relations between the opposing participants as to make the return to peace—short of a Carthaginian peace—extremely difficult if not impossible. The other is that extermination, peace of the Carthaginian variety, is not a permissible objective of international violence; if it were, all legal limitations would be entirely pointless.

On another level of abstraction and realism, reference may be made to such objectives as the maintenance or furtherance of varying contending systems or conceptions of world public order, compatible, in theory or in specific interpretation, in greater or lesser degree with the values of a free society. The variation in systems or conceptions of world public order is observably both "vertical"—through time—and "horizontal"—through differing areas of the world at a given time. "Vertical" variation [106] is perhaps most dramatically illustrated in the changes, over the last century or so, in conceptions of the requirements of world public order exhibited in the formulation of the distinction between permissible and nonpermissible resort to coercion and of the corollary notion of permissible discrimination between belligerents by neutrals. The doctrines of the last century

103. Cf. Kunz, "The Geneva Conventions of August 12, 1949," in *Law and Politics in the World Community* 279, 283 (Lipsky, ed., 1953).

104. See Department of the Army, *The Law of Land Warfare* par. 2 (FM 27-10, 1956); Department of the Navy, *The Law of Naval Warfare* par. 200 (1955).

105. Quoted in Boggs, "National Claims in Adjacent Seas," 41 *Geographical Rev.* 185, 208 note 29 (1951).

106. See, generally, Vinogradoff, "Historical Types of International Law," 1 *Bibliotheca Visseriana* 3 (1923).

on "measures short of war," on war as a "prerogative right" of sovereign states, on the "juridical equality" of belligerents, and on the neutral's "duty of impartiality," in substantial effect permitted the relative strength of participants to determine issues between them; [107] decision-makers, in other words, honored the assertion of exclusive rather than inclusive values. In contrast, in contemporary prescriptions attempting to ensure that force be employed only in response to unlawful force, emphasis is placed upon more inclusive values. "Horizontal" variation, or the simultaneous plurality of demanded systems or conceptions of world public order, is a candid fact of international life.[108] The antagonism and competition between the major

107. Thus, with respect to reprisals as "measures short of war," it has been observed that "in modern times [after the eighteenth century] the effective use of reprisals is confined to the Greater Powers in their relations with the smaller. . . . Reprisal . . . is only practised against small or weak Powers by others which fear little harm from the utmost step they can take. So confident, indeed, are they of the superiority of the force they can bring to bear that they take it for granted that the State against which they have proceeded will quickly bow to the logic of facts, and, not making a difficulty of its wounded dignity, will hurry on to concessions in order to secure relief from the measures of coercion." Maccoby, "Reprisals as a Measure of Redress Short of War," 2 *Camb. L. J.* 60, 69 (1924). Some publicists have regarded the doctrine of reprisals, in permitting relative power to resolve issues, as embodying a policy of limiting the extent of, and involvement in, violence. See Hall, *International Law* 434 (Higgins, 8th. ed., 1924); Holland, *Letters to the Times upon War and Neutrality, 1881–1920,* 14 (3d ed., 1921). See also Hindmarsh, *Force in Peace* 73–4, 87–8, 93–4 (1933); 2 Westlake, *International Law* 52 (1907): "A war between civilised states is begun because one at least of the parties makes some demand with which the other does not comply, or some complaint of which the other gives no explanation regarded by the first as satisfactory. International law says its last word on that point when it pronounces the demand or the complaint to be legitimate or illegitimate, and, if possible, offers arbitration. If the parties are not content with this, the want of organisation in the world of states compels the law which was concerned with their dispute to stand aside while they fight the quarrel out." "The outbreak of war removes the controversy out of which it arose from the domain of law. It will be settled at the peace on such terms as the superiority of force decides. . . ." Id. at 29.

108. Cf. Stone, *Legal Controls* 57–64, who somewhat understates the point when he writes that "the hypothesis that there are at least two international communities and legal orders cannot yet, however, be regarded as proved." See also Smith, *The Crisis in the Law of Nations* c. 2 (1947); Kunz, "Pluralismo de Sistemas Legales y de Valores y el Derecho Internacional," 3 *Revista de Derecho y Ciencias Sociales* 33 (Argentina. 1956–1957); Schwarzenberger, "The Impact

systems or conceptions—frequently described in such broad terms as, on one hand, "western, Christian, liberal-democratic" and, on the other, "Marxist, totalitarian, popular-democratic"—reflect basic power conflicts in the world arena. It is no dark secret that decision-makers who are proponents of a totalitarian world public order constantly assert and promote their totalitarian goals by appropriate specific interpretations in concrete cases.

The more specific policy objectives of different authoritative decision-makers and the precise operational meanings they give to the more abstract goals of community policy can of course be determined only by the detailed study of particular decisions through time about major recurring problems. The range of specific objectives and interpretations will be indicated in some detail at a later point.[109]

Conditions

The conditions under which authoritative decisions are taken obviously include all those same variables of the world power process that affect the process of coercion. Among the factors that bear immediately upon the prescription and application of community policy are common expectations as to the character and efficiency of

---

of the East-West Rift on International Law," 36 *Tr. Grotius Soc.* 229 (1950); Wilk, "International Law and Global Ideological Conflict: Reflections on the Universality of International Law," 45 *A.J.I.L.* 648 (1951); Martin, "Universalism and Regionalism in International Law and Organization," 7 *Cursos Monographicos, Academia Interamericana de Derecho Comparado e International* 375 (1959). Cf. also the related observations made by Lyon-Caen, "International Law and the Co-Existence, in a State of Peace, of States with Opposing Political Systems," 79 *Journal du Droit International* 49, 55 (1952), who emphasizes that "the structure of the world is no longer homogeneous in character; there are now several types of States," and urges that "international law must adjust their co-existence." In this connection, see the important point made by De Luna in "Fundamentación del Derecho Internacional," 60 *Revista del Derecho Internacional* 210, 248 (Cuba, 1952): "Todo derecho, como fenómeno cultural que es, se afirma y cae con una determinada cultura. Y como el derecho internacional pretende regular la comunidad humana entera, presupone un minimo de unidad cultural del mundo para poder subsistir. Ahora bien, esta unidad en nuestros días no existe, ha sido rota en mil pedazos, porque no hay cultura donde no hay principios comunes a que apelar, y es evidente que hoy el mundo, en lo cultural como en lo político, está por lo menos dividido en dos bloques."

109. See text at notes 141–237 infra.

the technique and technology of violence.[110] It may be recalled, for purposes of illustrating the impact of such expectations on the structure of prescription, that historically only weapons regarded as obsolete, marginal or indecisive, and militarily inefficient—weapons which did not or could not be expected to yield a substantial net military advantage after discounting the concomitant destruction of values, such as poisoned arms and expanding bullets—have successfully been proscribed.[111] The continuing failure, despite their awesome destructiveness, to achieve authoritative community prohibition of the use of basic energy weapons, the military ineffectiveness of which has still to be demonstrated, lends confirmation to historical experience.

Expectations of particular decision-makers as to the probable effectiveness of, or compliance with, projected regulation constitute another factor affecting the prescription and, more particularly, the application of policy in specific cases.[112] Such expectations in turn frequently depend on at least two other related factors. One factor is

110. "[The Hague Regulations] were written in a day when armies traveled on foot, in horse-drawn vehicles and on railroad trains; the automobile was in its Ford Model T stage. Use of the airplane as an instrument of war was merely a dream. The atomic bomb was beyond the realms of imagination. Concentration of industry into huge organizations transcending national boundaries had barely begun. Blockades were the principal means of 'economic warfare.' 'Total warfare' only became a reality in the recent conflict. These developments make plain the necessity of appraising the conduct of defendants with relation to the circumstances and conditions of their environment. Guilt, or the extent thereof, may not be determined theoretically or abstractly. Reasonable and practical standards must be considered." "The Flick Trial," 9 *Law Reports of Trials of War Criminals* 23 (1949).

111. Royse, *Aerial Bombardment and the International Regulations of Warfare* 141–6 (1928); Stone, *Legal Controls* 551; Borchard, "The Atomic Bomb," 40 *A.J.I.L.* 161, 165, (1946).

112. The wide discretion given to the Security Council by Art. 39 of the Charter, and to the General Assembly by Art. 11 and the "Uniting For Peace" resolution, leaves these organs ample opportunity to take this factor into account. A similar point was made by Judge Lauterpacht with respect to the Assembly of the League of Nations: "[T]he factors which may legitimately enter into the exercise of discretion are not only the scope and nature of the acts of force with which the League is confronted, but also the general political situation, including the actual prospects of the effectiveness of the League's action following upon the finding that resort to war has taken place." Lauterpacht, " 'Resort to War' and the Interpretation of the Covenant during the Manchurian Dispute," 28 *A.J.I.L.* 43, 54 (1934).

the decision-makers' estimate of the amount of effective power available to support an application of policy. This estimate is itself a function of their appraisal of the structural features of the world arena existing at a given time; [113] in less abstract terms, the decision-makers seek to anticipate who will support, who will attack, and who will ignore the decision if one is taken. The other is the estimation of decision-makers of the possible costs of making and enforcing a decision. Costs may take the shape of expanded involvement, measured in terms of both the number of opponents and the geographic locale of violence, and of grievously increased destruction of values. The operation of these factors has been demonstrated in the Korean,[114] Suez, and Hungarian cases.[115]

113. Cf. Wright, "The Prevention of Aggression," 50 id. at 514, 516 (1956). In 1937, the British Secretary of State for Foreign Affairs, explaining in the course of a debate in the House of Commons the failure of the League Assembly, the Brussels Conference, and Britain to adopt definitive sanctions against Japan, then conducting large-scale military operations against China, stated:

> We were told that in the Far East to-day we ought to be upholding the rule of law. . . . If Hon. Members opposite are advocating sanctions . . . I would remind them that there are two possible forms of sanctions—the ineffective, which are not worth putting on, and the effective, which means the risk, if not the certainty, of war. I say deliberately that nobody could contemplate any action of that kind in the Far East unless they are convinced that they have overwhelming force to back their policy.
>
> Do right Hon. Gentlemen opposite really think that the League of Nations to-day, with only two great naval Powers in it, ourselves and France, has got that overwhelming force? It must be perfectly clear to every one that that overwhelming force does not exist.

Quoted in 1 *Survey of International Affairs 1937,* 292–3 (Royal Institute of Int. Affairs, 1938).

114. Goodrich and Simons, *The United Nations and the Maintenance of International Peace and Security* 365 (1955). In the Assembly discussions on the draft of the resolution condemning the People's Republic of China as an aggressor, the Syrian representative argued that adoption of the draft resolution would not end the Korean war but would be more likely to extend it and that, should the war be extended, the United Nations would have to fight a population of about 800 million. The Indian delegate said that he would vote against the draft for the reason that it would prolong hostilities in Korea indefinitely and might expand the conflict into a global war. See *Y.B. of the United Nations 1951,* 217–24. Goodrich and Simons point out that considerations such as these resulted in delaying the condemnation of the People's Republic of China.

115. In the Suez case the resolutions of the General Assembly calling for a cease-fire and withdrawal of Israeli, British, and French forces from Egyptian

Still another factor influencing the prescription and application of policy is the state of expectations of various participants as to the possibilities of effective decision-making by the organized world community—the dependability, in other words, of reliance upon world community intervention. It is common knowledge that low estimates of such possibilities, induced by the adoption of the Yalta voting formula among other things, led to the insertion of Article 51 in the

---

territory, U.N. Gen. Ass., Res. Nos. 997, 999, 1002, U.N. Gen. Ass., *Off. Rec.,* 1st Emer. Spec. Sess., Plenary Mtg. and Annexes, Agenda Item No. 5, at 33–4 (1956), were supported by the United States, the Soviet Union, and most of the other member states. Together with other factors, such support resulted in compliance with the resolutions.

In the case of Hungary, the resolutions condemning the Soviet armed repression of the Hungarian people were much more strongly worded. U.N. Gen. Ass., Res. Nos. 1004, 1005, 1006, U.N. Gen. Ass., *Off. Rec.,* 2d Emer. Spec. Sess., Annexes, Agenda Item No. 5, at 6–7 (1956); but the polar powers confronted each other in opposition, and realistic expectations of effectiveness were minimal. Doubts as to the probable effectiveness of the resolutions were expressed by Indonesia, among others, whose representative said:

> Sentiments of sympathy, of anger and of condemnation of one another have been expressed. . . . We respect all those sentiments and feelings, many of which, indeed, we share. If, however, we ask the Assembly to take a decision, the prime consideration should be whether, after the adoption of [Res. 1004] . . . on 4 November, the adoption of another draft resolution would really contribute further to the solution of the situation, even though it might satisfy our sentiments and feelings. . . . With all respect to the sentiment and principles which are expressed in this draft resolution, in all fairness we do have honest doubts whether this draft resolution, if adopted, would have the effect it seeks to achieve.

Id. at 67. See also the statements of the representatives of India, Ceylon, and Burma, id. at 68, 71, 72.

The so-called double standard of the United Nations is largely attributable to the differential operation of these factors in different situations. There is less than adequate appreciation of this fact in Green, "The Double Standard of the United Nations," 11 *Y.B. of World Affairs* 104 (1957). Cf. Hoffman, "Sisyphus and the Avalanche: The United Nations, Egypt and Hungary," 11 *Int. Organization* 446 (1957), which offers perceptive discussion of these factors.

It may be observed, in addition, that in the current debate on the question of "defining aggression," one of the arguments against definition is that under conditions of prevailing expectations of possibly excessive costs of enforcing a decision, a "definition of aggression" may be "more dangerous than useful" and that it may be sound, even essential policy to "refrain from branding as an aggressor one of the parties to the dispute." See the statements of the Netherlands representative, U.N. Gen. Ass., *Off. Rec.,* 8th Sess., 6th Comm. 7–8 (1953).

Charter of the United Nations, which recognized individual and collective self-defense, and since then, to the elaboration of the permission of collective self-defense in numerous treaties establishing regional organizations.[116] The realism of such estimates will continue, it may be expected, to be of intense relevance both for participants deciding on an appropriate response to coercion and for external decision-makers passing upon the lawfulness of a participant's claim to respond to coercion under the name of self-defense.[117]

Methods

The methods by which authoritative decision-makers attempt to regulate the process of coercion include certain special functions or procedures by which they continually formulate, reformulate, and ap-

116. See Beckett, *The North Atlantic Treaty, the Brussels Treaty, and the Charter of the United Nations* (1950); Goodrich and Hambro, *Charter of the United Nations: Commentary and Documents* 297–9 (2d rev. ed., 1949); Bebr, "Regional Organizations: A United Nations Problem," 49 *A.J.I.L.* 166 (1955); Kelsen, "The North Atlantic Defense Treaty and the Charter of the United Nations," 19 *Acta Scandinavica Juris Gentium* 41 (1949); Kelsen, "Collective Security and Collective Self-Defense under the Charter of the United Nations," 42 *A.J.I.L.* 783 (1948); Kunz, "Individual and Collective Self-Defense in Article 51 of the Charter of the United Nations," 41 *A.J.I.L.* 872 (1947).

117. The operation of these expectations may be illustrated by the decision of the British Government to resort to armed force in Suez. The discussions in the House of Commons afford some insight into the considerations involved in the issuance of the ultimatum to the Israeli and Egyptian Governments. Mr. Maitland said: "We have heard the Leader of the Opposition . . . [propose] that nothing should be done until the Security Council had reached a decision. This proposition is put forward within a matter of days of another resort to the Security Council which produced no decision at all. It is put forward after some years of resort to the Security Council in many other matters that have produced no decision either. It is put forward in the light of the fact that on the one occasion when the Security Council did reach a decision nobody did anything about it." 558 H.C. Deb. (5th ser.) 1351–2 (1956).

The Foreign Secretary was even more explicit: "There is a fundamental point which this House and other countries will have to face. We have created a system of international law and order in which we have to face the fact that the Security Council is, first, frustrated by the veto and, secondly, that it cannot act immediately. In a sense, the policeman has his hands tied behind his back. He has to wait a long time before he is allowed to play his part. . . . We say that in the present international system, where the Security Council is subject to the veto, there must be the right for individual countries to intervene in an emergency to take action to defend their own nationals and their own interests." Id. at 1377.

ply policy with respect to the various major types of claims to initiate and exercise or avoid coercion. In most comprehensive statement, such policy functions or procedures might be described to include those of intelligence, recommending, prescribing, invoking, applying, appraising, and terminating.[118] In the interests of brevity, and because of the lack of institutional specialization in the performance of each of these functions in the law of war, as in international law generally, emphasis here will be confined to prescription and application.

PRESCRIPTION

The more obvious method by which the law of war is prescribed is by explicit agreement of the participants, as in great international conventions like those of the Hague and Geneva. It is commonly recognized, however, that the method of explicit agreement, particularly in the field of management of combat, has never been able to achieve much more in formulation than a general restatement of pre-existing consensus about relatively minor problems. Negotiators, seated about a conference table contemplating future wars and aware of the fluid nature of military technology and technique, imagine too many horrible contingencies, fantastic or realistic, about the security of their respective countries to permit much commitment.

Much more effective than explicit agreement in the prescription of the law of war has been the less easily observed, slow, customary shaping and development of general consensus or community expectation. Decision-makers confronted with difficult problems, frequently presented to them in terms of principles as vague and abstract as "the laws of humanity and the dictates of the public conscience" [119] and in terms of concepts and rules admitting of multiple interpretations, quite naturally have had recourse both to the experience of prior decision-makers and to community expectation about required or desired future practice and decision. The myth is that when cer-

118. See McDougal, "International Law, Power and Policy: A Contemporary Conception," 82 *Hague Recueil* 137, 177–8 (1953).

119. Preamble, "Respecting the Laws and Customs of War on Land," Hague Convention No. IV (1907). The tribunal in "The Krupp Trial," 10 *Law Reports of Trials of War Criminals* 133 (1949), declared that the preamble was "much more than a pious declaration," that it was a "legal yardstick" to be applied when specific conventional provisions did not cover specific cases.

tain practices are repeated or mutually tolerated over a period of time by a substantial number of decision-makers, in the context of certain common perspectives of "oughtness" or "authority," a certain customary rule or principle of law emerges.[120] On a more realistic level, the function of this myth is to permit and authorize a decision-maker to achieve a more rational balancing of past experience, contemporary realities, and future probabilities without appearing to create new policy. The process of customary development, considered as one of continual, creative readaption or reinterpretation of given prescription, whether conventional or customary, is particularly marked when it is in response to patterns of interaction, such as blockade and submarine and air warfare, which are themselves, because of altered conditions and fast-developing technology and technique, in a process of profound and rapid change.[121] In such cases, the rate of attrition or obsolescence of particular inherited rules may be accelerated and the emergence of new ones hastened.[122]

From this perspective, if by "law" one means to make any operational reference to probable or realistically expected decision, the continued characterization by some commentators of certain pre-1914 prescriptions as law, despite their practically universal non-observance in two world wars,[123] may at best be harmless nostalgia.

120. For formulations of the myth with particular reference to the law of war see "Trial of Altstotter," 6 *Law Reports of Trials of War Criminals* 35–8 (1948); "Trial of List," 8 id. at 53 (1949); "Trial of Von Leeb," 12 id. at 68, 69–70 (1949).

121. Smith, *The Crisis in the Law of Nations* cc. 1–5 (1947). The technical device commonly used in the last two world wars for bridging the gap between traditional prescription and contemporary practice was that of reprisals. The principal difficulty with this device is not so much its lack of complete ingenuousness as that it purported to leave the structures of formal doctrine intact, supposedly unaffected by the insistent pressure of changed conditions and the imperatives arising from these conditions. See Stone, *Legal Controls* 355 note 39, on the "legislative function" of reprisals. The central problem, which need not be obscured by disingenuous labels or by the requirements of propaganda warfare, is one of determining realistic expectations of probable future practice and decision. Cf. Rowson, "British Prize Law, 1939–1944," 61 *L.Q. Rev.* 49, 57 (1945); Smith, supra at 16.

122. Cf. "Trial of Altstotter," 6 *Law Reports of Trials of War Criminals* 35 (1948).

123. See, e.g., Tucker, *The Law of War and Neutrality at Sea* 305, 315–17 (1957), discussing the lawfulness of the establishment of war zones by means of minefields and of "long-distance" blockades.

Such pre-1914 prescriptions may indeed possibly be regarded as "authority" in some cases in the future; but if they are, it will not be because they were once prescribed by certain earlier decision-makers for a bygone world, but because future decision-makers decide that they embody precisely the detailed limitations upon violence thought appropriate, in common interest, for future wars, total or limited, nuclear or non-nuclear.

APPLICATION AND SANCTION

The application of the prescriptions of the law of war to specific problems may be by any of the officials indicated above, international or national, and occurs in a variety of contexts—from general assemblies and international tribunals to foreign offices and battlefields. So great is the recognized common interest of all participants in the observance of the law of war that certain traditional principles on allocation of jurisdiction confer upon the courts of all belligerents—perhaps all states belligerent or nonbelligerent [124] and not merely those of the belligerent in whose territory the acts were committed or whose nationals are involved—power to try individuals held before them for violations of that law.[125] Reflecting the same unity of

124. See Cowles, "Universality of Jurisdiction over War Crimes," 33 *Calif. L. Rev.* 177 (1945); 15 *Law Reports of Trials of War Criminals* 26 (1949). See also "Trial of Altstotter," 6 id. at 37–8 (1948).

125. Tucker, note 123 supra at 154–5; Baxter, "The Municipal and International Law Bases of Jurisdiction over War Crimes," 28 *Brit. Y.B. I. L.* 390–2 (1951); Brand, "The War Crimes Trials and the Laws of War," 26 *Brit. Y.B. I. L.* 414–16 (1949). In "Trial of List," 8 *Law Reports of Trials of War Criminals* 54 (1949), the tribunal said: "An international crime is such an act universally recognized as criminal, which is considered a grave matter of international concern and for some valid reason cannot be left within the exclusive jurisdiction of the state that would have control over it under ordinary circumstances. The inherent nature of a war crime is ordinarily itself sufficient justification for jurisdiction to attach in the courts of the belligerent into whose hands the alleged criminal has fallen. . . . [War crimes] are punishable by the country where the crime was committed or by the belligerent into whose hands the criminals have fallen, the jurisdiction being concurrent."

See the 1949 Geneva Conventions, which require each party to search for persons alleged to have committed "grave breaches" of the conventions and to "bring such persons, regardless of their nationality, before its own courts." Wounded and Sick Convention, Art. 49; Wounded, Sick, and Shipwrecked Convention, Art. 50; Prisoners of War Convention, Art. 129; Civilians Convention, Art. 146.

interest, the municipal codes, statutes, ordinances, and regulations of many states embody into their national law, for administration as other national law is administered, prescriptions about the conduct of warfare and nonparticipation in warfare which, if not always identical, are at least comparable in policy with the prescriptions of the community of states.[126]

Sanctions for enforcement raise perhaps the only issue, in application, which requires special elaboration. The opinion has been so often urged that the law of war is not law at all that it may be worth while to observe that the effective sanction which supports the law of war is the same sanction which supports all law: the common interest of the participants in an arena.[127] The common interest which sustains the law of war is the interest of all participants in economy in the use of force—in the minimization of the unnecessary destruction of values. Unnecessary destruction of values constitutes uneconomical use of force not only because it involves, by definition, a dissipation of base values which yields no military advantage; [128] it will also, by operation of the condition of reciprocity, result in the offending belligerent sustaining a positive disadvantage in the shape of at least an equal amount of destruction of its own values. By stimulating hatred in the enemy and strengthening his will to resist, it will in addition frequently compel the expenditure of much larger amounts of force than would otherwise have been necessary to secure the same objective.[129] Economy in the use of force is thus a matter of shared

126. See, e.g., Uniform Code of Military Justice, 64 Stat. 108 (1950), 50 U.S.C. §§ 551–741 (1952); Department of the Army, *The Law of Land Warfare* (FM 27–10, 1956); Department of the Navy, *The Law of Naval Warfare* (1957); United Kingdom, *Manual of Military Law* (9th ed., 1956); *Codes de justice militaire: Armées de terre et de mer* (Petits Codes, Dalloz, ed., 1957). National statutes and regulations on neutrality are collected in Jessup and Deak, *Neutrality Laws, Regulations and Treaties* (1939).

127. Cf. Corbett, *Law and Society in the Relations of States* 13 (1951).

128. Indication of the kinds of calculations in which economy of force manifests itself may be found in Cagle and Manson, *The Sea War in Korea,* 333–4, 352–3 (U. S. Naval Institute, 1957). "The cost of a 5-inch shell at the end of the Korean pipeline was approximately $200," Admiral Gingrich, commander of Task Force 95, is reported to have said, and "unless it did that much damage, we were hurting ourselves more than the enemy" (id. at 352).

129. The results of the policies of Nazi Germany in occupied areas of the Soviet Union during World War II offer excellent illustration. The unbelievably savage and ruthless treatment of Soviet prisoners of war and the civilian popula-

interest in self-restraint, and it is this general sanction which finds its detailed expression in all the varying procedural modalities of collective measures for redress by international organizations, including the employment of all instruments of coercion, of war crimes trials during or after war by international or national courts and military commissions, of reprisal procedures in the course of hostilities, and of diplomatic negotiations or interpositions with respect to claims for damages.

Compelling testimony to the effectiveness of the sanction of self-interest comes from the German archives made public at Nuremberg in the form of certain memoranda prepared by the "Operational Staff of the Armed Forces [Wehrmacht]." [130] These documents commented upon and assessed a proposal, made apparently at the last stages of the war, that Germany denounce its international obligations concerning the conduct of war. After listing the international conventions to which Germany was a party, the documents reviewed in minute detail the possible consequences of denunciation, methodically calculating expected advantages and disadvantages, and uniformly concluded that the disadvantages far outweighed possible advantages. In the course of its discussion, one of these remarkable documents stated:

> (1) Strictly formally, a denunciation of the agreements is not possible. The conventions concerning P.W. and wounded provide for no denunciation, the Hague Convention admits a denunciation only if one year's notice is given.
> (2) On the basis of the practice of states in the wars of the last centuries, there exists the "International Law of Usage" which cannot be done away with unilaterally. It comprises the latest principles of a humane conduct of war; it is not laid down in

---

tion drove the inhabitants and stragglers from the Red Army to join the partisan movements, which correspondingly grew in effectiveness until they controlled large areas behind German lines. The German policies of absolute terror and extermination also resulted in the forfeiture of the opportunities offered by the nationalistic aspirations of the Ukrainians and Byelorussians and by their hopes for a better and freer life under Hitler's "New Order." A recent comprehensive study is Dallin, *German Rule in Russia 1941–1945: A Study of Occupation Policies* (1957).

130. Memoranda Nos. 313/45, Feb. 20, 1945, 1859/45, Feb. 21, 1945, 1825/45, Feb. 20, 1945, in *Nazi Conspiracy and Aggression* 894–905 (Supp. A, 1947).

writing. To respect it is however considered a prerequisite for membership [in] the community of states. (Prohibition on misusing the flag of truce, killing of defenseless women and children, etc.)

Consequently Germany will by no means free herself from this essential obligation of the laws of war by a denunciation of the conventions on the laws of war.[131]

Recently, there has been much discussion of the existence of a "nuclear stalemate," comprised, it is said, of a relative parity between the two "superpowers" in capacity to inflict annihilating destruction on each other through "saturation" with nuclear explosives, and of a common military inability either completely to defend against contemporary delivery systems or completely to destroy the other's capabilities for retaliation. The implications of such a stalemate have also been considered in terms of the necessity, in view of the exorbitant costs of total war, of a strategy of "limited war." [132] The reference commonly given to "limited war" has been that of exercises of military violence in which the participants mutually limit their objectives to determinate ones susceptible of negotiated settlement and in which the aggregate destruction of values is kept at a correspondingly low level by reciprocal limitations upon weapons, areas of operations, or objects of attack. The point of present emphasis is that the possibilities of "limited war" appear to depend in large measure upon observance of the same principle which, as indicated before, traditionally has sustained a law of war, the principle of economy in the exercise of force. Thus Professor Osgood states the point of theory involved succinctly:

131. Memorandum No. 313/45, Feb. 20, 1945, in id. at 895.

132. See, e.g., *Military Policy and National Security* (Kaufmann ed., 1956); Kissinger, *Nuclear Weapons and Foreign Policy* (1957); Osgood, *Limited War: The Challenge to American Strategy* (1957); *On Limiting Atomic War* (Royal Institute of Int. Affairs, 1956); Aron, "A Half-Century of Limited War?" 12 *Bull. Atomic Scientists* 99 (1956); Buzzard, Slessor and Lowenthal, "The H-Bomb: Massive Retaliation or Graduated Deterrence," 32 *International Aff.* 148 (1956); Hoag, "Nato: Deterrent or Shield?" 36 *Foreign Aff.* 278 (1958); King, "Nuclear Plenty and Limited War," 35 id. at 238 (1957); Kissinger, "Force and Diplomacy in the Nuclear Age," 34 id. at 349 (1956); Slessor, "The Great Deterrent and Its Limitations," 12 *Bull. Atomic Scientists* 140 (1956); Teller, "Alternatives for Security," 36 *Foreign Aff.* 201 (1958). But cf. de Seversky, "A Forecast and a Warning: No More Little Wars," *This Week Magazine,* March 23, 1958, p. 8.

> [A]s an examination of the interaction between military means and political ends will show, the proportionate use of force is a necessary condition for the limitation and effective control of war.[133]
>
> In the light of this proportion between the dimensions of warfare and its susceptibility to political control, the importance of preserving an economy of force is apparent. For if modern warfare tends to exceed the bounds of political control as it increases in magnitude, then it is essential to limit force to a scale that is no greater than necessary to achieve the objectives at stake. By the same token, if war becomes more susceptible to political control in proportion as its dimensions are moderated, then the economy of force is an essential condition of the primacy of politics in war.[134]

Similarly, Professor Kissinger makes explicit the application of this principle to the contemporary hope that, if there must be war, it be only limited war.

> The argument in favor of the possibility of limited war is that both sides have a common and overwhelming interest in preventing it from spreading. The fear that an all-out thermonuclear war might lead to the disintegration of the social structure offers an opportunity to set limits to both war and diplomacy.[135]

If, then, the assumption of "nuclear stalemate" and the hope for only limited war are more than illusion, there will continue to be, in the principle which establishes their contact with reality, some sanction for a law of war.

THE ROLE OF RULES

With more general reference to the whole process of authoritative decision, one point already mentioned may perhaps bear further emphasis. Observers have too often assumed that it is the function of inherited legal rules to point definitely and precisely to certain preordained conclusions. The difficulty with this assumption is that it seeks to impose too great a burden upon man's frail tools of thought

133. Osgood, note 132 supra at 18.

134. Id. at 26.

135. Kissinger, *Nuclear Weapons and Foreign Policy* 144 (1957).

and communication and an impossible rigidity upon the processes of both decision and social change. The fact is that the rules of the law of war, like other legal rules, are commonly formulated in pairs of complementary opposites and are composed of a relatively few basic terms of highly variable reference.[136] The complementarity in form and comprehensiveness of reference of such rules are indispensable to the rational search for and application of policy to a world of acts and events which presents itself to the decision-maker, not in terms of neat symmetrical dichotomies or trichotomies, but in terms of innumerable gradations and alternations from one end of a continuum to the other; the spectrum makes available to a decision-maker not one inevitable doom but multiple alternative choices. The realistic function of those rules, considered as a whole, is, accordingly, not mechanically to dictate specific decision but to guide the attention of decision-makers to significant variable factors in typical recurring contexts of decision, to serve as summary indices to relevant crystallized community expectations,[137] and, hence, to permit creative and adaptive, instead of arbitrary and irrational, decisions.

136. The phenomenon of polarity in the syntax of prescriptions is by no means unique to the law of war, nor even to international law generally. See Cardozo, "Paradoxes of Legal Science," in *Selected Writings of Benjamin Nathan Cardozo* 252 (Hall, ed., 1947). The same phenomenon has been more recently observed in the field of constitutional law: "His [Thomas Reed Powell's] thinking was infused also, as I have suggested, by the principle of polarity, finding in each of two opposing propositions an element of validity which when combined will produce a more serviceable guide than either principle standing alone. Interstate commerce must not be taxed by the states; interstate commerce may be made to pay its way. A state may exclude a foreign corporation from local business; a state may not condition the admission of a foreign corporation on its relinquishment of a constitutional right. The power to tax involves the power to destroy; the legislative motive for a tax is immaterial. In the control of public carriers a state may not regulate interstate commerce; a state has undoubted power to protect the safety of its inhabitants. These abstractions, arrayed in intransigent hostility like robot sentinels facing each other across a border, can become useful guardians on either hand in the climb to truth if they can be made to march together. Somehow the lifeblood of the concrete problem tempers the mechanical arrogance of abstractions." Freund, "Thomas Reed Powell," 69 *Harv. L. Rev.* 800, 802–3 (1956). Application has also been made of the notion of polarity in the more rarefied region of legal philosophy. See Cohen, *Reason and Law* 4, 6–7 (1950).

137. Each particular rule, however, points to certain specific factors and policies, and the significance of any specific factor or policy in a given case depends upon its interrelation with other factors and policies, including the pres-

The most comprehensive study of this process of decision, established by the public order of the world community for regulating international coercion and for minimizing the destruction of values in such coercion, would require the sustained systematic performance, with respect to each of the seven major types of controversies outlined earlier, of the several intellectual tasks we have noted as indispensable to policy-oriented inquiry. These may be briefly restated as including: the detailed clarification of the world community policies at stake in the prescriptions and procedures about permissible and nonpermissible coercion and the lawfulness or unlawfulness of particular exercises of coercion; the identification and description of trends in decisions with respect to all such problems and of the shifting constellations of variables that bear upon decision; the critical projection of observable trends and the estimation of the probable shape of future decision; the appraisal of both trends in the past and probable developments in the future in terms of their consistency with clarified policies; and the search for alternatives in prescription and procedure better designed to secure the preferred goals of maximum human dignity and minimum destruction of human values.

All this chapter attempts, however, in introducing the chapters to follow, is briefly to observe, with respect to each of the several types of controversies, some of the fundamental policies which authoritative decision-makers have in the past labored to secure in passing upon the lawfulness of specific claims to exercise or defend against coercion, and to make certain suggestions, tentative and impressionistic, as to possible lines of further clarification of the requirements of rational community policy with respect to various types of particular controversies.[138] As the factors that affect decision in the world arena shift toward inclusive rather than exclusive determination of community policy, the basic policies at stake in characterizations of coercion as permissible or impermissible may, hopefully, be clarified to the advantage of a public order of freedom, and the complementary policies appropriate in each type of controversy may be more sharply delineated and balanced in favor of humanitarian-

ence or absence of such other factors and policies, in total context. Cf. the formulation of the functions of rules or principles of interpretation in "The Law of Treaties," in *Harvard Research on International Law* 937–8 (1935).

138. In the chapters that follow, we attempt a more detailed development of community policies about some of the major types of controversies.

ism. The principal difficulty in past efforts to clarify and formulate such policies has stemmed largely from conditions of decentralization in the world arena. The elementary degree of organization of authority and centralization of effective power, in the very arena of interaction for the regulation of which policies are sought to be prescribed and applied,[139] has thus put the highest premium upon the effective competence of each state by its own unilateral decision and action to preserve and defend its security.[140]

This characteristic decentralization, exhibited most obviously in the lack of specialized institutions for the continuous and effective clarification and application of community policy about coercion, has infected with formidable ambiguity both the characterization of unlawful coercion and the detailed prescriptions of the fundamental policy of minimum destruction of values. Decentralization has thus resulted in the relatively heavier weighting of the set of policies, such as those embodied in self-defense and military necessity, conferring upon participants a broad unilateral discretion to secure and perpetuate their exclusive values, rather than upon the complementary set of policies emphasizing the more inclusive claims of minimum destruction and humanitarianism. As conviction of the common interest in postponing Armageddon grows, and slow, if tortuous and scarcely observable, progress is made toward more effective organization and centralization in the world arena, the hope that may be held out is that the set of policies embodying the restraint of coercion and the promotion of humanitarianism may rise in the balance and that the scope of permissible coercion may gradually be attenuated and more exacting standards of humanity formulated and applied.

MAJOR PROBLEMS AND GENERAL PRINCIPLES: THE COMMON INTEREST IN MINIMUM DESTRUCTION OF VALUES

Community Prohibition of Resort to Coercion

The most difficult problem which today confronts world public order is that of characterizing and preventing unlawful violence. The

139. See Kelsen, *Collective Security under International Law* 1–39 (1957).

140. The decentralization of the international system, a condition under which each state was responsible for its own defense, made it necessary at times to have recourse to anticipatory self-defense. Fenwick, *International Law* 231 (3d ed., 1948).

history is familiar how over the centuries—through *bellum iustum*, the Covenant of the League of Nations, the Pact of Paris, the judgments at Nuremberg and Tokyo, and the Charter of the United Nations—the public order of the world community has at long last come to a prohibition of certain coercion as a method of international change and to a distinction between permissible and nonpermissible coercion.[141] It is equally well known that before this prohibition and distinction were achieved, and the supporting principles of community concern and collective responsibility institutionalized,[142] however weakly, traditional doctrine recognized in each state an uncontrolled faculty, as a sovereign competence and prerogative to prosecute its rights, real or imagined, by recourse to coercion and violence.[143] Such doctrine of course reflected the then dominant patterns of multipolarity and power balancing in the world arena and the completely decentralized and unorganized character of the community of states, as well as the atomistic conceptions of state security and the limitations of the available military technology.

The basic complementary policies embodied in the contemporary prescriptions on recourse to coercion are reasonably clear. In its prohibition of certain coercion, the community attempts to effect a policy of promoting change through procedures of peaceful persuasion. The assumption that underlies this policy is that coercion and violence, necessarily entailing the destruction of values, are not suitable instrumentalities for asserting and prosecuting claims for change.[144] In characterizing certain other coercion as permissible,

141. See Martin, *Collective Security: A Progress Report* (1952); Pompe, *Aggressive War, an International Crime* (1953); Wehberg, *The Outlawry of War* (Zeydel, trans., 1931); Komarnicki, "La Définition de l'aggresseur dans le droit international moderne," 75 *Hague Recueil* 1 (1949); Tucker, "The Interpretation of War under Present International Law," 4 *Int. L.Q.* 11 (1951); Von Elbe, "The Evolution of the Concept of the Just War in International Law," 33 *A.J.I.L.* 665 (1939); Waldock, "The Regulation of the Use of Force by Individual States in International Law," 81 *Hague Recueil* 455 (1952).

142. See Hogan, *International Conflict and Collective Security: The Principle of Concern in International Organization* (1955).

143. See Shotwell, *War as an Instrument of National Policy* 14 (1929); cf. Pompe, note 141 supra at 138–52; 1 Wright, *A Study of War* 331, 335–41 (1942); McNair, "Collective Security," 17 *Brit. Y.B. I. L.* 150, 151 (1936); Nussbaum, "Just War—A Legal Concept?" 42 *Mich. L. Rev.* 453, 476 (1943).

144. Thus the Nuremberg Tribunal, echoing Dubois' "omne bellum in se malum et illicitum," quoted in Possony, "Peace Enforcement," 55 *Yale L. J.* 910,

the community seeks quite rationally to utilize coercion as an instrument of order by authorizing its use for community police actions, and acknowledges the still low degree of organization attained by permitting individual and collective self-defense as a response to unlawful coercion.[145] The technical legal concepts by which such policies are sought, sometimes summed up as an attempt to secure and maintain a "community monopoly of force," [146] are equally complementary: for characterizing nonpermissible coercion, there are such phrases as "war of aggression," "crimes against peace," "threats to the peace," "breach of the peace," "acts of aggression," "threat or use of force," "intervention," and so on; for designating permissible coercion the terms are "self-defense," "collective self-defense," "police action," "enforcement measures," "reprisal," and so forth.

In the framing of the United Nations Charter the deliberate choice was made to keep these technical characterizations as ambiguous as they appear.[147] For the past decade, however, a tremendous resurgence of agitation for their clarification has appeared. The principal effort has so far centered about a "definition of aggression," upon the assumption that if aggression is clarified, self-defense and justifiable police action will not be far behind. Many definitions, both official and unofficial, have been offered in many bodies, both official and unofficial. Some definitions are enumerative in approach, attempting a catalogue of concrete situations of aggression and reciting such "first shot" items as a declaration of war, invasion, bombardment, landing of troops and supporting of armed bands.[148] Others are generic or

912 (1946), said: "War is essentially an evil thing. Its consequences are not confined to the belligerents alone but affect the whole world. To initiate a war of aggression . . . is the supreme international crime differing only from other war crimes in that it contains within itself the accumulated evil of the whole." "Opinion and Judgment," in *Nazi Conspiracy and Aggression* 16 (1947).

145. Cf. Kelsen, note 139 supra at 25.

146. Kelsen, *Principles of International Law* 13–15 (1952).

147. See Report of the Rapporteur (Boncour) of Comm. III/3 to Comm. III of the San Francisco Conference, 12 U.N.C.I.O., *Docs.* 505 (1945); Goodrich and Hambro, *Charter of the United Nations: Commentary and Documents* 263–6 (2d rev. ed., 1949).

148. The example par excellence of an enumerative definition is that proposed by the Soviet Union, found, in its more recent form, in U.N. Doc. No. A/AC.77/L.4 (1957). The Soviet draft definition finds its prototype in the London Conventions for the Definition of Aggression of 1933, 147 *League of Na-*

catch-all formulations seeking to cover any threat or use of force by one state against another, in any manner, open or covert, and whatever the weapons, for any purpose other than for self-defense or police action.[149] Still other definitions endeavor to combine the enumerative and generic approaches.[150] Amid all this intellectual contention, one strongly held view—the present official position of the governments of the United States and the United Kingdom—is that all attempt at definition is futile, that all definitions would restrict the freedom of decision-making organs of the United Nations to determine aggression from the particular and peculiar circumstances of each instance of coercion.[151]

It is of course as futile to seek a reificatory, absolutist, and all-sufficing definition of aggression as of any other legal concept or word.[152] But the impossibility of absolute precision does not necessarily render complete confusion desirable. In this most fundamental problem of all, as in lesser problems, legal principles might be formulated which would serve the same function that other legal principles serve—that of bringing to the focus of attention of a decision-maker

---

tions Treaty Series 67, 77 (1933); 148 id. at 211, and in the Draft Act prepared by the 1933 Geneva Disarmament Conference, Committee on Security Questions, Conference for the Reduction and Limitation of Armaments [1933], "Politis Report," 2 *Conf. Docs.* (1935.IX.4) 679–90 (1935).

149. See, e.g., the draft definitions that were submitted to the International Law Commission by Mr. Alfaro, U.N. Doc. No. A/CN.4/L.31, at 27 (1951); Mr. Amado, U.N. Doc. No. A/CN.4/L.6 (1951); Mr. Cordova, U.N. Doc. No. A/CN.4/L.10 (1951); Mr. Yepes, U.N. Doc. No. A/CN.4/L.12 (1951). See also the Iraqi draft definition, U.N. Doc. No. A/AC.77/L.13, Annex II, at 5–6 (1957); Alfaro, "La cuestión de la definicíon de la agresión," 59 *Revista de Derecho Internacional* 361 (Cuba 1951).

150. The draft definitions proposed in 1956 by Iran and Panama, U.N. Doc. No. A/AC.77/L.13, Annex II, at 4–5 (1957); Paraguay, id. at 3–4; The Dominican Republic, Mexico, Paraguay, and Peru, id. at 9–10, are the more recent examples. Earlier ones include the formulations submitted by Mexico and Bolivia. U.N. Doc. No. A./AC.66/L.11, Annex (1953).

151. See the statements of the representative of the United States (Mr. Klutznick) in the Sixth Committee of the General Assembly, U.N. Doc. No. A/C.6/SR.519, at 14–18 (1957), and of the representative of the United Kingdom (Mr. Vallet), U.N. Doc. No. A/C.6/SR.523, at 2–5 (1957). See also Fitzmaurice, "The Definition of Aggression," 1 *Int. and Comp. Law Q.* 137 (1952).

152. Cf. Dias, "Mechanism of Definition as Applied to International Law," *Camb. L. J.* 215, 219 (1954).

relevant factors in context which should rationally affect decision.[153] From this perspective, the basic task is one of categorizing such variable contextual factors with respect to the distinction between permissible and nonpermissible coercion. Inquiry of the kind recommended above into the processes of coercion and decision suggests that such a categorization might include interrelated factors like the following:

a. The chronological factor of priority in resort to coercion of substantial degree, not in terms simply of the "first shot" but of all modes of coercion.[154]

153. It is sometimes suggested that the clarification of legal principles has no significant part to play in the prevention of catastrophic violence. The prevention of such violence, the argument runs, must depend upon new dispositions of effective power and not upon rearrangements of authoritative words.

This argument underestimates the degree to which a careful clarification of authoritative community goals may aid in securing the necessary sustaining dispositions of effective power. One of the lessons of contemporary science about human behavior is that it helps in creating the conditions necessary for the achievement of a goal to have the goal more sharply delineated. The clarification in detail of distinctions between lawful and unlawful coercion will not, of course, of itself establish all the necessary conditions for restraint of unlawful coercion. But it may perform the very necessary task of outlining the major contours of the effects sought—in terms of which alternative choices in the rearrangement of effective power and in the adoption of new modalities in practice must be appraised. The clarification of community goals about "aggression" need not retard and might even stimulate the establishment of more effective institutions for the performance of various necessary policy functions, the adoption of more effective programs in economic development and trade, the more general promotion of human rights and freedom of inquiry and communication, and the creation of progressively more comprehensive regional organizations.

154. The element of priority in time has been stressed by Spiropoulos, who regards it as "logically inherent in any notion of aggression. Aggression is presumably: acting as first." U.N. Doc. No. A/CN.4/44, at 65 (1951). See also the statements of Politis in "Records of the Conference for the Reduction and Limitation of Armaments," 2 *Minutes of the Gen. Comm.* 500 (League of Nations, Ser. B, 1933). Priority can, of course, be determined only within a specific delimited time sequence. The delimitation of the relevant time sequence is primarily a function of the definer's choice of the material causative factors. To give in all cases exclusive significance to the "first shot"—to overt military violence—may be grossly to underestimate the potentialities of all the contemporary modes of exercising coercion, both military and nonmilitary. On the "first shot" test, Judge Moore dryly observed that "the law does not require a man

b. The occasion for the coercion—whether the purpose exhibited by the initiator, objectively ascertained, is to attack and acquire values held by the target-state or to conserve and protect its own values, and whether the initiator seeks exclusive or inclusive values.

c. The type and intensity or the consequentiality of the coercion threatened or exercised.[155]

d. The realism of expectations created in the target-state as to the necessity, or imminence of necessity, of resort to counter-coercion for the maintenance of its freedom of decision-making and of its territorial base.[156]

---

who believes himself to be in danger to assume that his adversary is a bad shot." 6 Moore, *Collected Papers* 445 (1944).

155. There was some appreciation of the relevance of this factor in the discussions in the 1956 Special Committee. Certain delegates argued that "since certain degrees could be said to exist in the use of force and not all of them were serious enough to describe as aggression . . . the use of force had to be sufficiently serious to constitute aggression." It was urged, in particular, that "frontier incidents" would have to be excluded from the possible forms of aggression. U.N. Doc. No. A/AC.77/L.13, at 19 (1957). Similarly, many delegates advanced the view that "economic or ideological aggression did not entitle individual States to the same defensive action as did armed attack," id. at 22, the premise being, it appears, that "economic and ideological aggression" do not exhibit the same intensity of coercion as does "armed attack."

Recognition of the importance of the factor of consequentiality, as well as of the complementary factor of proportionality, seems implicit in the proposal of the Netherlands representative that the committee address itself to defining and clarifying the term "armed attack" as used in the U.N. Charter, Art. 51. "The crucial point," in the view of the Netherlands representative, "was to determine the cases of the use of armed force in which a State might go to war in self-defense." He observed further that in cases of "border incidents," a state could resort to "limited action in self-defense," based on its function "to maintain law and order in its territory." U.N. Doc. No. A/AC.77/L.13, at 42 (1957). See also id. at 49, 58, 59; and the view of the Iraqi delegate that the Soviet draft definition "lacked a distinction between acts of force which did constitute aggression and acts of force which did not," and that "the gravity of the act and of the situation in which it was happening should be taken into account." Id. at 50.

156. Cf. Pompe, *Aggressive War, an International Crime* 102–4 (1953), whose views were adopted and elaborated by the Netherlands representative in the 1956 Special Committee. The Netherlands representative urged that the criterion distinguishing armed attack from other uses of force not entitling the target state "to take the action provided for in Art. 51 [was] . . . the use of force in such circumstances that the victim-State had no means other than military to

e. The type and intensity or degree of proportionality of the coercive response of the target-state to the coercion initiated against it.

f. The relative willingness of the contending participants to accept community intervention for the cessation of violence and nonviolent procedures for settlement.[157]

g. The type and purpose of the decision demanded from an authoritative decision-maker.[158]

h. The probable effectiveness and costs of decision.[159]

Still another factor, somewhat less obvious, perhaps deserves no

---

preserve its territorial integrity or political independence. In case the use of force was such that United Nations intervention could provide sufficient protection, an armed attack within the meaning of Article 51 did not exist." U.N. Doc. No. A/AC.77/L.13, at 63–4 (1957). See also Röling, "On Aggression, on International Criminal Law, on International Criminal Jurisdiction," 2 *Nederlands Tijdschrift voor Internationaal Recht* 167 (1955); "The Report of De Brouckère," in *Documents of the Preparatory Commission for the Disarmament Conference,* League of Nations, Ser. 3, Pt. 93, at 100–1 (Doc. No. C.740.M.479.1926.IX) (1926); U.N. Doc. No. A/AC.66/L.11, at 20 (1953).

157. The U.N. Charter, Art. 40 authorizes the Security Council, for the purpose of preventing "an aggravation of the situation," to "call upon the parties concerned to comply with such provisional measures as it deems necessary or desirable," and to "take account of failure to comply with such provisional measures." The same power has been exercised by the General Assembly under the "Uniting For Peace" resolution. See U.N. Gen. Ass., Res. No. 378(V), U.N. Gen. Ass., *Off. Rec.,* 5th Sess., Plenary 308 (1950), entitled "Duties of States Upon Outbreak of Hostilities." Cf. Professor Wright's suggestion that refusal "to accept an armistice proposed in accordance with a procedure which [a state] has accepted to implement its no-force obligation" may be taken as a test of aggression. Wright, "The Concept of Aggression in International Law," 29 *A.J.I.L.* 373, 395 (1935). See also Wright, "The Test of Aggression in the Italo-Ethiopian War," 30 id. at 45 (1936).

158. The discussions in the General Assembly and in the 1953 and 1956 Special Committees on the question of defining aggression indicate growing recognition that criteria of aggression may differ as the types and purposes of decision differ. See, e.g., U.N. Gen. Ass., Res. No. 599(VI), U.N. Gen. Ass., *Off. Rec.,* 6th Sess., Plenary 368 (1952); U.N. Gen. Ass. Res. No. 688(VII) U.N. Gen. Ass. *Off. Rec.,* 7th Sess., Plenary 408 (1952); U.N. Doc. No. A/AC.66/L.11, at 34–35 (1953); U.N. Doc. No. A/AC.77/L.13, at 36 (1957). See also Pompe (note 156 above), at 66–71, 95–115; Stone, *Legal Controls* 331, 333, conceding that criteria for purposes of "peace enforcement against states" and criteria for purposes of "punishment of individuals" may vary, but denying that a "workable definition" is available to meet either purpose.

159. See notes 112–15 supra and accompanying text,

less attention: the anticipated impact of a proposed decision on the values of the system of world public order to which the decision-maker adheres. The debates in the United Nations show clearly that representatives of states adhering to a totalitarian world public order consistently assess proposals on this basis. From a perspective which postulates the desirability of maintaining and furthering a public order honoring human freedom, the suggestion may be ventured that so long as competing systems of world public order remain, it may at best be simple utopian idealism for decision-makers committed to nontotalitarian conceptions of world public order to reject that factor as of no relevance at all.[160]

Different decision-makers with different responsibilities do and must, of course, weight varying factors differently in differing contexts. The function of the United Nations representative in preventing or repressing aggression and in activating the machinery of collective security, the function of the official of a nation-state in deciding upon the necessity of countering coercion, and the function of the judge on an international tribunal charged with allocating criminal liabilities after the cessation of violence are obviously quite different. The judge imposing penalties may have to consider many

160. This proposal that a decision-maker take into account the anticipated impact of alternatives in decision upon the values of the system of world public order to which he subscribes has encountered the objections that it ignores that "justice is blind" and requires a decision-maker to abandon impartiality for identification with one or the other of the contending participants. The answer is that the symbol of justice as a blind goddess, balancing scales evenly between unknown parties, comes from the assumed relevance of analogy to a completed legal system—that is, to municipal systems, exhibiting a single inclusive public order and a high degree of consensus among members about how values should be shaped and shared. The analogy scarcely appears apt when it is considered, as we have emphasized, that the contemporary world arena exhibits not one completed, inclusive public order but a number of incomplete, exclusive, contending orders, each with its own perspectives about law and about how values should be shaped and shared. The rational course for a decision-maker subscribing to the values of freedom, who locates himself in time and conceives his task to be that of moving an incomplete public order of freedom still further toward completion in practice as well as in theory, would appear to be to appraise carefully the significance of all the factors in any particular context which may affect movement toward or away from the order he seeks. To permit decision to be controlled mechanically by the presumed dictates of an inappropriate analogy from a very different public order, especially when representatives of opposing world orders do not so handicap themselves, could be suicidal.

mitigating and perhaps exculpating circumstances; he may require a high degree of proof without weakening any deterrent effect of criminal sanctions. But in a world in which the major powers are continuously observing each other and calculating every change and proposal for change in terms of possible effects upon relative fighting potential, ready to act upon the split second with all contemporary instruments of vast destruction,[161] the United Nations representative and the state official must be authorized to act quickly and upon less exacting requirements of proof, if authority is to have any substantial purpose. The traditional requirements imposed upon resort to self-defense—a realistic expectation of instant, imminent military attack and carefully calculated proportionality in response—may, in more particular, require some redefinition to take into account the potentialities of the newer technology of violence.[162] From this perspective, the emphasis in the United Nations Charter upon "armed attack" as the precipitating event for the legitimate recourse to self-defense may appear most unrealistic.

161. The possibility and perils of a surprise attack appear to be enhanced as the velocity and destructiveness of contemporary weapons systems increase. The chilling possibilities of mistakes in identification may also increase. Hanson Baldwin writes that there have been instances when the United States Strategic Air Command bombers, carrying nuclear explosives, were ordered on an emergency takeoff after radar screens registered what appeared to be large numbers of unidentified planes approaching United States bases. In the case of ballistic missiles, Mr. Baldwin observed that recall after launching is impossible and that the period of control, in the sense of capacity to destroy the missile in flight, is measured in minutes. *N.Y. Times,* Feb. 4, 1958, p. 16, cols. 5–6.

162. At least two points about contemporary weapons require consideration. One is that missile weapons make necessary a very short "reaction time"—the time required for reacting with defensive and offensive measures to enemy attack or threat of attack. It has been estimated that present radar systems can give at most fifteen to twenty minutes warning of an attack by means of missiles. Hanson Baldwin, id. Feb. 5, 1958, p. 14, col. 2; "International Security: The Military Aspect," in *Special Studies Report* II, 56 (Rockefeller Bros. Fund, 1958). Obviously, there may be very little time and opportunity for calculation of proportionality. The second point is the possibility that, under certain conditions, the initial attacks may prove decisive. See Beukema, "Warfare and Military Organization," in *Modern World Politics* 374, 378 (Kalijarvi, ed., 1953). While this possibility may be curtailed, so far as concerns the superpowers vis-à-vis each other and to the extent that an "atomic stalemate" exists and is maintained, it cannot be entirely ruled out, even as between the superpowers. The equilibrium represented by an "atomic stalemate" is extremely delicate and precarious.

Community Regulation of Participation in Coercion

The consideration of community regulation of participation involves two closely interrelated but perhaps distinguishable problems: the first requires a determination of the degree of common responsibility available for the maintenance of public order and of the extent to which nonparticipation is permissible; and the second requires a determination, in whatever degree nonparticipation is permissible, of the relative rights and duties of belligerents and nonparticipants in particular situations.

With respect to the first problem, the technical doctrines and detailed rules of nineteenth-century neutrality sought to limit involvement in, and the spatial extension of, violence. These doctrines and rules were originally formulated in a multipolar arena of participants of relatively equal power [163] and, as already suggested, were but one expression of an overriding policy of permitting, in an unorganized and decentralized community of states, the resolution of issues by the relative strength of the contending participants. The most basic premise of the whole structure of prescription and doctrine was that recourse to violence was an exercise of the discretionary competence of a sovereign state and that other states were not entitled to sit in judgment upon the legitimacy of either belligerent's cause.[164]

Again, however, developments in recent decades have caused once hallowed doctrines to atrophy. The emergence of a community prohibition upon recourse to violence, supported by commitments

163. See, generally, Jessup and Deak, "The Origins," in 1 *Neutrality: Its History, Economics and Law* (1935); Phillips and Reede, "The Napoleonic Period," in 2 id. (1936). The structure of the arena permitted the operation of power balancing of which the possibilities of nonparticipation were a function. See Morgenthau, "The Problem of Neutrality," 7 *U. Kan. City L. Rev.* 109, 112–16 (1939); Morgenthau, "The Resurrection of Neutrality in Europe," 33 *Am. Pol. Sci. Rev.* 473, 480–3 (1939); Wright, "International Law and Power Politics," 2 *Measure* 123, 126 (1951); Wright, "The Present Status of Neutrality," 34 *A.J.I.L.* 391, 410–14 (1940).

164. Brierly, *The Outlook for International Law* 25–6 (1944); 2 Oppenheim-Lauterpacht 639, 644; Politis, *Neutrality and Peace* 4–14, 83–4 (1936); Komarnicki, "The Place of Neutrality in the Modern System of International Law," 80 *Hague Recueil* 399, 411–12 (1952); Lauterpacht, "Neutrality and Collective Security," 2 *Politica* 133, 146 (1936).

as in the United Nations Charter to a common responsibility for the maintenance of public order, have destroyed the more important policy premises of traditional doctrines of neutrality and raised grave questions of the degree to which shared responsibility can endure claims of impartiality. The words of the United Nations Charter do authorize the Security Council [165] and perhaps even the General Assembly, if certain provisions are appropriately interpreted,[166] to call upon both member and nonmember states to participate in varying degree in measures designed to repress violence authoritatively characterized as unlawful.

Nonetheless, to suppose that either claims to nonparticipation or the doctrines of neutrality have entirely departed would be extremely rash. Groupings of "uncommitted" states insisting upon "neutralism" in differing degrees have appeared, and recognition of the increasingly massive destructive capabilities of contemporary weapons makes a policy of seeking to avoid involvement in coercion and violence appear considerably more attractive than it did not too long ago.[167] Moreover, most observers agree that the formal prescriptions of the Charter leave many gaps through which permissible nonparticipation may still claim to assert itself.[168] Because of the

165. U.N. Charter, Art. 2, pars. 5, 6; id., Art. 25; id. c. VII.

166. U.N. Charter, Art. 2, pars. 5, 6; id., Arts. 10, 11, 12, 24, par. 1. The "Uniting for Peace" Resolution, U.N. Gen. Ass., Res. No. 377(V), U.N. Gen. Ass., *Off. Rec.*, 5th Sess., Plenary 302 (1950), has been the subject of controversy in which much erudition and exegetical talent have been expended. See, e.g., Kelsen, *Recent Trends in the United Nations* 959–90 (1950); Stone, *Legal Controls* 266–78; Andrassy, "Uniting for Peace," 50 *A.J.I.L.* 563 (1956). The controversy as to the "constitutionality" of the resolution may have become largely academic. In the Suez and Hungarian cases the Security Council itself invoked the resolution and called the General Assembly into emergency sessions.

167. Cf. Morgenthau, "Neutrality and Neutralism," 11 *Y.B. of World Affairs* 47, 67–75 (1957).

168. See, e.g., the analyses set out in 2 Oppenheim-Lauterpacht 645–52; Tucker, *The Law of War and Neutrality at Sea* 171–80 (1957); Komarnicki, "The Problem of Neutrality under the United Nations Charter," 38 *Tr. Grotius Soc.* 77 (1952); Lalive, "International Organization and Neutrality," 24 *Brit. Y.B. I.L.* 72 (1947); Taubenfeld, "International Actions and Neutrality," 47 *A.J.I.L.* 377 (1953). The possibility of permanent neutrality for a member also exists, where such neutrality is accepted by the permanent members, as in the case of Austria. See Kunz, "Austria's Permanent Neutrality," 50 *A.J.I.L.* 418 (1956); Verdross, "Austria's Permanent Neutrality and the United Nations Organization," 50 id. at 61.

veto, the Security Council may not be able to reach a decision or, if it does, may call for participation by only a few states or in differing degree. The powers of the General Assembly have been generally disputed, as well as the powers of the organization as a whole with respect to nonmembers. A state demanding the advantages of nonparticipation may, accordingly, still be able to do so with at least the vestments of respectable authority; that it is able to do so is again but a reflection of the rudimentary character of the organization and primitive recognition of common interest observable in the world arena.

Thus the second problem about participation must often be faced, that of determining the relative rights and duties of belligerents and nonparticipants. Traditionally, authoritative decision-makers have sought to reconcile and accommodate the contraposed policies of military effectiveness, in terms of permitting a belligerent to effect the isolation of its opponent, and of minimizing unnecessary disruptions of the value processes of nonparticipating states.[169] The reconciliation is achieved through complementary concepts: on the one hand, "rights of belligerents," "duties of neutrals," "angary and requisition," "blockade," "contraband," "unneutral service," and "ultimate destination"; on the other, "rights of neutrals," "duties of belligerents," "inviolability of neutral territory," "ineffective blockade," and "freedom of the seas." Some of these technical doctrines and the detailed policies they embody conceivably will survive into the future. What is certain, however, is that to whatever degree they do survive, they will be refashioned by specific practical interpretations to fit the special conditions and demands of future wars, with their own peculiar limits or lack of limits.

One further point that perhaps may be given emphasis is that here, as with the problem of nonpermissible resort to coercion, a decision-maker sharing the values of a nontotalitarian world public order might again rationally take into account the probable consequences for such values of any particular decision demanded. Neither

169. Cf. Jessup, "Today and Tomorrow," in 4 *Neutrality: Its History, Economics and Law* 12–13 (1936); Morgenthau, "Neutrality and Neutralism," 11 *Y.B. of World Affairs* 47, 52, 53 (1957). In c. 2 Professor Jessup makes the point that economic motives and interests frequently underlie the respective claims and countering claims of belligerents and neutrals. See also Castrén, *The Present Law of War and Neutrality* 425–7 (1954).

the unfortunate circumstance that the United Nations cannot reach a "binding" decision in a particular case nor the inability or unwillingness of some states to assume a full share of responsibility for the maintenance of public order requires a state to demand all the rights and assume all the duties of traditional neutrality. A resolution of the General Assembly, coupled with the general commitment of members embodied in Article 2(5) of the Charter, may be construed to authorize a state to appraise the lawfulness of each belligerent's cause and accordingly to discriminate in its demands.[170] In such decision and discrimination, the effects of any proposed resolution on the values of a world public order honoring freedom need not be left unconsidered.

Regulation of the Conduct of Hostilities

In the regulation of hostilities, the patterns of specific controversy to which authority must respond are established by the reciprocal claims of the participants to apply violence against each other's bases of power, by employing certain combatants and weapons, in certain areas of operation, against certain objects of attack.

For resolving such controversies, authoritative decision-makers bring to bear the familiar complementary policies of military necessity and humanitarianism.[171] In all the many varying contexts, these polar policies struggle for recognition and ascendancy or compromise: permissible destruction is characterized in such technical terms as "combatant," "unprivileged belligerency," "military objective," "permissible weapon," "war booty," and "legitimate reprisals"; non-

170. See Martin, *Collective Security: A Progress Report* 146 (1952); 2 Oppenheim-Lauterpacht 652; Komarnicki, "The Problem of Neutrality under the United Nations Charter," 38 *Tr. Grotius Soc.* 77, 85–6 (1952); Woolsey, "The Uniting for Peace Resolution of the United Nations," 45 *A.J.I.L.* 129, 134 (1951). Even the failure of the Assembly to arrive at a recommendation need not mean lack of formal authoritative bases for permissive participation and discrimination. Residual bases may be available in Art. 51 of the Charter and the Pact of Paris. See 2 Oppenheim-Lauterpacht 651; Lalive, note 168 supra at 81–2; Komarnicki, "The Place of Neutrality in the Modern System of International Law," 80 *Hague Recueil* 399, 480–2 (1952).

171. Explicit recognition of the complementary, rather than contradictory, character of these principles may be found in Department of the Navy, *Law of Naval Warfare* pars. 220(a), (b) (1957), quoted in Tucker, note 168 supra at 369 note 11. See also Dunbar, "The Significance of Military Necessity in the Law of War," 67 *Jurid. Rev.* 201, 212 (1955).

permissible destruction is described in such terms as "noncombatants," "civilian immunity," "open city," "nonmilitary objective" and "unlawful confiscation."

The key concept in this structure of doctrine is of course that of military necessity, which affects both the formulation of general prescriptions and their concrete application in particular instances. In a form of statement which adds a few words to the general principle of economy in the exercise of force, this concept may be said to authorize such destruction, and only such destruction, as is necessary, relevant, and proportionate to the prompt realization of legitimate belligerent objectives.[172] Since it is not feasible, as a practical matter, to quantify and to measure precisely the amount of destruction necessary, the fundamental policy embraced in this concept must be modestly expressed as the minimizing of unnecessary destruction of values. Because the law of war is designed for the benefit of all mankind and not merely of certain belligerents, most observers agree, further, that this most basic policy of the minimum unnecessary destruction of values applies to all forms of hostilities, irrespective of the characterization of the resort to violence as lawful or unlawful; [173] of the formal character of one or the other participant as an

172. Comparable formulations abound in the literature. See, e.g., Hall, *International Law* 83 (Higgins ed., 1924): "When violence is permitted at all, the amount which is permissible is that which is necessary to attain the object proposed. The measure of the violence which is permitted in war is therefore that which is required to reduce the enemy to terms." 3 Phillimore, *Commentaries upon International Law* 78 (3d ed., 1885): "The great principle upon which all these rules are framed, is that of, on the one hand, compelling the enemy to do justice as speedily as possible, and, on the other hand, of abstaining from the infliction of all injuries both upon the subjects of the enemy, and upon the Government and subjects of third powers, which do not, certainly and clearly, tend to the accomplishment of this object." Birkenhead, *International Law* 218 (Moelwyn-Hughes, ed., 1927): "The general principle must always be observed that only such violence is permissible as is reasonably proportionate to the object to be attained." A very recent, comprehensive, and insightful exploration of the principle of military necessity appears in O'Brien, "Legitimate Military Necessity in Nuclear War," 2 *World Polity* 35 (1960).

173. Lauterpacht, "Rules of War in an Unlawful War," *Law and Politics in the World Community* 89 (Lipsky, ed., 1953); Lauterpacht, "The Limits of the Operation of the Laws of War," 30 *Brit. Y.B. I.L.* 206 (1953). In the first article, Judge Lauterpacht expressed certain qualifications as to the applicability of the law of war in an unlawful war, at least one of which—that only "laws of warfare in the strict sense of the word," as distinguished from rules relating to the acquisition of title to property, are so applicable—he discarded in the

intrastate rebel group or unrecognized government or authority,[174] or international organization; [175] of the intensity of the violence and its extension in time and space; [176] and of recognition or nonrecognition of the existence of a technical state of war.[177]

---

second article. See also Tucker, note 168 supra at 4–11; Kunz, "The Law of War," 50 *A.J.I.L.* 313, 317–19 (1956). As to the decisions of the war crimes tribunals on this point, see, e.g., "Trial of List," 8 *Law Reports of Trials of War Criminals* 34, 59 (1949); "Trial of Alstotter," 6 id. at 1, 52 (1948); "Trial of Von Leeb," 12 id. at 1, 123–6 (1949); *Re* Christiansen, *Annual Digest 1948,* Case No. 121.

174. While in traditional law, recognition by the legitimate government of the belligerency of the rebel groups has been regarded as a formal condition for the applicability of the law of war, there is recent awareness that the fundamental policy of minimum unnecessary destruction of values is independent, in its application, of a formal recognition of belligerency. Thus, although the 1949 Geneva Conventions do not purport to be applicable as such in civil wars, they set forth minimum standards to be observed by each party to an "armed conflict not of an international character occurring in the territory of one of the High Contracting Parties." Art. 3 of all four Conventions.

Again, Art. 13 of the Wounded and Sick Convention, and Art. 4 of the Prisoners of War Convention, include, among the persons entitled to their protection, "members of regular armed forces who profess allegiance to a Government or an authority not recognized by the Detaining Power."

175. See Jessup, *A Modern Law of Nations* 213 (1948); 2 Oppenheim-Lauterpacht 224–5; Baxter, "The Role of Law in Modern War," 47 *Proc. Am. Soc. I. L.* 90 (1953); Kunz, "The Law of War," 50 *A.J.I.L.* 313, 319–20 (1956). See also Taubenfeld, "International Armed Forces and the Rules of War," 45 *A.J.I.L.* 671, 676–9 (1951), who, however, makes the cryptic statement that "all in all, it cannot be said that the laws of war, in their old form, are prima facie binding on international forces on a strictly legal basis." Cf. Wright, "The Outlawry of War and the Law of War," 47 *A.J.I.L.* 365, 374–5 (1953); Committee on Study of Legal Problems of the United Nations, "Should the Laws of War Apply to United Nations Enforcement Action?" 46 *Proc. Am. Soc. I. L.* 216 (1952).

176. Kunz, "The Law of War," 50 *A.J.I.L.* 313, 321 (1956); see Grob, *The Relativity of War and Peace* 217–18 (1949).

177. Article 2 of all four 1949 Geneva Conventions declares the Conventions applicable to "all cases of declared war or of any other armed conflict which may arise between two or more of the High Contracting Parties, even if the state of war is not recognized by one of them." This provision apparently does not cover a situation, such as the Sino-Japanese hostilities in 1937, where both parties refuse to acknowledge the existence of a state of war. See Kunz, "The Geneva Conventions of August 12, 1949," in *Law and Politics in the World Community* 305 (Lipsky, ed., 1953). But see Yingling and Ginnane, "The Geneva Conventions of 1949," 46 *A.J.I.L.* 393, 394 (1952).

The basic difficulty in this fundamental policy principle of military necessity is reasonably obvious. It contains an inherent and infinitely manipulatable obscurity in its reference to the "legitimate" objectives of violence.[178] The basic principles and most of the prescriptions on the management of hostilities were first formulated before the public order of the world community, by imposing a prohibition upon resort to violence and distinguishing between permissible and nonpermissible violence, began to seek to regulate the objectives of violence. Thus, in their formulations of the principle of military necessity, commentators have frequently referred to belligerents' objectives in terms of military aims so expansive

178. The obscurity is rooted in the difficulty in distinguishing the total political objectives of a belligerent in resorting to coercion from specific military objectives sought in the course of conducting hostilities. The total political purposes of a belligerent may be characterized as impermissible in the sense that the initial resort to coercion is regarded as unlawful. This does not mean, however, that authoritative decision-makers either do or should deny to such a belligerent, because of the nonpermissible character of its total purposes, the application of the principle of military necessity in determining the lawfulness or unlawfulness of specific acts done during the course of hostilities. Cf. Wright, "The Outlawry of War and the Law of War," 47 *A.J.I.L.* 365, 371 note 28 (1953). The problem of determining whether a state has by its total political purposes and acts breached the community prohibition upon resort to violence is very different from the problem of determining the responsibility of individuals for specific acts of destruction. Though failing in its efforts to prevent unlawful resort to violence, the general community of states may still seek to secure a policy of minimizing unnecessary destruction of values during hostilities and, for that end, impose the same standards of humanitarianism upon both the belligerent exercising lawful defense or engaging in police action and the aggressor-belligerent. In some limited contexts of active combat, a distinction may be drawn, in appraising the necessity for specific acts of violence, between total political purposes and specific limited operational military objectives, such as the capture and occupation of a particular locality and the advance to or retreat from a particular line or zone, and necessity measured against those specific limited military objectives. See, e.g., *United States v. List,* 11 *Trials of War Criminals before the Nuremberg Military Tribunals* 759, 1295–7 (1949); *United States v. Von Leeb,* id. at 462, 541, involving charges of unnecessary devastation, where the necessity for the devastation was measured against the specific military purpose of successful retreat in the face of advancing Russian forces; the accused were found not guilty. In other contexts, however, the distinction becomes difficult to make. Consider the continuing debate about the legal justification of strategic bombardment and of the decision to drop the atomic bomb on Hiroshima and Nagasaki.

as to cover every possible objective: "the overpowering and utter defeat of the enemy," [179] "complete surrender," [180] "complete submission," [181] or "victory." [182] But the world arena presents little effective agreement on the legitimate objectives of coercion and violence; agreement is unlikely so long as rival systems of world public order, totalitarian and free, compete for supremacy. The further clarification of the detailed limits of permissible violence in the conduct of hostilities must depend upon further clarification of permissible objectives in resort to violence.[183]

The best that can be done by way of clarification is to review the compromises between military necessity and humanitarianism which earlier authoritative decision-makers have effected in the various

179. 2 Oppenheim-Lauterpacht 225.

180. Downey, "The Law of War and Military Necessity," 47 *A.J.I.L.* 251, 254 (1953).

181. 3 Hyde, *International Law* 1801 (2d rev. ed., 1945). The old War Department Field Manual, FM 27-10, Department of War, *Rules of Land Warfare* pars. 22–3 (FM 27-10, 1940), used the same term. The new FM 27-10, Department of the Army, *Law of Land Warfare* par. 3 (FM 27-10, 1956), states that "The law of war . . . requires that belligerents refrain from employing any kind or degree of violence which is not actually necessary for military purposes." Department of the Navy, *The Law of Naval Warfare* par. 220(a) (1957), on the other hand, speaks of military necessity as permitting "a belligerent to apply only that degree and kind of regulated force, not otherwise prohibited by the laws of war, required for the partial or complete submission of the enemy with the least possible expenditure of time, life and physical resources."

182. Stone, *Legal Controls* 351.

183. See infra, chs. 3 and 5. It is obvious enough that any particular quantum of instrumental violence can be appraised as necessary or unnecessary, not in vacuo, but only in context and in relation to a determined purpose or objective. If characterization of violence in terms of lawfulness or unlawfulness depends upon appraisal of necessity, the purpose or objective must be relevant in that characterization. The problem of indicating the purpose or objective against which necessity is to be measured, however, is not eliminated by frequently difficult distinctions between military purposes and ultimate political purposes. Military purposes are not fixed constants; they are, at least in broad outline, determined and controlled by the character and scope of the political purposes of the belligerent. See note 92 supra. The narrower or broader the scope of political objectives characterized as permissible, the narrower or broader will be the legitimate military purposes, and as legitimate military purposes are narrowed, the quantum of violence necessary for their achievement, and hence, in general principle, lawful, tends to diminish. See note 178 supra; cf. Tucker, *The Law of War and Neutrality at Sea* 49 (1957).

types of controversies arising out of the conduct of hostilities and to suggest alternatives in compromise which may be more compatible with the values of a free society in the world arena probably emerging. Detailed clarification could extend into volumes; this chapter will only touch quickly a few major points.

COMBATANTS

Decision-makers have sought to protect combatants against surprise [184] and to limit the involvement of individuals in war and their subjection to direct attack [185] by confining permissible combatancy, carrying with it a right to admission to prisoner-of-war status upon capture, generally to a well-defined category of individuals—members of the public armed forces of participating states exhibiting certain prescribed indicia. The realism of this policy may differ as future wars are total or limited.

AREAS OF OPERATION

The delimitation of permissible areas of operation is based on deference to claims of nonparticipant states to "inviolability" of their territory, waters, and airspace. However, the nonparticipant's tolerance of, or inability to prevent, unilateral violation of its territory may convert such territory into a permissible area of operation.[186] The recent Geneva Conventions and contemporary discussions of limited war raise the possibility of establishing, by mutual agreement, zones of immunity in the territories of participants for

184. Belligerents are, it is said, entiled to know who their enemies are. See *The German War Book* 61 (Morgan, trans., 1915); Cowles, "Recent Practical Aspects of the Laws of War," 18 *Tul. L. Rev.* 121, 133 (1943). See also Winfield, *The Foundations and Future of International Law* 70 (1941).

185. The immunity from direct attack accorded by traditional law to the noncombatant individual assumed that that individual was a harmless nonparticipant. Fenwick, *International Law* 554 (3d ed., 1948); Hall, *International Law* (Higgins, ed., 1924); 3 Hyde, *International Law* 1799 (2d rev. ed., 1945).

186. See 3 Hyde, *International Law* 2337–9, 2340–1 (2d rev. ed., 1945); 2 Oppenheim-Lauterpacht 678–80; Smith, *The Law and Custom of the Sea* 145 (2d ed., 1950). See also *Coenca Brothers v. German State, Annual Digest 1927–1928,* Case No. 389; The *Anna Maria, Annual Digest 1946,* Case No. 174; The *Tinos* and other vessels, in Garner, *Prize Law during the World War* 228–30 (1927). The last two cases involved conversion of neutral waters into a permissible area of operations for purposes of exercise of the right of capture.

the special protection of certain classes of individuals.[187] The policy of limiting the involvement of states and individuals in war is here again evident.

WEAPONS

The permissible or nonpermissible character of the employment of a particular weapon or mode of attack has in broad principle been made by decision-makers to turn upon the proportionality between the deprivation of values incidental to the use of the weapon or mode of attack and the military advantage accruing to the belligerent user.[188] As already mentioned, only weapons whose use has resulted in incidental value deprivations obviously superfluous and grossly disproportionate to the ensuing military advantage have been characterized as nonpermissible and effectively outlawed.[189] Since such weapons are by definition militarily inefficient—value deprivations necessitate the expenditure of force—the compromise in favor of military necessity is obvious.

In particular, it may be noted that the argument about the supposed nonpermissible character of nuclear weapons is derived principally by analogy from earlier prescriptions about poisonous gas, poisoned arms and other weapons causing disproportionate suffering.[190] Analogies are important, however, only so far as the policies

187. See Art. 23 of the Wounded and Sick Convention, Arts. 14, 15 of the Civilians Convention, and the Draft Agreements relating to Hospital Zones and Localities annexed to both conventions.

188. Hall, *International Law* 635–6 (Higgins, ed., 1924), who also observed that "the amount of destruction or suffering which may be caused is immaterial if the result obtained is conceived to be proportionate"; 1 Garner, *International Law and the World War* 282 (1920); 3 Hyde, *International Law* 1813–18 (2d rev. ed., 1945); Spaight, *War Rights on Land* 76–7 (1911). Conventional expression of the general principle involved is found in the Declaration of St. Petersburg of 1868 and Art. 23(e) of the Hague Regulations.

189. See text at note 111 supra. The determination of what value deprivations may be designated as "incidental" may, of course, present perplexing difficulties. These difficulties include the demarcation of the boundaries of a physical target and the variable capability of weapons and modalities of attack for confining destruction within such boundaries. Where the target selected is not possessed of spatial dimensions, such as "enemy morale," the possibility of determining the incidental character of deprivations may reach the vanishing point.

190. See Sack, "ABC—Atomic, Biological, Chemical Warfare in International

they suggest are relevant; and analogies here suggest only the requirements, again, of compromise between military necessity and humanitarianism. In the context of the contemporary world arena, a very strong case would have to be made to establish that no possible uses of nuclear and thermonuclear weapons could conceivably be within the scope of military necessity for objectives legitimate by standards making reference to human dignity. The very difficulty in securing explicit agreement about the effective control of such weapons must suggest expectations of their military effectiveness and the perils of relying upon any alleged limitations derived from analogies. The rational position would appear to be that the lawfulness of any particular use or type of use of nuclear and thermonuclear weapons must be judged, like the use of any weapon or technique of warfare, by the level of destruction effected—in other words, by its reasonableness in the total context of a particular use.[191]

OBJECTS OF ATTACK

Under traditional doctrines, belligerents have been granted a wide discretion in selecting and attacking the opponent's bases of power —human, material, or institutional—which, in substantial degree, are being used for belligerent purposes. When the purposes of attack

Law," 10 *Law. Guild Rev.* 161 (1950). Stone, *Legal Controls* 343, states that "radio-active substances are clearly 'poisonous' or at least 'analogous substances' in any functional sense" and that they "in a sense, cause injuries and inevitable death beyond the needs of military operations." See also Spaight, *Air Power and War Rights* 275–6 (3d ed., 1947); Moore, "The Present State of International Law," in *Report of the 46th Conference, International Law Association* 12, 31 (1954). The recent "Text of Statement by Leaders of 81 Communist Parties After Meeting in Moscow" (*N.Y. Times,* Dec. 7, 1960, pp. 14–17), describing "peaceful coexistence" as a temporary tactic and insisting upon the legality of "national-liberation wars," makes this idiosyncratic interpretation completely explicit.

191. Cf. Tucker, note 183 supra at 55, who distinguishes between uses "against military objectives in the proximity of the non-combatant population" and uses "exclusively against military forces in the field or naval forces at sea." It may also be noted that the yield of nuclear explosives is subject to control and that low-yield weapons adapted to tactical uses are now commonplace. See Reinhardt and Kintner, *Atomic Weapons in Land Combat* (1953). We share the common humanitarian hope that such weapons may eventually be outlawed. The humanitarian realist must recognize, however, that successful outlawry will depend upon consensus and effective multilateral implementation.

have been achieved, however, and the objects of attack deprived of their character as effective bases of enemy power, the principle of humanitarianism becomes applicable and makes further violence, already militarily unnecessary, nonpermissible.[192] Such is the principal burden of the recent Geneva Conventions.

Special questions have sometimes been raised about the law of air warfare—in particular, about legal limitations on strategic bombardment—in connection with this problem of permissible objects of attack. While the determination of what, in specific contexts, may legitimately be regarded as a military objective involves some difficulties, air warfare would not appear to present any unique issues: the purpose and level of destruction obtained are of prime importance to legal policy, not the modality of delivery. The advent of ballistic missiles, which can be launched from the surface or beneath the surface of land or sea and from the air, will perhaps serve to underscore the irrelevance of traditional distinctions about modality of delivery.[193] It is possible, nevertheless, that all modalities of destruction, not merely strategic air power, may remain subject to one overriding inhibition which Judge Lauterpacht has described as "an absolute rule of law." He writes:

> [I]t is in [the] prohibition, which is a clear rule of law, of intentional terrorization—or destruction—of the civilian population as an avowed or obvious object of attack that lies the last

192. Arts. 23(c), (d) of the Hague Regulations; Hall, *International Law* 473 (Higgins, ed., 1924); 2 Oppenheim-Lauterpacht 338; 2 Wheaton, *International Law* 165 (Keith, ed., 1944). On the criminality of refusing quarter see "The Abbaye Ardenne Case," 4 *Law Reports of Trials of War Criminals* 97 (1948); "Trial of Von Ruchteschell," 9 id. at 83 (1949).

Even Clausewitz, who is not commonly accused of being a humanitarian, wrote: "The military forces must be destroyed, that is to say, put into such a condition that they can no longer continue to fight. We take this opportunity to explain that . . . the expression 'the destruction of the enemy's military forces' is to be understood only in this sense." Clausewitz, *On War* 19 (Jolles trans., 1943).

193. It may be, however, that intercontinental ballistic missiles when combined with high-yield dirty thermonuclear warheads cannot, with the present low capabilities of guidance systems for precision, be used without forfeiting all possibilities of keeping some limits on destruction. Such weapon systems may reduce the conception of purpose and level of destruction—reasonableness in the total context of particular uses—to marginal utility.

vestige of the claim that war can be legally regulated at all. Without that irreducible principle of restraint there is no limit to the licence and depravity of force. . . . It is clear that admission of a right to resort to the creation of terror among the civilian population as being a legitimate object *per se* would inevitably mean the actual and formal end of the law of warfare. For that reason, so long as the assumption is allowed to subsist that there is a law of war, the prohibition of the weapon of terror not incidental to lawful operations must be regarded as an absolute rule of law.[194]

The essentially modest character of this "absolute rule" needs no underlining.[195]

REPRISALS AND SUPERIOR ORDERS

A comprehensive presentation would survey the detailed policies and decisions on the various defenses which an individual accused of violating the law of war may interpose to shield himself from criminal punishment—such as "military necessity" in its most specific sense, reprisals, official capacity, and superior orders. Perhaps reprisals and superior orders, however, merit a few words in this introductory statement.

Reprisals may be described as violent measures which would otherwise be unlawful, invoked as a response to and a sanction against the prior unlawful violence of the enemy. While reprisals have frequently been the subject of extravagant claims, it is a mistake to regard the doctrine of reprisals as a denial of law or of the possibility of law.[196] The world public order, on the contrary, authorizes re-

194. Lauterpacht, "The Problem of the Revision of the Law of War," 29 *Brit. Y.B. I. L.* 360–9 (1952).

195. One difficulty is that, conceding the lawfulness of certain political and strategic objectives, certain forms of "terrorization," such as terror bombing, when carried out under certain circumstances and within certain limitations, might conceivably result in less aggregate destruction of values than other alternatives in the application of violence. It has also been difficult in practice to distinguish the effects of the bombing of cities for purposes of destroying military installations and transportation and communications systems from those of bombing for purposes of terror. Where nuclear explosives are used, it may be even more difficult to make this distinction.

196. It comes too close to such a view to say, as Professor Hyde did, that "when opposing belligerents reciprocate in dealing with each other as the law

prisals as a last desperate measure to secure law-conforming behavior. The first effort of such order is to prevent change by violent procedures; when that effort fails, resort is next had to the law of war to minimize the inevitable destruction of values; when observance of the law of war breaks down, the only immediate recourse of the injured is to reprisals in the hope of creating expectations in the enemy of the desirability of a return to observance of that law. Other decision-makers may, of course, have an opportunity to review the judgment of the acting belligerent as to the propriety of the occasion and proportionality of the response in reprisal, but in a world arena, organized as at present, no effective alternative to such immediate administration of reciprocities in benefit and injury is apparent.

The somewhat vague formulation of principle governing superior orders represents what clearly is a compromise between the requirements of maintaining military discipline in armies [197] and the necessity of securing enforcement of law through the imposition of individual criminal responsibility. Were both official capacity or "act of state" and superior orders, as formulated in their most absolute assertions,[198] unconditionally accepted as absolving defenses, there would be little left of a law of war; for superior orders would result in an indefinite regressive transmission of responsibility until the very apex of the authority and control structure in the belligerent state is reached,[199] while "act of state" would serve to shield those

---

forbids, their conduct is extra-legal and finds no proper place in a system of law purporting to govern the conduct of States at war." 3 Hyde, *International Law* 1841 (2d rev. ed., 1945). See also Stone, *Legal Controls* 354, where the sweeping statement is made that belligerents' duty to observe the law of war is "not absolute but conditional" on reciprocation. Cf. Westlake's view that the unlawful acts of its enemy do not loose a belligerent from law but entrust it with a right to redress of a violated obligation. 2 Westlake, *International Law* 114–15 (1907).

197. See "Trial of Von Leeb," 12 *Law Reports of Trials of War Criminals* 73 (1949).

198. See, e.g., Manner, "The Legal Nature and Punishment of Criminal Acts of Violence Contrary to the Laws of War," 37 *A.J.I.L.* 407, 416–18 (1943); Schick, "War Criminals and the Law of the United Nations," 7 *U. Toronto L. J.* 27, 45 (1947–1948).

199. See "Trial of Von Leeb," 12 *Law Reports of Trials of War Criminals* 71 (1949); Lauterpacht, "The Law of Nations and the Punishment of War Crimes," 21 *Brit. Y.B. I. L.* 58, 70 (1944). See also Glueck, *War Criminals: Their Prosecution and Punishment* 141 (1944); Berger, "The Legal Nature of War

who stand at the top of the structure. The present flexible doctrine has at least the virtue of authorizing a decision-maker to take into account in any particular situation relevant variables, such as the patency or obscurity of the illegal character of the order, the relative positions in the hierarchy of command of both the superior issuing the order and the subordinate complying with it, the time of the commission of the offense, and the specific tactical military situation at such time.[200]

Belligerent Occupation

In this context, one of the participants has so far succeeded in his active exercise of violence as to acquire, establish, and solidify effective control over portions of the territory of the other. The reduction of enemy territory and of its people and resources to the firm possession of a belligerent deprives the enemy of their use as effective bases of power. The occupant then seeks to police and utilize the captured bases of power so as to sustain and augment his own means of carrying on combat in still unoccupied areas. In this time period, after successful invasion but before final victory, the expectations of all parties about future permanent authority in the area are obscure; but some temporary authority must be conceded, and the inhabitants, for whom life must go on, present against the occupant counter-demands for continuity and minimum dislocation of their value processes.

Here again, as in the context of active combat, the basic policy consistently sought by authoritative decision-makers is an equilibrium between the requirements of military necessity and humanity, or the minimum unnecessary destruction of values. The applicable prescriptions on the one hand concede authority to the occupant

---

Crimes and the Problem of Superior Command," 38 *Am. Pol. Sci. Rev.* 1203 (1944); Sack, "Punishment of War Criminals and the Defence of Superior Orders," 60 *L. Q. Rev.* 63 (1944); Wright, "War Crimes under International Law," 62 *L. Q. Rev.* 40, 45 (1946).

200. See, e.g., "Trial of Von Leeb," 12 *Law Reports of Trials of War Criminals* 71–4 (1949); "Trial of Masuda," 1 id. at 71 (1947), 5 id. at 18–19 (1948); "Trial of Greifelt," 13 id. at 1, 69 (1949); "Trial of Milch," 7 id. at 42 (1948). See also Dunbar, "Some Aspects of the Problem of Superior Orders in the Law of War," 63 *Jurid. Rev.* 234, 251, 253–5, 261 (1951).

to safeguard his military security by policing the occupied area and punishing inhabitants who commit hostile acts directed against him and, on the other hand, require him to respect the lives, loyalties, and, in general, the human dignity of the inhabitants. In like manner, while the relevant prescriptions permit the occupant to secure the satisfaction of his military needs out of the resources and labor of the occupied territory, they simultaneously restrict the permissible extent and character of that utilization in deference to the domestic needs and loyalties of the inhabitants. The familiar technical terms for incorporating one set of policies include "belligerent occupation," "maintenance of *vie publique,*" "war treason," and "requisitions and contributions"; the opposing policies are expressed by "premature annexation," "usurpation of sovereignty," "unlawful alteration of fundamental institutions," "unlawful subversion of allegiance," and "disproportionate requisitions and contributions."

For some illustration of the details of the continuing complementarity of policy and prescription, some of the more important provisions of the 1949 Geneva Civilians Convention, which supplements the 1907 Hague Regulations in concise formulation of both inherited principles and new prescriptions, may be mentioned. The Civilians Convention prohibits the cruder forms of violence and brutality, such as extermination, murder, torture, corporal punishment, mutilation, and scientific experiments; [201] vicarious punishment, such as collective penalties, reprisals against inhabitants and their property, and the taking of hostages; [202] and individual deportations and mass forcible transfers of the population to the home country of the occupant.[203] The Convention enjoins respect for "the persons [of the inhabitants], their honour, their family rights, their religious convictions and practices, and their manners and customs" and demands special protection for women against rape, enforced prostitution, and any form of indecent assault.[204]

201. Art. 32. For general surveys of the Civilians Convention, see Gutteridge, "The Protection of Civilians in Occupied Territory," 5 *Y.B. of World Affairs* 290, 297–308 (1951); Gutteridge, "The Rights and Obligations of an Occupying Power," 6 id. at 149, 160–9 (1952).

202. Arts. 33, 34.

203. Art. 49, par. 1.

204. Art. 27.

At the same time, however, the Convention permits the occupant to take such measures of control and security in regard to the inhabitants as may be "necessary as a result of the war." [205] For "imperative military reasons," for instance, the occupant may require the total or partial evacuation of a given area [206] and "for imperative reasons of security," he may confine the inhabitants to assigned residences or intern them.[207] More generally, the occupant is permitted by the Convention to subject the inhabitants to regulations essential to the security of the occupant and the members and property and communications of the occupation forces or administration,[208] and to punish with imprisonment or death, after judicial proceedings complying with certain minimum procedural standards of fairness,[209] those who violate such regulations.

Among the more pressing problems in this area is the treatment of inhabitants who join guerrilla or partisan forces or resistance movements. Guerrilla forces and their operations have in the past been characterized by mobility, stealth and secrecy, and an ability to sink at will into the protective anonymity of the civilian population.[210] It is these characteristics of guerrilla techniques that occupants have found vastly annoying, dangerous, and difficult to counter. Presumably because of the peculiar danger to the occupant's security posed by guerrilla forces, both traditional law and the Geneva Civilians Convention have left the occupant free to visit death on captured inhabitants who are members of such forces.[211] All that the

205. Ibid.

206. Art. 49, par. 2.

207. Art. 78.

208. Art. 64, par. 2.

209. Arts. 65–77 constitute a rough and ready code of criminal law and procedure applicable in cases of violations of the occupant's security legislation.

210. For description of guerrilla techniques and tactics, see Levy, *Guerrilla Warfare* (1942); Miksche, *Secret Forces: The Technique of Underground Movements* cc. 2, 3 (1950).

211. The tribunal in "Trial of List," 8 *Law Reports of Trials of War Criminals* 34, 58 (1949), asserted that "in no other way can an army guard and protect itself from the gadfly tactics of such armed resistance" and that "members of such resistance forces must accept the increased risks involved in this mode of fighting." The war crimes tribunals commonly held that civilians not exhibiting the indicia set forth in Art. 1 of the Hague Regulations were not permissible combatants and that their execution, as such, did not constitute a war

Civilians Convention does is to require a previous judicial determination of the fact of participation in guerrilla activities.[212]

The 1949 Geneva Prisoners of War Convention does now include among the categories of captured persons entitled to prisoner-of-war treatment members of "organized resistance movements belonging to a Party to the conflict and operating in or outside their own territory, even if this territory is occupied." [213] The revolutionary character of this rule is, however, less real than apparent. For the same convention requires members of organized resistance movements to exhibit all the indicia of legitimate combatancy—responsible command; a fixed, distinctive, recognizable sign; open carrying of arms; and observance of the laws of war. Compliance with all these requirements by members of guerrilla or resistance movements without discarding their character as secret underground forces seems difficult indeed.[214] Thus, whether a consistent application of the fundamental community policy of minimizing unnecessary destruction of values would not require the reassessment of the position in law of resistance movements, and possibly their legitimation and admission of members to prisoner-of-war status, still appears open to question. Experience in previous major wars would seem to point both to the military effectiveness of resistance movements in immobilizing and compelling dispersion of occupation troops and in disrupting the

---

crime. See, e.g., "Trial of Von Leeb," 12 id. at 85–6 (1949); "Trial of Ohashi," 5 id. at 27–9 (1948); "Trial of Bruns," 3 id. at 21 (1948).

212. See Arts. 64–75. Article 68 does limit the imposition of the death penalty to cases of espionage, "serious acts of sabotage" and "intentional offenses which have caused the death of one or more persons," and adds the condition that "such offenses were punishable by death under the law of the occupied territory in force before the occupation began." The requirement of judicial determination of participation in guerrilla activities had been laid down by the war crimes tribunals. The execution of persons charged with sabotage and guerrilla warfare, without such previous determination or trial, was punished as a war crime. See, e.g., "Trial of Shinohara," 5 *Law Reports of Trials of War Criminals* 32 (1948); "Trial of Motosuke," 13 id. at 129–30 (1949); "Trial of Hisakasu," 5 id. at 70 (1948); "Trial of Altstotter," 6 id. at 96–104 (1948).

213. Art. 4(A) (2).

214. Cf. Stone, *Legal Controls* 565. See also Baxter, "So-Called 'Unprivileged Belligerency': Spies, Guerrillas, and Saboteurs," 28 *Brit. Y.B. I. L.* 323, 327–8, 336–7 (1951); Ford, "Resistance Movements in Occupied Territory," 3 *Nederlands Tijdschrift voor International Recht* 355, 379 (1956).

highly complex logistics of modern war, and to the minimal deterrent value of expectations of death upon capture.[215] If the military utility of partisan war does substantially outweigh the value deprivations incident to capture, and if the threatened value deprivations are, in point of fact, ineffective to secure the occupant against guerrilla attacks by inhabitants, the assertion might be made with some degree of plausibility that such deprivations of values are unnecessary and pointless.[216] The realism of any new line of compromise between the competing policies will, of course, differ as future wars are total or limited.

Prisoners of War

Since prisoners of war constitute bases of enemy power already effectively neutralized by capture, the further direct application of violence against them would result in a destruction of values without

215. See, e.g., Furniss, *American Military Policy* 413–23 (1957); Stone, *Legal Controls* 564; Donovan, "Secret Movements, Espionage and Treachery," in *Modern World Politics* 308, 324 (Kalijarvi, ed., 1953); Baxter, "So-Called 'Unprivileged Belligerency': Spies, Guerrillas, and Saboteurs," 28 *Brit. Y.B. I. L.* 323, 334 (1951); Kueder, " 'Territorial War': The New Concept of Resistance," 32 *Foreign Aff.* 91 (1953); Papagos, "Guerrilla Warfare," 30 id. at 215 (1952). For an account of the guerrilla or resistance movements in occupied Europe during World War II see *Hitler's Europe, Survey of International Affairs 1939–1946,* 327–37 (Italy), 419–34 (France), 561–8 (Poland), 650–72 (Yugoslavia) (Royal Institute of Int. Affairs, 1954). See also Dallin, *German Rule in Russia 1941–1945: A Study in Occupation Policies* (1957). The very intensity and widespread character of guerrilla war in the occupied countries testify to the weak deterrent effect, if any, of execution and torture upon capture. Neither the German nor the Japanese occupation forces were particularly lenient with captured guerrillas or partisans. The current experience of the French armies in Algeria and their continuing inability—despite fierce repressive measures—to stop Algerian guerrilla rebels tend to sustain the point made.

216. Of course, the more effective guerrilla warfare becomes the more insistent becomes the occupant's interest in effectively combatting it. What we suggest is that denial of prisoner-of-war rights may be an uneconomical and inefficient way of dealing with guerrillas. Cf. the observation in Stone, *Legal Controls* 567 note 25, that "a belligerent may often find it preferable to offer guerrillas the privileged status of prisoners of war if they surrender, rather than to expend the resources necessary to overcome and destroy them by force." See also Von Glahn, *The Occupation of Enemy Territory* 52 (1957); Baxter, "So-Called 'Unprivileged Belligerency': Spies, Guerrillas, and Saboteurs," 28 *Brit. Y.B. I. L.* 323, 337 (1951).

military significance.[217] Nonetheless, the captor-belligerent does assert claims to exercise coercive control over prisoners of war for certain purposes, such as the maintenance of his military advantage through their continued neutralization and the utilization of their labor. On the other hand, the captive personnel as well as their home state make countering demands for enjoyment of certain minimum values during captivity.

That the prescriptions applicable here, codified in the 1949 Geneva Prisoners of War Convention, represent once more an attempted balancing of the same polar policies sought by authoritative decision-makers in other contexts is clear. The Geneva Convention seeks to extend the humanitarian benefits of prisoner-of-war treatment by attempting to catch as many as possible in its categorization of those entitled to such treatment. The categories include, aside from members of the regular armed forces, militias, volunteer corps, and guerrillas who exhibit the prescribed marks of permissible combatants, the armed forces of an unrecognized power, civilian contractors and aircraft crews, war correspondents, members of labor and welfare units, crew members of merchantmen and civil aircraft, and participants in a *levy en masse*.[218] But deferring to the security needs of the captor power, the Convention leaves it free to deny prisoner-of-war status to spies, saboteurs, deserters from its own forces, traitors, and perhaps parole violators. Similarly, while the Convention requires that prisoners of war must at all times be humanely treated and protected from mental and physical violence and immunized from reprisals,[219] prescribing in minute specification the details of the required standard of treatment, prisoners of war are declared subject to the laws, regulations, and orders of the captor power, violation of which renders them liable to disciplinary or penal,

217. Under the general principle of military necessity, as that principle was formulated above, there can, of course, be no necessity for killing prisoners of war who have ceased to be effective units of enemy power. It is perhaps for the purpose of shielding this rule of general protection from eroding exceptions that operational necessity which may in varying degree be generated by pressure from forces other than the captured personnel is not accepted as a defense to a charge of killing such prisoners. See, e.g., "Trial of Thiele and Steinert," 3 *Law Reports of Trials of War Criminals* 56 (1948). See also Department of the Army, *The Law of Land Warfare* par. 85 (FM 27-10, 1956).

218. Art. 4.

219. Art. 13.

judicial sanctions.[220] Again, though the Convention obliges the captor power to respect the loyalties and human dignity of the captured personnel, it permits the captor to augment his resources by exacting compulsory labor from prisoners of war for certain projects which, while not of a distinctly military character, are of substantial value to his over-all war effort.[221]

Among the problems of contemporary interest involving prisoners of war is that of compulsory repatriation. The Convention states that captured personnel "shall be released and repatriated without delay after the cessation of hostilities." [222] During the Korean armistice negotiations, a very large number of communist prisoners held by the United Nations Command refused to be repatriated to North Korea and the People's Republic of China. Mr. Vishinsky demanded the repatriation of each and every prisoner, including the unwilling, and insisted vehemently that Article 118 was a "clear" and "categoric formula," a "principle of international law," which needed no interpretation.[223] He pointed at the same time to Article 7, which provides that prisoners "may in no circumstances renounce in part or in entirety the rights secured to them by the present Convention." The position officially taken by the United Nations was that neither the general prescriptions of international law nor the particular ones of the Geneva Convention required the United Nations forcibly to repatriate prisoners unwilling to go home. The submission has been made that this stand is sustained by a realistic conception of the nature and functions of the familiar principles of interpretation and by the independent right of states to grant asylum, and that it is the conclusion compelled by a deep commitment to humanitarianism and the goal values of a free world society.[224] Such submission seems persuasive. No set of words can, apart from context, have any one "clear," "unambiguous," or "literal" meaning that of itself compulsorily determines decision, whatever the particular circumstances

220. Art. 82.

221. Arts. 49–50.

222. Art. 118.

223. U.N. Gen. Ass., *Off. Rec.*, 7th Sess., 1st Comm. 37 (1952–1953).

224. Charmatz and Wit, "Repatriation of Prisoners of War and the 1949 Geneva Convention," 62 *Yale L. J.* 391 (1953). See also Gutteridge, "The Repatriation of Prisoners of War," 2 *Int. and Comp. Law Q.* 207 (1953); Mayda, "The Korean Repatriation Problem and International Law," 47 *A.J.I.L.* 414 (1953); Schapiro, "Repatriation of Deserters," 29 *Brit. Y.B. I. L.* 310 (1952).

may be. A rational theory of interpretation must recognize that treaty words acquire meaning in specific controversies only from context and in terms of the major purposes and demands of the parties to the treaty.[225] There is no question that the major purpose of Articles 118 and 7 was humanitarian in character—for the benefit of the prisoners, to prevent abuse by coerced retention or waiver—and that forcible repatriation despite the prisoners' well-founded expectations of severe deprivations upon return does not serve that purpose.

Enemy Persons and Property within a Belligerent's Territory

The problem arises largely with respect to enemy persons and property found within the territory of a belligerent or its allies upon the outbreak of hostilities. The characterization, it is important to note, is of "enemy" persons and property and not of "alien nationals." Recognition is developing that the niceties of "nationality" law, devised for other purposes, have less relevance to purposes of control of an enemy's bases of power than factual loyalties and group membership, which transcend both national boundaries and technical niceties.[226]

225. For amplification and documentation of this theme, see McDougal and Gardner, "The Veto and the Charter: An Interpretation for Survival," 60 *Yale L. J.* 258 (1951).

226. See Domke, *Trading with the Enemy in World War II,* 46–51 (1943). See also Lafitte, *The Internment of Aliens* 35 (1940), who, speaking primarily of the refugees from Nazi Germany, urged that "we discriminate, not between Britons and 'aliens,' or between 'friendly aliens' and 'enemy aliens' in the present way, but between those who stand for freedom and those who stand for tyranny in every country. This division cuts right across all nationalities. The real 'aliens' are the 'Nazis of the soul' of all countries, including our own. . . . Our real friends are not to be determined by tests of birthplace, nationality or language, but by their past and present conduct in the struggle against authoritarian forms of government." See also the United States' Emergency Detention Act of 1950, 64 Stat. 1019 (1950), 50 U.S.C. §§ 811–26 (1952), which authorizes, in cases of an "internal security emergency" brought about by invasion, declaration of war, or insurrection in aid of a foreign enemy, the apprehension and detention of any person "as to whom there is reasonable ground to believe that such person probably will engage in, or probably will conspire with others to engage in, acts of espionage or sabotage"; the United Kingdom's Emergency Powers (Defence) Act, 1939, 2 and 3 Geo. 6, c. 62, § 1(2) (a).

Upon control of enemy persons found in a belligerent's territory, international law would appear to interpose but few limits. Complementary policies are here again contraposed and compromised in terms of the security needs of the belligerent [227] and of the human rights of the individual. Whether even in time of peace, however, the alien national is entitled to protection by standards of civilized justice or merely to equal treatment with nationals is still debated. For nationals of the belligerent, the common assumption is that international law offers no protection, other than in relatively obsolete doctrines of humanitarian intervention. When violence breaks out, restraints may a fortiori be even more modest, unless the Nuremberg judgment be thought to afford some degree of protection by its limited concept of crimes against humanity.[228] The recent unprotested practice of states presents such measures as the registration and compulsory detention of aliens, or detailed regulation of their activities, and, in some instances, even sterner measures for nationals.[229] The 1949 Geneva Civilians Convention does seek to establish a modicum of human rights for alien nationals caught in the hands of belligerents,[230] but it yields, as was of course necessary, to the security interests of the belligerent, as determined, in the first instance, by the belligerent himself.[231]

The protection which international law affords to enemy property found in a belligerent's territory is disputed. Unquestionably, a belligerent may seize and apply such property to its purposes during war. Whether international law imposes upon the belligerent a duty either to restore or to pay for such property after the termination of hostilities, however, has recently been questioned. A number of reputable writers have, in surveying past practices, been able to find such a duty.[232] But this finding seems to represent both a somewhat

227. Stone, *Legal Controls* 443–4.

228. See Schwelb, "Crimes against Humanity," 23 *Brit. Y.B. I.L.* 178 (1946).

229. The cause célèbre is, of course, the detention and relocation of Japanese-Americans in World War II. See Rostow, "The Japanese-American Cases—A Disaster," 54 *Yale L. J.* 489 (1945); Note, "Alien Enemies and Japanese Americans: A Problem of Wartime Controls," 51 id. at 1318 (1942).

230. Arts. 13–46.

231. See, e.g., Arts. 5, 41.

232. Borchard, "The Treatment of Enemy Property," 34 *Geo. L. J.* 389 (1946); Jessup, "Enemy Property," 49 *A.J.I.L.* 57 (1955); Sommerich, "A Brief against Confiscation," 11 *Law and Contemp. Prob.* 152 (1945). See also Castrén, *The Present Law of War and Neutrality* 118–19 (1953); Reeves, "Is Confiscation of

selective reading of past practice and a projection of future decision which appears highly optimistic when the variables which are likely to affect such decision are considered. It would seem most difficult to find, in realistic observation of the varied practice and opinion in the past, a crystallized community expectation of a duty to return property.[233]

The basic policies are commonly posed in terms of the inviolability of private property and individual rights and the encouragement of the worldwide circulation of capital on the one hand, and of the interests of the belligerent and the maintenance of certain standards of world order on the other. Such basic policies, all in a measure persuasive, are best debated not in the abstract but with reference to specific controversies in context. Among the many different factors in a particular context which might rationally affect policy choice may be listed such items and considerations as the types and characteristics of owners of claimed property; the prior use of the property, as an instrument of economic warfare or otherwise; the degree to which the property was controlled by the enemy state; the type of world public order the enemy state seeks to establish, totalitarian or free; the relation of the war waged to the public order of the organized community; possible future uses of the property and its relation to the security of the state; and any needs for recoupment for war damage by the enemy. When such factors are reviewed in particular context, the possibility of a realistic determination of the probable effects of alternative decisions upon both commerce and security is enhanced.

Termination of the Process of Coercion

In terminating the process of coercion, belligerents seek to disengage themselves and return to persuasion as a mode of interaction. Factually, the context of decelerating coercion may present the par-

---

Enemy Assets in the National Interest of the United States?" 40 *Va. L. Rev.* 1029 (1954); Wright, "War Claims: What of the Future?" 16 *Law and Contemp. Prob.* 543 (1951).

233. See Corbett, *Law and Society in the Relations of States* 216 (1951); 2 Oppenheim-Lauterpacht 326–31; Stone, *Legal Controls* 435; "Report of the Special Committee to Study the Dirksen Bill," in Section of International and Comparative Law, American Bar Assoc., *Proceedings* 52 (1955); Rubin, "The 'Inviolability' of Enemy Private Property," 11 *Law and Contemp. Prob.* 166 (1945). See also Schisgall, *The Enemy Property Issue* (Public Affairs Pam. No. 246, 1957), which collects the arguments for and against return.

ticipants in many differing degrees of intensity of combat, in many different postures of relative victory and defeat, in many different degrees of consensus, both tacit and explicit, about the cessation of coercion and subject in varying degree to the intervention of third states or international organizations.

In so complex a process, many difficult legal problems naturally arise from the contraposed claims of the participants. Between belligerents, problems arise over the timing of the cessation of hostilities, the repatriation of prisoners, the restoration of territory and property taken, the cession of territory and property, responsibility for unlawful destruction and violence, the resumption of treaty obligations and peaceful procedures generally, and so on. Between belligerents and nonparticipants, the questions concern responsibility for unlawful destruction, the repatriation of property looted and smuggled by the enemy, and the restoration of normal peaceful intercourse. Private individuals and groups, acting sometimes across and sometimes within national boundaries, contest the continuing enforceability of agreements, the restoration of property taken and transferred by the enemy, and the interpretation of "duration of war" clauses in private agreements. Between individuals and belligerent states, freedom from personal restraint, amnesty, the release or return of property sequestered or vested, and the liquidation of various internal wartime controls are relevant questions. And between different branches of the government within the same state, decisions to continue or terminate extraordinary war powers must be made.

The sources of policy upon which authoritative decision-makers will draw for the solution of such diverse controversies are many and varying. It is futile to subsume all these problems, of such different policy import, under a few vague principles about the "termination of war," [234] as is commonly done.[235] About many of these problems,

234. See, e.g., Castrén, note 232 supra at 132–7; 2 Oppenheim-Lauterpacht 596–620; Stone, *Legal Controls* 639–46.

235. On the parallel subsumption of disparate problems under the label of "the commencement of war" see Ch. 2. Just as discussions on the commencement of war have frequently been concerned with determination of the beginning of a "state of war," so discussions on the termination of war have commonly centered on ascertainment of the cessation of the "state of war." The most that efforts at clarification of the different "termination" problems have thus far achieved is the recognition that the "date of termination of a war according to

international law has had little or nothing to say, and decision is appropriately founded in national law. Even for problems appropriately regarded as in the domain of international concern, however, there has been very little development of customary international law. Practice, apart from explicit agreement, has been so diverse that contention abounds on most problems as to what authoritative expectation requires. The result has been that belligerents, insofar as their foresight and degree of consensus have permitted, have sought to prescribe for termination problems by agreement as explicit as possible in truces, armistices [236] and treaties of peace.[237] The most important law governing the termination of coercion is thus, perhaps, those fundamental principles for the interpretation of agreements mentioned in the discussion of repatriation of prisoners of war. The continuing importance of such principles might be further demonstrated by reference to the controversy between the Egyptians and Israelis as to the meaning of their uneasy armistice.

THE COMMON INTEREST IN AN INCLUSIVE PUBLIC ORDER OF FREEDOM

In projecting these broad outlines of policy-oriented inquiry, and in offering certain possible clarifications of some of the more fundamental policies, we have sought neither to minimize nor to

---

a particular State's municipal law" does not necessarily coincide with the date of termination "under international law." See Stone, *Legal Controls* 643; Hudson, "The Duration of the War between the United States and Germany," 39 *Harv. L. Rev.* 1020 (1926); Kunz, "Ending the War with Germany," 46 *A.J.I.L.* 114, 118–19 (1952); Note, "Judicial Determination of the End of the War," 47 *Col. L. Rev.* 255 (1947), distinguishing between "termination of war under international law," "termination of wartime legislation" and "effects of termination of war on private legal relations."

For surveys of cases on "termination of war" for various municipal purposes see Roberts, "Litigation Involving 'Termination of War,'" 43 *Ky. L. J.* 199 (1955); Note, "Termination of a War," 4 *Wyo. L. J.* 115 (1949). See also French, "The End of the War," 15 *Geo. Wash. L. Rev.* 191 (1947).

236. See, generally, Maurice, *The Armistices of 1918* (1943); Graham, "Two Armistices and a Surrender," 40 *A.J.I.L.* 148 (1946); Graham, "Armistices—1944 Style," 39 id. at 286 (1945).

237. See, generally, Fitzmaurice, "The Juridical Clauses of the Peace Treaties," 73 *Hague Recueil* 259 (1948); Metzger, "The Liberal Japanese Peace Treaty," 37 *Corn. L. Q.* 382 (1952).

exaggerate the potential role of law in controlling and regulating international coercion. The contemporary world arena exhibits, unfortunately, all too many factors which tend to confer upon the attitude of cynical disenchantment with law at least the appearance of realism:

> neither the leaders nor the peoples of the world have yet effectively recognized a common interest in economizing the use of force or in establishing appropriate institutions for securing such interest;
>
> the public order presented by the world arena is composed not of a single inclusive order, moved by common policies, but of several competing, exclusive orders, moved by the most disparate policies;
>
> the policies which move some of these contending world public orders reject not only the values of human dignity, implicit in the principle of economy of force, but even the very distinction between means and ends;
>
> contemporary technology makes possible a concentration and application of naked force hitherto inconceivable even in megalomania's wildest dreams; and so on.

The cumulative import of contemporary scientific analysis and observation of factors affecting individual and collective choices is, however, that over a period of time most men do and can act to maximize their values, conscious and unconscious, and that such values include, if not a large measure of humanitarianism for their fellow man, at least a demand for self-preservation.[238] The world

238. See note 95 supra. See also *Personality in Nature, Society and Culture* (Kluckhohn, Murray, and Schneider ed., 1955); Parsons, *The Structure of Social Action* (2d ed., 1949); Stagner and Karwoski, *Psychology* (1952). That men generally tend to act to maximize their values is a premise basic in contemporary theories of economic analysis, see Little, *A Critique of Welfare Economics* (1950); Samuelson, *Foundations of Economic Analysis* (1948); and in the theories of games and of decision-making, see *The Policy Sciences* (Lerner and Lasswell, ed., 1951); Luce and Raiffa, *Games and Decisions* (1957); Von Newmann and Morgenstern, *Theory of Games and Economic Behavior* (3d ed., 1953); Lasswell, "Current Studies of the Decision Process: Automation versus Creativity," 8 *Western Pol. Q.* 381 (1955).

arena, fortunately, exhibits certain factors, countervailing the pessimistic, which suggest that the hope of an increasing role for authority in the control and regulation of international coercion is not entirely illusory:

> the peoples of the world, and especially their leaders, have begun to recognize the imperative need to establish at least minimum controls to lessen the risk of their common destruction by miscalculation or inadvertence, whatever the system of world order demanded;
>
> the peoples of the world may be observed further, beyond demand for survival, to express increasing common demands for many shared values and increasingly to exhibit recognition of their common interdependence in the achievement of such values;
>
> despite the contending public orders, there is a slow trend toward inclusive rather than exclusive determination of global policy on some problems, as well as some movement toward the expansion and improvement of specialized institutions for the performance of policy functions;
>
> some observers are beginning to perceive that the almost inconceivable concentration of force made possible by modern technology might, by appropriately shared perspectives, be brought to the support rather than the destruction of an inclusive public order; and so on.

From these tentative initial clarifications of a common interest in survival and other values could come a more comprehensive and creative clarification of the common interest of all peoples of the world in effective community monopolization of force behind an inclusive public order of safety, freedom, and abundance and in a wide sharing of responsibility for the maintenance of such order. From such comprehensive clarification of common interest could come the detailed initiatives and dispositions of effective power necessary to invention and establishment of the appropriate institutions and procedures for securing and preserving such interest. To these ends, lawyers may most effectively contribute, in performing their special roles in the clarification of common interest and invention of alternatives, not by the repetitive reiteration of over-optimistic faith in inherited ambiguous technicalities, but by the systematic application of certain important emphases:

> that clarity in thought requires a careful distinction of the processes of coercion from the processes of authoritative decision;
>
> that rationality in decision and recommendation demands that one pierce through technical rules and concepts to the underlying fundamental policies and continually appraise such rules and concepts in terms of contemporary and projected policies;
>
> that both relevant policies and technical rules are commonly and necessarily formulated in pairs of opposites and that the appropriate function of such formulations is not to dictate decision but to guide decision-makers to all the factors in a context which should be taken into account in making rational decision; and, finally,
>
> that responsible decision-makers who share the values of a free society may appropriately give effect to such values not only in their formulation of principles but also in their specific interpretations and applications.

It is by the consistent maintenance of these emphases, in the employment of all his special intellectual skills for inquiry into the basic specific problems of international coercion, that the lawyer who values human dignity may make his richest contribution to moving the general community of mankind from its present incomplete and disorganized structures and processes of authority, harassed by contending exclusive orders, toward a more inclusive world public order in which the values of a safe, free, and abundant society are honored not merely in theory but in practice.

In the chapters that follow we seek, with appropriate humility, to maintain these emphases in detailed inquiry into certain most urgent contemporary problems.

2. THE INITIATION OF COERCION: A MULTITEMPORAL ANALYSIS

Inquiry about the legal regulation of international coercion commonly begins with discussion of the many and disparate problems frequently subsumed under headings like "The Initiation of War," "The Commencement of War," "The Legal Meaning of War," and "State and Effects of War," or under the simple query, "When does war exist (or begin)?" The orthodox debates here have been concerned mainly with determination of the beginning in time of a "legal state of war." They have usually centered on the necessity and the relative technical effect of a somewhat mystical *animus belligerendi,* manifested either in the shape of a formal declaration of war or some other modality, and of physical acts of coercion for the creation of such "state of war." The confusion in these debates arises from a shifting reference to and emphasis on the subjective *animus* of participants and the realities of their coercive practices, as well as to certain assumed consequences of such *animus* or practices, without relating either the *animus* or the practices to the larger context of any particular instance of international coercion and to the major community policies sought by authoritative decision-makers with respect to various specific problems in such context.[1]

Some publicists, for example, have rigorously insisted that *animus belligerendi* on the part of either the initiating or responding state is the prime requisite which must be unequivocally revealed and without which not "war," or a "state of war," but only "reprisals," or "intervention," or some other "measure short of war" may be

1. The perspectives from which we write are briefly indicated supra pp. 11–39 and in the editorial "Peace and War: Factual Continuum with Multiple Legal Consequences," 49 *A.J.I.L.* 63 (1955).

First published in 52 *A.J.I.L.* 241–59 (1958). Reprinted with permission.

regarded as having been initiated. The formulation of this view achieved by Lord McNair about three decades ago is now classical:

> A state of war arises in International Law (a) at the moment, if any, specified in a declaration of war; or (b) if none is specified, then immediately upon the communication of a declaration of war; or (c) upon the commission of an act of force, under the authority of a State, which is done *animo belligerendi,* or which, being done *sine animo belligerendi* but by way of reprisals or intervention, the other State elects to regard as creating a state of war, either by repelling force by force or in some other way; retroactive effect being given to this election, so that the state of war arises on the commission of the first act of force.[2]

Other writers, in contrast, have de-emphasized the subjectivities of the participants and regard the commencement of "material war" as

2. "The Legal Meaning of War and the Relation of War to Reprisals," 11 *Tr. Grotius Soc.* 45 (1925). Among those who have shared this view is Quincy Wright, who wrote: "War begins when any state of the world manifests its intention to make war by some overt act, which may take the form of an act of war, a declaration of war or some ultimatum with a time limit—the existence of war is not dependent upon the type of operations undertaken by the belligerents." "Changes in the Concept of War," 18 *A.J.I.L.* 758–9 (1924). Later, Professor Wright submitted that where both belligerents disclaim an intention to make "war," "a state of war does not exist until such time as third states recognize that it does." "When Does War Exist?" 26 id. 366 (1932). How and with respect to what problems the intention of a third state is relevant in interbelligerent relations is not explained.

In his Report on the Legal Position Arising from the Enforcement in Time of Peace of the Measures of Economic Pressure Indicated in Article 16 of the Covenant, Particularly by a Maritime Blockade, 8 League of Nations *Off. J.* 834 (1927), the Secretary-General of the League said: "from the legal point of view, the existence of a state of war between two states depends upon their intention and not upon the nature of their acts. Accordingly, measures of coercion, however drastic, which are not intended to create and are not regarded by the State to which they are applied as creating a state of war, do not legally establish a relation of war between the States concerned."

Similar statements may be found in Lawrence, *The Principles of International Law* 309 (7th ed., Winfield, 1928); 2 Westlake, *International Law* 1–2 (1907); Castrén, *The Present Law of War and Neutrality* 31–4 (1954); 2 Møller, *International Law in Peace and War* 156 (trans. Pratt, 1935). Professor Eagleton, too, seems to have shared this view: see his "Acts of War," 35 *A.J.I.L.* 321 (1941). Cf. Starke, *An Introduction to International Law* 363 (3rd ed., 1954).

simultaneously inducing a "legal status of war." Among the more recent expressions of this position is Professor Kelsen's:

> A state of war in the true and full sense of the term is brought about only by acts of war, that is to say, by the use of armed force; and only such a state may be, but need not necessarily be, terminated by a peace treaty. Consequently war is a specific action, not a status. From the point of view of international law, the most important fact is the resort to war, and that means resort to an action, not resort to a status. Some writers consider the intention to make war, the *animus belligerendi,* of the state or states involved in war as essential. *Animus belligerendi* means the intention to wage war. But this can only be the intention to perform acts of war, that is to say, to use armed force, with all the consequences international law attaches to the use of armed force.[3]

Still others have attempted, in interpreting the pattern of commitments under the Covenant of the League of Nations, to combine both these "subjective" and "objective" theories of "war" and assert that, while ordinarily *animus belligerendi* must be present for a "state of war" to commence,

> if acts of force are sufficiently serious and long continued, then, even if both sides disclaim any *animus belligerendi* and refuse to admit that a state of war has arisen between them, there comes a point at which the law must say to the parties, you are refusing to recognize the facts; your actions are of a kind which it is the policy of the law to characterize as war; and therefore,

3. *Principles of International Law* 27 (1952). The protagonists of this side of the debate include Risley, *The Law of War* 81–2 (1897); Baty, "Abuse of Terms: 'Recognition'; 'War,'" 30 *A.J.I.L.* 398 (1936); Ronan, "English and American Courts and the Definition of War," 31 *A.J.I.L.* 642 (1937); Green, "The Nature of the 'War' in Korea," 4 *Int. L. Q.* 468 (1951); Pye, "The Legal Status of the Korean Hostilities," 45 *Geo. L. J.* 48–51 (1956). Cf. Hall, *International Law* 444–5 (8th ed., Pearce Higgins, 1924). Professors Borchard and Stowell appeared to have favored this side: see Borchard, "'War' and 'Peace,'" 27 *A.J.I.L.* 114 (1933), and "When Did War Begin?" 47 *Col. L. Rev.* 742 (1947); and Stowell, *International Law* 491 (1931). Professor Hyde expressed the same view as Lord McNair (3 *International Law* 1693–5 [rev. ed., 1945]), but proposed at the same time that "the character of the acts committed rather than the design of the actors should, and probably will be, regarded as decisive of the legal result." (Id., 1688).

whatever you choose to say about it, you have in fact set up a state of things which in the eye of the law is a state of war.[4]

It should be observed that these formulations, like the comparable definitions of "war" which abound in the literature, make implicit, ambiguous, and indiscriminate references to both the "facts" of coercion and certain asserted "legal consequences" of such facts—to both the precipitating events of resort to, and exercise of, international coercion and the responses of authoritative decision-makers to such events. In sum, their reference is, without discrimination of different particular types of claims, to both the processes of factual coercion and the processes of legal authority. There is apparent in these formulations, premised as they are on the ancient dichotomous categorization of "war" and "peace," no recognition that the initiation of coercion generates, not one unitary problem of ascertaining a precise moment in time for the beginning of a singularly elusive and all-sufficing "legal state of war," [5] but rather a whole series of complex problems. The problems created in any particular instance of coercion, as will appear below, call for the resolution of very different types of conflicting claims asserted by various parties upon the initial stages of the process of coercion, and raise greatly differ-

4. Brierly, "International Law and Resort to Armed Force," 4 *Camb. L. J.* 313 (1932). Cf. Lauterpacht, "'Resort to War' and the Interpretation of the Covenant During the Manchurian Dispute," 28 *A.J.I.L.* 43 (1934), who does not accept the "intention" theory of "war," but at the same time suggests that "war" is not necessarily synonymous with the use of "armed force." These so-called "subjective" and "objective" theories are summarized and discussed in Eagleton, "The Attempt to Define War," *Int. Conciliation,* No. 291, p. 258 et seq. (1933), and in Williams, *Some Aspects of the Covenant of the League of Nations* 298 et seq. (1934).

5. Professor Wright stated the traditional point succinctly: "the incidence of an act or declaration converting the state of peace into a state of war establishes a division in time before which acts of war are illegal and after which they are legal between belligerents . . ." "Changes in the Concept of War," 18 *A.J.I.L.* 757 (1924). Hence, traditionally, juristic effort has been directed toward determining what acts or declarations convert "the state of peace" into a "state of war." And see Déak, "Computation of Time in International Law," 20 *A.J.I.L.* 506–8, 514 (1926) for a plea, made with great seriousness, that the exact date, hour, and minute for the beginning of a "state of war" be specified for the reason that "this changes profoundly the juridical situation of each country" (at 506).

ing issues of legal policy for the different officials who must reach a decision.

Increasing dissatisfaction with the traditional answers to the traditional question is in modest measure displayed in the recent literature of international law. A number of scholars have sought, with varying degrees of success, to bring significant clarification into the use of basic terms. Dr. Grob, for instance, rejects with deserved ridicule the absolutistic notion of "war in the legal sense" and of a "legal state of war." He contends that what must be looked for is not "one over-all legal definition of war" but rather a "variety of legal definitions." [6] Each "legal definition" he would formulate in relation to, and after ascertainment of, "the particular intent and purpose" of the specific "rule of law on war" which happens to be under consideration at a given time. The question whether any particular exercise of coercion "constitutes" "war" or not must, in his view, to be meaningful, specify a particular rule of law in relation to which the "existence of war" may be affirmed or denied.[7] In his analysis, to affirm or deny that a set of events marks the beginning or existence of "war" is to assert that the specified rule of law is or is not applicable to such events. The same exercise of coercion, which may "legally constitute" "war" in relation to one rule of law on war, obviously need not at the same stage "constitute" "war" in the sense of another rule; hence the relativity of which he speaks.[8] The applicability or nonapplicability of a given rule to given facts, Dr. Grob explains, "depends upon its [the rule's] intent and purposes. It is the business of interpretation to furnish that answer. It cannot be gleaned from anywhere else." [9] Thus, for Dr. Grob, the basic task is reduced to the "interpretation" of legal technicality.

Considerably more restraint and diffidence are exhibited by Professor Stone in his efforts at clarification. He still speaks of a "necessity," in view of the "wide ranging legal effects of war," of determining "*the* moment of its legal commencement." The problem, to

6. *The Relativity of War and Peace* 189 (1949).

7. Id., 202.

8. Id., 303: "Operations, as they progress . . . begin to be war legally at diverse points of time. The question 'when does war legally begin?' thus requires not one but several answers." See also Id., 192, 194, 221–4, 318.

9. Id., 204.

him, is "plain enough." "War commences," Professor Stone writes, "when facts come into existence which satisfy the [above] definition of war." [10] Since his definition of war is no more revolutionary than a rephrasing of the "intention" or "subjective theory" of "war," he adheres closely to Lord McNair's formulation quoted earlier. That he does not escape the ambiguity resulting from a dual and simultaneous reference to "facts" and "legal consequences" is perhaps most clearly shown in his casual remark that "war begins with the earliest *operative event.*" [11] Professor Stone, however, departs from the wholly conventional treatment of the initiation of coercion in two respects. First, he recognizes that "the moment" of commencement of war "on the international level" need not necessarily coincide with the beginning of war for differing "municipal legal purposes." [12] Secondly, in the course of discussing the "legal consequences of *undeclared* hostilities," he suggests that clarity in the question of "war or no war" may be approached by recognizing that varying answers may be given as "the purposes for which an answer is sought" vary.[13] He refers, as Dr. Grob did, to the purpose of individual rules or sets of rules of war law, and of individual provisions of such instruments as the Pact of Paris and the Charter of the United Nations. Unlike Dr. Grob,[14] however, he confines his suggestions to

10. *Legal Controls of International Conflict* 310 (1954). His definition of war is "a relation of one or more governments to at least one other government, in which at least one of such governments no longer permits its relations with the other or others to be governed by the laws of peace." (at 304.)

11. Id., 310, note 75. It is of course the authorities who must decide what facts are operative.

12. Id., 310–11, 311, note 78. He gives some indication of what he means by "municipal legal purposes": "It has become . . . a matter of legislative prudence to fix explicitly the beginning and end of war for the purpose at hand in each major field of legislative endeavor. They may, for example, be fixed at one point in relation to wartime emergency powers, in another for regulation of private legal relations, and this even though the legislature may seem to have left the matter open." (at 311.) Cf. Corbett, *Law and Society in the Relations of States* 213–13 (1951); and Green, "Armed Conflict, War, and Self-Defence," 6 *Archiv des Völkerrechts* 387, 424, 438 (1957).

13. Stone, supra note 10 at 312. Professor Stone almost deprecates his own contribution, insisting that its value is "rather *de lege ferenda* than as a description of existing law," and describing his observations as "most tentative" and "by no means coherent with each other." (at 313.)

14. See Grob, supra note 6 at 283–302.

situations where the contending participants not only fail to issue formal declarations of war but also disclaim an intent to engage in war and describe their coercive operations by some other words.[15] The assumption of Professor Stone seems to be that the relativity of "war or no war" is precluded by a declaration of intent by either belligerent and that as soon as such a declaration is made, there can be but one unvarying answer, whatever "the purposes for which an answer is sought" may be.

While recognizing that some measure of clarification has been achieved by both scholars, a measure which was anticipated by Judge Hudson,[16] it may be observed that both appear unduly preoccupied with the technical rules on which they have focused rather than on particular problems, particular policies, and particular decision-makers. The task of clarification, as will be indicated below, involves deeper difficulties than either Dr. Grob or Professor Stone recognizes. It calls, contrary to the suggestion of the former, for much more than ascertaining the "legal meaning" of words used in particular formulations of prescriptions or the "exact intent and purpose" of the formulators.[17] It demands, notwithstanding the suggestion of the latter, that an inquirer go behind pronouncements of intent to the factual and policy problems which are just as varied and complex when such rituals are performed as when they are foregone. Both scholars exhibit little awareness of the number and complexity of the variables in the interrelated but distinguishable processes of coercion and of decision.[18] They do not emphasize, in particular, that the application or nonapplication of a particular rule to a particular situation of fact, if inquiry is to go beyond abstract and normatively ambiguous statements,[19] must be viewed as the outcome of a deci-

15. Stone, supra note 10 at 312.

16. See his "The Duration of the War Between the United States and Germany," 39 *Harv. L. Rev.* 1020 at 1020–21 (1926).

17. Dr. Grob conceives the basic task to be that of ascertaining the "legal reality," "the truth" and "legal meaning" of the "two central, all important terms 'war' and 'peace' " (at 36), of determining "what the rules of law on war mean" (at 188). His demand for "legal answers" leads him to say that "Arguing with *facts* alone will not do. Mere *facts* prove nothing" (at 201; italics in the original). The conceptualism of his study thus does not extend to the clear relation of the facts of coercion and the process of decision.

18. Ch. 1 suggests one mode of outlining these processes.

19. For exposition of what is characterized as normative-ambiguity, see Lass-

sional process, and that such outcome can scarcely be meaningfully studied unless the decision-maker (the applier) is identified, his policy objectives clearly articulated, and the various conditions and the procedures of application specified.[20] Both scholars stop short of the effort to arrive at a comprehensive guiding theory for inquiry into the problems, policies, and prescriptions relating to the initiation of coercion and violence. The several intellectual tasks indispensable to the achievement of deeper insight into the processes of coercion and decision and of closer approximation to community and preferred goals remain unperformed.[21]

Preoccupation with legal technicality is even more intense in Dr. Kotzsch's recent study.[22] Dr. Kotzsch, addressing himself as Professor Stone did to the problem of "war without a declaration of war," works out at labored length a distinction between "war in the material sense" and "war in the formal sense." "Formal war," in his sense, is no more than the "legal state of war" as conceived in all its rigor in traditional theory, while "material war" includes all factual situations of military conflict of some duration and extent (as distinguished from isolated acts of violence) where, through disclaimer or lack of a showing of *animus belligerendi,* no "legal state of war" is regarded as established. The main difference to which he points is in terms of "legal consequences" and lies in the extent of application of the law of war: "formal war" automatically brings about the full operation of all the rules of war and neutrality; "material war," on the other hand, as "institutionalized in the province of international law," initiates only a "selective" application of those rules.[23] The

well and McDougal, "Legal Education and Public Policy: Professional Training in the Public Interest," 52 *Yale L. J.* 203, 266–7 (1943).

20. Amplification of this general point is offered in McDougal, "Law As a Process of Decision: A Policy-Oriented Approach To Legal Study," 1 *Natural Law Forum* 53, 54–8, 64–8 (1956); and id., "The Comparative Study of Law For Value Purposes: Value Clarification As An Instrument of Democratic World Order," 61 *Yale L. J.* 915 (1952), 1 *A.J. Comp. Law* 24 (1952). See also Lasswell, "Current Studies of the Decision Process: Automation versus Creativity," 8 *Western Pol. Q.* 381 (1955); and *The Policy Sciences* (Lerner and Lasswell, eds. 1951). For an introduction to the theory of decision-making, see Bross, *Design For Decision* (1953).

21. Cf. supra p. 10.

22. *The Concept of War in Contemporary History and International Law* (1956).

23. Id., 52–65, 234–5, 241–4. Dr. Kotzsch differentiates his distinction from

question "war or no war," he writes, following Dr. Grob, "henceforth must be specified by material or formal if a legal answer is sought." [24] In Dr. Kotzsch's scheme, there is not one intermediate status between "peace" and "war." There are instead, he asserts, two dichotomies—"peace" and "formal war," and "peace" and "material war." [25] The initiation of international coercion may thus mark the commencement of either "formal war" or of "material war," depending on whether or not there is an announced *animus belligerendi.* "War" having been split, so to speak, into the "formal" and "material," he states that it ("war") no longer necessarily implies "the integral application of the sum-total of the laws of war." [26] One of his main concerns appears to be to fashion a technical answer to belligerents' claims, which have been asserted in the past, to avoid the thrust of the law of war and neutrality by labeling their physical operations with some other name. Dr. Kotzsch's aspirations in his scholarly study are admirable. It would seem open to serious doubt,

---

that between "war in the legal sense" (war as a "legal condition") and "war in the material sense" (war as actual military operations) adverted to, for instance, by Professor Wright (supra note 2) in the following terms: "If we, however, replace the distinction of *war in the legal sense* and *war in the material sense* by that of *war in the formal sense* and *war in the material sense,* it is for the following reason: The former distinction implies the idea that *war in the legal sense* is of relevancy under international law whereas *war in the material sense* is not. This is not true. Both forms have obtained their meaning under international law. By customary international law legal consequences have been imputed to *war in the material sense. . . .*" (at 52.)

24. Id., 55.

25. Id., 241–4.

26. Supra note 22 at 243. Through his two dichotomies (or trichotomy), he also attempts to resolve the old debate on the "subjective" and "objective" tests of the beginning or existence of war by combining the two: "The concept of *war in the material and formal senses* pays regard to both the purely objective test of war and the subjective test, which is the essence of the status theory of war. It resolves the doctrinal conflict between the objective and subjective theories of war by the assumption that these theories are not mutually exclusive but complementary" (at 54–5). The minor point has been suggested above that such observations are apt to be no more than exercises in legal syntactics unless both the perspectives of participants and their physical operations are considered in the larger context of the particular instance of coercion involved. The major point is that Dr. Kotzsch's framework for inquiry seems to us less than completely adequate even for the modest goal he set for himself—"to *describe* the modern concept of war in general international law" (at 2; italics supplied).

however, whether its conceptualism, which is at times less than lucid, can offer more than minimal help in clarifying the problems of legal policy attendant upon the initiation of coercion and in increasing the incidence of rational decisions.

The first step, we submit, toward contact with reality is reference to, and careful orientation in, the factual process of coercion across national boundaries. In broad preliminary characterization, this process of coercion may be described, as has been indicated in detail in the previous chapter, in terms of various *participants* applying to each other coercion of alternately accelerating and decelerating degrees of intensity, for a wide range of *objectives,* utilizing *methods* which include the employment of all known distinctive strategies or instruments of policy, under the variable *conditions* of a world arena in continuous flux.[27] It may be emphasized that, in the course of this process of coercion, the participants assert against each other many varying claims respecting the lawfulness and unlawfulness of the particular coercive practices being utilized by or against them, invoking both world prescriptions and world opinion to fortify their respective assertions.

The description we suggest of factual coercion in terms of "process" is intended, however, not merely to convey a sense of the variety in participant, purpose, modality and claim, but also to stress the facts of *continuity*—continuity in coercive action and reaction and in assertion and counterassertion—and of *changing intensities in degree,* from the mildest to the most severe applications of coercion. Between the two extremes of "pure" peace and "total" war, the states of the world arena may in these terms be observed continuously to engage each other for power and other values, by all instruments of policy, in a *continuum* of degrees in coercive practices, ranging from the least intense to the most intense.[28] From this orientation, to speak of

27. Compare Wright, "International Conflict and the United Nations," 10 *World Politics* 24, 34–44 (1957), who describes the processes of conflict among states in terms of the *parties,* their *relations,* and the *field* in which conflicts occur.

28. The point is made more or less explicitly in any number of studies on international relations; see, e.g., Haas and Whiting, *Dynamics of International Relations,* c. 3 (1956); Morgenthau, *Politics Among Nations,* cc. 3–6 (2nd ed., 1954); Strausz-Hupé and Possony, *International Relations,* cc. 1–3 (2nd ed., 1954); Schwarzenberger, *Power Politics* 17 and cc. 6–12 (1951); Kalijarvi and Associates, *Modern World Politics,* c. 3 (3rd ed., 1953). On the fluctuations and

the initiation of coercion is to refer to those stages of the factual process at which coercion is still at a relatively low degree of intensity but accelerating toward the peak intensity of maximum destructive use of the military instrument.[29]

At such initiation stages of the coercion process, participants of all categories—including officials of the contending belligerents, officials of international organizations and of nonbelligerents (who are nonparticipants in the process of coercion but nevertheless assert certain claims), and individual nationals of both the belligerents and nonbelligerents—begin, as suggested, to make certain claims against each other. An indication of the rich complexity of the structure of claims made at initiation stages may be had even from impressionistic description.

Thus, in one type of controversy, a belligerent asserts, as against a target-state and international officials who are representatives of the world public order, claims to initiate highly coercive or violent strategies of modifying the existing world public order and the world distribution of power and other values. The assertion of these claims frequently marks the culmination of a longer or shorter period during which an intensifying degree of coercion was exerted by and against the claimant through nonmilitary instruments, or in which the dimensions of military force were kept short of open and substantial destruction. At a certain stage in intensity, officials of the target-state may respond with claims to employ retaliatory coercion in the name of self-defense. International officials may, for their part, make claims to competence to characterize such coercion and violence

---

periodicity of the magnitude of coercion and violence over long periods of history, see 3 Sorokin, *Social and Cultural Dynamics* 259–380 (1937).

29. Cf. 2 Wright, *A Study of War* 698 (1942): "[A]nalysis of the military, psychological, legal, and sociological manifestations of war suggests that all may be regarded as variables which reach a certain threshold of intensity in actual war. War may therefore be regarded from the standpoint of each belligerent as an extreme intensification of military activity, psychological tension, legal power, and social integration—an intensification which is not likely to result unless the enemy is approximately equal in material power." At 689: "[T]he time space continuum, which in a legal sense is designated a war, has not necessarily been accompanied by a unity or uniformity of intense military activity. While in international legal theory a state of war between two states begins and ends at definite moments of time, these moments have frequently been difficult to establish in practice."

as unlawful breaches of the public order of the world community and to take appropriate steps forcibly to redress such breaches.

Similarly, in another type of controversy, the belligerents, including both the attacking and defending states and, where community responsibility is successfully organized, international armed forces, make claims against each other to engage in the different component practices of military violence to secure their respective objectives. This general claim to employ the military instrument may be given operational meaning in terms of the detailed claims of each to apply violence in the capture or destruction of the other's bases of power by employing certain combatants with certain weapons, in certain areas of operations, and against certain objects of attack. The negating claim asserted in turn by each against the other is that the violence exerted is inhuman, unnecessary, or disproportionate, or, in more detail, that certain combatants are unauthorized, that certain weapons are unlawful, that certain areas of operations are beyond permissible bounds, and that certain objects may not legitimately be captured or destroyed. Both belligerents may also, before or after the outburst of military violence, claim to cut off, with varying degrees of completeness, diplomatic and consular relations and the commerce, communication, and transportation between them, and to terminate or continue observance of previous agreements with each other.

In still another type of controversy, representatives of the world public order claim, mostly after the stage of overt violence has been reached, competence to activate the commitments of third states to participate in organized community measures designed to repress violence characterized as unlawful. Nonbelligerents may respond favorably and claim a right to participate, or unfavorably and set up claims to avoid participation, in community sanctions procedures. Where the pattern of community responsibility fails, and the international officials are unable effectively to assert claims of authority, a second set of claims assumes special importance. Belligerents demand from third states nonparticipation and nonaugmentation of the other belligerent's power resources. Third states make countering demands for noninterference with their nationals, resources, and normal activities.

In a fourth type of controversy, each belligerent may be observed to begin, at points of varying time before or after the stage of active military hostilities, making claims to exercise more or less comprehensive control over the industry, commerce, labor, communications, transportation, price and consumption levels, private agreements and property, and personal activities of individuals within its own territory. Internal value processes are governmentalized in increasingly high degree, in the effort to organize, maximize, manage, and effectively utilize the belligerent's bases of power. Each belligerent further claims authority to define and discriminate between "enemy persons" and nonenemy persons, and to impose more rigid controls on the former's persons and property, both for preventing their utilization by the enemy belligerent and for satisfying its own military needs. The countering claim of "enemy persons" is for respect for their human dignity, loyalties, and property.

There is a fifth type of controversy where individuals assert against other individuals, at differing points along the *continuum* of coercion, certain claims and counterclaims, the most conspicuous of which are to require, or refrain from, or terminate, the honoring of certain commitments, and to certain specific interpretations of so-called "war clauses" in documents such as, for instance, insurance policies and charter parties. It is in connection with the latter type of claims that much of the judicial discussion on "When does (or did) war begin?" has taken place.[30] It is perhaps an index of the ex-

30. The "war clause" in life insurance policies is typically a clause excluding or limiting the liability of the insurer in case the insured dies as a result of, or while engaged in, service in the armed forces in "time of war." The wording of the "war clause" has, of course, varied in different policies. The technical issue, however, has usually been presented in the form of whether or not, at the time of the insured's death, there was "war" either between the state of the forum and another state or between foreign states.

The cases which arose in American courts during World War II commonly involved deaths which occurred on Dec. 7, 1941, during the attack by Japanese forces on Pearl Harbor. A group of cases—e.g. *West v. Palmetto State Life Ins. Co.*, 25 S.E. 2d 475 (1943), 202 S.C. 422; *Rosenau v. Idaho Mutual Benefit Assn.*, 145 Pac. 2d 227 (1944), 65 Idaho 408; *Savage v. Sun Life Insurance Co.*, 57 F. Supp. 620 (W.D. La., 1944); *Pang v. Sun Life Assurance Co.*, 37 Hawaii 208 (1945)—allowed recovery by the beneficiary, holding that because the U. S. Congress, to which the Constitution had allocated the power to declare war, had not declared war until Dec. 8, 1941, and had not made its declaration retroactive (as the President had requested) to Dec. 7, there was as yet no "state of war," or "war in the legal" or "constitutional sense," on the latter date. These cases relied on a concept that courts may not take judicial notice of the existence of

tent of the common confusion that it is precisely this type of private claim in the resolution of which the world prescriptions and fundamental world community policies relating to coercion are really largely, if not wholly, irrelevant. The basic problem raised by these claims is not that of distinguishing between permissible and non-permissible exercises of coercion, nor that of formulating distinctions between the "legal" and the "non-legal" senses of "war" or

---

a war until it is formally and officially declared by the Congress, and distinguished between an "act of war" and a "state of war." In *New York Life Ins. Co. v. Bennion,* 158 F. 2d 260 (C.C.A. 10th, 1946), 41 *A.J.I.L.* 680 (1947), cert. denied, 331 U. S. 811 (1947), noted in 56 *Yale L. J.* 746 (1947), however, the court, under an identical set of facts, denied recovery against the insurer, holding that the existence of a state of war was not dependent upon its formal declaration but was determinable from an appraisal of actualities, and that there had been a sufficient political determination (by the President) of the existence of war commencing with the attack on Pearl Harbor. Cf. *Stankus v. New York Life Ins. Co.,* 312 Mass. 366, 44 N.E. 2d 687 (1942), where the insured seaman died when the *USS Reuben James* was torpedoed by German submarines on Oct. 30, 1941; and *Vanderbilt v. Travelers Ins. Co.,* 112 Misc. 248, 184 N.Y.S. 54 (1920), where the insured lost his life when the *Lusitania* was sunk.

A similar set of life insurance cases arose out of deaths which occurred during the United Nations action in Korea. *Beley v. Pennsylvania Mutual Life Ins. Co.,* 373 Pa. 231, 95 A. 2d 202 (1953), and *Harding v. Pennsylvania Mutual Life Ins. Co.,* 171 Pa. Super. 236, 90 A. 2d 589, rehearing denied, 95 A. 2d 221 (1953), held that since war had not been declared by Congress, the conflict in Korea did not constitute a "war" in the "constitutional" or "legal" sense, and permitted recovery against the insurer. Other courts have taken the opposite stand in a long line of cases: e.g. *Stanberry v. Aetna Life Ins. Co.,* 26 N.J. Super. 498, 98 A. 2d 134 (1953); *Langlas v. Iowa Life Ins. Co.,* 245 Iowa 713, 63 N.W. 2d 885 (1954); *Gudewicz v. John Hancock Mutual Life Ins. Co.,* 331 Mass. 752, 122 N.E. 2d 900 (1954); *Christensen v. Sterling Ins. Co.,* 284 Pac. 2d 287 (1955); *Western Reserve Life Ins. Co. v. Meadows,* 152 Tex. 559, 261 S.W. 2d 554 (1953), cert. denied, 347 U.S. 928 (1954); *Lynch v. National Life and Accident Ins. Co.,* 278 S.W. 2d 32 (1955); *Weissman v. Metropolitan Life Ins. Co.,* 112 F. Supp. 420 (D.C.S.D. Cal., 1953); *Gagliormella v. Metropolitan Life Ins. Co.,* 122 F. Supp. 246 (D.C. Mass., 1954); *Carius v. New York Life Ins. Co.,* 124 F. Supp. 388 (D.C.S.D. Ill., 1954); and *Wilkinson v. Equitable Life Assurance Society,* 151 N.Y.S. 2d 1018 (1956).

For cases involving charter parties containing "war risk" clauses, see *Navios Corporation v. The Ulysses II,* 161 F. Supp. 932 (D.C. Md., 1958) affmd. 260 F. 2d 959 (1958), *Kawasaki Kisen Kabushiki Kaisha v. Bantham Steamship Co. Ltd.,* [1939] 2 K.B. 544, and *Spanish Government v. North of England Steamship Co. Ltd.,* [1938] 54 T.L.R. 852.

"blockade" or comparable terms, as Professor Stone seems to suggest,[31] but rather that of discerning and giving effect, within the limits of any overriding community policy, to the major purposes and expectations which the private parties to the document in question shared in their commitment and sought to project.[32]

31. Stone, *Legal Controls* 304, note 40; 310, note 77; 314, note 92.

32. It seems fairly obvious that the question of the commencement or existence of a "state of war," or "war in the legal sense," or simply "war," between two countries as determined for the very different purposes of the world public order is but of tangential, if any, relevance to this problem, which calls essentially for the application of familiar principles of interpretation. The approach adopted in the Bennion case (note 30 supra), where the court inquired into the expectations of the parties as to what risks would be excluded exemplifies the point we are making. The court said: "The subject matter of the contract was a risk assumed on the life of the insured by the Company, for a stipulated premium, and the use of the word war was obviously intended to denote a restriction or limitation upon the risk assumed. It is plain, therefore, that the definition given to the word war bears a direct relationship to the risk assumed. . . . Viewed in this light, it is also plain that when the parties used the word war, they had in mind the hazard to human life incident thereto" (158 F. 2d at 265). Obviously, the hazard to life was not dependent on a situation of military violence being characterized as a "war" or "state of war." This approach was adopted in the cases arising out of the Korean conflict starting from the Stanberry case (note 30 supra).

In the Navios case (note 30 supra), the charter party permitted either owner or charterer to cancel the charter "if war is declared against any present NATO countries." The court was of opinion that a speech delivered by President Nasser on Nov. 1, 1956, supported by a press statement issued on Nov. 3, 1956 by the Information Department of the Ministry of National Guidance of Egypt, "constituted a declaration of war even under the technical requirements of international law," and dismissed a libel for damages against the owner who had cancelled the charter. More importantly, the court found that one purpose of war clauses in charters was to permit the owner to take advantage of increased charter rates, and to make up for increased operating expenses, during conditions of conflict. The court also found that the Suez conflict, and more particularly the closing of the Canal, did cause an immediate shortage of ships and a sharp rise in freight rates.

In the Kawasaki Kisen Kabushiki Kaisha case (note 30 supra) the court refused to hold the steamship company liable for damages for canceling the charter-party under a clause authorizing such cancellation by either party "if war breaks out involving Japan." The court held in effect that the contingency provided for by the parties had occurred, despite the fact that neither Japan nor China (in 1937) had issued formal declarations of war and that the two countries maintained diplomatic relations with each other. Again, the risk that the parties

It is not, of course, meant to be suggested that in each and every context in which coercion is initiated, all the participants actually make all these types of claims. In any particular constellation of events, one or more of the participants may, for diverse reasons, refrain from asserting any one or more of the kinds of claims that such participants might otherwise be expected to assert. For instance, organs of international governmental organizations may restrain themselves from, or may postpone, characterizing exercises of coercion by a particular belligerent as nonpermissible, or calling for collective enforcement action, because of low estimates of the degree of probable conformity.[33] Again, because of expectations of excessive material and human costs which a military response may occasion, a target nation-state may decline to claim to meet force with force. The bloodless conquest of Czechoslovakia and the military occupation of Denmark by Nazi Germany in 1939 and 1940 are obvious examples of this situation.[34] A belligerent of negligible military capabilities and with relative security from military attack may also content itself with controlling enemy persons or taking enemy property within its territory and not claim actively to use the military instrument.

sought to provide against did not depend upon the presence or absence of "*animus belligerendi*" in either or both countries. The Master of the Rolls said: "I am unable to accept the suggestion that there is any technical meaning of the word 'war' for the purpose of the construction of this clause. . . . It seems to me that to suggest that, within the meaning of this charter party, war had not broken out involving Japan on the relevant date is to attribute to the parties to it a desire to import into their contract some obscure and uncertain technicalities of international law rather than the common sense of businessmen."

In the Spanish Government case (note 30 supra), Lewis, J., did say that the word "blockade" in a clause to the effect that the vessel would not be bound to proceed to "blockade ports," was used in its "strict legal sense." However, regardless of whether a "strict legal sense" or some other sense was to be imparted to "blockade," the court explicitly found that the risk provided against never materialized, that the announced intention of the Franco Government to blockade certain ports was never carried out, and that there was no greater danger or risk of interference with British vessels after the Nationalist announcement than before.

33. See infra Ch. 3, p. 296. Lauterpacht, supra note 4 at 55, 59 (on the Manchurian incident of 1931).

34. On the case of Czechoslovakia, see 3 *Survey of International Affairs, 1938* 247–88 (Royal Institute of Int. Affairs, 1953); on the occupation of Denmark, see *Hitler's Europe, Survey of International Affairs, 1939–1946* 519 et seq. (Royal Institute of Int. Affairs, 1954).

Certain Latin American countries which joined the Allied Powers in both world wars sequestered private German property without engaging in or contributing to actual military operations against Germany.[35]

The next step we recommend in the clarification of the ambiguous and confusing reference of the "commencement of war" is an equally careful orientation in the process of legal decision by which community intervention is organized in the attempt to regulate international coercion. This second process too may be described, in highest-level abstraction, as was indicated in detail in Chapter 1, in terms of certain *established decision-makers* seeking certain common policy *objectives* under the varying *conditions* of the world arena, by certain *methods* or *procedures* of formulating and applying authoritative prescriptions. From such perspective, it must be apparent that the great variety of claims asserted by varying parties at various points in the factual *continuum* of coercion, generate just as great a variety of policy problems, all traditionally lumped together under one simple label. It is to these "facts," claims, and problems, that the different decision-makers, who include officials of international governmental organizations and judges of international courts and arbitration tribunals, as well as civil and military officials of both belligerents and nonbelligerents, respond and attach "legal consequences" in the shape of decisions about the lawfulness or unlawfulness of any particular application or avoidance of coercion. The detailed issues of policy, as might be expected, commonly differ as the specific contexts and controversies differ.

With respect to the first type of initiation controversy—i.e., the belligerent *versus* target belligerent and international officials type of controversy—we may observe authoritative decision-makers to be seeking to prevent change through coercive procedures (or procedures involving a high degree of coercion), to promote change through noncoercive procedures (or procedures involving only a minimum degree of coercion) and to maintain a world public order of varying consistency with the values of a free society.[36] At the same

35. See Grob, supra note 6 at 293–4, and Kotzsch, supra note 22 at 248–50; see also *The War and the Neutrals, Survey of International Affairs, 1939–1946* 114–36 (Royal Institute of Int. Affairs, 1956).

36. We have, for the purpose of economy in expression, spoken of "the" public order of the world community. It is a fact of contemporary international life,

time, the community seeks to harness coercion to the maintenance of order by authorizing coercion as an individual, group, or community response to unauthorized coercion. These complementary policies are sought by invoking and applying, with varying degrees of success, fundamental prescriptions which discriminate between different coercive practices and characterize some as nonpermissible and others as permissible.

In the controversies between belligerents about the conduct of hostilities, the authoritative decision-makers bring to bear the familiar, equally complementary, principles of military necessity and humanitarianism. The basic effort is to minimize the unnecessary destruction of values through the application of a law of war sustained by the same principle which sustains the self-interest of belligerents—the principle of economy in the exercise of coercion and force.

In the confrontation of international officials or belligerents and nonbelligerents about participation, two sets of policies, corresponding to the two sets of claims we have noted, are successively sought by the established decision-makers. In the first, the community attempts to secure the maximum possible of common responsibility for repressing coercion authoritatively designated as unlawful by limiting the extent to which nonparticipation is permissible. The complementary policy of minimizing involvement and localizing the area of violence is urged by those who seek possible advantages in non-

---

however, that there is no single world public order as such, or a single conception thereof. There appear, rather, competing demanded conceptions of world public order and of international law, some of which are compatible with the postulated goal of wide sharing of values while others are not. See, e.g., the literature cited supra, Ch. 1, note 108.

On the Soviet conception of international law, see, e.g., Hazard, *Law and Social Change in the U.S.S.R.*, c. 11 (1953); id., *The Soviet Union and International Law* 189 et seq. (1950); Soloveitchik, "International Law as 'Instrument of Politics,'" 21 *U. of Kan. City L. Rev.* 169 (1953); Kulski, "The Soviet Interpretation of International Law," 49 *A.J.I.L.* 518 (1955); Schlesinger, *Soviet Legal Theory*, c. 10 (2nd ed., 1951); Taracouzio, *The Soviet Union and International Law* (1935); Kelsen, *The Communist Theory of Law* (1955).

On the Nazi German conception of international law, see Preuss, "National Socialist Conceptions of International Law," 29 *Am. Pol. Sci. Rev.* 594 (1935); Gott, "The National Socialist Theory of International Law," 32 *A.J.I.L.* 704 (1938); and Florin and Herz, "Bolshevist and National Socialist Doctrines of International Law," 7 *Social Research* 1 (1940).

participation. In the second set, authoritative decision-makers are seeking, in determining the relative rights and duties of belligerents and nonbelligerents, to adjust and balance the contraposed policies of military effectiveness, in terms of the isolation of the enemy belligerent, and of reducing to a minimum the consequent disruptions of the value processes of nonbelligerents.

In the fourth type of controversy which may arise in initiation contexts, i.e., belligerent vis-à-vis individuals in the belligerent's own territory, and in so far as the control of "enemy persons" is concerned, the competing policies to be reconciled refer to the security interests of the belligerent and to the human rights of "enemy" individuals. Respecting the control of enemy property, the basic policies discernible in the few vague and disputed limitations interposed by international law have been described in terms of the protection of private property and the encouragement of free worldwide circulation of wealth and of the satisfaction of the security and military needs of the belligerent. Substantially thc samc policies are at stake, though perhaps in differing degree, in the regulation and utilization by a belligerent of its own nationals and their property. Such policies are here, however, sought to be secured for the most part, if not wholly, through the medium of municipal rather than international prescription; decision-makers external to the state have imposed but few controls. The historic frame of reference for such problems is that which Professor Stone designated as "war" for "municipal legal purposes."

In the fifth type of controversy relating to initiation contexts—individuals against individuals—authoritative decision-makers, in regulating private transactions involving what might be called an "enemy element," seek an equilibrium between protection of the military interests of the belligerent and maintenance of the stability of expectations created by such transactions. Like the preceding context, this is much regulated by municipal law and policies vary greatly.

With such brief orientation in both the practices of coercion and the responses evoked from the various authoritative decision-makers, it may be possible to attempt some further clarification of the legal policy problems commonly associated with the initiation, as distinguished from the management and termination, of processes of coercion.

We have, assuming the perspective of the nonparticipant observer, described the process of coercion in terms of accelerating and decelerating degrees of intensity—that is, in terms of stages in a process of constant change. We have also noted that the participants in this process make different appeals to authority at different stages, to which appeals the established decision-makers of the world public order respond, invoking different sets of policies and supporting prescriptions in granting or denying such appeals. Considering both the differences in the claims presented to the authoritative decision-makers and the differences in the policies and prescriptions which such decision-makers deem relevant to the respective types of problems created by those claims, it would seem reasonably clear to an outside observer that there is no one, unique, and unitary "when" question that can be fruitfully asked about the application of authority in processes of coercion. To raise, as earlier text-writers have commonly done, one single, undifferentiated "when does war begin" question is to attempt at once to comprehend and transcend all the varying categories of problems, thus placing an impossible burden on communication. Accordingly, the general "when" question about the role of authority in coercion processes must be individualized and asked in respect of each specific type of problem. To put the point more positively, the allegedly unitary question must be dissolved into a number of more specific inquiries of how, in differing specified configurations of interrelated and variable factors, certain decision-makers may be expected to respond to certain characteristic claims as to the lawfulness or unlawfulness of certain exercises or avoidances of coercion. So conceived, a "when" question may be regarded as a semantically equivalent, if cryptic, way of referring to the peculiar constellation of all the elements in a given context which elicits certain responses from decision-makers. In this sense, the conventional question, "When does war exist (or begin)?" amounts, in equally conventional language, to the question, "What constitutes war?"

From these perspectives, to speak, for instance, of when coercion is prohibited (or when prescriptions on aggression, or threat to or breach of the peace, and self-defense become applicable) is only to refer to the totality of factors—like the chronological priority of resort to coercion; the type and intensity of the coercion exercised; the proportionality of the target-state's coercive response; the objectives of both the initiator and the target-states; the type and purpose of the decision demanded; the probability and costs of effective decision and so on—which decision-makers, explicitly or otherwise, take into account in characterizing certain applications of coercion as non-permissible. Similarly, to raise the question when nonparticipation is permissible (or when the rules on neutrality are applicable) is to pose for consideration the relative relevance for differing decision-makers of such factors as the formal commitments of the members of international security organizations, the procedures available for making operative such commitments, the nonmember status of a participant or nonparticipant, the character and degree of participation demanded, the intensity, spatial location, and extent of the violence involved, and the differences in power between the participants and nonparticipants. In like manner, to ask when certain modalities of combat are proscribed (or when certain rules on the conduct of hostilities become applicable) is to inquire into the relevant details of the level of destruction sought or secured, which, in varying specific contexts, may include among others: the character and authorization of combatants; the type, magnitude, and duration of the damage inflicted; the geographic locale of operations; the nature of the objects of attack and the degree to which they constitute effective enemy power bases; and the *quantum* of control achieved over such bases of enemy power. Again, to seek to determine when certain coercive controls may be taken by a participant over certain persons and resources in noncombat situations (or when rules, international or municipal, on the definition and treatment of "enemy" and non-"enemy" persons and property begin to be applicable) is to consider the shifting patterns, as presented to decision-makers, of such elements as expectations of impending violence; the formal allegiance and factual loyalties of individuals; the ownership of property, public or private; the degree of actual control by the enemy; the location, type, and possible uses of the property regulated; and the security and military needs of the acting participants. Finally, to inquire into when regulation of, or interference in, private transactions is permissible (or when certain rules on the effects of war on contracts become applicable) is to assess the impact on decisions of factors like the location of the parties in relation to the line of war; the time, *i.e.*, the stage in the coercion process, of the formation of the agreement; the stage of performance of the contract;

the effects of performance, in terms of the extent to which enemy resources may thereby be augmented or to which the belligerent's own resources may be diminished; and the timing of benefits.

From this partial listing, it would appear fairly obvious that authoritative decision-makers, in reaching decisions about these many different types of controversies, in fact respond not merely to assertions about time, i.e., the particular stage in the process of coercion, at which particular events occur, but also to the whole constellation of significant variables that make up the context of such assertions. The special significance to be accorded to the fact of the stage in the process of coercion is dependent upon the relation of such fact to the other equally important variables; the *datum* of time acquires relevance only within the other coordinates, as it were, of particular situations. Hence, as intimated above, "when" questions call for much more than a simple reference to the stage in coercive processes at which certain claims are made. They are appropriately posed, not in terms of the relation of some single factor, such as a declaration of *animus belligerendi* [37] or a cannon shot, to a calendar or clock, but

37. It is somewhat difficult to follow Professor Stone's position when he says that the 1907 Hague Convention III "lacks any substantial modern function" (*Legal Controls* 309, note 66), considering that he follows Lord McNair in assigning the time stated in a formal declaration of war (when made), or the time of its communication, as "the moment of its (war's) legal commencement" (id., 310).

It is true, however, that the Convention is pointless in so far as the prevention of surprise attacks is concerned; for the period of time between the communication of the declaration or ultimatum and the beginning of hostilities was left undetermined, such that even an infinitesimal space of time would apparently satisfy the requirement of "previous warning." See Hall, supra note 3 at 451–2. Westlake, supra note 2 at 267, noted that a "very moderate proposal" of a 24-hour interval made by the Netherlands' Delegation to the Conference of 1907 was rejected; contrast this with the fact that during the days of the ancient *jus fetiale,* provision was frequently made in declarations that hostilities would not begin till after 33 days (see 2 Phillipson, *The International Law and Custom of Ancient Greece and Rome* 200 (1911)). In our own age when rocket missiles and artificial satellites travel at velocities measured in tens of thousands of miles per hour, it would seem somewhat optimistic to suggest, as Professor Castrén does (supra note 2 at 99), that a "time of grace" or an "intermediary period" should be given in the future.

For the possible uses of a declaration of war in contexts other than the conduct of hostilities, see Eagleton, "The Form and Function of the Declaration of War," 32 *A.J.I.L.* 19 (1938).

in terms rather of the relations of the different factors *inter se* and to the policies of world public order regarded as material to the type of problem under consideration.

An authoritative decision-maker, in determining the legal import to be ascribed to any particular constellation of variables on any specific problem, may and does rationally take into account sequence relationships of "beforeness," "afterness" and "simultaneousness" among variables (and this is what we mean by "stage" in a process of coercion). Once such decision-maker has determined to attach certain "legal consequences" (or apply certain prescriptions) rather than others, to the "facts" of coercion alleged before him, he may equally rationally and casually assign a calendar date for the beginning of the ascription of the determined "consequences" (or for the applicability of the prescriptions determined). But the assignment of time he makes is a function of his reaction to all the factors constitutive of the specific context and hence varies from problem to problem. Irrationality comes in when some subsequent decision-maker or commentator seizes on one date so assigned for one problem, objectifies it into a monistic concept of *"the* commencement of war," and projects such concept as allegedly controlling for other problems in fact raising differing policy issues. Rationality, in fine, in the determination of "when war begins" requires not a marking of one or even a few dates in a calendar, nor a search for one decisive factor, for the applicability *in abstracto* of prescriptions, but rather the clarification of the requirements of general world community policies uniquely relevant to varying claims of authority at varying stages in coercion processes. A policy-oriented approach is not a single-factor but a multiple-factor approach; rational policy is not uni-temporal but multi-temporal.

Because of the difficulties thus indicated in isolating the special significance for decision that assertions about the stage in a coercion process may have from the cumulative impact of all the other factors on decision, it would accordingly appear more rational to study that factor, in so far as it does have, in a particular type of controversy, any special significance, in the course of more comprehensive inquiries into each of the various types of controversies. Such a mode of inquiry might begin with a more careful discrimination of the different types of major recurring controversies and proceed, within each type of controversy, to a more comprehensive itemization of the factors significantly affecting decision. From such contextual orientation, an inquirer might, it is to be hoped, much more effectively seek to perform the various intellectual tasks deemed essential to policy-oriented study, including, as specified in Chapter 1: the clarification of policies, the observation and comparison through time of past trends in decision, the identification in relative detail of the more significant conditioning elements, the projection of past trends into future probabilities, and the recommendation of preferred alternatives designed to secure the values of a free society.

3. RESORT TO COERCION: AGGRESSION AND SELF-DEFENSE IN POLICY PERSPECTIVE

The maintenance of public order—when public order is conceived in its minimal sense as community control and prevention of private violence—is commonly and appropriately regarded as the first indispensable function of any system of law.[1] The securing of a public order—understood in a broader sense as embracing the totality of a community's legally protected goal values and implementing institutions [2]—which seeks, beyond an effective community monopolization of force, the richest production and widest sharing of all

1. Recognition of the primacy of this function in the international as in municipal arenas is widely reflected in the literature. See, e.g., Waldock, "The Regulation of the Use of Force by Individual States in International Law," 81 *Hague Academie de Droit International, Recueil des Cours* (hereinafter cited as *Hague Recueil)* 455 (1952); Brierly, *The Basis of Obligation in International Law* 230 (1958); Pound, "A Survey of Social Interests," 57 *Harv. L. Rev.* 1, 17–18 (1943); Stone, *The Province and Function of Law* 454–5, 555, 559–60 (1950); Kelsen, *General Theory of Law and State* 21–2 (1954); cf. De Visscher, *Theory and Reality in Public International Law* 99 (Corbett, trans., 1957). Studies on primitive and ancient systems indicate that such communities accorded similar priority to control of disruptive violence. See, e.g., Hoebel, *The Law of Primitive Man* (1954); Llewellyn and Hoebel, *The Cheyenne Way* cc. 10–12 (1941); Maine, *Ancient Law* c. 10 (Everyman's ed., 1954); 1 Simpson and Stone, *Law and Society* 66–89, 284–97 (1948). See also Aberle et al., "The Functional Prerequisites of a Society," 60 *Ethics* 100, 103, 110 (1950).

2. For development of the reference assigned to a "system of public order," see McDougal and Lasswell, "The Identification and Appraisal of Diverse Systems of Public Order," 53 *A.J.I.L.* 1 (1959). See also Dession and Lasswell, "Public Order Under Law: The Role of the Advisor-Draftsman in the Formation of Code or Constitution," 65 *Yale L. J.* 174, 185 (1955); Dession. "The Technique of Public Order: Evolving Concepts of Criminal Law," 5 *Buffalo L. Rev.* 22, 23–4 (1955).

First published in 68 *Yale L. J.* 1057–1165 (1959). Reprinted with permission.

values, is today also commonly projected as appropriate aspiration by most mature territorial polities. The intimate interdependence of these two conceptions of public order is obvious. Effective prevention and repression of private violence are necessary prerequisites to establishing appropriate institutions for the most rewarding pursuit of other values. Conversely, a full opportunity to pursue individual and community values through peaceful procedures, by lessening predispositions to coercion and violence, may be expected to further the continued maintenance of minimum order.

Conspicuous features of the world social process today include the increasing unity of demand among most of the peoples of the world for achievement, in the international arena, of public order, in its widest as well as in its narrowest sense, and the increasing awareness that efficient world institutions for the optimum creation and distribution of values depend upon the securing of minimum order. Subjecting the processes of coercion and violence among nation-states to effective community controls is thus the most fundamental contemporary problem for all who seek a world public order honoring, in deed as in rhetoric, human freedom. This problem is not of course peculiar to our age, although the implications of continued failure, given the existing weapons of catastrophic destruction, are now perhaps unique. It had its origin with the first conception of a community of states under a common law.[3] When emerging territorially-based polities first began to constitute an international arena, the problem became, as it remains, the central one in international law.

This basic problem of legal regulation of resort to international coercion may perhaps be most economically outlined by recalling in briefest summary the related, but analytically separable, processes of coercion and legal decision.[4] In Chapter 1, we described the process of international coercion in terms of nation-states seeking the fulfillment of their value goals and applying to each other for that end

3. See Schiffer, *The Legal Community of Mankind* c. 2 (1954); Van Vollenhoven, *The Law of Peace* cc. 1–3 (1936); Van Vollenhoven, *The Three Stages in the Evolution of the Law of Nations* (1919); Van Vollenhoven, "Grotius and Geneva," in 6 *Bibliotheca Visseriana* 5 (1926); Smith, *The Crisis in the Law of Nations* 8 (1947).

4. A recommended mode of inquiry into these processes is spelled out in some detail in Ch. 1.

coercion of fluctuating degree of intensity, by all available instruments of policy, under all the constantly changing conditions in the world arena. We sought to indicate that some degree of coercion is almost continuously observable in the ordinary processes of state interaction for values,[5] and perhaps in all human interaction, whether the processes be confined within the boundaries of a single state or transcend state boundaries. In the course of this continuous process of coercion among states, as we also noted, contending participants make certain characteristic types of opposing claims about the lawfulness and unlawfulness of their respective exercises of coercion. The contraposed claims with which we are here more particularly concerned relate to the initiation of coercion. Generally, one participant asserts that it is lawful to employ highly intense coercion, or to accelerate the intensity of coercion previously exercised, against the opposing participant; and the opposing participant then maintains that such is unlawful initiation or acceleration of coercion and justifies defensive coercion. To these facts of initiative and response in coercion and these claims and counterclaims of lawfulness and unlawfulness, certain decision-makers, established by community perspectives as authoritative, respond by determining both the requirements or limits of authority in respect of the coercion and the appropriate community or unilateral countering measures. In fulfilling their community responsibility decision-makers commonly find it necessary to appraise particular exercises of coercion in terms of conformity to public-order goals, and when appropriate to characterize such exercises as permissible or impermissible. In the making of such appraisals and characterizations, the decision-makers seek to give effect to certain shared policy objectives. To this end they formulate and apply authoritative community prescriptions.

Complementary Prescriptions on Permissible and Nonpermissible Coercion

The contemporary world prescriptions about the application of coercion across state boundaries project in general terms a set of complementary policies designed, in ultimate effect, to secure and maintain an overriding policy of peaceful change and of minimizing

5. Cf. Aron, *On War* 8 (Anchor ed., 1959): "Relations between sovereign states may be more or less bellicose; they are never *essentially* or *ultimately* peaceful."

destruction of values. A principal purpose of modern efforts at comprehensive organization of the community of states has been to clarify a distinction between permissible and nonpermissible coercion and to establish the institutions and procedures thought indispensable and appropriate for sustaining that distinction. The Charter of the United Nations indicates, in broad strokes, the level of coercion that is sought to be prohibited: members are required—and this is declared a basic principle—to "refrain in their international relations from the threat or use of force against the territorial integrity or political independence of any state, or in any other manner inconsistent with the Purposes of the [organization]." [6] The positive aspect of this prohibition lies in the obligation of members to resolve their disputes "by peaceful means" that do not endanger "international peace and security, and justice." [7] The commitment of members to "refrain from the use or threat of force" is sometimes assumed by commentators to refer to the use or threat of armed or military force.[8]

6. U. N. Charter, Art. 2, par. 4.

7. U. N. Charter, Art. 2, par. 3. See also United Nations, *Systematic Survey of Treaties for the Pacific Settlement of Disputes 1928–1948* (1948) for indication of the frequency with which, and the specific forms in which, this obligation was assumed and affirmed before and after the U. N. Charter.

8. See, e.g., 2 Oppenheim, *International Law* 153 (7th ed., Lauterpacht, 1952) [hereinafter cited as Oppenheim-Lauterpacht]; Bentwich and Martin, *A Commentary on the Charter of the United Nations* 13 (1950); Goodrich and Hambro, *Charter of the United Nations* 104 (2d rev. ed., 1949); Waldock, "The Regulation of the Use of Force by Individual States in International Law," 81 *Hague Recueil* 455, 492 (1952); Bowett, *Self-Defence in International Law* 148 (1958).

The discussions and preparatory work at San Francisco appear somewhat confused and equivocal on this point and hardly yield conclusive indication of the correctness of the commentators' assumptions. For instance, while it is true that a Brazilian amendment to Article 2(4), one that would have added the words "and from the threat or use of economic measures," was rejected by the Drafting Subcommittee of Committee I/1, 6 *Documents of the U.N. Conference on International Organization* 334, 559 (1945) [hereinafter cited as U.N.C.I.O.], the Report of Committee 1 to Commission I stated that "The unilateral use of force or *similar coercive measures* is not authorized or admitted," id. at 400. (Emphasis added.) The commentators cited above commonly invoke the "ordinary connotation" and the "plain, common-sense meaning" of "force"—a criterion of interpretation which in other contexts is seldom regarded as conclusive.

See, further, Kelsen, "General International Law and the Law of the United Nations," in *The United Nations: Ten Years' Legal Progress* 4–5 (1956). He

The apparent implication, however, that employment of nonmilitary types of coercion was never meant to be prohibited, is subject to serious reservations. The authority of the Security Council to characterize particular coercion as a "threat to the peace," "breach of the peace," or "act of aggression," and to call for appropriate sanctioning measures, is not restricted, by the Charter at least, as to the modality of coercion that may be so characterized.[9] Beyond cavil, political and economic pressures may, in some particular contexts, endanger "international peace and security and justice" [10] when they assume such proportions and intensity as to generate a substantial likelihood of or need for a military response. In contrast with the differences of opinion about nonmilitary instruments, there is no question that the applications of armed force prohibited by the Charter include both the comprehensive and highly intense uses commonly associated with "war" and the less comprehensive and relatively milder exercises often described in the past as "measures short of war." [11] These affirmative obligations, subsequently and frequently reiterated in charters of regional governmental organizations,[12] are supplemented

---

suggests that "force" in Article 2(4) may be construed to refer to both "armed force" and "non-armed force."

9. U. N. Charter, Art. 39; see text accompanying note 103 infra. See, in this connection, the argument made by Professor Kelsen, supra note 8 at 11, that "Member states are not only under the obligations stipulated expressly in Article 2, paragraphs 3, 4, and 5, but also under the obligations to refrain from a threat to or breach of the peace stipulated in Article 39; . . ."

10. Stone, *Legal Controls of International Conflict* 286–7 (1954) suggests that in such cases, "forcible or coercive" measures may be regarded as violative of Article 2(3), if not Article 2(4), of the U. N. Charter.

11. See, e.g., Waldock, supra note 8 at 489; 2 Oppenheim-Lauterpacht 152, 184; Goodrich and Hambro, *Charter of the United Nations* 104 (2d rev. ed., 1949); Jessup, *A Modern Law of Nations* 169–77 (1948).

12. Citations to these regional treaties are collected in Ch. 1, note 100. See also Security Treaty Between Australia, New Zealand, and the United States, Art. 1 (1951) (text in 46 *A.J.I.L. Supp.* 93 (1952)); Mutual Assistance Pact Between Greece, Turkey, and Yugoslavia, Art. 1 (1954) (text in 49 id. *Supp.* 47 (1955)); Mutual Defense Treaty Between the United States and the Philippines, Art. 1 (1951) (text in Subcommittee on Disarmament, Senate Committee on Foreign Relations, *Disarmament and Security: A Collection of Documents 1919–1955*, 84th Cong., 2d Sess., 598 (1956)); Mutual Defense Treaty Between the United States and the Republic of Korea, Art. 1 (1953) (text in id. at 607); Mutual Defense

by the "Nuremberg principles" which were unanimously affirmed by the United Nations General Assembly as "principles of international law" [13] and which authorize the imposition of negative (criminal) sanctions on individual persons judicially ascertained to be responsible for the "planning, preparation, initiation or waging of a war of aggression or a war in violation of international treaties, agreements or assurances." [14]

The conception of permissible coercion, complementary to that of nonpermissible, is characterized by multiplicity of reference. One reference is to all coercion which is implicit in and concomitant to the ordinary interaction of states, and which does not rise to the level and degree of prohibited coercion.[15] Another and more common reference is to coercion of a high degree of intensity, including the most comprehensive and violent uses of military instruments, when employed in individual or group defense against unlawful coercion. States traditionally have claimed and reciprocally acknowledged a large competence to protect themselves by countering coercion with coercion. The United Nations Charter explicitly mentions and preserves this permission to resort to force in response to unauthorized coercion, describes it as an "inherent right," and recognizes that permissible coercion may be exercised by the target state individually, or by a collectivity of states, without prior authorization from the organized community (although, of course, subject to its subsequent appraisal). [16] A third reference is to coercion exercised in fulfillment of or in accordance with certain commitments and permissions of members to participate in police measures required or authorized by the general security organization to prevent or repress impermissible coercion. These measures of collective peace enforcement are designed to supplement the efforts of the participant or group of par-

---

Treaty Between the United States and the Republic of China, Art. 1 (1954) (text in id. at 608).

13. U.N. Gen. Ass., Res. No. 95(I), Gen. Ass., *Off. Rec.*, 1st Sess., Plenary 55 (1946).

14. Principle VI, Formulation of the Nuremberg Principles, Report of the International Law Commission covering its second session, June 5–July 29, 1950, in 2 *Y.B. of the Int. Law Comn. 1950* at 376.

15. This and the other references of permissible coercion are explored in relative detail in the second part of this chapter.

16. U. N. Charter, Art. 51.

ticipants determined by the community to have been exercising lawful defense.

The most elementary distinction that any system of law must make in attempting to secure minimum public order is thus today established by the world community in its fundamental prescriptions.[17] By contraposing the prohibition of unlawful coercion and the permission of lawful coercion, we seek to emphasize the complementarity and polarity of these prescriptions.[18] Contrary to the suggestion sometimes made,[19] to couple the prohibition with the permission is not to neutralize and nullify the prohibition. The world community's prescriptions about coercion, like other world prescriptions, march and must march in pairs of complementary opposites. An absolute interdiction of all coercion is scarcely conceivable, or if conceivable is hardly within the limits of the achieveable. A certain degree of coercion is almost always exhibited in all the value-institutional processes that take place in the world arena. Certainly the world social processes, characterized in terms of the dominant value

17. In the language of Professor Kelsen's system, the effect of establishing this distinction is to permit "war" to be characterized as either a "delict" or a "reaction against a delict [sanction]." See Kelsen, *Law and Peace* 34–55 (1942); Kelsen, *The Law of the United Nations* 707–8 (1950); Kelsen, *Principles of International Law* 33–5 (1952). See also Tucker, "The Interpretation of War Under Present International Law," 4 *Int. L.Q.* 11 (1951).

18. There is some recognition of this complementarity in, e.g., Stone, *Aggression and World Order* 75 and note 182 (1958); Lauterpacht, "The Pact of Paris and the Budapest Articles of Interpretation," 20 *Tr. Grotius Soc.* 178, 199 (1935); Williams, *Some Aspects of the Covenant of the League of Nations* 237 (1934). See also the American Note of June 23, 1928, issued during the drafting of the Briand-Kellogg Pact: "Express recognition by treaty of this inalienable right [of self-defence], however, gives rise to the same difficulty encountered in any effort to define aggression. It is the identical question approached from the other side. . . ." (Text in Miller, *The Peace Pact of Paris* 214 (1928).) In contrast, see Kelsen, *Collective Security Under International Law* 27–8 (1957), and Pompe, *Aggressive War: an International Crime* 55–60 (1953).

19. See, e.g., Stone, *Legal Controls of International Conflict* 243 (1954), who lists article 51 of the U. N. Charter among "clauses of escape and evasion from peaceful settlement and peace enforcement." Similarly, Professor Stone writes that "if these provisions [e.g., articles 2(3), 2(4), 39–50] were not qualified by other provisions [e.g., Article 51] of the Charter, and by the difficulties of operating them, they would virtually have established legal control over the resort of states to war, analogous to that of municipal law over the resort of citizens to private violence." Id. at 303.

at stake as power processes, pervasively and continuously manifest many aspects of coercion.[20] Further, not even the most highly centralized and effectively organized municipal public order attempts to prohibit private coercion absolutely; some provision for self-defense in residual, exceptional cases always remains.[21] In a decentralized world arena, in which the general community of states still lacks effective capacity to protect constituent states from unlawful coercion, it would seem a fortiori even less practicable to eliminate permissive self-defense and achieve a truly complete prohibition of coercion. Inasmuch as an absolute prohibition of coercion has not been feasible, the historical alternatives of the general community have been either to permit complete disorder or to aspire to minimum public order. Complete disorder, failure to forbid even the most intense and comprehensive destruction of values, is not only possible, but has in fact long characterized the perspectives of traditional international law. If, on the other hand, the deliberate choice is made to pursue at least a minimum of order in the world arena, the coercion that is to be prohibited clearly must be distinguished from that which is to be permitted.[22] The conceptions both of impermissible

20. Lasswell and Kaplan, *Power and Society* 98 (1950), point out that power can be described in terms of, *inter alia,* its degree of coerciveness which "depends on which values serve as the influence base (and function as positive or negative sanctions), and on the amounts of those values promised or threatened. . . . The exercise of power is simply the exercise of a high degree of coerciveness. When the values promised or threatened are sufficiently important to those over whom the influence is being exercised, the latter are being coerced: they are subjected to a power relationship." See also id. at 250–61.

21. Cf. Kelsen, *Collective Security Under International Law* 27 (1957). It is made clear in Jenks, *The Common Law of Mankind* 139–43 (1958) not only that all major legal systems recognize self-defense, but also that such systems exhibit an impressive uniformity with regard to the appropriate limiting principles. Dr. Jenks made reference to the common law, Canadian, French, German, Italian, Islamic, Hindu, Jewish, Chinese, Japanese, African, and Soviet systems.

22. Contrast the suggestions made in Cohn, "The System of Sanctions of Article 16 of the Covenant and the Future Role of Neutrality," in *Collective Security* 402 (Bourquin, ed., 1936):

> The system of sanctions should be directed against war as such, as a fact, without regard to its psychological basis. . . . [D]efensive war must be included as well as offensive war, so that the States not involved in the conflict may not be obligated to make a choice which would at the same time necessitate the moral condemnation of one of the Powers, but may simply

and of permissible coercion are thus necessary in the theoretical formulation of authoritative policy as well as in the practical application of that policy to interacting human groups.

The Basic Postulate of Peaceful Change

The fundamental policies embodied and projected in these prescriptions are, as indicated, complementary. In formulating, interpreting, and applying the prohibition of impermissible coercion, authoritative decision-makers of the world community attempt to regulate conflicting claims by states, on the one hand, to *effect* changes, and, on the other, to *avoid* changes in the patterns of power and other value allocation among the various nation-states.[23] The decision-makers seek to prevent coercive and violent unilateral modification and reconstruction of value patterns and, simultaneously, to encourage recourse to nonviolent, noncoercive methods of change and adjustment. This policy is instinct with a community recognition that coercion of provocative intensity and violence are not appropriate instruments for asserting and implementing claims to a reallocation of values; commonly intense coercive and violent unilateral redistribution of values in the world arena not only wastefully entails the expenditure of values for the destruction of values but also generates further value expenditure and destruction in the shape of a countering response.[24] The basic community policy might, there-

---

> be confronted with the state of war as a fact which must be prevented and combated [sic], in the common interest of all the nations. It is of little importance to determine who, from a purely formal standpoint, is playing the part of the aggressor. War is forbidden in all cases and for all parties. . . .

The singular want of realism in these suggestions is all the more conspicuous when it is recalled that they were addressed to the problem of making the League of Nations "more and more effective and universal."

23. As to this mode of generalizing the opposing claims, cf. Dunn, *Peaceful Change* 1–4 (1937).

24. "Indeed no more grave crimes can be conceived of than a conspiracy to wage a war of aggression or the waging of a war of aggression, for the conspiracy threatens the security of the peoples of the world, and the waging disrupts it. The probable result of such a conspiracy, and the inevitable result of its execution is that death and suffering will be inflicted on countless human beings." *Judgment of the International Military Tribunal for the Far East* 1142 (1948). The comparable, and more frequently quoted, passage from the judgment of the Nuremberg Tribunal appears in Office of U.S. Chief of Counsel for

fore, simply be generalized in terms of a demand for elemental public order and for the preservation of basic human values in the course of international change. In permitting, on the other hand, certain coercion as lawful, authoritative decision-makers seek to utilize coercion, under appropriate conditions, for the more effective securing of such minimum public order by authorizing community enforcement action and, in deference to the still poor degree of organization obtaining in the world arena, by conceding individual and group defense against breaches of public order. The assumption which underlies the permission of lawful coercion is, like that which underlies the prohibition of unlawful coercion, not that the value distribution map and the particular configuration of the international arena existent at any given time should be immunized from change but that the common interest in minimizing the destruction of values dictates that they should not be reconstructed through intense coercion or violence.

In an arena as decentralized, primitively organized, and afflicted with competing conceptions of preferred world public order as the existing world is, and in the absence of effective, specialized institutions for prescribing and applying community policy about coercion, the essential distinction between permissible and nonpermissible resort to coercion is, of course, difficult to apply in varying specific contexts of coercion. At a later stage in this chapter, we propose to canvass these difficulties and to indicate in some detail the range of contextual factors bearing upon application of the permissible-nonpermissible distinction. The point of present emphasis is that

---

Prosecution of Axis Criminality, *Nazi Conspiracy and Aggression, Opinion and Judgment* 16 (1947).

The character and capabilities of modern weapons have, of course, imparted new and sharper point to this humanitarian recognition. As Professor Dunn observes in "Peaceful Change Today," 11 *World Politics* 278–9 (1959):

> The recent spectacular developments in military weapons have sharply restricted the utility of coercion as a means of changing the *status quo*. The destructiveness of nuclear weapons is out of all proportion to any political gains that might be achieved by war. There is no certainty that even mild forms of coercion would not eventually lead to their use. Hence, whereas change by voluntary agreement is very difficult to achieve, change through the resort to forceful measures has in most cases become entirely too dangerous to contemplate.

neither difficulty of application nor the continuing high expectations of violence should obscure the indispensability of the distinction for securing both minimum order and the necessary conditions for a world public order of freedom and abundance. Withal the authoritative establishment of that distinction represents a substantial achievement.[25] The long perspective of history precludes casual deprecation of prescriptions which epitomize what has for centuries been a major aspiration of much of mankind—the institution of processes of authority, encompassing both prescriptions and procedures, that permit and encourage the production and sharing of values without the disruption of coercion and violence from across national boundaries.[26]

Emergence of the Fundamental Distinction: Bellum Iustum

These contemporary prescriptions have roots that reach far back into the Middle Ages when comparable efforts to distinguish between legitimate and nonlegitimate (*iustum* and *iniustum*) violence were made.[27] The gist of the conception of *bellum iustum,* as formu-

25. Cf. Jessup, "The Crime of Aggression and the Future of International Law," 62 *Pol. Sci. Q.* 1 (1947).

26. For surveys of the numerous peace plans, in which this ancient and continuing aspiration found expression, conceived and put forward from the days of Dubois at the beginning of the fourteenth century down to the establishment of the United Nations, see, e.g., Beales, *The History of Peace* (1931); Hemleben, *Plans for World Peace Through Six Centuries* (1943); Trueblood, *The Development of the Peace Idea* (1932); Wynner and Lloyd, *Searchlight on Peace Plans* (1944). See also *The Evolution of World-Peace* (Marvin, ed., 1921); Phelps, *The Anglo-American Peace Movement in the Mid-Nineteenth Century* (1930); Souleyman, *The Vision of World Peace in Seventeenth and Eighteenth-Century France* (1941). A brief summary is offered in Schwarzenberger, *The League of Nations and World Order* 7–18 (1936), and Possony, "Peace Enforcement," 55 *Yale L.J.* 910 (1946).

27. See, e.g., Ballis, *The Legal Position of War: Changes in Its Theory and Practice from Plato to Vattel* (1937); Butler and Maccoby, *The Development of International Law* 107–21 (1928); Eppstein, *The Catholic Tradition of the Law of Nations* cc. 4–5 (1935); Nussbaum, *A Concise History of the Law of Nations* cc. 3–4 (rev. ed., 1954); Pompe, *Aggressive War: an International Crime* 116–38 (1953); Scott, *The Catholic Conception of International Law* (1934); Wehberg, *The Outlawry of War* (Zeydel, trans., 1931); Von Elbe, "The Evolution of the Concept of the Just War in International Law," 33 *A.J.I.L.* 665 (1939). References to continental literature are compiled in Stone, *Legal Controls of International Conflict* 298–9 notes 6 and 9 (1954).

lated and systematized by the medieval theologians and jurists, was that resort to violence could be regarded as a legitimate procedure of self-help only if certain requirements relating to a belligerent's authority to make war (*auctoritas principis*), and to the objectives (*iusta causa*) and intent (*recta intentio*) of the belligerent, were met.[28] In this conception, the legitimate objectives of violence were limited to the redressing of "a wrong received," [29] a "wrong" "serious and commensurate with the losses the war would occasion" and "which cannot be repaired or avenged in any other way." [30] *"Iusta causa"* thus anticipated the requirements of consequentiality and necessity which seem implicit in present conceptions of permissible coercion.

The classical doctrine of *bellum iustum* may be seen to be comparable in policy with contemporary prescriptions. The doctrine incorporated a policy of limiting the incidence of violent change among the multitude of kingdoms and principalities that comprised the medieval European world.[31] In the context of the arena that existed at least in the later Middle Ages, *bellum iustum* and the

28. Systematization of the conception of *bellum iustum* in terms of these three general requisites was the work of St. Thomas Aquinas. The requirement of *auctoritas principis* was designed to exclude private violence. *Iusta causa* required the showing of fault on the part of the adverse party. *Recta intentio* was absent where the belligerent's motive was aggrandizement rather than "securing peace," "punishing evil-doers," and "uplifting the good." See Scott, *The Spanish Origin of International Law* Pt. 1, at 192 (1934). Suárez much later modified the Thomist doctrine by substituting for *recta intentio, debitus modus,* a proper mode of conducting a war. Suárez, "De Triplici Virtute Theologica," in 2 *Selections From Three Works* 805 (*Classics of International Law,* 1944). Grotius, beyond stating the just causes of war as defense, recovery of property, and punishment, added little to the scholastics' analysis. *De Iure Belli Ac Pacis* Bk. II, c. 1, s. II, 2, 171 (*Classics of International Law,* 1925).

29. Vitoria, "De Indis et De Iure Belli Relectiones," in Scott, *The Spanish Origin of International Law* at liv (1934). Vitoria expressly rejected extension of empire, differences of religion, and personal glory or advantage of the belligerent prince as just causes of war. Id. at liii–liv. See also Stanislai de Scarbimiria, *De Bellis Justis;* the Latin text, Polish translation and an English summary may be found in Ehrlich, *Polski Wyklad Prawa Wojny XV Wicku* (Warszawa, 1955).

30. Suárez, supra note 28 at 816; cf. Vitoria, supra note 29 at liv–lv: "Not every kind and degree of wrong can suffice for commencing a war. . . . As, then, the evils inflicted in war are all of a severe and atrocious character, such as slaughter and fire and devastation, it is not lawful for slight wrongs to pursue the authors of the wrongs with war, seeing that the degree of the punishment ought to correspond to the measure of the offence."

31. See Vitoria, supra note 29 at lxx.

policy it embodied seemed much more practicable of application than might be supposed from the epithets with which the doctrine has been described by some modern writers.[32] The Western world in the later Middle Ages exhibited a basic unity characterized, in its fundamental aspect, by one widely and deeply shared body of spiritual perspectives, a centralized ecclesiastical organization that transcended political boundaries, and a common overriding respect for the supreme ecclesiastical authority, the Papacy. The degree of unity and centralized organization of authority achieved by the Church was such that medieval Christendom has been described by scholars as an "international state." [33] The Papacy, whose authority was conceived as derived from a source independent of and higher than human volition, was regarded as competent to formulate and interpret general standards for the ordering of relations among temporal rulers, to intervene in disputes between them for the maintenance of peace and, in case of war, to pass judgment on the justness of a belligerent's cause.[34] Sanctioning procedures available for enforcing papal judgments included the pronouncement of excommunication and interdict which, in that age, entailed extensive material deprivations and, at times, even the deposition of an offending prince.[35]

Profound changes in the conditions of the medieval world—

32. Nussbaum, "Just War—A Legal Concept?," 42 *Mich. L. Rev.* 453 (1943); Kunz, "Bellum Justum and Bellum Legale," 45 *A.J.I.L.* 528 (1951); Kunz, *La Problematica Actual de las Leyes de la Guerra* 85 (1955).

33. See Krey, "The International State of the Middle Ages: Some Reasons for Its Failure," 28 *Am. Hist. Rev.* 7 (1927); cf. Figgis, *Studies of Political Thought from Gerson to Grotius 1414–1625,* at 4 (2d ed., 1923): "In the Middle Ages the Church was not a State, it was the State; the State or rather the civil authority (for a separate society was not recognized) was merely the police department of the Church." See also Hoffner, *La Etica Colonial Española del Siglo de Oro* 3–44 (Caballero, trans. 1957).

34. Schiffer, *The Legal Community of Mankind* c. 1 (1954); Gierke, *Political Theories of the Middle Ages* 9–21 (Maitland, trans., 1900) (especially at 14–15); Wright, *Medieval Internationalism* 18–50 (1930). See also 4 Carlyle and Carlyle, *A History of Medieval Political Theory in the West* 362 (1922); 5 id. 165–71 (1928); Eppstein, *The Catholic Tradition of the Law of Nations* c. 8 and app. I (1935); Nussbaum, *A Concise History of the Law of Nations* 17–21 (rev. ed., 1954); 1 Pereña Vicente, *Teoria de la Guerra en Francisco Suárez* 271–82 (1954).

35. 2 Carlyle and Carlyle, op. cit. supra note 34 at 200–6. For instances of excommunication and deposition of kings and princes by papal decree for breaking the peace, see 1 Walker, *A History of the Law of Nations* 92–3 (1899).

brought about by the Reformation with its disintegrating impact on the unity and authority of the Church, and by the consolidation of the effective power of territorial polities [36]—deeply affected the viability of *bellum iustum*. With the authority of the Papacy repudiated by many temporal rulers, there was no longer any supranational organ commonly acknowledged as competent to give judgment on the legitimacy of the cause asserted by a sovereign prince who resorted to violence. The absence of an effective central authority enabled each belligerent to be, in effect, his own and final judge; a prince's recourse to war was in fact likened by commentators to a decree of a law court against a defendant.[37] Thus, the question of the "subjective," as distinguished from the "objective," justice of a resort to violence, and the possibility and implications of an armed conflict being "subjectively" just on both sides, were much discussed. Neither Vitoria's conception of "invincible ignorance" as sufficient justification or Suárez' notion of "probabilism" [38] could infuse much vitality into the doctrine of *bellum iustum* in an arena where no effective decision-maker was generally accepted as authorized to apply it.[39] By the eighteenth century, Vattel could write that the rectitude of international violence was a question pertaining to the "necessary

36. Figgis, op. cit. supra note 33 at 55, summed up the changes as "a change from a world-empire to a territorial State, and from ecclesiastical to civil predominance." See also Lawrence, *International Law* 20–1 (7th ed., Winfield, 1928); Schiffer, *The Legal Community of Mankind* 27 (1954); Sturzo, *The International Community and the Right of War* c. 1 (Carter, trans., 1929); Nussbaum, *A Concise History of the Law of Nations* c. 4 (rev. ed., 1954).

37. The judicial analogy is especially discernible in the writings of Vitoria, supra note 29 at LV–LVI (1532), and Suárez, supra note 28 at 806 (1612). See also Scott, *The Catholic Conception of International Law* 39–41, 441–3 (1934); Husserl, "The Conception of War as a Legal Remedy," 12 *U. Chi. L. Rev.* 115, 258 (1945); Von Elbe, supra note 27 at 679.

38. See Scott, *The Catholic Conception of International Law* 48–9, 459–65 (1934); Butler and Maccoby, *The Development of International Law* 110–14 (1928); 1 Pereña Vicente, *Teoria de la Guerra en Francisco Suárez* 214–70 (1954).

39. It is in the light of Grotius' historic task of supplying secular principles to fill the void left by the shattering of medieval religious and ecclesiastical unity and of giving definitive form to the conception of a community of territorial states without centralized organs, but under a common law, that his use of the *bellum iustum* doctrine is to be considered. For a brief but excellent exposition of the function Grotius assigned to permissible coercion in his system, see Schiffer, *The Legal Community of Mankind* c. 2 (1954). Schiffer points out that Grotius himself was quite aware of the difficulties presented by the then existing arena conditions. Id. at 40–1, 46.

law of nations" addressed to the "conscience of sovereigns," and that the "voluntary" or "positive law of nations" derived from the practice of states drew no distinction between wars on the basis of the "intrinsic justice" of the respective belligerents' causes.[40]

Regression from Order: Decision by Relative Strength

In the theory and practice of international law during the nineteenth and early twentieth centuries, *bellum iustum* had for all practical purposes been brought to an unobtrusive demise. Resort to coercion was, in the view of most publicists and state officials of that century, the exercise of an attribute or prerogative of sovereignty the legitimacy of which nonparticpating states were not competent to judge.[41] Traditional international law included no prescription for controlling a resort to coercion or for characterizing coercion as permissible or nonpermissible; it attempted only the regulation and humanization of violence once violence had in fact been initiated. In theory, the contending belligerents stood on a plane of "juridical equality," and third states which chose not to participate were said to be under a "duty of impartiality" and nondiscrimination in their relations with both belligerents.[42] Consequently, as some scholars have observed,[43] a deep internal contradiction in the structure of world prescriptions developed: the right to independent existence, though classed as a fundamental right of states, did not include a prohibition against states waging war and destroying one another.

The international law of the nineteenth century may thus be seen to represent a policy of indifference,[44] as it were, to the common

40. Vattel, *The Law of Nations or the Principles of Natural Law,* 247, 305, 308 (Fenwick, trans. *Classics of International Law,* 1916).

41. See, e.g., Hall, *International Law* 51–2 (1st ed., 1880); Hershey, *The Essentials of International Public Law* 349, 351–2 (1912); Lawrence, *The Principles of International Law* 292 (2d ed., 1897); 2 Oppenheim, *International Law* 55–7 (1st ed., 1906); Risley, *The Law of War* 68–9 (1897). See also Pompe, *Aggressive War: an International Crime* 138–52 (1953); Wright, "Changes in the Conception of War," 18 *A.J.I.L.* 755 (1924).

42. Hall, *International Law* 52 (1st ed., 1880); Wheaton, *Elements of International Law* 697 (2d ed., Lawrence, 1863) (quoting Bynkershoek).

43. See Brierly, *The Outlook for International Law* 21 (1944); 2 Oppenheim-Lauterpacht 178–9; Tucker, "The Interpretation of War Under Present International Law," 4 *Int. L.Q.* 11, 13–4 (1951); 2 Wright, *A Study of War* 950 (1942).

44. Pompe, *Aggressive War: an International Crime* 138–9 (1953) speaks of a "period of indifference," existing "from the seventeenth to the twentieth centuries." On the main point in the text, see 2 Westlake, *International Law* 4

interest in restraining violence, and hence of permitting the speedy resolution of controversies between states simply on the basis of their relative strength. Its principal effort appeared to be to limit the spatial extension of violence through application of its "neutrality" rules, designed in theory to isolate the contending belligerents and practically tending to make superior indigenous strength decisive. Obviously, this policy manifests an acceptance of private coercion and violence as permissive methods not only of self-help and self-vindication for conserving values but also of effecting changes in the international distribution of values.[45] In this way, the doctrine and policy of traditional international law reflected the decentralized and unorganized character of the world arena of the eighteenth and nineteenth centuries, the multi-polar structure of that arena which permitted the operation of a system of power-balancing among the stronger states, the great movements of Western nationalism and the expansion of colonial empires, and the limitations of the contemporary technology of violence.[46]

There were, it is true, a few prescriptions that purported to govern noncomprehensive uses of coercion—coercion of limited dimensions for limited objectives—technically denominated as "reprisal," "inter-

(1907): "The truth is that when war enters on the scene all law that was previously concerned with the dispute retires, and a new law steps in, directed only to secure fair and not too inhuman fighting."

45. Judge Lauterpacht made this clear:

> Prior to that treaty [the 1928 General Treaty for the Renunciation of War] the system of international law, glaringly inconsistent in many matters, was symmetrical in one respect: while it made no provision for institutional peaceful change, it permitted war as an instrument for changing the existing legal position. Every State had the right, by formally going to war and thus risking its own existence, to alter the *status quo* either by annihilating the defeated opponent or by dictating to him the conditions of peace.

Lauterpacht, "The Legal Aspect," in *Peaceful Change—an International Problem* 139 (Manning, ed., 1937).

46. See, e.g., Claude, *Swords Into Plowshares: The Problems and Progress of International Organization* 19–34 (2nd ed. 1959); Liska, *International Equilibrium* c. 1 (1957); Wright, "International Law and the Balance of Power," 37 *A.J.I.L.* 97 (1943); Wright, "Accomplishments and Expectations of World Organization," 55 *Yale L.J.* 870 (1946). See particularly 1 Oppenheim, *International Law* 73–4, 185–6 (1st ed., 1905), in which the author conceived of the "existence of international law" as dependent upon "an equilibrium between the members of the Family of Nations."

vention," "pacific blockade," and so forth, and generically classed as "measures short of war." Without attempting any detailed exposition of the traditional theory about the coercive exercises deemed not to bring about the "legal consequences" compendiously, if confusingly, termed a "legal state of war," we may observe that the rules on "measures short of war" restricted the lawful application of limited coercion to cases in which a prior unlawful act, or a culpable failure to perform international obligations, was attributable to the state against which coercion was applied.[47] The limitations which these prescriptions sought to impose seem less real than ostensible: the initiating state could at any time designate its operations as "war" and avoid the thrust of the limitations. There is appropriate sarcasm in the analogy drawn by one scholar to a municipal enactment that punished petty thieving while condoning armed robbery.[48] "Measures short of war" were generally utilized only by participants with a very substantial power differential over their opponents.[49] The

47. Thus, for instance, the German-Portuguese Arbitration Tribunal in the *Naulilaa* case (1928) defined "reprisals" as "acts of self-help of the injured State, acts in retaliation for an unredressed act of the offending state contrary to international law" and stressed that "they will be illegal unless a previous act in violation of international law has furnished the justification." Briggs, *The Law of Nations* 951 (2d ed., 1952). The Tribunal specified two other requirements for the lawfulness of "reprisals"; they must "have been preceded by a request for redress which has been unavailing" and must not be "out of all proportion to the act which has motivated them." Id. at 953. See also Colbert, *Retaliation in International Law* (1948); Hall, *International Law* 433–43 (8th ed., Pearce Higgins, 1924); Hindmarsh, *Force in Peace* (1933); 2 Oppenheim-Lauterpacht 136–51.

48. Kelsen, *Law and Peace* 53 (1942). Compare Jessup, *A Modern Law of Nations* 157 (1948).

49. Maccoby, "Reprisals as a Measure of Redress Short of War," 2 *Camb. L.J.* 60, 69 (1924); Giraud, "Memorandum on Pacific Blockade up to the Time of the Foundation of the League of Nations," League of Nations, *Off. J.*, 7th Ass., 841, 842 (1927); Hindmarsh, *Force in Peace* 73–4, 87–8, 92–4 (1933); Westlake, "Reprisals and War," 25 *L.Q. Rev.* 127, 133 (1909). It seems an interesting commentary upon the change of perspectives exhibited in contemporary prohibitions of coercion that in 1897 Professor Holland could ask plaintively:

> Why, again, is it made a matter of reproach that a pacific blockade has almost always been employed, as a matter of fact, by strong against weak states? Unless weak states are to be allowed to shelter their wrong doing, or their persistence in a policy detrimental to the peace of the world, behind their weakness, they must be brought to reason either by forcible pressure

doctrines on "measures short of war," like other nineteenth-century international law doctrines, in fact constituted but one expression of the general policy which would localize the area of coercion and violence by permitting, in an unorganized world arena, a quick settlement through superior strength.[50] The tacit assumptions were that the weaker participant would readily perceive the futility of widening or prolonging the conflict and make haste to comply with the demands of its more powerful opponent, and that such demands would be kept so relatively modest as neither to create furious resistance on the part of the weaker state nor to excite the alarm of nonparticipants fearful of a serious imbalance of power in the arena.

The Fundamental Distinction Revived: From the Covenant to the Charter

The Covenant of the League of Nations represented the first significant break with the theory of traditional international law.[51] The Covenant set forth a broad undertaking of members to "respect . . .

> in time of peace, or by war. There can be little doubt which of these two methods is better adapted to oblige and enable a weak state to make concessions, which in any case are inevitable, with the least injury to itself and the least disturbance of the peace of the world.

Holland, *Studies in International Law* 141 (1898). See also Holland, *Letters to the Times Upon War and Neutrality, 1881–1920* at 14 (3d ed., 1921).

50. As Professor Briggs points out, "justifications were found in allegations that such hostile measures were, in reality, 'pacific' in character, since States, instead of exercising their legally unfettered right to resort to war, prevented the rise of general hostilities by confining their measures to a restricted *locale,* a particular bombardment, blockade or occupation of territory. That such measures of armed coercion did not always lead to war was due only to the preponderance of force on one side. . . ." Briggs, *The Law of Nations* 958 (2d ed., 1952); cf. Hall, *International Law* 434 (8th ed., Pearce Higgins, 1924).

51. There had been prior but minor and fragmentary efforts to establish some limitation on the *"jus ad bellum"* of traditional law. The Hague Convention II of 1907 prohibited the use of force for recovery of contract debts, save in case of refusal of the debtor state to arbitrate. The Bryan arbitration treaties imposed the duty not to begin hostilities before the report of the conciliation commissions provided for in such treaties. See generally White, "Limitation Upon the Initiation of War," 19 *Proc. Am. Soc. I.L.* 102–8 (1925). For a listing of the Bryan treaties, as well as of bilateral agreements between Latin American countries providing for recourse to arbitration or other peaceful modes of settlement before resorting to violence, see Harvard Research in International Law, "Rights and Duties of States in Case of Aggression," 33 *A.J.I.L. Supp.* 858–61 (1939).

the territorial integrity and existing political independence" of each other.[52] The specific obligations it imposed upon its members were, however, less comprehensive. "Resort to war" was, under the terms of the Covenant, unlawful in four cases: when made without prior submission of the dispute to arbitration or judicial settlement or to inquiry by the Council of the League; when begun before the expiration of three months after the arbitral award or judicial decision or Council report; when commenced against a member which had complied with such award or decision or recommendation of a unanimously adopted Council report; and, under certain circumstances, when initiated by a nonmember state against a member state.[53]

It was of course no mere historical accident that the break with traditional theory and the re-establishment of a distinction between permissible and nonpermissible resort to coercion coincided with the first attempt at a permanent, institutionalized organization of the community of states. The necessity for such organization was underscored by the collapse of the nineteenth-century system of power-balancing in Europe, a system that had become increasingly unstable and precarious as the number of effective territorial units of power gradually diminished. The bloodletting of World War I, the first conflict since the Napoleonic Wars to assume the proportions of "total war," generated widespread revulsion over the use of violence to secure national goals. Thus, promoting recourse to nonviolent procedures of change was a principal purpose infusing the prescriptions of the Covenant. In fact, prior recourse to nonviolent procedures was made a test of permissible coercion. The prevention of resort to violence was also sought in the Covenant by incorporating a "principle of delay," upon the hopeful assumption that the effect of time on contending participants would be a tranquilizing one.[54]

52. League of Nations Covenant, Art. 10.

53. League of Nations Covenant, Art. 12, paras. 1, 2; Arts. 13, 15, paras. 6, 7; Art. 17, paras. 1, 3; see Martin, *Collective Security* 90–3 (1952). To Professor Brierly, war under the circumstances listed above was "of a particularly heinous kind." 17 *Tr. Grotius Soc.* 77 (1931). The Eighth Assembly of the League unanimously approved a resolution declaring that *"all wars of aggression are, and always shall be, prohibited."* League of Nations, *Off. J.*, Spec. Supp. No. 54 at 155–6 (1927). The effect of this resolution upon the scope of the prohibitions of the Covenant was much debated.

54. Williams, *Some Aspects of the Covenant of the League of Nations* 137–8 (1934).

The Covenant prescribed what was in substance a three-month moratorium on violence after the chosen peaceful procedure had resulted in a decision; and it allowed a participant, upon the expiration of such moratorium, to implement by force of arms a decision in its favor against a noncomplying party.

The League's rudimental degree of organization, reflected in the modest scope of the Covenant's specific prohibitions of coercion, was most clearly exhibited in the decentralized character of the decision-making required for the application of those prohibitions. Each member of the League retained authority to characterize a particular exercise of coercion as one in breach of or consistent with the requirements of the Covenant and hence to render operative or inoperative its own commitments to participate in sanctioning procedures against an offending state. The authority of the League Council did not extend beyond that of formulating recommendations to the individual members.[55] The difficulties of application inherent in such decentralized decision-making were not relieved by the phraseology of the Covenant's prohibitions. "Resort to war" aroused confused contention as to the continuing legitimacy of force and violence if participants used some verbal symbol other than "war," such as "reprisal" or "intervention" or other "measure short of war," in designating their exercises of coercion, and if they disclaimed any intention to institute a "legal state of war." [56]

The formally modest limitations which the Covenant of the League placed on the *jus ad bellum* of traditional international law were sought to be extended, and the so-called "gaps" in the Covenant closed,[57] by the General Treaty for the Renunciation of War of 1928.

55. See Resolutions 4 and 6 of the Resolutions on the Economic Weapon adopted by the Assembly of the League on Oct. 4, 1921. League of Nations, *Off. J.*, Spec. Supp. No. 6 at 25. See also Williams, *Aspects of Modern International Law* 91 (1939); Williams, "Sanctions Under the Covenant," 17 Brit. *Y.B.I.L.* 130 (1936).

56. For a recent canvassing of the polemical literature on this point, see Kotzsch, *The Concept of War in Contemporary History and International Law* 154–71 (1956). This debate related to the so-called "subjective" or "intention" and "objective" theories of "war"; a possible mode of clarification is sketched in Ch. 2.

57. These "gaps" referred to cases in which unilateral resort to "war" (other than in self-defense) was not prohibited by the explicit language of the Covenant. See the list of "licit wars" conceivable under the Covenant set out in

This Pact of Paris (Kellogg-Briand Pact) condemned "recourse to war for the solution of international controversies" and set out comprehensive undertakings to renounce "war as an instrument of national policy" and to seek the resolution of "all disputes or conflicts, of whatever nature or whatever origin they may be" exclusively by "pacific means." The policy objectives of preventing violence and promoting noncoercive methods of adjustment were thus much more ambitiously formulated than in the League Covenant. That the Pact of Paris left intact the freedom of states to exercise violence in self-defense has at times been noted with some aspersion,[58] as though that in some way impaired the Pact's prohibition of "recourse to war." The fact is, of course, that self-defense is recognized in even the most advanced municipal public orders, and is indispensable in an arena as ineffectively organized as that of the present world, so long, at least, as the assumption prevails that an arena of plural participants should be maintained.[59] Some scholars have observed that the Pact of Paris

---

Eagleton, *International Government* 480 (3d ed., 1957). See also Martin, *Collective Security* 92–3 (1952). There had been, prior to the Pact of Paris, considerable efforts devoted to closing these "fissures" in the structure of authoritative prescription, the most notable effort being the drafting of the 1924 Geneva Protocol. Apropos of these efforts, Professor Brierly wrote in 1943 (and hence with the benefit of hindsight) that they "implied that if war came, there was a real danger that the aggressor would first carefully observe his Covenant obligations, and then take advantage of one of the gaps to enter on a war not expressly prohibited; this was formally possible, but it was always politically most improbable, and in fact none of the wars that have broken out since the Covenant came into force has begun that way." Brierly, *The Basis of Obligation in International Law* 283 (1958).

58. See, e.g., Pompe, *Aggressive War: an International Crime* 157, 159 (1953); Borchard, "The Multilateral Treaty for the Renunciation of War," 23 *A.J.I.L.* 116 (1929). See also Ferrell, *Peace in Their Time* 170–200 (1952). What could properly be objected to was not the "reservation" of self-defense but the excessively broad statement in the United States Note of June 23, 1928, that a state claiming self-defense "alone is competent to decide whether circumstances require recourse to war in self defense." (Text in Miller, *The Peace Pact of Paris* 213, 214 (1928).) Justice Pal in his dissenting judgment in the Tokyo Trial took that statement in a literal and absolute sense as making "the question whether a particular war is or is not in self defense . . . unjusticiable." Pal, *International Military Tribunal for the Far East* 35–48 (1953); see note 216 infra.

59. In laying stress upon self-defense here as elsewhere in this chapter, we have no intent to make a fetish of the nation-state as it is known today. It should be obvious that the only rational hope is the common one that a much

did not inhibit the "customary liberty [of states] to resort to war" to the extent that it prohibited "recourse to war" only as an instrument of "national" policy and only as between its signatories.[60] The importance of these observations need not be exaggerated. First, "recourse to war," as an instrument of "international" as distinguished from "national" policy, referred simply to the use of coercion in accordance with the mandates or authorization of the League Covenant to participate in sanctions against a Covenant-breaking state, in a word, to community-enforcement action.[61] Second, practically every nation-state in the world, certainly every state of any consequence in world-power processes, became a party to the Pact.

It is true, however, that the Pact, by retaining "war" as a term of art, failed to quiet the continued debate as to the permissibility of force that participants might verbally describe as a "measure short of war." [62] It was left to the Charter of the United Nations to resolve and make moot that debate by discarding the term "war" and employing in its stead the multiple references to "threat or use of force," "threat to the peace," "breach of the peace," and "act of aggression." Taken collectively, these phrases refer to a whole spectrum of degrees of intensity of coercion, including (so far as *force* is concerned) not

---

higher degree of effective organization may be secured in the world arena. We do, however, assume the desirability of some deconcentration and dispersal of power, both authoritative and effective, in the world. The contemporary nation-state is, of course, not the only possible organizational form that plural units of participation in world processes of power may take. The configuration of the world arena and the interrelations of global and subglobal (the more comprehensive and the less comprehensive) power processes are susceptible of nearly infinite detailed variation and the number of possible organizational patterns for allocating authoritative power between a center and balanced regions is indefinite.

60. See, e.g., Stone, *Legal Controls of International Conflict* 300 (1954).

61. 2 Oppenheim-Lauterpacht 182–3; Kelsen, *Law and Peace* 39 (1942) (*semble*). See also Pompe, *Aggressive War: an International Crime* 158 (1953), who writes that "war as an instrument of international policy is a *contradictio in terminis*. The international action against a lawbreaker, to enforce exactly those rules the Kellogg Pact preconised has . . . nothing but the laws of warfare in common with 'normal' interstate war, 'war as an instrument of national policy.' "

62. See Wehberg, *The Outlawry of War* 98–100 (Zeydel, trans. 1931); Brierly, "International Law and Resort to Armed Force," 4 *Camb. L.J.* 308 (1932); McNair, "Collective Security," 17 Brit. *Y.B.I.L.* 150, 157 (1936); Williams, "The Covenant of the League of Nations and War," 5 *Camb. L.J.* 1 (1933).

only "war," understood as extensive armed hostilities or the highest degree of destructive use of the military instrument, but also all those applications of force of a lesser intensity or magnitude that in the past had been characterized as "short of war." The Charter sought also to centralize the process of characterizing, for purposes of requiring or authorizing enforcement action, a particular exercise of coercion as permissible or nonpermissible, and to vest that function in the organized community itself.

THE CONCEPTIONS OF PERMISSIBLE AND IMPERMISSIBLE RESORT TO COERCION: MULTIFACTOR ANALYSIS FOR POLICY CLARIFICATION

PART I: THE CONCEPTION OF IMPERMISSIBLE RESORT TO COERCION

The Debate about Definitions

The decision of the framers of the United Nations Charter to leave such terms as "threat to the peace," "breach of the peace," and "act of aggression" ambiguous and comprehensive was a deliberate one.[63] In recent years, however, the failure of the optimistic hopes for great power cooperation and intensifying expectations of violence have caused renewed agitation for the clarification and elaboration of basic concepts. The continuing debates today, like those within the League of Nations, have centered principally on the question of "defining aggression." [64] Unfortunately, the efforts of the First and Sixth Committees, the political and legal committees, of the General

63. See the Report [on Chapter VIII, section B] of the Rapporteur of Committee 3 to Commission III. 12 U.N.C.I.O. 502, 505. The Committee, after rejecting the Bolivian and Philippine proposals for inserting an enumerative definition of aggression in the Charter (texts of the proposals in 3 U.N.C.I.O. 584, 538), decided "to leave to the Council the entire decision as to what constitutes a threat to peace, a breach of the peace, or an act of aggression." 12 U.N.C.I.O. 505. See also Russell and Muther, *A History of the United Nations Charter* 669–72 (1958).

64. The term "aggression" has been in very common use both in international agreements and in official statements of governments, at least since 1919. See Harvard Research in International Law, "Rights and Duties of States in Cases of Aggression," 33 *A.J.I.L. Supp.* 819, 848–55, 861–70 (1939).

Assembly, the International Law Commission, and the 1953 and 1956 Special Committees on Defining Aggression to formulate a generally acceptable "definition of aggression" have not been blessed with conspicuous success.[65] Representatives of nation-states engaged in the enterprise of defining aggression conceive of too many implications, real and unreal, for national security to permit much consensus either on any particular proposed verbalization of the conception of aggression or even on the utility of attempts at definition.

The principal formulations proposed have generally assumed one or the other, or a combination, of two main forms. The first consists of a more or less lengthy catalogue of stereotypes of aggressive acts. The formulation vigorously propounded by the Soviet Union—a formulation which grew from the five-item closed list of overt military acts incorporated in the 1933 London Conventions for the Definition of Aggression[66] to an open-ended fifteen-item inventory

65. See Stone, *Aggression and World Order* 27–77 (1958) for the most recent brief and spirited survey of these labors, including those in the League period, at definition up to the consideration of the Report of the 1956 Special Committee by the Sixth Committee of the General Assembly at its Twelfth Session (1957). See Report of the Sixth Committee, U.N. Gen. Ass., *Off. Rec.,* 12th Sess., Annexes, Agenda Item 54, at 2 (1957). By Resolution No. 1181(XII), the General Assembly established a committee to determine "when it would be appropriate for the General Assembly to consider again the question of defining aggression" which time would be "not earlier than the fourteenth session." Id. at 5–6. This committee decided to defer, "until April 1962," determination of an appropriate time for considering again the definition question, unless an "absolute majority" of its members subsequently call for an earlier meeting. *N. Y. Times,* April 18, 1959, p. 2, col. 7.

66. Signed by the Soviet Union, the Baltic states, some of the Balkan states, and Turkey and Persia. 147 *League of Nations Treaty Series* 66, 69 note 2 (1933); 148 id. 211 (1933); 27 *A.J.I.L.* Supp. 192–4 (1933). This was the same list that had been incorporated, upon a Soviet proposal, into the Draft Act Relating to the Definition of Aggression prepared by the 1933 Geneva Disarmament Conference, Committee on Security Questions, Conference for the Reduction and Limitation of Armaments (1933), *Politis Report,* Conf. D/C-G 108 (1935.IX.4 League of Nations Publications) 679–90 (1935). Subsequent treaties adopting this listing, verbatim or substantially, are enumerated in the Report by the Secretary-General, "Question of Defining Aggression," U.N. Gen. Ass., *Off. Rec.,* 7th Sess., Annexes, Agenda Item 54, p. 50, A/2211 (1952) [hereinafter cited as Report of the Secretary-General].

The interesting fact may be noted that, at the 1945 London Conference on war crimes, the United States proposed the inclusion of the Litvinov-Politis definition in the Charter of the International Military Tribunal. There the Soviet

of acts of military, "indirect," "economic," and "ideological" aggression in 1956 [67]—is perhaps the best-known species of this genus of definitions. The point of such an inventory is that the state "which first commits" one of the listed acts is to be declared the aggressor. More distinctively, the Soviet formulation includes a list of negative criteria, of acts which are not to be characterized as aggression and internal conditions which do not justify the commission of any act catalogued as aggressive. The most basic defect of the Soviet and other comparable definitions is an overemphasis on material acts of coercion and on a mechanistic conception of priority; concomitantly, they fail to take into account other factors which rationally are equally relevant, factors such as the nature of the objectives of the initiating and responding participants and the character or intensity of the coercion applied.[68]

The second major type of definition exhibits a different approach which rejects the technique of specific enumeration and seeks instead the construction of a broad and general formula that would comprehend all possible instances of aggression. Perhaps the broadest of these formulas was that submitted by Sr. Alfaro to the International Law Commission:

> Aggression is the threat or use of force by a State or Government against another State, in any manner, whatever the weapons employed and whether openly or otherwise for any reason or for any purpose other than individual or collective self-defense or in pursuance of a decision or recommendation by a competent organ of the United Nations.[69]

---

representative resolutely opposed such inclusion, stating that "when people speak about 'aggression,' they know what that means, but, when they come to define it, they come up against difficulties which it has not been possible to overcome up to the present time." See Report of Robert H. Jackson, U.S. Representative to the International Conference on Military Trials, U.S. Dep't of State, Pub. No. 3080, at 328 (1949).

67. U.N. Doc. No. A/AC.77/L.4 (1956); also in Report of the 1956 Special Committee on the Question of Defining Aggression, U.N. Gen. Ass., *Off. Rec.*, 12th Sess., Supp. No. 16 (A/3574), at 30–1 (1957) [hereinafter cited as Report of the 1956 Special Committee].

68. See text accompanying notes 131–49, 170–82 infra.

69. U.N. Doc. No. A/CN.4/L.31, at 27 (1951). See also Alfaro, "La Cuestión de la Definición de la Agresión," 59 *Revista de Derecho Internacional* 361

This formulation emphasizes the complementarity of aggression on the one hand and self-defense and collective peace enforcement on the other. It is, however, little more than a posing, in highest level abstraction, of the general problem involved, and offers no index for the guidance of decision-makers who must apply it in specific cases.[70] Only slightly less abstract is the definition achieved by Professor Scelle:

> Aggression is an offense against the peace and security of mankind. This offense consists in any resort to force contrary to the provisions of the Charter of the United Nations, for the purpose of modifying the state of positive international law in force or resulting in the disturbance of public order.[71]

Thus, Professor Scelle appropriately stresses the relevance of the character of the objective or purpose of the state resorting to force; but he fails to specify any operational index of the nonpermissible objective of modifying "the state of positive international law in force." In further illustration of this second major type of definition, the formulation incorporated in the Act of Chapultepec signed by all the American republics on March 8, 1945, may be noted. The act provides that

> [A]ny attempt on the part of a non-American state against the integrity or inviolability of the territory, the sovereignty or the political independence of an American State shall be considered an act of aggression against all the American States.[72]

(Cuba 1951). Comparable drafts were submitted to the Commission by Mr. Amado, U.N. Doc. No. A/CN.4/L.6 (1951); Mr. Cordova, U.N. Doc. No. A/CN.4/L.10 (1951); Mr. Hsu, U.N. Doc. No. A/CN.4/L.11 and Corr. 1 (1951); and Mr. Yepes, U.N. Doc. No. A/CN.4/L.12 (1951). A very similar draft was proposed by the Netherlands representative in the 1953 Special Committee. See Report of the Special Committee on the Question of Defining Aggression, U.N. Doc. No. A/AC.66/L.11, at 35 (1953) [hereinafter cited as Report of the 1953 Special Committee].

70. Cf. Fitzmaurice, "The Definition of Aggression," 1 *Int. and Comp. L.Q.* 137, 142–3 (1952).

71. U.N. Doc. No. A/CN.4/L.19 and Corr. 1 (1951).

72. 9 Hudson, *International Legislation* 286 (1950). A comparable treaty provision is found in the Finnish-Soviet peace treaty of 1939: "Any act of violence attacking the integrity and inviolability of the territory or the political independence of the other High Contracting Party shall be regarded as an act of

In contrast with Professor Scelle's definition, this act offers some indication of the character of the perspectives that make coercion and violence unlawful. It exhibits, however, little effort to clarify what operations, "attempts," when moved by these perspectives, may be characterized as aggression.

A third type of definition, the so-called "mixed" definition, seeks to combine both the enumerative and "broad-formula" approaches by appending an illustrative but nonexhaustive list of specific examples of aggression to a relatively abstract statement of general policy. Although the facile objection has been raised that such "mixed" definitions would only tend to cumulate the difficulties that the catalogue and abstract types of definition have individually presented,[73] the great majority of states that support the formulation of *some* definition have favored the "mixed" kind as a possible *via media*.[74] The draft definition submitted by Iran and Panama at the ninth session of the General Assembly is representative:

> 1. Aggression is the use of armed force by a State against another State for any purpose other than the exercise of the inherent right of individual or collective self-defense or in pursuance

---

aggression, even if it is committed without declaration of war and avoids warlike manifestations." 157 *League of Nations Treaty Series* 397.

If still another illustration of this general approach to definition were desired, the Harvard Research formulation may be adduced. The Harvard draft reads: "'Aggression' is a resort to armed force by a State when such a resort has been duly determined, by a means which that State is bound to accept, to constitute a violation of an obligation." Harvard Research in International Law, "Draft Convention on the Rights and Duties of States in Case of Aggression," Art. 1(c), 33 *A.J.I.L. Supp.* 827 (1939). The draft emphasizes the need for authoritative third-party determination but does not seek at all to indicate the factors that rationally may enter into a "due determination" of the lawfulness of a particular resort to armed force. From this perspective, the formulation amounts to little more than the tautologous statement that aggression is a prohibited resort to coercion.

73. See, e.g., the statement of the Belgian representative, U.N. Gen. Ass., *Off. Rec.*, 6th Comm., 6th Sess., 287th mtg., par. 34 (1952); Report of the 1953 Special Committee 14; Report of the Sixth Committee, U.N. Gen. Ass., *Off. Rec.*, 9th Sess., Annexes, Agenda Item No. 51, at 10 (1954); Report of the 1956 Special Committee 8–9.

74. Report of the Sixth Committee, U.N. Gen. Ass., *Off. Rec.*, 12th Sess., Annexes, Agenda Item 54, par. 21 (1957).

of a decision or recommendation of a competent organ of the United Nations.

2. In accordance with the foregoing definition, in addition to any other acts which such international bodies as may be called upon to determine the aggressor may declare to constitute aggression, the following are acts of aggression in all cases:

(a) Invasion by the armed forces of a State of territory belonging to another State or under the effective jurisdiction of another State;

(b) Armed attack against the territory, population or land, sea or air forces of a State by the land, sea or air forces of another State;

(c) Blockade of the coast or ports or any other part of the territory of a State by the land, sea or air forces of another State;

(d) The organization, or the encouragement of the organization, by a State, of armed bands within its territory or any other territory for incursions into the territory of another State, or the toleration of the organization of such bands in its own territory, or the toleration of the use by such armed bands of its territory as a base of operations or as a point of departure for incursions into the territory of another State, as well as direct participation in or support of such incursions.[75]

The Demand for Ad Hoc Decision

Throughout the course of this contention in the United Nations and even in the debates during the League period, one view consistently and energetically put forward has been that all definitions of whatever type are undesirable restrictions on the discretion of the appropriate decision-making organ. "[All] definition[s] delimit," it

75. This draft was resubmitted by Peru to the 1956 Special Committee. See Report of the 1956 Special Committee 31. See also the draft definition proposed by the Dominican Republic, Mexico, Paraguay, and Peru to the 1956 Special Committee, id. at 9–10, and the drafts submitted by China, Mexico, and Bolivia to the 1953 Special Committee, Report of the 1953 Special Committee, Annex 4–8.

is said, and make certain factors decisive while passing over other elements and circumstances that may be equally relevant.[76] The primary desideratum, in this view, is that the decision-maker should be unfettered by a priori rules and tests, and completely free to make *ad hoc* determinations upon appreciation of the peculiar elements of each specific situation of coercion.[77]

Recently, a distinguished scholar has undertaken to restate at detailed length, to document, and to build upon this view. Professor Stone inveighs mightily against those who, in his opinion, seek to

76. See Pompe, *Aggressive War: an International Crime* 80 (1953), summing up this view.

77. Such is the official view of the United States and United Kingdom governments as of now. See Ch. 1, note 151 and accompanying text. For a collection of statements of these and other governments urging this view in its many detailed forms, see Report of the Secretary-General 54–9. These arguments, which, as will be developed below, rest on a singular conception of the processes of decision-making, have been repeated uncritically ever since Sir Austen Chamberlain dropped his mot in the House of Commons about any definition of aggression being "a trap for the innocent and a sign-post for the guilty." Observations of His Majesty's Government in Great Britain on the Programme of Work of the Committee on Arbitration and Security, Minutes of the Second Sess. of the Committee on Arbitration and Security, League Doc. No. C.165.M.50.1928.IX, p. 176 (1928).

In the discussions of the 1956 Special Committee, the U.S. representative added a mildly astonishing ground: the limitations of the human mind. He said:

> It would be no remedy to say that any definition must, of course, be interpreted and applied in the light of circumstances. That would, in his opinion, be another way of saying that it was impossible to avoid appraising a threat or act of aggression in the light of the circumstances as a whole. Since each threat of aggression varied in its history and its facts in an infinite number of ways, it taxed human ingenuity and wisdom beyond reasonable limits to evolve a formula which would anticipate events and provide useful guidance.

Report of the 1956 Special Committee 12. The suggestion may not be inappropriate that the principal deficiency lies, not in the human intellect as such but in the character of the intellectual tools of analysis which thus far have been applied to the problem of clarification. The infinitude of the number of possible combinations of specific circumstances is scarcely unique to aggression and defense; it has not deterred other decision-makers, including both the Congress and the courts of the United States, from prescribing and applying policy with respect to any number of municipal problems.

find a "mechanical test of aggression, insulated from the merits of the situation in which States act," a test that would be "clear and precise enough for certain and automatic applications to all future situations," in short, a "juristic push-button device." [78] The purpose behind the continuing search for "precise definition" has been, as Professor Stone sees it, "to control determinations to be made when passions are aflame by advance criteria agreed upon before national passions were embroiled . . . ," [79] "to make it clear in advance of the particular crisis what the judgment will be and remove the agony and the conflict of national interests from the moment of decision." [80] The referent of the notion of aggression includes, he emphasizes, "a judgment of value, and in particular of justice"; [81] and if the application of a criterion of aggression is not to "outrage minimal levels of justice as between the contending Parties," that criterion "must allow consideration of the full socio-political context of the conduct under judgment." [82] But for it "to be *precise enough* to control the future judgment of aggression," the criterion must be "a violent abstraction from that full context of the crisis which consideration of the merits of the dispute would require to be taken into account." [83] Thus, the failure of states and scholars to achieve agreement on a definition is ascribed by Professor Stone, "at least in part," to "the impossibility of containing the unceasing struggle for a minimal justice in international relations within the straitjacket of precise formulae . . ." [84] Professor Stone makes explicit his conviction that a satisfactorily precise and certain definition is unattainable. Even if advance criteria were agreed upon, there will still be, he states, "additional elements of uncertainty of interpretation of the criteria themselves": [85] the "verbal formulation . . . still has to be interpreted and applied by the very organs whose unreliability is the reason for the formulation. . . ." [86]

78. Stone, *Aggression and World Order* 10–11 (1958).
79. Id. at 25.
80. Id. at 151–2.
81. Id. at 81.
82. Id. at 18.
83. Id. at 156.
84. Id. at 12.
85. Id. at 24.
86. Id. at 25.

Goal Clarification by Configurative Analysis: An Alternative Conception

The mechanistically conceived function of a "definition of aggression" which Professor Stone appropriately castigates is, in the light of what is known today about the processes of decision-making, a curious one indeed. To seek to construct a set of words that will automatically determine all future decisions and relieve human decision-makers of the anguish of choice and judgment in responding to events of coercion and opposed claims about coercion is, of course, a futile enterprise; to recognize its futility is, however, only the beginning of wisdom.[87] It is no more feasible or desirable to attempt to define aggression "once and for all" than it is so to define any other legal term or concept of international or municipal law. For observers with full awareness of the factors realistically affecting decision, the task of "defining aggression" is not appropriately conceived as one of searching for a precise, certain, and final verbal formula that would abolish the discretion of decision-makers and dictate specific decisions. It is rather, in broad outline, that of presenting to the focus of attention of the various officials who must reach a decision about the lawfulness or unlawfulness of coercion, the different variable factors and policies that, in differing contexts and under community perspectives, rationally bear upon their decisions; of indicating the interrelations of these factors and policies in context;

87. Today it is commonly recognized that the process of applying authoritative words in concrete instances requires creative choice. The late Judge Jerome Frank some three decades ago made classic disposition of the illusion of verbal absolutism. Frank, *Law and the Modern Mind* (1930). It is not the collocation of letters or concatenations of noises in verbal signs but rather the fundamental perspectives of decision-makers, seldom adequately expressed in brief technical definitions, which importantly affect decision (save, perhaps, for an occasional judicial robot). See, e.g., Rapaport, *Operational Philosophy* (1953); Probert, "Law, Logic and Communication," 9 *W. Res. L. Rev.* 129 (1958); Williams, "Language and the Law," 61 *L.Q. Rev.* 71 (1945).

It is not our brief that a short technical definition of aggression, if agreement on one were secured, would adequately serve community policy purposes. As Judge Lauterpacht has, however, suggested, because "no definition acts automatically," the objection that adoption of a definition of aggression would necessarily deprive governments and tribunals of "the freedom of appreciation of the merits of a particular situation" lacks thrust. 2 Oppenheim-Lauterpacht 189 note 2.

and, perhaps, of making some lower-order generalizations about the relative weighting of pertinent factors and policies in different contexts.[88] The task, again, is not so much to abolish, with quasi-magical

88. The task of clarifying general community objectives in the process of authoritative decision about the coercive relations of states is entirely comparable to that with respect to the consensual relations of states. For assistance and guidance in the application of agreements between states to specific instances of interaction, authoritative decision-makers over the centuries have developed a comprehensive set of principles of interpretation, including both content principles and principles of orderly inquiry. The content principles guide decision-makers to all the relevant features of the process of agreement (parties, objectives, situations, base values, preliminary negotiations, modes of expression, immediately indicated shared expectations of commitment, subsequent conduct, etc.) and of context (the embracing conditions of more general community processes) and offer certain tentative weightings to such features both in terms of the presumptive meanings that parties of the specified characteristics would attach to their expressions when affected by such features and in terms of certain relevant community policies. The principles of orderly inquiry prescribe the modalities of analysis by which an interpreter can get the most rational results in applying the content principles. Thus, in most general summation, the two sets of principles, taken together, require an interpreter to proceed as follows: first, to seek a preliminary orientation among possible inferences of shared expectation in community-wide ("plain" and "natural") meanings; next, to test these possible, preliminary inferences by logical (syntactical) principles for contradictions, ambiguities, and omissions; and, finally, to seek the closest possible approximation of the actual active expectations of the particular parties by a pragmatic and systematic examination of all of the relevant features of the process of agreement and its context, as such process and context might have been viewed by parties of the ascertained characteristics. Introduction to the literature may be had from materials referred to in note 255 infra.

Similarly, decision-makers who are asked to pass judgment upon the lawfulness or unlawfulness of acts of coercion have their attention directed to a series of *specialized events* that are provisionally designated by the parties (claimants) as "acts of aggression" or "acts of self-defense" (or otherwise). The problem confronting such decision-makers is to discover and assess the perspectives (conservatory or expansionist) of the parties who formulated and executed the coercive policies whose designation and lawfulness are in dispute. Whether the coercive policies in question are permissible or impermissible coercion depends in significant measure upon the *demands and expectations of the claimant parties* at the times of formulation and execution; and these expectations must be established and assessed both according to their "manifest" content and according to other features of the context which may be more indicative of actual demands and expectations.

What we urge here is the need for principles of interpretation of coercive

arrangements of words, conflicts of national interests (more or less myopically perceived) as it is to clarify common, long-term interests in the maintenance of minimal public order. To dissolve the problem into one of determining "justice" as between contending participants makes conscious efforts at more detailed clarification for policy guidance neither impossible nor dispensable. It can scarcely be assumed

---

policies, as for persuasive policies, to provide guidance for decision-makers. Such guidance might again take the form both of principles of content (pointing to and weighting the relevance of the important features of the process of coercion and its context) and of principles of orderly inquiry (outlining the sequence in which the components of process and context may most rationally be brought to the focus of attention of decision-makers). See Lasswell, "Clarifying Value Judgment: Principles of Content and Procedure," 1 *Inquiry* 87 (1958), for some amplification of these principles. Emphasizing the contextual basis of inference, such principles would systematically explore the way in which the specialized events of formation and execution of coercive policies are interrelated with the manifold events relevant to their characterization. Thus, beginning with the manifest content of the parties' demands and expectations as indicated by community-wide intelligence, such principles might provide for the orderly examination of the alleged demands and expectations on both sides of the controversy for contradictions, ambiguities, and omissions, and then outline a pragmatic appraisal of the actual, active perspectives of each set of parties in terms both of their special characteristics and of the intelligence in fact known to have been available to them.

In this chapter, we attempt both to outline some of the more important features of processes of coercion which may affect the actual perspectives of participants charged with "impermissible" and claiming "permissible" coercion and to relate these features by tentative general weightings to fundamental community policy. Any claimed perspectives may be appraised according to the typicality of the predispositions affecting them and their rational plausibility in context, and may be explored at many different levels of intelligence. The range of possibilities may be indicated by such questions as these:

a. Were the expectations of the claimants based upon the overwhelming concord of *public* and *secret* intelligence content?

b. If *public* intelligence was divided, were the bases of inference relied upon by the claimants more plausible at the time than the contradictions? (E.g., statements by elite "enemy" figures? Deeds of elite "enemy" figures? Statements and deeds of elite figures of third powers? Of our body politic? E.g., reputable commentators, investors?)

c. Were the *public* bases of inference overwhelmingly confirmed by the *secret* channels of intelligence?

d. If *public* bases were tenuous and the *secret* sources were contradictory, were the secret bases of inference more plausible at the time than the con-

that no policies of a lower level of abstraction than "justice" can be articulated and described. Nothing inherent in nature prevents the objective scholar from describing past applications of a distinction between permissible and impermissible coercion (it seems salutary to recall that there have been some), from identifying the variables that have conditioned and affected these applications, from making estimates of probable future applications, and from appraising both past and projected future applications in terms of their probable consequences upon the goal values of the kind of world public order the scholar prefers.[89]

Of course, every definition of aggression, as of any other legal term, is an abstraction; indeed, one of the principal lessons which contemporary studies on semantics and linguistics offer is that every verbalization, whether definitional or not, is an abstraction from the "unspeakable level of objective events." [90] It does not follow from this, however, that all verbalization about aggression, of whatever order of generalization, is futile and undesirable or creates any unique risk that decision-makers may be misled in particular cases and fail to take some relevant element of the "full context" into appropriate account. Such a risk seems inherent in the application of any general concept or standard of any legal system, if not all processes of human decision-making, authoritative or otherwise. That risk is more likely to be reduced to tolerable levels, and the incidence of rational decisions (in the sense of closer approximation of community-approved value

---

tradictions? (E.g., were the sources relied upon plausibly regarded as relatively trustworthy?)

e. If the *public* and *secret* bases of inference at the time were both tenuous, does subsequently available knowledge show that the inferences made by the claimants were actually correct?

It may be added that intellectual procedures of sufficient refinement are today available to permit increasingly relevant estimates at the different levels of intelligence of the actual perspectives of participants resorting to coercion. See, e.g., Hillsman, *Strategic Intelligence and National Decisions* (1956); Platt, *Strategic Intelligence Production* (1957); Ransom, *Central Intelligence and National Security* (1958). See also the literature referred to in note 129 infra.

89. These intellectual tasks relate to indispensable component operations in problem-solving processes. See Ch. 1, note 23.

90. Korzybski, *Science and Sanity* cc. 24–7 (2d ed., 1941). See also Hayakawa, *Language in Thought and Action* (1949); Morris, *Signs, Language and Behavior* (1946); Ogden and Richards, *The Meaning of Meaning* (10th ed., 1949).

goals) is more apt to be increased, by explicit, sustained, and systematic efforts at clarifying relevant variables and policies affecting decisions about coercion. Certainly it cannot be reduced by an approach that assumes a completely futilitarian attitude toward words, views each specific case of coercion in microcosm with no more than a few terms of highest level of abstraction, and relies upon calculation of momentary expediencies and, as it were, on visceral sensitivity.

Semantic Equivalents or Roses as Sweet

The suggestion has also been made that the notion of aggression is unimportant since the legal powers of the organized world community can be activated as well by any "threat to the peace" and "breach of the peace" as by any "act of aggression," and hence that any "supposed 'aggression' " can be "more easily brought home as a breach of the peace." [91] The addition, it is also said, of the "factual" terms "breach of peace" and "threat to the peace" makes it unnecessary to locate responsibility for aggression or to weigh equities before police action is undertaken by the organized community; the Security Council, indeed, is neither required nor authorized to wait until the "guilty party" has been identified beyond a reasonable doubt. The Council, the argument runs, has only to resolve a "simple question of fact"—whether or not an actual or imminent "threat to the peace" or "breach of peace" exists.[92] While some verbal symbol less emotionally charged than "aggression" may well be preferred, and while the scope of authority of United Nations organs is not dependent upon the use of one rather than another symbol, the point bears emphasis that the intellectual complexities that attend characterizing impermissible coercion are not successfully evaded simply by the substitution of less invidious labels. Even initial, noncoercive, community intervention for conciliation and settlement requires guidance by an understanding of fundamental long-term goals, guidance not likely to be secured by verbal legerdemain.[93] With respect to the

91. Stone, *Aggression and World Order* 22–3, 152 (1958).

92. Eagleton, *International Government* 525 (3d ed., 1957); Martin, *Collective Security* 118 (1952). See also the statement of Dr. Pasvolsky, *Hearings before the Senate Committee on Foreign Relations, Charter of the United Nations,* 79th Cong., 1st Sess., 282 (1945).

93. We recognize that different types of decisions reflecting different degrees of community involvement may be taken in the application and implementation of fundamental community policy about recourse to coercion, from traditional

security organs of the United Nations, the problem of characterizing coercion in particular cases as permissible or nonpermissible is principally one of determining the appropriate direction or target of the collective repressive action that is decided upon for the organization or recommended to the several states; [94] it arises when noncoercive

---

exercises of diplomacy in "good offices," through collective conciliation and political pressure, to collective military enforcement action. Differing emphases upon different specific factors and policies may be appropriate in varying types of decision.

The kind of process of clarification that is suggested in this chapter is intended to be of assistance in the making of any type of decision. The assumption made is that consideration of goals is relevant to any kind of decision-making which purports to affect the future. Whatever the specific type of decision and whatever the degree of involvement of the general community, continuous and purposeful focus upon long-term goals and policies may help in promoting rationality in decision. Certainly, orderly intellectual procedures for examining contextual factors and policies need not interfere with or impede the negotiation of a compromise or settlement. All we urge is that such compromise or settlement should be as rational, in terms of basic community goal and policy, as particular circumstances may permit.

When the general community of states is most deeply involved, as when collective military action is required or authorized, the need for systematic reference to and appraisal of relevant factors and policies in context is most obvious. In insisting that the most serious decision the general community may make be explicitly related to fundamental goals, we are not recommending the making of facile judgments about guilt or blameworthiness for their own sake. Any decision to engage in collective enforcement that does not impose a plague upon both houses must rest upon some assumption about an appropriate allocation of responsibility. Rational decision requires conscious, ordered, and goal-oriented examination of such assumptions.

94. Cf. Professor Bourquin in *Collective Security* 329 (Bourquin, ed., 1936):

> Why is the need felt of determining the guilty party? It is not for the pleasure of attributing blame or praise; it is because the point of departure is the idea that the aggression must be repressed, that sanctions must be applied to the guilty and aid brought to the victim or victims.
>
> The problem of the determination of the aggressor is of capital importance; it is a problem leading to a practical consequence, tending to set in motion a social reaction against one of the States in conflict, and to secure to the other the advantage of the protection of the society. . . . [T]he determination of the aggressor . . . is an act of reprobation, tending to designate, among the States in conflict, the one against which sanctions are to be applied.

See also Royal Institute of International Affairs, *International Sanctions* 13 (1938): "The international community, if it would apply coercion for the resto-

community intervention has failed, and it persists as long as one or both of the contending participants refuses to cease acts of coercion. Thus, although characterization for coercive intervention may in some measure be forestalled through successful collective conciliation and compliance by both participants with injunctions to cease and desist, the replacement of "aggression" with some other nonemotive words of the same level of abstraction offers little guidance toward rational decision, even in the diplomacy of conciliation, once the problem has arisen. In fact, commonly implicit in arguments such as those noted above is a facile analogy drawn from municipal law situations: a municipal peace officer separates two individuals who are in violent conflict and brings them before a court for a determination of their rights and liabilities.[95] The appropriateness of this analogy in an arena such as that of the contemporary world is, obviously, highly questionable. While, in point of theory, the United Nations as keeper of the international peace may have competence to coerce both contending participants into stopping hostilities, with the exception of peripheral situations involving only small powers of negligible military capability, the dispatch of international armed

---

ration of order, must reach some conclusion as to guilt before using either economic pressure or military action as in either case it would be necessary to inflict material loss, possibly on large populations, in order to restore peace." See also Braatöy, "The Quest for Treaty Definitions of Aggression," 5 *Acta Scandinavica Juris Gentium* 29, 35 (1934).

The point we seek to underscore—the irrelevance of the particular term employed in making the characterization—may be illustrated by the Security Council resolutions of June 25 and 27, 1950, (S/1501 and S/1511) in the Korean case. The Council there used the term "breach of the peace" which neither prevented nor dispensed with the Council's discriminating between the North Korean authorities and the Republic of Korea and recommending assistance to the latter as against the former. It should be obvious that "threat to the peace" and "breach of the peace" are, in this sense, little more than functional equivalents of "act of aggression" and call for the same act of judgment if coercive enforcement measures are at all to be taken.

95. The analogy is explicitly developed in Kopelmanas, "The Problem of Aggression and the Prevention of War," 31 *A.J.I.L.* 244, 253–6 (1937). Jessup, *A Modern Law of Nations* 196–7 (1948) envisaged the aerial bombardment of the "positions" of both belligerents who refuse to heed a U.N. call for cease-fire and withdrawal of troops, but conceded that where the fighting continues despite such bombardment, the U.N. would have to decide against whom sanctions are to be applied. The suggestion of a preliminary air bombardment by "international air contingents" must today seem quaint.

forces to do battle with both participants does not presently seem a significant possibility.

From this perspective, the basic intellectual task is one of categorizing the variable contextual factors and policies which relate to the distinction between permissible and impermissible coercion for the guidance of differing particular decision-makers.[96] The burden of this task is not so much the distillation of brief, black-letter definitions for authoritative projection in treaty or other form as it is the clarification of a process of intellectual analysis by which responsible decision-makers may discipline themselves for the consideration of relevant factors and policies.

We are hopeful enough to believe that to attempt to clarify the community policies at stake in this most fundamental of all problems is not entirely futile, and that these policies can be clarified and refined in sufficient operational detail to give significant guidance to the various officials who must respond to varying specific controversies.[97] We are acutely aware that the formulation and assignment

96. See the insightful suggestion made by the United States representative (Maktos) in the 1953 Special Committee that "instead of trying to establish a general formula which would probably be incomplete, it would be better to offer the competent organs of the United Nations, and in the first place the Security Council, a list of factors to be taken into account in deciding a given case." Unfortunately, although some other members of the Committee "thought this idea constructive and worth examining," the suggestion apparently was not followed up in subsequent discussions in later committees by either the U.S. representative or other delegates. The objection raised by the Polish delegate in the 1953 Special Committee that "such a list of factors could only circumvent the important problem of clearly defining aggression and would serve no useful purpose" indicates less than adequate grasp of the character of the task involved. See Report of the 1953 Special Committee 14.

97. The suggestion is sometimes made that for decision-makers to discipline their judgment by a comprehensive "check list" of factors would mean protracted debate and delay when prompt action may be of the utmost importance. It is not, however, our contention that decision-makers must consider each and every factor in minutest detail in every single case. The specific factors upon which inquiry, in a given case, should center and the degree of detail to which such inquiry should be carried, are a function of the particular context to which the decision-maker is responding, including the type of decision to be made. An appropriate metaphor is that of the telescope: the inquiry may be compressed or drawn out as particular contexts may require. But however insistent may be the demand for prompt action, some reference to relevant factors and policies in context must be made if the decision is to make any pretense toward being a rational one, that is, related to the securing of both long-term and short-

of operational meaning to policies which, while inherent in the structure of authoritative myth, are there expressed only in the highest order of abstraction, may be most difficult in some particular contexts. There is no way of escaping these intellectual difficulties, just as there is no avoiding the uniquely human problem of choice which all decision-makers ultimately must face. We do not purport to have any magic means of coercing the raw living flow of events into imaginary absolutes of word-categories. We do not seek an impossible perfectionism of complete and permanent precision. Our belief is that here, as in other problems of international law, both approximations of policy clarification and rough practical judgments to promote clarified policies are possible, and that perfection is as unnecessary as it is unattainable.

It may be useful to anticipate in summary manner the mode of inquiry that we recommend for detailed clarification of community policies about both nonpermissible coercion and permissible coercion. We propose, as a step preliminary but indispensable to clarity, to identify the different types of decision-makers from whom a judgment as to the lawfulness of particular applications of coercion may come to be demanded, to locate their differing positions in the structure of authority, and to note differences in function, in purpose, and in the conditions under which they operate. Next, we shall consider the method of analysis which is relevant when decision-makers are confronted with claims that a certain act or series of acts of coercion is impermissible, and which may enable them to identify and focus upon the more important factors that in various specific contexts may rationally condition or affect a characterization of coercion as nonpermissible. Finally we will suggest a rough and tentative categorization which includes such interrelated items as: the factor of priority in exercise of substantial coercion; the relative size and strength of the contending parties; the nature of their objectives; the conditions under which coercion is applied; the methods employed; the effects achieved; their relative willingness to accept community intervention; and expectations about the effectiveness and costs of decision.

---

term community goals. The reluctance to become explicit about such factors and policies may occasionally be only a reflection in actual operation of the destructive skepticism that minimizes or denies the role of authority, and its efforts to achieve policy clarification, in power processes.

It is well to stress in advance that the significance of any particular factor or set of factors is relative and may be expected to vary from particular context to context. The significance of any factor is in principal measure a function of its location in the whole constellation of variables in a specific context, and of the interrelations of these variables.

Typically, the set of events with which a decision-maker is confronted includes not only a claim of impermissible coercion but also a countering claim by the participant charged with unlawful resort to coercion that it was in fact acting in lawful defense. It is thus necessary to examine in systematic detail the coercion applied by each party upon the other. Claims of lawful defense involve factors which are comparable to, and just as complex as, those raised by charges of unlawful coercion. Parallel analysis is called for and this we propose also to outline.

The Differing Functions of Different Decision-Makers

The first indispensable requirement is to identify the types of decision-makers who may, on different occasions, be confronted with conflicting claims about the lawfulness of particular coercive acts and to whom differing configurations of factors may make a difference. A general categorization must include officials of international governmental organizations; judges of courts or tribunals, national or international, permanent or specially constituted; and officials of nation-states.[98]

98. See the related categorization achieved in the 1956 Special Committee of the various functions which a definition (or definitions) of aggression may perform and which differ as the decision-makers utilizing such definition (or definitions) differ: (a) guidance for U.N. organs in carrying out the task of safeguarding international peace; (b) guidance for members claiming self-defense; (c) guidance for an international tribunal punishing individuals under the Draft Code of Offences against the Peace and Security of Mankind; (d) possible functions in relation to disarmament arrangements and regulation of atomic weapons. Report of the 1956 Special Committee 5–7. It should be noted that (d) was raised in the form of a call for postponement of discussions on aggression until "the results of disarmament negotiations were known." See also Stone, *Aggression and World Order* 23, 137–9 (1958), who focuses only upon functions (a) and (c). Compare Pompe, *Aggressive War: an International Crime* 66–71 (1953) and Wright, "The Prevention of Aggression," 50 *A.J.I.L.* 514, 520 (1956). Earlier and somewhat fragmentary recognition of this variation in function is found in the Report of the 1953 Special Committee 32–5; U.N. Gen. Ass., Res. No.

Officials of the United Nations offer the most convenient illustration of the first type. The principal function of the United Nations, and the relevant one for present purposes, is expressed thus in the Charter: "to maintain international peace and security, and to that end: to take effective collective measures for the prevention and removal of threats to the peace, and for the suppression of acts of aggression or other breaches of the peace . . ." [99] In practice, responsibility for the exercise of this security or peace-enforcement function is shared by the Security Council and the General Assembly. Although the Charter assigns "primary responsibility" to the Council,[100] the Assembly has formally and effectively claimed authority to exercise that function when the Council is veto-bound.[101] The competence of the United Nations to deal with situations of coercion is comprehensive. The exercises of coercion which the Security Council may determine to be impermissible and whose prevention or suppression may be sought through measures of community coercion are characterized only in such broad formal terms as "threat to the peace," "breach of the peace," and "act of aggression." Neither the authority of the Council to require or recommend in a particular case collective enforcement action, nor the type, military or political and economic, of enforcement measures that may be required or recommended, is made contingent upon the particular technical

---

599(VI), U.N. Gen. Ass., *Off. Rec.*, 6th Sess., Plenary 368 (1952); U.N. Gen. Ass., Res. No. 688(VII), U.N. Gen. Ass., *Off. Rec.*, 7th Sess., Plenary 408 (1952).

99. U. N. Charter, Art. 1, par. 1.

100. U. N. Charter, Art. 24.

101. Under the "Uniting For Peace" Resolution, U.N. Gen. Ass., Res. No. 377(V), U.N. Gen. Ass., *Off. Rec.*, 5th Sess., Plenary 302 (1950). In the light of the effective structural modifications which the organization has undergone, the debates about the "legality" and "constitutionality" of the "Uniting For Peace" Resolution appear remarkably detached from reality. The effects of the "process of structural evolution" have been summed up in the following terms:

> [T]he principle of differentiation of function, as between the Security Council and the General Assembly, has been cast into the discard. The scheme of division of labor, involving the supervisory Assembly and the specialized Councils, has tended to break down. The concept of decentralization has given way to a situation in which the General Assembly is the dominant organ within the United Nations.

Tenth Report of the Commission to Study the Organization of Peace, *Strengthening the United Nations* 26 (1957).

nomenclature invoked. Except, perhaps, to the extent that "threat to the peace" may be thought implicitly to convey the notion of a lower degree of coercion than "breach of the peace,"[102] the possible references of these phrases (and of "act of aggression")—in terms of the kinds and intensities of coercion that may be determined to be non-permissible—are deliberately left indeterminate. Distinguished authorities have accordingly emphasized that the Council's authority to order or call for enforcement action is not conditioned upon a finding of a use or threat of *armed* force in violation of Article 2(4) of the Charter.[103] It would then seem a clear inference that the Council may designate as unlawful coercion that which is applied by other than military instrumentalities and which has not reached the level of open military violence.

The conditions under which the United Nations has exercised or attempted to exercise its peace enforcement functions have usually been characterized either by overt military hostilities or by high or rising expectations of violence. The corresponding objectives of community intervention in these situations may be expressed, in most general description, as to prevent accelerating coercion from reaching the intensity of overt violence, and, where that stage has already been reached, to effect the termination of unlawful violence. Beyond these objectives, the organized community may also seek to bring about conditions calculated to prevent the recurrence of violence. The measures adopted to this end may be partial and provisional arrangements. Thus, in the Suez affair, for example, a United Nations Emergency Force[104] was stationed in the Gaza area to preclude further incursions of guerrilla forces across belligerent lines. In some instances the measures may extend to complete and final settlement of the original dispute as in the 1932 Peruvian-Colombian conflict over the Leticia trapezium.[105]

Both the objectives sought in efforts at peace enforcement and the

102. See Wright, "The Prevention of Aggression," 50 *A.J.I.L.* 514, 524–6 (1956).

103. See 2 Oppenheim-Lauterpacht 163–64; Kelsen, *The Law of the United Nations* 726–31 (1950). See also Bowett, *Self-Defence in International Law* 147, 176 (1958); Tucker, "The Interpretation of War Under Present International Law," 4 *Int. L.Q.* 11, 25 (1951).

104. U.N. Gen. Ass., Res. Nos. 1000 (ES-1), 1001 (ES-1), U.N. Gen. Ass., *Off. Rec.*, 1st Emer. Spec. Sess., Supp. No. 1 (A/3354) (1956).

105. See 2 Walters, *A History of the League of Nations* 536–40 (1952).

conditions that commonly attend such efforts place a considerable premium upon expeditious action by the organized community, a premium which tends to increase as capabilities of modern weaponry and techniques of coercion mature. Despite modern means of communication, and sometimes because of their character, difficulties of objectively ascertaining facts and of verifying proclaimed purposes may be compounded. If the exercise of authority and the application of community enforcement measures are not to be prejudiced, or conceivably entirely nullified, the United Nations must obviously be authorized to act quickly and upon less rigorous standards of evidence than those appropriately demanded of other decision-making bodies, such as judicial tribunals, or of scholarly historians writing a hundred years *post facto*. To put the point most comprehensively, shifting concatenations of relevant factors may be appraised by the security organization differently from other decision-makers who have different functions and purposes and who speak under different conditions.[106]

Judges of tribunals may also have occasion to pass upon the permissibility of resort to coercion in particular cases. The tribunals may be municipal in character, that is, unilaterally established, as were the Chinese War Crimes Military Tribunal[107] and the Polish Supreme National Tribunal for trial of war criminals,[108] or international, that is, established by multilateral agreement, as were the International Military Tribunal (the Nuremberg court) and the International Military Tribunal for the Far East.[109] They may be

106. It might, for more specific instance, be suggested that the organized community may appropriately consider itself as authorized to intervene with measures of varying scope and severity in contexts of intense and accelerating coercion, even before the stage of critical intensity is reached, when the target state may itself be authorized to react militarily.

107. See "Trial of Takashi Sakai," 14 *Law Reports of Trials of War Criminals* 1 (1949).

108. See "Trial of Greiser," 13 id. 70. Mention may also be made of the military tribunals and courts established by each of the occupying powers in Germany in its respective zone, pursuant to Control Council Law No. 10. These tribunals and courts had jurisdiction to try, *inter alia,* alleged crimes against peace. See 15 id. 39–43.

109. The aptness of the adjective "international" as applied to the Nuremberg and Tokyo Tribunals has been impugned by some scholars. Kelsen, *Principles of International Law* 238 (1952) contends that the Nuremberg Tribunal was not an "international" tribunal but a "common tribunal" of the Allied

temporary *ad hoc* creations or, as a higher degree of organization is achieved in the world arena, permanent institutions.[110] The function of these judicial bodies is not the enforcement of peace among nations but rather the determination of the criminal responsibility of individual persons for unlawful resort to coercion. The individuals brought before these tribunals would commonly be political, military, or economic elites, in other words, the top effective decision-makers of the state which breached the prohibition of unlawful coercion.[111] The objectives embodied in the imposition of criminal punishment upon these types of individuals may, but need not, differ from, and may include, all the ordinary purposes for which criminal justice is administered in municipal public orders.[112]

The Judgment of the Nuremberg Tribunal, it may be recalled, evoked much learned, if at times confused, contention about the "criminality" as distinguished from the "illegality" of aggressive war under international law. This contention has, today, been largely

---

Powers on the ground that the Axis Powers were not parties to the London Agreement. Schwarzenberger, "The Judgment of Nuremberg," 21 *Tul. L. Rev.* 329, 338 (1947), wrote that it was "more akin to a joint tribunal under municipal law than to an international tribunal in the normal sense of the word." Anent this preoccupation with word-labels, what is important, it may be suggested, is that those tribunals were established by multilateral agreement and that they invoked and sought to apply inclusive policies. It is hardly practical to stipulate an absolute "universality" as the only possible reference of "international."

110. Such as the proposed international criminal court. See Report of the Committee on International Criminal Jurisdiction, U.N. Gen. Ass., *Off. Rec.*, 7th Sess., Supp. No. 11 (A/2136) (1952); Report of the 1953 Committee on International Criminal Jurisdiction, U.N. Gen. Ass., *Off. Rec.*, 9th Sess., Supp. No. 12 (A/2645) (1954). The problems that confront contemporary efforts to establish such an institution are of course vast and complex, and a high probability of realization in the near or foreseeable future is difficult to posit. See Stone, *Legal Controls of International Conflict* 378–9 (1954); Report by Sandstrom on the Question of International Criminal Jurisdiction, 2 *Y.B. of the Int. Law Comn. 1950,* at 18. But approval may be given to the continuation of efforts to clarify the conditions under which such probability may be increased.

111. See "High Command Trial," 12 *Law Reports of Trials of War Criminals* 1, 69–70 (1949); "Krupp Trial," 10 id. at 127–28; "I. G. Farben Trial," id. at 37–8.

112. For an excellent, recent inquiry into these purposes, see Lasswell and Donnelly, "The Continuing Debate Over Responsibility: An Introduction to Isolating the Condemnation Sanction," 68 *Yale L.J.* 869 (1959).

muted. Perhaps few will doubt that the present corpus of authoritative myth permits the punishment of individual persons responsible for impermissible recourse to violence, and that the real problem is creating appropriate international institutions and sustaining perspectives and dispositions of effective power for the implementation of authority. It may be observed in this connection that the charters and judgments of the Nuremberg and Tokyo Tribunals as well as the International Law Commission's formulation of the "Nuremberg principles" refer to individual criminal responsibility in the context of a "war of aggression," [113] that is, impermissible coercion that has reached the dimensions and intensity of overt and extensive military violence. The Draft Code of Offenses Against the Peace and Security of Mankind would extend the policy involved to "any act of aggression" [114] and thereby include unlawful coercion falling short of naked, armed violence. The realism of this projection obviously depends in considerable degree upon the extent to which an effective community monopoly of force is secured in the international arena.

Realistically, the judicial attribution of criminal responsibility can, of course, be carried out only after the termination of violence, and only upon the assumption that the state identified as having unlawfully exercised coercion has been so far forcefully subdued as to permit the arrest and seizure of its leaders and top policymakers. With respect to coercion that has not matured into open military violence, it is conceivable—though history as yet offers no precedent—that a revolutionary elite may emerge in the offending state, capture power and surrender the ousted elite for trial or try them in its own courts. The point of emphasis, however, is that, with either the termination of violence or the subsidence of expectations of violence, judges inquiring into individual guilt would not experience the same

113. See "Charter of the International Military Tribunal," Art. 6(a), in 1 *Trials of War Criminals Before the Nuremberg Military Tribunals* at XI (1949); "Charter of the International Military Tribunal For the Far East, Art. 5(a), in *Judgment of the International Military Tribunal For the Far East, Annexes* 21 (1948); "Formulation of the Nuremberg Principles," Principles I & VI, 2 *Y.B. of the Int. Law Comn. 1950,* at 374, 376.

114. Article 2(1); Report of the International Law Commission Covering the Work of its Sixth Session, June 3–July 28, 1954, U.N. Gen. Ass., *Off. Rec.,* Supp. No. 9 (A/2693), at 11 (1954). For brief general comment, see Johnson, "The Draft Code of Offenses Against the Peace and Security of Mankind," 4 *Int. and Comp. L.Q.* 445 (1955).

insistent need for quick decision that presses upon the security organs of the organized community. The judges may and appropriately do require more exacting degrees and procedures of proof.[115] Difficulties of fact-finding may be substantially relieved by access which the judges presumably would have to the secret files and archives of the accused leaders of the subdued state, and by other evidence not available to the preceding decision-makers. The judicial organs would have full opportunity for more extended inquiry into the relevant factors in context; the relevant context might indeed be defined, and the significant segment of time delimited, somewhat differently for purposes of individual punishment than for purposes of peace enforcement. In particular, in the weighing of equities and apportionment of blame, close consideration can be given to the subjectivities of the individuals accused—in terms of the degree of voluntary and purposeful participation in the making of decisions unlawfully to engage in coercion—[116] which may be pleaded in mitigation or exculpation of responsibility.

The third group of authorized decision-makers is composed of the officials of nation-states who make judgments about the lawfulness of coercion for a number of differing purposes. First, state officials must be continually appraising that degree of constraint, usually minimal, exercised in the ordinary course of interaction with other states. These officials must also assess and decide upon an appropriate response to any drastically accelerated coercion that may be applied

115. A wide-ranging survey and evaluation, encompassing the procedures utilized in both trials for crimes against peace and trials for "conventional" war crimes, is presented in Tsai, "Judicial Administration of the Law of War: Procedures in War Crimes Trials," 1957 (unpublished thesis in Yale Law Library).

116. Cf. Pompe, *Aggressive War: an International Crime* 252 (1953). In the Krupp trial, Judge Anderson stressed that for conviction there

> must be knowledge of facts and circumstances which would enable the particular individual to determine not only that there was a concrete plan to initiate and wage war, but that the contemplated conflict would be a war of aggression and hence criminal. Such knowledge being shown, it must be further established that the accused participated in the plan with the felonious intent to aid in the accomplishment of the criminal objective. In the individual crime of aggressive war or conspiracy to that end as contra-distinguished to the international delinquency of a state in resorting to hostilities, the individual intention is of major importance.

10 *Law Reports of Trials of War Criminals* 123 (1949).

against their states. Third, in the event that one or both security organs of the organized community, the Security Council and the General Assembly, are unable to arrive at a characterization of coercion exercised by two contending participants, individual third states may need to decide about permissive discrimination and participation on the basis of such residuary authority as the Pact of Paris.[117] States, finally, which are parties to collective defense arrangements must make determinations as to the occurrence of a *casus foederis,* and must appraise a party's claim for assistance in collective self-defense.

We focus here upon officials of a state against which highly intense coercion has been exercised. Such officials, in responding to coercion with coercion and in asserting a claim to act in self-defense, in fact make a determination that the coercion to which they respond constitutes an unlawful breach of world public order. A determination of this sort is and must be provisional. It is a *claim* to self-redress without prior authorization from the organized community, and is subject to review and appraisal by that community.[118] In the uncertain interval, however, between initiation of substantial coercion and subsequent determination by the organized community, the individual state must be conceded competence to respond quickly if response is to serve the purpose of protection. The need for celerity in decision may be even more pressing, the perils of delay more portentous, for the target state than for the general security organization. Thus, the target state may appropriately be regarded as authorized to act upon a prima facie evaluation of the coercion exercised against it, and on standards of proof at least no more demanding than those upon which decision-makers responsible for the enforcement of peace may find it necessary to act.

The Analysis of Alleged Initiating Coercion

We turn now to the mode of analysis we suggest as relevant for inquiring into contextual factors that influence decisions about the lawfulness of coercion. The order in which we proceed to analysis of these factors reflects requirements of convenience in exposition rather than a posited hierarchy of intrinsic importance.

117. On residual bases of permissive discrimination and participation, see the references cited in Ch. 1, note 170.

118. See text accompanying notes 213–17 infra.

PRIORITY IN THE EXERCISE OF SUBSTANTIAL COERCION

There has been much discussion in the United Nations committees that have sought to define aggression of a purported "principle of priority" or, as it is sometimes called, a "principle of the initial act." [119] This discussion has, however, been characterized in large degree by misdirection; it has focused too much upon a reference to the chronological priority of some single, "precisely defined," physical act, divorced from the subjectivities of attack or defense accompanying the act. Much of the argument has centered about the "principle of priority" incorporated in the enumerative Soviet draft definition: the stipulation that of two contending participants, that party is the aggressor which first commits any of the acts specifically catalogued as aggressive acts. Some have urged that this particular "priority principle" furnishes the only available criterion for distinguishing a prohibited act of aggression from permissible self-defense. "None of the acts mentioned in the USSR draft resolution," the Ukrainian SSR delegate explained, "amounted to aggression *per se*. Two acts might be the same in the military sense yet from the legal point of view, one would be an act of aggression and the second legitimate retaliation [*sic*]. Aggression would inevitably be the first act, which induced or provoked the second." [120] From an antithetical perspective, the representative of the United Kingdom asserted with equal confidence that "the question of which State was 'first' to commit a certain act was basically irrelevant and that everything depended essentially upon the circumstances." [121] More re-

119. See, e.g., Report of the Sixth Committee, U.N. Gen. Ass., *Off. Rec.*, 9th Sess., Annexes, Agenda Item 51, at 11–12 (1954); Report of the 1956 Special Committee 9–10; Report of the Sixth Committee, U.N. Gen. Ass., *Off. Rec.*, 12th Sess., Annexes, Agenda Item 54, at 4 (1957).

120. U.N. Doc. No. A/C.6/SR. 408, at 13 (1954); cf. "Report of the [Politis] Committee on Security Questions, Conference for the Reduction and Limitation of Armaments," (1933) 2 *Conf. Docs.* (1935.IX.4) 680 (1935) ("The chronological order of the facts is decisive here."). See also the statements of Politis in the Records of the Conference for the Reduction and Limitation of Armaments, 2 *Minutes of the General Commission* 500 (League of Nations, Ser. B 1933).

121. U.N. Doc. No. A/C.6/SR.406, at 8 (1954). The United Kingdom delegate, curiously enough, went on to echo the argument made by the Soviet Union in the 1945 London Conference and stated that "Everyone could recognize aggression when it occurred and the matter should be left at that. . . ." Id. at 9. As to the argument referred to in the text, see also Report of the 1956 Special Committee 9.

cently, it has been appropriately emphasized that the "tasks of evaluation" involved in a determination of aggression "simply cannot be performed by limiting consideration to the occurrence of a precisely defined act, at a particular moment, in insulation from the broader context of the relations of the States concerned." [122]

The factor of priority cannot lightly be dismissed as wholly irrelevant to judgments about permissibility or impermissibility of coercion. A conception of priority is implicit in the very notion of impermissible coercion; [123] what community policy seeks to prohibit is resort to certain coercion, not responding coercion in necessary protection of values. Completely to reject the relevance of priority is thus, in substance, to reject the fundamental community policy of limiting permissible change to change by peaceful procedures only.[124]

122. Stone, *Aggression and World Order* 70–1 (1958).

123. Cf. Spiropoulos, "Second Report on the Draft Code of Offences Against the Peace and Security of Mankind," 2 *Y.B. of the Int. Law Comn. 1951,* at 43, 67. The same point was stressed by the Netherlands representative to the 1956 Special Committee: "[T]he priority principle was inherent in every definition dealing with armed attack and self-defense. The only problem was to what kind of acts the priority principle was related." Report of the 1956 Special Committee 19. Even the United Kingdom delegate conceded that "it was self-evident that for a legitimate exercise of the right of self-defence something must have first happened to call it into play." Ibid.

124. Stone, *Aggression and World Order* 71 (1958) appears to come perilously close to such a position. Professor Stone writes:

> This difficulty was increased to the point of caricature by the express provision in the Soviet draft that virtually no considerations whatsoever "political, strategic or economic", nor in particular any of a rather exhaustive list of provocative invasions by the "victim" of the "attacker's" legal rights and legitimate interests, could justify the attack. In a state of the world in which there is usually no other possible means of vindicating rights and interests, this is rather like proposing a municipal legal order in which the only law which is enforced is a law forbidding physical trespass against the realty or person of another.

See also id. at 43, 95, 100. The list of nonjustifying circumstances incorporated in the Soviet definition is, of course, in some of its items, open to serious objection. But Professor Stone himself failed to indicate what "legal rights and legitimate interests," other than the right and interest in defending against "physical trespass against [one's] realty or person" may or should be permitted to be "vindicated" by unilateral force. It may be well to recall that that prohibition is the first indispensable law of any public order. And it is travesty of customary international law to analogize the general community of states to a "municipal society [where] no means whatever existed for changing the law except with the

It is, on the other hand, equally obvious that to assign exclusive relevance to a "principle of priority" whose reference is limited to the timing of a particular "precisely defined" operation indexed, as in the Soviet list, as aggressive, is hardly more rationally designed to secure the fundamental community policies at stake; such a unifactor test ignores the significance of subjectivities or objectives of coercion which must be considered when ascertaining responsibility for breaches of basic policy.

Any conception of priority takes on meaning and must be appraised in terms of the fundamental policies to be served, policies which in considerable measure determine the categories of phenomena to be observed and considered in terms of their sequential relationships of anteriority, simultaneity, and posteriority. Priority, in other words, can here as in other types of problems be ascertained only within a temporal sequence which the decision-maker deems relevant. To delimit the relevant sequence in time necessarily involves specifying the kind of behavior (subjectivities and operations) that may be characterized as unlawful. This specification obviously depends upon the policies the decision-maker seeks to realize. Determination of priority can lapse into an infinitely regressive historical excursion only when the decision-maker is unclear about basic policy or in fact secretly rejects the minimum policy which demands that no change shall be effected through intense coercion and violence.

The diverging views in the United Nations about priority have been inspired by deep discontent with the attempt to utilize, for purposes of fixing responsibility for breach of the public order, a much too mechanistic rule relating single "precisely defined" operations in abstract chronological sequence. The conception of priority that would determine community policy simply by the chronology of individual physical acts without reference to any other contextual factor was appropriately rejected. The rejection of this notion, however, at times came too close to denying any relevance to conceptions of priority. For proper clarification, neither priority in conducting a specified operation alone nor priority in certain subjectivities unattended by operations is crucial. What is crucial is, rather, priority in the exercise by certain operations and with certain perspectives, of

---

consent of *every* individual member of the society." Id. at 71 note 164. (Emphasis added.)

destructive coercion which reasonably creates in the target state—as reasonableness can be tested by third parties—expectations that it must react with violence to conserve its own values.[125] A physical operation alone, considered simply as an act of coercion, is deaf, dumb, and blind to policy and yields no necessary indication of its impact on demanded policies. The question of priority is, we submit, appropriately posed not in terms of marking the exact date or hour of some one physical act, such as the landing of a battalion or the firing of a cannon, but in terms of ascertaining initiative in creating, by certain operations impelled by certain perspectives, the stipulated realistic expectations as to the requirements for protecting values. Subjectivities about coercion are, of course, no more open to direct observation than are subjectivities about persuasion and agreement, and must often be inferred from operations; but inference is no more impossible with respect to coercion than with respect to agreement. Inference about subjectivities, in processes of coercion as of agreement, may and must be drawn from many different particular operations, not merely from one, and from the varying configurations of the specific operations performed by each participant in detailed contexts, including the relative chronological sequence of individual operations.[126] A judgment as to priority thus requires, if chronology is to serve fundamental community policy, appraising and relating to a calendar or clock whole constellations of factors, encompassing both acts and qualifying perspectives, exhibited in the coercion exercised by the respective participants.

THE CHARACTERISTICS OF PARTICIPANTS

In considering the relevance of the character and constitution of participants for determining the lawfulness or unlawfulness of coer-

125. We are here anticipating inquiries made below; see text accompanying notes 170–9 infra. This conception of priority does not compel an infinite regress in historical search for responsibility. The thrust is upon initiative in creating expectations in a contemporary context of a need for military reaction. Difficulty in finding a "time of beginning" for determining responsibility—that is, selecting the appropriate target of community intervention—only arises where one does not accept the basic postulate of no change through too intense coercion or assumes the impossibility of clarifying standards for identifying too intense coercion for expansionist purposes.

126. See note 88 supra. With respect to processes of agreement, see also notes 254–5 infra.

cion, it is necessary to recall that the nation-state is still the major type of participant in world processes of coercion and ordinarily commands control of armed forces, the power base which permits the application of the most intense degree of coercion. The relative size and power of a state which is alleged to have unlawfully initiated coercion, that is, its size and power in relation to that of its opponent, may serve as indices of the real, as distinguished from the proclaimed, objectives of each participant, of the intensity of coercion exercised by each (particularly before the stage of open military violence is reached), of the realism of asserted expectations that violence is necessary for protection, and hence of the probable situs of responsibility. The more conspicuous the disparity in relative fighting capability, appraised in terms of both forces-in-being and potential for war, the more easily inferences of responsibility may be drawn. Both common sense and the history of such wars as the Italo-Abyssinian war, the Sino-Japanese conflicts of 1931 and 1937, and the Soviet-Finnish war of 1939 suggest that, in the ordinary course of events, a state with a low level of fighting capability is not likely to initiate highly intense coercion against a much more powerful state. A plea of self-defense has a characteristically implausible ring when uttered by a great power against a weak or disorganized or primitive state.[127]

In weighing relative power and strength, account must be taken of the capabilities not only of the immediately contending participants but also of those defined by each participant as its allies or potential allies. The external structure of identifications that each participant projects, indeed the very configuration of the world arena, may thus be relevant. In the current world, however, the significance of an appraisal of relative capability may depend upon the extent to which the patterns of power move toward diversification rather than toward a simple, rigid bipolarity. Inquiry into such identification structures may yield a more direct indication of the character of the objectives

127. There may, however, be cases of small and weak states deliberately engaging in attacks of a minor and diminutive scale, largely of nuisance value, against a more powerful state. This may be illustrated by the recent incidents at the ill-defined Yemen-Aden border where, it was reported, Yemeni troops with a few field guns and machine guns fired at British forces in the Aden protectorate. British forces reacted by bombing and strafing Yemeni gun positions. The United Kingdom, in a letter to the U.N. Secretary-General, stated that the British air action was taken under Article 51 of the U. N. Charter. *N. Y. Times,* May 8, 1958, p. 13, col. 5; p. 34, col. 5.

or purposes of the respective participants by revealing the kind of world public order each demands, whether it be one which requires the subordination or destruction of independent power centers or one which seeks peaceful coordination and cooperation in a pluralistic arena.

The nature of the internal structures of authority and control in each of the contending states may also suggest relevant probabilities. A distinguished scholar has submitted that "among factors which appear to influence the war-likeness of a state are the degrees of constitutionalism, federalism, division of powers and democracy established in its political constitution." [128] The degree to which both

128. 2 Wright, *A Study of War* 833–48 (1942). See also id. at 1164, 1168, 1172, where some generalizations about possible interrelations of economic structure and warlikeness are attempted. More than half a century before Professor Wright wrote, a comparable insight into the relation between internal value systems and external policies of states was offered by F. de Martens:

> I have tried to show the existence of a connection between the internal system and external relations of each country in successive historical periods from antiquity to our times and I have reached the conclusion that when civil and political rights in a State are based on respect for human personality and its inalienable prerogatives, the foreign policy of the government seeks as a natural result to protect the legitimate interests of the nation in its external affairs in upholding order and right abroad and in encouraging every attempt to spread the benefits of civilisation throughout the world. Such a foreign policy should generally produce firmly established peaceful relations and respect for the acquired rights of others. On the other hand, relations with states where human personality enjoys no rights but is oppressed, surrendered to arbitrary caprice, and subject to brutal force cannot be established on a firm basis or develop.

1 *Traité de Droit International* at ii–iii (Leo, trans., 1883), as translated and quoted in Jenks, *The Common Law of Mankind* 73 (1958).

More recent studies sustain these insights. E.g., Loewenstein, *Political Reconstruction* 86 (1946):

> The distinction [between a political democracy and an autocracy] acquires point when applied to the system of international relations. There is an interrelationship or, it may be said, a causality between form of government and world peace or world organization; and the two are identical, as we have learned the hard way. In the simplest and least controversial terms, a nation organized as a political democracy is more inclined to cooperate peacefully with other nations, and is less prone to resort to violence and war, than one organized as an autocracy.

Id. at 90: "But the causality between autocracy and war does not end here. A government which has come to power and must maintain itself by internal

authoritative and effective power are shared by several organs of government and the extent to which a system of power-balancing is maintained within a state, as well as the character and composition of the ruling elite and of predominating symbols,[129] appear in the present world to have some impact on the capacity and likelihood of a state undertaking arbitrarily to resort to force and violence. It is significant that the states which have been explicitly determined by an international organization or tribunal to have unlawfully resorted to force and violence were commonly totalitarian in internal structure: Fascist Italy, prewar Japan, Soviet Russia, Nazi Germany, North Korea, and the People's Republic of China. Again, it does not seem unreasonable to suppose that the internal characteristics of a state, like its external identifications, reflect in certain measure the kind of public order it projects in the international arena and hence the nature of the objectives that motivate it.[130]

THE NATURE OF PARTICIPANTS' OBJECTIVES

In the United Nations committees that sought to define aggression, certain delegations contended that the objectives or purposes or "sub-

---

violence cannot be expected to behave peacefully towards other countries." See also Neumann, *Permanent Revolution* (1942); Arendt, *The Origins of Totalitarianism* 394–6, 427–8 (1951); Friedrich and Brzezinski, *Totalitarian Dictatorship and Autocracy* 57–68 (1956); Moskowitz, *Human Rights and World Order* 87–8 (1958).

129. The significance for war and peace of the character and composition of elites and of dominant symbols are explored in, e.g., Abrahamsen, *Men, Mind and Power* (1945); Bluemel, *War, Politics, and Insanity* (1948); Lasswell, Lerner and De Sola Pool, *The Comparative Study of Symbols* (1952); Lasswell, Lerner and Rothwell, *The Comparative Study of Elites* (1952); Lasswell, *Power and Personality* (1948). Contemporary techniques of content analysis appear promising and may provide operational indices for elite and symbol factors and trends bearing on the use (or nonuse) of coercion and violence. Recent suggestive studies include De Sola Pool, *Symbols of Democracy* (1952); De Sola Pool, *Symbols of Internationalism* (1951); Lasswell, Leites and Associates, *Language of Politics: Studies in Quantitative Semantics* (1949).

130. We are not, it might be made explicit, suggesting that nontotalitarian states can never be guilty of prohibited coercion and violence. See also note 156 infra. The suggestion made is simply that in examining a participant's publicly asserted perspectives for their realism or spuriousness, inquiry may appropriately extend to the authority and control arrangements, the system of public order, maintained within such participant and projected in the world arena.

jective motives" [131] of a participant charged with having unlawfully initiated coercion were not to be considered in determining the lawfulness of coercion. This view was urged principally in connection with the supposed merits of the enumerative Soviet definition. "The Soviet draft," the representative of Roumania stated, "rightly excluded the subjective element, *animo aggressionis*. The aggressor would, of course, always maintain that whatever his actions, his intention had not been to attack but merely to defend himself or to forestall aggression. Hence no opportunity should be given to the aggressor to plead alleged good intentions." [132] A comparable view was submitted by the Iranian delegate who objected to the inclusion of a reference to "territorial integrity and political independence" in a joint Iran-Panama draft. He argued that this language introduced a "subjective element" and that "the effect of the act, rather than the intention of the aggressor, should be the decisive factor in determining aggression . . ." [133]

The objectives or subjectivities of participants (or, more precisely, of the top effective decision-makers in participating states) cannot, as suggested earlier, be wholly disregarded in characterizing coercion

131. We speak of "objectives" or "purposes" as referring to preferred and actively sought configurations of events. For purposes of clarity, this reference should be distinguished from that frequently given to "aggressive intention" or "*animus aggressionis*"—the deliberate, rather than merely inadvertent or accidental, initiation of violence. The latter reference is made explicit in, e.g., the Report of the Secretary-General 68. Inadvertent or accidental initiation may, for instance, occur where a state, mistaking weather or freakish electronic disturbances on radar screens for approaching hostile missiles, reacts by launching its own missiles. The Secretary-General's report pointed to a historical example: during the Second World War, Allied bombs meant for enemy territory fell on Swiss towns.

Purpose can of course be projected only by human beings. It is not easy to appreciate the fine subtleties about "State *mens rea*" spun in Stone, *Aggression and World Order* 141 (1958). An appropriate conception of top formal and effective decision-makers may go far in clearing such alleged difficulties. The tribunal in the High Command Trial explained that "war whether it be lawful or unlawful is the implementation of a national policy. If the policy under which it is initiated is criminal in its intent and purpose it is so because the individuals at the policy making level had a criminal intent and purpose in determining the policy." "The German High Command Trial," 12 *Law Reports of Trials of War Criminals* 67 (1949).

132. U.N. Doc. No. A/C.6/SR.520, at 11 (1957).

133. U.N. Doc. No. A/C.6/SR.416, at 9 (1954).

as impermissible. Fundamental community policy does not seek to prohibit all coercion, nor even all highly intense coercion; it explicitly permits coercion for certain purposes, such as that necessary to protect certain indispensable values and to enforce certain community decisions. A participant should not, of course, be allowed to escape responsibility by simply asserting some secret legitimate intention that is belied by any reasonable construction of its acts. This is only to say that proclaimed objectives must be distinguished from objectives sought in fact, and that verbal proclamations alone do not offer conclusive indications of the purposes actually pursued. In the exercise of coercion, as in the making of agreements, the purposes or subjectivities of a participant must be "objectively" ascertained; they are, it may again be emphasized, appropriately inferred from acts and the effects of acts, the totality of a participant's operations, verbal and nonverbal, considered in detailed context. From this perspective, the dichotomy posed by the representative of Iran between the "effect of the act" and the "intention of the [actor]" or, as formulated by Dr. Pompe, between the "purport of the act" and the "purpose of the actor," [134] appears unreal. To speak of the "purport of the act" apart from the purpose of flesh-and-blood actors is like, in Professor Williams' figure, "speaking of the grin without the Cheshire cat." [135] The available quanta and kinds of evidence from which inference as to purposes is to be drawn may obviously differ as decision-makers differ in function, objective, and operating condition. The point which we would emphasize, however, is that the purposes that impel an exercise of coercion must be relevant to policy, whatever the specific controversy and whoever the decision-maker purporting to apply community prescription.[136]

In authoritative myth and doctrine, the nature of objectives or purposes that may not lawfully be sought through destructive coercion is characterized only in terms of a very high level of generality. Article 2(4) of the United Nations Charter prohibits the threat or

134. Pompe, *Aggressive War: an International Crime* 103–4 (1953).

135. Williams, "Language and the Law," 61 *L.Q. Rev.* 71, 83 (1945).

136. "Whether," the tribunal in the High Command Case said, "a war be lawful, or aggressive and therefore unlawful under International Law, is and can be determined only from a consideration of the factors that entered into its initiation. In the intent and purpose for which it is planned, prepared, initiated and waged is to be found its lawfulness or unlawfulness." "Trial of Von Leeb," 12 *Law Reports of Trials of War Criminals* 67 (1949).

use of force "against the territorial integrity or political independence of any state, or in any other manner inconsistent with the Purposes of the United Nations." "Territorial integrity" and "political independence," phrases which, it is well known, were inserted in the original Dumbarton Oaks draft at San Francisco upon the insistent behest of small states,[137] are classical, technical terms embracing in summary reference the most important bases of state power, the values or interests whose impairment and destruction are sought to be prohibited and, correlatively, whose necessary protection by coercion is permitted. "Political independence" is commonly taken most comprehensively to refer to the freedom of decision-making or self-direction customarily demanded by state officials.[138] Impairment of "political independence," as an attack upon the institutional arrangements of authority and control in the target state, thus involves substantial curtailment of the freedom of decision-making through the effective and drastic reduction of the number of alternative policies open at tolerable costs to the officials of that state. It may further consist of an attempt to reconstruct the process of decision in the target state, to modify the composition or membership of the ruling elite group, and, perhaps, to dislodge that group completely and to substitute another more acceptable to the attacking state. The reference commonly assigned to "territorial integrity," on the other hand, is that control which state officials hold over a certain geographic resource base and the peoples there located. Impairment of "territorial integrity" as an objective of coercion thus implies that control over all or part of a state's physical and demographic resources will be reduced or eliminated. The appropriate emphasis is upon effective control or possession rather than upon formal recognized title,[139] for

137. Goodrich and Hambro, *Charter of the United Nations* 103 (2d rev. ed., 1949); see 6 U.N.C.I.O. 557, 720.

138. Cf. Pompe, op. cit. supra note 134 at 106: "Political independence opposes the other classic aim of war: the imposition of one's will upon the attacked State." See also Goodrich and Hambro, op. cit. supra note 137 at 105.

139. See Bowett, *Self-Defence in International Law* 34–6 (1958). The reference to effective control or possession is made not only in the Draft Act prepared by the 1933 Geneva Disarmament Conference and the 1947 Rio Treaty cited by Bowett, but also in, e.g., the definition of aggression proposed by Bolivia to the 1953 Special Committee, which included "the invasion by one State of the territory of another State across the frontiers established by treaties or judicial or arbitral decisions and demarcated in accordance therewith, or, in the

community policy seeks change only by peaceful modalities, a policy whose applicability is not contingent upon lack of disputation about the formal "legal status" of the area involved or upon the recognition of an opponent's technical "statehood." Initiating coercion intended to accomplish factual modification in resource distribution is prohibited.

The phrase "or in any other manner inconsistent with the Purposes of the United Nations" was designed to emphasize the inclusiveness of the basic policy and to "insure that there should be no loophole." [140] Since the purposes of the United Nations are formulated in

---

absence of marked frontiers, an invasion affecting territories under the effective jurisdiction of a State. . . ." U.N. Doc. No. A/AC.66/L.9 (1953); Draft Submitted by Iran and Panama, Report of the 1956 Special Committee 31; Draft Proposed by Mexico, id. at 32–3; Joint Draft Proposal of the Dominican Republic, Mexico, Paraguay, and Peru, id. at 33.

140. 6 U.N.C.I.O. 335. Contrast the singular reading of Article 2(4) by Professor Stone: "Article 2(4) does *not* forbid 'the threat or use of force' *simpliciter;* it forbids it only when directed 'against the territorial integrity or political independence of any State, or in any other manner inconsistent with the purposes of the United Nations.' " He goes on to suggest, in effect, that "the use of force for the vindication of rights" (i.e., other than in self-defense) "where no other means exist," is not inconsistent with either Article 2(4) or 2(3), and that a "blanket prohibition" is difficult "to reconcile" with the words "and justice" found in Article 2(3). Stone, *Aggression and World Order* 95 (1958). It may be noted that what Professor Stone seeks to demolish by this argument is "the extreme view of Article 2(4) prohibiting resort to force by States for the vindication of their rights, save in reaction to armed attack or pursuant to collective decisions. . . ." Id. at 98.

A partial and preliminary answer is that the "extreme view" with which Professor Stone grapples is, to the extent that it purports to limit the reference of permissible self-defense to defense against overt military violence, largely a straw man. Such a limitation of reference represents a highly selective reading of the drafting history of Article 51 and other relevant articles of the U. N. Charter, as well as a projection of doubtful realism. Further, appropriate application of the requirements of necessity and proportionality of response should provide adequate answers to alleged difficulties of having "to submit in default of collective action, to all kinds of illegality, injustice and inhumanity as long as these do not take the specific form of an 'armed attack' under Article 51." Id. at 99.

One principal difficulty with Professor Stone's view is that it misconceives the purpose and scope of Articles 2(3), 2(4), and 1(1) and treats too casually the preparatory work on these articles. Thus, for instance, he assumes that the inclusion of "territorial integrity" and "political independence" in Article 2(4) somehow had a limiting effect upon the prohibition there projected. Contrast such broad terms as "to maintain international peace and security," "to develop friendly relations among nations," and "to achieve international cooperation in solving international problems," [141] the omnibus phrase may be seen to include in its reference an indeterminate number of possible objectives which are, on the one hand, less ambitious in scope than the total destruction of the "territorial integrity" or "political independence" of the target state and which are, on the other hand, different from the objectives embodied in "legitimate self-defense" and enforcement of decisions of the organization.[142]

The appraisal of the objectives of a participant alleged to have resorted to unlawful coercion would, of course, present no difficulties if the participant explicitly and publicly declared its intention to de-

---

the observation made in Bowett, *Self-Defence in International Law* 151 (1958) that the "origin [of those words] is found in the desire of the smaller powers to secure some express guarantee of their territorial integrity and political independence; the introduction of this phrase at San Francisco had not, as its purpose, the qualifying of the obligation. . . ." See also 2 Oppenheim-Lauterpacht 154; 6 U.N.C.I.O. 334–5, 400, 564. Again, Professor Stone makes too much of the insertion of "and justice" in Article 2(3). "[A]nd justice" was meant to refer to the terms of the disposition and settlement of a dispute—in other words, the settlement should not only not threaten the peace and security of others but should also be just; it was not intended to qualify "by peaceful means." 6 U.N.C.I.O. 399. The location of the phrase "in conformity with the principles of justice and international law" in Article 1(1) was carefully chosen precisely with such a purpose in mind. See 6 U.N.C.I.O. 203, 245–6, 318, 394–5, 422. There is absolutely nothing to suggest that the unilateral use of force for vindication of rights (other than in self-defense) in the name of "justice" was intended to be permitted. But the cumulative effect of Professor Stone's view (*Aggression and World Order* 100 (1958)) is to place an enormous premium upon the unilateral determination and vindication of "justice" by resort to force.

141. U. N. Charter, Art. 1.

142. The comprehensive reference of this omnibus phrase makes it, we submit, all the more clear that Article 2(4) is—notwithstanding Professor Stone's valiant exegetics—appropriately interpreted to exclude the unilateral use of force other than in permissible self-defense, in particular, the recourse to force for the protection or vindication of lesser rights and interests than those involved in "territorial integrity" and "political independence." Schachter, "The Enforcement of International Judicial and Arbitral Decisions," 54 *A.J.I.L.* 1, 14–17 (1960), offers strong support for this submission. Detailed, multiple-factor or configurative analysis such as is recommended in this book remains, however, as necessary for distinguishing the lawful use of force in self-defense from its unlawful use for lesser purposes as it is for discriminating between lawful self-defense and prohibited aggression.

stroy the "territorial integrity" or "political independence" of its opponent. Such open explicit declarations, however, are bound to be rare.[143] The more usual case has been, and in all probability will remain, that in which actual objectives are not so candidly expressed. For characterizing actual as distinguished from publicly declared purposes, and for considering the concordance of actual purposes with the fundamental policies outlined in the Charter, certain general factors relating to such purposes may, we submit, be usefully examined. Some suggested categorizations are considered below.

Consequentiality

The comprehensiveness or consequentiality of the objectives, considered in terms of the nature, scope, and relative importance (to each participant) of the values a given state seeks to affect, is of obvious, if preliminary, significance. The spectrum of possible objectives ranges from the most modest to the most comprehensive. The degree of consequentiality of particular objectives is commonly related in roughly direct proportion to the intensity of the coercion applied to secure an objective; [144] and both these factors taken together bear upon the degree of realism attributable to the target state's expectation that it must react with violence. Objectives of relative inconsequentiality may be expected to involve no more than a low degree of coercion and may thus be but an incident of the ordinary intercourse of states arousing no appreciable expectations of a need for countering violence. Although, in principle, the authority of the security organs of the general community may be said to extend to these cases, they would not ordinarily be expected to seize upon such minimal coercion as conduct appropriately calling for community intervention. A certain degree of consequentiality is, as a practical matter, an implicit condition for an exercise of the policing functions of the organized community. On the other hand, objectives that approach the upper extremes of consequentiality, such as the total destruction of the "territorial integrity" and "political independence" of the target state, require for their achievement the application of highly intense coercion. An objective of this sort arouses

143. In the Suez case, the Israeli representative to the U.N. argued that the Egyptian Government had made unequivocal and public statements of a purpose to destroy and eliminate Israel. See U.N. Gen. Ass., *Off. Rec.*, 1st Emer. Spec. Sess. 21–3 (1956).

144. See Ch. 1, pp. 33–6.

strong expectations of a necessity for violence in response. The more comprehensive the objective and the more intense the coercion initiated, the easier it may be to arrive at a rational determination of impermissibility.

Extension or Conservation

A major category clearly discernible in the prescriptions of the Charter is that of extension or conservation; a participant charged with unlawfully initiating coercion may be seeking to expand its value resources by attacking and acquiring values held by its opponent or to conserve and maintain its own values against acquisition by its opponent. Characterizing objectives in these terms is obviously required by the fundamental policy of the community respecting permissible modes of change. International change in an arena exhibiting in high degree "position scarcity" and "resource scarcity" [145] realistically involves a reallocation of values among the participants concerned, and reallocation commonly means expansion for the one and diminution for the other.[146] It is perhaps just as obvious that this distinction, to be meaningful in determinations of lawfulness, must be considered in conjunction with both the relative consequentiality of the values involved and the degree of coercion employed to acquire or conserve those same values.[147]

In partial reiteration, for the overriding purpose of securing public order in its most elementary sense, basic community policy seeks to protect from destructive unilateral reconstruction those patterns of value allocation that actually exist and manifest at least a minimum degree of stability. Such patterns need not entirely coincide with those which other, less critical, policies and prescriptions, or

145. See id. at 785 note 50.

146. See generally Bloomfield, *Evolution or Revolution? The United Nations and the Problem of Peaceful Territorial Change* (1957); Dunn, *Peaceful Change* (1937); *Peaceful Change* (Manning, ed., 1937).

147. This posing of complementary categories need not imply any rigid dichotomy nor any assumption about the existence of an absolute "zero-line" between conservation and extension, with one party invariably and wholly located on one side of the line and its opponent always and entirely on the other side. "Pure" cases are bound to be few. What matters is the relative position of each party with respect to the other in the particular context considered; differentiation of degrees—with one party so much more conservationist and the other so much more expansionist—is sufficient for the making of practical judgments of policy.

perspectives of "justice and equity," may require. It is not a theme of an international law of human dignity that our inherited distribution of values among peoples accords completely with humanity's noblest conceptions of justice, nor is it an expectation of such an international law that no future wrongs against peoples will be done. The dominant theme is only that both a more just distribution of values and the revindication of future wrongs must be effected by less primitive methods than the destruction of peoples and resources. While in particular cases it may be difficult to draw lines between conservation and revindication, between defense and redress, it is necessary to continue an attempt to make a practical judgment because there is in their impact upon policy a crucial difference, a difference arising from the interposition of the community's elemental interest in minimum order.

Inclusiveness or Exclusiveness

The relative inclusiveness or exclusiveness of the objectives that move a participant may also be relevant in appraising the lawfulness of coercion. Objectives manifest inclusivity to the extent that they admit of widespread participation in the sharing of the values involved, that is, to the extent the values are sought on behalf of other states, or possibly of the entire community of states, as well. Exclusivity, on the other hand, marks objectives which preclude a sharing of the demanded values, with the acting participant seeking unilateral control thereof. Inquiry into the degree of inclusiveness or exclusiveness of belligerent purposes thus entails inquiry into the degree of comprehensiveness of a participant's "self-system" or external structure of identification. But much more than a mechanical counting of heads on each side is involved, for members of a coalition may quite possibly have as little in common as a collective enemy. Objectives of coercion may range from the most exclusive, such as conquest and annexation of the target state, to the most inclusive, such as participation in community peace-enforcement action.[148] The more exclusive a participant's objectives are, that is, the closer their approximation to a program of self-aggrandizement, the less difficult it may be to assess their impact on that fundamental policy which seeks to ensure "that armed force shall not be used, save in the com-

148. Some illustrations are suggested on pp. 16–17 supra.

mon interest." [149] Consideration of relative inclusiveness or exclusiveness may find particular application in appraising the objectives of subsequent participants—participants other than the states originally involved in the conflict situation—who intervene under a claim of collective defense. The legitimate objectives envisaged in the permission of collective defense are inclusive in nature; they comprise a demand for common safety. Appraisal of the objectives of subsequent participants would of course present little difficulty when the organized community had previously achieved, through either of its security organs, a characterization of the original coercion. The aims of later participants may then be measured against the previous characterization for concordance or contrariety, for sustainment or defiance.

THE CONTEXT OF CONDITIONS

We have previously generalized the relevant conditions under which an allegedly unlawful resort to coercion takes place so as to embrace all the variable interacting components of a world power process.[150] The more important factors of fairly obvious significance to our present problem of appraising lawfulness include expectations about the nature of the available technology of violence, and about the relative probabilities of effective community intervention, and the kind of public order demanded by the respective participants.

The expectations of the participant accused of unlawful coercion as to the character of the technology of violence available to, and the relative vulnerability of, itself, its allies, opponents, and potential opponents may partially explain both the participant's objectives and its expectations concerning the necessity and costs of recourse to violence. We have adverted to the capability of some contemporary weapons systems for quick and comprehensive destruction. Possessors of these weapons enjoy an overwhelming advantage over those without them. This disparity makes it difficult to give credence to a claim that violence is necessary to protect the stronger against the weaker participant. In the event of an armed conflict between powers possess-

149. U. N. Charter, Preamble. In the apt words of Lord McNair, force is sought to be "collectivized, denationalized." McNair, "Collective Security," 17 Brit. *Y.B.I.L.* 150, 161 (1936).

150. See pp. 20–7 supra.

ing them, these weapons may conceivably make, under certain present circumstances, surprise and the first strikes "decisive"; they may thus place a considerable premium on an effective capacity to counter an expected blow by an anticipatory thrust.[151] In these and analogous circumstances, to the extent that an imminently impending attack is realistically expected, seizing the initiative in the actual exercise of violence need not be incompatible with perspectives of lawful defense. The same velocity and destructiveness of contemporary weapons, by reducing to a few minutes the time available for accurate ascertainment of an approaching attack and of the identity of the attacker and by correspondingly increasing the need for instant reaction,[152] may further make so-called "accidental war" a significant possibility,[153] a possibility not likely to be reduced by the continuing de-

151. The conference convened at Geneva Nov. 10, 1958, between Western and Communist Powers, for exploring technical means of preventing or detecting surprise attacks, strongly suggests continuing concern over such a possibility. Proposals and counterproposals have been made for specific detection systems against specific weapons that can be used in massive surprise attacks. *N. Y. Times,* Nov. 25, 1958, p. 1, col. 5; id., Nov. 29, 1958, p. 1, cols. 7–8. The factors that contribute to this possibility, that is, that make the effectiveness of both offensive and defensive capabilities sensitive to who strikes first, are ably discussed in Rathjens, "Deterrence and Defense," 14 *Bull. Atomic Scientists* 225 (1958) and Schelling, "Surprise Attack and Disarmament" in *NATO and American Security* 176 (Knorr ed., 1959). See also Brooks, "Surprise in the Missile Era," 11 *Air Univ. Q. Rev.* 76 (1959); Brodie, "The Anatomy of Deterrence," 11 *World Politics* 173 (1959); Phillips, "The Growing Missile Gap," *The Reporter,* Jan. 1959, p. 10; Puleston, "Should the United States Ever Strike the First Blow?," *U.S. News and World Report,* Dec. 13, 1957, pp. 64–6. It does not seem impossible that technological factors of weapons development may overtake cultural perspectives which predispose a nation to accept the "first blow."

152. See Shelton, "Impact of the Ballistic Missile on Defense," in *U.S. Air Force Report on the Ballistic Missile* 127 (Gatz. ed., 1958); Sheridan, "Impact of the Ballistic Missile on Warfare," id. at 139.

153. See Leghorn, "The Problem of Accidental War," 14 *Bull. Atomic Scientists* 205 (1958); Rabinowitz, "Accidental War, Missiles and World Community," id. at 202. The very necessity for maintaining deterrence capabilities tends to increase the possibility of accidents. Wohlstetter, "The Delicate Balance of Terror," 37 *Foreign Aff.* 211, 231 (1959):

> A deterrent strategy is aimed at a rational enemy. Without a deterrent, general war is likely. With it, however, war might still occur.
>
> In order to reduce the risk of a rational act of aggression, we are being forced to undertake measures (increased alertness, dispersal, mobility) which,

velopment of new weapons systems.[154] "Accidental war," understood as violent action impelled by a misapprehension that an attack has been launched, raises problems that may be inescapable in a primitively organized world which lives under the shadow of ever more fearful instruments of destruction.

Common estimations of participants as to the dependability of timely and effective intervention by the organized community, estimates which obviously reflect the degree of organization and integration achieved in the world arena, may have a significant bearing upon the reasonableness of asserted expectations that violence was necessary for self-protection. When the prevailing estimations of the possibility of such intervention are low, there are evident difficulties in requiring a participant to wait very long, in a context of rapidly accelerating coercion, before responding with violence. These expectations also have particular relevance for officials and members of regional security organizations, established precisely because those expectations were low, who must respond to demands for assistance made in the name of collective defense. Furthermore, to tribunals determining the criminal responsibility of particular members of an accused elite, these expectations may present themselves as possible mitigating circumstances.

In a world marked by deep, continuing conflict among differing conceptions or systems of world public order, it is no longer revolutionary to suggest that the kind of public order demanded by a participant charged with unlawful coercion is a factor relevant to a decision on permissibility. The suggestion amounts to this: that decision-makers rationally should take account of the probable effects of various alternative decisions upon the values of the system of world

---

to a significant extent, increase the risk of an irrational or unintentional act of war.

A recent comprehensive but preliminary study explores five categories of events that may precipitate "accidental war": (1) defense systems accidents; (2) human aberrations; (3) unintended spread of limited war; (4) catalytic war; (5) diplomatic and military miscalculations. See Cummins and others, "Accidental War: Some Dangers in the 1960's," reprinted in 106 *Cong. Rec.* 15080, Aug. 12, 1960.

154. Such as the submarine-ballistic-missile complex, as to which see Brinckloe, "Missile Navy," 84 *U.S. Naval Inst. Proc.* No. 2, at 23 (1958); Garthoff, "Sea Power in Soviet Strategy," id. at 85; and the report by Witkin on ballistic missiles capable of being launched from sea and air, *N. Y. Times,* Jan. 14, 1959, p. 12.

order to which they are committed. There is growing recognition that conflict between competing conceptions or demanded systems in fact deeply affects both the prescription and application of policy on recourse to coercion, as on other problems.[155] Clarification of fundamental policy about permissible and impermissible coercion requires clarification of the permissible and impermissible objectives of coercion. Differing conceptions of world order which incorporate different perspectives about law, human nature, and human society, and appropriate patterns for the production and sharing of values, define differently the objectives or occasions that, in terms of each system, legitimate the use of coercion and violence. The Soviet doctrine of "just" and "unjust" war offers an important illustration:

> (a) *Just* wars, wars that are not wars of conquest but wars of liberation, waged to defend the people from foreign attack and from attempts to enslave them, or to liberate the people from

155. Citations to the growing body of relevant literature are collected in Ch. 1, note 108, and McDougal and Lasswell, "The Identification and Appraisal of Diverse Systems of Public Order," 53 *A.J.I.L.* 1 note 1 (1959). See also, Pinto, "International Law and Coexistence," 82 *Journal Du Droit International* 307 (1955); Schwarzenberger, "Scope and Limits of International Legislation," in *Gegenwartsprobleme des Internationalen Rechtes und der Rechtsphilosophie, Festschrift für Rudolf Laun* 65 (1953); Berlia, "International Law and Russo-American Coexistence," 79 *Journal du Droit International* 27 (1952); International Law Assoc., American Branch, "Report of the Committee on Peaceful Co-existence," in *Proceedings and Committee Reports* 85 (1957–1958); International Law Ass'n, N.Y.U. Conference, *Report of the Rapporteur* [Radojkovic] *of the Committee of Co-existence* (1958).

The suggestion made above that probable impact upon values should be considered appears implicit in Professor Goodrich's eloquent warning:

> [T]he United Nations cannot be satisfied with a role which is basically neutral as to values. It must seek to preserve the peace by harmonizing the policies and actions of states, but always on terms which will represent progress toward the achievement of those values for which the United Nations stands. These constitute the life blood of the Organization and unless it is loyal to them, and continually seeks to bring their fulfillment nearer by its actions, it loses its vital force and becomes a piece of lifeless machinery that can easily and properly be dispensed with once it has served or failed to serve its utilitarian purpose.

Goodrich, *The United Nations* 330 (1959). Three pages earlier, Professor Goodrich had observed that "Unlike nationalism, Communism offers as part of its basic ideology the promise of an integrated world community, but the goal to be achieved and the path to it are not those of the Charter." Id. at 327.

capitalist slavery, or, lastly, to liberate colonies and dependent countries from the yoke of imperialism; and

(b) *Unjust* wars, wars of conquest, waged to conquer and enslave foreign countries and foreign nations.[156]

With such differences as to the legitimate purposes of coercion and violence existing,[157] universal consensus on any clarification of policy

156. *History of the Communist Party of the Soviet Union (Bolsheviks), Short Course* 167–8 (ed. Commission of the Central Committee of the C.P.S.U. [B], 1939). In the 1950 sessions of the U.N. General Assembly's Sixth Committee, the Netherlands representative observed that under the above Soviet doctrine, "there would be two fundamentally different concepts of aggression. On the one hand, the [U.N.] Charter forbade a change in the *status quo* brought about by armed force. On the other hand, there was the view that wars could be fought to achieve an ideological purpose." The reply of the Soviet representative was characteristic: "[F]rom the actual description given by the great Lenin and the great Stalin of just, non-aggressive wars, it followed that they were not aggressive wars but wars of liberation, whereas unjust wars were always wars of aggression." U.N. Gen. Ass., *Off. Rec.*, 5th Sess., 6th Comm. 135, 157 (1950).

For a more recent statement, note the speech delivered by Premier Khrushchev at Leipzig on March 7, 1959, where he is reported to have said, after stressing that "the military power of the Communist bloc is greater than that of the 'imperialists' ": "We recognize the right of using strength in dealing with the imperialists. When you talk with the imperialists, morals are not enough. You must be supported by strength." *N. Y. Herald Tribune,* March 8, 1959, p. 14, col. 4.

Lest the contrary impression arise by default, it may be made clear that, in contrast with the quoted Soviet doctrine, we make no proposal for incorporation of a double or multiple standard in the conception of permissible coercion. The policy we recommend is, on the contrary, that of demand for effective universality, for the uniform application to all participants of a basic policy that excludes the acquisition or expansion of values by coercion and violence. In urging the explicit examination of the fundamental public order perspectives of participants, in particular their definitions of the legitimate purposes of coercion, the hope is precisely that decision-makers may thereby escape the double standard which in specific interpretations may be created against those who do not accept as permissible the use of coercion for expansion. We think of the interest to be clarified, the demand for change by noncoercive and nonviolent procedures only, as a general community interest, as the long-term interest of all individual states, and recognize that there must be a promise of reciprocity from states who reject totalitarian conceptions of world order. It does not need elaborate demonstration that this interest has special significance for the newly emergent, the small, or the weak territorial communities who comprise the bulk of the peoples of the world and who cannot even hope by their individual resources to maintain their identities as distinct and self-directed participants in the contemporary arena as against powerful states which may seek self-expansion.

157. In further illustration of such differences, the doctrine of *jihad,* so im-

must seem unlikely except, perhaps, on the level of rhetoric of a sufficiently high order of generality. Furthermore, whatever the consensus achieved on an abstract verbal formulation, differences in specific interpretation and application are to be expected. In point of fact, even a cursory review of the records of the General Assembly and Security Council and of the United Nations committees on defining aggression reveals that both the draft definitions of aggression —in particular, the types of specific indices of aggression and of nonexculpating circumstances—and the specific interpretations of broad prescription in particular cases that have been urged by states projecting totalitarian systems of world order, are constantly designed to enhance the strategies, and promote movement toward the goal values, of their systems. In these circumstances, for decision-makers committed to a system of world order that seeks to honor human dignity either to dismiss as totally irrelevant the probable impact of possible alternative resolutions upon the values embodied in such system, or else to assume a nonexistent universality, may be only to engage in traumatic self-delusion. Even in today's extreme crisis, however, we do not recommend that expansion by violence be held permissible for the half-world or regions or states adhering to nontotalitarian systems of public order. Any violent expansion involves a destruction of values that is, we submit, incompatible with the overriding conception of human dignity.

Any clarification of permissible and impermissible purposes of coercion must obviously be sustained by a certain minimum community of interest and sharing of values. In last resort, all law must depend for its efficacy upon the common interest and shared values of the participants in the arena to be regulated. From the perspective of proclaimed doctrine—postulating an implacable hostility and irreconcilable conflict between the Communist world and the Western

---

portant in traditional Islamic law, may be noted. Islamic law theory divided the world into the *dār al-Islam* (abode or territory of Islam) and the *dār al-harb* (abode or territory of war). *Jihad* imported an obligation upon the Moslem state to transform the latter into the former by war as well as by other means. Khadduri, *War and Peace in the Law of Islam* 51–73 (1955); Khadduri, "International Law," in 1 *Law in the Middle East* 353–4, 359 (Khadduri and Liebesny, ed., 1955). For an authoritative statement of the dynamic contemporary purposes and aspirations projected for the Islamic world, see Nasser, *Egypt's Liberation: The Philosophy of the Revolution* 81–114 (1955).

"bourgeois, capitalist" world, and explicitly envisaging the eventual liquidation of the latter at the most economic speed—a serious question arises whether the necessary community of values remains between leaders and peoples committed to such a doctrine and other peoples.[158] From the more realistic perspective of the conditions that must eventually affect specific demand, however, there may be discernible at least an immediate mutual interest in continued survival. The fundamental import of the conditions of power which, in the contemporary global arena, manifest themselves in a precarious equilibrium of capacity for inflicting fearful destruction, is that the proponents of one system cannot destroy by violence the proponents of the other without bringing their own world to enduring radioactive ruin.[159] As peoples dedicated to freedom maintain this last and nar-

158. See, e.g., Goodman, *The Soviet Design for a World State* (1960); Possony, *A Century of Conflict* (1953); Aaron and Reynolds, "Peaceful Coexistence and Peaceful Cooperation," 4 *Political Studies* 283 (1956); Cottrell and Dougherty, "Hungary and the Soviet Idea of War," 16 *Russian Rev.* No. 4, at 17 (1957); Lissitzyn, "Soviet Interpretation and Application of International Law," 8 *Naval War College Rev.* No. 5, at 33 (1956); Strausz-Hupé, "Protracted Conflict: A New Look at Communist Strategy," 2 *Orbis* 13 (1958); Triska, "A Model for Study for Soviet Foreign Policy," 52 *Am. Pol. Sci. Rev.* 64 (1958). Compare Hula, "The Question of Russian Objectives," in *East-West Negotiations* 52 (Washington Center of Foreign Policy Research, 1958).

In his Leipzig speech, as reported in the *N. Y. Times,* March 8, 1959, p. 3, col. 4, Premier Khrushchev affirmed that "if there is a new war—one could start in a small way—it will end with the downfall of capitalism," and that "even the blind will see what is white and what is black and they will see that for the world there are not two ways but only one way—the way of communism." Premier Khrushchev is here reiterating the theme of systemic revolution which he, Adlai Stevenson reported, had previously expressed:

> You must understand, Mr. Stevenson, that we live in an epoch when one system is giving way to another. When you established your republican system in the eighteenth century, the English did not like it. Now, too, a process is taking place in which the peoples want to live under a new system of society; and it is necessary that one agree and reconcile himself with this fact. The process should take place without interference.

N.Y. Times, Aug. 28, 1959, p. 6, col. 1.

159. The type of situation that may be referred to here has been characterized in terms of "determinate," meaning calculable, but "unlimited" risks associated with the prosecution of "unlimited objectives," that is, objectives "related to survival." See King, "The Rationale of Agreement Between Nuclear Powers —A Method of Analysis," in *East-West Negotiations* 38, 42 (Washington Center

row common ground, they may cherish the hope that others will recognize such common ground and that it may slowly be widened to include sharing of other values sufficient to sustain a common policy against coercion.

THE MODALITIES OF COERCION

In considering the relevance of the methods used by a participant who allegedly has initiated unlawful coercion, it may be recalled that, while armed force has for centuries been the classical instrumentality of coercion between states and still remains the ultimate means of applying the most intense coercion, it is today a commonplace that all instruments of policy—military, ideological, economic, and political—can be and are being used to achieve varying degrees of coercive effect. The burden of the experience of recent decades is that many objectives for which armed force was used in an earlier day may now frequently be realized, or at least substantially facilitated, by highly developed nonmilitary techniques of coercion without open violence. Of principal importance in this connection are the exercises of coercion emphasizing political or ideological instruments, with military instruments in a muted and background role, commonly referred to as "indirect aggression" and frequently described as more dangerous than the "direct" or military type of aggression. A chief characteristic of "indirect aggression" appears to be the vicarious commission of hostile acts by the aggressor state through the medium of third-party groups located within the target state and composed either of foreigners or nationals of the target ostensibly acting on their own initiative.[160] The hostile acts may include the giving of aid and support and, frequently, strategic and tactical direction to rebellious internal groups. The classic postwar case is that of the Greek Communist guerrillas to whom Albania, Bulgaria, Yugoslavia, and Roumania furnished both open military aid and the use of their territory as a base for military operations against the constitutional Greek Government and also as a safe refuge in tactical

---

of Foreign Policy Research, 1958). King suggests that in this situation, negotiations "indicating mutual recognition of the stand off and a mutual resolve not to challenge the *status quo*" might be useful. Id. at 47. The sensitivity and precariousness of the equilibrium is underscored by, e.g., Wohlstetter, "The Delicate Balance of Terror," 37 *Foreign Aff.* 211 (1959).

160. Report of the Secretary-General 72.

defeat.[161] The assistance given to internal groups may frequently assume more covert and subtle forms including the training, exportation, and financing of leaders and specialists in subversion, sabotage, infiltration, fomentation of civil violence, and *coups d'état*. "Indirect aggression," disguised as a purely domestic change,[162] presents peculiar difficulties for external decision-makers. The organized community may suddenly be confronted with a *fait accompli,* as in the case of Czechoslovakia in 1948, which may leave as an alternative to passive acquiescence only the improbable prospect of collective coercion against the victim state in an effort to dislodge the new revolutionary elite. Persuasive evidence of common fear and expectations of the effectiveness of "indirect aggression" may be found not only in the repeated proposals specifically to include condemnation of its use in a definition of aggression but also in declarations of the United Nations General Assembly. In the "Peace through Deeds" Resolution, the General Assembly did "solemnly reaffirm" that "whatever the weapons used, any aggression, whether committed openly, or by fomenting civil strife in the interests of a foreign Power, or otherwise, is the gravest of all crimes against peace and security throughout the world." [163] In a world exhibiting in ever increasing numbers military

161. In Resolution No. 193(III), the General Assembly declared that "the continued aid given by Albania, Bulgaria and Yugoslavia to the Greek guerrillas endangers peace in the Balkans. and is inconsistent with the purposes and principles of the Charter of the United Nations." U.N. Gen. Ass., *Off. Rec.,* 3d Sess., Part I, Resolutions 18, 19 (1948). The Assembly later recommended that all U.N. members and "all other States . . . take into account, in their relations with Albania and Bulgaria, the extent to which those two countries henceforth abide by the recommendations of the General Assembly in their relations with Greece." U.N. Gen. Ass., Res. No. 288(IV), U.N. Gen. Ass., *Off. Rec.,* 4th Sess., Resolution 9 (1949). Detailed findings of fact are contained in the Reports of the U.N. Special Committee on the Balkans; U.N. Gen. Ass., *Off. Rec.,* 3d Sess., Supp. No. 8 (A/574) (1948); U.N. Gen. Ass., *Off. Rec.,* 4th Sess., Supp. No. 8 (A/935) (1949).

162. See, e.g., with respect to capture of Czechoslovakia in 1948, the statements of the Soviet representative in the Security Council invoking Article 2(7) of the U.N. Charter on "domestic jurisdiction" on behalf of the Czech Communist Government. U.N. Sec. Council, *Off. Rec.,* 3d Yr, No. 56, at 2–21 (1948). For exposition of the circumstances surrounding the seizure of power and the techniques employed by the Communists in Czechoslovakia, see the statements of the U.S. representative, id. at 25–33. See also Possony, *A Century of Conflict* 292–5 (1953) and, more generally, Seton-Watson, *The Eastern European Revolution* (1951).

163. Resolution No. 380(V), U.N. Gen. Ass., *Off. Rec.,* 5th Sess., Supp. No. 20

weapons of awesome capability for destruction and in which the possibility of avoiding or limiting the use of such weapons once violence breaks out remains problematical, there is growing awareness that recourse to military force even of the "conventional" type may impose unacceptable risks of grievously exorbitant costs. Consequently, increasingly frequent resort to methods of "indirect aggression" may be anticipated since they provide more economical means of achieving unlawful objectives. The most serious problem confronting adherents to systems of world order which seek to honor freedom may thus be to devise appropriate procedures for identifying and countering unlawful attack disguised as internal change.[164]

(A/1775), at 13 (1950). See also Resolution No. 381(V), id. at 14. Cf. The "Essentials of Peace" Resolution where the Assembly condemned "any threats or acts, direct or indirect, aimed at impairing the freedom, independence or integrity of any State, or at fomenting civil strife and subverting the will of the people in any State." Resolution No. 290(IV), U.N. Gen. Ass., *Off. Rec.*, 4th Sess., Resolutions 13 (1949). See also the formulations achieved by the International Law Commission in the "Draft Code of Offenses Against the Peace and Security of Mankind," Arts. 2(4), 2(5), and 2(6); Report of the International Law Commission, 6th Sess., U.N. Gen. Ass., *Off. Rec.*, 9th Sess., Supp. No. 9 (A/2693), at 11 (1954).

164. This problem of coping with "indirect aggression" presents the difficult task of distinguishing between (a) situations in which there is significant intervention in a factual sense, whatever the precise modalities, by external elites, and (b) rebellion situations which are wholly or primarily of genuinely indigenous initiation and management. This distinction must be attempted because of the differences in the relevant fundamental community policies.

The type of situation in which an external elite attacks a body politic by use of internal agents poses no new policy problem. Highly intense attacks through such instrumentalities, of such impact as to create in the target state a reasonable expectation that it must resort to the military instrument (and, for instance, strike at the bases of operations maintained in the external elite's border zones) to preserve its independence and territorial integrity, are just as inimical to minimum world public order as any other mode of attack. The fact that attacking external principals utilize and receive aid from internal agents merely adds a new dimension to the threat, and neither the target state nor the general community should be required to make too nice discriminations of the degrees of threat from the "outside" and from the "inside." For dealing with this type of situation, all the provisions of the U. N. Charter and other documents referred to above are entirely relevant.

Situations where rebellion is of indigenous stimulation and genuine internal direction pose more difficulty. One of the basic premises of a world arena composed of states is that territorial communities of peoples whose interactions most

In connection with efforts to clarify the meaning of "indirect" or nonmilitary types of aggression, particular proposals have been made for formulating a definition of "economic aggression." Concern for this form of coercion is revealed by a number of proposals; however,

---

directly and immediately affect each other may establish their own internal public order, with whatever specific goal values and implementing institutions they choose. The presumption in favor of "self-determination" by appropriately responsible communities is in substance a presumption in favor of the human rights—the private choice—of individuals. In the increasingly interdependent contemporary world, however, no community lives entirely alone. When the balance of global power teeters precariously between two poles, or a few major centers of concentration, what begins as honest home-grown violence may easily become a spreading conflagration affected with the deepest international interest. In such situations, initial preference for self-direction of lesser communities should of course yield to the necessities of the larger community interest in securing even a minimum of public order. Fortunately, the U. N. Charter affords adequate authority for the continued surveillance of coercion which begins as internal rebellion and for general community intervention when such appears necessary. Note the very broad language of Articles 14 and 34 of the U. N. Charter. Cf., further, the recent United Nations actions in respect of the internal disorders in the Congo, which actions included the organization and dispatch of a United Nations Force for the Congo to the disturbed region. See the first report of the Secretary-General to the Security Council on the Congo situation. *N. Y. Times,* July 19, 1960, p. 4.

In particular instances, it may not, of course, be at all easy to determine whether internal violence is merely disguised external attack or genuine indigenous revolt. Rebellions may be of many different kinds and occur in many differing contexts under varying conditions. The recourse of the responsible decision-makers must again be to systematic and careful examination of all the factors that make up the coercion in its context, at all possible levels of intelligence. The more obvious observation of lines of communication and movements of persons and material may again be supplemented by inquiry into more subtle and covert factors, such as: the relation, if any, of the internal disturbance to claimed world revolutionary movements; the differential allegiance of various internal groups to varying competing systems of world public order; the degree of sharing of power admitted in internal structures of public order; the degree to which internal practices, institutionalized or not, constitute "provocative conditions" by denial of human rights to minorities or even whole populations; and so on. The presumption against general community regulation of indigenous violence is, it must always be recalled, a presumption in favor of human rights. When the factual bases for such presumption are nonexistent or fail, the presumption may, much as in the traditional doctrines of humanitarian intervention, be required to give way to more inclusive policies.

Confusion in discussions of these problems may further arise from failure to

they have tended to be idiosyncratic and are frequently characterized by formidable abstraction and ambiguity. For instance, the draft definition formulated by Bolivia provides in part that:

> 3. . . . unilateral action whereby a state is deprived of economic resources derived from the proper conduct of international trade or its basic economy is endangered so that its security is affected and it is unable to act in its own defense or to cooperate in the collective defense of peace shall likewise be deemed to constitute an act of aggression.[165]

---

distinguish attack by external aggrandizing elites upon a target state, through the medium of internal groups, from assistance to a state, upon request of its constitutional government, in maintaining internal order. In respect of the latter, it is sometimes necessary to recall that traditional international law imposed no prohibition upon the rendering of aid to an independent and duly constituted government, inside its own territory, for quelling internal disturbances and it seems difficult, save perhaps where such government has consistently and ruthlessly denied the most basic human rights to its own people, to find such a prohibition in the U. N. Charter. It was only where rebel groups had been able to maintain prolonged civil strife, waging general hostilities and occupying substantial territory, that some modification of the liberties of the constitutional government was sought under the somewhat elusive customary law doctrines on "belligerency" and "insurgency." See Fitzmaurice, "The General Principles of International Law Considered From the Standpoint of the Rule of Law," 92 *Hague Recueil* 1, 177–9 (1957). The suggestion has on occasion been made that when the stage of substantial success is reached by rebels, provisions of the U.N. Charter (e.g., Article 2(4)) may be supplied to impose comparable limitation upon requests by the *de jure* government for external aid. In this connection, see Wright, "United States Intervention in the Lebanon," 53 *A.J.I.L.* 112, 119–25 (1959). The basic policy at stake is, as indicated above, the preservation of the genuine self-direction of territorial communities and not the restraining of peoples from changing their governments. The long experience under the older "belligerency" and "insurgency" doctrines, however elusive those technical formulations may have been, may possibly afford relevant guidance to contemporary decision-makers who must cope with this problem in appraising the genuineness and degree of internal changes in authority and effective control.

165. U.N. Doc. No. A/AC.66/L.9 (1953). Compare Article 16 of the Charter of the Organization of American States which prohibits "the use of coercive measures of an economic or political character in order to force the sovereign will of another State and obtain from it advantages of any kind." (Text in 46 *A.J.I.L. Supp.* 43, 47 (1952).) Clearly similar to Article 16 of the O.A.S. Charter is Article 2(9) of the "Draft Code of Offenses Against the Peace and Security of Mankind," supra note 163 at 11.

Bolivia's concern over "economic aggression" has not been wholly academic. Dumping of cheap tin on the world markets by the Soviet Union, resulting first

Other proposals include the suggestion of the Afghan representative that closing the "historical trade route of a land-locked country or creating difficulty in the way of free and normal trade and commerce" should be condemned as "economic aggression." [166] The delegate of Pakistan urged that to deprive riparian states of their rights with respect to international rivers was an act of "economic aggression." [167] The most extravagant formulation is that in the Soviet draft which includes "measures of economic pressure violating [another state's] sovereignty and economic independence and threatening the base of its economic life." [168] None of these proposals have met with much enthusiasm, partly because of the fear that their inclusion in a definition of aggression "might suggest the right to go to war in self defense" against "economic aggression." [169] An appropriate application of the principle of proportionality would com-

---

in the downward revision of export quotas under the International Tin Agreement and later in the collapse of price levels, led Bolivia to raise a charge of "economic aggression" against the Soviet Union. Bolivia's economy depends in very considerable measure upon her production of tin. *N. Y. Times,* May 6, 1958, p. 17, col. 3; id., Oct. 2, 1958, p. 29. Bowett, *Self-Defence in International Law* 106 n.3 (1958) cites examples of cases where complaints were made to the Security Council of various forms of "economic aggression."

More recently, Cuba has charged the United States with "economic aggression" for reducing the Cuban sugar quota, representing the share of the United States sugar market normally allotted to Cuban producers. See the statement of the Cuban representative to the U. N. Security Council made on July 18, 1960; *N. Y. Times,* July 19, 1960, p. 8, cols. 1–2. The Security Council referred the Cuban charges to the Organization of American States; id., July 20, 1960, p. 1, col. 4.

166. U.N. Gen. Ass., *Off. Rec.,* 12th Sess., 6th Comm. 50 (1957).

167. Id. at 62.

168. Report of the 1956 Special Committee 30. The items listed in the Soviet draft as constituting "economic aggression" and "ideological aggression," as well as most of the nonexculpating circumstances specified are, of course, designed to serve the purposes of political warfare.

Still another illustration of the type of proposal that has been made, formally or informally, in respect of "economic aggression," is the suggestion of the Syrian representative in the 1953 Special Committee that: "If a great Power made exorbitant demands in return for the assistance it gave to a weak nation, it was acting contrary to the spirit of the Charter. When those demands threatened the independence of the country concerned, they amounted to aggression." Report of the 1953 Special Committee 25.

169. Report of the 1956 Special Committee 8; see also Report of the 1953 Special Committee 27.

monly rule out "war" or extensive violence as a legitimate response to economic coercion which, in many contexts, may be merely of the kind and level inescapable in the ordinary relations of states. Yet, however tendentious and destructive of initiative and freedom in ordinary intercourse these proposals may be, their very submission reflects a recognition that, with the development and refinement of methods of economic warfare, the flow of goods and services in the international arena can be so managed as to inflict a substantial measure of coercion upon a target state and that, with increasingly tight economic interdependences, the vulnerability of most states to economic coercion tends to increase.

Awareness of the potentialities of all instruments of coercion may indicate that what is of particular importance for decision-makers is not the specific modality or even combinations of modalities employed, considered in typological abstraction, but rather the level and scope of intensity achieved by the employment of any one or more modalities in whatever combination or sequence. The relevance of the kinds of instruments utilized by a participant is rather limited: it lies primarily in the rough and ready indication—precise quantification not presently being practicable—which it affords, first, of the level of coercion being applied, second (in equally gross terms), of the relative proportionality of the response in coercion, and, third (though indirectly), of the nature and comprehensiveness of the participant's subjectivities.

THE EFFECTS SECURED

Dimensions of Coercion

That the effects achieved by the employment of coercion constitute a factor of the highest relevance for a determination of lawfulness requires only brief demonstration. Community policy addresses itself not to objectives and intentions as psychological phenomena alone but rather to such objectives and intentions in action, to their materialization in concrete relations between peoples, to the impact of the coercive pursuit of such purposes upon value processes in the world of time and space. We principally refer to the intensity and magnitude of the coercion—its consequences upon the values of the target state—actually achieved in the process alleged to have been initiated unlawfully. Just as in the appraisal of the consequentiality of objectives, the most comprehensive and detailed appraisal of the consequentiality of the achieved coercion involves consideration of factors like the number and kinds of values of which the target state is deprived, the relative importance of these values to the target state, and the scope of value deprivations, including both the geographical range and temporal dimension of the damage. The spectrum of possible degrees of consequentiality is obviously a very wide one.

From perspectives either of realistic descriptions of the past or of projections into the probable future, it will be seen that not every intensity and magnitude of coercion may be characterized as impermissible, whether the purpose be to specify the appropriate precipitating event for lawful recourse to the military instrument in self-defense, or to initiate coercive repression by the organized community, or to impose criminal punishment upon particular individuals. As has been suggested before, a certain degree of coercion is inevitable in states' day-to-day interactions for values. Fundamental community policy does not seek to reach and prohibit this coercion, as indeed it cannot without attempting to impose moral perfection, not to mention social stagnation, on humanity.

There remains the problem of clarifying the intensity and magnitude of coercion that, for varying purposes, may appropriately be characterized as impermissible. The discussions in the United Nations committees on aggression show increasing awareness of the need for clarification. "To constitute aggression," the delegate from Iran stated, "the use of force must be sufficiently serious; otherwise the door would be open to dangerous abuses by States claiming to be acting in self-defense." [170] The Iraqi representative was even more

170. U.N. Doc. No. A/C.6/SR.405, at 3 (1954). The Iranian representative was here echoing what the de Brouckère Report of 1926 had observed:

> Every act of violence does not necessarily justify its victim in resorting to war. If a detachment of soldiers goes a few yards over the frontier in a colony remote from any vital centre . . . then it cannot be maintained that . . . the invaded country has *reasonable grounds* for mobilising its army and marching upon the enemy capital. . . . [The invaded country] could not be so released [from its obligations under the League Covenant] unless it were the victim of a *flagrant aggression of such a serious character that it would obviously be dangerous not to retaliate at once.*

Documents of the Preparatory Commission For the Disarmament Conference, League of Nations, Series III, at 101 (1927). (Emphasis added.)

Cf. the effort to clarify a distinction between a "frontier incident" listed as a nonexculpating circumstance in the Litvinov-Politis definitions and an "act

explicit in explaining that, under his country's draft definition, which took account of "both the purpose and the effect of the act in question," "the material factor was the gravity of the act, judged by its scale and intensity." [171] Similarly, in the 1956 Special Committee, the Netherlands proposed that the Committee dedicate itself to clarifying "armed attack" as used in Article 51 of the Charter. The Netherlands representative stressed that "the place of Article 51 in Chapter VII indicated clearly that small-scale hostilities connected with border incidents fell outside the scope of that Article," and that the "crucial problem" was "to find the criterion distinguishing armed attack from any other use of force, which did not entitle the [target] State to take the action provided for in Article 51." [172]

The Critical Intensities of Coercion—The Test of Impact Upon Expectations

In indicating the resulting levels of coercion that are of crucial importance for the application of community policy, it is necessary to refer to a continuum of degrees of coercion, extending from the mildest through an ascending scale of intensity and scope to the most intense. Coercion located at the upper ranges of this hypothetical scale of scope and intensity presents little difficulty. Open and extensive military violence inflicting substantial destruction upon both peoples and resources, the principal constituent bases of state power, clearly represents a prohibited intensity of coercion. The sudden unilateral intensification to such high intensities of a process in which coercion had been at the ordinary minimum level justifies, almost by definition, a reaction on the part of the target state with war in self-defense. The handful of cases in which the League of Nations achieved an explicit determination of impermissibility involved highly destructive uses of the military instrument: the Chaco War,[173]

---

of aggression," made in the Report of the Secretary-General 62: "[T]he first salient feature to note is that [a frontier incident] is on a small physical scale, the forces involved being too slight to enable an invasion or attack to be carried out. This criterion, however, would not be a very strict one: What amount of force would have to be used to constitute something which was no longer an incident but an aggression?"

171. Report of the 1956 Special Committee 22.

172. Id. at 24.

173. Upon the acceptance by Bolivia and rejection by Paraguay of the formal recommendations of the League Assembly for the settlement of the Chaco dis-

the Sino-Japanese (Manchurian) War,[174] the Italo-Abyssinian War,[175] and the Soviet-Finnish War.[176] Similarly, most of the cases arising after 1945 in which either Article 2(4) or 39 of the Charter was explicitly or implicitly invoked, whether in their submission or in the proposals and decisions concerning them, involved overt and substantial uses of armed force: the Indonesian (II), the Palestinian, the Korean, the Guatemalan, the Suez, and Hungarian cases.[177] Of course, the cases of coercion dealt with and penalized by both the Nuremberg and Tokyo International Military Tribunals were principally cases of the most severe and extensive armed hostilities. The reference of such descriptive words as "substantial" and "extensive," in terms of particular quanta of military force, may of course be variable,[178] inasmuch as they are a function of, among other things, the fighting capability of both the attacking and the target states.

---

pute, the Assembly recommended that the arms embargo, which had previously been imposed as against both parties, be lifted for the benefit of Bolivia and maintained against Paraguay. See League of Nations, *Off. J.*, Spec. Supp. No. 133, at 49 (1935); id., Spec. Supp. No. 134, at 56–57; id., Spec. Supp. No. 135, at 22, 26.

174. See id., Spec. Supp. No. 112, at 22 (1933), where the Assembly adopted unanimously (Japan's negative vote was not counted; there was one abstention) the Lytton Report finding Japan responsible for resorting to war in violation of the League Covenant. The text of the Report is found in id. at 56–76.

175. See League of Nations, *Off. J.*, 16th Yr, 1223–5 (1935).

176. See League of Nations, *Off. J.*, 20th Yr, 505–8, 531–41 (1939).

177. See 2 *Repertory of Practice of United Nations Organs* 334–8 (1955).

178. At Tokyo, in reply to the indictment charging aggression by Japan against the Soviet Union in the Lake Khassan (1938) and Khalkin Gol (1939) areas, the defense contended that the operations in both these areas were mere "border incidents caused by uncertainty as to the boundaries." In the Lake Khassan area, the Japanese attacked first with "a small number of troops probably not exceeding one company," and later with "the main forces of one division." The fighting continued for about two weeks and resulted in the Japanese troops being "practically wiped out." The tribunal stated that "the attack having been planned and undertaken with *substantial forces* cannot be regarded as a mere clash between border patrols." *Judgment of the International Military Tribunal for the Far East* 833–4 (1948). (Emphasis added.) The fighting at the Khalkin Gol area was described by the tribunal as being on an "extensive scale," with aircraft, artillery, and tanks being committed, and resulting in more than 50,000 casualties for the Japanese and 9,000 for the Soviet Union. The tribunal again rejected the defense that the fighting was no more than a "border incident." Id. at 840. In both cases, the objective of the Japanese forces was shown to be seizure of strategically important territory.

As the level of coercion under consideration moves away from the upper extreme toward the lower end of the putative scale of intensity and scope,[179] when, in other words, a process of accelerating coercion has not reached the stage of open and extensive violence, the problem assumes some complexity. Despite the focus upon applications of armed force in Article 2(4) of the Charter, severe destructive uses of the military instrument do not exhaust the competence of the community to intervene with appropriate police measures. A sufficiently flexible test of the crucial intensity and scope may be reached, we suggest, by considering the impact of the coercion exercised upon the expectation structure of the target state. In these terms, the key effect is creation in the target state of reasonable expectations, as third-party observers may determine reasonableness, that it must forthwith respond with exercises of military force if it is to maintain its primary values, customarily described as "territorial integrity and political independence." If the coercion brought to bear by whatever modality or combination of modalities (falling short of open and extensive violence) is of such order and proportions as reasonably to bring about expectations in the target state of the insufficiency of nonmilitary countermeasures and of an immediate necessity for a military response, our submission is that a characterization of such coercion as impermissible may appropriately be made.[180] When this stage is reached in a developing process of coercion, to require the target

179. Contexts located at the lower extreme of the hypothetical scale may perhaps be illustrated by the Spanish Question. In that case, the subcommittee created by the U. N. Security Council reported that, since no "threat to peace," no "breach of the peace," and no "act of aggression" had been established, the Council had no jurisdiction to require or authorize enforcement measures against the Franco regime, but that a "potential threat to the peace" might be found. See U.N. Sec. Council, *Off. Rec.,* 1st Yr, 1st series, Spec. Supp. 1–12 (1946). Whatever coercion existed was largely of the order of a "moral affront" arising from the disreputable origin and activities of the Franco government.

180. Cf. the specification, proposed by the Netherlands representative, of the intensity of military coercion that would warrant determination of an "armed attack" for purposes of Article 51 of the U. N. Charter, in Report of the 1956 Special Committee 24–5. See also the statements of the same representative in Report of the 1953 Special Committee 20; Pompe, *Aggressive War: an International Crime* 111 (1953). Both Dr. Pompe and the Netherlands representative, however, limited the reference of aggression to coercion by *military* instruments; obviously, we make no such postulation about the types of instruments by which coercion may be accelerated to such an intensity.

state to delay its reaction further may be to compel it to forego effective defense and submit to its own destruction. At this stage, conditions of fact, high expectations of impending violence, will have been generated, requiring immediate intervention by the organized community to prevent the consummation of the attacking state's objectives. Before this stage is reached, the destructive use of armed force would, by application of the proportionality principle, be precluded *per definitionem* as a legitimate response. In such anterior stages, collective coercive measures, as distinguished from collective conciliation, by the organized community may be both improbable and impolitic. The location of the crucial stage in any particular process of coercion or the determination of the reasonableness of the target state's expectations as to the need for reacting with military force must clearly depend in large measure upon an appraisal of the other factors detailed above. With specific reference to contexts of "indirect aggression," the capabilities of the target state appraised in such terms as the strength of its internal authority and control structures, the stability or vulnerability of its economic basis, its military power resources, and the ideological cohesiveness or homogeneity of its people, may be of special importance.

The clearest and most common illustration of impermissible intensities is that involving a serious direct threat of an imminent, large-scale, military attack, such as that employed by Nazi Germany against Austria, Czechoslovakia, and Denmark in 1938–1940.[181] The possible scope of application of the recommended test of intensity need not, however, be limited to contexts in which the target state is put under the apprehension that intensifying coercion is about to culminate in hostile armed violence. The thrust of contemporary concern about "indirect aggression," "economic aggression," and so on, is that the skillful management and combination of economic, ideological and diplomatic strategies, against a background and implicit threat of military violence, may achieve degrees of coercion that leave no effective alternative to the target state but a military strike (alone or with its allies). The cumulative intensity or value consequences of the coercion applied rather than the particular modality or modalities of application is of primary significance for legal policy; the modality need not be a conclusive index to the de-

181. See the judgment of the International Military Tribunal at Nuremberg, *Nazi Conspiracy and Aggression, Opinion and Judgment* 21–7, 38 (1947).

gree of intensity actually secured. In many and perhaps most contexts, economic, political, and ideological measures may result only in relatively low-level coercion calling for denial of reciprocities or for impositions of retaliation other than the application of extensive military force. In some contexts, however, they may in fact be so intense and swiftly effective as to preclude successful resistance on the part of the target state.[182]

182. A conception of aggression limited to aggression by overt military means assumes that coercion emphasizing other instruments of policy may not in any context present the same danger to territorial integrity and independence that armed violence may. This assumption is as unnecessary as it may be hazardous. Cf. the point well stressed in Bowett, *Self-Defence in International Law* 24 (1958):

> [W]hen the delict does not involve force or the threat of force, it would similarly seem arbitrary to deny to the defending state the right to use force in defence of its rights as a matter of fixed principle. . . . [T]here is something to be said for the view that economic or ideological aggression can be as detrimental to a state's security and, if illegal, as dangerous a violation of the state's essential rights as the use or threat of force. The relevance of any distinction between delicts involving force and those not so doing lies, in our submission, in the requirement of proportionality. The use of force as a reaction to a delict not involving force will scarcely ever be "proportionate," but there is no rule of law to say it can never be so. . . .

To accept Dr. Bowett's position is not to open a Pandora's box of real as distinguished from supposed evils. The tests of "necessity" and "proportionality" are not in any greater degree susceptible of abuse here than in other contexts, if the reviewing decision-makers desire to safeguard them from subverting misuse. Susceptibility to abuse is a common property of all legal standards and rules.

To the above suggestion that a response with armed force to coercion which has not assumed the form of overt military violence may, in certain contexts exhibiting the crucial intensity, be reasonable and appropriate, objection is occasionally raised also upon the ground that, the conditions of the contemporary arena being what they are, especially with the growing diffusion of the techniques of nuclear destruction, global or general war may result from such defensive armed action. One difficulty with this argument is that it may prove too much. A military response to coercion which has in fact taken the shape of open violence presents the same possibility of a spreading conflagration and expanding destruction, but it has never been seriously contended that, in such case, armed responding coercion may not lawfully be exercised. It would seem very difficult to suppose that that possibility is overwhelmingly greater in the first than in the second type of situation.

In final comment, the alternative to the suggestion made above—that is, to reject a right of self-defense in any and all contexts not exhibiting overt vio-

ACCEPTANCE OR REJECTION OF COMMUNITY PROCEDURES

Still another factor of some relevance to judgments about the lawfulness of coercion is the relative willingness of the contending participants to accept community procedures for the cessation of hostilities already begun and for the nonviolent settlement of the underlying dispute. That this factor *is* relevant has long been recognized. It was in fact adopted as a test of aggression in a number of conventions drafted under the auspices of the League of Nations, all of which conventions, however, failed of ratification. The Geneva Protocol of 1924, for instance, required the League Council to enjoin an armistice upon the belligerents and prescribed that any belligerent refusing to accept the armistice or violating its terms "shall be deemed an aggressor" against whom sanctions were to be applied.[183] Similarly, the 1931 General Convention for Improving the Means of Preventing War raised a prima facie presumption of responsibility for aggression—"resort to war" within the meaning of Article 16 of the League Covenant—against the party failing to comply with provisional measures ordered by the Council.[184] The United Nations Charter, while also expressly recognizing the relevancy of this factor, is less mechanical in its terms. The Security Council is authorized, for the purpose of preventing "an aggravation of the situation," to call upon the parties concerned to comply with provisional measures,

---

lence and even against the most intense uses of nonmilitary instruments—may, under the same conditions of the present world, amount to requiring a target state to assume a suicidal posture.

183. Art. 10; League of Nations, *Off. J.*, Spec. Supp. No. 24, at 136, 138–9 (1924). It may be noted that in the summary of "factors [which] may provide the elements of a just decision" about aggression drawn by a Special Committee of the Temporary Mixed Commission For the Reduction of Armaments, there was included: "(e) Refusal of either of the parties to withdraw their armed forces behind a line or lines indicated by the Council." Commentary on the Definition of a Case of Aggression, League of Nations, *Off. J.*, Spec. Supp. No. 16, at 184–5 (1923). The formulation proffered by Professor Wright in 1935 turned wholly upon this factor of refusal to accept an armistice. Wright, "The Concept of Aggression in International Law," 29 *A.J.I.L.* 373, 395 (1935). In 1957, he spoke of a "strong presumption" of lawfulness arising when a state "has indicated willingness to accept a cease-fire order of a United Nations organ. . . ." Wright, "The Legality of Intervention Under the United Nations Charter," 51 *Proc. Am. Soc. I.L.* 79, 87 (1957).

184. Art. 5; League of Nations, *Off. J.*, Spec. Supp. No. 93, at 242 (1931).

including not only "cease fires," truces, and armistices but also arrangements for the withdrawal of armed forces from particular areas and the establishment of demilitarized zones, and to "take account of failure to comply with such provisional measures." [185] The 1950 General Assembly resolution on the "Duties of States in the event of the Outbreak of Hostilities" [186] offers still further acknowledgment that attitudes toward community intervention may be of help in determinations of responsibility. The resolution recommended that each participant promptly and publicly declare its readiness, upon assurances of reciprocity, to "discontinue all military operations and withdraw all its military forces" that have entered the territory of another; and provided that such a declaration, or a failure to make one, may "be taken into account in any determination of responsibility for the breach of the peace or act of aggression in the case under consideration and in all relevant proceedings before the appropriate organs of the United Nations." The practices of both the Security Council and the General Assembly offer at least a few instances in which failure to comply with provisional measures appears to have been weighed in characterizing coercion as impermissible. These include the condemnation of the attack by North Korea against the Republic of Korea,[187] the designation of the People's Re-

185. U. N. Charter, Art. 40. See also Art. 7 of the Inter-American Treaty of Reciprocal Assistance (Rio Pact) of 1947; text in Sub-Committee on Disarmament, Senate Committee on Foreign Relations, *Disarmament and Security: A Collection of Documents 1919–55*, 84th Cong., 2d Sess., 651 (1956).

186. Resolution No. 378(V), U.N. Gen. Ass., *Off. Rec.*, 5th Sess., Supp. No. 20 (A/1775), at 12–13 (1950).

187. In its Resolution of June 25, 1950, the Security Council called "for the immediate cessation of hostilities" and called "upon the authorities of North Korea to withdraw forthwith their armed forces to the 38th parallel." U.N. Sec. Council, *Off. Rec.*, 5th Yr, No. 15, at 13–14 (1950). In its June 27, 1950 Resolution, the Council "noted . . . that the authorities in North Korea have neither ceased hostilities nor withdrawn their armed forces to the 38th parallel. . . ." Id. No. 16, at 4. See also the statement of the Belgian representative in U.N. Gen. Ass., *Off. Rec.*, 5th Sess., 1st Comm. (412th mtg.), p. 419 (1950): "Secondly, as the Yugoslav representative had pointed out in the Security Council, the behaviour of the two opposing parties must be taken into account. While the Government of the Republic of Korea had appealed to the United Nations at the outbreak of hostilities and had accepted in principle the cease-fire order of the Security Council, the Government of North Korea had simply declared that

public of China as an aggressor in Korea,[188] and the determination of the existence of a "threat to the peace" in Palestine.[189]

The significance of relative willingness to accept community intervention is principally derived from the indication it gives of the real as distinguished from the ostensible objectives sought by a participant. Just as conduct subsequent to agreement is commonly honored in principles of treaty interpretation, conduct subsequent to the initiation of coercion is relevant in gauging the realistic subjectivities of the contending states. The special application of this principle here is that a refusal to observe an order addressed to both parties to cease using violence is inconsistent with a professed purpose merely to maintain and defend one's own values. Conversely, a willingness to cease hostilities is evidence of good faith and negates an imputed objective to expand values by violent means. When a participant charged with unlawfully initiating coercion accepts and implements arrangements for cessation of hostilities, it removes the necessity for defense expressly or tacitly pleaded by the opposing participant. Accordingly, if the latter rejects these arrangements, it tends to show that the asserted necessity was unreal in the first place. Disregard of provisional measures, however, does not offer conclusive indication of the unlawful character of a participant's objectives. The initial attacks may, in a particular situation, have created a serious

---

the Security Council's order was illegal. The Government of the USSR and the Central People's Government of the People's Republic of China had maligned that order in their Press and ignored it officially for two months, all the while chanting the praises of the army of North Korea for its victories."

188. Resolution No. 498(V), U.N. Gen. Ass., *Off. Rec.*, 5th Sess., Supp. No. 20A (A/1775/Add. 1) (1951). In this resolution, the Assembly noted "that the Central People's Government of the People's Republic of China has not accepted United Nations proposals to bring about a cessation of hostilities in Korea with a view to peaceful settlement. . . ."

189. Resolution of July 15, 1948; U.N. Sec. Council, *Off. Rec.*, 3d Yr, Supp. for July at 76 (1948). The Council, in this resolution, "[took] into consideration that the Provisional Government of Israel has indicated its acceptance in principle of a prolongation of the truce in Palestine; that the states members of the Arab League have rejected successive appeals of the United Nations Mediator and of the Security Council . . . for the prolongation of the truce in Palestine . . . ," ordered a cease-fire, and declared that "failure by any of the Governments or authorities concerned to comply . . . would demonstrate the existence of a breach of the peace within the meaning of Article 39. . . ."

imbalance of power or placed the target state in a specially vulnerable strategic position with respect to the attacking state, a position or imbalance which may be frozen by the imposition of a "cease fire" or truce. In the absence of international armed forces able effectively and decisively to aid the complying party in redressing such a disadvantage in the event that hostilities are resumed, failure to comply promptly with provisional measures called for by the organized community need not always be incompatible with perspectives of defense.[190] Response to provisional measures must, like all other factors, be appraised in conjunction with every other factor.

EXPECTATIONS ABOUT EFFECTIVENESS OF DECISION

The final item in the constellation of relevant factors of which explicit mention may be made is the state of expectations of decision-makers as to the degree of conformity that probably can be secured to a particular demanded decision. This factor, of special significance to officials of international security organizations, is frequently a function of the officials' calculations of the degree of common responsibility and the amount of effective power that realistically can and will be organized to sustain a characterization of impermissibility if one is made, as well as of their expectations about the probable costs of an application, or nonapplication, of policy.[191] That this factor does in fact bear upon decisions to characterize or to refrain from characterizing impermissible coercion [192] obviously reflects the still rudimentary degree of effective organization which the general community of states has achieved and the dependence of the organized community upon the bases of power made available to it by member states.

190. Cf. Pompe, *Aggressive War: an International Crime* 96–7 (1953). See the discussions preceding the adoption by the General Assembly of the Resolution on "Duties of States Upon the Outbreak of Hostilities" (note 186 supra). U.N. Gen. Ass., *Off. Rec.,* 5th Sess., 1st Comm., 249–81 et passim (1950).

191. Some illustration is offered in Ch. 1, notes 113–15 and accompanying text. See also Goodrich, *The United Nations* 164–8, 176–88 (1959).

192. It also bears upon the prospects of securing substantial consensus upon any particular formulation of prohibited coercion. Among the arguments presented against "defining aggression" was that "the international situation had placed greater emphasis on the functions of conciliation and mediation of the United Nations rather than on the coercive function. Member states were reluctant to undertake collective military action for fear of provoking a third

PART II: THE CONCEPTION OF PERMISSIBLE COERCION

As indicated above, the conception of permissible coercion may usefully be assigned a threefold reference. First, there is a relatively low-level coercion which is "normal" and perhaps ineradicable in the ordinary value processes taking place across state boundaries and which includes all coercion not accelerated to the levels of intensity and magnitude that signal impermissible coercion. Secondly, there is the coercion of relatively great scope and intensity, including the most intense and extensive violence, that is exercised in necessary response to and defense against impermissible coercion by others. Lastly, there are police measures of varying degrees of comprehensiveness and intensity applied by or under the authorization of the organized community of states.

Admittedly, various specific acts encompassed in the first type of coercion, "ordinary coercion," may constitute international wrongs other than aggression which legitimatize responses in the form of denying reciprocities and imposing retaliations other than destructive uses of the military instrument. Such acts may contravene community prescriptions and policies other and less fundamental than those concerned with the securing of minimum public order and the promotion of peaceful modalities of international change, and entail "legal consequences" differing from those we have detailed above.[193]

world war." Report of the Sixth Committee, U.N. Gen. Ass., *Off. Rec.*, 12th Sess., Annexes, Agenda Item 54, at 3 (1957).

193. In referring to such coercive acts as "permissible," we do so only in the sense that they do not assume the intensity and dimensions requiring application of international prescriptions about aggression and self-defense. We do not intend to suggest that such coercive acts may not appropriately by characterized by an arbitral tribunal, for instance, as unlawful, "tortious," or "internationally delinquent" acts in requiring, for instance, financial indemnification, as to which, see, e.g., 1 Schwarzenberger, *International Law* cc. 31–36 (3rd ed., 1957). Cf. the distinction well expressed in Fitzmaurice, "The Foundations of the Authority of International Law and the Problem of Enforcement," 19 *Modern L. Rev.* 1, 5 (1956):

> It is not against law-breaking as such that [U. N. Charter provisions] . . . are directed, but against that particular type of law-breaking that takes the form of an act of aggression or of committing a breach of the peace. Now it is possible to violate a large part of international law in all sorts of different ways, and to commit breaches of treaties right and left, without ever

We focus in subsequent discussion upon the second and third references of permissible coercion.

The specific contexts of interstate conflict which may confront authoritative decision-makers commonly include both measures of coercion and measures of counter or opposing coercion. These processes of coercion and counter coercion give rise to opposed claims that, on the one hand, the coercion applied is unlawful,

---

having recourse to aggression or breaking the peace or even threatening a breach of the peace.

It is also a source of confusion in relevant community policy that lesser deprivations or minor interferences are sometimes assimilated to greater deprivations or major interferences under labels as encompassing as "intervention." The literature frequently fails to make indispensable distinctions. E.g.: the facts of state interaction are not distinguished from the responses of established decision-makers in application of authority to such interaction; among facts, beneficial interdetermination is not differentiated from detrimental interference (as benefit or detriment may be assessed by a third-party observer or decision-maker); among detrimental interferences, major assaults upon indispensable bases of power are not distinguished from minor injury to local pride and sensibility; and among claimed lawful responses to injurious interference, unilateral reprisal for primarily exclusive purposes is not differentiated from general community measures in support of inclusive policies. See, e.g., Gould, *An Introduction to International Law,* 596–7, c. 19 passim (1957); Thomas and Thomas, *Non-Intervention* (1956); Lador-Lederer, "General Report on Zenith and Decay of the Doctrine of Non-Intervention of States in the Internal Affairs of Other States," 59th *Int. Cong. Comp. Law* (Brussels, 1958).

The principles we consider in this chapter are those designed to assist in identifying the major deprivations and in clarifying the conditions under which coercive responses, of differing institutional modality, may be appropriate with regard to community policy for securing basic order. Comprehensive consideration and identification of all possible types of lesser deprivation and of the remedies appropriate for them would take us beyond reasonable compass. It may suffice to register that we share the common view that the prescriptions and policies embodied in the U. N. Charter forbid the unilateral use of force and violence by way of reprisal for lesser wrongs or "tortious" conduct. See, e.g., Bowett, *Self-Defence in International Law* 13–14 (1958); Brierly, *The Law of Nations* 324–6 (5th ed., 1955); Waldock, "The Regulation of the Use of Force by Individual States in International Law," 81 *Hague Recueil* 455, 493 (1952). The overwhelming common interest in basic order, and the exorbitant potential costs of exercises of force by contemporary weapons, would appear to counterbalance losses states may occasionally incur from lesser wrongs left inadequately redressed because of deficiencies in available remedial procedures or the limited ability of a poorly organized community to create effective remedies for all wrongs.

initiating coercion and that, on the other, the coercion is lawful self-defense. When the respective contending participants are viewed in turn, each may be seen commonly to assert both claims simultaneously: that its opponent has unlawfully initiated coercion and that it is itself responding with coercion in self-defense. Obviously, an external decision-maker must make coordinated inquiry into and assessment of both the coercion claimed to be prohibited aggression and the coercion claimed to be permissible defense. The theme of complementarity is thus a dominant one manifesting itself both in the contraposition of claims asserted in practice and in the necessities of rational analysis by decision-makers.

Self-Defense Distinguishable From Other Exercises of Coercion

For clarity in thought, that coercion which is claimed to be in defense against unlawful attack or threat against independence or territorial integrity must be distinguished sharply from certain other types of asserted coercion which differ greatly in modality, purpose, specific context, and relevant community policy but which also are frequently put forward under the name of self-defense. The claims with which we are primarily concerned here are claims to exercise highly intense coercion in response to what is alleged to be unlawfully initiated coercion. The other distinguishable types of assertions include claims by one belligerent that it is lawful to apply coercion against a nonparticipant state in response to or anticipation of some operation by the opposing belligerent in the nonparticipant's territory. They also include claims to exercise, for varying purposes, limited and occasional jurisdiction over portions of the oceans and the superincumbent airspace.

CLAIMS OF SELF-DEFENSE

The first type—claims to employ highly intense coercion in defense against allegedly impermissible coercion—may be conveniently subcategorized according to the imminence and intensity of the coercion to which response is to be made. Most conspicuous perhaps are claims to respond with force to intense coercion that is immediate and current and that may be of varying degrees of comprehensiveness and continuity. Such is the claim which a target state makes when reacting violently to military blows initiated and delivered against it; the United States' declaration of war following the attack by

Japanese air forces on Pearl Harbor is a familiar example.[194] Claims to resort to force in anticipation and prevention of intense coercion are only slightly less prominent. The coercion anticipated may, in the expectations of the claimant, be of varying degrees of imminence or remoteness. Claims have been made, for instance, to initiate pre-emptive violence under allegedly high expectations of imminent or impending military attack. Israel's claim that its invasion of Egyptian territory in 1956 was defensive in character being, among other things, in anticipation of an "all-out attempt to eliminate Israel by force" [195] presents one contemporary illustration. The notion of anticipatory defense has at times been given extravagant unilateral interpretation by claimant states. In the past, states have asserted claims to pre-empt and counter by armed force not only imminently expected eruptions of military violence but also more or less remote possibilities of attack. They have asserted, in other words, the need to preclude a context of "conditions which, if allowed to develop, might become in time a source of danger." [196] What states have in effect

194. The U.S. declaration referred to "the Imperial Government of Japan [having] committed unprovoked acts of war against the Government and the people of the United States of America." 55 Stat. 795 (1941).

195. See the statements of the Israeli representative in the General Assembly. U.N. Gen. Ass., *Off. Rec.,* 1st Emer. Spec. Sess. 61 (1956). The "inherent right of self-defense" was explicitly invoked by the same representative. Id. at 22–3.

196. Fenwick, *International Law* 231 (3d ed., 1948). Claims of this type were most prominent in the eighteenth and nineteenth centuries and are of course to be viewed in the context of the system of power balancing that prevailed in the Europe of those eras. Such claims were frequently justified by the claimants in terms of maintenance of equilibrium. The assumption was basic in such system of power balancing that conditions which resulted in marked preponderance of power of one participant were conditions of potential danger to all the other participants in the arena. See Liska, *International Equilibrium* c. 1 (1957); Wright, "The Prevention of Aggression," 50 *A.J.I.L* 514, 516–17 (1956). Secretary of State Elihu Root spoke of the struggle to preserve the balance of power in Europe as depending upon the principle that affirms "the right of every sovereign state to protect itself by preventing a condition of affairs in which it will be too late to protect itself." Root, "The Real Monroe Doctrine," in *Addresses on International Subjects* 105, 111 (Bacon and Scott, ed., 1916).

It need not be supposed, however, that such claims, or analogous ones, have entirely departed from the international arena. See, for instance, the Soviet attempt to justify its invasion of eastern Poland in 1939 on the basis, among others, of self-defense. Ginsburgs, "A Case Study in the Soviet Use of International Law: Eastern Poland in 1939," 52 *A.J.I.L.* 69, 75–6 (1958). See also the

claimed in these assertions, sometimes under an invocation of "self-preservation," is a competence forcibly to protect their values by forestalling processes which, they argue, may in the future develop into highly intense coercion or violence. Hence they seek to strike while these processes still embody only a low level of coercion.

ASSERTIONS OF COERCION AGAINST THIRD STATES

Claims by a belligerent to use force against a third state—a non-participant in the original conflict—in order to prevent or counter some anticipated hostile operation by the opposing belligerent in the territory of the third state, have been made under differing words: "self-defense," "self-preservation," "right of necessity," "necessity in self-preservation" and so on. The force employed against the third state under these assertions has varied widely in intensity, scope, and continuity, from isolated acts to full-scale invasion and occupation of the third state's territory. The classic illustration of a single limited application of force was the seizure of the Danish fleet in 1807 by British naval forces, following a severe bombardment of Copenhagen, to prevent acquisition of the fleet by Napoleon.[197] A comparable instance arose in 1940 when the British destroyed the French fleet at Mers-el-Kebir and Oran to preclude capture of the fleet by German forces.[198] Assertion of more comprehensive claims of this type may be documented by reference to the German invasions of Belgium in World War I and of Norway in World War II. In 1914, in its ultimatum demanding permission for German troops to march through Belgium, Germany declared that it was "essential for [her] self-defense that she should anticipate" what was alleged to be a French intention to mount an attack through Belgian territory.[199] In 1946, it was contended by the defense at Nuremberg that "Germany was compelled to attack Norway to forestall an Allied invasion

---

claims made by Pakistan in connection with the entry of Pakistani troops into Kashmir in 1948. U.N. Sec. Council, *Off. Rec.*, 5th Yr, 464th mtg. 1–40 passim (1950).

197. Hall, *International Law* 326–8 (8th ed., Higgins, 1924); Karlsrud, "The Seizure of the Danish Fleet, 1807," 32 *A.J.I.L.* 280 (1938).

198. 1 Oppenheim-Lauterpacht 270–1; *The Initial Triumph of the Axis, Survey of International Affairs 1939–1946*, at 209–11 (Royal Institute of Int. Affairs, 1958).

199. 2 Garner, *International Law and the World War* 188–9 (1920).

and [that] her action was therefore preventive." [200] Another comprehensive (though less extravagant) claim was the Anglo-Soviet occupation of Iran in 1941 to prevent further German infiltration and "fifth column" activities.[201]

ASSERTIONS OF TEMPORARY AND LIMITED AUTHORITY ON THE HIGH SEAS

Claims of the third type, frequently asserted with an invocation of "self-defense," or "self-protection," or "security," or "general security," comprehend a rich variety of particular claims to exercise limited or temporary and episodic authority over certain events on the high seas and in the airspace above the high seas. Of the specific claims of this type, some relate to the maintenance and protection of the military security interests of the claimant state: unilateral establishment of "Air Defense Identification Zones" extending hundreds of miles seaward; placement of radar warning platforms in contiguous areas of the high seas; surveillance, visitation, and search of vessels in contiguous zone areas; establishment beyond territorial waters of "defensive areas" in which navigation is limited or temporarily excluded; and temporary exclusive use of high-seas areas for weapons testing and maneuvers.[202] Other specific claims that relate to the protection of coastal interests other than military security —claims for customs inspection, antismuggling controls, conservation and exclusive exploitation of mineral and organic marine resources—have also been frequently couched in the language of "self-defense" or "self-protection" or "security." [203] These claims are of

200. Office of U.S. Chief of Counsel for Prosecution of Axis Criminality, *Nazi Conspiracy and Aggression, Opinion and Judgment* 36 (1947). The same claim was made with respect to the German invasion of Belgium, the Netherlands, and Luxembourg in 1940, both at Nuremberg, id. at 40, and at the commencement of the invasion, *The Initial Triumph of the Axis, Survey of International Affairs 1939–1946,* at 159 (Royal Institute of Int. Affairs, 1958).

201. See Kirk, *The Middle East in the War, Survey of International Affairs 1939–1946,* at 129–41 (Royal Institute of Int. Affairs, 1952).

202. For detailed documentation and analysis of these claims, see McDougal and Schlei, "The Hydrogen Bomb Tests in Perspective: Lawful Measures for Security," 64 *Yale L.J.* 648, 666–82 (1955); McDougal and Burke, "Crisis in the Law of the Sea: Community Perspectives Versus National Egoism," 67 *Yale L.J.* 539, 553–4, 563–4, 581–8 (1958). See also the convenient listing of the claims in Boggs, "National Claims in Adjacent Seas," 41 *Geographical Rev.* 185 (1951).

203. See Bowett, *Self-Defence in International Law* c. 4 (1958); Jessup, *The*

course supported by threats of deprivation, as are all claims to state authority. But they constitute exercises of coercion of such a relatively low level of intensity and magnitude as frequently to be indistinguishable from the ordinary coercion inescapable in a world of states interacting and competing for values. Further, they are general in character in that they are commonly directed not against a particular target state defined as an enemy but rather against all other states.

DIFFERENCES IN POLICY ISSUES

While the three broad types of claims are often made under the same or similar verbal designations and while there may be some overlap between the first and second types, the specific demands made commonly refer to different activities moved by varying purposes, arising in varied contexts, and posing greatly different issues of community policy. Indiscriminately to group the several types of claims together and to subsume them under some single verbal rubric such as "self-defense" or "necessity" or "self-preservation" may tend only to conceal their disparity in activity, purpose, context, and policy and possibly to induce confusion.[204]

In respect of claims to exercise highly intense coercion in response to prohibited aggression, the fundamental community policy at stake is the common interest of all the world's peoples in securing a minimum of public order. This most basic policy seeks to preserve an existing distribution of values among states against modification by destructive coercion and to that end permits the unilateral use of

---

Law of Territorial Waters and Maritime Jurisdiction c. 2 (1927); Memorandum on the Regime of the High Seas (Gidel), U.N. Doc. No. A/CN.4/32, at 45 (1950).

204. Subsumption of disparate things under a common rubric is observable not only in the rhetoric of claims but also in some of the learned literature. See, e.g., Cheng, *General Principles of Law* 29–102 (1953); Hall, *International Law* 322–6 (8th ed., Pearce Higgins, 1924); Rodick, *The Doctrine of Necessity in International Law* (1928); Weiden, "Necessity in International Law," 24 *Tr. Grotius Soc.* 105 (1938). Bowett attempts to establish a distinction, *intra* the third broad group of claims, between "defence of [a state's] security" by exercise of "the right of self-defence upon the high seas adjacent to its territory" on the one hand, and, on the other, "protection of certain essential interests of the state" with respect to which "customary rights of a jurisdictional character" may have developed; when the latter "customary rights" "exist," there is, in his view, no need to invoke the former. Bowett, op. cit. supra note 203 at 86.

force and other intense coercion only in necessary reaction to coercive reconstruction. In the contemporary world, low expectations as to the effective competence of the general organization of states to protect individual members, among many other factors, make indispensable the permission of some self-defense. Even in an arena with a much higher degree of effective organization than the present world exhibits, self-defense must, if experience in municipal arenas can be projected,[205] still be regarded as an emergency, interim authorization subsisting until the public force of the organized community is effectively brought to bear.

In contrast, the distinctive characteristic of the claims to apply coercion against a third state is that coercion is claimed as permissible against a state which has not attacked the claimant. Such claims, when they are something more than veils for aggrandizement, are moved by the claimant's expectations that certain hostile operations will imminently be carried on by its opponent in the territory of the third state and that the third state will be unable or unwilling to prevent those hostile operations. In short, the claimant seeks to anticipate or counter such hostile conduct. The relevant context is not simply one of the claimant-belligerent initiating coercion against the third state but rather the broader one of continuing coercion between the claimant-belligerent and the opposing belligerent. The claims against the third party are made in the course of and as an incident in an on-going process of highly intense coercion. The community policy most immediately involved is not merely that emphasizing peaceful change; it extends to the limitation of the area of involvement and limitation of the aggregate destruction of values. The problem is that of accommodating the contraposed policies of securing military effectiveness and of minimizing the disruption of the value processes of nonparticipating states. The relevant prescriptions applicable to implement these policies include not merely the prohibition of aggression and the permission of self-defense, but also the rules on the rights and duties of belligerents and neutrals.[206] In

205. See note 21 supra.

206. The specific rules directly relevant include those on the belligerents' duty to respect and the neutral's duty to preserve the "inviolability" of neutral territory, waters, and airspace and those relating to the conversion of such territory, waters, and airspace into permissible areas of hostile operations by the neutral's tolerance of or inability to prevent their violation by one of the bellig-

view of these differences, we suggest that these claims—to the extent that the supporting expectations relating to imminent enemy operations in the third state's territory and such third state's inability or unwillingness to prevent those operations are determined to be genuine and reasonable—are more appropriately considered under the second major problem of the international law of coercion, that is, the regulation of participation in coercion. If, of course, the claimant's expectations prove fictitious, the assertion of force against the third state may, when the other detailed variables noted earlier are considered, be characterized as a new, unlawful initiation of coercion. Such is implicit in the Nuremberg Tribunal's rejection of the defense's claim respecting Germany's invasion of Norway, as well as of Belgium, the Netherlands, and Luxembourg.[207]

---

erents. See, e.g., Castren, *The Present Law of War and Neutrality* 442–3, 462–3 (1953); Hall, op. cit. supra note 204 at 721–4; 2 Oppenheim-Lauterpacht 678–80; 3 Hyde, *International Law* 2337–9, 2340–1 (2d rev. ed., 1945); "The Anna Maria," *Annual Digest 1946,* Case No. 174; *Coenca Brothers v. German State, Annual Digest 1928–29,* Case No. 389.

It may be noted that after the German invasion of Belgium in World War I, Germany sought to justify her actions in terms other than those of "self-defense," "self-preservation," and "necessity." Charges were made that, before the delivery of the German ultimatum, France had already violated Belgian neutrality with the consent of the Belgian Government. 2 Garner, *International Law and the World War* 203–6 (1920). Similarly, the Allied occupation of Saloniki and other measures taken against Greece when it was still a neutral in the same war were sought to be justified upon the ground that Greek territory was long used as a source of supplies and a base of operations by Germany with the approval of the Greek Government. Id. at 254–5.

207. Although the evidence submitted at Nuremberg indicated that there had in fact been an Allied plan to occupy harbors and airports in western Norway, it also appeared that at the time of the German invasion of Norway, Germany did not know of this Allied plan and in fact ruled it out as a serious possibility. As the tribunal pointed out, anticipation and pre-emption of an Allied landing was not, in point of fact, the precipitating purpose of the invasion of Norway which Germany had projected and prepared long before the Allied Powers found it necessary to plan a landing. Office of U.S. Chief of Counsel for Prosecution of Axis Criminality, *Nazi Conspiracy and Aggression, Opinion and Judgment* 35–8 (1947).

Similarly, with respect to the German invasion of Belgium, Holland, and Luxembourg, the Allied Powers agreed, one month before such invasion, to "press for a preventive entry of their troops into Belgium." Belgium, however, rejected their demand and publicly reiterated its determination to maintain its neutrality. The German decision to attack the Low Countries had been taken, again,

The problems raised by claims to exercise limited or occasional jurisdiction on the high seas and superjacent airspace are completely distinct from those raised by the claims to respond to unlawful initiating coercion and to employ coercion against a third state. Although often urged in the rhetoric of "self-defense" or "self-protection," these claims to prescribe and apply authority to certain events for many differing purposes, are commonly made not in contexts of high level interstate coercion but in those phases of the persuasion-coercion continuum in which persuasion is still relatively dominant. The general community policy here most directly at stake is not the maintenance of world public order, in its minimum sense; it is, rather, the promotion of the fullest, conserving, peaceful use of such great common resources as the oceans by achieving the most economic balance possible between the special exclusive demands of coastal states and other special claimants and the general inclusive demands of the other members of the community of states.[208] Authorized decision-makers seek to secure this common interest by formulating and applying the bodies of authoritative myth commonly referred to as the "law of the sea" and the "law of the air." These domains of doctrine and practice are obviously distinct from, for instance, the prohibitions and permissions about coercion established in the United Nations Charter. The type and range of conditioning variables of which account must be taken in determining the reasonableness (in detailed context) of, for example, a claim to a contiguous zone, are very different from the kinds of variable factors that bear upon the necessity and proportionality of an assertion of extensive violence in self-defense. In fine, claims of jurisdiction and those of defensive violence have too little in common to warrant their continued subsumption under a single label.[209]

---

long before the Allies sought permission for "preventive entry." Id. at 39–40; *The Initial Triumph of the Axis, Survey of International Affairs 1939–1946,* at 125–6, 155–8 (Royal Institute of Int. Affairs, 1958).

208. Amplification is offered in McDougal and Burke, supra note 202; McDougal and Schlei, supra note 202. Cf. the formulation expressed in Memorandum (Gidel), supra note 203 at 10. Cf. Sorensen, "Law of the Sea," *Int. Conciliation* No. 520, at 198–9 (1958), the force of whose criticism is impaired by failure to recognize possibilities of genuine integrative solutions in which all gain and none lose.

209. In McDougal and Schlei, supra note 202 at 674–88, 686, it was suggested that the nuclear weapons tests by the United States off the Pacific atolls could

Self-Defense

THE REQUIREMENTS OF SELF-DEFENSE: NECESSITY AND PROPORTIONALITY

These preliminary distinctions make it possible now to focus more sharply upon the class of claims with which we are immediately concerned—claims to use highly intense coercion in defense against what is claimed to be impermissible initiating coercion. The principal requirements which the "customary law" of self-defense makes prerequisite to the lawful assertion of these claims are commonly summarized in terms of necessity and proportionality. For the protection of the general community against extravagant claims, the standard of required necessity has been habitually cast in language so abstractly restrictive as almost, if read literally, to impose paralysis. Such is the clear import of the classical peroration of Secretary of State Webster in the *Caroline* case—that there must be shown a "necessity of self defense, instant, overwhelming, leaving no choice of means and no moment for deliberation." [210] The requirement of

be justified both as reasonable measures in the interests of "security" and as "in substance a claim *to prepare for* self-defense." (Emphasis added.) In so far as this suggestion depends upon the traditional technical conception of "self-defense," it may be regarded as an "over-kill." In conducting these tests, the United States was not employing the military instrument against any opponent state. The United States was rather seeking to assert merely a temporary, exclusive control or jurisdiction over a portion of a common, shared resource, the Pacific Ocean. To establish the lawfulness of the United States' claim, it is necessary only to establish its reasonableness by traditional criteria of the law of the sea. This necessary "reasonableness," it was suggested, is primarily indicated by the deeply vital importance of the tests to the security of the United States, and indeed of all free peoples, as contrasted with the minimal and temporary interference with shared interests in navigation and fishing. The same essential community policy of maintaining a basic public order in which peoples are free from attack and threats of attack, underlies of course both the broader concession of jurisdiction for "security" purposes, authorizing lesser interferences with less fundamental interests of others and the narrower permission of "self-defense" authorizing the application of military force in response to major and grievous threats; and comparable tests of necessity and proportionality, in sum of "reasonableness," are relevant in applications of both concepts. The latter concept, that of "self-defense," simply is not necessary, by Occam's razor, to sustain lesser interferences.

210. Mr. Webster to Mr. Fox, April 24, 1841, in 29 *British and Foreign State Papers* 1129, 1138 (1840–1841). See generally Jennings, "The Caroline and Mc-

proportionality which, as we shall develop below, is but another application of the principle of economy in coercion, is frequently expressed in equally abstract terms. One example is M. de Brouckère's formulation: "Legitimate defense implies the adoption of measures proportionate to the seriousness of the attack and justified by the imminence of the danger." [211] There is, however, increasing recognition that the requirements of necessity and proportionality as ancillary prescriptions (in slightly lower-order generalization) of the basic community policy prohibiting change by violence, can ultimately be subjected only to that most comprehensive and fundamental test of all law, reasonableness in particular context.[212] What remains to be stressed is that reasonableness in particular context does not mean arbitrariness in decision but in fact its exact opposite, the disciplined ascription of policy import to varying factors in appraising their operational and functional significance for community goals in given instances of coercion.

THE DECISION-MAKERS: PROVISIONAL CHARACTERIZATION AND SUBSEQUENT REVIEW

The authoritative decision-makers whom community expectation establishes to pass upon coercion claimed to be in response to prior coercion from others are of course the same decision-makers who assess the coercion which is alleged to be prohibited aggression. But the determination of whether the coercion directed against a target state constitutes unlawful initiating coercion and therefore justifies an assertion of responding coercion in self-defense is, in the first instance, made by the target-state claimant itself. Competence to make an initial and provisional determination without previous authorization from the organized community must be conceded to the claimant pending the completion of a much more viable world public order. "To wait," Professor Brierly explained, "for authority

---

Leod Cases," 32 *A.J.I.L.* 82 (1938). Cf. Professor Wright's formulation: "[T]he plea of defense will justify otherwise illegal action only if the action was taken to *prevent* an *immediately impending, irreparable injury* and *for that purpose alone.*" Wright, "The Meaning of the Pact of Paris," 27 *A.J.I.L.* 39, 54 (1933).

211. Report of de Brouckère, supra note 170.

212. Cf. Schwarzenberger, *Report on Some Aspects of the Principle of Self-Defence in the Charter of the United Nations and the Topics Covered by the Dubravnik Resolution* 23 (Int. Law Assoc., 1958).

to act from any outside body may mean disaster." [213] The recommendation of a distinguished scholar that even "a true war of defense" should be permitted only as a "war of sanctions" by delegation from and with the prior permission of the organized community [214] must, despite the modern technology of communications, seem unreal and utopian. The inevitable time-lag between initiation of highly intense coercion and appropriate determination and authorization by the general security organization, and the ever present possibility of the organization's failure to reach any determination at all, make such a recommendation potentially disastrous for defending states. The provisional characterization of the target state—its assertion of a claim of self-defense—must, however, be subject to subsequent appraisal by other, external, decision-makers, both international and national. The statement that the acting state "alone is competent to decide whether the circumstances require recourse to war in self defense" [215] cannot be taken literally without in effect repudiating fundamental community policy.[216] Thus, the general

213. Brierly, *The Law of Nations* 320 (5th ed., 1955).

214. Wehberg, *The Outlawry of War* 100–3 (Zeydel, trans., 1931).

215. Identic Note of the Government of the United States, June 23, 1928. (Text in Miller, *The Peace Pact of Paris* 213–14 (1928).)

216. At the Tokyo Trial (as at Nuremberg) the defense relied on Secretary Kellogg's note in contending that, under the Pact of Paris: "(4) the nation resorting to measures of self-defense was to be the sole judge on the question of self-defense, (5) that the question of self-defense was not to be submitted to any tribunal, (6) that no nation should have anything to do with deciding the question of self-defense regarding the action of any other nation unless such action constituted an attack on itself." Takayanagi, *The Tokio Trials and International Law* 36–7 (1948). The Tribunal rejected this argument, saying: "Under the most liberal interpretation of the Kellogg-Briand Pact, the right of self-defence does not confer upon the State resorting to war the authority to make a final determination upon the justification for its action. Any other interpretation would nullify the Pact; and this Tribunal does not believe that the Powers in concluding the Pact intended to make an empty gesture." *Judgment of the International Military Tribunal for the Far East* 68 (1948). See also 2 Oppenheim-Lauterpacht 187–88; Lauterpacht, *The Function of Law in the International Community* 179–82 (1933); Wright, supra note 210 at 41–50. Professor Brierly stressed that "the practice of states decisively rejects the view that a state need only declare its own action to be defensive for that action to become defensive as a matter of law. . . . [I]t is clear that the defensive or non-defensive character of any state's action is universally regarded as a question capable of determination by an objective examination of the relevant facts." Brierly, *The Law of Nations* 320–1 (5th ed., 1955).

competence of both the Security Council and the General Assembly to characterize impermissible coercion necessarily implies that the participant claiming to exercise coercion in self-defense does so at its peril. The same implication flows from Article 51 of the United Nations Charter, which requires that measures taken under claim of self-defense be immediately reported to the Council and which explicitly reserves the "authority and responsibility" of the Council "to take at any time such action as it deems necessary in order to maintain or restore international peace and security." [217]

THE APPRAISAL OF ALLEGED DEFENDING COERCION

Inquiry into the factors that are relevant to an appraisal of coercion claimed to be permissible self-defense parallels our earlier inquiry into factors that rationally bear upon judgments about impermissible initiating coercion. Accordingly the same categories of variables, that is, *participants, objectives, methods, conditions* and *effects,* are equally useful in this examination. Likewise, all the factors elicited in our analysis of initiating coercion are equally relevant to the appraisal of coercion alleged to be lawful defense. The principal emphasis here, however, must be upon the need of relating particular factors to the requirements of necessity and proportionality.

The Characteristics of Participants

At the outset, there may arise the problem of identifying participant groups, to whose mutual applications of coercion and violence the community policy and prescriptions distinguishing between permissible and impermissible coercion may appropriately be applicable. Allegations of impermissible coercion and accompanying claims to use intense coercion in self-defense have been made not only by officials of bodies politic universally recognized as nation-states but also by officials of territorial communities and governmental organizations not formally recognized as states by their opponents and, at times, by some members of the community of states as well. The Arab-Israeli conflict in Palestine in 1948 and the Korean war of 1950 afford familiar illustrations. The Jewish Agency for Palestine, even before issuing the proclamation on establishing an independent state of Israel, raised a charge of aggression against Trans-Jordan and Egypt before the United Nations Security Council and, at least in-

217. See Jessup, *A Modern Law of Nations* 165 (1948).

ferentially, claimed a right to self-defense.[218] The Arab states refused to recognize Israel as a state and indeed asserted that, with the termination of the British Mandate, Palestine had become an independent nation in which the Jews constituted a rebellious minority.[219] In the Korean conflict, neither of the initial participants—the Republic of Korea and the North Korean People's Republic—recognized the other as a state. The Soviet Union argued to the United Nations that the exercise of violence in Korea could not be characterized as unlawful coercion since the conflict was an internal or civil one and the Charter prescriptions are not applicable to coercion between two groups within a single state.[220] The decisions reached by the United Nations in the Palestine and Korean cases [221] suggest that conflicts involving a newly organized territorial body politic, or conflicts between two distinct territorial units which the community expects to be relatively permanent, are, for purposes of policy about coercion, to be treated as conflicts between established states. Thus, the applicability of basic community policy about minimum public order in the world arena and competence to defend against unlawful violence are not dependent upon formal recognition of the technical statehood of the claimant-group by the opposing participant.[222] This conclusion is but an obvious corollary of effective community policy;

218. See the letter of the Jewish Agency for Palestine to the President of the Security Council, May 14, 1948, and the statements of the representative of the Jewish Agency, U.N. Sec. Council, *Off. Rec.*, 3d Yr, No. 66, 292d mtg. 2, 4–7 (1948).

219. See, e.g., the statements of the representative of the Arab Higher Committee, id. at 7–9, and the statements of the Egyptian delegate, U.N. Sec. Council, *Off. Rec.*, 3d Yr, No. 68, 294–5th mtgs. 5, 8–9 (1948).

220. U.N. Sec. Council, *Off. Rec.*, 5th Yr, No. 24, 482d mtg. 6–10 (1950). See the answering arguments made by the United Kingdom representative, id. No. 28, 486th mtg. 4–6 (1950).

221. As to the Palestine case, see the Resolutions of May 22, 1948, U.N. Sec. Council, *Off. Rec.*, 3d Yr, Supp. for May at 97 (1948), and of July 15, 1948, id. Supp. for July at 76 (1948). As to the Korean case, see note 187 supra.

222. For indication of the complexities of policy relating to internal strife within bodies politic, see note 164 supra. Our emphasis here is merely that rational community policy must be directed to the coercive interactions of territorially organized communities of consequential size, whatever the "lawfulness" of their origin and whatever the prior niceties in the presence or absence of the ceremony of recognition. This necessity appears acknowledged in measure even in the older doctrines of "belligerence" and "insurgency." See, e.g., Lauterpacht, *Recognition in International Law* (1947).

a contrary view would permit the thrust of fundamental policy to be avoided by the simple device of refusing to perform a ceremonial ritual. It is not the ceremony of recognition by others that constitutes a group an effective, self-directed, territorially organized community, but the facts of the world power process.

The Nature of Claimants' Objectives

The objectives of the participant claiming self-defense may best be examined in terms of the same factors found useful for inquiry into the objectives of the participant claimed to have unlawfully initiated coercion: extension or conservation, degree of consequentiality, and the degree of inclusivity or exclusivity. The first two factors may require some additional discussion.

Limitation of Permissible Conservation. Characterization of the real objectives of the claimant in terms of extension or conservation is most directly related to the requirements of permissible self-defense. The very conception of self-defense implies that the purpose of the defender is to conserve its values rather than to extend them through acquiring or destroying values held by the opposing participant. Conservation, as the legitimate objective of self-defense, is commonly referred to by commentators in such terms as "stopping or preventing" [223] or repelling "any imminent or present invasion of the rights [of the defender]." [224] Such confining language is doubtless intended to induce restraint in the assertion of claims to self-defense.[225] Nonetheless, a rational appraisal of particular purposes must depend upon a consideration of all relevant conditioning factors in particular detailed contexts, including especially the condition of necessity which impelled the response in coercion. Permissible objectives of self-defense against massive military attack and invasion, for instance, need not necessarily be limited to stopping and repelling or pushing back invading enemy troops to their own side of the frontier; realistically, the necessity to which the target-claimant is responding may

223. Waldock, "The Regulation of the Use of Force by Individual States in International Law," 81 *Hague Recueil* 455, 464 (1952).

224. Schwarzenberger, "The Fundamental Principles of International Law," 87 *Hague Recueil* 195, 335 (1955).

225. "[T]here is a natural temptation, when force has been resorted to, to continue its use after the needs of defence have been fairly met." Brierly, *The Law of Nations* 316 (5th ed., 1955).

not, in the circumstances of a particular case, be wholly terminated merely by repulsion of the enemy invasion, and may reasonably require counter-invasion of the enemy's own territory.[226]

The problem of clarifying the permissible limits of conservation as the only legitimate objective of self-defense may perhaps be put in sharper focus by referring to the objectives of the Allied (United Nations) Powers in World War II. Allied objectives, as formulated and developed in the course of the prolonged struggle, were not limited to physically stopping or repelling the aggressive violence exercised by the Axis Powers.[227] Prominent among these purposes was the comprehensive, long-term aim of preventing any recurrence of aggression by Germany and Japan. This aim was sought by imposing upon the entire territory of the enemy states what might be called "therapeutic" occupation—occupation designed to permit the modification and reconstruction of certain basic enemy political, economic, social, and legal institutions, the reorientation of mass and elite perspectives, the removal or limitation of enemy potential for war, and so forth.[228] From the perspective of prediction, perhaps this and other objectives of comparable degrees of comprehensiveness will not present a serious problem of legal policy if certain conditions of power are secured in the future. Such conditions include at the minimum, first, the achievement and maintenance of a rough equilibrium between the polar powers in capacity for delivering as well as in vulnerability to annihilating thermonuclear destruction; second,

226. Cf. Schwarzenberger, "The Fundamental Principles of International Law," 87 *Hague Recueil* 195, 334 (1955). The factual question, from the perspective of an independent observer, is whether the repulsion of the enemy invasion, together with calculations as to the probable costs of mounting another attack, have effectively modified the expectation and demand structure of the enemy elite. The question would in measure depend upon the comprehensiveness of and the value assigned by such elite to their original objectives.

227. See generally 1 *War and Peace Aims of the United Nations—September 1, 1939–December 31, 1942* (Holborn, ed., 1943); 2 id.—*January 1, 1943–September 1, 1945* (1948).

228. See, e.g., Friedrich and Associates, *American Experiences in Military Government in World War II* cc. 1–2, 12 (1948); Loewenstein, "Law and the Legislative Process in Occupied Germany," 57 *Yale L.J.* 724 (1948); Loewenstein, "Reconstruction of the Administration of Justice in American-Occupied Germany," 61 *Harv. L. Rev.* 419 (1948); Plischke, "Denazification Law and Procedure," 41 *A.J.I.L.* 807 (1947); U.S. Dept. of State, Pub. No. 2671, Far Eastern Series, *Occupation of Japan: Policy and Progress* 17 (1946).

the recognition by both powers of their common interest in keeping coercion below a ruinous level of destruction; and third, the constant awareness by the powers of the close relation that prospects of limiting violence bear to limitation of the moving purposes of violence.[229] To the extent, in other words, that the hope that only limited war may take place is realism, the deliberate postulation and prosecution, by defending as well as by attacking states, of objectives as comprehensive as those of the Allied powers may become unlikely. From perspectives of preference, competence to pursue and implement an objective of ensuring against recurrence of aggression in the more or less remote future by "therapeutic" reconstruction of the institutions and fundamental demand and identification patterns of the defeated aggressor more appropriately belongs to the organized community of states. Such measures should be exercisable only by, or under an unambiguous authorization from, the entire community, rather than impliedly included in the permission of self-defense.[230] A restrictive definition of the scope of permissible conservation that excludes this and similar "pedagogic" [231] objectives accords both with the Charter's conception of self-defense as an interim and emergency authorization, and with the imperatives of limiting the dimensions of violence. The viability of such definition, we are aware, depends upon the degree of effective, centralized organization secured in the arena, and upon the degree of success achieved in establishing and maintaining the supporting arrangements of power.

Consequentiality of Values Conserved. Characterization of the particular objectives of a claimant as conservation rather than extension need not be conclusive as to the lawfulness of the coercion exercised;

229. The principal reference here is to the conditions of so-called "mutual deterrence" and "limited war." See supra pp. 55–6. See also Appadorai, *The Use of Force in International Relations* 19–20 (1958).

230. In respect of the comprehensive Allied objectives of reconstruction in the last world war, it is relevant to point to the observation made by Dr. Yokota: "[T]he very fact that the 51 allied nations opposing the Axis in the last war, represented the overwhelming majority of all the nations of the world, may be considered as the imposition of an ultimate sanction by the international community." Yokota, "War as an International Crime," in *Foundamental* [sic] *Problems of International Law, Festschrift für Jean Spiropoulos* 453, 458 (1957).

231. The term is borrowed from Kecskemeti, *Strategic Surrender: The Politics of Victory and Defeat* 239 (1958). Mr. Kecskemeti makes able inquiry into some aspects of the problem of limitation of objectives.

such objectives must also, among other relevant, considerations, be appraised for the degree of consequentiality of the values sought to be protected and conserved. The values which states have on occasion sought to conserve and protect present a wide spectrum in degree of consequentiality; they range from the most trifling to the most fundamental. In this connection, certain propositions, derived by distinguished scholars as inferences from the judgment of the International Court of Justice in the *Corfu Channel* (*Merits*) case,[232] appear to confuse the milder coercion unavoidable in the relation of states with intense attacks upon independence and territorial integrity. In the view of Professor Waldock, the court held, among other things, that:

> [A] threat and, indeed, use of force—the demonstration of naval force in Albania's territorial waters—is not contrary to Article 2(4) *when it is in affirmation of rights which have been illegally and forcibly denied.*[233]

More recently, Dr. Schwarzenberger has written:

> [The] case appears to suggest three propositions regarding the interpretation of Paragraph 4 of Article 2 and Article 51 of the Charter of the United Nations:
>
> (1) The exercise of a right for the purpose of testing whether it is threatened by armed attack, and in such strength as to discourage the repetition of such an attack or its prompt repulsion is not an illegal threat under Paragraph 4 of Article 2 of the Charter of the United Nations. More specifically, it does not deprive a passage through an international strait of its innocent character.
>
> . . .
>
> (3) If it is legal to take precautionary measures of the kind discussed, it must be compatible with the international quasi-order of the United Nations to take *armed action in self defense against any actual armed interference with the enjoyment of rights under international law.*[234]

232. 1949 *I.C.J. Rep.* 5.

233. Waldock, supra note 223 at 500.

234. Schwarzenberger, *Report on Some Aspects of the Principle of Self-Defence*

These generalizations, as Dr. Schwarzenberger concedes, rest on the assumption that Articles 2(4) and 51 of the Charter were applicable to the situation presented by the passage of British warships through the channel on October 22, 1946, and are derived wholly from the failure of the court to characterize their passage as violative of Article 2(4). It is difficult to find much basis in the judgment for this assumption and derivation, since neither Article 2(4) nor Article 51 was mentioned by the court, and the plea of self-defense was never raised by the United Kingdom as a justification for the passage of its warships on October 22, 1946.[235] The complete silence of the court on this matter is, at the very least, ambiguous. It is equally explainable by the contrary assumption—that the court did not regard Article 2(4) and the permission of self-defense as bearing upon the particular case. The issues raised and conclusions reached by the court in the *Corfu* case seem too narrowly drawn to support, by process of necessary implication, the inferences urged.

The extrapolations under discussion appear open to yet more fundamental objections. To the extent that they seem to suggest, for failure of appropriate qualification, that the enjoyment of *any* "right under international law," without regard for any other factor such as the consequentiality of the "right" involved, may be "affirmed" or defended by the employment of force, the formulations submitted by Dr. Schwarzenberger[236] and Professor Waldock come perilously

---

in the Charter of the United Nations and the Topics Covered by the Dubrovnik Resolution 24 (Int. Law Assoc. 1958). (Emphasis added.) The same reading of Corfu has apparently been urged by still another British writer: see Fitzmaurice, "The General Principles of International Law Considered from the Standpoint of the Rule of Law," 92 *Hague Recueil* 1, 171–2 (1957).

235. The pleas of "self-defence and self-redress" and of "self-help" were made by the United Kingdom agent with respect to the sweeping of the Channel on Nov. 12–13, 1946 ("Operation Retail"). See 2 *Corfu Channel Case—Pleadings, Oral Arguments, and Documents* 280–4 (I.C.J. 1950); 3 id. at 293–7; 4 id. at 572–92. The pleas were rejected by the Court. The passage of Oct. 22, 1946, was sought to be justified by the U.K. agent not in terms of "self-defence" or "self-help" but as being "fully within the right of innocent passage." 3 id. at 293. See also 2 id. at 301. It may also be noted that the specific right involved was the right of innocent passage *by warships* and that such a right can neither be exercised in the first instance nor subsequently "affirmed" without instrumentalities of force, i.e., warships, being used.

236. Dr. Schwarzenberger had previously written that: "This prerequisite [that the need must be overwhelming] limits self defence to action in protection

close to emasculating the basic community policy on minimum public order. The need for imposing limits on the kind and character of "rights" or values that may legitimately be defended by highly intense coercion must seem obvious. The denial, even by "actual armed interference," of inconsequential or trivial "rights" or value claims warrants proper reciprocities, retaliations, and remedies other than high-level coercion. It is not necessary to invoke self-defense to sustain ordinary reciprocities and retaliations against such tortious conduct of another state, in other words, in contexts in which the level of coercion falls far short of highly intense and destructive attack upon fundamental and indispensable values. If, as we suggest, the permission of self-defense is most appropriately conceived as a permission to exercise destructive coercion, a requirement of a certain degree of consequentiality in the values sought to be conserved by such coercion is a substantial, if implied, effect of the combined principles of necessity and proportionality.

The conception of requisite consequentiality can be assigned functional references only in particular contexts. On one level of abstraction, there would generally be no necessity for highly intense coercion—nor could such coercion be characterized as proportionate—except in response to an unambiguous and imminent threat or present imposition of severe deprivations of values so important that their loss or destruction will substantially impair the functioning of the territorially organized community or preclude its continued existence as a distinct polity. On another level of abstraction, a finding that appropriate standards of consequentiality have been met may be most easily reached when the claimant shows the particular "rights" or values or interests threatened or attacked to be indispensable components of its "territorial integrity" or "political independence." As our discussion of impermissible coercion indicated, the primary reference of the words "territorial integrity" and "political independ-

---

of *vital, or at least important, rights or interests* and precludes such action in cases of merely formal or trivial breaches of international law." Schwarzenberger, "The Fundamental Principles of International Law," 87 *Hague Recueil* 195, 333 (1955). (Emphasis added.) Barely five pages later, however, he also wrote that "The [Corfu] Judgment clarifies beyond doubt that the prohibition of the use of force in Paragraph 4 of Article 2 of the Charter does not preclude action in self defence, as distinction from self help at large, against the forcible denial of *any* right." Id. at 339. (Emphasis added.)

ence" is to the more important bases of community power. These bases are comprised of a community's continuing, comprehensive control over its geographical base and physical resources, over its people, and over its institutions. This control over institutions extends to both the integrity and continuity of the community's internal arrangements of authority and effective power and its freedom of self-direction and self-commitment in customary interaction with other communities. In considering the reasonableness of asserted expectations about the serious impact of a threat or deprivation of particular values upon a claimant's "territorial integrity" or "political independence," the territorial location of the values affected may have an obvious relevance. If a threat or an actual deprivation is directed, for instance, against the person or property of a stray national or two in some distant land, it would seem most unlikely, even if carried out by violence, to have any appreciable effect upon the fundamental bases of power of the home state.[237] But if, on the other hand, the values threatened or attacked are located within the community's territorial base, a strong presumption that fundamental power bases are significantly affected may be appropriate. There seems, in gross illustration, an evident distinction between the sinking of a small boat in some internal river of China [238] and the destruction of eight battleships in Pearl Harbor. We do not, of course, mean to suggest that geographical situs has anything like conclusive significance.[239] What we suggest is that the relation of the particular value or interest affected to the essential bases of community power is a capital aspect of consequentiality, and physical location of the value or interest may be one index to that relationship.

The Modalities of Response

The methods the claimant of self-defense employs in exercising coercion may, like those employed by the participant charged with having initiated unlawful aggression, comprise any one or all—in

237. Cf. Bowett, *Self-Defence in International Law* 93 (1958).

238. E.g., the sinking of the *U.S.S. Panay* on the Yangtze River by Japanese aircraft. See 15 *Bull. of Int. News* 9 (1938).

239. Thus the relevance of geographical location may be relatively minimal in cases of attack upon a state's strategic military bases situated in third countries. For an exploration of the importance of overseas bases for the military security of the United States under present power conditions and current strategic doctrines, see Hoopes, "Overseas Bases in American Strategy," 37 *Foreign Aff.* 69 (1958).

combinations and sequences of varying emphases—of the policy instrumentalities familiarly categorized as diplomacy, mass communication, control over goods and services, and armed force. Here again the relevance of modality lies principally in its utility as a crude and prima facie indicator of the general level of intensity reached by the coercion claimed to be in self-defense and, in equally rough evaluation, of the proportionality or disproportionality of the allegedly responsive coercion when measured against the necessity created by the initial coercion.[240] Military violence is of course easily distinguishable from nonmilitary coercion; the distinction is, in terms of susceptibility to direct or optical observation, similar to the popular subdistinction between "conventional" arms and "nuclear" weapons. But, in the regulation of resort to coercion just as in regulation of the conduct of combat, rational policy is and must be primarily concerned not with modality as such but with the effects of coercion, the level of intensity and scope, actually obtained in particular contexts. Appraisal of the level of coercion exercised in specific contexts and of the degree of proportionality exhibited is not rationally limited to application of a single-factor test of modality.

Conditions and the Expectation of Necessity

Inquiry may next be directed to the conditions under which coercion claimed to be in self-defense is exercised. The conditions we noted as relevant for scrutinizing allegedly unlawful coercion, con-

240. As to the possible function of modality as a quick index of intensity, cf. Nitze, *Symmetry and Intensity of Great Power Involvement in Limited Wars*, Military Policy Papers 55 (Washington Center of Foreign Policy Research 1958):

> [T]he means actually employed can be roughly graded as to intensity. One can start with normal diplomatic and political support; go on to more intense advice and propaganda support; to the furnishing of economic and military supplies and the active training of personnel; to manpower support in gradations from volunteers to participation by satellites or allies on to direct and open military participation by the great power itself; and the military participation by the major power can be graded from air and sea support to direct participation by all services; the weapons used by the supporting forces can be conventional, tactical atomic, or without restriction; the geographic area subject to hostilities can be expanded by gradations to any given approximation to a global conflict. The possible gradations and combinations of gradations do not fall neatly on a linear scale of intensity. It is, however, generally meaningful to say that one set of means involves a greater intensity of major power intervention than some other set of means.

ditions including both the general elements pervasive in power processes in the world arena and certain particular conditions of more direct significance, are, again, of equal relevance for reviewing assertions of self-defense. The most important condition that must be investigated is the degree of necessity—as that necessity is perceived and evaluated by the target-claimant and incorporated in the pattern of its expectations—which, in the particular instance, impels the claim to use intense responding coercion.[241] All other conditions must be assessed for their bearing upon this fundamental condition of necessity. Since necessity is generated by and represents the total impact of the opposing participant's application of coercion upon the claimant's expectations about the costs of conserving and protecting its values, an appraisal of the condition of necessity must involve an estimate of the entire coercion applied by the opposing participant. The most comprehensive specification of functional indices of necessity must logically include all the factors we have detailed for considering coercion alleged to be prohibited aggression. The relative size and power of the participant charged, the nature and consequentiality of its objectives, the character of its internal institutional structures, the kind of world public order it demands, the intensity and magnitude of the coercion applied, its expectations about effective community intervention, all are relevant. The tight complementarity of the conceptions of permissible and impermissible coercion and the interdependence of the factors comprising a detailed context may once again be underscored.

241. What must, in other words, be ascertained and appraised by a third-party decision-maker are the claimant's perceptions and evaluations that culminated in assertion of the claim. It has been emphasized in Sprout and Sprout, "Environmental Factors in the Study of International Politics," 1 *J. of Conflict Resolution* 309, 319 (1957) that "what matters in policy-making is how the milieu appears to the policy-maker, not how it appears to some sideline analyst or how it might appear to a hypothetical omniscient observer." Id. at 324: "If the problem is to explain or to predict a policy decision, the analyst has to answer such questions as: What environmental factors (or aspects of the situation) did the decision-maker [claimant] recognize and consider to be significant? What *use* did he make of his environmental *knowledge* in defining what was to be attempted and the means to be employed?"

For an antithetical perspective, see Schwarzenberger, "The Principle of Self-Defence in International Judicial Practice," in *Estudios de Derecho Internacional: Homenaje al Profesor Camilo Barcia Trelles* 213, 216 (Universidad de Santiago de Compostela, 1958), referring to "putative self-defence."

The Exacting Standard of Customary Law. The structure of traditional prescription has established a standard of justifying necessity commonly referred to in exacting terms. A high degree of necessity—a "great and immediate" necessity,[242] "direct and immediate," [243] "compelling and instant" [244]—was prerequisite to a characterization of coercion as "legitimate self-defense." Necessity that assumed the shape of an actual and current application of violence presented little difficulty. It was of course the purpose of high requirements of necessity to contain and restrict the assertion of claims to apply preemptive violence, that is when the necessity pleaded consisted of alleged expectations of an attack which had yet actually to erupt. In the *Caroline* case, it will be recalled, the British claim with which Secretary of State Webster was confronted was an assertion of anticipatory defense.[245] There is a whole continuum of degrees of imminence or remoteness in future time, from the most imminent to the most remote, which, in the expectations of the claimant of self-defense, may characterize an expected attack. Decision-makers sought to limit lawful anticipatory defense by projecting a customary requirement that the expected attack exhibit so high a degree of imminence as to preclude effective resort by the intended victim to non-violent modalities of response.

One illustration of the application of the customary-law standard of necessity for anticipatory defense is offered in the judgment of the International Military Tribunal for the Far East in respect of the war waged by Japan against the Netherlands. Japan contended that "inasmuch as the Netherlands took the initiative in declaring war on Japan, the war which followed [could] not be described as a war of aggression by Japan." [246] The Netherlands declared war on Japan on December 8, 1941, before the actual invasion of the Netherlands East Indies by Japanese troops and before the issuance of the Japanese declaration of war against the Netherlands, both of which took place on January 11, 1942. The evidence showed, however, that as

242. 1 Westlake, *International Law* 300 (1904).

243. Lawrence, *The Principles of International Law* 118 (2d ed., 1897).

244. Schwarzenberger, "The Fundamental Principles of International Law," 87 *Hague Recueil* 195, 334 (1955).

245. Note 210 supra.

246. *Judgment of the International Military Tribunal for the Far East* 994 (1948).

early as November 5, 1941, the Imperial General Headquarters had issued to the Japanese Navy operational orders for the attacks upon the Netherlands East Indies, as well as the Philippines and British Malaya,[247] and that on December 1, 1941, an Imperial Conference had formally decided that Japan would "open hostilities against the United States, Great Britain and the Netherlands." [248] The Tribunal held that the Netherlands, "being fully apprised of the *imminence* of the attack," had declared war against Japan "in self defense." [249] Similarly, the International Military Tribunal at Nuremberg, in rejecting a defense argument that the German invasion of Norway was "preventive" in character and designed to anticipate an Allied landing in Norway, pointed out that the German plans for invasion were not in fact made to forestall an *"imminent"* Allied landing, and that, at best, such plans could only prevent an Allied occupation "at some future time." [250] The documentary evidence submitted to the Tribunal did indicate that there was a "definite" Allied plan to occupy harbors and airports in Norway. The Tribunal found, however, that the expectations of Germany at the time of launching the invasion did not as a matter of fact include a belief that Britain was about to land troops in Norway.[251]

Maintenance of Customary-Law Standard in the U.N. Charter. It is against the background of the high degree of necessity required in traditional prescription that Article 51 of the United Nations Charter should be considered. Article 51 states in full:

> Nothing in the present Charter shall impair the inherent right of individual or collective self defense if an armed attack occurs against a Member of the United Nations, until the Security Council has taken the measures necessary to maintain international peace and security. Measures taken by Members in the exercise of this right of self defense shall be immediately reported to the Security Council and shall not in any way affect the authority and responsibility of the Security Council under the present Charter to take at any time such action as it deems

247. Id. at 964–6.
248. Id. at 976–8.
249. Id. at 995.
250. Office of U.S. Chief of Counsel for Prosecution of Axis Criminality, *Nazi Conspiracy and Aggression, Opinion and Judgment* 37 (1947).
251. See note 207 supra.

necessary in order to maintain or restore international peace and security.

There has been considerable contention about the impact of this article upon the standard of required necessity projected in the customary law of self-defense. Some scholars have taken the view that Article 51 demands an even higher degree of necessity than customary law for the characterization of coercion as permissible defense, that it limits justifying necessity to an "armed attack" as distinguished both from an expected attack of whatever degree of imminence and from applications of nonmilitary types of intense coercion, and that it absolutely forbids any anticipatory self-defense. For instance, Professor Kunz, insisting that Article 51 provides a "clear and unambiguous text," wrote, in characteristic exegesis:

> [F]or this right [of self-defense under Article 51] does not exist against any form of aggression which does not constitute "armed attack." Secondly, this term means something that has taken place. Article 51 prohibits "preventive war." The "threat of aggression" does not justify self-defense under Article 51. Now in municipal law self-defense is justified against an actual danger, but it is sufficient that the danger is *imminent.* The "imminent" armed attack does not suffice under Article 51.[252]

Most recently, Dr. Ninčić has argued from the canon *exceptiones sunt strictissimae interpretationis* that:

> [T]his means that nothing less than an armed attack shall constitute an *act-condition* for the exercise of the right of self-defense within the meaning of Article 51 (i.e. "subversion" and . . . "ideological" or "economic aggression" does not warrant armed action on the basis of Article 51). It further stipulates that *the armed attack must precede the exercise of the right of self-defense,* that only an armed attack which has actually materialized, which has "occurred" shall warrant a resort to self-defense. This clearly and explicitly rules out the permissibility of any "anticipatory" exercise of the right of self-defense, i.e. resort to armed force "in anticipation of an armed attack." [253]

252. Kunz, "Individual and Collective Self-Defense in Article 51 of the Charter of the United Nations," 41 *A.J.I.L.* 872, 878 (1947).

253. Reply from Dr. Ninčić, in Schwarzenberger, *Report on Some Aspects of of the Principle of Self-Defence in the Charter of the United Nations and the*

The major difficulties with this reading of what appears to be an inept piece of draftsmanship are twofold. In the first place, neither Article 51 nor any other word formula can have, apart from context, any single "clear and unambiguous" or "popular, natural and ordinary" meaning that predetermines decision in infinitely varying particular controversies.[254] The task of treaty interpretation, especially the interpretation of constitutional documents devised, as was the United Nations Charter, for the developing future, is not one of discovering and extracting from isolated words some mystical pre-existent, reified meaning but rather one of giving that meaning to both words and acts, in total context, which is required by the principal, general purposes and demands projected by the parties to the agreement.[255] For determining these major purposes and demands, a rational process of interpretation permits recourse to all available indices of shared expectation, including, in particular, that which Professor Kunz casually de-emphasized,[256] the preparatory work on

---

Topics Covered by the Dubrovnik Resolution 69 (Int. Law Assoc., 1958). (Emphasis in the original.) Professor Kunz and Dr. Ninčić have not been alone in their position on this matter. See Kelsen, *The Law of the United Nations* 797–8 (1950); Martin, *Collective Security* 169 (1952); 2 Oppenheim-Lauterpacht 156; Tucker, "The Interpretation of War Under Present International Law," 4 *Int. L.Q.* 11, 29–30 (1951).

254. Of the numerous eloquent exposures of the fundamental flaw of such a view, it suffices to quote Pollux, "The Interpretation of the Charter," 23 Brit. *Y.B.I.L.* 54, 67 (1946):

> It does not seem very helpful to state that "the ordinary methods of interpretation" shall be used in order to determine the "clear" meaning, "the plain terms," the "natural," "grammatical," "logical," "categorical," or "ordinary" meaning of one or more words. These terms beg the question for two reasons. In the first place, there may be words which have no such fixed meaning, and secondly, words may be used in a sense quite different from the usual one. Moreover, the foregoing expressions are not really at all informative. In practice they usually veil the process whereby a person, a court, or another body reaches a certain conclusion which inclines them to regard a particular meaning as the natural and plain meaning of a given word.

255. Some development of this general point is offered in McDougal and Gardner, "The Veto and the Charter: An Interpretation for Survival," 60 *Yale L.J.* 258 (1951). See also Hudson, *The Permanent Court of International Justice 1920–1942*, at 641–5 (1943); 2 Hyde, *International Law* 1468–72 (2d rev. ed., 1945); Harvard Research in International Law, "The Law of Treaties," 29 *A.J.I.L. Supp.* 937–71 (1935); Stone, "Fictional Elements in Treaty Interpretation—A Study in the International Judicial Process," 1 *Sydney L. Rev.* 344 (1955).

256. Supra note 252 at 873.

the agreement. Such a process of interpretation would, moreover, seek to bring within the attention frame of the interpreter and applier not just one element of a context suggested by one rule or principle of interpretation, such as that upon which Dr. Ninčić relied, but all the relevant variable factors of a particular context. It is of common record in the preparatory work on the Charter that Article 51 was not drafted for the purpose of deliberately narrowing the customary-law permission of self-defense against a current or imminent unlawful attack by raising the required degree of necessity. The moving purpose was, rather, to accommodate regional security organizations (most specifically the Inter-American system envisioned by the Act of Chapultepec) within the Charter's scheme of centralized, global collective security, and to preserve the functioning of these regional systems from the frustration of vetoes cast in the Security Council.[257] Further, in the process of formulating the prohibition of unilateral coercion contained in Article 2(4), it was made quite clear at San Francisco that the traditional permission of self-defense was not intended to be abridged and attenuated but, on the contrary, to be reserved and maintained. Committee 1/I stressed in its report,[258] which was approved by both Commission I and the Plenary Conference,[259] that "The unilateral use of force or similar

257. See 12 U.N.C.I.O. 680–2; 11 id. 52–9. See also, e.g., Bowett, *Self-Defence in International Law* 182–4 (1958); Goodrich and Hambro, *Charter of the United Nations* 297–9 (2d rev. ed., 1949); Russell and Muther, *A History of the United Nations Charter* 688–704 (1958); Bebr, "Regional Organizations: A United Nations Problem," 49 *A.J.I.L.* 166 (1955); Lleras Camargo, "El Sistema Regional Americano," 1 *Revista Colombiano de Derecho Internacional* No. 2, at 5 (1947). Professor Kunz himself was quite familiar with the purpose that lay behind Article 51. See Kunz, supra note 252, at 872–3; Kunz, "The Inter-American System and the United Nations Organization," 39 *A.J.I.L.* 758 (1945).

The Dumbarton Oaks Proposals, it may also be recalled, contained no provision at all on self-defense. At Dumbarton Oaks, in connection with a question raised by China as to who was to determine whether a state claiming self-defense was using force consistently with the purpose and principles of the projected organization, "it was agreed that the Charter could not deny the inherent right of self-defense against aggression. . . ." Russell and Muther, op. cit. supra at 465–6. See also id. at 599.

258. Report of Rapporteur of Committee 1 to Commission I, as adopted by Committee 1/I, 6 U.N.C.I.O. 446, 459.

259. See Verbatim Minutes of Fifth Meeting of Commission I, 6 U.N.C.I.O. 202, 204; Report of Rapporteur of Commission I to Plenary Session, id. at 245, 247. For the approval of this Report by the Plenary Conference, see Verbatim Minutes of the Ninth Plenary Session, 1 id. at 612, 620.

coercive measures is not authorized or admitted. The use of arms in legitimate self defense remains admitted and unimpaired."

More comprehensively considered, the principle of restrictive interpretation, of which *exceptiones sunt strictissimae interpretationis* is but one variant, may, with at least equal cogency, be invoked against the position Dr. Ninčić has taken. "Legitimate self-defense," encompassing anticipatory defense, has long been honored in traditional authoritative myth as one of the fundamental "rights of sovereign states." In accordance with one variant of the principle of restrictive interpretation, limitations or derogations from sovereign competence are not lightly to be assumed.[260] The view urged by Ninčić proceeds

260. On the principles of restrictive interpretation, see, e.g., the North Atlantic Coast Fisheries Case, in Briggs, *The Law of Nations* 313, 315 (2d ed., 1952); Fiore, *International Law Codified* 345 (Borchard, trans., 1918); Hall, *International Law* 394–5 (8th ed., Pearce Higgins, 1924); 2 Phillimore, *Commentaries Upon International Law* 110, 111–13 (3d ed., 1882); Fitzmaurice, "The Law and Procedure of the International Court of Justice: Treaty Interpretation and Certain Other Treaty Points," 28 *Brit. Y.B.I.L.* 1, 22 (1956). Sir Gerald attaches a curious label on this principle—"subsidiary interpretative finding."

In most comprehensive and accurate formulation, the principle of restrictive interpretation is a full complement of the principle of effectiveness, or interpretation by major purposes. Each principle serves merely to weight certain features of the process of agreement, as bases of interference of the shared expectations of the parties, for the guidance of decision-makers, and both principles are designed to preserve the integrity of the agreement-making process as an instrument by which states may securely project policies as to their future interrelations. The principle of effectiveness is a positive formulation that, when unfolding events inevitably lay bare contradictions, gaps, and omissions in the reference of an agreement, such deficiencies must be remedied by an interpretation best designed to promote the more general, essential purposes of the parties. The principle of restrictive interpretation is a negative formulation that the clarification of contradictions, completion of gaps, and resolution of ambiguities should not be carried beyond what is absolutely necessary to implementation of major purposes and should not be extended to imposing new purposes and unnecessary detailed obligations upon the parties.

For determining the shared expectations of the parties with respect to Article 51 of the United Nations Charter, the two principles, or formulations, fortunately reinforce each other in indicating a single conclusion. It is scarcely conceivable, as developed in our text, that the major "security" purposes of the parties to the Charter could in contemporary conditions be adequately, if at all, served by an intepretation which would reduce "self-defense" to assumption of the posture of the sitting duck. Similarly, to require the parties to the Charter to give up their traditional right of self-defense for so illusory a return would

from the hypothesis that self-defense is an "exception" whose recognition tends to nullify the "general rule" of prohibition of coercion and which must therefore be confined within the narrowest of limits. Even apart from the essential complementarity of prohibited and permissible coercion to which we have so very often adverted, the permission of self-defense embodied in customary prescription cannot of itself, if appropriately applied, render ineffective or illusive either the fundamental community policy against change by destructive coercion projected in the Charter, or the peace-maintaining functions of the United Nations. As noted above, customary prescription has always required a high degree of necessity—specifically, in the case of an anticipated attack, a high degree of imminence—to support the lawfulness of intense responding coercion. One index of the required condition of necessity is precisely the degree of opportunity for effective recourse to nonviolent modes of response and adjustment, including invocation of the collective conciliation functions of the United Nations. Furthermore, permitting defense against an imminently expected attack does not, any more than permitting defense against an actual current attack, impair or dilute the "authority and responsibility" of the organized community "to maintain or restore international peace and security." [261] Whether the events that precipitate the claim of self-defense constitute an actual, current attack or an imminently impending attack, the claim remains subject to the reviewing authority of the organized community. Finally, the continuing refusal of most of the members of the United Nations to accept the Soviet or Litvinov-Politis type of definition of aggression appears significant. If the members did concur in the narrow con-

certainly be to impose upon them deprivations nowhere clearly stipulated by the records of the Charter, and, in conformity with a policy of protecting the integrity of agreements, should not be done.

261. U. N. Charter, Art. 51. Professor Kunz and Dr. Ninčić are in effect purporting to discover in Article 51 words not written there in printer's ink. They interpret the phrase "if an armed attack occurs" as if it read "if, and only if, an armed attack occurs." A proposition that "if A, then B" is *not* equivalent to, and does *not* necessarily imply, the proposition that "if, and only if, A, then B." To read one proposition for the other, or to imply the latter from the former, may be the result of a policy choice, conscious or otherwise, or of innocent reliance upon the question-begging Latinism *inclusio unius est exclusio alterius;* such identification or implication is assuredly not a compulsion of logic. If a policy choice is in fact made, it should be so articulated as to permit its assessment.

struction of Article 51, if their demands and expectations were that the justifying conditions of necessity for self-defense should be and have been limited to an "armed attack" and that responding coercion must in all circumstances be postponed until unlawful coercion has exploded into destructive violence, then the Soviet first-shot test of aggression would have been embraced, it might be supposed, as a matter of course.[262]

The second major difficulty with a narrow reading of Article 51 is that it requires a serious underestimation of the potentialities both of the newer military weapons systems and of the contemporary techniques of nonmilitary coercion. If, in scholarly interpretation of authoritative myth, any operational reference is seriously intended to be made to realistically expected practice and decision, an attempt to limit permissible defense to that against an actual "armed attack," when increases in the capacity of modern weapons systems for velocity and destruction are reported almost daily in the front pages of newspapers, reflects a surpassing optimism. In these circumstances, "to cut down," Professor Waldock suggests forcefully, "the customary right of self defense beyond even the *Caroline* doctrine does not make sense. . . ."[263]

262. That acceptance of the construction of Article 51 objected to above would logically require adoption of the Soviet first-shot definition of aggression was made clear by the Soviet representatives to the U.N. committees in defining aggression. See, e.g., the statement of the Ukrainian SSR delegate that "the negative reference to the right of self-defense in operative paragraph 1 [of the draft definition submitted by Iran and Panama] did not stress the point that defensive measures were only permitted after an act armed attack [sic] had been committed by the opposing party. The draft resolution of Iran and Panama thus obscured the essence of Article 51 of the Charter, while the Soviet proposal was the perfect complement of that Article." U.N. Gen. Ass., *Off. Rec.*, 12th Sess., 6th Comm. 59 (1957).

263. Waldock, "The Regulation of the Use of Force by Individual States in International Law," 81 *Hague Recueil* 455, 498 (1952). This indicates a major difficulty in the position taken in Tucker, "Force and Foreign Policy," 47 *Yale Rev.* 374 (1958). Professor Tucker would compel policy-makers to choose between deference to "standards set by the United Nations Charter" and the achievement of "American security" and "preservation of Western interests." Id. at 379. He assumes the wholly unnecessary view that what the U. N. Charter prescribes is the excessively narrow construction of Article 51, id. at 375, and proceeds to describe such a "doctrine" as "divorced from political reality," id. at 380. There are other dichotomies drawn by Professor Tucker—such as "national interests" and "international standards," "renunciation of force" and "interna-

For illustration of the tergiversations and curious distinctions that become necessary in any attempt to accommodate the position insisted upon by, *inter alia,* Professor Kunz and Dr. Ninčić, with the actualities and potentialities of the contemporary technology of violence, reference may be made to the recommendations of Dr. Singh.[264] While vigorously stressing that "the sole condition on which the right [of self-defense] can be exercised is restricted to an armed attack," [265] Dr. Singh, recognizing at the same time that "in nuclear warfare time is of the very essence," [266] proposes a conception of "armed attack" that would permit the target state to respond with violence at some time before an attack is actually delivered or physically felt in its territorial domain. He writes:

> [I]f the provisions of Article 51 are carefully examined, it would appear that what is necessary to invoke the right of self defense is an *armed attack* and not the actual, physical violation of the territories of the State. . . . [A]s long as it can be proved that the aggressor State with the definite intention of launching an armed attack on a victim member-State has pulled the trigger and thereby taken the last proximate act on its side which is necessary for the commission of the offense of an armed attack, the requirements of Article 51 may be said to have been fulfilled even though physical violation of the territories by the armed forces may as yet have not taken place.[267]

Thus, Dr. Singh illustrates, submarines known to the target state "as a result of secret intelligence" to be about to undertake a nuclear attack may be attacked and destroyed "as soon as," but not before, they leave the territorial waters of the aggressor state. Similarly, the moment an initiating state has allowed its aircraft "to take off" and its guided missiles "to be shot," such instrumentalities of attack may

---

tional order," "security" and "survival," "justice" and "order"—which others may find difficult to make with the same confidence. For a presentation somewhat more concerned with community perspectives of authority, see his earlier article, "The Interpretation of War Under Present International Law," 4 *Int. L.Q.* 11 (1951).

264. Singh, "The Right of Self-Defence in Relation to the Use of Nuclear Weapons," 5 *Indian Yb. of Int. Affairs* 3 (1956).

265. Id. at 24.

266. Id. at 24–5. See also id. at 18.

267. Id. at 25.

be "repelled" by the target state. The justification offered is in terms of a *locus poenitentiae* admitted by "the general principles of law":

> before the submarine fleet had left territorial waters, there was the possibility of the aggressor state changing its mind and hence it may be premature to attack the fleet while still within the territorial limits of the aggressor state.[268]

It is not difficult to achieve the impression that these lines between "attack" and "actual preparation for the mounting of the attack" are largely unreal and arbitrary. On the one hand, imaginary boundaries on the sea and in the air have no necessary realistic relation to the limits of a hypothetical *locus poenitentiae*. On the other hand, considering the state and potentialities of modern telecommunications and guidance systems, there may in fact be no "last irrevocable act"—in respect of the instrumentalities Dr. Singh referred to: submarines, aircraft, and guided missiles—short of dropping or exploding a nuclear weapon. Thus, the whole tenor and effect of consistently requiring a "last irrevocable act" would seem to be to compel the target state to defer its reaction until it would no longer be possible to repel an attack and avoid damage to itself. In case of delivery by ballistic (as distinguished from guided) missiles, whose trajectory is traversed in a matter of minutes and against which effective repulsion measures have yet to be devised, it should be even clearer that to require postponement of response until after the "last irrevocable act" is in effect to reduce self-defense to the possible infliction, if enough defenders survive, of retaliatory damage upon the enemy. It is precisely this probable effect that gives to the narrowly restrictive construction of Article 51, when appraised for future application, a strong air of romanticism.

In particular connection with exercises emphasizing nonmilitary forms of attack, we have suggested that, in many contexts, the use of political, economic, and ideological instrumentalities may indeed result in no more than a modest degree of coercion, a degree which may constitute part of the ordinary coercion implicit in the power and other value processes in the world arena. To say, however, that Article 51 limits the appropriate precipitating event for lawful self-defense to an "*armed* attack" is in effect to suppose that in no pos-

268. Id. at 26.

sible context can applications of nonmilitary types of coercion (where armed force is kept to a background role) take on efficacy, intensity, and proportions comparable to those of an "armed attack" and thus present an analogous condition of necessity. Apart from the extreme difficulty of establishing realistic factual bases for that supposition, the conclusion places too great a strain upon the single secondary factor of modality—military violence. A rational appraisal of necessity demands much more than simple ascertainment of the modality of the initiating coercion. The expectations which the contending participants create in each other are a function not only of the simple fact that the military instrument has or has not been overtly used but also of the degree and kind of use to which all other instrumentalities of policy are being put. What must be assessed is the cumulative impact of all the means of coercion utilized; policy-oriented analysis must be *configurative* analysis. The kind, intensity, and dimension of political, economic, or ideological pressure applied may, through this analysis, serve in some contexts as relevant indices of the imminence or remoteness of an allegedly expected armed attack.

Effects and the Proportionality of Responding Coercion

We turn, finally, to appraisal of the effects of coercion claimed to be in self-defense. The principal reference here is to the degree of intensity and scope exhibited in this coercion—factors long recognized to be of special relevance in judgments about the lawfulness of particular claims to self-defense. It is primarily in terms of its magnitude and intensity—the consequentiality of its effects—that alleged responding coercion must be examined for its "proportionality." "Proportionality" which, like "necessity," is customarily established as a prerequisite for characterizing coercion as lawful defense, is sometimes described in terms of a required relation between the alleged initiating coercion and the supposed responding coercion: the (quantum of) responding coercion must, in rough approximation, be reasonably related or comparable to the (quantum of) initiating coercion.[269] It is useful to make completely explicit that concealed

269. See, e.g., the formulation in the report of de Brouckère quoted in text accompanying note 211 supra. Weightman, "Self-Defense in International Law," 37 *Va. L. Rev.* 1095, 1097 (1951), summarizing the conclusions of Giraud, "La Theorie de la Legitime Defense," 49 *Hague Recueil* 691 (1934), and Jenks, *The Common Law of Mankind* 141–3 (1958), observe that proportionality is a common requirement of self-defense in municipal systems. See also Sancho Izquierdo,

in this shorthand formulation of the requirement of proportionality are references to both the permissible objectives of self-defense and the condition of necessity that evoked the response in coercion. Proportionality in coercion constitutes a requirement that responding coercion be limited in intensity and magnitude to what is reasonably necessary promptly to secure the permissible objectives of self-defense.[270] For present purposes, these objectives may be most comprehensively generalized as the conserving of important values by compelling the opposing participant to terminate the condition which necessitates responsive coercion. Put a little differently, the objective is to cause the initiating participant to diminish its coer-

---

"La Guerra Defensiva y la Doctrina de la Legitima Defensa," in 3 *La Guerra Moderna* 29, 41, 51–3 (Universidad de Zaragoza 1956) and Jiménez de Aréchaga, "La Legitima Defensa Individual en la Carta de las Naciones Unidas," in *Estudios de Derecho Internacional: Homenaje al Profesor Camilo Barcia Trelles* 325, 337 (Universidad de Santiago de Compostela, 1958).

Kunz, "Individual and Collective Self Defense in Article 51 of the Charter of the United Nations," 41 *A.J.I.L.* 872, 878 (1947), made the astonishing statement that "If 'armed attack' means illegal armed attack it means, on the other hand, any illegal armed attack, even a small border incident; necessity or proportionality are no conditions for the exercise of self-defense under Art. 51." This of course reduces fundamental community policy to nonexistence. To say, further, that even a few shots across a border give rise to a right of self-defense, while maintaining that the most imminent threat of massive violence does not, is to make an absolutistic fetish of certain irrelevant aspects of modality.

270. This mode of formulating the proportionality principle, which would relate the response directly to legitimate objectives of defense rather than mediately to the stimulus of initiating coercion, may acquire new significance should contemporary possibilities of achieving instrumentalities of coercion that would incapacitate without killing, maiming, or otherwise producing permanent incapacity, be realized. The possibility of securing such instruments in the form, for instance, of a "P-bomb" (paralysis bomb) or a "P-beam" (paralyzing beam), as one approach to the "problem of harmonizing considerations of humanity with the use of whatever coercion cannot be avoided," was referred to in Lasswell, "The Political Science of Science: An Inquiry into the Possible Reconciliation of Mastery and Freedom," 50 *Am. Pol. Sci. Rev.* 961, 968 (1956). More recently, the U. S. Army is reported to have "held out the hope" that chemical and biological agents with such capabilities "could prevent small wars or help win nearly bloodless victories in a big conflict." Among the items specifically mentioned are means of producing temporary blindness, a "debilitating disease" "that would not kill but would leave enemies listless," and "psycho-chemicals" that would induce temporary "irrational behaviour" (such as trying to "fly across a room"). *N. Y. Times,* May 10, 1958, p. 10, col. 3. See infra.

cion to the more tolerable levels of "ordinary coercion." This is the import of Secretary of State Webster's somewhat cryptic statement that "nothing unreasonable or excessive [must be done], since the act, justified by the necessity of self defense, must be limited by that necessity and kept clearly within it." [271] Thus articulated, the principle of proportionality is seen as but one specific form of the more general principle of economy in coercion [272] and as a logical corollary of the fundamental community policy against change by destructive modes. Coercion that is grossly in excess of what, in a particular context, may be reasonably required for conservation of values against a particular attack, or that is obviously irrelevant or unrelated to this purpose, itself constitutes an unlawful initiation of coercive or violent change.

From this perspective, it should be evident that an appropriate appraisal of the magnitude and intensity of an exercise of self-defense for its proportionality—a determination, in other words, of the amount of coercion reasonably necessary in a particular instance for achieving the lawful purpose of self-defense—requires functional reference to all the various factors relating to the opponent's allegedly aggressive coercion as well as to all the other factors relating to the claimant's coercion, which together comprise a detailed context.

271. Note 210 supra.

272. Some amplification of this principle may be found in Ch. 1, pp. 35–6. As a reading of the literature there referred to will indicate, the conception of proportionality or economy in coercion has acquired increased significance as recognition of the difficulties of keeping violence limited has grown. The conception, put in one form or another, appears to underlie many of the current theories of "graduated deterrence" and "limited war" strategies. It is perhaps most conspicuous in proposals on "proportional" or "measured deterrence" which envisage almost mechanical equilibration of response and attack, for example, response by delivering the same number of bombs on the attacker's cities as that detonated by the attacker on the replier's cities. See Amster, "Design for Deterrence," 12 *Bull. Atomic Scientists* 164 (1956); Sherwin, "Securing Peace Through Military Technology," id. at 159. The soundness of exclusive reliance upon a theory of "massive deterrence," i.e., where deterrence from *any* initial act is sought to be effected by the very disproportion of the promised reaction, under present power conditions, has been insistently questioned. See, e.g., Nitze, "Symmetry and Intensity of Great Power Involvement in Limited Wars," in *Military Policy Papers* 55 (Washington Center of Foreign Policy Research, 1958). See also Kaplan, "The Calculus of Nuclear Deterrence," 1 *World Politics,* 20 (1958), and Kaplan, *The Strategy of Limited Retaliation* (Policy Memorandum No. 19, Center for International Studies, Princeton University [1959]).

More particularly, the determination of proportionality is not, as is sometimes suggested, necessarily exhausted by ascertaining the qualitative similarity or dissimilarity of the weapons employed by one and the other contending participant. It has been urged, for instance, that a lawful defense against an attack executed with "conventional" weapons may not utilize "unconventional" or nuclear weapons; the use of nuclear arms, the argument runs, would be a disproportionate and excessive reaction.[273] We have repeatedly indicated that modality may be useful as a quick index to intensity and scope. But, as we have just as frequently suggested, modality is no more than a prima facie rule of thumb which cannot dispense with more detailed inquiry into the consequentiality of coercion, and which must be taken in conjunction with all other relevant variable factors. Thus, in particular respect of the "conventional-nuclear" dichotomy, it would, we suggest, be an extremely hazardous prediction to say (as Dr. Singh appears in effect to be saying) that in no possible set of events will an authorized decision-maker regard the use of nuclear weapons—the "yield" of which, it should be recalled, is subject to control and may vary enormously—as reasonably necessary to stop and turn back an attack initiated with "conventional" weapons. It is perhaps symptomatic that Dr. Singh himself would concede one "possible exception": when the target state, "facing certain defeat, with a view to upholding the law and to prevent the aggressor from becoming victorious, after giving full trial to permissible weapons, uses prohibited nuclear weapons as a last resort against the law-breaker." [274]

Collective Self-Defense

The permission of collective self-defense recognized in Article 51 of the United Nations Charter has, in the context of continuing conflict between the major demanded systems of world public order and of consequently low expectations about the reliability of effective intervention by the organized community, acquired special promi-

273. Singh, "The Right of Self-Defence in Relation to the Use of Nuclear Weapons," 5 *Indian Yb. of Int. Affairs* 3, 32–4 (1956). Cf. the statement of the Indian representative in U.N. Gen. Ass., *Off. Rec.*, 12th Sess., 6th Comm. 54 (1957): "If the use of atomic weapons was declared illegal, even in self-defence, any state which used them to defend itself against an attack using conventional weapons would become an aggressor. It was a general principle that self-defence must be legitimate and must be proportionate to the attack."

274. Singh, supra note 273, at 33.

nence and importance. That importance, of course, flows from the faculty afforded by Article 51 of taking collective action in defense against initiating coercion without need of securing prior authorization from the general security organization. The last decade or so has seen the proliferation of regional defense arrangements or organizations which has culminated in the emergence of two principal sets of opposing, mutually exclusive, agreements that impart, in substantial effect, formal expression to the contemporary phenomena of systemic conflict and of polarizing power in the world arena. There are, on the one hand, the agreements among Western and Western-oriented states, such as the Inter-American Treaty of Reciprocal Assistance of 1947, the Brussels Treaty of 1948, the North Atlantic Treaty of 1949, the Pacific Security (ANZUS) Treaty of 1951, and the Southeast Asia Collective Defense Treaty of 1954.[275] On the other hand, there are the Warsaw Treaty of 1955 between the Soviet Union and her protected states,[276] the Treaty of Friendship, Alliance and Mutual Assistance of 1950 between the Soviet Union and the People's Republic of China,[277] and the network of bilateral treaties of the Soviet Union with Bulgaria,[278] Roumania,[279] Hungary[280] and Finland,[281] and of the protected Eastern European states *inter se*.[282] In addition to these major groupings, there is the Joint Defense and Economic Cooperation Treaty of 1950 between the members of the Arab League.[283] These regional arrangements or organizations to-

275. See note 12 supra. The text of the Brussels Treaty may be found in 43 *A.J.I.L. Supp.* 59 (1949). See generally Royal Institute of International Affairs, *Atlantic Alliance: Nato's Role in the Free World* (1952); Royal Institute of International Affairs, *Collective Defense in Southeast Asia: The Manila Treaty and Its Implications* (1956).

276. 49 *A.J.I.L. Supp.* 194 (1955).

277. 44 *A.J.I.L. Supp.* 84 (1950).

278. 48 *United Nations Treaty Series* 142 (1950).

279. 48 *United Nations Treaty Series* 196 (1950).

280. 48 *United Nations Treaty Series* 170 (1950).

281. 48 *United Nations Treaty Series* 156 (1950).

282. 1 U.S. Dept. of State, *Documents and State Papers* 238–49 (1948); id. at 681 (1949). On the Soviet network of treaties generally, see Kulski, "The Soviet System of Collective Security Compared with the Western System," 44 *A.J.I.L.* 453 (1950); Schapiro, "The Post War Treaties of the Soviet Union," 4 *Y.B. of World Affairs* 130 (1950); Yakobson, "World Security and Regional Arrangements—Soviet Position," 44 *Proc. Am. Soc.* I.L. 15 (1950).

283. 49 *A.J.I.L. Supp.* 51 (1955).

gether embrace a very substantial number of the countries of the world that have any power capability. Some scholars have eloquently deplored that "the right to collective self defense has been used to emasculate the world organization in favor of regional organization"[284] and that "collective self defense" and "collective security" are poles apart, "as distant from each other as order is from chaos."[285] These lamentations appear to assume that only that security is collective which is also universal and to ignore that not the permission of collective self-defense but the rising power and the dynamics of totalitarian world orders have imperiled the aspiration for universal security. The real point of the development of regional defense arrangements and organization is the increased recognition that, the facts of contemporary international life being what they are, defense must be collective if it is not to be an exercise in individual suicide.

Establishment of a collective defense organization represents a claim to prepare for collective defense. Objection to treaties establishing such organizations has, in the past, been made upon the ground that the permission of self-defense, whether individual or collective, is available only at the precise moment of "armed attack," and that apprehension of attack does not justify military preparations.[286] It is not necessary to take this objection seriously; the permission of self-defense, particularly under the conditions posed by the present technology and techniques of coercion, must be quite meaningless if read to exclude peacetime preparatory arrangements to meet coercion. Claims to the actual exercise of coercion in collective self-defense are of more important concern to the present

284. Levi, *Fundamentals of World Organization* 84 (1950).

285. Stone, *Legal Controls of International Conflict* 264 (1954). See also Wolfers, "Collective Security and the War in Korea," 43 *Yale Rev.* 481 (1954), where the assertion is made that the action taken in Korea was "collective self-defense" rather than "collective security," at least on the part of the United States, upon the theory that the United States had vital "national interests" in taking the action it did. For Dr. Wolfers, no concerted action may appropriately be described as "collective security" unless the members participating "actually chose the long run advantage at the expense of immediate security." Id. at 485.

286. See the statement issued by the Soviet Ministry of Foreign Affairs on Jan. 29, 1949, asserting the nonconformity of the North Atlantic Treaty with the U. N. Charter. 3 *Int. Organization* 400–6 (1949). See also Schick, "The North Atlantic Treaty and the Problem of Peace," 62 *Juridical Rev.* 26, 49 (1950).

inquiry. Review and appraisal of the lawfulness of these claims present no special or unique intellectual difficulties. Exactly the same kind of multiple-factor analysis we have recommended for passing upon coercion claimed to be in individual self-defense seems necessary for making judgments about coercion avowed to be in group self-defense, and all the categories of detailed factors relevant for the one are in general relevant for the other. It remains necessary, however, to deal with a few objections to the entire concept of collective self-defense and, in so doing, to examine certain factors that relate peculiarly to claims of group defense.

The deprecatory attitude toward collective self-defense begins with a strong preoccupation with a dogmatic conception limited to the defense of single, territorially-organized polities like those which broke away from feudalism several centuries ago. This preoccupation is evident in Professor Kelsen's analysis:

> [Self-defense] is a right of the attacked or threatened individual or state, and of no other individual or state. Article 51 confers the right to use force not only upon the attacked state but also upon other states which unite with the attacked state in order to assist it in its defense. This is probably the meaning of the term "collective self defense." If so, the term "collective self defense" is not quite correct. It is certainly collective "defense," but not collective "self"-defense. . . . [T]he action on the part of the states which are not attacked, but only assist the attacked state against its aggressor, is not exactly self-defense.[287]

The strictures of Professor Stone are comparable:

> [U]nder general international law, a State has no right of "self-defense" in respect of an armed attack upon a third state. The very notion of *collective* self-defense seems contradictory, except as resorted to by two or more victims simultaneously attacked by the same Power.[288]

The most recent detailed statement on collective self-defense is built upon the same limited conception. The "essence" of collective self-defense "properly termed," Dr. Bowett writes, is "that the partici-

287. Kelsen, *The Law of the United Nations* 792 (1950).

288. Stone, *Legal Controls of International Conflict* 245 (1954).

pants base their action on a violation of their own legally protected rights or interests." [289] Upon this premise, Dr. Bowett submits that:

> [T]he situation which the Charter envisages by the term is . . . a situation in which each participating state bases its participation in collective action on its own right of self-defense. It does not, therefore, generally extend the right of self-defense to any state which desires to associate itself in the defense of a state acting in self-defense.[290]
>
> . . .
>
> The intervening state which has no legal right in the security of the actual victim, which has not itself the right of self-defense, must justify its action as being in the nature of a sanction; it is not self-defense, individual or collective.[291]

The most fundamental difficulties in these formulations are twofold. The first lies in the implicit or explicit assumption that only single nation-states are authorized to claim self-defense, that, in other words, the "self" which may be defended is simply, as indicated, that of the particular form of body-politic inherited from the decay of feudalism. That assumption leads almost inevitably to a misconception of the core problem—identification of the "self" which may lawfully claim to exercise defending coercion. A claim of collective self-defense arises whenever a number of traditional bodies-politic asserting certain common demands for security as well as common expectations that such security can be achieved only by larger cooperative efforts, and purporting to define their respective identification structures so as to create a common overlap and interlock, confront an opponent, and present themselves to the rest of the general community as one unified group or collectivity for purposes of security and defense.[292] Each member of the group in effect asserts, singly and in combination, defense of the new and more comprehen-

289. Bowett, *Self-Defence in International Law* 206 (1958).

290. Id. at 216.

291. Id. at 217.

292. Cf. the formulation of the "general rationale behind collective defense" in King, "Collective Defense: The Military Commitment," in *Military Policy Papers* 25, 28 (Washington Center of Foreign Policy Research, 1958). See also Haas, "Regional Integration and National Policy," *Int. Conciliation* No. 513 (1957).

sive "self." The question is whether the comprehensive group of collective "self" projected for purposes of security should be accepted by authorized decision-makers and be entitled to lawful defense. In view of the power processes existing in the world arena, a group "self" that comprehends several traditional territorial polities need no more be dismissed as a "legal fiction" than a "self" consisting of only one such polity. It can indeed be dismissed as a "legal fiction" only if the prior, question-begging assumption is made that the individual "self" of a particular nation-state is a constant for all purposes and may alone be protected and maintained by lawful coercion. The identifications which human beings make, the "self" systems which they establish for many different purposes, may be of many differing degrees of geographical range and scope; [293] the territorial state, as we know it today, is only one such system for certain particular purposes. Groupings of states, regional or functional, constituted in many varied degrees of organization and integration, are familiarly recognized as authorized participants for equally varied purposes in many authority processes.[294] There is no compelling reason why they may not or should not be recognized as authorized

293. Introduction to "self" or identification systems is provided in Lasswell and Kaplan, *Power and Society* 11–13, 30–1 (1950). On the state considered as one (among many) system of interlocking identifications, see Lasswell, *Psychopathology and Politics* c. 13 (1930). For the social psychological bases and processes of "self" formation, see the influential accounts in Cooley, *Human Nature and the Social Order* (1902) and *Social Organization* (1909) (both reprinted *sub nom. The Two Major Works of Charles H. Cooley* (1956)); Mead, *Mind, Self and Society* (1934). See also Krech and Crutchfield, *Theory and Problems of Social Psychology* (1948); Sherif and Cantril, *The Psychology of Ego-Involvements* (1947). A recent discussion of the processes and conditions of community formation, the construction and integration of a larger "self," among several states in a particular geographical region, is found in Deutsch and Associates, *Political Community and the North Atlantic Area* (1957). See further Deutsch, *Political Community at the International Level: Problems of Definition and Measurement* (1954).

294. For indication of the range of relevant organizations, see, e.g., Eagleton, *International Government* (3d ed., 1957); Hill, *International Organization* (1952); Leonard, *International Organization* (1951); Mangone, *A Short History of International Organization* (1954); Jenks, "Co-ordination in International Organization: An Introductory Survey," 28 Brit. *Y.B.I.L.* 29 (1951); Potter, "World Institutions," in *The World Community* 259 (Wright, ed., 1948); Bebr, "Regional Organizations: Their Functions and Potentialities in the World Community," 1951 (unpublished thesis in Yale Law Library).

units of claim and participation for the most important purpose of all, defense and security. If the provision for collective self-defense in the United Nations Charter has any point, it is the recognition that, in particular contexts, an unlawful attack upon one component of a group may, in its objectives, dimensions, and probable effects, so involve and endanger the whole as to make prompt response by the group necessary, meet, and reasonable. Community authority joins, we submit, with realistic observation in recognizing that the "self" systems by and on behalf of which claims to exercise defending coercion may be reasonably asserted may exhibit differing measures of comprehensiveness. These systems range from the primary "self" of a single state, through a more comprehensive group "self" established by two or a few states, to the most inclusive "self" that may be organized in a particular situation and which may include the bulk of the community of states.

The second principal difficulty is the apparent failure to perceive that the same fundamental community policy runs through all the varying specific forms that permissible coercion may assume.[294a] "Individual self-defense," "collective self-defense," "regional enforcement action," and "collective security action" or "police action" are indeed but differing remedial techniques and institutional modalities designed to secure the first and most basic policy of any legal system: the prevention and suppression of unilateral change by destructive coercion and thereby the maintenance of those conditions of minimum order indispensable for the continued and fruitful functioning of all human value processes. In these terms, "individual self-defense" and "police action" represent the opposed ends of a spectrum of degrees of community involvement and participation in the forcible redress of breaches of world public order. "Collective self-defense" and "regional enforcement action" refer to the degrees of involvement in the middle ranges of the spectrum where more than one nation-state but less than the whole or the bulk of the community is engaged in the task of securing public order. Thus a wide variation may exist, first, in the range and comprehensiveness of the "self" on behalf of which the exercise of lawful coercion may be claimed, and, second, in the specific institutional techniques by which primary community policy may be implemented.

294a. This failure is illustrated in Skubiszewski, "The Postwar Alliances of Poland and the United Nations Charter," 53 *A.J.I.L.* 613 (1959), esp. 633.

We do not mean to suggest that, in terms of the more particular requirements of common, unifying, fundamental policy, differences may not exist between "individual self-defense," "collective self-defense," and "collective security action" (the last including both "regional enforcement action" and more general "community police action"). Broad, basic policy must be adapted to the varying specific types of contexts in which it is to be secured by the varying institutional modes of implementation. Thus, the differences in the structure and comprehensiveness of the "participant" or "self" may rationally require differences in appraisal of the other constituent factors of a particular context. For instance, in assessing the conditions under which collective self-defense is asserted, it may be appropriate to require a higher degree of imminence of attack and more exacting evidence of compelling necessity for coercive response by the group as such than would be reasonably demanded if the responding participant were a single state. The larger "self" of a group-participant ordinarily means greater bases of power at its disposal and, vis-à-vis a single opponent state, a substantial preponderance of force. Indeed a major, if somewhat obvious, premise of the multiplication in recent decades of collective defense arrangements and organizations is that a consolidated and coordinated group is less easily threatened than a lone and isolated state. Again, the limitations on the scope of permissible objectives of self-defense, individual or group, in which force is asserted without previous specific authorization from the organized general community, need not necessarily be regarded as restricting the competence of the organization itself inclusively to determine upon more comprehensive objectives for police action.

From this perspective, Dr. Bowett's focus upon the "individual right" of self-defense of each single participating state would seem essentially misdirected. It is not, we submit, an atomistic inquiry into the existence of an "individual right" to self-defense in each component member of a group-claimant, but rather a determination of the reasonableness of coercion by the group considered as a unified whole, as a collective "self," that is demanded by basic policy and prescription. Reasonableness here, as in individual self-defense, refers to the total configuration of relevant variables in context, and depends, in broadest statement, upon the character of the objectives sought by the group and the necessity for and proportionality of the group response. Appraisal of the real as distinguished from the proclaimed goals of the group-claimant involves appraisal of the genuineness of the asserted common identifications for defense and security. It also necessitates an evaluation of the realism of the avowed expectation that the defense and security interdependences of the members are such that an attack upon any member seriously prejudices the security of every other member.[295] A first step in the determination of reasonableness (that is, lawfulness) is thus an inquiry into the substantiality of the collective "self" alleged for security and defense, and into whether a purported grouping for common protection is in reality a façade for other unlawfully expansive purposes.

For similar reasons, the dilemma Dr. Bowett constructs between, on the one hand, the necessity of showing an "individual right" of self-defense in each element of a group-participant and, on the other hand, the imposition of inaction, however dire the emergency, until previous authorization for "collective security" or "police action" is obtained from the organized community,[296] appears specious. Dr. Bowett himself recognizes the probable "serious disadvantages" which acceptance of his analysis would entail "once we assume the impotency of the competent organs of the United Nations": "piecemeal aggression" whereby "each victim would fall in turn with no hope of assistance from friendly nations." [297] Dr. Bowett insists, however, that these consequences are reasons for "questioning the political wisdom" of the Charter scheme, *not* for "extending and distorting the legal concept of self defence." [298] He adds that neither the "political conditions of post war" nor the numerous collective defense treaties adverted to earlier "can alter the concept of self defence." [299] Moreover, under the "Uniting For Peace" Resolution, the argument continues, the inability of the United Nations to authorize "collective [security] action" can no longer be assumed.[300] It is difficult to ascribe much force to this plea for maintaining the purity of a particular past conception of self-defense. Outside the celestial abode of

295. Dr. Bowett approaches this view in stating that "the important question is always, in final analysis, whether an attack upon one state in fact threatens the security of the other." Bowett, *Self-Defence in International Law* 238 (1958).

296. Id. at 239–43.

297. Id. at 245.

298. Id. at 246.

299. Id. at 241.

300. Id. at 246.

juristic concepts, in the world of time and space where the global processes of power are located, it must seem a curious conviction that this concept of self-defense must remain unaltered despite profound changes in the conditions and features of those processes. A "legal concept" of self-defense, like any other legal concept, can be given empirical reference only in terms of who, for what purposes and under what conditions, uses and applies the concept. The expectations both of the general community and of particular authorized decision-makers about lawfulness (that is, reasonableness) do and must change through time as the conditions of use and application change. Fortunately, with the "Uniting For Peace" Resolution, a somewhat higher exponent can be placed on the probability of obtaining an authorization—a characterization of the permissibility of particular coercion—by the organized community. This very expectation, however, makes it all the more difficult to concede point to Dr. Bowett's version of collective self-defense. A group claim of self-defense, no less than an individual claim, remains subject to review by the organized community. It is to the necessities arising in the interim between initiation of the unlawful coercion and subsequent authorization or characterization that the permission of self-defense, individual or group, addresses itself. A final indication of the extent to which Dr. Bowett's analysis escapes contact with reality lies in the character of the alternatives that he offers for meeting those necessities: disarmament and world federation.[301]

Community Police Action

The third and final reference of permissible coercion is to police or enforcement action. It is sometimes suggested with undertones of cynicism that "police action" in fact means going to "war." [302] In the sense that police action undertaken by or on behalf of the organized general community may be as immediately destructive of values as an

301. Id. at 247. We do not, it may be added, seek to disparage these alternatives as long-term goals. What is open to grave doubt is the probability of their realization in the (now) discernible future and the wisdom of rejecting group defense while those goals as yet remain out of reach.

302. The suggestion appears, with varying nuances in reference, in, e.g., Appadorai, *The Use of Force in International Relations* 98–9 (1958); Wolfers, "Collective Security and The War in Korea," 43 *Yale Rev.* 481, 484 (1954). See also Borchard, "The Impracticability of 'Enforcing' Peace," 55 *Yale L.J.* 966 (1946).

unauthorized application of violence, this is true. But the inclusive policy at stake in police action is the exact opposite of the exclusive purpose projected in unauthorized violence. The one is the overriding community policy of establishing and maintaining that minimum order in which all value processes may peacefully go forward; the other is unilateral expansion by force that directly repudiates and attacks minimum order. Whatever the similarity in the physical destruction wrought or in the instrumentalities of policy employed, significant differentiation is to be found in the identifications of the participants and the nature of their objectives.

The agreements envisaged in Article 43 of the United Nations Charter, agreements for the supply of "armed forces, assistance and facilities" to the Security Council, have never been concluded, and in all likelihood will not be concluded in the foreseeable future. Furthermore, the probability of unanimity among the permanent members of the Council—except, perhaps, in a conflict between small powers not involving any appreciable interest of the polar powers—seems apt to remain negligible. As a result, the participants in a police action probably will consist of individual members or groups of members acting as agents of the organized community upon the basis of a permissive authorization or delegation from the General Assembly. The operative assumption behind any police action is thus that the organization has succeeded in characterizing coercion in a particular case as impermissible.

The appropriate objectives of a particular police action are to be determined by the security organization itself. The ample range of U.N. authority in this regard is indicated by the high level of generality with which the grant of competence is formulated in the Charter: "to maintain or restore international peace and security." [303] On the one hand, police action cannot, without making nonsense of fundamental community policy, seek the destruction of the political independence and the disposition of the territory and other values of the aggressor state for the exclusive aggrandizement of the participating members. On the other hand, the restrictions in respect of permissible conservation customarily established for unilateral self-defense need not be regarded as necessarily applicable to police ac-

303. U.N. Charter, Art. 39. See also Article 1(1). In Article 24(2), it is stipulated that "in discharging these duties the Security Council shall act in accordance with the Purposes and Principles of the United Nations."

tion authorized by the organized community. The significant policy difference would seem to lie in the inclusive character both of the identifications of the participants and of the decision process by which the appropriate objectives of a specific police action are formulated and established.[304] More specifically, neither the Charter of the United Nations nor other basic authoritative policy would preclude the organization from setting, in a particular case, objectives for police action more comprehensive than the mere "repelling" or "halting" of the unlawful attack. Authority, for instance, may well be conceded to the organized community to reconstruct those basic institutions of the target aggressor-state which outrage all conceptions of human dignity, or otherwise to modify conditions which, in reasonable expectation, may give rise to future violations of public order.[305] For a public order committed to human dignity, however, a fundamental constitutional principle is that individuals must not be coerced beyond a level reasonably necessary to maintain the order itself. In addition, objectives may be limited by the differential operation in differing cases, or even in differing stages of the same case, of the cost factor—the expectations of the general community about the tolerable or unbearable character of the probable costs of achieving a particular objective.

The experience in Korea affords documentation of the effect of this cost factor upon the definition of objectives. The Security Council resolution of June 27, 1950,[306] after noting that the North Korean authorities had "neither ceased hostilities nor withdrawn their armed forces to the 38th parallel," recommended assistance to the Republic of Korea "to repel the armed attack and to restore international

304. From this viewpoint, the related controversy, aroused by the very broadness and generality of the authority granted by the Charter, as to whether the organization is "bound" by "principles of justice and international law" in the characterization of prohibited coercion and the application of sanctions, appears largely unreal. The details of this contention may be found in Kelsen, "Collective Security and Collective Self-Defense Under the Charter of the United Nations," 42 *A.J.I.L.* 783 (1948); Kelsen, "Sanctions in International Law Under the Charter of the United Nations," 31 *Iowa L. Rev.* 499 (1946); Tucker, "The Interpretation of War Under Present International Law," 4 *Int. L.Q.* 11, 25–7 (1951). See also Schick, "Peace on Trial—A Study of Defence in International Organization," 2 *Western Pol. Q.* 1, 13–15 (1949).

305. Cf. the argument on desirability of such authority made in Loewenstein, *Political Reconstruction* (1946).

306. U.N. Sec. Council, *Off. Rec.*, 5th Yr, No. 16, at 4 (1950).

peace and security in the area." Later, on October 7, 1950, with the military position of the United Nations forces dramatically improved and the North Korean armies being pushed back toward the 38th parallel, the General Assembly asserted authority to determine upon a general objective that went beyond the mere repulsion of the unlawful North Korean attack. The Assembly authorized the United Nations forces to take "all appropriate steps . . . to ensure conditions of stability *throughout Korea,*" as well as "all constituent acts . . . including the holding of elections, under the auspices of the United Nations, for the *establishment of a unified, independent and democratic government in the sovereign State of Korea.*" [307] Upon the initiation of massive unlawful intervention by the "People's Republic of China," however, and the change in the prevailing expectations, realistic or otherwise, of the members about the costs and risks of pursuing the objective of unification, the General Assembly redefined and re-interpreted that objective in the following more modest terms: "to bring about a cessation of hostilities in Korea and the achievement of United Nations objectives in Korea by peaceful means. . . ." [308]

Police action may be carried out, like any other coercion, by all the familiar instrumentalities of policy, and may present a considerable variety in the kind and extent of participation and assistance undertaken by various members. For clarity, police action in this sense—the application of coercive sanctions against a participant inclusively determined to have initiated prohibited coercion—must be distinguished from the operations of an international "police force" like the "United Nations Emergency Force" created during the Suez crisis of 1956.[309] While the mere presence of the UNEF in the conflict

307. Res. No. 376(V), U.N. Gen. Ass., *Off. Rec.,* 5th Sess., Supp. No. 20 (A/1775) at 9 (1950). (Emphasis supplied.)

308. Res. No. 498(V), U.N. Gen. Ass., *Off. Rec.,* 5th Sess., Supp. No. 20A (A/1775/Add. 1) at 1 (1951). See also Res. No. 500(V), id. at 2; No. 711(VII)A, id. 7th Sess., Supp. No. 20B (A/2361/Add.2) at 1 (1953); Goodrich, *Korea, A Study of U.S. Policy in the United Nations* cc. 5–8 (1956); Goodrich, "Korea: Collective Measures Against Aggression," *Int. Conciliation* No. 494 (1953); Wright, "Collective Security in the Light of the Korean Experience," 45 *Proc. Am. Soc. I.L.* 165, 171–5 (1951).

309. Res. No. 1000 (ES-1), U.N. Gen. Ass., *Off. Rec.,* 1st Emer. Spec. Sess., Supp. No. 1 (A/3354) at 2 (1956). See generally Goodrich and Rosner, "The United Nations Emergency Force," 11 *Int. Organization* 413 (1957).

area may have induced restraint in the contending belligerents, it was neither designed nor equipped actually to exercise force and to "influence the military balance" against an identified violator.[310] Its functions were limited to supervising and policing the cease-fire and withdrawal of forces called for by the General Assembly. The modest character of these functions is perhaps most clearly indicated by the fact that the consent of the country in whose territory they were to be performed was regarded by the organization as indispensable.[311] In making this distinction between "police action" and a UNEF-type of "police force," we do not mean to minimize the latter. There are, on the contrary, a number of conceivable situations in which such a "police force" can be a valuable device for the localization of conflict.[312]

In contrast with the customary-law permission of unilateral self-defense, the competence of the organized community to order or authorize police action is not circumscribed by Charter specification of a required degree or condition of necessity. No specific standard has been accepted as authoritative for the organization in "determining the existence of" the appropriate precipitating events—"a threat to the peace," "breach of the peace," "act of aggression"—for requiring or authorizing coercive action to "maintain or restore international peace and security." It is precisely for rationality in such determinations, for maintenance of the most delicate adjustment of specific decision to fundamental community policy, that configurative analysis of changing contexts of coercion, by appropriate standards like those recommended above, is most essential. The conditions under which, in a particular instance, police action is authorized by

310. Second and Final Report of the Secretary-General on the Plan for an Emergency International United Nations Force, U.N. Gen. Ass., *Off. Rec.*, 1st Emer. Spec. Sess., Annexes, Agenda Item 5, at 19, 20 (1956).

311. The Secretary-General stated, id. par. 9, that "While the General Assembly is enabled to *establish* the Force with the consent of those parties which contribute units to the Force, it could not request the Force to be *stationed* or *operate* on the territory of a given country without the consent of the Government of that country." This was approved by the General Assembly. Res. No. 1001 (ES-1), U.N. Gen. Ass., *Off. Rec.* 1st Emer. Spec. Sess., Supp. No. 1 (A/3354) at 3 (1956).

312. See Frye, *A United Nations Peace Force* cc. 7–9 (1957); Nitze, "Where and under What Circumstances Might a United Nations Police Force be Useful in the Future?," in Frye, op cit. supra at 111; Munro, "Can the United Nations Enforce Peace?" 38 *Foreign Aff.* 209 (1960).

the organization may exhibit a very high and even an extreme necessity for arresting an unlawful attack and for aiding the victim. As a practical matter, participation in police action carries with it burdens and risks which states do not lightly assume. There are, as a result, built-in safeguards against premature or officious initiation of police action. Indeed, the constant danger to world public order is not that police action may be precipitously taken in circumstances of actually inadequate necessity, but that it may not be taken at all.

Policy Clarification a First Step Toward Minimum Public Order

The main purpose of this chapter has been to establish that, even in the contemporary cloven and disjointed world, it is both intellectually possible and practically indispensable for peoples genuinely dedicated to the values of human dignity to clarify in some detail a rational community policy concerning resort to international coercion. The principal emphases comprising our theme have been:

that in a world of accelerating interdependences with respect to all values, minimum order—in the sense of freedom from expectations of unauthorized violence and coercion—is as indispensable in the general community of states as it is in single states to an order of freedom and abundance in the production and sharing of values;

that existing world prescriptions, expressed in the United Nations Charter and other authoritative pronouncements and judgments, and accepted, formally at least, with near universality, make the necessary distinction between permissible and nonpermissible coercion and project a basic policy which seeks to prohibit the use of intense coercion as an instrument of international change, that is, for purposes of extension rather than defense of values;

that by orderly examination of processes of coercion in context, with appropriate significance being accorded to principal features such as *participants, objectives, methods, conditions* and *effects,* an observer or decision-maker may, in particular instances, make the specific interpretations of basic community policy best designed to promote the values of human dignity and progress toward a more complete international order in which these values are more secure;

that from perspectives seeking movement toward a world order of human dignity, the coercion characterized as "nonpermissible"—and prohibited in general community prescription as "acts of aggression," "breaches of the peace," "threats to the peace," and so on—is most rationally conceived as extending to all coercion, by whatever instrument or combination of instruments, military and other, which is directed with requisite intensity against such substantial bases of power as the "territorial integrity" and "political independence" of the target state;

that, from similar perspectives, the coercion characterized as "permissible" and authorized by the general community in the cause of "self-defense," should be limited to responses to initiating coercion that is so intense as to have created in the target state reasonable expectations, as those expectations may be reviewed by others, that a military reaction was indispensably necessary to protect such consequential bases of power as "territorial integrity" and "political independence";

that general community measures—from gestures of conciliation to armed police action—as well as individual self-defense, collective self-defense, and regional enforcement are all appropriately regarded as modes of securing, and as being limited by, the same basic policy of minimum change by coercion, and that explicit focus upon basic policies, with constant relation to the principal features of processes of coercion in context, is as helpful to appropriate decision by one authoritative decision-maker as by another, whatever the degree of community involvement and action;

and, finally, that the explicit examination and weighting of major features in processes of coercion in terms of relation to values of human dignity, and the explicit appraisal of alternatives in decision for their relative impact upon a projected public order of these values are, far from being an abnegation of law, in fact of the very essence of a reasoned decision grounded, without dependence upon a transcendent metaphysic, in the most persuasive authority our world today offers—the most deeply held demands and expectations of peoples about the kind of public order in which they wish to live.

It has not been our purpose, by all this emphasis upon the importance of clarifying basic community policies, to underestimate the importance of such other tasks as the evaluation and invention of structures of authority and sanctioning procedures for the more effective application of basic policies. The assumption upon which we have proceeded is, rather, that clarity about fundamental goals and policies, about principal premises and the type of public order demanded, so insistently and continuously affects choices about authority structures and sanctioning procedures that it affords an economical first focus of attention. The primacy of basic policies over institutional modalities is the primacy of ends over means: the possible models for improving structures of authority and implementing procedures that could be projected, in the absence of systematic clarification of fundamental policies, are countless; further, very different structures and procedures may in some contexts serve the same policies; and comparable structures and procedures may in other contexts serve very different policies. Conversely, however, it must be recognized that available means and knowledge of means affect the rational choice of ends and, hence, that the potentialities and limitations of achievable and known structures of authority and sanctioning techniques affect the realism with which basic policies can be projected and maintained. The most fateful challenge to lawyers and scholars in our time may, accordingly, be seen to embrace the dual tasks of inventing the structures of authority and sanctioning procedures designed most economically to move the peoples of the world from our immediate, precarious balance of terror toward minimum security and a more complete world public order of human dignity, and after investigating controlling conditions, of recommending the measures in communication and other action most effectively calculated to affect the predispositions of leaders and peoples to accept these structures and procedures and to put them into practice.

4. COMMUNITY SANCTIONING PROCESS AND MINIMUM ORDER

The "establishment of a civil society which generally administers the law" has been described as "mankind's most difficult problem." [1] In a community of states afflicted with clashing conceptions of the appropriate ends of law and civil society, whose largest arena is a military arena of multiplying devices that promise both infernal destruction and access to the heavens, the establishment of a society generally administering a law adequately expressing the deepest aspirations of the world's peoples for freedom, security, and abundance —the establishment, in other words, of a world public order of human dignity—is truly a problem of the most heroic proportions.

In the preceding chapter, it was pointed out that one indispensable prerequisite to the achievement of such a world public order is the securing of minimum order, understood as freedom from expectations of severe deprivations by unauthorized coercion and violence. A principle of minimum order, it was observed, has been embodied in the authoritative prescriptions of contemporary international law. This principle makes the necessary distinction between permissible and nonpermissible resort to coercion and projects a fundamental policy prohibiting the employment of intense coercion as an instrumentality of international change. By explicit, systematic, and contextual examination of processes of international coercion and by the careful relation of the major features of such processes to the values of human dignity, this fundamental community policy may, we sought to emphasize, be clarified, interpreted, and applied in particular instances of coercion, in ways designed to enhance movement toward a more inclusive international order in which the values of human dignity are more firmly held and fully achieved.

Important as it is, the problem of clarification of basic community

1. Friedrich, *Inevitable Peace* 61 (1948). The thought is ascribed to Kant.

policy about minimum order does not of course exhaust the requirements for establishing such order. The problem of implementing the principle of minimum order, of putting it into controlling practice, is equally important and vastly more difficult. It scarcely needs documentation that the efficacy, or limitations, of available and achievable processes, the structures of authority and the sanctioning techniques and procedures by which minimum order may be sought to be maintained, inevitably affect the viability and realism of the basic policy and, hence, the prospects of progress toward the world order preferred. In a world exhibiting in increasing degree interdependences in the attainment of security and all other demanded values, the degree of success, or the lack of it, in effectively implementing basic order, is commonly thought to bear in a most intimate manner upon the shape and course of global community processes and upon the very survival of large parts of mankind.

Securing basic order among self-directed territorial polities has never been a simple problem. It has not been a simple problem even, as the history of Western Europe shows, in a highly diversified arena where the multiple units of participation share substantially the same general conceptions about appropriate shaping and distribution of values and the same kind of ideological and cultural presuppositions. The problem is made infinitely more difficult in the present global arena, with its simplified configurations of effective power, by the existence of, and conflict between, differing systems of public order embodying different demands about allocations of values and different views about the nature and ends of man. One fundamental source of difficulty has been the different effective attitudes of the major contending systems toward the legitimacy of coercion and violence for realizing their respective postulated goals, and hence toward the possibilities of genuine peaceful cooperation. The devotion to the principle of minimum order of dynamic totalitarian orders seeking completion and fulfillment on transnational and global scales has been and, in the absence of fundamental change in the overriding demands and expectations, will continue to be, largely limited to the realm of rhetoric. It does not lessen the difficulties that the totalitarian orders also make demands for incompatible institutional practices for the production and distribution of values other than power.

The establishment of basic order across state lines, as a most general objective, embraces, as will be developed below, a range of more specific, interrelated, security goals. These goals have included the prevention of potential breaches of public order by bringing about conditions calculated to predispose effective decision-makers to noncoercive, nonviolent, strategies of change; the deterrence of threatened impending disruptions of basic order by creating in the threatening state expectations of severe deprivations that cancel and outweigh the anticipated gains from the proposed coercion and violence; the repression of disruptions and the restoration of public order by compelling the disrupter to withdraw its challenge and terminate its unlawful coercion; the rehabilitation of the area of disturbance by the repairing of damage resulting from the violation of basic order and by the resumption of ordinary community processes; and finally, the initiation of important structural changes in the basic institutions of the violator state as well as in the constitution of the global arena itself, designed to reduce the probability of future disruptions of minimum order. The implementation of minimum order may thus be described, in most general statement, as the obtaining, in particular situations and in the aggregate flow of situations, of outcomes of a higher degree of conformity with the security goals of prevention, deterrence, restoration, rehabilitation, and reconstruction. The problem encompasses not only the invention and establishment of institutionalized sanctioning practices—the authority structures and procedures—appropriate to varying contexts, but also, and more fundamentally, the creation and fostering of the necessary predispositions in effective decision-makers to put such structures and procedures into operation.

The quest for minimum order by and among nations is scarcely a uniquely modern problem. The effective establishment of such order has been an enduring aspiration of many peoples, ancient and modern, and a historic concern of many scholars and statesmen of many ages and many lands. One manifestation of this perennial preoccupation has been the formulation, through several centuries past, of numerous plans and projects for avoiding or reducing violence and keeping the peace between political communities.[2] These peace plans

2. For introduction to these plans and projects, see the survey literature referred to supra, Ch. 3, note 26. See also Darby, *International Tribunals: A Collection of the Various Schemes which have been propounded; and of Instances since 1815* (3rd ed., 1899); York, *Leagues of Nations: Ancient, Mediaeval, and Modern* (1919).

and projects have uniformly stressed the need for more comprehensive organization and for a higher degree of integration than that observed by their formulators in the international arena of their own ages. They have most frequently consisted of blueprints, varying in specificity and complexity of detail, for particular organizational structures of differing scope and level of centralization and specialization. At least one plan proposed the achievement of order and peace by the conversion of the arena from a pluralistic to a monolithic one. Dante in *De Monarchia* envisioned the establishment of a unified world-state under the secular rule of one supreme prince.[3] Most of the plans recorded in history, however, projected the coming together of the several nations in a league equipped with common supranational organs. Thus, Pierre Dubois urged in the first decade of the fourteenth century a federation of Christian states with a council of nations authorized to resolve all disputes among members. A power resorting to violence was, in his plan, to be the target of concerted military action by the general council.[4] The seventeenth century *Grand Dessein* variously attributed to Henry IV of France or to his minister, the Duc de Sully, the "classical project of international organization," [5] contemplated a similar general council of Christian Europe, supported by a number of smaller or inferior regional councils, accommodating conflicting interests, pacifying members' quarrels, and generally regulating the civil and political life of Europe.[6] It provided also for international armed forces to be contributed by and maintained at the expense of the members. Other plans, like that of William Ladd in the nineteenth century, recommended, in addition to a world "congress" or "parliament," an internation judicial organ to which disputes would be referred. Ladd explicitly rejected the use of force for enforcing the judgments of such tribunal, proposing exclusive reliance upon "the influence of moral power." [7] There is a host of still other particular proposals which may

3. Henry, *The De Monarchia of Dante Alighieri* (1904).

4. See Hemleben, *Plans for World Peace Through Six Centuries* 1–4 (1943).

5. Hemleben, supra, note 4, at 31 so characterized it. Hemleben was quoting Scott, *Introduction to William Ladd, An Essay on a Congress of Nations for the Adjustment of International Disputes Without Resort to Arms,* xiv, xv (1916).

6. *Sully's Grand Design of Henry IV, From the Memoirs of Maximilian de Béthune duc de Sully* (1559–1641) (Grotius Soc. Pub.: Texts for Students of International Relations, No. 2, 1921).

7. Ladd, *An Essay on a Congress of Nations for the Adjustment of Inter-*

be recalled—those of Crucé,[8] Erasmus,[9] Penn,[10] Saint-Pierre,[11] Rousseau,[12] Bentham,[13] Kant,[14] Saint-Simon,[15] Jay,[16] Lorimer,[17] and so on.

It is thus obvious that there has been no dearth in history of specific detailed designs for international authority structures and functions; these seem, in the language of Professor Goodrich, "not too difficult to draw." [18] The historic concern of scholars and reformers with the problem of minimum order, however, has perhaps been too much confined to the elaboration of such blueprints. It has not as yet generally extended to the consideration of the conditions, environmental and predispositional, essential for actually establishing and effectively maintaining order through the particular proposed union or federation of nations, nor to the formulation of strategies for bringing about such conditions. There is strong but not wholly unjustified sarcasm in the observation of Frederick II of Prussia upon the detailed "Project for Perpetual Peace" of the Abbé de Saint-Pierre: "The thing is most practicable, for its success all

---

national Disputes without Resort to Arms (Carnegie Endowment for International Peace, 1916).

8. *The New Cyneas of Émeric Crucé* (Balch, ed. and trans., 1909).

9. Erasmus, *The Complaint of Peace; to which is added, Antipolemus; or The Plea of Reason, Religion, and Humanity, Against War* (1st Amer. ed., 1813).

10. Penn, "An Essay Towards the Present and Future Peace of Europe by the Establishment of an European Diet, Parliament or Estates" (1693), reprinted in *Int. Conciliation,* No. 394, p. 569 (1943).

11. De Saint-Pierre, *Selections from the second edition of the Abrégé du Projet de Paix Perpétuelle,* 1738 (Bellot, trans., Grotius Soc. Pub.: Texts for Students of International Relations, No. 5, 1927).

12. Rousseau, *A Project of Perpetual Peace* (Nuttall, trans., 1927).

13. *Jeremy Bentham's Plan For an Universal and Perpetual Peace* (Grotius Soc. Pub.: Texts for Students of International Relations, No. 6, 1927).

14. Kant, *Perpetual Peace: A Philosophical Essay* (Campbell Smith, trans., 1903).

15. Saint-Simon, *De La Réorganisation de la Société Européenne ou de la Nécessité et des Moyens de Rassembler les Peuples de l'Europe en un Seul Corps Politique en Conservant a Chacun son Independance Nationale* (Octobre 1814) (Bibliothèque Romantique, Paris, 1925).

16. Jay, *War and Peace: The Evils of the First and a Plan for Preserving the Last* (Carnegie Endowment for International Peace, 1919).

17. 2 Lorimer, *The Institutes of the Law of Nations,* Bk. V, esp. c. IV, pp. 279–87 (1884).

18. Goodrich, "The Amount of World Organization Necessary and Possible," 55 *Yale L.J.* 950, 956 (1946).

that is lacking is the consent of Europe and a few similar trifles." [19] Frederick's comment is not without its contemporary point. The specification and refinement of institutional detail, rather than inquiry into the relevant variable conditions that affect implementation and consideration of strategies for manipulating and restructuring such variables, continues to absorb a large measure of the skills and energies of many scholars.[20]

Still other misconceptions relating to the implementation or sanctioning of minimum order, and indeed of international law generally, continue to affect the realism with which a more perfect international order is demanded and sought. There is, firstly, what may be called the mistaking of a part for the whole, the focussing upon one, or a few, particular and isolated forms or aspects of sanctions rather than upon the entirety of a dynamic process of sanctions. Sometimes the principal focus has been upon a single, specific security goal in casual neglect of the full range of relevant particular goals and of the interdependence of each with every other goal. For instance, in terms of the fivefold characterization of more specific sanctioning objectives referred to above, the immediate, short-term goals of deterrence (of disruptions of public order) and restoration (of the disrupted public order) are sometimes de-emphasized and deprecated and the long-term objective of prevention (of conditions that tend to mature in violence) assigned exclusive validity. In this vein, Professor Possony has written:

> The major objection to peace enforcement is, therefore, that it attacks only the symptoms, but not the causes of war. Private warfare was not ended by a strong central government alone; in the course of five centuries, it vanished together with feudal

19. Aldington, *Letters of Voltaire and Frederic the Great* 160 (1927) as cited in Possony, "Peace Enforcement," 55 *Yale L.J.* 910, 917 (1946).

20. The most recent instance is Clark and Sohn, *World Peace Through World Law* (2nd ed., rev., 1960). Some notion of the kinds and variety of contemporary proposals and projects being made and elaborated by different individuals and organizations may be had from DeRusett, *Strengthening the Framework of Peace: A Study of Current Proposals For Amending, Developing, or Replacing Present International Institutions for the Maintenance of Peace* (Royal Institute of Int. Affairs, 1950); Committee on the "Principles of an Effective Free World Order," *A Study of Existing Plans for World Order* (Amer. Bar Assn., 1951); Wilcox and Marcy, *Proposals For Changes in the United Nations* (1955).

> society and medieval technology, which provided knights and lords with military strength. Wars are due to social, economic, ideological, and political "incompatibility"; [21] . . .
>
> Since war was an integral part of the society as we have known it in history, the conclusion seems unavoidable that war cannot quickly be abolished unless a new type of society without fundamental cleavages is created.[22]

The minor suggestion may not be inappropriate that unless the requirements of deterrence and of restoration are met as they arise in the here and now, the need and the possibility of preventing violence by bringing about a new, more integrated, world society may become distantly ephemeral. The major point is that the rationality of a focus upon one or another specific goal is, in any particular case, a function of the fundamental perspectives of effective decision-makers with respect to that and all the other relevant goals, as well as of the other component features of the sanctioning process and its larger context.

At other times, the major emphasis has been on some particular environmental feature, like the high and still rapidly increasing level of armaments of various powers, or the relative geographic proximity of counter-poised armed forces,[23] to the elimination of which central importance is ascribed. Thus, Mr. Noel-Baker wrote with passionate conviction:

> These proposals [for disarmament] are not "starry eyed" idealism. They are plain, realistic common sense. The romanticists are those who still believe that modern armaments can make a nation safe. There is no military defence today for any nation except in drastic measures of disarmament, embodied in a multilateral treaty to which all governments subscribe. From the first day that this treaty enters into force, and the UN inspectors take up their posts in the countries which they will control, the security of every nation will at once, and notably, be

21. Possony, supra note 19 at 948.

22. Id., 949.

23. Emphasis upon this specific factor gave rise to the recent debate about "disengagement" of Soviet and Western forces in Europe. See Kennan, "Disengagement Revisited," 37 *Foreign Aff.* 187 (1959); Acheson, "The Illusion of Disengagement," 36 id. 371 (1958).

> increased. The acceptance of inspection means the end of military secrets; it is the greatest of the "surrenders of sovereignty" which disarmament must mean; but, in itself, it will do much to end the "nightmare fear" of sudden and unprovoked attack; it will gradually, but profoundly, change the whole character of the international relations between states.[24]

It is entirely possible to share the basic aspiration exhibited here while observing that the significance, positive or negative, for minimum world order of any particular environmental condition—including comparative levels of armament—need not be regarded as an inherent attribute nor as a predetermined and inevitable consequence of such condition. The importance of an environmental factor lies rather in its impact upon the effective perspectives of the participants and its relation to every other feature of the sanctioning process in context. Even vast armaments, in other words, may be ambivalent in their effects upon the probabilities of basic order;[25] they, like every other condition, must be assayed contextually.

At still other times, the focus of scholarly attention is narrowly confined to one kind of strategy employed for implementation purposes—to wit, negative sanctions, that is, a strategy for securing conformity through imposition of deprivations. The focus has sometimes been even more sharply limited to one type of negative sanction—organized deprivational techniques, such as economic blockade or military action by international armed forces.[26] The rational im-

24. Noel-Baker, *The Arms Race: A Programme for World Disarmament* 561–2 (Oceana ed., 1960).

25. Cf. the cogent suggestion made by Schelling, *Toward a General Theory of Conflict Applicable to International Relations* 33 (Rand P-1648, March 19, 1959): "If we take 'disarmament' not in its traditional and literal sense of reducing the aggregate level of armaments (measured somehow) but rather as a generic term covering measures to reduce the *likelihood* of war, we have to inquire whether a disarmament scheme is likely to be more successful if it involves more arms, less arms, or different types of arms. An important condition of a successful 'disarmament' scheme is that it should lead to some kind of stable equilibrium, or at least one not too unstable." The possible ambivalence of modern armaments is explicitly and optimistically noted in Claude, *Swords Into Plowshares: The Problems and Progress of International Organization* 299–300 (2nd ed., 1959).

26. Focus upon negative sanctions was observable in the activities of the League of Nations throughout most of its life. See, generally, *International*

portance of emphasis upon one rather than another specific kind of sanctioning technique may, again, be expected to be quite relative and dependent upon the shape and distribution of both capabilities and effective perspectives about its employment, or nonemployment, in a particular constellation of conditions.

A second kind of misconception concerns the role of force in international sanctions processes. In its simplest form, this is the assumption that force is not an appropriate instrumentality for maintaining minimum order in the world. This assumption, which has long been a fundamental article of the pacifist's faith,[26a] has been used to deplore organization for collective security in general and peace enforcement in particular. For instance, it has been contended that

> 2. *Proposals for the Use of Force to Maintain Security Have Been Outgrowths of the War Spirit and Are in Effect War Plans, Not Peace Plans.*
>
> . . .
>
> 9. *Force Has Been a Disruptive, Not a Cohesive Influence in International Organization.*
>
> Whether employed by Germany, or Italy, or Japan, or Poland, or Russia, or France or the numerous small countries who followed their example in defiance of the League; or whether used by the nations who seek to maintain the *status quo* which the League sought to freeze—by the United States, and Britain, and Russia, and France, and their many satellites—there is only one outcome of force. Breakdown! Disruption! [27]

Sanctions (Royal Institute of Int. Affairs, 1938); Brierly, "Sanctions," 17 *Tr. Grotius Soc.* 67 (1932); Williams, "Sanctions Under the Covenant," 17 *Brit. Y.B.I.L.* 130 (1936). Thus, during the League period, "sanctions" meant to most the application of economic embargoes. To the more visionary, "sanctions" sometimes also embraced "international police force." See, e.g., Wehberg, *Theory and Practice of International Policing* (1935); Bryn Thomas, *An International Police Force* (1936).

26a. We are aware of the many shades and differing varieties of pacifist beliefs; however, refusal of participation, on grounds of principle, in violent civil and international conflicts appears to be a recurrent emphasis. See Sharp, "The Meanings of Non-Violence: A Typology" (Revised), 3 *J. Conflict Resolution* 41 (1959).

27. Freeman, *Coercion of States in International Organizations* 55, 57 (1944),

The same assumption, with a slight variation in nuance of reference, may be seen both to underlie and pervade the view urged by Professor Niemeyer:

> States, units of supreme government in human society, are by inherent necessity the highest, most powerful and most efficient organizations in the sphere of social order. Accordingly there can be no effective pressure against a state except by another state. This means that to base international law ultimately on the threat of sanctions is equivalent to basing it on the action, and interest in action, of some great power. This was precisely the fundamental defect of the League scheme, and the reason why it failed in all its practical tests. The same inherent weakness will characterize any system of international order which ultimately relies on force. . . . there is only one form in which compulsion can be employed against these territorial units . . .: war. . . .
>
> Consequently an international order which depends on force as its *ultima ratio* is a permanent source of international struggle rather than a medium of order.[28]

To adopt a priori this assumption of the incompatibility of force and law is in effect to reject the conception of minimum order that has prevailed in every territorial community, including the more mature and liberal humanitarian polities. The burden of that conception, it may be recalled, is not that the use of force is in itself necessarily unlawful but that force is lawfully used only when exercised to sustain community order. The application of force, of course, involves the same deprivations of physical values whether the application be characterized as lawful or unlawful, as in support or in repudiation of community authority. No government of a mod-

---

italics in the original; see also Freeman and Paullin, *Coercion of States: in Federal Unions* (1943) and Paullin, *Introduction to Non-Violence* (1944). Cf. the contention made in Joyce, *Red Cross International and the Strategy of Peace* 198 (1959): "that the resort to military force to meet dangerous situations—especially when they arise in other peoples' countries—defeats its own purpose and destroys the very basis of peaceful action through the United Nations machinery of mutual adjustment."

28. Niemeyer, *Law Without Force, The Function of Politics in International Law* 21–2 (1941).

ern state has, however, to our knowledge, thought it feasible deliberately to abjure the right to employ force when indispensable for maintaining order and the very bonds of internal community life. What municipal orders, including those most dedicated to the principle of consent, have commonly sought is not the elimination of force from the ambit of human experience but rather the effective monopolization of force by the community. It is hence difficult to concede validity to a demand that force for the maintenance of minimum order be abjured in the international arena, unless, indeed, it be postulated that a higher, more exacting, morality can be expected of men when associated together in political communities than from men acting simply as individual personalities. By designating as "war" even that force which is exercised to defend and sustain processes of authority and basic world order, those who deprecate or minimize potential collective sanctions even impose upon sanctioners the invidium and all the moral aversion aroused by a label that for decades has been used to refer to unlawful force.[29] This is to reverse the common signification of words and in effect to proclaim as irrelevant the characteristics of conformity or nonconformity to public order, sustainment of or attack upon authoritative community policy.

Objections to forcible sanctions like those noted above may occasionally proceed from another misconception even more nihilistic in its implications—that it is not in fact possible to distinguish between force that is in concordance with and force that repudiates community authority, between the violator and the enforcer of public order, by criteria transcending the narrow and exclusive interests of the decision-maker drawing the distinction. Professor Borchard, for instance, after describing the "seekers of a new world order" as

29. See supra, p. 253. Cf. Buell, in *Are Sanctions Necessary to International Organization?* 19 (Pamphlet No. 82–83, Foreign Policy Assn., 1932): "There is a fundamental difference between military force used by a state for the prosecution of national objectives—which is what happens when war occurs—and the use of force by states under international organization after all efforts at peaceful settlement have failed and a state has formally been adjudged guilty of having violated its obligations and embarked on illegal war. Ethically and legally the use of force by a state to advance interests to which a legal claim has not been established is in an entirely different category from the use of coercion by the world community to protect one of its members from aggression. Even if the imposition of economic sanctions should result in armed clashes, which is unlikely, such clashes could not properly be called 'war'."

"romantic chasers of the international rainbow" and the enforcement of peace "by war" as an "essentially anarchistic process," [30] contended that

> To [the identification of peace with the status quo] we owe the chameleonic epithet "aggressor" which is applied selectively to those particular disturbers of the status quo whom the dominant states happen to dislike. . . . It is responsible for the doctrine of sanctions, designed to bend nations to the will of the ruling group and carrying behind it a whole flood of evils.[31]

This view amounts in practical substance to the a priori rejection of the very conception of minimum order, the first principle of any public order, and, logically, requires regression to what historically has been the only alternative principle—that of arbitrament by naked power. The intellectual complexities of achieving specific interpretations of the basic principle which are rational from the perspective of common and overriding interests, rather than peculiar and momentary expediencies, are not of course to be minimized. The appropriate recourse, however, is scarcely the discarding of the principle itself as a mere piece of cynicism. It is rather the clarification of shared, fundamental interests and the recommending of an ordered mode of analysis for ascribing operational meaning to such interests in particular contexts.

The misconceptions of which we speak may extend still further to the denial that there are available any sanctions for prohibitions of international coercion and for international law generally. Translated literally, such a denial would appear a flat conclusion that coercion or force cannot successfully be exerted against a territorial body politic. This of course is absurd upon its face; force has in fact been applied against states, even unto the destruction of Carthage. Hence, the common accompanying view that has been seriously urged is that "war," understood as overt and extensive exercises of force, cannot properly be described as a sanction for international law because force is as likely to be invoked for purposes other than enforcement of law and because the outcome of "war" is uncertain,

30. Borchard, "The Impracticability of Enforcing Peace," 55 *Yale L.J.* 966, 967 (1946).

31. Id., 971. See also Moore, "An Appeal to Reason," in 6 *Collected Papers of John Bassett Moore* 416, 444–8 (1944).

no guarantee being possible that the sanctioner of public order shall always prevail. Thus, adopting the very limited conceptions about decision-makers, processes of authoritative decision, and sanctions characteristic of the analytical school of jurisprudence, Professor Patterson writes:

> Do they [the norms of international law] have a sanction like that of a legal sanction? In my judgment, they do not. O. W. Holmes, rejecting Austin's view that international law is not properly designated as law, suggested that "war" is a sanction of international law. But nations do not go to war merely, if at all, because of violations of international law; . . .[32]

The circumstance that force has in the past been, and may in the future be, unilaterally used in violation of basic community order certainly does not mean that it has not or cannot be exercised in defense and protection of community order. In the international as in municipal arenas force is in itself ambiguous and neutral to policy; it is an *instrument* for realizing policy, a means of action, and may be employed in conformity with authoritative community policy in exactly the same degree that it may be used in repudiation of such policy. Similarly, the uncertainty of outcomes need not militate against considering force as a sanction for basic order. The reduction of such uncertainty to negligible levels has been a primary purpose of historic efforts to improve the procedures of organized deprivational sanctions, which as yet remain very rudimentary.

The obvious point of stress, however, is that the force at the disposal of a potential target state and of its allies importantly affects the calculations of potential violators. It is true, as sometimes is pointed out,[33] that although in previous centuries the use of force constituted a "recognized method of enforcing international law," today, because of the contemporary prescriptions of the United Nations Charter and other documents on permissible and nonpermissible coercion, force may lawfully be used as a sanction, not for international law generally, but only for that very part of it which estab-

32. Patterson, *Jurisprudence: Men and Ideas of the Law* 176 (1953). See also MacIver, "Some Implications of a Democratic International Order," 1 *J. of Legal and Pol. Sociology* 5, 6–8 (1942).

33. Fitzmaurice, "The Foundations of the Authority of International Law and the Problem of Enforcement," 19 *Modern L. Rev.* 1, 3–4 (1956).

lishes the prohibition of resort to force and coercion and the permissions of self-defense and enforcement action. Force is lawfully exercised only in necessary response to and redress of violations of minimum order. It does not necessarily follow, however, that the rest of international law has been rendered "unenforceable by direct action." [34] For the enforcement of prescriptions less fundamental than that of minimum public order, for responding to violations of rights less consequential than destructive attack upon the essential bases of state power commonly referred to as "territorial integrity" and "political independence," there are other appropriate reciprocities and remedies, other "direct action," than the invocation of violence. It is scarcely a revolutionary observation that military weapons do not exhaust the arsenal of policy instruments, that the lashing out with force is not the only conceivable and certainly not necessarily a rational response to each and every one of a wide variety of possible "tortious" or "internationally delinquent" acts.

The position that there are no legal sanctions for international law, illustrated above by Professor Patterson, on occasion derives support and supplement from the view that the "real" sanctions for international law lie in "public opinion." The classical statement of this view is that of Secretary Elihu Root:

> [T]here is a consciousness that in the most important affairs of nations, in their political status, the success of their undertakings and their process of development, there is an indefinite and almost mysterious influence exercised by the general opinion of the world regarding the nation's character and conduct. The greatest and strongest governments recognize this influence and act with reference to it . . .
>
> This is independent of any calculation upon a physical enforcement of the opinion of others. It is difficult to say just why such opinion is of importance, because it is always difficult to analyze the action of moral forces; but it remains true and is universally recognized that the nation which has with it the moral force of the world's approval is strong, and the nation which rests under the world's condemnation is weak, however great its material power.[35]

34. Id., 5.

35. Root, "The Sanction of International Law," in *Addresses on International*

All law must of course finally depend for its viability and efficacy upon a fundamental, minimum consensus among the participants in the arena for which it is projected.[36] Policies authoritatively prescribed are most effective where they substantially express, and are supported by, confluences in the basic perspectives—the deeply held and shared demands, identifications, and expectations—of the peoples subjected to them. In this sense, public opinion is the ultimate and indispensable sanction for all law. From this, nonetheless, no necessary conclusion flows that for securing the effectiveness of any particular legal prescription in a concrete situation, exclusive reliance must be placed upon the inscrutable and automatic workings of amorphous opinion and sentiment. It has not been so in municipal public orders even in those with relatively well informed and culturally and ideologically homogeneous populations; it need not be so in the general community of states. There are, and this will be developed below, in the international arena potential processes in which the perspectives of peoples, their opinion and sentiment, may be marshaled and channeled and made efficacious in appropriate structures of authority and sanctioning procedures, processes in which all values may be managed and used, both in organized and unorganized modalities, to offer indulgences or to impose deprivations, for the obtaining of outcomes conforming to community order. Finally, it may be added, the sustaining perspectives of peoples are not isolated autonomous phenomena but are continually being affected, reinforced, or reshaped, by the extent to which they achieve effective expression in sanctioning processes.

All these misconceptions about sanctions are related, finally, in reciprocal interdetermination, to certain fundamental misconceptions about the "nature" and "binding force" of international law. There is of course a great variety of conceptions of law but most formulations include some reference to a requirement of effectiveness or enforceability. Conceptions of effectiveness or enforceability commonly depend upon conceptions of sanctions, in other words, of appropriate means of securing the effectiveness of law. The widely

---

Subjects by Elihu Root 30–1 (Bacon and Scott, eds., 1916). See also Pearce Higgins, *The Binding Force of International Law* (1910).

36. Cf. Brierly, "Law, Justice and War," in *The Basis of Obligation in International Law and Other Papers by the late James Leslie Brierly* 265 (Lauterpacht and Waldock, eds., 1958).

known position which characterized the analytical school of jurisprudence—that international law is "not law properly so-called" but only "positive moral rules which are laws improperly so called" [37]—is perhaps still the best illustration of how restricted conceptions of sanctions, and of authority processes generally, lead to equally restricted notions about the legal or nonlegal nature of international law. Austin, it may be recalled, limited the reference of "legal sanction" to an eventual evil annexed to a command proceeding from a determinate political superior.[38]

The direct connection between conceptions of sanctions and the realism of inquiries for the "binding force" of international law is well indicated in Sir Gerald Fitzmaurice's recent essay cited earlier. After stating that the bulk of international law has become unenforceable by "direct action," Sir Gerald proceeded to say that

> Fortunately . . . international law has never, in practice, been more than partly dependent for its authority on the possibility of its physical enforcement . . .
>
> The real foundation of the authority of international law resides similarly in the fact that the States making up the international society recognize it as binding upon them, and, moreover, as a system that *ipso facto* binds them *as* members of that society irrespective of their individual wills.
>
> But this is not the end of the matter.
>
> . . . [I]nternational law could derive no authority from its acceptance by States as binding, or States would not give that acceptance, unless it were felt by them to be in fact inherently binding.[39]

Pressing his inquiry for "precisely what it is in the ultimate and juridical sense, that makes international law a binding system," Sir Gerald noted, after the manner of Professor Brierly,[40] the cir-

37. See Austin, *The Province of Jurisprudence Determined and the Uses of the Study of Jurisprudence* 133–42 (Library of Ideas, ed., 1954).

38. Id., 133.

39. Fitzmaurice, supra note 33 at 8. Sir Gerald appears on occasion to equate "authority" and mere prestige, and at other times to treat "authority" and "effective control" as equivalents. The references of "binding" and of "obligation" are left as mysterious as in the older literature.

40. See Brierly, *The Basis of Obligation in International Law and Other Papers,* c. 1 (Lauterpacht and Waldock, eds., 1958); and Brierly, *The Law of*

cularity and infinite regression necessarily encountered in efforts to find a *"juridical* answer." He concluded, like Professor Brierly, that the "ultimate source of validity" must be looked for "beyond law," "in some non-juridical ground or field," such as "justice."[41]

To continue this quest for some "binding force" or "basis of obligation" by derivational logic is not, it may be suggested, the only possible and certainly not necessarily the most meaningful way of clarifying the problem of sanction either for minimum order or for international law generally. Neither Professor Brierly nor Sir Gerald made crystal clear whether "binding force" or "basis of obligation" was used to refer to effective control or to authority.

Where reference is made to effective control, infinite regression is no necessary result. Effective control is a function of the interrelation of many different variables that occur in world processes of power and these are susceptible of empirical investigation. The general empirical question is what factors or variables affect the choices of community-established decision-makers to conform or not to conform to the requirements of community policy. Where reference is

---

Nations 50–7 (5th ed., 1955). See also Ross, *Constitution of the United Nations* 31 (1950).

Both Professor Brierly and Sir Gerald reject "consent" as a "basis of obligation," alleging that its acceptance would involve circularity in reasoning. Thus, Professor Brierly writes: "For consent cannot of itself create an obligation; it can do so only within a system of law which declares that consent duly given, as in a treaty or a contract, shall be binding upon the party consenting. To say that the rule *pacta sunt servanda* is itself founded on consent is to argue in a circle." (*The Law of Nations* 54 [5th ed., 1955]).

This would appear to confuse different levels of abstraction and contexts in the reference of the word consent. Consent to the maintenance of a general system is at one level of abstraction and consent to the prescription or application of specific rules is at another. The consent of the effective participants in a system is obviously necessary to the continued maintenance of the system, but this does not mean that particular participants may not on occasion be required by the comprehensive network of reciprocities and potential retaliations in the system to conform to particular policies to which they have not explicitly consented.

41. Fitzmaurice, supra note 33 at 12. See also Fitzmaurice, "The General Principles of International Law Considered from the Standpoint of the Rule of Law," 92 *Hague Recueil* 5, 40–7 (1957) where Sir Gerald ends up with *"ubi societas ibi jus."* The "juridical conscience of humanity" is a similarly favored abstraction; see Johnson, "The Effect of Resolutions of the General Assembly of the United Nations," 32 *Brit. Y.B.I.L.* 97, 115–16 (1955–1956).

made to authority, infinite regression is equally unnecessary. The active and prevailing expectations of the members of a community about how decisions should be taken—and these are what is commonly meant by authority—like other variables affecting decisions admit of empirical inquiry. The consequential way of relating specific decisions to such expectations is not by derivations ascending to higher and higher abstractions but rather by detailed specification descending the ladder of abstraction to the concrete phases of social processes.[42]

When the factors that bear upon decisions about conformity to the requirements of authority are empirically investigated, they may be seen to refer to whole processes in contexts of interdependence where, through the operation of the principle of maximization, expectations of reciprocity and retaliation play a pervasive, organizing role. Amorphous, transcendental notions of an "inherent binding force" and "basis of obligation" may be useful in the exhortation of the conscience of peoples. Propositions cast in the solemn terms of "binding obligation" probably do in measure commit and engage peoples' consciences. The suggestion we make, however, is that the clarification of fundamental policy and the explicit relating of specific alternatives in decision to the basic demands, expectations, and identifications of peoples constitute, again because of the postulate of maximization, much the more effective way of organizing, channeling, and harnessing their perspectives to the implementation of minimum order and as well of international law generally.

In view of the various kinds of misconceptions which, in varying forms, pervade much of the literature, the most important immediate task, it appears to us, is not the attempted discovery and elaboration of new and hopefully "permanent" panaceas in either specific institutional structure or technical principle and procedure. It is rather the formulation and development of a more comprehensive conception of a sanctioning process that will facilitate the continuous employment of all necessary intellectual skills in the invention and evaluation of the detailed strategies rationally designed for securing practicable immediate, mid-range, and long-term goals in continually changing contexts of conditioning factors. This more modest task is in principal measure one of achieving organizing and

42. See Lasswell, "Clarifying Value Judgment: Principles of Content and Procedure," 1 *Inquiry* 87 (1958).

synthesizing conceptions and an analytical framework that will promote insight into the multiple interrelated conditions, both environmental and predispositional, which affect the choices made by human decision-makers relating to the establishment and maintenance of basic order. It may be but homely wisdom that some mode of identifying and characterizing such conditions in at least provisional terms, and of viewing them configuratively in all their relatedness in impact upon the decisions actually made, is an essential preliminary to the development of the strategies necessary for managing and modifying them in the hope of increasing the probability of outcomes compatible with minimum public order. The important suggestion has recently been made by Professor Strausz-Hupé and his associates that among the principal reasons for the enormous gains registered by the Communists in the last few decades has been their "ability to conceive of the struggle for power—its terms, its theater, its methods and its goals—in larger dimensions than their opponents." [43] Communist strategy, he observes, "derives from a superior understanding of the total historic situation." [44] The suggestion we would essay is that the approach of contextuality should not be left to the monopoly of the strategists of totalitarianism and that increased chances of success in securing basic order as a precondition for a wider international public order of human dignity may depend upon the ability of potential sanctioners to think of *this* struggle in equally large and contextual terms.

We seek, hence, in the succeeding pages to approach the task indicated by first constructing a generalized model or theoretical image of sanctioning processes across state lines, abstracting both from the manifold details observable in the international arena through time and from potential aspects and possible combinations and permutations of detail. Next we will attempt to draw forth some general principles or considerations, necessarily of a relatively abstract character, for improved management of sanctions processes. We propose then to offer, in terms of the generalized image of sanctions and of the recommended general principles of sanctions strategy, a brief review both of the major defects discernible in the constitutive aspects of contemporary sanctioning processes and of some of the proposals presently being made for removal of these defects.

43. Strausz-Hupé and others, *Protracted Conflict* 29 (1959).
44. Id., 1.

Only illustrative and impressionistic depiction is of course here possible; prolonged and detailed presentation must be left to more specialized inquiry. In the final section of this chapter, we seek to make a few tentative and general suggestions about the basic requirements of pragmatic programs for affecting the relevant predispositions of effective decision-makers. Most appropriately conceived, such programs would envisage the weakening and subverting of warping, parochial biases and the strengthening of the predispositions, or the creation of new ones, appropriate to each step from where we are now toward the more effective maintenance of minimum order and, ultimately, toward a world where the values of human dignity are more widely shared.

THE POTENTIAL SANCTIONING PROCESS AND ITS CONTEXT OF CONDITIONS

In this chapter, we use the term "sanctioning process" most comprehensively to refer to all phases of the process of authoritative decision in the international community by which implementation of the fundamental principle of minimum order is sought. The reference we make is not limited to strategies—deprivational or indulgent with respect to particular values—designed to secure conformity to specific authoritative applications of this principle.[45] We refer as well to the whole process of authoritative decision, exclusive of the particular exercises of the prescribing function [45a] by which the prin-

45. The emphasis in the above formulation is upon the perspective of the manipulator. Equally inclusive statements suggesting this and other standpoints are made in Wild, *Sanctions and Treaty Enforcement* (1934); e.g., at 57: "[S]anction of law signifies the means of ensuring enforcement or the means of inducing observance of law"; at 61: "The sanctions of international law are what tend to make a state abide by the law; if it does not, certain consequences implicit in the sanction are the likely result and a state must make its choice." Contrast the definition framed in Sloan, "Comparative International and Municipal Law Sanctions," 27 *Neb. L. Rev.* 1, 2 (1947).

45a. With such exercises of the prescribing function we have sought to deal comprehensively in the preceding chapter. It should require no argument that the effectiveness with which the prescribing function is performed, with respect to both minimum order and other problems, is a variable which must substantially affect the success obtainable in specific applications of the principle of minimum order. A similarly broad conception of sanctions is suggested in Kelsen, *Collective Security* 101 (1956): "The term 'sanction' can have different meanings. In its widest sense, it means any measure taken in support of a social

ciple of minimum order is projected, in so far as such process bears upon the effectiveness with which the application function is performed. All phases of the more comprehensive process—participants, objectives, situations, bases of power, strategies, outcomes and effects —are appropriately regarded, in our submission, as within the ambit of "sanctioning process" to the extent that they affect either policy choices in specific applications or the degree to which such policy choices are, or can be, put into controlling practice. Implementation obviously involves the assumption that the policy to be implemented has gone through the phase of authoritative articulation both as a general prescription and, in appropriate specific cases, as a characterization of particular coercion in relation to the general prescription. We propose in the succeeding pages to outline, in at least its most salient features, this process of implementing or sanctioning the basic policy of minimum order. A speculative construct of the sanctions process may help in the more refined performance of the scientific task of observing, identifying, and describing the various categories of events, subjective and nonsubjective, which in their continuous interplay shape authoritative responses to exercises of coercion, actual or anticipated, across political boundaries. A model of what an eminent anthropologist has called "systems of relevant concatenation" [46] should also be helpful not only in the appraising of both the trends observed in historical experience in the administration of sanctions and contemporary projects for reform and improvement, but also in the disciplined invention of alternatives in both the principles and procedures of implementation.

PARTICIPANTS

The principal categories of formally authorized participants in the process of sanctions are the same as those in other processes of decision

---

order regulating human behavior. The purpose of a sanction is to bring about that behavior which, according to the opinion of the social authority, is useful to society and hence is considered to be in conformity with the social order; and to prevent that behavior which, according to the opinion of the social authority, is harmful to society and hence is considered to be contrary to the social order." The narrower conception of "legal sanctions" offered by Professor Kelsen is that of "coercive reactions against a violation of the law." In the compass of his book, however, he pays the greater deference to the broader definition.

46. Malinowsky, "Man's Culture and Man's Behavior," 29 *Sigma Xi Q.* 182, 183 (1941).

in the international arena. These include not only officials of international governmental organizations, especially security organizations of differing territorial compass and judges of such international tribunals as may be established or have occasion to deal with problems relating to sanctions, but also officials of individual nation-states. The point may bear some emphasis that to limit the reference of sanctions to measures taken by an international organization is both unnecessary and arbitrary and that community-authorized action by individual states, whether alone or in concert, in response to prohibited resort to coercion may quite appropriately be embraced in such reference. As was observed in the preceding chapter the same fundamental community policy of securing minimum order runs through all the differing particular institutional modalities that permissible coercion may assume: from "individual self-defense," through "collective self-defense" and "regional enforcement action," to more general "collective security action" or "police action." [47] In the present poorly organized world arena, individual member states of the general community of states play many differentiated roles as potential sanctioners.

A comprehensive listing of participants would of course include more than the authorized officials noted above. Ultimately, all groups and entities which play effective roles in power processes in the world arena, may in fact participate in the process of sanctions by intervening and acting in any one or more of its functional phases. Cartels furnish an obvious illustration; they may significantly contribute to either the efficacy of enforcement or the evasion of economic sanctions measures. International non-governmental organizations specialized to the shaping and distribution of values like education and skill and rectitude may importantly affect the degree to which the long-range sanctions goals and strategies of influencing and re-shaping relevant predispositional factors can be successfully achieved. To keep the model we project to manageable proportions, however, our principal concern will be with states and organizations of states.

The characteristics of participants or potential sanctioners which are of most immediate importance to us consist, in very general statement, of the structures of perspectives which condition and move the effective decision-makers in initiating and participating, or in declin-

47. Supra, p. 250. Contrast Goodhart, in 35 *Tr. Grotius Soc.* at 15 (1950).

ing to initiate or participate, in measures designed to establish and maintain minimum order. Such perspectives act upon the environmental context which prevails in particular sanctions situations, or more precisely, that portion of the context coming within the frame of attention of the decision-maker, and give rise to outcomes of varying compatibility with basic community policy. The relevant perspectives may be said to include all patterns or clusters of subjectivities relating to the public order system which the decision-makers, in making such choices, visualize themselves as protecting and fulfilling. In outlining at least the major contours of these patterns, for possible guidance in the detailed investigation and mapping which must eventually be done, it is useful conceptually to break down the patterns—which may or may not be internally consistent—into their component demands, identifications, and expectations.[48]

We think of "demands" as designating expressions of valuation, more particularly, of preference and positive commitment varying in intensity. They may be described as comprised of the values sought and of the practices assumed to embody those values.[49] Demands may hence relate to any or all values as well as to any or all modes of shaping and allocating values, and may be made on behalf of a particular segment or the whole of the self-structure of the demanding person. The first inquiry is of course to the shape and contents of the demands, as these might be reported by a non-participant observer, which particular decision-makers bring to the consideration of the implementation of minimum order. The next problem is that of the detailed relation of these demands to the values of a public order of human dignity and, more specifically, to minimum order as a prerequisite condition to the securing of such a public order on a larger scale in the world arena. In their farthest reach, inquiries such as these would require the delineation and appraisal of the entire system of public order actually demanded by the potential sanctioners.[50] Inquiry, however, could come to a focus upon demands relating to the legitimacy of the use of coercion and violence as

48. This breakdown is derived from Lasswell and Kaplan, *Power and Society* 25 (1950).

49. Id., 17–18.

50. A conspectus for such inquiries is offered in McDougal and Lasswell, "The Identification and Appraisal of Diverse Systems of Public Order," 53 *A.J.I.L.* (1959).

means of acquiring values; specific demands may range all the way from complete acceptance to complete rejection of intense coercion or violence for the acquisition of values. It is perhaps obvious that the demands best suited to support the implementation of minimum order are those which start from the insistence upon persuasion as the principal modality of value change that is appropriate in a world order of human dignity and from the recognition that the maintenance of minimum order is an indispensable requirement of such world order.

The word "identification" is commonly used to refer both to the process by which a person or individual ego comes to regard and symbolize himself as part of an aggregate or group and to the group or aggregate with which the person symbolically unites himself.[51] The identifications of an individual considered together with the core of the self (the "primary ego") constitute his self-system. The charting in detail of the perspectives of effective decision-makers must include the ascertainment of the configuration of their self-systems, of how, in other words, they perceive themselves as included in or excluded from differing groups, both geographic and functional. The interdependence of identification and demand is close and real. Identifications depend upon the number, intensity, and patterning of shared demands; unity of demand enhances the establishment and strengthening of identifications. Demands in turn are always put forward in the name of the self-structure or some segment thereof. The operative identifications of potential sanctioners may be characterized by many varying degrees of inclusivity or exclusivity, of plurality and diversity, or singularity and simplicity. A definition of the boundaries of the self marked by a high degree of exclusivity and by monistic simplicity may frequently manifest itself in rejection of involvement in and responsibility for efforts to prevent or deter or redress breaches of public order; the potential sanctioner may not be able to identify with a community sufficiently comprehensive effectively to apply sanctions to the target state. Where, on the other hand, their identifications are more inclusively drawn in scope and exhibit in considerable measure a complex pluralism, potential sanctioners may be more likely to see their selves as sig-

51. Lasswell and Kaplan, supra note 48 at 11–13. See also Lasswell, "Nations and Classes: The Symbols of Identification," in *Reader in Public Opinion and Communication* 28 (Enlarged ed., Berelson and Janowitz, 1953).

nificantly involved and committed to the securing or restoring of minimum order; the potential sanctioner thus identifies with a community sufficiently large to be effective. The most appropriate identifications for the sustaining of basic order would thus appear to be those which are most comprehensive in breadth and reach, embracing all of mankind, and which are greatest in number and multifariousness, embracing not only territorial communities of differing scope, from the most local to the entire globe, but also functional organizations specialized to many differing values.[52]

"Expectations" comprise the third principal component of patterns of perspectives. By expectations we mean assumptions about events wherever located in the continuum of time. They include both beliefs about the past and forecasts of the shape of the future; and the former of course find some reflection in the latter. Expectation statements are descriptive propositions in the sense that they represent neither demand for any value nor identification with any person or group.[53] The most general relevant expectations of any participant are, however, that participant's assumptions with respect to the conditions under which it can best achieve its demanded values.

Of the innumerable specific expectations about innumerable matters which potential sanctioners may bring to the consideration of choices relating to minimum order,[54] the more relevant may in-

52. See, in this connection, Lasswell, "World Loyalty," in *The World Community* 200 (Wright, ed., 1948). Guetzkow, *Multiple Loyalties: Theoretical Approach to a Problem in International Organization* 61 (1955) offers highly suggestive formulations as implications of his conception of multiple loyalties:

> (1) Loyalty is not a single entity—once used up, then exhausted. It is, rather, an expandable quantity which can be generated in increasing amounts towards a variety of objects. Thus, there is no need to think that increases in loyalty to a supranational group necessarily mean decreases in loyalty to the nation-state.
>
> . . .
>
> (3) The exclusiveness norm seems to be the greatest barrier to expanding loyalties where a barrier exists. But to build a new loyalty one need not necessarily destroy other loyalties.

53. Lasswell and Kaplan, supra note 48 at 21.

54. The range of potentially relevant kinds of expectations is suggested in the illustrative listing of "attitudinal factors that might affect international relations" presented in Kelman, "Societal, Attitudinal and Structural Factors in International Relations," 11 *J. Social Issues* 42, 46 (1955): "attitudes towards

clude their expectations about the probable success or failure of the particular implementing or sanctioning measures proposed. This set of expectations would be comprised of their estimations of the dimensions of the challenge to public order, the prohibited coercion, sought to be avoided and forestalled or repressed and undone. It would also include their anticipations of who, among the other potential sanctioners, will respond to that challenge by cooperating and participating in appropriate sanctioning measures, who will ignore the challenge and refuse to participate in such measures, and who will aggravate the challenge by aligning themselves with the challenger. It would embrace, finally, their assessment of the relative strength available to each probable grouping of participants. Another set of relevant expectations is concerned with the probable future of the system of international order to the protection and fulfillment of which potential sanctioners regard themselves as committed. Perceptions of the future, realistic or not, may be expected to affect not only the strategies employed to bring about or to avoid the prospects perceived but also the intensity of commitment to the public order system involved. Perhaps the most crucial cluster of expectations would be the convictions of the effective decision-makers about the security or insecurity of their own individual value positions within their respective political communities and about the probable impact, upon their access and control over values, of participation or nonparticipation in various measures designed to secure minimum order. The postulate of maximization strongly indicates that expectations of being personally better off, that is, of maintaining and improving their total value position, or of being worse off, that is, of sustaining a net loss of values, by adopting one or another of various alternative courses of conduct will have a profound, even controlling, influence upon the actual choices made by political leaders about the implementation of basic order. More generally, the same postulate would

---

other nations (often based on traditions of long standing); attitudes towards internationalism in general . . . international organization, specific international bodies; attitudes towards one's own nation, its destiny, its honor, its sovereignty; general attitudes relating to the perception of threat . . . ; values or ideologies regarding war and violence, regarding alternative ways of resolving conflicts; expectations about war and assumptions about its inevitability; images of war and military life (such as the glamorization of war as an exciting experience, or as a test of heroism)."

also suggest that anticipations of effective decision-makers about their own location in the kind of value structures expected in an international order of human dignity, to the extent such anticipations can be made, will affect their decisions relating to the establishment and completion of such a world order.

A consideration of rather obvious importance is the degree of realism exhibited in the expectational structure of the decision-makers. Realism in expectations depends to a considerable extent upon the kind of information that reaches the focus of attention. Political leaders may in differing measure and under different conditions be effectively alienated from the possibilities of obtaining comprehensive and realistic information; their exposure to the flow of communications may be more or less restricted and selective. Their expectations may thus be, in extreme cases, nightmarish fantasies, or they may bear reasonably close correspondence with the events as a disinterested observer would report them. Rational choice is of course possible only to the extent that the expectations of the choosing person are characterized more by the latter than by the former condition.[55]

Objectives

The fundamental objective of establishing and maintaining minimum public order in the international arena may be characterized,

55. An important aspect of this general problem is examined in Boulding, "National Images and International Systems," 3 *J. Conflict Resolution* 120 (1959). Note, in particular, Professor Boulding's distinction between "real" and "illusory" incompatibility of images. See, further, Scott, "Rationality and Non-Rationality of International Attitudes," 2 id. 8 (1958); and Buchanan and Cantril, *How Nations See Each Other: A Study in Public Opinion* (1953).

The series of "National Studies on International Organization" sponsored by the Carnegie Endowment for International Peace is noteworthy in this regard. The studies, 20-odd in number, seek to depict the expectations and attitudes of an educated group, presumably representative in some degree within each of the countries surveyed, with respect to the United Nations, its problems, functions, and prospects. The importance of considering those sets of attitudes and expectations is suggested by Professor MacIver in his "summing-up" volume—*The Nations and the United Nations* 7 (1959): "It is when policy-makers, wrapped in their own subjectivities, fail to take into the reckoning the subjectivities of others that their calculations are most likely to go awry." General comment is offered in Hoffmann, "National Attitudes and International Order: The National Studies on International Organization," 13 *Int. Organization* 189 (1959).

in a somewhat lower order of abstraction, in terms of a series of more particular goals or images of projected "states of affairs," of "sets of specifications" the comprehensive realization of which may be designated as achievement of the basic objective.[56] There is little mystery about the general shape of these states of affairs which, in differing contexts, may appropriately be sought in a rational sanctioning process.

We refer first to the *prevention* of breaches of minimum public order which has of course historically been a primordial purpose of inter-governmental security organizations. It may be well to recall a primary emphasis of contemporary studies of the sociology and psychology of international conflict and violence that there is no need to postulate any unifactor explanation, any single, sufficient "cause" or "condition" of war which must be excised and eliminated if peace is to be secured.[57] Prevention embraces a great variety of measures and activities designed, over a varying range of time, significantly to reduce the probability of states frequently resorting to intense coercion and violence as modes of changing the distribution of values existing at any given time. This mode of referring to prevention as an objective of sanctioning or implementing processes is intended to emphasize the central importance of bringing about in effective decision-makers a structure of perspectives marked both by strong preference for noncoercive, nonviolent procedures of change and by expectations that change by such methods is possible, practical, and economic—perspectives, in other words, which predispose political leaders to acceptance of minimum order as a principle of action. So conceived, there may be subsumed under prevention an

56. Snyder, Bruck and Sapin, *Decision-making as an Approach to the Study of International Politics* 51 (1954).

57. This emphasis upon the multiplicity of the conditions or factors that bear upon the probable incidence of violence is observable, with particular clarity, in the current maps for research on "war and peace." See e.g. Kelman, supra note 54; Wright, "The Peaceful Adjustment of International Relations: Problems and Research Approaches," 11 *J. Social Issues* 3 (1955); Cottrell, "Research to Establish the Conditions for Peace," 11 ibid. 13; Angell, "Governments and Peoples as Foci for Peace-Oriented Research," 11 ibid. 36; Van Wagenen, *Research in the International Organization Field: Some Notes on a Possible Focus* (Center for Research on World Political Institutions, Pub. No. 1, Princeton Univ., 1952).

Contrast Sorokin, "The Cause of War and Conditions of a Lasting Peace," in *Approaches to World Peace* 88 (Bryson, Finkelstein, and MacIver, eds., 1944).

indefinite number of more detailed goals relating, directly or indirectly, to the kinds of predispositions about the use of coercion and violence required by the minimum order principle. For instance, the formation and shaping of such predispositions may be directly sought by appropriately affecting the content and orientation of processes of communication and education.[58] Less direct but no less important influence upon predispositions has been sought through the modification of various environmental conditions which are thought to bear upon such predispositions. The particular goals of attempts at environmental alteration have included the lowering of tension levels and of the intensity of expectations of violence by diverse means. There are, thus, the historical and perennial aims of arresting the continuous processes of accumulation and expansion in military weaponry, and the reduction of and institution of some controls over the aggregate level of armaments.[59] Another kind of pre-

58. This is, of course, the so-called "minds-of-men" theory about the control of international conflict. The preamble of the Constitution of the United Nations Educational, Scientific and Cultural Organization states: "That since wars begin in the minds of men, it is in the minds of men that the defenses of peace must be constructed; . . ." "The most important thing to be observed about the minds-of-men theory," Professor Dunn points out in *War and the Minds of Men* 10 (1950), "is that it is primarily a theory of communication and learning. It asserts that, if only the right things are communicated by some people to some other people, a change can be effected in the attitudes of nations toward each other that will make a durable peace possible. This is a technical proposition which rests upon our knowledge of the processes of using ideas or symbols to modify the behavior of men."

59. Of a mountainous literature on disarmament, see, for a sketch of historical efforts, Wehberg, *The Limitation of Armaments* (1921). Accounts of contemporary negotiations on disarmament may be had from: Nogee, "The Diplomacy of Disarmament," *Int. Conciliation,* No. 526, p. 235 (1960); Noel-Baker, *The Arms Race: A Programme for World Disarmament* 181–234 (Oceana ed., 1960); U.S. Dept. of State, *Disarmament: The Intensified Effort 1955–1958* (Pub. No. 6676, General Foreign Policy Series 131, 1958); Subcommittee on Disarmament, Committee on Foreign Relations, U.S. Senate, *Control and Reduction of Armaments—Final Report,* 85th Cong., 2nd Sess. (1958); Id., *Handbook on Arms Control and Related Problems in Europe: Excerpts and Summaries of Official and Unofficial Proposals,* 86th Cong., 1st Sess. (1959); *Disarmament Developments, Spring 1960, Hearing before a Subcommittee of the Committee on Foreign Relations,* U.S. Senate, 86th Cong., 2nd Sess. (1960).

A useful statement of the psychological dynamics of an arms race may be found in Singer, "Threat-Perception and the Armament-Tension Dilemma," 2 *J. Conflict Resolution* 90 (1958). A theoretical analysis of varying proposals for

ventive activity is the establishment of more adequate structures of authority—principles and procedures—for peaceful change and dispute settlement and, generally, for the inclusive prescription and effective application of community policy for constantly changing conditions.[60] Again, the relieving of festering human rights situations and the promotion of human rights generally have been important objectives of international organizations, upon the hopeful assumption that the one eliminates a condition provocative of both internal violence and external intervention while the other reinforces mass inclinations toward peace.[61] The improvement of standards of economic and social welfare throughout the world generally and, in particular, in underdeveloped countries and regions, has been an especial concern of a variety of international organizations which perceive some connection between depressed standards of living and the probabilities of international conflict.[62] Efforts addressed to the raising of common levels of welfare are at the same time designed, in hopeful expectation, to bring about the improvement of the techniques and enlargement of the areas of functional cooperation among nations. The hope "functionalists" postulate is that strong habits of peaceful cooperation will, almost surreptitiously, thereby be fostered.[63] Most authoritative expression of the above component

---

total disarmament, arms control, armed stability, qualitative and quantitative competition is essayed in Burns, "A Graphical Approach to Some Problems of the Arms Race," 3 id. 326 (1959).

60. See, generally, Claude, *Swords into Plowshares: The Problems and Progress of International Organization*, c. 11 (2nd ed., 1959); Bloomfield, *Evolution or Revolution? The United Nations and the Problem of Peaceful Territorial Change* (1957); Goodrich and Simons, *The United Nations and the Maintenance of International Peace and Security*, cc. 9–13 (1955). Various proposed improvements in the institutions and procedures of pacific settlement are summarized in Wilcox and Marcy, *Proposals for Changes in the United Nations*, c. 5 (1955).

61. A good recent statement of these assumptions is Moskowitz, *Human Rights and World Order* (1958). See also McDougal and Leighton, "The Rights of Man in the World Community: Constitutional Illusions Versus Rational Action," 59 *Yale L.J.* 60, 64–6 (1949) and the literature there collected.

62. The most comprehensive presentation and summary of activities of international organizations in this field is Asher and others, *The United Nations and the Promotion of the General Welfare* (1957).

63. A quick exposition of the assumptions and problems of "functionalism" as an "approach to peace" may be had from Claude, supra note 60 at c. 16. The classic statement of the "functionalist" creed is Mitrany, *A Working Peace Sys-*

goals of prevention is furnished by Article 55 of the Charter of the United Nations:

> With a view to the creation of conditions of stability and well-being which are necessary for peaceful and friendly relations among nations based on respect for the principle of equal rights and self-determination of peoples, the United Nations shall promote:
>
> (a) higher standards of living, full employment, and conditions of economic and social progress and development;
>
> (b) solutions of international economic, social, health, and related problems; and international cultural and educational cooperation; and
>
> (c) universal respect for, and observance of, human rights and fundamental freedoms for all without distinction as to race, sex, language, or religion.

Deterrence, like prevention, relates to an act in the future. Unlike prevention, however, which is a long-term proposition, deterrence is concerned with a threat or challenge to minimum order that has emerged and been clearly posed and imminently promised. Deterrence envisages the influencing of the decision that the potential violator will make by affecting his expectations of how the sanctioner will behave and respond. The potential violator is informed that the reaction of the sanctioner will be contingent upon and determined by his, the potential violator's, choice. The sanctioners seek to modify the calculations of the challenger as to the probable consequences of particular available alternatives—e.g. executing his threat or withdrawing it and making some other proposal—in such a way as to lead the challenger, in the light of his modified evaluations, to choose the alternative of abstention and withdrawal demanded by the sanctioners.[64] The hypothesis of maximization suggests that the chal-

---

tem: An Argument for the Functional Development of International Organization (Royal Institute of Int. Affairs, 1944); see also Mitrany, *The Progress of International Government* (1933). Friedmann, "Limits of Functionalism in International Organization," 10 *Y.B. of World Affairs* 256 (1956) offers some evaluation.

64. A general theory of deterrence is essayed in Schelling, *The Strategy of Conflict,* cc. 1, 4–6 (1960). Recent studies include Milburn, "What Constitutes

lenger may be constrained to revise his previous calculations by generating in him expectations that the response to the carrying out of his threat will impose upon him deprivations which will neutralize and offset the gains he expects from such execution. Most briefly put, deterrence involves the credible communication to the potential violator of the uneconomic character of a decision to disrupt minimum order. Some such conception of deterrence may be seen to underlie not only the contemporary assumptions about the posture of "nuclear stalemate" imposed upon the two polar powers, but also the unorganized balancing of power so familiar in preceding centuries and the institutionalized collective security arrangements of the present one. Deterrent capacity, that is, the capacity effectively to compel a potential violator to re-evaluate his probable losses and gains, has characteristically been sought in collective security organizations through the establishment of a pattern of commitments by member states to make their individual bases of power available for the administration of deprivations in case a threatened violation is carried out.

It may be noted that in point of theory the challenger's computations of probable losses and gains may be revised, as it were, either on the debit or on the credit side. The challenger may be deterred from resorting to military violence by a threat of deprivations that will make the costs of achieving his objective exorbitant, or by a promise of an indulgence that will approximate the net gain he expects from the use of violence.[65] The experience both in Europe and in Asia in the last several decades suggests, however, that the abstention from violence achieved by an offer of satisfacton, widely termed "appeasement," tends to be quite transitory and that the point of satiety tends to be pushed further back by the very attempt at satisfaction. In terms of impact upon the fundamental community policy, satisfaction frequently signals not deterrence from unlawful violence but the consummation of prohibited coercion. We subscribe

---

Effective Deterrence?" 3 *J. Conflict Resolution* 138 (1959); Snyder, "Deterrence and Power," 4 id., 163 (1960); Burns, "From Balance to Deterrence," 9 *World Politics* 494 (1957); Brodie, *Strategy in the Nuclear Age,* c. 8 (1959).

65. Snyder, *Deterrence by Denial and Punishment* (Research Monograph No. 1, Center of International Studies, 1959) seeks to distinguish "deterrence by punishment" or the infliction of deprivations, and "deterrence by denial" or the blocking of the expected gain.

to the common view that "deterrence by satisfaction" of impermissible demands is appropriately excluded from the objectives of a rational sanctioning process.

The sanctioners may, for a variety of reasons, be unable to constitute their promise of response a decisive factor in the potential violator's calculus of expected costs and gains. There may be a failure to convey the promise credibly and authentically to the potential violator, or the potential violator may have a low capability for realistic estimation of probabilities, or the processes of communication to the potential violator may be subject to garbling and distortion.[66] Whatever the reason may be, where the potential violator is not effectively deterred and basic order is in fact breached by an unlawful resort to coercion, another sanctions objective assumes immediate relevance.

By *restoration* of disrupted public order, we mean the application of responding coercion for the purpose of compelling the violator to reduce the intensity and scope of the coercion unlawfully initiated to more tolerable "ordinary" levels, and thus to terminate and withdraw his challenge to basic order. Restoration may involve the actual infliction of severe deprivations, as distinguished from the promise thereof in a situation of attempted deterrence, and thereby the raising of the cost factor by such an exponent as clearly to demonstrate the unprofitableness of continuing the unlawful coercion. Efforts addressed to the restoration or redress of the public order may be seen to be, in an important sense, the continuation of the efforts at restructuring the perspectives of the violator, efforts that, in preceding stages of the sanctioning process, characterized the objectives of prevention and deterrence.[67] It is, moreover, not only the violator's perspectives relating to the specific instance of coercion involved that are sought to be reached; his perspectives, and those of decision-makers in third states, about the use of coercion *in the future* are likewise intended to be affected. Thus, one assumption which appears to underlie the projection of restoration as an essential objective of collective security organization is that failure to redress a breach of public order tends to increase the probable future incidence of other breaches by cumulating and reinforcing both the

66. See Schelling, supra note 64 at 16.

67. Cf. the observation offered in Snyder, supra note 64 at 166 that "deterrence operates *in* war as well as *before* war."

predispositions and capacity of the successful violator to engage in prohibited coercion and by stimulating like-minded political elites in other states to similar enterprises.

To the extent that the sanctioners succeed in their efforts to compel deceleration and termination of the prohibited coercion, it becomes necessary to consider a fourth sanctions objective—that of *rehabilitation,* or the reparation of the destruction of values sustained because of the disruption of public order. As important as it is in itself, the simple humanitarian relieving of human suffering and want in war-ravaged areas is not, however, the only relevant dimension of rehabilitation. Rehabilitation as a proper objective in sanctioning processes also embraces the facilitating of resumption, as between all the participants, of the "ordinary" community processes, processes where persuasion once again is the predominant mode of interaction.[68] It contemplates also the avoidance of internal conditions of widespread economic and social disorder which massive destruction of capital resources and resulting severe depression of customary living standards are likely to bring about if the necessary means for replacement are not furnished. The view has been widely held that such conditions where left for long unrepaired and unameliorated tend to foster predispositions toward violence and the establishment or re-establishment of totalitarian systems of public order, both of which may be portentous of renewed danger for the maintenance of basic world order. Rehabilitation may thus be seen to be concerned again with structures of perspectives and environmental factors relating to the future of minimum order in the world. It is perhaps obvious that the above conditions of future danger to public order may arise both in the state which was the original target of the prohibited coercion and in the violator state; indeed, the likelihood of such conditions occurring may be greater in a state that has previously resorted to unlawful violence. Hence, although rehabilitation is most commonly taken to refer to damage suffered by the former, the term as here used may refer also to the losses inflicted upon the latter by the sanctioners in the course of restoring public order.

The carrying out of the rehabilitation objective would of course involve the formulation of some criteria for distributing the costs thereof. In that formulation, the factor of capacity to pay may in

68. This is also, it may be noted, one of the objectives embodied in the law on conduct of hostilities, i.e., the rules of war.

some cases loom more importantly than the factor of responsibility for the violation of public order, at least during the period of initial outlay.[69] Such may be the case not only in a conflict of major proportions where the violator sustains crushing damage but also in a "limited war" situation like that of the Korean war where the violator is repulsed but retains considerable armed strength. In the Korean war, the costs of rehabilitating the Republic of Korea were distributed and assessed through the United Nations.

Reconstruction is still another objective that in certain situations may become appropriate and feasible in sanctioning processes. We use "reconstruction" to designate the long-term purpose of avoiding the recurrence of prohibited coercion by modifying or reorganizing or eliminating particular structures and processes of authority and control within the violator state which are regarded as having in the past created, and as likely again to create in the future, perspectives and conditions especially dangerous to the maintenance of basic order. Such, for instance, was the aim sought by the Allied Powers after the Second World War in the "de-nazification" program in Germany and in the "democratization" of Japan. A comparable objective was set forth by the United Nations at one stage of the Korean conflict: "the establishment of a unified, independent and democratic government in the sovereign State of Korea." [70] Reconstruction, thus conceived, obviously merges into prevention, the first sanctions objective referred to above. We speak of reconstruction where important and basic, i.e., structural, changes in the power and other value-institutional processes in the violator state are sought to be effected in the hope of fostering through time the predispositions and environment appropriate to peaceful interaction and competition in the world arena. Prevention refers to efforts primarily carried out, in relation to individual territorial communities, within pre-existing structures and processes. Because of the comprehensiveness of reconstruction as an objective of sanctions policy, its prosecution may be expected to require a very considerable investment of force where the violator state is a substantial power. The experience of the Allied

69. Brown and Opie, *American Foreign Assistance* (1953), provides an account of the rehabilitation programs, after World War II, in which the United States participated directly or through the United Nations.

70. Res. No. 376(V), U.N. Gen. Ass., *Off. Rec.*, 5th Sess., Supp. No. 20 (A/1775) at 9 (1950).

Powers in the Second World War on the one hand and of the United Nations forces in the Korean war on the other, underscores the somewhat obvious lesson that reconstruction is likely to become practicable only where the sanctioners achieve a position of such preponderant strength, and so far subdue the violator state, as to permit them to exercise effective control over the entire territory of the violator state. To put the point most generally, in contexts where the factors that in the contemporary world arena make urgent the hope for "limited war only" are operative, they may make reconstruction an uneconomical objective at least when measured against the immediate prospects of spreading or intensifying destruction, and hence require its abandonment or indefinite deferment.

Situations

The sanctioning process goes forward in the world arena in both unorganized and organized situations. The patterns of decision-making and participation, the particular security objectives sought, the character and relative distribution of the power bases at the disposal of the participants, the combinations and sequences of strategies employed, may all differ in varying measure as the particular situation considered is organized or unorganized.

The unorganized sanctioning situation has historically been most characteristic of international law.[71] The principal reference here is to those noninstitutionalized practices and procedures of reciprocity and retaliation which have been pervasive aspects of the interaction of states.[72] In most abstract generalization, reciprocity, em-

71. Thus, Professor Brierly observed: "[T]he real difference in this respect between municipal and international law is not that the one is sanctioned and the other is not, but that in the one the sanctions are organized in a systematic procedure and that in the other they are left indeterminate. The true problem for consideration is therefore not whether we should try to *create* sanctions for international law, but whether we should try to organize them in a system." Brierly, "Sanctions in International Law," in *The Basis of Obligation in International Law and Other Papers of the late James Leslie Brierly* 202 (Lauterpacht and Waldock, eds., 1958).

72. See Keeton and Schwarzenberger, *Making International Law Work* 40–3 (2nd ed., 1946). The organizing and stabilizing role that reciprocity and mutuality play both within and among communities without centralized and specialized organs of enforcement was several decades ago observed by Professor Malinowski. In his *Crime and Custom in Savage Society* 31–2 (1926), he summarized: "We can see now that a narrow and rigid conception of the problem—a definition of 'law' as the machinery of carrying out justice in cases of trespass—would

bracing both the bestowal of benefit for benefit and the infliction of injury for injury, may be said to involve the establishment of a relation of dependence or contingency between the choices of the parties concerned, who are, each with respect to the other, potential sanctioner and potential violator. This patterning of the action of one upon the action, past or prospective, of the other, this interdetermination of decisions, is designed to affect each party's expectations about the losses and gains to be derived from various alternatives of conduct and, through the operation of the maximization principle, to maintain common adherence to that course which benefits both.

Conspicuous examples of the successful functioning of the practices and procedures of reciprocity may be found in the law of diplomatic immunities, the law of the sea, and in the resolution of the many differing types of controversies which are commonly subsumed under the imprecise label of "private international law." [73] Specific illustration of the way in which anticipations of probable reciprocities and retaliations enter into the consideration and shaping of particular decision and conduct in these areas is offered by the case of the Iranian Minister at Elkton, Maryland. The Iranian Minister to the United States was arrested in 1935 in Elkton for disorderly conduct following the arrest of his chauffeur for a violation of local traffic laws. The charge against the Minister was dismissed two hours later and the offending police officers were dropped from the service. In expressing the apologies of the United States Government over the incident, the Secretary of State said:

> It should be obvious that the unhampered conduct of official relations between countries and the avoidance of friction and

---

leave on one side all the phenomena to which we have referred. In all the facts described, the element or aspect of law, that is of effective social constraint, consists in the complex arrangements which make people keep to their obligations. Among them the most important is the manner in which many transactions are linked into chains of mutual services, every one of them having to be repaid at some later date." At 23: "[E]very chain of reciprocity is made the more binding by being part and parcel of a whole system of mutualities."

73. See the series of articles on reciprocity by Professor Lenhoff—"Reciprocity in Function: A Problem of Conflict of Laws, Constitutional Law, and International Law," 15 *U. Pitt. L. Rev.* 44 (1953); "Reciprocity: The Legal Aspect of a Perennial Idea," 49 *Nw. U. L. Rev.* 619, 752 (1954–1955); and "Reciprocity and the Law of Foreign Judgments: A Historical-Critical Analysis," 16 *La. L. Rev.* 465 (1956).

> misunderstandings which may lead to serious consequences are dependent in large measure upon a strict observance of the law of nations regarding diplomatic immunity. If we are to be in a position to demand proper treatment of our own representatives abroad, we must accord such treatment to foreign representatives in this country, and this Government has no intention of departing from its obligations under international law in this respect.[74]

Similar and very recent recognition of the effective pressures toward reciprocal tolerance and mutual self-restraint that inhere in world processes of interaction is exhibited in the important case of *Romero v. International Terminal Operating Co.*[75] There, the United States Supreme Court refused to apply the Jones Act to the claims brought by a Spanish seaman who had been injured on board a Spanish vessel in the port of New York, at Hoboken. In dismissing the claims against the Spanish ship-owner, Mr. Justice Frankfurter said:

> But in the absence of a contrary congressional direction, we must apply those principles of choice of law that are consonant with the needs of a general federal maritime law and with due recognition of our self-regarding respect for the relevant interests of foreign nations in the regulation of maritime commerce as part of the legitimate concern of the international community. These principles do not depend upon a mechanical application of a doctrine like that of *lex loci delicti commissi.* The controlling considerations are the interacting interests of the United States and of foreign countries . . .
>
> [The] rule [*of lex loci delicti commissi*] does not fit the accommodations that become relevant in fair and prudent regard for the interests of foreign nations in the regulation of their own ships and their own nationals, and the effect upon our

74. Briggs, *The Law of Nations: Cases, Documents, and Notes* 773 (2nd ed., 1952). In *Salm v. Frazier,* ibid. 776, the Court of Appeals of Rouen, France, underscored the reciprocity principle in these terms: "Considering that the principle of immunity from jurisdiction, which does not allow summoning diplomatic agents before courts of countries other than their own, is founded on the interest that states maintaining diplomatic relations with each other have in reciprocally guarantying the respect and independence of their representatives;."

75. 358 U.S. 354 (1959), rehearing denied 359 U.S. 962 (1959).

> interests of our treatment of the legitimate interests of foreign nations.[76]

Beyond the impact of promise and expectation of reciprocity upon particular decisions, the broader suggestion has been made that it is largely by the process of accumulation and stabilization, with the passage of time, of patterns of uniformities in mutual benefit and reciprocal restraint that rules of customary international law have been formulated and developed. "[There are] two functions," Professor Lenhoff has written insightfully,

> which are exercised by reciprocity in the field of international law. On the one hand, it is used for the purpose of championing progressive ideas, and on the other hand, it supplies a rationale for their acceptance and helps to bring about their transformation into general international law.
>
> Taking a historical view, we see the emergence of a process of law-making without the compulsory power of a superior legislature; . . .[77]
>
> [T]he acceptance of a specified pattern of future conduct, unless it is imposed on a weaker or defeated State by a more powerful one, has resulted only from the mutual interests of States in its observance. In the long run, the great gap in international law which results from the absence of a common authority, has, to a good part, been bridged by the reciprocal interest of the states in the observance of certain rules. . . .[78]
>
> [I]dentity of interest lies at the root of the reciprocal acceptance of the same rule as one of law.[79]

The examples above are drawn from "peacetime" problems and relate to contexts where only a relatively low degree of coercion is exhibited. Even with respect to the problem of high intensity coercion, however, calculations of probable reciprocity in unorganized situations exert, if less conspicuously, an equally important and pervasive influence. Indeed, since it is in this type of problem that

76. 358 U.S. 354, 382–4. See, also, *Lauritzen v. Larsen,* 345 U.S. 571 (1953).

77. Lenhoff, "Reciprocity: The Legal Aspect of a Perennial Idea," 49 *Nw. U. L. Rev.* 619, 624 (1954–1955).

78. Ibid., 622–3.

79. Ibid., 627.

the stakes are highest, effective decision-makers, to the extent that they are capable of dealing with probabilities, may be expected to give the closest consideration to such calculations.[80] The best known historical example is that system of power balancing which prevailed in Western Europe for several centuries. That system, it might be recalled, was characterized by a plurality of great states exhibiting low power differentials *inter se,* each seeking to increase its own power and other values but ready, singly or in combination with others, to oppose any individual state or coalition of states that sought the forcible unification of the arena or a predominant position within it.[81] The common assumption was that through the functioning of the network of expectations about mutual confrontation and net advantages and disadvantages, an equilibrium level would be reached and maintained where each of the great powers achieved an optimum position in respect of security and other values that could not economically be improved by resort to violence. The smaller states, it was also assumed, would incidentally benefit from the restraint thus imposed upon the great powers by the dynamics of equilibrium. A special aspect of the imperatives of reciprocal restraint was that action against a big power threatening imbalance could not be carried to the point of eliminating that power completely and reducing the number of effective actors without endangering the stability of the entire system.[82]

Consideration of comparable probabilities may be seen to infuse much of the widespread contemporary assumption that the two polar powers are locked in thermonuclear stalemate. Observers point to the ability of both the United States and the Soviet Union to visit upon each other intolerable and scarcely imaginable destruction and to the present inability of each to achieve invulnerability from such destruction.[83] These factors impinge upon the demands and expectations of both, generating compulsions to mutual restraint at least

80. Cf. Schwarzenberger, *Power Politics: A Study of International Society* 208–9 (2nd rev. ed., 1951).

81. Kaplan, *System and Process in International Politics* 22–36 (1957) offers important discussion of the "essential rules" of the "balance of power" system abstracted and generalized from the European experience.

82. See id., 24, 25; see also Kaplan, "Theoretical Inquiry and the Balance of Power," 14 *Y.B. of World Affairs* 19 (1960).

83. Some of the relevant literature is collected supra, p. 55. See, further, the material referred to infra, pp. 375–76.

from the resort to such apocalyptic violence; and negotiations proceed in a hundred unorganized situations. Every current conception of "limited war," every proposal for a strategy of "graduated deterrence" or "limited retaliation," is grounded upon recognition of the imperatives of reciprocity.

Situations of organized implementation of sanctions, while not characteristic of international law in the past, have had a measure of illustration. The panorama here embraces entities and groupings that may vary widely in degree of organization and institutionalization, as in geographic compass and in functional scope. It comprises both a very informal and poorly institutionalized arrangement like the nineteenth-century Concert of Europe [84] and an elaborate and complex structure with a multiplicity of organs and affiliated bodies like the United Nations. It includes global security organizations typified by the League of Nations and the United Nations—both of which, it is sometimes salutary to recall, have had some success in certain kinds of sanctioning contexts—as well as organizations of lesser territorial comprehension like the Organization of American States. The institutions covered may be general purpose organizations, once again like the United Nations, through which the full range of security objectives, short-term and long-term, may be sought to be implemented in differing contexts; or they may be organizations specialized to one of those objectives or, more commonly, to a particular aspect or segment of one objective, such as the United Nations Educational, Scientific and Cultural Organization (Unesco) and other international agencies concerned with "functional cooperation" in processes where the principal value at stake is something other than power.

The movement toward international institutions in our century was impelled in considerable part by the common belief that for the securing of basic public order, organization in processes of implementation was essential, that organized sanctions would be more effective than unorganized ones. The establishment of the League of Nations was, in a principal sense, an effort to remedy the uncertainty

84. See Claude, *Swords into Plowshares: The Problems and Progress of International Organization* 23–8 (2nd ed., 1959). An excellent recent study is Kissinger, *A World Restored: Metternich, Castlereagh and the Problems of Peace 1812–22* (1957). See also Nicholson, *The Congress of Vienna—A Study in Allied Unity: 1812–1822* (1946).

in operation that marked the preceding unorganized balance-of-power system, the moral ambiguities which were most prominently exhibited in the "compensations" at the expense of small states resorted to in maintaining or restoring an equilibrium level in the relative power of the big states, and its inability to adjust to the changed conditions and enlarged arena of international politics.[85]

Base Values

The base or instrumental values that may be at the disposal of sanctioners are of course the same generically as those that may be available to violators or potential violators. The point, which has been suggested earlier, bears some further emphasis that control over any value may in appropriate occasions be exercised and used by effective decision-makers for the achieving of sanctioning effects as easily and to the same extent as for the prosecution of prohibited purposes. Comprehensive inquiry must extend to the base values of both the major types of participants in sanctioning processes—intergovernmental organizations and nation-states.

We begin with the base values at the disposal of international governmental organizations seeking one or more of the security goals earlier outlined. For inquiry into the bases of power of an organization of states, it is useful to distinguish between the base values which are continuously available to, and subject to the control of, the organization itself and those values which member states may in particular instances bring to the support of the organization for the achievement of certain particular objectives.

Concerning the base values at the continuing disposal of the organization, a most important base of power, for intergovernmental organizations as for the governments of individual states, is authority itself. By authority we here refer to community-wide expectations that the organization is established to make certain decisions in accordance with certain criteria and through certain procedures. It is familiar knowledge to students of community processes that not only does effective power often in time become invested with authority but also that quite commonly authority, when deeply established in the perspectives both of effective decision-makers and of the general

85. See e.g. Claude, supra note 84 at cc. 1–3; Liska, *International Equilibrium* (1957); 2 Wright, *A Study of War*, c. 20 (1942).

populace, in turn becomes a dynamic base of effective power.[86] The authority conferred upon an intergovernmental organization by the member states may of course vary, from organization to organization, in scope, domain, and weight. The scope of competence, as the term is here used, is the range of values that an organization is authorized to affect by its decisions. The domain of competence refers to the number of persons or participants whose interrelations the organization may be authorized to affect through its decisions. Weight of competence may be used to designate the degree of participation in decision-making processes, especially as indicated by the range and efficiency of the procedures, by which the organization is authorized to apply and make effective its substantive competence.[87]

The broad scope of authority that may be assigned to an international security organization is best illustrated in the Charter of the United Nations. The authority of the United Nations may be exercised to affect all values, in obvious contrast with the more limited competences of its affiliated agencies—such as the World Health Organization, the Food and Agricultural Organization, and so on—which are each specialized to a particular value process or combination of value processes. Thus, the grant of competence made to the General Assembly embraces such matters as general "cooperation in the maintenance of international peace and security" including "disarmament and the regulation of armaments"; [88] international cooperation in the political, economic, social, cultural, educational, and health fields; [89] the promotion of human rights; [90] and the protection and development of the inhabitants of non-self-governing and trust territories.[91] The domain of authority that an international

86. Lasswell and Kaplan, *Power and Society* 134 (1950): "Possession of authority is itself a basis for participation in the making of decisions—authority is never completely powerless—but the weight of power which it commands depends on the stress toward political action in the domain of power. In situations of minimal conflict the Crown does not exercise effective power *merely* because it is the Crown; as tension mounts, however, authoritativeness itself comes to have more and more weight."

87. For this usage of terms, see ibid., 77, 134.

88. Art. 11(1), U. N. Charter.

89. Art. 13(1) and (2), id.

90. Art. 55, id.

91. Arts. 73–91, id.

organization disposes may consist of a handful of states members, like that of the South East Asia Treaty Organization; or of all the states in a distinct geographic region, like the Organization of American States; or may extend, as in the case of the United Nations, to the vast majority of the political communities of the world and even, in respect of the maintenance of basic order, to nonmember states. The variation in the weight of competence conferred upon an international organization may be similarly substantial. For instance, the weight of United Nations' authority is rather less than might be supposed considering its impressive scope and domain. Apart from control over its internal organization and procedure, the admission and expulsion of members and its budgetary functions, the authority functions of the General Assembly are confined to discussion, to initiation of studies, and to the making of recommendations.[92] The Charter does authorize the Security Council to prescribe certain policies and apply the necessary and appropriate negative sanctions

92. Arts. 4(2), 6, 17, 20–22, id. The significance of the low weight of the Assembly's authority need not, however, be overstated. The weaknesses of the Assembly's authority as a base of power, including the fact that it is not in continuous session, have been substantially mitigated in practice. In the first place, the distinction between the "nonbinding" nature of the recommendations of the General Assembly and the "binding force" of certain decisions of the Security Council has not been as profound as might be thought, particularly since the Organization has not been in a position to compel its members to carry out its decisions whether designated as "binding" or not. It may be recalled that the United Nations action in Korea was in response to a recommendation. See, generally, Vallat, "The General Assembly and the Security Council of the United Nations," 29 *Brit. Y.B.J.L.* 63 (1952); Sloan, "The Binding Force of a Recommendation of the General Assembly of the United Nations," 25 id. 1 (1948); Johnson, "The Effect of Resolutions of the General Assembly of the United Nations," 32 id. 97 (1955–1956).

In the second place, a decision of the Security Council to delete an item from its agenda in favor of the Assembly is in practice treated as a procedural decision, not subject to the veto. The Assembly has not in fact been excluded from acting in the international peace and security field despite the Security Council's "primary responsibility."

In the third place, the Assembly has devised three methods that taken together keep it continuously active: keeping its Committee on Political and Security Questions in session after the full Assembly recesses; an Interim Committee; and provision for meeting in emergency special session within 24 hours of a request by the Security Council or the Organization's membership, under the "Uniting for Peace" Resolution.

in case of a violation of minimum order; but, and this is commonplace observation, the character of the decision-making procedures authorized for the Council, together with the continuing failure of members to conclude the agreements for the supply of armed forces and facilities envisaged in Article 43 of the Charter, practically assure that the substantive competence of the Security Council will not be made operative against a permanent member or a state protected by it.[93] Some contrast is furnished by the Organ of Consultation of the OAS which is authorized to determine upon collective measures against unlawful attack by a two-thirds vote of the member states.[94]

In addition to the authority granted it, or which it achieves, an intergovernmental organization may utilize other values continuously at its disposal as bases for influencing the behavior of states and implementing basic order. Thus, military *power* is a base value for the North Atlantic Treaty Organization (NATO) which has armed forces assigned to it and brought under its operational command as well as forces earmarked for its use in the event of mobilization or overt hostilities.[95] Influence and power may be based on control over *wealth* resources and processes, such as that which the United Nations disposes either directly through, for example, the Special Fund for economic development, or through its specialized agencies like the International Bank for Reconstruction and Development, the International Monetary Fund, and the International Finance Corporation (IFC).[96] The fund of *skills,* represented by its officials and personnel, available to an international organization is a base value the character and amount of which may profoundly affect the effective ability of the organization to influence the policies of individual states.[97] The disposition of technological skills, as in the United

93. See, e.g., Goodrich and Simons, *The United Nations and the Maintenance of International Peace and Security,* c. 14 (1955).

94. See Arts. 8, 9, 17, "Inter-American Treaty of Reciprocal Assistance," 43 *A.J.I.L. Supp.* 56–7 (1949).

95. See *Facts About Nato,* c. BI, p. 2 (NATO Information Service, Paris, 1957).

96. Concise accounts of the establishment, functions, and activities of these entities and agencies may be had from *Everyman's United Nations,* 197–200, 488–502 (6th ed., 1959). There is also the projected International Development Association which is supposed to make "soft" loans to underdeveloped countries for development projects. *N. Y. Times,* Feb. 1, 1960, p. 11, col. 1.

97. The literature about international civil service is large and growing. Representative citations: Ranshofen-Wertheimer, *The International Secretariat*

Nations Expanded Technical Assistance Program, may similarly be a significant source of influence.[98] *Enlightenment* is available as a base of power to international organizations which again like the United Nations engage extensively in intelligence functions. The organization may act as a forum where members can inform each other and the rest of the world of facts, of their policies and estimations of the future, and even of their idiosyncratic biases; it may also carry out fact-finding through investigation commissions in particular disputes or situations involving danger to basic order; and it may conduct and make available special studies on particular problems, the existing conditions and the available alternatives, in areas of its general or specialized concern. "International agencies," Robert Asher wrote in summing up and appraising their welfare activities, "by bringing additional data and differing viewpoints to the attention of member countries, modify assessments by members of their own national interests." [99] An international organization may also seek to base power and influence upon *rectitude* by acting as the "open conscience of the world" and appealing to and focussing the moral sensibilities of peoples through, for instance, the public determination and condemnation of unlawful behavior, the announcement of suspension or even expulsion of members, and clarion calls for various sanctions measures. International organizations may build prestige and influence upon the *well-being* they dispense in successfully carrying out programs for the improvement of medical care, the prevention of disease, the raising of nutrition levels, the care of infants and the aged, the melioration of working conditions and so forth, all of which bear in some degree upon the prospects of public order.[100] *Loyalty* to communities larger than nation-states presents

(1945); Schwebel, *The Secretary-General of the United Nations* (1952); Scott, "The World's Civil Service," *Int. Conciliation,* No. 496, p. 259 (1954); Loveday, *Reflections on International Administration* (1956).

98. See, generally, Sharp, *International Technical Assistance* (1952). Some notion of the range and extent of the disposition of technical skills the U.N. program effects may be secured from "The Expanded Programme of Technical Assistance: A Statistical Summary of Activities from July 1950–May 1960," *Technical Assistance Newsletter,* No. 64 (June–July 1960).

99. Asher and others, *The United Nations and the Promotion of the General Welfare* 1077 (1957).

100. See id., cc. 11–12. See also Gorove, "International Cooperation in Promoting Health" (unpublished J.S.D. dissertation, Yale Law Library, 1952).

the most comprehensive potentialities as a base of power for international organizations which constantly seek to build and reinforce such sentiments by the circulation of appropriate symbols and by achieving efficiency in all their functions.

The second type of base values available to international governmental organizations includes those which member states may on particular occasions bring to the support of the organization for the securing of particular purposes. In the present rudimentary stage of world organization, the base values states make available commonly constitute the major proportion of the power and influence bases which a particular organization can bring to bear in a specific crisis situation. The various intergovernmental organizations, in particular the United Nations, are in ultimate analysis no more and no less than what the effective consensus of the members will permit and what individual members are willing to allocate and expend for the achievement of the organizations' objectives. This is of course but to underscore once more the crucial importance of bringing about in the political elites of individual nation-states the appropriate structure of perspectives necessary for making effective use of the available sanctioning institutions.

The base values available to nation-states for employment in sanctioning processes, whether such states are acting independently (*qua* states) in situations of varying degrees of organization or acting (*qua* members) in support of an international governmental organization, embrace of course all those characteristic bases of power upon which states depend in their effective relations with other states and other types of participants. For consideration of total or aggregate potentialities, the ordinary bases of state power are conveniently categorized in terms of control over people, control over resources, and control over institutional arrangements.[100a]

States characteristically assert a continuous and comprehensive control over certain peoples, whom they define as their "nationals," this control being manifested both in a cumulation of specific assertions of state authority against the individual human beings claimed

100a. A good statement of the elements or bases of state power is provided in Washington Center of Foreign Policy Research (Johns Hopkins Univ.), *Developments in Military Technology and the Impact on United States Strategy and Foreign Policy,* 32–43 (A Study [No. 8] Prepared at the Request of the Committee on Foreign Relations, U. S. Senate, 86th Cong., 1st Sess., Dec. 6. 1959).

as well as in claims against other states for the protection and control of such individuals. The continuing importance of people as a base of power, despite the contemporary technology of automation, scarcely needs documentation. It still requires a large population, a population with diversified skills, and a population loyal to the dominant symbols of the body politic, to achieve and sustain the economic productivity and military potential necessary to great national power. Similarly, states make certain claims to the exclusive, all-purpose control, of indefinite duration in time, over certain resources—a specified portion of the land surface of the globe together with its surrounding waters and the superjacent airspace—as its "territory." That the size, strategic location, and resource potential, both mineral and organic, of the geographic base of a political community are a fundamental dimension of its power is perhaps axiomatic. States, finally, base their power on control over certain institutions, including both internal structures and processes of decision-making and external patterns of practice in relation to other territorial communities. Concerning internal institutions, it may be noted that the effective power of a state depends not only upon its available quanta of skilled and loyal manpower and the richness of its resource environment, but also upon its freedom of decision in determining and managing specific institutional practices for utilizing such manpower and resources and upon the efficiency of these institutions. With respect to external practices, it may be further noted that not only freedom from external interference but also the degree of support forthcoming from allies are important aspects of a state's power. All these bases of power nation-states may bring to bear in varying sanctions situations, whatever the degree of community involvement and participation in the enterprise of securing basic order—that is, irrespective of whether states act as unilateral sanctioners acting under their own responsibility in individual or collective defense, or as members of a regional or general security organization exercising the mandate or authorization of the organization.

It remains only to add that for states which are members of an intergovernmental organization—these include, with respect to the United Nations, the great bulk of the states of the world—such membership is itself an additional basis of influence and power. Membership affords a state opportunities to affect in some degree the extent and manner of disposition which the organization makes both of the base values at its continuous disposal and of those brought to it on occasion. Further, by virtue of its membership in an international organization, a state can avail itself of a convenient forum for bringing its own power bases to bear more fully upon the other member states. Thus, the persistent pressure for admittance to membership in the United Nations exercised (directly or through proxies) by states which were not original members of the organization suggests that something more than participation in empty ceremonial is thought to be at stake. Just as an international governmental organization is, through the membership of states, able to avail itself of some of the base values held by individual member states, so also, and conversely, admission to membership in an intergovernmental organization means the acquisition by the new member of some access to the base values at the disposal of the organization.

Strategies

Most succinctly described, a strategy is a course of action designed to manage base values for the achievement of policy objectives. We seek here to highlight the instrumental aspect of strategy: the same types of strategies that are employed by a state in challenging and disrupting basic order are available to sanctioners for protecting and supporting basic order. With respect to strategies, as with the base values which are manipulated according to defined strategies, it is in the relation of objectives to fundamental community policy that significant difference is to be found. It is hence possible and convenient to employ in outlining a model of sanctions processes the same fourfold categorization of strategies or instruments for realizing policy earlier used in sketching processes of international coercion—diplomatic strategy, ideological strategy, economic strategy, and military strategy.[101] Sanctioners may of course employ these policy instruments singly or in combinations of differing emphases, with each instrument complementing and supporting every other instrument, to induce by the proffering of indulgences or to constrain by the imposing of deprivations certain kinds of outcomes demanded as concordant with the requirements of basic order.

Diplomatic strategy

Diplomatic strategy aims at the influencing of agreement and the projection of shared policy among the ruling elites of nation-states. It is concerned with the methods or operations and routes by which

101. Supra, pp. 27–33.

these elites communicate with each other and constitutes a direct and continuing instrumentality for affecting the choices and behavior of elites.[102] More specific aims of diplomatic strategy in sanctions situations may be described in the same terms used earlier to refer generally to the kinds of particular objectives appropriate in a rational sanctioning process.

Prevention

The aim of diplomatic activity may be to prevent and forestall situations which present increased probabilities of a participant resorting to violence. Thus, sanctioners may bring their diplomacy to bear upon parties to a dispute to induce recourse to arbitral procedures or may inject themselves into the arena of the dispute as mediators or conciliators or simply as officious friends.[103] A strategy of diplomacy may also look more generally toward the improvement of the available principles and procedures of peaceful dispute settlement. Prevention diplomacy may simultaneously aim at the making of agreements for the limitation or reduction of armaments. Recent diplomatic oratory even projects, with varying degrees of seriousness, "general and complete" or "comprehensive" disarmament[104] and the immediate release of resources which have been devoted to the production of ever more fearful weapons to more peaceful enterprises like economic development and social welfare. A closely related objective of diplomacy, of particular importance in the contemporary

102. See, generally, Morgenthau, "The Permanent Values in the Old Diplomacy," in *Diplomacy in a Changing World* 10 (Kertesz and Fitzsimons, eds., 1959); Pearson, *Diplomacy in the Nuclear Age* (1959).

103. Schelling, *The Strategy of Conflict* 143–5 (1960) presents a thoughtful analysis of the functions of mediators as an element in game theory.

104. See the statement by Premier Khrushchev before, the United Nations General Assembly, Sept. 18, 1959; extract reproduced as appendix to Noel-Baker, *The Arms Race: A Programme for World Disarmament* 583–5 (Oceana ed., 1960). A brief summary of the discussion at the 14th session of the General Assembly appears in *United Nations Action on Disarmament,* Subcommittee on Disarmament, Committee on Foreign Relations, U. S. Senate, 86th Cong., 2nd Sess. (Feb. 22, 1960). Resolution No. 1378 (XIV) of the General Assembly refers to "the goal of general and complete disarmament under effective international control." U.N. Gen. Ass., *Off. Rec.,* 14th Sess., Supp. No. 16 (A/4354), p. 3 (1959). See also the "Western Five-Nation Proposal for General Disarmament," submitted to the ten-nation disarmament conference convened in Geneva on Mar. 16, 1960; text in *N. Y. Times,* Mar. 15, 1960, p. 8.

arena, is the establishment of procedures for safeguarding against—understood as the early detection of—surprise attacks and the cessation, under appropriate controls and inspection, of testing of nuclear and thermonuclear explosives. It does not seem necessary here to seek to resolve the so-called "arms-tension dilemma," that is, whether high armament levels, weapons testing and the consideration of preemptive strikes are a cause or an effect of high-level tensions and expectations of violence.[105] Arms and tension levels appear to have a reciprocal, mutually reinforcing tendency and a preventive strategy of diplomacy must address itself to a reduction of both sides of the equation, as it were.

Deterrence

The purpose of diplomatic communication may be the more immediate one of constraining a challenger to abstain from pressing and executing its challenge to basic order. Sanctioners may employ all the channels and techniques of diplomacy both to ascertain the valuation assigned by a challenger to the objective it seeks by prohibited coercion, and convincingly to communicate to the challenger that their response will be such as significantly to alter the indulgence-deprivation ratio and wipe out the gain expected by the challenger from its violation of basic order.[106] Supplementary aspects of a diplomatic strategy of deterrence are the obtaining of commitments from third-party states either to participate in carrying out the response promised, or to withhold or terminate support for the challenger in case it discounts the promise of response.

Restoration

Among the strategies employed, somewhat paradoxically, for the restoration of public order that has in fact been violated is the severance of diplomatic relations. The measure contemplates the withdrawing by sanctioners of their heads of diplomatic missions, diplomatic missions, trade agencies and consular officials and personnel stationed in the territory of the violator state and the requir-

105. See Singer, "Threat-Perception and the Armament-Tension Dilemma," 2 *J. Conflict Resolution* 90 (1958).

106. The problems of communication between participants in deterrence situations are explored in Schelling, *The Strategy of Conflict* 74–80, 146–150 (1960). Appropriate stress is laid on the necessity for keeping channels of communication open.

ing of the latter to withdraw its own representatives from the sanctioning states.[107] Where intergovernmental organizations are concerned, the termination of relations may take the form of suspension or expulsion of the violator state from membership in the organization. The best known instance is perhaps the expulsion of the Soviet Union from the League of Nations in 1939 after a finding that the Soviet Union had violated the Covenant of the League in attacking Finland.[108] Such measures as these serve in principal part as means of registering the moral censure and indignation of the sanctioning states and members of the organization. When applied as isolated sanctions gestures, or as substitutes for other, more exacting, strategies whose burdens the sanctioners are not willing to assume, the severance of diplomatic relations and the termination of membership rights are of course likely to have but negligible impact upon the violator's coercive policies, save, perhaps, where the elites of the offending state are peculiarly sensitive to moral pressure. These diplomatic practices are most appropriately exercised in conjunction with the other types of sanctions strategies which permit the application of higher degrees of responding coercion.

Closely akin to the above measures is the nonrecognition of "changes" brought about by coercion in violation of public order, a strategy of diplomacy widely known a few decades ago as the "Stimson Doctrine." [109] There is distinguished support for the view that this Doctrine, which affirms that changes in the international distribution of values wrought by resort to intense coercion and violence should not be recognized, "legitimized" and given effect by the rest of the general community of states, is but a logical corollary of the fundamental policy principle prohibiting such resort to coercion and

107. See Art. 41, U. N. Charter; also, *Report of the Collective Measures Committee,* U.N. Gen. Ass., *Off. Rec.,* 6th Sess., Supp. No. 13, p. 5 (A/1891) (1951), hereafter cited as *First Report of the Collective Measures Committee.* Recent illustration is supplied by the action of the Organization of American States authorizing diplomatic (and economic) sanctions against the Trujillo government in the Dominican Republic. *N. Y. Times,* Aug. 21, 1960, p. 1. Pursuant to this action, the U.S. withdrew its diplomatic representative from the Dominican Republic. Id. Aug. 27, 1960, p. 1.

108. See League of Nations, *Off. J.,* 20th Yr., 531–41 (1939).

109. See *First Report of the Collective Measures Committee,* 5; and the Note of Secretary Stimson to China and Japan, Jan. 7, 1932, text in *Int. Conciliation* No. 293, p. 413 (1933).

violence.[110] This corollary policy has even, at least in one region of the world, been expressed in the terms of an explicit commitment: the Charter of the Organization of American States stipulates, as one of the "fundamental duties" of states, that "no territorial acquisitions or special advantages obtained either by force or by other means of coercion shall be recognized." [111] The "changes" (the "fruits of aggression" in Secretary Stimson's phrase) respecting which nonrecognition may be invoked, may include both the outright annexation of territory, such as the annexation of Ethiopia by Italy in 1936, of Austria and the Sudetenland by Germany in 1938, and of the Baltic states by the Soviet Union in 1940, and the establishment of new "puppet states," such as "Manchukuo" created by Japan, "Slovakia" set up by Germany, and "Croatia" fathered by Italy.[112] The "satel-

110. In 1932, twelve members of the Council of the League of Nations pointed out to Japan that from the terms of Article 10 of the League Covenant, it followed "that no infringement of the territorial integrity and no change in the political independence of any member of the League brought about in disregard of this article ought to be recognized as valid and effectual by members of the League of Nations." League of Nations, *Off. J.*, 12th Yr., Part I, p. 384 (1932). The resolution of Mar. 11, 1932 of the League Assembly was more forthright: "It is incumbent upon the Members of the League of Nations not to recognize any situation, treaty or agreement which may be brought about by means contrary to the Covenant of the League of Nations or to the Pact of Paris." Id., Spec. Supp. No. 101, pp. 87–8 (1932). See Brierly, "The Meaning and Legal Effect of the Resolution of the League of Nations of March 11, 1932," 16 *Brit. Y.B.I.L.* 159 (1935).

See, further, the precedents collected and discussed in Sharp, *Nonrecognition as a Legal Obligation 1775–1934* (1934); also, Garner, "Non-recognition of Illegal Territorial Annexations and Claims to Sovereignty," 30 *A.J.I.L.* 679 (1936). Perhaps the best-known formulation is Art. 5 of the "Budapest Articles of Interpretation of the Pact of Paris," International Law Association, *Report of the 38th Conference* 67–8 (Budapest, 1934). Less well-known is Art. 11 of the "Draft Declaration of the Rights and Duties of States," in 1948–1949 *U.N. Yearbook* 949.

111. Art. 17, O.A.S. Charter; text in Subcommittee on Disarmament, Senate Committee on Foreign Relations, *Disarmament and Security: A Collection of Documents 1919–1955,* 84th Cong., 2d Sess., 162 (1956).

112. Langer, *Seizure of Territory: The Stimson Doctrine and Related Principles in Legal Theory and Diplomatic Practice* (1947) offers a convenient summary of practice relating to nonrecognition of territorial changes.

One technical expression of nonrecognition policy is set out in Art. 4(2) of the "Harvard Draft Convention on the Rights and Duties of States in Case of Aggression": "situations created by an aggressor's use of armed force do not

lite" government maintained by the effective control of a big power through many various mechanisms presents a more recent type of veiling device.

A strategy of nonrecognition commonly involves the exclusion of the unrecognized entity from access to certain arenas of formal authority. Denial of access to arenas external to any particular state results from such operations as exclusion from membership in international organizations, from participation in international conferences, and from accession to international conventions.[113] Exclusion from *fora* internal to the nonrecognizing states is effected by refusal to enter into diplomatic relations with the unrecognized entity[114] and by denial of access to national courts. Moreover, the sanctioners may refuse to give effect within their territorial jurisdiction to governmental acts of, as well as acts performed under a claim of authority from, the unrecognized state or government.[115] Illustration is offered by the *Maret*[116] where the court rejected a claim to the ownership of the vessel made on the basis of a decree of the "Soviet Republic of Estonia" purporting to transfer ownership of all vessels owned by Estonian nationals to a state agency. The "Soviet Republic of Estonia" had been created by the Soviet Union after annexing Estonia and had been explicitly refused recognition by the United States. The court said:

> When the fact of nonrecognition of a foreign sovereign and nonrecognition of its decrees by our Executive is demonstrated as in the case at bar, the courts of this country may not examine

change sovereignty or other legal rights over territory." 33 *A.J.I.L. Supp.* 889 (1939). See, in this connection, McMahon, *Conquest and International Law* (1940); compare Briggs, "Nonrecognition of Title by Conquest and Limitations on the Doctrine," 34 *Proc. Am. Soc. I.L.* 72 (1940).

113. See *First Report of the Collective Measures Committee*. The above kinds of measures were recommended to members of the League of Nations in connection with the Japanese conquest of Manchuria; see the "Recommendations of the Advisory Committee of the League of Nations," addressed to all governments on June 7, 1933, text in *Int. Conciliation* No. 293, pp. 455–8 (1933).

114. See Langer, supra note 112 at 101–2; Sharp, supra note 110 at 197–205.

115. See, e.g., Lauterpacht, *Recognition in International Law* 142 et seq. (1947); Chen, *The International Law of Recognition* 133 et seq. (1951); Note: "The Legal Effects of Non-recognition of Governments," 36 *Minn. L. Rev.* 769 (1952).

116. 145 F. 2d 431 (3rd Cir. 1944).

the effect of decrees of the unrecognized foreign sovereign and determine rights in property, subject to the jurisdiction of the examining court, upon the basis of those decrees. A policy of nonrecognition when demonstrated by the Executive must be deemed to be as affirmative and positive in effect as a policy of recognition.[117]

The sanctioners may, further, refuse to treat the public property of the dispossessed state or government, which is found within their territories, as having been acquired by the unrecognized entity.[118]

It is perhaps obvious that where exercised to the exclusion and in lieu of any other sanctions strategy, nonrecognition, like the termination of diplomatic relations and of rights of membership in intergovernmental organizations, can hardly be expected to achieve a high degree of coercive effect against a powerful violator state.[119] It has indeed been suggested by Judge Lauterpacht that the "principal function [of nonrecognition] must, more accurately, be conceived as a somewhat symbolic instrument for upholding the challenged authority of international law." [120] Nonrecognition, however, is but one

117. 145 F. 2d at 442. See also *Latvian State Cargo and Passenger S.S. Line v. Clark,* 80 F. Supp. 863 (D.C., 1948), aff'md. 188 F. 2d 1000 (D.C. Cir., 1951).

118. See Langer, supra note 112 at 107.

119. This point was most frequently urged in the decade preceding the Second World War when nonrecognition was frequently looked upon as an inexpensive exercise of moral indignation that dispensed with any obligation to take more strenuous and significant sanctioning activity. The low degree of effectiveness of nonrecognition as an isolated gesture made the Stimson doctrine an easy target for "realist" critics. See, e.g., Moore, "Fifty Years of International Law," 50 *Harvard L. Rev.* 395, 436 (1937); Williams, "Some Thoughts on the Doctrine of Recognition in International Law," 47 id. 776, 791–2 (1934); Borchard and Morrison, "The Doctrine of Nonrecognition," in *Legal Problems in the Far Eastern Conflict* 157 (Institute of Pacific Relations, 1941).

120. Supra note 115 at 433. Judge Lauterpacht went so far as to suggest that the nonrecognition doctrine be limited to a withholding of *"de jure* recognition," that inconvenience and hardship may be avoided by permitting *"de facto* recognition." Id., 432–3. Cf. Sharp, supra note 110 at 205.

Refusal to enter into diplomatic relations as a mode of dramatizing protest against a certain state of affairs finds recent illustration in the determination of the German Federal Republic not to "extend diplomatic recognition to any country that maintained diplomatic relations with Communist East Germany." "To do so," Chancellor Adenauer is reported to have maintained, "would mean giving legal sanction to the division of Germany." *N. Y. Times,* Oct. 14, 1959, p. 11, col. 1.

of a whole arsenal of sanctions techniques and is most meaningful when considered as a concomitant to military and economic measures. Moreover, the potentialities of *collective* nonrecognition have yet to be explored in practice and the suggestion has been made that "in a more adequately organized international community," the sanction of nonrecognition should gain in force and reality.[121]

Rehabilitation

The use of diplomacy is, almost by definition, indispensable in the termination phases of the process of coercively restoring public order when early and orderly transition to the processes of peaceful interaction becomes a principal objective. Diplomatic activity may in these stages be oriented toward the making of agreements, between sanctioners *inter se* as between sanctioners and violators, about the reparation or replacement of values destroyed in the course of the process being terminated and about the appropriate incidence of the economic costs of such reparation. Negotiations may also be concerned with the rehabilitation of the human resources, as it were, of both sanctioners and violators and aim at the release and repatriation of the captured personnel held by each side.

Reconstruction

Sanctioners may employ all the arts and operations of diplomacy in seeking to bring about important changes both in the structure of the arena of world politics and in the basic value and institutional processes internal to the violator state. Optimally, such changes are designed not only to prevent the recurrence of disruptions of basic order, but also to move the system of world order, which sanctioners regard themselves as protecting, toward a greater measure of fulfillment or completion. The objective of a strategy of diplomacy may be, for instance, at the termination of global upheavals in 1945 as in 1918 to introduce changes in world processes of authoritative and effective decision-making by the creation of new, more effective, international organizations or by the restructuring and the reinforcing of pre-existing ones. From the perspectives of an international law of human dignity, principal reliance should be placed upon diplomatic-ideologic methods—understood in broadest sense as the

121. Jessup, *A Modern Law of Nations* 162 (1948). Cf. Middlebush, "Non-Recognition as a Sanction of International Law," 27 *Proc. Am. Soc. I.L.* 40 (1933).

procedures of persuasion—rather than upon naked imposition under indefinite military occupation in fostering changes in the basic value patterns and institutions of defeated violator states.

IDEOLOGICAL STRATEGY

Ideological strategy is oriented toward the influencing of the attitudes of large groups.[122] The target groups may consist of the domestic audience of the strategists' nation-state as well as external audiences in other states. The techniques of ideological strategy relate principally to the selection of symbols to be circulated in the target audience and to the establishment and maintenance of centers and channels of communication through which the symbols chosen are put into circulation. Suitable symbols may be chosen with a view to affecting the expectations, demands, and identifications of people in the audience, to creating attitudes—that is, stresses or tendencies to the commission of acts by which a particular perspective is externalized [123]—and to channeling and directing the existing tension as well as the expected response of the audience. The practitioners of ideological strategy may utilize both official and nonofficial centers of dissemination, whether located within or outside the strategists' own state. The external centers include not only public (e.g. diplomatic establishments, information agencies) and private agencies in a foreign state, but also the invaluable *fora* of governmental and of nongovernmental international organizations. The communication channels most distinctive of ideological practices are, of course, the mass media—the printed page, radio, cinema, television. It is notorious, however, that strategists also frequently employ individual human beings as open or covert carriers of symbols and collectors of intelligence across political boundaries.

Prevention

An ideological strategy of sanctions may, in very broad statement, aim at creating and giving wide currency to symbols, slogans, and doctrines which are favorable to the maintenance of basic order and to the fulfillment of the public order being protected. Sanctioners, for instance, may seek to plant and cultivate in the masses of various

122. Introduction to ideological or communications strategy may be secured from *Reader in Public Opinion and Communication* (enlarged ed., Berelson and Janowitz, 1953); and *Mass Communications* (Schramm, ed., 1949).

123. Lasswell and Kaplan, *Power and Society* 25 (1950).

states (especially those which may appear to be potential violator states, e.g., the "dissatisfied," "dynamic" states) demands for recourse to nonviolent modes of dispute settlement, for functional cooperation with other countries and international organizations, for reductions of military expenditures, for increase of production of civilian or consumer goods, and so on. Ideological practices may also be employed in the effort to widen the effective identifications of peoples, in domestic as in external audiences, to initiate and build up favorable attitudes and loyalties to symbols referring to communities and organizations more inclusive than the nation-state.[124] By multiplying the audience's exposure to such symbols and appropriate statements, sentiments of positive identification with these communities and organizations, and with mankind as a whole, may be fostered, which sentiments may in turn increase the likelihood that many acts of policy will be shaped less by the extremes of parochially conceived "national interests" than by the larger perspectives of a peaceful international community.[125] An important aspect of a strategy of prevention is the influencing of the shape of popular and elite expectations about the future, including the conditions of both minimum and optimum order in the world arena, the common and realistic assumption being that long-range expectations are a sig-

124. This has been an important aspect of the work of the United Nations Educational, Scientific and Cultural Organization (Unesco). See Laves and Thomson, *Unesco: Purpose, Progress, Prospects,* cc. 10–12 (1957); Huxley, *Unesco: Its Purposes and Philosophy* (1947); Tripp, "Unesco in Perspective," *Int. Conciliation* No. 497, p. 323 (1954); Ascher, "The Development of Unesco's Program," 4 *Int. Organization* 12 (1950). Special mention may be made of Unesco's efforts to promote the cooperative revision of textbooks, in particular history textbooks—an enterprise with at least two decades of history prior to Unesco—with a view to modifying those tending to disseminate distorted, negative images of other nations or to impede sentiments for international cooperation, and so forth. See Laves and Thomson, 230–6; and Lauwerys, *History Textbooks and International Understanding* (Unesco, 1953). See also Lowie, "Parochialism and Historical Instruction," in *Learning and World Peace* 89 (Bryson, Finkelstein and MacIver, eds., 1948).

125. See Lasswell, "World Loyalty," in *The World Community* 200 (Wright, ed., 1948); also Dunn, *War and the Minds of Men* 71–92 (1950). Professor Dunn distinguishes three tasks: (a) raising of levels of (realistic) information; (b) modification of conscious attitudes and opinions; and (c) alteration of deeply embedded or unconsciously held attitudes and motivations. The most difficult, of course, is the third task.

nificant factor for policy and behavior. Thus, such a strategy may aim at the weakening and modification of expectations of violence, and of beliefs in the "inevitability" of war, which may tend to set in motion spiraling sequences of apparently confirmatory acts and thence may proceed to devastating self-fulfillment.[126]

Deterrence

Serious disruptions of basic order rarely spring full blown from the brows of political elites. There is frequently a longer or shorter period of accelerating coercion and deepening crisis during which the threat to minimum order is posed and perceived with increasing clarity and immediacy. In this stage, strategists may employ ideological means (which ordinarily involve a time lag between initiation and impact) for deterrent purposes. The aim of ideological activity may, for instance, be to reduce the bases of power upon which the potential challenger can confidently rely in his calculations by, for example, undermining mass support for his challenge in countries allied to him. At the same time, sanctioners may seek elsewhere to organize and mobilize popular support for resistance to the expected attack upon public order and to line up other states in opposition to the challenger.

Restoration

In the course and as part of action to repress attacks upon basic order, all the techniques of psychological and propaganda warfare which belligerents employ to achieve maximum impact upon the "will to fight" of an enemy belligerent are available to sanctioners. These techniques are, of course, ancillary to the use of military and other instruments which are principally addressed to the reduction of the enemy's (violator's) physical capabilities for fighting. The weakening of the "will to fight," as an aim of the ideological strategy of sanctioners (as of the participant offending against public order), includes, more specifically, interference with: the making and implementing of foreign policy and internal governance by the opposing political elite; the selection and execution of military operations, and the maintenance of command over the armed forces, by the military leaders; the willingness of military leaders, armed forces, and the working population to follow the political elite; and the willing-

126. See Lasswell, "'Inevitable War': A Problem in the Control of Long-Range Expectations," 2 *World Politics* 1 (1949).

ness of both military leaders and personnel to fight.[127] Thus, propaganda specialists may seek to induce selected target audiences in both the working and fighting population of the violator state to abstain from, or to minimize or discontinue, participation in the enterprise of unlawful war. The propagandists may aim to affect the identifications of these audiences, to detach from the audiences' operative identification systems the elites responsible for plunging the nation into war, and hence to withdraw support from these elites. For this purpose, the development and increase of "privatization" in the target groups may be encouraged by stressing the senselessness of the destruction of war and the importance of the individual listener's own values, such as his personal well-being, which are threatened by the efforts of his political leaders to realize their demands. Appropriate emphasis may be placed upon the deprivations of rectitude which these elites' decision to attack public order imposed upon the entire nation. The target audiences may be urged affirmatively to cooperate with the forces of the sanctioners by all kinds of deviant, politically significant behavior. The effective modification of the internal decision processes in the violator state may in some cases be encouraged by supporting the formation and activities of counter elite groups which in certain circumstances may even succeed in capturing power and ousting the elites who initiated the war. The specific detailed aims, themes, and practices of propaganda and psychological warfare would of course differ as the particular situations of both strategists and target groups differ.[128]

Reconstruction

The use of strategies specialized to the management of symbols may be particularly prominent in efforts at reconstruction, whether what is attempted to be reconstructed is the important political and social institutions of a defeated violator state or the patterns of participation and organization in the world arena.

In most general statement, the reconstruction of the internal social order of an offender state envisages, whatever else it may include, both the suppression and elimination of the peculiar symbols and practices that contributed and led to the violation of basic order and

127. Speier, "Psychological Warfare Reconsidered," in *Propaganda in War and Crisis* 463, 466–72 (Lerner, ed., 1951).

128. See the literature referred to infra, pp. 611–14.

that hence are regarded as especially dangerous for the future maintenance of order, and the circulation of new symbols and establishment of new practices more compatible with and conducive to peaceful interaction and cooperation. In the case of Germany after World War II, for instance, extirpation of Nazi symbols and institutions was sought by such means as the liquidation of the Nazi Party together with all "its subordinate organizations, affiliated associations and supervised organizations, and of all Nazi public institutions created as instruments of Nazi domination";[129] the repeal of all laws that embodied and protected Nazi ideology and militarism; and the removal from public office and from positions of responsibility in private enterprises of members and active supporters of the Nazi Party. All communications propagating militarist and Nazi doctrines, especially racial hatred, were excluded from all mass media, including church pulpits, and expunged from courses of instruction and textbooks in schools and universities. The use and display of Nazi insignia, uniforms, salutes, flags, anthems, and similar paraphernalia was prohibited. Further, streets, parks, bridges, buildings, and so on, which had been named after persons or objects associated with Nazism, were given less evocative designations. With the delegitimation of Nazi symbols and practices, new ones, such as "freedom of the press," "freedom of religion," "equality," "independent judiciary," were made positive symbols and systematically disseminated as part of comprehensive programs of "democratization" and "reeducation."[130]

129. Section XI, par. 39, "Agreement between the United States, the United Kingdom, the Union of Soviet Socialist Republics, and the Provisional Government of the French Republic on Additional Requirements to be Imposed on Germany," signed Sept. 20, 1945; text in 8 *Documents on American Foreign Relations July 1, 1945–December 31, 1946,* 189, 197 (1948).

130. On the "de-nazification" program of the occupation government in Germany, see, in addition to the materials cited supra, Ch. 3, note 228. Griffith, "Denazification in the United States Zone of Germany," 267 *Annals* 68 (1950); Gimbel, "American Denazification and German Local Politics 1945–1949: A Case Study in Marburg," 54 *Am. Pol. Sci. Rev.* 83 (1960). The problems relating to modification of a totalitarian elite structure are explored in Edinger, "Post-Totalitarian Leadership: Elites in the German Federal Republic," 54 id. 58 (1960).

For recent accounts of the "democratization" program in Japan during the occupation period, see Baerwald, *The Purge of Japanese Leaders Under the Occupation* (1959); Kawai, *Japan's American Interlude* (1960).

Ideological strategists may be assigned the deeply vital task of securing enlightened popular support for projects that look to the more effective and integrated organization of "security"—understood as the "demand for the maintenance of a public order which affords full opportunities to preserve and increase all values by peaceful procedures, free from more than a minimum level of coercion or threats of such coercion." [130a] Not the least important aspects of this task is the process of maintaining at the focus of public attention, and of sentimentalizing, appropriate symbols of identification with and demand for more effective international security organizations.

ECONOMIC STRATEGY

Economic strategy seeks to affect all phases—production, conservation, distribution, consumption—of wealth processes. It is concerned with methods of and facilities for managing a flow of capital, goods, and services across national boundaries.

Prevention

The prevention of conditions which are thought potentially dangerous for minimum order among nations underlies, with varying degrees of explicitness, much of the international economic policy of various mature, industrial states as well as the programs of many international economic organizations. By common agreement, the economic and social development of the underdeveloped countries, embracing some 1.6 billion peoples, most of them newly emerged from colonial status, is regarded as among the most important current problems of the world. When viewed in the context of the contemporary world power processes, the gap between demanded and actual levels of production and consumption in these modernizing communities and the "revolution of expectations" sweeping across them, appear to have significant potential implications for basic order.[131] From perspectives oriented to both the securing of minimum

130a. McDougal and Lasswell, "The Identification and Appraisal of Diverse Systems of Public Order," 53 *A.J.I.L.* 1, 23 (1959).

131. Asher and Associates, *The United Nations and Promotion of the General Welfare* 582 (1957): "The pressing problems of the underdeveloped countries have been elevated to the international level, not because they involve international transactions, but because they are common to a large number of countries, because those countries individually and collectively lack the resources to solve them, and because failure to solve them—or at least failure to move

order and to movement toward an optimum international order of human dignity, the potential outcomes of disorder that the process of modernization may hold appear to have at least two aspects. Firstly, the frustration and failure to achieve quickly enough the mass demands for higher levels of living, whatever the sources of failure may be, may explode into civil disorder which may be exploited, fanned, and spread by an outside power intervening at a strategic moment. The dynamics of the transitional process may, secondly, lead the elites in these communities to establish totalitarian and police-state patterns of political and social-economic controls. They may come to believe, in the words of Mr. Brzezinski, that "[p]luralism, the basis of democracy, [is] an awkward impediment to the monolithic unity essential to success" [132] in the enterprise of industrialization. Given the conditions of conflict between systems of international order, the implications of such a development need little elaboration.

Economic strategies for assisting transitional communities toward development and modernity include the now familiar programs for pooling and making available the technological and administrative skills of the economically mature countries to such communities and for imparting such skills to the people of the recipient community. Provision for a continuing and expanded flow of international capi-

---

energetically and perceptibly in the direction of solutions—is widely believed to threaten the peace and security of the world as a whole."

Cf. Kindleberger, *The Implications of Differential Economic Development* (International Relations Conference, Northwestern University, April, 1959) notes the ambivalent implications of economic development for international relations and the spectrum of possible consequences, including consequences dangerous for basic order (esp. at p. 36). Staley, *The Future of the Underdeveloped Countries,* c. 4 (1954) submits that no simple, one-to-one, relation is observable between economic development and democracy and peacefulness. He summarizes (at 58): "For each of these objectives ("improved material livelihood," "freedom for the human spirit," and "peace and security") economic development of the underdeveloped areas is an essential condition. It is not, however, a sufficient condition for any of them, since economic development does not of itself guarantee the kind of society and government which will bring a wide distribution of economic goods, or freedom, or security and peace."

132. Brzezinski, "The Politics of Underdevelopment," 9 *World Politics* 55, 63 (1956). See also Parkinson, "Social Dynamics of Underdeveloped Countries," 14 *Y.B. of World Affairs* 207 (1960). Hagen, A General Framework for Analyzing Economic Growth (Conference on Research for the Improvement of Development Assistance Programs and Operations, Brookings Inst., 1961) is comprehensive and thoughtful.

tal into the modernizing countries to assist in the long-term financing of carefully planned and diversified development programs is an equally important aspect of preventive economic strategy. Scarcely less important are the reorganization of feudalistic patterns in agriculture, the achievement of high and stable levels of employment, the relating of production potential to the international economy, and avoidance of the international spread of depressions. Still another aspect is the coordination of the multiplying number of national and international agencies engaged in economic assistance programs.[133]

133. Center For International Studies (M.I.T.), *Economic, Social, and Political Change in the Underdeveloped Countries and Its Implications for United States Policy* (A Study [No. 12] Prepared at the Request of the Committee on Foreign Relations, U. S. Senate, 86th Cong., 2d Sess., Mar. 30, 1960) sets forth an excellent comprehensive formulation of United States interest in relation to the development of the modernizing communities. With the elision of a few words, set off in brackets, and with an appropriate substitution for "our,' the statement expresses, we believe, a shared interest of communities seeking an international order of human dignity. The formulation follows: (at p. 10)

". . . It is in our interest to see emerge out of the transition processes nation states which—

1. Maintain effective independence, [especially of powers hostile or potentially hostile to the United States].

2. Do not resort to violence in their relations with other states. The development of modern weapons has made the outbreak of violence anywhere in the world exceedingly dangerous for all nations, especially because of the opportunities it opens for intervention by Communist or other extremist powers.

3. Maintain effective and orderly government internally without resort to totalitarian controls. The effort to impose rigid controls is likely to produce tensions within a society which cannot indefinitely be contained. If internal conflict erupts, intervention by an outside power and the consequent spread of violence become a serious threat. Our interest therefore lies in the emergence of institutions for the wielding and transfer of power by consent of major groups; this is essentially what we mean by the creation of "democratic" forms of government.

4. Are capable of progressively meeting the aspirations of all major classes of their people. This is a condition which must be met if the first three objectives are to have much chance of realization.

5. Are willing to cooperate in those measures of international economic, political, and social control necessary to the functioning of an interdependent world community.

6. Accept the principles of an open society whose members are en-

Restoration

When the over-all strategic objective of sanctioners is the constraining of a violator state to terminate its unlawful coercion, there are available to sanctioners a host of techniques of economic warfare for enhancement of their relative economic strength as against the violator. On a somewhat lower level of abstraction, economic warfare strategists seek to isolate the economic entity comprised by the violator (enemy) state from access to the flow of outside resources and services, to eliminate its economic influence in third states as in the strategists' country, and to interfere with its efficient use of its own internal resources. The complementary aim is to increase the strategists' own access to and secure influence over the resources and services obtainable from third states.[134]

Perhaps most prominent among the particular strategies of economic warfare are commodity and financial controls. Commodity controls are addressed to the severance or regulation of both the trade of the sanctioners and of third states or neutrals with the violator (enemy) state. They may involve the imposition of an embargo on direct exports from the sanctioners to the violator state and on direct imports by the sanctioners from the violator, the prevention of re-exportation or transshipment from neutral countries of goods from the sanctioners to the violator state or vice versa, and the regulation of the neutral countries' "own" or direct trade with the violator state.[135] An embargo on exports, whether total or selec-

couraged to exchange ideas, goods, values, and experience with the rest of the world."

The same study presents some recommended strategies, economic and other, for seeking achievement of the clarified interest. With respect to these strategies, see the superb book, Millikan and Rostow, *A Proposal: Key to an Effective Foreign Policy* (1957). See also Maxwell Graduate School of Citizenship and Public Affairs (Syracuse Univ.), *The Operational Aspects of United States Foreign Policy,* 30–50 (A Study [No. 6] Prepared at the Request of the Committee on Foreign Relations, U. S. Senate, 86th Cong., 1st Sess., Nov. 11, 1959) where related strategies are worked out in some detail. Myrdal, *An International Economy: Problems and Prospects,* cc. 9, 11–13 (1956) and *The Emerging Nations* (Millikan and Blackmer, eds., 1961) deal with the special problems of underdeveloped countries.

134. On economic warfare generally, see the literature referred to supra, Ch. 1, note 83.

135. See *First Report of the Collective Measures Committee* 11–13. The chief historical examples of embargoes imposed against a violator state determined by

tive, is intended to weaken the target (violator) state directly by the withholding of supplies from it while an embargo on imports is calculated to deprive the offending state of the foreign exchange it needs to finance its purchases from abroad.[136] Embargoes are enforced and supplemented by ancillary controls on communications and sea, air, and land transportation lines and facilities. Control over re-exportation from neutrals as well as over direct neutral trade with the enemy (violator) state may be sought through techniques of modern contraband and blockade control made familiar in the two world wars and including pre-emptive purchases in neutral countries and "blacklisting." [137]

Financial controls may consist in stopping the international movement of capital to the violator state through, for instance, the denial of loans and credits—whether sought directly or through intervening third parties and whether the funds or credits involved be public or private—and the suspension of payments. They may also take the

---

the organized community of states remain the economic sanctions taken against Italy by members of the League of Nations and the embargo on strategic materials called for by the U. N. General Assembly against the Peoples' Republic of China. On the first, see e.g., Atwater, *Administration of Export and Import Embargoes by Member States of the League of Nations 1935–1936* (Geneva Studies, Vol. 9 [1938]); and Highley, *The Actions of the States Members of the League of Nations in Application of Sanctions Against Italy 1935–1936* (1938). Strange, "The Strategic Trade Embargoes: Sense or Nonsense?" 12 *Y.B. of World Affairs* 55 (1958) offers pungent criticism, of uneven value, of the strategic embargoes enforced by Western powers against the Soviet-Chinese bloc.

A more recent invocation of trade embargoes for sanctioning purposes is the action of the conference of independent African states that convened at Addis Ababa in June, 1960. In protest against the "shameful policy of racial discrimination" in South Africa, the conference called upon its members to apply a series of trade sanctions including the boycotting of all South African goods, the closing of member states' ports to all South African flag vessels, prohibiting ships flying member states' flags from entering South African ports, and refusing landing and passage facilities to all South African aircraft. *N. Y. Times,* June 25, 1960, p. 1, col. 6. Ghana, on July 29, 1960, became the first to implement this resolution by imposing a total embargo on goods originating in South Africa and the closure of all Ghanaian airports and seaports to South African ships and planes, and by forbidding entry of South Africans who do not declare their opposition to "apartheid." Id., July 30, 1960, p. 1, col. 1.

136. *First Report of the Collective Measures Committee* 12–13.

137. See *International Sanctions* 98–100 (Royal Institute of Int. Affairs, 1938). Blockade and contraband control methods are discussed infra, p. 477 et seq.

form of blocking or freezing assets of the violator state and its nationals. Like the import embargo, these financial measures are designed to reduce the purchasing power abroad of the target state.[138]

Other types of economic warfare techniques are available to strategists for interfering with and possibly undermining the internal controls established by the violator over its economic and financial resources. These techniques include measures for generating inflationary pressures on domestic price levels such as, for instance, drying up supplies of essential materials, promoting speculation in commodity exchanges, inciting work stoppages, and so on. They also embrace measures for reducing the foreign exchange resources of the target state such as, for instance, the dissipation of foreign assets by the promotion of smuggling, the stimulation of capital flight, and the depression of the foreign value of the target's currency by promotion of black market operations in such currency and deliberate selling at progressively lower rates of exchange.[139]

These techniques directed against the economy of the violator state may commonly be supplemented both by measures of positive assistance to the state which was the initial target of unlawful coercion, that is, the participant determined to be acting in permissible self-defense, and by measures of positive inducement to nonparticipant states. Economic assistance to the defending participant may take the form of outright transfers of supplies and services or of extension of loans or grants and subsidies to bolster its ability to resist.[140] The League of Nations draft Convention on Financial Assistance of 1930, it may be recalled, provided for authorization of loans to victim states

138. See *First Report of the Collective Measures Committee* 13–14; Royal Institute of Int. Affairs, "Sanctions," in *Collective Security* 358, 359 (Bourquin, ed., 1936); Naudin, "Economic and Financial Sanctions and Assistance in Case of International Conflicts," in id., 348; *International Sanctions* 76–7 (Royal Institute of Int. Affairs, 1938). Eckel, "The Military Effectiveness of Economic Sanctions," in *Boycotts and Peace: Report by the Committee on Economic Sanctions* 150 (Clark, ed., 1932) suggests that any effective credit embargo would have to take the broad form of prohibition of trading with the enemy. The financial measures taken against Italy in 1935–1936 are reported in League of Nations, *Off. J.*, Spec. Supp. No. 145, pp. 16, 45, 122.

139. See Wu, *Economic Warfare* 139–44 (1952).

140. *First Report of the Collective Measures Committee* 8; see also Williams, "The Coming of Economic Sanctions into American Practice," 37 *A.J.I.L.* 386, 392 (1943).

and the guaranteeing of the servicing of such loans by members of the League.[141] Economic strategists may also seek to relieve hostile pressures on the victim state by improving its access to raw materials and by removing trade barriers. Economic aid and inducement may be offered to nonparticipant states in the effort to divert and reorient their trade away from the violator state and toward the sanctioners. Pre-emptive or preclusive buying, referred to above, is one particular species of diversion measure. All the procedures and practices of "foreign aid" developed since World War II may also be utilized for diversion and reorientation of neutral trade.[142]

The effectiveness of these economic sanctions strategies in a given situation is, of course, a function of many variables. The relative vulnerability of the target (violator) state to the impact of these strategies is affected by such interrelated factors as the degree of its industrial development and the extent of its dependence upon foreign trade. Countries which are highly developed industrially may rely heavily upon foreign trade for markets or raw materials and sometimes for both, and hence may be particularly vulnerable to imposition of embargoes. A state with a larger agrarian sector may be only slightly affected by an embargo on food or raw materials but its warmaking potential may be drastically reduced by cutting off its access to arms and strategic materials. Conversely, an arms embargo may be largely ineffective against a heavily industrialized country.[143] It is, moreover, possible for an intending offender state to cushion the impact of economic sanctions measures by creating a substantial time lag between the initial application and the felt effects through such standard means as anticipatory stockpiling, rationing, and resort to substitutes as well as through widening of its effective resource base by quickly overrunning a contiguous state.[144] The point we would again stress, however, is that, with the possible exception of conflicts involving only small, marginal powers, the economic methods noted above are most usefully regarded not (as in the League period) as cheap substitutes for military enforcement action but as

141. Text in 5 Hudson, *International Legislation* 751 (1936).

142. Representative citations are collected supra, Ch. 1, notes 87–8.

143. *First Report of the Collective Measures Committee* 6–7; see also *International Sanctions* 24–6 (Royal Institute of Int. Affairs, 1938); Eckel, supra note 138 at 255.

144. *First Report of the Collective Measures Committee* 7; also Mackay, "Military Effectiveness of Economic Sanctions," in *Collective Security* 339 (Bourquin, ed., 1936); Martin, *Collective Security: A Progress Report* 152 (1952).

an integral, if partial, aspect of a combined strategy of sanctions that employs all available instruments.

Rehabilitation and Reconstruction

Even before the termination of measures applied for "rolling back" the participant which unlawfully resorted to coercion, the planning and undertaking of rehabilitation operations become important. These operations may envisage the channeling of capital and resources into both emergency relief programs designed to provide the minimum subsistence necessary to remedy or avoid starvation, disease, and extreme destitution, and projects for longer-term, post-hostilities economic aid and development of the devastated country. The very extent of devastation may make opportune the consideration, not merely of re-establishing the pre-hostilities economic structure and facilities, but also of substantially modifying such facilities and structure and establishing a new economic and social order that promises higher stable levels of production and wider distribution and that would generally be closer to the requirements of a public order of human dignity. In the Korean case, for instance, the United Nations, in addition to providing immediate relief, sought, in the words of a recent commentator, "to lay the ground work for a model democratic economy that would adequately reflect the highest principles of the United Nations." [145] The program of the United Nations Korean Reconstruction Agency included long-range projects for rehabilitating and developing "agriculture, manufacturing, electric-power production, transportation, mining, housing, education, and health, sanitation and welfare." [146]

MILITARY STRATEGY

Most generally put, military policy aims at affecting the intentions and capabilities of elites by the management of manpower and other instrumentalities specialized to the application of violence. Like all other means of policy, it may be directed toward varying specific objects.

Deterrence

The aim of a military strategy of sanctions may be to influence the elites threatening unlawful violence by confronting them with

145. Asher and others, *The United Nations and the Promotion of the General Welfare* 216 (1957).

146. Id., 219.

the will and capability to exercise counter-violence which will impose unacceptable costs. From this perspective, the strategy of military sanctions reaches optimum effectiveness when it renders unnecessary the actual exercise of violence. The specific practices of military deterrence have included such time-honored devices as the pointed announcement or demonstration of new weapons endowed with increased efficiency for destruction, and the timely holding of maneuvers or exercises by armed forces in areas strategically contiguous to the threatening state.[146a]

Restoration

Compelling a violator state to withdraw its forces to its own side of a border and to terminate prohibited coercion has frequently required the employment of armed force in supplementation and support of nonmilitary instruments. There is little need to refer at any length to the particular practices embraced in the active application of violence by sanctioners (as by any other participant). Perhaps all that need be observed is that in a rational process of sanctions (as in any rational process of coercion), contextual considerations influence the selection of specific strategic and tactical military objectives as well as the choice of weapon and its mode of utilization. For sanctioners, an important part of the relevant context relates to the future maintenance of public order.

CORRECTIVE STRATEGIES DIRECTED AGAINST INDIVIDUALS AND NONGOVERNMENTAL GROUPS

We add a fifth category of strategies to cover those sanctioning practices which may be directed, not so much against whole bodies politic as units of participation in world power processes, as against particular identified individuals and groups within a target body politic. These practices are principally illustrated by the subjection to negative (deprivational) sanctions of particular individuals specified as criminally responsible for a violation of the fundamental prescriptions on minimal order. Though the projection of a community policy imposing individual responsibility for impermissible coercion can be expected to increase the probabilities of conformity

146a. For a historical account of the use of these deterrence practices, see Vagts, *Defense and Diplomacy: The Soldier and the Conduct of Foreign Relations,* c. 7 "Armed Demonstrations" (1956).

with public order, negative sanctions can of course be actually applied only where strategies aimed at the restoration of order have been successful to such a degree as to permit sanctioners to acquire and exercise control over the bodies of those individuals. Doubt is sometimes expressed as to whether in the future, as it will probably develop, there will realistically be many opportunities for the exercise of criminal sanctions against individuals for violation of the prohibitions of unlawful coercion. It may, however, not be inappropriate to observe that the judicial application of the principle of individual criminal responsibility is but one more technique for seeking implementation of basic order which may be availed of whenever opportune combinations of circumstances present themselves. In a world assuming a more substantial measure of organization and integration, the relevant principle may be expected to acquire new importance.

For selection of appropriate targets of criminal sanctions, sanctioners may of course draw upon the principles commonly applied in municipal public orders. Perhaps the most important target-selection principle that emerged from the decisions in post-World War II cases is that only individuals who ranked in the top policy-formulating levels of the authority and control structures of the violator state should be held liable to these deprivations. A major objective projected was deterrence of possible future violations of basic order, and maximum deterrent impact was sought by focussing on those individuals whose decisions were actually necessary for unleashing unlawful violence. For instance the term "waging [aggressive war]" was restrictively interpreted both by the International Military Tribunal and subsequent tribunals at Nuremberg as referring only to the activities of individuals who held very high positions in the military or economic or administrative structures of the defeated violator state.[147]

147. The tribunal in "The Krupp Trial," 10 *Law Reports of Trials of War Criminals* at 127–8 (1949) said: "[I]f the threat of punishment deters [the top policy makers and leaders], there will be no war and the object of the law will have been accomplished. Upon the other hand, if the threat to the policy-makers, leaders and their collaborators proves of no avail, is it reasonable to conclude that the law contemplates that the threat of post-war punishment—held out to the mass of the people will prove effective?" See also the other cases referred to supra, Ch. 1, note 28.

It may also be recalled that the Nuremberg Charter authorized the Tribunal conclusively to determine the criminality of a group or organization, the effect of such a determination being to render membership therein an offense indictable before the courts of a signatory power.[148] The Tribunal carefully circumscribed its competence, the grant of which appeared to have been motivated by considerations of procedural expediency [149] and took particular account of "well settled legal principles one of the most important of which is that criminal guilt is personal, and that mass punishments should be avoided." [150] The Tribunal said:

> Since the declaration with respect to the organizations and groups will, as has been pointed out, fix the criminality of its members, that definition should exclude persons who had no knowledge of the criminal purposes or acts of the organization and those who were drafted by the State for membership, unless they were personally implicated in the commission of acts declared criminal by Article 6 of the Charter as members of the organization. Membership alone is not enough to come within the scope of these declarations.[151]

To hold a member responsible, in effect, for the criminal activities of his organization, the Tribunal in fact required evidence of conduct showing active identification with the organization's aims. Not the collectivity purely and simply as such, but rather a specified portion of its membership was thus defined as the appropriate target for criminal sanctions. It remains to add that other kinds of depriva-

148. Arts. 9–10, in *The Charter and Judgment of the Nurnberg Tribunal—History and Analysis,* 93–4 (U.N. Doc. No. A/CN.4/5 [1949]).

149. See the statement of the American Chief Prosecutor in 1 *Trial of Major War Criminals before the International Military Tribunal at Nuremberg* 144 (1947).

150. "Judgment of the International Military Tribunal at Nuremberg," in 41 *A.J.I.L.* at 251 (1947).

151. Ibid. In each of the four cases where a declaration of criminality resulted—Leadership Corps of the Nazi Party, id., 256; *Die Geheime Staatspolizei* (Gestapo) and *Der Sicherheitsdienst der Reichführer SS* (SD), id., 262; and S.S., id., 266–7—the tribunal explicitly based its finding upon participation of the organization concerned in war crimes and crimes against humanity. There appears, however, nothing to suggest that participation in crimes against peace could not give rise, in an appropriate case, to such a finding.

tions may be directed against the whole organization or association declared criminal. The group itself may be abolished and its assets forfeited, for example.[152]

Outcomes and Effects

We mean by "outcomes" the immediate results obtained in particular situations—the decisions actually taken in implementation of basic policy—by participants engaging in sanctioning activities. These outcomes may be described and appraised in terms of both the degree to which the specific objectives projected by the sanctioners are actually realized and of the extent to which the results obtained are conformable to the requirements of protecting and fulfilling the overriding goals of a world public order of human dignity. "Effects" refer to the longer-term or structural consequences of the aggregate flow of sanctioning activities upon the power and other value processes in the international arena. The assessment of the effects of sanctioning processes may again be made in terms of the degree to which a world order of human dignity is thereby moved toward completion and fulfillment.

The Context of Conditions

The conditions, establishing the context within which the sanctioning process sketched above proceeds, may be economically categorized for inquiry under two principal groupings—the one of predispositional factors, and the other of environmental factors. It seems scarcely necessary to add that these groupings refer not to completely separate and autonomous sets of phenomena, but rather to interrelated categories of events, the significance of each event for basic

152. See Control Council Law No. 2, "Providing for the Termination and Liquidation of the Nazi Organizations," Allied Control Authority, Germany, *Enactments and Approved Papers of the Control Council and Coordinating Committee,* Vol. 1, p. 131 (1945).

Distinguishable from the above are the somewhat metaphysical debates about the "criminal responsibility" of the violator state. The niceties of these debates may be obtained from Wright, "International Law and Guilt by Association," 43 *A.J.I.L.* 746 (1949); De Vabre, *Memorandum for the Commission for the Progressive Development of International Law and Its Codification,* U.N. Doc. No. A/AC.10/34 (27 May 1947); and Sottile, "The Problem of the Creation of a Permanent International Criminal Court," 29 *Revue de Droit International de Sciences Diplomatiques et Politiques* 267, 329–46 (1951).

order being a function of its location in a particular constellation and of its relation to every other component of such constellation.

The factors designated as predispositional include all conditions that relate to the structures of perspectives which decision-makers, i.e., the potential sanctioners, bring with them to the making of choices about the implementation of minimal order and which are externalized in such choices. These perspectives—the patterns of demand, identification, and expectation—of potential sanctioners, like those of every other individual, are channeled through and are continually being affected and shaped by aggregates of factors that in shorthand reference may be dominated as *culture, class, interest, personality,* and *crisis* factors.

"Culture" is used most comprehensively to refer to patternings of peoples' values and institutions, which are of such distinctiveness as readily to be brought into contrast with each other.[153] Contemporary anthropologists employ the concept for both descriptive and explanatory purposes. Thus, Professors Kluckhohn and Kelly speak of culture in the descriptive sense as "a historically derived system of explicit and implicit designs for living, which tends to be shared by all or specially designated members of a group." [154] They use culture in an explanatory sense to embrace "those historically created selective processes which channel men's reactions both to internal and to external stimuli." [155] Perhaps the most useful concept for lawyers is the "functional" theory developed by Professor Malinowski, who stressed that

> [C]ulture is clearly the fullest context of all human activities. It is the vast instrumentality through which man achieves his ends. . . . Thus, culture is at the same time the minimum mechanism for the satisfaction of the most elementary needs of man's animal nature, and also an ever-developing, ever-increas-

153. Some amplification is offered in Lasswell and McDougal, "Law, Science and Policy," Pt. II, 9–10 (unpublished mimeographed materials, Yale Law School, 1954); see, further, Lasswell, "Person, Personality, Group, Culture," 2 *Psychiatry: Journal of the Biology and Pathology of Interpersonal Relations* 533 (1939).

154. Kluckhohn and Kelly, "The Concept of Culture," in *The Science of Man in the World Crisis* 78, 98 (Linton ed., 1945).

155. Id., 84.

> ing system of new ends, new values, and new creative possibilities.[156]
>
> [C]ulture determines the situation, the place, and the time for the physiological act. It delimits it by general conditions as to what is licit or illicit, attractive or repulsive, decent or opprobrious. Although the act itself, as defined in terms of anatomy, physiology and interaction with the environment, is constant, its prerequisites as well as its consequences change profoundly.[157]

It seems difficult to overestimate the extent to which the culture of a community conditions and molds, on both the conscious and unconscious levels, the perspectives, attitudes, and behavior of the individuals comprising the community.[158] Inquiry of the kind we suggest must of course focus upon the impact of cultural factors upon the aspects or segments of the systems of perspectives which relate to the achievement and maintenance of basic order and which find expression in political behavior. Attitudes toward violence and toward coercion in general, for instance, that prevail in and are characteristic of a particular culture may be expected to find some re-

156. Malinowski, "Man's Culture and Man's Behavior," 29 *Sigma Xi Q.* 182 (1941).

157. Id., 192. See further Malinowski, "The Group and the Individual in Functional Analysis," 44 *Am. J. Sociology* 938, 963 (1939): "In the genetic approach, the functionalist demands that, in field work and theory alike, the formation of such collective attitudes and formed dispositions as taste, skill, principle, dogma, and value be stated in terms of both individual and group. No mental attitude or bodily skill can be understood without reference both to the innate individual and organic endowment and to the cultural influences by which it is shaped." The definitive statement of Professor Malinowski's theory of functionalism is found in his *A Scientific Theory of Culture and Other Essays* (1944).

158. Cf. Dunn, *War and the Minds of Men* 47 (1950) who adverts to the fact that cultural factors make uniformities in expected response possible: "Since most of his predispositions came from his cultural community, [an individual's] behavior tends to follow a pattern common to other members of the community. Hence it is possible to observe many uniformities of responses to ideas among those who belong to particular groups and subgroups. These uniformities can serve as useful guides in appraising the probable effectiveness of proposed communications programs." The programs Professor Dunn refers to are programs for affecting the predispositions of individuals relating to the maintenance of peace.

flection in the responses to international violence of decision-makers located within the culture-area. The same culturally determined attitudes may also be thought to affect the probabilities of the decision-makers themselves resorting to unlawful unilateral coercion. Reasonable expectations about the shape of such responses and the incidence of such probabilities may differ depending upon, for example, whether the community's culture emphasizes pacifism and a deep respect for all forms of life or the power and the glory of a nation of conquering warriors.[159]

The word "class" is used to designate the position of an individual in terms of control over a specified value or over values generally. It may refer at the same time to a major aggregate of individuals who stand in approximately the same relation to the shaping and distribution of particular values.[160] That class position, actual as well as expectancy, commonly bears upon the predispositions and effective perspectives of decision-makers, like other individuals, would seem no more than a common-sense assumption.[161] An ideology aspiring to effective establishment on a global scale has been built upon this assumption. Inquiry here may again appropriately center on the relation of class position (in respect of power or any other value or set of values important in the community) to those perspectives of the political elite which relate to the maintenance of minimum order. Of general importance in this regard are the expectations of the elite (the potential sanctioners) as to whether their own individual class position as well as the fortunes of their class group as a whole will be maintained and even improved, or will decline and deteriorate, by participation in particular sanctioning activities, be they long-term preventive measures or restorative measures in the here and now. Active participation, especially in restoration or enforcement activity, may, for instance, impose substantial burdens upon the population which, in the estimation of the political elite, realistic or unrealistic, may lead to diminution of popular support and even loss of position in authority and control structures. In such circumstance, desire to maintain class position on the part of

159. A recent suggestive study is Galtung, "Pacifism from a Sociological Point of View," 3 *J. Conflict Resolution* 67 (1959).

160. Lasswell and Kaplan, *Power and Society* 62 (1950).

161. *Class, Status and Power: A Reader in Social Stratification* (Bendix and Lipset, eds., 1953) affords introduction to the relevant issues and literature.

the elite can be expected to lead to general reluctance to undertake such activity and to demands for nonparticipation.

When used most generally, the word "interests" refers to both patterns of demands and the supporting expectations about the conditions under which such demands may be achieved.[162] When a collection or aggregate of persons is organized for the satisfaction of a shared interest, one may speak of an interest group.[163] Elites in a territorial community may commonly be members of one or more interest groups, and a crucial point for inquiry must be how membership in a given interest group affects perspectives relating to the extent to which basic order may and should be secured.[164] Put a little more concretely, relevant inquiry may be concerned with whether or not, or in what measure, the expectations of the effective decision-makers as to the conditions necessary or appropriate for realizing their projected demands include initiation of or participation in measures for implementing minimum order. It was, for example, widely assumed a few decades ago that certain special interest groups, like those engaged in the manufacture and marketing of instrumentalities of violence, could not be expected to oppose national policies (of their own or other countries) involving recourse to armed force.[165] Perhaps not unrelated to this assumption is the question currently being debated in some quarters with differing degrees of seriousness, whether a mature industrial democracy, a substantial sector of the economy of which is devoted to the production of modern military weapons, can—should it suddenly agree to disarmament measures—convert to the production of other kinds of goods without severe economic dislocation or disruption. Professional specialists in the management of violence constitute another interest aggregate whose wholehearted commitment to the prevention of international violence has sometimes been regarded with dubiety.[166]

162. Lasswell and Kaplan, *Power and Society* 23 (1950).

163. Id., 40.

164. Dunn, supra note 158 at 55–70 explores the implications raised by interest and class stratification for communications strategies.

165. See Special Committee on Investigation of the Munitions Industry of the United States, U. S. Senate, *Munitions Industry,* Report No. 944, 74th Cong., 2nd Sess., part 3 (1936); also Beard, *The Devil Theory of War* (1936).

166. See, generally, Vagts, *A History of Militarism, Civilian and Military* (rev. ed., 1959). Among recent studies of the military profession as an interest

Any model of a sanctioning process, as of any other social process, that aspires to reasonable comprehensiveness must make some reference to personality factors. The importance of personality factors in affecting social processes is today widely recognized. The basic, organizing value orientations, practices, and dynamisms characteristic of an individual are, most concisely, what we mean by personality. In respect of an individual human being considered as a personality system, an initial broad distinction is drawn between character and aptitude. The character system embraces both the self-system and the energy-system. The self-system comprises the conscious pattern of perspectives relating to the basic values of the individual, and may be organized around one dominant value exercising profound effect upon the character or may be oriented to plural values. The energy-system may facilitate the self-system or be in opposition to it; the reference is to the degree to which the energies of the total personality are at the command of the self-system and the extent to which they are dissipated and lost in inner conflicts of the character. The aptitude system is composed of potential skills which may variously depend upon inherited characteristics or mainly upon experience. The aptitudes of an individual person are of course continually being affected by his energies and perspectives. "Dynamisms" is the psychologist's term for the devices employed by a personality system for coping with anxiety.[167]

It is perhaps a commonplace that the personality system of an individual member of an elite or sub-elite group affects his perspectives relating to the use of coercion and violence between nations.[168] In the kind of world we live in today, the potential impact of per-

---

group and of militarism and antimilitarism are Janowitz, *The Professional Soldier: A Social and Political Portrait* (1960) and Ekirch, *The Civilian and the Military* (1956).

167. The definition and distinctions here presented are developed in Lasswell and McDougal, *Law, Science and Policy,* Part II, c. 3 (unpublished mimeographed materials, Yale Law School, 1954). See also Lasswell, supra note 153; and Kardiner, "The Concept of Basic Personality Structure as an Operational Tool in the Social Sciences," *The Science of Man in the World Crisis* 107 (Linton, ed., 1945). Frankel, "Rational Decision-Making in Foreign Policy," 14 *Y.B. of World Affairs* 40 (1960) offers some comment on the influence of personality factors on rationality in elite decision-making.

168. The relationship of personality structure to perspectives about power and influence is discussed in Lasswell, *Power and Personality* (1948) and Lasswell, *Psychopathology and Politics* (Compass ed., 1960). See, further, Lasswell,

sonality factors is not easily overstated. Personality disorders in the ruling elite of a great power that, for instance, render it unable to make the necessary identifications to demand and support minimum order, or that significantly reduce capacity to deal realistically with nice probabilities of reciprocity,[169] may conceivably plunge the world into the thermonuclear chasm. Even the anxieties and defenses of a technician on lonely watch before a radar screen have suddenly become of great moment for vast numbers of people. The relevance of inquiry into personality factors extends, beyond the consequences of pathological tendencies in persons strategically located, to identification of the kinds of personality traits that may be more likely to lead to effective commitment to basic order and hence should be promoted both in the community at large and, more particularly, the sub-elite groups from which the top elite are recruited.

The remaining category of predispositional factors which we designate as "crisis" factors refers to conflict situations characterized by high levels of expectation of violence.[170] Relevant inquiry may once again focus upon the effects of a situation reaching crisis level upon the predispositions bearing on the implementation of basic order. The shock of exposure to crisis may, for instance, precipitate and harden a determination to "do something" to stop a threatening challenger or may, on the contrary, dissolve whatever previous inclination there may have been to participate in sanctioning activity.[171] This ambiguous effect of changing crisis level has been underscored by Professor Wright, who observed that:

"The Selective Effect of Personality on Political Participation," in *Studies in the Scope and Method of "The Authoritarian Personality"* 197 (Christie and Jahoda, eds., 1954), and Lasswell, "Political Constitution and Character," 46 *Psychoanalysis and the Psycho-Analytic Review*, No. 4 (1960). McNeil, "Psychology and Aggression," 3 *J. Conflict Resolution* 195 (1959) is a recent survey-inquiry into the psychological bases of aggressive perspectives and behavior generally.

169. Schelling, *The Strategy of Conflict* 13–14 (1960) characterizes this capacity—"an ability to perceive alternatives and to calculate with probabilities"—as an aspect of "rationality" of decision-makers.

170. Lasswell and Kaplan, *Power and Society* 242 (1950).

171. The response of the United Nations, with the leadership of the United States, to the North Korean attack on the Republic of Korea illustrates the one type of reaction. The other type is exemplified in the rush toward neutrality in Europe and the United States after the collapse of League sanctions against Italy and Germany's march into the Rhineland in 1936. On Mar. 31, 1938, Mr. Herbert Hoover stated upon returning from a trip to Europe: "Every phase

> In crisis situations the policies of states not immediately threatened might be supposed to give an adequate consideration to the long-run tendencies of action, but such states have tended toward policies of irresponsible neutrality. In proportion as the crisis deepens, states behave in ways which are considered necessary for the immediate security of each but which, like a panic in a theater fire or a stock-market collapse, actually involve all in common ruin.
>
> Crisis situations might be used to promote united efforts to remedy genuine grievances and to establish universal principles. On such occasions rapid progress might be made toward permanently stabilizing peace if suitable leadership were followed, as it was in the United States in 1787. On the other hand, failure to follow such leadership may mean a long-time worsening of the situation, as happened after World War I.[172]

It may also be noted that crisis level may affect the other four categories of predispositional factors; important questions relate to the impact of repetitive and prolonged crises upon the culture of the community, upon class structure and interest groupings, and upon the stability of the internal environment or characters of people.

The second principal group of conditioning factors, designated as environmental, embraces in its widest reach all the component features of world processes of power. We have in earlier pages sketched in somewhat impressionistic lines these component features which comprise the larger context within which processes of authoritative decision making (sanctioning processes being a sub-process thereof) take place across political boundaries.[173] Here we intend only to make brief reference to a few features that appear to be of direct significance for the probable effectiveness of sanctioning activity. An important preliminary distinction may be drawn between environmental factors which are explicitly brought into the focus of attention of potential sanctioners (the "*milieu*") and those factors which are not (the "surroundings").[174] These two classes of factors

of this picture should harden our resolve that we keep out of other people's wars. Nations in Europe need to be convinced that this is our policy." Quoted in 2 Wright, *A Study of War* 1329 (1942).

172. Id., 1331.

173. See supra, Ch. 1.

174. The distinction is made in Lasswell, "World Loyalty," in *The World Community* 215 (Wright, ed., 1948).

may obviously be expected to differ in their consequential impact upon the ensuing outcomes and effects.

The structures of perspectives of decision-makers comprise, as we have previously observed, their most important characteristics. From the standpoint of the decision-makers in a given state, the character of the perspectives held by decision-makers in other states or, more precisely, the *incidence* and *distribution* across state lines of perspectives that demand and support, perspectives that conflict with, and perspectives that ignore, the securing of basic order, are themselves environmental factors. Whether, for instance, in a given situation the determination to apply sanctioning measures is enthusiastically asserted by the political leaders of a large number of great and small states or is, contrariwise, hesitantly suggested by the officials of one or two marginal powers may be expected to influence the decision of potential sanctioners in any specified state. Again, it may reasonably be supposed to make a difference to the decision-makers of a particular state whether the determination to resort to (or desist from, and even to resist) the application of sanctions is announced by a powerful contiguous nation or by a geographically distant country. In this connection, it may be noted how important it is for decision-makers to keep informed about these factors of incidence and distribution of perspectives, about the elements that in turn affect incidence and distribution, and about the trends that manifest themselves with respect to all such factors and elements. Ways are needed for providing a continuing flow of intelligence that will permit the charting, as it were, of prevailing effective perspectives and the plotting of trend curves, on the basis of which rational policy choices can be made by potential sanctioners.[175]

The relative distribution, as between sanctioners or potential sanctioners and violators or potential violators, of the resources and capabilities upon which power is commonly based is another feature of the environment that confronts the decision-makers in any given body politic. Considered most comprehensively, this environmental factor embraces in reference all the features and configurations of power obtaining in the international arena which constantly impinge upon a decision-maker's estimations of the probable effectiveness of a projected application of sanctions.[176] It may be observed

175. See the recommendation for establishment of a world attention and attitude survey put forward in id., 224–5.

176. Summary reference is made to these features, supra, pp. 45–9. An eco-

in this regard that a recent commentator engaging in the exercise of appraising "collective security as an approach to peace," has suggested that among certain "objective requirements of collective security" are conditions of "power diffusion." Professor Claude writes:

> The basic importance of the objective conditions of power diffusion and organizational comprehensiveness lies in the fact that collective security assumes the possibility of creating such an imbalance of power in favor of the upholders of world order that aggression will be prevented by the certainty of defeat or defeated by the minimal efforts of collective forces. This assumption may be invalidated by the inadequate diffusion of power. If the power configuration is such that no state commands more than, say, ten percent of the world's strength, the possibility is open for collective security to mobilize up to ninety percent against it, a very comfortable margin. If, however, one state controls a very substantial portion of global power resources, forty-five percent, for instance, the collective matching of its strength is doubtful and the massing of overwhelming power against it manifestly impossible.[177]

Making reference to contemporary patterns of polarizing power, Professor Claude goes on to speculate on whether "collective security" has been thereby "doomed to irrelevance in the twentieth century." [178] The distribution of capabilities, that is, the degree of diffusion or polarization of power in the world arena is, of course, as we have noted, relevant to choices about the application of sanctions. It seems open to doubt, however, whether the postulation of "overwhelming power" vis-à-vis a violator or potential violator as a *sine qua non* for preventing or defeating unlawful coercion is not a counsel of impossible perfectionism. Thus, contemporary studies on military policy suggest—indeed, the entire military posture of the

---

nomical description of the more important trends with respect to these features is available in Maxwell Graduate School of Citizenship and Public Affairs (Syracuse Univ.), *The Operational Aspects of United States Foreign Policy* 8–29 (A Study [No. 6] Prepared at the Request of the Committee on Foreign Relations, U. S. Senate, 86th Cong., 1st Sess., Nov. 11, 1959).

177. Claude, *Swords into Plowshares: The Problems and Progress of International Organization* 265 (2nd ed., 1959).

178. Id., 283.

non-Communist world, as well as its hopes for continued survival, are based upon the assumption—that the imposition of deterrent restraints upon the Communist pole of power is possible even in the absence of overwhelming superiority against such pole and that what is indispensable is rather the maintenance of equilibrium in capabilities for both massive retaliatory strikes and more carefully tailored applications of violence.[179] In terms of the indulgence-deprivation ratio analysis referred to earlier, the establishment of a situation of deterrence involves the creation in the potential violator of expectations of net loss, that is, of an excess of expected deprivations over expected indulgences. For creating these expectations, a vast and staggering power differential, the capacity for "massive overpowering" of the potential violator, while desirable and comforting, need not be absolutely essential. The invention of basic energy weapons and new delivery systems is commonly thought to have made it possible to impose unacceptable costs even upon a giant or superpower.

Another environmental factor, of especial relevance for the preventive implementation of minimal order, relates to what Professor Dunn described as the "growing belief that we are at last coming into the possession of knowledge and techniques that will enable us to influence men's political behavior in desired directions and so exercise a greater control over international events." [180] Over fairly recent decades, the social sciences in general and those disciplines called the behavioral and policy sciences in particular, have exhibited substantial development and now seem to promise new and deeper consequential understanding of the processes that underlie and affect the choices and behavior of human beings, as well as of the processes of communication between human beings, both as individuals and in groups.[181] Sharper and more sophisticated intellectual tools, fundamental theory, and data, according increasingly full recognition of the contextual character of human behavior, and whose imaginative use may make possible the manipulative modification of some seg-

179. See supra, Ch. 1, note 132.

180. Dunn, *War and the Minds of Men* 3 (1950).

181. *The Policy Sciences: Recent Developments in Scope and Method* (Lerner and Lasswell, eds., 1951), *The State of the Social Sciences* (White, ed., 1956) and *The Human Meaning of the Social Sciences* (Lerner, ed., 1959) afford some notion of the present state and prospects of the behavioral and policy sciences.

ments of context, are being made available. While it is of course possible to overstate the present development and the potentialities of the social sciences,[182] they do offer some basis for the hope that, for the first time in his history, man may be able to understand the factors that lead him to seek the destruction of his own kind; with such understanding, he may achieve a meaningful measure of control over at least some of those factors.

RECAPITULATION: SOME RECOMMENDED PRINCIPLES OF SANCTIONS STRATEGY

Building upon this detailed examination of past, and potentially future, sanctioning procedures, we recapitulate by formulating principles designed to serve as guidelines for the optimum employment of sanctions strategy.[183] The focus is upon concrete problems that arise in the flow of interrelationships within the world arena. We are leaving to one side, or de-emphasizing, the questions that would arise if a world constitutional convention were called into being for the purpose of designing a new or drastically revised charter for the governance of the world community. As matters stand today, issues connected with sanction strategy characteristically arise within the framework of particular disputes, or of anticipated controversies among nation-states. Hence principles of strategy are most directly addressed to officials of international governmental organizations and to the officials of nation-states who are most immediately confronted by situations in which sanctioning policies must be applied.[184] For

182. Waltz, *Man, The State and War: A Theoretical Analysis,* c. 3 (1959) has some forceful words to say about the "failure of behavioral scientists as prescribers for peace." It is less than clear whether Dr. Waltz's own "three images" of international conflict advances consequential analysis beyond the point that he believes behavioral scientists to have reached (or stopped).

183. These principles were worked out in collaboration with Professor Harold Lasswell and the formulation here presented is largely his drafting.

184. Some conception of the sophistication with which totalitarians utilize principles of strategy appropriately designed to secure their own goals and objectives may be had from, e.g., Strausz-Hupé and others, *Protracted Conflict* (1959); Leites, *A Study of Bolshevism* (1953); and Selznick, *The Organizational Weapon: A Study of Bolshevik Strategy and Tactics* (1952). It may be appropriate to recall that principles of strategy are, by their nature, instrumental principles, that they relate to the management and disposition of base values for achieving goals, and that the same general kinds of strategies may frequently

the most part our principles are related to the application phase of the world decision process, though no attempt is made to delimit the problems too strictly.

For present purposes the principles of sanctioning which we recommend may be conveniently dichotomized as principles of *content* and principles of *procedure*. The principles of content are designed to indicate relevant criteria for rational decision by spotlighting the more important features of the total context to be taken into account. Procedural principles are designed to suggest the most pertinent order for the consideration of content during the course of examining any problem. It may perhaps bear emphasis that all of these principles are to be interpreted in relation to each other and that none of them are to be construed as purporting to dictate particular outcomes irrespective of contextual factors. Further, the principles are intended to be suggestive, and not exhaustive, of useful principles.

Principles of Content for Sanctions Problems

THE GOAL PRINCIPLE

However urgent the necessity for action, or however protracted potential preoccupation with particular situations may be, details are to be assessed according to their significance for the overriding goal values sought to be maximized by the use of sanctions. In the long run we recommend that the strategy of sanctioning be integrated with the fundamental aim of promoting the long-term goal of human dignity on the most inclusive scale possible. More specifically, sanctioning objectives can be distinguished, in terms of the categories hitherto developed in some detail, as follows:

a. The objective of prevention.

   Within the current framework of the world arena, decision-makers can be influenced, to some extent, to regard themselves—and all with whom they are identified—as better off by abstaining from breaches of order than by initiating deviations.

---

be employed to achieve vastly differing types of goals. The need for such principles is well stated in Morgenstern, *The Question of National Defense* 264 (1959).

b. The objective of deterrence.

The dominant objective when the probability is high that breaches of order will occur.

c. The objective of restoration.

Breaches have already taken place.

d. The objective of rehabilitation.

The value positions of individuals and groups have been damaged and further loss is unavoidable unless many values are made immediately available to those who have suffered deprivation.

e. The objective of reconstruction.

The fundamental institutions of the world community can be brought into more direct harmony with the overriding goal.

THE FACTUAL PRINCIPLE

The provisional specification of objectives within the overriding goal requires continual adjustment in the light of factual information and estimates of the future.

a. Trend information.

Provides knowledge of the trend toward or away from goals and objectives in the perspectives and operational activities of decision-makers and bodies politic as a whole in the world arena and in every sub-arena.

b. Scientific information.

Provides knowledge of the factors which account for the trends.

c. Projective estimates.

Assuming that present policies are continued, what are the probable future developments pertinent to the goal values sought?

THE EVALUATIVE PRINCIPLE

The task of sanctioning policy includes the inventing and assessment of alternative courses of conduct. Policies call for value losses or risks (threatened losses) at various stages; policies may bring value gains and reductions of risks (avoided deprivations) at various stages.

The following principles of evaluation pertain to particular components of the sanctioning process:

a. Participants.

(1) A fundamental goal affecting the choice of sanctioners is the development of comprehensive acceptance of responsibility among all members of the world community for the measures of sanctioning required to protect and fulfill the most inclusive approximation possible of a world public order of human dignity.

(a) States should be encouraged to support sanctioning procedures by both unilateral and multilateral decision;

(b) In order to strengthen official action, fullest use should be made of nonofficial groups (parties, pressure groups, and other associations) and individuals.

(2) Degrees of responsibility for participation in sanctioning measures can properly vary within a broad range from active support to passive abstinence from interference with collective programs. Among factors affecting responsibility are these:

(a) degree of local value involvement in situation;

(b) readiness and capacity for action.

(3) The composition of the most active sanctioning groups can wisely be designed to strengthen the components within the targets of sanction who are disposed to accept community judgment. For example:

(a) Provide formal or tacit representatives of the widest system of public order who enjoy reputations for genuine regard for the principles involved;

(b) Utilize sanctioning elements with which it is likely that most components will positively (rather than negatively) identify.

(4) Targets of sanction can properly include individuals as well as groups.

(a) Individual violators of public order, who have had the opportunity and capability to be educated by exposure to community norms, are properly regarded as fully responsible for what they do.

(b) Individual violators who have not had the opportunity and capability to acquire community norms should be subjected to corrective measures in proportion to their threat to community values.

b. Objectives.

(1) As indicated in the statement of "the goal principle" and "the factual principle," the specification of appropriate practicable objectives in a concrete problem situation is to be made in the light of both goals and facts.

(2) In harmony with the fundamental conception of human dignity, middle-range and immediate objectives must rely upon persuasive rather than coercive measures, save when coercion by targets of sanction promises to impose relatively enduring limitations upon the use of persuasion. Coercion is solely appropriate in order to limit coercion in the community context.

c. Situations.

(1) Since acute sanctioning problems are especially prone to arise in military rather than in civilian arenas, it is obvious that conditions which sustain the world military arena must ultimately be changed. Among these basic factors are expectations that large-scale coercion will continue in the immediate future, and that voluntary agreement for a civic arena is impossible. No simple means are available for altering these expectations, though we regard them as subject to change.

(2) Even within the framework of a military arena, the probability of violations of public order can be reduced if the decision process is so organized that norms of public order are clear, decision-making structures are integrated in advance, and provocative situations are not allowed to build up to crisis intensity.

(a) Clear allocations of responsibility are needed for the performance of all policy functions connected with sanctions, including intelligence (and planning), recommending, prescribing, invoking, applying, appraising, terminating.

(b) In view of the relative decentralization of effective power, sanctioning processes in the world arena require advance arrangements to harmonize and coordinate the contributions to public order which can be made from different geographical areas—provincial, regional, hemispheric.

(c) Since comprehensive organized authority does not exist, the success or failure of sanctioning is especially conditioned by unorganized interactions of reciprocity and retaliation.

Effective sanctions are those that mobilize within nation-states support beyond official organs.

d. Base Values.

(1) Provision should be made for the control by sanctioners of base values proportionate to the problems confronted in the maintenance of public order.

(2) The burdens upon particular sanctioners should be adjusted according to their capacity and to the magnitude of the values immediately at stake for each.

(3) Strategies should be devised which, considering total impact upon all community value patterns and institutional practices, keep at a minimum the net cost of employing community base values either to adapt to unchangeable conditions or to adjust modifiable conditions to objectives.

(a) To the extent possible, reliance should be placed upon the use of base values which are most economical of community resources, such as those (enlightenment, skill, rectitude) which rely primarily upon the use of communication.

e. Strategies.

(1) Despite the emphasis that must continue to be put upon value deprivation (including threatened as well as actual loss), sanctioning strategists have value indulgences at their disposal. A balanced program of positive and negative components is preferable to excessive reliance upon negative elements, since an ultimate aim is to reduce coercion in the world arena and the ultimate consequences of coercion are frequently unpredictable.

(2) Strategies require specialization according to the dominant objective whether it be prevention, deterrence, restoration, rehabilitation, or reconstruction. All instruments of policy are

available in various combinations—diplomatic, ideological, economic, military—and are to be employed with the full context of goal and fact in mind.

(3) Some sanctioning problems can be satisfactorily dealt with by strategies that involve minimum publicity and relatively few participants. When wider publicity and participation is called for, one aim of strategy is to build community consensus by involving as many as possible in sanctioning programs.

f. Outcomes.

Decision outcomes involve in varying degrees all seven phases (intelligence, recommending, prescribing, invoking, applying, appraising, terminating) of the decision process. The policy aim is to harmonize the use of all functions most effectively.

g. Effects.

Since the value and institutional consequences of decision go beyond immediate targets of sanction and the most active sanctioners, effects are to be appraised aggregatively in terms of overriding goals of policy.

Principles of Procedure in the Sanctioning Process

1. The first step in any sanctioning process is to make a preliminary and provisional estimate of the objectives predominantly involved in the situation.

a. The time to be taken by community decision-makers depends upon the magnitude of the deprivations involved, an assessment that depends upon events to date and estimates of the future. More specifically:

(1) Who regards himself as suffering deprivation (actual, potential) by violations of public order attributed to whom? What values are at stake? In what magnitude? What normative prescriptions are alleged to have been breached? What operational activities related to the situation have occurred and are pending?

(2) Who regards himself as imposing deprivations upon others (actual, potential) which the other party stigmatizes as a violation of public order? Does he accept or reject the attribution? In terms of what prescriptive norms?

(3) What measures if any have already been taken by what decision-makers other than the participants most immediately involved? What results to date and what prospective results?

2. If the objective is *prevention:*
Since the urgency of preventive measures is less than in connection with the objectives referred to below, the role of recommending, prescribing, and appraising can be relatively greater.

3. If the pertinent objective is *deterrence,* the decision phases may be employed as follows:

(1) Intelligence.

(a) If avoidance of publicity is estimated to increase the chances of favorable outcomes, do not disseminate information relating to the threat, and cooperate informally in minimizing its magnitude.

(b) If the prospects of a satisfactory outcome are perceived as low, or as dependent in part upon reactions throughout the world arena, multiply the number of those who are informed of the true magnitude of the problem.

(2) Recommendation.

(a) If informal measures are likely to succeed, formal recommendations for the resolution of the immediate situation are to be avoided.

(b) If formal recommendations are likely to prove effective, they should be made promptly and upon the largest basis of possible consensus.

(3) Prescription.

(a) Since formal processes of prescription are unwieldy in crisis situations, it is rarely practicable to initiate new general prescriptions to cope with an emergency. Nevertheless, it may be practicable for community decision-makers having the widest consensual base to reaffirm existing prescriptions which are regarded as pertinent to the current problem.

(4) Invocation.

(a) If the chances of a successful outcome by informal means are high, avoid complicating the situation by formally invoking prescriptions in reference to the conduct of particular participants.

(b) If the prospects of success by informal means are low, arrange for prompt characterization of the situation (or of special participants) as violating the requirements of public order.

(5) Application.

(a) If measures short of application are likely to succeed, they are preferable.

(b) If full-scale measures of application are indicated, it is important that they be used without delay and preferably according to procedures well understood in advance.

(6) Appraisal.

(a) In the rush of crisis, appraisal and intelligence functions merge, since the success or failure of official initiatives must be subject to continual assessment.

(b) However, if past appraisals of official action have been executed in detail, they may provide a source of guidance for the immediate situation.

(7) Termination.

(a) Since termination is a decision phase that can often be more quickly executed than prescription, decision-makers may be able to influence current crises effectively by declaring an end to provocative and outmoded policies.

4. If the pertinent objective is *restoration:*
The procedures mentioned in connection with deterrence are relevant here. Restoration adds the additional complication that what is provisionally regarded as a flagrant violation of territory may have occurred, for instance, and further violations may be in immediate prospect. Promptness of action—informal and formal—may be the prime condition of success in "rolling back" a destructive operation and restoring a previous state of nonviolence.

5. If the pertinent objective is *rehabilitation:*
Efforts at rehabilitation can begin as soon as deprivations begin to be imposed. During active hostilities, the principal targets of rehabilitative efforts are human beings; when hostilities subside, capital reequipment is a chief aim. We note that rehabilitative activities, by dramatizing the cost of coercion, have some influence upon restoration and other objectives of sanction policy.

6. If the objective is *reconstruction:*

Since the long-run goal is to reconstruct the world arena, it is always present. But at some periods opportunities are made available for sweeping changes in the social structure of various communities. This is often the case at the end of war, or when successful revolutions have taken place. Reliance needs to be put upon intelligence planning and recommendation to keep reconstruction aims at the focus of attention of decision-makers.

MAJOR DEFECTS IN CONTEMPORARY SANCTIONING PROCESS

It could only be a work of mordant supererogation, in the present stage of crisis and state of scholarly concern, for us here to elaborate in detail the defects of the sanctioning process of the contemporary world arena.[185] These defects have been amply reviewed by others in all necessary detail and from many different perspectives of appraisal.[186] Some recall of the major outlines of inadequacy in the

185. Center for International Affairs (Harvard), *Ideology and Foreign Affairs* (A study [No. 10] Prepared at the Request of the Committee on Foreign Relations, U. S. Senate, 86th Cong., 2nd Sess., Jan. 17, 1960) 66 summarizes: "The liberal dream of a world of nation-states willing to pool their power against any aggressor instead of resorting to traditional balancing policies, ready to settle their disputes by peaceful means and to work together within a league of sovereign nations—this dream which inspired Wilson survives only as a hope for the future rather than as a faith in the present."

The defects in the sanctioning process itself, with which we are here concerned, may be distinguished from the misconceptions in theory *about* sanctioning process, with which we were concerned above—though misconceptions in theory may, of course (we emphasize again), contribute to defects in process.

186. For insightful surveys of the inadequacies, for sanctioning purposes, of traditional customary international law, see Dickinson, *Law and Peace* (1951) and Brierly, *The Law of Nations* (5th ed., 1955). Further detail and references may be found in Kunz, "Sanctions in International Law," 54 *A.J.I.L.* 324 (1960); Corbett, *Law and Society in the Relations of States* (1951) and *Law in Diplomacy* (1959); Reuter, *International Institutions* (1958); Herz, *International Politics in the Atomic Age* (1959); McClure, *World Legal Order* (1960); Gould, *An Introduction to International Law* (1957); Bloomfield, *Law, Politics, and International Disputes* (1958).

The defects of contemporary international governmental organization in sanctioning process are reviewed in all necessary detail in abundant sources, including: Goodrich, *The United Nations* (1959); Goodrich and Simons, *The United Nations and the Maintenance of International Peace and Security* (1955);

general community's processes of authoritative decision in implementation of basic minimum order may, however, serve to underscore the emphasis we seek to give to the importance of a disciplined, contextual, adaptive approach to the problem of sanctions.[187] The features of the general community's processes of authoritative decision with which we are primarily concerned are, of course, the constitutive features—that is, the more important decisions which establish competence, as contrasted with the vast flow of particular decisions in exercise of competence. It is the constitutive features of the general community's processes of decision which identify authoritative decision-makers, project fundamental community objectives, establish structures of authority, provide for bases of power in authority and other values, stipulate and legitimize the use of different strategies in persuasion and coercion, and facilitate outcomes in decision with respect to all necessary authority functions; and it is all these features, combined in process, which importantly affect the particular decisions in application or nonapplication of appropriate sanctions and, hence, the community's successes and failures in the maintenance of minimum order.[188] The constitutive features of the

---

Claude, *Swords into Plowshares* (2nd ed., 1959); Wilcox and Marcy, *Proposals for Changes in the United Nations* (1955); *Compilation of Staff Studies Prepared for the Use of the Subcommittee on the United Nations Charter of the Committee on Foreign Relations,* pursuant to S. Res. 126, 83rd Cong., Aug. 2, 1954 (1955); Lissitzyn, *The International Court of Justice* (1951); Haviland, *The Political Role of the General Assembly* (1951); Arechaga, *Voting and the Handling of Disputes in the Security Council* (1950); Frye, *A United Nations Peace Force* (1957); Jessup, "Parliamentary Diplomacy," 89 *Hague Recueil* 181 (1957); Schachter, "The Enforcement of International Judicial and Arbitral Decisions" 54 *A.J.I.L.* 1 (1960); Schwarzenberger, "Reflections on the Law of International Institutions," 13 *Current Legal Problems* 276 (1960). Green, "Gentlemen's Agreements and the Security Council," 13 *Current Legal Problems* 255 (1960).

See also the National Studies on International Organization sponsored by the Carnegie Endowment for International Peace. Review and references are offered by Haas, "The Comparative Study of the United Nations," 12 *World Politics* 298 (1960) and Hoffman, "National Attitudes and International Order: The National Studies on International Organization," 13 *Int. Organization* 189 (1959). MacIver, *The Nations and the United Nations* (1959) is particularly helpful.

187. Were it not for some invidious connotations of the word, we would say "opportunistic" rather than "adaptive."

188. What is meant by constitutive process, as distinguished from particular

contemporary general community's processes of authoritative decision are the outcomes of important prescriptive decisions, taken both by derivation of "customary" expectations from past uniformities in behavior and by the making and interpretation of comprehensive multilateral agreements, such as in the United Nations Charter and the constitutions of the great host of other international organizations. The most convenient mode of organizing a brief review of major defects would, accordingly, appear to be a phase-by-phase analysis of constitutive process, making with respect to each phase appropriate reference to both customary derivations and charter prescriptions. Thus, we proceed:

Decision-makers

The most comprehensive participation in community processes of authoritative decision is still reserved to the territorially organized bodies politic called "nation-states." Only very partial roles are accorded the other participants in world processes of effective power: dependent territorial communities, international governmental organizations, political parties, pressure groups, private associations, and individual human beings.

Constitutive prescriptions afford no guarantee of participation even to the territorial communities commonly regarded as nation-states. Exclusive and arbitrary decisions about "recognition," membership, representation, and credentials are authorized, which not infrequently bar large segments of mankind from the privileges and responsibilities of participation.

Requirements for statehood—that is, for eligibility for the most comprehensive participation—bear little relation to effective capabilities for the discharge of community responsibility either in the maintenance of minimum order or in the production and sharing of other values. The principle of equality requires, further, that states of vastly differing capabilities be given precisely the same compre-

---

exercises of constitutive competence in specific sanctioning decisions, may perhaps be gathered from Ross, *Constitution of the United Nations: Analysis of Structure and Function* (1950) and Jenks, "Some Constitutional Problems of International Organizations," 22 *Brit. Y.B.I.L.* 11 (1945).

The sanctioning process as a whole of course includes, as indicated in our survey of potential process above, both the constitutive decisions and the decisions in particular application.

hensive role in decision, irrespective of the consequences for maintenance of responsibility.

Community Objectives Projected

The most fatal defect in world constitutive process is in the absence among many effective elites about the globe, despite the broad promises of the United Nations Charter, of a genuine commitment to the principle of minimum order. Many *pro forma* commitments to the sustaining goal values of a world public order of human dignity are obviously even less genuine. The deeds in practice too often belie the words of authority.

The prudent humanitarian may, as we have already emphasized, reasonably doubt whether the totalitarian elites of the world have, despite the new threats of nuclear weapons and intercontinental ballistic missiles, abandoned their long-cherished goals of attaining world domination by any means, coercive included, to which they can turn their hand.[189] Thus, Professor Goodrich finds a most important "cause of United Nations weakness" in "Communism," which projects "an integrated world community" very different from the aspiration of the United Nations Charter. "While the Soviet Union, the chief Communist member of the United Nations, was," he writes, "one of the original sponsors of the Organization and professes full and explicit acceptance of its principles and purposes, it is obvious that its interpretation of these purposes and principles and its interest in the Organization differ fundamentally from those of the leading Western democracies." [190] Still another commentator more bluntly documents, at book length in the most minute detail, the thesis that among the Soviets the "idea of the withering away of the state has itself withered away" to be replaced by the goal of a "Soviet world state," totally directing and controlling man "in his body, mind, and spirit," in "the most extravagantly coercive, caste-ridden world state ever conceived in the mind of man." [191]

The genuineness of the commitment to minimum order even in

189. Some review of persisting attitudes is offered in Kennan, "Peaceful Coexistence," 38 *Foreign Aff.* 171 (1960). See also "Peking on Coexistence," 38 *Foreign Aff.* 676 (1960).

190. Goodrich, *The United Nations* 327 (1959).

191. Goodman, *The Soviet Design for a World State* 471, 472 (1960).

the Western democracies is, further, sometimes questioned. Thus, Professor Claude writes:

> Men, by and large, are still unprepared to act as if they believe in the indivisibility of peace; they are not ready to acknowledge the primacy of a global community and to assume the identity of national interests with the universal interest; they are not willing to accept the risks of commitment to defend any victim against any aggressor under unforeseeable circumstances in accordance with the decision of an international agency which is independent of national control; they are not prepared to bet their national life upon the proposition that the international community will faithfully and effectually safeguard their security; they are not confident that they can forego the autonomous pursuit of national strength and the discretionary formulation of national policy for dealing with future contingencies.[192]

Certainly, even in the Western democracies one finds, as we emphasized by way of introduction, the greatest confusion about the more specific, sub-goals of minimum order—prevention, deterrence, restoration, rehabilitation, and reconstruction—and much running off in all directions, as well as oscillation and vacillation in no direction.

Structures of Authority

Established structures of authority, despite their proliferation, bear little relation to the distribution of effective power, or potentialities of the natural environment, and afford inadequate opportunity for the responsible performance of the various authority functions indispensable to the clarification and implementation of general community interest.

The more important structures remain at the decentralized, national level and are largely unorganized, subject to unilateral disruption by exclusive decision.

192. Claude, *Swords into Plowshares* 285 (2nd ed., 1959). Cf. Liska, *International Equilibrium* 14 (1957). Sometimes one finds, in the most unexpected places, a nihilistic denial of even the "very concept of community interest." See, for example, Sorensen, "The Law of the Sea" 199 (1958), *Int. Conciliation* No. 520, a publication of the Carnegie Endowment for International Peace.

Structures at the international level, even including the host of new international governmental organizations and agencies, are most rudimentary. Legislative and executive institutions are not even admitted in name and the acknowledged judicial institutions are in measure a parody of model requirements. The institutions, organs, and agencies established, on a scale aspiring toward global, for the more modest tasks of investigation, discussion, and recommendation are insufficient even for these tasks and are imperfectly coordinated and interrelated.

Structures of authority established at regional levels, though increasing, are sometimes directed more toward partisan than general community objectives, and do not reflect a rational regional organization of the world by accepted criteria of community planning for the greater production and wider distribution of values.[193]

Access to national structures of authority by all participants—other nation-states, international governmental organizations, parties, pressure groups, private associations, and individuals—is at the sufferance of the exclusive decision of the territorial sovereign. Even the most general purpose international governmental organization, the United Nations, is made dependent, in discharge of its high responsibilities, upon the consent of a state for admission to its territorial domain.

Access to international structures of authority remains largely the prerogative of nation-states and international governmental organizations. Other participants—parties, pressure groups, private associations, and individuals—are accorded a differential, and highly inadequate, access to different structures for different purposes. Perhaps the most notable failures are in the inadequacies of access to judicial institutions provided for individuals and private associations.

Participation by nation-states in both unorganized and organized interactions with other states is regarded as voluntary, and complete withdrawal from participation is authorized.

Bases of Power

Nation-states continue to reserve to themselves control, by unilateral and exclusive decision, over most of the important bases of

193. Haas, "The Challenge of Regionalism," 12 *Int. Organization* 440 (1958) offers an introduction to contemporary attitudes and literature. See also Deutsch, *Nationalism and Social Communication* (1953).

effective power which can be employed to sustain general community authority. This is most obvious with respect to control over resources (territory, technology, etc.), people (residents, armed forces, etc.), and the institutional practices of the territorial community by which values are shaped and shared. It is no less true with respect to *authority* itself as a base value. States remain reluctant to delegate even their inclusive, shared competence—that competence which is authorized by the general community and exercised in the name of and on behalf of the general community—to international governmental organizations.

The competence which is in fact conferred upon international governmental organizations is inadequate in many ways. The most striking inadequacy, as will be developed below, relates to the authority functions established. Competence with respect to the intelligence and recommending functions is increasingly easily conferred and inferred, but competence for the prescribing and applying, and even invoking, functions is still very zealously guarded. Thus, the important innovatory competence of the United Nations—in the Security Council and General Assembly—with respect to violations of minimum order is so hemmed in by procedural and voting requirements (veto or special majority) that its exercise is made extremely difficult. On occasion competence in form granted, such as to the International Court of Justice, is in fact not granted because of permissible reservations to compulsory jurisdiction.

The competence commonly accorded international governmental organizations is further limited in terms of the kinds of participants in effective power processes which the organization may directly affect or make sanctioning targets. Thus, only occasionally, as in war crimes trials, may individuals be made directly subject to intergovernmental organization sanctions.

The limits of the competence accorded international governmental organizations in terms of the kinds of values they may control are no less exigent. It is a common lament that, with the failure in implementation of Article 43 of the Charter, the United Nations has only the most modest military forces at its direct disposal. The armaments held in the exclusive discretion of states, still refusing any serious considerations of disarmament, make any immediately conceivable forces at the direct disposal of the general community appear infinitesimal. Similarly, the general community organization is neither given control over any productive resources of its own nor accorded direct access, by taxation or otherwise, to the wealth processes of the member territorial communities. The potential advantages of a general community organization in employing such values as enlightenment, respect, loyalty, and rectitude for sanctioning purposes are not infrequently lost in the ambiguities of provisions granting competence and in the failures in coordination of authorized structures.

Cutting across the whole of the inclusive competence, unorganized and organized, of the general community are certain specter-like concepts of limitation, according priority to the exclusive competence of particular states. The service so long performed by the concepts of "sovereignty," "equality," "independence," and so on, in perpetuating the "divisions" of the world now has succor in Article 2(7) of the United Nations Charter, precluding the organization from intervening "in matters which are essentially within the domestic jurisdiction of any state." Were these concepts in limitation, old or new, construed—in an interdependent world in which matters of international concern and domestic concern, in a factual sense, are wholly and irrevocably commingled—to authorize each particular state by its own exclusive decision to determine the matters within its domestic concern, they could, of course, mean the complete negation of obligation.[194] Fortunately, in practice the concepts are regarded as expressing little more than a vague, intimidating threat.

Strategies

Authoritative control over the various instruments of policy—military, diplomatic, economic, and ideological—of course closely attends control over the effective bases of power which condition their use and is, hence, still largely reserved to exclusive decision by particular states. Little provision is made in global constitutional order either for the direct employment by international governmental organizations of the various instruments or for the effective coordination of the exclusive decisions by particular states in support of community sanctions policy. The largely investigatory and advisory competence conferred upon international organs is not adequate to achieve a rational specialization of instruments toward the more particular goals of prevention, deterrence, restoration, re-

194. See Ross, *Constitution of the United Nations: Analysis of Structure and Functions* 129 (1950) for a critique which deserves much wider attention.

habilitation, and reconstruction or to establish comprehensive and continuous programs for securing such specialized goals.

In the absence of implementation of Article 43 of the United Nations Charter, the general community has had placed at its disposal only the token military forces of the United Nations Emergency Force. As promising as is the experience in the Middle East and the Congo with this new community "police force," it is obvious that much more direct control over a more potent military instrument is necessary if the United Nations is effectively to serve its overriding security purposes.[195]

The contribution which international organization is authorized to make by use of the diplomatic instrument remains largely that of providing *fora* for old and new exercises of the instrument by the officials of nation-states. Question has been raised whether the new forms of public "parliamentary diplomacy" in fact promote the responsible outcomes in "agreement" most rationally designed to sustain minimum order.[196]

With respect to the economic instrument, much competence of wide scope has been conferred upon international organization, such as in the United Nations Charter (e.g. Article 41) for sanctioning deterrent and restoration policies and in a multitude of provisions in many different organizational charters for promoting preventive, rehabilitation, and reconstruction policies. Most of this competence is, however, either restricted by procedural and voting difficulties or confined to intelligence and recommendation.[197] The competence granted is clearly minimal in its weight in relation to need.

It is, however, with respect to the ideological (perhaps better "informational") instrument that least competence has been conferred upon international organization. Professor Dunn puts the matter in sharpest summary:

> There is no international communication system, as such, that can be mobilized to influence the masses of men in all countries for a particular purpose.[198]

195. Cf. Munro, "Can the United Nations Enforce Peace?" 38 *Foreign Aff.* 209 (1960).

196. Jessup, "Parliamentary Diplomacy," 89 *Hague Recueil* 181 (1957) indicates both potentialities and dangers.

197. Asher and Associates, *The United Nations and Promotion of the General Welfare* (1957) describes both achievements and difficulties.

198. Dunn, *War and the Minds of Men* 71 (1950).

The consequence is:

> There are no international agencies today which are empowered to communicate directly with the people of a particular country to induce them to take some attitude that is not in accord with the national policies of that country.[199]

Quite consistently, the ideological instrument is not even mentioned in the comprehensive reports upon sanctions by the Collective Measures Committee.[200]

Outcomes

Techniques both for harmonizing exclusive national decisions and for achieving inclusive decisions within international governmental organizations remain most primitive. The traditional requirement of customary international law for harmonizing exclusive decision has been that of unanimity. Though this requirement of unanimity appears to be disappearing from the charters of international organizations, special majorities and even vetoes are still not infrequently stipulated. The most notorious example is, of course, the veto and double veto accorded the permanent members of the United Nations Security Council in certain situations before the Council. The important point is that special majorities and vetoes authorize a minority, on occasion even of one, to determine sanctioning policy for the whole general community. Inaction is as fraught with policy consequences as action and the failure to achieve decision may be the most significant kind of decision. Conversely, as already indicated, when decisions are taken by voting units as disparate in population and other bases of power as contemporary nation-states, even decisions by ordinary majority voting may be in fact "minority" decisions with little relation to the realistic possibilities of either immediate sanctioning action or the long-term maintenance of minimum order.

More detailed inadequacies for achieving outcomes in decision may be noted in relation to the several authority functions:

199. Id., 32.

200. *Report of the Collective Measures Committee,* U.N. Gen. Ass., *Off. Rec.,* 6th Sess., Supp. No. 13 (A/1891) (1951); id., 7th Sess., Supp. No. 17 (A/2215) (1952).

PRESCRIPTION

The unanimity requirement, of course, dominates the negotiation of agreement, the most common instrument of explicit policy projection, and but modest progress has been made away from the notion that even great constitutional charters cannot bind nonmembers. The derivation of "customary" prescription from past uniformities in behavior, despite the myth to the contrary, avoids this difficulty, but the technique is one subject to many vagaries in interpretation, "glacial" in its time dimension,[201] and highly suspected by the many new nation-states who have had little direct participation in the past uniformities of behavior from which implicit policies are sought.

Some competence to prescribe is, of course, conferred upon the International Court of Justice and the United Nations Security Council by virtue of the functions for which they are established. The intelligence and recommending competence conferred upon all the principal organs of the United Nations shows some promise, further, of development under conditions of crisis toward a meager equivalence of prescriptive function. Such largely interstitial and precarious competence is, however, but a poor substitute for an effective legislative body with appropriate powers for promoting minimum order and its necessary conditions.

The special conferences of nation-states called on occasion to legislate with respect to immediate, urgent problems, because of their focus upon isolated problems and necessary concern for unanimity, too often succeed in prescribing, if any common interest, only the lowest comon denominator of interest. The dramatic failures in the 1958 and 1960 Geneva conferences on the law of the sea bear eloquent witness.[202]

The inherited prescriptions of contemporary international law offer, further, few clarifications in terms of detailed principles of content and procedure, such as we have sought to outline with respect to the distinction between permissible and impermissible coercion and the maintenance of minimum order.

201. Dickinson, *Law and Peace* 117 (1951) suggests that custom "grows glacially."

202. McDougal, Burke and Vlasic, "The Maintenance of Public Order at Sea and the Nationality of Ships," 53 *A.J.I.L.* 25 (1960) documents some of the difficulties in such conferences.

INTELLIGENCE

The broad competence commonly accorded international governmental organizations, whether by explicit grant or implied derivation, to obtain, process, and disseminate information tends to be somewhat illusory. The competence accorded is seldom adequate for piercing the façade of an obstructionist state. Compulsory powers to procure information from governments, private associations, and individuals are conspicuously wanting. Little obligation is imposed upon organizations to make investigation. Still less obligation is imposed upon governments and others to take relevant findings into account. The great, open-conscience-of-the-world, *fora* of international governmental organizations for the potential enlightenment of all mankind in the making of rational decisions, permit of easy transformation into mere platforms for promotion of partial interests.

RECOMMENDING

The recommending function, for promotion and advocacy of specific policy alternatives, is perhaps the most honored of all functions in inclusive competence. In consequence of their effective control, most of the participants in the world power process demand and receive authoritative roles in performance of this function. It is a competence, further, which is frequently granted international governmental organizations as a substitute for genuine prescriptive power. The difficulty is, as we have seen, that while such competence does tend on occasion to approximate that of prescription, the safeguards necessary to discipline competence to the service of community interest are lacking.

INVOKING

Competence to invoke the application in particular instances of inclusive community prescription is differentially accorded to different effective power participants in different arenas. This competence has been greatly augmented in the United Nations structure, but many participants are still precluded from taking direct initiative in many arenas. The most obvious example is in the denial to private associations and individuals of access to the International Court of Justice or equivalent comprehensive institutions.

APPLICATION

The application of inclusive community prescription in particular instances remains largely within the highly decentralized competence of particular nation-states. State officials act both within the institutional structures of their own states and in countless day-to-day interactions, organized and unorganized, with the officials of other states. The "absence of an authority [that is, of disinterested third-party authority] to declare what the law is at any given time, how it applies to a given situation or dispute, and what the appropriate sanction may be" is commonly regarded as a most basic defect in international law.[203] "In the absence of such an authority, and failing agreement between the states at variance on these points," writes Professor Leo Gross in full fidelity to tradition, "each state has a right to interpret the law, the right of auto-interpretation, as it might be called."[204] This right of "auto-interpretation," with its potentiality of many conflicting interpretations, extends, unfortunately, beyond derivations of customary international law, even to the application of great constitutional charters, like that of the United Nations.

The provision of a third-party role in such traditional procedures as those of good offices, mediation, conciliation, and arbitration—even with the new structures of authority in the United Nations—is still on an *ad hoc* basis and subject to unilateral rejection or termination by the contending participants.

The acceptance by states of the jurisdiction of the International Court of Justice is wholly discretionary, and many purported acceptances of compulsory jurisdiction are in fact so qualified as to make commitment nominal or nonexistent. The most notorious reservation, which regrettably has had the flattery of considerable emulation, is that of the United States, excepting "matters which are essentially within the domestic jurisdiction of the United States of America as determined by the United States of America."[205]

203. Gross, "States as Organs of International Law and the Problem of Autointerpretation," in *Law and Politics in the World Community* 76–7 (Lipsky, ed., 1953).

204. Id.

205. The text of the reservation appears in Sohn, *Cases on World Law* 169 (1950). Thorough discussion of the general problem is offered by Briggs, "Res-

The competence conferred upon the principal organs of the United Nations with respect to the pacific settlement and adjustment of disputes, while in terms broad, is severely limited in many ways, such as with respect to the types of disputes which may be considered, the authority functions which may be exercised, and the obligation of states to respect or support decision.

The competence conferred upon these same organs of the United Nations with respect to "breaches of the peace, threats to the peace, and acts of aggression," though the most promising innovation of our time, has proved to be too limited in weight because of voting and procedural requirements, and has been deprived of practical effectiveness because of the failure of the states to supply the organization with military forces. The system of permissive participation which has replaced the originally projected enforcement procedures and measures has obvious weaknesses.

APPRAISAL

Assessment of the successes and failures of inclusive community prescriptions and applications is generally subsumed under the intelligence function and shares all the inadequacies of that function.

TERMINATION

In the absence of centralized legislative institutions and of courts of genuine compulsory jurisdiction, the general community's constitutive processes make little explicit provision for a competence to terminate prescriptions and arrangements effected under the authority of prescriptions. The consent which establishes agreements can, of course, disestablish them, but a terminating consent is not always forthcoming even under drastically changed conditions. The competence for unilateral termination authorized by the doctrine of *rebus sic stantibus* is a subject of bitter contention both as to scope and modality. Though the principal organs of the United Nations in exercise of their recommending functions may in fact ease transition from old to new policies, the lack of explicit authorization and specialized machinery greatly impedes their performance. It has been often noted that this failure to establish an appropriate centralized

---

ervations to the Acceptance of Compulsory Jurisdiction of the International Court of Justice," 93 *Hague Recueil* 223, 309 (1958).

competence for promoting and effecting peaceful change has many dire consequences, not the least of which is the comfort it affords for the ill-founded notion that international law serves only to protect the status quo.[206]

PROPOSALS FOR IMPROVEMENT MULTIPLICITOUS AND PARTIAL

The proposals currently being made for remedy of all these defects in the general community's constitutive process are, of course, multiplicitous and largely ineffectual. The literature of both unofficial and official concern and suggestion is mountainous.[207] The more significant proposals differ greatly in scope, design, and realism. Some proposals, such as those of the Chicago Group [208] and of Messrs. Clark

206. Cf. Ross, *Constitution of the United Nations: Analysis of Structure and Function* 157 (1950). See also Bloomfield, *Evolution or Revolution?: The United Nations and the Problem of Peaceful Change* (1957).

207. Many of the citations in notes 1–20 and 186, supra, are equally relevant here. The most comprehensive review of contemporary proposals is perhaps Wilcox and Marcy, *Proposals for Changes in the United Nations* (1955), making extensive use of the studies of the Subcommittee on the United Nations Charter of the United States Senate (hereinafter cited as Wilcox and Marcy). Incisive, and uncommonly realistic, appraisal of many proposals is offered in Claude, *Swords into Plowshares* (2nd ed., 1959).

A recent collection of proposals is offered in Foreign Affairs Division, Legislative Reference Service, Library of Congress, *Strengthening Free World Security* (A Collection of Excerpts and Bibliographies Printed for the Use of the Committee on Foreign Relations, U. S. Senate, 86th Cong., 2nd Sess., July 26, 1960).

The proposal made by Chairman Khrushchev in September 1960, before the General Assembly, for restructuring the office of the Secretary-General of the United Nations is based upon an explicit denial of common interest which transcends Communist, free world, and neutralist countries. (See *N. Y. Times,* Sept. 24, 1960, pp. 6, 8, and 7 *United Nations Review* 37 (1960); the theme of lack of common interest was elaborated in a later statement, quoted in *N. Y. Times,* Oct. 4, 1960, p. 19.) Proposals of this type are of course appropriately regarded, not as alternatives genuinely designed to promote a world public order of human dignity, but rather as expressions of perspectives inimical to the establishment of such an order, constituting a condition which the proponents of human dignity must confront.

208. Hutchins and Associates, *Preliminary Draft of a World Constitution* (1948).

and Sohn,[209] are explicitly designed to be all-comprehensive: thus the latter insist, with appropriate detailed recommendations, that "besides universal and complete disarmament, nothing less will suffice than a comprehensive plan whereby there would be established on a world scale institutions corresponding to those which have been found essential for the maintenance of law and order in local communities and nations." [210] Other proposals—viewing the problem, as the men from Hindustan viewed the elephant, in parts—recommend only bits of detail ("gimmicks") in institution, principle, or procedure: a new court or police force, a new principle of human rights or definition of aggression, or a new form of compulsory jurisdiction with universal writ. Some proposals seek a complete overhauling of existing global power and other value processes, while others would not substantially alter the present system. Some proposals limit their imaginative projections to existing municipal or national models; others soar in the outer realms of fantasy about new techniques. Considered comprehensively, the proposals all share a common modest regard for the conditions under which they are likely to be accepted and for the relevance of the context of conditions to the rational choice of legal technique. Few of the proposals exhibit sufficient awareness of context, particularly of the time dimension, to specify the details of immediate, mid-range, and long-term measures toward acceptance and implementation. The character and range of contemporary proposals may perhaps be most economically indicated by a brief, impressionistic sampling, again phase by phase of constitutive process.

Decision-makers

Proposals commonly insist upon the universalization of the participation of all mankind in the general community's processes of authoritative decision. Some would achieve this indirectly by requiring the universal membership of territorially organized communities in appropriate international organizations. Others would seek to achieve a more direct participation by abolishing the nation-state system and establishing a monolithic, centralized structure of authority or "world government." More fully specified proposals in-

209. Clark and Sohn, *World Peace Through World Law* (2nd rev. ed., 1960) (hereinafter referred to as Clark and Sohn).

210. Id., xi.

clude prohibiting the expulsion or withdrawal of territorial communities from international organizations and the granting to private associations and individuals of increased access to the structures of international authority.

Community Objectives Projected

The range extends from the most comprehensive values of a world public order of human dignity, including both minimum and optimum order, to the most limited conception of minimum order, that is, merely the prevention of unauthorized violence. Whatever the range, the recommendations are, of course, for genuine acceptance exhibited by deeds along with words.

Specifications of subordinate goals and implementing practices are at many different degrees of abstraction. Thus, Clark and Sohn stipulate that "the powers of the world organization should be restricted to matters directly related to the maintenance of peace," [211] without specifying in detail how "matters directly related to the maintenance of peace" are operationally to be distinguished from other matters.

Structures of Authority

The most ambitious proposals project centralized legislative, executive, judicial, and administrative institutions of global, and most recently of outer space, reach. Many proposals include a more rational regional organization of the world. Specifications include new parliaments, new courts (criminal, human rights, equity, and so on), new executive offices, and new specialized agencies.

Less ambitious proposals dabble with the United Nations structures and procedures—reconstructing the principal organs and improving coordination between them, conceding the Secretary-General new functions, subordinating the specialized agencies, and so on.

Bases of Power

A principal design in most proposals is to augment the authority of inclusive decision. Thus, Clark and Sohn insist upon the need for "the law of a world authority, i.e. law which would be uniformly applicable to all nations and all individuals in the world and which would definitely forbid violence or the threat of it as a means for

211. Id., xvii.

dealing with any international dispute." [212] Many proposals suggest that a new, extensive competence be conferred upon "world" or "supranational" organs "to enact, interpret and enforce world law." [213]

Some proposals demand an increase in inclusive authority over the effective bases of power. The plans for "world" or "international" police or other military forces are legion.[214] Disarmament proposals, recommending national disarmament in many different degrees and of many different kinds, flood even the daily newspapers.[215] Proposals designed to enhance inclusive authority over resources embrace such resources as those of the oceans and ocean beds, of the polar regions, and of outer space and include the internationalization of the control of nuclear energy. Proposals to confer upon international organization the taxing power or its equivalent are not uncommon.

The suggestion is sometimes made, further, that Article 2(7) of the United Nations Charter, formulating the "domestic jurisdiction" limitation upon inclusive decision, should be explicitly restricted in the scope of its application.[216] More pragmatic measures in contemporary restrictive interpretation include the recommendation of new covenants between states to protect the "human rights" of individuals against their own states, to protect minorities of many different kinds, and to establish new rights of self-determination among peoples.[217]

Strategies

The tendency, explicit or implicit, of most of the more comprehensive proposals is to enhance competence for inclusive decision with respect to all instruments of strategy. The provision of armed forces directly at the disposal of international organization, along with national disarmament, would obviously establish a new com-

212. Id., xv.

213. Wilcox and Marcy, 58.

214. Clark and Sohn 164 specify elaborate details. See also Schwarzenberger, "Problems of a United Nations Force," 13 *Current Legal Problems* 247 (1959).

215. The complexities which would attend serious proposals are well indicated in Melman, *Inspection for Disarmament* (1958) and Henkin, *Arms Control and Inspection in American Law* (1958). Cf. the special issue of *Daedalus* (The Journal of the American Academy of Arts and Sciences), Fall 1960.

216. Wilcox and Marcy, 257, 260.

217. Lauterpacht, *International Law and Human Rights* (1950); Moskowitz, *Human Rights and World Order* (1958).

petence over the military instrument. Many of the proposals with respect to reorganization of the structures of authority of international organization, including provision of new access to authority for many participants in effective power processes, would drastically alter the present relatively exclusive control of particular nation-states over the diplomatic instrument. Proposals for the improvement of inclusive control over the economic instrument are most explicit: they extend comprehensively to practically every detailed phase of wealth processes transcending nation-state lines, and especially emphasize the provision of positive assistance in facilitation of economic growth.[218] Improvements in competence over the ideological instrument are implicit in proposals for strengthening the intelligence and recommending functions of international organizations, in the proposed covenants on freedom of information and inquiry, and in designs to expand the activities of Unesco.

Outcomes

It is with respect to procedures for achieving outcomes in inclusive decision, "voting," that proposals for improvement have completely run riot. The most "supranational" proposals project world assemblies in which individuals are elected on a global basis and vote as individuals. Slightly less reconstructive proposals suggest a rational reorganization of the territorial regions of the world, with voting variously weighted. Still other proposals do not attempt to reconstitute existing nation-states, but suggest allocation of voting competence in accordance with many varying combinations of such factors as population, literacy, experience with democratic institutions, national wealth, productivity, and military strength.[219] Less ambitious proposals seek to improve the functioning of United Nations organs by the removal or limitation of vetoes, by expansion of

218. For comprehensive bibliography see U. S. Department of State, External Research Report, *Research on Underdevelopment: Assessment and Inventory on Research on Economic, Social and Political Problems of Underdeveloped Areas* (1960).

Gardner, "New Directions in U. S. Foreign Policy" (Foreign Policy Association, Headline Series, No. 133, 1959) offers discussion and references from both international and national perspectives. See also Miller, "American Participation in Multinational Economic Institutions: A Problem in Constitutional Law and Policy," 1959 *Wash. U.L.Q.* 325 (1959).

219. Wilcox and Marcy, 354 et seq.; Sohn, *Cases and Materials on United Nations Law* (1956) c. 3.

the concept of "procedural matters," and by provisions for simple majority voting by existing states.

We note briefly suggestions with respect to varying particular authority functions:

PRESCRIPTION

It is commonly recommended that a "constitutive" competence should be explicitly recognized in the general community of states and that the fundamental charters of international organizations be regarded as binding even dissenters. This is the mode of adoption urged for various new constitutional principles, such as Clark and Sohn's "clearly stated law against violence." [220] Proposals for conferring direct "legislative" competence upon international organization differ greatly in the competence they would confer. The Clark and Sohn proposal is for a "legislative power" strictly limited to "matters directly related to the maintenance of peace." [221]

Proposals for the clarification and codification of inherited principles of public and private international law have long been popular in theory, but—despite much effort—neglected in fact.

INTELLIGENCE

Among the more promising proposals are those for increasing the independent investigatory competence of international governmental organizations and for employment of citizens of the traditionally "neutral" countries in multilateral measures designed to preclude surprise attacks.

RECOMMENDING

Many observers continue to advocate expansion of the recommending competence of international governmental organizations, especially with reference to problems in economic, social, and cultural development.

INVOKING

The more significant changes proposed would accord private associations and individuals a new access to international courts and other inclusive structures of authority.

220. Clark and Sohn, xv.

221. Id., xii.

APPLICATION

It is proposed from many sides that the competence of the International Court of Justice be greatly expanded, with compulsory jurisdiction not only over states but also over other participants in world processes of effective power.[222] Reservations to the Court's jurisdiction, such as that of the United States with respect to matters determined by it to be within its domestic jurisdiction, are subjected to especial criticism. One strongly supported proposal is that the Court be made the ultimate, authoritative interpreter of the United Nations Charter and other great constitutive agreements.

Suggestions for enlargement of the competence of international governmental organizations in the peaceful adjustment and settlement of disputes take many different forms, including drastic changes in both parliamentary and executive procedures. The role of such organizations in the application of authority to breaches of minimum order would be greatly enhanced by changes in voting requirements and by provision of direct and continuous control over military forces.

The application of inclusive prescriptions within the internal structures of authority of particular states would be expedited by proposed new international agreements precluding change in national constitutions requiring the internal application of inclusive prescriptions.[223]

TERMINATION

The provision of a new specialized, inclusive competence for terminating international prescriptions and arrangements effected under their authority has been a highly favored recommendation of publicists since World War I, and continues to receive widespread endorsement.[224]

It is not our intention to suggest that all these multiplicitous proposals to which we thus allude are without merit. Many of the pro-

222. Wilcox and Marcy, 380.

223. *Survey of International Law,* Memorandum submitted by the Secretary-General, U.N. Gen. Ass., Int. Law Comm. (1948) 23 (commonly attributed to the late Sir Hersch Lauterpacht).

224. Wilcox and Marcy, c. XV. Dunn, "Peaceful Change Today," 11 *World Politics* 278 (1959).

posals, on the contrary, exhibit not only a genuine dedication to the common interest but also the highest professional skill, and the mere propagation of awareness that there are legal techniques available which might be employed to mitigate danger may serve some role in creating the necessary predispositions in peoples to take appropriate measures. It is, however, our very strong conviction that most of these proposals are partial, in the sense indicated above that they place too much emphasis upon functionally equivalent legal techniques, and too little emphasis upon the conditions which must affect the acceptance of any appropriate techniques and upon the necessary relevance of such conditions to the rational recommendation of particular techniques. Thus, the insistence of Clark and Sohn that "if the world really wants peace," it must adopt "a comprehensive and interrelated system" [225] of the general character that they propose, and Mr. Clark's further assumption that peoples' increasing recognition of risk in the contemporary world make the imminent adoption of some such system highly probable,[226] appear somewhat facile. The historic ineffectuality of most proposals to improve the general community's sanctioning process would appear to derive from the paralyzing and destructive contention of incompatible public orders in "the framework of a divided world"—a framework or "basic configuration" which "has persisted since prehistory and throughout history to this day" and which includes "the expectation of violent coercion" ("the expectation that violence will in all probability continue as a means of coping with many conflicts in world politics"), the "pattern of parochial rather than universal identification" ("the effective identification of the self with small groups or with large social formations, like nation-states, which are less inclusive than mankind"), and "the ethical imperative to coerce" ("the demand upon the self to make whatever sacrifices are required to establish or extend the position of authoritative power for less than universal groups").[227] It was only in recognition of the contemporary manifesta-

225. Clark and Sohn, xii.

226. Id., xliv.

227. The summary and quoted words are from Lasswell, "The Main Trends in the World Picture," address, Sixteenth Conference on Science, Philosophy, and Religion, The Jewish Theological Seminary of America (to be published in the proceedings of the conference). Lasswell, *World Politics and Personal Insecurity* (1935) spells out the detailed interrelations and consequences of the historic syndromes.

tion of this historic configuration of contending world public orders that a Subcommittee of the United States Senate Committee on Foreign Relations, after several years of systematic study of numerous proposals for improvement of the enforcement provisions of the United Nations Charter, concluded: "The subcommittee cannot escape the conclusion that under present international circumstances most of these suggestions have not taken full account of the reality of the tensions which exist between the free world and the Communist world." [228] The most immediately relevant tasks of scholars and others concerned for the establishment of inclusive sanctioning processes appropriate to a world public order of freedom, security, and abundance would thus appear to lie, not so much in the invention and evaluation of specific new legal techniques, as in the design and execution of appropriate alternatives in communication and collaboration for promoting the necessary changes in the perspectives of the effective decision-makers of the world.

RECOMMENDED ALTERNATIVES IN COMMUNICATION AND COLLABORATION

From an objective vantage point, certainly the most conspicuous fact about contemporary world social process must be the common interest of all peoples, whatever the comprehensive public order to which they adhere, in the maintenance of minimum order. The precarious balance of terror today dominating the world arena—a balance in which each of the contending polar powers has, or will shortly have, the capability, irrespective of which strikes first, to destroy the other and perhaps to render the whole globe uninhabitable, and in which it is realistically expected that even the smaller powers will soon have only slightly less awesome capability—offers but little assurance that it can be kept in balance.[229] "The worst of all possible cold-war worlds," Dr. Oskar Morganstern appropriately summarizes, "is a self-generating arms race feeding upon a rapidly advancing technology, each country progressing at a different rate kept secret

228. Subcommittee on the United Nations Charter, Final Report of the Committee on Foreign Relations, Review of the United Nations Charter (U. S. Senate, 84th Cong., 2nd Sess., Apr. 9, 1956) 13.

229. Cf. Wohlstetter, "The Delicate Balance of Terror," 37 *Foreign Aff.* 211 (1959); Burns, "Disarmament or the Balance of Terror," 12 *World Politics* 132 (1959).

from the other." [230] In this context, in which accident or miscalculation may play as destructive a role as malevolent intent, the common interest of all men, without regard for their political or ideological affiliations, in mere survival establishes a common interest in minimum order.

The task of highest priority, in such context, for every one genuinely committed to the goal values of a world public order of human dignity would, accordingly, appear to be that of creating in all peoples of the world the perspectives necessary both to their realistic understanding of this common interest and to their acceptance and initiation of the detailed measures in sanctioning process appropriately designed to secure such interest. It is, as we have seen, the conflicting, confused, and disoriented perspectives of peoples—such as the syndromes in expectations of violence, patterns of parochial identification, and demands for domination—and not the inexorable requirements of environmental factors, which keep alive the contention of world orders, with such appalling threat for all mankind. The maximization postulate—that men act within their capabilities to maximize their values—suggests that by appropriate modifications in perspectives the peoples of the world can be encouraged to move toward both the establishment of a more effective constitutive process and the making of more rational specific sanctioning decisions. It is common ground of both historical knowledge and contemporary science that the factors—culture, class, interest, personality, and crisis—which most directly condition peoples' perspectives can be changed and managed to promote constructive rather than destructive perspectives. Promising alternatives in communication and collaboration designed to promote the perspectives appropriate to the maintenance of minimum order and, with minimum order, opportunity for peaceful progress toward a more comprehensive public order of human dignity, have long been recommended by competent specialists upon different instruments of policy and different value processes, and await employment in sufficiently comprehensive, integrated, and disciplined programs. The "means available for changing men's attitudes" are as open, in slight adaptation of the language and thought of Professor Frederick Dunn, to those who seek to main-

230. Morgenstern, "Goal: An Armed, Inspected, Open World," *Fortune* 93 (July, 1960).

tain minimum order and to promote a world public order of human dignity as "to those who pursue irresponsible power." [231]

The major kinds of perspectives—expectations, identifications, and demands—required for promoting progress toward a more effective community sanctioning process, though already indicated in some detail, may be briefly recapitulated. The proponents of human dignity must, in the first instance, establish in themselves and others credible expectations that they do accept the principle of minimum order—that force and intense coercion are not to be used for the expansion of values—and that the peaceful cooperation of all peoples in the greater production and wider sharing of all values compatible with human dignity is not only possible, but perhaps even the price of survival. The falsity of totalitarian myth, with its overemphasis on a single factor as dominating human motivation and social change and its prediction of inevitable total war, must be exposed.[232] Conversely, the proponents of human dignity must make it equally clear that they have suffered no loss of nerve and that, when attacked in violation of public order, they have both the will and capability to defend their values by force.[233] The expectations which must be established in all effective decision-makers are, in sum, the expectations that they, and all with whom they identify, have more to gain and less to lose by genuine peaceful cooperation than by breaches of minimum order. The identifications best designed to sustain comprehensive minimum order are, as previously noted, those which

231. The precise words of Dunn, *War and the Minds of Men* xiii (1950) are: "The means available for changing men's attitudes are open to those who seek to restore international order as well as to those who pursue irresponsible power."

232. Professor George Catlin, referring to Karl Marx, has appropriately written: "Here, by an odd irony, it is the very prophet of the economic determination of history and of the inevitable material dialectic who is the most striking example of how an ideology can by the force and the psychological appeal of its ideas, sway a considerable portion of the human race." Catlin, "The Effect of Politics upon Trends in Philosophical and Religious Thought," address, Sixteenth Conference on Science, Philosophy, and Religion, Jewish Theological Seminary of America (1960).

233. With Lord Russell's bland equation of totalitarian ideology and human dignity values as causes of danger, contrast Mr. Hugh Gaitskell's careful analysis of conditions and alternatives. Russell, "The Case for Neutralism," *New York Times Magazine* 10 (July 24, 1960) and Gaitskell, "And the Case Against It," id. 11.

most nearly embrace all mankind and achieve pluralistic expression in both functional and territorial associations. The demands which require strengthening are, of course, those which emphasize persuasion and cooperation, as contrasted with coercion and domination, in the modalities of shaping and sharing values and which insist upon the greater production and wider sharing of all values compatible with human dignity.

The potentialities that inhere in the planned management of the factors most importantly affecting peoples' perspectives, though infrequently employed in support of comprehensive minimum order, have within recent decades become of almost commonplace knowledge. Techniques are available by which peoples may both liberate themselves from the parochial and destructive biases established by the different factors and, more positively, even employ such factors in the promotion of the appropriate universal, constructive perspectives.[234] Modern communications media make it possible, further, that all men may share in this common enterprise of emancipation and construction. The constraining biases of particular *culture* may be weakened by acquisition of an increasing self-consciousness of one's own culture and a deeper understanding of other cultures. Cultural factors may be made to support comprehensive minimum order by appropriate emphasis upon the primacy of goal values, which most cultures share, and the potential equivalence in service or disservice to basic goal values of many different institutional practices, which may appropriately vary in desirable experimentation with different cultural patterns. The warping influence of *class* may be discounted by focussing explicit attention upon the tendency of all classes—upper, middle, lower—to take decisions for their own benefit, rather than in the common interest. The distortions of the Marxian myth which make this tendency the all-important factor in social change require, however, explicit rejection. The class factor may be employed positively by the maintenance in theory and fact of a mobile, caste-free society, encouraging both movement upward and long-term equality. The divisive effects of special *interests,* in different functional or areal groups, may be minimized by exposure of too limited perceptions of interest and insistence upon the rational priority of more comprehensive, long-term interests. The im-

234. See citations in notes 153–75 supra.

portance of developing multiple interests, including numerous competing and balancing pressure groups, may be stressed in positive programs to yoke special interest to the common good. The destructive consequences of pathological traits in *personality* may be lessened by acquiring insight, at whatever depth may be necessary, into the basic value orientations and dynamisms of the self, along with a deeper understanding of others. In positive programs relating to the personality factor the tremendous resources of modern science could be brought to bear upon the rearing and education of healthier personalities. The traumatic effects of exposure to *crisis* may be mitigated by precisely the same type of awareness and insight which is effective with respect to the other factors; positive programs may include measures designed to prevent, avoid, and postpone direct confrontations in crisis situations.

The successful management, in progressive movement toward minimum world public order, of conditioning factors so pervasive, stubborn, and complex must, of course, depend upon a tremendous "common constructive effort," [235] in both organized and unorganized situations, by all persons genuinely committed to human dignity values, addressing all accessible constituencies and seizing upon every appropriate opportunity for effective intervention. In such a "common constructive effort," direct communications only, by specialized signs such as words, cannot—the point may bear emphasis—reasonably be expected to be enough. The potentialities of direct communications, however great, cannot be adequate to the immense task of persuading the peoples of the world to discard their parochial, destructive perspectives for the necessary, more universal, constructive perspectives. An infantile faith, all too frequently exhibited by the adult, in the omnipotence of mere words, authoritative or other, has never been more irrelevant. The communications which are required, if the various significant conditioning factors are to be effectively influenced in appropriate directions, include not only the mediation of subjectivities by specialized signs, but also the deeper mediations which occur in acts of collaboration, as when people freely work together for shared ends. The point has been well put by Millikan and Rostow:

235. The quoted words are from Millikan and Rostow, *A Proposal: Key to an Effective Foreign Policy* 66 (1957).

> Ideology, values, and principles of political organization can be much more quickly grasped and promoted through programs of common action than through debate or "education." [236]

The contributions which rational employment of the different instruments of policy—military, economic, ideological, and diplomatic—might make to comprehensive programs in communication and collaboration, beyond the contributions to specific sanctioning practice already recited, are easily indicated. Thus, with respect to the *military instrument,* there has within the United States in recent years arisen a tremendous, burgeoning literature about how, from purely national perspectives, this instrument can be effectively employed for the objective of deterrence.[237] Comparable effort, premised explicitly upon broader community perspectives and with wider participation, could contribute significantly both to the desired enlargement of community perspectives and to useful innovation in community organization and specific sanctioning practice. Similarly, specialists upon the management of the *economic instrument* are projecting, again largely from national perspectives, comprehensive and elaborately detailed programs for promoting the emancipation and modernization of the less developed areas of the world.[238] With some broadening of the perspectives postulated and of bases in participation, these programs, too, could be adapted in their planning and execution to more general community purposes. Comprehensive models for the systematic employment of the *ideological instrument* are, unfortunately, not so plentiful, but some brilliant preliminary analyses have been made, and the potentialities need no new elab-

236. Id., 38.

237. Representative studies include Schelling, *The Strategy of Conflict* (1960); Morgenstern, *The Question of National Defense* (1958); Brodie, *Strategy in the Missile Age* (1959); Kahn, *The Nature and Feasibility of War and Deterrence* (1960).

238. One very important study, highly suggestive of what might be achieved from broader perspectives, is Center For International Studies (M.I.T.), *Economic, Social, and Political Change in the Underdeveloped Countries and Its Implications for United States Policy* (A Study [No. 12] Prepared at the Request of the Committee on Foreign Relations, U. S. Senate, 86th Cong., 2nd Sess., Mar. 30, 1960). Cf. Millikan and Rostow, *A Proposal: Key to an Effective Foreign Policy* (1957); Ward, "The Economic Revolution," *The Saturday Evening Post* 43 (May 14, 1960).

oration.[239] Perhaps the most convincing demonstration, finally, of the potentialities in the skilled use of the *diplomatic instrument* in shaping general community perspectives, as well as in implementing specific sanctioning decisions, comes not from scholarly books, but from the performance of United Nations officials in various delicate contemporary contexts.[240]

The effects in support of desired sanctioning process that might be achieved by comprehensive programs in the shaping and sharing of many different, important base values are no less obvious. Thus, *power* processes may be managed to establish in support of inclusive decision the military strength indispensable to many sanctioning objectives,[241] and assistance can be given to particular territorial communities in modernizing and democratizing their processes of authoritative decision for a more responsible participation in external affairs and the more secure internal protection of human dignity values. The processes of *enlightenment* can be expanded to make more effective provision of the information required for rational decision in power processes and for the modernization and improvement of other value processes. An impressive case has been made that an "open world" must henceforth be necessary to even the most minimal security of any people.[242] The processes of *respect* can be adapted to bestow recognition for merit in performance in the common interest and to preclude the arbitrary discriminations irrelevant to

239. The best statement of possibilities is Dunn, *War and the Minds of Men* (1950). Cf. Wright, "Project for a World Intelligence Center," 1 *J. Conflict Resolution* 93 (1957); Claude, *Swords into Plowshares* c. 14 (2nd ed., 1959); Tripp, "Unesco in Perspective," *Int. Conciliation* No. 497 (1954).

240. The more positive contributions of the neo-realists, such as Kennan, Corbett, and Morgenthau, are to be found in their emphasis upon the potentialities of the diplomatic instrument. See Kennan, *American Diplomacy 1900–1950* (1951); Corbett, *Law in Diplomacy* (1959); Morgenthau, *Politics Among Nations* (3rd ed., 1960). For a great variety of views, see Kertesz and Fitzsimons (eds.), *Diplomacy in a Changing World* (1959).

The great need is for study in "task force" proportions of the potentialities that might inhere in a comprehensive, integrated program for action, explicitly based upon general community perspectives and placing an appropriate emphasis upon all four instruments of policy.

241. The necessity for this position in military strength is cogently stated by Morgenstern and Brodie, supra note 237.

242. Morgenstern, supra note 230.

merit, which breed psychopathic personalities, with predispositions to violence. *Wealth* processes could be expanded, by appropriate assistance to particular communities and a rational division of labor, to take advantage of a developing technology in the production of the goods and services necessary to maintain continually rising standards of living and to provide employment on respected jobs. The process for maintaining *well-being,* especially health and physical integrity, could be guided toward standards facilitating the fullest and freest participation in all value processes; full use might be made of contemporary knowledge about how patterns in child rearing affect personality. Effective programs, training and other, might be devised and afforded for the encouragement and protection of the *skills* necessary to maintain and operate value processes compatible with human dignity in the contemporary world. Processes for the cultivation of *rectitude* can be directed toward a consensus, tolerant of many different modes of derivation in religion and secular philosophy in conceptions of right and wrong, which creates a sense of common responsibility and sustains institutions appropriate to human dignity values. Freedom for private association and intimate human relations can be provided which will foster the widening identifications of peoples and promote the larger *loyalties* necessary to a comprehensive and effective world public order.[243]

The only note of reassurance upon which it is possible for us to conclude is, thus, that today, perhaps for the first time, it is within the means of man to establish the necessary conditions of minimum public order on a global scale. The means today available include both the fantastic potentialities of a continuously developing technology for both communication and collaboration and the new scientific knowledge about the various factors which importantly condition "the wellsprings of individual human behavior." [244] How much even these ample means will be augmented by increasing access to the resources of outer space is still beyond the reach of plausible fantasy. In such a context, it is conceivable that even the present

243. Lasswell, "World Loyalty" in Wright (ed.) *The World Community* (1948) outlines a program for promoting more comprehensive loyalties.

244. The quoted words are attributed to Dr. Leonard Carmichael by Stanford Research Institute, *United States Foreign Policy* (A Study [No. 2] Prepared at the Request of the Committee on Foreign Relations, U. S. Senate, 86th Cong., 1st Sess., Sept., 1959).

apparently insuperable difficulties in securing and policing disarmament could be made to yield to a comprehensive, systematic, and unceasing effort by the proponents of human dignity credibly to communicate to the peoples of the world that they are in fact genuinely committed to, and possess the capability of, making all the benefits of modern civilization available to all mankind. The appropriate emphasis upon both alternatives and possibilities is perhaps that of Herman Kahn, of the Rand Corporation:

> The tools actually or potentially available to the analyst, planner, and decision-maker, both organizational and technical, are many times better than anything we have had before. It is just barely possible that with determined efforts by large numbers of responsible people we can achieve enough to make a significant difference.[245]

245. Kahn, *The Nature and Feasibility of War and Deterrence* 46 (1960). The same conclusion is more comprehensively documented in Kahn, *On Thermonuclear War* (1960). The volume by Arens and Lasswell, *In Defense of Public Order: The Emerging Field of Sanction Law* (1961) offers a comprehensive conception of sanctioning process, with focus primarily upon the internal public order of states.

5. PARTICIPATION AND NONPARTICIPATION IN COERCION: NEUTRALITY IN CONTEXT

INTRODUCTION

The fundamental policy issues at stake in the law of neutrality are enshrouded in the modern literature in an unusually rich profusion of terms of shifting and ill-defined reference: "nonbelligerency," "status of nonparticipation," "absolute neutrality," "differential neutrality," "qualified neutrality," "benevolent neutrality," "permanent neutrality," and so on. In some instances, the principal reference of these and other similar terms appears to be to the physical activities of belligerents and third states in processes of coercion; in others, to the claims to the invocation and application of authority made by the belligerents and third parties against each other and to the varied supporting justifications in legal technicality; and in still other instances, to certain responses of authoritative decision-makers in the past. With respect to the problem of regulating participation in coercion, as with respect to other problems of the law of war, it is thus necessary for both clarity in thought and rationality in policy intellectually to keep distinct the differing processes of factual interaction, of claim, and of authoritative decision.

The Interactions of Belligerents and Nonparticipants

What we speak of as a process of interaction between belligerents and third parties, that is, between those who participate and those who do not participate in exercises of intense coercion and violence, may be regarded as an aspect of the more general processes of international coercion.[1] Here, we seek to identify and very briefly to

1. It will be noted that we employ the concept of "participation" with reference also to the sanctioning processes and distinguish between participation

consider some of the factors in processes of coercion which peculiarly bear upon problems relating to participation and nonparticipation in such coercion and which may rationally affect policy about these problems. We proceed, once again, phase by phase.

The *participants* in a given process of coercion may or may not include the organized community itself or particular nation-states acting under an authorization and on behalf of the organized community of states. The organized community, in other words, may or may not have reached a characterization of the coercion in terms of its permissibility. Each contingency entails various possible implications in determining the more detailed commitments of individual states, as members of a general security organization, respecting participation in the enforcement or restoration of basic order.[2] The participants, again, may include a revolutionary group—which may or may not be principally of indigenous origin and direction—seeking to capture control of the state apparatus. Where the rebel group is determined to be primarily and substantially a genuinely internal community movement, certain policies and prescriptions relating to intervention and participation of external elites on one or the other side, not necessarily identical with those applicable in conflicts between other types of participants, become relevant.[3]

The conflict *situations* within the context of which the relations between belligerents and nonparticipants take place, may be characterized most broadly in terms of the dimensions of the conflict. In its geographic extension, the conflict may range from a world war in which the great majority of the states of the world are belligerents, to a local, bilateral application of violence in which the rest of the

---

in making basic characterization and implementing decisions, and participation in the detailed activities of enforcement. The context of particular uses of "participation" should make our intended reference in such uses clear.

2. Some of these implications are explored infra, pp. 410–18.

3. Some indication of the kinds of legal policy issues that relate to the determination of the genuineness of an alleged internal movement, and to the international regulation of a genuinely internal conflict, is offered supra, Ch. 1, note 164. See also Wright, "International Law and Civil Strife," 53 *Proc. Am. Soc. I. L.* 145 (1959); Falk, "The United States and the Doctrine of Nonintervention in the Internal Affairs of Independent States," 5 *How. L. J.* 163 (1959); Wright, "Recognition, Intervention and Ideologies," 7 *Indian Yb. of Int. Affairs* 89 (1958); Wright, "The Legality of Intervention Under the United Nations Charter," 51 *Proc. Am. Soc. I. L.* 70 (1957).

world are nonparticipants. The kinds of specific claims and counterclaims that are asserted and tolerated by belligerents and nonparticipants respectively, may be expected to differ as the particular conflict approaches one or the other extreme. The total or limited character of the conflict—understood in terms of the comprehensiveness of the objectives sought, and the importance assigned to these objectives, by each of the contending belligerents, as well as the level of destruction being inflicted by each upon the other belligerent—likewise deeply affects the relationships of belligerents and nonparticipants. Belligerents, for instance, engaged in a conflict which approaches total proportions and in which they conceive their very existence as separate political communities to be at stake, have not, historically, exhibited punctilious regard and great sympathy for claims of nonparticipant states to continue or expand a lucrative prewar commerce with the opposing belligerents.[4] The relevant situations may also manifest varying degrees of confrontation between particular belligerents and particular nonparticipants. The reference intended here embraces not only the relative geographic location of a belligerent vis-à-vis a nonparticipant but also the nature, intensity, and frequency of their prewar interaction, commercial and otherwise. The kinds of claims about the specific belligerent-nonparticipant relationships that may be expected to be made by and against a nonparticipant physically contiguous to either or both belligerents, or who has long had substantial and important economic relations, ideological affiliations, and cultural and social ties with one or the other belligerent, would of course differ from claims that may be asserted by and against a country geographically remote from the locale of conflict and with but negligible intercourse with both belligerents. Where there is only a nominal degree of confrontation

4. With respect to neutral claims about wartime commerce, Professor Jessup has trenchantly observed: "If the neutrals had in reality been content to continue their normal peacetime trade, many of the conflicts with the belligerents would not have taken place and the law of neutrality might have been shaped quite differently." *Today and Tomorrow* 23 [Neutrality: Its History, Economics and Laws, Vol. IV, 1936]. "[Neutrals] have sought to grasp the momentary inflated profits of the war boom, unwilling to hold themselves down to a normal economic life even in so far as normality is possible under such circumstances. Their complaints, their quarrels with the belligerents and their frequently resulting involvement in the war, have resulted from their insistence upon entering the economic conflict." Id., p. 34.

—Pakistan, for instance, with respect to a war between Guatemala and Costa Rica—there may realistically be no occasion for many of the claims relating to specific relationships, as distinguished from claims relating to assumption of responsibility for maintaining public order, to be made.

Belligerents and nonparticipants may differ in many varying degrees in the number and weight of the *bases of power* available to each. It has been frequently observed that as a matter of history the relative strength of belligerents and nonparticipants in a given conflict has exercised an important conditioning effect upon the probabilities of success in avoiding participation in such conflict. The capacity of a nonparticipant to convince a belligerent that the costs of disregarding claims to avoid involvement would offset the expected strategic or tactical advantage, has commonly had direct bearing upon the prospects of belligerent deference to such claims.[5] At times, what was important was the capability and determination of the nonparticipant to resist an act of violence with violence and thereby to constitute itself a significant factor in the military calculations of the belligerent exerting pressure. At other times, the ability to withhold or destroy scarce resources or services useful for the waging of war was decisive. The dependence of one or both belligerents upon scarce and vital commodities or communication links controlled by a nonparticipant has been an important aspect of the latter's power.[6] In the Second World War, for instance, the uninterrupted flow of Swedish iron ore and steel products was worth more to Nazi Germany than the possible advantages that she might have secured in a costly attack against Sweden during which the iron mines could easily have been wrecked.[7] Common expectations about

5. See e.g. Morgenthau, "The Problem of Neutrality," 7 *U. Kan. City L. Rev.* 109 (1939); id., "The Resurrection of Neutrality in Europe, 33 *Am. Pol. Sci. Rev.* 473 (1939); Warren, "What Are the Rights of Neutrals Now, in Practice?" 27 *Proc. Am. Soc. I. L.* 128 (1933); Preuss, "The Concepts of Neutrality and Nonbelligerency," 218 *Annals* 97 (1941); Friedmann, "International Law and the Present War," 3 *Modern L. Rev.* 177 (1940).

6. These points are developed in a recent excellent study: Fox, *The Power of Small States* (1959). See, in particular, Mrs. Fox's last chapter for a notable listing of factors affecting the probable success of small neutrals in absorbing and resisting the pressures of powerful belligerents.

7. Fox, op. cit., supra note 6 at 5–6. Switzerland was in an analogous situation: "If invaded, the Swiss could have destroyed the tunnels and passes in

relative strength, it has also been recognized, influenced the location of the moving line of compromise and equilibrium between the characteristic demands and counterdemands of participants and nonparticipants and, through time, affected those patterns of reciprocal claims and tolerances widely known as the rights and duties of belligerents and neutrals. A recent historian of the law of neutrality has indeed suggested, in pertinent summary of historical experience, that relative strength was the determinative factor in the shaping of these patterns:

> The outcome of the struggle to establish such a modus vivendi [between belligerents and neutrals] has at all times been entirely dependent upon the economic and military strength, the strategic position and the perspicacity and persistence of the two sides. In short, the rules of neutrality are products of two forces pulling in opposite directions, the final result being determined by the relative bargaining power of the parties.[8]

It may be added that the same expectations about the distribution of power bases between nonparticipants and the organized community of states on the one hand, and the belligerents (more particularly, the belligerent authoritatively identified as having breached basic order) on the other, also affect the making of claims relating to responsibility for redressing such breach.

The *strategies*—the instrumentalities and techniques of coercion—that the opposing belligerents employ against each other may pose particular problems and special dangers for nonparticipants. Most obvious and dramatic are the dangers and problems arising from the belligerent use of weapons whose physical effects are not always confined to the territorial domain of the target belligerent. Among these weapons are nuclear and thermonuclear explosives and chemical and bacteriological agents. The detonation of nuclear and thermonuclear explosives produces, under certain conditions and along with other effects, residual radiation consisting partly in the radioactivity induced in certain elements of soil and sea by the capture of neutrons and partly in the fallout or subsidence of radioactive particles from

---

the Alps so useful to Germany's communication with its Italian partner." Ibid., p. 5.

8. Orvik, *The Decline of Neutrality 1914–1941*, 13 (1953).

the column or cloud formed in the explosion.[9] Scientists distinguish between, on the one hand, "local" fallout or nuclear bomb debris consisting chiefly of larger particles which descend to earth "in a matter of hours" and travel downwind "not more than a few hundred miles" from the center of the burst and, on the other hand, "world-wide" fallout of very fine residues that remain suspended in the atmosphere, are carried over vast distances and slowly deposited on the earth's surface.[10] People in nonparticipant states, whether contiguous to or remote from the nuclear target areas, would hence be exposed to the somatic and genetic effects of basic-energy weapons. Comparable problems may conceivably arise for nonparticipant states adjoining either or both belligerents from the use of biological and chemical weapons the techniques for the dissemination of which remain sensitive to atmospheric conditions. Distribution techniques for biologicals include, it has been reported, the use of "aerosol sprays" which "have covered very large areas," and reduction to "very fine powders" which, like pollen, "can be distributed over great distances."[11] Where live micro-organisms and viruses of artificially intensified virulence are used, the spread of infection through unsuspecting human carriers or through infected crop exports may be very difficult to cope with, even with quarantine controls at neutral borders and ports and may possibly require the closing of such borders to both cargo and human transit. Scientists have also begun

9. *The Effect of Nuclear Weapons* 408 (Glasstone, ed., 1957).

10. Ibid., 446–9. See, of the voluminous literature on fallout and, generally, on the somatic and genetic effects of nuclear explosives: *Biological and Environmental Effects of Nuclear War,* Hearings before the Special Subcommittee on Radiation of the Joint Committee on Atomic Energy, 86th Cong., 1st Sess., June 22–26, 1959; *Fallout From Nuclear Weapons Tests,* Hearings before the Special Subcommittee on Radiation of the Joint Committee on Atomic Energy, 86th Cong., 1st Sess., May 5–8, 1959. For both of these Hearings, there is a convenient Summary-Analysis. See also Lapp, "Local Fallout Radioactivity," 15 *Bull. Atomic Scientists* 181 (1959).

11. Chisholm, "Biological Warfare: Demand for Answers," 15 *Bull. Atomic Scientists* 209, 209–10 (1959). See also the Statement on Biological and Chemical Warfare of the fifth International Conference of Scientists at Pugwash, text in 15 id. 337 (1959). Cf. Washington Center of Foreign Policy Research, *Developments in Military Technology and Their Impact on United States Strategy and Foreign Policy* 71–2 (A Study [No. 8] prepared at the request of the Committee on Foreign Relations, U. S. Senate, 86th Cong., 1st Sess., Dec. 6, 1959). Chemical and biological warfare is discussed infra, Ch. 6.

to talk about the possibilities of developing and using techniques of weather modification and climate control as weapons.[12] The problems that such uses may present to nonparticipants are still but barely imaginable. Nonetheless, there seems little reason to suppose they will be less real and difficult than those now discernible in nuclear and biological warfare.

Somewhat more prosaic are the problems that employment of economic warfare methods, developed to a high degree of refinement in the last two world wars, have raised for nonparticipating states. Economic warfare, as will be developed below,[13] though ultimately directed against the enemy belligerent, is frequently immediately directed against nonparticipating states constituting, as they do, the only external sources of supply upon which the enemy belligerent can draw.

The *conditions* that constitute the larger context within which processes of international coercion take place also compose the framework and background of processes of interaction between belligerents and nonparticipants. Certain of these conditions warrant particular, if abbreviated, mention for their probable influence upon prospects of noninvolvement in given conflicts, and upon the kinds of claims likely to be asserted therein.

The first of these conditions refers to the contemporary contention between the principal demanded systems of world order, concretised in the continuing conflict between the United States and the Soviet Union. Considered most comprehensively, the relevant reference is to the entire structure and configuration of the arena of international politics. As we have more than once observed, among the most ob-

12. *Developments in Military Technology,* supra note 11, p. 76: "Further in the future [i.e. post-1970's] appear such achievements as that of effective climate control, which the late John von Neumann prophesied with some justice may make all our present difficulties seem simple. Such a technique, it has been said with authority, might allow one adversary to put great and effective pressure on another without invasion of the opponent's territory by men or weapons." See also Stanford Research Institute, *Possible Nonmilitary Scientific Developments and Their Potential Impact on Foreign Policy Problems of the United States,* 20–3 (A Study [No. 2] prepared at the request of the Committee on Foreign Relations, U. S. Senate, 86th Cong., 1st Sess., Sept. 1959); and Anderson, "Toward Greater [Weather] Control: High Risks, High Stakes," in *Science and Resources: Prospects and Implications of Technological Advance* 54 (Jarrett, ed., 1959).

13. Infra, p. 477.

vious characteristics of the international arena in the first decade or so after the Second World War was the trend toward the polarization of power around two major poles. In a world where this trend reached completion, in a world of absolute and rigid bipolarity, the prospects of noninvolvement, in case of a major collision between the centers of power, would seem insubstantial indeed. In more recent years, however, as the Soviet Union achieved parity and stalemate in nuclear and thermonuclear capability, the polarizing trend appears to have decelerated in some degree. Unstable combinations of "uncommitted" countries, composed largely of newly independent, economically underdeveloped communities, have emerged, resisting the attraction of and definitive alignment with one or the other pole. Within the Western, as within the Soviet, grouping, some states have tended to move toward the periphery of their respective systems.[14]

We briefly recapitulate these features of the contemporary world arena to recall and highlight one lesson from the history of Western Europe in the eighteenth and nineteenth centuries to which political scientists and historians have frequently pointed as relevant. The lesson, partly obscured by the relative peace and quiet of the nineteenth century after the Napoleonic wars, is that realistic expectations of avoiding involvement in an armed conflict, particularly with respect to the smaller powers, were, in important measure, related to the degree of pluralism exhibited in the prevailing patterns of power and dependent upon the continued operation of power-balancing processes.[15] The protection which small states derived from their position between particular great powers or combinations of

14. See supra, pp. 21–3. Further, see Center for International Affairs (Harvard University), *Ideology and Foreign Affairs,* passim and more particularly pp. 61–5 (A Study [No. 10] prepared at the request of the Committee on Foreign Relations, U. S. Senate, Jan. 17, 1960). Accounts of perspectives and conditions in particular countries and regions include: Thomson, "Burmese Neutralism," 72 *Pol. Sci. Q.* 261 (1957); Zartman, "Neutralism and Neutrality in Scandinavia," 7 *Western Pol. Q.* 125 (1954); Stevens, "Arab Neutralism and Bandung," 11 *Middle East J.* 139 (1957).

15. The lesson is conveyed in, e.g., Wright, "The Present Status of Neutrality," 34 *A.J.I.L.* 391 (1940); Morgenthau, "The Problem of Neutrality," 7 *U. Kan. City L. Rev.* 109 (1939); Schwarzenberger, "The 'Aid Britain' Bill and the Law of Neutrality," 27 *Tr. Grotius Soc.* 1 (1941); Graham, "Great Powers and Small States," in *Peace, Security and the United Nations* (Morgenthau, ed., 1946). More recently, the same lesson has been stressed by Hägglöf, "A Test of Neutrality: Sweden in the Second World War," 36 *International Aff.* 153 (1960).

great powers depended upon the maintenance of a common interest among the great powers both to refrain from interfering with and incorporating the small states and to prevent such interference or incorporation by the opposing power or combination.[16] To put the point most broadly, the probabilities of noninvolvement in a given conflict appear to be a function of, among other factors, the general configuration of the arena and of the maintenance of a relative equilibrium of power between the belligerents *inter se,* as well as between the belligerents and nonparticipants.

Another contextual condition that should be noted relates to the character and requirements of the contemporary technology of violence. The waging of modern war commonly requires the utilization and expenditure of vast amounts of resources, skills, and capital. In past wars, particularly those of major proportions and prolonged duration, belligerents have sought to augment their own resources by obtaining access to the resource base and industrial capacity of neutral states and at the same time to deny such access to the enemy. Thus, the control of and interference with neutral commerce have commonly formed an important part of a belligerent's war effort and accounted for the bulk of the controversies between belligerents and neutrals with which the law of neutrality has been concerned. The advent of strategic nuclear air and missile power has generated some discussion about its probable effects upon the wartime military significance of both possession of and access to industrial capacity and resources. In a war between nuclear powers where strategic bombardment with multimegaton explosives is resorted to at the very outset of hostilities, the military forces and products in being may be expected to take on overriding importance. Such a war, it has been frequently assumed in the Western world, may leave little effective opportunity to transform indigenous industrial potential into military power *in esse,* or *a fortiori* to tap the potential of a neutral.[17]

16. Wright, *Problems of Stability and Progress in International Relations* 252–5 (1954).

17. E.g., in its study on *Developments in Military Technology,* supra note 11, the Washington Center of Foreign Policy Research said, at p. 36: "The wartime military significance of the American asset in industrial potential has rapidly diminished, however, in recent years with the rise of strategic nuclear air power. No longer is there any assurance that this vast potential can be transformed into an arsenal for war after hostilities have begun. Then, if strategic air power is brought into action at the start of a war, the industrial contribution to the

Upon this assumption, it might be supposed that there would perhaps be lesser occasion for the belligerent-neutral controversies relating to economic warfare, made familiar by the last two world wars, to arise. Indeed, when considered against the consequences of such a holocaust for large portions of mankind, whatever controversies about specific belligerent-neutral relationships may conceivably arise would seem pale and trifling. The suggestion has also been made that with the continuation of present trends in military technology toward increased air and ground mobility and toward shrinkage of the size and weight of nuclear ammunition (i.e. "tactical" nuclear weapons), even limited or localized conflicts involving the polar powers may in the future be "nuclearized" and may be more rapidly initiated, fought, and terminated than, for instance, the Korean conflict.[18] Assuming the realism of such a projection, the probabilities of claims and counterclaims about economic warfare arising in these types of "limited, nuclear" wars may, it might again be supposed, logically tend to diminish should the compression of the time dimension of such wars through "nuclearization" be drastic enough. Emphasis might in such cases shift to other kinds of controversies: for instance, controversies about compensation for damages suffered by nonparticipants from the effects of nuclear weapons exploded in adjoining belligerent territory.

Assumptions such as these about the possible duration of future conflicts must, however, remain conjectural. It seems an especially relevant observation that postulations about the brevity of future nuclear wars do not appear to form part of recent published Soviet military doctrine. On the contrary, Soviet military theoreticians have in print stressed the view that future major wars, including nuclear wars, will "inevitably" be of substantial duration.[19] When

---

power equation must be measured in terms of its military product already in existence at the outset." See also Brodie, *Strategy in the Missile Age,* 402 (1959). Cf. the argument on the continuing importance of war potential in Knorr, *The War Potential of Nations* c. 1 (1956).

18. *Developments in Military Technology,* supra note 11 at 78, 84.

19. Col. Baz, "Soviet Military Science on the Character of Contemporary War," *The Military Herald,* No. 6, June 1958, translated and reproduced in Garthoff, *The Soviet Image of Future War,* Appendix A, p. 93 (1959) wrote: "[T]he armed forces of the two sides, and the scale of the arena of armed conflict under contemporary conditions, are so great that one could scarcely conclude a war in a short period. Even the appearance of atomic and hydrogen

this view is considered in conjunction with the equally heavy emphasis laid by the same theoreticians upon the economic aspect of military strategic planning and upon "an adequate economic base" for war,[20] it does not seem an unreasonable inference that Soviet strategists do not necessarily assume the obsolescence of economic warfare. Perhaps the only suggestion which can be made with some confidence, at any rate by those whose professional training does not lie in the field of military science, is that it is principally in so-called "conventional" wars, whether they be "limited" wars between great powers who reciprocally refrain from invoking their strategic nuclear capabilities or conflicts between nonnuclear powers, that the policies and prescriptions on the relations of belligerents and neutrals may be expected to be of continued relevance.[21]

A third condition of pervasive significance, for the making of claims between belligerents and nonparticipants as for the making of decisions about these claims, relates to the extent to which the internal economic and social value processes of states are subjected to public organization and management. Different states exhibit differing degrees of governmentalization. On the one hand, totalitarian public orders are, almost *per definitionem,* nearly completely governmentalized and regimented. On the other hand, it is scarcely revolutionary to observe that even in democratic communities, the area of the governmental sector in the economy and in social welfare activity—the measure of state planning, participation, control, and supervision—has expanded substantially since the last century.[22] The impact of the high common level of governmentalization in internal social and economic organization, in nonparticipant as in belligerent states, upon the realism and continued viability of certain prescriptions of the law of neutrality will be considered in later pages.[23]

---

weapons, and IRBM's and ICBM's, cannot secure the swift destruction of such massive armed forces, and consequently not the conclusion of the war. Moreover, the use of those weapons by both sides will more likely lead to extending the duration of the war than to speeding it. Hence, while in the past major wars could be short or long, in our time all major wars inevitably assume a rather drawn-out character." See also Dinerstein, *War and the Soviet Union,* c. 7 (1959).

20. See Garthoff, supra note 19 at c. 2.

21. Cf. Tucker, *The Law of War and Neutrality at Sea* 218 note 50 (1957).

22. See supra, Ch. 1, notes 71–2 and accompanying text.

23. Infra, p. 438 ff.

The Complex of Claims about Participation and Nonparticipation

The making of assertions and counterassertions about the requirements and permissions of authoritative community policy occurs in every phase of the course of interaction between belligerents and nonparticipants. The persons who take part in this process of claim include, most prominently, the officials and representatives of the belligerent and nonparticipating states and those of international security organizations. The representatives of nongovernmental associations as well as private individuals may also, for important if limited purposes, sometimes assume the role of claimants. Thus, asserting that they bear the nationality of nonparticipant states, they have in many cases contested, before the prize courts of a belligerent or an international tribunal or claims commission, the lawfulness of some belligerent seizure or interference with property claimed by them.[24] In making their claims, the differing categories of claimants of course seek to invoke and obtain the application of community perspectives of authority for securing their respective value demands. Most briefly put, these demands refer, in the case of belligerent claimants, to all the objectives for the realization of which they have engaged in war; in the case of nonparticipant claimants, to the avoidance of the consequences of the coercive policies that the contending belligerents reciprocally prosecute; and in the case of the organized community, the restoration and maintenance of minimum public order.

The most salient types of claims which are made and which, when juxtaposed with the appropriate contrapuntal assertion, compose the principal problems of the law of neutrality, may be conveniently grouped under two broad headings. The first heading comprehends claims relating to the assumption of responsibility for the restoration and maintenance of basic public order; the second comprises claims about specific belligerent-nonparticipant relationships during processes of coercion.

The principal affirmative assertions subsumed in the first group may be generalized in terms of a claim that third states—i.e., states

24. Stone, *Legal Controls of International Conflict,* 534 (rev. ed., 1959). On the *locus standi* of an enemy alien before a prize court, see id. 534–5 and Colombos, *A Treatise on the Law of Prize* 349–55 (3rd ed., 1949).

other than the initiator and target—are required or authorized to assume responsibility for the maintenance and restoration of minimum public order. Assumption and discharge of responsibility here means discrimination in favor of and the giving of assistance to the belligerent authoritatively determined to be acting in lawful defense, by a variety of measures which may embrace active military participation in collective enforcement action as well as more passive economic and other nonmilitary aid. The major countervailing claims commonly take the form of a negative assertion that third states are not required and may lawfully refuse to assume such responsibility or to make such discrimination, and that they may adopt the same posture of impartiality and indifference vis-à-vis both belligerents which was writ so large in the nineteenth-century law of neutrality. The problem may be viewed, in its more fundamental aspects, as one of determining the authoritatively required specific content of commitments respecting the implementation of basic order which comprise a collective security system.

The second broad grouping covers the claims made in the course of interaction between one or the other belligerent and third states which, whatever may be regarded as the extent of permissible nonparticipation in a particular set of events, in fact take part in the process of coercion only in limited degree and refrain from taking direct part in the waging of hostilities. For convenience in the presentation and analysis that will be attempted in succeeding sections, these specific claims may be organized under three subheadings: (a) claims by belligerents against nonparticipants; (b) claims by nonparticipants against belligerents, and (c) claims by a belligerent to regulate or stop the economic intercourse of nonparticipants with the opposing belligerent. In preliminary general characterization, the most important claims which belligerents have customarily asserted against nonparticipants are that the latter abstain from rendering direct aid to enemy belligerents and that they prevent the utilization of their territory or resource bases by enemy belligerents. The responding assertions made by the nonparticipants against belligerents not only counter the specific claims of belligerents but also include a demand that the latter observe the requirements of minimum public order vis-à-vis the former and refrain from interfering with neutral territory, resources, and nationals. As a matter of logic in classification, the third subcategory of claims would of course be comprehended in the first. Claims to impose economic isolation upon the enemy by the employment of differing control techniques have, however, been of so considerable importance in previous conflicts as to warrant separate treatment.

It should be obvious from the previous references to phases of belligerent-nonparticipant interaction that all the factors and elements which at once comprise and shape the course of such interaction, also act upon and condition the making of claims about participation and nonparticipation. Particular mention may, however, be usefully made of certain other conditions directly bearing upon this process of claim and counterclaim.

The first of these conditions refers to the fundamental change in the authoritative myth of the general community of states signaled by the emergence of the contemporary prescriptions prohibiting resort to international coercion and violence. Belligerent claims for abstention and impartiality on the part of nonparticipants and the whole structure of doctrine and rule of the nineteenth-century law of neutrality depended, for their fundamental premise, upon the conception of war as a "prerogative right" of sovereign states.[25] In that conception, it may be recalled, recourse to violence was no more than a manifestation of an essential attribute of "sovereign statehood," a disposition of state power in the exercise of a discretionary faculty with respect to the lawfulness of which community authority had nothing to say. Third states were regarded as incompetent to pass upon the legitimacy of either belligerent's cause and from this incompetency was thought to follow a legal obligation of impartiality and nondiscrimination in their relations with the contending belligerents.[26] These traditional doctrines about war and neutrality were, we have previously observed,[27] the formal expressions of the operations of the "classical" balancing of power and of great-power supremacy.

25. See supra, Ch. 3; see also Lauterpacht, "Neutrality and Collective Security," 2 *Politica* 133, 146 (1936); 2 Oppenheim, *International Law* 639, 664 (7th ed., Lauterpacht, 1952); 7 Hackworth, *Digest of International Law* 670–1 (1943); Fenwick, *International Law* 611 (3rd ed., 1948).

26. The relation between the conception of "absolute neutrality" and that of an "unrestricted right of war" is stressed in e.g. Komarnicki, "The Place of Neutrality in the Modern System of International Law," 80 *Hague Recueil* 399, 411–12 (1952) and in Politis, *Neutrality and Peace* 83–4 (1936). Professor Stone also suggested that the conception of neutrality was "not unconnected with the acceptance of the view that the binding force of international law derives only from the consent of states." Op. cit. supra note 24 at 380.

27. Supra, pp. 391–2.

The establishment, at least in authoritative prescription, of a principle of minimum order thus marks a revolutionary modification in perspectives of authority. Contemporary international law does seek to regulate recourse to coercion and violence and does distinguish between lawful and unlawful recourse. The outbreak of international coercion and violence is regarded as a matter of legitimate and most basic concern to the rest of the general community of states. With erosion of the policy basis of the traditional doctrines of neutrality,[28] a different conception about the appropriate posture of third states emerged, and other claims than for abstention and nondiscrimination—that is, claims for participation and differential treatment—began to be asserted.

The second condition, closely related to the first, refers to the organization of international security through which the minimum order principle is sought to be implemented and administered. In some of its more important aspects, the problem of legal regulation of resort to international violence may be viewed as essentially a question of the relations of third states to those engaged in the application of violence. The practical significance of the principle of minimum order and the distinction it imports between lawful and unlawful coercion may be expressed in terms of the variable positions that become incumbent upon or permissible to all other states in consequence of an invocation and application of that principle and distinction.[29] So long as an unregulated competence to make war was recognized, an unlimited right to refrain from participation

28. Judge Lauterpacht spoke of this policy basis as the "principal explanation and justification" of the law of neutrality "conceived as an attitude of absolute impartiality," and characterized the establishment of the distinction between permissible and nonpermissible resort to coercion as having "reestablished the historic foundation of qualified—discriminatory and discriminating—neutrality." Lauterpacht, "The Rules of War in an Unlawful War," in *Law and Politics in the World Community* 110 (Lipsky, ed., 1953). See also Dehn, "The Effect of the United Nations Charter on the Development of International Law with Special Reference to the Status of Neutrality and the Hague and Geneva Conventions," in 41st *Report of the International Law Association* 39, 42 (1946).

29. Hogan, *International Violence and Third States since the World War* (1941). Cf. Lauterpacht, "The Grotian Tradition in International Law," 23 *Brit. Y.B.I.L.* 1, 39 (1946): "It is theoretically possible for international law to declare that some wars are illegal and criminal and yet to lay down that the neutral states not involved in the war must act with absolute detachment in relation both to the aggressor and to his victim. The legal consistency of such

and to adopt a posture of impartiality was likewise acknowledged in third states. In contrast, organized collective security is in substance a pattern of commitments to participate in collective action directed against the belligerent authoritatively determined to have unlawfully resorted to violence; it is, put a little differently, an organization of common responsibility for the securing of minimum order. Implicit in this system are the principles of community concern and of discrimination and differential treatment [30] which are, of course, the antitheses of the principles of abstention and impartiality regarded as basic in the traditional law of neutrality. Considered as general formulations of policy, collective security and neutrality are, Judge Lauterpacht wrote, "mutually exclusive" and "inherently antagonistic and antinomous." [31] It is within the framework of the organization of collective security that claims *not* to be

a system of international law would be questionable; its ethical impropriety would be obvious."

30. The principle of community concern was given broad and vigorous formulation by Professor Wright in "The Lend-Lease Bill and International Law," 35 *A.J.I.L.* 305, 313 (1941): "A community of nations, however, cannot exist unless each of the members recognizes that it has a concern in the observance of the common law by all the others. Impartial treatment of the law observer and the law violator is a repudiation of such concern. Therefore, impartiality, in the presence of hostilities undertaken in violation of international obligation, is a denial of the existence of a community of nations and a repudiation of international law." See also Politis, *Neutrality and Peace* 3 (1936). Comparable perspectives had been expressed much earlier by Westlake and Lorimer. 2 Westlake, *International Law* 161–2 (1907): "There is no general duty of maintaining the condition of neutrality. On the contrary, the general duty of every member of a society is to promote justice within it, and peace only on the footing of justice, such being the peace which alone is of much value or likely to be durable. . . . [N]eutrality is not morally justifiable unless intervention in the war is unlikely to promote justice or could do so only at a ruinous cost to the neutral." 2 Lorimer, *The Institutes of the Law of Nations* 129 (1884): "An attitude of indifference between rational entities, whether individual or corporate, bound together as they are by the links of reciprocal rights and duties, if it can be called a relation at all, is an anti-jural relation, and I neither share nor envy the opinion of those who would voluntarily purchase peace at such a price." The antithetical viewpoint was presented, in the language of advocacy, in Borchard and Lage, *Neutrality for the United States* (2d ed., 1940). These contrasting positions, it may be noted, have in their broad outlines recurred in more recent polemics about "neutralism."

31. "Neutrality and Collective Security," 2 *Politica* 133, 149 (1935). In "Neutrality and the Covenant of the League," in *Collective Security* 430 (Bourquin, ed., 1937), he described collective security as "nothing less than a system the

neutral—i.e. claims that participation is required or authorized—are asserted. Claims *to be* neutral—i.e. claims that nonparticipation is authorized or even required—are, on the other hand, to be expected where the pattern of commitments is incomplete, whether the incompleteness be in the number of states pledged or in the variety of situations in which the commitments are determined to be operative.[32] The precise impact of a particular organization of security upon both claims *not* to be and claims to be neutral in differing situations thus depends upon the scope of the specific commitments (and permissions) that comprise the collective security organization.

A third condition warranting particular mention bears connection with the second: the state of common expectations of claimants about the probable effectiveness of the existing organization of collective security. The relation of these expectations to the incidence of claims about assumption of responsibility for restoration of minimum order may be gleaned from almost any standard history of the League of Nations and of the United Nations. Unfavorable estimates of the effective ability of the organized community to maintain and implement basic order have tended to bring about increased assertion, at least among smaller powers, of claims to avoid participation. Expectations of a low and declining degree of effectiveness may activate a process of emasculatory interpretation by which the scope of specific commitments is increasingly reduced. It is of course irony that this contraction of commitments and assertion of claims to be neutral in turn tend to depress still further the common estimations of the probability of effective collective action and to accelerate disintegrative processes.

The Process of Decision with Respect to Participation and Nonparticipation

The process of authoritative decision with respect to participation and nonparticipation in coercion exhibits much the same features

members of which mutually agree not to be neutral in cases in which one of the members of the system is attacked by another through unlawful resort to force or war." See also Thompson, "Collective Security Re-examined," 47 *Am. Pol. Sci. Rev.* 753, 755 (1953).

32. McLaughlin, "Legislative Neutrality in the United States," 22 *Minn. L. Rev.* 603, 629–30 (1938).

as with respect to the other problems of the international law of coercion. The *decision-makers* established in community authority include, once more, officials and representatives of international security organizations, members of international arbitration tribunals and claims commissions which may be set up by agreement of the conflicting claimants, and the national officials of both the belligerent and nonparticipating states. The last mentioned category prominently includes judges of national courts sitting in prize,[33] the officials and agents of ministries or boards of economic warfare,[34] and, though today somewhat less conspicuously, naval officers on contraband and blockade patrol duty. It is sometimes suggested that in view of the elementary degree of effective centralization exhibited by the general community of states and of the pervasive influence of factors like relative strength and systemic conflict, there are really no objective decision-makers projected by the community for resolution of the problems of participation and nonparticipation in coercion. The requirement of an international law of human dignity, however, with respect to coercive as to noncoercive processes, is not so much for an "objective" or "disinterested" decision-maker, in the sense of one neutral or insensitive to values, as it is for a decision-maker who can be expected to clarify and implement inclusive, shared interests rather than exclusive, parochially defined demands.

The *objectives* which these authoritative decision-makers have

33. On prize courts generally, see Stone, *Legal Controls of International Conflict* 522–44 (Rev. ed., 1959) and Colombos, *A Treatise on the Law of Prize* cc. 1–2 (3rd ed., 1949).

On the Egyptian Prize Court at Alexandria, see generally Ahmed Safwat Bey, "The Egyptian Prize Court: Organization and Procedure," 5 *Revue Egyptienne de Droit International* 28 (1949). The Court was charged to "apply the rules of public international law and, in their absence . . . the principles of equity." *The Field,* Egyptian Prize Court, *Int. Law Rep. 1950,* Case No. 108, p. 345, 346.

Professor Stone, op. cit., 543–4, in discussing the question of what law [British] prize courts apply, evokes the staple controversies about the relation of municipal law and international law and appears to have aligned himself with the "dualists" against the "monists." An alternative conception is offered in McDougal, "The Impact of International Law Upon National Law: A Policy-Oriented Perspective," 4 *S.D.L. Rev.* 25 (1959).

34. Medlicott, *The Economic Blockade,* Vol. 1 (1952) and Vol. 2 (1959) promises to become the classical account of the organization, functioning, and activities of British, and later Anglo-American, economic warfare agencies in the last world war.

sought in passing upon controversies about participation include two sets of goals that, on one level of generality, may be seen to be the same as those sought in other contexts. The first and, it may be recalled, the more recent of these objectives is the achievement and maintenance of minimum public order among nations by attempting to establish and secure the assumption of that common responsibility indispensable for preventing disruptions of order and restoring order when disrupted. The second general and historically much older goal is the mitigating and minimizing of the destruction of values which inevitably attends the breakdown of minimum public order. This latter goal embraces at least two interrelated component policies. The first component, most commonly designated as humanitarianism and explicitly related to the requirements of human dignity, is a demand that the moral and physical integrity of peoples be respected, that they be treated with the least possible coercion and violence. The second component is a demand for restraint and economy in attack upon—as in the expenditure of—resources, in other words that resources be not wantonly and senselessly destroyed and that permanent impairment and exhaustion be avoided. In contexts of neutrality, these components of the objective of minimum destruction have traditionally been given more distinctive particular expression in equally interrelated policies designed to restrict the geographic dimensions of violence and to permit the maintenance in economic operation of the internal community processes of specific nonparticipating states. Decision-makers in applying the traditional law of neutrality sought to limit the extension of a conflict by requiring abstention and impartiality from third states, thereby permitting inequality between belligerents in indigenous power and in thoroughness of previous preparation to play a decisive role for the expeditious resolution of issues.

The *strategies* that community-established decision-makers employ in attempting to regulate participation and to realize the broad objectives outlined above consist, in most comprehensive reference, of all the functions and procedures for the projecting and implementing of authoritative policy with respect to claims about the avoidance and minimization of coercion.[35] We focus upon the procedures and functions of prescription and application.

35. A summary statement of these policy functions may be found in McDougal, supra note 33 at 40–2. Lasswell, *The Decision Process: Seven Categories*

Community policies about the incidence of responsibility for the securing of basic order have historically and appropriately been prescribed through the medium of multilateral conventions assuming the stature of constitutional documents of the world community.[36] It has been through the Covenant of the League of Nations and the Charter of the United Nations, which set forth systems of commitments of individual states both to refrain from unlawful coercion and to join in community responses to such coercion, that shared responsibility for basic order has been sought to be organized. We propose to consider in later pages some of the details of these attempts to organize common responsibility and collective security. The strategy of explicit agreement has also been employed in the prescription of policy about specific interactions of belligerents and nonparticipants. Unlike the Covenant and the Charter, however, the multilateral conventions about belligerent and neutral rights and duties—including, most prominently, Hague Conventions V and XIII, 1907,[37] and the Havana Convention of 1928[38]—for the most part merely collected and systematized in print the policies already prescribed through the much slower and less visible processes of customary law. It seems relevant to observe that because these policies about the particular relationships of belligerent and nonparticipant were crystallized in authoritative prescription long before the recent revival of the principle of minimum order and its incorporation into

---

of Functional Analysis (Bureau of Governmental Research, Univ. of Maryland, 1956) presents a more extended treatment.

36. The appropriateness of the medium of conventions relates not only to preferences for strategies of persuasion over strategies of coercion but also to the pluralistic structure of the world arena. Cf. what has been expressed as one of the "underlying assumptions" of the United Nations system for maintenance of peace and security: "(3) at the present stage of world political development, the organization of this common action must take the form of voluntary cooperation between governments, not of action dictated by a world government." Goodrich and Simons, *The United Nations and the Maintenance of International Peace and Security* 11 (1955).

37. The texts of Convention V, 1907, Respecting the Rights and Duties of Neutral Powers and Persons in Case of War on Land, and of Convention XIII, 1907, Concerning the Rights and Duties of Neutral Powers in Naval War, may be found in *The Hague Conventions and Declarations of 1899 and 1907*, 133, 209 (2nd ed., Scott, 1915) respectively.

38. Convention on Maritime Neutrality, adopted at Habana, Feb. 20, 1928; 4 Hudson, *International Legislation* 2401 (1931).

the corpus of international law, there arises the need for achieving accommodation of the former to the overriding requirements of the latter.

The application of legal policy to claims about involvement proceeds in contexts as diverse as the *fora* of international organizations, prize proceedings, and administrative determination in contraband control ports. With more particular respect to the sanctions which are invoked in processes of application, it may be observed that in the matter of securing common responsibility for basic order, neither the Covenant of the League of Nations nor the Charter of the United Nations provided any specialized technique or device for enforcing the commitments of members there projected. Indeed, in this problem perhaps more so than in any other problem, it must be evident that the sanction which sustains common responsibility is the sanction of recognized shared interest and that no special gadget in technical procedure or institutional organization can take the place of constant awareness of the security interdependences which, like it or not, bind the states of the world.

Turning to the specific relationships of belligerent and nonparticipant, it may be noted, firstly, that the activities and interferences of a belligerent in neutral territory may assume such scope and intensity as appropriately to be characterized as a breach of minimum order. By violating a neutral state, an aggressor-belligerent may compound its offense and commit a new and separate act of aggression.[39] In such situations, the permission of self-defense becomes available to the target neutral and the whole panoply of sanctioning measures contemplated in the United Nations Charter becomes relevant. On the other hand, where the aid and sustenance given by a third state to a belligerent authoritatively identified as a violator of basic order reaches such significant and potentially decisive proportions as to amount to substantial participation, the third state may be identified with the original violator-belligerent and itself treated as a new aggressor.[40] In either case, estimations of the relative strength of

39. Thus, the violations of the neutrality of Norway, Belgium, the Netherlands, and Luxembourg by Germany in the last world war were regarded by the Nuremberg Tribunal as distinguishable and separate acts of aggression; see supra, Ch. 3.

40. This was what the General Assembly did in Resolution No. 498(V), Feb. 1, 1951, U.N. Gen. Ass., *Off. Rec.*, Fifth Sess., Supp. No. 20A, p. 1 (1951), holding that the People's Republic of China had engaged in aggression in Korea.

belligerent and nonparticipant may be expected to affect the deterrent value of a threat of full-scale participation or involvement.

Belligerent interferences which do not reach the consequentiality of a breach of minimum order present no unique difficulty; the nonparticipant is authorized to apply in reprisal appropriate reciprocities and retaliations.[41] Similarly, the refusal of a nonparticipant to carry out the duties of abstention and prevention discussed below may authorize the injured belligerent to engage in proportionate counter-deprivation. In particular connection with neutral duties of prevention, it may be noted that the scope of the requirement imposed upon a nonparticipant of preventing belligerent operations within its territory has traditionally been defined with such qualifying terms as "due diligence," [42] "as the means at its disposal allow," [43] and "all the vigilance within [its] power." [44] Because of these restrictive definitions in conventional law,[45] the belligerent may not, it is some-

41. The nonparticipant may, for instance, deny to the offending belligerent what it may have previously permitted to both belligerents; sojourn in the neutral's ports for refueling and revictualing is the example commonly given. See, in this connection, Article 9 of Hague Convention XIII, 1907. Historical examples of neutral retaliation are collected in Harvard Research in International Law, "Rights and Duties of Neutral States in Naval and Aerial War," 33 *A.J.I.L.* Supp. 330–3 (1939). In its comment, the Harvard Research suggested a limitation on neutral reprisals, stating that such reprisals "must not be violation of any absolute neutral duty. Thus, the neutral State would not be entitled, even as a measure of reprisal against belligerent A to permit vessels of belligerent B to be outfitted in its ports, or itself to furnish arms and munitions to belligerent B. If the neutral State desires to go so far in its opposition to the conduct of belligerent A, it abandons its neutrality and becomes a participant in the war." The possibility of distinguishing the absolute from any other type of neutral duty would seem open to doubt. The lawfulness of the neutral act of reprisal would depend largely upon satisfaction of the requirements of necessity and proportionality; factual full-scale involvement is, at least in part, dependent upon the response of the original offending belligerent against whom reprisals are invoked.

42. Treaty of Washington between the United States and Great Britain, of May 8, 1871; text in 2 *A Collection of Neutrality Laws, Regulations and Treaties of Various Countries,* 1368 (Deak and Jessup, eds., 1939).

43. Hague Convention XIII, Article 25.

44. Havana Convention of 1928, Article 26.

45. In *The Cysne, Annual Digest 1929–1930,* Case No. 287, the German-Portuguese Mixed Arbitral Tribunal stressed that reprisals may be directed against neutrals only for violation of obligations incumbent upon them. The tribunal said (at 490):

times said, lawfully subject the nonparticipant to reprisals for its inability to restrain the opposing belligerent from engaging in prohibited utilization of neutral territory.[46] At the same time, however, publicists recognizing the serious disadvantage that the weakness of a neutral may impose upon one belligerent write that the "scope of the belligerent's duty to abstain from committing hostile acts against enemy forces within neutral waters [is] limited, in principle, by the effectiveness with which the neutral state can enforce its rights." [47]

Preferences in doctrinal justification may of course differ. But it should be evident that, in this specific context and in terms of impact upon policy, the distinction between permitting an invocation of "reprisals" and building into, as it were, the belligerent's duty a condition of neutral effectiveness is singularly insubstantial. Exactly the same net result is achieved by one and the other modality of justification. That result is that a belligerent is authorized in appropriate cases of necessity, created by either neutral unwillingness or incapacity to prevent hostile acts of the opposing belligerent, to protect its military interests by entering neutral territory and there

---

"There is no legal justification for reprisals except when they have been provoked by an act contrary to international law. This means that they are not admissible except against the State held guilty of the original violation of international law. It is conceivable that such legitimate reprisals may indirectly injure the subjects of the innocent neutral. . . . But in the present case, the reprisals were aimed directly and deliberately against neutral subjects. As Portugal had not violated, in relation to Germany, any rule of international law, acts of reprisals directed against her were contrary to international law."

The restrictive definitions of duty of course facilitated neutral allegations in specific cases that no duty had been breached. See infra note 47.

46. E.g. Harvard Research, supra note 41 at 419–20. The related question of the lawfulness of interbelligerent reprisals affecting neutral rights is realistically a question of the lawfulness of the techniques and practices of embargoing commerce with the enemy employed in the last two world wars. See infra, p. 477 ff.

47. E.g. Tucker, *The Law of War and Neutrality at Sea* 223–4 (1957). Professor Tucker presents this interpretation in the hope of resolving the "seeming incongruity" created by, on the one hand, the qualified nature of the neutral's duty of prevention and, on the other, by belligerent invocation of "reprisals" in responding to situations brought about by a weak neutral's inability to prevent violations of its neutrality by the opposing belligerent. "This characterization [of reprisals]," he writes, "is mistaken, since the neutral, in using the means at its disposal, has fulfilled its duty. But although the neutral state has not violated its duty, it is equally true that the belligerent, in taking hostile measures, has not violated the rights of the neutral." (at 223).

taking the measures necessary for countering such hostile operations.[48] In a word, the belligerent becomes authorized to convert neutral territory, at least temporarily, into a permissible area of operations.[49]

The process of decision with respect to the problems of participation is affected by all the contextual *conditions* that influence the course of factual interaction of belligerents and neutrals, as well as by the conditions that impinge upon the claims and counterclaims they respectively make. It may not be amiss, however, very briefly to reiterate some of the conditions that set the over-all limits of authoritative decision.

Perhaps the condition most fundamental for the legal regulation of participation is another factor in formal authority: the recent change in the structure of authoritative perspectives about permissible and impermissible coercion and the emergence of the minimum order principle.[50] The historical nexus between, on the one hand, the kinds of policies projected with respect to the initiation of coercion and violence and, on the other hand, the kinds of policies projected with respect to participation or nonparticipation by third states, was long ago brought into clear relief in the differing positions taken by Grotius and Bynkershoek. Grotius, having laid stress on a distinction between *bellum iustum* and *bellum iniustum,* could not

48. See 2 Oppenheim, *International Law* 678–80 (7th ed., Lauterpacht, 1952); Smith, *The Law and Custom of the Sea* 181 (3rd ed., 1959); 3 Hyde, *International Law* 2337–9, 2340–1 (2nd rev. ed., 1945); Colombos, *A Treatise on the Law of Prize* 277 (3rd ed., 1949).

49. Some illustration is provided by *The Anna Maria, Annual Digest 1946,* Case No. 174. The *Anna Maria* was an Italian vessel captured by Allied (Free French) forces in the Tunisian port of Sousse. In condemning the vessel and passing upon the question of whether capture could lawfully be effected in a port of Tunis, a "neutral protected state," the French *Conseil des Prises* said: "[T]he presence of German and Italian forces, and the series of warlike acts committed by them in the waters and on the territory of Tunis, had made these waters and that territory a theatre of operations where the right of capture could be exercised." To the same effect is *The Impero,* id., Case No. 173. See also *Coenca Brothers v. German State,* in Green, *International Law through the Cases,* 667 (1951) where the Greco-German Mixed Arbitral Tribunal held that the occupation of Salonika by the Allied Powers in World War I, when Greece was neutral, "entitled Germany to take even on Greek soil any acts of war necessary for her defense" (at 668).

50. Supra, p. 397.

speak of absolute impartiality, except where there was doubt on which side justice lay. He urged instead differential treatment upon the basis of that distinction:

> [I]t is the duty of those who keep out of war to do nothing whereby he who supports a wicked cause may be rendered more powerful, or whereby the movements of him who wages a just war may be hampered, according to what we have said above. In a doubtful matter, however, those at peace should show themselves impartial to either side in permitting transit, in furnishing supplies to troops, and in not assisting those under siege.[51]

In contrast, Bynkershoek, who had rejected the conception of *bellum iustum,* advised that

> In my judgment, the question of justice and injustice does not concern the neutral, and it is not his duty to sit in judgment between his friends who may be fighting each other, and to grant or deny anything to either belligerent through considerations of the relative degree of justice. If I am a neutral I may not lend aid to one to an extent that brings injury to the other.[52]

The translation of the new principle of minimum order into a community monopoly of coercion that is sustained by effective and continuing commitments of states in an appropriate sharing of authority is, as we have previously noted, made extraordinarily difficult by the condition of systemic conflict in an international arena still largely dominated by two great agglomerations of power. It is well to recall that the structure and content of inherited prescription themselves reflect the general features and conformation of the arena in which they emerged.[53] The traditional law of neutrality was

51. *De Jure Belli Ac Pacis,* Bk. III, Ch. 17, S.3, Classics of International Law, Vol. 2, p. 786 (Kelsey trans., 1925). The position of Vattel is less than clear. Although he had excluded the doctrine of *bellum iustum* from the "positive law of nations" (supra, Ch. 3), he nonetheless wrote: "It is lawful and praiseworthy to assist in every way a nation who is carrying on a just war; and such assistance even becomes a duty for every nation which can give it without injury to itself. But no assistance may be given to one who wages an unjust war." *The Law of Nations or The Principles of Natural Law,* Bk. III, Ch. 6, S.83, Classics of International Law, p. 262 (Fenwick trans., 1916).

52. *Quaestionum Juris Publici, Libri Duo,* Bk. I, Ch. 9, Classics of International Law, Vol. 2, p. 61 (Frank trans., 1930).

53. Jessup and Deak, *The Origins* 3–19 (Neutrality: Its History, Economics

formulated and developed in an arena characterized by a greater degree of pluralism in patterns of effective power than that observable today. Hague Conventions V and XIII of 1907 on the rights and duties of neutral powers in land and naval war codified the customs and practices of a period dominated by several great powers which roughly approximated each other in strength, and which, through the fluid and informal processes known as the "classical" or "traditional" balance of power, restrained each other from achieving hegemony and forcible unification of the arena. This body of prescriptions at the same time gave expression to the principal social, economic, and military conceptions and characteristics of that period. The received law of neutrality did not then escape the pervading impact of historical context any more than it can do so today.

THE POLICIES OF MINIMUM ORDER AND MINIMUM DESTRUCTION OF VALUES IN CONTEXTS OF NONPARTICIPATION

From such broad orientation in the processes of interaction, claim, and decision, it may now perhaps be possible to attempt in some detail the consideration and recommendation of appropriate policies for the resolution of the different controversies arising between states about nonparticipation. In a community which genuinely accepts the principle of minimum order, the most important task for authoritative policy is that of organizing an assumption of responsibility and a sharing of burdens adequate to achieve and preserve such order. Adequate organization of responsibility and rational distribution of burdens require that each particular controversy about the acceptance or rejection of participation and about specific belligerent–neutral relationships be constantly related to both basic policies, the maintenance of minimum order and the minimization of destruction of values. Both these fundamental general policies are at stake in each of the principal types of participation problems.

Policies Relating to Minimum Order

The policies which we conceive as most appropriately projected with respect to the problem of maintaining minimum order may be

---

and Law, Vol. 1 [1935]) offer a summary of the factors that historically affected the early development of the law of neutrality (i.e., up to the Peace of Westphalia).

conveniently considered in terms of two general situations. In the first situation, the organized community of states succeeds in characterizing particular coercion in terms of its lawfulness. The second situation is marked by the failure or absence of characterization by the organized community of the lawfulness of coercion.

SITUATIONS IN WHICH THE ORGANIZED COMMUNITY CHARACTERIZES THE LAWFULNESS OF COERCION

The characterization by the organized community to which we refer includes, in terms of technical procedure, not merely "binding" decision or determination by the Security Council of the United Nations under Article 39 of the Charter, but also a "recommendation" by either the Security Council or the General Assembly. In situations in which such characterization is achieved, the policy we recommend is, very generally put, that of the widest possible requirement and assumption of responsibility by the members of the organized community for restoring minimum order. In a community which projects democracy in patterns of value production and sharing, the principle of minimum order would seem most appropriately sustained by a principle of common responsibility. Common responsibility here means not only wide participation in the making of the basic characterization decision and of implementing determinations, but also wide willingness to place at the disposal of community-established sanctioners the bases of power that, in differing amounts and kinds, may be necessary in differing particular situations for effective enforcement.[53a] One purpose of a strategy of widening participation is of course to increase the probabilities that the necessary counterbalancing, and possibly preponderating, power will be marshaled and brought to bear against the belligerent disrupting public order (who frequently is stronger than the defending belligerent).[54]

53a. In its first report, the Collective Measures Committee established by the U. N. General Assembly wrote down among its "general conclusions": "6. The ability and readiness of States to contribute armed forces and other assistance and facilities in support of United Nations collective action are essential to an effective security system. 7. United Nations collective action, to be most effective, should be as nearly universal as possible. Contributions to and support of United Nations measures should come from the maximum number of States." U.N. Gen. Ass., *Off. Rec.*, 6th Sess., Supp. No. 13 (A/1891) p. 33 (1951).

54. Compare the emphasis laid upon ability to mobilize an overwhelming superiority of power vis-à-vis any potential violator as a postulated "objective

Every organization of collective security may itself be viewed as an institutional device both for assembling and organizing base values made available by members into an equilibrium and potential preponderance of power, and for distributing the burdens of securing basic order.

The requirements of the complementary fundamental policy of minimum destruction of values are perhaps best considered in connection with the suggestion sometimes made that securing the widest possible participation—a demand which seems implicit in any collective security system—means the conversion of every conflict into a world war. For instance, Dr. Liska wrote:

> [A]n apriori legal system may reject the use of force totally only to expand it into a total war by all when challenged.
>
> . . .
>
> Once aggression has been committed, however, collective security seems to be a perfect medium for spreading the conflict. The balance of power with the aid of neutrality is supposed to promote localization of strife; under collective security, the premise of the indivisibility of peace implies general mobilization of all members against the aggressors, making a limited war possible only against minor states.[55]

Taken literally, and carried to the logical extreme which it suggests, this contention would seem to deny the reasonableness (and hence the lawfulness) of the use of force for maintaining and restoring order in the international arena. We noted in the preceding

---

requirement" of "collective security" in Claude, *Swords into Plowshares: The Problems and Progress of International Organization* 264–7 (2nd ed., 1959).

55. Liska, *International Equilibrium* 79–80 (1957); see also Hula, "Fundamentals of Collective Security," 24 *Social Research* 1, 3 (1957). This view was also stressed by Professor Coppola, in his paper on "The Idea of Collective Security," in *Collective Security* 144, 146 (Bourquin, ed., 1936). Professor Coppola wrote, in seeking to demonstrate that "collective security" was "anti-historic," "anti-human," and "impossible": "a particular war would be transformed, always and necessarily, into a world war—a strange way of advancing the cause of peace." It need not be irrelevant that his paper was submitted for the *Centro Italiano di Alti Studi Internazionali*, a governmental institution, and that in 1936 the Italo-Ethiopian war was under consideration by the League of Nations.

chapter that some use of force has commonly been found necessary for the preserving of public order even in the more mature national societies.[56] The forcible subduing of outlaws by municipal police, as the hanging or imprisonment for murder, clearly increases the sum total of lives lost and other values destroyed at a given period of time; but few seriously suggest that municipal police forces should be disbanded or that punishment of some kind does not or cannot serve public order.

With more particular reference to the possibility of spreading conflict—a risk which may be realistically calculated and perhaps reduced by careful strategic planning and sensitive timing but which must ultimately be faced in any event—it is no part of the necessary expectations of a policy of wide participation that the total military capability of every member be mobilized for general and absolute war and automatically brandished and wielded in each and every case. Because, as indicated above, the problems of regulating participation in processes of coercion are integral with the more general problem of sanctions, the principles of sanctions strategies earlier outlined find direct application in these problems. The very practical dictates of these principles of strategy here happily reinforce and coincide with the more specific requirements of the general policy of minimum destruction of values. Thus, a major import of these principles taken together is that collective coercion for restoration of public order, like all sanctioning activities, is rationally to be tailored to the dimensions of the unlawful coercion and to the requirements of compelling, as quickly and economically as possible, the deceleration and termination of such unlawful coercion. The overriding principle of economy in coercion, in particular, demands that the quantum of collective responding coercion should not be grossly disproportionate to what is rendered necessary by the scope of the specific assault upon basic order that must be met.[57] There is, moreover, not just one but a whole spectrum of degrees of possible participation, from all-out assistance with armed force to many differing uses of the economic, ideological, and diplomatic instruments of policy.[58] As the United Nations Charter itself recognizes, it is hardly

56. Supra, Ch. 3.

57. Supra, Ch. 4.

58. Various degrees of participation lower in the scale than all-out military assistance have frequently been referred to by means of the term "nonbel-

practical to demand the same measure and form of participation from each member state.[59] The distribution, in other words, among the individual members of the burdens involved in the optimum effort necessary in a given case, may reasonably take into account differing capabilities and contemporaneous needs, as well as peculiar

---

ligerency." See e.g. Stone, *Legal Controls of International Conflict* 402–7 (Rev. ed., 1959); Greenspan, *The Modern Law of Land Warfare* 529–30 (1959) who also noted that Article 4(B)(2) of the 1949 Geneva Prisoners of War Convention requires "neutral or non-belligerent" powers to give prisoner of war treatment to certain persons; Wilson, " 'Non-belligerency' in Relation to the Terminology of Neutrality," 35 *A.J.I.L.* 121 (1941); Coudert, "Nonbelligerency in International Law," 29 *Va. L. Rev.* 143 (1942). Professors Kunz ("Neutrality and the European War 1939–1940," 39 *Mich. L. Rev.* 719, 747 [1941]), Briggs (*The Law of Nations* 1041 [2nd ed., 1952]), Bishop (*International Law* 684 [1953]), and Borchard ("War, Neutrality and Non-belligerency," 35 *A.J.I.L.* 618 [1941]) denied that "nonbelligerency" was a "legal status" and argued for maintenance of the categories "neutrality" and "belligerency." The disrepute into which the term "nonbelligerency" fell during World War II is partly attributable to the fact that it was principally invoked by states assisting the aggressor belligerent (i.e., Nazi Germany), e.g. Italy and Spain. The terms commonly used or proposed for referring to authorized participation in nonmilitary *sanctions* were "qualified neutrality," "differential neutrality," "benevolent neutrality" and so on. See, on this terminological morass, Komarnicki, "The Place of Neutrality in the Modern System of International Law," 80 *Hague Recueil* 399, 419–44 (1952). The legal policy problem—i.e. what degree of participation may be required or authorized—is not, of course, resolved by the use of one or any other term.

59. Infra p. 428. There was comparable recognition of this in the League of Nations. Resolution 9 of the Resolutions on the Economic Weapon adopted by the Assembly of the League on October 4, 1921 provided that:

> All States must be treated alike as regards the application of the measures of economic pressure, with the following reservations:
>
> (a) It may be necessary to recommend the execution of special measures by certain states;
>
> (b) If it is thought desirable to postpone, wholly or partially, in the case of certain States, the effective application of the economic sanctions laid down in Article 16, such postponement shall not be permitted except in so far as it is desirable for the success of the common plan of action, or reduces to a minimum the losses and embarrassments which may be entailed in the case of certain Members of the League by the application of the sanctions.

League of Nations, *Off. J.*, Spec. Supp. No. 6, at 25 (1921).

factors like physical proximity to one or the other, or both, belligerents.

Where a state is unable or unwilling to assume a share in the burdens of direct and affirmative participation, the posture most consistent with the implementation of basic order is, we submit, that of discrimination, in favor of the forces of the active sanctioners and against the offending belligerent, in other, more passive, ways. A policy of discrimination may, for instance, take the form of permitting the use of the territory of the third state as a base for operations against the offending belligerent or of allowing the transit of sanctioners' forces through such territory.[60] In its minimal requirements, the posture of discrimination means that the third state should not hamper the efforts of those applying sanctions and should simultaneously abstain from rendering any aid to the violator-belligerent. The latter requirement is particularly worthy of note for it constitutes the indispensable minimum demand which an organized community must make of its members and exemption from which cannot be envisaged without making nonsense of the fundamental principle of basic order. The further point must also be made that this demand is not necessarily satisfied by application of traditional neutrality law. As will be developed later, certain prescriptions of that law, far from consistently embodying a duty of abstention for neutrals, in effect permit the furnishing of certain forms of assistance, not always inconsequential, to belligerents.

SITUATIONS IN WHICH THE ORGANIZED COMMUNITY DOES NOT CHARACTERIZE THE LAWFULNESS OF COERCION

It has been suggested by a distinguished scholar that in situations marked by the absence or failure of characterization by the organized community, individual states should withhold judgment on the merits of the respective causes of the contending belligerents and maintain an "international quarantine" on the conflict. Professor Jessup writes:

60. Grotius long ago wrote that passage through its territory should be granted by a third state to the belligerent engaged in a just war, and denied to the belligerent resorting to an unjust war. *De Jure Belli Ac Pacis,* Bk. II, Ch. 2, S.13, 1–4, Classics of International Law, Vol. 2, pp. 196–9 (Kelsey trans., 1925). And see Art. 16(3) of the Covenant of the League of Nations.

> If the legal position of nonparticipants in the conflict is to be regulated by some international agreement short of a return to the old status of war and neutrality, it would be disastrous to agree that every state may decide for itself which of the two contestants is in the right and may govern its conduct according to its own decision, even if it were agreed that they would not actually support one or the other side by force. The ensuing conflict among Members of the United Nations would be destructive of the ordered world community which the Charter and any modern law of nations must seek to preserve. . . .
>
> There is no alternative except to extend throughout the duration of the conflict the system of impartial blockade against both parties to the fighting.[61]

A more recent observer makes comparable recommendation:

> The danger of states proceeding on their own initiative is that divergent characterization may be made, either by single states, groups of states, or even different organizations for collective self-defence. . . .
>
> [T]he only proper course for states which are not themselves placed in the necessity of self-defence, is for those states to abstain from intervention or discrimination until such time as a competent organ of the United Nations has determined what measures are necessary for the maintenance of international peace and security, and what part those states shall take in these measures.[62]

The above position, attractively logical as it may seem, does not exhaust the field of possible policy alternatives. We would, in this type of situation, project a policy not of uniformly and inflexibly requiring suspension of judgment, but rather of permitting the assumption of responsibility by individual states. The responsibility to be assumed here may seem, in a sense, a heavier one including as it

61. Jessup, *A Modern Law of Nations* 205 (1948). See also Jessup, *Today and Tomorrow* 118–213 (Neutrality: Its History, Economics and Law, Vol. 4, 1936); Hyde, "International Cooperation for Neutrality," 85 *U. Pa. L. Rev.* 344 (1937); Woolsey, "Problems of American Neutrality," 34 *Proc. Am. Soc. I.L.* 21 (1940); and Cohn, *Neo-Neutrality* (Keller and Jenson trans., 1939) for comparable pre-World War II proposals for interneutral cooperation.

62. Bowett, *Self-Defence in International Law* 180 (1958).

does the making of the necessary characterization in application of the fundamental prohibition of coercion as well as the implementation of this characterization by appropriate discrimination between offending belligerent and target. Appropriate discrimination may range, as observed earlier, from affirmative participation in all its possible gradations in scope and variety on the side of the defending belligerent to the passive denial of assistance to the offending belligerent.

The characterization is of course made by an individual state at its own peril. It partakes, in other words, of the nature of a provisional determination in precisely the same way that a claim of self-defense does,[63] and remains subject both to the contemporaneous appraisal of other individual states and to the subsequent review the organized community may eventually exercise. The risk, which Dr. Bowett stressed, of "making an authoritative determination which may, in the outcome, prove wrong," [64] need no more be decisive of the impolicy of allowing individual initiative in the making of provisional discriminations between offending belligerents and defending targets than it is of the improvidence of permitting initial determination by claimants of the legitimacy of claimed self-defense. A policy of permitting individual initiative is, of course, again like the policy of allowing self-defense, susceptible to perverting abuse; but this susceptibility is an attribute common to all legal policy, doctrine, or rule. The relation between individual assumption of responsibility and claims of self-defense would indeed seem closer than casual analogy. For provisional characterizations of coercion made upon the individual responsibility of particular states may, as a practical matter, be expected frequently to assume the shape of claims to exercise collective self-defense. The assumption of responsibility always entails costs in base values expended and losses sustained. To the extent that what is announced as an assumption of responsibility is not a mere façade for an act of aggression by the third state, the probabilities of acceptance of these costs would seem, in realistic expectation, greatest where the acting (third) state perceives the security of a collectivity with which it deeply identifies to have been immediately and seriously involved. The policy bases of an

63. Supra, pp. 217 ff.

64. Bowett, supra note 62 at 180.

assumption of individual responsibility thus includes, and may in particular cases be indistinguishable from, those underlying a reasonable (lawful) claim of collective self-defense.[65] The more perceptive states might nonetheless note that, in the long run, all are involved, for the securing of their major values, in the continuous and comprehensive maintenance of fundamental order and that the threads which in the contemporary world link peoples together in a common destiny are long and many.

Apprehension that divergent individual characterizations may result in the spreading of a conflict looms large in Professor Jessup's and Dr. Bowett's recommendations. Expectations that, in a given case, the conflagration may expand and raise to exorbitant levels the costs—in terms of aggregate destruction of both immediate and long-term community values—of implementing the minimum order principle are, of course, a relevant factor. The policy we suggest need not be insensitive to this factor. In this, as in the preceding type of situation, all the more particular requirements of the policy of minimum destruction and all the strategic principles of sanctions policy have direct relevancy. One of these principles and requirements is precisely that of economy in the outlay of base values, which principle enjoins realistic appreciation of the limits, in specific circumstances, of effective action in keeping to a minimum the net costs of securing basic order. It is, however, somewhat less than self-evident that expectations of vastly increased destruction and of uneconomical cost levels will arise in each and every case or that they will exhibit the same high degree of realism apparently postulated in the passages quoted above. There would appear room for doubt whether these overriding realistic expectations are the necessary, or even the most probable, consequences of a policy permitting decentralized responsibility for enforcement action so as to warrant an

65. Supra, pp. 244–52. The fact that the acting state was moved partly and even mainly because of its appreciation of a direct and serious threat to its own security as part of a collective self that might not include the entire community of states, need not detract from its action as an assumption of responsibility for basic public order. The important thing is that its action sustains an inclusive community interest. The community-wide interest involved is, of course, not so much an interest in the continued existence of any particular body politic as it is an interest in the maintenance of orderly and peaceful relations among states generally.

undifferentiated demand for "quarantine" in each case. The image evoked by Professor Jessup and Dr. Bowett of the dangers of third states zealous and impatient to enforce order with all good faith but innocently arriving at divergent conclusions about the appropriate location of guilt for the violation of public order may occasionally seem more romantic than real. On the other hand, situations may arise where to require collective inaction in the absence of a centralized characterization may have precisely the effect of increasing the aggregate value losses both of the participants and the community at large. Put more positively, to permit decentralized responsibility is not necessarily to invoke total chaos; decentralized characterization, where fundamental goals are genuinely shared, may exhibit a surprising degree of uniformity and could result in the maintenance of order.

Policies about Specific Belligerent-Nonparticipant Relationships

In problems raised by specific relationships of belligerents and third states which decline active participation in processes of coercion, the basic policies at stake are, as in the preceding type of problem, the broad complementary ones of minimum order and minimum destruction of values. In the present type of problem, the policy of minimum order assumes the more particular form of promoting and securing the military effectiveness of the defending and other belligerents engaged in authorized enforcement action, by requiring the isolation of the violator-belligerent from external sources of aid and supply and by permitting the belligerent sanctioners to enforce such isolation. The counterpoised policy envisages depressing to minimal levels the value losses accompanying processes of coercion, by promoting the limitation of the locale of interbelligerent operations and by protecting the continued normal functioning of the value processes of the nonparticipating states. The concrete requirements of these contraposed policies may obviously conflict in specific instances and have to be balanced continually against each other in the differing particular contexts which will be reviewed below.

It will be noted that the international law of neutrality of the nineteenth century had itself sought the balancing and adjustment of the military interests of each belligerent and the neutrals' interest in avoiding disruption of their internal community processes and external commercial activities.[66] A basic contemporary problem is, as intimated earlier, the accommodation of the specific compromises of belligerent and neutral interests embodied in the detailed prescriptions of the traditional law to the necessities of the newer and overriding policy of minimum order. Where asserted by belligerents acting on behalf of and under an authorization from the general community of states, the claims against nonparticipants for abstention from aid to the opposing belligerent and for prevention of utilization of neutral bases of power by such opposing belligerent, which have been honored in traditional law, have certainly not diminished in authority. Indeed, the authority of these claims may be enhanced, and more rigorous standards of neutral abstention and prevention appropriately entailed, by the requirement or authorization of at least passive discrimination against a violator-belligerent. On the other hand, in view of the same requirement or authorization of discrimination, the same claims for abstention and prevention, when made by a belligerent authoritatively determined, in centralized or decentralized characterization, to have resorted to unlawful aggression, may possibly be regarded as having declined in authority. Nonetheless, the imperatives of potential retaliation factually open to the aggressor-belligerent as to the sanctioners may, in particular situations, impose upon a nonparticipating state a very practical necessity for uniformity in observance of abstention and prevention. Because, in other words, mutuality in benefits may on occasion be a condition for securing what humanitarianism is possible, the policy of minimum destruction similarly may still authorize the state in declining participation in permissive enforcement to apply, vis-à-vis both the aggressors and the sanctioners, the duties of abstention and prevention.[67]

66. Cf. Jessup and Deak, supra note 53 at xii; Castren, *The Present Law of War and Neutrality* 426–7 (1954).

67. Lauterpacht, "Rules of Warfare in an Unlawful War," in *Law and Politics in the World Community,* 111 (Lipsky, ed., 1953). Judge Lauterpacht adds (ibid.) that "[T]here is nothing—save, perhaps, the victory of the aggressor—to prevent the courts and other organs of neutral states from drawing *after the war* the appropriate consequences from the fact that the war was illegal on the part of one belligerent and could therefore confer no lasting rights upon him." (Emphasis added.)

HISTORIC EXPERIENCE IN SECURING MINIMUM ORDER AND MINIMUM DESTRUCTION IN CONTEXTS OF CLAIMED NONPARTICIPATION

We propose now to turn to a somewhat summary review of past experience, as well as to an exploration of some of the factors which shaped such experience, with respect to the two major kinds of problems posed in the regulation of participation in coercive processes. In considering the first kind of problem, that is, the establishment and assumption of inclusive responsibility for maintaining basic order, we shall review principally the efforts represented by the Covenant of the League of Nations, and the Charter of the United Nations. In considering the second type of problem, that is, those arising out of the factual interactions of belligerents and nonparticipants, we shall examine the more important trends observable in relation to the principal claims of belligerents against nonparticipants, the principal claims of nonparticipants against belligerents, and the claim to embargo neutral commercial intercourse with an opposing belligerent.

The Quest for Shared Responsibility for Minimum Order: Neutrality and the Organization of Collective Security

While, as earlier observed, neutrality and collective security are, in basic conception and at highest level abstraction, antithetical, realistically it must be anticipated that claims to nonparticipation will continue to be made and that justification for such claims will continue to be sought in terms of authority. Hence, particular claims respecting responsibility for minimum order must be related to the specific commitments that constitute a given organization of collective security. We consider briefly the undertakings comprised in the two historical attempts in our century comprehensively to organize international security.

THE COVENANT OF THE LEAGUE AND THE PACT OF PARIS

The specific prohibitions of the Covenant of the League of Nations against recourse to coercion and violence were, it may be recalled, relatively modest ones. The applicability of the members' undertakings respecting the exercise of sanctions was limited to the four cases of "resort to war" prohibited by the Covenant's terms.[68] We have also pointed to the decentralization under the scheme of the Covenant of the authority to characterize particular coercion as in conformity with or in breach of the Covenant's prescriptions against "resort to war." [69] Thus, the commitment of members to participate in sanctions, i.e., the obligation imported by Article 16 of the Covenant to apply economic and financial measures against a Covenant-breaker, was a facultative one. Authority to activate its own commitment was reserved by each member unto itself. A claim to avoid participation could hence be asserted by the simple expedient of passing *sub-silentio* controversies about the lawfulness of a particular "resort to war" and the resulting recommendations of the League Council.[70] Finally, it may be noted that even the facultative obligation of the members did not embrace more than the employment of nonmilitary sanctions, like the severance of commercial and financial relations, the sharing of the costs of these measures, and the affording of passage through their territory to members' forces.[71] A member could, however, at its option invoke military sanctions: in the technical vocabulary of the League, "[t]he unilateral action of the defaulting state [could] not create a state of war; it merely entitle[d] the other members of the League to resort to acts of war or to declare themselves in a state of war with the Covenant-breaking state." [72]

It is thus obvious that the commitments of members of the League were set at a very modest level and that consequently there was ample room for assertion of claims of nonparticipation. In the war between Greece and Turkey in 1921, for example, in which the League Council took the passive stance of a spectator, a collective

68. Supra, p. 138 ff. Thus, apart from these four cases, the question of permissible nonparticipation did not arise; Lauterpacht, "Neutrality and Collective Security," 2 *Politica* 133, 135–6; Bustamante, *Manual de Derecho Internacional Publico* 573–4 (1942). See also, generally, Graham, "The Effect of the League of Nations Covenant on the Theory and Practice of Neutrality," 15 *Calif. L. Rev.* 357 (1927) and Kunz, "The Covenant of the League of Nations and Neutrality," 29 *Proc. Am. Soc. I.L.* 36 (1935).

69. Supra, p. 138 ff.

70. Cf. De LaPradelle, "The Evolution of Neutrality," in *Collective Security* 405–6 (Bourquin, ed., 1936); see also Orvik, *The Decline of Neutrality, 1914–1941*, 124–31 (1953).

71. Art. 16, Covenant of the League of Nations.

72. Resolution 3 of the Resolutions on the Economic Weapon, supra note 59 at 24.

declaration of neutrality was issued by the Allied Powers.[73] In the Chaco conflict, after Paraguay decided to declare the existence of a state of war with Bolivia, both being members of the League, declarations of neutrality followed from all the neighboring states—Argentina, Brazil, Chile, Peru, and Uruguay—some of which were also members of the League.[74] In the Italo-Ethiopian war, three members—Albania, Austria, and Hungary—refused to agree with the conclusion reached by the League Council as to Italy's violations of her obligations under the Covenant. Endorsement of the Council's conclusions would have required the three countries to apply sanctions against Italy, "a state to which they had so many reasons to be grateful." [75]

There were, further, concluded during the League period certain treaties, multilateral as well as bilateral, that envisaged the assertion of claims to nonparticipation by both members and nonmembers of the League in possible future conflicts. Among the best known multilateral agreements was the 1922 Nine-Power Treaty, signed by the United States and eight members of the League. The Treaty provided, among other things, that the parties (except China) "agree fully to respect China's rights as a neutral in time of war to which China is not a party," and that China "when she is a neutral," "will observe the obligations of a neutral." [76] Another multipartite agreement was the 1928 Havana Convention on Maritime Neutrality adopted by the Sixth International Conference of American States and ratified by at least five League members. A number of states also entered into bilateral treaties providing for the assumption of the posture of neutrality in the event of an attack upon one or the other signatory by a third state.[77]

In the decade before the outbreak of World War II, with the failure of the League to prevent the rearmament of Germany under the National Socialists, the expansion of Japan into Continental Asia,

73. 48 *Journal du Droit International* 433 (1921).

74. See 2 Walters, *A History of the League of Nations* 530 (1952). The texts of these neutrality declarations may be found in *A Collection of Neutrality Laws, Regulations, and Treaties of Various Countries,* 2 vols. (Deak and Jessup, eds., 1939): Argentina–9; Brazil–92; Chile–357; Peru–873; Uruguay–1269.

75. 2 Walters, supra note 74 at 656.

76. 38 *League of Nations Treaty Series* 278, 283.

77. Some of these treaties are reproduced in their relevant provisions in *A Collection of Neutrality Laws,* supra, note 74 at 1506, 1508, 1511–17.

and the Italian conquest of Ethiopia, expectations of the effectiveness of the League declined steadily until the vanishing point was reached. Claims to avoid participation in the impending conflict were multiplied and asserted with a vigor begotten of desperation. The members' already tenuous commitments under Article 16 respecting the application of economic and financial sanctions were further de-emphasized and attenuated. On July 1, 1936, the governments of seven European states—Denmark, Finland, the Netherlands, Norway, Spain, Sweden, and Switzerland—declared, with classic indirection, that "so long as the Covenant as a whole is applied only incompletely and inconsistently, [they were] obliged to bear that fact in mind in connection with the application of Article 16." [78] On January 31, 1938, the situation was described with greater explicitness by the Swedish delegate to the League:

> By the force of events, without any amendment of the Covenant, a practice has become established whereby Members of the League do not consider themselves bound to take coercive action against an aggressor State.[79]

Two years later, the Swedish and Norwegian governments made concrete application of this view. They rejected the request of the Allied Powers for permission for passage of an expeditionary force to Finland through their territories,[80] which request was made under

78. League of Nations, *Off. J.*, Spec. Supp. No. 154, at 19 (1936). The declarants also used language suggestive of a possible intent to invoke *rebus sic stantibus:* "The aggravation of the international situation and the cases of resort to force that have occurred during the last few years, in violation of the Covenant of the League, have given rise in our countries to some doubt whether the conditions in which they undertook the obligations contained in the Covenant still exist to any satisfactory extent."

79. League of Nations, *Off. J.*, Spec. Supp. No. 180, at 9–10 (1938). See, on the Declaration of Copenhagen of July 23, 1938, Orvik, *The Decline of Neutrality, 1914–1941,* 185–7 (1953). The statement of the Swedish delegate was echoed by the majority of the members in the 19th Assembly; League of Nations, *Records of the Plenary Meetings of the Assembly,* 3rd, 4th, and 5th meetings, passim (1938). See, generally, Morgenthau, "The Resurrection of Neutrality in Europe," 33 *Am. Pol. Sci. Rev.* 473 (1939).

80. See Fox, *The Power of Small States,* 92–4 (1959); *The War and the Neutrals, Survey of International Affairs 1939–1946,* 173–7 (Royal Institute of International Affairs, 1956); *Norway and the War, September 1939–December 1940, Documents on International Affairs,* 30–3 (Royal Institute of International Affairs, 1941).

the resolution of the League condemning the Soviet attack on Finland and urging members to provide Finland with material and humanitarian assistance.[81] Upon the outbreak of large-scale hostilities in September, 1939, a large number of states, including many members of the League, issued declarations of neutrality.[82] For instance, twenty-one American republics issued, on October 3, 1939, a declaration "reaffirm[ing their] status of general neutrality" and setting forth common standards for their relations with the belligerents.[83]

The Pact of Paris (General Treaty for the Renunciation of War, 1928) did not establish a new collective security system. The signatory states did not assume any commitments to impose sanctions upon a violator of the Pact, the identification of which remained, as under the League Covenant, a decentralized function. Nonparticipation, in other words, was under the Pact always a permissible alternative in policy. It need not be supposed, however, that the Pact had no impact upon the structure of authoritative policy. By the very broadness of its prohibition of "war as an instrument of national policy," it eroded, to a greater degree than did the League Covenant, the principal premise of the traditional law of neutrality.[84] Distinguished scholars have taken the view that the Pact constitutes a general authorization or permission to parties to discriminate against a signatory state which breaches its obligation not to have recourse to war and to assist the defending state by a variety of measures extending to the use of armed force.[85] The Pact, so conceived, extended and made available to states not members of the League of Nations the League system of permissive participation in

81. League of Nations, *Off. J.*, 20th Yr. 540 (1939).

82. These neutrality declarations and proclamations are listed and reproduced in 143 *British and Foreign State Papers* (1939).

83. The text of the declaration may be found in 34 *A.J.I.L. Supp.* 10 (1940).

84. 2 Oppenheim, *International Law* 643 (7th ed., Lauterpacht, 1952).

85. This view was carefully formulated in Article 4 of the famous "Budapest Articles of Interpretation," *38th Report of the International Law Association,* 67 (1934). Cf. the categorization in the "Harvard Draft Convention on the Rights and Duties of States in Case of Aggression," embodying a graduated scale of participation: "co-defending states," "supporting states," and "other states." 33 *A.J.I.L. Supp.* 828–30 (1939).

Dehn, "The Problem of Neutrality," 31 *Tr. Grotius Soc.* 139, 144–5 (1945) went further and asserted an *obligation* under the Pact of Paris to discriminate in favor of and assist the defending state. It appears difficult to document this view in the practice of states in the decade before the outbreak of World War II.

lawful responding coercion. The technical arguments commonly urged in support of this interpretation have variously rested upon the principle of "*ex iniuria ius non oritur*" and upon the principle of "community concern" in combination with the conception of "reprisals." [86] Whatever one's preference in supporting doctrine may be, the point bears emphasis that one possible interpretation of the Pact of Paris makes available an adequate basis in authority for the policy earlier adverted to of permitting, in the absence of a centralized characterization of the lawfulness of specific coercion, individual assumption of responsibility for implementation of minimum order.

The best known historical instances of claims to engage in discrimination between aggressor and defending belligerents, upon the basis of the authorization furnished by the Pact of Paris, are still the exchange of destroyers for air and naval bases entered into by the United States and the United Kingdom in 1940 [87] and the Lend-Lease Act approved by the United States Congress on March 11, 1941.[88] The Lend-Lease Act, it may be recalled, authorized the manufacture or procurement of, and the transfer of title to, or other disposition of, any "defense article" for the benefit of "the government of any country whose defense the President deem[ed] vital to the defense of the United States." The Act further authorized the testing and repair of "defense articles" as well as the communication of defense information respecting such articles to such government. Mr. Justice Robert H. Jackson, then Attorney-General, elaborated upon the authority for permissive discrimination made available by the Pact of Paris, to which authority both the House and Senate Com-

86. The principal technical justifications are illustrated in, e.g.: Dehn, supra note 85; Wright, "Neutrality and Neutral Rights Following the Pact of Paris for the Renunciation of War," 24 *Proc. Am. Soc. I.L.* 79 (1930); Wright, "Permissive Sanctions Against Aggression," 36 *A.J.I.L.* 103 (1942); Politis, *Neutrality and Peace* 58 et seq. (1936); Garner, "The Outlook for the Law of War and Neutrality," 22 *Tr. Grotius Soc.* 1 (1936); Cassin, in *Collective Security* 439 (Bourquin, ed., 1936); McNair, "Collective Security," 17 *Brit. Y.B.I.L.* 150, 158 (1936); Schwarzenberger, "The 'Aid Britain' Bill and the Law of Neutrality," 27 *Tr. Grotius Soc.* 1 (1941); 2 Oppenheim, *International Law* 644–5 (7th ed., Lauterpacht, 1952); Kelsen, *Principles of International Law* 86–7 (1952); Tucker, *The Law of War and Neutrality at Sea* 168 (1957).

87. The texts of the diplomatic notes exchanged by the United States and United Kingdom governments may be found in 34 *A.J.I.L. Supp.* 184 (1940).

88. 55 *Stat.* 31; also in 35 *A.J.I.L. Supp.* 76 (1941).

mittees on Foreign Relations had explicitly referred in approving the Act:[89]

> [The Pact of Paris and the Argentine Anti-War Treaty] did not impose upon the signatories *the duty* of discriminating against an aggressor, but it conferred upon them *the right* to act in that manner. This right they are indisputably entitled to exercise as guardians both of their own interests and of the wider international community.[90]
>
> [S]uch an interpretation of international law is not only proper but necessary if it is not to be a boon to the lawless and the aggressive. A system of international law which can impose no penalty on a law-breaker and also forbids other states to aid the victim would be self-defeating and would not help even a little to realize mankind's hope for enduring peace.[91]

It is a sobering commentary upon contemporary capabilities and prospects for organizing basic international order that two decades have deprived Mr. Justice Jackson's words of neither cogency nor urgency.

89. *H. Rep. No. 18,* 77th Cong., 1st Sess., pp. 5–6 (1941); *S. Rep. No. 45,* 77th Cong., 1st Sess., p. 4 (1941).

Bowett, *Self-Defence in International Law* 165–7 (1958) labors to demonstrate that "there is little or no evidence that the United States ever deemed herself *obliged* to assist Great Britain by reason only of the fact that Great Britain waged a war of individual and collective self-defence again flagrant aggression" (165; emphasis added). In view of the *permissive* character of discrimination in favor of the defending state under the Pact of Paris, a point well understood in both the House and Senate Reports, the relevancy of Dr. Bowett's thesis is less than apparent. It is, in particular, difficult to discover anything in *H. Rep. No. 18* that supports Dr. Bowett's remarkable assertion that "the House Committee's own report *corrects* [Secretary Stimson's] liberal view [on permissive discrimination under the Paris Pact] in soundly basing the United States policy on the assumption that the U.S. would throughout be acting in her own defence." (167; emphasis added). The constant contraposing of self-defense and sanctions, whether permissive or obligatory, observable throughout Dr. Bowett's chapter on "Neutrality and Self-defence," suggests once more a failure to note the fundamental unity and continuity of policy that underlies these and all other forms of permissible coercion. Supra, pp. 248–53.

90. "Address of Robert H. Jackson, Attorney-General of the United States, Inter American Bar Association, Havana, Cuba, March 27, 1941," 35 *A.J.I.L.* 348, 354 (1941); italics in the original.

91. Id., 358.

THE PRESENT ORGANIZATION OF SECURITY: THE UNITED NATIONS

The level of the collective security commitment sought to be established and stabilized by the United Nations' founding fathers at San Francisco was, in important respects, substantially higher that that initially projected in the League Covenant. In the first place, the prohibition of coercion embodied in the Charter was cast in more comprehensive terms than the Covenant's. The Charter's characterization of unlawful coercion, as we observed in an earlier chapter,[92] assumed the form, not of a list of unlawful cases of "resort to war," but rather of multiple terms of sweeping and unspecified reference, such as "threat to the peace," "breach of the peace," and "act of aggression." The conceivable range of situations in which members' commitments to participate in sanctioning measures might be made applicable was thus correspondingly broader. Secondly, the function of identifying the appropriate target of those measures was sought to be centralized and located in the organization itself. Centralization of the characterization process was complemented by an explicit undertaking to implement any particular characterization. Article 25 of the Charter sets out this undertaking:

> The Members of the United Nations agree to accept and carry out the decisions of the Security Council in accordance with the present Charter.

The undertaking is reiterated in somewhat broader terms, and appropriately included among the basic principles of the organization, by Article 2(5):

> All members shall give the United Nations every assistance in any action it takes in accordance with this Charter, and shall refrain from giving assistance to any state against which the United Nations is taking preventive or enforcement action.

It may be observed that the organization was granted competence to vary, in differing particular situations, the actual operative scope of the general commitment. Both the extent and kind of participation and the number of members enjoined to participate may differ as the strategic and tactical requirements of varying specific contexts

92. Supra, Ch. 3.

of coercion, as well as the location and capabilities of and degree of benefit to individual members, differ. For instance, under the original scheme of the Charter, "measures not involving the use of armed force," i.e. employment of diplomatic, ideological, and economic instruments, could be enjoined upon some members, while "action by air, sea and land forces" could be assigned to certain other members.[93] Further, where the disruption of basic order occurs in an area covered by a regional arrangement, the Council is authorized to utilize the regional agency and commission it or its members to undertake restorative measures under the Council's authority and on behalf of the organized general community.[94]

From the above brief sketch it is clear that, in terms of the system of commitments conceived at San Francisco, permissible claims of nonparticipation are authorized to be asserted by members only to the extent that their commitments are not in fact made operative in particular cases by an injunction to participate in some degree. In such cases they are in effect exempted *pro tanto* from affirmative participation. Even for nonparticipants so exempted, there always remains the last and minimum obligation to "refrain from giving assistance" to the offending belligerent.[95]

The events and circumstances of systemic conflict in the postwar world, a matter of recent history too familiar to require recitation, soon revealed the instability of the high level of commitment set in the Charter and released a cumulation of effective downward pressure.[96] The curve, as it were, of permissible nonparticipation

93. Arts. 41, 42, and 48(1), U. N. Charter; see Goodrich and Hambro, *Charter of the United Nations* 294 (2nd rev. ed., 1949); Kelsen, supra note 86 and 88; and Bentwich and Martin, *A Commentary on the Charter of the United Nations* 104 (1950).

94. Art. 53, U.N. Charter. Lalive, "International Organization and Neutrality," 24 *Brit. Y.B.I.L.* 72, 82 (1947) suggests that, in such case, third states (not members of the regional organization) might even be obliged to refrain from participation.

95. See 2 Oppenheim, *International Law* 650 (7th ed., Lauterpacht, 1952); Taubenfeld, "International Actions and Neutrality," 47 *A.J.I.L.* 377 (1953); Tucker, supra, note 86 at 173; Lalive, supra note 94 at 83; Kelsen, supra note 86 at 87–8; Martin, *Collective Security: A Progress Report* 18 (1952).

96. See Liska, *International Equilibrium,* c. 3 (1957) who develops an "integrative approach in multiple-equilibrium terms" to the problems of organizing collective security. He applies equilibrium analysis to, *inter alia,* the commitments of members, distinguishing between the commitment to individual self-restraint and the commitment to mutual assistance in collective intervention.

correspondingly rose. Thus, the commitment to take part in military enforcement activity by making armed forces available to the Security Council appears in practice to have been construed as being contingent upon the conclusion of the special agreements between Council and contributing member contemplated in Article 43 of the Charter.[97] No special agreement has been entered into and there appear no appreciable prospects for any in the probable future. Even in the Korean case, it may be recalled, the Security Council's call was cast in the language of recommendation.

The process of attrition of commitments did not stop there. As the rising incidence of Soviet vetoes in the Security Council forced a shift in the organization's center of gravity to the General Assembly,[98] the operative scope of the collective security commitment declined to even lower levels. As observed in the preceding chapter, the weight (as distinguished from the scope and domain) of the General Assembly's competence is limited and principally consists in discussion and the making of recommendations; it does not include authority to *prescribe* and *require* affirmative participation even in the milder "measures not involving the use of armed force." [99] Claims to avoid participation in such collective measures against an identified violator as may be recommended and urged by the General Assembly may hence be asserted and sustained, in point of legal technicality, as permissible.

An Assembly resolution determining a prohibited recourse to coercion and violence and recommending the giving of assistance to the defending belligerent is, however, not without consequences for legal policy: it constitutes an authoritative, centralized characterization and affords adequate authorization for permissive implementation and discrimination, individual or concerted, in favor of the

97. At San Francisco, the Sponsoring Powers assured the members that none would be required to contribute forces, assistance, or facilities in excess of the amounts promised in the projected special agreements. See Report of the Rapporteur for Chapter VIII, Section B, 12 U.N.C.I.O. *Docs.* 508 (1945). See also Martin, supra note 95 at 159; Tucker, supra note 86 at 172 note 16; Wortley, "The Veto and the Security Provisions of the Charter," 23 *Brit. Y.B.I.L.* 95, 107–8 (1946).

98. Useful accounts of this constitutional development may be secured from Goodrich, *The United Nations* 117–28 (1959); and Claude, *Swords into Plowshares: The Problems and Progress of International Organization* 171–81 (2nd ed., 1959).

99. Supra, Ch. 4.

defending belligerent.[100] Such was the interpretation given in practice to the 1951 resolution of the Assembly determining that the People's Republic of China was engaged in aggression in Korea and calling upon "all states and authorities" both to "lend every assistance to the United Nations action in Korea" and to "refrain from giving any assistance to the aggressors in Korea." [101] The succeeding Assembly recommendation for imposition of an arms and strategic materials embargo against the People's Republics of China and North Korea was similarly interpreted as supplying a base of authority for permissive discrimination.[102]

The level of commitment originally projected at San Francisco has thus in effect been depressed to that which had characterized the League system in its last decade. The observation may be made with some emphasis, however, that for members of the United Nations which do not choose to assume responsibility for permissive enforcement, the fullness of neutral rights envisaged in the nineteenth century law is still not available. The residuary commitment under Article 2(5) to abstain from "giving assistance to any state against which the United Nations is taking preventive or enforcement action" is not, it is believed, impaired by the permissive character of participation in Assembly-recommended sanctions.[103] A consistent

100. Bowett, *Self-Defence in International Law* 178 (1958) admits this point, albeit with apparent reluctance. See, further, Komarnicki, "The Problem of Neutrality Under the United Nations Charter," 38 *Tr. Grotius Soc.* 77, 85–6 and Martin, supra note 95 at 146.

Judge Lauterpacht stresses, in this connection, the residual responsibility of member states: "However, the failure of the Security Council to arrive at a decision does not necessarily relieve the members of the United Nations of all initiative or responsibility in the matter. There is nothing in the Charter which obliges them to maintain an attitude of full neutrality in such cases." He goes on to suggest the right of collective self-defense (Art. 51) and the Pact of Paris as formal bases for permissive action on the part of third states. 2 Oppenheim-Lauterpacht 651.

101. Resolution No. 498(V), U.N. Gen. Ass., *Off. Rec.,* 5th Sess., Supp. No. 20A (A/1775/Add.1), p. 1 (1951).

102. Resolution No. 500(V), id., p. 2. Thirty-seven member states reported to the Additional Measures Committee that they had taken action to implement the resolution. Three other members stated they did not export or re-export arms and strategic materials to the People's Republic of China. 1951 *U.N. Yearbook* 228–9.

103. Taubenfeld, supra note 95 at 390, note 80 and 395, appears also to suggest this view.

application of this commitment may require, for instance, that nonparticipating members deny permission to warships of the offender state to refuel or revictual or undergo repairs in their ports. Further, it does not seem an unreasonable view that the same commitment imports an obligation of nonparticipating members to prevent their private nationals from exporting arms and materials of war to the identified aggressor, an obligation not imposed by the traditional law of neutrality.

The suggestion is sometimes made that this residual obligation in Article 2(5) is "limited by the phrase 'preventive or enforcement action' " which "can only refer to action ordered or authorized by the Security Council under Chapter VII or Art. 53(1)" [104] and that the "collective measures" referred to in the Uniting for Peace resolution, "though authorized by Art. 1(1), are probably different from 'enforcement action' taken by the S.C. or under its direction." [105] To the extent that they go beyond affirming the permissive nature of collective measures authorized by the Assembly, and tend to insinuate the permissibility of claims to frustrate such measures by the rendering of assistance to the violator belligerent, the above suggestions appear to us as singularly unfortunate. They would reduce to absurd irrelevancy the authority and security functions of the organization, which in present context substantially are exercised by the Assembly. Without meaning to resuscitate the learned controversies on Charter exegetics that the 1950 Uniting For Peace Resolution aroused, it seems sufficient to observe that the practice of the organization itself,[106] reflecting the process of structural modification in the past decade, joins with a rational conception of interpretation that seeks to give effect to principal purposes and major expectations [107] in sustaining the authority and responsibility of the General Assembly where the Security Council is veto-bound and paralysed. The same process of interpretation by major purposes, which rarely

104. Bowett, *Self-Defence in International Law* 178 (1958).

105. Ibid., note 2. Tucker, *The Law of War and Neutrality at Sea* 19–20 (1957) makes comparable suggestion.

106. In the Korean, Suez, Hungarian, and Lebanese cases; see Goodrich, *The United Nations* 179–82 (1959); and Petersen, "The Uses of the Uniting For Peace Resolution Since 1950," 13 *Int. Organization* 219 (1959).

107. One such approach to interpretation is outlined and documented in McDougal and Gardner, "The Veto and the Charter: An Interpretation for Survival," 60 *Yale L.J.* 258 (1951).

regards statistical incidence of particular collocations of letters as conclusive,[108] sustains the view that permissive participation in collective measures authorised by the Assembly may appropriately be regarded as constituting, "no less than the obligatory action enjoined by a Council decision," "preventive or enforcement action" by "the United Nations" for the purposes of Article 2(5). The factor of overriding significance for community policy is, in our submission, identity in inclusive purpose.[109]

The problem of regulating participation and nonparticipation by states not members of the general security organization has been discussed with animation by textwriters. Much of this discussion has commonly centered around *pacta tertiis nec nocent nec prosunt* and its application with respect to the United Nations Charter. Without seeking to rehearse details, the broad point may be made that controversies in the relations of a handful of nonmembers vis-à-vis the organization constituted by the overwhelming bulk of the nations of the world are not adequately resolved by simple invocation of the *pacta tertiis* maxim. There is something bizarre about treating the Charter of the United Nations, the constitutional act of the world community (or the vast part thereof), as if it had no larger implications for humanity than, for instance, a real estate mortgage. Much more appropriate is the kind of policy perspective outlined by the International Court of Justice in the Reparations for Injuries case,[110]

108. See, for instance, the argument presented in Beckett, *The North Atlantic Treaty, The Brussels Treaty and the Charter of the United Nations* 7–8 (1950), upon which Bowett, supra note 105, apparently relied. It might also be noted that Sir Eric Beckett's essay was written before the controversies about the authority of the General Assembly respecting the maintenance of peace and security arose, and that his principal purpose appeared to be something other than the examination of such authority.

109. Contrast Tucker, supra note 105 at 20 who lays decisive stress upon certain assumptions about the lack of "binding force" in Assembly resolution: "Although a considerable degree of coordination may be achieved among the national armed forces of Member states acting in response to General Assembly recommendations made under the 'Uniting For Peace' Resolution, the present character of such recommendations does not appear to allow the conclusion that these forces may be considered as acting 'on behalf' of the United Nations."

110. The Court said: "[The United Nations] could not carry out the intentions of its founders if it was devoid of international personality. It must be acknowledged that its Members, by entrusting certain functions to it, with the attendant duties and responsibilities, have clothed it with the competence re-

the perspective that stresses the requirements of functional effectiveness. The same perspective may be seen to infuse the grant of authority to the organization to ensure that nonmembers act in accordance with the principles of the Charter "so far as may be necessary for the maintenance of international peace and security." [111]

It would seem a clear inference from this provision that the organization is authorized in general community expectation to take steps to prevent a nonmember from furnishing assistance to and discriminating in favor of the identified violator.[112] The resolutions of the General Assembly in the case of Korea—when nonmembers were more numerous and included more states of consequential power position than today—suggest its acceptance of this inference.[113] The Assembly resolution determining the People's Republic of China to have committed aggression in Korea called upon "all States and authorities" to deny assistance to the aggressors. Similarly, the resolution recommending the application of an embargo upon arms and strategic materials against the offending belligerents addressed

---

quired to enable those functions to be effectively discharged." With more particular regard to nonmembers, the Court ruled that "fifty states, representing the vast majority of the members of the international community, had the power, in conformity with international law, to bring into being an entity possessing objective international personality, and not merely personality recognized by them alone, together with capacity to bring international claims." 1949 *I.C.J. Rep.* 174, 179, 185.

111. Art. 2(6), U.N. Charter. At San Francisco, it may be recalled, the Uruguayan delegate proposed reconsideration of this paragraph of the Dumbarton Oaks Draft; his proposal was overwhelmingly defeated. The Belgian delegate stated that this was a most important provision, that the Organization should not be paralyzed by a nonmember state invoking the Hague Conventions, and that the Organization, being the authorized expression of the international legal community, could ignore demands made by nonmembers (presumably under the Hague Conventions). The Australian representative agreed it was a difficult provision to enforce but that it was an essential one. See Summary Report of the twelfth meeting of Committee I/1, 6 U.N.C.I.O. *Docs.* 348 (1945).

112. 2 Oppenheim-Lauterpacht 119, 652; Martin, *Collective Security: A Progress Report* 17 (1952); and Kelsen, *Law of the United Nations* 106–7 (1950) support this inference.

113. Other cases include the Indonesian question, the Corfu Channel case between the United Kingdom and Albania, the Spanish question, and the threats to the independence of Greece arising from actions of Albania, Bulgaria, Romania, and Yugoslavia.

itself to "every State." Five nonmembers, it may be added, expressly undertook to comply with the resolution calling for an embargo.[114]

The more ambitious suggestion sometimes made that the organization may require nonmembers to engage in affirmative participation in collective sanctioning measures,[115] must, at a time when the effective commitments of members themselves have been depressed to minimal levels and prevailing expectations limited to permissive enforcement, seem a largely unprofitable point for speculation. Moreover, even if the state of common expectations were different, there appears room for doubting whether a postulated authority to require affirmative participation from nonmembers would assume critical importance in the probable future. Nine states remain outside the organization—Federal Republic of Germany, Liechtenstein, Monaco, Republic of Korea, Republic of Vietnam, San Marino, Switzerland, the Vatican City, and the People's Republic of China; twelve, if the German Democratic Republic and the People's Republics of North Korea and of North Vietnam are regarded as independent political units and counted. With respect to most of these, it would seem probable that their participation, or nonparticipation, in conceivable future conflicts would not importantly affect the outcome of enforcement action. The posture of the Federal Republic of Germany and that of the People's Republic of China would, it may be expected, constitute significant factors in estimations of probable effectiveness of such enforcement action. The point of practical importance, however, would appear to be that, on the one hand, the Federal Republic of Germany is a member of the North Atlantic Treaty Organization, while, on the other hand, to suppose that the People's Republic of China would presently support any United Nations enforcement action must seem unduly sanguine. The new nations in the African continent which are in the process of emerging from a dependent status seem most likely to seek, as the other newly established states in Asia and Africa did commonly and eagerly seek,

114. The reports of states, members and nonmembers, on action taken by them in respect of the embargo are summed up in 1951 *U.N. Yearbook* 228–9.

115. See, e.g., the interpretation suggested by Professor Kelsen to the effect that all the obligations of member states, including obligations relating to affirmative participation in enforcement measures, were incorporated, by way of Article 2(2), into Article 2(6) and imposed upon nonmembers. Kelsen, *Law of the United Nations* 75–6, 85–6, 108 (1950); also Kelsen, "Membership in the United Nations," 46 *Col. L. Rev.* 391, 394, 410–11 (1946).

admission to the organization as a kind of collective imprimatur upon their claims to act as distinct units of participation in the world power process. It may, nonetheless, be added, in final observation, that nonmembers are at liberty to engage in permissive participation and to cooperate with members applying collective measures.[116]

Specific Relationships of Belligerents and Nonparticipants: The Balance of Military Effectiveness and Noninvolvement

Because of the progressive attenuation of the scope of the commitment to collective responsibility and the consequent ample room for permissive claims of nonparticipation, the second general problem—that of determining appropriate relations between belligerents and nonparticipants—must frequently be faced. The specific relations of belligerents and nonparticipants in the course of an ongoing process of coercion may be broadly generalized as a complex of claims and counterclaims relating to control and utilization of bases of power—territory, people, and resources—of the nonparticipants. These claims and counterclaims, hypostatized as rights and duties, exhibit a complementarity that may impart an impression of *elegantia juris*, of conceptual symmetry. In point of history, however, the line of contact has not been established by logical derivations of decision-makers. It has, rather, been gradually delineated by compromise, balancing, and adjustment, a process heavily influenced by such pragmatic factors as power differentials of belligerents vis-à-vis nonparticipants both in particular wars and in historical series of wars; the intensity, geographical extension, and time duration of wars; the available techniques and instrumentalities of coercion; and the prevailing conceptions and doctrines of conflict management.

It may be noted at the outset that the pattern of controversy constituted by the complex of claims and counterclaims is, in contrast with the patterns observable in most of the other areas of the law of war, a trilateral one. The same set of events that generates a claim by one belligerent against a nonparticipant ($B_1 \rightarrow N$) may occasion not only a countering assertion by the nonparticipant ($B_1 \leftarrow N$) but also a separate, principal claim by the nonparticipant against the op-

116. In the Korean case, at least two nonmember states furnished or offered to furnish military units, medical and other services and supplies, and funds, to the U.N. Command; U.N. Doc. A/1822 and Addenda 1–5, June 25, 1951.

posing belligerent ($N \rightarrow B_2$). The opposing belligerent may of course in turn assert a counterdemand against the nonparticipant disputing, for example, the latter's characterization of events ($N \leftarrow B_2$). Further, in respect again of the same constellation of events, the first belligerent may, with or without making a previous claim against the nonparticipant, assert authority to proceed directly against its enemy ($B_1 \rightarrow B_2$).

CLAIMS OF BELLIGERENTS AGAINST NONPARTICIPANTS

The many detailed assertions customarily made by belligerents against nonparticipants may be precursively described in terms of two principal types of claims. The first type of claim is that nonparticipants abstain from direct aid and support to the opposing belligerent. In countering assertion, a nonparticipant may deny that its acts amount to giving direct aid and support to the opposing belligerent, or may invoke the bifurcation of neutral state and neutral national which pervades the traditional law and claim that the acts of assistance are those of its private nationals.

The second principal type of belligerent claim relates to the policing of the territorial domain of a nonparticipant and primarily comprises a demand that the nonparticipant prevent the utilization of its territory, people, and resources by the opposing belligerent. Replication by the nonparticipant to this kind of belligerent claim may assume differing particular forms. The nonparticipant may, for instance, claim authority to allow utilization of its territory for humanitarian purposes which produce no significant impact upon the military balance between the belligerents. Where the belligerent claim specifically relates to the use by its opponent of the manpower resources of the nonparticipant, the opposing claim of the nonparticipant may be that its nationals serving with the other belligerent are "volunteers." Again, the nonparticipant may in effect simply plead in opposition that its "duty of prevention" is not without limits and assert that it has exhausted "the means at its disposal" in seeking to prevent unlawful utilization by the other belligerent. This latter kind of counter assertion may in turn bring about the supplementary, albeit distinct, belligerent claim to authority to anticipate or respond, in the nonparticipant's territory, to its opponent's unlawful exercises in such territory.

The preliminary point may also be made that the succeeding discussion of the principal types of belligerent claims should be regarded as generally qualified by the considerations and submissions outlined above in connection with the problem of securing common responsibility for implementing basic order. More specifically, contemporary international law makes available to nonparticipants a broad authority to discriminate against the belligerent authoritatively determined to have breached the fundamental prescriptions against unlawful resort to violence. Nonparticipants (i.e. third states who do not engage in military participation) may, in other words, assert permissible discrimination in comprehensive counterclaim in respect of any particular demand, for abstention as for prevention, that the offending belligerent may make against them.

Abstention from Aid to Enemy Belligerent

We turn to a somewhat summary consideration of the first principal type of belligerent demand. These belligerent claims have included most prominently demands for abstention by nonparticipants from supplying, directly or indirectly, an opposing belligerent with "war-ships, ammunition, or war material of any kind whatever." [117] Withholding or denial by the nonparticipant of loans and credit, of the use of its public agencies, and of its industrial, transportation, and communication facilities, and *a fortiori* of the services of its public armed forces, has similarly been customarily demanded by belligerents.[118] Illustration of the last specific claim is afforded by the case of the "Blue Division" which, during the Second World War, was raised by the Spanish Government and dispatched to the Russian front for service with the German armies. Although some of the seventeen thousand men of the Division are reported to have been genuine volunteers, the great bulk appeared to be soldiers of the regular Spanish armed forces.[119] The Allied (United Nations) Powers protested this action as a violation of neutral duty and demanded withdrawal of the Division by the Spanish Government. In

117. Art. 6, Hague Convention XIII; Art. 16, Havana Convention.

118. 3 Hyde, *International Law* 2231–2 (2nd rev. ed., 1954).

119. See *The War and the Neutrals, Survey of International Affairs, 1939–1946*, 285 (Royal Institute of International Affairs, 1956); Fox, *The Power of Small States* 160 (1959); Latimer, "Spain: Foreign Relations and Policy Since 1940," 19 *Bull. of Int. News* 1013 (1942).

1943, the Division was withdrawn and returned to Spain, although some of the volunteers stayed and were organized into a "Spanish Legion" under German command.[120]

The assertions of nonparticipants made in opposition to belligerent demands for abstention and withdrawal frequently included averments that the activities sought to be stopped were activities, not of the nonparticipant states themselves, but of their private nationals and inhabitants. These averments were commonly accompanied by disclaimers of responsibility for such private activities and of any requirement in legal authority to prevent and suppress them.[121] These claims were customarily honored in the theory and practice of the inherited international law of neutrality, succinctly summarized on this point by Hague Convention XIII of 1907 in the following terms:

> A neutral Power is not bound to prevent the export or transit, for the use of either belligerent, of arms, ammunition, or, in general, of anything which could be of use to an army or fleet.[122]

It is by now almost commonplace to point out that the dichotomy between the nonparticipant state and its private inhabitants imported in the prescriptions of traditional law had historically for its principal policy foundation the particular conceptions of public order, of economic organization and social structure, that prevailed in Western Europe and America in the last century.[123] In these conceptions, frequently characterized in such terms as "laissez faire," "economic individualism," and "liberalism," the functions thought appropriate and permissible for the governmental organization were limited in number and closely circumscribed in scope. Regulation of the internal economic processes of production and distribution and of foreign trade was not one of those functions; in the postulates of classical economics and liberalism, this was an area left to private initiative and enterprise and to the operation of "impersonal," "au-

120. *The War and the Neutrals,* supra note 119 at 301, 302; Fox, supra note 119 at 169, 173–4.

121. See e.g. the correspondence and other documents collected in 7 Hackworth, *Digest of International Law* 610–21 (1943).

122. Art. 7, Hague Convention XIII; see also Art. 7, Hague Convention V; and Art. 22, Havana Convention.

123. See Stone, *Legal Controls of International Conflict* 408 (rev. ed., 1959); Smith, *The Crisis in the Law of Nations* 27–8 (1947).

tomatic," "market forces." It may be observed, however, that these prescriptions expressed a policy of permitting the continued functioning of the internal wealth processes and external economic relationships of the people of the nonparticipant state; to this extent, they embodied the more general policy principle of humanitarianism, or the conservation of values in time of war.

Today, of course, the foundations of the inherited distinction have been substantially eroded. Governmentalization of community processes is, in larger or lesser degree, exhibited in all municipal public orders and the observable trend continues to be one of expanding levels of organized official activity and control.[124] There has been, in most abstract characterization, a proliferation in the functions acquired by or thrust upon states and a corresponding vast extension of the area in fact subjected to public control and regulation. In more particular reference to the domestic economic processes and international trade of totalitarian public orders, comprising nigh half of the peoples of the world, government officials of course exercise at all times complete and exclusive control over every stage and aspect of the production and distribution, as of the exportation and importation, of all goods and services.[125] Even in nontotalitarian orders, however, governments commonly exercise extensive control over the movements of capital, goods, and services across their boundaries, utilizing a large variety of control techniques and devices, such as exchange controls, tariffs, import quotas, export licensing, bilateral balancing of trade, and the like.[126] In periods of crisis and

124. E.g., Friedmann, "Some Impacts of Social Organization on International Law," 50 *A.J.I.L.* 475 (1956); Friedmann, "The Growth of State Control Over the Individual and Its Effect Upon the Rules of International State Responsibility," 19 *Brit. Y.B.I.L.* 118 (1938).

125. Spulber, "The Soviet-Bloc Foreign Trade System," 24 *Law and Contemp. Prob.* 420 (1959); and Mikesell and Wells, "State Trading in the Sino-Soviet Bloc," id., 435 offer recent surveys of the extent and operation of state control over the foreign export and import trade of the Communist world.

126. See, for comparable surveys of foreign trade practice in Western countries, Fensterwald, "United States Policies toward State Trading," 24 *Law and Contemp. Prob.* 369 (1959) and Ouin, "State Trading in Western Europe," id., 398. Trade controls established by the United States in a context of systemic conflict are discussed in Silverstone, "The Export Control Act of 1949: Extraterritorial Enforcement," 107 *U. Pa. L. Rev.* 331 (1959). A wide ranging general inquiry is undertaken in Miller, "Foreign Trade and the 'Security State': A Study of Conflicting National Policies," 7 *J. Pub. L.* 37 (1958).

emergency, i.e., of overt violence or high expectations of violence, public control is commonly intensified and broadened such that the private (nongovernmental) entities and individuals involved in an act of exportation or importation may actually be little more than nominal participants.[127] The crucial points are that decisions on the important aspects of foreign trade—direction, content, volume, financing, and so forth—are either made by government officials directly or are subject to their approval and that the private parties in fact function as instrumentalities of state policy.

It seems an important observation that both state trading, understood as trading by state organs in a country with a centrally planned economy, and the comprehensive governmental controls on the trading activities of private persons and associations, are basic and indispensable instruments of economic warfare.[128] It seems equally important to stress that these instruments are utilized not only by belligerents but also by nonparticipants, and that, since the last world war at least, the exercise by nonparticipants of effective control over the commercial and trading operations of their inhabitants forms part of the common expectations of belligerents which in fact rely upon neutral assumption of such control. Belligerent reliance upon control by the nonparticipant state over its own traders is perhaps best illustrated by the "war trade agreements" concluded for example between the Allied Powers and European neutral states in World War II.[129] These agreements indeed commonly set forth among other provisions an explicit undertaking by the neutral state to control, by means of a system of export licensing or otherwise, the commodities the importation of which the Allied Powers undertook to allow, and to prevent the re-exportation of such commodities to the Axis Powers.[130] These "war trade agreements" moreover specified the

127. The point is appropriately stressed in Tucker, *The Law of War and Neutrality at Sea* 211 (1957). A useful account of trade controls and policies adopted by both Allied and Axis Powers in the last world war may be found in Chalmers, *World Trade Policies: the Changing Panorama, 1920–1953,* 181–327 (1953). Materials on regulation of trade and industry during the First World War are compiled in *Readings in the Economics of War,* 254–303 (Clark, Hamilton, and Moulton, eds., 1918).

128. See the excellent study by Allen, "State Trading and Economic Warfare," 24 *Law and Contemp. Prob.* 256 (1959).

129. See infra, pp. 513–15.

130. 1 Medlicott, *The Economic Blockade,* 664–5 (1952).

kinds and volume of goods to be imported into, and those to be exported from, the nonparticipant state. Neutral states in World War II, it might further be noted, sometimes entered into trade agreements with both sets of belligerents, the terms of an agreement with one side being commonly affected by the terms of a previous or projected agreement with the other side.[131]

In the light of these developments, certain inferences, we submit, suggest themselves as appropriate. One is that a state should not be permitted to avoid the thrust of the duty of abstention by the somewhat transparent expedient of acting through a trading organ or corporation that is established, owned, and controlled by the state itself and that can be regarded as separate from the state only in the most rarefied regions of juristic conceptualism. The corporate veil is too thin to cover the naked impact of the nonparticipant's acts upon the military balance between the belligerents.[132] The absurdity of any

131. Sweden, for example, and Turkey and Norway (while still a neutral) concluded war trade agreements with the Allied Powers and as well with Germany, each seeking to relieve pressure on itself by playing off each belligerent against the other. See Fox, *The power of Small States,* cc. 2, 4–5 (1959); 2 Medlicott, *The Economic Blockade* cc. 6, 8 (1959).

132. Preuss, "Some Effects of Governmental Controls on Neutral Duties," 31 *Proc. Am. Soc. I.L.* 108, 117–18 (1937). The general formulation offered by Professor Preuss was: "A neutral government performs an unneutral act whenever it engages in commercial or financial intercourse with a belligerent which, if engaged in by a private individual, would legitimately expose such individuals to belligerent penalties for trade in contraband, carriage of contraband, breach of blockade, or unneutral service." (116).

Castren, *The Present Law of War and Neutrality* 475 (1943) and the Harvard Research, "Rights and Duties of Neutral States in Naval and Aerial War," 33 *A.J.I.L. Supp.* at 239 (1939) make comparable formulations. With more specific respect to publicly-owned neutral vessels, Rowson, "Prize Law During the Second World War," 24 *Brit. Y.B.I.L.* 160, 178 (1947) and McNair, "Legal Aspects of State Shipping," 34 *Tr. Grotius Soc.* 31, 45–7 (1949) submit that such vessels would be good prize if shown to have carried contraband, or breached blockade and so forth. Tucker, *The Law of War and Neutrality at Sea* 214 (1957) appears much more diffident and finds even a right to visit and search, let alone the seizure and condemnation, of such vessels "by no means certain."

In connection with the use of the corporate device by pretended neutrals, it may be noted that the Economic Agreement of Feb. 11, 1940 between Nazi Germany and the Soviet Union contained a "Confidential Protocol" in which the Soviet Government undertook to "instruct the proper Soviet commercial organization to enter into negotiations with the German organizations and firms designated by the Government of the German Reich in regard to the purchase

other construction is heightened by the assertion of claims by countries in which foreign trade is a complete state monopoly to immunity from the ordinary procedures of belligerent inspection and verification of neutral trade. The Soviet Union, it may be recalled, in protesting on October 25, 1939 the Allied contraband control system, asserted the public and state-owned character of its merchant vessels which therefore "should not be subjected to any measures of compulsion such as are applied to private merchant vessels." [133] Whatever view may be taken on the problem of immunities for public instrumentalities engaged in commercial activities in time of peace, it must be obvious that to extend the principles and doctrines of state immunities to cover the Soviet claim is to reduce any duty of abstention to a vacuous curiosity. The policies that underlie the law on state immunities are completely different from those which are projected in the law of neutrality.

The second inference which may be recommended is that other nonparticipant states, not operating under a completely governmentalized economy but exercising comprehensive control over foreign trade, are appropriately held responsible for the exportation of arms, munitions, and other war or strategic materials to a belligerent by their private inhabitants. From a perspective, again, which pays primary regard to substantive impact, what appears decisive is that (with occasional exceptions arising from the audacity and enterprise of smugglers) a shipment of strategic or war materials can only be effected with the consent and approval of the nonparticipant government, and that such consent and approval manifested through the issuance of a license constitute, in every sense meaningful to

---

by the Soviet Union of metals and other goods in third countries and in regard to the sale of these metals and goods to Germany." *Documents on German Foreign Policy 1918–1945*, Series D (1937–1945), Vol. 8: *The War Years, September 4, 1939–March 18, 1940*, pp. 788–9 (1954).

133. 1 Medlicott, *The Economic Blockade* 319 (1952). Professor Medlicott adds that the Soviet Union apparently did not wish to put the case to a test and discreetly withdrew Soviet ships from areas where they might be subjected to contraband control. Soviet vessels were thenceforth largely concentrated in the Pacific. (Id. at 320). Two ships, the *Selenga* and the *Vladimir Mayakovsky*, were intercepted in January and February, 1940, the second with a load of copper consigned to Vladivostok. *The War and the Neutrals, Survey of International Affairs 1939–1946*, 15 (Royal Institute of Int. Affairs, 1956).

policy, participation in the act of exportation.[134] The suggestion, most briefly put, is that responsibility must bear reasonable relation to actual control.

The formulations outlined above, in requiring the nonparticipant both to abstain, as a composite body politic or as any lesser organ or entity, from supplying an opposing belligerent with the wherewithal of war and to assume responsibility commensurate with its effective authority for preventing similar acts of supply by its inhabitants, obviously place a high value upon the military interests of belligerents.[135] We do not, however, mean to suggest that these interests

134. Cf. Smith, *The Crisis in the Law of Nations* 28–9 (1947). Tucker, supra note 132 at 215 appears to have adopted this position.

135. This kind of formulation meets, it is believed, the purported thrust of contentions sometimes made that "simply to apply the Hague rules of abstention to state trading states . . . would tend to penalize a socialized or semisocialized country in its international operations." Friedmann, "Changing Social Arrangements in State-Trading States and Their Effect on International Law," 24 *Law and Contemp. Prob.* 350, 355 (1959) referring to and reiterating his suggestion made over two decades ago in supra note 124. The same suggestion is taken up, but without re-examination, in Greenspan, *The Modern Law of Land Warfare* 550 (1959).

Stone, *Legal Controls of International Conflict* 408–12 (rev. ed., 1959) does not dispute, and indeed strongly emphasizes, the trends toward governmentalization of both domestic economic processes and foreign trade that we noted above. Professor Stone, however, presents a recommendation that differs in important part from that essayed above: that "trading activity of neutral Governments with belligerents should be assimilated to private trading in both respects. First, that the duty of the neutral Government not to supply arms, munitions, or to grant loans should be abolished. Second, that the ships, and cargoes, and other instrumentalities of the neutral government engaged in such trade should be subject to the ordinary penalties for contraband carriage . . . and should not enjoy (while involved in such trade) the immunities ordinarily enjoyed by State owned ships and property" (413). It may be observed that these two specific suggestions bear no necessary relation of mutual dependency; the second is, as a matter of fact, embraced in the formulation suggested above in our text. It is Professor Stone's first submission that is, we believe, open to profound objection.

The formulation presented in the text must, it is well to make explicit, be related to the recommendations offered in respect of the first and overriding problem of securing common responsibility for maintaining basic order. See supra, p. 409 ff. The importance of relating recommendations about supply of war material to belligerents to recommendations about responsibility for mini-

alone are relevant to policy and specific decision. Rational policy and decision require the accommodation of belligerent interests with the competing demands of nonparticipants for maintenance of their "normal" economic processes. This accommodation is, it is believed, most appropriately sought through application of a contextual conception of war materials or contraband. Anticipating the discussion presented below,[136] it may be observed that the determination of what, in a particular given conflict, may appropriately be characterized as war materials or contraband itself requires the careful relation by decision-makers of the specific features of such conflict in context to the contraposed policies of military effectiveness and maintenance of economic well-being. Particular characterizations may be expected to differ as the features and conditions of particular conflicts differ. It is by no means clear that the experience on this matter in the last world war must necessarily be extrapolated in simple linear projection; characterizations reasonable in a World War II type of conflict may conceivably be wholly unnecessary and inapt in another, more limited, kind of war. Finally, it may be observed that war trade agreements appear to make available a device for achieving flexible and *ad hoc* specifications, as well as modification, of the above structure of belligerent and nonparticipant rights and duties in at least some situations.[137]

---

mum order may perhaps be best illustrated by means of Professor Stone's proposal for abolition of the neutral duty of abstention from supplying war material. This proposal was, in effect, pre-empted by Mr. Vishinsky in the discussion at the U.N. General Assembly on the intervention of the People's Republic of China in the Korean War. Mr. Vishinsky said:

> Article 7 of [Hague Convention V, 1907] states: A neutral Power is not called upon to prevent the export or transport, on behalf of one or other of the belligerents, of arms, munitions of war, or, in general, of anything which can be of use to an army or fleet. Thus, the Central People's Government of the People's Republic of China cannot be held responsible for, or charged with, having violated the principles of international law, even if it has supplied its Korean brethren with armaments . . . [U]nder article 7 it is clearly absurd to bring charges against a government of a neutral Power on the grounds that it has provided one of the belligerent parties with armaments, so that can in no way be regarded as a breach of neutrality.

U.N. Gen. Ass., *Off. Rec.*, 5th Sess., Plenary 592 (1950).

136. Infra, p. 481 et seq.

137. The suggestion is perhaps most conveniently documented by means of

Prevention of Enemy Utilization of Nonparticipant's Bases of Power

The second principal type of belligerent demand relates to the occurrence or the expectation of occurrence of certain events within the geographic base—including the territorial waters and airspace—of a nonparticipant state. These events, occurrence of which belligerents demand that nonparticipants prevent, may consist of, firstly, activities of opposing belligerents or, secondly, activities of nationals and inhabitants of the nonparticipant. In preliminary and general reference, the kinds of belligerent activities here embraced, and which decision-makers have traditionally regarded nonparticipants as obliged to prevent, consist in the utilization of their territory as an "area of operations" or "base of operations." The activities of individual persons, which nonparticipants were similarly required in traditional law to prevent, were technically characterized as acts amounting to "direct military aid" to a belligerent.

The basic policies that may be seen to be at stake in the regulation and prevention of belligerent utilization of neutral bases of power are again, as in the problem of neutral abstention from aid to a belligerent, the securing of military effectiveness and the minimizing of destruction of nonparticipants' values. Belligerent effectiveness is sought to be served by requiring the prevention, counteraction, re-

---

the war trade agreement concluded by Britain and Sweden on Dec. 7, 1939. This agreement provided, among other things, that Sweden would be entitled to export indigenous products up to the level of her 1938 export figures which were adopted as representing her "normal" trade. Of chief importance among Swedish indigenous products was high-grade iron ore, certainly a contraband item in the last world war. More than seventy per cent of Sweden's iron-ore exports before the war had gone to Germany, a fact well known, and of considerable concern, to Britain. The *quid pro quo* included, along with certain other things, the continuation of the Swedish supply to the Allied Powers of such items as aircraft parts, special steel castings, and ferrochrome, also clearly contraband. See 1 Medlicott, *The Economic Blockade* 141–52 (1952).

Another illustration is furnished by the trilateral arrangement the Norwegian government secured from Britain in the Anglo-Norwegian war trade agreement negotiations. Norway offered ten extra tankers, beyond those promised in a previous shipping agreement, for the use of Britain. In return, Britain agreed to the exportation by Norway of 50,000 tons of fresh fish (food being a conditional contraband item in the British list) to Germany beyond the "normal" (1938) export figures. Germany, in turn, promised to deliver the guns and munitions Norway desired. Id., 162; Fox, *The Power of Small States* 89 (1959).

pression, and nullification of acts, within neutral territory, that disadvantage one belligerent and hence tend to disturb the interbelligerent balance of power. The effective prevention and nullification of such acts at the same time promote the countervailing policy in precluding exposure of the nonparticipant to involvement and attack by the disadvantaged belligerent and permitting maintenance of the integrity and continuity of the normal community processes in the nonparticipant state. It is in deference to the comprehensive exclusive competence to control all the processes within its territorial base which a nonparticipant state as an independent body politic asserts, that prevention of belligerent utilization is, in the first instance, imposed as a duty upon the nonparticipant.[138]

Belligerent Operations in a Nonparticipant's Territory. We begin with the prevention of belligerent operations in a nonparticipant's territory.

Utilization of a nonparticipant's territory as an "area of operations" may be somewhat impressionistically described as referring to all belligerent exercises therein which constitute the conduct of or immediate preparation for armed hostilities, including exercise of the procedures of visit, search, and capture of enemy vessels.[139] Officials of the nonparticipant state are authorized and indeed required to anticipate and respond to such belligerent operations with force where necessary and to redress the balance by, for example, securing the release or return of a prize captured within its waters and restoring the same to the other belligerent.[140] Among the kinds of specific acts commonly included in the category here considered is the use of nonparticipant territory for the transporting of armed forces and *materiel de guerre*. Perhaps the widest known instance of this type of proscribed use is the German transit traffic through Sweden in the last world war. After completion of the German cam-

138. Cf. 3 Hyde, *International Law* 2226, 2237 (2nd rev. ed., 1945); Fenwick, *International Law* 648 (3rd ed., 1948).

139. See Art. 2, Hague Convention XIII and Arts. 2, 26, Havana Convention.

140. See Art. 3, Hague Convention XIII. Familiar World War I cases include *The Pellworm* [1920], p. 347, a German vessel captured by British cruisers in Dutch waters and claimed by the Dutch Government before the British prize court; *The Dusseldorf* [1920] A.C. 1034 and *The Valeria* [1921] 1 A.C. 477, both being German ships taken by British forces in Norwegian waters, the release of which Norway demanded. The classic case is *The Florida* 101 U.S. 37 (1879).

paign in Norway, and yielding to strong German pressure, Sweden concluded an agreement with Germany permitting the passage through Swedish soil of German troops "on leave" and war material en route either from Germany to Norway or vice versa, or from one point in Norway to another. The Swedish Government also permitted, upon the commencement of the German invasion of the Soviet Union, the passage of a German division from Norway through Sweden to Finland.[141] Another slightly less well-known instance of belligerent transit in the last world war was the transporting of supplies of war material between Germany and Italy through Swiss territory. During the long and costly campaign in Italy, the Allied Powers vainly sought from the Swiss Government the termination, or at least the limitation, of this transit traffic.[142] There would seem little doubt that the Allied Powers' protests in those cases, asserting Sweden's and Switzerland's obligation to prevent such uses of their respective territories, accurately reflected the requirements of the law of neutrality.

In opposition to these belligerent demands for prevention of transit and comparable uses of neutral territory,[142a] nonparticipants occasionally assert authority to permit such uses for humanitarian purposes. Humanitarian use is best exemplified in the passage of the wounded and sick of belligerent forces, which passage nonparticipants have long been authorized by customary law to grant.[143] It is perhaps obvious that permission for such passage may in fact be of some value and assistance to the requesting belligerent; pressure upon its transportation lines will to that extent be relieved. In this specific context, however, the requirements of humanitarian policy are commonly regarded as outweighing whatever military disadvan-

141. A concise account is available in *The War and the Neutrals, Survey of International Affairs 1939–1946,* 183–9 (Royal Institute of Int. Affairs, 1956). See also Joesten, "Phases in Swedish Neutrality," 23 *Foreign Aff.* 324, 326–7 (1945).

142. *The War and the Neutrals,* supra note 141 at 80–1.

142a. It may also be noted that on July 6, 1960, during his visit to Austria, Premier Khrushchev warned that "the presence of foreign rocket bases in northern Italy, should they be used against the socialist countries, would presuppose a violation of Austrian neutrality" and that the Soviet Union "would not remain idle" if it considered Austrian neutrality violated. *N. Y. Times,* July 7, 1960. This statement seems difficult to reconcile with what has hitherto been the Soviet position on the freedom of outer space.

143. Art. 14, Hague Convention V.

tage may accrue to the other belligerent from the temporary reduction of load pressure on its opponent's communication system.

A similar weighting in favor of the policy of minimum destruction of values is observable in the practice frequently referred to as "neutral asylum." The practice consists in the grant by the nonparticipant, at its discretion, of access and refuge in its territory to private individuals, members of the public forces of either belligerent, and prisoners of war whether escaped or escorted. Switzerland, for example, gave asylum during World War II to large numbers of assorted refugees and fugitives: French troops after the fall of France in 1940, Italian soldiers in 1943, escaped prisoners of war of many differing nationalities, Jews and other civilians fleeing from the German occupation of their homelands, and so forth.[144] Where asylum is granted to members of a belligerent's public forces, the military interests of the opposing belligerent—who is prevented thereby from pursuing and capturing such forces—are accorded weight by the requirement imposed upon the nonparticipant to disarm and intern such forces for the duration of the war and by that means to insure against their further employment as elements of military power.[145] Curiously enough, conventional law prescribes no comparable requirement in respect of escaped prisoners of war. The nonparticipant may permit their departure and return to their own country where,

144. See *The War and the Neutrals,* supra note 141 at 225.

145. Art. 11, Hague Convention V. See 2 Oppenheim-Lauterpacht 719–25. A minimum standard of treatment for these internees is established by Art. 4(B)(2) of the 1949 Geneva Prisoners of War Convention. This provision generally prescribes prisoner-of-war treatment for such internees "without prejudice to any more favorable treatment which these [neutral or non-belligerent] Powers may choose to give." Some elaboration will be found in Greenspan, *The Modern Law of Land Warfare* 555–60 (1959). The position accorded by Switzerland in World War II to interned members of belligerent armies who were granted asylum is described in *Slubicki v. Commissioners of Police of the Canton of Berne, Annual Digest 1941–1942,* Case No. 182.

Exposition of the provisions of the 1949 Geneva Conventions on the Wounded and Sick, and on the Wounded, Sick, and Shipwrecked, relating to asylum on neutral territory is offered in Greenspan, op. cit., 564–9.

The question of reimbursement of expenses incurred by a neutral in interning and maintaining members of armed forces given asylum is discussed in Freeman, "Non-Belligerent's Right to Compensation for Internment of Foreign Military Personnel," 53 *A.J.I.L.* 638 (1959).

presumably, they may rejoin the armed forces.[146] It perhaps may be assumed that very few belligerents are so casual in their watch over prisoners of war as to permit mass escapes and that escaped prisoners will constitute no more than a mere trickle without appreciable military significance. In view, however, of the tremendous importance in contemporary military establishments of technical personnel with highly specialized skills, nuclear physicists and rocket engineers for instance, some nice discriminations in the exercise of authority respecting repatriation of escaped prisoners of war may with reason perhaps be demanded from nonparticipants in the future.

It may be noted, in further connection with "neutral asylum," that at the terminal stages of the Second World War, the issue was raised by the Allied Powers whether a nonparticipant's authority to grant asylum to private persons and public forces should not be interpreted as excluding those against whom reasonable ground existed for believing they had committed violations of the law of war.[147] The Allied Powers several times requested the Swiss Government, for example, for assurances that war criminals would not gain immunity by fleeing into Switzerland. The Swiss Government's position stressed its claim of comprehensive and exclusive competence over admission of fugitives but appeared to accept the gist of the Allies' view:

> [The] Federal Council intends to exercise [the] unquestioned right of [a] sovereign state to give asylum to fugitives whom it considers worthy thereof. It does not, however, feel disposed—even in cases involving risk of death—to authorize without examination refuge on Swiss territory to all those who may re-

146. Art. 13, Hague Convention V; see *Stepczynski v. Secretary-General of the U.N., Int. Law Rep. 1956,* 609 where the Tribunal ruled that "from the moment the complainant entered Switzerland as an escaped prisoner of war, he was *ipso facto* free . . . [and] could apply for permission to leave Switzerland at any time . . ." (at 610). See also Wilson, "Escaped Prisoners of War in Neutral Jurisdiction," 35 *A.J.I.L.* 519 (1941) where the suggestion is made that escaped prisoners of war should be interned by the neutral granting asylum.

147. See, e.g., the statement of Secretary of State Hull on Sept. 28, 1944, and the statements of the governments of Argentina, Ireland, Portugal, Spain, Sweden, and Switzerland, in 7 *Documents on American Foreign Relations, July 1944–June 1945,* 252–5 (1947).

> quest it as the number of fugitives therein has already reached disturbing proportions. It is obvious in particular that asylum could not be granted . . . to persons . . . who have committed acts contrary to the laws of war or whose past gives evidence of conceptions incompatible with fundamental traditions of law and humanity.[148]

Without seeking to canvass the details of post-World War II experience, the problem may be seen to involve, in addition to the ordinary policies at stake in the international law of asylum and extradition, an inclusive, community-wide, interest in securing effective sanctioning processes for sustaining the principles of minimum order and of minimum unnecessary destruction in warfare.[149] While the optimum line of development is probably toward a permanent international tribunal with criminal jurisdicton, common recognition of an inclusive competence of neutrals as well as of belligerents to try and punish offenders against the law of war, under the "universality" principle of jurisdiction, may also significantly mitigate the problem of effectiveness of sanctions. Questions relating to fairness and convenience in procedural and evidentiary matters may, however, remain.

Belligerent utilization of the territorial waters, as contrasted with both the land surface and the airspace, of a nonparticipant for transit purposes presents problems of some complexity. It may be observed that the trilateral relationships between belligerent, opposing belligerent, and nonparticipant give rise to two distinguishable but interrelated sets of claims.

The first set of claims comprises, on the one hand, a claim by one belligerent to use neutral territorial waters for the "innocent passage" of its warships. The nonparticipant coastal state, on the other hand, asserts in opposition a comprehensive authority over its maritime belt to regulate all passage of warships and even altogether to prohibit such passage, albeit "innocent." The claim to a right of

148. Ibid., 254–5.

149. See Lauterpacht, "The Law of Nations and the Punishment of War Crimes," 21 *Brit. Y.B.I.L.* 58, 86–95 (1944); Morgenstern, "Asylum for War Criminals, Quislings and Traitors," 25 id. 382 (1948); and Neumann, "Neutral States and the Extradition of War Criminals," 45 *A.J.I.L.* 495 (1951). Cf. Garcia-Mora, "The Present Status of Political Offenses in the Law of Extradition and Asylum," 14 *U. Pitts. L. Rev.* 371, 390–6 (1953).

innocent passage for belligerent warships was asserted, for example, by the United Kingdom in a comment it made on May 23, 1939 upon the Neutrality Regulations issued by Norway: [150]

> While His Majesty's Government do not deny that there may in special circumstances be a right to refuse to belligerent warships entry into neutral territorial waters, they have always maintained and must continue to maintain the existence of such a right of entry for the purposes of innocent passage, and they are not aware of any case in which it has been refused by neutrals to belligerents for this purpose.[151]

"The object of this reservation," a later British note explained, "was, of course, to maintain the principle of the right of innocent passage." [152] The extreme opposing claim is exemplified in the Netherlands' World War I neutrality proclamation which prohibited "the passage of belligerent warships . . . through Netherlands waters situated within the territorial waters." [153] In protesting the internment of a German submarine, the German Government stated among other things that, since belligerent warships had under international law a right of innocent passage through neutral waters, the Dutch Proclamation could not lawfully be interpreted to exclude all passage. The reply of the Dutch Government confirmed the intent to forbid even "mere passage" and insisted that international law did not forbid neutrals from closing off their territorial waters and denying any passage to belligerent warships.[154]

It does not seem necessary to dwell at length on the details of this problem. The observation might nevertheless be made that, con-

150. The Neutrality Regulations issued by Norway may be found in 32 *A.J.I.L. Supp.* 154 (1938).

151. Quoted in the statement issued by the British Foreign Office, Feb. 27, 1940, in *Norway and the War, Documents on International Affairs* 37 (Royal Institute of Int. Affairs, 1941).

152. Viscount Halifax to Monsieur Colban, 15 March 1940, reproduced in MacChesney, *Situation, Documents and Commentary on Recent Developments in the International Law of the Sea* 46 (1957).

153. The text of the proclamation will be found in 2 *A Collection of Neutrality Laws, Regulations and Treaties of Various Countries* 802 (Deak and Jessup, eds. 1939).

154. See Vandenbosch, *The Neutrality of the Netherlands During the World War* 88–9 (1927).

sidering the still fluid state of both learned opinion and community expectations about a right of innocent passage for warships in time of peace,[155] it must *a fortiori* appear even more difficult to document in terms of crystallized general expectations the British and German assertions of such a right in time of war, save perhaps—it has been suggested [156]—in the case of international canals and straits. Because, however, many nonparticipants permit *some* passage by belligerent warships through their territorial waters, the more important problem relates, not to neutral authority to prohibit any and all passage, but rather to the scope of neutral authority to permit certain passage or, put in correlative form, the extent of a nonparticipant's duty to prevent certain other passage. It is this problem that is raised by the second set of claim and counterclaim.

The second pair of claims, with which we are most immediately concerned here, embraces demands made by and between the nonparticipant coastal state and the other or opposing belligerent, i.e., the opponent of the belligerent seeking or exercising passage. The demand of this other belligerent is that the nonparticipant forbid and prevent passage of its enemy's war vessels which imposes a disadvantage upon the claimant. Nonparticipants have in countering assertion claimed that the exercises complained of constitute innocuous transit which nonparticipants are authorized to permit and hence have no duty to prevent.

The complex of competing interests at stake in this specific context is quickly summarized. The claimant belligerent has clearly an interest in seeking out, attacking, and destroying its enemy's naval

155. The 1958 Geneva Convention on the Territorial Sea and the Contiguous Zone has scarcely served definitively to fix expectations and quiet all the controversies of the doctors relating to this particular point. See, of the flood of recent accounts and commentaries on this and the other 1958 Conventions, Jessup, "The United Nations Conference on the Law of the Sea," 59 *Col. L. Rev.* 234, 247–8 (1959); Fitzmaurice, "Some Results of the Geneva Conference on the Law of the Sea. Part I—The Territorial Sea and Contiguous Zone and Related Topics," 8 *Int. and Comp. Law Q.* 73, 98–103 (1959); Sorensen, "Law of the Sea," *Int. Conciliation,* No. 520, p. 195, 235 (1958). For outstanding recent inquiry and analysis, see Burke, *Comprehensive State Authority Over Ocean Areas: A Policy Perspective,* c. 2 (unpublished J.S.D. thesis, Yale Law Library, 1959).

156. Baxter, "Passage of Ships Through International Waterways in Time of War," 31 *Brit. Y.B.I.L.* 187 (1954).

power. Its enemy's interest in securing safe navigation for its war vessels is equally obvious. The interests of the coastal nonparticipant state consists, on the other hand, in the safeguarding of its land-based community processes from the possible serious consequences of a naval engagement in close proximity to its shores, and in the avoidance of the more comprehensive impact of involvement in the war as a full-fledged belligerent. These are the clashing interests that are sought to be adjusted in relevant compromise by application of the "mere passage" and "base of naval operations" rules.

Article 10 of Hague Convention XIII, 1907, sets forth the first rule: "The neutrality of a Power is not affected by the mere passage through its territorial waters of warships or prizes belonging to belligerents." The implications which appear to follow from this sibylline language are that the nonparticipant is authorized, though not required, to permit the "mere passage" of a belligerent's warships and that the nonparticipant is required to prevent the activities of such warships which go beyond "mere passage." [157] The other prescription is embodied in Article 5 of the same Convention which prohibits belligerents from "us[ing] neutral ports and waters as a base of naval operations against their adversaries . . ." "Mere passage" and "base of naval operations" may be seen to be polar opposites and to embrace in factual reference a whole spectrum of kinds of activities by warships.[158] The characterization of a particular kind of activity in terms of permissibility or impermissibility is, we submit, most appropriately conceived of as a function of the various detailed factors and conditions that comprise a specific context. Some of these factors and conditions almost naturally suggest themselves: the kind of warship involved; the character of the route proposed or taken; the character of the waters traversed; the frequency of use; the duration of particular uses; the relative strength of the contending belligerents in naval surface as in subsurface power and in air, including missile power; and so on. The relevancy of these and analogous factors lies principally in their utility, when carefully appraised, as bases of inference as to the strategic and tactical objectives of particular passages, the impact—in terms of the degree

157. Tucker, *The Law of War and Neutrality at Sea,* 233 (1957).

158. Cf. MacChesney, supra note 152 at 18 discussing the relationship between Article 10 and Article 5.

of disadvantage imposed—upon the military position of the belligerent demanding prevention, and the probable effects upon the security and other interests of the nonparticipant coastal state.

The *cause célèbre* of the *Altmark* affords illustration of how some of these factors may be considered and appraised in a particular situation. The *Altmark,*[159] it may be recalled, was a German naval auxiliary vessel carrying some 300 British officers and seamen as prisoners of war. It entered Norwegian territorial waters at Trondheim Fjord, on February 14, 1940 and sailed down the maritime belt of Norway for about 400 miles en route to Germany. On February 16, 1940 it was stopped by British warships. The British request, addressed to the commander of the Norwegian torpedo-boats escorting the *Altmark,* that the *Altmark* be brought under joint British and Norwegian escort to Bergen for full examination was refused. The British warships then forced the *Altmark* into Jössing Fjord where it was boarded. The British prisoners were released, transferred to a British warship, and taken to England. The Norwegian Government protested the acts of the British warships in its territorial and internal waters as a violation of its neutrality, alleging, along with other contentions, that since the *Altmark* had not called at any Norwegian port, it had been engaged all throughout in "mere passage," and that consequently the Norwegian Government had not had to decide what to do with the vessel and the prisoners.[160] The reply of the British Government laid stress on, among other things, the character of the route taken and, to all appearances, proposed to be completed by the *Altmark* and the duration of its passage as indicating the objective of such passage:

> "Innocent passage," which it was the object of Article 10 to allow, means passage through such territorial waters as would form part of the ship's normal course from the point of departure to her destination, and in particular through such terri-

159. The facts are recited at some length in the note of 15 March 1940 of Viscount Halifax to Monsieur Colban, supra note 152 at 37–40. A summary of the facts may be found in 7 Hackworth, *Digest of International Law* 568–9 (1943); this summary is reproduced in MacChesney, supra note 152 at 7–8. A brief account is also set out in Waldock, "The Release of the Altmark's Prisoners," 24 *Brit. Y.B.I.L.* 216, 218–19 (1947).

160. Official statement by the Norwegian Government, Feb. 25, 1940, in *Norway and the War,* supra note 151 at 35–6.

torial waters as form part of straits which provide access from one area of the sea to another.

. . .

[T]he Norwegian Government will not suggest that the circuitous route taken by the *Altmark* bears any relation whatever to the course normally adopted by shipping proceeding from the Atlantic north-about to Germany. The sole and the admitted object with which the *Altmark* took this highly remarkable course was to conclude her warlike operations under the protection of Norwegian neutrality for a distance of several hundred miles and a period of more than three days, so as to escape the fate which awaited her on the high seas at the hands of the British Fleet; . . .[161]

It is difficult to ascribe much force to the construction of Article 10 of Hague Convention XIII, 1907, urged by Norway, a construction that would equate "mere passage" with *continuous* passage as distinguished from passage that is interrupted by entry and call at a coastal port. There appears no necessary or even usual relation between the physical continuity, or discontinuity, of a warship's passage and the potentiality, or lack thereof, of such passage for disadvantage to the other belligerent or for danger to the nonparticipant coastal state, the preclusion of which must seem the principal purpose projected in Articles 5 and 10.[162] As the British note suggests, somewhat cryptically, to permit belligerent passage through neutral territorial waters for purposes of refuge and securing immunity from attack is significantly to disturb the relative positions of the belligerents vis-à-vis each other. By such permission and tolerance, the neutral state would in effect be neutralizing and nullifying the relative

161. Viscount Halifax to Monsieur Colban, supra note 152 at 44, 45.

162. Cf. the construction of "mere" or "innocent passage" in MacChesney, supra note 152 at 19: "It must be an innocent passage for bona fide purposes of navigation rather than for escape or asylum. The passage must also be innocent in the sense that it does not prejudice either the security interests of the coastal state, or the interests of the opposing belligerent in preventing passage beyond the type agreed to in Article X. A passage that increased the burden of surveillance or the likelihood of embroiling the neutral in hostilities would certainly prejudice the security interests of the neutral coastal state." Professor MacChesney lines up the writers arrayed on each side of the question in the *Altmark;* ibid., 8–10.

superiority of the other belligerent in naval or air power and preventing such belligerent from securing outcomes it could otherwise realistically expect to achieve.

The degree of disadvantage thus imposed upon the other belligerent may of course be expected to differ as the detailed features of specific situations differ. The impact upon such other belligerent may vary, for example, with the kind of war vessel allowed refuge from attack. Thus, refuge for submarines, which today may be used not only for destroying maritime commerce but also for strategic missile bombardment, might reasonably be regarded as creating a particularly clear and heavy disadvantage for the opposing belligerent as well as special dangers for the coastal nonparticipant.[163] The practice of many states, embodied in their neutrality regulations,[164] of prohibiting or subjecting to special restrictions the entry or passage of belligerent submarines in territorial waters, reflects recognition of such special difficulties and dangers. It may be, as is sometimes suggested, that "belligerent passage through neutral waters always forms part of naval operations and therefore can always be interpreted as conferring some sort of advantage upon the belligerent which makes use of neutral territorial waters." [165] So long, however, as it remains necessary to make discriminations as to de-

163. In 1918, as Professor Waldock noted, supra note 159 at 234–5, the British and United States Governments protested the use of Norwegian territorial waters by German submarines for purposes of safe passage to and from their areas of operations in the Atlantic. The ordinary routes of the U-boats had been closed by means of the Allied mine barrage in the North Sea. The United States Government stated that such use "could justly be regarded" as converting Norwegian territorial waters to a "base of naval operations," and urged Norway to mine its waters. Norway eventually laid down the minefields desired by the Allied Powers.

It might be added, in connection with the factor of impact upon the neutral coastal state's interests, that the use of nuclear depth charges by the disadvantaged belligerent against its opponent's submarines taking refuge in neutral waters could result in comprehensive damage to the neutral. Coastal fisheries, for instance, might be rendered unexploitable at least for some time.

164. See Harvard Research, "Rights and Duties of Neutral States in Naval and Aerial War," 33 *A.J.I.L. Supp.* 432–5 (1939).

The 1958 Geneva Convention on the Territorial Sea and Contiguous Zone requires submarines passing through the territorial waters of a state to navigate on the surface and to display their flag; Art. 14(6), text in 52 *A.J.I.L.* 834 (1958).

165. Tucker, *The Law of War and Neutrality at Sea* 235, note 84 (1957).

grees of disadvantage,[166] the general submission may be made that the nonparticipant is appropriately required to prevent belligerent passage (physically continuous or otherwise) through its territorial waters which is of such a character as to create reasonable expectations on the part of the other belligerent that it must forcibly intervene and terminate such passage to avoid consequential harm to its military position. By "reasonableness" we mean reasonableness as third-party observers and decision-makers, appraising contextual factors, may determine it. Where these expectations are generated in the other belligerent, a corresponding degree of danger of involvement arises for the nonparticipant permitting the passage. The measure of its duty of prevention is thus unavoidably in part a function of the nonparticipant's estimate of the probable limits of belligerent tolerance.

We turn to the second broad category of belligerent activity the prevention of which is demanded from the nonparticipant: the utilization of its territory as a "base of operations." In comprehensive conception, the conversion of neutral territory into a "base of operations" has been described in terms of its use as "a source or station from which a belligerent State as such augments its power of doing harm to the enemy." [167] It will be seen, however, that this conception is rarely carried through consistently in the customary law and practice of neutrality. Historically, belligerent-nonparticipant controversies in this area have centered around a limited number of relatively well-defined species of acts.

One species of acts that decision-makers have customarily required nonparticipants to prevent and belligerents to abstain from consists of the drawing of military manpower from the nonparticipant's human resources. This act, characterized by Professor Hyde as "the origination and organization of military and naval forces," has included all efforts of a belligerent to enlist, commission, hire, or induce persons of whatever nationality to enter upon its service.[168] Such efforts may be difficult to police since it is not frequently to be

166. The necessity being imposed by failure or unwillingness to deny *all* passage through neutral territorial waters to belligerent warships. Recommendation for total denial or drastic restriction of passage has been made in, e.g., 3 Hyde, *International Law* 2312 (2nd rev. ed., 1945).

167. Id., 2249.

168. Id., 2238–40; Art. 4, Hague Convention V.

expected that recruitment would be conducted with the same openness and conspicuousness shown by the French Minister to the United States, M. Genêt, who issued military commissions in 1793 to American citizens to fit out and man privateers and to cruise against British merchantmen.[169] The requirement of prevention of recruitment, a matter of moment in earlier centuries when privateers and foreign mercenaries were important components of the public forces of states,[170] would seem of limited applicability in an era of mass citizen armies. Conceivably, however, the prescription may acquire new point should belligerents, particularly states below the first order of power, seek to draw from third states the scientific and technical personnel necessary to develop, manufacture, and handle the highly complex contemporary weapons systems. Closely comparable to the recruitment of manpower are the fitting out, arming, and commissioning, within the nonparticipant's territory, of war vessels [171] and military aircraft [172] for participation in military operations against the opposing belligerent. This situation—that is, of units of belligerent naval (and, today, of air) power being built and equipped in neutral territory and from there essaying forth to do battle with the enemy—is the classic illustration of what the "base of operations" rule was designed to preclude.

Another species of belligerent activity traditionally regarded as

169. See Hall, *International Law* 705–7 (8th ed., Pearce Higgins, 1924); 7 Moore, *Digest of International Law* 886–8.

See, however, the recent announcement of the opening of a recruiting office by the National Union in the United Arab Republic for recruitment of volunteers for service in Algeria on the side of the Algerian rebels. It was reported that the Union—an official body chosen in nationwide elections "as a first step toward the selection of a national assembly"—had "one fully equipped division in mind." *N. Y. Times,* March 23, 1960, p. 1, col. 8.

170. See Preston, Wise and Werner, *Men in Arms: A History of Warfare and Its Interrelationships with Western Society* c. 7 (1956); and Ropp, *War in the Modern World* 36–42 (1959) for historical accounts.

171. Art. 8, Hague Convention XIII. The *Alabama* Claims is too well known to require more than casual mention; in Briggs, *The Law of Nations* 1026 (2nd ed., 1952).

172. See Art. 46, "Hague Rules of Air Warfare, General Report of the Commission of Jurists to Consider and Report upon the Revision of the Rules of Warfare," Feb. 11, 1923; text in 32 *A.J.I.L. Supp.* 36 (1938). Cf. Art. 99 of the "Harvard Draft Convention, Rights and Duties of Neutral States in Naval and Aerial War," supra, note 164.

falling within the "base of operations" principle relates to the use of neutral territory for military communications purposes. Specifically, customary law required a nonparticipant to prevent belligerents from establishing and operating radio stations in its territory and transmitting military information through such means.[173] In addition, there has developed the supplementary practice of nonparticipants of prohibiting the use by belligerent vessels, while on neutral waters, of their radio apparatus, save in case of distress.[174] The situation sought to be avoided by this requirement and practice was principally that of the maintenance of command and communications posts in neutral refuges from which a belligerent could direct the operations of its forces on land and sea. It is illustrative of the lack of consistency in the patterns of traditional rules referred to above that no comparable requirement is imposed to prevent the belligerent construction and operation of, and transmission of military information through, means of telecommunications other than radio, such as telephone (land), telegraph and submarine cables.[175] Moreover, traditional law imposed no duty to prevent and control the use by belligerents, even for the communication of military orders and intelligence, of the telecommunication—including wireless—systems and facilities owned and operated either by the nonparticipant gov-

173. Art. 3, Hague Convention V; Art. 5, Hague Convention XIII; Art. 4(b), Havana Convention. See also Arts. 3, 4, and 6, "Hague Rules for the Control of Radio in Time of War, General Report of the Commission of Jurists," supra note 172.

174. References to national neutrality regulations forbidding such use are collected in Harvard Research, supra note 164 at 272–4. See also 3 Hyde, *International Law* 2259 (2nd rev. ed., 1945).

175. Certain bases for distinguishing between radio and other media utilizing wires or cables were offered by Secretary Bryan in 1915. The first related to the possibility of belligerent interruption of the process of transmitting information; cables could be cut, while wireless communication could not. This is, of course, without point today since radio transmission is easily "jammed." The second was that radio permitted communication with belligerent warships at sea and the direction of their movements from neutral territory which hence became a base of naval operations; such communication with and direction of warships at sea was not possible in the case of telegraph or submarine cables. This distinction was, even in 1915, more ingenious than real. For information transmitted by cables could easily be relayed by belligerents' radio stations to their ships at sea. Secretary Bryan's letter is excerpted in Harvard Research, supra note 164 at 269. The above arguments strongly reflected British and French views (ibid.).

ernment or private companies and individuals.[176] This absence of duty in respect of belligerent use of neutral-owned systems and facilities obviously dulled the point of the prohibition against belligerents constructing and operating their own stations in neutral territory. Practice on this matter appears to have overtaken conventional prescription, and the trend discernible in the last two world wars is toward increasing recognition of a duty to control and regulate all radio, and probably telegraph, stations within neutral territory to prevent the communication of military information to the belligerents.[177] Postal communications, however, are still not the subject of any requirement of prevention or control. Anent the probable future utility and applicability of these prescriptions, it may be speculated that in future wars involving belligerents with space capabilities, the perfection and use of communications and reconnaissance satellite vehicles [178] may significantly reduce the occasions for utilization of neutral territory and facilities for communications purposes and hence for assertion of demands for neutral prevention.

The failure of traditional law consistently to carry through in its specifics the broad prohibition of use of a nonparticipant's territory as a "base of operations" is perhaps most clearly observable in the regulation of the use of neutral ports by belligerent war vessels. Customary law imposed no requirement upon a nonparticipant to prevent the entry and stay of belligerent war vessels in its ports; at the same time no duty to permit such entry and stay, save in cases of distress, was recognized.[179] Nonparticipants have characteristically asserted a wide competence to control access to their ports, occasionally prescribing complete exclusion of belligerent war vessels,[180] and to determine the conditions under which access is granted to such

176. Art. 8, Hague Convention V.

177. See Harvard Research, supra note 164 at 276–9; also De Wolf, "Telecommunications and Neutrality," 30 *A.J.I.L.* 117 (1936).

178. The potentialities of artificial satellite systems for communications and reconnaissance purposes are discussed in *Developments in Military Technology,* supra note 11 at 72–5. See also *Space Handbook: Astronautics and Its Applications,* Staff Report of the Select Committee on Astronautics and Space Exploration, 86th Cong., 2nd Sess., 171–91, 202–4 (1959). The actual use of reconnaissance satellite vehicles has commenced with Tiros I.

179. Tucker, *The Law of War and Neutrality at Sea* 240 (1957).

180. States which have in the past prescribed total exclusion, subject to the usual exceptions of entry in distress etc., are listed in Harvard Research, supra note 164 at 428.

vessels. One of these conditions relates to the duration of stay. Under Article 12 of Hague Convention XIII, 1907, which reflects common practice, the ordinary permissible period of sojourn of belligerent war vessels in neutral ports is limited to twenty-four hours. The stringency of this limitation is, however, less real than apparent for exceptions are available for permitting a longer stay in cases that matter to the belligerent flag state. Thus, aside from delay arising from stress of weather, a longer stay may be granted where the vessel has been damaged until such condition is remedied.[181] In the case of the *Admiral Graf Spee* in 1939, for instance, the Uruguayan Government gave the German commander three days to repair the damage inflicted by the guns of British warships.[182] In 1914 and 1915, the United States Government allowed the German gunboat *Geier* three weeks for repairs, the battleship *Prinz Eitel Freidrich* fourteen working days, and the cruiser *Kronprinz Wilhelm* six working days.[183] Moreover, where the refueling and revictualing of belligerent warships in accordance with the nonparticipant's municipal regulations are not completed within twenty-four hours, then permissible stay may be extended another twenty-four hours.[184]

As indicated in the preceding paragraph, nonparticipants commonly claim authority not only to permit simple entry and stay—which, in the case of a warship being pursued and hunted by enemy forces, means at least temporary relief—but also to allow the vessel to undergo repairs, to take on fuel, and to revictual. It is scarcely a profound observation that such authority is in effect authority to permit a belligerent to derive from neutral territory assistance and sustenance which is not always militarily insubstantial. Thus, to permit a warship to carry out repairs, even though the repairs be limited to those "absolutely necessary to render them seaworthy," [185] is at least to allow it to survive as a unit of belligerent strength and

181. Art. 14, Hague Convention XIII; Art. 5, par. 3, Havana Convention.

182. *The Uruguayan Blue Book* 38 (Ministry of Foreign Affairs, Republic of Uruguay, 1940).

183. See 3 Hyde, *International Law* 2269 (2nd rev. ed., 1945).

184. Art. 19, Hague Convention XIII; Art. 5, par. 4, Havana Convention. The arbitrator in *The Attilio Regolo, Annual Digest, 1947,* Case No. 137, observed that Article 19, Hague Convention XIII, imposed no obligation on the neutral to give active assistance in ensuring fuel supplies for the belligerent warships which it admits into its ports, and that fueling was a right which the captain of the warship may exercise by recourse to the market.

185. Art. 17, Hague Convention XIII.

to return to its home base. There is partial recognition of this point in the practice of some states of distinguishing between damage inflicted by enemy action and damage brought about by weather conditions, and of permitting repair only of the latter kind.[186] Again, to permit a warship to fill up its bunkers with fuel, or even merely to refuel up to the "nearest home port" level, and to replenish its food supplies up to the "peace [time] standard," is to enable the ship to engage in hostile operations against its enemy.[187] The military value of entry and stay in neutral ports is not necessarily contingent upon frequency of resort.[188]

It is thus clear that maritime states have not in practice accepted the implications for prevention which with strictest logic may be derived from general principle. In line with the direction of the principal policy recommendation essayed earlier, that is, toward discrimination by third states between belligerents upon the basis of the fundamental principle of minimum order and abstention from aid to the belligerent acting in breach of this principle, the suggestion may be submitted that the area left to the exclusive competence of the nonparticipant should be reduced, and that more exacting duties of prevention may appropriately be demanded from nonparticipants to ensure that no assistance of any military significance is afforded to the offending belligerent. It may additionally be noted that even apart from the imperative of abstention from aid to violator belligerents, proposals continue to be made for the

186. See Harvard Research, supra note 164 at 470–2; Art. 9, Havana Convention. Tucker, *The Law of War and Neutrality at Sea* 244 (1957) finds that the "tendency" of neutral states is "clearly" toward forbidding the repair of battle damage.

187. Art. 19, par. 2, Hague Convention XIII. The tactical opportunities opened up for belligerent warships by permitting their refueling and revictualing have been stressed in, e.g., 3 Hyde, *International Law* 2266 (2nd rev. ed., 1945) and Harvard Research, supra note 164 at 473, 476.

188. Contrast Hall, *International Law* 724–5 (8th ed., Pearce Higgins, 1924): "[C]ontinued use is above all things the crucial test of a base, both as a matter of fact and as fixing a neutral with responsibility for acts in themselves innocent or ambiguous. A neutral has no right to infer evil intent from a single innocent act performed by a belligerent armed force; but if he finds that it is repeated several times, and that it has always prepared the way for warlike operations, he may be fairly expected to assume that a like consequence is intended in all cases to follow and he ought therefore to prevent its being done within his territory."

reduction of what has been called the "excessive license embodied in the Hague Convention of 1907." [189] For instance, the demands of humanity might be met, Professor Hyde suggested, by allowing entrance to belligerent warships in distress, and the military interests of the opposing belligerent might be simultaneously protected by requiring internment of the vessel and complement.[190]

Activities of Individuals in a Nonparticipant's Territory. We turn next to demands for the prevention of certain activities of individuals in a nonparticipant's territory which disadvantageously affect a belligerent. Here again, practice may be seen to fall far short of principle. The duty of prevention recognized in customary law by no means covered all acts of individuals which in their impact were advantageous to one and detrimental to the other belligerent.

Belligerent demands for prevention have historically centered around two closely similar kinds of acts of individual persons. There are, firstly, such acts as the construction, fitting out, and arming of war vessels, as well as the conversion or adaptation of merchantmen into war vessels, "to the order of a belligerent," and the launching of any such vessel from neutral territory. After the famous *Alabama Claims* award of 1872,[191] there was no question that customary law required a nonparticipant to prevent such activities. At the same time, however, customary law imposed no requirement upon a nonparticipant to prevent individuals within its territory either from selling warships to a belligerent or from building such craft for the purpose of selling them to a belligerent. This curious distinction, which, on the one hand, assimilates the construction of a warship "to the order of a belligerent" to the proscribed utilization of neutral territory as a "base of operations" and, on the other hand, identifies the construction of the same warship with the aim of selling it to a belligerent with the permissible manufacture and export of "con-

189. 3 Hyde, supra note 187 at 2266.

190. Ibid. Cf. Smith, *The Law and Custom of the Sea* 189–90 (3rd ed., 1959). The matter may, of course, decline in importance when nuclear-powered warships, both surface and submersible, become more common.

191. Briggs, *The Law of Nations* 1026 (2nd ed., 1952). The full text of the award is contained in 1 Moore, *History and Digest of the Arbitrations to Which the United States Has Been a Party* 653–9 (1898). The three Rules of the Treaty of Washington, May 8, 1871, in 2 *A Collection of Neutrality Laws, Regulations and Treaties of Various Countries* 1368 (Deak and Jessup, eds., 1939), are embodied in Art. 8, Hague Convention XIII.

traband," has been described, with considerable restraint, as "hair-splitting." [192] The recommendation that we make is, in line with what has above been submitted with respect to the exportation of war materials, that the nonparticipant be required to take responsibility for such acts of its inhabitants and to prevent the furnishing of war-ships, as of other war material, to a belligerent without regard to the details and the timing of contractual transactions.

Belligerent demands for prevention relate, secondly, to the combination and organization of individuals in a nonparticipant's territory for the purpose of undertaking military operations against one or the other belligerent. The common claim of belligerents is that the nonparticipant has a duty to prevent persons within its jurisdiction from so combining and organizing into units of hostile military power, in much the same way that it is required to prevent the opposing belligerent government from recruiting troops from the neutral's population.[192a] A principal assertion frequently made in opposition by the nonparticipant is that the individuals involved are volunteers whose participation in military operations the nonparticipant is not required to forbid and prevent.

The problems raised by the making of these claims and countering claims in modern context may be economically illustrated by reference to the fairly recent controversies that arose during the Russo-Finnish war of 1939 and the intervention of the People's Republic of China in the Korean conflict of 1950. On January 5, 1940, the Soviet Government officially protested certain "actions of the Swedish authorities directed against the U.S.S.R." as "inconsistent with Sweden's policy of neutrality." The Soviet Government claimed, among other things, that "certain [Swedish] official persons [were] openly taking part in the organization of military assistance for the [Finnish] Government," that 47 "recruiting stations" had been opened in Sweden "under the patronage of Swedish authorities," and that "up to 10,000 'volunteers' " so recruited had arrived in Finland from Sweden. The Swedish Government stated in reply that the recruitment of volunteers was undertaken "on private initiative only," that Swedish governmental organs were not cooperating in the recruitment of volunteers, that no officers or enlisted men of the

192. 2 Oppenheim-Lauterpacht 714.

192a. The duty to prevent recruitment of troops is embodied in Arts. 4 and 5, Hague Convention V.

Swedish army were taking part as volunteers in the Finnish war, and finally that the figures cited by the Soviet Government were inaccurate.[193] Subsequent postwar accounts indicate that Sweden had indeed permitted the recruitment of volunteers in her territory and from her population, and that about 9000 fully armed and equipped volunteers had crossed the Gulf of Bothnia and served with the Finnish army.[194]

More recently, a somewhat different view on the question of volunteers was taken by the Soviet Union. In the discussions at the United Nations which followed the sudden and vast outpouring of Chinese forces into Korea in November, 1950, it was urged with great seriousness by the Soviet delegate that those forces were composed wholly of volunteers. Mr. Vishinsky argued insistently that

> In reality, there has been no invasion of Korea by the armed forces of the People's Republic of China . . . since that government has no armed forces in Korea. It has never sent such forces there and is not sending them.
>
> . . .
>
> In righteous indignation ["against United States aggression in Korea"], large numbers of Chinese are going voluntarily to the aid of the Korean people.
>
> . . . [T]he attempt . . . to depict the position and the action taken by the Central People's Government of the People's Republic of China as some kind of armed intervention by the Central People's Government in Korea, is completely unfounded. Such an interpretation of the question is at variance

193. See the *Narkomindel* (People's Commissariat for Foreign Affairs) statement on "Soviet Relations with Sweden and Norway," Jan. 15, 1940, in 3 *Soviet Documents on Foreign Policy 1933–1941,* 416–20 (Degras, ed., Royal Institute of Int. Affairs, 1953). The same charges were made by the Soviet Government against Norway, and the Norwegian Government's reply was substantially the same as that of the Swedish Government.

194. *The War and the Neutrals, Survey of International Affairs 1939–1946,* 175 (Royal Institute of International Affairs, 1956). Fox, *The Power of Small States* 123 (1959) speaks of "over 8000 volunteers," "many of them from the ranks of the Swedish reserves." Mrs. Fox writes further that the Swedish Government "granted permission for the passage of volunteers organized in England and France so long as these were not on active service with the Allied forces, went in small groups, and received their equipment after arrival" (ibid.). See also Joesten, "Phases in Swedish Neutrality," 23 *Foreign Aff.* 324, 325 (1945).

> with all the facts . . . and it is contrary to the principles of international law and the international agreements bearing on this question.[195]

Quoting Article 6 of Hague Convention V, 1907, Mr. Vishinsky drew the conclusion that

> The Central People's Government . . . can in no way be held responsible for any volunteers who may be fighting side by side with the Korean People's army of liberation.[196]

The primary focus of inquiry in controversies about the activities of persons claimed to be volunteers has characteristically been on the degree and extent of governmental control and participation. Clearly, there may be a broad range of possible degrees of governmental participation and control. At one end of the continuum, effective governmental control over the initiation, direction, and management of these activities may be so complete as to render the use of the term "volunteers" no more than an inept and transparent effort to disguise the operations of public armed forces of a state and to avoid the thrust of the fundamental prohibition of aggression. In such a situation, the problem resolves itself into one of applying the principle of minimum order. In situations located at the other extreme of free private choice on the part of the individuals involved, governmental participation is limited to tolerance and permissive acquiescence. It was historically to this type of situation that Article 6 of Hague Convention V, 1907, was addressed and here the principal problem would seem one of determining what may appropriately be demanded from the nonparticipant by way of preventive measures.[197]

Article 6 provides that "The responsibility of a neutral Power is not engaged by the fact of persons crossing the frontier separately to offer their services to one of the belligerents." The military interest of a belligerent in making sure that the human, as other, resources of a nonparticipant do not become available to its enemy, has been adverted to above. It should be observed that the consequences, for this interest, of volunteers from neutral territory have

195. U.N. Gen. Ass., *Off. Rec.*, 5th Sess., Plenary 590, 592 (1950).

196. Id., p. 592.

197. See, generally, Brownlie, "Volunteers and the Law of War and Neutrality," 5 *Int. and Comp. Law Q.* 570 (1956) and Garcia-Mora, "International Law and the Law of Hostile Military Expeditions," 27 *Fordham L. Rev.* 309 (1958).

no necessary relation either to the manner of their departure—"separately" (*isolement*) or "simultaneously" in more or less organized groups—or to the degree of private choice (or, conversely, the extent of governmental compulsion) which attends their military enterprise. On the other hand, Article 6 reflects a policy of permitting individual persons to give, where governmental officials may or will not, free expression to their preference as between the contending belligerents, whether the motivation of such preference be commercial or ideological.

Indeed, as commentators have observed, Article 6 had for its principal presuppositions the same notions of political order and economic and social organization that underlay Article 7 (on the exportation of war materials by private entities) and which defined most restrictively the "proper" scope of governmental action.[198] The same condition pointed to in connection with Article 7—the increasingly high common level of governmentalization in internal community processes—must hence be also noted here. It is reflective of the large control today commonly exercised by governments over movement of their peoples that many states unilaterally forbid, either by standing statute or *ad hoc* neutrality regulation, the enlistment of their nationals in the armed forces of foreign belligerent states. It would in fact seem difficult to imagine how, in a reasonably well organized state, any sizeable number of people can leave for the purpose of serving with belligerent armies abroad without the knowledge and consent of state officials. Moreover, some states have, by means of multilateral conventions, undertaken to prevent their nationals from joining the forces of a belligerent and participating in hostilities.[199] In line, once more, with our basic recommendation on the establishment of common responsibility for minimum order and on discrimination between belligerents, a nonparticipant may, it is submitted, appropriately be required to assume responsibility for preventing its inhabitants from augmenting the ranks of the belligerent determined by the organized community to have unlawfully

198. Brownlie, supra note 197 at 577; Garcia-Mora, supra note 197 at 325.

199. Brownlie, supra note 197 at 575–7 collects references to these conventions, as well as to municipal statutes and regulations prohibiting enlistment of nationals in foreign armed forces. See Curtis, "The Law of Hostile Military Expeditions as Applied by the United States," 8 *A.J.I.L.* 1, 224 (1914) for earlier American practice.

resorted to violence.[200] At the same time, the nonparticipant, being authorized to take part in permissive sanctioning measures, may *a fortiori* be regarded as competent to permit its inhabitants to serve with the forces engaged in such enforcement activity where more extensive governmental participation is declined.[201]

The activities of neutral nationals which may significantly affect the military interests of a belligerent are not of course limited to enlistment in the armed forces of the opposing belligerent. These activities include, for instance, the performance of what is technically designated as "unneutral service." "Unneutral service" has principally been given a maritime reference [202] embracing such activities of privately owned neutral vessels as sailing under the orders or immediate control, or in the exclusive employment, of a belligerent or its agent; sailing under the convoy of a belligerent's warships; transporting members of a belligerent's armed forces and the like. Customary law authorized a belligerent to treat private neutral vessels

200. The Peruvian representative (Belaunde), during the discussions in the Korean case, stressed perceptively that:

> It mattered little whether or not the troops resisting the United Nations' action to establish the rule of law and the right of the peoples to self-determination were volunteers since the neighboring countries were in any case under a legal as well as a moral obligation to prevent any action contrary to that undertaken by the United Nations, which was acting on behalf of all mankind. Consequently, the argument based on the application of the 1907 Convention was wholly irrelevant . . .

U.N. Gen. Ass., *Off. Rec.*, 5th Sess., 1st Comm. 407 (1950).

201. This suggestion is also essayed in Brownlie, supra note 197 at 579. It may be noted, however, that certain forms of what may be called humanitarian participation by neutral persons are permitted in the 1949 Geneva Conventions. The Wounded and Sick Convention provides in Article 27 that a Red Cross Society of a neutral country may lend the assistance of its medical units to a belligerent, with the consent of both the neutral and such belligerent, and that such assistance may not be regarded as interference in the conflict. The Wounded, Sick and Shipwrecked Convention, in Article 25, provides for protection of hospital ships which are used by the Red Cross Society or by other relief societies and private persons of neutral countries, and which are placed under the control of one of the belligerents.

202. Stone, *Legal Controls of International Conflict* 512 (rev. ed., 1959) makes the noteworthy suggestion that "unneutral service" seems to be a "residual category remaining after the specific heads of contraband and blockade became differentiated."

engaged in these activities as assimilated to the merchant marine or naval forces of its enemy and hence to subject them to capture and condemnation or, in proper cases, to sinking at sight.[203]

CLAIMS OF NONPARTICIPANTS AGAINST BELLIGERENTS

The principal affirmative claims that nonparticipants make against belligerents may be very generally described in terms of a demand that both belligerent sides observe toward the nonparticipants the requirements of the principle of minimum public order. The requirements of minimum order embrace, in this context, not only the refraining from direct attack upon the nonparticipant and its bases of power but also desistance from interbelligerent activities in neutral territory that result in harm and injury for the nonparticipant. From a slightly different viewpoint, nonparticipants may be seen to be demanding from both the contending belligerents that they abstain from those exercises and activities which each belligerent requires the nonparticipant to prevent and restrain the other belligerent from carrying out.

Specific claims of nonparticipants include, most importantly, a demand that belligerents refrain from carrying their hostile operations into the territorial domain of the nonparticipant and an accompanying assertion of authority to exclude the entry of belligerent forces into such domain. With particular reference to naval warfare,

203. The most recent canvassing of the detailed requirements of the law on unneutral service is in Tucker, *The Law of War and Neutrality at Sea* 318–31 (1957). 2 Oppenheim-Lauterpacht 745–51 and Smith, *The Law and Custom of the Sea* 131–7 (3rd ed., 1959) set forth summaries. The term "analogues of contraband" was used by the older texts; e.g., Hall, *International Law* 817–35 (8th ed., Pearce Higgins, 1924).

Examples of World War II cases where the doctrine of unneutral service was invoked to support condemnation in prize are *The Leontios Teryazos, Annual Digest, 1943–1945,* Case No. 167, and *The Gragesberg,* id., Case No. 195, both decided by the German Prize Court at Hamburg. The first was a Greek ship chartered by the British Ministry of Food to carry wheat from Montreal to Bordeaux; the second was a Swedish vessel chartered by a French Government agency to bring coal from Newcastle to Le Havre and Rouen. Cf. *The Captain Manoli* and *The Lea Lott,* infra note 301, decided by the Egyptian Prize Court at Alexandria, where the charterer of the neutral (Liberian and West German) vessels involved was an Israeli company. The Court did not require evidence as to whether the charterer company was in fact subject to the control of the Israeli Government.

nonparticipant coastal states have claimed authority to protect their security generally and the integrity of their landbased community processes by excluding belligerent operations not only from their territorial waters [204] but also from areas of the high seas adjacent to their maritime belt. The most prominent example of neutral claims to establish a special contiguous zone for safeguarding lives and property in the neutral coastal state from the impact of belligerent operations is still the Declaration of Panama of October 3, 1939 by the American Republics. The Declaration marked out a neutral protective zone which enveloped the American continents and extended seaward for several hundred miles beyond the belt claimed by the declarants as territorial waters. In the Declaration, it was stated that

> As a measure of continental self-protection, the American Republics, so long as they maintain their neutrality, are as of inherent right entitled to have those waters adjacent to the American continent, which they regard as of primary concern and direct utility in their relations, free from the commission of any hostile act by any non-American belligerent nation, whether such hostile act be attempted or made from land, sea or air.[205]

In their replies to the protest which the American Republics made following the *Admiral Graf Spee* incident, both the Allied Powers and Germany rejected the duty of belligerent abstention envisaged in the Declaration.[206] Notwithstanding this rejection, recent decades have shown a very wide claim to and acceptance of the concept of the contiguous zone and, more specifically, of the concept of a contiguous zone for security purposes. Indeed the interest in security has been one of the interests most frequently sought to be protected

204. Art. 1, Hague Convention XIII; Art. 3, Havana Convention.

205. 7 *Dept. of State Bull.* 331 (1939); also in 34 *A.J.I.L. Supp.* 17 (1940). For general comment, see Fenwick, "The Declaration of Panama," 34 *A.J.I.L.* 116 (1940); Brown, "Protective Jurisdiction," 34 id. 112; and Masterson, "The Hemisphere Zone of Security and the Law," 26 *A.B.A.J.* 860 (1940). Cf. Wright, "Rights and Duties Under International Law as affected by the United States Neutrality Act and the Resolutions of Panama," 34 *A.J.I.L.* 238, 246–8 (1940).

206. The replies of the British, French, and German Governments may be found in 7 Hackworth, *Digest of International Law* 704–8 (1943).

through the device of the contiguous zone.[207] That such a contiguous zone from which exercises of conflict are sought to be excluded may be a wholly reasonable and hence lawful measure for avoiding injurious impact upon the people and processes of the nonparticipant coastal state [208] should be fairly evident in an age where long-range weapons and such items as nuclear depth charges and other nuclear ammunition and "homing" torpedoes have become commonplace.

The demand for exclusion of belligerent activities extends to activities in the airspace superjacent on the land mass and waters of the nonparticipant. Terrestrial gravity imparts obvious urgency to this demand and probably accounts for the absence of any practice analogous to that of permitting "mere passage" to belligerent warships through neutral territorial waters.[209] In the last two world wars, it was the substantially uniform practice of nonparticipants to prohibit the entry of belligerent military aircraft into neutral airspace,

207. Documentation and analysis are offered in McDougal and Schlei, "The Hydrogen Bomb Tests in Perspective: Lawful Measures for Security," 64 *Yale L.J.* 648, 666–82 (1955); McDougal and Burke, "Crisis in the Law of the Sea: Community Perspectives versus National Egoism," 67 *Yale L.J.* 539, 553–4, 581–5 (1958). Harvard Research, "Rights and Duties of Neutral Powers in Naval and Aerial War," 33 *A.J.I.L.* Supp. 343–8 (1939) collects references to municipal statutes and regulations by which "many maritime states claimed for purposes of neutrality a belt of marginal waters more than three miles in width."

The second cited article discusses the International Law Commission's 1956 draft which omitted mention of "security" among the range of interests a state is authorized to protect in contiguous areas. The 1958 Geneva Convention on the Territorial Sea and the Contiguous Zone, which in Article 24 followed the Commission draft, is appraised in Burke, *Comprehensive State Authority over Ocean Areas: A Policy Perspective,* c. 5 (unpublished J.S.D. thesis, Yale Law Library, 1959). It should be noted that the 1958 Convention does not purport to deal with contiguous zones for security purposes in contexts of war.

208. The formulations of the "Harvard Draft Convention," supra note 207, are worth quoting: Art. 18: "A belligerent shall not engage in hostile operations on, under, or over the high seas so near to the territory of a neutral State as to endanger life or property therein." Art. 19: "A belligerent shall not permit its warships or military aircraft to hover off the coasts of a neutral State in such a manner as to harass the commerce or industry of that State."

209. There were, in World War II, recurrent incidents in which Allied bombs, intended for German targets, fell upon Swiss territory. See *The War and the Neutrals, Survey of International Affairs 1939–1946,* 224–5 (Royal Institute of Int. Affairs, 1956).

to resist such entry even by firing upon the offending aircraft where necessary, to compel the aircraft to land where entry is nonetheless effected, and to intern both the plane and its crew.[210] Nonparticipants, moreover, drew no distinction between deliberate entry and entry by inadvertence whether resulting from navigational error or from atmospheric conditions.[211] The one probable exception that appears to have been given some recognition in recent conventions refers to hospital aircraft or "flying ambulances," entry of which may be authorized by the nonparticipant.[212] The use of long-range missiles in war may, it might be noted, conceivably give rise to a comparable demand for exclusion. The possible pattern of future practice on this matter can of course only be speculated upon. Among the variables which may affect the shape of such pattern would seem such factors as the physical characteristics of the missile (e.g., the degree to which it is subject to control after launching), the extent of possible danger to the subjacent neutral state, and the availability of means of repelling or destroying the missiles in flight.

That modern weapons whose reach may extend well beyond an immediate area of combat may present new and special dangers for nonparticipants was adverted to in an earlier section. It was observed, more particularly, that the explosion of fission and fusion weapons may expose people in neutral territory to certain deleterious somatic and genetic effects.[213] In this connection, it has been sug-

210. 7 Hackworth, *Digest of International Law* 549–57 (1943) and Spaight, *Air Power and War Rights* 420–9 (3rd ed., 1947) describe the practice in the two world wars. Art. 95 of the "Harvard Research Draft Convention," supra note 207 is a succinct summary of the customary requirements that have emerged on this matter; see also Art. 40 and 42, "Hague Rules of Aerial Warfare of 1923," in 32 *A.J.I.L.* Supp. 34, 36 (1938).

211. Spaight, supra note 210; 2 Oppenheim-Lauterpacht 725; Castren, *The Present Law of War and Neutrality* 589, 591 (1954). See also Lissitzyn, "The Treatment of Aerial Intruders in Recent Practice and International Law," 47 *A.J.I.L.* 559, 562–3 (1953).

212. See Art. 37, "Geneva Convention for the Amelioration of the Condition of the Wounded and Sick in Armed Forces in the Field," 12 Aug. 1949, text in Dept. of the Army, *Treaties Governing Land Warfare,* 24 (Pam. 27–1 1956), and Art. 40, "Geneva Convention for Amelioration of the Condition of the Wounded, Sick and Shipwrecked Members of Armed Forces at Sea," 12 Aug. 1949, ibid., 48. See also Art. 17, "Hague Rules of Aerial Warfare of 1923," in 32 *A.J.I.L.* Supp. 20 (1938).

213. Supra, p. 388–9.

gested by a recent commentator that so to expose the peoples of nonparticipant states amounts to an unlawful conversion of their territory into an area of operations in violation of neutral rights. Dr. Singh wrote, building upon Professor Oppenheim's distinction between the "region of war" and the "theater of war," [214]

> [I]n international law no place which is not within the region of war can be made a theater of war or subjected to its operational effects. If the theater of war shifts, or its evil effects spread to a place beyond the region of war, hostilities must be said to be unlawfully taking place on neutral territory. . . . With the unpredictable and indiscriminate effects of nuclear bombardment, . . . [the] effects can spread to any part of the globe, affecting neutral States and permanently neutralized territories. . . . [T]he use of nuclear weapons in circumstances in which the user knows that it is bound to injure neutral States, must be considered as a violation of international law and, if it involves the killing of innocent neutrals, a clear war crime.[215]

Dr. Singh went on to state that the aggrieved neutral has both a "remedial right to compensation" and a "right to treat the menace of radioactive fall-out as a hostile act of the belligerent and resort to a declaration of war." [216]

The preliminary point suggests itself that Dr. Singh's premise about international law requiring the immunization, so to speak, of neutral states from the "operational effects" of war appears to have been too broadly drawn. To document such a requirement, in the absolutistic form that Dr. Singh attempts to give it, would seem difficult indeed. Thus, in the realm of economic warfare, it must be obvious that the authority conceded by the law of war to a belligerent to embargo neutral commerce with the enemy belligerent may have very substantial "operational effects" upon the neutral community.[217] Further, as has been observed above, the nonparticipant's tolerance

214. See 2 Oppenheim-Lauterpacht 236–47.

215. Singh, *Nuclear Weapons and International Law* 106 (1959). There appears some novelty in Dr. Singh's description of the "region of war" as "the area of land, sea or air *which falls under the territorial control of the belligerents* within which hostilities have to be confined . . ." Id. 105; italics supplied. Contrast Professor Oppenheim's definition in 2 Oppenheim-Lauterpacht 237.

216. Singh, supra note 215 at 239.

217. See infra, p. 477 et seq.

of or inability to prevent hostile operations within its territorial domain by one belligerent may authorize the other belligerent in effect to convert such domain into a permissible area of operations and hence to subject the nonparticipant, in a most direct manner, to the "operational effects" of war.[218]

The more important observation that may be made, however, is that, assuming a future decision-maker of even modest sophistication, the factors which rationally may be taken into account in passing upon neutral claims for compensation for damage from nuclear explosions, or upon claims to resort to violence because of such damage, need not be exhausted by the one consideration Dr. Singh points to, i.e. the knowledge of the (presumably identifiable) user that the weapon was "bound to injure neutral states." Potentially relevant factors may include, for example, the degree of necessity under which the user found itself in the particular use involved; the relation of the user's political objectives to the public order of the organized world community; the extent to which the neutral claimant was authorized to remain neutral; the type of damage complained of; the incidence of the ascertainable damage, that is, whether the damage was limited to the neutral or shared by the user and the rest of the world, and so forth.

Other kinds of claims that nonparticipants have made against belligerents relate to the protection of the persons and property of the nonparticipants' nationals found outside their territory. These claims have commonly been claims for compensation for damage allegedly imposed upon such nationals by belligerent operations. In general, neutral nationals can come in contact with a belligerent in three situations: when residing in such belligerent's territorial domain; when residing in the territory of the opposing belligerent or in territory occupied by it; and when found on the high seas. In the first two situations, neutral nationals are commonly regarded by each belligerent as having "cast their lot" with the respective local civilian populations. Thus, in the belligerent's territorial domain, they are in practice subjected to the ordinary wartime burdens the belligerent sovereign imposes on its own citizens, such as the payment of special wartime taxes and the compulsory rendition of services of a police or administrative character.[219] So far as concerns compulsory

218. See supra, p. 405–7.

219. See 3 Hyde, *International Law* 1755–58 (2nd rev. ed., 1945); Fenwick,

service in the armed forces, however, there is respectable authority for the view that the belligerent sovereign may not require such service from neutral nationals.[220] The United States position on this matter, it may be noted, is that a belligerent is authorized to require military service from neutral aliens as a condition for their continued eligibility for naturalization, and perhaps even for their continued residence in the belligerent's territory.[221] Neutral nationals are, moreover, in effect required to share in the risks and damages of war. While neutral nationals, as such, are not of course permissible objects of attack, arbitral tribunals and claims commissions have commonly refused to award compensation for damages determined to be incidental to operations of war which are not violative of the law of war.[222] With respect, finally, to neutral nationals on the high seas, it needs only to be noted that claims for damages here have related principally to the lawfulness of "unrestricted" submarine, air, and mine warfare and of the establishment of war zones. Consideration of these matters is attempted in the succeeding chapter.

International Law 629 (3rd ed., 1948); Hall, *International Law,* 901–2 (8th ed., Pearce Higgins, 1924). And see Art. 18(b), Hague Convention V, 1907.

In re X and Mrs. X, *Int. Law Rep.* 1950, Case No. 99, the French *Conseil d'État* upheld the application, to a Swiss national residing in France, of an Ordinance providing for confiscation of profits derived from commercial relations with the enemy (German) forces during the last world war.

It should be noted that the 1949 "Geneva Convention Relative to the Protection of Civilian Persons in time of war," text in Dept. of the Army, *Treaties Governing Land Warfare,* 135 (Pam. 27–1, Dec. 1956), includes in its categorization of protected persons (Art. 4) neutral nationals in the territory of, or territory occupied by, a belligerent, when the neutral state of which they are nationals have no "normal diplomatic representation" with such belligerent.

220. Fenwick, supra note 219 at 629; Hall, supra note 219 at 587. See also Parry, "International Law and the Conscription of Non-Nationals," 31 *Brit. Y.B.I.L.* 437 (1954).

221. See 3 Hyde, supra note 219 at 1744–55 and Fitzhugh, "The Drafting of Neutral Aliens by the United States," 36 *A.J.I.L.* 369 (1942). See the Selective Service Act of 1940, sec. 3(a), 54 *Stat.* 885 (1940), 50 U.S.C.A. App. § 303(a), now 50 U.S.C. App. § 454a; and *U.S. v. Bussoz* 218 F. 2d 683 (9th Cir. 1955); *Brownell v. Rasmussen* 235 F. 2d 527 (D.C.Cir., 1956); *Machado v. McGrath* 193 F. 2d 706 (1951) cert. denied 342 U.S. 948, 72 S.Ct. 557, 96 L. ed. 705 (1952); *In re* Molo, 107 F. Supp. 137 (D.C.S.D.N.Y., 1952).

222. Harvard Research, supra note 207 at 386–91 collects the relevant decisions and awards. See also Freeman, "Responsibility of States for Unlawful Acts of Their Armed Forces," 88 *Hague Recueil* 267, 293–311 (1955).

Turning briefly to claims relating to property of neutral nationals, three situations may again be roughly distinguished upon the basis of the location of the property involved. The taking of neutral property located in a belligerent's own territory raises issues customarily discussed in terms of a "right of angary." [223] The destruction or capture and condemnation of neutral property found on the high seas are of course problems of the law of contraband, blockade, and

223. The "right of angary" is of very ancient lineage; see Bullock, "Angary," 3 *Brit. Y.B.I.L.* 90 (1922–1923); Albrecht, "Requisitions of Private Neutral Property, Especially of Ships," in Henckels and Crocker, *Memorandum of Authorities on the Law of Angary* 25–8 (1918). Briefly put, most authors write that (a) an appropriate exercise of angary requires some urgent need of the belligerent for such property in the waging of the war, and (b) the belligerent has a duty to pay compensation to the neutral owners. 3 Hyde, supra note 219 at 1758–64, 2 Oppenheim-Lauterpacht 762; Bullock, supra at 129; Fenwick, supra note 219 at 629–30; Alessandri, "El Derecho de Angaria: su Aplicacion por los Tribunales Chilenos,' 7 *Cursos Monograficos* 597 (Academia Inter-Americana de Derecho Comparado e Internacional, 1959). The close analogy between expropriation in time of peace and angary in time of war may be noted; indeed, angary would seem not inappropriately regarded as expropriation in time of war. The fact of war obviates any need for a special showing of the element of "public purpose."

Among the more spectacular exercises of angary was the taking over by the United States of eighty-seven Dutch ships in American harbors on March 20, 1918; see 12 *A.J.I.L. Supp.* 259 (1918), and S.S. *Merak* and *Texel, Annual Digest 1923–1924,* Case No. 226 where the U.S.–Germany Mixed Claims Commission affirmed the lawfulness of the taking. Similar takings have been effected by *neutral* states perhaps in anticipation of full participation. See the *Idle Foreign Vessels Act of 1941,* 55 *Stat.* 242 under which the U.S. Government on June 6, 1941, assumed possession of half a million tons of foreign shipping in its ports. It has been debated among publicists whether this was "angary" or, alternatively, "requisition"; see 2 Oppenheim-Lauterpacht 765 and Woolsey, "The Taking of Foreign Ships in American Ports," 35 *A.J.I.L.* 497 (1941); compare the decision of the Mexican Supreme Court in *Lorenzo v. Gobierno, Annual Digest 1941–1942,* Case No. 181. The substantiality of this debate is itself open to doubt.

It might be noted finally that neutral-owned property within the belligerent's territorial domain has been subjected to belligerent taking whether such property was brought into such domain by the owner voluntarily, or involuntarily, or even over the owner's protest. See *The Zamora* (1916) 2 A.C.77; *Commercial and Estates Co. of Egypt v. Ball* 36 Times L.R. 526 (1920); *Commercial and Estates Co. of Egypt v. Board of Trade* [1925] 1 K.B. 271; and *The Pomona, Annual Digest, 1938–1940,* Case No. 219. See, generally, Lauterpacht, "Angary and Requisition of Neutral Property," 27 *Brit. Y.B.I.L.* 455 (1950).

unneutral service, and appropriately dealt with under those headings. The location of neutral property in enemy territory or enemy-occupied territory raises a presumption, as it were, of incorporation and employment in the community processes of the enemy belligerent and, for many purposes, such property is simply assimilated to enemy property.[224] With respect to claims for compensation for damage to or destruction of such neutral property arising from belligerent activities, decision-makers have frequently invoked, much as in claims relating to the persons of neutral nationals, the conception of "incidental damage," refusing compensation where the damage or destruction is determined to be incidental to lawful belligerent operations.[225]

CLAIMS OF BELLIGERENTS TO EMBARGO ECONOMIC INTERCOURSE WITH THE ENEMY

The final type of claim we consider relates to the demands by belligerents to control, or to embargo in varying degree, the flow of commerce to enemies which may enhance fighting potential. To achieve such control or embargo, a belligerent's efforts must obviously be directed toward affecting and interdicting the commerce of neutrals with the enemy. The entire stoppage of, or comprehensive embargo upon, the flow of goods and services to the enemy—a function traditionally regarded as peculiarly within the province of seapower—has in many wars been a major belligerent objective.[226] In the last two global wars, the waging of which necessitated staggering quantities of supplies and materials and a massive industrial production base, it was an especially vital objective. It is sometimes suggested, as earlier noted, that to the extent future major wars may tend to be nuclear wars, the interdiction of economic intercourse with the enemy may decline in importance. It is scarcely possible, however, to be dogmatic about the requirements of possible future

224. See, e.g., 2 Oppenheim-Lauterpacht 280–4.

225. Id., 444; Stone, *Legal Controls of International Conflict* 437 (1954). See also supra note 222; and Greenspan, *The Modern Law of Land Warfare* 575–80 (1959).

226. See Brodie, *A Guide to Naval Strategy* cc. 1, 4 (4th ed., 1958); *American Sea Power Since 1775*, c. 18 (Westcott, ed., 1947); Bacon and McMurtrie, *Modern Naval Strategy* c. 3 (1940); and Cranwell, *The Destiny of Sea Power* (1941). A common theme of these writers is the strategic importance of establishing command of the sea that permits control of communications and commerce.

armed conflicts and since wars other than a short and sharp exchange of annihilating nuclear blows remain distinct possibilities, the problems relating to interference with or destruction of commerce cannot yet safely be left to historians of international law.

The assertion of the general belligerent claim to embargo economic intercourse with the enemy contemplates the performance by the claimant of three distinguishable tasks. The first is that of characterizing the goods whose flow the claimant seeks to prohibit or control. In concrete cases, this task involves, in its preliminary aspect, the determination of the enemy or neutral character or ownership of the goods under consideration. In its substantive aspects, the task of characterization requires appraisal of the relation of the goods to the military potential and effectiveness of the enemy, which appraisal is made through application of doctrines about "contraband." The second task is that of actually stopping the flow of enemy imports determined to be likely to increase the fighting capabilities of the enemy as well as the flow of enemy exports to neutrals. Belligerents have resorted for the performance of this task to a variety of methods which differ in comprehensiveness of scope and effect and in details of military application; the range is from the occasional visit and search of individual vessels, through narrowly projected naval blockades and more comprehensive "war zones," to the most comprehensive administrative techniques of economic warfare. The third task concerns the disposition of the goods and of the carrying craft, the principal alternative possibilities being destruction, condemnation, requisition, or release.

Summarily anticipating the arguments developed below, we may note that there is little ground for controversy about the permissibility, in certain contexts, of the belligerent objective of completely embargoing commercial relationships of neutrals with the enemy. It is the lawfulness of certain measures, which became familiar in the two world wars, and which were designed to result in such embargo, that some commentators curiously continue to debate. Thus, building upon the frequent invocation of the technical doctrine of "reprisals" by the belligerents as they put into effect these measures for interdiction and control, Professor Tucker concludes his assessment of these measures by insisting that

> [T]here is room for asserting that from the standpoint of a formal legal analysis it is unnecessary to go beyond an examina-

> tion of the legitimacy of the measures reviewed in preceding pages, *as measures of reprisal;* that whatever judgment is made concerning the legitimacy of these measures, as measures of reprisal, it cannot affect the continued validity of the law governing blockade. If this position is adopted it would appear that the traditional law remains—on the whole—unchanged. . . .[227]

From any perspective that seeks to transcend concern with the syntactic elegance of a "formal legal analysis" and to relate past experience to probable future decision in comparable contexts, it would seem evident that, despite the disingenuous use by belligerents of technical labels, the traditional law has not remained virginally intact. The embargo measures repetitively applied in the two world wars realistically involve something more than the exceptional, emergency response to a violation of an unquestioned authoritative prescription which the conception of "reprisals" ordinarily connotes.[228] The nearly universal nonobservance in two global wars of certain nineteenth-century prescriptions which these measures reflect strongly suggest, on the contrary, the clear emergence and crystallization of the particular expectations of uniformities and rightness in decision commonly called law—or, in other words, the growth and development of new patterns of customary law.[229]

From a realistic perspective, what may appropriately be emphasized is that all the various control measures—from visit and search at sea to administrative certification at source—are but differing modalities, with varying procedures and detailed effects, invented in response to differing conditions of application, for achieving the same objective of denying the enemy commerce which might benefit him.[230] To appraise the lawfulness of the newer modalities, devised to meet new conditions of warfare, in terms of the requirements pro-

227. Tucker, *The Law of War and Neutrality at Sea* 316 (1957). While Professor Tucker acknowledges that "the more realistic view" was to look upon "recent belligerent practice . . . as a thinly veiled endeavour to replace the traditional law through the instrument of reprisals" (ibid.), it appears clear that he espouses the view quoted in the text. See id., at 317.

228. See Colbert, *Retaliation in International Law* 194–8 (1948) and the remarkable account in 1 Medlicott, *The Economic Blockade* 112–14 (1952) of the antecedents of the Nov. 27, 1939 Reprisals Order-in-Council.

229. See 2 Oppenheim-Lauterpacht 796–7; Stone, *Legal Controls of International Conflict* 508–10 (rev. ed., 1959).

230. See infra, p. 488 ff.

jected in traditional law for an older modality developed under very different conditions,[231] is to impose an impossible rigidity upon the processes of customary development and largely to doom such appraisal to irrelevance. The lawfulness of these modern measures is, we suggest, most appropriately regarded as a function of the detailed factors that compose particular contexts; appraisal of lawfulness demands, not the extrapolation of the technical exigencies of one specific method characteristic of an earlier era, but rather simply the determination of reasonableness in particular contexts.[232] The types of contextual factors which such a determination would note in comprehensive reference include the peculiar imperatives of military necessity and effectiveness, respecting the use of a particular modality, imposed by the prevailing state of military technology and technique; the degree of interference with or destruction of neutral values entailed by the employment of such modality; the comprehensiveness of the war, that is, whether the conflict approaches totality, in number and range of participants as in level of intensity, or is of more limited proportions; the success or failure of characterization by the organized community of the lawfulness of the particular process of coercion, the nature of the political objectives sought by the belligerent user and their relation to the fundamental policies projected by the world community about such objectives; and so on. This kind of determination makes possible the individualization of judgment as to each modality and dispenses with both blanket denials and blanket affirmations of legitimacy.

The individualizing of judgment, more importantly, permits the careful consideration, weighing, and adjustment of the requirements, in the specific context being examined, of the competing policies of securing the military effectiveness of efforts to maintain minimum order and of minimizing the disruption of neutral values. That belligerents engaged in community-required or -authorized enforcement action may lawfully seek to impose a more or less comprehensive embargo upon commercial intercourse with the violator-belligerent

231. E.g. Tucker, *The Law of War and Neutrality at Sea* 296–317 (1957).

232. Cf. the emphasis on a test of reasonableness, in relation to interbelligerent "reprisals" affecting neutral claims, developed by British prize courts in, e.g., *The Leonora* [1919] 3 B. & C. Pr. Cas. 385, 398; *The Stigstad* [1919] 3 id., 347, 351–2; *The Noordam* (No. 2) [1920] 3 id. 599, 606; and *The Zamora* [1916] 2 A.C. 77, 98.

appears hardly open to controversy. Among the sanctioning measures "not involving the use of armed force" explicitly envisaged in Article 41 of the United Nations Charter is the "complete or partial interruption of economic relations." It is a somewhat more complex question whether the same claim may legitimately be asserted by the violator-belligerent and enforced against neutrals' trading with the sanctioner-belligerents. In answer to this question, the general suggestion may be essayed that where mutuality is, in realistic expectation, a condition for effectiveness in securing both minimum order and minimum destruction, authoritative policy might properly be interpreted as providing for such mutuality. Thus, a weak neutral geographically within the military reach of a powerful violator-belligerent might, for instance, in contrast with neutrals more happily situated, be authorized to recognize a very practical necessity for conceding equality of rights to the violator-belligerent in respect of the interruption of its commerce with the sanctioner-belligerents.[233]

The Characterization of Goods: Contraband

In major part the substantive task of characterizing the goods the flow of which the belligerent seeks to control is performed through the formulation, reformulation, and application of certain conceptions and doctrines about "contraband." These conceptions and doctrines are of ancient lineage; the three-fold categorization set down in the Declaration of London of 1909 goes back to Grotius.[234] In their factual reference, these categorizations of traditional law relate to the differing degrees of relevancy that differing goods have for the war effort of the enemy. Thus, "absolute contraband" embraced things which were specialized to, and hence of the highest relevance for, the exercise of war-like violence: arms and munitions, military and naval stores, and the like.[235] "Conditional contraband" referred

233. Supra, note 67. See also Lauterpacht, "The Limits of the Operation of the Law of War," 30 *Brit. Y.B.I.L.* 206, 238–9 (1953); cf. Wright, "The New Law of War and Neutrality," in *Varia Juris Gentium: Liber Amicorum J.P.A. François* 412, 422 (1959).

234. *De Jure Belli ac Pacis, Libri Tres,* Bk. III, Ch. I, S. 5, 2 Classics of International Law, p. 602 (Kelsey Trans., 1924). A proper sense of the antiquity of these doctrines and distinctions is imparted by Kulsrud, *Maritime Neutrality to 1780* (1936).

235. Arts. 22–23, Declaration Concerning the Laws of Naval Warfare, Signed at London, Feb. 26, 1909, text in 2 *A Collection of Neutrality Laws, Regulations and Treaties of Various Countries* 1380 (Deak and Jessup, eds., 1939);

to goods of equivocal relevance being "susceptible of use in war as well as for purposes of peace"; [236] although military uses did not exhaust their possible utility, such goods could under certain circumstances be of great value to a belligerent for the waging of war. "Free articles" were those not relevant at all to belligerent activity, being incapable of use in war; [237] they were, in traditional theory, not subject to capture and condemnation.

An essential part of the conception of contraband was the enemy or hostile destination of the goods so characterized. Condemnation of goods categorized as "absolute contraband" was authorized upon a showing that they were destined for enemy or enemy-controlled territory. The character of such goods raised a presumption that they would in fact be used for the waging of war. Condemnation of "conditional contraband" items required the resolution of the ambiguity inhering in their susceptibility to both military and nonmilitary types of uses, by a further showing that they were destined for military uses. Dedication to such uses was presumed from proof of consignment to the governmental authorities or public force of the enemy, or to places of obviously military character such as naval or army bases.[238]

By the projection of these distinctions and categories, the traditional law of contraband sought to provide for the balancing and compromise of the military interests of the claimant-belligerent and the neutrals' demands for continuation of their external commercial relations. It is perhaps evident that here, as in other contexts, the line of compromise is not a simple and static one. Except with respect to the more obviously martial items exclusively useful for the application of violence, the location or configuration of the line of compromise may in particular cases appropriately be expected to vary as the technology, objectives, and other conditions of particular conflicts vary. The U. S. Law of Naval Warfare puts the point succinctly:

---

hereinafter cited as the Declaration of London. Art. 22 listed goods which could be treated as contraband of war without notice; all other articles "exclusively used for war" could be made absolute contraband by a special declaration and notification to other governments under Art. 23. See also, generally, Pyke, *The Law of Contraband of War* (1915).

236. Art. 24, Declaration of London.

237. Arts. 27–28, id.

238. Arts. 30–31, 33–35, id. Smith, *The Law and Custom of the Sea* 146–7 (3rd ed., 1959).

> The precise nature of a belligerent's contraband list may vary according to the particular circumstances of the armed conflict.[239]

Thus, in wars of the proportions and characteristics of World War I and World War II, the line of compromise has by practice been located so near to one (the belligerent's) end of the spectrum as in effect to reduce the very notion of compromise to marginal utility. This is the gist of the observation very frequently made that the character and requirements of "total war" tend to blur and wipe away the traditional distinctions between absolute and conditional contraband and between contraband and noncontraband. In the limited or duel wars of the eighteenth and nineteenth centuries, the range of articles of decisive significance for belligerents was distinctly limited. The requirements of modern armies engaged in large-scale and prolonged hostilities seem, in contrast, to defy enumeration.[240] Further, as new weapons and instruments of violence are invented and made operational, new materials, or materials formerly thought nonuseful or innocuous, may become "strategic" or even "critical." The net result is that it has in such context become increasingly difficult to point with any great confidence to any particular article or material as "not susceptible of use in war." [241]

239. U.S. Law of Naval Warfare, s. 631(b), reproduced as an appendix to Tucker, *The Law of War and Neutrality at Sea* (1957).

240. See, e.g., Stone, *Legal Controls of International Conflict* 481–3 (rev. ed., 1959); Smith, *The Crisis in the Law of Nations* 54 (1947). Einzig, *Economic Warfare* 5 (1940) observes that the increase in the material requirements of war due to the mechanization of armed forces enhanced the relative importance of the economic factor among the factors affecting the outcome of a war. See Wu, *Economic Warfare* 10–11 (1952) criticizing what he calls "the strategic materials fallacy," i.e., that in order to prevent assistance to an enemy, it was sufficient to prevent supplies of "strategic materials" from reaching such enemy. Dr. Wu refers to this as a "pre-total war" concept.

241. The list of "free articles" in the Declaration of London was obsolete even at the time it was first drawn up. This list included such items as metallic ores, rubber, raw cotton, nitrates and phosphates, wool and hemp, and chronometers. "Consider, for instance," Mr. Arnold-Forster wrote, "the non-contraband list [of the Declaration of London]. It put iron ore on the free list, so that all such ore would be free to pass straight through a British blockade to Krupp's munition works at Essen. Yet the foundation of modern war is steel . . . Rubber for motor tyres was on the free list, although . . . much of the mobility of modern armies depends on motor transport. The Declaration authorized

This result is reflected in the fact that the contraband lists of both the Allied Powers and Germany in the last world war were composed, not of catalogues of specific items, but rather of sets of categories cast in language of such comprehensiveness and generality as to permit the easy subsumption of practically any article the capturing power might wish to condemn.[242] The same development, it may parenthetically be noted, had the effect of pre-empting the utility for belligerents of the doctrine of "infection" which authorized the condemnation of innocuous goods because of concurrent carriage of contraband articles.[243]

There are other aspects of the two world wars that at once reflected and powerfully aided the attentuation of the distinctions of the traditional law of contraband. The conduct of war required each belligerent state to utilize and control practically every member of its population as an element of power; significant participation in war was no longer confined to members of the public armed forces. Thus, the distinction between combatant and noncombatant imported by the conception of "conditional contraband," in this context, tended in increasingly high degree to be factitious.[244] In more

---

seizure of guns and shells but not the metal for making them; explosives might be seized but not cotton or nitrates." Arnold-Forster, *The New Freedom of the Seas* 42–3 (1942). See also Percy, *Maritime Trade in War* 40 (1930). In the First World War, the British Government repudiated the Declaration of London completely; see the Maritime Rights Order-in-Council, 1916, in 7 Hackworth 40.

242. For the British and German contraband lists issued in 1939, see 7 Hackworth 24–6; since the German, French, and Italian lists followed the British one very closely, in effect the major European belligerents had a common contraband list. See Rowson, "Prize Law During the Second World War," 24 *Brit. Y.B.I.L.* 160, 187–8 (1947). Lip service was paid to the notion of conditional contraband, that category being formally retained; foodstuffs, clothing, and materials used for their manufacture were there included. Actually, no distinction was made in practice. In *The Sidi Ifni, Annual Digest 1943–1945,* Case No. 197, it was held by the Judicial Committee of the Privy Council that all foodstuffs, of necessity, would assist in the warlike operations of the enemy. They were regularly condemned upon proof of enemy destination.

243. Rowson, supra note 242 at 195.

244. E.g., 2 Oppenheim-Lauterpacht 207–8. Garner, "Violations of Maritime Law by the Allied Powers During the World War," 25 *A.J.I.L.* 26, 33 (1931) points out that "the original distinction between the two kinds of contraband rested on the assumption that it was possible to control the destination of conditional so as to insure that it would reach only the civil population of the

specific illustration, use or consumption by civilians engaged in war industries became more and more difficult to distinguish from use or consumption by members of the regular armed forces; such use became in consequential sense use in war. Further, the governments at war commonly assumed control over practically every aspect of the production and distribution of goods within their territories, as well as over the importation and exportation of commodities and supplies, and of course assigned priority to the requirements of the armed forces.[245] Thus, each belligerent could confidently assume that some part, if not all, of goods brought into enemy territory would be utilized by the enemy's armed forces, or release an equivalent volume for utilization by such forces.[246] Finally, it may be noted that the fact that goods were not consigned to a military or naval port or base had no significance at all so far as concerned the de-

---

belligerent and would not, therefore, subserve, directly at least, his military interests."

245. See, e.g., Lederer, "War Economics," in *War in Our Time* 206, 215 et seq. (Speier and Kahler, eds., 1939); Percy, *Maritime Trade in War* 41 (1930); Burnham, *Total War: The Economic Theory of a War Economy* (1943); Basch, *The New Economic Warfare* (1941) especially at p. 44, where he observes that under the economic impact of total war, the internal economic structures of totalitarian and nontotalitarian states tended to become essentially similar; *Introduction to War Economics* (Neal, ed., 1942); *Economic Problems of War* (Steiner, ed., 1942); Pigou, *The Political Economy of War* (rev. ed., 1951); Filipetti, *Industrial Production in Time of War* (1943); *Economic Mobilization and Stabilization* (Chandler and Wallace, eds., 1951).

246. British prize courts acted upon this assumption. In *Part Cargo ex S.S. Monte Contes, Annual Digest 1943–1945,* Case No. 196, the Judicial Committee of the Privy Council took judicial notice that the government of Italy, as ruler of a totalitarian state, would take the conditionally contraband goods (a large consignment of canned fish) for its own use or disposal in whatever way would best further its total war effort. In *The Alwaki,* id. *1938–1940,* Case No. 223, foodstuffs were condemned upon proof of German decrees which "impose government control on all these articles and prescribe that they are automatically seized at the moment of crossing the frontier or . . . at the moment of coming into the customs house." In *The Nailsea Court* (id., *1946,* Case No. 182) the French *Conseil des Prises* held that "the measures taken by the German government to ensure the control and equitable distribution of home grown and imported foodstuffs must mean that these articles of conditioned contraband, if destined for German territory, are intended for the German state itself or for its administration."

termination of probabilities of use by armed forces.[247] That circumstance may have been meaningful in earlier centuries when inland transportation and communication systems were so primitive, or practically nonexistent, that consignment to a nonmilitary port furnished some assurance that the goods consigned would be there consumed by noncombatants.[248] Considering the subverting impact upon distinctions in traditional doctrine that contemporary conditions of application in global conflicts appear to have had, it should be possible to avoid the tedious disputation respecting the applicability of the "continuous voyage" or "ultimate destination" doctrine in cases of "conditional contraband." Of much more importance is the recognition that in such conflicts each belligerent state, in taking complete control of the import trade in wartime and prohibiting the purchase of goods which do not serve its belligerent effort, itself characterizes what is and what is not useful to it in war, and that the opposing belligerent may therefore seek with considerable reason to capture all goods the importation of which was not forbidden by the other belligerent.[249]

As we have earlier suggested, there appears little necessity for assuming all future wars must take on the dimensions and characteristics of World Wars I and II. More limited conflicts appear possible, whether they be "brushfire" affairs or experimental skirmishes between great powers or small wars between small states. In these types of conflicts, it seems conceivable that the appropriate line of compromise may move away from the belligerent's end of the spectrum and toward the other end. In conflicts involving the great powers and which the great powers seek to keep limited, deliberately

247. Fenwick, *International Law* 638 (3rd ed., 1948). Besides, a certificate from the Admiralty that the port of consignment is a military or naval base is apt to be treated as conclusive by the prize court; see *The Wirpi, Annual Digest 1943–1945,* Case No. 207, decided by the German prize court of Hamburg.

See further, Tucker, *The Law of War and Neutrality at Sea* 269 note 10 (1957) briefly recounting the steps leading to abandonment by both sides, in World War I, of attempts to distinguish between requirements about destination in absolute and destination in conditional contraband.

248. See the *Jonge Margaretha* (1799) 1 C. Rob. 189, a famous old case dealing with the condemnation of Dutch cheeses consigned to Brest, then a French naval port. The Prize Court said that had the cheeses been destined to a "general commercial port," they would not have been condemned since they would be intended for "civil use."

249. See Smith, *The Crisis in the Law of Nations* 55 (1947).

to refrain from comprehensive characterization of contraband, and from imposition of total embargoes upon neutral commerce with the opposing great power, may possibly constitute one aspect of efforts (that is, serve as one mode of communicating an intention) to maintain limits and avoid "totalization" of the conflict.[250] In small wars between small states, the interests of the rest of the general community may possibly require more restrictive definitions of contraband. Cases appear conceivable where contraband may appropriately be required to be limited to guns and munitions, and other specialized tools of violence.

We have thus far been considering the characterization of goods the flow of which *into* enemy territory belligerents seek to control. It remains very briefly to consider goods the flow of which *from* enemy

250. It may be noted that the embargo recommended by the U.N. General Assembly against the People's Republic of China in the Korean war—commonly regarded as a "limited war"—was limited to arms, munitions, nuclear material, etc. Resolution No. 500(V), U.N. Gen. Ass., *Off. Rec.*, 5th Sess., Supp. No. 20A (A/1775/Add.1), p. 2 (1951).

The original contraband list issued in 1950 by the Egyptian Government in connection with the Arab-Israeli conflict was similarly limited to "war contraband." "War contraband" was defined to include the following:

> (1) Arms, munitions, war material and their appurtenances, explosives, and explosive substances of every kind;
>
> (2) Chemicals, drugs, apparatus and instruments capable of being utilized for chemical warfare;
>
> (3) Fuel of every kind;
>
> (4) Aircraft, ships and spares for either;
>
> (5) Motor vehicles and trailers necessary for military forces;
>
> (6) Cash, ingots of gold and silver, negotiable securities and metals, raw materials, planks, machinery, and other objects necessary to its manufacture or adaptable to that purpose.

Art. 10, Decree on the procedure of ship and airplane searches and of seizure of contraband goods in connection with the Palestine War, Feb. 6, 1950, in U.N.S.C., *Off. Rec.*, 9th Yr., Supp. for Jan.–March 1954, p. 7 (1954). In November 1953, however, a seventh paragraph was added which read:

> Foodstuffs and all other commodities which are likely to strengthen the war potential of the Zionists in Palestine in any way whatever.

Id., p. 9. On the scope and effects of the Egyptian blockade in the Suez Canal, see e.g., Dinitz, "The Legal Aspects of the Egyptian Blockade of the Suez Canal," 45 *Georgetown L.J.* 169, 171–3 (1956–1957); Gross, "Passage Through the Suez Canal of Israel-Bound Cargo and Israeli Ships," 51 *A.J.I.L.* 530, 538–40 (1957); U.N.S.C., *Off. Rec.*, 9th Yr., 658th, 659th, and 661st mtgs. (1954) passim.

territory belligerents similarly seek to control. It suffices here to observe that in the control of enemy exports, no distinction and categories comparable to those in the control of contraband have historically developed.[251] The principal purpose sought in controlling and embargoing enemy exports has been that of preventing the enemy from earning foreign exchange necessary for financing its imports and hostile operations abroad.[252] For the securing of this purpose, the warlike or innocuous character of the enemy exports intercepted would clearly have little or no relevance.

The Stopping of the Flow of Goods

Traditional Modalities: Visit and Search and Blockade. The principal traditional naval procedures for stopping the flow of commerce which might benefit the enemy were visit, search, and capture at sea and blockade. The one was directed at particular enemy or neutral vessels anywhere upon the oceans, save in neutral territorial waters; the other was moved by the more comprehensive objective of denying to all vessels access to and from more or less defined portions of enemy coastal waters.

We turn first, and very briefly, to the procedures of visit, search, and seizure. These time-honored naval operations, which are adequately described elsewhere,[253] had for their purpose the ascertainment of the relevant characteristics—such as neutral or enemy character, nature, destination, and origin—of vessel and cargo. It scarcely needs demonstration to show that the successful exercise of

251. Historically, the bases in authority of enemy export control consisted of the law of blockade, which permitted all goods going in or *out* of the blockaded area, and of the general right to capture enemy property on the high seas. In respect of the latter, the principal controversies that arose were focussed upon determination of enemy ownership and upon the application of Article 2 of the Declaration of Paris of 1856 relating to enemy goods on neutral ships, rather than upon the substantive character of the goods.

252. Fenwick, *International Law* 636–7 (3rd ed., 1948); Gordon and Dangerfield, *The Hidden Weapon* 40 et seq. (1947); Einzig, *Economic Warfare 1939–1940*, 15–16 (1941); Wu, *Economic Warfare* 248–9 (1952).

253. For a succinct statement of the procedures of visit and search, as developed by custom and bilateral treaties in the 18th and 19th centuries, see Art. 53 of the "Harvard Draft Convention on the Rights and Duties of Neutral Powers in Naval and Aerial War," 33 *A.J.I.L. Supp.* 535–6.

See also Tucker, *The Law of War and Neutrality at Sea* 336–8 (1957) for another exposition.

these procedures at sea, in the context of modern naval and air warfare, presents the most formidable difficulties. The warship attempting to stop, board, and search a suspected enemy or neutral vessel becomes, in the course of such attempt, highly vulnerable to air and submarine attack. Moreover, the size of present-day ocean carriers and the volume of cargo carried make any inspection of cargo that goes beyond the perfunctory examination of shipping manifests practically impossible without modern dock facilities. Serious efforts at verification of enemy or neutral character of ship, as of cargo origin and destination, are of course not any more feasible as shipside operations than the detection of goods of a contraband nature. In response to these difficulties, there developed the belligerent practice of intercepting and diverting suspected merchantmen to designated control ports where fuller examination of cargo and carrier could be undertaken.[254] That this practice of diversion was sustained by reasonable necessity would seem difficult to controvert.[255] If the lawfulness of diversion for search under circumstances of reasonable suspicion be conceded, there would appear no reason why, under comparable circumstances, diversion before visit—that is, without a formal boarding of the suspected craft—should not similarly be conceded as permissible. The purpose of visit is to permit determination of the existence of grounds for search and detention.

254. Tucker, supra note 253 at 338–40; 2 Oppenheim-Lauterpacht 854; Frascona, *Visit, Search and Seizure on the High Seas* 78–81 (1938). Cf. Jessup, *Today and Tomorrow* 72 (Neutrality: Its History, Economics and Law, Vol. 4, 1936). The ancient practice, which was developed in the days of privateers, apparently prohibited "breaking bulk" and restricted search to an examination of the ship's papers. The Harvard Research, supra note 253 at 546–7, noted that this rule was considered obsolete by most states, but that search at sea was in any case only a process of sampling. Jessup, loc. cit., suggested that diversion would have been unnecessary if the old rule against "breaking bulk" were retained.

255. But see Trimble, "Violations of Maritime Law by the Allied Powers During the World War," 24 *A.J.I.L.* 79, 97–8 (1930); 3 Hyde, *International Law* 1967–8 (2nd rev. ed., 1945); and Warren, "Lawless Maritime Warfare," 18 *Foreign Aff.* 424, 432–3 (1940) for characterizations of diversion as "illegal and unjustified." For affirmations by British courts of the lawfulness of diversion for search at control ports, see: *The Mim* (1947) 2 All E.R. 476, *Annual Digest 1947,* Case No. 134. *The Bernisse* and *The Elve* (1921) 1 A.C. 458, *Annual Digest 1919–1922,* Case No. 346; and *Netherlands American Steam Navigation Co. v. H. M. Procurator General* (1926) 1 K.B. 84, *Annual Digest 1925–1926,* Case No. 370.

Since, in the usual case, evidence justifying search will previously have been secured through naval and commercial intelligence methods by the belligerent ordering diversion, visitation would seem of little more than ceremonial significance.[256] Diversion and search are perhaps most appropriately regarded as supplementary naval procedures for policing the embargo measures discussed below, and are largely reserved for the exceptional cases where administrative sanctioning procedures fail to secure compliance.

More comprehensive in reach than the simple visit and search of individual suspected vessels, but today subject to the same dangers and technological difficulties, is the equally time-honored technique of maritime blockade.

The traditional law of blockade embodied in the Declaration of Paris of 1856 [257] and the Declaration of London of 1909 projected certain "conditions of validity," or requirements for lawfulness, which are susceptible of summary statement. "Effectiveness" was frequently referred to in terms of maintenance of a force capable of preventing access to—entry into as well as exit from—the blockaded area.[258] Somewhat less abstractly, "effectiveness" was commonly interpreted to require an indeterminate number of ships of war so situated as to bring about reasonable expectations that a vessel seeking to breach the blockade would probably be captured. A second requirement was that of authoritative competence to establish a blockade, a competence regarded as limited to the officials of the belligerent power, including, most prominently, its naval authorities.[259] The third requisite was a formal declaration of the establish-

256. Tucker, supra note 253 at 342; Smith, "Aircraft and Commerce in War," 17 *Brit. Y.B.I.L.* 37, 41 (1936). But see Jessup, "The Diversion of Merchantmen," 34 *A.J.I.L.* 312 (1940).

257. Text in 2 *A Collection of Neutrality Laws, Regulations and Treaties of Various Countries* 1473 (Deak and Jessup, eds., 1939).

258. Art. 4, Declaration of Paris of 1856; Arts. 2–3, Declaration of London of 1909.

259. See U.S. *Law of Naval Warfare,* s. 632(b). Thus, "unrecognized insurgents" or rebels have at times been held unauthorized to establish a maritime blockade. See 3 Hyde, *International Law* 2183–8 (2nd rev. ed., 1945). The most recent but nontypical example is furnished by the Spanish Civil War, where recognition of belligerency was withheld by the Nyon Arrangement from *both* contestants. The result was that the powers signing the Nyon Arrangement refused to recognize the blockades established by *both* sides and other interferences with foreign shipping outside the three-mile limit. See Padelford, "For-

ment of blockade and its communication to nonparticipant states. The declaration had to set forth certain data of special importance to neutrals, such as the geographical location and limits of the area blockaded, the time for commencement of effectiveness, and the days of grace allowed to neutral vessels to leave the area affected.[260] Fourthly, the blockade was required to be limited to enemy coasts and ports and could not be extended to control access to neutral coasts and ports.[261] There was, lastly, the requirement of impartiality of application; denial of access was to be enforced against ships of all nations, including, more particularly, ships of the blockading belligerent.[262]

The maritime situation originally referred to in these conditions and requirements was that of a cordon of surface cruisers hovering a few miles off the enemy coast. It was indeed sometimes insisted that a closed and stationary cordon, as distinguished from cruising patrols, was essential and that a blockade maintained by the latter was "fictitious," i.e. a "paper," and hence ineffective, blockade.[263] Such a situation is perhaps still susceptible of re-creation in a conflict between a great power and a very weak one. The only reported instance of a maritime blockade of the "close-in" type during the Second World War was that instituted by the Soviet Union against Finland in the Russo-Finnish war of 1939.[264] The blockades declared and

---

eign Shipping During the Spanish Civil War," 32 *A.J.I.L.* 264 (1939). And see *Spanish Government v. North of England Steamship Co. Ltd., Annual Digest 1938–1940,* Case No. 30 and *Tatem v. Gamboa,* id., Case No. 31. This situation is to be distinguished from the closure of ports in the control of insurgents by decree of the legitimate government; see Dickinson, "The Closure of Ports in Control of Insurgents," 24 *A.J.I.L.* 69 (1930).

260. Arts. 8–9, 11–12, Declaration of London of 1909.

261. Arts. 1, 18, id.

262. Art. 5, id. Neutral warships, however, may be allowed to enter and leave a blockaded port; Art. 6, id. The purpose of the requirement is to preclude blockades for the purpose of furthering the blockader's own trade at the expense of neutrals. See, for example, the controversy between Britain and the United States in the First World War over the increase of British exports to the same countries from which American ships were barred by the British blockade; Turlington, *The World War Period* 55–8 (Neutrality: Its History, Economics, and Law, Vol. III, 1936).

263. See references collected in Harvard Research, "Rights and Duties of Neutral Powers in Naval and Aerial War," 33 *A.J.I.L. Supp.* 711 (1939).

264. See 16 *Bull. of Int. News* 1426 (1939).

established in accordance with the above conditions by the Allied Powers in the First World War were quite minor operations against coasts without modern fortifications: German East Africa, the Cameroons, Bulgaria on the Aegean Sea, Asia Minor, Kiauchau in China, and a few others.[265] The Korean war of 1950 suggests that in a limited war involving great powers, the traditional type of maritime blockade may also still be militarily feasible. In the Korean conflict, United Nations naval forces did establish command of the sea and carried out blockade operations against enemy-held coasts much along the lines of classical sea power. It must, however, be noted that the Soviet Government, which was in effect fighting the war by proxy, chose not to commit any of its submarines and aircraft against the United Nations forces, and contented itself with furnishing mines and small- and medium-caliber coastal guns to the North Koreans.[266] In a major war between great powers, the old technique of naval blockade does clearly appear obsolete. A surface squadron that attempted to employ it against the coasts of an enemy great power would not only be confronted by magnetic, acoustic, pressure, and other types of mines and long-range shore batteries but also present a choice target for attack by submarines, aircraft, and missiles.

It was in partial response to the challenge of mines, submarines, and air weapons that the so-called "long-distance" blockade was evolved.[267] In its purely naval reference, a "long-distance" blockade meant the closing and patrolling of strategic high seas areas many hundreds of miles from the enemy coast. Thus, in the two world wars, the naval aspects of the blockade against Germany consisted primarily of controlling the northern and southern approaches of the North Sea. Considering, however, the progressive development of the fighting power and operational range of air and undersea craft, the distance from enemy coasts at which blockading operations by surface naval vessels can take place seems likely to increase. The difficulties posed by a rapidly developing military technology

265. See 2 Garner, *International Law and the World War* 318–19 (1920); and Turlington, supra note 262 at 35–6.

266. See Brodie, *A Guide to Naval Strategy* 236, 244 (1959); Cagle and Manson, *The Sea War in Korea* 283 (1957).

267. See 2 Oppenheim-Lauterpacht 791–2; Stone, *Legal Controls of International Conflict* 508–10 (rev. ed., 1959); 2 Garner, supra note 265 at 327–8; Colombos, *The International Law of the Sea* 670–1 (4th rev. ed., 1959); Malkin, "Blockade in Modern Conditions," 3 *Brit. Y.B.I.L.* 87 (1922–1923).

are not relieved when one considers the possible tactical uses of nuclear explosives.

It was also in response to these changed conditions of military technology and combat operations that instrumentalities other than surface cruisers were resorted to for physically controlling the flow of commerce with the enemy. The principal instrumentalities employed for this purpose in the last two world wars were the mine, the submarine, and aircraft. Frequently all three weapons were utilized to supplement one another and occasional surface naval patrols. With respect to the use of these devices for controlling physical access to designated coasts, a recent commentator has written, with insistent emphasis,

> [T]he effectiveness required of valid blockades cannot be secured by means violative of other firmly established rules. The element of danger associated with an effective blockade is therefore to be understood in terms of a liability to seizure and eventual condemnation, though not in terms of a liability to destruction upon entrance into the forbidden area. But there is nothing in the traditional law preventing the use either of submarines or of aircraft in maintaining a naval blockade, so long as their employment does not thereby result in a violation of the rules applicable to surface vessels.[268]

Referring specifically to the establishment by belligerents of war zones through which passage was either prohibited or restricted and made dangerous by use of any of the three weapons noted above, Professor Tucker reiterates his view:

> There is no basis for the belief that the requirement of effectiveness, demanded of lawful blockades, can be met simply by using any means in order to render dangerous the passage of neutral vessels through areas of the high seas declared to be "blockaded." [269]

Clearly, by requiring that the use of all other instrumentalities conform to the requirements originally projected for surface squadrons, there is in effect registered a comprehensive denial of the possibility of their legitimate use for blockade purposes. For it should be evi-

268. Tucker, *The Law of War and Neutrality at Sea* 289 (1957).
269. Id., 298.

dent even upon casual observation that, of itself, a minefield can never, and submarines and aircraft only in very exceptional cases, meet the requirements for a cordon of surface vessels. The position taken by Professor Tucker would appear to represent an inadequate generalization of past experience and perspectives and, so far as concerns estimations of probable future practice and decision in comparable contexts, substantially to have escaped contact with reality.[270]

The experience of two global wars realistically indicates, as we have earlier noted, that the imposition of embargoes of varying degrees of comprehensiveness has become part of those expectations of uniformities and rightness called customary law. The lawfulness of the objective of embargoing, more or less comprehensively, commerce with the enemy being thus established, the lawfulness of any particular modality of achieving this objective in possible future contexts rationally depends upon appraisal of the relative destructiveness of such modality as compared to any other available alternative modality, rather than upon conformity to practices technologically obsolete. Such an appraisal, essentially an appraisal of reasonableness in detailed contexts, entails the careful relation of specific components of contexts to the relevant competing policies of military effectiveness and minimum destruction of values.

To illustrate, with particular reference to the establishment of war zones where stretches of the ocean are sown with mines, the important general consideration would seem to be that mines, as an instrumentality of blockade, need not be more destructive of neutral values than surface war vessels. More specifically, the strategic importance, in the particular war in question, of the objective of stopping the stream of commerce with the enemy; the details of the particular use of mined war zones, including the specific disposition of the mines; the economics made possible in time, effort, and commitment of surface craft; the giving or withholding and timing of

270. Cf. the projections offered in Powers, "Blockade: For Winning Without Killing," 84 *U.S. Naval Inst. Proc.* No. 8, p. 61, 65 (1958).

Contrast also Art. 73 of the "Harvard Draft Convention," supra note 263 at 714: "For the purpose of establishment and maintenance of a blockade, a belligerent must use surface or submarine vessels or aircraft, and may also use fixed obstacles and anchored contact mines which become harmless on becoming unanchored."

notification of neutrals—all appear factors appropriately included in the assaying of reasonableness. Thus, as the Allied Powers used them in the last world wars,[271] minefields functioned strategically as blockade devices by channeling shipping in particular parts of the ocean to predetermined routes for subjection to contraband and export control procedures. Both effectiveness and minimum destruction were served by giving notice to neutrals of the extent and location of the minefields and of the safe passages through them or of the procedures to be followed for obtaining safe passage. Neutral compliance, evidenced by keeping clear of the war zone or by using the safe passage through it, permitted the carrying on of the genuinely interneutral trade as distinguished from commerce with the enemy. The neutral vessel which ignored the notice and which would presumably do so only if engaged in commerce with the enemy of course became liable to destruction in the minefield. It is not clear, however, why this liability to destruction from exploding mines should be regarded any differently from the liability to destruction from a surface cruiser's fire which a neutral vessel incurs in seeking to escape inspection. It is, at any rate, only by the examination of the above and other types of detailed factors in the use of minefields as in the use of submarines and aircraft, that rational discriminations can be made as to the lawfulness (reasonableness) of particular, newer instrumentalities for securing the requirement of effectiveness in interdiction of passage.

Changing conditions of military technology and combat operations were not the only source of strain on the traditional law of blockade. The observation may be made that even a "long-distance" blockade by surface war vessels would seem inadequate to prevent penetration and carriage of goods by aircraft and submarines. During the Second World War, while Italy was still nominally a neutral, the

271. For summary accounts of practice in the two world wars, see 3 Hyde, *International Law* 1941–7 (2nd rev. ed., 1945); 2 Garner, supra note 265 at 320–51; Turlington, supra note 262 at 36–48; Spaight, *Air Power and War Rights* 493–4 (3rd ed., 1947); Bailey, *The Policy of the United States Towards the Neutrals, 1917–1918,* 408–17 (1942) esp. on the vast North Sea mine barrage.

The obsolete character of Art. 2 of Hague Convention VIII, 1907, text in *The Hague Conventions and Declarations of 1899 and 1907,* 151 (2nd ed., Scott, 1915), prohibiting the laying of automatic contact mines off enemy coasts and ports for "the sole object of intercepting commercial shipping" is commonly conceded.

LATI (*Linee Aeree Trancontinentali Italiene*) carried goods of small bulk and high strategic value—such as platinum, mica, industrial diamonds—into Germany from South America, Spain, and other neutrals.[272] The example of the "Berlin Airlift" of 1948–1949 suggests, moreover, that goods which can be transported and kept flowing through aircraft need not be insignificant in volume.[273] With respect to submarines, cargoes of such critical materials as rubber, wolfram, molybdenum, and tin were also transported into Germany by specially converted German, Italian, and Japanese submarines.[274] Much larger, nuclear-powered, cargo submarines may probably be expected in the not-too-distant future.[275] Of course, it has been suggested by distinguished commentators that the "effectiveness" of a naval blockade is not affected by the failure to interdict access by enemy or neutral aircraft (and, presumably, submarines).[276] In the sense that a neutral surface vessel would probably not be allowed by a prize court to escape condemnation for breach of blockade upon the defense that neutral aircraft succeeded in reaching the opposing belligerent's territory, this is true. The point that bears stress, however, is that techniques other than the traditional ones of maritime blockade are essential if commerce moved by means other than surface ships is successfully to be embargoed.

One of the "conditions of validity," it will be recalled, was that a blockade could not extend to the coasts and ports of adjacent neutrals. That scrupulous observance of a literal interpretation of this requirement was likely to result in substantial nullification of efforts to blockade or embargo commerce useful to the enemy was clearly indicated by the experience in the two global wars. When it first emerged in customary law, the requirement might have been a reasonable limitation of belligerent claims. Even so, in modern

272. *The War and the Neutrals, Survey of International Affairs 1939–1946*, 62 (Royal Institute of Int. Affairs, 1956).

273. Smith, *The Law and Custom of the Sea* 170 (3rd ed., 1959). And see, generally, Davison, *The Berlin Blockade: A Study in Cold War Politics* (1958).

274. See 2 Medlicott, *The Economic Blockade* c. 15 (1959).

275. Cohen, "The Future of the Submarine," 38 *Foreign Aff.* 110, 118–20 (1959); Galantin, "The Future of Nuclear-Powered Submarines," 84 *U.S. Naval Inst. Proc.* No. 6, p. 23 (1958).

276. 2 Oppenheim-Lauterpacht 781. See also Harvard Research, supra note 263 at 711; and the comment on Art. 53 (i) of the Hague Rules of Aerial Warfare of 1923, in 32 *A.J.I.L. Supp.* 47–8 (1938).

contexts, a blockaded belligerent flanked by adjoining neutrals and connected by modern and highly organized land transportation systems would have but little difficulty in exporting and importing goods through the ports of the neutrals. It may indeed be seen that a strict construction of this "condition of validity" would render grievously difficult the institution and maintenance of an effective embargo against any save a purely insular state, like Japan or the United Kingdom.[277] An embargo to be really effective must establish a barrier coextensive and coincident with the territorial boundaries of the target belligerent. To limit a lawful embargo to the traditional reach of a maritime blockade is, accordingly, in modern context, to insure the serious inadequacy of the embargo. A simple maritime blockade, even if extended to control access to adjacent neutral coasts, obviously cannot interdict commerce across land boundaries. The historical transformation of the traditional, essentially naval, practice into a wide arsenal of techniques for managing "economics" as a weapon is but realistic recognition of these facts.

It is important briefly to consider two principles developed in supplementation of the traditional laws of contraband, visit and search, and blockade. The first principle is that of ultimate enemy destination and is concerned with the control of imports into enemy territory. The second principle is that of ultimate or real enemy origin and is concerned with the control of exports from enemy territory.

The Problem of Ultimate Destination. The determination of the hostile or innocent destination of goods would present no difficulties where the shipping documents set forth such destination as enemy or enemy-occupied territory. Save in cases of goods shipped before a sudden and unexpected outbreak of war, such a situation would of course be wholly exceptional. The difficulties arise in the much more common case where the destination stated in the shipping papers is a port in neutral territory adjacent to the enemy belligerent and an intention in either the shipper or consignee of record to forward the goods from neutral to enemy territory exists or is suspected. The process of carriage is split, as it were, into two

277. Colombos, *The International Law of the Sea* 669–70 (4th rev. ed., 1959); Percy, *Maritime Trade in War* 34–5 (1930); Jack, *Studies in Economic Warfare* 79 (1941).

phases: from neutral to neutral territory, and from neutral to enemy territory. The device of interposing a neutral port to negative the element of hostile destination would clearly nullify belligerent claims to intercept and seize enemy imports, or at least intensify the strain on the belligerent's contraband control system by requiring the belligerent again to intercept the goods at the second phase, unless the decision-maker undertook to look beyond the ostensible or intermediate to the real or ultimate destination, to pierce, in other words, the veil of shipping bills. This is precisely what a prize court does in applying, in appropriate cases, the doctrine of continuous voyage. In condemning goods seized and captured while still in the first phase of its voyage, that is, while en route to the intervening neutral port, the court puts together and characterizes as one integral process of transmission what the neutral trader had sundered. The mode of shipment contemplated for the second phase of the carriage is without bearing on the question of destination.[278] In the famous *Springbok* [279] case, the contraband goods were intended to be shipped from British Nassau by a smaller, swifter vessel to the Confederate coast, while in the equally well-known case of the *Peterhoff*,[280] the goods were to be transported from the Mexican port of Matamoras overland to Texas. In both cases, the contraband goods were declared good prize.

It may be noted that the neutral technique of splitting voyages—a technique with a very long history [281]—is susceptible of many

278. A distinction between carriage by sea and carriage by land in the second stage of a process of importation was previously made by those who had argued that the doctrine of continuous voyage was not applicable in case of blockades. The *Peterhoff* case, infra, was cited as support, since there the Court refused to condemn *noncontraband* goods, although such goods, together with the contraband ones, were destined ultimately for Texas, the blockade by the Federal forces not being extended to Matamoras. As 2 Garner, supra note 265 at 333 points out, it is illogical and unreasonable to make the means of transportation, rather than intent or effect, the real test. In the First World War the distinction was explicitly provided against in the Order-in-Council of July 7, 1916 (text in Ritchie, *The Navicert System During the World War* 54–6 [1938]), while in the Second World War, it was simply disregarded.

279. 72 U.S. (5 Wall.) 1 (1866).

280. 72 U.S. (5 Wall.) 28 (1866).

281. Historical accounts are offered in Mootham, "The Doctrine of Continuous Voyage, 1756–1815," 8 *Brit. Y.B.I.L.* 62 (1927); Davies, "Enemy Property and Ultimate Destination During the Anglo-Dutch Wars, 1664–7 and 1672–4,"

variations and refinements. Thus, to heighten the difficulties of detection, the voyage may be split into more than two parts. The course of transmission from neutral to enemy territory may be made highly circuitous by arranging for several intermediate neutral ports, or several changes of hands within one or more ports, before final re-exportation to the enemy.[282] Another variation consists in the simple diversion of the goods at sea and the omission altogether of the ostensible neutral destination. This procedure, it has been reported, was used by the Chinese communist forces during the recent civil war to draw materials from territory controlled by the Nationalist Government forces. A third variation is presented by transfer to another carrier at sea or just off a neutral port or waters, without physical landing of the goods. This procedure was reportedly utilized by Hong Kong merchants who exported to the People's Republic of China, during the Korean war, prohibited strategic materials by way of Bombay and other neutral ports.[283]

In the context of application of authority by a prize court, the problem of ultimate destination is always one of proof: what factors, in what collocation, give rise to a reasonable inference of ultimate enemy destination? During the Napoleonic era, at which time our inherited rules crystallized, the ordinary method of securing proof consisted of visitation of the ship at sea, the examination of its papers, and interrogation of crew and passengers.[284] Under present circumstances, such a procedure would, of course, as observed earlier, be less than adequate, not because forgers of shipping documents have grown in numbers or in artfulness,[285] but rather because the com-

15 id. 21 (1934). See also Pares, *Colonial Blockade and Neutral Rights 1739–1763* (1938).

282. Wu, *Economic Warfare* 22 (1952) . At pp. 20–8, Dr. Wu discusses the complex procedures required by efforts to control re-exports from neutral territories.

283. Id., 20. The Additional Measures Committee established by the U. N. General Assembly was particularly concerned over the circumvention of the recommended embargo against the People's Republic of China by means of transshipment or re-exportation. The General Assembly's resolution on the embargo, incorporating the Committee's recommendation, urged (every state) to "prevent by all means within its jurisdiction the circumvention of controls on shipments applied by other states pursuant to the present Resolution." 1951 *U.N. Yearbook,* 226, 228.

284. Smith, *The Law and Custom of the Sea* 153 (3rd ed., 1959).

285. On the use of false or duplicate papers and other fraudulent practices, standard tactics of smugglers during the Napoleonic wars, see Phillips and

plexity of the processes and institutions of modern commerce and financing has made discovery of covert enemy destination or interest much too difficult adequately to be performed by casual visit and search at sea.[286] It is here that the technical significance—i.e. for a prize court—of the newer procedures of economic warfare, described below, embracing navicerts, ship warrants, mail certs, and the like, is to be found. The failure of the carrier or shipper to produce such documents was regarded as creating a presumption of hostile destination which, if not rebutted by the trader or carrier, sufficed to support condemnation of the goods in question.[287] The function of collecting intelligence was thus in effect transferred from boarding officers and principally vested in ministries or boards of economic warfare and their agents.

Actually, the necessity for proof of hostile destination is not, or is no longer, as pressing as might be supposed.[288] Previously, such proof was indispensable because condemnation was indispensable for effective stoppage of the flow of goods. Unless a decree of condemnation was forthcoming, the goods had eventually to be released to the owner and there was nothing to prevent him from attempting reshipment to the enemy. Thus, the goods, unless a second interception was effected and more adequate proof of hostile destination obtained, could still reach the enemy. In the *Falk*,[289] however, the Judicial Committee of the Privy Council laid down the ruling that an order for the release of goods seized in prize operated only to place the owner in possession of such goods within the belligerent's

---

Reede, *The Napoleonic Period* (Neutrality: Its History, Economics and Law, Vol. II, 1936) 44, 111, 165.

286. Tucker, *The Law of War and Neutrality at Sea* 271 (1957). Cf. Jessup, *Today and Tomorrow* 65–72 (Neutrality: Its History, Economics and Law, Vol. IV, 1936) emphasizing the venerable age of the neutral trader's practice of using simulated documentation.

287. See infra, p. 512. Rowson, "Prize Law During the Second World War," 24 *Brit. Y.B.I.L.* 160, 196–7 made the interesting observation that these techniques of economic warfare might be considered as merely new rules "of a procedural character," such that invocation of the doctrine of reprisals would seem unnecessary. He said: "a more adequate foundation seems to be the inherent right of every state to issue legislation governing the procedure of its own prize courts."

288. See Fitzmaurice, "Some Aspects of Modern Contraband Control and the Law of Prize," 22 *Brit. Y.B.I.L.* 73, 77–8 (1945).

289. [1921] 3 B. & C. Pr. Cas. 955, 966.

territory and did not in itself authorize the owner to remove them from the territory of the forum. The ordinary legislation on exports, which in time of war commonly provided for stringent export controls, thus became applicable to these goods.[290] Moreover, as the same tribunal had ruled in *The Zamora,* the goods could be ordered requisitioned, or sold in case of perishables, provided that certain conditions were met. These conditions were:

> First, the vessel or goods in question must be urgently required for use in connection with the defense of the realm, the prosecution of the war, or other matters involving national security. Secondly, there must be a real question to be tried, so that it would be improper to order an immediate release. And thirdly, the right must be enforced by application to the prize court, which must determine judicially whether, under the particular circumstances of the case, the right is exercisable.[291]

Where these requirements were satisfied and compulsory preemption held authorized, the claim of the owner was limited to the release of the proceeds in case of eventual success in showing ultimate innocent destination. Thus, the capturing power may either acquire the goods for its own use or at least preclude their acquisition by the enemy by preventing removal from its territory. The suggestion may hence not be inappropriate that with the *Falk* and *Zamora* rulings, judicial verification of ultimate hostile destination is probably not likely to prove a crucial problem in the future.

The Problem of Ultimate Origin. The determination of the ultimate origin of goods for purposes of enemy export control would obviously pose no problem if enemy-owned exports were sent abroad from enemy ports in enemy ships. In such cases, the general belligerent right to capture enemy property on the high seas would be an adequate basis in authority for embargoing such goods.[292] Enemy exports, however, may be carried on neutral vessels departing from neutral ports, and may in addition frequently be neutral-owned before shipment.

This was the type of situation that the British Reprisals Order-in-

290. Fitzmaurice, supra note 288 at 75–7.

291. [1916] 2 A.C. 77, 106.

292. See Smith, *The Law and Custom of the Sea* 157 (3rd ed., 1959).

Council of November 27, 1939,[293] was designed to meet. This Order required that all goods loaded in enemy or enemy-controlled ports, and all goods which, although not on board a vessel sailing from such ports, were of enemy origin or ownership, be discharged at a British or Allied port. Vessels outward bound from Germany, or from countries to which Germany had access, were required to obtain "certificates of origin and interest" for their cargoes. These certificates were issued by British consuls upon satisfactory showing that the goods had not been produced in enemy territory, and that no enemy or "blacklisted" person or firm had any interest in it.[294] In the case of goods manufactured in a neutral country, the certificate was not issued unless such goods contained no more than the permissible maximum percentage of "enemy content." [295] "Enemy content" referred to the portion of the total value of an article manufactured in a neutral country which had been contributed by enemy material or labor; the permissible maximum percentage differed with differing types of goods and ranged from five to twenty-five per cent. Because a high proportion of the raw materials used in manufacture in the neutral countries adjoining Germany came from Germany, it would have been impossible for the adjacent neutrals to maintain any export trade unless some "enemy content" in neutral exports were tolerated by the Allied Powers. An exception to the regulation requiring a certificate was provided for the exportation of enemy goods which had been ordered under a long-term contract and paid for in advance and which could be shipped only after the lapse of a considerable period of time. Blocking the exportation of such goods would obviously benefit only Germany.[296]

Respecting the enforcement of this Order-in-Council, noncertified goods diverted to or discharged at Allied control ports were placed in the custody of a prize court. If the court found these goods to be of enemy origin or ownership, they were detained, or sold and the proceeds held for account of the owner "until the conclusion of peace," or, more commonly, ordered to be requisitioned for govern-

293. Gt. Brit., Statutory Rules and Orders, 1939, No. 1709, p. 3606; also in 7 Hackworth, *Digest of International Law* 138. For the corresponding order in the First World War, see the Order-in-Council of Feb. 16, 1917, in ibid., 137–8.

294. See 1 Medlicott, *The Economic Blockade* 116–17 (1952).

295. Gordon and Dangerfield, *The Hidden Weapon*, 41–2 (1947); Wu, *Economic Warfare* 249 (1952).

296. 1 Medlicott, *The Economic Blockade* 116 (1952).

ment use. Thus, instead of condemnation which had been the ordinary penalty under traditional law for breach of a maritime blockade, compulsory pre-emption served in effect as the sanction for export control. However, the Reprisals Order-in-Council of July 31, 1940,[297] issued following the occupation of the Low Countries and the further diminution in the number of neutrals, subsequently declared goods of enemy origin or ownership, and ships carrying such goods, liable to condemnation in prize.

Generally speaking, the problem of ultimate origin in export control parallels that of ultimate destination in contraband (import) control. The enemy belligerent seeks to evade export control by interposing neutrals between itself and the capturing belligerent. The exporting (enemy) belligerent may, more specifically, seek to interpose a neutral vessel, an adjacent neutral country or port, or neutral ownership, or possibly all three, in the attempt to defeat its opponent's claims to capture. We consider these devices *seriatim.*

In loading its exports on a neutral vessel, and in asserting the immunity of such goods from capture, an enemy belligerent invoked the provisions of the Declaration of Paris of 1856. Article 2 of the Declaration provided that "the neutral flag covers enemy goods, with the exception of contraband of war." This provision, it may be recalled, was among those set aside in the two world wars by the Allied Powers through Reprisals Orders-in-Council and by their opponents through simple practice to the contrary. Even apart from these developments, however, the scope of protection afforded to enemy exports by Article 2 was, from one perspective, attenuated almost to the vanishing point. Article 2 had been interpreted by most publicists, as well as by courts, as referring to and protecting only privately owned enemy goods.[298] The public property of belligerents had always been regarded as a legitimate object for capture and condemnation, in much the same way that the law of war booty authorized the taking of such property on land.[299] This distinction between public and private enemy property, like the distinction

297. Art. 4, Statutory Rules and Orders, 1940, No. 1436, in 7 Hackworth, *Digest of International Law* 141–2 (1943).

298. Smith, "The Declaration of Paris in Modern War," 55 *Law. Q. Rev.* 237, 238–42 (1939) canvasses learned opinion, judicial decision, and contemporaneous interpretation. But cf. 2 Oppenheim-Lauterpacht 461 note 1. For the diplomatic history of the Declaration, see Malkin, "The Inner History of the Declaration of Paris," 8 *Brit. Y.B.I.L.* 1 (1927).

299. See infra, Ch. 6.

between acts of neutral governments and acts of private neutral nationals, rested on certain nineteenth-century conceptions and institutions of social organization and political economy. It should hence be obvious that the same developments that have rendered the latter distinction anachronistic—in particular, the extension of state ownership and vast multiplication of state controls over economic processes and, generally, the common employment of state trading practices—have also, in large measure, vitiated the former distinction. The extensive export and exchange controls exercised by all belligerent governments underscore state participation in wartime commerce as an economic fact. Certainly at least in case of belligerents engaged in major conflicts, no export trade would be permitted that was not calculated to enhance capacity to carry on the struggle.[300] Most importantly, the foreign exchange earned by such export trade was subject to the control and disposition of the belligerent government and it was, as noted earlier, precisely the principal object of export control to prevent the acquisition and building up of foreign credits by the opposing belligerent. In net result, there is, under this view, little by way of enemy exports that cannot, with considerable realism, be regarded as public enemy property removed from the cover of the Declaration of Paris.[301]

300. 2 Medlicott, *The Economic Blockade* 31 (1959) observed: "Great Britain [in World War II] had to maintain some export trade in order to secure the currency resources needed for purchases of food and raw material abroad; this trade was under complete governmental control and was in no sense a mere matter of private profit. Otherwise export trade was ruthlessly abandoned."

301. Smith, supra note 298 at 249: "If we are again confronted with the facts for which the Declaration laid down the law, then that law must be applied to those facts. That is to say, if we can discover a genuine enemy private merchant carrying on his own trade in his own way for his own profit, then we must admit that his non-contraband goods carried in neutral ships are immune from capture at sea. Under the conditions of the modern socialistic world such person is not easily to be found. In the books of the last generation he was commonly called the 'innocent merchant,' and the disappearance of this phrase from the literature of our day has its own significance. To-day he has become a disciplined individual mobilised in the vast military organization of the totalitarian State. It would be a defiance both of the letter and the spirit of the Declaration of Paris to bring within its protection the mobilised forces of the enemy."

Quite apart from the above qualification of the scope of the Declaration of Paris (Art. 3), there are other restrictions which have been developed by judicial interpretation. These are discussed in some detail in Stone, *Legal Controls of International Conflict* 466–8 (rev. ed., 1959).

Cf. the decision of the Prize Court in Alexandria in *The Marine Cap, Annual*

By the interposition of a neutral country or port, the enemy exporter seeks to divide the outgoing voyage into two or more phases, from enemy to neutral and from neutral to neutral territory, in precisely the same way that the neutral trader attempts to split the incoming voyage in ultimate enemy destination. To meet this device, prize courts have utilized certain familiar doctrines such as those relating to the passing of property while *in transitu*. In *The United States,*[302] for instance, Sir Samuel Evans held that the *in transitu* doctrine, which prohibited the alteration of enemy character of goods while in the course of carriage, applied not only to one part of the carriage but to the whole of the journey, that is, from the original point of shipment or exportation to the ultimate neutral destination. The goods in question had been shipped overland from Leipzig to Copenhagen, and then at Copenhagen loaded on board a Danish vessel bound for New York City. The relevant transit began when the goods began their journey and, in this case, the journey started not when the goods were put on board the vessel at Copenhagen but rather when they were shipped from Leipzig. The enemy character of the goods was held to have survived transshipment at a neutral port and the goods declared good prize. Thus, the court integrated what the enemy exporter sought to sever into stages, which, it need not escape notice, was precisely the same effect achieved by application of the doctrine of ultimate enemy destination. The *in transitu* doctrine has also been applied by prize courts to defeat transshipment of enemy goods from an enemy to a neutral

---

Digest 1949, Case No. 202. The Prize Court there refused to condemn certain cargo from Israel shipped on an American vessel and consigned to persons in the United States, although enemy export control regulations had been issued by the Egyptian Government. The Court invoked Art. 2 of the Declaration of Paris and in the course of its opinion noted that "the Direction of June 6, 1948 [the enemy export control regulations] was not made with the object of following the procedure of reprisals in the first place, because there did not exist [in the Palestine conflict] a blockade on a large scale . . ." It is, however, open to doubt whether this reaffirmation of Art. 2 of the Declaration of Paris is more real than apparent. See, for example, *The Captain Manoli,* in 15 *Revue Egyptienne de Droit International* 186 (1959) and *The Lea Lott,* 16 December 1959 (typewritten copy made available by Judge Jasper Y. Brinton) where the Alexandria Prize Court held in effect that a neutral ship sailing under a charter to an enemy (Israeli) company loses the "benefit of its neutrality" with the result that its flag is ineffective to protect enemy goods.

302. [1917] 2 B. & C. Pr. Cas. 525. *Semble* the decision of Lord Sterndale in *The Dirigo* [1919] 3 ibid. 439.

ship. In *The Jeanne*,[303] the same judge, Sir Samuel Evans, declared that goods which had been transferred from an enemy ship to a neutral vessel, and which were seized after such transfer, were appropriately considered as still *in transitu* and, in effect, as still on board the enemy vessel. The neutral ship was regarded as a vessel employed by the enemy, much as if the enemy ship had approached port and used the neutral ship as a lighter in waters too shallow for the enemy vessel itself.

The interposition of neutral ownership constitutes a somewhat more complex problem. Prize courts have employed doctrines and tests relating to enemy character for the ascertainment of the fictitious or genuine nature of the asserted neutral ownership. In *The Proton* [304] and *The Hamborne*,[305] for instance, the court in substance held that where the evidence indicated that the neutral purchaser was, in point of fact, acting as an agent of the enemy exporter, the vesting of ownership in such purchaser was properly regarded as merely apparent and would not be permitted to disguise the real enemy origin of the goods. The clearest case would probably be that of a purchase and exportation or re-exportation by a firm chartered in a neutral country but controlled by enemy nationals. Condemnation, however, upon the ground that the goods were really of enemy ownership—in other words, that the neutral person's ownership was merely ostensible—presented no novel technical problem. It was the condemnation of goods which were, by all the relevant tests of actual control and effective disposition, of real and genuine and not merely ostensible neutral ownership, but which were of enemy origin, that raised the problem of adequacy of traditional authority. Further, in so far as the *in transitu* doctrine was a doctrine about the persistence of enemy character or ownership, it was subject to the same difficulty.[306] Where real and genuine neutral ownership was acquired

303. [1916] 2 B. & C. Pr. Cas. 227. See also *The Alga, Annual Digest 1949*, Case No. 209, decided by the Prize Court of Alexandria.

304. [1918] 3 B. & C. Pr. Cas. 125.

305. [1917] 3 B. & C. Pr. Cas. 80, affirmed (1919) 3 id. 279.

306. See, e.g., *The Noordam* (No. 2) [1919] 3 B. & C. Pr. Cas. 488 where Lord Sterndale held that the "bona fide" sale and delivery of securities by their German owners to Dutch purchasers, either in Germany or Holland, served to negative their "enemy origin." The result was that when the securities were seized while being forwarded to the United States by the Dutch purchasers, they had become exempt from condemnation. There is probably here a confounding of

before the relevant course of transit (however defined in geographic terms) started, the *in transitu* doctrine furnished no authorization for condemnation at all.

It must be evident that the efforts to control and interdict enemy exports must fail if neutral ownership is allowed to intervene decisively in the process of transmission from enemy exporter to the final neutral consignee. This is of course the same problem of re-exportation by neutrals that, in the field of contraband (import) control, the doctrine of ultimate enemy destination was developed to meet. Just as in contraband control neutral ownership is held irrelevant and ultimate enemy destination ascribed controlling significance, so also in export control, we submit, when it is militarily important to belligerents to stop the accumulation of enemy credits abroad, ultimate enemy origin should be regarded as the basic consideration and neutral ownership held equally immaterial. The conception of integral, continuous voyage or transportation, which may be seen to embody a principle of effectiveness, may be as necessary and reasonable in one as in the other type of situation.[307] That the process of transmission is outward from, rather than inward to, the enemy country, does not, in and of itself and without regard to the policy of military necessity and effectiveness, impress one as a manifestly rational basis for distinction. Clearly, in contexts of major conflicts, the interdiction of enemy exports may be as important in the over-all strategy of belligerents as the interdiction of enemy imports.

It may be concluded, finally, that the expansionist developments in the law of contraband referred to earlier, and the principle or doctrine of ultimate enemy destination together constitute an adequate basis in authority for a comprehensive embargo or blockade

---

ownership for origin. In effect, Lord Sterndale refused to consider as continuous the transit from Germany to the United States, but looked only to the latter portion thereof, i.e., from Holland to the U.S.

The above difficulty is probably mitigated by another doctrine utilized by prize courts: that transfers *in transitu* from enemy to neutral ownership, if done "in fraud of" the capturing belligerent, may not be set up against the captor; e.g., *The Bawean* [1918] P. 59. The mitigation, however, is only partial for the taking of "actual" possession by the neutral transferee has been held to terminate the process of transit and in effect to defeat the claim of the captor. See the analysis in Stone, *Legal Controls of International Conflict* 472–4 (rev. ed., 1959).

307. Cf. Tucker, *The Law of War and Neutrality at Sea* 312 (1957).

inward. Their cumulative effect is to permit a belligerent to seize and condemn practically all goods whose real or final destination is, or may reasonably be presumed to be, an enemy belligerent's territory. Thus, a major distinction established in traditional theory between the law of contraband and the law of blockade—that is, that while the law of contraband authorized capture only of goods characterized as enhancing enemy fighting potential, the law of blockade permitted capture of all goods flowing into the blockaded region across the line of blockade—tended to disappear. To such extent, the law of contraband has been adapted to perform the functions of the law of blockade, avoiding the narrow geographical limitations projected in the latter.[308] This development at the same time deprived both Article 19 of the Declaration of London stipulating the inapplicability of the doctrine of continuous voyage or ultimate enemy destination to blockades, and the debates which ensued thereafter, of any substantial point. One other important difference frequently pointed to between the traditional law of contraband and of blockade was that the law of contraband was authority for seizure of enemy imports only, while the law of blockade authorized the severance both of the import and the export trade of the enemy.[309] Thus, even the enlarged conception of contraband provided no authority for seizure and condemnation of goods originating from enemy territory, i.e. for a blockade outward. It is here of course that what is above referred to as a principle of ultimate enemy origin,[310] a principle which we believe may be distilled from the practice of belligerents in the last two global wars, assumes functional importance. The modern conception of contraband and the principles of ultimate

308. Rowson, "Modern Blockade: Some Legal Aspects," 23 *Brit. Y.B.I.L.* 346, 350 (1946); Smith, *The Crisis in the Law of Nations* 59 (1947). Earlier recognition of this resulting partial equivalency of function may be found in Hall, *The Law of Naval Warfare* 226–7 (2nd ed., 1921). See also "Neutrals and Naval Economic Warfare," 16 *Bull. of Int. News* 1033 (1939) and Lovitt, "Survey of Economic Policy Toward the European Neutrals," 13 *Dept. of State Bull.* 777 (1945).

309. See Rowson, "Prize Law During the Second World War," 24 *Brit. Y.B.I.L.* 160, 193 (1947); Malkin, "Blockade in Modern Conditions," 3 id. 87, 93 (1922–1923); Colombos, *A Treatise on the Law of Prize* 267–8 (3rd ed., 1949).

310. In 2 Oppenheim-Lauterpacht 797, Judge Lauterpacht spoke of a principle of "ultimate origin."

enemy destination and of ultimate enemy origin, when conjoined, and supported by a general requirement of effectiveness and reasonableness in particular context, may be seen to present a complete basis in structures of legal authority for the maintenance of comprehensive embargo. These principles are in a sense but slightly lower-order specifications of what Judge Lauterpacht has felicitously generalized as

> The latent principle of the law of blockade, namely, that the belligerent who possesses effective command of the sea is entitled to deprive his opponent of the use thereof for the purpose either of navigation by his own vessels or of conveying on neutral vessels such goods as are destined to or originate from him.[311]

Administrative Methods of Commerce Control: Economic Warfare Practices. The final and ultimate response to the difficulties of embargoing commerce with the enemy imposed by modern conditions of military operations, of weapons and transport technology, and of "total war" generally, consisted, in the two world wars, in the development of certain techniques commonly and loosely described as "economic warfare." The primary focus of these techniques, which sought to establish control at the source of the flow of goods and services, shifted from the sea and Allied ports to the neutral ports of exportation.

One of the most important of these techniques was the navicert system, devised by the Allied Powers during World War I and further elaborated and extended in World War II. A cargo navicert was a commercial passport or "letter of assurance" issued by the British mission in a neutral exporting country in respect of a particular consignment of goods which, at the time of issuance, did not appear liable to seizure as contraband.[312] Goods covered by a navicert

311. Id., 796–7.

312. See Ritchie, *The Navicert System During the World War* (1938); Siney, *The Allied Blockade of Germany 1914–1916,* 139–44 (1957); 1 Medlicott, *The Economic Blockade,* 94–101, 343–50, 436–42 (1952); 2 id. cc. V and XIV (1959). Cf. the "certificates of neutrality" proposed in Art. 41 and Annex II of the "Harvard Draft Convention." These certificates are to be issued by the government of the neutral state from which the merchant ship is to begin its voyage, and countersigned by officials of any other neutral state at whose ports the ship

could count on favorable treatment by the control services. If, however, they were carried on a vessel with other unnavicerted cargo, the navicerted goods would naturally be subject to any delays applying to the whole ship. The full benefits of the system could therefore be enjoyed only by ships with "ship navicerts," which were certificates issued to the master when the whole cargo was covered by navicerts.[313] The inconvenience, delay, and expense that could be avoided by means of navicerts were such as to create in neutral shippers a strong inclination to make use of the system. Shipowners, in turn, would refuse to carry uncertified cargo, since even one single consignment of such cargo on board would disentitle the vessel to a ship navicert and render her subject to diversion. This attitude of shipowners was strengthened by the common refusal of consignors, for the same reasons, to ship their goods on a vessel not qualified for a ship navicert. The net effect of these mutually reinforcing expectations was the widespread use of navicerts and the practical impossibility of shipping unnavicerted goods.[314] By 1941, the system had been extended to cover all cargoes consigned to every neutral European port, to Morocco, the Atlantic Islands, and to Iraq and Iran.[315]

Navicerts, it should be evident, were a device for controlling the inward flow of goods toward a blockaded zone, that is, for controlling the imports of neutrals adjacent to the enemy belligerent. Much the same system of certification, and the same machinery for sanctions, was employed for controlling goods flowing outward, that is, the exports of adjacent neutrals. Succinctly, "certificates of origin and

---

calls. It is doubtful whether belligerents will frequently be inclined to repose such absolute trust in the good faith of neutral governments.

It may be observed that the system of certification or passes was not entirely new even in the First World War; some analogous procedure has been occasionally used in the 16th–18th centuries. See Rowson, "Prize Law During the Second World War," 24 *Brit. Y.B.I.L.* 160, 197 (1947); Jessup and Deak, *The Origins* 188 et seq. (Neutrality: Its History, Economics and Law, Vol. I, 1936).

313. 1 Medlicott, *The Economic Blockade* 94 (1952). At 2 id. 160–3, Professor Medlicott observed that the system of navicerts and ship navicerts also permitted the exercise by the Allied Powers of passenger and crew control. See also Salter, *Allied Shipping Control* (1921).

314. Fitzmaurice, "Some Aspects of Modern Contraband Control and the Law of Prize," 22 *Brit. Y.B.I.L.* 73, 84 (1945); Lovitt, "The Allied Blockade," 11 *Dept. of State Bull.* 597 (1944).

315. See Moos, "The Navicert in World War II," 38 *A.J.I.L.* 115 (1944).

interest" were to enemy export control what navicerts were to enemy import (contraband) control.

The system of navicerts reduced in very significant degree the necessity for resorting to the older procedures of visit and search and of deviation to control ports; indeed, it functioned in large measure as a substitute for these procedures.[316] As between the neutral trader and the belligerent administering the embargo, certification at source appeared more effective and more economical of both belligerent effort and neutral values than the older procedures. To the neutral shipper or consignee, the system was useful because it permitted the fixing of expectations as to whether a particular shipment was likely to be held up or allowed to proceed to its destination with minimum delay. Compliance with navicert regulations also enabled the neutral shipper to save the cost of insurance against the risk of detention and delay. As for the belligerent, the system, properly administered, made possible a much tighter method of contraband control and at the same time allowed a significant saving in the naval forces that would otherwise have been necessary for enforcement. Air and submarine warfare made this economy a consideration of importance.

It must be noted that the possession of a cargo or ship navicert was not, in Allied practice, an absolute guarantee against interception and seizure by the contraband control or naval authorities or condemnation by the prize court. New facts might have intervened since the issuance of the navicerts: [317] the destination of the ship or goods, to take an obvious instance, might have become an enemy or enemy-occupied one since the commencement of the voyage. Thus, in *The Selandia* [318] and *Goods ex S.S. Maro* [319] cases, goods consigned to France were seized by the British control services on the ground that after the fall of France and the Armistice of 1940, their destina-

316. See 2 Medlicott, *The Economic Blockade* 637–9 (1959); also Harvard Research, "Rights and Duties of Neutral States in Naval and Aerial War," 33 *A.J.I.L. Supp.* at 508, 511 (1939).

317. Fitzmaurice, supra note 314 at 83.

318. *Annual Digest 1938–1940,* Case No. 218, decided by the Supreme Court of South Africa.

319. *Annual Digest 1941–1942,* Case No. 179, decided by the Colonial Admiralty Court in Ceylon. More recent cases to the same effect include *The Orsia, Annual Digest 1949,* Case No. 206, and *The Hemland,* id., Case No. 215, both decided by the Prize Court in Alexandria, and *The Sado Maru* [1947] 1 All E.R. 430.

tion had become hostile. Further, occasional interceptions and diversions might be effected by naval patrols to provide a continuing deterrent against surreptitious carriage of uncertified cargo.[320]

The possession of a navicert was not of course allowed as a defense against seizure and condemnation where the cargo was shown actually to consist of contraband. In the somewhat spectacular case of *The Monte Albertia,*[321] the prize court condemned cargo although duly covered by navicerts. The cargo included containers which were discovered to have false bottoms and to have stored therein smuggled discs of platinum. On the other hand, the absence of a navicert did not automatically result in the condemnation of the goods or ship. The Reprisals Order-in-Council of July 31, 1940[322] provided that absence of a navicert gave rise to rebuttable presumptions of carriage of contraband or goods of enemy ownership or origin in the case of a ship, and of enemy destination in the case of cargo. Although in point of theory the presumption, if not displaced by evidence of the shipper or shipowner, could suffice for condemnation by the prize court, actually, it is reported, in no case was a decree of condemnation rested on the above presumption alone. The absence of a navicert was in practice treated by the Allied prize courts as only one of many possible grounds of suspicion.[323]

A navicert saved a neutral trader and shipowner considerable inconvenience. But its possession also made the vessel liable to seizure and condemnation by the opposing belligerent for unneutral service or hostile assistance. This was the doctrine announced by the German Supreme Prize Tribunal in the case of the *Ole Wegger.*[324] The tribunal observed that ship navicerts and warrants were a measure of

320. Gordon and Dangerfield, *The Hidden Weapon* 37 (1947).

321. See 2 Medlicott, *The Economic Blockade* 442 (1959).

322. Statutory Rules and Orders, 1940, No. 1436, in 7 Hackworth, *Digest of International Law* 141–2 (1943).

323. See Fitzmaurice, supra note 314 at 87–9; Rowson, "Prize Law During the Second World War," 24 *Brit. Y.B.I.L.* 160, 197–8 (1947). And see *The Monte Contes, Annual Digest 1943–1945,* Case No. 196 and *The Sidi Ifni,* id., Case No. 197. Cf. the decision of the *Conseil des Prises* in *The Mount Taurus,* id. *1946,* Case No. 183 which held that the refusal of a navicert did not suffice to show that the consignee Swiss firms were "suspect in character or conduct."

324. *Annual Digest 1943–1945,* Case No. 193. Rowson, supra note 323 at 180 observed that the Japanese view was even harsher: the neutral merchantman was to be treated as an enemy vessel.

economic warfare aimed at placing under enemy [British] control those ships which were not yet in enemy [British] hands. The submission of vessels to this control aided and facilitated the economic war waged by the enemy, removing the necessity of direct application of military force and enabling the enemy to determine in advance what voyages would be unobjectionable. Neutral shipowners and traders were apt, therefore, to be caught between a British Scylla and a German Charybdis.

The navicert system provided the means for enforcement of another technique of control, commonly denominated as "rationing of neutrals." Briefly expressed, the basic assumption was that only by limiting imports to nonparticipant states adjoining enemy territory to quantities sufficient merely for their own necessities would it be possible to ensure that no substantial portion thereof would reach the enemy.[325] Failing this limitation, one of two things could be expected to follow. Firstly, the goods imported would either be transshipped forthwith, or in the case of raw materials, processed or transformed, and then exported to the enemy belligerent. Secondly, if the imported goods should be actually utilized or consumed in the neutral state, the importation would operate to displace and release for exportation to the enemy belligerent a corresponding quantity of the same or similar indigenous goods.

The "rationing" system was put into effect in the last war by means of War Trade Agreements negotiated with the individual nonparticipant countries.[326] The agreements negotiated by the Allied Powers, though varying in specific detail, commonly included,

325. Fitzmaurice, supra note 314 at 89; Fenwick, *International Law* 640–1 (3rd ed., 1948); and see the Statement of the Measures Adopted to Intercept the Seaborne Commerce of the Enemy, Parliamentary Paper, Misc. No. 2 (1916) Cmd. 8145, in Ritchie, *The Navicert System During the World War* 28, 34–5 (1938).

326. Detailed description of the "rationing" system and war trade agreement with various neutrals may be secured from Medlicott, *The Economic Blockade* Vols. 1 and 2, passim. For World War I practice, see Siney, *The Allied Blockade of Germany 1914–1916*, cc. 5 and 8 (1957) and Guichard, *The Naval Blockade 1914–1918* (1930). The imposition of these "rationing agreements" was made possible not only by the existence of blockade and contraband controls but also by the fact that the Allied Powers controlled most of the important sources of supply outside Europe; see Lovitt, supra note 308 at 778. Thus Allied export controls were used partially to enforce the "rationing agreements."

in one form or another, two conditions designed to meet each of the possible situations indicated above. Firstly, the nonparticipants agreed to the establishment of import quotas for most of the goods they normally bought abroad. The quotas were set at levels designed to permit satisfaction of the neutrals' own needs but to leave no surplus for re-export. Quotas which were ordinarily based on normal prewar net imports from sources overseas were generally fixed on a quarterly basis for each commodity, that is, the quotas set maximum limits on the importation of that commodity during each three-month period. When those limits were reached, no further imports would be navicerted by the Allied contraband control service. Secondly, each nonparticipant undertook not to re-export to the enemy any goods received through the blockade as part of the agreed quota. Further, they agreed not to export to the enemy "similar goods" produced entirely in their own territory, nor goods processed in their territory and containing a certain proportion of an imported commodity. It may be observed that the nonparticipants, by undertaking to guarantee the nonhostile destination of its imports, were in effect enforcing the contraband control or blockade regulations of one belligerent against the other belligerent.

These War Trade Agreements were supplemented by separate agreements entered into with important private neutral firms, or associations of firms, engaged either in exporting from outside Europe to the neutrals adjacent to Germany or in importing from Europe.[327] The British Ministry of Economic Warfare agreed to provide special facilities for the passage of the firms' consignments through the contraband control subject, however, to the reservation of belligerent rights. In turn, the firms bound themselves to refrain from selling to or buying from the enemy and to obtain guarantees of neutral destination or consumption from purchasers. In some cases, the neutral firms even undertook to sell only to such persons and in such quantities as the Ministry would approve. Further, the neutral firms commonly agreed to submit to administrative pro-

327. 1 Medlicott, *The Economic Blockade* 102 et seq. (1952). The best known agreements made by the Allied Powers in World War I were the arrangements with the Netherlands Overseas Trust and the *Société Suisse de Surveillance Economique*. See Turlington, *The World War Period* 134 et seq. and 217 et seq. (Neutrality: Its History, Economics and Laws, Vol. III, 1936); and Siney, supra note 326 at c. 5.

cedures specified by the Ministry, such as inspection by Allied government accounts and submission of sales statements. These agreements gave the Ministry access to important sources of commercial intelligence and enabled it to wield a significant measure of control over the companies' operations and even over the recruitment and tenure of their personnel.

The formal nexus between the law of contraband and blockade and the "rationing of neutrals" may be seen to lie in the principle of ultimate enemy destination. The importance of a "rationing" agreement for a prize tribunal lay in the presumption of ultimate enemy destination which was generated by evidence that the neutral's imports clearly exceeded its normal domestic requirements specified in the agreed quota.[328] Whether or not this presumption of enemy destination based on comparative import figures would alone suffice for condemnation of the particular consignment before the prize court was, in British prize law, less than clear. What was clear was that a "statistical case," much like the absence of a navicert, was regarded as shifting to the neutral claimant the onus of showing actual innocent destination.[329] What was also clear was that such practice signaled the further refinement and extension of the doctrine of ultimate enemy destination. The impact of "rationing" practices upon doctrine is well and forcefully summed up by Professor Stone:

> The Court [in *The Kim*] regarded the cargoes of contraband as caught by the doctrine regardless of whether it went forward to the enemy in its original form, or as a manufactured or part manufactured product; regardless, indeed, in the final resort, of whether this particular cargo went forward *in any form whatsoever*. It was sufficient to implicate *this* cargo if some goods of

328. Colombos, *The International Law of the Sea* 620–1 (4th rev. ed., 1959); Fitzmaurice, supra note 314 at 91–5. See *The Kim and other vessels* (1915) 1 B. & C. Pr. Cas. 405, where 4 ships carried to Copenhagen within less than a month more than 13 times the quantity of lard imported annually into Denmark for each of the 3 years preceding the war; *The Baron Stjernblad* (1917) 3 B. & C. Pr. Cas. 17, where it was shown that Swedish imports of cocoa beans had increased tenfold since the war; and *The Kronprinzessin Victoria* (1918) 3 B. & C. Pr. Cas. 247, where statistical evidence showed that Swedish imports of coffee had jumped to 6 times the normal prewar figure.

329. *The Urna*, 3 B. & C. Pr. Cas. 595 (1920).

> the class would go forward to the enemy, and that the entry of this cargo into the neutral country would enable such other goods to be released to the enemy. The question, in short, was no longer one of any individual's intention concerning this particular assignment. It was more a generalized inquiry into statistical probability, as to the trends in the foreign trade of the neutral with regard to this kind of goods. . . . The doctrine of ultimate enemy destination became a vital strategic manoeuvre in emerging economic warfare, of which the chiefs of staff were economists.[330]

Certain subsidiary or auxiliary control methods were developed by the Allied Powers to buttress and enforce the "rationing of neutrals" and the navicert system. One of these was the ship warrant scheme.[331] The ship warrant was a document issued to each neutral vessel whose owner had given satisfactory undertakings to do what the British Government required of him. The owner agreed to comply with economic warfare, or blockade and contraband, regulations and, in particular, that his ships would not sail to or from the designated navicert areas without a ship navicert. The British Ministry of Economic Warfare, in return, guaranteed his ships access to British-controlled resources and facilities all over the world which included insurance, credit, bunkers, stores and charts, and dry docking and repairing. Access to these facilities was denied to *all* ships of a

330. Stone, *Legal Controls of International Conflict* 489 (rev. ed., 1959); see also Tucker, *The Law of War and Neutrality at Sea* 274–5 (1957). In *The Bonna* (1918) 3 B. & C. Pr. Cas. 163 at 168 the Admiralty Division of the English High Court of Justice said: ". . . if it were established that raw materials were imported by a neutral for the manufacture of margarine with an intention to supply the enemy with the manufactured article, I should be prepared to hold that the doctrine of continuous voyage applied so as to make such raw materials subject to condemnation as conditional contraband with an enemy destination. I should go even further, and hold that if it were shown that in a neutral country particular manufacture[rs] of margarine were acting in combination with particular producers or vendors of butter, and . . . the object of their combination was to produce the margarine in order to send the butter to the enemy, the same doctrine would be applicable with the same results." See also *The Maria* decided by the German Supreme Prize Court (trans. in 10 *A.J.I.L.* 927 [1916]). Cf. Harvard Research, supra note 316 at 527.

331. See 1 Medlicott, *The Economic Blockade* 442 et seq. (1952); Gordon and Dangerfield, *The Hidden Weapon* 37–8 (1947); Wu, *Economic Warfare* 247–8 (1952).

ship-owner, including those operating outside the navicert areas, the moment *any* of these ships violated the conditions of the warrant. The selective manipulation and administration of its control over these facilities, vital to the shipping industry, gave to the British government not only a very considerable bargaining power but also strong sanctions for violations of the undertakings embodied in a ship warrant. After the United States entered the war, that power became well nigh overwhelming. The ship warrant scheme, it may also be noted, was important to the Allies not only for interdicting sea-borne commerce with the enemy, but also for the securing of bottoms for the carriage of Allied cargo.

The mechanics of control over the mentioned facilities, sometimes designated as "interference by sovereign right," [332] may be described briefly. The measure known as bunker control, which was inaugurated in the First World War, consisted primarily in the imposition of conditions for the licensing of supplies of coal and fuel oil for neutral ships in Allied ports.[333] Generally, these conditions were that no vessel owned or controlled by the owner of the ship receiving bunkers would be chartered to an enemy national, or to other persons without notification to the Allied authorities, and that no such vessel would trade in any port in enemy territory, or carry cargo or enemy subjects of military age to or from enemy territory. The effectiveness which characterized bunker control was attributable to the fact that nearly all bunker depots in the world were either in Allied territory or were dependent on supplies from such territory. Credit control was exercised by issuance to all banks and financial institutions in Allied territory of government instructions requiring as a condition for the opening of a line of credit that the goods, whose shipment was sought to be financed thereby, would be carried on a warrant-holding ship.[334] Compliance with such instructions was very much in the interests of the banks themselves, which would have been ill advised to grant credit against goods on ships subject to the disabilities of nonwarrant-holders. Insurance control consisted in refusing coverage

332. Turlington, supra note 327 at 67 explained this language by suggesting a lack of international law rules which neutrals may invoke against the belligerent's selective manipulation of these facilities within its own territory.

333. Id., 73; 1 Medlicott, *The Economic Blockade* 443–5 (1952); Bailey, *The Policy of the United States Towards the Neutrals, 1917–1918,* 339–40 (1942).

334. 1 Medlicott, *The Economic Blockade* 445–6 (1952).

to ships not provided with a ship warrant.[335] Allied companies inserted in all hull policies, whether marine or war, a warranty to the effect that during the period of coverage, the owners of the vessels insured would be possessed of a ship warrant. The same warranty was contained in all policies insuring other shipowners' interests, including port and repairing risks. The pre-eminence and combined weight of British and American companies in the world of finance permitted credit and insurance control to reach very high degrees of effectiveness.

Another control or economic warfare technique used in close support of the foregoing ones was "black listing." The "black list" (termed by the British as Statutory List, by the Americans as Proclaimed List) consisted of a collection of names of neutral persons and firms known to be or strongly suspected of, furnishing aid and comfort to the enemy by trafficking with him.[336] Each belligerent, by means of trading-with-the-enemy legislation, prohibited its own nationals from entering into any commercial or financial transaction with a listed person or firm, which was thereby assimilated to "enemy person." Banks could not grant credit to, or perform any service for, listed persons or firms. Business companies could not buy from them, nor sell to them, transport goods for them, use their brokerage, insurance, or shipping facilities, advertise in their newspapers, or even rent space in buildings owned by them.[337] Furthermore, the full weight of Allied controls over bunkers, insurance, credit, port and repair facilities [338] was brought to bear against listed persons and firms. The coercive power of the "black list" was such that a mere threat of listing often sufficed to compel compliance from obstinate neutrals with the regulations of the contraband control and blockade authorities. The comprehensiveness of the deprivations entailed by

335. Id., 22–3, 125–6, 446.

336. Details of listing are available in Wu, *Economic Warfare* 48–52 (1952); Turlington, supra 327 at 80 et seq.; Bailey, supra note 333 at 349–50; 1 Medlicott, *The Economic Blockade* 124–7 (1952); 2 id. 134–52 (1959).

337. Gordon and Dangerfield, *The Hidden Weapon* 153 (1947).

338. 1 Medlicott, *The Economic Blockade* 21–2 (1952). In addition to the "black list" proper, there was also an unpublished "grey list," which included the doubtful cases. British firms were required to apply to the Ministry of Economic Warfare for advice before entering into any transaction with firms on the "grey list." Einzig, *Economic Warfare 1939–1940,* 60 (1941); and Bidwell, "Our Economic Warfare," 20 *Foreign Aff.* 421, 427 (1942).

listing made the provision of adequate safeguards against hasty and arbitrary inclusion a matter of serious concern for the neutral trader, as for the belligerent itself anxious to avoid inflaming the neutral government or pushing it into the arms of the enemy. At the same time, the closest scrutiny was necessary for the detection and prevention of evasive practices, such as the successive creation of "dummy" corporations. It is perhaps apparent that in a conflict between belligerents of roughly equal economic power, where both resort to listing, a neutral trader is likely to get caught in an unenviable dilemma.

One other technique, utilized by both the Allied and the Axis Powers, remains to be mentioned—pre-emption or preclusive buying. This method was employed in World War II to meet the specialized economic warfare situations presented by Spain, Portugal, and Turkey, where for peculiar political and military reasons, the more ordinary measures like "rationing" and "blacklisting" could not successfully be employed.[339] The objectives of preclusive buying were simple: to deny to the enemy the strategic mineral and agricultural products of a neutral, and secondarily, to obtain those products for the belligerent purchaser's own use. The main tactic employed, that of attempting to dry up the market by large volume purchases, required a very deep pocket. Such purchases inevitably resulted in sharply increased prices, which in turn stimulated a corresponding expansion of production. The spiraling of price levels was, however, deliberately sought and maintained by the Allied purchasers as a supplementary means of forcing competing German buyers off the market and of draining the limited German reserves of foreign exchange. Other tactics resorted to include the buying and closing of producing properties or sources of supply; destroying or sabotaging the sources bought by the enemy; and diverting the produce of those sources by bribery and even robbery or "highjacking." The effectiveness of preclusive buying as a weapon of economic warfare, judged by the experience of the last war, appears to be at best uncertain. The weapon, it may be noted, is one of last resort, even for the belligerent with superior financial resources.[340]

339. 1 Medlicott, *The Economic Blockade* c. 15, 18 (1952) and 2 id., cc. 4, 8, 10–11, 18–20 (1959) passim offer an excellent account of allied pre-emption strategy in the differing adjacent neutral countries.

340. Wu, *Economic Warfare* 83–5 (1952); Gordon and Dangerfield, *The Hidden Weapon* 126–8 (1947).

6. COMMUNITY REGULATION OF COMBAT SITUATIONS

By "combat situations" we mean the specific contexts within a process of coercion principally characterized by the actual and active application of violence between contending belligerents. Combat situations represent those stages of an ongoing process in which, after a longer or shorter period of acceleration and cumulation, peak intensities of coercion are reached in the confrontation and contention of opposing units of power. Though all instruments of policy are commonly employed in such stages, these situations exhibit, as their most prominent single physical feature, the overt and destructive use of military instruments.

The major claims to the applications of authority that belligerents characteristically make with respect to these situations or stages may be distributed under two principal headings. The first grouping embraces claims that, in broad generalization, relate to the lawfulness of the detailed practices of violence by which each belligerent seeks to deprive the opposing belligerent of its bases of power and thereby to compel acceptance of and compliance with the demands each asserts against the other. The second grouping comprises claims made by particular officials of a belligerent government or members of its public forces, typically in the specialized context of a judicial trial, in defense against allegations of violations of the international law on the conduct of hostilities. It may perhaps be made explicit that the distribution of claims in terms of these groupings is intended primarily to serve the requirements of convenience in policy-oriented exposition.

The first group covers claims made with respect to almost every feature of contexts of combat. Thus, claims are made about the applicability or nonapplicability of the rules of warfare in various types of situations in which violence is exercised. Secondly, there are claims asserted with respect to the employment of persons and machines as units of participation in combat. A third type of claim relates to the areas or zones in which combat operations are conducted. Fourthly, claims are put forward with respect to the selection of objects as targets of attack. A fifth category is composed of claims about the use of certain instrumentalities or methods of application of violence. Within each sub-group, it is sometimes useful to distinguish between the primary claim or assumption of authority to carry out a certain activity, and the countering assertion that negates the lawfulness or legitimacy of such activity. The countering assertion may, further, preface the making of another, affirmative, claim to administer (otherwise unlawful) retaliations for the purpose of compelling the opposing belligerent to terminate the activity the legitimacy of which the claimant denies.

The second group covers assertions commonly made in connection with the judicial determination of individual criminal responsibility for alleged breaches of the combatant law of war. These assertions refer to certain circumstances which, the accused urges, should be given effect for the purpose of avoiding or mitigating the imposition of punishment. The most important of these are the assertions that the operations taken or ordered by the accused were justified by "military necessity"; that such operations were measures of "legitimate reprisal"; that the accused acted under the compulsion of and in compliance with "superior orders"; and that the accused, in taking or ordering such operations, was "acting in an official capacity."

MILITARY NECESSITY AND MINIMUM DESTRUCTION OF VALUES

Throughout the sets of specific rules of warfare that authoritative decision-makers seek to prescribe and apply to specific problems framed by the claims sketched above, the familiar policies of military necessity and minimum destruction of values may be seen to recur continuously as basic themes. Recognition of the fundamental character of these policies has perhaps been more consistent and more explicit in the regulation of the conduct of hostilities than in most of the other areas of the law of war. Thus, it is commonly stated in the learned literature that three basic principles underlie the more detailed prescriptions of combatant law: the principle of military necessity, the principle of humanity, and the principle of chivalry.[1] The principle of chivalry would seem little more than a somewhat romantic inheritance from the Medieval Ages when combat between mailed knights was surrounded by symbolic and ritualistic formalities.[2] In an age increasingly marked by mechanized and automated warfare, the scope of application of chivalry as a principle distinct from humanity may very probably be expected to diminish in corresponding measure. The customary formulations of the remaining two principles in complementary terms and at highest level of abstraction appear, of course, at first glance, as largely tautologous: the principle of military necessity is said to be "subject to the principles of humanity [and chivalry]," while the principle of humanity is assumed to preclude only such kind or degree of violence as is "not actually necessary." Here, however, as in most of the other domains of the law of war, and of the law of nations generally, complementary general principles serve the important function of spotlighting broad categories of competing considerations that must be taken into account by decision-makers aspiring to rationality. What at highest level abstraction may appear to be tautologous opposites may, in contexts of specific application of policies, be indispensable preliminaries to, and anticipations of, inquiries for detailed factors of contexts and their appropriate relation to overriding community goals.

The principle of military necessity and the principle of humanity may each be seen to express a genuine, inclusive interest of states and peoples. Each territorial community has a most direct and immediate

1. See e.g., 2 Oppenheim, *International Law* 227 (7th ed., Lauterpacht, 1952); hereafter cited as Oppenheim-Lauterpacht; Greenspan, *The Modern Law of Land Warfare* 313–16 (1959); Dept. of the Army, *The Law of Land Warfare*, par. 3(a) (FM 27-10, 1956); Judge Advocate General's School, *Law of Land Warfare* 5–8 (1943); 2 Wheaton, *International Law* 165 (7th ed., Keith, 1944); Fenwick, *International Law* 546–8 (3rd ed., 1948); Hall, *International Law* 83–4 (8th ed., Pearce Higgins, 1924); Tucker, *The Law of War and Neutrality at Sea* 45–50 (1957).

2. Stone, *Legal Controls of International Conflict* 337 (1954), "[t]he ideal of chivalry, moving though its occasional manifestations may be even today, never really retained any robust independence of life after the general decay of the feudal society which produced it and the rise of explosive weapons for killing and maiming at a distance." It should be remembered too that the rules of chivalrous warfare applied only to contests between knights, and not to attacks on peasant foot soldiers or on pagan or Moslem warriors. See Speier, *Social Order and the Risks of War* 224 (1952).

interest in maintaining its security, that is, in protecting the integrity of its fundamental bases of power and the continued functioning of its internal social processes from the obtrusion of unlawful violence. Each such community has consequently an interest in authority to exercise the force indispensable and appropriate for maintaining or re-establishing its security. Each territorial polity has at the same time an interest in reducing to minimal levels the destruction of values, both of itself and others, that attends such efforts. As we have earlier indicated, this interest has at least two interrelated, component elements. The first element is expressed in the demands, characteristic of a public order of human dignity, that the least possible coercion—not to mention violence—be applied to individual human beings, and that all authorized control over human beings be oriented toward strategies of persuasion with widest possible participation in decision, rather than toward strategies of coercion. The second equally pragmatic element is that of demand for economy in the outlay and expenditure of resources and other base values for safeguarding or restoring security. There is no ineluctable necessity for postulating the priority of one of these basic, complementary interests over the other. The point which does bear emphasis is that the whole process of authoritative decision with respect to combat situations is a continuous effort to adjust and accommodate the specific requirements of both these interests in a series of concrete contexts. Historically, of course, the line of compromise has, more frequently than not, tended to be located closer to the polar terminus of military necessity than to that of humanity.[2a] Paradoxical as it may seem, the observation may not be inappropriate, however, that contemporary weapons whose destructiveness almost surpasses understanding may yet tend to push the line of compromise more toward the other terminus.

2a. Cf. the analysis essayed in Schwarzenberger, "Functions and Foundations of the Laws of War," 44 *Archiv für Rechts- und Sozial Philosophie* 351 (1958). Dr. Schwarzenberger categorizes the rules of warfare into four groups and locates those groups along the continuum from "standard of civilization" (humanity or minimum destruction) to "necessities of war" (military necessity). See also Dunbar, "The Significance of Military Necessity in the Law of War," 67 *Jurid. Rev.* 201, 211–12 (1955). After some hesitation about the relevancy of the "orthodox concept of military necessity in the law of war" in contemporary context, Dr. Dunbar lays appropriate stress on the notion of equilibration between military necessity and humanity.

The content which has traditionally been written into the concept of military necessity is the policy of permitting the exercise of that violence necessary for the prompt realization of legitimate belligerent objectives. In terms of a theoretical image of the process of combat, one can of course conceive of the achievement of a clearly specified objective as requiring, under a given set of conditions, and at a given moment, the application of a particular (and no larger) amount of violence for a particular (and no longer) period of time against a particular base of enemy power. In point of practical fact, however, no such perfection is achievable. The actual determinations of the lawfulness of particular exercises of violence, by military commanders on the spot as by war crimes tribunals reviewing the decisions of commanders, go forward in contexts of variables which, even when they can be identified, are hardly susceptible of precise quantification and measurement.

In a slightly lower order of abstraction, the conception of necessary violence is said to embrace two related but perhaps distinguishable requirements: the one of relevancy and the other of proportionality. Destruction is characterized as irrelevant when it is not directed toward the achievement of the legitimate objective specified. Clearly, such destruction is unnecessary in respect of such objective. Put a little differently, the relevancy of destruction refers to "the degree to to which there was a definite and forseeable connection between the act committed and the alleged military necessity." [3] Irrelevant destruction includes, in somewhat obvious illustration, death and devastation inflicted upon an occupied region to gratify the private pathological appetites of the local garrison commander. Proportionality is commonly taken to refer to the relation between the amount of destruction effected and the military value of the objective sought in the operation being appraised.[4] Disproportionate destruction is thus, almost by definition, unnecessary destruction. Just as disproportion includes in its reference a whole continuum of degrees, so relevancy is a relative thing. All that can be derived from past formulations and experience is that the disproportion should be minimal and not

3. O'Brien, "The Meaning of 'Military Necessity' in International Law," 1 *World Polity* 109, 141 (1957).

4. A good recent formulation of proportionality may be found in Art. 8 of the International Committee of the Red Cross, *Draft Rules for the Limitation of the Dangers Incurred by the Civilian Population in Time of War* (Geneva, 1956).

gross, and that the connection between the destruction actually imposed and the objective postulated by the destroyer should be reasonably proximate and not remote.[5]

The formulations noted above, which are scarcely novel, have frequently seemed obscure. The obscurity has stemmed in considerable part from the difficulty of clarifying the conception of "legitimate belligerent objectives." Necessity, like its component concepts of relevancy and proportionality, is a relational concept. To speak of necessity (or lack of necessity) is simultaneously to raise the question: necessary (or unnecessary) for what? A particular combat operation, comprising the application of a certain amount of violence, can be appraised as necessary or unnecessary only in relation to the attainment of a specified objective. Obviously, further clarification of the principle of military necessity is, in corresponding part, contingent upon specification of legitimate belligerent objectives.

In search of clarification, publicists have attempted to distinguish between, on the one hand, the political purposes—the particular distribution or redistribution of power and other values—that a belligerent seeks to bring about in resorting to violence and, on the other hand, the military objectives, designated in varying levels of specificity, which may be sought in the course of conducting hostilities. Distinguished commentators have on occasion sought some stability of reference in their formulations of military necessity by limiting such references to military objectives only, in strategic or tactical sense.[6] These efforts, however, have not been conspicuously successful.

Two interrelated factors appear to explain the tendency toward futility. Firstly, traditional international law, that is, the law before the modest re-emergence of the distinction between prohibited and permitted recourse to violence in the prescriptions of the Covenant of the League of Nations, did not seek to prescribe any limits upon the scope and contents of the political or ultimate purposes for which belligerents were authorized to apply violence. Secondly, military

5. As Winfield, *The Foundations and the Future of International Law* 59 (1941) put it: "War is . . . essentially a brutal and inhuman affair, however we view it. The remark is trite enough, but it must be emphasized in order to understand that the Laws of War can at best do no more than modify the brutality and inhumanity of it; they cannot eliminate those characteristics."

6. Among the most recent and explicit of these efforts is that of Dr. O'Brien, supra note 3 at 142, 148.

objectives are commonly not autonomous phenomena. At least in wars moved by more than the mere pathological desire for senseless destruction, the objectives of military strategy are shaped, certainly in their outer limits if not in specific detail, by the political purposes of the belligerent.[7] It is not easy to see how military objectives could be evaluated as legitimate or nonlegitimate save in terms of their relation to some broader political purpose postulated as legitimate. To put the point comprehensively, it is most difficult rationally to appraise the necessity of a particular exercise of violence without relating it to a wider context of which it is part—a context which includes a series of objectives, each of a higher or lower order of generality, with the more general affecting and determining the more specific. In the absence in traditional law of restrictions upon the ultimate political purposes that could lawfully be prosecuted through violence,[8] limits sought to be introduced at some lower level tended to regress until a criterion was reached which made no distinction.

The formulations of Professor Oppenheim offer economic illustration of the futility of efforts at clarification under such circumstances. Professor Oppenheim distinguished between several levels of belligerent objectives: (a) the "objects" or "ends of war" referring to the ultimate political purposes of belligerents; (b) the "purpose of war"; and (c) the "aims of land and sea warfare," including, for example, "occupation of enemy territory," [9] "defeat of the enemy navy, annihilation of the enemy merchant fleet," and so on.[10] He wrote:

> . . . the objects of war must not be confounded with the purpose of war. Whereas the purpose is always the same—namely, *the overpowering and utter defeat of the opponent*—the ends may be different in each case. At the beginning of the war its objects are determined by its cause or causes. But they may undergo alteration, or at least modification, with its progress and development. *Apart from specific treaty obligations, no moral or legal duty exists for a belligerent to stop the war when his opponent is ready to concede the object for which war was made.*[11]
>
> . . .

7. Supra, pp. 33 ff.
8. Supra, pp. 74 ff.
9. 2 Oppenheim-Lauterpacht 336.
10. Id., 458.
11. Id., 225; italics supplied.

> [W]hatever the ends of war may be, they can only be realized by one belligerent overpowering the other. *Such a defeat as compels the vanquished to comply with any demand the victor may choose to make is the purpose of war.* Victory is necessary in order to overpower the enemy; and it is this necessity which has been invoked as justifying all the horrors of war, the sacrifice of human life, and the destruction of property and devastation of territory. . . .[12]

The statement of the principle of military necessity Professor Oppenheim accordingly arrived at was:

> [T]he principle that a belligerent is justified in applying any amount and any kind of force which is necessary for the realization of the purpose of war—namely, *the overpowering of the opponent.*[13]

It does not need elaborate demonstration to show that to write into the principle of military necessity a conception of the legitimate "purpose of war" which, like that quoted above, is so comprehensive and open-ended as to permit subsumption of practically any particular political purpose and combat aim, is substantially to render illusive any limitation upon military necessity.

Contemporary international law, hopefully, offers new potentiality for significant clarification. In the principle of minimum order, newly resurrected in the Charter of the United Nations and other authoritative formulations distinguishing between permissible and impermissible resort to coercion, may, it is believed, be found new limits to give new specificity to the principle of military necessity. In our examination of this fundamental distinction,[14] it was observed generally that permissible coercion is limited in its reference to coercion exercised, in necessary defense of public order, by an individual

12. Id., 208–9; italics supplied.

13. Id., 227; italics supplied. Comparable formulations may be found in the literature cited in Ch. 1 (notes 179–82). Cf. the formulation in Marin, "The Evolution and Present Status of the Laws of War," 92 *Hague Recueil* 633, 638–9 (1957) where the "principle of necessity" is said to "justif[y] violence and ruses within the limits where violence and ruses are absolutely indispensable in order to fulfill the aim of wars, that is *to reduce the adversary to impotence.*" Emphasis added.

14. Supra, Ch. 3.

state as by a group or the general community of states. It was there submitted, somewhat more specifically, that from perspectives seeking progress toward a world order of human dignity, the legitimate purposes of coercion and violence are most appropriately conceived as restricted to responding to, repelling, and compelling the termination of, highly intense initiating coercion directed against such consequential bases of power as "territorial integrity" and "political independence." The suggestion we now urge is that, by relating any specific exercise of violence to the permissible objectives of lawful defense of minimum public order, it may be possible to give anchor to the search for clarification of military necessity and to stop the indefinite regression of limits sought to be placed upon such conception. The principle of military necessity may, in these terms, accordingly be said to permit the exercise of that violence which is indispensably necessary (proportionate and relevant) for promptly repelling and terminating highly intense initiating coercion against "territorial integrity" or "political independence"—indispensably necessary, in a word, for successful defense or community enforcement actions.

The submission essayed above—that the limited political objectives legitimate by contemporary international law should be incorporated into the principle of military necessity—is *not* intended to suggest that the aggressor-belligerent should be denied the benefits of the laws of warfare and that every particular exercise of violence by the forces of such belligerent in the course of hostilities should be held unlawful and a war crime.[15] The thrust of our submission is rather that even the belligerent put under the necessity of self-defense or participating in community enforcement action must be restricted to narrowly defined objectives and required to shape and limit his violence conformably with such objectives. Certainly, rational policy oriented toward a public order of human dignity could concede no greater license in the conduct of violence to the aggressor-belligerent. Conversely, both the requirements of the humanity principle and the imperatives of effective sanctions for law about the management of combat demand that the violator-belligerent and the defending belligerent together be held to the same standard of necessity in hostilities. The suggestion made is simply that that standard must be the restrictive one appropriate to permissible defense.

15. Compare O'Brien, supra note 3 at 142, 147–8.

Demand for limitation of violence, implicit in efforts to clarify the principle of military necessity, is itself a cardinal aspect of the contrapuntal principle of humanity. Humanity, or humanitarianism, imports much more than the "soft sentimentality" or the "mere reflection of contemporary prejudices on ethical questions" to which this principle is sometimes assumed to refer.[16] When conceived, as earlier suggested, as one manifestation of a profound preference—however justified in terms of religion, secular philosophy, sociology, psychology, or otherwise—for the shaping and sharing of values by noncoercive, rather than coercive, modes, the principle of humanity may be seen to be a basic postulate of any international law of human dignity.[17] This fundamental preference is indeed reflected in various technical expressions. One expression may be found in the frequent insistence among the English-speaking writers (in self-conscious differentiation from the pre-1914 German publicists who gave unfortunate prominence to the so-called *"Kriegsraison* theory") that the general principle of military necessity is circumscribed by the more specific prescriptions of the rules of warfare.[18] A more contemporary reflection is in the principle of economy of force, the growing interest in which has coincided with increasing recognition of the exorbitant potential costs of comprehensive violence.[19] Still other expressions are found even among those who verbally reject the humanity or humanitarian principle. Thus, the same commentator who describes the term "humanity" "and its derivatives" as "much too vague," and characterizes "humanitarianism" as "tend[ing] to mean 'soft sentimentality,' " writes:

> Military necessity and permissible violence are limited, not only by the laws of war, but also by the more general but no less important commands of the natural law.[20]

16. O'Brien, supra note 3 at 152–3.

17. See, generally, McDougal, "Perspectives For an International Law of Human Dignity," 53 *Proc. Am. Soc. I.L.* 107 (1959).

18. See e.g. 2 Westlake, *International Law* 57 (1907); Downey, "The Law of War and Military Necessity," 47 *A.J.I.L.* 251 (1953); 2 Oppenheim-Lauterpacht 232–3; Greenspan, *The Modern Law of Land Warfare* 314 (1959). See also Dept. of the Army, *The Law of Land Warfare,* par. 3(a) (FM 27-10, July, 1956).

19. See supra, Ch. 1. See also, generally, Baldwin, "A New Look at the Law of War: Limited War and Field Manual 27-10," 4 *Military Law Rev.* 1 (Dept. of the Army Pamphlet No. 27-100-4, Apr. 1959).

20. O'Brien, supra note 3 at 152.

In its second capital aspect, that is, as a demand for economy in the use of a belligerent's own human and material resources for achieving its legitimate objectives, the principle of humanity is of course a counsel of efficiency. Conjoining its principal aspects, the principle may be regarded as dictating the choice, from among possible alternatives, of that operation or course of action which promises most by way of economy in both base values expended and in value losses imposed upon the opposing belligerent.

The principles of military necessity and of humanity may be synthesized and generalized on a still higher level of abstraction in terms of a single and overriding conception of minimum unnecessary destruction. Historically, however, it may be observed that authoritative decision-makers seek to consider and compromise the competing requirements of each principle in varying specific contexts. In succeeding sections, we propose to review the differing compromises achieved by past decision in differing kinds of contexts in the process of combat. We shall review first the controversies pertaining to the substantive requirements of military necessity and humanity in hostilities contexts, and then turn to a consideration of the defenses commonly raised against allegations of violations of such requirements.

THE SUBSTANTIVE REQUIREMENTS OF MILITARY NECESSITY AND MINIMUM DESTRUCTION OF VALUES IN COMBAT: TRENDS IN APPLICATION OF THE RULES OF WARFARE

Claims with Respect to Applicability of the Basic Policies in Certain Situations

We begin with the controversies relating to the applicability of the rules of warfare—the international law on the management of combat—in certain types of situations. The major kinds of situations here referred to are two: (a) situations in which the resort to violence by one or more belligerents is characterized as impermissible; and (b) situations in which entities or groups other than states are involved as major participants. Two other bases of categorization are of somewhat lesser importance: the dimensions of the hostilities; and the disclaimer or nonrecognition of the existence of a technical "state of war."

Turning to the first type of situation, assertions have been made that the laws of warfare should not be held applicable in respect of a belligerent authoritatively determined to have been guilty of resorting to an unlawful war of aggression. The gist of this assertion is that the violator-belligerent should be regarded as dispossessed of the "rights of belligerents" including, more particularly, the "right to legitimate military necessity." The logical consequences of this argument were made explicit by the Chief French and British Prosecutors before the International Military Tribunal at Nuremberg. M. François de Menthon said:

> What does this [the Kellogg-Briand Pact] mean, if not that all acts committed as a consequence of this aggression for the carrying on of the struggle thus undertaken will cease to have the juridical character of acts of war?
>
> . . .
>
> Acts committed in the execution of a war are assaults on persons and goods which are themselves prohibited but are sanctioned in all legislations. The state of war could make them legitimate only if the war itself was legitimate. Inasmuch as this is no longer the case, since the Kellogg-Briand Pact, these acts become purely and simply common law crimes. . . . [A]ny recourse to war is a recourse to means which are in themselves criminal.[21]

Sir Hartley Shawcross, in closely comparable argument in his closing address, stated:

> The killing of combatants in war is justifiable, both in International and in Municipal laws, only where the war itself is legal. But where a war is illegal, . . . there is nothing to justify the killing, and these murders are not to be distinguished from those of any other lawless robber bands.[22]

Much the same submission was made by the Prosecution at the International Military Tribunal for the Far East. The Prosecution included in the indictment several charges of murder and conspiracy to commit murder, separately from and in addition to the charges of waging and conspiracy to wage unlawful war, upon the ground that

21. 5 *Trial of the Major War Criminals before the International Military Tribunal, Proceedings 9 Jan.–21 Jan. 1946,* p. 387 (1947).

22. *Nazi Conspiracy and Aggression, Supplement A,* pp. 86–7 (1947).

"the waging of aggressive war was unlawful and involved unlawful killing which is murder." [23]

That the prospects of effectively securing the limitation of violence sought by the basic policies of military necessity and humanity and by their divers specifications in the rules of warfare are contingent upon reciprocity, should be fairly obvious. While there have been cases where one belligerent limited its warfare more than its opponent did, in a war of any substantial duration between belligerents having the same or similar means and weapons, reciprocal treatment tends to develop.[24] The violence exercised by one and the other belligerent tend, so to speak, sympathetically to settle upon a common level. The inherent structure and conditions of the sanctioning process, here clearly built into processes of combat, require that each belligerent concede a measure of humanity to the other in order to secure a corresponding measure unto itself, and that, consequently, application of the rules of warfare be made independently of the characterization of one or the other belligerent's resort to violence as nonpermissible. The violator-belligerent, as indicated earlier, can scarcely rationally be regarded as having, by its own unlawful recourse to violence, freed itself from duties of restraint in the detailed exercise of such violence. At the same time, however, he must remain entitled, if the sanctions of promised reciprocity and threatened retaliation are to be effective, to claim observance of equal restraint from the defending belligerent.[25]

Such, in bold strokes, was the view adopted by many war crimes

23. *Judgment of the International Military Tribunal for the Far East,* Part A, Ch. II, p. 34 (1948).

24. See Speier, *Social Order and the Risks of War* 229 (1952).

25. E.g., Lauterpacht, "Rules of War in an Unlawful War," in *Law and Politics in the World Community* 89 (Lipsky, ed., 1953); Lauterpacht, "The Limits of the Operation of the Law of War," 30 *Brit. Y.B.I.L.* 206 (1953); Tucker, *The Law of War and Neutrality at Sea* 4–11 (1957); Schwarzenberger, "Legal Effects of Illegal War," in *Volkerrecht und Rechtliches Weltbild: Festschrift für Alfred Verdross* 243 (1960); and Kunz, "The Laws of War," 50 *A.J.I.L.* 313, 317–19 (1956).

See also Draper, *The Red Cross Conventions* 8–9, 97–8 (1958) where the interesting suggestion is made that Article I common to all four Geneva Conventions of 1949 has the effect of requiring equal application of the benefits and burdens of the Conventions in respect of aggressor and defender. Art. 1 reads: "The High Contracting Parties undertake to respect and to ensure respect for the present Convention in all circumstances."

tribunals after World War II. The International Military Tribunal at Nuremberg did not explicitly deal with the argument put forward by Sir Hartley Shawcross and M. de Menthon, but it is clear from the judgment as a whole that their argument was not accepted. The International Military Tribunal at Tokyo reached the same result by turning on a purportedly procedural point: it held that counts of murder, or of conspiracy to commit murder, were not properly charged separately from the counts of waging, or of conspiracy to wage, aggressive war.[26] The United States Military Tribunal established under Control Council Law No. 10 was much more explicit in rejecting the prosecutors' argument. Some illustrative decisions of this Tribunal may be indicated. In *United States v. List et al.*, the prosecution contended that since Germany's wars against Greece and Yugoslavia were aggressive wars, the German occupation troops were there unlawfully and gained no "rights" whatever as an occupant. The Tribunal met this contention by saying:

> For the purposes of this discussion, we accept the statement as true that the wars against Yugoslavia and Greece were in direct violation of the Kellogg-Briand Pact and were therefore criminal in character. But it does not follow that every act by the German occupation forces against person or property is a crime or that any or every act undertaken by the population of the occupied country against the German occupation forces thereby became legitimate defence . . .[27]

The same tribunal, in *United States v. Altstötter*,[28] again refused to consider as relevant the criminal nature of Germany's aggression in determining whether the harsh German penal laws and the court decisions rendered under those laws constituted war crimes or crimes against humanity. The Tribunal was unable to accept the conclusion that every German soldier who marched under orders into occupied territory, or who fought in his homeland, was a criminal and a murderer. It was pointed out by the Tribunal that if this view were accepted, the rules of warfare would no longer be the criteria of un-

26. *Judgment of the International Military Tribunal for the Far East,* Part A, Ch. II, p. 36 (1948).

27. 8 *Law Reports of Trials of War Criminals* 34, 59 (1948), hereafter cited as *War Crimes Reports.*

28. 6 id. 1, 52 (1948).

lawful conduct in hostilities and that the pronouncement of guilt in any particular case would be reduced to a mere formality. In *United States v. Von Leeb,*[29] the Tribunal impliedly held that the defense of military necessity was available even to an officer of the aggressor-belligerent, to justify, in a proper case, destruction in occupied territory.

Other courts took what amounted substantially to the same position. The Dutch Special Court at Arnheim, in *re Christiansen,*[30] held that the prescriptions of international law regulating the methods of warfare and occupation of enemy territory make no distinction between wars started legally and those started illegally. An aggressor-occupant was consequently entitled to punish acts of resistance on the part of the inhabitants, and in so doing could invoke the "legal grounds of impunity" afforded by the laws of war. Similarly, the Dutch Special Court of Cassation, in the *Trial of Willy Zuehlke,*[31] declared that "it is going too far" to consider as war crimes all acts committed against the Netherlands and Netherlanders by the German forces during the war solely on the ground of the illegal nature of that war. The Supreme Court of Denmark also appears to have adopted this view.[32] German courts have explicitly done so,[33] as was perhaps to be expected.

We consider next situations in which the major contending participants include entities other than nation-states. The kind of situation traditionally envisaged in the course of development of the rules of warfare is, of course, a conflict in which the participants on both sides are nation-states. Controversies about the applicability of the rules of warfare arise, however, with respect to situations involving either a group not previously regarded as constituting an independent territorial community or an organization of states.

The first and more complex case is that of "civil war," that is, a genuinely internal conflict within a nation-state in which a counter-

29. 12 id. 1, 123–6 (1949).

30. *Annual Digest, 1948,* Case No. 121.

31. 14 *War Crimes Reports* 139, 144 (1948).

32. *Blue Star Line v. Burmeister and Wain* (*The Adelaide Star*) *Annual Digest, 1948,* Case No. 126. See Ross, "Denmark's Legal Status During the Occupation," 1 *Jus Gentium* 1 (1949).

33. General Devastation (Germany) Case, Oberlandesgericht of Dresden, *Annual Digest 1948,* Case No. 124; *In re* Garbe, Oberlandesgericht of Kiel, id., Case No. 125.

elite group either seeks forcibly to organize a new political unit separate from the old body politic, or to capture effective control of existing governmental structures. It is useful to keep distinct two sets of assertions that the legitimate or constitutional government fighting a civil war commonly makes. One type of claim is made vis-à-vis third states and the organized community of states and typically involves the invocation of "domestic jurisdiction." [34] The other type of assertion—and it is upon this that we here focus—is addressed to the rebels. This latter kind of claim may be broadly described as an assumption of competence to maintain or restore the supremacy of the constitutional government by enforcing its municipal statutes relating to rebellion. The rebel group may, for its part, demand, as against both the constitutional government and third states, to be treated as a regular belligerent community and, as such, authorized to exercise violence in accordance with the rules of warfare and entitled to the protection of those rules.

The physical characteristics of exercises of violence and their effects upon people and resources are of course the same, assuming violence of comparable proportions, in an internal as in an international conflict. It would thus seem fairly obvious that what has been generalized above as a fundamental policy of minimum unnecessary destruction is equally vital and applicable in one as in the other type of conflict. At least for the purposes of regulating the mutual applications of violence and of reducing destruction of values, the character of one of the participants as a rebel group, and therefore criminal under municipal law, should be regarded as immaterial. Reciprocity clearly remains an imperative condition for securing restraint. As the conflict assumes greater and greater proportions, and as the rebel forces achieve an increasing degree of success, the interest of the constitutional government in observing the rules of warfare may be expected to gain in clarity and depth.[35]

34. See e.g., Goodrich and Simons, *The United Nations and the Maintenance of International Peace and Security* 115–17, 269–70 (1955); Dejany, "Competence of the General Assembly in the Tunisian-Moroccan Questions," 47 *Proc. Am. Soc. I.L.* 53 (1953); Wright, "International Law and the United Nations," 5 *Cursos Monographicos, Academia Interamericana de Derecho Comparado e Internacional* 319, 362–84 (1956). A recent survey of United Nations treatment of this claim is offered in Rajan, *United Nations and Domestic Jurisdiction* 179–259 (1958).

35. Lauterpacht, *Recognition in International Law* 245 (1947): "A clearly

The customary law on this matter has frequently seemed somewhat impalpable. It is commonly assumed that the applicability of the rules of warfare, or, more particularly, the availability of the protection of such rules to the rebels, accompanies or follows the recognition by the constitutional government of the belligerency of the rebels.[35a] Recognition by third states of the belligerency of the rebels, however discreetly and appropriately timed such recognition may be, does not, it is said, impose an obligation upon the constitutional government to concede to the rebels the protection of the laws of warfare and to refrain from hanging them as ordinary criminals forthwith upon capture. The structure of customary law included no clear and generally accepted prescription requiring the constitutional government to accord recognition to the rebel forces even when they had achieved a substantial measure of success.[36] Customary law in effect conceded the constitutional government a large freedom to restore and maintain its effective control, a freedom practically unregulated save, perhaps, by amorphous doctrines on "humanitarian intervention" on the part of third states, and more recently by broad human-rights commitments and standards.

The Geneva Conventions of 1949 on the protection of war victims mark a noteworthy step in the establishment of authoritative policy for the regulation of violence in internal conflicts. While these conventions do not purport to be applicable as such in civil wars, they do set forth certain minimum standards to be observed by "each Party" to an armed conflict "not of an international character" occurring in the territory of a contracting party.[37] The Conventions

---

ascertained state of hostilities on a sufficiently large scale, willed as war at least by one of the parties, creates *suo vigore* a condition in which the rules of warfare become operative. . . . Once a situation has been created which, but for the constitutional law of the state concerned, is indistinguishable from war, practice suggests that international law ought to step in in order to fulfill the same function which it performs in wars between sovereign States, namely, to humanize and regularize the conduct of hostilities as between the parties." To achieve this Professor Lauterpacht suggested that the legitimate government be regarded as under a duty to recognize the insurgents as a belligerent party (at 246).

35a. Greenspan, *The Modern Law of Land Warfare* 19–20 (1959).

36. Lauterpacht, supra note 35 at 246; see also 2 Oppenheim-Lauterpacht 209–10.

37. Art. 3 of all four Conventions. This article was adopted as a compromise,

provide, generally, that persons taking no active part in the hostilities, including members of armed forces who have surrendered or been rendered *hors de combat,* shall in all circumstances be treated humanely without distinctions based on race, religion, sex, birth, or similar criteria. More particularly, they prohibit murder, mutilation, torture, the taking of hostages, outrages upon personal dignity, and the passing of sentences and carrying out of executions without prior judicial action surrounded by guarantees "recognized as indispensable by civilized peoples." They further require that the wounded and sick be collected and cared for. The Conventions also specify, however, that application of the above provisions "shall not affect the legal status of the Parties to the conflict." [38] The inference drawn by commentators is that compliance by the legitimate government with these standards does not constitute implied recognition of the rebels as a belligerent party,[39] such that the former remains entitled to try

---

the Conference being unable to decide on any of the three general propositions submitted to it. These propositions were: (a) that the conventions should be applicable in all cases of internal armed conflicts; (b) that they should not be applicable in any such conflict; (c) that they should be applicable only in a conflict of certain proportions and characteristics. See Yingling and Ginnane, "The Geneva Conventions of 1949," 46 *A.J.I.L.* 395–6 (1952); also *Summary Report of the Work of the Conference of Government Experts for the Study of the Conventions for the Protection of War Victims* (International Committee of the Red Cross, Geneva, 1947) p. 6.

See also Art. 2(b) of the International Committee of the Red Cross, *Draft Rules for the Limitation of the Dangers Incurred by the Civilian Population in Time of War* (Geneva, 1956).

38. Art. 3.

39. 2 Oppenheim-Lauterpacht 211; Kunz, "The Geneva Conventions of August 12, 1949," in *Law and Politics in the World Community* 308 (Lipsky, ed., 1953); Gutteridge, "The Geneva Conventions of 1949," 26 *Brit. Y.B.I.L.* 301 (1949).

There is some controversy as to whether recognition of the belligerency of the rebels, however effected, converts the internal conflict into one of "an international character," removes such conflict from the purview of Article 3 of the Conventions, and makes the Conventions applicable in their entirety (as well as the rest of the law of war). See 2 Oppenheim-Lauterpacht 370–1; compare Draper, *The Red Cross Conventions* 16 (1958). Because of the difference in the scope and details of protection afforded by Article 3, on the one hand, and by the full Conventions, on the other, the matter need not be academic. One difficulty suggested by Col. Draper's negative answer is that, under such view, Article 3 would be less favorable to the persons it seeks to protect than customary law

captured rebels for treason and rebellion, that is, in effect, to deny them the treatment accorded to prisoners of war in a conflict between nation-states. Expectations of trial and punishment as traitors or rebels upon capture or defeat are not likely to increase the probabilities of effective restraint on the part of the revolutionary forces in their hostile activities. On the other hand, the interest of the constitutional government in authority to maintain or restore its supremacy cannot reasonably be entirely disregarded. Perhaps all that can be projected with prima facie realism is that both the humanity principle and the practical conditions for securing this principle require the deferment of treason trials until the issue of success or failure is resolved and, pending the resolution of this issue, the observance by both parties of at least the minimum standards of the Geneva Conventions.[40]

The second case concerns armed conflicts in which international governmental organizations, global or regional, are major participants. The specific situations here referred to include collective military enforcement action required or authorized by the Security Council or the General Assembly of the United Nations, as well as collective action by members of regional defense organizations. There seems little reason to doubt that reciprocity is as necessary in this type of situation as in ordinary interstate hostilities if the fundamental principle of minimum unnecessary destruction is to be secured. From such perspective, an affirmative answer appears the only possible answer to the question of whether or not the rules of warfare should be regarded as applicable in such situations.[41]

It has sometimes been suggested, however, that with respect to col-

---

under which, once recognition of belligerency was granted by the constitutional government, the laws of war (including, presumably, the Geneva Convention) became clearly applicable.

40. Cf. 2 Oppenheim-Lauterpacht 211. In *Ford v. Surget,* 97 U.S. 594 at 605 (1878), the Court said: "To the Confederate Government was conceded, in the interests of humanity, and to prevent the cruelties of reprisals and retaliation, such belligerent rights as belonged, under the law of nations, to the armies of independent governments engaged in war against each other."

41. Jessup, *A Modern Law of Nations* 213 (1948); Baxter, "The Role of Law in Modern War," 47 *Proc. Am. Soc. I.L.* 90 (1953); Kunz, "The Laws of War," 50 *A.J.I.L.* 313, 319–29 (1956). Cf. Taubenfeld, "International Armed Forces and the Rules of War," 45 *A.J.I.L.* 671, 676–9 (1951).

lective enforcement action required or authorized by the United Nations, account should be taken of the "superior legal and moral position" of the organized community of states. Police measures by or on behalf of the organized community are, it is said, different from wars between nation-states which are "units of equal legal status." From this premise, the proposal has been made that the United Nations should deal selectively with the laws of war, observing those which may "seem to fit its purposes," adding new ones, and disregarding those "incompatible with its purposes." [42] No criterion for selection has, however, been put forward, save, perhaps, the "principle of humanity." [43] It must be observed that the principle of humanity, when understood in terms of the minimization of destruction of values, underlies, together with the complementary principle of military necessity, the entire body of combatant law. It does not seem to require laborious demonstration to show that, at least in this limited context, such "superior legal and moral position," like the impermissible character of the resort to violence, should be held irrelevant. Certainly it does not diminish the practical necessity for reciprocity. That necessity is not removed, and applicability of the rules of warfare avoided, by attaching a label other than "war" to the

42. Committee on Study of Legal Problems of the United Nations, "Should the Laws of War Apply to United Nations Enforcement Action?" 46 *Proc. Am. Soc. I.L.* 216 (1952).

43. Wright, "The Outlawry of War and the Law of War," 47 *A.J.I.L.* 365, 374–6 (1953) suggested selective application of the "law of war" on the basis of the following classification: "(1) [rules] which confer new powers on belligerents; (2) [rules] which impose liabilities upon belligerents; (3) [rules] which confer individual rights on soldiers and civilians; (4) [rules] which impose individual liabilities on soldiers and civilians; (5) [rules] which define the extent to which the United Nations can authorize action by states which go beyond belligerent rights."

In a subsequent paper, Professor Wright laid great emphasis upon a dichotomy between "humanitarian prohibitions" and "military permissions." He wrote: "Apparently the main opposition to discrimination as between the aggressor and the defender has been the fear that it would brutalize war and particularly that it would reduce military occupation by an aggressor to a state of anarchy. As noted, this idea has arisen from failure to distinguish the humanitarian prohibitions of the law of war from its military permissions." Wright, "The New Law of War and Neutrality," in *Varia Juris Gentium: Liber Amicorum J.P.A. François* 412, 422 (1959).

combat situation considered, whether the label be upgraded ("police or enforcement" action) or downgraded ("reprisals," "intervention," "punitive action," etc.).[44]

Practice in the Korean war provides scant support for the proposal of a specially privileged position for United Nations forces. On the contrary, the United Nations Command and the United States in its capacity as the Unified Command declared that United Nations forces were under instructions to observe at all times, and had observed, the provisions of the Hague Regulations and the Geneva Conventions of 1949.[45] The North Korean Government itself gave at least verbal deference to the same Conventions.[46]

It remains only briefly to observe that the applicability of the overriding principle of minimum unnecessary destruction of values, and of its specific expressions in the rules of warfare, is rationally not dependent upon either the intensity or scope of any particular hostilities, or upon the recognition by one or both parties of a technical "state of war." While the dimensions of a given conflict may of course bear upon the shape of particular decisions in specific contexts, obviously, whether the violence is "total" or limited, global or local, prolonged or short, there is need for regulating and mitigating its impact upon value processes.

If the Geneva Conventions of 1949 on the protection of war victims reflect any trend at all with respect to this matter, it is one of universal applicability in situations exhibiting the one fundamental factor of destructive use of military instruments. Thus, Article 2 common to all four conventions has abandoned the *clausula si omnes*

44. Cf. Grob, *The Relativity of War and Peace* 215–18 (1949). This is not to suggest that the facts of coalition war may not pose peculiar problems. Such problems may include, for example, the inventing of procedures facilitating the location and allocation of responsibility for observance and enforcement of the rules of warfare. More particularly, as Professor Baxter has observed, there are the problems of determining the Detaining Power who would be charged with custody of prisoners of war, and of apportioning occupational responsibilities among members of the organization or coalition. Specific procedures would of course vary with the degree of integration of the military command structure established. See Baxter, "Constitutional Forms and Some Legal Problems of International Military Command," 29 *Brit. Y.B.I.L.* 325, 352–9 (1952).

45. Letter dated 5 July 1951, from the Representative of the United States of America (Warren R. Austin) to the Secretary-General of the United Nations 25 *Dept. of State Bull.* 189–90 (1951).

46. See Taubenfeld, supra note 41 at 678.

found in the Hague Conventions and Declarations,[47] providing, as it does, that

> Although one of the Powers in conflict may not be a party to the present Convention, the Powers who are Parties thereto shall remain bound by it in their mutual relations. They shall, furthermore, be bound by the Convention in relation to the said Power, if the latter accepts and applies the provisions thereof.

This provision renders unnecessary the circuitous technique of determining that the conventional rules invoked had so hardened into customary prescription as to be applicable in a conflict where one or more of the participants were not parties to the conventions.[48] Article 2 further declares:

> In addition to the provisions which shall be implemented in peace time, the present Convention shall apply to all cases of declared war or of *any other armed conflict* which may arise between two or more of the High Contracting Parties, *even if the state of war is not recognized by one of them.*

The article strongly indicates the irrelevance, for the purposes of regulation of combat situations, of an issuance or omission of a declaration of war, as well as of recognition or disclaimer of the existence of a "state of war." [49] All four Conventions, it may be noted finally,

47. Hague Conventions (1907) IV (Art. 2); V (Art. 20); VI (Art. 6); VII (Art. 7); VIII (Art. 7); IX (Art. 8); X (Art. 18); XI (Art. 9); XII (Art. 51). Also Hague Declarations XIV (1907) on Projectiles from Balloons; IV(2) (1899) on Asphyxiating Gases; IV(3) (1899) on Expanding Bullets.

48. The Nuremberg Tribunal, in answering the Defense contention that Hague Convention IV was inapplicable because of the "general participation" clause, said: "the convention expressly stated that it was an attempt 'to revise the general laws and customs of war,' which it thus recognized to be then existing, but by 1939 these rules laid down in the convention were recognized by all civilized nations, and were regarded as being declaratory of the laws and customs of war . . ." *Nazi Conspiracy and Aggression, Opinion and Judgment* (1947) 83. See also "The Krupp Trial," 10 *War Crimes Reports* 69 at 133 (1948). In "The High Command Trial," 12 *War Crimes Reports* at 87–93 (1948), the Tribunal felt compelled to run through the Hague and Geneva Conventions to determine which *specific prohibitions* had become "expression(s) of the accepted views of civilized nations."

49. There is some dispute as to whether disclaimer of a "state of war" by *both* belligerents, as China and Japan so disclaimed in 1937, may be regarded

provide that denunciation by a Contracting Party in the course of a conflict will not take effect until after "peace has been concluded" and after operations relating to the release, repatriation, and resettlement of protected persons are completed.[50] The trend toward comprehensive applicability thus manifested in all these provisions reflects increasing awareness that the rules of warfare, both conventional and customary, comprise standards of human rights for contexts of violence. "It is important," Professor Kunz writes, "to emphasize that the laws of war in general and the Geneva Conventions in particular are a chapter in the international protection of human rights. . . . The dignity of and respect for the human personality is the very basis of the Geneva Conventions." [51]

Claims with Respect to Permissible Combatants

The controversies respecting permissible combatancy may be most generally described in terms of the contraposition of, on the one hand, primary claims to exercise violence through the employment of differing groups of persons organized in varying degrees and ways, and, on the other, of opposed claims to counter and safeguard against the activities of such groups by denying to them upon capture the privileged treatment of prisoners of war. We mean by "permissible combatants" those persons who, upon capture, must be accorded all the rights conventionally provided for prisoners of war. "Nonpermissible combatants" refers to those persons whose activities are assumed to pose special dangers to the opposing belligerent and upon whom, in the event of capture, the opposing belligerent is regarded as

---

as coming within the purview of Article 2. See Kunz, "The Geneva Conventions of August 12, 1949," in *Law and Politics in the World Community* 279, 305 (Lipsky, ed., 1953); contrast Yingling and Ginnane, "The Geneva Conventions of 1949," 46 *A.J.I.L.* 393, 394 (1952).

50. Art. 63, Wounded and Sick Convention; Art. 62, Wounded, Sick and Shipwrecked Convention; Art. 142, Prisoners of War Convention; Art. 158, Civilians Convention.

51. Kunz, supra note 49 at 283. See also 2 Oppenheim-Lauterpacht 211 note 3 and Pictet, "The New Geneva Conventions for the Protection of War Victims," 45 *A.J.I.L.* 462 (1951). *The British Manual of Military Law,* Part III, p. 2 (1958) which was prepared by Judge Lauterpacht, includes among the purposes of the law of war the "safeguarding (of) certain fundamental human rights of persons who fall into the hands of the enemy . . ." See, further, Art. 15(1) and (2) of the European Convention on Human Rights; text in 45 *A.J.I.L. Supp.* 24 (1951).

authorized, after certain procedures of identification, to impose execution or lesser deprivation.

The policies sought to be effectuated in the rules of warfare about permissible and nonpermissible combatants exhibit the twin, complementary aspects of humanity and military necessity. The particular manifestation of the humanity principle in this context may perhaps be made most explicit by anticipating a closely related distinction that refers, as will be developed below, to people as permissible objects of attack: the distinction between combatants and noncombatants. The immunity from direct attack provided in traditional law for the noncombatant individual was conditioned upon that individual remaining an innocuous nonparticipant.[52] It may be recalled that in the eighteenth and much of the nineteenth centuries, when our inherited rules of warfare were in process of development and crystallization, the significant participation of individuals in war was in principal measure limited to actual, weapon-in-hand combatancy.[53] Thus, in confining combatancy generally to relatively well-

52. See Hall, *International Law* 611 (8th ed., Pearce Higgins, 1924); 3 Hyde, *International Law* 1798–9 (2nd rev. ed., 1945); Fenwick, *International Law* 554 (3rd ed., 1948).

The so-called Rousseau-Portalis doctrine provided some theoretical underpinning for the combatant-noncombatant dichotomy. 2 Wheaton, *International Law* 170 (7th ed., Keith 1944); Higgins, *War and the Private Citizen* 13 (1912). "War," said Portalis in 1801 on opening the French Prize Court, borrowing heavily from Rouseau (*Social Contract,* Bk. I, c. 4), "is a relation of state to state, and not of individual to individual. Between two or more belligerent nations the private persons of whom those nations are composed are only enemies by accident; they are not so as men, they are not so even as citizens, they are so only as soldiers." Quoted in Hall, supra, p. 86; see also Edmunds, "The Laws of War: Their Rise in the Nineteenth Century and Their Collapse in the Twentieth," 15 *Va. L. Rev.* 327–8 (1929).

This conception, while it in time became commonplace in the writings of continental publicists, was rejected by British and American writers. E.g. 2 Westlake, *International Law* 37–8 (1907); Art 20 of the "Instructions for the Government of Armies of the United States in the Field, 1863" ("Lieber's Code"), in JAG's School, *Law of Land Warfare* 159 (1943). More accurately the doctrine was not accepted for all purposes; the individual was assimilated to his state for some purposes, while for others he was not.

53. In 1801, the armies of most of the European countries still consisted of professional soldiers and mercenaries; the idea of the "nation in arms" and of universal conscription had been introduced in revolutionary France only a few years back. See 1 Wright, *A Study of War* 295–7 (1942); Speier, *Social Order and the Risks of War* 230 (1952).

defined categories of persons, such as members of the public armed forces, the rules of warfare may be seen to reflect a policy of limiting the involvement—that is, the participation and hence subjection to direct violence—of individuals in war. These limitative requirements at the same time sought to serve the military and security interests of belligerents and belligerent-occupants. The traditional law, in prescribing certain indicia of permissible combatancy, required combatants to present themselves as open enemies.[54] Where a belligerent is able to determine who are involved as hostile participants, it is able both to protect itself by avoiding being taken by surprise and to refrain from attacking the nonhostile civilians, having *ex hypothesi* no need to do so. Where, on the other hand, belligerents are unable to distinguish the hostile from the nonhostile and to secure themselves from the former, they have been disposed to react with harsh reprisal measures and to draw the whole population into the struggle.[55]

COMBATANCY IN LAND WARFARE: ORGANIZED AND UNORGANIZED COMBATANTS

The groups of people that in fact engage in combat operations may differ greatly in degree or extent of organization. In the uppermost ranges of a hypothetical scale of organization are, of course, the regular armed forces of a belligerent state and it is by these forces that hostilities have ordinarily and largely been carried on in the past. The major characteristics of armed forces are that they embody the highest degree of organization, are provided with external or discernible signs permitting ready identification, and commonly are so under the effective operational and disciplinary control of the state as to afford the enemy reasonable assurance of observance by its members of the rules of war. They constitute an instrument specialized to the exercise of violence and are most adapted to doing so conformably with legal restraints; they represent the principal category of permissible combatants. Regular armed forces may consist of a permanent, standing army, or of militias or volunteer corps, or both; the composition of the forces, determined by internal legisla-

54. See the literature cited in Ch. 1, note 184.

55. Bordwell, *The Law of War between Belligerents* 231–2 (1908); cf. Spaight, *Air Power and War Rights* 76 (3rd ed., 1947).

tion, is in this regard immaterial.[56] The term regular armed forces, includes, of course, not only land but also naval and air units.

There are certain kinds of individuals who accompany the armed forces but are not combatant members of the same, in the sense that they do not themselves oppose the enemy arms in hand. These include war correspondents, supply contractors, civilian members of military aircraft crews, and members of labor units and welfare services. These persons, so long as properly authorized by the armed forces they accompany, are likewise entitled to treatment as prisoners of war.[57] Personnel of medical service units and chaplains who are retained rather than released by the capturing power, are also entitled as a minimum to the benefits of prisoner-of-war treatment.[58] Similarly, captured crew members of the enemy mercantile marine and civil aircraft may claim the same benefits,[59] unless released on a formal pledge not to enter the enemy's public service during the war.[60] The activities of the merchant marine and civil airlines in war are commonly so closely related to the belligerent's military effort, furnishing indispensable logistical support, that their members are properly assimilated to the armed forces upon capture.

Participants in combat processes often include persons less formally organized than the regular armed forces. These persons are generally designated as irregular troops. Within the broad category of irregular troops, the possible variation in extent of organization of particular bodies of troops is substantial. At one extreme are paramilitary units like the British Home Guard, the Belgian *Guard Civique* and German *Volksturm* established during World War II by express legislation and subject to control of military authorities

56. 2 Oppenheim-Lauterpacht 255; JAG's School, *Law of Land Warfare* 15 (1943).

57. See Art. 4A(4), Geneva Prisoners of War Convention of 1949.

58. See Art. 33, id. See also Wilson, "Status of Chaplains With Armed Forces," 37 *A.J.I.L.* 490 (1943).

59. Art. 4A(5), Geneva Prisoners of War Convention.

60. Under Arts. 6–7, Hague Convention XI of 1907, which set forth the "more favorable treatment" referred to in the Geneva Convention. This parole privilege was practically a dead letter, merchant marine crews being treated either as prisoners of war (by Britain) or as civilian internees (by the United States and Germany). See Commission of Government Experts for the Study of Conventions for the Protection of War Victims, *Preliminary Documents Submitted by the International Committee of the Red Cross,* Vol. II, pp. 7–8 (Geneva, 1947).

and in this respect practically indistinguishable from the regular armed forces. Members of such units ordinarily display the indices of legitimate combatants specified in the Hague Regulations and carried over into the 1949 Geneva Prisoners of War Convention: command by a person responsible for subordinates, possession of a "fixed distinctive sign recognizable at a distance," carrying arms openly and observance of the laws and customs of war. To the extent that they do display these indicia, it is clear they may not lawfully be denied prisoner-of-war status [61] by a capturing power.

At the other extreme is the *levy en masse,* the undirected, spontaneous, and therefore unorganized civilian reaction to the approach of invading enemy forces.[62] The unorganized character of the uprising commonly makes compliance with the first two requisites of responsible command and distinctive emblem impossible. The conventional rules have accordingly exempted *levies* from these two requirements, without, however, dispensing with the other conditions of carrying arms openly and observance of the laws of warfare.[63] The protection accorded to impromptu combatants by legitimation of the *levy en masse,* a concession to the perspectives of patriotic nationalism which presumably motivate the uprising, was actually a very restricted one. *Levies* did not, in the first place, cover the case of isolated individuals committing hostile acts intended to impede the enemy's advance.[64] In the second place, the scope of that protection was limited to an uprising which was a response to invasion, not occupation, to an uprising, in other words, which explodes before the enemy succeeds in establishing its effective control over the territory

61. 2 Oppenheim-Lauterpacht 256; Stone, *Legal Controls of International Conflict* 568–9 (1954). And see Jones, "Status of the Home Guard in International Law," 57 *L. Q. Rev.* 212 (1941). In "The Trial of Josef Hangobl," 14 *War Crimes Reports* 86 (1945), the accused was a member of an Austrian civilian defense organization called *Gauwehrmannschaft* which had no distinctive emblem. He had shot an American airman who had bailed out and landed in Austrian territory. The prosecution charged he was not a "lawful belligerent." The General Military Court at Dachau found Hangobl guilty, without, however, an explicit ruling on his status.

62. Art. 2, Hague Regulations; Art. 4A(6), Geneva Prisoners of War Convention of 1949.

63. See the *German War Book* 62–3 (Morgan trans., 1915) for the German view which apparently required compliance with all four requisites.

64. Spaight, supra note 55 at 52; JAG's School, *Law of Land Warfare* 19 (1943).

of the inhabitants.[65] Professor Oppenheim suggested that such protection was even more restricted, and drew a refined distinction between "approach of the enemy" and "invasion."[66] It hardly needs mention that modern techniques of mechanized warfare make very difficult the marking off with definite and precise lines various stages in an onrushing process of assault and combat. These same techniques render *levies* pitifully ineffective militarily and indicate that *levies* will not occur frequently in the future.

The experience of the last war suggests, however, that a comparable situation may arise in the terminal phases of belligerent occupation: a sudden upsurge of the civil population upon advance of *liberating* (the returning sovereigns' or his allies') forces and in the face of the retreating occupant's troops. A decision[67] of the French Permanent Military Tribunal at Dijon appears to suggest that in such situations, just as in a *levy* upon approach of an advancing enemy, civilians may become permissible combatants. A retreating German column reached the town of Autun where it engaged a force composed of regular French troops and some members of the French Forces of the Interior. Three members of the F.F.I. were captured by the Germans and summarily executed. The charge against Bauer et al. alleged "murder" of these three "prisoners of war." Article 2 of the Hague Regulations was invoked by the prosecution, stating that the F.F.I. troops had fought the "invading" forces "without having had time to organize themselves." The Tribunal found the accused guilty of the charge. The inference suggested by the decision would seem to be that portions of territory in which the occupant is deprived, by the presence of enemy military forces, of actual means of effective normal administration, is no longer "occupied" within the meaning of Article 2, though his effective control may not yet have completely disintegrated. Inhabitants then resorting to arms would appear entitled to the rights of prisoners of war, so long as they comply with the two requisites of carrying arms openly and observing the laws of war.[68]

65. See Greenspan, *The Modern Law of Land Warfare* 63 (1959). Contrast Bordwell, supra note 55 at 233 (1908) who suggested that *levies* in occupied territory displaying the required indicia are appropriately held entitled to regular combatant rights.

66. 2 Oppenheim-Lauterpacht 258.

67. "Trial of Bauer," 8 *War Crimes Reports* 15 (1945).

68. Id. 17–18; see also 2 Oppenheim-Lauterpacht 214. Fitzmaurice, "The

Along the line between the two extremes of well organized paramilitary units on the one hand, and unorganized, unpremeditated *levies en masse* on the other, are bodies of irregular troops most frequently operating in belligerent-occupied territory or in areas behind enemy lines, and commonly called "guerrillas" or "partisans." It is useful to distinguish guerrillas from units of the regular armed forces, identifiable as such, which are detached from the main body of such forces for special missions in enemy-held territory and which employ combat tactics loosely described as "guerrilla warfare" and characterized chiefly by stealth and suddenness.[69] Further, the term "guerrillas" is not intended to include in reference the remnants of defeated armies which continue to fight after a *general* surrender or *debellatio* both of their own government and of their co-belligerents. The activities of these remnant forces present problems of legal policy which are not conveniently subsumed under the heading of "combat situations." [70]

Guerrilla forces commonly fail to exhibit all the characteristics that belligerents have habitually required as prerequisites for admission to the category of permissible combatants. Subordination to a responsible commander has perhaps been easy enough. It is in fact difficult to see how guerrillas could function at all as a military force unless such subordination were first achieved. Compliance with the other traditional requisites of permissible combatancy, however, is commonly rendered very difficult by the very nature of guerrilla

---

Juridical Clauses of the Peace Treaties," 73 *Hague Recueil* 259, 277 (1948): "Now, when a country is under enemy occupation but is being so to speak *re*-invaded by its own forces, or those of its allies, the same situation occurs as it were in reverse. Once again the country is being invaded, though by its own forces, once again fighting is going on *in* the country, and again the occupation is being contested and challenged. It is difficult to see why, in such circumstances, the civilian population should not be entitled to take up arms against the occupying enemy on the same general basis as they did or could have done at the time of the original invasion."

69. Spaight, *War Rights on Land,* 61 (1911) and 2 Wheaton, *International Law* 175 (7th ed., Keith, 1944) appear to have referred to this kind of situation when they wrote that "guerrilla warfare" was "perfectly legitimate." See, further, *British Manual of Military Law,* Part III, 38 (1958).

70. See Nurick and Barrett, "Legality of Guerrilla Forces Under the Laws of War," 40 *A.J.I.L.* 563 (1946); and JAG's School, *Law of Land Warfare* 21–2 (1943).

operations. Carrying arms openly and displaying "fixed, distinctive and recognizable signs" would clearly often preclude the secrecy and tactical surprise essential to the success of guerrilla warfare.[71] The requirement respecting signs is, of course, imprecise and abstract; the distance at which the sign must be recognizable is not specifically prescribed. The required sign, while it need not be a complete and conspicuous uniform, should, many observers agree, be "something which cannot be instantly taken off or assumed at will, thus enabling a combatant to appear a peaceful citizen one moment and a soldier the next." [72] The partisan with an irremovable identifiable mark will not be able to sink at his convenience into the general class of innocuous civilians, which procedure has been the usual defense against capture. Similarly, while observance of the laws of war would seem a reasonable requirement, the conditions under which guerrilla operations are carried out are not commonly propitious for adherence to some of those rules. For instance, the need for high mobility and for a frequently shifting headquarters as well as shortage of food and other supplies, are not calculated to encourage guerrilla troops to encumber themselves by taking prisoners.[73] Frequently, they can only seek to inflict the maximum damage their limited means and opportunities may permit, and having so inflicted destruction to vanish forthwith. Inferiority in manpower, equipment, and organization, when combined with a strong and deeply felt demand for national liberation from a military conqueror, has rarely been conducive to restraint in warfare.[74] Where guerrilla forces succeed in securing control over a certain area of land and in establishing a territorial base of operations, they would perhaps be better able to conform to the rules on prisoners of war. To the extent that they do so succeed, however, they will have discarded their character of secret underground forces.[75]

71. See, with respect to guerrilla techniques, the references cited in Ch. 1, note 210. See also Ney, "Guerrilla War and Modern Strategy," 2 *Orbis* 66 (1958); that guerrilla methods change but little and slowly is indicated in the earlier account found in Callwell, *Small Wars: Their Principles and Practice* 125–49 (3rd ed., 1906).

72. Greenspan, *The Modern Law of Land Warfare* 59 (1959).

73. Cf. 3 Hyde, *International Law* 1797 (2nd rev. ed., 1945).

74. Speier, *Social Order and the Risks of War* 225 (1952).

75. In the International Committee of the Red Cross, *Summary Report of the Work of the Conference of Government Experts for the Study of the Conven-*

Turning to a summary review of decisions rendered after the last world war by various tribunals, it may be observed that the problem of permissible combatancy by partisan forces arose in two distinguishable types of cases. The first type of case was a trial for war crimes. The summary execution of large numbers of civilians was frequently charged as a war crime. A defense commonly raised was that the civilians executed had been guilty of hostile guerrilla or sabotage activities in occupied territory and were therefore illegitimate combatants whom the Axis occupants had the right to punish by execution. The war crimes tribunals held, with marked uniformity, that civilians or partisans failing to manifest the indicia set forth in Article 1 of the Hague Regulations were not permissible belligerents such that their execution, as such, did not constitute a war crime.[76] The same tribunals did impose, however, the qualifying requirement that persons charged by the enemy belligerent with sabotage or guerrilla warfare were in all cases entitled to a judicial determination, attended by certain minimum procedural safeguards, of their factual status as saboteurs and guerrillas. It was, the tribunals held, the denial of such judicial determination to the persons so charged that rendered their killing a war crime.[77] There appears here no dis-

---

tions for the Protection of War Victims 39 (Geneva, 1947), among the proposed conditions for legitimation of guerrilla combatants was that they should gain "effective, albeit temporary, control of a region." This condition was objected to on the ground that "it would render the whole system ineffective," and was dropped from the final text of Art. 4 of the Geneva Prisoners of War Convention.

In *In re* Ohlendorf ("The *Einsatzgruppen* Trial") *Annual Digest 1948,* Case No. 217 at 662, the U. S. Military Tribunal said: "in many of the areas where the *Einsatzgruppen* operated, the so-called partisans had wrested considerable territory from the occupant, and . . . military combat action of some dimensions was required to reoccupy those areas. In belligerent occupation, the occupying power does not hold enemy territory by virtue of any legal right. . . . In reconquering enemy territory which the occupant had lost to the enemy, he is not carrying out a police performance but a regular act of war. The enemy combatants in this case are, of course, also carrying out a war performance. They must, on their part, obey the laws and customs of warfare, and if they do, and they are captured, they are entitled to the status and rights of prisoners of war."

76. See the cases cited in Ch. 1, note 211.

77. See "Trial of Shinohara," 5 *War Crimes Reports* 32 (1946); "Trial of Motosuke," 13 id. 126 at 129–30 (1948). Respecting the kinds of facts that suffice to show denial of a fair trial, see "Trial of Hisakasu," 5 id. 70 et seq. (1946),

cernible trend toward assimilation of partisans to members of the regular armed forces. On the contrary it was stressed, in the *List* case, in language that disregarded even the distinction between "unlawful" and "unprivileged" combatancy proposed by some commentators, that

> [t]he rule is established that a civilian who aids, abets or participates in the fighting is liable to punishment as a war criminal under the laws of war. Fighting is legitimate only for the combatant personnel of a country. It is only this group that is entitled to treatment as prisoners of war and incurs no liability beyond detention after capture or surrender.[78]

Clearly, the security needs of belligerents and belligerent-occupants were given strong and preponderating weight.

The second type of case dealt with what might compendiously be called the internal or municipal legal effects of acts of partisan groups. These cases, decided by ordinary civil tribunals of the constitutional sovereign on whose behalf guerrilla warfare was waged during the last war, were concerned with such noncombat situations as the interpretation of insurance contracts and the recovery of property seized by partisans, and are therefore but obliquely relevant to our principal inquiry. They are, however, interesting since they indicate that, for certain purposes other than the punishment of war criminals, partisans may be regarded as perfectly legitimate combatants. Death or destruction wrought by partisans, for example, have been held to constitute "acts of war" within the meaning of clauses in insurance policies either covering or excluding loss due to "war." [79]

"Trial of Altstotter," 6 id. at 96–104 (1947), and 15 id. 111–13, 161–6. In "The High Command Trial," the Tribunal declared criminal the issuance of the "Barbarossa Jurisdiction Order," which in part provided that inhabitants of occupied territories in the East suspected of hostile activity against the occupant were not to be tried by military commissions or courts-martial, but to be brought before any officer who would decide whether they would be shot or not. 12 *War Crimes Reports* at 29, 82–3 (1948).

See also *In re* von Lewinsky (called von Manstein) *Annual Digest 1949,* Case No. 192.

78. 8 *War Crimes Reports* at 58 (1948).

79. *Von Hoeve de Feyter v. Fire Insurance Co.,* District Court, Dordrecht, Holland, *Annual Digest 1947,* Case No. 81; *Drenthina v. Insurance Co.,* District Court, Rotterdam, Holland, id. *1948,* Case No. 132; *Cie d'Assurance v. Vve Ca-*

Further, seizure of the property of traitors and collaborators by guerrillas has been held in effect to be nonactionable to the same extent and under the same conditions as seizure by regular armed forces.[80] It is obvious that in this type of situation, the necessity for and difficulties of accommodating the conflicting interests of opposing belligerents are not present. To the extent that any policy broader than the narrow necessities of the specific decisions can be distilled from these cases, it is perhaps that of encouraging the participation of inhabitants in the defense of their country by giving some legal recognition to patriotic motivations. Such policy objective seems discernible in the declaration of the Dutch court in *Van Hoeve de Feyter v. Fire Insurance Co. of 1859, Ltd.*:

> Taking into account the total character of modern war, it was impossible to confine the notion of acts of war to acts committed by organized armies levied and maintained by the State. The civilian population had a part in the conduct of the war. . . . In such a case, acts of war must include acts of persons who, either individually or organized in an underground resistance movement, inflicted losses on the enemy in agreement with, or by order of the lawful government . . . by committing acts of resistance or of sabotage. . . . *It was not even necessary that the lawful government should have expressed its wishes to that effect. It was enough if the perpetrators acted from patriotic motives in the spirit of the general principles which inspired the conduct of war on the part of their government.*[81]

The point may thus summarily be made that different decision-makers, in different contexts and for differing purposes, appro-

---

banel, Court of Appeal, Montpellier, France, id. *1946,* Case No. 95; *Peeterbroek v. Assurances Générales de Paris,* Tribunal Civil de Huy, Belgium, id. *1496,* Case No. 98; *Smulders v. Société Anonyme "La Royale Belge,"* Civil Court of Liège, Belgium, id. *1943–1945,* Case No. 102. Cf. *Saporiti v. S.A. Infortuni Milano,* Court of First Instance of Milan, Italy, id. *1948,* Case No. 130; *Marissal v. Mutuelle Générale Française Accidents,* Court of Cassation, France, *Int. Law Rep. 1950,* Case No. 109; *Beccarini v. Societa La Sicurta,* Court of Cassation, Italy, id., Case No. 111.

80. *Baffico v. Calleri,* Court of Appeals of Turin, Italy, *Annual Digest 1948,* Case No. 128; *Ostino v. Fantini,* Court of First Instance of Turin, Italy, id., Case No. 129.

81. *Annual Digest 1947,* Case No. 81 at p. 170. Emphasis added.

priately come to very diverse conclusions about the permissibility of guerrilla combatancy.

The Geneva Prisoners of War and Civilians Conventions of 1949 remain briefly to be considered. All that the Civilians Convention has done is, firstly, to adopt the requirement laid down by the war crimes tribunals that the fact of participation in guerrilla or partisan activities must be judicially determined; and secondly, to specify the minimum procedural guarantees of fairness to be followed in such judicial determinations.[82] The Prisoners of War Convention lists among those entitled to be treated as prisoners of war the members of "organized resistance movements, belonging to a Party to the conflict and operating in or outside their own territory, even if this territory is occupied." [83] It might be supposed that this provision makes permissible combatants out of guerrilla and partisan forces in territory under belligerent occupation. This legitimation is, however, likely to be largely unreal. For the Convention continues to demand from organized guerrillas and partisans all the requisites of permissible combatancy prescribed in the 1907 Hague Regulations. As indicated previously, it is scarcely realistic to expect that many partisan groups will be able in future wars to conform to all these requisites: their characteristic tactics and operating conditions make such conformity very difficult.[84]

The need for retaining unqualifiedly all the traditional requisites appears less than self-evident. It has been observed, for instance, that even regular combatants often have no rifles or other easily visible weapons, but are equipped with certain small arms like machine pistols, hand grenades, and the like, which may be carried under the uniform.[85] Dressmarks, it has also been suggested, should not be demanded in all cases. Where the "organized resistance movement" comprises substantial numbers of men divided into large bands, the fact that a large group is operating together in a specific tactical confrontation with the forces of the opposing belligerent would seem to distinguish it sufficiently as a body from the general class of the non-

82. Arts. 64–77, Geneva Civilians Convention of 1949.

83. Art. 4A(2), Geneva Prisoners of War Convention of 1949.

84. Relevant citations are collected in Ch. 1, note 214. See also Krafft, "The Present Position of the Red Cross Geneva Conventions," 37 *Tr. Grotius Soc.* 131, 136–7 (1951).

85. See Commission of Government Experts, supra note 60 at 6–7.

combatant population.[86] Individual members might be supplied with identity cards certifying their combatant character when captured singly or in small detachments. Admission to belligerent privileges should perhaps in such cases depend solely on subordination to a responsible commander, that is, one who is capable of enforcing and does actually enforce observance by his men of the rules of war.

It has, within recent years, been argued with both energy and erudition that hostilities by guerrilla forces are not internationally criminal acts in the sense that they are not violative of "any positive prohibition of international law." [87] Guerrillas and partisans are not, it is said, "unlawful" belligerents but, rather, "unprivileged" belligerents. There is, Professor Baxter submitted, a "fundamental" distinction between "acts punishable under international law and acts with respect to which international law affords no protection." [88] Hostilities by guerrillas fall, in his view, within the latter class; because of the dangers such hostilities present to the opposing belligerent, international law simply does not prohibit the captor from denying to captured guerrillas the treatment required for prisoners of war. There appears some room for doubt whether this exercise in technical theory, and its proposed application to the combatancy of guerrilla and partisan forces, amount to anything more than a complicated mode of recommending a compromise that takes only a modest step in its aspiration toward a greater humanity in the conduct of war. The distinction Professor Baxter appears to make is that between the comprehensive responsibility to the general community through an indefinite period of time beyond termination of hostilities which is commonly imposed for war crimes under the principle of universality of jurisdiction, and a more limited responsibility (or perhaps vulnerability) to a particular opposing belligerent confined to the period of hostilities during which such belligerent has continuing control over the captured combatant.[89] This is a distinc-

86. Cf. Hall, *International Law* 619 (8th ed., Pearce Higgins, 1924).

87. Baxter, "So-called 'Unprivileged Belligerency': Spies, Guerrillas, and Saboteurs," 28 *Brit. Y.B.I.L.* 323 (1951). The argument has been picked up by Stone, *Legal Controls* 562–70; see also Castberg, "Franc Tireur Warfare," in *Varia Juris Gentium: Liber Amicorum J.P.A. Francois* 81 (1959).

88. Baxter, supra note 87 at 340.

89. See his Note on "The Municipal and International Law Basis of Jurisdiction over War Crimes," 28 *Brit. Y.B.I.L.* 382, 391–3 (1951) where Professor Baxter, in outlining the distinction noted above, refers to what he calls "col-

tion which, despite its theoretical elegance and reach toward humanity, can offer but little protection to captured partisans. Captured partisans are as dead by enforcement of the one responsibility as by the other.

Perhaps the more fundamental question that should be raised is whether a consistent application of the basic principle of minimum unnecessary destruction of values would not require a re-evaluation of the line of compromise embodied in the 1907 Hague Regulations and the 1949 Geneva Conventions in respect of guerrilla or partisan forces or resistance movements as permissible combatants. The factors that may be relevant to such a reassessment seem myriad and only a few can be highlighted here. Expectations about the military effectiveness of guerrilla warfare are perhaps of primary relevance. The experience of the Axis occupants in the last world war in, for instance, Yugoslavia, Russia, France, and the Philippines, as well as the extensive efforts devoted by the Allied Powers to the organizing, coordinating, training, and arming of the underground movements in various occupied countries, suggest that the military value of such movements was far from insignificant. Guerrilla operations were developed into a distinct technique of warfare behind enemy lines, effective in tying down troops for garrison duty and compelling the commitment and dispersal of occupation forces, disrupting lines of communication and sources of supply, ambushing and destroying occasional patrols and isolated posts and so forth.[90] That comparable effectiveness can be secured in future wars, and even in some nuclear wars, would seem an assumption underlying the organization of the so-called "Special Forces" units in the armed forces of the United States, for example. The particular task of these "Special Forces," it

---

lateral legal problems." These problems lie at the very core of Professor Baxter's distinction, as we understand it, for it is in respect of these problems (rather than the regulation of guerrilla warfare) that the distinction makes any difference.

90. See the literature referred to in Ch. 1, note 215. For accounts and analyses of guerrilla operations in World War II, see e.g., Hart, "United States Employment of Underground Forces," 26 *Military Rev.* (U.S. Army Command and General Staff College), No. 1, p. 52 (1946); Peers, "Guerrilla Operations in Northern Burma," 28 id. No. 3, p. 10 and No. 4, p. 12 (1948); Harris, "Partisan Operations," 30 id. No. 5, p. 10 (1950). Lowry, "Could It Happen?" 36 id. No. 12, p. 33 (1957) offers suggestions on guerrilla warfare within the United States in case of enemy occupation.

has been reported, is to organize, equip, and direct large-scale guerrilla forces in occupied territory, particularly in Asia.[91] It seems relevant also to note that in any future war where ideological instruments are committed in significant degree, the civil population will be subject to strong pressures for participation in the conflict.[92]

The impact of guerrilla war upon the opposing belligerent or belligerent-occupant must of course also be taken into account. The more widespread and effective guerrilla activities become, the graver becomes the danger to the enemy belligerent's security interests and perhaps the greater will be its reluctance to accord prisoner-of-war status to captured partisans. Considering that reprisals against the civil population of the enemy are now prohibited by the Geneva

91. *N. Y. Times,* Feb. 23, 1960, p. 1, col. 6.

92. Lieber had denounced guerrillas, declaring that they "almost always degenerate into simple robbers or brigands," because "they cannot otherwise subsist than by rapine." (See 3 Hyde 1797.) Cowles, "Universality of Jurisdiction over War Crimes," 33 *Calif. L. Rev.* 177, 181 (1945) identified guerrillas with "pirates" and "bandits." Baxter, supra note 87 at 335 correctly pointed out that "Patriotism, nationalism, allegiance to some sort of political authority have replaced the desire for loot, which has traditionally been attributed to the guerrilla, in motivating civilians to take an active part in warfare." (at 337–8 note 4): "Although some guerrillas may engage in banditry and thereby become guilty of the war crimes of murder, plunder, and wanton destruction, it is somewhat naive to suppose that a desire for blood and booty for their own sakes is the sole well spring of such warfare. . . ."

It does not seem irrelevant to note that recourse to underground resistance and partisan warfare form part of the Soviet conception of a "peoples' war." Kozhevnikov, *International Law* c. 10 (Moscow, 1957) writes: "From the point of view of established custom, partisan warfare on territory occupied by the aggressor is absolutely legal. Partisans are combatants. Partisan struggle presents itself as a type of peoples' war, and such a character may be had only by a justified war." (translated from the Russian text by T. P. Jakaboski, of the second-year class, Yale Law School, 1960)

See Trainin, "Questions of Guerrilla Warfare in the Law of War," 40 *A.J.I.L.* 534 (1946); also Kulski, "Some Soviet Comments on International Law," 45 *A.J.I.L.* 347–9 (1951). Hazard, *Law and Social Change in the U.S.S.R.* 290 (1953) observed that revision of the Hague Regulations in the light of the experience of the Soviet civilians who had served effectively as guerrillas in occupied Ukraine was demanded by Soviet legal scholars. The matter of guerrilla warfare was inevitably related to revolutionary aims, it having become "a form of national struggle against the exploitation of imperialist powers." A useful descriptive account is Dixon and Heilbrunn, *Communist Guerrilla Warfare* (1954).

Civilians Convention,[93] the question might plausibly be raised whether to legitimize partisan warfare would not be seriously to cripple the opposing belligerent in maintaining its security. Another kind of factor that rationally calls for consideration is the extent to which the denial of prisoner-of-war status—i.e., execution upon capture and ascertainment of participation in guerrilla activities—is, in realistic expectation, effective to deter resort to partisan warfare. The deterrent value of the threatened deprivations may, of course, itself be a function of other specific factors, such as the degree of ideological commitment of the population and the ruthlessness of the occupant. The widespread recourse to guerrilla warfare in the last world war despite the common practice of executing captured guerrillas, and despite even the extremely harsh reprisals inflicted by the Axis occupying powers upon the general populace of occupied regions, suggest that the effectiveness of denial of prisoner-of-war rights as a deterrent countermeasure cannot lightly be assumed. The dimensions—total or limited—of the future conflicts in which any new line of compromise will have to be applied constitute still another factor. The degree of realism of any particular proposed line may be expected to differ in differing types of conflict.

As earlier indicated, units of regular forces assigned special tasks commonly behind enemy lines should be distinguished from guerrilla or partisan forces. The former were illustrated *par excellence* in the last world war by the British "Commandos" and the American "Rangers." These were specially trained troops, members of regular armed forces, frequently landed or parachuted on enemy or enemy-occupied territory to carry out specialized missions such as the destruction of vital supply and communication lines. The techniques of operation employed by these special troops did not differ essentially from those of partisans: clandestine methods designed to secure maximum surprise and shock impact. These methods sometimes included the use of civilian clothing under the troops' regular uniforms, with the expectation that upon performance of their task, the shedding of the outer uniforms would facilitate escape and return to their own lines. War crimes tribunals after World War II consistently held that the execution, pursuant to the German "Commando" Order of August 18, 1942, of "commando" troops which had carried on their operations and had been captured while in uniform,

93. Art. 33.

was a war crime.[94] From these cases, commentators have drawn the inference that where "commandos" are taken while in civilian clothes, the captor-belligerent may, after a judicial determination of the facts, refuse to treat them as prisoners of war, in effect assimilate them to guerrillas, and execute them.[95] The "clear criminality" of the German "Commando" Order lay, it is said, in the fact that it applied to all "commando" troops whether taken in uniform or not.[96] It would seem evident that "commando" tactics which are calculated to prevent detection and alarm until the very last moment before eruption of the attack in effect deny to the enemy the advantage the traditional law on permissible combatancy sought to confer upon him by requiring ready identifiability. The unreality of determinations which permit life and death to hinge upon a man's garb is accentuated when one considers that combat military uniforms today are deliberately designed to enhance invisibility by visual integration into the immediate environment. Uniforms or dressmarks might have been a meaningful test of belligerent qualifications in days when each knight had his own crest and colors, or when military dress was more spectacularly cut and colored. In

94. See "Trial of Dostler," 1 *War Crimes Reports* 22 (1945), involving the killing of 15 American soldiers who had been landed 250 miles behind enemy lines in Italy, in uniform, to destroy a tunnel and railway lines; "Trial of Buck," 5 id. 39 (1946), concerning the execution without trial of, *inter alia,* 6 members of the British Special Air Service Regiment sent to coordinate the activities of the Maquis with Allied operations; "Trial of Golkel," 5 id. 45 (1946) concerning the summary killing of 8 members of the same British unit engaged in the same mission; "Trial of Von Falkenhorst," 11 id. 18 (1946) involving the execution of British and Norwegian "commandos" captured on raids on Norway. In the last-mentioned case, the "commandos" had ordinary skiing attire under their uniforms, presumably for purposes of evading capture after completion of the raids. They were captured while still in uniform. Their status would probably have been held to be that of "war traitors" had they been taken after shedding their uniforms; see Baxter, supra note 87 at 341. This point was not, however, touched upon by the tribunal.

95. See 2 Oppenheim-Lauterpacht 575–6; Baxter, supra note 87 at 339–40. See also Dept. of the Army, *The Law of Land Warfare,* pars. 63 and 74 (FM 27–10, July 1956).

96. See annotation to "The Von Falkenhorst Case," 11 *War Crimes Reports* at 28. "The Trial of Skorzeny," 9 id. 90 (1947) affords some support for the above view. Detailed comment and speculation are offered in Koessler, "International Law on Use of Enemy Uniforms as a Stratagem and the Acquittal in the Skorzeny Case," 24 *Mo. L. Rev.* 16 (1959).

modern war where insignia or dress afford little, if any, protection against surprise, the rationality of this rule-of-thumb on permissible combatants must be regarded as open to serious doubt.

Spies form another class of combatants who have customarily been denied prisoner-of-war status upon capture. Article 29 of the Hague Regulation requires three elements to constitute an individual a belligerent spy: the obtaining or seeking to obtain information for the use of a hostile belligerent; doing so clandestinely or under false pretences; and doing so in the "zone of operations" of a belligerent. The gist of espionage, it is often said, is the use of dissimulation and false pretences; thus, the wearing of a uniform in the case of an alleged military spy, or acting openly in case of an alleged civilian spy, operates to negative such element.[97] In respect to the required locale of acts of espionage, it might be observed that with the development of air weapons and the use of airborne troops, the conception of a "zone of operations," as distinguished, for example, from a "zone of the interior" tends increasingly to be imprecise of reference.[98] The commonplace fact is that espionage and counterespionage activities may be and are carried on throughout the territories of belligerents as of nonbelligerents.

The traditional law clearly placed a preponderating weight upon military interests in permitting the capturing belligerent to execute captured spies. This weighting is frequently explained in terms of some theory of deterrence; the special dangers spies pose for the opposing belligerent are regarded as justifying such belligerent in imposing special risks upon those engaging in such enterprise.[99] Some

97. Art. 29, second par., Hague Regulations. See also Spaight, *War Rights on Land* 203–4 (1911) and Hall, *International Law* 650 (8th ed., Pearce Higgins, 1924). See, further *In re Wuistaz, Annual Digest 1948,* Case No. 127, where the French Court of Cassation held that since the accused had joined the German paramilitary *Todt* Organization and wore its uniform, he could not be treated as a spy.

98. In *U.S. ex rel. Wessels v. McDonald,* 265 Fed. 754, 763 (D.C.E.D.N.Y. 1920) the court held that the port of New York was within the "zone of operations" for the purposes of Art. 29 of the Hague Regulations: "With the progress made in obtaining ways and means for devastation and destruction, the territory of the United States was certainly within the field of active operations."

99. Dept. of the Army, *The Law of Land Warfare,* par. 77 (FM 27–10, July 1956): "Spies are punished, not as violators of the laws of war, but to render that method of obtaining information as dangerous, difficult, and ineffective as possible." Also, Baxter, supra note 87 at 329–30, 333; and McKinney, "Spies and

deference to the countervailing policy of minimum destruction of values is, however, observable in Articles 30 and 31 of the Hague Regulations which seek in measure to limit the special risks that belligerents may impose. Article 30 requires a judicial determination of the fact of having engaged in espionage. The execution of an alleged spy without such previous trial subjects the captors to liability for a war crime.[100] Article 31 provides for what might be regarded as a prescriptive period: upon successfully rejoining his own forces, the spy may no longer be held liable for his acts of espionage.[101]

COMBATANCY IN SEA AND AIR WARFARE: MECHANICAL UNITS OF COMBAT

The problems of permissible combatancy we have thus far considered have related peculiarly to land warfare. Comparable problems have arisen in sea and air warfare. In hostilities on land, the ultimate unit of military power has, in common conception, been the individual soldier. In sea and air war, it is for some purposes convenient to conceive of the unit of combat as constituted by a machine

---

Traitors," 12 *Ill. L. Rev.* 591 at 603 (1918). See Koessler, "The International Law on the Punishment of Belligerent Spies: A Legal Paradox," 5 *Crim. L. Rev.* (N.Y.) 21 (1958) for the curious argument that if, and so long as, the employment of spies by a belligerent is "lawful" under international law, it is a "paradox" to say that a captured spy may be "lawfully" tried and executed by the opposing belligerent.

100. See "Trial of Rohde," 5 *War Crimes Reports* 54, 56–8 (1946); and "Trial of Sandrock," 1 id. 35, 43–4 (1945).

101. See *In re* Rieger *Annual Digest 1948,* Case No. 152, where the French Court of Cassation upheld the decision of the Military Tribunal of Strasbourg to the effect that Rieger, not having been captured *flagrante delicto,* could not be held for espionage. Rieger, a German officer, had, in civilian disguise, acted as a spy in both Northern and Southern Zones from 1941–1944. In 1944, he was transferred to the German forces in Denmark. He was arrested in 1946 after demobilization.

Strangely enough, this immunity for past acts is supposed to be limited to military spies; see 2 Oppenheim-Lauterpacht 424–5, and McKinney, supra note 99 at 601–2. Professor Baxter, supra note 87 at 331, seeks to explain this limitation of punishment by suggesting that "[o]nce the act [of espionage] is completed, the deterrent purpose of the death penalty has no room for operation." As Koessler, supra note 99 at 32–3 notes, however, deterrence is appropriately addressed to potential future spies rather than to the spy who has successfully completed his task and rejoined his own forces. The prescriptive period in effect diminishes the risk, and hence the deterrent influence, of the death penalty.

—a vessel or aircraft—operated commonly by a number of individuals acting as a coordinated team. The qualifications of permissible combatants in sea and air warfare have principally related to the machines themselves and the national emblems or signs affixed thereto. The uniform worn by the individual seamen and airmen has thus not been given the same crucial significance it has in land warfare.[102] Where captured individuals are able to show membership in the regular naval or air forces of a belligerent, that is, where the requisite public authorization is present, their individual clothing would appear largely a matter of indifference; they are regarded as entitled to prisoner-of-war status. Thus, there is respectable authority for the view that airmen forced to bail out on enemy territory, who assume civilian disguise in the effort to evade capture and who are captured in such disguise, are nevertheless entitled to prisoner-of-war status.[103] They would, of course, have to show upon trial that they are neither spies nor saboteurs.

Hostilities at sea are, in general, carried on by belligerents' regular navies corresponding to the regular armies employed for combat on land. Just as regular land forces are often supplemented by irregular militia, so also belligerents frequently add to their regular naval strength by making use of privately owned vessels. A few centuries ago, augmentation of naval forces was effected by issuing letters of marque to privateers.[104] While privateering is today primarily of antiquarian interest, analogous practices have developed which have much the same functional effect: the conversion of merchantmen into warships and the arming of merchantmen for "defensive purposes." More importantly, the latter practice among others tended to subvert the traditional line of compromise between military necessity and humanity with respect to permissible combatants in maritime warfare.

The requisites to which converted merchantmen must conform in order to be recognized as permissible naval combatants are closely

102. Cf. Spaight, *Air Power and War Rights* 77 (3rd ed., 1947).

103. See id. 99–104; "Trial of Schonfield," 11 *War Crimes Reports* 64, 73 (1946); "Trial of Sandrock," 1 id. 35, 43–4 (1945). Cf. Art. 15 of the Hague Rules of Aerial Warfare; text in Commission of Jurists to Consider and Report Upon the Revision of the Rules of Warfare, General Report, 32 *A.J.I.L. Supp.* 12 (1938).

104. A recent history of the law of privateering is Azcarraga y de Bustamante, *El Corso Maritimo* (1950).

similar to those prescribed for combatants in land war. Hague Convention VII of 1907 [105] requires that the converted ship be placed under the direct authority, immediate control, and responsibility of the flag state which must, in its roster of warships, give notice of the conversion. Its captain must be a duly commissioned officer of the war fleet (as distinguished from the merchant marine), and its crew subject to naval discipline. The converted ship is required to exhibit the distinguishing marks of the regular national navy. It must, finally, observe the rules of warfare. These requirements implicitly sought, much as in land warfare, to protect the opposing belligerents' naval and commercial fleets from surprise attacks from vessels which had previously held themselves out as noncombatants. The requirement of ready identifiability purported at the same time to promote the humanitarian limitation of violence by permitting the opposing belligerent to distinguish ordinary merchantmen from both regular and converted warships. In traditional combatant law, it should be noted, distinctions were made between the treatment appropriate for enemy merchant ships and the treatment allowable for enemy war vessels. The other requirements also had a humanitarian aspect in providing against recrudescence of the tendencies toward private plunder and the abuses arising from lack of public control and naval discipline which characterized privateers and which, eventually, in conjunction with other factors, led to the abolition of privateering.[106]

It remains briefly to note two controversies in which commentators frequently engage in respect of conversion. The first relates to the lawfulness of conversion on the high seas. The British in the First World War contended that conversion on the high seas would present sudden and unexpected dangers to the opposing belligerent's maritime commerce.[107] The matter proved to be of little practical moment.[108] Save in the case of merchant ships originally built with a

105. Convention VII Relating to the Conversion of Merchant Ships into Warships; text in *The Hague Conventions and Declarations of 1899 and 1907,* 146 (2nd ed., Scott, 1915).

106. See Fenwick, *International Law* 584 (3rd ed., 1948); Hall, *The Law of Naval Warfare* 51 (1921).

107. See Higgins, *War and the Private Citizen* 142–3 (1912); 3 Hyde, *International Law* 1925 (2nd rev. ed., 1945). But British practice, without notable logic, recognized the legitimacy of conversion on the high seas of captured enemy merchant vessels; see Stone, *Legal Controls* 577 note 38.

108. There are very few cases of conversion on the high seas actually reported.

view to future conversion and already carrying, in anticipation of an outbreak of hostilities, guns to be assembled and mounted, conversion on the high seas is rarely a practicable enterprise. The second controversy relates to reconversion of a converted warship back to a merchantman. Reconversion may suggest an analogy with guerrilla war on land. But the analogy would seem superficial. For, in maritime war, both enemy merchantmen and warships are, in differing degrees, legitimate objects of belligerent endeavor. The interests of the belligerent flag state will probably lead it to advertise the fact of reconversion. It would indeed appear that it is in contexts of neutrality—i.e., of specific belligerent-neutral relationships—that reconversion may, if at all, give rise to questions of some interest.[109]

The second practice adverted to above—the "defensive" arming of merchant vessels—represents a revival, purportedly in response to the use of converted cruisers,[110] of an ancient usage that had disappeared with the abolition of privateering and the development of modern naval forces.[111] The familiar controversies here have been marked by somewhat disingenuous use of words which have tended to obscure the really important development. On the one hand, it was frequently asserted that merchantmen, much like the civilian non-

In World War I, only two German merchant ships were actually converted outside German waters: the *Kronprinz Wilhelm* and the *Cap Trafalgar,* the former having left New York immediately before war was declared, and the latter having sailed from the River Plate about three weeks later. See Hall, supra note 106 at 52; Colombos, *The International Law of the Sea* 455–6 (4th rev. ed., 1959), hereafter cited as Colombos, *Law of the Sea.* There are no similar reported instances in the last war.

109. The Havana Convention on Maritime Neutrality of 1928 (4 Hudson, *International Legislation* 2401), in Art. 13, sets forth the requirements to be conformed to by reconverted merchantmen in order to be entitled to the hospitality of neutral ports. The requisites are, briefly, that the vessel has not previously violated the neutrality of the port state, that the reconversion was done in ports of the belligerent or his allies, that the reconversion is genuine and notified to other states and that the vessel will not again be converted into a warship. See "The Kronprinz Wilhelm and other vessels," *Annual Digest 1929–1930,* Case No. 300 at 512 where the suggestion was made that to permit reconversion for the purpose of avoiding imminent capture by the other belligerent or internment by the neutral may run counter to the neutral's duties of abstention and prevention.

110. 3 Hyde, *International Law* 1925 and note 3 (2nd rev. ed., 1945).

111. The classic study is that of Higgins, "Defensively Armed Merchantmen" in *Studies in International Law and Relations* 239 (1928).

combatant in land war, were not authorized to carry on "offensive" operations against the enemy.[112] This assertion probably meant only that the merchant vessel when armed was not to go out of its way to seek battle with enemy warships or to attempt to capture enemy merchantmen. The likelihood of such attempts occurring was of course never very great. On the other hand, it was insisted, in particular by British writers, that the merchant ships of a belligerent had an "immemorial right to resist" attack by enemy forces.[113] The construction of this "right to resist" urged by the same writers and by the British Government was singularly liberal. Attack was said to include the attempt to capture, and the attempt to capture included the attempt to exercise visit and search.[114] In net effect, an armed merchantman was, under this view, entitled to start firing upon being sighted and approached by an enemy force.

What these assertions about a "right to resist" or a "right of self-defense" of merchant ships tended to obscure was that the arming of belligerents' merchantmen, which in World War II was resorted to by practically all the participants, was in principal part a reflection of

112. Fenwick, *International Law* 585 (3rd ed., 1948); Hall, *International Law,* 630 (8th ed., Pearce Higgins, 1924). And see Bellot, "The Right of a Belligerent Merchantman to Attack," 7 *Tr. Grotius Soc.* 43 (1922).

113. Higgins, supra note 111 at 250–7; Colombos, *Law of the Sea* 456–9; Hall, supra note 106 at 53–6. Germany apparently denied the existence of this right to resist. In the celebrated case of Captain Fryatt, the Germans executed Fryatt who had tried to ram with his unarmed merchant ship a U-boat attempting to visit his ship. Fryatt was sentenced as a "sea *franc tireur.*" See 1 Garner, *International Law and the World War* 407–13 (1920).

114. Hall, supra note 106 at 54. Cf. Higgins, supra note 111 at 273–4: "The right to resist capture includes the right to resist visit and search, and the latter includes the right to resist approach. As soon as the belligerent merchant ship is aware that an enemy warship shows an intention to effect its capture, that is the moment for the defensive-offensive to commence."

The British "Instructions Regarding Submarines" of Feb. 25, 1915, par. 3, provided that: "If a submarine is obviously pursuing a ship, by day, and it is evident to the master that she has hostile intentions, the ship pursued should open fire in self defense, notwithstanding the submarine may not have committed a definite hostile act such as firing a gun or torpedo." The Instructions of Oct. 20, 1915 elaborated: "it may be presumed that any submarine or aircraft which deliberately approaches or pursues a merchant vessel does so with hostile intention. In such cases fire may be opened in self defense . . . to prevent the hostile craft closing to a range at which resistance to a sudden attack with bomb or torpedo would be impossible." 6 Hackworth, *Digest of International Law* 494–5 (1943).

certain conditions that characterized protracted and large-scale wars in the modern world. The first condition was the emergence of the submarine as an effective instrument for commerce destruction. The submarine of the last two world wars was a relatively slow and thinly armored craft and, once surfaced, vulnerable to the "defensive" armament of merchant ships. Obviously, the British view while permitting merchant vessels to "defend" themselves against submarines in turn encouraged "unrestricted" submarine warfare. The second condition related to the vast requirements of modern war in materials and resources and to the consequent vital need for maintaining supply and communication lines across oceans. The arming of merchant vessels carrying goods important for the belligerent's war effort permitted economies in the surface naval craft that would otherwise be necessary for escort duty. In these circumstances, and so far as concerns the combatancy and hence liability to direct attack of the vessel itself, efforts to distinguish between the regular warship and the "defensively" armed merchantmen appear in increasingly high degree unreal.[115] This impression is not relieved when one recalls that the British Admiralty, in its Handbook of Instructions to the Merchant Navy, not only gave orders to all merchantmen to send position reports by radio upon sighting submarines, thereby integrating merchant ships into the warning system of naval intelligence, but also instructions to ram submarines where possible.[116] Finally, it seems not without significance that the 1949 Geneva Prisoners of War Convention, in granting prisoner-of-war status to the individual crew members of the merchant marine of belligerent parties, makes no distinction between armed and unarmed, nor between "defensively" armed and "offensively" armed, merchant ships.[117]

115. See Tucker, *The Law of War and Neutrality at Sea* 42 (1957); Smith, *The Law and Custom of the Sea* 105 (3rd ed., 1959). Borchard, "Armed Merchantmen," 34 *A.J.I.L.* 110 (1940) emphasized that: "the immunity of the merchant ship from unwarned attack was directly associated with its inability to attack or endanger a warship. This disability became masked when armorplate was introduced on warships. But when merchant ships became speedy, powerful and armed and the vulnerable submarine appeared on the scene, the reason for immunity from unwarned attack disappeared. It is elementary that an armed belligerent merchant ship, especially when under orders to attack submarines at sight, is a fighting ship, subject to all the dangers of the belligerent character. . . ."

116. See *Nazi Conspiracy and Aggression, Opinion and Judgment* 139 (1947).

117. Such distinctions, however, need to be considered in another type of

The Hague Rules of Aerial Warfare of 1923 proposed requirements of permissible combatancy in air war closely comparable to those established for land and sea warfare. These draft rules required, for instance, military aircraft to bear external marks indicating their nationality and military character.[118] These external marks were required to be fixed and unalterable in flight, "as large as practicable," and "visible from above, from below, and from each side." [119] Only belligerent military aircraft were, under the Rules, authorized to engage in hostilities.[120] The Commission of Jurists emphasized that

> A clear distinction must be made between aircraft which form part of the combatant forces in time of war and those which do not. Each class must be easily recognizable; this is essential if the immunities to which non-combatant aircraft are entitled are to be respected.[121]

. . .

The immunities which a belligerent is bound to respect in the

---

context, that is, in neutrality contexts relating to specific belligerent-neutral relationships. It may be recalled that the traditional law of neutrality provided for certain restrictions upon the facilities which neutral states may open to belligerent warships in neutral ports. Whether the neutral coastal state adopted the policy of permitting limited sojourn or the policy of complete exclusion, the assimilation of armed belligerent merchantmen to belligerent warships would substantially hamper seaborne trade between the neutral and the belligerent flag state. Moreover, since most belligerent maritime states armed their merchantships in the last two world wars, such assimilation would have the practical effect of cutting off all commerce between the neutral and the belligerents. As was indicated in the preceding chapter (supra, p. 477), neutrals have not commonly been willing to cease all trading with belligerents. Neutral states, save Holland in the First (but not in the Second) World War, have accordingly employed the convenient but elusive and tenuous distinction between "offensive" and "defensive" armament. See e.g. Colombos, *Law of the Sea* 459–60. One's recommendation upon this point clearly must depend upon the character of one's recommendations in respect of belligerent-neutral trade in general.

118. Art. 3. Art. 14 also required military aircraft to be under the command of an officer or enlisted man of the armed services and the crew to be "exclusively military." Art. 15 incorporates the requirement of a recognizable, fixed distinctive emblem in respect of the crew members when separated from the aircraft.

119. Art. 7.

120. Arts. 13, 16.

121. *General Report,* supra note 103 at 13.

non-combatant impose upon the non-combatant a corresponding obligation not to take part in hostilities. This principle applies equally to aerial warfare.[122]

The draft Rules thus evidently sought to project much the same policy of preventing surprise and limiting involvement in combat by requiring ready identifiability that the traditional law sought in respect of combatancy in land and sea warfare. It should be noted, however, that while painted insignia or marks on belligerent aircraft may have been quite adequate means of identification in the earlier decades of aircraft development, such insignia or markings have tended, as modern aircraft gained rapidly in speed and operating altitude, to become irrelevant in accelerating degree to the task of identification by defending ground forces. In the last world war, aircraft identification from the ground was frequently effected through discernment of the distinctive shapes of differing types of belligerents' warplanes, rather than through visual observation of painted marks. The difficulties of identification through such markings become even greater in the case of contemporary jet aircraft capable of velocities several times the speed of sound and of extremely high altitudes. When, finally, ballistic missiles are considered, the policy itself of preventing surprise and limiting destruction by requiring ready identifiability may be seen to reach a vanishing point in relevancy.

Building upon the analogy provided by naval warfare, the Hague Rules of Aerial Warfare of 1923 authorized the conversion of private into public military aircraft "within the jurisdiction" of the flag state, but not on the high seas.[123] It is not easy to see how conversion could be effected on the high seas, unless, perhaps, it be done on an aircraft carrier which, however, would presumably be "within the jurisdiction" of the flag state. In most cases, conversion would probably mean incorporation into the military air transport and reconnaissance systems, since present-day fighter or bomber craft are highly specialized machines.[124] For this reason, it may be added, the arming of private aircraft, which the Hague Air Rules provided against, is not likely to become an important problem.

122. Id. at 18.

123. Art. 9.

124. See Spaight, *Air Power and War Rights* 395–6 (3rd ed., 1947).

Claims With Respect to Permissible Areas of Operations

We consider next certain claims concerning the delineation of the field within which the opposing belligerents may legitimately conduct their hostile operations. The principal problem here involved may be most generally framed in terms of, on the one hand, claims of belligerents to carry on their war effort and mutual applications of violence wherever it may become militarily necessary to do so, and, on the other hand, demands of nonparticipating states that belligerents refrain from engaging in such activities and applications in neutral territory, waters, and airspace. A second problem is that of the establishment of zones of immunity within areas of operation determined to be permissible under the first problem.

"Region of War" and "Theater of War"

With respect to the first problem, the geographical limits of the permissible areas of operation in any given conflict have historically been set by the presence and number of neutral states. In general, belligerent activities may be legitimately conducted anywhere in the globe save in the territory, waters, and airspace of nonparticipant states and in areas specially neutralized by international convention. As access to outer space is secured and expanded, a new, extraterrestrial dimension may be added to areas of belligerent operations. In thus excluding neutral countries from the permissible area of operations, customary laws give specific expression to the general humanity principle in terms of a policy of limiting the destruction of values by limiting the locale of violence. The requirements of the competing principle of military necessity are accommodated by permitting, under specialized circumstances, at least temporary conversion of neutral territory (including waters and airspace) into a permissible area of operations. As indicated in the previous chapter,[125] where a nonparticipant is unable or unwilling to prevent one belligerent from carrying on hostile activities within neutral territory, or from utilizing such territory as a "base of operations," the opposing belligerent, seriously disadvantaged by neutral failure or weakness, becomes authorized to enter neutral territory and there to take the necessary measures to counter and stop the hostile activities.

125. Supra, p. 406.

For indicating preferences about the extent of permissible areas of operation, it is useful to recall the distinction drawn by Professor Oppenheim between the "region of war" and the "theater of war."[126] "Region of war" was defined by Professor Oppenheim to refer to those portions of the globe where belligerents may "prepare for and execute" hostile acts. The particular part of such "region of war" where, at any specified time, violence is actually being exercised, was designated as a "theater of war." The further restriction of areas where actual military violence would be permissible would seem no more revolutionary than any other extrapolation of the policy principle of minimum destruction of values. Development in this direction will probably require the establishment of special protective zones by neutrals along the lines set by the Declaration of Panama of 1939.[127] The prospects of effective delimitation will, of course, in realistic expectation, be affected by the number and strength of the nonparticipants relative to the belligerents.

A contrasting recommendation as to the "region of war" is required by the policy, put forward in the chapter on neutrality, of securing the widest possible assumption of responsibility for the maintenance of minimum order.[128] For this policy envisages the enlargement of the area from which the needed manpower and other bases of power may be drawn, assembled, organized, and deployed for the restoration and implementation of minimum public order.

ZONES OF IMMUNITY WITHIN PERMISSIBLE AREAS OF OPERATION

The *ad hoc* creation of limited zones or enclaves of immunity within areas where the conduct of operations would otherwise be permissible throughout, is envisaged in the 1949 Geneva Conventions on the Protection of War Victims. The Wounded and Sick Convention and the Civilians Convention provide for the optional establishment, before or after the outbreak of hostilities, of hospital and safety zones and localities by the belligerents within their respective territories, as well as in territory belligerently occupied by one or the other party.[129] The Conventions further contemplate the conclu-

126. 2 Oppenheim-Lauterpacht 237.

127. Supra, p. 470.

128. Supra, p. 409 ff.

129. Art. 23, Wounded and Sick Convention; Art. 14, Civilians Convention.

sion of special agreements between the contending belligerents, upon the outbreak or during the course of hostilities, providing for the mutual recognition of the zones and localities they may have created. To facilitate the conclusion of such *ad hoc* interbelligerent agreements, the Conventions have each annexed draft model agreements.

The categories of persons sought to be benefited by this procedure are the wounded and sick permissible combatants, aged civilian persons, children under fifteen years of age, expectant mothers, and mothers of children under seven.[130] The hospital and safety zones and localities where these protected persons are to be brought must be marked clearly with the Red Cross emblem and are not under any circumstances to be made targets of attack by the opposing belligerent.[131] The zones of immunity are thus most obviously humanitarian in their motivation. At the same time, however, the military interests of the opposing belligerent are accommodated by prescribing compliance with requirements designed to render such zones completely innocuous and hence militarily worthless targets. Thus, no person residing in such zone may perform, either within or without the zone, any work directly connected with military operations or the production of war material.[132] The zones may comprise only a small portion of the territory of belligerents, and must be thinly populated in relation to the possibilities of accommodation. They must be free from all "military objectives" including industrial and administrative establishments. For their own protection, the zones must be "far removed" from such objectives and must not be situated in areas which "may become important for the conduct of the war." [133] Moreover, the communications and transport lines within

---

The idea of safety zones is not new. See e.g. the "Draft Convention for the Protection of Civilian Populations Against New Engines of War," Arts. 10–21, prepared by the International Law Commission in 1938; *Report of the International Law Association, Fortieth Conference, Amsterdam* 41 et seq. (1938).

130. Art. 23, Wounded and Sick Convention; Art. 14, Civilians Convention.

131. Art. 11, Draft Agreement relating to Hospital Zones and Localities, Annex I to the Wounded and Sick Convention. An identical draft agreement is annexed to the Civilians Convention.

132. Art. 2, Draft Agreements.

133. Art. 4, id. The Draft Convention on Hospital Localities and Zones prepared by the International Red Cross in 1938 specified a surrounding zone of 5 kilometers depth, free from all military units and establishments connected with national defense; Commission of Government Experts, supra note 60 at Vol. I,

the zone may not be used by military personnel or material, even though it be only in transit. Finally, the zones may in no case be defended by military means.[134] The verification and supervision of the observance of these conditions are to be entrusted to Special Commissions consisting of representatives of both sides.[135]

The Civilians Convention further provides that any party to a conflict may propose to its opponent the establishment of "neutralized zones" in regions where active combat is actually taking place. These zones are intended for the protection of certain members of the population of *both* belligerents without distinction: the wounded and sick combatants or noncombatants; and civilians who do not participate in hostilities nor perform any work "of a military character." The geographic location, administration, supervision, and duration of neutralization of the zones are to be fixed by written agreement of the belligerents.[136]

There are some reported instances of successful establishment of immunity zones in recent wars. Japan, for example, in 1937 and 1938, agreed to the setting up of sanctuary areas or refugee zones, where civilians would be spared from bombardment, in Shanghai, Hankow, and other densely populated Chinese cities. The zones were supervised by international committees composed of representatives of the major foreign nationality groups residing in those cities. Japan, it was reported, carefully respected the sanctuary areas to the benefit of many hundreds of thousands of Chinese civilians.[137] During the Second World War, proposals made by the International Committee of the Red Cross to both belligerent sides for the creation of comparable safety localities met with much less success.[138]

---

p. 84. Five kilometers is of course inadequate in nuclear and thermonuclear warfare.

134. Art. 5, Draft Agreements.

135. Arts. 7–10, id.

136. Art. 15, Civilians Convention. See also Art. 16, International Committee of the Red Cross, *Draft Rules for the Limitation of the Dangers Incurred by the Civilian Population in Time of War* (Geneva, 1956) which provides for the establishment and demilitarization of "open towns."

137. See Spaight, supra note 124 at 256–7.

138. Commission of Government Experts, supra note 60 at Vol. III, p. 43: "Upon the outbreak of hostilities, the International Committee approached the belligerent powers on Sept. 9, Sept. 13, and Oct. 21, 1939 recommending the creation of Safety Localities and Zones for the protection of certain categories

The establishment of zones of immunity would seem so eminently humane and mutually advantageous in its conservation of values and economizing of force that it might be a matter for wonder why belligerents have not more generally resorted to it. As indicated above, the primary purpose of such zones is the shielding of protected persons from bombardment by land or other forces. It may not be inappropriate to suggest that the difficulties involved in the securing of agreement to such zones are difficulties relating to civilian morale as a legitimate object of attack.[139] The willingness or unwillingness of different belligerents to recognize immunity zones may be in measure a function of differing expectations about the practicability and the military value of shattering civilian morale by bombardment. It might, finally, be added that high-yield, multimegaton fission and fusion weapons may make effective protection through immunity zones quite problematical.

Claims With Respect to Permissible Objects of Attack

Put in broadest terms, the central policy problem in the legal regulation of combat situations is that of determining the level or degree of permissible destruction in differing situations. Assuming a given number of combatants (or units of combat) functioning in a given area of operations, the level of destruction which is lawfully exercisable may be conceptualized as a resultant of two interrelated kinds of variables—the number and nature of the objects of attack, and the character of the instruments of attack. We turn first to objects of attack.

The principal primary claim each belligerent makes in this respect is to select certain objects as targets for destruction or capture. The common contraposed assertion is that the targets selected by the op-

---

of the civilian population. The German Government stated their readiness, subject to reciprocity, to examine the creation of such zones, but their attitude, which was brought to the notice of other governments, met with no response. On March 14, 1944, in view of the development of aerial warfare, with its daily toll of defenceless children, old people and women, the International Committee made a final appeal to Governments to afford immunity in Safety Zones to defenceless non-combatants who could in no wise contribute to any warlike effort. The reception of this appeal by the Governments concerned, although favorable in principle, precluded any attempt at securing a positive result."

139. Infra, p. 652 ff.

posing belligerent are legally immune in greater or lesser degree from destructive violence or capture. The underlying principles which seek to regulate target selection are, once again, the principle of military necessity and of minimum destruction of values. Military necessity finds expression in the specific prescriptions that, most generally characterized, permit the exercise of violence against objects constituting substantial bases of effective enemy power and utilized in prosecuting or resisting the political demands at stake in the conflict. The countervailing humanity principle is observable in the limitations that operate to prohibit both the projection of violence against objects which are not substantial elements of enemy power, and the continuation of violence against objects already rendered ineffective, through disablement or capture, as enemy power bases. The familiar threefold categorization of people, resources, and institutions is employed below for convenience in presentation.

ENEMY PERSONS AS OBJECTS OF ATTACK

The population of a belligerent state, taken collectively, composes one of the foundations of its power. Different segments of the population, however, bear varying relationships to state power; different segments may exhibit a wide variation in the degree to which they comprise effective elements or bases of belligerent power. Thus, while the English and American publicists who rejected the Rousseau-Portalis conception of war insist that each national of a belligerent is the enemy of every national of the opposing belligerent,[140] an application of violence reasonable as against one class of enemy persons may be wholly inappropriate as against another class of enemy persons. In high-level generalization, enemy persons are permissible objects of attack to the extent and so long as they form substantial and effective bases of enemy power.

The persons who form the chief and indispensable base of effective enemy power are the members of the opposing belligerent's public armed forces. The combatant members of such forces are, of course, permissible targets of attack. The noncombatant personnel, to the extent that they refrain from participation in actual fighting, are not liable to direct assault as distinguished from the incidental

140. See e.g., 2 Oppenheim-Lauterpacht 205; 2 Westlake, *International Law* 32 et seq. (1907); Hall, *International Law* 88–9 (8th ed., Pearce Higgins, 1924); Fenwick, *International Law* 548 (3rd ed., 1948).

consequences of military operations. The purpose of attack is achieved by killing or wounding members of the armed forces, or by capturing them. Where the unit of combat is an armed and manned machine, the objective of attack is gained primarily by destroying or disabling the machine. Thus, in naval warfare, enemy warships, including perhaps naval auxiliaries, may be sunk on sight.[141] In air warfare, enemy military aircraft, whether fighters, bombers, or transports, may be destroyed from the ground or sea or shot down from the sky. But once the stage of attack or assault has passed and its purpose has been realized, the further exercise of violence against the defeated members of the enemy forces becomes unnecessary. The death or captivity of such members renders their continued effective military use by the enemy belligerent impossible.[142]

It is here that the law about permissible targets of attack assumes a modest function of proscribing violence already unnecessary. In this phase, a mass of detailed conventional prescriptions on the treatment of prisoners of war and the care of the wounded and sick become operative. With the exposition and analysis of these specifics, however, we are not here concerned. It suffices for immediate purposes to dwell on the general point that members of the enemy armed forces who have come under the power of a belligerent no longer constitute permissible objects of violence, such that subsequent violence directed against them is internationally illegal and criminal. The Hague Regulations declare that:

> In addition to the prohibitions provided by special Conventions, it is especially forbidden—
>
> (c) To kill or wound an enemy who, having laid down his arms, or no longer having means of defence, has surrendered at discretion.
>
> (d) To declare that no quarter will be given.[143]

141. E.g., Smith, *The Law and Custom of the Sea* 104 (3rd ed., 1959); 2 Oppenheim-Lauterpacht 465–6.

142. Cf. 2 Wheaton *International Law* 165 (7th ed., Keith, 1944): "On any theory of war . . . , neither person nor property should be injured or damaged, if the legitimate purpose of the belligerent is not thereby clearly promoted, and the overcoming of his enemy not facilitated. . . . The purpose of a belligerent is obviously attained if he puts *hors de combat* the adversary; the infliction of unnecessary suffering is not indispensable to achieve this object."

143. Art. 23, Hague Regulations.

In the *Abbaye Ardenne* case,[144] a military tribunal condemned the commander of an S.S. (*Schutzstaffeln der NSDAP*) regiment to death for having incited and counseled his men to deny quarter to Allied troops. Denial of quarter consisted in refusal to take prisoners, that is, to discontinue violence after the enemy combatants had become unable or unwilling to resist further and to that extent had come under the power of the attacking forces. *The Trial of Von Ruchtechell*[145] affords illustration of denial of quarter in maritime warfare. The accused, who was captain of a German surface raider, was charged with having prolonged his attack after the enemy had indicated surrender. After five minutes of heavy fire from the raider, the target, a British merchantman, stopped its engines, acknowledged the raider's signal not to use its radio, and hoisted an answering pennant. The raider nevertheless continued firing for fifteen minutes, injuring the British crew trying to abandon ship. In another specification of the same charge of denying quarter, the target merchant ship did not stop upon being attacked but began to sink while still moving. Its captain signaled with a torch that he was abandoning ship. The raider disregarded these signals and, again, continued its firing. The accused was held guilty on the first but not on the second count, apparently because the second victim had not given an unequivocal manifestation of surrender or desire for quarter.

It may be observed that in case of close and sustained combat in land war, where the signal of surrender is postponed and resistance continued to the very last moment, quarter may in practice be difficult to grant.[146] Unlike a warship, an attacking body of troops is not subject to instantaneous control. A similar difficulty may be presented where some members of an enemy land force continue to fire despite the giving of a surrender signal by their commander.[147]

144. 4 *War Crimes Reports* 97 (1945). The International Military Tribunal considered as a war crime the act of Jodl in signing an order which stated that Hitler would not accept an offer of surrender of Leningrad or Moscow, insisting on the contrary that they be completely destroyed. *Nazi Conspiracy and Aggression: Opinion and Judgment* 151.

145. 9 *War Crimes Reports* 82. In this case, the Prosecutor explicitly pointed out to the court that the question of legality of the attack without warning was not involved.

146. See Spaight, *War Rights on Land* 91 (1911); JAG's School, *Law of Land Warfare* 32–3 (1943).

147. See 2 Oppenheim-Lauterpacht 339 and note 3.

Determination of the particular time when further violence becomes nonpermissible is thus a matter of rough practical judgment. But once the rushing momentum of attack has subsided, difficulties of determination disappear.

The judgment of the International Military Tribunal at Nuremberg[148] and numerous decisions of other war crimes tribunals[149] leave no possible doubt that the killing of prisoners of war, without lawful cause, is punishable as a war crime. The "lawful cause" may only be either an offense committed during captivity, or a war crime perpetrated prior to the prisoner's capture; in either case, the prisoner is entitled to a fair judicial trial.[150] Lesser violence, like the physical ill-treatment and torture of prisoners of war, similarly constitute war crimes.[151] Acts of ill-treatment that have been held to be criminally punishable include the denial to prisoners of the minimum conditions conducive to life and health,[152] the exposure to acts of violence, insults, and public curiosity of the civil popula-

148. *Nazi Conspiracy and Aggression: Opinion and Judgment* 57 et seq. (1947).

149. E.g., "Trial of Masuda" ("The Jaluit Atoll Case"), 1 *War Crimes Reports* 71 (1945); Trial of Amberger," 1 *id.* 81 (1946); "Trial of Heyer" ("The Essen Lynching Case"), 1 id. 88 (1945); "Trial of Thiele and Steinert," 3 id. 56 (1945); "Trial of Bury and Hafner," 3 id. 62 (1945); "Trial of Rauer," 4 id. 113 (1946); "Trial of Schosser," 3 id. 65 (1945).

150. The procedural safeguards prescribed in trials for offenses against the captor's security regulations, committed during captivity, are found in Part II, Sec. VI, Ch. III (Arts. 82–108) of the Geneva Prisoners of War Convention of 1949.

As to trials of prisoners of war for war crimes committed prior to capture, see e.g., "Trial of Hisakasu," 5 *War Crimes Reports* 66 at 70 et seq. (1946); Trial of Rauter," 14 id. 89 at 114 et seq. (1949); and 15 id. 99–100.

In "The Trial of Baba Masao," 11 *War Crimes Reports* 56 (1947), Allied prisoners of war were forcibly evacuated from Sandakan, Borneo to Ranau in the interior. The forced march resulted in the death of practically all the prisoners, the rest being shot upon reaching Ranau. The defense pleaded that the evacuation was an operational necessity as the original camp was near the seashore and an allied landing was anticipated. Allied troops did in fact land there, two months after the evacuation. The court found the accused guilty. In "The Trial of Thiele and Steinert," 3 id. 56 (1945), the accused, who were part of a unit closely surrounded by U.S. troops, killed an American prisoner of war. The tribunal rejected their plea of military necessity.

151. See e.g. "Trial of Weis" ("The Dachau Concentration Camp Trial,") 11 id. 5 (1945); "Trial of Chuichi," 11 id. 62 (1946).

152. "Trial of Heering," 11 id. 79 (1946).

tion,[153] the use of prisoners as shields for advancing troops,[154] and their subjection to cruel and inhuman medical experiments.[155]

Violence directed against the bodies of enemy dead is even more clearly useless and militarily unnecessary. Conventional prescriptions require belligerents to collect the dead and to provide honorable burial or cremation.[156] It may be noted in this connection that some cases of mutilation of prisoners' bodies and of cannibalism came up before war crimes tribunals after World War II. In the *Schmid* case,[157] for instance, the accused had severed the head of a dead American airman, boiled the head to remove skin and flesh, bleached the skull, and kept it on his desk. The court rejected his plea that he had used the skull for instructional purposes. In the cases involving cannibalism by Japanese troops it does not appear that a plea of necessity to avoid death by starvation was ever raised. In each case a conviction was handed down by the courts.[158]

The exercise of violence against defeated members of enemy forces who survive attack and combat but who are not reduced to effective captivity has occasionally raised problems of some complexity. Special conventions require belligerents to search for and collect the wounded and sick in land war,[159] and the wounded, sick, and shipwrecked in naval war,[160] to ensure their protection and adequate care. In maritime warfare, however, where the duty to make reasonable efforts to rescue survivors is obviously especially urgent, compliance with this duty may paradoxically become particularly difficult. The characteristics of the attacking war vessel and the tactical operational situation at or immediately after the attack may, for instance, present obstacles to the collection of survivors (who would thereby become prisoners of war) which are not necessarily unreal. Thus, submarines during the last world wars were small, cramped, and slow crafts which, when surfaced, presented choice targets for air or

153. "Trial of Maelzer," 11 id. 53 (1946).

154. "Trial of Von Leeb," 12 id. 1 at 104–5 (1948); "Trial of Student," 4 id. 118 (1946).

155. *Nazi Conspiracy and Aggression, Opinion and Judgment* 61 (1947).

156. Art. 17, Wounded and Sick Convention; Art. 20, Wounded, Sick and Shipwrecked Convention.

157. 13 *War Crimes Reports* 151 (1947).

158. See 13 id. at 152.

159. Art. 15, Wounded and Sick Convention.

160. Art. 18, Wounded, Sick and Shipwrecked Convention.

sea action and which, consequently, were ill adapted to the rescuing of survivors of submarine attacks. The Second World War, however, saw the assertion of what, in effect, were belligerent claims not only to desist from efforts at rescue but also to treat the survivors of sunken ships who could not be taken prisoners by the attacking submarine as continuing to be permissible objects of violence. The underlying assumption appeared to be that survivors rescued by the enemy belligerent will later rejoin the enemy naval forces or merchant marine and once again constitute bases of enemy power.

In the so-called "Laconia Order," the German U-Boat Command ordered that, among other things,

> (1) No attempt of any kind must be made at rescuing members of ships sunk, and this includes picking up persons in the water and putting them in life boats, righting capsized life boats, and handing over food and water. These are absolutely forbidden. Rescue measures contradict the most primitive demands of warfare that crews and ships should be destroyed.[161]

The International Military Tribunal at Nuremberg found, in its judgment with respect to Admiral Doenitz, that the "Laconia Order" was "ambiguous," and it was unable to hold that Doenitz had deliberately ordered the affirmative killing, as distinguished from the mere abandonment, of survivors.[162] In the subsequent *Moehle* case,[163] however, the court held the accused guilty of a war crime for transmitting the same Order to subordinate U-boat commanders. The court felt, it appears, that the "ambiguity" was removed when the accused, in passing on the Order, commented upon it and gave examples which must necessarily have led the subordinate commanders to believe that the policy of the Naval High Command required the killing of surviving crew members. Finally, in the famous *Peleus* Trial,[164] the Tribunal condemned the crew members of a German submarine as guilty of a war crime for machine-gunning

161. 5 *Trial of the Major War Criminals before the International Military Tribunal, Proceedings 9 Jan.–21 Jan. 1946,* p. 238 (1947).

162. *Nazi Conspiracy and Aggression, Opinion and Judgment* 140 (1947).

163. 9 *War Crimes Reports* 75 (1946).

164. 1 id. 1 (1945); see also *The Peleus Trial* (Cameron, ed., 1948). And see *"The Llandovery Castle,* Germany, Reichsgericht," *Annual Digest 1923–1924,* Case No. 235.

and hurling grenades at the survivors of an Allied merchantman the submarine had sunk.

A closely comparable situation has been commonplace in aerial warfare: airmen bailing out from disabled craft. The last world war afforded many instances of German and Japanese aircraft, and at times ground forces, firing upon Allied pilots in the process of parachute descent. In the case of airmen falling upon territory held by the opposing belligerent, to attack them in the course of descent would appear clearly unnecessary violence. The appropriate assumption would be that the airmen would be captured by the ground troops at any event.[165] The lawfulness of attack from the air upon airmen falling upon their *home* territory has been debated by the commentators and it is difficult to discover any clear consensus in the practice of the last world war.[166] Unless missiles completely replace manned aircraft in the future, the possibility cannot, perhaps, be ruled out that the military value of trained pilots, who represent a much larger belligerent investment of skills, money, time, and energy than the ordinary infantryman, may give rise to a custom permit-

165. Spaight, *Air Power and War Rights* 155–64 (3rd ed. 1947).

166. The unratified Hague Air Rules of 1923, in Art. 20, do not make any distinction: "When an aircraft has been disabled the occupants, when endeavoring to escape by means of a parachute, must not be attacked in the course of their descent." See also 2 Oppenheim-Lauterpacht 521. Spaight, supra note 165 at 135, however, says that it is "perfectly legitimate" for an airman to attack an opponent who has crashed in the latter's own territory, though the latter may hold up or wave his hands. If Spaight's view be accepted, it is not easy to distinguish this case from attack while the opponent is descending by parachute on his own territory. Stone, *Legal Controls* 615, suggests that "the practice of the Second [World War] gave a general license to shoot an airman who baled out of a disabled machine." He then laments as "callousness towards air crews as opposed to soldiers and sailors as well as civilians" this "general license" to refuse quarter. It is not clear whether Professor Stone meant to suggest that a permissive rule has emerged. Spaight, whose account of belligerent practice he cited, himself makes no such suggestion.

Dept. of the Army, *The Law of Land Warfare* par. 30 (FM 27–10, July 1956) provides: "The law of war does not prohibit firing upon paratroops or other persons who are or appear to be bound upon hostile missions while such persons are descending by parachute. Persons other than those mentioned in the preceding sentence who are descending by parachute from disabled aircraft may not be fired upon." Cf. *British Manual of Military Law,* Part III, par. 119 n.b. (1958). These provisions appear to refer to ground forces firing upon enemy airmen falling upon hostile territory.

ting attack in case of descent upon their own territory. On the other hand, there may be, as Dr. Spaight observed,[167] a military advantage to be derived from not discouraging enemy airmen from readily taking to their parachutes, a recourse presumably preferable to bitter combat to the end.

We turn to enemy persons in enemy territory who are not members of the armed forces of the enemy belligerent. The distinction between enemy combatant and noncombatant (or civilian) persons has been designated as "the vital principle of the modern law of war" [168] and the "foundation and the vital source of those limitations on the destruction of life and property with which our boasted civilization is synonymous." [169] Appraisal of this distinction has not, it may be noted, been unmixed. It has, for example, been said that the separation of armies and peaceful inhabitants into two distinct classes was "perhaps the greatest triumph of International Law." [170] The same separation has, however, in sharp contrast, been denounced as "in itself, illusory and immoral," upon the ground that to conceive of war "as affecting only certain elements of the population" was "an incentive to war." [171] Whichever view is taken, it bears some emphasis that the time-honored combatant-civilian dichotomy, and the immunity from direct attack it imported for civilians, rested upon certain premises and historical conditions which may no longer obtain in their pristine vigor. The first assumption of civilian immunity was civilian innocuousness.[172] Civilians were not, in the postulations of traditional law, permissible objects of attack because, and to the extent that, they were not significant participants in the belligerent effort. The principle of civilian immunity reflected,

167. Supra, note 165 at 163.

168. Moore, *International Law and Some Current Illusions* viii (1924).

169. Id., 6.

170. Spaight, *War Rights on Land,* 37 (1911).

171. 2 Wheaton, *International Law* 171 (7th ed., Keith, 1944).

172. Supra, p. 543. In *Damson v. Germany, Annual Digest 1925–1926,* Case No. 330, at 437, Parker, Umpire of the U.S.–Germany Mixed Claims Commissions, said: "If the activities of such nationals were at the time aimed at the direct furtherance of a military operation against Germany or her allies, then, although they may not be nominally enrolled in the military organization of that State so as to have a military status for all purposes affecting their domestic relation between them and their government, they cannot be held to have been 'civilians' or a part of the 'civilian population' of their respective nations within the meaning of the [reparations provisions of the] treaty [of Versailles]."

secondly, the limitations of the military technology available during the period of development of our inherited laws of warfare. As will be indicated at somewhat greater length below,[173] civilians behind the line of battle or beyond the immediate zone of combat were said to be legally immune from direct attack because, in point of fact, there were no military means for directly reaching them. In contexts where civilians could be reached even by indirect ways, as by impoverishment through capture of their property at sea, the protection of the civilian immunity principle tended to be relaxed.

Appraisal of the operable scope of the principle of civilian immunity in modern combat situations requires appraisal of the extent to which these assumptions and conditions have persisted. With respect to the first assumption, it is quite commonplace to note that "innocuous" and "innocent" have become increasingly unreal when applied to the general population of belligerents engaged in major conflicts.[174] It may be, as Judge Moore suggested,[175] that some part of the civil population had always, in centuries past, supplied the professional combatants by growing their food and forging their weapons, and that to such extent had commonly been participants and not quite "innocent." Civilian participation in modern major wars has, however, been so much greater in scope and depth as to be qualitatively different. Conflicts, for example, of the World War I and II type were characterized by the comprehensive mobilization, direction, and utilization of the energies of the civil population in the production of the instruments and material of war.[176] The iden-

173. Infra, p. 606–7.

174. The learned literature reflects wide recognition that the general population has tended to lose its innocence in war. See 2 Oppenheim-Lauterpacht 207–8; Smith, *The Crisis in the Law of Nations* 75–7 (1947); Nurick, "The Distinction Between Combatant and Noncombatant in the Law of War," 39 *A.J.I.L.* 680–2 (1945); Friedmann, "International Law and the Present War," 26 *Tr. Grotius Soc.* 223 (1940); Schwarzenberger, *A Manual of International Law* 82 (2nd ed., 1950).

175. Supra, note 168 at 8–9; cf. Baty, *The Canons of International Law* 464–5 (1930).

176. Of the voluminous literature on the extent to which the substance, human and material, of a nation is organized and committed in wars of such type, see, e.g.: U. S. Civilian Production Administration, *Industrial Mobilization for War,* Vol. I: *Program and Administration* (Washington, D.C., 1947); Hancock and Gowing, *British War Economy* (1949); Klein, *Germany's Economic Preparations for War* (1959). 1 Wright, *A Study of War* 306–7 (1942); Lederer, "War

tifications and demands of the civilian masses were likewise organized, harnessed, and managed for the support of the war effort.[177] In other words, the civil population, or a considerable proportion of it, in fact constituted an indispensable base of effective belligerent power. With respect to the second condition, it only needs to be noted at this stage that the last two global wars saw the development of instruments for delivering violence straight to any point in enemy territory. Air power made it possible, for the first time in history, for a belligerent to reach and attack the industrial and economic bases of its enemy's war effort without need of first capturing and occupying the territory on which such bases were located. The potentialities aircraft seemed to offer were quickly recognized and, indeed, overstated in doctrines of strategic air power that envisaged the visitation of maximum damage in the shortest possible time upon industrial centers which, of course, were population centers as well. Thus, belligerents not only regarded themselves as possessed of a cogent reason for striking at the general population of the enemy but were also equipped with the means of doing so. In net result, the enemy population was defined as a militarily appropriate target of attack.[178]

Economics," in *War in Our Time* 206 (Speier and Kähler, eds., 1939); Burnham, *Total War: The Economic Theory of a War Economy* (1943); "Organizing for Total War," 220 *Annals* (1942).

177. The interdependence between the armed services and the supporting civilian production forces of belligerents engaged in such conflicts was stressed by the prophets of "total war." Thus Ludendorff, *The Nation at War* 25 (Rappaport, trans., 1936) describing the character of "totalitarian war," wrote: "The armed forces are rooted in the nation, are a constituent part of it, and in totalitarian war the strength of these forces will be in accordance with the physical, economic, and psychical strength of the people"; (at 16): "The nature of a totalitarian war postulates that it can be waged only when the existence of the entire nation is actually being threatened, and the latter is really determined to wage such a war." Cf. Speier, *Social Order and the Risks of War* 253 (1952).

This phenomenon in "total war" of course runs counter to the principle set forth in the preamble of the Declaration of St. Petersburg of 1868 that "the only legitimate object which states should set before themselves during war is to weaken the *military forces* of the enemy." Emphasis supplied.

178. See Falls, *A Hundred Years of War* 392, 394 (1953); Aron, *The Century of Total War* 19, 41 (1954). The question of general immunity for the civil population (as distinguished from the armed forces) in the enemy belligerent's territory is, in a functional sense, primarily a question of the lawfulness of

In possible future major wars where nuclear weapons are committed at the outset, it has been suggested, as we noted in the previous chapter,[179] that there may be little opportunity and occasion for converting industrial potential into combat power in being. The civil population, in other words, may in such a conflict not represent bases of belligerent power to the same extent and in the same sense as in World War II. Unfortunately, the very destructiveness of strategic nuclear bombardment which appears to make the drastic compression of time possible at the same time renders this development poor comfort. As "hard cover" or strategic concealment of retaliatory forces is gradually achieved, and as both missile and nuclear "plenty" is attained, whole communities may become increasingly likely to be targets should deterrence break down and hostilities actually erupt between the polar powers. It is perhaps in "limited wars," where belligerents deliberately refrain from exercising their strategic nuclear capabilities, that some possibilities remain of a reinvigoration of the civilian immunity principle. For it is most difficult to conceive of a conflict between nuclear powers remaining "limited" once the economy and general population of the opponent are directly attacked. Similar possibilities may remain in conflicts between belligerents without nuclear capabilities.

Whatever the vicissitudes to which the traditional principle of civilian immunity may in modern wars be subjected in contexts involving enemy persons in enemy territory, one point bears continued stress. This point is that, when a belligerent has succeeded in depriving the enemy of the use of its civil population as a base of power by the military occupation of its territory, continued violence against such population becomes unmistakably unlawful. It was indeed historically in this context that the conception of civilian immunity from warlike violence developed, powerfully aided, we noted, by the primitive, "two-dimensional," nature of the war technology of earlier centuries.[180] It is in this context that the conception most

---

strategic target area bombing, terror bombardment, and of uses of mass destruction weapons. See supra, p. 652, where some discussion of these instrumentalities and modes of attack is offered.

179. Supra, p. 392.

180. Smith, supra note 174 at 70: "Since all war was two-dimensional, it followed that an army normally did not come into contact with the enemy civil population until after victory had been achieved and a town or other place

clearly retains continued validity. We have in mind here, of course, not the forcible measures that may reasonably be necessary for the policing of occupied territory. We principally refer, rather, to that kind of unspeakable violence which National Socialist Germany in the last world war inflicted upon occupied regions in the name of anti-Semitic, racial and *lebensraum* policies. The ruthless and methodical extermination of peoples already rendered innocuous by control through belligerent occupation presents none of the legal and moral ambiguities that strategic bombardment of cities containing "military objectives"—however broadly conceived—entailed.

The methods of extermination or "biological war" used by Nazi Germany were numerous and varied. Two achieved special prominence by the very magnitude of the horror they inflicted: the *Einsatzgruppen* and the concentration camps. The *Einsatzgruppen* were special S.S. (*Schutzstaffeln Nationalsozialistischen Deutschen Arbeiterpartei*) units that accompanied the German Army during the invasion and occupation of Soviet Russia, with the general mission of ensuring "political security" in the occupied areas. As conceived and executed, this mission involved the immediate slaughter of all Jews and certain other specified categories including gypsies and Communist Party officials. In Russia alone, approximately one million Jews and others were killed by the *Einsatzgruppen*.[181] The concentration camps accounted for several other millions; Auschwitz in Poland alone disposed of two and a half million by means of gas chambers.[182] The extent of the deliberate destruction of human life was, in the words of the tribunal in the *Trial of Ohlendorff*,

---

had been occupied. When the authors prohibit, as they all do, the massacre of noncombatants, this is what they mean, that it is unlawful to kill the peaceful inhabitants of an occupied place after the place has been captured." See also Lawrence, *The Principles of International Law* 371–2 (7th ed., Winfield, 1928).

181. "Trial of Ohlendorf" ("The *Einsatzgruppen* Case"), 4 *Trials of War Criminals Before the Nuernberg Military Tribunals Under Control Council Law No. 10* (hereafter cited as *Trials of War Criminals*) 3 at 427 et seq. (1947). On the criminality of the German racial policies, see also "Trial of Greifelt" ("The RuSHA Case"), 4 and 5 *Trials of War Criminals* (1948); and "Trial of Pohl," 5 *Trials of War Criminals* 195 (1947).

182. See "Trial of Kramer" ("The Belsen Trial") 2 *War Crimes Reports* 3 (1945); also *The Belsen Trial* (Phillips, ed., 1949); "Trial of Weis" ("The Dachau Concentration Camp Trial") 11 id. 5 (1945).

> so beyond the experience of normal man and the range of man-made phenomena that only the most complete judicial inquiry, and the most exhaustive trial, could verify and confirm them. Although the principal accusation is murder, and unhappily, man has been killing man ever since the days of Cain, the charge of purposeful homicide in this case reaches such fantastic proportions and surpasses such credible limits that believability must be bolstered with assurance a hundred times repeated.[183]

The defense counsel asserted in *Ohlendorff* that the defendants had acted in "presumed self-defense on behalf of a third party" and under conditions of "presumed necessity" for such acts, that is, that they had *assumed* that the existence of Germany was threatened by the "Jewish problem" and by Bolshevism and that the mass killings were "necessary" to solve the two problems.[184] The tribunal emphatically rejected that assertion, declaring that the accused's acts could not "by the widest stretch of the imagination" be justified as self-defense on behalf of Germany.

It may be observed that the treatment administered to the "racially inferior" inhabitants of occupied territories was in some instances not completely without claimed relation to military interests. Experiments at the Dachau concentration camp, for instance, were carried out for the benefit of the *Luftwaffe,* in order to investigate the limits of human endurance at high altitudes, and to determine the most effective treatment of flyers who had been severely frozen. Other experiments, for the benefit of the *Wehrmacht,* were made to determine the effectiveness of sulfanilamide, to study bone, muscle, and nerve regeneration and bone transplantation, to find an effective cure for mustard gas wounds and phosphorous burns, and to test the effects of certain poisoned weapons. The tribunal in the *Medical* case [185] found that these experiments, which resulted in death and terrible agony for thousands, were "conducted as an integral part of the total war effort." Among the defenses there raised was a plea of "national emergency," based upon the plight of the German

183. IV *Trials of War Criminals* 411–12 (1947).

184. Id., at 462–4.

185. "Trial of Brandt" 2 *Trials of War Criminals* 181 (1947); see also "Trial of Milch," 2 id. at 773 et seq., 7 *War Crimes Reports* 27 at 35–7 (1947).

forces in the East where the Russian winter allegedly aggravated the danger of wound infection, threatened the survival of the wounded, and sapped the fighting strength of the troops.[186] The tribunal in effect rejected this plea in laying down as "absolutely essential" the completely voluntary consent of the human subject. Experimentation without that consent, and certain other requisites necessary to satisfy "moral, ethical and legal concepts," was declared a war crime.[187] The plea of necessity was not taken seriously by the court. Even if there had been a showing that the nationals of the offending belligerent, or animals, would not have made equally good subjects of experiment, there is little doubt that the decision would have been the same.[188]

Thus, in quick recapitulation, the rules of warfare on people as objects of attack prohibit destruction which has become superfluous through attainment of the purposes of attack. In contexts of attack, that is, the actual violent contact between opposing forces, military requirements are inevitably heavily favored. It is largely after control over enemy troops or enemy territory has more or less crystallized in the belligerent attacker that the minimizing of value destruction acquires preponderance of weight. That the prescriptions about instruments and methods of attack which have unmistakably survived into the present are few and highly general, while those about the treatment of prisoners of war, the wounded and sick and ship-

186. See extracts from the final plea for defendant Gebhart, 2 *Trials of War Criminals* at 5 et seq. (1947).

187. The requisites for permissible medical experiments are set forth in 2 *Trials of War Criminals* 181–2, and in 7 *War Crimes Reports* 49–50. One argument presented by the defense was that some of the experimental subjects had been offenders sentenced to death, and that a state had power, "in the broad interest of alleviating human suffering," to provide for experiments to be carried out on such prisoners without their consent. The tribunal held that "Whatever may be the right of a state with reference to its own citizens, it is certain that such legislation may not be extended so as to permit the practice upon nationals of other countries. . . ." Further, it held that while the laws of war may recognize the validity of execution of spies, "war rebels" and resistance workers, that did not mean such persons could be made involuntary subjects of experiments. 2 *Trials of War Criminals* at 224, 227 (1947).

188. Art. 32 of the Geneva Civilians Convention prohibits the infliction of physical suffering or extermination of protected persons, including murder, torture, corporal punishment, mutilation, and medical or scientific experiments not necessitated by the medical treatment of a protected person.

wrecked, and enemy civilians are numerous and detailed, is no fortuitous accident.

ENEMY RESOURCES AS OBJECTS OF ATTACK

An enemy belligerent can, as a matter of broad theory, be effectually disarmed by being deprived of either its human or its material bases of power.[189] Since war cannot be waged without the utilization and expenditure of material resources, it has commonly been a major claim of belligerents to deprive the enemy of its control over resources by destroying or capturing such resources. A secondary claim is to the utilization of captured enemy resources for augmentation of the captor's own war effort.

Belligerent claims with respect to enemy resources are perhaps most conveniently categorized according to the location of the resource or property involved. Enemy property may be found (a) in the claimant-belligerent's own territory; (b) on the high seas; (c) in enemy territory; and (d) in regions belligerently occupied. Enemy property in (a) presents a noncombat situation outside the scope of the present chapter; enemy property in (d) is considered in the succeeding chapter on belligerent occupation. We focus here upon enemy property in the (b) and (c) locations.

Enemy Property on the High Seas

We include in "enemy property" a reference to both enemy ships and enemy goods. Enemy goods may of course be carried either on enemy ships or on neutral ships. We have, in the preceding chapter on neutrality, dealt with enemy goods on neutral ships.[190] Accordingly, it is with enemy ships, and enemy goods on enemy ships, that the present section is concerned. Generally formulated, the primary belligerent claim with respect to enemy ships and enemy goods on enemy ships is a claim to capture or destroy such property. One kind of claim traditionally asserted in opposition relates to the appro-

189. Rodgers, "Suggestions As to Changes in the International Law for Maritime War," 17 *A.J.I.L.* 3 (1927): "The attempt may be directly by means of bloodshed, or indirectly by attack on the enemy's means of economic support. Either attack will bring forth the most strenuous resistance. Destruction of hostile property and the enemy's economic means of livelihood will be as efficient in subduing him as bloodshed. Thus attack on property has always appeared as a normal and reasonable form of warfare."

190. Supra, p. 501 ff.

priate procedures for taking or attacking. Thus, a countering assertion commonly made until World War II was that merchantmen could not lawfully be attacked and sunk at sight. A second kind of countering assertion is that the vessel captured or destroyed belongs to a class legally exempt from capture or destruction.

A significant difference between the permissible treatment of enemy property at sea and that of enemy property on land may be noted at the outset. The traditional rules relating to land warfare, particularly those relating to belligerent occupation, embody a broad distinction between public and private property and project a general immunity for the latter from seizure and appropriation subject to certain circumstances of necessity. The laws of naval warfare provide for no comparable immunity for private enemy property at sea. This difference in permissible treatment appears to reflect differing requirements of belligerent necessities. Military occupation of enemy territory serves effectually to terminate the enemy belligerent's control over property within the occupied area and hence precludes further utilization by the enemy. At sea, however, termination of enemy control and use is obtainable only through capture or destruction of the property—vessel and goods—itself.[191] Thus, control and disruption of enemy seaborne communications and commerce has commonly been a prime objective of sea warfare, being fruits of what naval strategists designate as "command of the sea." Mighty battle fleets have clashed for control of the movement of the common freighter and tanker.[192] The seizure or sinking of enemy merchantmen has been, in wars past, too efficacious a means of warfare and the continued flow of goods too vital for enemy fighting strength for the great naval powers to relinquish such means and to accept a general immunity for private property at sea.[193] The military effectiveness of commerce destruction is manifested in the avidity with which belligerent powers with weaker navies and merchant marine

191. See Lawrence, supra note 190 at 481–2. Mr. Choate, the American delegate to the Second Hague Conference in 1907, had attempted to draw a "perfect analogy" between the treatment of private property in land and in sea warfare, and urged acceptance of a rule of immunity in both. See *American Addresses at the Second Hague Peace Conference* 11–12 (Scott, ed., 1910).

192. See e.g., Brodie, *A Guide to Naval Strategy* c. 4 (4th ed., 1958); Smith, *The Law and Custom of the Sea* 130–1 (3rd ed., 1950); *American Sea Power Since 1775*, 269–71 (Westcott, ed., 1947).

193. 2 Oppenheim-Lauterpacht 462–4; see also Colombos, *Law of the Sea* 486–90 for presentation of the time-honored British view.

have frequently sought to employ neutral merchantmen to sustain a flow of goods across oceans. Traditional theory in effect assimilates the individual enemy shipper or carrier to his state for purposes of naval warfare.

Clearly, enemy ships and enemy goods, public or private, represent legitimate objects of attack. Traditional law, however, giving expression to the counterpoised principle of minimum destruction of values, sought to regulate the procedures of attack and appropriation. In contradistinction to warships, which, as the ordinary or "regular" combatants in naval war, could be sunk at sight by any instrument available to the attacker, merchantmen were in traditional law liable to direct violence only when attempting to resist capture. The "equities of the unarmed merchantman's crew," it is said,[194] intervened to prohibit sinking at sight. Capture, in other words, was projected as the normal recourse against enemy merchant vessels, destruction of the captured vessel being permitted only in exceptional circumstances where conveyance to a home port of the captor was not militarily feasible and then only after provision had been made for the safety of crew, passengers, and papers.[195] Customary law further required the captor to bring the captured vessel before a prize court for condemnation as good prize. Even in case of destruction, a determination in prize of the justifiable nature of the act of destruction was required. This requirement as to appropriation procedure was designed for the protection of neutral claims to goods carried by the captured or destroyed prize, in line with the provision of the Declaration of Paris of 1856 that "neutral goods, with the exception of contraband of war, [were] not liable to capture under the enemy's flag." [196] With the indefinite expansion of the notion of contraband, the requirement of a decree in prize was, of course,

194. 3 Hyde, *International Law* 1990 et seq. (2nd rev. ed., 1945).

195. See U.S. Law of Naval Warfare, par. 503(b)(2); text in appendix to Tucker, *The Law of War and Neutrality at Sea* (1957). A succinct statement of the customary law prior to World War I may be found in Smith, *The Destruction of Merchant Ships Under International Law* (1917).

196. Text in 2 *A Collection of Neutrality Laws, Regulations and Treaties of Various Countries* 1473–4 (Jessup and Deak, eds., 1939). Where the prize court finds that destruction of the enemy prize was justifiable, neutral owners of cargo on board are not deemed entitled to any indemnification or compensation. See 2 Oppenheim-Lauterpacht 488; and *The Glitra* and *The Indian Prince,* decided by the German Supreme Prize Court in the First World War (trans.) 10 *A.J.I.L.* 921, 930 (1916).

destined to be little more than a somewhat cumbersome formality.

The more important problem, however, concerns the extent to which compliance with the customary law requirement of capture rather than destruction remains feasible under conditions of modern war at sea. It need hardly be mentioned that the interests of the attacking belligerent are normally served by capturing, instead of destroying, enemy merchantmen and by conveying them to a home or friendly port. That ships are valuable war resources even in the age of aircraft needs little documentation. Self-interest may thus ordinarily be expected to move the attacker toward restraint, so long as it perceives an opportunity to take and utilize a prize in comparative safety. The incidence of such opportunity drastically declined in the two world wars. As suggested earlier, the operating characteristics of the instruments of attack commonly utilized in sea warfare, notably the submarine and including aircraft and mines, were not conducive to observance of customary law. The difficulties of conformity by these instruments were compounded by the methods adopted for countering the threat to shipping posed by such instruments. The arming of merchantmen has been adverted to above. It remains to note another practice developed for defense of shipping—the convoying of merchantmen.[197] Convoying consisted of herding freighters together in groups which were then provided with escorts of warships. The strength of the escort varied with the importance the belligerent assigned to the cargo; sometimes a few destroyers were enough, while at other times whole battle fleets were used. The convoy system was usually supplemented by the attaching of fire power directly to the merchant ships convoyed. Each ship was armed with a 5-inch or 6-inch gun and smaller anti-aircraft armament. A convoy of several dozens of merchantmen each so armed represented, with its naval escorts, a considerable concentration of fire which made highly perilous an attack, let alone an attempt to capture, by a commerce raider whether it was a surface or submersible vessel or an aircraft. Sometimes, it may be added, the escort force included fighter planes

197. Good accounts of shipping defense practices in World War II may be found in e.g. Brodie, supra note 192 at c. 5; Anderson, "The Protection of Commerce in War," 78 *U.S. Naval Inst. Proc.* 881 (1952); and see generally, Richmond, *War at Sea Today* (1942); Richmond, *The Naval Role in Modern Warfare* (1940); Russel, *Sea Shepherds* (1941); and Creswell, *Sea Warfare: 1939–1945* cc. 2, 6 (1950).

mounted on catapults attached to the deck of merchantmen. Thus, when considered together with the military importance which belligerents placed upon the interruption and severance of enemy transport and communication lines at sea, it is scarcely a matter for wonder that, in the practice of both sides in the last war, merchantmen were in fact regarded as regular combatants and subjected to sinking at sight.[198]

198. In respect of this practice, 3 Hyde, *International Law* 1991 (2nd rev. ed., 1945) said: "It is not believed, however, that the indirect harm to be wrought in consequence of [letting enemy merchantmen] escape equals that to be anticipated from the deliberate disregard and destruction of the lives of the occupants of the ship. Claims of military necessity still fail to turn the scales of justice." That the belligerents in the last war did not act upon this assumption is clear from the fact that the Allied Powers lost about 23 million tons of shipping, while Japan lost 9 million tons, from 1939–1945; see Anderson, supra note 197 at 881, 887.

Contrast with Professor Hyde's position the broad conclusion drawn by Smith, *The Crisis in the Law of Nations* 62 (1947): "[I]t becomes clearly impossible for the old distinctions still to be drawn between the warship and the privately owned merchant vessel. Here again, the law can do nothing but adjust itself to the facts, and the belligerent must be allowed to sink at sight every ship which he encounters under the enemy flag."

Apparently more modest than Dr. Smith's wide-ranging statement is the U.S. Law of Naval Warfare, par. 503(b)(3) which provides:

> (3) Destruction of Enemy Merchant Vessels Prior [sic] to Capture. Enemy merchant vessels may be attacked and destroyed, either with or without prior warning, in any of the following circumstances:
> 1. Actively resisting visit and search or capture.
> 2. Refusing to stop upon being duly summoned.
> 3. Sailing under convoy of enemy warships or enemy military aircraft.
> 4. If armed, and there is reason to believe that such armament has been used, or is intended for use, offensively against an enemy.
> 5. If incorporated into, or assisting in any way, the intelligence system of an enemy's armed forces.
> 6. If acting in any capacity as a naval or military auxiliary to an enemy's armed forces.

It might, however, be an exacting task to find many enemy merchantmen, in any major war where commerce destruction became important, that would not be subsumable under (3) or (4) or (5) or (6).

Smith, in *The Law and Custom of the Sea* 87 (2nd ed., 1950), makes the interesting observation that after the Allied Powers adopted the policy of attacking all enemy ships without warning, either from the sea or air, the vessels attacked were described as "enemy supply ships" in the official communiqués,

A second, and perhaps more enduring, manifestation of the minimum destruction principle is found in the provision for immunity from attack and capture for certain types of enemy vessels. The most important of these is the hospital ship. Hague Convention X of 1907 envisaged, it is said, hospital ships accompanying battle fleets, waiting at the edge of the battle zone while naval combat raged, and then hastening in at the termination of the engagement to give speedy succor to the disabled and drowning.[199] In the last world war, however, the main activity of hospital ships consisted of the ferrying of wounded and sick from overseas areas to home bases and the carrying of medical supplies on the outward voyage.[200] This change of activity is recognized in the 1949 Geneva Wounded, Sick and Shipwrecked Convention which defines military hospital ships as ships built or equipped "specially and wholely with a view to assisting the wounded, sick and shipwrecked, to treating them and to transporting them." [201] These ships, the Convention continues, "may in no circumstances be attacked or captured but shall at all times be respected and protected." [202] They are required to afford relief and assistance "without distinction as of nationality." [203]

The Geneva Convention, as may be expected, takes ample account of the countervailing military interests of belligerents. Thus, belligerents may prevent the possible re-employment of the wounded and sick and shipwrecked in war duties upon recovery or return, by demanding their surrender and removal from hospital ships and

---

"thus assimilating them to colliers and other vessels directly engaged in the service of enemy forces." The United States Navy Department, in justifying the wartime decision to wage "unrestricted air and submarine warfare" against Japan, declared that "The conditions under which Japan employed her so called merchant shipping were such that it would be impossible to distinguish between 'merchant ships' and Japanese Army and Navy auxiliaries." See Bishop, *International Law—Cases and Materials* 608 (1953).

199. See Higgins, "Hospital Ships and the Carriage of Passengers and Crews of Destroyed Prizes," 26 *L. Q. Rev.* 408 (1910).

200. Mossop, "Hospital Ships in the Second World War," 24 *Brit. Y.B.I.L.* 401 (1947).

201. Art. 22.

202. Id. Arts. 24 and 25 of the same Convention provide for the same protection for hospital ships utilized by National Red Cross Societies or private persons or officially recognized relief societies of either belligerent or neutral countries, provided, in the latter case, the ships are placed under the control of one of the parties to the conflict.

203. Art. 30, Geneva Wounded, Sick and Shipwrecked Convention of 1949.

thereafter treating them as prisoners of war.[204] In 1944 and 1945, for example, the Allied Powers diverted the German hospital ships *Tubingen* and *Gradisca* to Allied ports and made prisoners of war of the 4000 or so enemy wounded and sick these ships had taken on at Salonica.[205] As a condition for continuing immunity from attack, hospital ships may not, under the Convention, be used for "any military purpose," [206] nor for acts "harmful to the enemy." [207] The Convention more specifically prohibits the possession and use of secret codes.[208] Hospital ships, furthermore, may not hamper the military operations of belligerents authorized to order them off. In 1944, the Allied Powers invoked this authority, which was conceded in the 1907 as in the 1949 Convention, in refusing to allow a German hospital ship to enter Brest, then under attack, upon the ground that the presence of the ship would inconvenience the attacking forces.[209] Finally, it may be noted, the Geneva Convention recognizes in belligerents a broad authority to control and search hospital ships.[210]

The immunity provided for hospital ships has been extended by the 1949 Geneva Conventions to medical aircraft exclusively used for the removal of the wounded, sick, and shipwrecked, and the transporting of medical personnel and equipment. To preclude the use of medical aircraft for reconnaissance purposes, flights over enemy or enemy-occupied territory are prohibited unless otherwise agreed upon.[211]

Other categories of vessels immune from attack and capture under

204. Art. 14, id.; the article adds a proviso, however, "that the wounded and sick are in a fit state to be moved and that the warship can provide adequate facilities for necessary medical treatment."

205. Mossop, supra note 200 at 405; 2 Oppenheim-Lauterpacht 501–2.

206. Art. 30, Geneva Wounded, Sick and Shipwrecked Convention of 1949.

207. Art. 34, id.

208. Art. 34, second par., id. In 1944, Allied forces seized the *Rostock,* a German hospital ship hastily converted from a warship in the besieged part of Bordeaux, having found her carrying code books and orders to engage in weather reporting. Mossop, supra note 200 at 404. And see *The Ophelia,* 1 B & C Pr. Cas. 210 (1915) where Sir Samuel Evans condemned a German hospital ship after a showing that its books and documents had been destroyed and that the ship had sent coded wireless messages.

209. Mossop, supra note 200 at 406.

210. Art. 31, Geneva Wounded, Sick and Shipwrecked Convention of 1949.

211. Art. 36, Wounded and Sick Convention; Art. 39, Wounded, Sick and Shipwrecked Convention.

conventional prescriptions—i.e. Hague Convention XI of 1907—are craft used exclusively for "fishing along the coast" and "small boats employed in local trade." [212] These exceptions seem survivals from a period when publicists could still aptly speak of "cultivators of the soil or mechanics" as "inoffensive." [213]

Even coastwise fishing and trade do in measure contribute to a belligerent's war effort, the former by augmenting the food supply and the latter by relieving internal transport lines of some load pressure. Prize courts and other decision-makers have consequently been careful to confine the exemptions within restrictive limits which assured that the military value of the exemptions remained insignificant.[214] For instance, vessels engaged in "deep sea fishing" far from their home ports have been held as not immune from capture.[215] A fishing craft bringing in 50 barrels of *salted* herring was found to be engaged in a "commercial enterprise" and not entitled to immunity.[216] Mr. Justice Gray in the classic *Paquete Habana* had spoken of "considerations of humanity to a poor and industrious order of men . . . unarmed, and honestly pursuing their peaceful calling of catching and bringing in *fresh* fish." [217] In the Korean war, the naval forces of the United Nations Command interdicted all fishing, inshore as well as offshore, by North Koreans. The assumption appeared to be that the tremendous importance of fish in the national diet of Koreans invested fishing with strategic military importance, which took the matter of immunity out of the traditional rationale of charity toward a small and characteristically depressed occupa-

212. Art. 3, Hague Convention XI, 1907, Relative to Certain Restrictions With Regard to the Exercise of the Right of Capture in Naval War.

213. Hall, *International Law* 536 (8th ed., Pearce Higgins, 1924).

214. Stone, *Legal Controls* 586: "These limitations on the exemption have increased in importance, for with the modern role of strategic bombing of internal communications, the value to the war effort of coastal steamer traffic has greatly increased. If all cabotage (sic) had been within the Convention, this exemption would probably have called for overhaul in the light of modern conditions"; (note 104): "Such a problem may indeed exist as to coastal fisheries in view of the great importance to the food supply of locally caught fish."

215. *The Fred Neumann,* France, Conseil des Prises, *Annual Digest 1946,* Case No. 175; and *The Stoer* 5 Ll. P.C. 18 (1916).

216. *The Berlin* 1 B & C Pr. Cas. 29 (1914). It is a matter for speculation whether ten small vessels bringing in five barrels each of *fresh* fish would constitute a "commercial enterprise."

217. 175 U.S. 677, 708 (1899).

tional group.[218] The exemption of coastwise shipping has been held unavailable to vessels of more than 5 tons' weight,[219] and to tugs and lighters although mainly used in port.[220] Finally, the immunity of both fishing and coastal shipping vessels, however small, is forfeited "as soon as they take any part whatever in hostilities." [221] Some illustration is furnished by the *Mahbrouck* [222] where fishing craft that had been used for revictualing ships in blockaded ports were held good prize. More common, perhaps, has been the use of coastal fishing or trading vessels for intelligence and warning purposes.[222a]

A final class of vessels exempted by Hague Convention XI comprises ships engaged in "religious, scientific or philanthropic missions." [223] It may be doubted whether this exemption is of much use today. It has not been invoked on behalf of ships on "religious or scientific missions" in the last two world wars, while prize courts in World War I interpreted "philanthropic mission" so narrowly as to render the exemption largely unreal. In the *Paklat,*[224] for example, a British prize court refused to consider as "philanthropic" the carriage of German women and children refugees from Tsingtao to Tientsin in China, the embarkation taking place six days before the declaration of a blockade of Tsingtao. The ship was to be used to house the refugees at Tientsin. Again, in the *Haelen,*[225] a German

218. See Cagle and Manson, *The Sea War in Korea* 296 (1957).

219. See Garner, *Prize Law During the World War* 251–3 (1927).

220. Floating Craft of the Deutsches Kohlen-Depot, Port Said 2 B & C Pr. Cas. 439 (1916) affirmed under title of *H.M. Procurator in Egypt v. Deutsches Kohlen Depot Gesellschaft* 3 id. 264 (1918). Neither does the exemption include yachts; *The Elvira* III 1 Ll. P.C. (2nd) 8 (1940); cf. *The Bernina, Annual Digest, Supp. Vol. 1919–1942,* Case No. 145.

221. See *The Impero,* France, Conseil des Prises, *Annual Digest 1946,* Case No. 173.

222. See Garner, supra note 219 at 629.

222a. See, for recent illustration, the case of the *S.S. Doron* decided by the Alexandria Prize Court, 15 *Revue Egyptienne de Droit International* 184 (1959). The *Doron* was an Israeli trawler captured in "territorial waters of the Arab Republic," and found to have on board a powerful wireless transmitter and receiver, a bathometer, and cases of "luminous signals which are ordinarily not used by fishing boats." (at 185). The boat was declared good prize.

223. Art. 4.

224. 1 B & C Pr. Cas. 515 (1915).

225. See Colombos, *The Law of Prize* 167 (3rd ed., 1949); and 6 Hackworth, *Digest of International Law* 546 (1943).

prize court condemned a Belgian ship chartered to carry wheat from Montreal to the Relief Commission in Belgium for the consumption of "starving women and children." The court held that a ship, to be immune, must have been engaged in humanitarian work prior to, as well as during, the war, a requirement not found in Hague Convention XI. However, immunity may still be conferred *ad hoc,* by specific agreement of contending belligerents, on cartel ships engaged in transporting exchanged prisoners of war.[226] It is manifestly to the mutual interest of belligerents to refrain from attacking each other's cartel ships.

It remains very briefly to note that the inherited rules of warfare provided for immunity for enemy goods on the high seas in certain cases. The first of these is the immunity from capture and condemnation the Declaration of Paris of 1856 conferred upon enemy goods when carried on neutral ships. As indicated in the preceding chapter,[227] more recent practice in the matter of contraband and enemy export control, and the emergence of a principle of ultimate enemy origin, have resulted in quiet demise of the "free ships free goods" rule. The second provision for immunity relates to postal correspondence. Hague Convention XI of 1907 stipulated that "the postal correspondence of neutrals or belligerents, whatever its official or private character may be, found on the high seas on board a neutral or enemy ship, is inviolable." [228] The inviolability of postal correspondence on board an enemy vessel became entirely supposititious in the last world war since sinking at sight was the common treatment administered to the vessel itself.[229] As to the immunity of postal correspondence on neutral ships, it seems sufficient to observe that such inviolability was not in practice interpreted to include exemption from belligerent censorship and search for preventing transmission of military intelligence or contraband goods through the mails.[230]

226. 2 Oppenheim-Lauterpacht 542; Colombos, *Law of the Sea* 540–1.

227. Supra, p. 508–9.

228. Art. 1.

229. Cf. Tucker, *The Law of War and Neutrality at Sea* 91 (1957).

230. Id. 92–4. See the British note of Jan. 16, 1940, in reply to the American protest of Dec. 22, 1939 against the censorship of mails carried on ships diverted to British control ports; 6 Hackworth 620–2. And see generally, Eagleton, "Interference with American Mails," 34 *A.J.I.L.* 315 (1940); and Colombos, *Law of the Sea* 545–9.

Enemy Property in Enemy Territory

We turn to a consideration of claims about the treatment of enemy property on enemy territory not yet reduced to belligerent occupation. Three kinds of specific claims are distinguishable in this area: (a) claims about the taking of enemy property as booty of war; (b) claims about permissible devastation; and (c) claims about permissible destruction in active combat or engagement.

Booty of War. The law of war booty, which is concerned with the appropriation of enemy property on land, is said to correspond to the law of prize concerned with the appropriation of enemy property found on the high seas.[231] The law of war booty, however, has in practice been of much less importance than prize law. One reason is perhaps the relative shortness of the time segment during which the law of war booty is applicable: the period of combat preceding the firm establishment of that effective control which constitutes belligerent occupation. Claims to take and utilize enemy property are more commonly asserted after effective capture of the enemy's territory than during the process of capturing such territory. It might also be observed that, unlike the procedure in captures in prize, belligerents do not commonly provide for special tribunals to pass upon questions of booty or no booty. These questions are ordinarily passed upon, at least in the first instance, by civil affairs officers of the capturing armies.

Customary law permitted belligerents to augment their resources by seizing enemy movable property left on the battlefield by the unsuccessful opponent. No particular procedure of appropriation was prescribed; discovery and "firm possession" sufficed, it was said, to produce the technical effect of "vesting title" in the appropriating belligerent.[232] The conservatory limitations projected were two. The

231. Smith, "Booty of War," 23 *Brit. Y.B.I.L.* 228 (1946).

232. See *Young v. United States,* 97 U.S. 39 (1878), *Oakes v. United States,* 174 U.S. 778 (1899). Office of Military Government for Germany (U.S.), Legal Division, *Selected Opinions,* Vol. IX, p. 60 (1947): "a belligerent does not acquire title to enemy public movable property until he has reduced it to firm possession. It appears that 'firm possession' requires some manifestation of intention to seize and retain the property involved and some affirmative act or declaration of a possessory or custodial nature with respect to the property. The

first established a distinction between public and private movable property. While all enemy public movables, whether warlike or innocuous in character, abandoned on the battlefield could be appropriated by the successful belligerent, enemy private movables, with the exception of arms, military papers, and the like, were protected from seizure.[233] The second limiting requirement was that booty of war became the property of the capturing belligerent, not of the individual soldier who in fact found it.[234] The purpose of this requirement was of course to insure against private plundering by soldiers, in historical contrast with the customary license of earlier times when the promise of booty was regarded as a necessary stimulant of martial enthusiasm in mercenary troops.[235]

It need not escape notice that in the kind of context contemplated by customary law—that of a battlefield freshly won—the exemption

circumstances which will satisfy these two elements of firm possession will, of course, vary in each case."

See, further, *De Deckere v. Belgian State,* Court of Appeal of Ghent, Belgium, *Int. Law Rep. 1955,* p. 930 where the Court ruled that a provision in the 1940 Belgian-German Protocol of Surrender requiring the handing over of stocks for the Belgian army to German authorities did not by itself have the effect of transferring title over such stocks to the German forces, and that title in booty passes only by effective possession.

233. See 2 Oppenheim-Lauterpacht 401–2; Lawrence, *The Principles of International Law* 407–8 (7th ed., Winfield, 1928); Dept. of the Army, *Law of Land Warfare,* par. 59 (FM 27-10, July 1956). For the qualified immunity of certain categories of movables—the material of mobile medical units and of fixed medical establishments, and transports of wounded and sick or of medical equipment—see Arts. 33 and 35 of the Geneva Wounded and Sick Convention of 1949.

234. *Law of Land Warfare,* supra note 233 at par. 396; Downey, "Captured Enemy Property: Booty of War and Seized Enemy Property," 44 *A.J.I.L.* 488 (1950). Thus, a soldier who found a box of francs in an abandoned enemy regimental headquarters, and who kept and used the same to buy money orders sent to his wife, was convicted by a court-martial for violation of Art. 80 of the U.S. Articles of War (10 U.S.C. 1552). See 4 *Bull. Judge Adv. Gen. of the Army* 338 (1945); also id. at 389–90.

235. See Nussbaum, *A Concise History of the Law of Nations* 69 (rev. ed., 1954); Butler and Maccoby, *The Development of International Law* 121 (1928). Vitoria had taught that it was "not unlawful in itself" to give up a city to the soldiery to sack if that was necessary "for the conduct of the war or as a deterrent to the enemy or as a spur to the courage of the troops." "De Jure Belli" S. 52 in Scott, *The Spanish Origin of International Law,* Part I, *Francisco de Vitoria and His Law of Nations,* p. lxviii (1954).

of private enemy property was of limited significance, embracing principally the personal belongings of enemy troops taken prisoner, the confiscation of which was in any case forbidden by the familiar rules on treatment of prisoners of war.[236] The conception of armed combat embodied in the customary law of war booty went back to the Napoleonic era when contending armies assembled in a confined area and fought for a day or two for possession of the field. This conception, of course, has found scant reflection in the actualities of modern war, whether the war be one of fixed positions (or trench warfare) as in the First World War, or one of fluid maneuver as in the Second.

The kind of situation in which claims to take enemy property as booty were asserted in the recent global wars was commonly that of an army leaving behind it, in retreat before a superior force, stocks of arms, munitions, supplies, and other material the removal or destruction of which had been prevented by lack of time. Such situations arose in the last war both at the initial invasion of enemy territory and at reinvasion by returning forces seeking to recover territory previously lost to the enemy. Because no particular prescription by agreement specifically covered the above situation, and because no battlefields of the 18th- and 19th-century type envisaged in the customary rule on booty of war were encountered, the Allied armed forces in Europe (or part of them) in World War II undertook to apply Article 53 of the Hague Regulations.[237] Article 53, which strictly speaking formed part of the law of belligerent occupation rather than of combatant law, authorized a belligerent to appropriate enemy public movables "which may be used for operations of the war," as well as privately owned means of transportation and communication and "all kinds of ammunition of war," subject, in the latter case, to restoration or compensation "when peace is made." [238]

236. Art. 18, par. 1 of the Geneva Prisoners of War Convention of 1949.

237. See Smith, supra note 231 at 228 et seq. Freeman, in "General Note on the Law of War Booty," 40 *A.J.I.L.* 797 (1946) uses the term "booty" to cover both "property found in the battle field" and property in occupied enemy territory. Compare Downey, supra note 234.

238. It may be noted that American commanders who, during hostilities, required the surrender by the civil population of all binoculars, cameras, and radios preferred to invoke military necessity under Art. 23(g) of the Hague Regulations which makes no mention of any obligation of compensation. The

The Allied forces found vast quantities of material left by the German armies retreating into Germany. Much of this material had been taken from occupied territories by the German troops in occupation. The Allied forces treated as enemy public movables the material and goods the German occupation forces had, in accordance with the law of belligerent occupation, seized or requisitioned.[239] As a practical matter, all materials and goods useful to the Allied armed forces were taken and utilized. Where a subsequent investigation showed that such materials and goods had not been lawfully requisitioned by the German occupant and had therefore remained the property of the original individual owner, the goods and materials were treated as having been ex post facto requisitioned by the Allied forces as military occupants. Thus, "in practice," Dr. H. A. Smith wrote, "questions of booty normally presented themselves as issues between civilian claimants and military authorities." [240]

Permissible Devastation. More difficult, perhaps, than the problem of booty of war is the characterization of devastation or widespread destruction of enemy property in terms of permissibility or impermissibility. Publicists have argued that devastation "pure and simple, as an end in itself, as a self-contained measure of war," is illegitimate under the laws of war.[241] This, however, is only to insist that devastation, like other forms of destruction of values inflicted in the process of combat, must not be militarily irrelevant, that it must have a "reasonably close connection" [242] with the securing of legitimate

theory was that such instruments could be used by the enemy for intelligence purposes. The military government authorities rejected the civilians' claims for compensation. See *Selected Opinions,* supra note 232 at Vol. X, pp. 48–50.

239. See the Le Havre Currency Case mentioned by Smith, supra note 231 at 232–3, where 34.25 million francs which the German commander at Le Havre had obtained on an overdraft from the Bank of France, and which were captured by Allied invasion forces, were held to be good booty. The money had become German state property at the time of capture.

240. Smith, supra note 231 at 234–5.

241. Spaight, *War Rights on Land* 112 (1911). Cf. 2 Wheaton, *International Law* 213 (7th ed., Keith, 1944): "[T]o destroy for the mere purpose of inflicting pecuniary loss is unlawful; gratuitous ravage is not warranted by military necessity." *U.S. v. List,* 11 *Trials of War Criminals* at 1243, 8 *War Crimes Reports* at 66 (1948): "[International law] does not admit of wanton devastation of a district or the wilful infliction of suffering upon its inhabitants for the sake of suffering alone. . . ."

242. *Law of Land Warfare,* supra note 233 at par. 56.

belligerent objectives in order to be lawful. Devastation must, in the language of the Hague Regulations, be "imperatively demanded by the necessities of war." [243]

Devastation may of course occur in diverse kinds of contexts. We distinguish, and postpone consideration of, devastation inflicted by air or missile power in interior areas, beyond or behind the locale of active land combat, for the purpose of undermining the enemy's collective will to fight.[244] With respect to devastation in occupied territory, appreciation by the occupant of his own self-interest ordinarily prevents him from destroying what is already in his power and subject to his utilization. It is perhaps by way of reprisal for partisan activities that an occupant is most apt to impose devastation in the territory he controls; the problems of policy here involved are, however, more conveniently examined elsewhere.[245] There remains the question of permissible devastation in, firstly, contexts of actual violent contact between opposing land forces and, secondly, in contexts immediately preceding or following such violent contact. The first kind of context is discussed in a succeeding subsection; our focus here is upon the second kind.

In broad generalization, the common assumption has been that devastation which is a concomitant of ordinary military action may be regarded as necessary and hence permissible.[246] The usual textbook examples include the burning down of buildings and cutting of trees to strengthen a defensive position, the demolishing of the suburbs of a defended city or town to facilitate attack or defense (by, for instance, obtaining a clear field of fire), and the firing of towns to cover the retreat of an army.[247] It is the last-named situation that war crimes tribunals after World War II had occasion to consider,

243. Art. 23(g).

244. Infra, p. 652 ff.

245. Infra, Ch. 7.

246. Committee I of the U. N. War Crimes Commission, in determining which cases of alleged war crimes would be actually prosecuted, often had to decide whether a given set of facts involving destruction of property was a war crime or whether the destruction was justified by military necessity. The general test applied was "whether military operations were in progress, or were imminent." See *History of the United Nations War Crimes Commission and the Development of the Laws of War* 488 (1948).

247. *Law of Land Warfare,* supra note 233 at par. 56; Hall, *International Law* 645 (8th ed., Pearce Higgins, 1924); 2 Wheaton, *International Law* 214 (7th ed., Keith, 1944); Lawrence, *The Principles of International Law* 534–5 (7th ed., Winfield, 1928).

and their decisions offer some illustration of the kinds of specific factors and tactical conditions that bear upon the appraisal of particular cases of devastation as militarily necessary or unnecessary.

In *U.S. v. List,*[248] General Rendulic, commander-in-chief of the German XXth Mountain Army in Norway, was charged with ordering acts of devastation "not justified by military necessity" in the Norwegian province of Finmark. In October, 1944, Rendulic ordered the evacuation of the entire population of the province and the destruction of all food stocks that could not be removed, of all houses and installations that could afford any shelter, and of all means of transport and communication.[249] About a month before, Finland had negotiated a separate peace with the Soviet Union and demanded that the German troops withdraw from Finnish territory within two weeks. The result was that the German armies had to fight their way out of Finland and to retreat into Norway under constant attack by special Russian ski troops. Rendulic was aware that two or three land routes were open to the pursuing Russians as well as a sea route to a point behind German lines. He had limited means of acquiring intelligence as to the Russians' actual movements, for the extreme cold and short days made air reconnaissance almost impossible. The purpose in creating a devastated zone appeared to be the protection of the southern flank of the German forces in Norway. Under these conditions, the tribunal held that Rendulic was justified in believing that "urgent military necessity" warranted the decision to carry out a "scorched earth" policy in Finmark.[250]

In *U.S. v. Von Leeb,*[251] seven German generals, all on the level of army or army group commander, were likewise indicted for the "wanton destruction of cities, towns and villages not justified by military necessity." In each instance, the devastation was carried out, with characteristic thoroughness, in Soviet territory by German troops retreating in the face of advancing Russian forces. The kind of operational situation in which each of the accused generals had ordered devastation was markedly similar to the situation in which Rendulic had acted in the Finmark case. In both cases, the acts of destruction

248. 11 *Trials of War Criminals* 759; 8 *War Crimes Reports* 34 (1948).

249. The text of Rendulic's order, as well as Jodl's directive in pursuance of which Rendulic acted, are reproduced in 11 *Trials of War Criminals* at 1113–17.

250. 11 *Trials of War Criminals* 1295–7; 8 *War Crimes Reports* 67–9.

251. 10 and 11 *Trials of War Criminals;* 12 *War Crimes Reports* 1 (1948).

were carried out in anticipation of the enemy advancing through the devastated zones within a relatively short time, Russian attacks presumably continuing all the while. In both cases, however, the recorded evidence failed to show the exact proximity of the Russians at the time the devastation was effected. Again, in both cases, the destruction took place in winter time when accommodation and shelter were, given the nature of a Russian winter, of utmost military importance.[252] The lack of such shelter could with reason be expected to impede the progress and lower the combat efficiency of the Russian troops. As in the Finmark case, the devastation was preceded by the forcible evacuation of the civil population. The targets, in other words, were resources only, not people, although in the *Von Leeb* case, some persons appeared to have died in the course of evacuation. If people had been deliberately destroyed simultaneously with the installations, the decisions might conceivably have been otherwise. Moreover, in both *List* and *Von Leeb,* the devastation was not of a nature or intensity calculated to cast a "permanent or long enduring blight" [253] on the area affected. If it had been, again the

252. An order issued by defendant Woehler concerning operational strategy in the east, dated 3 Jan. 1942, ran thus: "But if. . . where I order a withdrawal, each town and village is burned down and the hearths and chimneys are demolished, then the enemy who has broken through between the localities, will also be surely annihilated. For even the Russian cannot live in winter without the protection of buildings or of constructed positions." 11 *Trials of War Criminals* at 307.

Defendant Reinhardt had also issued an order authorizing individual soldiers to confiscate winter clothing like felt boots and warm gloves from the population. The tribunal held that, although the evidence on the charge of plunder and spoliation showed great ruthlessness, "we are not satisfied that it shows, beyond a reasonable doubt, acts that were not justified by military necessity." Id. at 609.

The devastation carried out also by retreating Germans, in the First World War in France, which aroused widespread condemnation, occurred in the spring of 1917 and autumn of 1918. See 1 Garner, *International Law and the World War* 315–28 (1920).

253. The phrase is Professor Hyde's; 3 Hyde, *International Law* 1808 (2nd rev. ed., 1945). "Long enduring blight" now appears literally possible through so-called "radiological warfare." "Radiological warfare" is used to refer to the dissemination of isotopes of varying "half-lives" derived either from a controlled reactor or from the fallout deliberately induced by a nuclear or thermonuclear explosion. See *Research in CBR,* H. Rep. 815, Committee on Science and Astronautics, U.S. House of Rep., 86th Cong., 1st. Sess., pp. 8–9 (1959).

tribunal might have decided that the possible defeat of the German armies would not suffice to offset the prolonged destruction of values. As it was, not one of the defendants was found guilty of the devastation charge. Said the tribunal:

> Defendants in this case were in many instances in retreat under arduous conditions wherein their commands were in serious danger of being cut off. Under such circumstances, a commander must necessarily make quick decisions to meet the particular situation of his command. A great deal of latitude must be accorded to him . . .[254]

Apparently the tribunal felt that given the tactical or operational conditions obtaining at the time the devastation orders were issued, some presumption of sufficient necessity operated in favor of the military decision-maker, a presumption the prosecution must rebut.

> What constitutes devastation beyond military necessity in these situations requires detailed proof of an operational and tactical nature.[255]

It may be noted that the presumption is in effect a formidable obstacle to conviction. Even where the prosecution succeeds in presenting "detailed proof," the tribunal might still, as in the *List* case, consider the facts sufficient to warrant the military commander's belief in the necessity of the devastation.

Permissible Destruction in Active Combat. If the necessary destruction of enemy property, public and private, is permissible in situations of strategic withdrawal or disengagement and of preparation for imminent contact with enemy forces, such property must *a*

254. 11 *Trials of War Criminals* at 541.

255. Ibid. Lauterpacht, "The Law of Nations and the Punishment of War Crimes," 21 *Brit. Y.B.I.L.* 74 (1944): "Total war has altered the complexion of many a rule. At a time when the 'scorched earth' policy, with regard to the belligerent's own territory, has become part of a widespread practice, general destruction of property ordered as an incident of broad military strategy will not properly form the subject matter of a criminal indictment."

Compare *In re* von Lewinski (called von Manstein) *Annual Digest 1949,* Case No. 192, where the British military court at Hamburg convicted the accused on a charge of devastation under analogous circumstances of strategic withdrawal in the face of advancing Soviet forces.

fortiori be liable to similar destruction where the opposing forces have actually established violent contact. The primary reference intended here is to what has more familiarly been designated as enemy property in assault, siege, and bombardment. The traditional laws of war project no detailed policies especially applicable in assault considered apart from the bombardment that usually precedes or accompanies it. There is only the broad principle that destruction which clearly exceeds the limits of military necessity, as such limits may be determined in particular tactical situations, becomes impermissible.[256] After the target locality is carried by assault, however, when further violence becomes unnecessary, the prohibition of pillage and plunder becomes applicable.[257] The rule against pillage and looting, it may be noted, provides excellent illustration of the perceptive observation made by Admiral Rodgers that while:

> [I]t pleases us to call [the] rules of war humanitarian . . . really they fulfill a double object—as towards the individual enemy, these restrictive rules are humane; as towards one's own organized forces in the field, these restrictives promote discipline and efficiency.[258]

With respect to siege (or, in more recent military rhetoric, encirclement) and bombardment, the handful of traditional prescriptions which purport to be applicable appear historically to have been largely shaped by the methods and system of warfare and the technology of bombardment available during the inception and maturation of those prescriptions. Bombardment by means of air and space weapons is examined below under the later heading of "Claims with Respect to Permissible Instruments and Means of Attack"; for the moment, and somewhat arbitrarily, we consider only siege and bombardment in land and sea warfare.

The Brussels Code of 1874 had provided that "fortified places" were alone liable to be besieged and that towns and villages which were "open and undefended" could not lawfully be bombarded.[259]

256. 2 Oppenheim-Lauterpacht 417–19; Dept. of the Army, *Law of Land Warfare,* par. 41 (FM 27-10, July 1956); cf. *British Manual of Military Law,* Part III, par. 287 (1958).

257. Art. 28, Hague Regulations.

258. Rodgers, "Suggestions as to Changes in the International Law for Maritime War," 17 *A.J.I.L.* 1, 4 (1923).

259. Text in 65 *British and Foreign State Papers* 1083 (1873–1874).

This provision reflected the state of military strategy and tactics during the preceding two or three centuries when operations on land were commonly focussed around particular fortified points or areas. Battles, with accompanying bombardment, ordinarily involved the investment of some such fortified point or town and the counter-effort to break the siege.[260] The range of artillery then in use was very limited and had the effect of localizing military operations to the area actually occupied by forces in the course of battle. The zone of operations, in other words, comprised only the particular fortified place besieged and bombarded. Within this zone of active combat operations, practically exerything that came within the range of artillery fire could, according to belligerent usage, legitimately be destroyed. Thus, in case of a fortified town, the town itself as distinguished from the fortifications and battlements, could, where necessary, be destroyed by chain shot, red-hot balls, and the like.[261] Outside the fortresses and fortified towns, the country lay "open and undefended" and bombardment was entirely pointless.

The Hague Regulations of 1899 and 1907 substituted "defended place" for the old "unfortified place" as the test for permissible bombardment. They prohibited bombardment of towns, villages, dwellings, or buildings "which are undefended." [262] By that time, the striking power and effective range of artillery had been substantially increased. Operations no longer centered upon the taking or defending of individual fortified points. Extended lines of forts and works were instead employed to defend—i.e., bar access to—towns themselves unfortified.[263] Inside the zone of operations or defended areas,

260. See Spaulding, Nickerson and Wright, *Warfare—A Study of Military Methods* 516 (1937).

261. At the Brussels Conference, the Belgian delegate presented a petition addressed to the Belgian Government by the inhabitants of Antwerp against the bombardment of inhabited quarters, even of fortified towns. The German delegate requested that it be set down in the Protocol that bombardment being one of the most efficacious means of attaining the object of a war, it would be impossible to yield to the petition. In the final text, nothing was said about immunity of residential quarters. See 65 *British and Foreign State Papers* 1082 (1873–1874). Hall, *International Law* 646–7 (8th ed., Pearce Higgins, 1924) considered the practice as one of "peculiar cruelty," but admitted it was sanctioned by usage. See also Vattel, *The Law of Nations or the Principles of Natural Law* (trans. Fenwick, Classics of International Law, 1916) Bk. III, c. 9, s. 169, p. 294.

262. Art. 25, Hague Regulations.

263. See Royse, *Aerial Bombardment and the International Regulation of*

the infliction of widespread destruction was deemed permissible "as one of the means of impressing upon the authorities the advisability of surrender." [264] Outside the area of combat activity, bombardment was unnecessary in the case of contiguous undefended places and towns open *ex hypothesi* to capture and occupation,[265] and impossible so far as concerned towns and places in the hinterland well beyond the still limited reach of artillery.

Thus, in respect of enemy property (and persons) located within the zone of ongoing land combat, the requirements of military operations have clearly been heavily weighted over the principle of civilian immunity. No general immunity for such property upon the basis simply of its private ownership or "nonmilitary" character has been recognized in the practice of belligerents. The conservatory restrictions which have been established at least in authoritative projection have been grounded rather upon the dedication of

Warfare 156–7 (1928). *Law of Land Warfare,* supra note 256 at par. 40 defines "defended places" as including: "(a) a fort or fortified place; (b) a city or town surrounded by detached defense positions, which is considered jointly with such defense positions as an indivisible whole; (c) a place which is occupied by a combatant military force or through which such a force is passing. The occupation of such a place by medical units alone is not sufficient to make it a defended place." See also *British Manual of Military Law,* Part III, par. 289 (1958).

Some details on the increase in the range of artillery from the 15th to the 20th centuries are offered in Spaulding, et al., supra note 260 at 498 et seq.; also Morgenthau, *Politics Among Nations* 349–51 (2nd ed., 1954).

264. 2 Oppenheim-Lauterpacht 421; Spaight, *War Rights on Land* 164 (1911). Spaight (at 158) speaks of a "certain solidarity between the garrison and the residents" and of assimilation of a defended city to a fortress. That civilians within a zone of operations have not been regarded as entitled to special immunity is made even clearer by the fact that they may be fired upon by a besieging force to prevent their flight from an invested area. The theory is that they would help consume the provisions of the besieged territory and hasten the surrender thereof. This is what happened in the siege of Leningrad where German artillery bombarded Russian civilians attempting to flee from the city. The tribunal in the *Von Leeb* case held that such an extreme measure was not criminal; 2 *Trials of War Criminals* at 563 (1948). The tribunal relied on 3 Hyde, 1802–3.

265. 2 Westlake, *International Law* 77 (1907); Royse, supra note 263 at 162. It might be noted, however, that even undefended places could lawfully be bombarded to destroy military stores, factories, and the like which a land force may not, for some tactical reason, be able to occupy. See 2 Oppenheim-Lauterpacht 420; Holland, *Studies in International Law* 110 (1898); and Spaight, supra note 264 at 170.

particular property to nonhostile purposes regarded as especially valuable to the general community of mankind—religious, cultural, charitable, and humanitarian. These restrictions are, as might be expected, not absolute. Thus, the Hague Regulations of 1907 enjoin belligerents to spare "buildings dedicated to religion, art, science, or charitable purposes, historic monuments, hospitals, and places where the sick and wounded are collected," "as far as possible." [266] Similarly, the 1954 Hague Convention for the Protection of Cultural Property in the Event of Armed Conflict requires each party to respect and to refrain from attacking "cultural property," including especially designated refuges for "cultural property," located in the territory of its opponent. The Convention at the same time permits "waiver" of this obligation, "where military necessity imperatively requires such a waiver," [267] and the withdrawal of the special immunity accorded to refuges of "cultural property" in "exceptional cases of unavoidable military necessity." [268] The qualification of military necessity in this type of context has, as a matter of historical expectation, related not only to the actual use to which such property is put by the opposing belligerent and the physical or tactical conditions under which the attack is executed and delivered, but also to the technological capabilities and limitations of the ordinance employed in the attack.

The preponderating weight placed upon the military interests of belligerents by rules which permit them to take full advantage of the capabilities of weapons is once more manifested in the context of naval bombardment. Naval bombardment represents the use of

266. Art. 27, Hague Regulations.

267. Art. 4, Final Act of the Intergovernmental Conference on the Protection of Cultural Property in the Event of Armed Conflict, The Hague, 1954.

268. Art. 11, id. See, generally, Noblecourt, *Protection of Cultural Property in the Event of Armed Conflict* (Unesco trans., 1958). See the Treaty on the Protection of Artistic and Scientific Institutions and Historic Monuments (Roerich Pact) of Apr. 15, 1935 (7 Hudson, *International Legislation* 56; 167 *League of Nations Treaty Series* 289) to which the United States and certain Latin American states are parties. The treaty accords a neutralized and protected status to historic monuments, museums, scientific, artistic, educational, and cultural institutions, and to the personnel thereof. See also the Treaty on the Protection of Movable Property of Historic Value, of Apr. 15, 1935 (7 Hudson, supra 59) in force between certain Central and South American states, providing that such movables may not be treated as spoils of war (Art. 8). Hollander, *The International Law of Art* c. 1 (1959) contains anecdotal material of mixed value.

ordnance mounted on mobile, seagoing platforms which permit circumvention of enemy defense lines on land and assault upon coastal areas well behind such lines. Hague Convention IX Concerning Bombardment by Naval Forces in Time of War, 1907, permitted naval forces to destroy by bombardment "military works, military or naval establishments, depots of arms or war *matériel,* workshops or plants which could be utilized for the needs of the hostile fleet or army, and the ships of war in the harbor" although situated in *undefended* towns and ports.[269] In effecting such bombardment, the naval commander was absolved from responsibility for "any unavoidable damage" but was required to "take all due measures in order that the [undefended] town may suffer as little harm as possible." It need not escape notice that the clause "workshops or plants which could be utilized for the needs of the hostile fleet or army" is, in contexts of wars like the two world wars, susceptible of, and has in practice been given, a latitudinarian construction which tends to make the injunction to the naval commander largely hortatory. At any event, where the town or port was *defended,* no obligation, it has been said by commentators, rested upon the commander to restrict the bombardment to the kinds of objectives indicated in the Convention.[270]

The discrepancy between the requirements respecting *undefended* towns in land and in naval warfare was explained at the Hague Conference in terms of the inability of a naval force, in contrast with a land army, to occupy such towns or, most often, even to take temporary possession for the purpose of destroying the military objectives specified.[271] Whether characterized as defended or undefended—a distinction which, in respect of a coastal state possessed of air power, must seem difficult of application—the coastal areas bombarded, which may be far behind the locale of land combat, are in practical effect comprehended within a temporary zone of operation delineated by the range of the ships' guns. The mobile warship has thus been

269. Art. 2.

270. Spaight, *Air Power and the Cities* 105 (1930); and id., "The Doctrine of Air Force Necessity," 6 *Brit. Y.B.I.L.* 3 (1925).

271. See the "Report of the Second Subcommission to the Third Commission on the Regulations Concerning the Bombardment by Naval Forces in Time of War," in *Proceedings of the Hague Peace Conferences: The Conference of 1907* (trans. of official texts, 1921), Vol. 3, p. 359.

regarded as possessed of the faculty of creating operational zones wherever it goes, within which zones the presence of enemy civilian persons and property has not been allowed seriously to embarrass the destruction of military objectives.[272] Some accommodation of the minimum destruction principle is sought by requiring, as in land bombardment, the naval commander to spare "as far as possible" buildings devoted to and actually used for religious, cultural, and humanitarian purposes.[273]

ENEMY INSTITUTIONS AS OBJECTS OF ATTACK

A belligerent's bases of power are values that are expected to be available during a continued sequence of time for use by the belligerent in achieving its postulated objectives. This expectation is obvious enough in respect of the two preceding categories of "people" and "resources"; it is clear, though more subtle and covert, in relation to "institutions." In its most comprehensive sense, an institution is a pattern of practices, and embraces in reference any organized activity of people using resources to achieve values.[274] By enemy institutions we mean both the internal patterns of practices adopted by an enemy belligerent state and the external patterns maintained by such state in its relations with other territorial polities. It has already been observed that the power of a belligerent state depends not only upon the raw manpower and resources at its disposition, but also upon the efficiency and stability of the structures and procedures of authoritative and effective decision-making by which such resources and manpower are disposed for belligerent objectives.[275] In respect of external institutions, the degree and firmness of support a belligerent secures from its allies constitute vital items in calculations of its strength by itself and by its opponent.

It is perhaps evident that when persons (those located in key au-

272. Royse, supra note 263 at 164. This faculty finds particular reflection in the fact that in many cases in the last world war, naval bombardment was employed as the initial step to so-called amphibious operations involving the landing of troops on an enemy coast.

273. Art. 5, Hague Convention IX of 1907. Art. 6, id., requires the naval commander, "if the military situation permits," to do his "utmost" to give warning of the bombardment.

274. See Lasswell and Kaplan, *Power and Society* 47–8 (1950).

275. E.g., *Foundations of National Power*, c. 4 (2nd ed., Sprout and Sprout, 1951); Morgenthau, *Politics Among Nations*, c. 9 (2nd ed., 1954).

thority and control positions) and resources (public or private), that is, the material bases of institutions, are captured or destroyed, the institutions themselves are in effect attacked. The destruction, for instance, of public buildings and of means of communication will inevitably interfere with the functioning of governmental institutions. We seek here, however, to consider attack upon institutions apart from violence specifically directed against people and resources.

In general, belligerents seek to attack the internal authority and control institutions of the enemy by modifying and subverting the supporting structure of loyalties predominant in the enemy society.[276] The loyalty structure—the sentimentalized demands and identifications [277]—of the enemy population influences the extent to which, on the behavioral level, voluntary cooperation displaces or strengthens habit, public praise or censure, and severe deprivations as modes of social control. The structure and intensity of loyalties at the same time reflect and indicate the degree to which, in popular expectations, the obtaining institutions satisfy the demands of the population; they are, in other words, both cause and reflection of the stability or instability of existing institutional patterns. The subversion of loyalty structures is, in turn, commonly sought by altering the expectations of the population about the rectitude or the continuing efficiency and success of these institutions.

All types of instrumentalities of policy may of course be employed in attacking the enemy loyalties—the collective will to fight—that sustain the enemy political elite's decisions about recourse to, waging, and continuing the war.[278] "Area bombardment" by military airpower, for example, was employed in the last world war for such purpose.[279] It is, however, the ideological instrument that is specialized to the modification and disruption of loyalty patterns or, more generally, patterns of perspectives, by the management of a flow of signs and symbols. The employment of the ideological instrument, involving both the use of mass communication media and

276. See Speier, "Morale and Propaganda," in *Propaganda in War and Crisis* 3 (Lerner ed., 1951).

277. Lasswell and Kaplan, supra note 274 at 24.

278. Lasswell, "Political and Psychological Warfare," in *Propaganda in War and Crisis* 261 (Lerner, ed., 1951). See also Dyer, *The Weapon on the Wall: Rethinking Psychological Warfare* (1959).

279. Infra, p. 654.

the coordinated handling of the other types of instruments to maximize impact upon the will to fight, in contexts of continuing military violence, is commonly designated as "psychological warfare."

The broad objective of "psychological warfare" vis-à-vis the enemy audience—elite and mass—may be described in terms of induction of dissension, defeatism, and defection in the enemy camp.[280] It hardly needs mention that in recent wars the target audience included not only the armed forces but also the civilian population of the enemy. Belligerents have frequently assumed that the dependence of the soldier upon the civilian worker for the implements of modern war, the intensified relation, in other words, between military effort and industrial and agricultural production, has made the loyalties and morale of the enemy civilian worker a militarily important target.[281] Just as belligerents mobilize, coordinate, and harness civilian activities for enhancement of belligerent objectives, so also do they seek to integrate civilian loyalties and organize them around overriding symbols of the national political community. Inevitably, the opposing belligerent seeks to weaken, diffuse, and diversify these integrated loyalties and to erode the civilians' will to work and will to obey their political elite.[282]

The methods utilized in seeking to manipulate enemy expectations about and evaluations of their authority and control institutions include what psychological warfare specialists or propagandists refer to as the "substitution" of collective loyalties and the "de-collectivization" or "privatization" of individuals.[283] The first calls for com-

280. See Whitton, "Propaganda and International Law," 72 *Hague Recueil* 545, 558–60 (1948); Lutz, "World War Propaganda," in *Public Opinion and World Politics* 157 (Wright ed., 1933). Representative citations to the recent literature on psychological warfare are collected in supra, Ch. 1, note 78. A listing of typical political-military and military objectives in psychological warfare is provided in Daugherty and Janowitz, *A Psychological Warfare Casebook* 342, 372–3 (Tech. Memo. ORO-T-360, 1958).

281. E.g., Carlson, "Ideopolitics," in *Modern World Politics* 234, 245 (2nd ed., Kalijarvi, 1953); Stowell, "The Laws of War and the Atomic Bomb," 39 *A.J.I.L.* 784, 785 (1945).

282. Speier, "Psychological Warfare Reconsidered," in *Propaganda in War and Crisis* 463, 466–72 (Lerner ed., 1951) offers an analysis of the common term "will to resist."

283. See Speier, supra note 276 at 20–3. See further, in connection with methods, Becker, "The Nature and Consequences of Black Propaganda," 14 *Am. Soc. Rev.* 221 (1949), and Doob, "The Strategies of Psychological Warfare,"

munications emphasizing or dramatizing subsidiary or submerged loyalties in the hope of nullifying and displacing loyalties to the ruling political elite. In the First World War, for example, the Allied Powers attempted to arouse in non-Prussian German soldiers separatist sentiments against Prussia. They sought similar aims in propaganda addressed to troops of the Austro-Hungarian Empire and Polish soldiers, while the Germans hoped to capitalize upon ancient Irish-English feuds.[284] In the Second World War, the Japanese forces tried to exploit the demands for independence in the former colonial territories in southeastern Asia and to channel such demand against the Allied colonial powers. "Privatization" of individuals involves communications which stress fear of both meaningless death and death for a worthless or unattainable cause and which appeal to the elemental "visceral drives." These communications are commonly supplemented by fervent assurances of good treatment for deserters and prisoners of war, as well as, in the case of the general civil population, not only of nonenslavement but also a new and undreamed-of prosperity. In possible future wars between protagonists adhering to different systems of world public order, intensified use of these and other methods of psychological and ideological warfare must in all probability be expected.

Both the customary and conventional law about combat situations exhibit practically no prescription specifically addressed to the use of ideological weapons in war. The only generalization which can be made with any confidence is that belligerents have in practice regarded the corruption and incitement of either enemy troops or enemy civilians to surrender or revolution as a permissible means of warfare.[285] It might be noted, however, that the traditional law of

---

13 *Public Op. Q.* 635 (1949–50). The latter attempts a schematic categorization of types of PW strategies and of the variables that affect the course or configuration of each type.

284. See Mock and Larson, *Words That Won the War* 257–62 (1939); Lasswell, *Propaganda Technique in the World War* 167–77 (1927).

285. See 2 Oppenheim-Lauterpacht 426–8; 3 Hyde, *International Law* 1838–9, (2nd rev. ed., 1945); Dept. of the Army, *Law of Land Warfare,* par. 49 (FM 27-10, July 1956); Murty, *The International Regulation of the Ideological Instrument of Coercion* cc. 6–7 (unpublished thesis in Yale Law Library, 1957).

In Spaight, *War Rights on Land* 149–50 (1911), a distinction was attempted to be drawn between enemy troops and enemy civilians, incitement of the latter to revolt being supposedly illegitimate: "The modern principle of the distinctive

belligerent occupation requires the occupant to respect the allegiance and fundamental institutions of the inhabitants. Thus, attack upon enemy loyalties and institutions, at least attack by such gross means as the exaction of oaths of allegiance to the occupant and impressment into his armed forces, may be said to become impermissible with respect to enemy population under the power of the attacking belligerent.[286] Finally, it may be observed that psychological warfare exercised through the manipulation of a stream of verbal and nonverbal symbols is commonly much less destructive of values than other modes of attack upon enemy institutions and morale. Even so, some effects produced by ideological instruments in, for example, the systematic vilification of the enemy and all that he stands for, or in the "brainwashing" of prisoners, may outlive the particular war in which these practices are resorted to and may militate against achievement of a durable and sensible peace.[287] The possible prolongation of damage would seem one reason for some community regulation of the permissible contents of propaganda.

Claims With Respect to Permissible Instruments and Means of Attack

The last half-century or so, through the increased industrialization of society and the mobilization of science, has seen the rapid acceleration of the process of inventing and developing new instruments specialized to the application of violence and of improving the older, inherited ones. The culmination in our epoch of this development with the achievement of thermonuclear explosives, chemical and biological weapons, and of new delivery systems, bring into sharp and urgent focus problems relating to the legitimacy of the use of these and other contemporary instrumentalities.

In approaching these problems, it is especially necessary to have a

---

status of combatants and noncombatants supplies a criterion for deciding the question. If a commander demands that the civil inhabitants of a hostile country occupied by him shall refrain from all participation in the war, he can not fairly or logically try to excite a revolt among those residing in the territory occupied by their own troops and administered by their national Government." However, in Spaight, *Air Power and War Rights* 333 (3rd ed., 1947), a different view appears to have been adopted. And see Art. 21 of the Hague Air Rules of 1923.

286. Infra, p. 802.

287. Cf. Carlson, supra note 281 at 247.

sense of history. New weapons of war frequently meet initial hostility and execration from moral theologians, lawyers, and military men, the latter because of vested interests in the current means of war. Pope Innocent III issued a decretum forbidding the use against Christians of the crossbow or arbalest and of siege engines for hurling projectiles such as the ballista.[288] The Second Lateran Council of the Church (1139) solemnly denounced the crossbow as "deadly and odious to God." [289] When firearms first made their appearance, those who used them were granted no quarter when captured. The Chevalier Bayard, it is recounted, when lying mortally wounded by an harquebus shot, gave thanks to the Lord that he had never shown mercy to a musketeer.[290] The bayonet too was for a long time looked upon with detestation that frequently manifested itself in denial of quarter to troops using the weapon.[291] Objections were also made when red-hot shot, split-shot, chain-shot, and *mitraille* were introduced; treaties are recorded in which some of these things were forbidden.[292] While these examples may seem quaint today, they illustrate the natural tendency of those whose expectations are shattered by a "technological surprise" to denounce as "cruel," "inhuman," and "illegal," and to seek to outlaw, the new and unfamiliar weapon. Yet clearly novelty in itself cannot rationally be equated with illegality.[293]

Here too, as in the other areas of the combatant law of war previously examined, the fundamental policy of minimum unnecessary destruction may be seen to underlie questions of legitimacy. Thus, the gist of the wisdom of the commentators is that where the suffer-

288. See Bordwell, *The Law of War Between Belligerents* 21–2 (1908). Belli, *De Re Militari et Bello Tractatus* (trans. Nutting, Classics of International Law, Vol. II, 1936), Part VII, c. 3, p. 186.

289. See Nussbaum, *A Concise History of the Law of Nations* 18 (rev. ed., 1954).

290. Walker, *A History of the Law of Nations,* Vol. 1, p. 190, note 1 (1899).

291. Maine, *International Law* 140 (1888). See also Nef, *War and Human Progress* 251–5 (1950), who calls the bayonet "the most terrifying of all the weapons introduced during the age of limited warfare."

292. Holland, *Lectures on International Law* 317 (Walker and Walker, eds., 1933).

293. 1 Garner, *International Law and the World War* 282 (1920) observed: "The employment of new and powerful inventions of destruction or of new methods is, of course, not to be condemned and ruled out merely because they are new or because they are more effective than those formerly employed, as a few sentimentalists in every age have wished to do."

ing or deprivation of values incidental to the use of a particular weapon is not excessively disproportionate to the military advantage accruing to the belligerent user, the violence and the weapon by which it is effected may be regarded as permissible. All war instruments are "cruel" and "inhuman" in the sense that they cause destruction and human suffering. It is not, however, the simple fact of destruction, nor even the amount thereof, that is relevant in the appraisal of such instruments; it is rather the needlessness, the superfluity of harm, the gross imbalance between the military result and the incidental injury that is commonly regarded as decisive of illegitimacy. For instance, Hall observed:

> the amount of destruction or suffering which may be caused is immaterial if the result obtained is conceived to be proportionate.[294]

Dr. Spaight put the matter lucidly, and bluntly:

> It is really by its fruits that the engine of war is judged. The test of lawfulness of any weapon or projectile is practically the answer one can give to the question—What is its "bag"? Does it disable so many of the enemy that the military end thus gained condones the suffering it causes?
>
> Today, a commander has an acknowledged war right to use any weapon or explosive which, however terrible and ghastly its effects, is capable of putting out of action such a number of the enemy as to justify the incidental mutilation of individuals.[295]

Similarly, Professor Hyde pointed out as "the underlying legal principle"

> whether the blows to be inflicted by new instrumentalities such as those designed and employed in the course of World War I possess a military value which outweighs in significance the severity and magnitude of the suffering caused by their use and likely to be incidentally felt by non-combatants.[296]

294. *International Law* 636–7 (8th ed., Pearce Higgins, 1924).

295. *War Rights on Land* 76–7 (1911).

296. 3 *International Law* 1814 (2nd rev. ed., 1945). Comparable formulations are made in 1 Garner, supra note 293 at 282; Lawrence, *The Principles of International Law* 528, 533 (7th ed., Winfield, 1928); and 2 Oppenheim-Lauterpacht 340.

The problem so posed is thus a highly pragmatic one of determining the substantiality of the net military advantage, the military gain, as it were, yielded by particular typical uses of a specific instrument after discounting the attendant costs in values. Costs in values include, in comprehensive reference, both the expenditures of base values incurred and the value losses inflicted upon the enemy. In casting the general problem in these terms, it is not easy to avoid creating an impression of cynicism. It is useful nonetheless to bear in mind the lesson admirably stressed by Dr. Royse and others more than three decades ago; that historically the community of nations has never yet succeeded in outlawing any weapon which was of substantial net military utility.[297] Weapon parity may of course in particular situations induce reciprocal abstinence, but in general only weapons which were militarily ineffective or inefficient, or which were of marginal or indecisive military value and obsolete, or which were not deemed vital to the military establishments of one or more great powers, have been successfully prohibited.[298]

The experience of the Hague Peace Conferences of 1899 and 1907 affords illuminating documentation. In the First Hague Conference, it was proposed that no powders (the propulsion force of projectiles as distinguished from the bursting or explosive charge)

297. Royse, *Aerial Bombardment and the International Regulation of Warfare* (1928).

Cf. Rodgers, "Suggestions as to Changes in the International Law for Maritime Warfare," 17 *A.J.I.L.* 11 (1923): "If experience is a guide, new weapons of war can never be abolished by law if they are serviceable; the most that can be done is to limit their use in accordance with such accepted principles as to the proper incidence of warfare on peoples and individuals as under the stress of war emotions we shall be able to agree to call sportsmanlike, humanitarian, and in accordance with fair play. . . . [I]f the new inventions will be serviceable in war to subdue the organized armed strength of the hostile nation and overcome national opposition in and behind the hostile lines, they will be so used and the rule of war will recognize them." See also Borchard, "The Atomic Bomb," 40 *A.J.I.L.* 161, 165 (1946).

The kinds of component considerations that enter into appraisal of military effectiveness of weapons are suggested in Edson, "Weapons Systems in Relation to Foreign Policy," in *National Security in the Nuclear Age* 6 (Center for International Relations and Area Studies, Univ. of Minn., 1958) *sub nom.* "functional parameters of a weapons system."

298. Royse, supra note 297 at 141–6; Stone, *Legal Controls* 551.

more powerful than those already in use should be permitted.[299] The proposal was unanimously rejected, after Captain Crozier of the American delegation pointed out that more powerful powders might be invented which would cause less injury to the gun barrel and thus be more efficient and economical.[300] Similarly, the proposals that no new high explosives, field and naval guns, muskets, and naval armor plate superior to the types then existing should be used were all rejected.[301] Clearly none of the great powers were willing to accept prohibitions and restrictions with regard to possible military improvements when potentialities of increased efficiency were involved.

The fate of the Russian attempt to prohibit the use of submarine torpedo boats and similar weapons in sea warfare is likewise revealing. There had already been some anticipations of the military effectiveness of such weapons in the American Civil War, and in the Sino-French (1884) and Sino-Japanese (1895) wars.[302] The small powers like the Netherlands, Sweden, Norway, and Turkey considered the submarine torpedo boat a cheap defensive weapon of the weak and refused to outlaw it. The big powers (save France), however, possessed of strong surface navies were willing to interdict the submarine if unanimity could be achieved, which unanimity was not

299. See the Russian Circular of Jan. 11, 1899 (Dec. 30, 1898, Old Style) by Comte Mouravieff, in 2 *The Hague Peace Conferences of 1899 and 1907* 3–5 (Scott, ed., 1909).

300. See the "Report of Captain Crozier to the Commission of the U.S.A. to the International Conference at the Hague regarding the work of the First Committee of the Conference and its Subcommittee," in 2 id. at 29.

301. Ibid., at 30–2. And see the "Report Presented in the Name of the First Subcommission by General Den Beer Poortugael," in *Proceedings of the Hague Peace Conferences: the Conference of 1899* 284–91 (trans. of official texts; Scott, ed., 1920). Said Captain Crozier, very candidly: "The general spirit of the proposals that have received the favorable support of the subcommission is a spirit of tolerance with regard to methods tending to increase the efficacy of means of making war and a spirit of restriction with regard to methods which, without being necessary from the standpoint of efficiency, have seemed needlessly cruel. . . . If we examine these decisions, it seems that when we have not imposed the restriction, it is the 'efficacy' that we have wished to safeguard, even at the risk of increasing suffering." (at 354).

302. See Huidobro Toro, *El Submarino Ante El Derecho Internacional* 16 (1936); and Royse, supra note 297 at 14.

forthcoming.[303] At the Second Hague Conference no similar prohibition was proposed. The Russo-Japanese War of 1904 had shown quite clearly that the submarine torpedo boat had been developed into an efficient instrument with great destructive capability. The only restriction approved was that torpedoes which had missed their target, i.e., after they were militarily valueless, must become harmless.[304]

POISON AND POISONED ARMS

Consideration of the kinds of instruments of war the Hague Conferences did succeed in formally prohibiting is equally instructive. The first of these was poison and poisoned arms.[305] From the time the bow and javelin became obsolete, no recorded instance appears of the use of poisoned arms, projectiles, or bullets in war by modern armies.[306] Obviously, bullets kill and disable with or without smearing with poison. With respect to poison itself, as distinguished from both poisoned arms and poisonous or toxic gases, its sole practical use in modern wars was perhaps the rendering of water supplies unusable. In the First World War, retreating German troops in the African theater of operations were alleged to have "poisoned" or polluted water sources with animal carcasses and cattle dung. Germany claimed that warning and notification of the pollution was given.[307] The legitimacy of this measure was debated in the learned literature.[308] Yet it might be noted that diversion of water supplies

303. See *Proceedings,* supra note 301 at 367–8. The statements of the delegates of the various countries are summarized in 7 Moore, *Digest of International Law* 367–8 (1906).

304. Art. 1(3), Hague Convention VIII Relative to the Laying of Automatic Submarine Contact Mines.

305. Art. 23(a), Hague Regulations.

306. Germany, however, was experimenting with the use of poison and poisoned bullets during the last war, and used human persons as subjects. See "Trial of Brandt," 2 *Trials of War Criminals* at 178 (1947).

307. For details, see 1 Garner, supra note 293 at 388–92.

308. Lawrence, supra note 296 at 542 and 1 Garner, supra note 293 at 291 suggest that where the civil population is dependent upon the wells contaminated, the measure is impermissible, even though warning is given. 2 Oppenheim-Lauterpacht 340 note 5 condemns it unqualifiedly.

The old *Rules of Land Warfare,* par. 28 (FM 27-10, 1940) provided that the rule against use of poison "does not prohibit measures . . . to contaminate

in the context of sieges was commonly regarded as permissible and it would seem difficult to draw meaningful functional distinctions between diversion and pollution with notice. Notice deprived the act of pollution, whatever the polluting agent or substance employed, of the element of clandestineness and secrecy popularly associated with the use of poison. If large-scale devastation by retreating force may be permissible, it is not easy to see why contamination of water supplies in the same or comparable kind of tactical situation should be regarded differently. Under certain circumstances, potable water may become a most vital war material.

EXPANDING AND EXPLODING BULLETS AND INCENDIARIES

A second kind of weapon the Hague Conference of 1899 prohibited was the expanding bullet—the so-called "dumdum" bullet.[309] These bullets flattened easily upon contact with the human body and tore great jagged wounds. As such they caused aggravated suffering without producing a compensating military advantage. Expanding or incised bullets were, moreover, both injurious to the rifle barrel and inaccurate at the distance at which modern battles were fought. They had hence been discarded for the much more accurate steel-nosed bullet which rendered a target equally *hors de combat*.[310] Being both obsolete and inefficient, they were successfully outlawed.

The Hague Conferences did not explicitly deal with exploding and incendiary bullets. About forty years earlier, the Russians had

---

sources of water by placing dead animals therein or otherwise, provided such contamination is evident or the enemy is informed thereof." In the new *Law of Land Warfare,* par. 37(b) (FM 27-10, July 1956), this statement was dropped; the reasons for dropping it are stated in the 1 Mar. 1954 revision, par. 217b to be that conditions of warfare may not permit notification to the enemy, and that the notices may be destroyed by the elements or third parties, and that anyway this measure of war will hardly assume "any substantial importance in the future." Cf. the *British Manual of Military Law,* Part III, par. 112 (1958).

309. Declaration (IV, 3) Concerning Expanding Bullets, of July 29, 1899.

310. See Royse, supra note 297 at 141–2. It should be noted, however, that Britain had been using expansive bullets against savage tribesmen who, she claimed, could not be stopped by ordinary bullets. Only Britain and the United States did not vote for the Declaration; see the "Report of Captain Crozier," supra note 300 at 34. During the First World War, each side charged the other with using expanding bullets; there was, however, no satisfactory evidence that either side had actually done so. See 1 Garner, supra note 293 at 263–70.

developed a bullet which exploded upon hitting either a hard or yielding surface.[311] It had not actually been used in war when the St. Petersburg Declaration of 1868 condemned the use of "any projectile of less weight than 400 grammes, which is explosive, or is charged with fulminating or inflammable substances." [312] When directed against human targets, the explosive bullet was closely similar in its effects to the expanding bullet and hence was commonly regarded as covered by the general interdiction of the Hague Regulations of "arms, projectiles or material calculated to cause unnecessary suffering." The prohibition was observed in practice until the First World War when it was suddenly discovered that the proscribed bullet was an efficient weapon in air warfare. Explosive or incendiary bullets were found useful in setting on fire and destroying airplanes, dirigibles, and balloons. Initially, Germany threatened to execute captured Allied pilots using the new ammunition, but very soon the German air force was using the same ammunition.[313] By 1923, the Commission of Jurists to Consider and Report Upon the Revision of the Rules of Warfare declared that the use of tracer, incendiary, or explosive projectiles "by or against aircraft" was permissible.[314] The universal use of these bullets in the last war and the lack of any protest strongly suggest their legitimation, and the desuetude of the prohibition at least in aerial war.[315] It may be noted that the last war

311. Bordwell, *The Law of War Between Belligerents* 87 (1908).

312. Text in Holland, *The Laws of War on Land* (1908). The Declaration of St. Petersburg marked the first appearance of conventional rules explicitly founded on the principle "which measures the illegality of weapons not by their destructiveness, but by the amount of unnecessary suffering they inflict." See Lawrence, supra note 296 at 529–30.

313. See Spaight, *Air Power and War Rights* 204–13 (3rd ed., 1947).

314. Art. 18, Hague Rules of Aerial Warfare of 1923. The same statement was made by the International Law Association in Art. 8 of the "Draft Convention for the Protection of Civilian Persons Against New Engines of War," *Report of the International Law Association, Fortieth Conference, Amsterdam* 44 (1938).

315. Professor Lauterpacht in 2 Oppenheim-Lauterpacht 520–1 admits that "in so far as the resort to such weapons serves primarily the purpose of disabling enemy aircraft, it will be difficult to insist on the full application of these prohibitions to air warfare. This is notwithstanding the fact that the use of such projectiles against aircraft may entail upon its occupants a degree of suffering whose infliction has been rightly stigmatized as inhuman." Cf. Stone, *Legal Controls* 552 note 27.

saw the development of rocket projectiles which seem closely analogous to explosive bullets. Fired from mobile ground launchers, aircraft, as well as from ships, they proved highly efficient against tanks, ships, submarines, and ground installations. The weight of the rocket is well beyond the 400-gram minimum limit specified for explosive projectiles in the St. Petersburg Declaration.[316]

The flamethrower or "liquid fire projector" may also be noted. This weapon, when introduced by the Germans in World War I, was denounced by the French as an "abominable method" and a "refinement of barbarity." [317] In alleged reprisal, the Allied powers soon adopted the instrument, and by the Second World War it had become a familiar weapon of the infantry and tank corps. When directed against enemy personnel as such, liquid fire, it is said, causes "needless suffering." [318] The flamethrower, however, like the napalm (jellied gasoline) bomb, was principally developed and used in World War II and in Korea, for reduction of bunkers and other installations and emplaced positions where ordinary high explosive (TNT) was not effective, for attacking tanks, and for routing out enemy snipers from densely wooded areas.[319] Certainly, in these types of situations, the flamethrower and the napalm bomb can hardly be said to be any less permissible than regular artillery shells. Here, as in the case of incendiary and explosive bullets, the nature and situation of the target would seem the factors of decisive significance.[320]

316. The rockets with which modern arsenals are stocked vary in size from, in the case of United States forces, the 3.5-inch projectile fired from a portable launcher to the giant intercontinental or global range missiles. See Worley, *A Digest of New Developments in Army Weapons, Tactics, Organization, and Equipment* 22–3 (1958).

317. 1 Garner, *International Law and the World War* 288 (1920).

318. 2 Oppenheim-Lauterpacht 340 note 3 declared that "There is no doubt that this practice was unlawful, because it causes 'unnecessary injury.' " 1 Garner, supra note 317 at 288 suggested a different view: "While the effect may be more deadly than bullets or shells, we can hardly say that it is any the less permissible. Indeed, owing to its very limited radius of action and the visibility of the flame, the chances of escape are greater. . . ." Lawrence, supra note 296 at 533 took an inconclusive position. Compare Art. 8(V) of the International Law Association's "Draft Convention," supra note 314 which would except from a prohibition of the use of incendiary weapons "appliances, such as flame projectors, used to attack individual combatants by fire."

319. See Worley, supra note 316 at 223.

320. Dept. of the Army, *Law of Land Warfare,* par. 36 (FM 27-10, July 1956) lays appropriate stress on these factors: "The use of weapons which employ fire,

SUBMARINE AND LAND MINES

Another weapon the Hague Conferences sought to regulate was the submarine automatic contact mine which was at the time the only available type of submarine mine. The British delegation to the 1907 Conference proposed first a total prohibition upon the employment of unanchored mines, but later suggested a qualified prohibition that would permit the launching of such mines "during a naval combat." The British delegation also proposed that the laying of anchored mines save in the territorial waters and in contiguous zones of the belligerents, and, in particular, the use of mines for purposes of blockade, be forbidden.[321] Automatic contact mines, however, had already been employed in naval war as long ago as the Crimean War.[322] The Russo-Japanese war had suggested the great potentialities of mines; the Japanese lost two out of six battleships in a single day due to anchored mines. The German delegation, indeed, described the mine as "an indispensable means of warfare" and explicitly envisaged its use against blockade cruisers.[323] The British proposals were rejected and all the Conference produced was Convention VIII, the chief prescription of which was that anchored mines must become innocuous upon detachment from their moorings, and unanchored mines within an hour after launching.[324] It might be noted that the military significance of free mines drifting away from the anticipated path of an oncoming enemy naval force, as well as of mines that undesignedly broke loose, was problematical. On the other hand, such drifting or loosed mines presented serious dangers to neutral shipping, which dangers could last beyond the period of hostilities.[325]

---

such as tracer ammunition, flame throwers, napalm and other incendiary agents, against targets requiring their use is not violative of international law. They should not, however, be employed in such a way as to cause unnecessary suffering to individuals." Cf. *British Manual of Military Law,* Part III, par. 110, note 1 (1958).

321. *Proceedings of the Hague Peace Conferences: The Conference of 1907,* Vol. 3, pp. 383–5, 404–5 (Scott, ed., 1921). See also Higgins, *The Hague Peace Conferences* 329 et seq. (1909).

322. See Brodie, *A Guide to Naval Strategy* 71–2 (4th ed., 1958).

323. *Proceedings,* supra note 321 at 380–1.

324. Art. 1(1) and (2) of Hague Convention VIII of 1907 Relative to the Laying of Automatic Submarine Contact Mines.

325. See Royse, supra note 297 at 145. It was in fact the damage which China

With respect to the employment of mines as blockade instrumentalities, Hague Convention VIII of 1907 contained a provision requiring that mines not be laid off enemy ports and coasts "with the *sole* object of intercepting *commercial* shipping." [326] The practice in the two world wars in the matter of war zones proved this provision singularly futile. Mines were effectively and widely used in the form of minefields or barrages that made access to and passage through designated ocean areas extremely hazardous.[327] Minefields were of course frequently supplemented by surface and subsurface vessels as well as by aircraft. It may be observed that exclusionary effects were achieved simultaneously against enemy and neutral vessels. Thus, war zones enforced by mines and other instruments constituted the assertion of two distinguishable claims.[328] Vis-à-vis neutrals, they represented a claim to control and embargo commerce with the enemy; war zones were, in other words, a technique of enforcing blockade controls. We have in the preceding chapter referred to the kinds of factors that appear rationally to call for consideration in appraisals of the reasonableness, and hence lawfulness, of such mode of imposing commerce controls. It might be stressed, however, as a requirement of the minimum destruction principle that adequate notice of the establishment of such zones should be given to neutral shipping and that provision be made for safe passage of ships determined to be engaged in genuinely interneutral, i.e. appropriately navicerted, trade.[329] The development of so-called influence mines, which include magnetic, acoustic, and pressure

---

continued to suffer from loose, live mines several years after the Russo-Japanese war that prompted the efforts of the Hague Conference to regulate such weapons. See Higgins, supra note 321 at 328–9. Art. 5 of the Convention requires that, at the close of the war, each party must remove the mines it has laid.

326. Art. 2 of Hague Convention VIII. Emphasis added. This was the innocuous end result of the original British proposal that the use of submarine automatic contact mines to establish or maintain a commercial blockade be forbidden. Higgins, supra note 321 at 329.

327. Exposition on the strategic use of mines may be secured from Gwynne, "The Submarine Mine in Naval Warfare," in *Evolution of Sea Power* 133 (Domville-Fife, ed., 1939), and from Rairden, "The Importance of Mine Warfare," 78 *U.S. Naval Inst. Proc.* 847 (1952).

328. Cf. 2 Oppenheim-Lauterpacht 682.

329. Cf. Stone, *Legal Controls* 574.

mines and which do not require actual contact for activation but simply a certain proximity to a vessel,[330] make provision for notification and safe lanes for neutrals even more urgent.

Vis-à-vis the enemy belligerent, mined war zones or mine barrages represented a claim to exercise combat by a distinct method of naval warfare. Belligerent practice in the first and second wars suggest the acceptance of such barrages or fields, designed to restrict the operational mobility of surface and submersible craft, as permissible instruments of combat. When in the First World War, in November, 1914, the British Admiralty first declared the whole North Sea a "military area" and invested the area with minefields, it invoked the pleas of reprisals and of protection against the indiscriminate sowing of mines on certain trade routes on the high seas.[331] The German response, which consisted of declaring all the waters surrounding Britain including all of the English Channel an "area of war," was itself sought to be justified as a counterreprisal.[332] When the United States participated in the laying of the great North Sea mine barrage between Scotland and Norway, the plea of reprisals was dropped and the purpose of the barrage stated simply as the prevention of passage of enemy submarines to and from the Atlantic Ocean by the northern route through the North Sea.[333] Early in the last war, in December, 1939, the British announced that minefields would be laid off the east coast of Britain as protection against the unnotified sowing by the Germans. Subsequently, further minefields were established which closed the Skagerrak and the Kattegat, and practically all of the Baltic Sea. A war zone was laid athwart the mouth of the Baltic, from a point near the Dutch coast to the Norwegian coast. Further, the whole German Baltic coast was covered by mines. The southern approaches to the English Channel, embracing 150,000 square miles of water, were also declared a "danger area." Certain areas of the Mediterranean were similarly covered by minefields laid by both the Allied and Axis Powers. Britain, for example, exten-

330. Brodie, supra note 322 at 72.

331. Note from the British Foreign Office to British Ambassader in Washington; presented to the Secretary of State, Nov. 3, 1914, *U.S. Foreign Relations 1914, Supp.* 464.

332. Imperial Chancellor's Proclamation, as given by the German Ambassador to the Secretary of State, Feb. 4, 1915, *U.S. Foreign Relations 1915, Supp.* 96.

333. See Note from Secretary of State to the Chargé at Norway, Aug. 27, 1918, *U.S. Foreign Relations 1918, Supp.* Vol. 2, p. 1764–5.

sively mined Italian coastal areas up to 30 miles from the coastline.[334] More recent use of mine warfare is illustrated in the Korean war where the North Koreans utilized both moored minefields and free floating mines to protect their coasts from the operations of the United Nations naval forces. The military effect of these Communist mines was far from negligible.[335]

In contrast with the submarine mine, the *land* mine has rather curiously failed to give rise to either controversies or established prescriptions relating to the permissibility of their use. About a hundred years ago, during the American Civil War, Generals Sheridan and Slocum vigorously protested as unlawful the planting of explosives on roads by retiring Confederate armies.[336] No similar protests appear to have been made in more recent wars. Land mines are commonly utilized to slow down pursuing forces and are emplaced as part of defense fortifications. Land mines, like submarine mines, are deliberately concealed from visual observation. Indeed, land mines are sometimes disguised as attractive and unoffensive objects, colloquially known as "booby traps." While some have perceived a rough analogy here with the clandestineness of poison or with the employment of treachery,[337] belligerents have not raised serious question in respect of the permissibility of "booby traps." The employment of land mines has in practice been treated as a permissible ruse of war.

SUBMARINE CRAFT

The submarine as a weapon of war has raised important, continuing legal issues. In the two global wars, the submarine was limited in its military functions to direct attack upon warships and upon the maritime logistics of the enemy belligerent. In contemporary military establishments, the submarine has been adapted and

334. 6 Hackworth, *Digest of International Law* (1943) 510 et seq.; U.S. Naval War College, *International Law Documents* 1943, 59 et seq.; Stone, *Legal Controls* 573 and note 11.

335. See Cagle and Manson, "Wonsan: The Battle of the Mines," 83 *U.S. Naval Inst. Proc.* 598 (1957).

336. Spaight, *War Rights on Land* 81–2 (1911).

337. Greenspan, *The Modern Law of Land Warfare* 363 (1959) condemns "booby traps" on the ground that they are "indiscriminate in dealing out death and injury" and are "more nearly related to the devices of an assassin than the arms of a soldier, . . ."

equipped for a new function—that of strategic bombardment. In the future, the submarine may also be utilized not only as an instrumentality of active combat but also as a military cargo carrier. The submarine as a cargo carrier does not appear likely to present any new and special problem of policy. The employment of the submarine-ballistic missile system for strategic bombardment purposes raises issues appropriately subsumed under a later heading. Those issues relate, it will be seen, primarily to the level of destruction imposed rather than to the peculiar modality or weapons system utilized. It is, of course, upon the utilization of the submarine for commerce destruction that controversies about the requirements of legal authority have been focussed.

These controversies, we have previously observed, were rooted in the inability of the submarine to comply with the traditional procedures of attack and capture at sea: of warning or summons, visit, search, and seizure and conveyance to a home port for adjudication in prize. We have also adverted to the methods adopted for defense of surface shipping which imposed high risks upon submarine craft attempting to observe those procedures. It may bear some reiteration that the physical characteristics of the weapon itself normally precluded observance of the time-honored procedures. A fragile craft by surface warship standards, the submarine commonly relied upon its ability to approach and attack unseen—an ability, it should be noted, now distinctly limited by the development of ultrasensitive sonar devices. The submarine was incapable of taking aboard any substantial number of the crew and passengers of target ships, and of sparing personnel for a prize crew. At the same time, the lifeboats of the attacked ships would only rarely constitute the "place of safety" in which customary law required the crew, passengers, and papers to be put in cases where destruction rather than capture was appropriate.[338]

During the years between the First and Second World War, it was frequently asserted by commentators that the technological char-

338. Wilson, "The Submarine and Place of Safety," 35 *A.J.I.L.* 496, 497 (1941) suggested that "Safety commensurate with that enjoyed by passengers and crew before the destruction of their vessels would seem to be the measure demanded. This does not imply the same comforts or conveniences, but the same absence of risk to life."

acteristics of the submarine did not exonerate a belligerent employing it from the duty of conforming to "the humane rules adopted in naval warfare." [339] The crux of the matter was of course that these rules were established when naval fleets consisted wholly of surface vessels such that the peculiar limitations of submersible craft could not have been considered. The unratified Treaty of Washington of 1922, reflecting the commentators' assertion, insisted that, if a submarine could not capture a merchantman in accordance with the customary prescriptions, "the existing law of nations" required it to desist from attack and to permit the merchant vessel to pass unharmed.[340] Similarly, Article 22 of the London Naval Treaty of 1930,[341] later incorporated into the London Procès-Verbal on Rules of Submarine Warfare of 1936,[342] declared that submarines must conform to the rules to which surface vessels are subject. There was always a brittle romanticism about these conventions and it surprised few that the treaty structure crumbled upon the first touch of war. These treaties in substance sought Utopianlike to outlaw the submarine, for the conditions imposed all but prohibited its militarily effective use.

It is now entirely commonplace to note that the submarine is an effective and vital weapon particularly when employed against insular states dependent on overseas communications and supply routes.[343] With it, Germany twice brought Britain to precarious teeter on the edge of disaster. In the First World War, German submarines destroyed more than 11 million tons of Allied and neutral

339. See e.g., Colombos, *Law of the Sea* 446–7; Mori, *The Submarine in War: A Study of Relevant Rules and Problems* 72–3 (1931); Lawrence, *The Principles of International Law* 519–20 (7th ed., Winfield 1928); Hall, *The Law of Naval Warfare* 69–70 (1921); 1 Garner, supra note 317 at 378–80. "Report of the Committee on the Legal Status of Submarines," 14 *Tr. Grotius Soc.* 155 (1928); Hall, "Submarine Warfare," 5 *Tr. Grotius Soc.* 83 (1919); cf. Huidobro Toro, supra note 302 at 41–3; Barnes, "Submarine Warfare and International Law," 2 *World Polity* 121 (1960).

340. Art. 1(2); text in 2 Hudson, *International Legislation* 794.

341. Text in 5 id. 394.

342. Text in 7 id. 490. See also Art. 12 of the *Projecto de Codificacion del Empleo del Submarino en la Guerra* (1929) prepared by the Centro de Estudios de Derecho Internacional Publico of the Universidad de Buenos Aires.

343. See, e.g., Usborne, "Influence of the Submarine on Naval Warfare," in *Evolution of Sea Power* 34 (Domville-Fife, ed., 1939); Low, *The Submarine at War* (1942); and Eliot, "The Submarine War," 21 *Foreign Aff.* 385 (1943).

shipping, which was more than 80 per cent of all the shipping lost.[344] At the peak of the submarine campaign in April, 1917, when Germany had only 125 operative submarines at any one time, Britain lost more than 900,000 tons in a single month. In the Second World War, when there were 400 operative German submarines, submarines accounted for 69 per cent of the total tonnage (23 million) lost by the Allied Powers. In the Pacific, American submarines sank about 60 per cent of the total of 9 million tons of Japanese shipping destroyed by the end of hostilities. It is true that with new antisubmarine warfare (ASW) devices and techniques[345] and with the vast shipbuilding resources of the United States, the Allied Powers did succeed in eventually mastering the submarine menace. To assume, however, that the weapon is no longer an effective one would be hazardous to an extreme.[346] On the contrary, the fact that with a U-boat fleet which in tonnage could not begin to compare with the opposing surface navies, the Germans succeeded in four years of war in sinking more ships than the entire British merchant marine had at the beginning of the war, and the further fact that the Japanese failed to stop the American submarines, indicate that only a giant power can bring the weapon under control.[347] Furthermore, the development of submarines powered by nuclear energy and whose submerged operating range is limited only by human factors can hardly be taken as an omen of military obsolescence.[348] Finally, there may be noted the

344. The above and succeeding figures are taken from Anderson, "The Protection of Commerce in War," 78 *U.S. Naval Inst. Proc.* 881 (1952).

345. Contemporary methods of ASW are described in Danis, "Offensive ASW: Fundamental to Defense," 83 id. 583 (1957).

346. Dr. Bush made the cautionary statement, more than a decade ago, in *Modern Arms and Free Men* 69 (1949): "The fact that emerges is that the day of the submarine is by no means over. If we entered a war soon, against a technically and industrially strong enemy, and if that enemy could effectively apply modern devices at sea, we should have the whole job of overcoming the submarine to do over again on a new and unattractive basis. Again we should face the severe threat that a nearly immune submarine fleet might determine the outcome of the war in favor of the enemy. Many of the successful methods of the last war are now obsolete against the truly modern submarine. There is no cure-all."

347. Brodie, *A Guide to Naval Strategy* 150 (4th ed., 1958).

348. See Galantin, "The Future of Nuclear-Powered Submarines," 84 *U.S. Naval Inst. Proc.* No. 6, p. 23 (1958); also Beavers, "Sea Power and Geopolitics in the Missile Age," 85 id. No. 6, p. 41 (1959).

heavy emphasis placed by one of the polar powers, the Soviet Union, upon a large and powerful submarine fleet.[349]

The submarine's capacity for destruction of life and property should be viewed in conjunction with the military importance of severing an enemy's supply and transport lines, thereby depriving him of the means with which to carry on war. If the "annihilation of the enemy's commerce" be postulated, as some of the very commentators who demanded compliance with surface-ship rules did so postulate, as "one of the great aims of naval warfare," [350] to expect belligerents with or without surface navies to give up an effective commerce destruction weapon can scarcely qualify as realism.[351] It does not seem especially helpful to deprecate the "attempt to change existing principles" as an "attempt to avoid the consequences of naval weakness." [352] The experience of the Second World War when even belligerents with powerful surface navies and air forces, and with a tradition of respect for international law, found it necessary to engage in unrestricted submarine warfare [353] strongly suggests that

349. See MacIntyre, "The Soviet Submarine Threat," in *The Soviet Navy* 168 (Saunders, ed., 1958). Garthoff, *Soviet Strategy in the Nuclear Age* 203 (1958) observes that, in Soviet naval strategy, the interdiction of sea communications between Western Europe and America by means of submarines continues to be regarded as of major importance even in a future general war.

350. Colombos, *Law of the Sea* 487.

351. Cf. Stone, *Legal Controls* 604–7.

352. Colombos, *Law of the Sea* 447. See also Higgins, "Submarine Warfare," 1 *Brit. Y.B.I.L.* 149 (1920–1921). The tacit assumption was, of course, that the submarine was not a proper component of naval strength.

353. See the Judgment of the International Military Tribunal at Nuremberg, in *Nazi Conspiracy and Aggression: Opinion and Judgment* 140 (1947).

As Judge Lauterpacht suggested in "The Problem of the Revision of the Law of War," 29 *Brit. Y.B.I.L.* 360, 374 (1952), the problem of "unrestricted submarine warfare" is but an aspect of the more general question relating to the viability of the combatant-noncombatant distinction in modern war. 1 Garner, *International Law and the World War* 378 (1920) argued that: "The rule (in respect to providing for the safety of crews and passengers) was adopted for the protection of innocent noncombatants, not for the benefit of belligerents, and it cannot be admitted that the invention of new instruments repeals or modifies the rule. The use of the instrument must be adjusted to the requirements of the law of nations and of humanity and not they to the instrument." No one disputes the desirability of this exemplary demand. But the legal regulation of international violence, if it is to amount to something more than edification, must be based on facts. And, while it may be a dubious commentary on human

change in pre-existing principles can no longer be so casually dismissed.

It is, of course, possible, notwithstanding the broad considerations indicated above, that particular encounters between submarines and merchantmen may occur under tactical circumstances in which compliance with the conventional procedures may be reasonably demanded from the submarine commander. The encounter, for instance, may involve a lone, unescorted merchantman away from the ordinary trade routes and from the immediate reach of enemy surface warships or aircraft. In such instance, warning to the target ship and opportunity for crew and passengers to abandon ship, and perhaps even to notify potential rescuers, before sinking the target need not pose grievous risks for the submarine. The submarine's security may ordinarily be adequately served in these circumstances by immediate departure from the scene of the attack. Most generally put, appraisals of lawfulness of submarine warfare must be appraisals of specific operational situations; the balancing of the requirements of military necessity and of minimum destruction must be a weighing of features of the detailed contexts of particular encounters.

Apart from such specific situations which, in conflicts of the World War I and II type, are likely to be exceptional, it is also conceivable that conditions may be re-created in future wars which permit some restraint in submarine warfare. Our principal reference here is to "limited-war" conflicts where the opposing belligerents mutually refrain from exercising their full capabilities for destruction. Unrestricted commerce destruction by submarines has been a hallmark of conflicts that approached totality in dimensions, and successful limitation of a conflict once recourse to such form of hostilities is had would seem largely problematical. Thus, it need not be pure fantasy to suppose that in limited conflicts—which *ex hypothesi* do not call for the full mobilization of the economic and military potential of participants—belligerents may tacitly agree to employ submarines against regular naval forces only. Indeed, refraining from unrestricted submarine warfare against enemy merchantmen may be precisely one way of signaling an intention to keep a conflict limited. Finally, in wars which remain limited because one or both bel-

---

nature, history and the practice of belligerents appear to indicate that it is the law of nations and of humanity that will have to be adjusted, if indeed they have not yet been so, to the requirements of effective use of submarines.

ligerents are not capable of anything else, observance of many of the traditional limitative rules may be quite feasible militarily. Where, for instance, an opposing belligerent is not possessed of either the surface naval or air power necessary for antisubmarine warfare and defense of shipping, the sinking of enemy merchantmen without warning by the belligerent disposing of submarines may be very difficult to characterize as necessary and lawful.

CHEMICAL WEAPONS

We turn now to the weapons and methods of mass destruction which are distinctive of modern total war. These instrumentalities promise to make possible the infliction of total violence on whole populations and lend an appalling literalness to what was once merely a propagandist's phrase—war of annihilation. Here, perhaps, the basic policy of minimum unnecessary destruction of values underlying legal controls on the application of violence approaches a point of diminishing utility. The vastly amplified range and intensity of destruction which employment of these weapons brings about is commonly expected simultaneously to entail greater civilian damage, the military relevance of which may in greater or lesser degree be remote. The very conception of military effectiveness, let alone the question of substantial proportionality, becomes increasingly refractory to disciplined inquiry.

We consider first the regulation of the gas weapon, use of which is commonly referred to under the broad term "chemical warfare."

The Hague Conference of 1899 had produced a Declaration of agreement "to abstain from the use of projectiles the sole object of which is the diffusion of asphyxiating or deleterious gases." [354] At that time, however, no practical gas shell had as yet been developed, such that necessarily the Declaration was adopted

> in ignorance of the facts as to whether the results would be of a decisive character, or whether injuries in excess of that necessary to attain the end of warfare, the immediate disabling of the enemy, would be inflicted.[355]

354. Text in *The Hague Conventions and Declarations of 1899 and 1907* 225 (2nd ed., Scott, 1915).

355. "Report of Captain Mahan to the Commission of the United States to the International Conference at the Hague," in 2 *The Hague Peace Conferences of 1899 and 1907* 37 (Scott, ed., 1909).

The military potentialities of poison gas were soon revealed. The Germans initiated the use of gas in the First World War, avoiding the letter of the Hague Declaration by employing canisters fixed to the ground and relying on the wind to waft the gas clouds over the Allied trenches. The Allied Powers soon retaliated, using bombs, projectiles, and cylinders, and toward the end of the war gas attacks became a fairly common means of warfare.[356]

After World War I came a series of attempts to outlaw the gas weapon. In the peace treaties with the defeated Central Powers, the Allied Powers uniformly included a provision to the effect that "the use of asphyxiating, poisonous or other gases and all analogous liquids, materials or devices being prohibited," their manufacture and importation was forbidden in the defeated states.[357] The Treaty of Washington of 1922 reiterated this prohibition and declared that poison gas "[had] been justly condemned by the general opinion of the civilized world." [358] This Treaty, however, never came into force for failure of French ratification. Subsequently, the Geneva Protocol for the Prohibition of the Use in War of Asphyxiating, Poisonous or other Gases and of Bacteriological Methods of Warfare of 1925 incorporated the same prohibition set forth in exactly the same language.[359] This Protocol, which was ratified by numerous states in-

356. For details, see 1 Garner, supra note 353 at 271–8.

357. Art. 171 of the Treaty of Versailles (with Germany), 3 *U.S. Treaties, Conventions, International Acts etc. 1910–1923* 3402; Art. 119 of the Treaty of Trianon (with Hungary) 3 id. 3577–8; Art. 135 of the Treaty of St. Germain-en-Laye (with Austria) 3 id. 3192; Art. 82 of the Treaty of Neuilly (with Bulgaria) 112 *British Foreign and State Papers* 801 (1919); Art. 176 of the Treaty of Sèvres (with Turkey) 113 id. 690 (1920); Art. 2(1) of the Treaty of Berlin (U.S. and Germany) 3 *U.S. Treaties, Conventions, International Acts etc. 1910–1923* 2598.

358. Art. 5 of the Treaty relating to the Use of Submarines and Noxious Gases in Warfare, Washington, Feb. 6, 1922, 2 Hudson, *International Legislation* 797.

359. Text in 3 Hudson, *International Legislation* 1670. Cf. Art. 39 of the Draft Convention prepared by the Preparatory Commission for the Disarmament Conference C.687. M.288.1930.IX (1930.IX.8) p. 26: "The . . . Parties undertake *subject to reciprocity,* to abstain from the use in war of asphyxiating, poisonous or similar gases, and of all analogous liquids, substances, or processes. They undertake *unreservedly* to abstain from the use of all bacteriological methods of warfare." (italics supplied). See also the resolution adopted by the Council of the League of Nations in connection with charges of gas warfare made by China against Japan in 1938 declaring that "the use of toxic gases is

cluding most of the great powers (but not the United States and Japan), considered together with the Declaration and treaties noted above, and with certain derivations from Article 23(a) of the 1907 Hague Regulations forbidding the use of poison and poisoned arms, is assumed by commentators to have become declaratory of customary international law.[360]

In contrast with the experience of the First World War, the Second did not see any authenticated substantial or large-scale use of the gas weapon. Japan, it has been reported, executed "a large number of small gas attacks" against Chinese forces from 1937 to 1943.[361] The fact that both the Allied and the Axis Powers had enormous stocks of lethal chemical agents available suggests that the threat of and capacity for reciprocation,[362] rather than doubt as to the destructive capability of the weapon, lay behind the self-restraint of the belligerents. This impression is heightened when one recalls that the armies of Fascist Italy had used gas against the barefooted Ethiopians,[363] while Germany employed it to exterminate several millions of the hapless inhabitants of occupied regions. Weapon parity may thus apparently neutralize the military value that abstractly might be ascribed to a particular weapon.

The prohibition of the use of "asphyxiating, poisonous or other gases, and of all analogous liquids, materials or devices," is not, it may be noted, susceptible of easy rationalization. The basis of the prohibitory rule has been said by distinguished authority to be that poison gas causes cruel and superfluous suffering in the process of

---

a method of war condemned by international law." League of Nations, *Off. J.*, 19th Yr., 378 (1938).

360. See Schwarzenberger, *The Legality of Nuclear Weapons* 38 (1958); 2 Oppenheim-Lauterpacht 344; Stone, *Legal Controls* 556. Dept. of the Army, *Law of Land Warfare,* par. 38 (FM 27-10, July 1956) states that because it was not ratified by the United States, the Geneva Protocol is "not binding on this country."

361. See *Research in CBR* (Chemical, Bacteriological, and Radiological Warfare), H. Rep. 815, Committee on Science and Astronautics, U.S. House of Rep., 86th Cong., 1st. Sess., 4 (1959).

362. On June 8, 1943, President Roosevelt declared that gas would not be resorted to unless it was first used by enemies of the United States. See 8 *Dept. of State Bull.* 507 (1943).

363. See the documents collected and the discussion in the Council of the League, League of Nations, *Off. J.*, 17th Yr., 362–486 (1936) passim.

rendering enemy forces *hors de combat.*[364] It would seem an exacting task, in comparative analysis of alternative weapons, adequately to document this assertion.[365] It may be noted that differing casualty or war gases differ in their physiological effects. There are, for instance, choking gases (asphyxiants) such as phosgene and diphosgene which accumulate in the lungs and drown the target; blood gases, such as hydrogen cyanide and arsine, which enter the blood stream through the lungs and stop the transfer of oxygen in the blood; blister gases (vesicants), such as mustard and lewisite, which blister the skin and attack internal organs; and nerve gases, such as Tabun (GA) and Sarin (GB) which disrupt nerve signals to the muscles.[366] Nerve gases are perhaps presently the fastest acting and most lethal agents, while asphyxiants and blood gases can apparently be tailored in their concentration and dissemination as to accelerate their effects. There appears considerable room for controversy whether quick death through these chemical agents is necessarily more cruel, in its physiological or neurological aspects, than the crushing blast effects of high explosive.[367] Yet, somewhat curiously, the one excites in

364. See 2 Oppenheim-Lauterpacht 344; U. S. Naval War College, *International Law Situations* 102, 106 (1935); 1 Garner, supra note 353 at 282.

365. The relative humanity or inhumanity of the gas weapon, in terms of World War I experience, was debated in the interwar period. Mills, "Chemical Warfare," 10 *Foreign Aff.* 444 (1932) argued that gas was "the most humane weapon" then in existence, and pointed to the low percentage of deaths among gas casualties in the First World War—2% in the American army, 3.3% in the British. But see Woker, "The Effects of Chemical Warfare, With Reference to the Statistics of Gas Warfare," in *Chemical Warfare—Report of Papers Read at an International Conference at Frankfurt am Main, 1929,* 35 (1930); also Fradkin, "Chemical Warfare—Its Possibilities and Probabilities," *Int. Conciliation* No. 248, p. 113 (1929). One difficulty with Mills' argument is that no distinction between the various kinds of gases is made.

366. See, e.g., *Research in CBR,* supra note 361 at 5–7; Dubinin, "Potentialities of Chemical Warfare," 16 *Bull. Atomic Scientists* 250 (1960); Waitt, *Gas Warfare* (1942); Wachtel, *Chemical Warfare* (1941).

367. Writing before the Geneva Gas Protocol was framed, Lawrence, *The Principles of International Law* 351 (7th ed., Winfield, 1928) observed: "It is not easy to see how quick asphyxiation exceeds in cruelty the blowing of a human body to pieces by the bursting of a shell. Slow torture by chemical methods might well be forbidden; but immediate death after inhaling deleterious fumes is comparable to drowning which is often the fate of seamen in a naval engagement." His editor added (at 532) that "if gas kills a combatant almost immediately, or puts him out of action, without needless pain or permanent evil

popular emotions intense aversion and indignation while the other is contemplated with relative equanimity. The supposition is sometimes made, further, that poison gas is appropriately forbidden precisely because of its deadly effects. This supposition is in effect an invocation of the St. Petersburg Declaration of 1868 which provided that: "the only legitimate object which states should endeavor to accomplish during war is to weaken the military forces of the enemy; [t]hat for this purpose it is sufficient to disable the greatest possible number of men; [t]hat this object would be exceeded by the employment of arms which uselessly aggravate the sufferings of disabled men, or render their death inevitable; . . ." It is perhaps evident that well-aimed firearms no less than well-handled artillery do render death inevitable for target troops. Few have suggested, nevertheless, that the laws of war require soldiers to fire only at the limbs, for example, of enemy troops.[368]

The second, and perhaps more important, point is that the present conventional prohibition is cast in language of such inclusive compass as to permit future interpreters mechanically to subsume thereunder even nonlethal chemical agents, which produce merely temporary if distressing effects entailing no enduring damage to the human organism. The so-called "riot-control" gases, like tear (lachrymators), vomiting (emetics), and sneezing (sternutators) gases, which may be extremely useful in some tactical situations, afford old and well-known illustrations of such agents. Much more recent are the incapacitating agents which, until five or six years ago, were almost entirely unknown. Incapacitating agents are generally grouped into two: agents which produce temporary physical disability like paralysis, blindness, or deafness; and agents, called "psycho-chemicals," which bring about temporary and reversible mental aberration. The physical incapacitating agents impose neither pain nor permanent aftereffects; varying dosage permits recovery within a few hours or a

---

results, it is not unnecessarily cruel." Cf. Birkenhead, *International Law* 221 (6th ed., Moelwyn-Hughes, 1927).

368. It might also be noted that protective masks and devices are available against gas attacks which, consequently, can hardly be said to render death inevitable. Worley, *A Digest of New Developments in Army Weapons, Tactics, Organisation and Equipment* 218–19 (1958) reports development of "a gas-aerosol filter material called fiber diffusion board, which will provide protection from all known chemical and biological warfare agents. It will also furnish a certain degree of protection against radiological agents."

few days. For at least one agent, an antidote is reported which brings immediate recovery. Some psycho-chemicals are said to induce a drastic reversal of character in the subject, while others render the subjects unable to carry out "simple commands" or perform "normal tasks" and at the same time unaware of their own abnormal behavior.[369] Incapacitating agents appear to hold forth great military promise. From the perspective of the minimum destruction principle they may hopefully be regarded as more humane weapons which eventually may conceivably permit the resolution of issues between belligerents without imposition of physical suffering or destruction of material resources. These new substances, in fine, will require the making of discriminations and distinctions in the application, or reformulation, of the current prohibition of the gas weapon.

BIOLOGICAL WEAPONS

The Geneva Protocol of 1925, referred to above, after reiterating a prohibition of gas warfare, goes on to declare that the states parties "agree to extend this prohibition to the use of bacteriological methods of warfare." Although this Protocol is the only treaty law on the matter, it is sometimes suggested that the prohibition of bacteriological warfare is now part of customary law.[370] The derivations from the Hague Regulation rule forbidding the use of poison and poisoned arms relied upon in making this suggestion are not, as is indicated below, wholly free from difficulties and it remains controversial whether a general prescription has emerged that is operative not only as against the forty-odd nations which have ratified the Protocol but also as against those which have not, such as the United States.[371]

369. *Research in CBR,* supra note 361 at 9–11. See also Summerson, "More on Chemical Warfare," 16 *Bull. Atomic Scientists* 252 (1960); and Cousins, "CBR v. Man," *Saturday Review,* July 23, 1960, pp. 9, 10–11.

370. Schwarzenberger, supra note 360 at 38. Cf. Greenspan, *The Modern Law of Land Warfare* 359 (1959).

371. Stone, *Legal Controls* 557. This failure of ratification by the United States proved mildly embarrassing when attention was drawn to that fact in the United Nations by Soviet Russia in connection with the latter's charges, wholly unsubstantiated, that the United States had employed germ warfare in Korea. See 27 *Dept. of State Bull.* 32 (1952) for the responding statement by the Deputy U.S. Representative to the United Nations. When the United States called for an investigation by the International Committee of the Red Cross, the World Health Organization, or the United Nations, Soviet Russia

Germ warfare has not as yet been used on any significant scale.[372] The military efficiency of differing "bacteriological methods of warfare" is consequently still an unknown factor. There are five groups of pathogenic micro-organisms from which, it is reported, biological agents are likely to be drawn: fungi; protozoa, such as those causing malaria and amoebic dysentery; bacteria causing, for instance, cholera, bubonic plague, and anthrax; rickettsia, including typhus; and viruses such as those of influenza and psittacosis. A sixth group of potential agents comprises toxins produced by micro-organisms.[373] It also appears that biological agents may be directed against plant and nonhuman animal life as well as against humans; [374] bacteriological warfare, in other words, may be employed against food sources of the enemy belligerent. While such measures may be brought under the literal language of the Geneva Protocol, they may, in their effects, be functionally analogous to an ordinary food blockade such as was applied by the Allied Powers in the two world wars. Various ways of disseminating biological agents in a target area are reported feasible, from covert introduction by saboteurs to delivery by air-

---

thoughtfully vetoed the proposal. See generally, Gross, "The Soviet Germ Warfare Campaign: A Case History," 28 id. 612 (1953).

372. A Soviet military tribunal, in 1949, convicted a number of Japanese nationals on a charge of having prepared and used bacteriological warfare against the "Mongolian People's Republic" in 1939. See 2 Oppenheim-Lauterpacht 343 note 2. In an announcement on Mar. 31, 1942, China accused Japan of dropping wheat and rice grains, paper, cotton wadding, and other articles supposed to have been impregnated with bubonic plague bacilli. 2 *Inter-Allied Review* 95–6 (1942). Merck, "Official Report [to the Secretary of War] on Biological Warfare," 2 *Bull. Atomic Scientists* No. 6, p. 16 (1946), though mentioning German and Japanese experiments with bacterial warfare, conveys the impression that the Japanese had not actually resorted to this means of warfare.

A brief history is offered in Rosebury, "Some Historical Considerations," 16 *Bull. Atomic Scientists* 227, 227–31 (1960). Dr. Rosebury includes in his survey a short summary of the Report issued by the so-called "International Scientific Commission for the Investigation of the Facts Concerning Bacterial Warfare in Korea and China" at Peking, in 1952. It is a matter for regret that Dr. Rosebury did not undertake to evaluate the authenticity and veracity of the statements made in this Report, beyond reporting that these statements were "categorically denied by American authorities" and that depositions made by U.S. prisoners of war were repudiated upon return of these persons to the U.S.

373. See *Research in CBR,* supra note 361 at 7–8; Kaplan, "Communicable Diseases and Epidemics," 16 *Bull. Atomic Scientists* 237 (1960).

374. See Bawden, "Plant Diseases," 16 id. 247.

craft or missiles.[375] A distinctive characteristic of the biological weapon is that its potentialities are not necessarily exhausted upon initial impact. A germ-laden canister that induces an epidemic has been likened to a bomb that explodes again and again; biological agents may, like fire, be self-propagating.[376]

The same general points made above in respect of the gas weapon seem applicable in respect of the biological weapon. It need not be assumed, for instance, that cholera induces any more unnecessary suffering than bullets or shell fragments. The virulence of biological agents is susceptible of selective control; it can be immensely intensified to promote quick fatalities or reduced to insure nonlethality. Nonlethal biological agents that distress and disable but neither make death inevitable nor impose permanent injury may, like incapacitating chemical agents, nonetheless be construed to be within the comprehensive sweep of the Geneva Protocol. Possibly it was the belief that the effects of biological warfare agents could not be confined to the fighting forces, and the expectation that it would be employed, if at all, against the civil population generally, which led to the verbally unqualified prohibition. The complete protection of the general population is manifestly extremely difficult; large-scale biological warfare may place an unbearable strain upon the medical and hygienic facilities of belligerents.[377] Whatever the historical reason for the inclusive scope of the Protocol's language,

375. E.g., Fothergill, "The BW Threat," 16 id. 244; Langmuir, "The Potentialities of Biological Warfare Against Man—An Epidemiological Appraisal," 66 *Public Health Reports* 387 (1951); Rosebury, *Peace or Pestilence* (1949); Rosebury and Associates, *Experimental Airborne Infection* (1947); and Merck, Fred, Baldwin and Sarles, *Implications of Biological Warfare,* U.S. Dept. of State Publication No. 2661, Vol. 1, Part Y, p. 65 et seq. (1946).

376. McLean, book review in 5 *Bull. Atomic Scientists* 353 (1949); cf. Possony, *Strategic Air Power: The Pattern of Dynamic Security* 143 (1949), who adds that if used in addition to other aerial weapons, the bacterial weapon would greatly increase the effectiveness of strategic bombing.

377. See Rosebury, supra note 375 at 120–35; Possony, supra note 376 at 143. See also the summaries of papers delivered at the "Symposium on Chemical and Biological Defenses in Perspective" of the American Chemical Society, Apr., 1960, reported *sub nom.* "Defenses Against CW and BW," 16 *Bull. Atomic Scientists* 254 (1960). Matilla Gomez, "Orientaciones Modernes en la Guerra Biologica," in 4 *La Guerra Moderna* 227, 247 (Univ. de Zaragoza, 1957) underscores the terror and panic-producing capabilities of biological warfare, which, among other things, may intensify impact upon the general population.

today, in disregard of the broad range of differing possible specific measures designated by a single undifferentiated term, the employment of "bacteriological methods of warfare," like the use of gas, is widely assumed to be a particularly disgraceful and odious activity. Thus, paradoxically, cultural stereotypes may prevent the development and use of instrumentalities that involve much less destruction of physical values than the older and more familiar projectiles loaded with high explosives.[378] Again, as in the case of gas, projection of a more discriminatingly worded prohibition may become important in the future.

AIR AND SPACE WEAPONS

We consider next the difficult problems raised by bombardment with air, and comparable weapons. For purposes of convenience in exposition, these problems are grouped under two headings: the one of claims relating to the permissible targets of aerial bombardment; and the other of claims relating to the permissible conduct of aerial bombardment. While we here speak of *aerial* bombardment, similar or analogous kinds of problems may be expected to arise from the use of *space* weapons—including long-range ballistic missiles and artificial satellites[378a]—against earthbound targets. Similarly, much of what is suggested below would appear equally applicable whether

378. Cf. the thesis of Rothschild, "Germs and Gas: The Weapons Nobody Dares Talk About," *Harper's Magazine* 28 (June, 1959). General Rothschild was, before retirement, Commanding General of the Chemical Research and Development Command, U. S. Army.

378a. The possibility of bombardment by means of missiles is now a notorious fact of life. The present utility of artificial satellite vehicles as a weapons delivery system seems less clear. See, for instance, Washington Center of Foreign Policy Research, *Developments in Military Technology and Their Impact on United States Strategy and Foreign Policy* 74 (A Study [No. 8] prepared at the request of the Committee on Foreign Relations, U. S. Senate, 86th Cong., 1st Sess., Dec. 6, 1959): "Bombing from satellites, which is so frequently suggested, appears feasible but of great difficulty and marginal value in comparison with existing and anticipated land-, sea-, and air-based missile systems; unmanned satellite bombers might have eventual utility as a supplementary deterrent system, but they would have to possess almost unprecedented qualities of mechanical reliability." See, further, *Space Handbook: Astronautics and Its Applications,* Staff Report of the Select Committee on Astronautics and Space Exploration, U. S. House of Rep., 85th Cong., 2nd Sess., 207–8 (1959).

the bombs are filled with "conventional" (TNT) or nuclear and thermonuclear explosives.

There is a marked paucity of conventional prescriptions for regulation of claims to subject particular targets to bombardment from the air. The paucity of community authority indeed extends to the whole field of aerial warfare. Hague Declaration XIV of 1907, which sought to prohibit the discharge of projectiles and explosives "from balloons or by other new methods of a similar nature" for a period "extending to the close of the Third Peace Conference," and which today would seem most quaint, was not even formally in effect during the last two world wars.[379] The Hague Rules of Aerial Warfare of 1923 were never adopted by an international conference and hence never ratified by any state.[379a] The 1956 Draft Rules for the Limitation of the Dangers Incurred by the Civilian Population in Time of War, prepared by the International Committee of the Red Cross, have yet to be given the form of a draft convention for consideration by some future international conference.[380] Both the 1923 Hague Rules of Aerial Warfare and the 1956 Draft Rules (ICRC) raise, however, the more important issues which need to be explored.[381]

379. Text in *The Hague Conventions and Declarations of 1899 and 1907* 220 (2nd ed., Scott, 1915). It is significant that the identical declaration of 1899, effective for a period of 5 years, was ratified by all the great powers except Britain. Royse, *Aerial Bombardment and the International Regulation of Warfare* cc. 2–3 (1928) passim, emphasized that at the time of the First Conference, only free balloons had been experimented with and had proved thoroughly inefficient, while by 1907 rigid or dirigible airships had been shown as practical machines.

379a. On these Rules, generally, see Rodgers, "The Laws of War Concerning Aviation and Radio," 17 *A.J.I.L.* 629 (1923); and Moore, "Rules of Warfare: Aircraft and Radio," in 6 *Collected Papers of John Bassett Moore* 140 (1944).

380. For general comment, see Kunz, "The 1956 Draft Rules of the International Committee of the Red Cross at the New Delhi Conference," 53 *A.J.I.L.* 132 (1959).

381. The jurisprudence of the war crimes tribunals offer practically no help at all. There are no records of trials where allegations of illegal conduct of aerial war were made. Although the Nuremberg Charter included among war crimes the "wanton destruction of cities, towns or villages, or devastation not justified by military necessity," the indiscriminate bombing of Allied cities by the Germans was not made the subject of a charge against any of the major German war criminals; 15 *War Crimes Reports* 110. There seems to be only one case of a conviction for a war crime connected with aerial warfare. A Jap-

Practically the only conventional provision that purports to regulate target selection in aerial bombardment is Article 25 of the 1907 Hague Regulations on land warfare to which we have previously adverted. The article stipulates that "the attack or bombardment, by whatever means, of towns, villages, dwellings, or buildings which are undefended is prohibited." Save for the phrase "by whatever means," the same rule cast in exactly the same language had been set forth in the 1899 Hague Regulations. The addition of "by whatever means" was, commentators commonly agree, designed by the Conference of 1907 to embrace aircraft.[382] In assessing the realism of extending the test of "undefended" towns to air bombardment, it is important to recall that first "unfortified" and later "undefended" towns were in the law of land warfare exempted from bombardment by reason of the cumulative factors of limited land artillery range and susceptibility to belligerent occupation. The inappositeness of the conception of "undefended" towns when applied in respect of the air weapon is indicated, on the one hand, by the fact that the

---

anese military commission had tried and sentenced to death two American airmen shot down in an urban area bombing attack on Osaka and Kobe, citing the Hague Air Rules and a resolution of the Disarmament Conference of 1932. An American military commission reversed the Japanese judgment and sentenced the Japanese judicial officer to death. The ground for the American decision is obscure. See Miller, "War Crimes Trials at Yokohama," 15 *Brooklyn L. Rev.* 191 at 207 (1949).

382. Stone, *Legal Controls* 621. Higgins, *The Hague Peace Conferences* 269–70 (1909). Illustrations of attempts to regulate air bombardment by the rules of land bombardment are found in the decisions of the Greco-German Mixed Arbitral Tribunal in *Coenca Brothers v. Germany, Annual Digest 1927–1928,* Case No. 389, and *Kiriadolou v. Germany,* id., *1929–1930,* Case No. 301. In these cases, the tribunal applied Art. 26 of the Hague Regulations, requiring the officer in charge of bombardment to "do all in his power" to give prior notification to the enemy "except in cases of assault," to the air bombing of Salonica and Bucharest by German planes in the First World War. It is interesting to note that in the Second World War, at least in the strategic bombardment of Japan, and in the Korean hostilities, warning was often given before air attacks were undertaken. See *U.S. Strategic Bombing Survey. The Effects of Strategic Bombing on Japan's War Economy* 38 (1946); and *Third Report of the United Nations Command Operations in Korea for the Period 1 to 15 August 1950,* U.N. Doc. S/1576 (Sept. 4, 1950), p. 7.

The question of notice or warning seems, however, peripheral to the main problems of either target selection or "indiscriminate" bombardment.

effective reach of contemporary aircraft is exponentially greater than that of even the largest field gun in existence. On the other hand, no part of the territory behind the lines established by enemy land armies could in any sense be said to be open to occupation by fighter or bomber aircraft as such. Moreover, belligerent aircraft penetrating enemy airspace have to contend with antiaircraft guns and missiles as well as interceptor planes long before they reach a particular target locality in the enemy hinterland. Analogy with warships appeared in consequence much more appropriate and it has been the naval warfare test of "military objectives" rather than "undefended places" which most commentators have approved and which belligerents have in practice invoked and purported to apply.[383]

The characterization of particular potential targets of air bombardment as legitimate "military objectives" is a task of considerable complexity embracing as it does in microcosm all the problems of adjusting the requirements of military necessity and minimum destruction. The Hague Rules of Aerial Warfare of 1923 offer both a broad generalization of policy and a number of specifications. "Aerial bombardment," Article 24(1) reads, "is legitimate only when directed at a military objective, that is to say, an object of which the destruction or injury would constitute a distinct military advantage to the belligerent." The categories of objectives specified in the Hague Rules seem studiedly few in number:

> Military forces; military works, military establishments or depots; factories constituting important and well-known centers engaged in the manufacture of arms, ammunition or distinctively

383. See e.g., Spaight, *Air Power and War Rights* 221 (3rd ed., 1947); Stone, *Legal Controls* 621, 623; Garner, "International Regulation of Air Warfare," 3 *Air L. Rev.* 103, 118–29 (1932); Spaight, "Air Bombardment," 4 *Brit. Y.B.I.L.* 21, 22–3 (1923–1924); Jennings, "Open Towns," 22 id. 258, 260–1 (1945).

The United Nations War Crimes Commission, in drawing up lists of persons against whom it had prima facie evidence of commission of a war crime, refused to decide whether in the light of modern warfare bombardment of "undefended places" came within the notion of war crimes. See *History of the United Nations War Crimes Commission and the Development of the Laws of War* 492–3 (1948). Instead, the Commission adopted the military objective doctrine and uniformly rejected charges of illegal bombardment where the evidence before it showed that the bombarded locality contained military objectives; see 15 *War Crimes Reports* 110 note 2.

military supplies; lines of communications or transportation used for military purposes.[384]

In general conception, the task of characterizing particular persons and things as permissible targets of aerial bombardment is, like the task of determining appropriate targets for other weapons and means of attack, one of categorizing the relationship of particular objects to the war effort of the enemy. More precisely put, it is one of determining the extent to which such objects constitute and are utilized as effective bases of enemy power. This task, it may be noted, is entirely comparable to that of characterizing the flow of goods to the enemy as contraband for purposes of naval interception and economic warfare. The full range of possible degrees of utility as military power bases is clearly a wide one. The objects enumerated in the 1923 Hague Rules may be thought of as clustered about one end of the spectrum, and controversy has been rare as to belligerent authority to destroy such objects. Controversies begin when one moves away from this end of the spectrum toward the opposite end. The location of particular objects along the continuum, in other words, the appreciation of the substantiality of any particular degree of military utility exhibited by specific objects, is of course dependent upon the particular dimension and characteristics of particular conflicts and the shape of prevailing conceptions of military strategy and tactics. In an all-out attrition conflict like the last world war where belligerents mobilize and harness the vast part of their economies to their war effort, objects or installations *not* of significant military utility may be expected to be much fewer in number and kind than, for example, in a limited conflict between Egypt and Israel. Thus, the problem that in World War II preoccupied strategic air staffs was frequently in practice not so much whether a particular factory or complex of factories was or was not appropriately characterized as a "military objective." It was rather the determination of the appropriate target priority to be assigned to such installations as acknowledged military objectives, selectivity being necessary for maximizing total impact upon the structure of the enemy's war economy.[385] The same kind of practice may be quite unnecessary and

384. Art. 24(2).

385. See Possony, *Strategic Air Power: The Pattern of Dynamic Security* 70–3 (1949).

unreasonable in other types of conflicts. A small war between Paraguay and Uruguay would seem an obvious hypothetical. Further, those who project a counterforce strategy in a conflict between nuclear powers suggest that the same characteristics of contemporary nuclear delivery systems which make force-in-being rather than industrial potential of supreme importance tend to render the general economy of the enemy a militarily unimportant and unattractive target system.[385a] It may be noted that there appears some recognition of the relativity of military utility in the 1956 Draft Rules (ICRC). Article 7 of these Rules, after providing for a catalogue of categories of permissible targets, adds that

> [E]ven, if [particular objects] belong to one of those categories, they cannot be considered as a military objective where their total or partial destruction, *in the circumstances ruling at the time,* offers no military advantage.

The second kind of claim relating to aerial bombardment—that is, claims about the conduct of such bombardment—raises the problem of confining destruction to permissible targets. This is the problem of "indiscriminate bombardment," back of which lies the assumption not only that certain things may not be characterized as legitimate "military objectives" but also that a legitimate "military objective" has definite and determinable dimensions in space.

Article 24 of the Hague Rules of Aerial Warfare of 1923, after setting forth a broad definition of "military objective" and listing some categories of "military objectives," provided:

> 3. The bombardment of cities, towns, villages, dwellings or buildings not in the immediate neighborhood of the operations of land forces is prohibited. In cases where the objectives specified in paragraph 2 are so situated that they cannot be bombarded without the indiscriminate bombardment of the civilian population, the aircraft must abstain from bombardment.
>
> 4. In the immediate neighborhood of the operations of land forces, the bombardment of cities, towns, villages, dwellings or buildings is legitimate provided there exists a reasonable presumption that the military concentration is sufficiently impor-

385a. See Richardson, "Atomic Bombs and War Damage," 4 *Orbis* 39 (1960).

tant to justify such bombardment, having regard to the danger thus caused to the civilian population.

These provisions distinguished between the bombardment of cities and installations, which are "in the immediate neighborhood" of land combat operations and the bombardment of cities and installations which are not so situated, and appeared to permit somewhat greater latitude to belligerents in the former than in the latter type of situation. The former involves what is frequently referred to as "tactical" air power which envisages the use of aircraft in close support of the operations of land forces. The targets of tactical air power are consequently commonly determined by the requirements of such operations and may consist of, for instance, a particularly stubborn emplacement, a detachment of tanks, or even attacking infantrymen. The latter type of situation involves so-called "strategic" air power which contemplates the destruction of targets independently of the activities of particular land forces. In this type of situation, the Hague Rules sought to require belligerents to abstain from attacking even admittedly military objectives where such objectives could not be attacked without "indiscriminate bombardment" of the civil populace.

Aerial bombs, like all explosive projectiles, create a zone of devastation around the point of impact, the diameter of the zone depending primarily upon the quantity and blasting power of the charge used.[386] Even if all the bombs dropped fall within the boundaries of the objective, a certain amount of destruction will be effected outside those boundaries. Such has been the case where bombs are filled with high explosive; so also in compounded measure in the case of incendiary agents. More importantly, however, not all the bombs can be expected to find their way to the target. Thus, notwithstanding the development of bombsights, radar devices and "pathfinder" techniques (for night attacks)[387] which were employed in World War II, it has been estimated that even under "favorable conditions," as much as one-third of the bombs delivered by aircraft may be expected to fall outside a target area of the size of "a large factory."[388] The factors that affect the percentage of misses are many and include

386. See Possony, supra note 385 at 53–6.

387. As to these techniques, see Harris, *Bomber Offensive* 199 et seq. (1947), also Hawton, *Night Bombing* 73 et seq. (1944).

388. Possony, supra note 385 at 55.

the bombing altitude, which in turn depends upon factors like the intensity of antiaircraft fire and the energy of the defending fighter aircraft; meteorological conditions; the size and disposition of the target; and the use of camouflage techniques to disguise targets. War production, moreover, like all industrial production, is usually carried on in or near populated centers since it is there that the necessary labor force, power, and transport facilities are available. This difficulty was compounded in the case of Japan in the last world war. Most Japanese urban homes were in fact small workshops where components and repair parts were produced for assembly in the large factories. To cut down the production of parts and to disorganize the large industries' supply system, it became necessary to destroy the workers' homes.[389] Finally, lines of communication and transportation, railroad yards and junctions, all of which are in varying degrees used for military purposes, are generally found in and running through centers of population. The point which bears underscoring is that air bombardment of military objectives almost inevitably entails some destruction of nonmilitary objects, i.e., civilian life and property. In this sense, aerial bombardment is always "indiscriminate." Thus, Article 24(c) and (d), above quoted,[390] would in effect have prohibited aerial bombardment in the vast majority of cases.[391] These provisions—which, it may be noticed, were more

389. This was one of the reasons why urban area attacks in Japan proved so effective. It has been estimated that these attacks by themselves reduced Japan's industrial output by about one-third. See *U.S. Strategic Bombing Survey, The Effects of Air Attacks on Japanese Urban Economy, Summary Report* 11–12, 19 (1947).

390. Cf. the more modest exhortation in a resolution adopted in 1938 by the Assembly of the League of Nations: "(3) Any attack on legitimate military objectives must be carried out in such a way that civilian populations in the neighborhood are not bombed through negligence." *Off. J.*, Sp. Supp. No. 182, p. 16 (1938).

391. Royse, supra note 379 at 228 et seq. Thus, Professors Lauterpacht (2 Oppenheim 526) and Garner (supra note 383 at 125) observed that only by total prohibition of any air bombardment can civilian immunity be completely respected. Belligerent practice has, of course, long ago demonstrated the idleness of such dream. More realistic, descriptively and in a predictive sense, is Professor Lauterpacht's statement (2 Oppenheim 525) to the effect that absolute immunity is not enjoyed by noncombatants, whose presence will not immunize military objectives where bombardment is not technologically feasible without incidental harm to noncombatants. See also Williams, "Legitimate Targets in Aerial Bombardment," 23 *A.J.I.L.* 577 (1929).

restrictive than the customary law on either land or naval warfare, in which bombardment may be just as "indiscriminate"[392]—would have practically outlawed any effective strategic use of aircraft.

It scarcely needs recounting that belligerents in the Second World War did not act in accordance with Article 24(c) and (d). At the outbreak of the war, Britain and France did announce their "firm desire to spare the civilian population" and prohibited their military commanders from bombarding "any except strictly military objectives in the narrowest sense of the word." Germany in turn proclaimed her "unqualified agreement" with the Allied declaration.[393] By 1940, however, Germany had "air blitzed" Polish, Norwegian, Yugoslav, Dutch, and British cities. In the same year, Britain had commenced limited resort to strategic target area bombing, where not individual objectives but rather designated target areas presumably containing a certain number and concentration of military objectives were aimed at.[394] By 1943, Allied strategic bombing had been intensified to the level of "saturation" of target areas sometimes comprising whole cities. Germany in turn had recourse to its so-called "revenge weapons"—"V-1" and "V-2"—which were simply launched in the general direction of London and other parts of England. Strategic air bombardment as thus conceived and executed inevitably involved considerable civilian destruction, that is to say,

392. 3 Hyde, *International Law* 1825 (2nd rev. ed., 1945).

393. These declarations were in response to President Roosevelt's appeal on Sept. 1, 1939 to both sides to refrain from air bombardment of "civilian populations or of unfortified cities." For the texts of the appeal and the replies, see 14 *Dept. of State Bull.* 181–2 (1939).

394. Spaight, in *Bombing Vindicated* 74 (1944), with singular abandon, characterized the British decision of May, 1940, to engage in such bombing as "splendid," "heroic," and as "self sacrificing" as Russia's decision to adopt the "scorched earth" policy. Liddell Hart, *The Revolution in Warfare* 92 (1947) asserted that the Germans commenced night attacks on London only in Sept., 1940, following six successive British raids on Berlin. The German attacks on Warsaw and Rotterdam he seemingly condoned as in conformity with "the old rules of siege bombardment," because they occurred when German troops were "fighting their way into these cities." Cf. Schwarzenberger, *Power Politics* 549 (2d rev. ed., 1951). It may be doubted whether chronological priority in this context is of any particular significance. A recent historical account of strategic air bombardment up to the Second World War is found in Lamarca, "La Aviacion en la Guerra," in 4 *La Guerra Moderna* 29 (Univ. de Zaragoza, 1957).

destruction of peoples and resources whose utility as bases of enemy military power was more or less indirect.

We do not intend to join the continuing debate over the lawfulness of target area or "carpet" bombing as practiced in World War II. It may, however, be useful to indicate, even if only in bold strokes, the types of factors that rationally may be taken into account in appraising differing particular bombardment contexts—bombardment by aircraft or by space vehicles, with "conventional" or nuclear explosives—and in seeking to apply therein the basic principles of military necessity and minimum destruction.

The 1956 Draft Rules (ICRC) offer suggestive general formulations of the relevant issue. Article 8 of the Draft Rules reads:

> The person responsible for ordering or launching an attack shall, first of all:
>
> (a) Make sure that the objective, or objectives, to be attacked are military objectives within the meaning of the present rules, and are duly identified.
>
> When the military advantage to be gained leaves the choice open between several objectives, he is required to select the one, an attack on which involves least danger for the civilian population:
>
> (b) Take into account the loss and destruction which the attack, even if carried out with the precautions prescribed under Article 9, is liable to inflict upon the civilian population.
>
> He is required to refrain from the attack, if, after due consideration, it is apparent that the loss and destruction would be disproportionate to the military advantage anticipated:
>
> (c) Whenever the circumstances allow, warn the civilian population in jeopardy, to enable it to take shelter.

Article 9 provides, in its first paragraph, that

> All possible precautions shall be taken, both in the choice of the weapons and methods to be used, and in the carrying out of an attack, to ensure that no losses or damage are caused to the civilian population in the vicinity of the objective, or to its dwellings, or that such losses or damage are at least reduced to a minimum.

The problem thus formulated from the perspective of an authoritative decision-maker reviewing a military commander's acts, is, most abstractly, one of determining proportionality between the military advantage derived from the destruction imposed upon the target, or upon the objectives located within the target area, and the concomitant deprivations of civilian values. Upon the assumption, as indicated earlier, that permissible military objectives have identifiable spatial dimensions, the question of proportionality [395] may perhaps be conveniently conceived in terms of the reasonableness of the degree, or extent, of disparity between the area actually destroyed in the particular bombing operation examined and the area physically occupied by the installations asserted to have been the target of such operation. The disparity may, in other words, be taken as a crude indicator of the extent of civilian damage.

Evaluation of the zone of disparity, as it were, appropriately involves inquiry into the kinds of values destroyed therein. The nonmilitary resources destroyed may, for instance, have been devoted to religious, cultural, and humanitarian uses that civilized communities commonly regard as specially valuable. On the other hand, it is frequently suggested that injuries and damage sustained in such zone by the labor force of a target war production plant should be discounted from estimates of the extent of civilian damage. Such work-

395. The notion of proportionality seems implicit in Art. 24(4) of the Hague Air Rules referring to bombing in operational zones. Garner, supra note 383 at 122, in connection with this provision, said that the "military damage" must be "compensatory" and sufficiently great to justify incidental or accessory civilian suffering. Spaight, *Air Power and the Cities* 102 (1930) expressed substantially the same idea of proportionality: "A military objective of vital importance will be bombed, notwithstanding the consequential effects, wherever found. There are objectives, however, which it cannot be of such moment to a belligerent to destroy that he is justified in shutting his eyes to the disastrous consequences that will be entailed upon harmless citizens by his attack."

The notion is at least as old as Grotius. Grotius declared that it was lawful to bombard a ship full of pirates or a house full of brigands even though there are within the same ship or house a "few" infants, women, etc. who are thereby endangered. Then he added: "We must also beware of what happens and what we forsee may happen, beyond our purpose, unless the good which our action has in view is much greater than the evil which is feared, or unless the good and the evil balance, the hope of the good is much greater than the fear of the evil." *De Jure Belli Ac Pacis* (trans. Kelsey, Classics of International Law, 1925) Bk. IV, c. I, IV, s. 102, p. 600–1.

ers, the suggestion runs, are "quasi-combatants" not entitled to claim immunity from direct attack.[396]

Other kinds of factors bearing upon appraisal of disparity relate to the operational conditions that attended delivery of the attack and shaped the degree of precision in aiming in fact achieved. These include, for example, the inherent or internal capabilities for precision of the weapon delivery system employed. In particular respect of ballistic missiles, it may be observed that steady improvements in guidance systems entail constantly increasing ability for precision.[396a] In contrast, the probable accuracy of bombardment from an orbiting satellite appears to be an unknown factor for the present. The great promise, however, that artificial satellites are reported to hold forth with respect to reconnaissance or the acquisition of target intelligence [396b] should make possible significant increases in the precision of both aircraft and missile bombardment. Other factors similarly affecting precision—such as the kind and efficacy of the defensive measures encountered, meteorological conditions, the size, location, and disposition of the target installations—have been alluded to above.

A third kind of factor to which the foregoing types need to be

396. Spaight, "Legitimate Objectives in Air Warfare," 21 *Brit. Y.B.I.L.* 161 (1944); id., "Noncombatants and Air Attack," 9 *Air L. Rev.* 372 (1938). Stone, *Legal Controls* 628 agrees, saying that the principle of civilian immunity "does not make sense" when offered to shield what he calls the "work force of military objectives." The writer of a Note on "Aerial Warfare and International Law," 28 *Va. L. Rev.* 516 at 525–6 and note 93 (1942) pushes the notion to the limits of its logic, and suggests that any distinction drawn between the position of munitions workers when actively engaged in their work and when they are in their homes, on the theory that in the latter case they are no different from the ordinary population, would be too tenuous. "A dead munition worker is effectively put out of the picture whether killed at home or at work." Cf. Garner, supra note 383 at 117 and note 30 and Smith, *The Crisis in the Law of Nations* 76–7 (1947).

396a. The accuracy of long-range missiles appears already to have overtaken the average accuracy achieved by World War II aircraft. In the recent Soviet missile tests, one missile was reported by the Soviet Government to have landed within one mile of the designated target area in the Pacific ocean after having been fired 7000 miles away. *N. Y. Times,* June 29, 1960, p. 1. A second rocket, it was also announced by the Soviet Government, achieved a range of 8078 miles and hit "directly at the determined point of landing." Id. July 8, 1960, p. 9.

396b. See *Developments in Military Technology,* supra note 378a at 73; and *Space Handbook,* supra note 378a at 171–85.

related is the military importance of the target, or, put a little more precisely, the attacker's estimate of the military importance assigned, realistically or unrealistically, to the target by the enemy. The specially vital importance of a particular target may perhaps not unreasonably be regarded as requiring or justifying an extended definition of the target area and its "saturation" in order to increase the probability of hitting and destroying the target. Bombardment resulting in many thousands of civilian casualties, for example, might not be regarded as excessive and unreasonable where indispensable to ensure destruction of nuclear delivery systems or of plants producing rocket missiles or nuclear explosives. The same quantum of destruction may at another time be characterized as grossly disproportionate if the objective were, say, a factory turning out leather belts for the infantry. The rough principle thought applicable is that the more vital the target is militarily, the greater the zone of disparity that may be condoned as incidental civilian damage. It seems hardly necessary to add that there is no scale of mechanical equivalency between military importance and civilian values and that judgments of approximation must satisfy the demands of community authority.

One assumption which may be seen to underlie the foregoing considerations is that, however relative and protean the conception of "military objective" must be, there remains a line beyond which its logic cannot be pushed without making nonsense of community policy about the limitation of violence. There is distinguished authority [397] for the view that that line is reached in bombardment for the generalized purpose of exercising psychological pressure upon the enemy—of "terrorizing" the civil community—with the ultimate aim of transmitting such pressure to the enemy political elite and compelling acceptance of the attacker's political demands.

Before and during World War II, current doctrine on strategic air power commonly associated with the Italian General Giulio Douhet, assumed the feasibility and effectiveness of such bombardment delivered from the air.[398] The basic assumptions seemed attractively simple. The elements of military power were twofold—the material fighting resources both potential and *in esse,* and the psychological-ideological factors comprising the collective predisposition or

397. Lauterpacht, "The Problem of the Revision of the Law of War," 29 *Brit. Y.B.I.L.* 378–9 (1952).

398. See Brodie, *Strategy in the Missile Age* c. 3 (1959).

will to fight and loosely summed up as "morale." The enemy might be disarmed, the assumption continued, by destroying one or the other element, for one avails little or nothing without the other.[399] Airpower made it technologically possible swiftly and decisively to shatter the enemy's will to fight. This mode of warfare clearly entailed the infliction of comprehensive violence. Douhet wrote:

> Tragic, too, to think that the decision in this kind of war must depend upon smashing the material and moral resources of a people caught in a frightful cataclysm which haunts them everywhere without cease until the final collapse of all social organization. Mercifully, the decision will be quick in this kind of war, since the decisive blows will be directed at civilians, that element of the countries at war least able to sustain.[400]

The First World War had seen some partial and tentative anticipations of Douhet's thesis. Hindenberg and Ludendorff candidly conceded that the German plane and zeppelin raids on London and other British and Allied cities had been for psychological purposes.[401] It was in the Second World War, however, that the above conceptions of strategic air warfare were put to deliberate and sustained application by both sides. Thus, the British Directive of October 29, 1942 on the subject of air warfare, after setting out such limitative instructions as "the intentional bombardment of civilian population, as such, [is] forbidden," concluded that these rules did *not* apply to air warfare against German, Italian, or Japanese territory. The Directive stated that

> consequent upon the enemy's adoption of a campaign of unrestricted air warfare, *the Cabinet have authorized a bombing policy which includes the attack on enemy morale . . .*[402]

399. See Possony, supra note 385 at 146–7; Spaight, *Air Power and War Rights* 34 (3rd ed., 1947).

400. *Command of the Air* 61 (Ferrari trans., 1942) as quoted in Brodie, supra note 398 at 98.

401. For the statement by Hindenberg and Ludendorff, see the "Consultation of MacDonogh," in *La Protection Des Populations Civiles Contre Les Bombardements* 64–5 (Geneva, 1930); see also Royse, supra note 379 at 214–16.

402. See International Committee of the Red Cross, *Draft Rules for the Limitation of the Dangers Incurred by the Civilian Population in Time of War*, p. 163, Annex IV (Geneva, 1956). Emphasis added.

At the Casablanca Conference of January, 1943, the primary purposes of air war against Germany were defined as:

> [T]he progressive destruction and dislocation of the German military, industrial, and economic system, and *the undermining of the morale of the German people to a point where their capacity for armed resistance is fatally weakened.*[403]

The extent to which the Allied Powers in fact regarded enemy civilian morale as an appropriate target of aerial attack is indicated by the fact that of the total bomb tonnage dropped in the European theater of operations (2,697,473 tons), 23.7 per cent (or 639,301 tons) was devoted to urban "area raids." [404] The term "area raids" denoted attacks having certain distinctive characteristics:

> [T]hey were made generally at night; they were directed against large cities; they were designed to spread destruction over a large area rather than to knock out any specific plant or installation; and *they were intended primarily to destroy morale, particularly that of the industrial worker.*[405]

403. 2 Craven and Cate, *The Army Air Forces in World War II* 305 (1949). Emphasis added.

404. *U.S. Strategic Bombing Survey, Over-all Report* (European War) 2 (1945). The breakdown of the rest of the tonnage by target systems is as follows:

32.1%—land transportation targets
11.1%—military
9.3%—oil, chemical and rubber
6.9%—airfields and airdromes
4.2%—naval and water transportation
2.0%—V-weapon launching sites
2.6%—miscellaneous manufacturing
1.8%—aircraft factories
6.3%—all other targets.

405. Id., 71; italics supplied. See also id., *The Effects of Strategic Bombing on the Japanese War Economy* 37–8 (1946) for the statement that the urban area incendiary attacks carried out by "superfortresses" had for their "preponderant purpose" "to secure the heaviest possible moral and shock effect by widespread attack upon the Japanese civilian population." For the practice during the interwar period, specifically in the Italo-Ethiopian War, the Spanish Civil War, and the Sino-Japanese War in 1937, see Spaight, supra note 399 at 254–6; Padelford, *International Law and Diplomacy in the Spanish Civil Strife* 129, 628 (1939) and 3 Hyde, *International Law* 1830–2 (2nd rev. ed., 1945).

Although no similar statistics on the tonnage of German bombs dropped on Allied cities are available, it may confidently be assumed that the same purpose lay behind the "blitz" on the English cities in 1940–1941 and the use of rocket missiles or "V-weapons" in 1944–1945.

One possible approach to the problem of terror bombardment as a means of moral pressure upon the enemy is to inquire, along the lines of suggested above, into the proportionality of the military effects yielded by such bombardment to the resulting destruction of civilian life and property. Appraisals of World War II experience (chiefly British, German, and Japanese experience) appear to indicate that terror attacks are at best of uncertain military value, if by military value one understands the extent to which the termination of a conflict is hastened by, in Dr. Brodie's words, "the direct pressure of public feeling." [406] The experience of Britain in 1940–1941 indicated, some observers believe, that terror bombardment is ambivalent in nature. It has been suggested that such bombardment may, under some circumstances, produce a reverse reaction and intensify propensities for combat, drain off guilt feelings (in case of a belligerent denounced by the general community as an aggressor), build up a desire for revenge, and enhance work diligence.[407] More commonly, of course, intense and sustained bombardment that works terrible execution in the general population depresses morale and produces acute emotional distress, heightened anxiety and fear.[408] Nonetheless, and this is one of the major lessons of World War II experience in military attack upon enemy morale, such effects may remain wholly confined to the attitude or opinion level and fail of manifestation in the form of overt, politically significant, behavior. Notwithstanding their impact upon morale, in other words, very high casualty rates need not bring about a popular movement for surrender nor directly influence the political elite to commence negotiations for surrender.[409] In a totalitarian country, the characteris-

406. Brodie, supra note 398 at 141.

407. Possony, supra note 385 at 150–1.

408. A careful inquiry into the psychological effects of air bombardment is offered in Janis, *Air War and Emotional Stress* (1951). An earlier study may be found in Vernon, "Psychological Effects of Air-Raids," 36 *J. of Abnormal and Social Psychology* 457 (1941).

409. See Ikle, *The Social Impact of Bomb Destruction* 198 (1958).

tic lack of any effective opposition to the regime may commonly mean the absence of any point or focus around which a surrender movement may crystallize and be organized.[410] Moreover, fear of the secret police may be more compelling than the war-weariness and anxiety induced by bombs; while the latter kill or maim by chance, the former do so with considerably more predictability.[411] Intensification of the attacks may yield no solution. On the one hand, there is evidence which suggests that after a certain "saturation" point is reached, further destruction may yield no correspondingly increased deterioration of morale, but actually some slight improvement thereof.[412] On the other hand, continuing massive destruction, which in fact destroys the morale and social organization of enemy masses to such an extent that the most primitive requirements of biological survival become the sole and overwhelming preoccupation, may be self-defeating. The enemy masses may become entirely incapable of the political behavior necessary to bring about the termination of the war.[413]

Whether or not the advent of theromonuclear explosives, whose casualty-creating capabilities immeasurably exceed those of "conventional" high explosives, may invalidate current assumptions about the military utility of morale bombardment remains speculative. Fortunately, our experience about the moral effects of basic-energy weapons is still limited. The imagined use of nuclear and thermonuclear weapons for terror bombardment evokes an image of death and desolation of such epic proportions that the mind recoils. Such use signals "absolute war" and perhaps compels abandonment of all hopes of limitation of violence save such limitation as may result from a quick termination of the war.

It is believed, with the late, authoritative Judge Lauterpacht, that objection [414] to the legitimation of terror bombardment of the gen-

410. Brodie, supra note 398 at 133–4.

411. Possony, supra note 385 at 148; cf. Harris, *Bomber Offensive* 78–9 (1947).

412. See *U.S. Strategic Bombing Survey, The Effects of Strategic Bombing on German Morale* I, p. 33–7 (1947); reprinted as "Social and Psychological Factors Affecting Morale," in *Propaganda in War and Crisis* 355 et seq. (Lerner, ed., 1951).

413. Possony, supra note 385 at 161.

414. Such objection has been given expression in e.g. Castren, *The Present Law of War and Neutrality* 404 (1953); Art. 22, Hague Rules of Aerial Warfare of 1923; 3 Hyde *International Law* 1829–30 (2nd rev. ed., 1945); Spaight, *Air*

eral population may be rested on grounds still more fundamental than the probable military inutility and uneconomical nature of such mode of warfare. To accept as lawful the deliberate terrorization of the enemy community by the infliction of large-scale destruction comes too close to rendering pointless all legal limitations on the exercise of violence. It bears some stress that we speak only of attacks upon morale by military instrumentalities. Enemy morale, whether of the armed combatants or of the general population, is not *in abstracto* an impermissible object of attack. None seriously suggest that attack upon enemy morale by means of a stream of selected communications is illegitimate. It may of course be true that a prohibition of the intentional violent dissemination of terror is apt to be tenuous and somewhat theoretical so long as effective consensus on a more restrictive conception of permissible physical "military objectives" than that which obtained in the practice of World War II is not achieved, and so long as strategic target area bombing is not unequivocally and effectively outlawed. In strategic bombardment, it remains possible, however, to require the minimization of unnecessary discrepancies between the dimensions of assigned target areas and those of the specific material establishments within such areas which are determined to be military objectives. Even this residual possibility is forfeited should terror bombardment be accepted as lawful. Annihilation of the enemy society itself would in effect have been accepted as a legitimate objective of belligerents. For annihilation could ensue if the process of terrorization is prosecuted long enough with powerful enough fusion weapons. Beyond such bounds, there appear no further possible policy limits.

The limitation which a learned commentator appears to have suggested—namely, that the morale of the "enemy's quasi-combatant workforce," but not that of "genuine civilians," may be regarded as a legitimate object of violence—would seem most difficult of application and perhaps apt to be numbered among the "escapes into verbal illusion" which the learned writer himself so forcefully deplored.[415] Contrary to the suggestion of Professor Stone, belligerents in the last world war did not act upon such distinction, as in fact they had

Power and War Rights 277 (3rd ed., 1947); Garner, "International Regulation of Air Warfare," 3 *Air L. Rev.* 103, 116 (1932); Manisty, "Aerial Warfare and the Laws of War," 7 *Tr. Grotius Soc.* 33 (1922).

415. Stone, *Legal Controls* 630–1.

no way of distinguishing, in their attacks upon whole cities, between the "quasi-combatant workforce" and "genuine civilians." Belligerents in practice considered the morale, not of the "quasi-combatant workforce" merely or as such, but of the population generally, as a military objective. If, further, to concede that the *morale* of war workers may be legitimately attacked by violent methods is to suggest something more than that the *persons* of war workers in the vicinity of physical military objectives are legitimate objects of attack,[416] it may not be entirely irrelevant to note that the best way of evoking paralyzing anxiety and distress in war workers may be precisely by killing off their wives and children and elderly folk. But these presumably would be included among Professor Stone's "genuine civilians." From such perspective, there would appear little reason for an attacker (apart from apprehension of reciprocity) to stop short of the slaughtering of prisoners of war and of inhabitants in

416. In Schwarzenberger, "The Law of Air Warfare and the Trend Towards Total War," 1 *U. of Malaya L. Rev.* 120, 135–6 (1959), a threefold classification of persons is put forward:

> (1) *Persons connected with* military operations or *the production of war materials. Whether members of the armed forces or civilians, these have become legitimate objects of warfare.*
>
> (2) Persons in target areas which consist of actual or likely theaters of war and objectives of the types illustrated in the Convention of 1949 and 1954. Irrespective of military or civilian status or occupation, persons in these areas are exposed to any hazards which, on grounds of necessities of war, befall these localities.
>
> (3) Persons who do not fall into Category (1) and are sufficiently remote from areas in Category (2). They are the only persons who may still expect immunity from acts of warfare. (Emphasis supplied)

Dr. Schwarzenberger, however, neglected to indicate how warworkers when remote from "areas in Category (2)," are in practice to be distinguished by a belligerent attacking from the air from other persons, i.e., nonwarworkers, similarly remote from "areas in Category (2)." It was this difficulty of distinguishing physically "quasi-combatants" and "genuine civilians" which led to the formulation in Article 6 of the 1956 Draft Rules (ICRC) that would prohibit attacks upon the civilian population for the purpose "of terrorizing it or for any other reason." The qualification recognized in this article relates to the spatial location of civilian persons: civilians "within or in close proximity to a military objective" are compelled to accept the risks involved in such a location. This, of course, comprises Dr. Schwarzenberger's "Category (2)."

See also, for discussion of the 1956 Draft Rules and underlying assumptions, De No Louis, "La Discriminacion entre Combatientes y Poblacion Civil en la Guerra Moderna," in 3 *La Guerra Moderna* 237 (Univ. de Zaragoza, 1956).

occupied regions, for such measures may be expected to induce profound shock in the entire enemy nation.

Observance of a prohibition of terror attacks may, as noted above, present practical difficulties. Among the possible avenues which efforts to reduce such difficulties may take is that opened up by the provisions of the 1949 Geneva Convention on safety zones and localities.[417] A closely comparable proposal relating to the establishment of "open towns" by mutual agreement is contained in the 1956 Draft Rules (ICRC).[418] The Draft Rules also envision a second and somewhat different avenue: the acceptance of obligations by each belligerent to protect its own civilian population by, in particular, removing them from the vicinity of military objectives and threatened areas.[419] The implementation of such an obligation to take "passive" precautions would not, of course, itself be free from difficulties, but the suggestion would seem deserving of further exploration.

NUCLEAR EXPLOSIVES

The destructive power of forces unleashed by the fission or fusion of atomic nuclei, exceeding by several orders of magnitude that of the largest high explosive bomb of World War II, makes it difficult to characterize nuclear and thermonuclear bombs as "just another weapon." Nonetheless, the basic policy issues involved in the use of these weapons in war are fundamentally the same issues raised by the other weapons or methods of mass destruction, including, in particular, strategic target area bombing. In respect of the one as in respect of the other, it is difficult to accept with much confidence absolute affirmations or blanket denials of legitimacy, however creditable the motivations of the persons affirming or denying. No clear and unmistakable consensus is observable either among commentators or governments on questions of lawfulness. The continuing attempts, however, by various governments and groups to "outlaw" nuclear weapons tend to sustain the impression that such weapons are regarded as permissible pending the achievement of agreement to the contrary.

Those who assert the illegitimacy of basic-energy weapons principally rely upon derivations and analogies from general principles

417. Supra, p. 569.
418. Art. 16.
419. Arts. 11–13.

and a handful of conventional prescriptions formulated long before these weapons become awesome realities. The first and oldest of these conventional prescriptions, which at the same time embodies a broad principle, is the preambulatory statement in the St. Petersburg Declaration of 1868 prohibiting the employment of weapons "which would uselessly aggravate the sufferings of disabled men, or render their death inevitable." A second provision invoked for the same purpose and entirely assimilable to the first clause of the St. Petersburg formulation, is Article 23(e) of the Hague Regulations of 1907 which "especially [forbids]" the employment of "arms, projectiles, or material calculated to cause unnecessary suffering." "It is submitted," Dr. Singh writes,

> that even if the blast and heat effects, which are also the concomitants of conventional TNT bombardment are accepted as legally unobjectionable and the area of destruction is also disregarded, the radio-active fall-out and the immediate nuclear radiation which not only wound, but cause various kinds of diseases ultimately resulting in death, would appear to come within the meaning of "employing arms calculated to cause unnecessary suffering" prohibited by Article 23(e).[420]

It is obvious that both Article 23(e) and the first clause of the St. Petersburg Declaration are but expressions of the basic principle that demands proportionality between military advantage and concomitant destruction. To invoke these conventional formulations of general principle is not, however, to dispense with the need of inquiring into anticipated advantage and expected deprivation and to relate one to the other. It would seem a demanding task—and this enterprise Dr. Singh did not embark upon—to demonstrate that in all possible and realistically expected types of situations, the value deprivations resulting from a nuclear explosion, of whatever magnitude, are out of all proportion to the military utility that may be conceived to accrue to the belligerent user.[421] The second clause of the St. Petersburg Declaration, as has been noted above, still awaits significant clarification. The reference cannot be merely to lethal as

420. Singh, *Nuclear Weapons and International Law* 150 (1959).

421. The justification offered, in the early postwar years, for the use of the bombs on Hiroshima and Nagasaki was that it saved the lives of countless Allied soldiers by making the invasion of Japan unnecessary. See Stimson, "The Decision to Use the Atomic Bomb," 3 *Bull. Atomic Scientists* 37 (1947). Stowell,

distinguished from nonlethal weapons. All weapons of war, from the bow and arrow to the rocket missile, when wielded under certain optimum conditions, can render death inevitable. Moreover, even assuming for a moment that the St. Petersburg Declaration was intended to embrace all lethal weapons, there is an infinite number of possible degrees of exposure to the effects—blast, thermal, and radiation—of nuclear weapons. At or below a certain threshold of exposure, the effects, including the radiation, are by no means inevitably lethal.[422] Dr. Spaight suggests the Declaration refers to arms whose effect is "to leave the individual wounded or otherwise affected with no hope of survival." [423] Whether this mode of paraphrasing the Declaration sheds much light on the problem seems open to doubt. The presence or absence of "hope of survival" in the

---

"The Laws of War and the Atomic Bomb," 39 *A.J.I.L.* 786 (1945) added that the bomb saved more civilian lives than it took plus thousands of Japanese soldiers. Stone, *Legal Controls* 343 apparently brushes aside "such life-saving by unheard of life-destruction" as having "little ethical merit." Cf. Phillips, "Air Warfare and Law," 21 *Geo. Wash. L. Rev.* 409 (1953).

More recent studies of the role played by the nuclear bombs in the Japanese decision to surrender indicate that their use did significantly influence the ending of the war, but tend to differ upon the precise weighting that may be ascribed to such use, as distinguished from the other, antecedent, circumstances that also affected this decision. See Brodie, *Strategy in the Missile Age* 139–42 (1959); Kecskemeti, *Strategic Surrender: The Politics of Victory and Defeat* c. 6 (1958); Butow, *Japan's Decision to Surrender* (1954).

422. See *The Effects of Nuclear Weapons* (Govt. Printing Office, 1957) which offers a lucid, relatively nontechnical treatment of the matter. The suggestion made in the text should be distinguished from the problem of the "maximum permissible dose" and "maximum permissible concentration," of radiation below which *no* somatic or genetic effects ensue. On this problem, see, generally, "The Nature of Radioactive Fall-out and Its Effects on Man," *Hearings before the Special Subcommittee on Radiation of the Joint Committee on Atomic Energy*, 85th Cong., 1st Sess., June, 1957; and "Fallout From Nuclear Weapons Test," id., 86th Cong., 1st Sess., May, 1959. In the *Summary-Analysis of the 1959 Hearings*, pp. 17–18 (August, 1959), the Joint Committee summed up the "general consensus concerning somatic and genetic effects" as:

> (a) For any given total dose, low dose rates are generally less effective than high dose rates in producing biological damage. (The possibility that this might be generally true was pointed out in the 1957 hearings.)
>
> (b) This difference in effectiveness related to radiation [sic] dose rate appears to apply to both somatic (nongenetic) and genetic consequences of radiation.

423. *Air Power and War Rights* 275 note 5 (3rd ed., 1947).

breast of a particular individual affected would appear to depend upon, *inter alia,* the gravity of the injury sustained (which in turn is a resultant of differing particular circumstances) and the availability of medical services. An individual who receives no more than a certain minimum roentgen dosage can, in exactly the same way as one wounded in the leg by a rifle bullet or bomb fragment, entertain "hope of survival."

Other treaty provisions that have been invoked in the effort to characterize nuclear and thermonuclear weapons as prohibited weapons are Article 23(a) of the Hague Regulations of 1907 and those of the Geneva Protocol of 1925. Article 23(a) forbids the use of "poison or poisoned arms," while the Geneva Protocol, it will be recalled, bans the use of "asphyxiating, poisonous or other gases, and of all analogous liquids, materials or devices." The judgment delivered by Professor Stone on the applicability of these provisions to nuclear weapons is not without categorical qualities, however illusory: "Radioactive substances are clearly 'poisonous' or at least 'analogous substances' in any functional sense." [424] The suggestion has been made by an observer that the tremendous blast and heat produced, rather than the release of neutrons and gamma rays or the dissemination of radioactive debris, account for the military importance of nuclear weapons and that the radiological consequences should be regarded as "incidental side effects." [425] Even so, the more important consideration would seem to be that the Hague rule against poison only codified a very ancient usage of war which in the main was expressive of a judgment of the prevailing culture rejecting clandestine methods of warfare as repugnant and amounting to treachery.[426] Radiation is of course an invisible process; but nuclear weapons are

424. Stone, *Legal Controls* 343; cf. Spaight, supra 423 at 275–6.

425. Phillips, supra note 421 at 410, 414.

426. See Grotius, *De Jure Belli Ac Pacis* (trans. Kelsey, Classics of International Law, 1925), Bk. III, Chaps. IV, XV–XVI, Vol. 2, pp. 651–2; also Vattel, *The Law of Nations or the Principles of Natural Law* (trans. Fenwick, Classics of International Law, 1916) Bk. III, Chap. VIII, s. 155–6, Vol. 3, pp. 288–9. Maine, *International Law* 135 (1888) said that the Greeks and Romans thought poisoning of food and water as worthy only of barbarians. He suggested as the origin of the feeling either the fact that poisoning was peculiarly painful (since arsenic apparently was the principal known efficacious poison in antiquity) or the idea that it did not constitute fair fighting.

As to the rule against poisoned weapons, suffice it to say that a rule historically

universally known to produce some amount of radiation and a nuclear or thermonuclear explosion can scarcely aptly be described as treacherously clandestine.

More recently, a distinguished scholar has put forward a somewhat broader formulation of what is described as "the true *ratio legis*" of the customary rule against poison and poisoned arms: "their use runs counter to the standard of civilization as understood by these sixteenth- and seventeenth-century humanists." [427] Building upon this view, Dr. Schwarzenberger writes:

> [A] fairly strong case can be made for the assimilation of radiation and radio-active fall-out to poison. If introduced into the body in sufficiently large doses, they produce symptoms which are indistinguishable from those of poisoning and inflict death or serious damage to health in, as Gentile would have put it, a manner more befitting demons than civilized human beings.[428]

The "true *ratio legis*" Dr. Schwarzenberger thus unearths appears but one more rendering of the broad principle of humanity. In seeking to bring nuclear weapons within the scope of the rule against poison, and apart from the alleged similarity in physiological effects between poisons and radiation—a matter not altogether free from doubt [429]—Dr. Schwarzenberger asserts rather than proves that uses of nuclear weapons necessarily collide with the humanity principle, that is, that their use inevitably entails disproportionate and unnecessary destruction of values. As we understand it, this is precisely the issue at stake. The allegorical language employed by Dr. Schwarzenberger may of course be interpreted to refer to popular abhorrence of the radiological effects of nuclear weapons, as a culture-fact, rather than to the rational relating of military utility to

---

directed against poisoned arrows and javelins can hardly be relied on as a basis for prohibition of nuclear and thermonuclear weapons.

427. Schwarzenberger, *The Legality of Nuclear Weapons* 33 (1958).

428. Id., 35. See also Singh, supra note 420 at 161–3.

429. Standard texts on toxicology embrace a great variety of substances of varying toxicity producing equally varied physiological symptoms and effects. There appears in fact no single set of symptoms that necessarily and invariably occurs upon ingestion of a toxic substance by a human and that, consequently, can be regarded as unique and distinctive to "poisoning." See, e.g. DuBois and Geiling, *Textbook of Toxicology* (1959).

concomitant destruction. If such reference was intended, it need only be noted that to lay much store by such popular revulsion, when the military postures of the great powers of the globe rest upon the expectation that these weapons will under certain circumstances be used, would seem hazardous indeed.

With respect to the 1925 Geneva Protocol, Dr. Schwarzenberger writes further:

> [T]he words "all analogous liquids, materials or devices" are so comprehensively phrased as to include any weapons of an analogous character, irrespective of whether they were known or in use at the time of the signature of the Protocol. If the radiation and fall-out effects of nuclear weapons can be likened to poison, all the more can they be likened to poison gas which is but an even more closely analogous species of the genus "poison." [430]

The omnibus phrase of the Protocol would seem either a frail reed to lean on, or one quite unnecessary. Prohibitions of specific weapons achieved in the past acquire relevance, in the evaluation of new weapons, only for the policies that infuse them. We have previously noted that the basic policy underlying the prohibition of poison gas was either the broad rule relating to unnecessary suffering of disabled combatants or the general principle of civilian immunity. For the first policy, it appears unnecessary to have recourse to the Protocol's omnibus phrase. For the second policy, any invocation of "analogy" here only means raising once more the fundamental and pervading issue of minimum unnecessary destruction of values. To assert the existence of a valid analogy does not by itself dissolve the question of whether or not, or in what types of situation, differing uses of a specific weapon may be regarded as resulting in gross, unnecessary, or irrelevant destruction of values. Most comprehensively put, to extrapolate past precedents by literalistic interpretation without explicit and operational examination of the policies at state is rather to beg than to justify the conclusion put forward.

The assumptions which may be seen to underlie the above exercises in analogical interpretation by Dr. Schwarzenberger and others are that words have absolutistic meanings which can be pro-

430. Schwarzenberger, supra note 427 at 38.

jected into the future without regard to original and contemporaneous contexts, and that future interpreters must accept these pristine meanings irrespective of facts and policies in contemporary context.[431] It does not seem necessary to belabor the inadequacy of this conception of the process of interpretation and it may suffice to suggest that individuals of one age who seek to control posterity by misplaced faith in the omnipotence of words of infinite abstraction are frequently destined to be disappointed. Thus, the effective decision-makers of the contemporary world seem no more likely to accept the nebulous derivations from past agreement and ancient usage considered above than they are to make in present context a new and explicit agreement by which to deny themselves all uses of so decisive a weapon.

It was suggested above that the kinds of considerations which rationally bear upon appraisal of target area bombing may also be relevant in appraisals of uses of nuclear explosives. The view is sometimes advanced, however, that while target area bombing is permissible, atom bombing must be held unlawful. A principal argument of the proponents of this view appears to be that bombardment with nuclear explosives renders completely impossible any discrimination between legitimate and nonlegitimate targets of attack; the implication *a contrario* is that such discrimination is practicable in target area bombardment with conventional high explosives.[432] The soundness of this argument cannot casually be assumed; for it is not easy to see how target area bombing, as conceived and executed during World War II, can be regarded as any less "indiscriminate" than a nuclear explosion.[433] The argument in effect rests upon a distinction that does not distinguish: a distinction between a single shattering blow and a drawn-out series of lesser attacks.[434] From the per-

431. The designation, popular in some parts of the world, of death by bullets as death by "lead poisoning" would appear to be based upon comparable criteria of interpretation. The principle of restrictive interpretation must of course impose a limit upon such expansive extrapolations. See the literature collected in supra, Ch. 3, note 260.

432. See Spaight, *Air Power and War Rights* 276 (3rd ed., 1947); also Singh, *Nuclear Weapons and International Law* 100, 191–2 (1959).

433. Lauterpacht, "The Problem of the Revision of the Law of War," 29 *Brit. Y.B.I.L.* 360, 369 (1952); cf. Phillips, supra note 421 at 408.

434. Cf. Smith, *The Crisis in the Law of Nations* 77–8 (1947) suggesting that

spective of fundamental policy, it is the level of impact upon the civilian population, rather than the number of times an operation is repeated, that would seem significant.

A second argument urged by Dr. Spaight relates to proportionality. In target area bombing, it is asserted, the zone subjected to assault is not out of proportion to the area physically occupied by the military objectives selected; in contrast, the assertion continues, in atom bombing the area affected is enormously enlarged and the disparity immense.[435] The reference to the proportionality of target area bombardment is, however, less an accurate description of past practice (a matter for factual verification) than an expression of one standard in terms of which particular target area bombing operations may be assessed. No compelling reason has been advanced why the same standard may not, in principle, rationally be projected for nuclear bombardment. Disparity between the area of devastation and the area actually occupied by a physical installation or cluster of installations characterized as military objectives might be minimized, for example, by confining the use of nuclear explosives to situations where the target area attains certain minimum dimensions, or by using bombs of lower yield—so-called "tactical" nuclear weapons—to destroy areas of lesser extent. Both the power of nuclear weapons and the specific manner of employment (e.g. an "air burst" as distinguished from a "surface burst") are subject to regulation and selection. Thus, the point that may be emphasized is that it is no more reasonable to say that nuclear bombing must in all cases be unlawful than it is to assert that strategic target area bombardment is always legitimate. Particular bombardment operations, of one as of the other kind, need to be examined in specific and detailed context.

The consistent application of a policy of minimum destruction requires consideration of certain special factors in cases of nuclear bombardment: the possible prolongation of damage beyond the period of hostilities, and the possible deposit of radioactive debris in nonparticipant states through the mechanism of fallout. The possibility of damage prolongation relates both to local radioactivity which under certain circumstances may be induced in such intensity

---

the difference between conventional and nuclear explosives is a matter of the time taken and the numbers engaged, and cannot serve as a basis for "a rational distinction of principle."

435. Spaight, supra note 432 at 274.

as to render an irradiated area impassable and uninhabitable for varying time periods, and to the genetic effects of irradiation in terms of impact on future offspring. Where a sufficient number of multimegaton "dirty" nuclear explosives are employed, nonparticipant countries coming within the fallout pattern may be exposed to the somatic and genetic effects of radiological agents. It may perhaps, however, still be possible to embrace these potential factors—they need not attend every single use of nuclear weapons[436]—within the kind of analytical framework considered above and to regard their incidence as requiring a showing of much more stringent necessity and a much larger military advantage than would otherwise be needed to redress the balance. In any event, the best hope for adequate protection of nonparticipants can be found not in distinctions between different types of weapons but in the more effective securing of minimum order.

The conclusion that thus suggests itself, however distressing it may be, is that processes of derivation and "analogy" from conventional rules and from inherited principles are hopelessly inadequate to sustain assertions, in realistic expectation of probable future decision, of a comprehensive prohibition in international law of the use of nuclear weapons.[437] Such a prohibition so devoutly to be wished for by all who cherish the values of human dignity, or perhaps even survival, must require more effective implementation. Perhaps the only limitation that can at present be projected with any

436. The *Summary-Analysis of Hearings on the Nature of Radioactive Fallout and Its Effects on Man,* Joint Committee on Atomic Energy, 85th Cong., 1st. Sess., p. 6 (August, 1957) listed the characteristics of nuclear weapon explosions that determine the nature and amount of fallout:

(1) The size of the explosion (that is, total energy yield, usually expressed as a certain number of kilotons or megatons of TNT explosive energy equivalent);

(2) The percentage of the total energy yield resulting from the fission process;

(3) The type of detonation (high in the air, near the ground, under water etc.);

(4) The nature of the surface material where the explosion takes place (water, rock, sand, coral etc.).

437. Cf. Lauterpacht, supra note 433 at 370; O'Brien, "Legitimate Military Necessity in Nuclear War," 2 *World Polity* 35 (1960), a comprehensive and profound consideration of basic issues.

plausibility is the ultimate one, that is, the prohibition of uses of these weapons for purposes of terrorization, in effect the annihilation, of the general enemy population. The difficulties involved in its practical observance to which we alluded in connection with strategic target area bombing with conventional explosives are not likely to diminish in respect of nuclear bombardment.

Here perhaps one approaches the limits of the logic of traditional community policy that we have traced in other areas of combatant law. A more promising alternative for limitation of nuclear violence may conceivably reside in the curious paradox that the capability and reciprocal promise of mutual annihilation is today widely regarded as a basic condition for keeping peace between the polar powers.[438] This paradox suggests with poignant clarity that effective control of and protection from nuclear weapons can be hopefully sought, not in scholarly extrapolations and derivations from past analogies, nor even in a new and unequivocal agreement outlawing these weapons, but rather in the achievement of a consensus of the kind considered earlier, in the context of a comprehensive and continuing sanctioning process, that sustains the principle of minimum order itself as well as a prohibition of nuclear weapons.

DECEIT IN COMBAT

We turn lastly, almost by way of anticlimax, to one other means of warfare—the utilization of deceit. Deceit has for centuries been a very common technique of war and in certain of its forms has always been regarded as permissible. Permissible deceit is principally manifested in military ruses and stratagems employed, for instance, to achieve tactical surprise by misleading the enemy as to one's own location, strength, and intentions, or to render attack unnecessary by inducing the enemy to surrender or evacuate a position held by him.[439] The invention of stratagems of course depends on the enter-

438. The relevant recent literature includes Brodie, *Strategy in the Missile Age* (1959); *NATO and American Security* (Knorr, ed., 1959); Schelling, *The Strategy of Conflict* (1960); Wohlstetter, "The Delicate Balance of Terror," 37 *Foreign Aff.* 211 (1959); Kahn, *The Nature and Feasibility of War and Deterrence* (P.1888 Rand Corp., Jan. 20, 1960).

439. See Art. 24, Hague Regulations. Dept. of the Army, *Law of Land Warfare* par. 51 (FM 27-10, July 1956) sets forth a suggestive listing of legitimate ruses, including, it is noteworthy, "psychological warfare activities."

Deceptive supply movements to mislead the enemy into believing in the arrival or relief of troop units were often used by the Russians in the last war;

prise and ingenuity of military commanders. Some regulation of this ingenuity and enterprise is attempted through projection of certain general limitations on the permissible use of deceit. Article 22(b) of the 1907 Hague Regulations prohibits belligerents from "kill[ing] or wound[ing] treacherously individuals belonging to the hostile nation or army." The line between perfidity and permissible deceit is obviously anything but sharp and precise. Halleck's test of an express or implied engagement to speak truthfully to the enemy [440] may seem quaint today when employment of psychological and political warfare techniques is commonplace. Nonetheless an important policy may be seen to underlie the prohibition of treachery—to maintain that residuum of good faith which makes possible some measure of humanitarian and reciprocally beneficial restraint and of pacific intercourse between belligerents, and without which no basis may remain for a return to peace short of total annihilation of one side.[441] This policy seems implicit in the prescription forbidding misuse of certain symbols having a recognized meaning like flags of truce and the distinctive emblem of the Geneva Conventions.[442]

---

see *Military Improvisations During the Russian Campaign,* 57 (Dept. of the Army Pamphlet No. 20–201, Aug., 1951). To deceive the enemy as to the time and place of an impending attack, the Russians would feign great activity in other sectors, moving troops and setting up dummy artillery, tanks, and aircraft therein, and carefully making visible tracks all the while. Running motors at night would simulate motorized columns on the move. See *Russian Combat Methods in World War II,* 88 (Dept. of the Army Pamphlet No. 20–230, Nov., 1950). For the use of "deception teams" to simulate the existence of whole armored divisions, see Cole, *The Lorraine Campaign* (*U.S. Army in World War II: European Theater of Operations*) 162 (1950). For an account of ruses employed in air warfare, see Spaight, supra note 432 at 169 et seq.

440. 1 Halleck, *International Law* 623 (4th Eng. ed., Baker, 1908). Cf. 3 Hyde 1811 who considers as the important characteristic of treachery the violation of an undertaking given to cause the enemy to refrain from violence he would otherwise surely exercise. Halleck's test is retained in *Law of Land Warfare,* supra note 439 at par. 50.

441. See *Law of Land Warfare,* id.; Stone, *Legal Controls* 561 note 80; and Spaight, supra note 432 at 170.

442. Art. 23(f), Hague Regulations; Arts. 42 and 44, Geneva Wounded and Sick Convention of 1949; Art. 44, Geneva Wounded, Sick and Shipwrecked Convention of 1949. In "Trial of Hagendorf," 13 *War Crimes Reports* 146 (1946), the accused was tried and convicted by an American Military Government court for having wrongfully used the Red Cross symbol in a combat zone by firing on American soldiers from an enemy ambulance displaying such symbol.

One species of ruse that has aroused some controversy is the use of enemy uniforms and enemy national symbols. Publicists and belligerents rarely dispute that the use of enemy uniforms and insignia during the course of combat may, under customary law, be countered by depriving the individual users of prisoner-of-war status upon capture. It has, however, sometimes been suggested that the use of such uniforms and symbols prior to actual combat is not unlawful.[443] Comparable assertions have been made in respect of naval warfare, and there is some practice to this effect, that to fly a neutral or enemy flag, so long as a warship strikes her true colors before commencing attack, is "perfectly legitimate."[444] The logic of these assertions is not self-evident. They are open to the interpretation that the ruse becomes impermissible only from the moment its further use is rendered unnecessary, the deceitful force or warship having been enabled to assume a posture favorable for attack. In land warfare, it is not frequently practical to expect forces to change their garb just before firing.[445] On the other hand, unless troops in enemy disguise actually engage in combat the enemy suffers no harm. In sea warfare,

443. E.g. Bordwell, *The Law of War Between Belligerents* 283 (1908), Hall, *International Law* 649 (8th ed., Pearce Higgins, 1924) and the writers cited in Jobst, "Is the Wearing of the Enemy's Uniform a Violation of the Laws of War?" 35 *A.J.I.L.* 436–7 note 12 (1941). Jobst, after a careful examination of the preparatory work of the Brussels Code and Hague Regulations and a survey of the more modern authorities, submitted that the "correct" and appropriate rule is that the use of enemy uniforms for purposes of deceit is unlawful, whether before or during combat. It may be noted that Russian soldiers frequently donned German uniforms in the last war; see *Russian Combat Methods in World War II,* supra note 439 at 88–9.

444. Hall, *The Law of Naval Warfare* 84–5 (1921); 2 Oppenheim-Lauterpacht 509–11; Winfield in Lawrence, *The Principles of International Law* 540 (7th ed., Winfield, 1928).

445. Cf. Spaight, *War Rights on Land* 105 (1911) who denies the existence of such a rule in the practice of belligerents. Hall, supra note 443, admits it to be a "curious arbitrary rule" but in effect asserts it to be a rule. Dept. of the Army, *Law of Land Warfare* par. 54 (FM 27-10, July 1956) follows Hall on this point, stating that "[I]t is certainly forbidden to employ them [national flags, insignia, and uniforms] during combat, but their use at other times is not forbidden." The decision of an American Military Court in "Trial of Skorzeny and others," 9 *War Crimes Reports* 90 (1947), apparently followed Hall's view. There, a special German brigade composed of English-speaking troops dressed in American military garb was formed and ordered to capture certain objectives behind Allied lines. The order could not be carried out; the brigade was attached to other units. The evidence showed only two cases of members of the brigade

the persistent use of neutral flags either by men-of-war or merchantmen would seem open to the additional objection that ships of the neutral flag state may thereby be exposed to grave dangers. The argument sometimes made that the ruse merely compels an attacking belligerent to follow the traditional verification procedures of visit and search [446] seems far from satisfactory, in the light of what has been noted in respect of the practicability of observance of these procedures. The fact is that submarines and aircraft rely on prima facie identification.[447]

SPECIFIC DEFENSES AGAINST ALLEGED VIOLATIONS OF THE RULES OF WARFARE

We turn to the second broad group of claims about the regulation of combat situations. This group embraces assertions made by individual officials of a belligerent body politic or by individual officers and members of its armed forces in defense against charges of having violated the substantive requirements of the combatant law of war. These claims are typically made in the context of a war crimes trial and have for their common purpose the avoidance or extenuation of criminal punishment, and relate to "military necessity," "legitimate reprisals," "superior orders," and "acting in an official capacity."

MILITARY NECESSITY

We have in the preceding sections used the phrase "military necessity" to refer to one of the two fundamental complementary policies that underlie the whole structure of the international law on hostilities. In the present section, the phrase is employed to designate the plea raised by an individual accused of violating particular rules

---

actually fighting in American uniforms. The court acquitted all the accused of the charge of improper use of American uniforms.

446. Hall, supra note 444 at 84.

447. Smith, *The Law and Custom of the Sea* 115–18 (3rd ed., 1959) strongly urged the abandonment of the practice by the British, noting that it gave Germany a plausible excuse for refusing to distinguish between Allied and neutral ships and for waging unrestricted warfare on both. The U.S. Neutrality Act of 1939, Art. 14(a) Pub. Res. No. 54, 76th Cong., 2d Sess., declared unlawful the use of the U.S. flag by foreign vessels; a sanction consisting of denial of entry into U.S. ports and waters for a period of 3 months was provided.

of warfare that certain circumstances existed which, in the specific instance, justified the disregard of those rules.[448]

The usual controversies in this area focus about two opposing views. The first view is embodied in the German doctrine of *Kriegsraison,* which it has become customary and even *de rigueur* for publicists to deplore and flagellate. In capsular form, this doctrine is to the effect that military necessity or, as it is sometimes called, the necessities of war (*Kriegsraison*) overrides and renders inoperative the ordinary laws and customs of war (*Kriegsmanier*).[449] Military necessity is, in this view, conceived as a kind of resolutory condition implied in all the particular prescriptions of the law of war. The second and opposing view would deny all importance to military necessity, narrowly conceived, save where it has been explicitly written into the conventional formulations of the rules of warfare. Under this view, military necessity is said to be unavailable as a legal excuse for violation of the rules of warfare, except where the specific rule alleged to have been violated verbally incorporates a qualifying reference to military necessity.

There is little doubt that *Kriegsraison,* as interpreted in German belligerent practice in the two world wars, does tend to reduce authoritative community policy to illusive platitude. Necessity surely is a matter of degree; but the slightest degree has on occasions sufficed, in German practice, for invocation of the doctrine. Necessity on such occasions came to mean relative expediency and comparative convenience and advantageousness.[450]

The opposing view commonly put forward with ringing condemnations of *Kriegsraison* does not, however, seem wholly free from difficulties. Referring specifically to the Regulations Respecting the

448. See Dunbar, "The Significance of Military Necessity in the Law of War," 67 *Jurid. Rev.* 201 (1955); Dunbar, "Military Necessity in War Crimes Trials," 29 *Brit. Y.B.I.L.* 442 (1952). O'Brien, "The Meaning of Military Necessity in International Law," 1 *World Polity* 109, 116 (1957) suggests that "military necessity" has been used "in a legal sense" in three ways: as an "exceptional justifying cause"; as an "overriding right or law"; as a "positive principle underlying the law."

449. A concise summary is offered in O'Brien, supra note 448 at 119–27.

450. The tribunal in "The Trial of Von Leeb," 12 *War Crimes Reports* at 93 declared that to define military necessity as a right to do anything that contributes to winning of a war would "eliminate all humanity and decency and all law from the conduct of war."

Laws and Customs of War on Land annexed to Hague Convention IV of 1907 (which, of course, do not embody the whole of the law of war), Professor Westlake wrote, in classic exposition of this view: "[M]ilitary necessity has been taken into account in framing the Regulations, and has not been left outside them, to control and limit their application in the circumstances which they embrace." [451] The conclusion which has been drawn from this view is that in no event and under no circumstances, however extreme, urgent, and dire, and even unto ultimate defeat, may observance of a verbally unqualified rule be lawfully dispensed with.[452] The standard thus put forward is indeed morally exacting. It has, however, never been adequately clarified what precisely is meant by saying that the framers of the Hague Regulations had already discounted military necessity. The ambiguity of "military necessity" here should not escape notice.

The preamble of Hague Convention IV, which Professor Westlake invoked, provides *inter alia:*

> According to the views of the High Contracting Parties, these provisions, the wording of which has been inspired by the desire to diminish the evils of war, so far as military necessities permit, are intended to serve as general rules of conduct for belligerents in their relation with each other and with populations.

The juxtaposition of "the desire to diminish the evils of war" with "military necessities" would seem to leave room for the interpretation that the Hague Conference was here only spotlighting "hu-

451. 2 Westlake, *International Law* 57 (1907); see also id. at 115–17. The conventional provisions explicitly qualified by military necessity include, in the Hague Regulations, Arts. 23(g), 26, 27, 33, 43, 51, and 54.

452. In "The Trial of List" ("The Hostages Case") 8 *War Crimes Reports* at 69 (1948), the Tribunal said: "The Hague Regulations are mandatory provisions of International Law. The prohibitions therein contained control and are superior to military necessities of the most urgent nature except where the Regulations themselves provide the contrary." Cf. Downey, "The Law of War and Military Necessity," 47 *A.J.I.L.* 251 (1953).

In the trial of von Manstein, the prosecution asserted that "if the necessities of war were an overriding consideration to be taken into account in regard to all the Articles of the Convention [IV of 1907] obviously it would be quite unnecessary to make a special provision to that effect in art. 23(g)." *Annual Digest 1949,* Case No. 192 at p. 512. It is suggested that if the express reservation of military necessity were left out in Art. 23(g) the article would have appeared

manity" and "military necessity" as fountainhead principles infusing the whole of the law of war, and pointing out that the former was limited by the latter.[453] If the Conference was in fact merely doing so and nothing more, then to suggest that "military necessity" was already discounted at the framing of specific rules may be either to state a tautology, or to assert a dogmatic preference for one of the two indissolubly complementary policies. But it is as utopian as it is undesirable to seek to proscribe the pervasive policy embodied in military necessity. The contrary construction, that is, that the Conference be regarded as discounting, not the basic policy of military necessity but rather the invocation of that policy as a specific defense in the infinitely varying circumstances under which a claim legally to be excused might be made with differing degrees of reasonableness, involves an assumption most difficult to indulge in. That assumption is that the Conference could have foreseen, and did foresee, all possible factual circumstances under which the particular rules would have to be applied and under which future wars would be fought, and that it appropriately concluded that in no conceivable operational context could their observance conflict with the imperious needs of survival which may confront particular forces. So to assume would be to attribute superhuman prescience to the Conference delegates and to place an impossible burden on their verbal formulations as instruments for communicating policy.

Whatever meaning is to be assigned to the postulated advance discounting of military necessity in the *formulation* of the Hague Regulations, decision-makers charged with the *application* of these rules

---

absurd. For then it would have read: "it is especially forbidden . . . (g) to destroy or seize the enemy's property."

453. The same passage is found in the preamble of Hague Convention II of 1899. In the Hague Conference of 1899, the preamble was simply adopted by the Conference unanimously, without any discussion which might serve to shed light on the "intent of the framers." See *Proceedings of the Hague Peace Conferences: The Conference of 1899* 207–8 (trans. of official texts; 1920). The preamble was drafted by the Second Subcommission of the Second Commission, which incorporated in it a declaration made by Martens, President of the Conference. That declaration ran thus: "The Conference is unanimous in thinking that it is extremely desirable that the usages of war be defined and regulated. In this spirit it has adopted a great number of provisions which have for their object the determination of the rights and of the duties of belligerents and populations and for their end a softening of the evils of war so far as military necessities permit." (ibid., 547–8.)

may, nonetheless, and doubtless commonly do, consider the circumstances of necessity which particular situations may exhibit. If the particular rule violation of which is charged in the indictment makes explicit reference to military necessity, the decision-maker must of course examine the facts alleged with respect to necessity. Even if the rule invoked is not explicitly qualified by military necessity, the decision-maker must nonetheless decide whether the particular constellation of facts in a specific occasion appropriately calls for application of such rule or whether the facts bring the case within the ambit of another rule.[454]

Professor Westlake's view, furthermore, assumes that it is possible to "generalize" necessity for all future circumstances. Under this view, taken seriously, the rules of warfare into which military necessity was not explicitly written would have to be regarded as absolute and impervious to change, not manifested through formal and centralized legislative procedures. Such a view requires a serious underestimation of the dynamic and contemporaneous character of the decision-making process called customary international law. In the sphere of naval warfare and maritime neutrality, the doctrine of reprisals was utilized to bridge the gap between traditional prescription and contemporary practice. Inquiry into whether a rationally limited doctrine of military necessity might not, in the

454. In the High Command case, the defendants were charged with, among other things, the "pillage," "plunder," and "spoliation" of public and private property in occupied territory. The charge was equivocally worded and might be made to fall under either Art. 23(g) referring to "destruction or seizure of property" or under Arts. 28 and 47 of the Hague Regulations dealing with "pillage." Art. 23(g) is explicitly qualified by military necessity; Arts. 28 and 47 are not. The specifications of this charge included the taking of all that could be moved and the burning of everything else in the course of evacuation of the areas involved by German troops and the civilian inhabitants, in anticipation of Russian advances. Further, the burning of towns and villages and seizure of livestock and food supplies therein, where those towns and villages were suspected of being used as bases of operations by partisans, was also charged. The tribunal apparently applied Art. 23(g) where acts specified were committed during the process of evacuating the localities affected. With respect to burning of towns and villages alleged to be partisan bases, the tribunal might have regarded the matter as one of reprisals (as did the tribunal in the Hostages case, 11 *Trials of War Criminals* at 1300 [1948]); the charge was not dealt with in a detailed fashion in the opinion. In any case, not one of the defendants was convicted on the pillage and plunder count; see 11 id. at 562, 577, 609, 618, 628, 680, 686 (1948).

interesting suggestion recently made,[455] serve a comparable function in respect of land and air warfare, may well be a worthwhile enterprise. Such an inquiry is, however, not likely to be enhanced by inspirational pronouncements stating goals which, while devoutly to be wished for, may realistically be unattainable until belligerents have commonly reached moral perfection.[456]

As indicated earlier, the German conception of military necessity came into disrepute when its logic was pushed too far and used to prove too much.[457] In both world wars, *Kriegsraison* was invoked in circumstances which very often fell so far short of any really stringent factual necessity, let alone survival, as such necessity or survival may be appraised by a nonparticipant observer, that it could be token only of a cynical disregard of legal restraint. A sampling of World War II cases affords ample documentation. In the trial of Alstoetter,[458] for instance, one of the defendants had proposed to the Reich Minister of Justice that German courts should try and convict Polish citizens upon a charge of "high treason" for having instituted, in Poland and before the war, judicial proceedings against Poles of German blood. This proposal, which was carried out, was defended on the ground of military necessity; the plea was of course rejected. The infamous medical experiments carried out with wanton brutality and cruelty on human subjects were also sought to be justified

455. The suggestion appears in Stone, *Legal Controls* 353 note 25.

456. E.g. the statement of the tribunal in the Hostages case, 11 *Trials of War Criminals* at 1272 (1948); "the rules of international law must be followed even if it results in the loss of a battle or even a war. Expediency or necessity cannot warrant their violation." In the Krupp case, 10 *War Crimes Reports* at 139 (1948), the court rationalized: "War is by definition a risky and hazardous business. . . . It is an essence of war that one or the other side must lose, and the experienced generals and statesmen knew this when they drafted the rules and customs of land warfare." The point is that belligerents may be expected to do their utmost to increase the probability that it is the other side that will lose.

457. Cf. 2 Garner, *International Law and the World War* 196–7 (1920) who with candor wrote: "Within reasonable limits, this much criticised theory is legally defensible; that is to say, a belligerent is justified in disregarding a rule of war whenever conformity to the rule would involve his destruction; but the German writers . . . have confused self preservation with mere strategical interest or convenience and have laid down the broad and unwarranted doctrine that observance of the laws of war is not required if conformity thereto interferes with the attainment of the object of war."

458. ("The Justice Trial") 2 *War Crimes Reports* 1, 19, 63 (1947).

by "military necessity." [459] Even the unbelievably ruthless extermination of millions of Jews, Poles, Russians, and gypsies and other inhabitants of occupied countries was blandly alleged to have been done out of necessity.[460] The killing of the children of these unfortunate ethnic groups was rationalized upon the theory that at some time in the future, when the children had grown up, they would threaten the security of Germany. In the *Peleus* case,[461] the massacre of the survivors of a sunken Allied merchantman by the attacking submarine's crew was asserted to have been demanded by military necessity. It appeared, however, that had the submarine commander been truly concerned over the security of his vessel against possible air attack, he could have left the scene of the sinking at once. Instead, he cruised around the site for five hours and disposed of the survivors clinging to life rafts and debris with machine-gun fire. Further, the massacre was foreseeably entirely futile as a means of concealing the sinking of the *Peleus,* for oil from the victim ship marked the site anyway.

The plea of military necessity was also invoked to defend the mass deportation of inhabitants of occupied territories for purposes of slave labor in Germany and the employment of prisoners of war in war production. In the *Krupp* trial,[462] for example, the defense argued that these measures were justified by the "great emergency" in which the German war economy found itself. It should be mentioned at once that these measures were, in their execution, innocent of the slightest concession to human life and dignity. The enslaved laborers and prisoners of war were transported and compelled to work under subhuman conditions and given food rations far below the minimum required to enable them to perform efficiently, and very often, even merely to sustain life.[463] Wages for labor done were

459. See *U.S. v. Brandt* ("The Medical Case"), 2 *Trials of War Criminals* at 5 et seq. (1947).

460. *U.S. v. Ohlendorf* ("The *Einsatzgruppen* Case"), 4 *Trials of War Criminals* at 462–4 (1947).

461. 1 *War Crimes Reports* 1 (1945).

462. 10 *War Crimes Reports* 138 (1948).

463. In *U.S. v. Pohl,* 5 *Trials of War Criminals* at 970 (1947), the tribunal said: "Slavery may exist even without torture. Slaves may be well fed, well clothed, and comfortably housed, but they are still slaves if without lawful process they are deprived of their freedom by forceful restraint. We might eliminate all proof of ill treatment, overlook the starvation, beatings, and other barbarous

of course out of the question. There is strong evidence [464] that Germany, throughout the war, never fully mobilized its available domestic manpower—particularly womanpower—for production for the armed forces. The output of civilian consumption goods, after initial restrictions which left the civilian standard of living at a "fairly comfortable" level well above that of the prewar depression years, was maintained at such level until the middle of 1944. There are even indications that local Nazi leaders resisted total mobilization to keep themselves popular with the people. The conclusion which suggests itself is that the use on a vast scale of enslaved foreign labor in the war industries enabled Germany to maintain throughout most of the war a high level of civilian production. The "great emergency" alleged would thus at any event have been most difficult to prove; convenience, expediency, and interest, perhaps, but certainly no overpowering necessity was shown.

In passing upon a claim of military necessity, the appropriate task of the decision-maker is not to determine whether, in the light of the facts as they appear to him in retrospect, sufficiently urgent military necessity "actually" or "objectively" existed. It is rather to estimate the military commander's reasonable appraisal of the features of a tactical situation as such features presumably appeared to the commander at the time of the acts complained of.[465] In reconstructing and assaying the impact of these facts as perceived by the commander in taking the military decision being reviewed, ac-

acts, but the admitted fact of slavery—compulsory uncompensated labor—would still remain. There is no such thing as benevolent slavery. Involuntary servitude, even if tempered by humane treatment, is still slavery." It might be noted, however, that Art. 52 of the Hague Regulations does permit requisition of services from inhabitants of occupied territories, which is really coerced labor. Compensation is of course required.

464. See *U.S. Strategic Bombing Survey, Over-all Report (European War)* 31 et seq. (1945). For detailed information and statistical tables on the extent to which German manpower was mobilized and the role which foreign workers and prisoners of war played in the German war economy see id., *The Effects of Strategic Bombing on the German War Economy* 29 et seq. (1945).

465. See "The Hostages Case," 8 *War Crimes Reports* at 68–9 (1948) where the tribunal absolved General Rendulic on the Finmark devastation charge, concluding that the operational conditions as they appeared to Rendulic at the relevant time were sufficient to warrant his belief that urgent military necessity required the devastation. See supra p. 602 for brief description of the facts involved.

count may rationally be taken of a number of factors, including, for instance, the location of the accused commander in the hierarchy or structure of command. The position of the officer charged in the military command structure may be expected to bear strongly upon the amount and character of the intelligence relating to the broader (in a relative sense, of course) or strategic military situation which may be presumed to have been available to such officer and upon which he presumably acted.[466] Where the unlawful acts alleged consist of or include the destruction of property, consideration should also be given to the military commander's estimate of the importance of the target, or, more precisely, the accused commander's estimate of his opponent's expectations about the importance of preserving the target intact. The intensity of enemy pressure at the time the military decision was made and executed may be a third significant factor. That the necessities of a specific situation, i.e., the intensity and direction of the enemy attack, were foreseen and plans to meet them were framed in advance need not render those necessities any less real. Finally, the ambiguity and controversial character of the rule alleged to have been violated, its seeming obsolescence or common uncertainty as to its continuing effect, may perhaps also be considered relevant.[467]

Legitimate Reprisals

The plea of legitimate reprisals is of the nature of a plea of confession and avoidance. Legitimate war reprisals refer to acts directed against the enemy which are conceded to be generally unlawful, but which constitute an authorized reaction to prior unlawful acts of the enemy for the purpose of deterring repetition of such antecedent acts.[468] The doctrine of reprisals thus permits the use of otherwise

466. See, for illustration of this point, the excerpt from the testimony of Rendulic in 11 *Trials of War Criminals* at 1127–8.

467. See "The Flick Trial," 9 *War Crimes Reports* at 23 (1947) for questioning statements by the Tribunal as to the impact of the new techniques of total war on the Hague Regulations, concluding that "these developments make plain the necessity of appraising the conduct of defendants with relation to the circumstances and conditions of their environment." And see in particular, Lauterpacht, "The Law of Nations and the Punishment of War Crimes," 21 *Brit. Y.B.I.L.* 58 at 74–5 (1944).

468. Cf. the formulations in 2 Oppenheim-Lauterpacht 561; Albrecht, "War Reprisals in the War Crimes Trials and in the Geneva Conventions of 1949,"

lawless violence as a response to lawless violence. It will be recalled that the general community of nations seeks, in first recourse, to prohibit international change by destructive coercion and for this purpose projects that most fundamental of principles—the principle of minimum order—and distinguishes between permissible and impermissible recourse to coercion. Where minimum public order is in fact breached by an unlawful resort to coercion, the general community nonetheless seeks to reduce to a minimum the destruction of values that inevitably attends hostilities by requiring observance of the combatant law of war. The permission of legitimate reprisals represents an effort to secure some humanitarianism on still a different level. Where in the course of hostilities the requirements of the law of war are disregarded and unnecessary or irrelevant destruction is inflicted, the doctrine of reprisals makes available the unorganized sanctioning procedures of reciprocity and retaliation for securing a return to the observance of the law of war.[469]

The common theme that runs through these successive lines of defense, so to say, of community authority is that of limiting the destruction of values in the interactions of states. It may, however, on occasion be necessary to become very explicit about the specialized manifestations of this common theme on each level of effort. In the trial of *Rauter,*[470] for example, the Netherlands Special Court of Cassation, in addressing itself to the problem of legitimate reprisals, indicated that the prior illegal act to which reprisal is an authorized response may consist of the initiation of a war of aggression. The Court said:

> It is indeed generally known and was convincingly established by the International Military Tribunal at Nuremberg . . . that the former German Reich unleashed against the Kingdom of the Netherlands, as against various other European states, an unlawful war of aggression, and by so doing violated international law, an international offence which in itself the Kingdom of the Netherlands was already justified in answering by taking reprisals against the aggressor.[471]

47 *A.J.I.L.* 590 (1953); Dept. of the Army, *Law of Land Warfare* par. 497(a) (FM 27–10, July 1956).

469. See Stowell, "Military Reprisals and the Sanctions of the Laws of War," 36 *A.J.I.L.* 643 (1942).

470. *Annual Digest 1949,* Case No. 193.

471. Id., at p. 539–40.

The Court here appears to suggest that the belligerent acting in self-defense becomes, upon this ground alone, entitled to engage in reprisals. There is, indeed, a strong parallel between the permission of self-defense and the permission of reprisals, for they exhibit as noted above an identity in basic policy theme and both doctrines authorize coercive response to unlawful coercion. The authorization of self-defense, however, refers to response to an impermissible *resort* to coercion while the reprisals doctrine authorizes response to particular instances of unlawful violence within an already initiated and *continuing* process of coercion. To combine and confuse the two doctrines (i.e. the first and third "lines of defense"), as the Netherlands Court appears in effect to do, and to suggest that the defending belligerent may by way of reprisal for the commencement of unlawful aggression disregard the rules of warfare, is to thwart the common underlying policy of minimum destruction. Such a view, further, seems idiosyncratic when considered in relation to the position taken in most of the war crimes cases after World War II that application of the rules of warfare should be independent of the characterization of a resort to violence as unlawful. Securing the minimum destruction principle requires that the reprisals doctrine become available to the defender only when the aggressor, subsequent to the violation of the prohibition against *resort* to violence, breaches the requirements of the law on *conduct* of violence.

In the first instance, of course, the legitimacy of a resort to reprisals is determined by each belligerent for itself. Each belligerent passes upon the conformity or disconformity of a prior act of its opponent with the international law on hostilities. The opposing belligerent will in turn judge for itself the legitimacy both of its original acts and of the measure alleged by the first belligerent to be a reprisal. The opposing belligerent is, in the nature of things, apt to find itself free to engage in counterreprisals. Thus, the possibility must be faced that an indefinitely spiraling process of reprisal, counterreprisal, and countercounterreprisal may under certain circumstances ensue. Obviously the doctrine of reprisals, like all authoritative policies, is vulnerable to perversion and abuse. By itself, however, this vulnerability cannot be decisive of the utility or desirability of the reprisals doctrine.[472] In the context of continuing hostilities, and until a comprehensive, centralized, and effective sanc-

472. Cf. Fenwick, *International Law* 580–1 (3rd ed., 1948); Baty, *The Canons of International Law* 463 (1930).

tions process is achieved in the world arena, belligerents have to police one another and enforce the laws of war against each other.

Community authority about reprisals establishes certain limiting requirements designed to reduce susceptibility to abuse. These requirements are conveniently considered under three headings: proportionality, selection of reprisal targets, and reprisal procedure.

Clarification of the conception of proportionality requires, at the outset, specification of the base in relation to which the response in reprisal must be proportional. It is frequently asserted that the requirement of proportionality refers to a relation between the original unlawful act and the retaliatory response. The response, it is said, must be proportional to the unlawful act that gave occasion for the response.[473] It may be suggested, however, that if reprisals are to signify something more than an adventitious "survival of *lex talionis*,"[474] they should be adapted and related, not so much to the past illegality but rather and primarily to the future purpose sought. It is a common emphasis that the legitimate purpose of reprisals is not the infliction of retribution but the deterrence of future lawlessness. From such emphasis, it would seem to follow that the kind and amount of permissible reprisal violence is that which is reasonably designed so to affect the enemy's expectations about the costs and gains of reiteration or continuation of his initial unlawful act as to induce the termination of and future abstention from such act. The quantum of permissible reprisal violence, so determined, may under certain circumstances conceivably be greater than that inflicted in the enemy's original unlawful act.[475] Upon the other hand, violence so gross as to have no reasonable relation to the postulated deterrent effect is appropriately characterized, not as a legitimate reprisal, but as a new and independent unlawful act. The requirement

473. E.g. 2 Oppenheim-Lauterpacht 563; Stone, *Legal Controls,* 354–5; Holland, *The Laws of War on Land* 61 (1908); *Law of Land Warfare,* supra note 468 at par. 497(3). As to proportionality in "peacetime" reprisals see the Naulilaa Incident Arbitration, in Bishop, *International Law: Cases and Materials* 561 (1953).

474. Spaight, *War Rights on Land* 462 (1911).

475. Speaking of "peacetime" reprisals, Colbert, *Retaliation in International Law* 76–80 (1948) suggests that the view of the tribunal in the Naulilaa Case is not supported by practice, and that states have actually proportioned the severity of reprisals "not to the extent of the damage already done but to the extent of the damage that might be anticipated in the future, should the consequences of illegal action not be sufficiently disastrous to deter repetition."

of proportionality in reprisals may thus be seen to be but one more manifestation of the pervasive policies of military necessity and minimum destruction.

In broadest terms, reprisal targets may be either persons or property. Turning first to persons, it must be observed that the law of reprisals projects immunity from reprisals for certain categories of individuals. The first category embraces prisoners of war. The exemption of prisoners of war from reprisals is set forth in the 1949 Geneva Prisoners of War Convention in unqualified language: "Measures of reprisal against prisoners of war are prohibited."[476] Thus, the common view is that even reprisals in kind—i.e., where the prior illegal enemy act itself consisted of maltreatment or killing of prisoners of war[477]—and so-called "prophylactic reprisals"—i.e., the deterrence of enemy action, *a fortiori* unlawful, by exposing prisoners to the anticipated effects thereof[478]—are included in the prohibition.

Before 1949, prisoners of war were practically the only exempt category of persons. The three other Geneva Conventions of 1949 greatly amplified the range of nonpermissible targets of reprisals. Under these conventions the categories of persons legally immune from reprisals include: the wounded and sick of armed forces in the field; the wounded, sick, and shipwrecked members of armed forces at sea; the personnel of medical units and establishments and hospital ships, including chaplains; enemy civilians found in a belligerent's own territory; and inhabitants of areas belligerently occupied.[479] The first three categories refer to the same persons already protected by the Prisoners of War Convention; in contrast, the last

476. Art. 13, par. 3. The prohibition covers all forms of reprisals though they may appear relatively slight, such as the interruption of mail privileges and handcuffing. See Commission of Government Experts for the Study of Conventions for the Protection of War Victims, *Preliminary Documents Submitted by the International Committee of the Red Cross,* Vol. 2, p. 13 (1947). See also "Trial of Dostler," 1 *War Crimes Reports* 22, 31 (1945) where this immunity of prisoners of war was given effect by the tribunal.

477. See Commission of Government Experts, supra note 476 at 13–14; cf. 2 Oppenheim-Lauterpacht 562–3 note 2.

478. Art. 23, Geneva Convention of 1949. On the practices of "prophylactic" or preventive reprisals, from the American Civil War up to the Anglo-Boer War, see Spaight, *War Rights on Land* 466 et seq. (1911). For the practice in the two world wars, see id., *Air Power and War Rights* 376 et seq. (3rd ed., 1947).

479. See Art. 46, Wounded and Sick Convention; Art. 47, Wounded, Sick and Shipwrecked Convention; Art. 33, Civilians Convention.

two are drastic innovations. The cumulative effect of the Geneva Conventions of 1949 is that all enemy persons who find themselves within a belligerent's effective control are immunized as targets of reprisal. Practically the only enemy persons who may still be lawfully subjected to reprisals are those on the high seas and in the enemy's own territory. In a sense, this is but a logical extension of the generalization, previously considered, that persons whose usefulness as bases of enemy power is precluded or has been terminated by belligerent control or capture cease to be legitimate objects of violence. In corresponding measure, however, the operation of reciprocity as a sanction of the law of war has been restricted. The immunity, it may be reiterated, is sweeping in scope: all reprisals are forbidden, however moderate the deprivations involved. Although from a humanitarian perspective, such immunity is of course desirable, there seems room for doubt as to whether the equipoise thus sought to be established between the principles of military necessity and humanity is realistically a durable one.[480]

Certain other restrictions on target selection in legitimate reprisals were laid down by war crimes tribunals after the last world war. While these restrictions have been superseded by the inclusive prohibition of the Geneva Conventions they may bear some mention. In *U.S. v. List,* the tribunal, speaking of "reprisals" against inhabitants of occupied territories, declared that there must be some reasonable connection between the targets of reprisals and the hostile acts sought to be deterred. Geographic proximity, for instance, may be required, upon the ground that reprisals directed against people in one locality for hostile acts committed in another can be expected to have little or no deterrent effect in the latter locality.[481] The other restriction is to the effect that selection of objects of reprisal may not be based simply on political, religious, or ethnic affiliations. The singling out of racial, religious, or political groups as special

480. Cf. Albrecht, supra note 468 at 614. Krafft, "The Present Position of the Red Cross Geneva Conventions," 37 *Tr. Grotius Soc.* 146 (1951), speaking of this article of the Civilians Convention, said: "It seems too good to be true. I even wonder if certain general principles contained in the Convention can be reconciled with the idea of war at all."

481. 11 *Trials of War Criminals* at 1250 (1948). See also *In re* Kappler, *Annual Digest 1948,* Case No. 151, p. 480 where the tribunal suggested that locality, office, association, or function may also constitute the necessary connection in certain cases.

targets of reprisal would, in the absence of a showing of some particular nexus between such group and the hostile acts committed or anticipated, be persuasive indication that the alleged reprisals are moved by some purpose other than deterrence and hence are illegitimate.[482]

Property, as the object of reprisals, may be appropriated or destroyed. From a policy perspective, property may be recommended rather than persons as reprisal targets, since wealth is perhaps commonly ranked lower than human life or liberty in most cultures. Reprisals against property involve lesser value deprivations and, where the object is appropriated rather than destroyed, afford an added increment of power for the actor-belligerent.[483] Conversely, perhaps, the deterrent impact of such measures on the enemy is likely to be smaller where both belligerents share the same pattern of value preferences. Conceivably, property reprisals against an enemy with a heavy surplus of manpower and which regards human life lightly, may be much more efficacious than retaliation on enemy persons.

There are certain classes of property for which the Geneva Conventions of 1949 provide immunity from reprisals. Thus, Article 33 of the Civilians Convention confers immunity upon the property of enemy aliens in a belligerent's territory, and upon the property of inhabitants of regions under belligerent occupation. Under this provision, orders like those issued by the German occupation forces in France for the burning of three farms for every German soldier killed by guerrillas and one farm for every German wounded would

482. As such they might be regarded as crimes against humanity. The description of this category of crimes found in Art. 6(c) of the Charter of the Nuremberg Tribunal included "persecutions on political, racial or religious grounds." In "The Trial of von Mackensen," 8 *War Crimes Reports* 2 (1945), the tribunal noted that of the 335 persons shot in the Ardeatine Caves massacre in reprisal for the Via Rosella explosion, 57 were Jews who had nothing to do with partisan activities and some of whom were not even Italians. The tribunal in the Hostages Case had intimated that nationality might in some situations be a sufficient basis for selection.

483. Colombos, *Law of the Sea* 678, 685 points out with understandable emphasis that the British retaliatory measures establishing blockade and contraband control were enforced in a manner that never violated the laws of humanity, in contrast with the German submarine and mine warfare, also alleged to be reprisals, which caused considerable loss of life and property both belligerent and neutral.

be clearly prohibited.[484] The buildings and equipment of medical units and establishments, mobile or fixed, and hospital ships, medical transports and aircraft—in general, property protected by the Conventions—are similarly immunized from reprisals.[485] It seems noteworthy that, until the conclusion of the Hague Convention for the Protection of Cultural Property in the Event of Armed Conflict of 1954, cultural and religious properties did not share this special protection save where they could be brought under the first-mentioned category, i.e., when they are the property of inhabitants of occupied territory. Under the 1954 Convention, cultural property registered in accordance with the Convention may not be subjected to reprisals.[485a] It may be doubted whether destruction of property of religious, historical, or cultural value is in any event likely to produce any significant deterrent effect. The selection of such property as reprisal targets lays the belligerent open to the charge of gratuitous vandalism and irrational vengeance and may enhance the morale of opponents. In the last world war,[486] the so-called "Baedeker raids" which were allegedly retaliatory bombing attacks by German air forces, and which were specially directed at historical monuments and buildings, museums, palaces, and other objects of cultural and artistic importance,[487] appeared to have been regarded by the Allied Powers as a wasteful expenditure of military energy.

The first requisite of reprisal procedure is that the retaliatory action must be authorized by a competent decision-maker. The decision-maker commonly is a military commander located somewhere in the military command structure. The United States *Law of Land Warfare* speaks of "the highest accessible military authority" but at the same time permits a "subordinate commander" in cases where "immediate action is demanded" to order reprisals on his own initiative and at his peril.[488] The required level of authority should

484. See "Trial of Holstein and others," 8 *War Crimes Reports* 22 (1947).

485. Supra, note 479.

485a. Art. 4(4).

486. See 1 Garner, *International Law and the World War* 437 et seq. (1920) for discussion of the excesses committed by the Germans in the First World War under the guise of reprisals, the most notable being the looting and burning of the University of Louvain.

487. See Spaight, *Air Power and War Rights* 286–7 (3rd ed., 1947).

488. Par. 497(d). *The British Manual of Military Law,* Part III, par. 645 (1958) provides only for reprisals "by order of a commander." Holland, supra

perhaps depend, in part at least, upon the character and magnitude of the original illegality and of the reprisal measure contemplated in response. The higher the authority, and the more detached from the immediate results of the enemy act denounced as unlawful, the greater would seem the guarantee against hasty, ill-advised, and arbitrary recourse to reprisals. In any event the ordinary soldier is clearly not regarded as competent to initiate reprisals on his own responsibility; as far as he is concerned, the defense of legitimate reprisal must be combined with that of superior orders.

The initial task of the competent decision-maker is the determination of the occurrence of a prior unlawful enemy act. The making of this determination involves two distinguishable tasks. The first task comprises the ascertainment of the physical events constituting the alleged enemy offense [489] and of the causal role played by the enemy

---

note 473 at 61 declared that except under "very special circumstances," a reprisal must be authorized by the Commander-in-Chief. The original Russian *Projet* submitted to the Brussels Conference of 1874 also required authorization by the commander-in-chief; 65 *British Foreign and State Papers* at 1102 (1873–1874). The Italian Military Tribunal in *In re* Kappler, *Annual Digest 1948,* Case No. 151 at 473 held that reprisals may be ordered "not only by those authorities of the State which represent it in International Law, but also by the Supreme Commander or by the Commander of a big unit."

489. The *British Manual of Military Law,* Part III, par. 643 (1958) provides that the prior illegality may consist of an act of the enemy government, its military commanders, or some other enemy individual. Cf. the theory set forth by the Netherlands Tribunal in "Trial of Rauter," 14 *War Crimes Reports* 89 (1949) that reprisals are justified only for violations by the enemy state acting through its competent organs and not for acts of individuals who are "irresponsible," that is, who were not, or could not be deemed as, acting in the name of the enemy state. The tribunal classified all the civilian inhabitants of an occupied territory as "irresponsible," such that hostile acts committed by the inhabitants against the occupant were not to be regarded as acts of the state itself. The ingenious net result was that no reprisal could lawfully be taken for those hostile acts. Contrast with this Dutch theory Westlake's view that enemy individuals are identified with their state not only in the execution of the reprisal, but also in the determination of a proper occasion for reprisals. Under Westlake's notion of a double process of identification, both the actor-individual and the reprisal target are assimilated to the enemy state. See *Collected Papers of John Westlake* 263 (1914). The Dutch court did not consider relevant the fact that hostile acts by populations are usually incited and directed by the legitimate exiled government.

in such events. Performance of this task is obviously indispensable even in situations where the safety of the troops requires immediate drastic action." [490] For necessity for immediate reprisals can scarcely arise before it becomes clear to the military commander that the enemy did bring about certain events which appear to be a violation of the law of war. The second task is that of characterizing the events attributable to the enemy in terms of concordance or conflict with the rules of warfare. The vagueness, ambiguity, and near obsolescence of many of the conventional rules may of course facilitate the imputation of unlawful conduct to the enemy, while at the same time compounding the difficulties which a decision-maker reviewing the military commander's determination must face.[491]

After the above determination is reached, a second requirement of lawful reprisal procedure becomes applicable: the exhaustion of available alternative methods of securing redress and future abstention.[492] The thrust of the requirement is that resort to the extraordinary remedy of reprisals must be necessary in high degree.[493] This requirement, which is again but one more expression of the policy that would minimize destruction of values, gains in urgency when one recalls that the burden of reprisals must ordinarily be sustained by nonoffending persons. Thus, effort must be bent toward the detection and apprehension of the actual offenders. A complaint may be lodged with the enemy, either directly or through the good offices of neutrals, and a demand made for some guarantee of nonrepetition and for punishment of the guilty persons. When, however, the delay attendant upon prior exhaustion of alternative procedures entails grave danger to the aggrieved belligerent, that requirement may be lawfully dispensed with.[494] Such a situation may arise, for in-

490. Dept. of the Army, *Law of Land Warfare,* par. 497(f) (FM 27-10, July 1956) states that "the rule requiring careful inquiry into the real occurrence will always be followed *unless* the safety of the troops requires immediate drastic action . . ." (italics supplied).

491. In "The Hostages Case," 11 *Trials of War Criminals* at 1274 (1948) the tribunal considered as a mitigating circumstance in favor of defendant List the uncodified and uncertain character of the law on hostages.

492. Albrecht, supra note 468 at 596–7; Holland, supra note 473 at 61.

493. Cf. Hall, *International Law* 497 (8th ed., Pearce Higgins, 1924).

494. 2 Oppenheim-Lauterpacht 562 note 2; Dept. of the Army, *Law of Land Warfare,* par. 497(b) (FM 27-10, July 1956); *British Manual of Military Law,* Part III, par. 646 (1958).

stance, where a prohibited but potentially decisive weapon of mass destruction is used by the enemy belligerent.

Public announcement to the enemy of retaliatory measures is another element of required reprisal procedure. The theory is that reprisals carried out in secret can have no deterrent effect and should, on that account, be deemed illegitimate.[495] The public declaration may be in the nature of an advance warning made even before the enemy actually employs illegitimate violence. While doubtless the threat of reciprocation is an implicit and constant factor that any belligerent contemplating a nonpermissible act must reckon with, an unequivocal assurance that swift retaliation will in fact ensue may have a special salutary inhibitive effect. For instance, President Roosevelt's announcement in 1943 that any use of gas by Germany against any of the Allied Powers would entail to a certainty reprisal in kind [496] probably had a stronger impact on Hitler than the assumed possibility that the Allies might resort to reprisals. Moreover, an advanced warning serves to stress the deterrent and to de-emphasize the merely retributive aspect of reprisals.

Although compliance with the requisites and limitations of the reprisals doctrine does authorize the aggrieved belligerent to take reprisals, whether or not they are actually resorted to depends on the belligerent's estimate of certain factors, military, political, and psychological in character. These factors may include his relative vulnerability to possible counterreprisals, whether they be lawful or not, and the probable impact of a reprisal on the enemy, neutrals, and the belligerent's own people. A reprisal, particularly when directed against the enemy civilian population, may conceivably result in strengthening the enemy's will to fight. It may also turn neutral opinion against the belligerent. When a belligerent is hard pressed, the diversion of military energy for reprisals may possibly prove uneconomical. On the other hand, recourse to reciprocity may have a positive effect on the morale of the belligerent's own people. These and similar factors must all enter into the calculations of the decision-maker.

495. See "The Hostages Case," 11 *Trials of War Criminals* at 1250–2 (1948); also "Trial of Bruns," 3 *War Crimes Reports* 19 (1946). The requirement of public notification was deemed particularly important in reprisals against inhabitants of occupied territories.

496. See 18 *Dept. of State Bull.* 507 (1943).

Superior Orders and Acts of Subordinates

The broad considerations of legal policy that underlie the problem of superior orders as a defense in a prosecution for violation of the rules of warfare require the usual balancing of the demands of military effectiveness and necessity and of minimum destruction. The efficiency and effectiveness of an army as a combat force depends to a great extent upon the disciplinary subordination of ranks within its hierarchical structure and the alacrity with which orders issued are executed. To reject the defense of superior orders is in effect to require subordinate personnel to pass judgment on the legality of orders emanating from their superior officers before complying with them; [497] this may be expected to have, it has been commonly argued, a deleterious effect on the conditions of discipline in the armed forces. The difficulties that inhere in this situation are magnified when a military unit is engaged in active operations and locked in combat with enemy forces, and disobedience or even hesitation is most likely to be met with summary and severe deprivations. The same reaction to noncompliance with a superior's orders may be expected although the armed force is not in immediate violent contact with the enemy. Indeed, the anticipation of such response is implicit in the notion and practice of military discipline.

There is, on the other hand, the necessity of enforcing the prescriptions of the law of war which are designed, as has time and again been emphasized, to minimize the destruction of human values in war and thereby to infuse a little humanity into what must be a brutal and bloody business. The acceptance of superior orders as an unqualified defense could all but render impossible the enforcement of these prescriptions by frustrating the imposition of individual criminal responsibility. It needs little reflection to see that the defense may result in an indefinitely regressive disavowal of responsibility until all save one or at most a handful of the most highly placed members of the political and military elite are absolved from liability.[498] The emasculatory impact of the defense is emphasized by

497. As the tribunal in "The High Command Case," 12 *War Crimes Reports* at 73 (1948) put it: "Orders are the basis upon which any army operates. It is basic to the discipline of an army that orders are issued to be carried out. Its discipline is built upon this principle. Without it, no army can be effective. . . ."

498. Relevant references are collected supra, Ch. 1, note 199.

the fact that those who have urged superior orders as a complete defense at the same time put forward the act-of-state doctrine as a protective shield for the top elite.[499] Thus, the inadequacy of either unqualified acceptance or simple rejection of the defense of superior orders, and the need for nice discriminations and compromises in achieving a workable equilibrium of the competing policy considerations, seem reasonably clear.

By way of preliminary clarification, it may be noted that the term "superior" has been interpreted to embrace in reference not only formal rank and authority but also effective physical or moral capacity to induce commission of an unlawful act.[500] "Orders" has in comparable fashion been effectively construed to include, in addition to instructions issued by particular officers, the requirements of the municipal law of a belligerent. The plea raised in several of the war crimes trials that the accused's acts were permissible or compulsory under the internal law of his state,[501] was treated by the tribunals in much the same way as the more orthodox "superior orders" defense. Finally, "superior orders" need not be exclusively limited to members of armed forces but may, in appropriate cases, be available to civilian personnel.[502]

Examination of the decisions of the war crimes tribunals indicates that by and large the plea of superior orders was assessed in the light of familiar criminal law principles relating to *mens rea* (culpable perspectives) as a basic condition of penal responsibility. Thus, where the court was satisfied that the accused did not in fact know of the illegal quality of the order he executed, he was not held accountable.[503] However, knowledge or lack of knowledge might be

499. For illustrative citations, see supra, Ch. 1, note 198. Cf. Kelsen, *Principles of International Law* 136 (1952) who considers superior orders as a problem of "criminal law, not of international law." To Kelsen, the only relevant question is whether the violation was or was not an "act of state."

500. See "The *Einsatzgruppen* Case," 2 *Trials of War Criminals* at 480 (1947); "Trial of Sadaiche," in 15 *War Crimes Reports* at 175.

501. E.g. "Trial of Altstotter," 7 *War Crimes Reports* at 48–9 (1947); "Trial of Wielen," 11 id. at 50 (1947).

502. See "Trial of Wagner," 3 War Crimes Reports at 54–5 (1946). One of the defendants, Lager, was a Public Prosecutor in the Special Court at Strasbourg. He was acquitted on the ground that he had acted under the orders of Gauleiter Wagner.

503. In "The Hostages Case," 8 *War Crimes Reports* at 50 (1948), the tribunal said: "If the illegality of the order was not known to the inferior and he could

inferred from the character of the order's contents.[504] Where the order was "illegal on its face" or "obviously unlawful," the accused, upon the assumption that although unlearned in the law of war he partook of a common humanity, was held liable. Illustrations of orders so characterized by the war crimes tribunals include orders for the killing or ill-treatment of prisoners of war,[505] the massacre of survivors of sunken ships,[506] and the mass extermination, torture, and mutilation of the civil population in occupied countries.[507] The extent to which knowledge may be imputed to the defendant may of course be affected by the rank he occupied. It would seem but rarely reasonable to ascribe the same degree of knowledge of the law of war to an ordinary enlisted man and, say, to an army group commander; an order "obviously illegal" to the latter may frequently not be so to the former.[508]

---

not reasonably have been expected to know of its illegality, no wrongful intent necessary to the commission of a crime exists and the inferior will be protected." Cf. Glueck, infra note 515 at 155–6. On the handling of the psychopathological aspects of *mens rea* by the war crimes tribunals, see Smith, "Mental Abnormality and Responsibility in International Criminal Law," 37 *Tr. Grotius Soc.* 99 (1951).

504. Cf. Dunbar, "Some Aspects of the Problem of Superior Orders in the Law of War," 63 *Jurid. Rev.* 253, 255 (1951).

505. See "Trial of Wielen," 11 *War Crimes Reports* at 47 (1947); "Trial of Renoth," 11 id. at 78 (1946); cf. *Rex v. Werner,* Supreme Court of South Africa, *Annual Digest 1947,* Case No. 93 which dealt with the killing of a German prisoner of war by his fellow prisoners, pursuant to an order by one of the latter who was a major.

506. "The *Peleus* Trial," 1 *War Crimes Reports* at 16 et seq. (1945). In *"The Llandovery Castle," Annual Digest 1923–1924,* Case No. 235 at p. 437–8, the German *Reichsgericht* held that while a military subordinate may ordinarily count on the legality of his superior's orders, he may not do so "if such an order is universally known to everybody, including the accused, to be without any doubt whatever against the law." Further, it declared that the killing of defenseless people in life boats was just such a case.

507. "The *Einsatzgruppen* Case," 4 *Trials of War Criminals* at 471 (1947); "The Belsen Trial," 2 *War Crimes Reports* 75–6, 79, 95–6, 108 (1945), cf. "Trial of Motomura," 13 *War Crimes Reports* at 144–5 (1947). In "Trial of Hans," 5 *War Crimes Reports* 82 (1947), the Norwegian Supreme Court held, in effect, that an order for the execution of civilians in occupied territory without a prior *judicial* trial and sentence was *not* an "obviously unlawful one" and acquitted the defendant. Cf. "Trial of Flesch," 6 *War Crimes Reports* 111 (1948), also decided by the Norwegian Supreme Court.

508. Dunbar, supra note 504 at 251; Koessler, "American War Crimes Trials in Europe," 39 *Geo. L.J.* 92–3 (1950). The tribunal in "The High Command

Where the accused's knowledge of the unlawful nature of the order he carried out was sustained by varying processes of proof, he was not permitted escape from liability by merely pleading superior orders. He could, however, set up an additional allegation of duress. There would seem implicit in the very conception of superior orders a certain degree of compulsion. Placing a heavy weighting upon the policy embodied in enforcement of the law of war, the war crimes tribunals commonly required a high degree of compulsion for exemption from liability. In the language of the International Military Tribunal at Nuremberg, duress, to be exempting, must in fact render "moral choice" impossible.[509] The Tribunal in the High Command case elaborated on this point:

> The defendants in this case who received obviously criminal orders were placed in a difficult position but servile compliance with orders clearly criminal for fear of some disadvantage or punishment not immediately threatened cannot be recognized as a defence . . . [T]here must be a showing of circumstances such that a reasonable man would apprehend that he was in such imminent physical peril as to deprive him of freedom to choose the right and refrain from the wrong.[510]

A second requirement for exempting duress was a showing that the harm actually inflicted by the accused's compliance with the unlawful order was not disproportionally greater than the personal

---

Case," 12 *War Crimes Reports* at 73 declared: "It is certainly not incumbent upon a soldier in a subordinate position to screen the orders of superiors for questionable points of legality. Within certain limitations, he has the right to assume that the orders of his superiors and the State which he serves and which are issued to him are in conformity with International Law." The tribunal, however, apparently considered "military commanders in the field with far reaching military responsibilities" as being in the same position.

509. *Nazi Conspiracy and Aggression: Opinion and Judgment* 53–4. The tribunal in "The I. G. Farben Case," 10 *War Crimes Reports* at 57 (1948), said: "We deduce that an order of a superior officer or a law or governmental decree will not justify the defence of necessity unless, in its operation, it is of a character to deprive the one to whom it is directed of a moral choice as to his course of action. It follows that the defence of necessity is not available where the party seeking to invoke it was, himself, responsible for the existence or execution of such order or decree, or where his participation went beyond the requirements thereof, or was the result of his own initiative."

510. 12 *War Crimes Reports* at 72 (1948). See also "The *Einsatzgruppen* Case," 4 *Trials of War Criminals* at 480 (1947).

deprivation anticipated from noncompliance.[511] A third, and potentially much more stringent, requirement indicated by the tribunal in the *Einsatzgruppen* case was that the accused must not have been "in accord with the principle and intent of the superior" who issued the illegal order. This requirement is open to the interpretation that the accused must have externally manifested his nonacquiescence in the illegality. The precise nature and extent of the required manifestation was not indicated by the tribunal; it only declared that to "rebel mentally" was not sufficient.[512]

Where the tribunal finds that the defendant knew or reasonably should have known that the order involved was illegitimate, and the elements of exempting duress noted above are not shown, superior orders may still be taken into account for mitigation of individual liability. The kinds of factors that may bear upon determination of the appropriate degree of extenuation include, for example, the time of the commission of the offense. In the trial of *Milch,*[513] the court appeared to have suggested that greater mitigating effect may be accorded to superior orders under wartime conditions than during times of peace. The weight of enemy military pressure at the time the offense was committed may also assume importance. In the

511. "The *Einsatzgruppen* Case," 4 *Trials of War Criminals* at 471 (1947): "It would not be an adequate excuse, for example, if a subordinate, under orders, killed a person known to be innocent, because by not obeying it he would himself risk a few days of confinement." Here, the crimes involved were the torture and extermination of several millions of persons in the occupied regions. The defendants showed no special circumstances constituting a grave and imminent peril to themselves should they have disobeyed their orders. On the contrary, they had voluntarily joined the *Einsatzkommandos* to whom the task of extermination had been entrusted. In "The Krupp Trial," 10 *War Crimes Reports* at 149 (1948), the court noted that probably the worst consequences which would have followed a refusal to follow orders to use slave labor in the Krupp factories would have been merely, for Krupp, the loss of his plant, and for the other defendants the ejection from their posts.

512. "The *Einsatzgruppen* Case," 4 *Trials of War Criminals* at 481. All the defendants had insisted that they were "shocked" by their orders to carry out the "final solution" of the "Jewish problem." None, however, had done anything about the matter. None had saved even one single Jew from death, an admission brought out in the cross-examination of the defendants.

513. 7 *War Crimes Reports* at 42 (1947). The court pointed out that Milch had participated in the terrorization, enslavement, and murder of Jews in Germany long before the outbreak of the war "at a time when there was no claim upon the loyalty of the defendant as a soldier to protect his homeland at war."

Jaluit Atoll case,[514] which involved an order for the killing of three American prisoners of war, the defense pointed out that at the time of the issuance of this order, the military situation of the Japanese forces at Jaluit was critical. The suggestion was that a more rigid discipline then prevailed than would normally have been the case. The relative positions in the military authority structure of both the individual issuing the order and of the recipient who executed it may also be usefully considered. The defense in the *Jaluit Atoll* case observed that the order to kill the three prisoners was issued directly by a rear admiral to the four other accused, one of whom was a lieutenant, one a warrant officer, and the other two ensigns.[515] It was there further alleged that Japanese troops were trained to regard a superior's orders as coming personally from the Emperor who occupied a unique position in Japanese national life. Perhaps the broader point may be made that the military organization and civilian bureaucracy in a totalitarian or police state seem much less likely to be tolerant of hesitancy or failure of obedience on the part of subordinate personnel than in a state with long experience in democratic procedures. It is, unfortunately, not clear what extenuating weight the court in the *Jaluit Atoll* and other cases gave to these factors. What might be stressed, however, is that the degree of compulsion that may accompany superior orders may differ markedly in varying situations and that in some contexts a subordinate may have much less effective opportunity to consider the legitimacy of a specific order than in others.

A fourth type of factor has been regarded as enhancing the mitigating effect of superior orders—the extent to which the accused sought to avoid executing the order or to thwart or soften its impact. In the trial of *Bauer*,[516] the court appeared to have considered the fact that

514. 1 *War Crimes Reports* at 74 (1945). See also 5 id. at 18–19.

515. In "The Trial of Greifelt," 13 *War Crimes Reports* 69 (1948), the tribunal took into consideration the fact that the defendants, members or organizations to which racial tasks (i.e., Germanization) were entrusted, were directly subject to Himmler. Koessler, supra note 508 at 92 suggested as important the question whether the superior involved was "just one rank higher up or towering in rank" as against the subordinate defendant. See also Glueck, *War Criminals: Their Prosecution and Punishment* 156–7 (1944) and Berger, "The Legal Nature of War Crimes and the Problem of Superior Command," 38 *Am. Pol. Sci. Rev.* 1203, 1206–7 (1944).

516. 8 *War Crimes Reports* at 16 and 21 (1945).

the accused Falten, a lieutenant who had received "categorical" orders from a colonel to execute captured prisoners, postponed the execution upon his own initiative and went back to the officer who had transmitted the orders to inquire "once more" whether the execution should be carried out. In the *Hostages* case,[517] the tribunal in passing sentence on one of the defendants took into account the circumstance that he had recognized "certain injustices and irregularities" in the reprisal policy and procedure ordered by his superiors and had "attempted to correct them." The Nuremberg International Military Tribunal observed that Speer had opposed Hitler's program of devastating some of the western occupied territories to the point of deliberately sabotaging it at considerable personal risk.[518]

The difficulties that attend appraisal of a plea of superior orders are magnified when this plea is combined with the defense of reprisals. An accused who pleads superior orders *cum* reprisals in effect admits that he knew or should have known of the illegal character of an order but asserts that the order was represented to him as a reprisal measure for some prior unlawful enemy act. The issue in such case is whether he may reasonably be required to determine the legitimacy of the reprisal. The making of such a determination—that is, to review the judgment of the superior officer that a proper occasion for reprisals had arisen—obviously requires not only knowledge of the law of war but also such information on the alleged illegality attributed to the enemy as would enable the accused to ascertain the actual occurrences, assess proportionality, and verify compliance with all the requirements of reprisal procedure.

Superior orders *cum* reprisals appears to have received little attention in war crimes jurisprudence. In the trial of *Von Falkenhorst,*[519] the accused was commander-in-chief of the German forces in Norway and had had about twenty years of senior service in the army. The order there involved was Hitler's so-called "Commando Order." The opening paragraph recited that the Allied Powers had been using methods of warfare prohibited by international conventions, and that in particular the "brutal and treacherous" commandos were

517. 8 *War Crimes Reports* at 75 (1948).

518. *Nazi Conspiracy and Aggression: Opinion and Judgment* 158–9 (1947).

519. 11 *War Crimes Reports* 18 (1946). See also *Trial of Nikolaus Von Falkenhorst* (Stevens, ed., 1949).

under orders to kill "defenceless prisoners." The Order required that quarter be refused to captured commandos whether taken in uniform or not, and explicitly threatened with a court-martial commanders and officers who failed to instruct their troops accordingly or who acted contrary to its provisions. The defense alleged that Von Falkenhorst "took this measure as a reprisal" and that he was not in a position to verify the facts set forth by Hitler. The tribunal found the accused guilty; as no opinion is recorded, the basis of the decision can only be speculated upon. It has been suggested that there were no facts upon which the court could find that the defendant "really believed" that the Order purported to be a reprisal.[520] One possible view of the case is that Von Falkenhorst could reasonably have been presumed by the tribunal to know, considering his long years of service, that the commandos were legitimate combatants at least when in uniform. Since Norway, where he was in command, was a frequent target of commando raids, he could have determined for himself that uniforms were in fact worn by the commandos on those raids and that therefore no basis for reprisals existed. He might also have been presumed to know that prisoners of war were by international convention immune from reprisals.[521] In the *Dover Castle* case,[522] decided by the German *Reichsgericht* in 1921, the accused U-boat commander, charged with sinking a British hospital ship, pleaded that he had merely carried out an order of the German Admiralty issued in the belief that the enemy were utilizing hospital ships for military purposes. The court ruled that the defendant was entitled to hold the opinion, upon information supplied by the German Admiralty, that the order was a legitimate reprisal measure. It seems a reasonable supposition that an ordinary submarine commander could hardly have been in a position to ascertain independently whether or not the enemy were in fact violating Hague Convention X. Probably all that can be gleaned from these cases is that the realism of requiring an accused to assess the legiti-

520. "Annotation," 11 *War Crimes Reports* 26–7.

521. In "The Trial of Dostler," 1 *War Crimes Reports* at 31 (1945) where the same "Commando Order" was involved, the combined plea of superior orders and reprisals was rejected by the tribunal, apparently on the basis of Art. 2(3) of the 1929 Geneva Prisoners of War Convention prohibiting reprisals on prisoners of war. Dostler was the commander of the 75th Army Corps in Italy and was probably presumed to be acquainted with the said provision of law.

522. *Annual Digest 1923–1924*, Case No. 231.

macy of an order presented to him as a reprisal depends, *inter alia,* upon the rank or authority of the accused.

Superior orders, whether alone or in conjunction with duress or reprisals, is appropriately raised by subordinate personnel who actually execute the orders. The superior officer from whom the unlawful order issued is, of course, himself criminally responsible.[523] A somewhat different but cognate question raised by what might be called the defense of "act of subordinates" is the legal accountability of the superior officer or commander for war crimes perpetrated by his subordinates on their own initiative and without an order from him. The *cause célèbre* is *In re Yamashita.*[524] Yamashita, the commanding general of the 14th Army Group of the Japanese forces in the Philippines, was charged before an American Military Commission with having "unlawfully disregarded and failed to discharge his duty as commander to control the operations of the members of his command, permitting them to commit brutal atrocities and other high crimes" against the civil population in occupied Philippine territory. In reviewing the sentence of death handed down by the Commission [525] the United States Supreme Court held, on the substance of the charge, that an army commander was burdened by the law of war with an affirmative duty "to take such appropriate measures as are within his power" to control the troops under his command and to prevent their violating the laws of war. Such a duty seems necessarily to imply an auxiliary duty to utilize available means of intelligence to discover the level of conduct of his troops.[526]

The same policy considerations that were observed to compete for ascendancy in "superior orders" may be seen to underlie "act of subordinates" or "command responsibility." The effective administration of a modern military organization requires a large degree of decentralization and delegation of authority and control.[527] While

523. 2 Oppenheim-Lauterpacht 572.

524. 327 U.S. 1 (1946); see also *Homma v. Patterson* 327 U.S. 759 (1946).

525. 4 *War Crimes Reports* 1 (1945).

526. See on this point Brand, "The War Crimes Trials and the Law of War," 26 *Brit. Y.B.I.L.* 425 (1949).

527. In "The High Command Case," 12 *War Crimes Reports* at 76 (1948), the tribunal said: "Military subordination is a comprehensive but not conclusive factor in fixing criminal responsibility. The authority, both administrative and military, of a commander and his criminal responsibility are related but by no means co-extensive. Modern war . . . entails a large measure of de-

means of communication between headquarters and field units and along the chain of command have been vastly improved, the degree of effective control actually wielded by a general officer high up in the structure of command over the detailed activities of subordinate units may vary in differing specific combat situations. The competing policy, on the other hand, of promoting the effective enforcement of the law of war demands that military commanders who are realistically in a position to exact compliance with the rules of warfare be required to take reasonable measures to control and discipline their soldiers.[528] In general, war crimes courts have tended to stress the necessities of military organization by requiring exacting proof of culpable perspectives on the part of the commander.[529] The tribunal in the *High Command* case said:

> There must be a personal dereliction. That can occur only where the act is directly traceable to him or where his failure to properly supervise his subordinates constitutes criminal negligence on his part. In the latter case it must be a personal neglect amounting to a wanton, immoral disregard of the action of his subordinates amounting to acquiescence.[530]

---

centralization. A high commander cannot keep completely informed of the details of military operations of subordinates and most assuredly not of every administrative measure."

528. Cf. 2 Oppenheim-Lauterpacht 572, 574. And see the majority opinion in *In re* Yamashita 327 U.S. at 15 where there appears an explicit recognition of this policy.

529. Since it is culpable failure to act that is the basis of liability, the decision-maker may often have to rely on processes of inference. In the Yamashita case, the Military Commission found that the war crimes committed by troops under Yamashita's command were so extensive and widespread, in space and time, that "they must either have been wilfully permitted by the accused or secretly ordered by the accused." 4 *War Crimes Reports* at 34 (1945) Other cases where "command responsibility" was applied, expressly or implicitly, are: "The Abbaye Ardenne Case," 4 *War Crimes Reports* 97 (1945); "Trial of Rauer," 4 id. 113 (1946); "Trial of Student," 4 id. 118 (1946); "Trial of Masao," 11 id. 56 (1947). See "Trial of Milch," 7 id. 35–7 (1947) where the tribunal, in determining the responsibility of Milch for illegal medical experiments, utilized notions closely analogous to those underlying "command responsibility." Cf. "Trial of Brandt," 2 *Trials of War Criminals* at 193–4 (1947).

530. 12 *War Crimes Reports* at 76 (1948). The rule of the Yamashita case is now incorporated into Dept. of the Army, *Law of Land Warfare,* par. 501 (FM 27-10, July 1956) and the *British Manual of Military Law,* Pt. III, par. 631

Acting in an Official Capacity

At the trial of the major German war criminals before the International Military Tribunal at Nuremberg, the defense invoked the doctrine of "act of state." Under that doctrine, acts of individuals done in their official capacity as representatives or organs of the state are "imputed" to the state itself. International legal responsibility for such acts, a distinguished scholar has contended, is located in the state and the individual actors may not be subjected to the jurisdiction of any tribunal without the consent of the state.[531] Though deference by one state to the official acts of another state may serve a useful function in other contexts—as, for instance, in facilitating peaceful and nonviolent intercourse among nation-states and individuals across their boundaries—it is abundantly clear that to extend its range of application to immunize individuals from responsibility for violations of the laws of war would reduce those laws to futile exhortations. The act-of-state doctrine would, at least as formulated by Professor Kelsen, in substance entail the entire negation of individual responsibility for violations of the rules of warfare. It would confer legal immunity not only upon heads of state, and

---

(1958). The criticisms which were directed against the *Yamashita* decision were primarily concerned with its procedural and evidential aspects, i.e. whether or not the defendant was accorded a "fair trial." See Reel, *The Case of General Yamashita* (1949) and the Review by Lyon, in 50 *Col. L. Rev.* 393 (1950); Snyder, "It's not Law—The War Guilt Trials," 38 *Ky. L.J.* 81 (1949); Guy, "The Defense of Yamashita," 4 *Wyo. L.J.* 153 (1949). See also Wright, "Due Process and International Law," 40 *A.J.I.L.* 398 (1946) and Kuhn, "International Law and National Legislation in the Trial of War Criminals—the Yamashita Case," 44 *A.J.I.L.* 559 (1950) for general comments on those facets of the case. The dissenting opinions of Justices Murphy and Rutledge revolved about those same aspects. It is significant that Justice Murphy said (327 U.S. at 40): "This is not to say that enemy commanders may escape punishment for clear and unlawful failures to prevent atrocities"; and (at 39): "Had there been some element of knowledge or direct connection with the atrocities the problem would be entirely different."

531. See Kelsen, "Collective and Individual Responsibility in International Law with Particular Regard to the Punishment of War Criminals," 31 *Calif. L. Rev.* 530 (1943); id., "Will the Judgment in the Nuremberg Trial Constitute a Precedent in International Law?" 1 *Int. L.Q.* 159–61 (1947); id., "Collective and Individual Responsibility for Acts of State in International Law," 1 *Jewish Y.B.I.L.* 226 (1948); id., *Principles of International Law* 117–19, 131–7 (1952).

highly placed state officials and administrators, military and civil, but also upon ordinary soldiers, whose acts, when performed "at the command or with the authorization of his government," Professor Kelsen regards as constituting "acts of state" too. If the minimization of destruction of values in war is to be realized through enforcement of the rules of warfare, these rules must be regarded as binding not on juristic constructions but on human persons.[532] That legal responsibility is inversely proportional to effective power is a bizarre proposition entirely inconsistent with the securing of minimum destruction.[533] The vast majority of the war crimes committed during the last war were not isolated or episodic acts done on the private initiative of common soldiers; they constituted, rather, by and large the systematic execution of policies formulated by those on the top levels of authority. To accord impunity to these officials would have rendered any effort at law enforcement largely farcical. Not deterrence from crime but inducement to crime is the result that may realistically be expected from pre-guaranteed immunity.[534]

In both the Nuremberg and Tokyo Charters [535] and in Law No. 10

532. Judge Lauterpacht, in "The Law of Nations and the Punishment of War Crimes," 21 *Brit. Y.B.I.L.* 58, 64–5 (1944), wrote with deliberate emphasis: "In no other sphere does the view that international law is binding only upon States and not upon individuals lead to more paradoxical consequences and nowhere has it in practice been rejected more emphatically than in the domain of the laws of war. . . . The immediate subjection of individuals to the rules of warfare entails, in the very nature of things, a responsibility of a criminal character."

533. See the "Report of Justice Jackson to the President of the United States, June 7, 1945," in *The Nuremberg Case—As Presented by R. H. Jackson* 8 (1947). Schwarzenberger, "War Crimes and the Problem of an International Criminal Court," 1 *Czechoslovak Y.B.I.L.* 73–5 (1942) remarked that the doctrine of immunity of heads of state does not extend to the time of war and does not, in particular, cover ex-heads of state. He pointed to the fact that a head of state who has fallen into the hands of the enemy is in exactly the same position as any prisoner of war. Cf. Wright, "War Criminals," 39 *A.J.I.L.* 268, 278 (1945). And see the "Report of the 1919 Commission on the Responsibility of the Authors of the War and on Enforcement of Penalties," 14 *A.J.I.L.* 95, 116–17 (1920) to which the American and Japanese delegates dissented (at 135–6, 152). The Japanese dissent is understandable enough since, in Japan, the Emperor was deemed to be of divine origin. See *History of the U.N. War Crimes Commission and the Development of the Laws of War* 265 note 2 (1948).

534. Glueck, supra note 515 at 136–7.

535. Art. 7, Nuremberg Charter; Art. 6, Tokyo Charter. The texts of these

of the Allied Control Council [536] for Germany, the defense of "act of state" was explicitly declared unavailable. The Nuremberg Tribunal declared:

> The principle of international law which, under certain circumstances, protects the representatives of a state, cannot be applied to acts which are condemned as criminal by international law. The authors of these acts cannot shelter themselves behind their official position in order to be freed from punishment in appropriate proceedings— He who violates the laws of war cannot obtain immunity while acting in pursuance of the authority of the State, if the State in authorizing action moves outside its competence under international Law.[537]

In at least two of the trials of the "minor" war criminals held after Nuremberg, the plea of "act of state" or acting in an official capacity was again raised by the accused and in both cases rejected by the tribunal.[538]

---

documents may be found in *History of the U.N. War Crimes Commission and the Development of the Law of War* 282 et seq. (1948). It may be noted that while in the Nuremberg Charter "official position" was declared as neither an exculpating nor a mitigating circumstance, the Toyko Charter apparently provides that it may be considered in mitigation of punishment. Principle III of the Nuremberg Principles declares: "The fact that a person who committed an act which constitutes a crime under international law acted as Head of State or responsible Government official does not relieve him from responsibility under international law." "Formulation of the Nuremberg Principles, Report of the International Law Commission covering its second session," in 2 *Y.B. of the Int. Law Comn. 1950,* 376.

536. Art. II, *Official Gazette of the Control Council For Germany* (1945), No. 22, p. 22.

537. *Nazi Conspiracy and Aggression: Opinion and Judgment* 53 (1947). Cf. Professor Wright's interesting thesis that an act of a government is not an "act of state" when it attempts to authorize an individual to do something beyond the state's competence in international law. Obviously, both the unlawful resort to violence and the illegitimate conduct of violence falls outside that competence. See Wright, "War Criminals," 39 *A.J.I.L.* 265–6 (1945). The theory appears to be that such acts are *ultra vires* the state, and that the individual actor becomes responsible. Id., "Legal Positivism and the Nuremberg Judgment," 42 id. 410–11 (1948). It must be noted that individual responsibility does not preclude responsibility of the state to respond with compensation. See Art. 3 of Hague Convention IV, 1907.

538. "Trial of Altstotter," 6 *War Crimes Reports* 60–1 (1947); "Trial of Greiser," 13 id. 117 (1946).

A somewhat analogous plea was submitted by the defense in the trial of Altstotetter.[539] The accused judges, prosecutors, and other officials in the Reich Ministry of Justice were charged with "judicial war crimes," i.e., the denial of access to impartial justice to inhabitants of occupied territories, participation in the enforcement of the "Night and Fog Decree," and, in general, the promotion of persecution of certain ethnic groups by means of their judicial office. The defense invoked on behalf of the Nazi judges the "Anglo-American doctrine of judicial immunity." The court vigorously rejected the plea, pointing out that the personal immunity of judges contemplated in that doctrine assumed "an independent judiciary administering impartial justice." So to characterize the court system in Nazi Germany would have outrageously taxed human language and belief, for the great majority of the judges enforced the dictates of the Party with fanatical rigor.

ADMINISTRATION OF THE LAW OF WAR: JURISDICTION AND PROCEDURE IN WAR CRIMES TRIALS

The main focus here adopted, as the organization of the foregoing materials will have indicated, is upon the judicial administration of the international law of hostilities. Other means for securing observance of these prescriptions than the trial and punishment of violators by war crimes tribunals may of course be available. Reprisals constitute an extraordinary remedy and an immediate sanction, the legitimacy of which in any specific instance must be regarded as subject to review by subsequent decision-makers. Protest may also be made to the offending belligerent, either directly or through the good offices of nonparticipant powers. The efficacy of this procedure in securing termination of allegedly unlawful conduct is not to be overestimated. Belligerents learned in the ways of political and psychological warfare are rarely ready to confess the illegality of any of their actions, nor even, probably, to permit an objective verification of the facts by nonparticipants.[540] Similarly,

539. 6 *War Crimes Reports* at 50 (1947).

540. Cf. Stone, *Legal Controls* 356–7. In the Korean war, for instance, North Korea consistently refused to permit the International Committee of the Red Cross to observe conditions in the prisoner-of-war camps, despite verbal adherence to the Geneva Convention of 1949. On the atrocities attributed to the

claims for compensation based on the international responsibility of belligerents for nonpermissible violence committed by their armed forces[541] cannot frequently be expected to prosper during hostilities. Realistically, the satisfaction of such claims is a function of the outcome of the war. The successful belligerent can always shift the economic burden of such claims (assuming that liability therefor is either admitted or otherwise determined by an authoritative decision-maker) to the defeated belligerent by the imposition of war indemnities upon the latter.

It would be disingenuous to gloss over the fact that effective power to prosecute and punish enemy war criminals is, in large measure, an attribute of victory. While hostilities are continuing, prosecutions, no matter how justified, are ordinarily likely to be postponed lest the enemy resort to punitive measures under color of reprisals.[542] The lack of mutuality is in part traceable to the poor and rudimentary degree of organization observable in the world arena. The Leipzig trials after World War I had indicated the difficulties involved in entrusting to a defeated state the task of administering the laws of war by trying and sentencing members of its own armed forces.[543] In 1920, the Allied Powers presented to the German Government a list containing the names of 896 accused. Upon vigorous German protest, a sample "abridged list" with only 45 names was delivered to the German Government, the accused to be tried before the Supreme Court of Leipzig. Of these, only 12 were actually subjected to trial and 6 eventually convicted. The two defendants who received the heaviest sentences (two years) later escaped from prison under cir-

---

North Koreans, see generally, *Hearings Before the Sub-Committee on Korean War Atrocities of the Committee on Government Operations*, U. S. Senate, 83rd Cong., 1st Sess., Dec. 3, 1953, Pts 1 and 2.

541. Art. 3, Hague Convention IV of 1907. 2 Oppenheim-Lauterpacht 593–4 observed that the principle of belligerent responsibility is not confined to breaches of the Hague Regulations but is applicable to violations of any of the laws of war.

542. In 1943, the Russians set up a military tribunal at Kharkov which tried several Germans and a Russian for war crimes. It should be remembered that the Germans treated Russian prisoners of war and civilian inhabitants with such unbelievable cruelty and brutality that the Russians probably felt that reprisals could not have made their lot any worse. On the Kharkov trial, see Glueck, supra note 515 at 62, 80.

543. See generally, Mullins, *The Leipzig Trials* (1923).

cumstances indicating official cooperation.[544] It is a matter for little wonder then, that after the last world war, the Allied Powers took into their own hands the business of war crimes prosecution.[545] Conversely, the delivery of Allied nationals who might have been guilty of war crimes for trial before tribunals of the defeated belligerents would appear to have been just as impolitic. While lack of mutuality is irrelevant so far as concerns the legal competence of a victorious belligerent to subject to trial and punishment enemy war criminals, it does, however, underscore the need for ensuring fair and impartial legal procedures, unvitiated by a predictable demand for vengeance, in determining individual guilt.[546] It is still occasionally suggested that the Nuremberg and other war crimes trials after World War II set a "bad precedent" for future wars, the future victors of which might not include the United States and its allies. One difficulty with this suggestion is, of course, that it may be merely optimistic to expect that "our" officers and men will be granted anything substantially approximating the standards set in the war crimes trials after World War II in respect of both the substantive law applied and the procedural safeguards followed. The "Nuremberg precedent" would seem infinitely more desirable than treating the accused as being, in the language of Professor Stone, "at the discretion of the aggrieved state." [547]

544. Glueck, supra note 515 at 31–4.

545. It should be added, however, that beginning in 1956 prosecutions were commenced in the municipal criminal courts of the Federal Republic of Germany against former Nazi officials and functionaries for common crimes, such as murder. At least some of these crimes are in all probability characterizable as violations of the law of war. Among those brought to trial, it is reported, are concentration camp officials and guards. It is also reported that a national coordinating agency, set up by the Justice Ministries of the eleven German states, announced that twenty trials involving 300 defendants were scheduled for 1960. *N.Y. Times,* Jan. 10, 1960, p. 11-E, cols. 7–8.

546. Judge Lauterpacht in 2 Oppenheim-Lauterpacht 584 note 3 suggests that neutral judges might be allowed to participate in municipal war crimes tribunals. He made the same suggestion in 1944, supra note 532 at 82, and further indicated that enemy assessors should also be allowed to sit in Allied tribunals. The Allied Powers did not think it convenient to adopt these suggestions. Dr. Schwarzenberger, in "The Judgment of Nuremberg," 21 *Tul. L. Rev.* 335 (1947) observed that while accused war criminals have no claim to be judged by neutral nationals or to have a co-national on the bench "much is to be said in favor of such additional guarantees of judicial impartiality."

547. Stone, *Legal Controls* 357.

War Crimes Tribunals and Bases of Jurisdiction

That a belligerent has competence to impose punishment on members of enemy armed forces who have breached the laws and customs of war has long been a part of customary international law. This doctrine could hardly be regarded as novel or revolutionary even before the First World War. It found early expression in the works of many of the classical writers—Vitoria,[548] Suarez,[549] Gentilis,[550] Grotius,[551] Vattel,[552] and Wolff [553] might be mentioned. At the Brussels Conference of 1874, the French delegate proposed the drafting of a uniform code dealing with the *penalties* to be imposed for infringements of the various rules of warfare.[554] This was an attempt, unhappily an unsuccessful one, to mitigate the rigors of the customary penalty which was death. Sir Henry Maine, writing in 1888, declared that:

> There is no doubt that at present the Manuals state the practice correctly, that quarter ought never to be refused to men who surrender, unless they have been guilty of some such violation of the customs of war as would of itself expose them to the penalty of death, and when so guilty they should whenever practicable be taken prisoners and put upon their trial before they are executed . . .[555]

548. *De Indis et de Jure Belli Relectiones* (trans. Bate, Classics of International Law, 1917) s. 19, fifth prop., p. 172.

549. "De Triplici Virtute Theologica," in *Selections From Three Works of Francisco Suárez, S.J.* (trans. Williams, Brown, and Waldron, Classics of International Law, 1944) 841.

550. *De Jure Belli Libri Tres* (trans. Rolfe, Classics of International Law, 1933, Vol. II) Bk. II, c. XVIII, p. 234.

551. *De Jure Belli Ac Pacis* (trans. Kelsey, Classics of International Law, 1925) Bk. III, c. XIV. I. 1, p. 761.

552. *The Law of Nations or the Principles of Natural Law* (trans. Fenwick, Classics of International Law, 1916) Bk. III, c. VIII, s. 141, p. 280.

553. *Jus Gentium Methodo Scientifica Pertractatum* (trans. Hemelt, Classics of International Law, 1934) s. 794, pp. 411–12. Schwarzenberger, supra note 546 at 330–1 refers to fourteenth- and fifteenth-century examples of war crimes trials.

554. See 65 *British Foreign and State Papers* 1107 (1847). And see Arts. 11–12 of the *Instructions For the Government of Armies of the United States in the Field* (1863).

555. *International Law* 154–5 (1888).

Professor Holland wrote, in 1908, that:

> Individuals offending against the laws of war are liable to such punishment as is prescribed by the military code of the belligerent into whose hands they may fall, or in default of such code, then to such punishment as may be ordered, in accordance with the laws and usages of war, by a military court.[556]

Thus, the competence of belligerents and the liability of individuals in this regard are beyond cavil. The rule has been too long and too well recognized for objections in terms of retroactivity or partiality to have any substance.

In the exercise of this competence, accused individuals may be subjected to the jurisdiction of international and municipal war crimes tribunals.[557] Both types of tribunals were utilized by the Allied Powers after the last world war. The "major war criminals" whose offenses had "no particular geographic location" [558] were tried before the International Military Tribunal at Nuremberg and the International Military Tribunal for the Far East, which tribunals represented the collective undertaking to do what each of the Allied Powers had competence to do by itself.[559] Necessarily they were *ad hoc* bodies; it is less clear whether it might not have been a politic measure to have included some neutral nationals among the judges.

Although *ad hoc* courts, even where exclusively composed of nationals of the victorious belligerents, need by no means be incapable of an impartial administration of the law of war, the appropriate goal is the establishment, by widespread consensus, of a permanent international court constituted in advance of hostilities, and having jurisdiction over nationals of both victors and vanquished.[560] Recourse to such a tribunal should effectively dispel suspicions of "victor's justice." Thus, while recognizing that the continuing sys-

556. *The Laws of War on Land* 59–60 (1908). And see Spaight, *War Rights on Land* 462–3 (1911).

557. See generally Glueck, "By What Tribunal Shall War Offenders Be Tried?" 56 *Harvard L. Rev.* 1059 (1943).

558. In accord with the Moscow Declaration of Oct. 30, 1943; text in 38 *A.J.I.L. Supp.* 7–8 (1944).

559. *Nazi Conspiracy and Aggression: Opinion and Judgment* 48 (1947).

560. Cf. 2 Oppenheim-Lauterpacht 585. See Pella, "Towards an International Criminal Court," 44 *A.J.I.L.* 42–7 (1950); and Wright, "Proposal For an International Criminal Court," 46 id. 63–5 (1952), who, together with a large number of writers, have underscored the appropriateness of such a goal.

temic conflict in the present world arena makes it difficult to place a high exponent on the probability of early success, concern for institutionalized procedures for the continuous clarification of common interest demands approval of efforts to bring about the creation of a permanent international criminal court. The International Law Commission [561] and the General Assembly of the United Nations,[562] it may be noted, recorded that they believed the establishment of such a court to be both "desirable" and "possible."

It is neither necessary nor possible here to discuss in any detail the multifarious and complex technical problems that might be involved in such establishment.[563] Some shortcomings of the draft statute for an international criminal court drawn up by the United Nations Committee on International Criminal Jurisdiction [564] may, however, be noted with some profit. In what appears to be a retrogression from the practice developed by the war crimes tribunals after the last war, the draft statute provides in Article 27 that before an accused individual may be tried, jurisdiction must have been conferred upon the court by the state of which the accused is a national and by the state in which the crime is alleged to have been committed. The consent of the first state has not been thought necessary in war crimes trials. During hostilities, such consent can hardly be expected; after hostilities, that of the defeated belligerent would

561. "Report of the International Law Commission covering its second session, June 5–July 29, 1950," in 2 *Y.B. of the Int. Law Comn. 1950,* 379.

562. Res. No. 489(V), U.N. Gen. Ass., *Off. Rec.,* 5th Sess., Resolutions, 77–8 (1950).

563. The problems of international criminal jurisdiction have spawned an awesome amount of literature, not a small part of which is of uncertain value. Some illustrative citations: Quintano Ripolles, *Tratado de Derecho Penal Internacional e Internacional Penal,* 2 tomas (1957); Alfaro, "Report on the Question of International Criminal Jurisdiction," in 2 *Y.B. of the Int. Law Comn. 1950* 1; Sandstrom, "Report on the Question of International Criminal Jurisdiction," in 2 id. 18; *Historical Survey of the Question of International Criminal Jurisdiction,* A/CN.4/7/Rev. 1 (1949); Pella, *Memorandum on the Establishment of an International Criminal Court,* U.N. Doc. A/AC.48/3 (1951); Sottile, "The Problem of the Creation of a Permanent International Criminal Court," 29 *Revue de Droit International de Sciences Diplomatiques et Politiques* 267 (1951).

564. Text of the draft Statute in Report of the Committee on International Criminal Jurisdiction, U.N. Gen. Ass., *Off. Rec.,* 7th Sess., Supp. No. 11, Annex I (GA/2136) (1952). Finch, "Draft Statute for an International Criminal Court," 46 *A.J.I.L.* 89 (1952) offers general comment.

be merely fictitious.[565] Respecting the consent of the state of the *locus delicti,* war crimes tribunals, as will be noted below, in approximating the principle of universality of jurisdiction have not regarded this consent as indispensable. The same material event or sequence of events that constitute a war crime might be claimed by two or more states, invoking both the "objective" and "subjective" territorial principles, as having taken place in their respective territories. To require the assent of all those states may be effectively to prevent the court's assumption of jurisdiction. The Revised Draft Statute of 1953,[566] in still further defect, deleted the provision in the 1951 Draft that permitted the General Assembly, or an international regional organization so authorized by the General Assembly, access to the proposed court. Under the Revised Draft, only states may institute criminal proceedings. It is thought, to the contrary, that a prosecution commenced by the organized world community itself may be an especially appropriate way of dramatizing the inclusive nature of the interests the law of war seeks to protect.

Each of the Allied Powers undertook to try "minor" war criminals before municipal, i.e., unilaterally established, tribunals. The assumption appears to have been that international law projected no prescription governing the kind of tribunal before which accused persons might be tried; [567] that there was no rule, for instance, re-

565. Wright, supra note 560 at 68 criticizes this provision as permitting a government, by simple refusal to confer jurisdiction, to immunize its national charged with international crimes and "thus does away with the principle, accepted in the Nuremberg Charter, that international criminal law is superior to national legislation."

566. Report of the 1953 Committee on International Criminal Jurisdiction, U.N. Gen. Ass., *Off. Rec.,* 9th Sess., Supp. No. 12 (A/2645) (1954).

567. Koessler, "American War Crimes Trials in Europe," 39 *Geo. L.J.* 18, 52 (1950) made this assumption very explicit: "Nothing in the present international law limits the discretion of a belligerent State in its decision as to whether the war crimes trials of captured enemy nationals should take place before its ordinary civil or military courts or before tribunals established *ad hoc,* including especially military commissions, and nothing in the present international law prevents a belligerent State from exercising its own judgment as to whether or not special rules of procedure, announced *ad hoc,* should prevail in those trials." Cf. Brierly, "The Nature of War Crimes Jurisdiction" (1944) reprinted in Brierly, *The Basis of Obligation in International Law and Other Papers,* c. 22 (Lauterpacht and Waldock, eds., 1958).

As to the effect of the Geneva Prisoners of War Convention of 1949, see infra p. 728.

quiring their trial by regular military courts and only by such courts. The matter was handled by means of regulations enacted individually by each of the belligerents and collectively by the four Occupying Powers acting through the Allied Control Council. As might have been expected, the resulting practice shows a substantial range of diversity in policies and procedures. Some states created new courts, military or civil, for the specific purpose of trying alleged war criminals. For instance, British military courts were established at Wuppertal, Hanover, and Hamburg by a Royal Warrant dated June 14, 1945,[568] while military commissions were set up by American theater commanders in Europe and Asia.[569] In contrast, Poland created a special civil "Supreme National Tribunal," [570] while Yugoslav and Czechoslovak legislation provided for specially appointed "People's County Courts" and "People's Courts" respectively.[571] A Luxembourg law provided for a special War Crimes Court having a mixed civil and military composition.[572] Other states referred cases of alleged war crimes to already existing military courts. A French Ordinance of August 28, 1944 provided for war crimes trials before the Permanent Military Tribunals and Military Appeal Tribunals which had previous jurisdiction over offenses by French armed forces personnel.[573] Still other states, like Norway and Denmark, entrusted war crimes cases to their ordinary, pre-existing, civil courts.[574]

The Allied Occupying Powers in Germany established military government courts which had jurisdiction over war crimes. As far as the American zone of occupation was concerned, these military government courts constituted *ad hoc,* that is, separately for each specific case, were in practical effect indistinguishable from the military commissions previously mentioned.[575] The war crimes proceedings

568. See 1 *War Crimes Reports* 105 et seq. The text of the Royal Warrant is annexed to Taylor, *Final Report to the Secretary of the Army on the Nuremberg War Crimes Trials Under Control Council Law No. 10* 254 (1949).

569. See 1 *War Crimes Reports* 111 et seq.

570. Decree of Jan. 22, 1946, 7 *War Crimes Reports* 83, 91–2.

571. 15 *War Crimes Reports* 36. The Netherlands too established special civil courts; see 11 id. 104–5.

572. Law of Aug. 2, 1947, 15 *War Crimes Reports* 31.

573. See 3 *War Crimes Reports* 93 et seq.

574. For the Norwegian law, see 3 *War Crimes Reports* 85; Danish law, 15 id., 31.

575. The American military government courts were set up under Ordinance

held before these courts are collectively known as the "Dachau trials." Further, pursuant to Law No. 10 of the Allied Control Council,[576] providing for the punishment of persons guilty of war crimes as well as of crimes against peace and against humanity, the United States set up special military tribunals at Nuremberg whose decisions collectively comprise the so-called "Nuremberg subsequent proceedings."[577] While in the American zone there were thus two distinct sets of war crimes tribunals, the British simply renamed their military government courts as "Control Commission Courts" and enlarged their jurisdiction to include crimes against peace and against humanity.[578] The French zone commander did the same thing without bothering to alter labels.[579]

With respect to the law applied by these courts, "the great cleavage," it is said, was between the charging of alleged war criminals with breaches of the international law of war, which was the Anglo-American practice, and their prosecution under municipal law for crimes defined in domestic penal codes and statutes, as was done in France and other continental European countries.[580] From one perspective this neat dichotomy is largely academic. So long as the kinds of physical acts for which the defendant is condemned are illegitimate under prescriptions of the law of war, the question whether it is "international law" or "municipal law" (or whether it is international law directly or international rules "transformed," in some recondite fashion, into municipal norms)[581] that is formally invoked

No. 2 issued by the Supreme Commander of the Allied Expeditionary Force; see 1 *War Crimes Reports* 122–4. And see Koessler, supra note 567 at 45–6.

576. Text appended to Taylor, supra note 568 at 250.

577. Ordinance No. 7, Military Government—Germany, U.S. Zone, Oct. 18, 1946; text in Taylor, supra note 568 at 286. See generally, Taylor, "The Nuremberg War Crimes Trials," *Int. Conciliation* No. 450, p. 243 (1949).

578. Ordinance No. 68, 15 *War Crimes Reports* 41.

579. Ordinance No. 36, id. 41–2.

580. Baxter, "The Municipal and International Law Basis of Jurisdiction Over War Crimes," 28 *Brit. Y.B.I.L.* 382 (1951).

581. For illustration of the most rigidly doctrinaire position on this matter, see Manner, "The Legal Nature and Punishment of Criminal Acts of Violence Contrary to the Laws of War," 37 *A.J.I.L.* 407 (1943). Manner, reasoning from his premise that individuals are not subjects of international law, insists that war crimes are not crimes against international law, but against the municipal laws of belligerent states. Cf. Stone, *Legal Controls* 357 who asserts that "international law did not itself make such violations by enemy individuals criminal.

and applied by the decision-maker would seem to be of limited substantive import. What may be emphasized is that acts committed in war by enemy civilians and members of armed forces may be punished as crimes under a belligerent's municipal law only to the extent that such acts are violative of the international law on the conduct of hostilities.[582] Clearly the rules of warfare would be pointless, with dissolution of both policies and sanctions, if every single act of war may by unilateral municipal fiat be made a common crime and every prisoner of war executed as a murderer. International law delineates the outer limits of the liability of supposed war criminals; and conformity with that law affords a complete defense for the violent acts charged.[583] This limitation of liability was explicitly recognized in the war crimes legislation of continental European countries. The French Ordinance of August 28, 1944, for instance, declared that those accused of war crimes

> shall be tried [by French Military Tribunals] *in accordance with the French laws in force,* and according to the provisions set out in the present Ordinance, *where such offenses,* even if committed at the time or under the pretext of an existing state of war, *are not justified by the laws and customs of war.*[584]

Substantially similar provisions were set forth in the Norwegian,[585] Danish,[586] Belgian,[587] Dutch,[588] Luxembourgian,[589] and Greek[590] laws on the subject.

Questions relating to the technical basis of jurisdiction of municipal tribunals over war crimes are perhaps best approached first from a descriptive standpoint. There are, it may be recalled, five general

---

What it did was to grant a liberty to a belligerent wronged by enemy illegalities to deal with the offending enemy individuals who came into its power."

582. Lauterpacht, "The Law of Nations and the Punishment of War Crimes," 21 *Brit. Y.B.I.L.* 58, 64, 66–7 (1944).

583. Cf. Garner, "Punishment of Offenders Against the Laws and Customs of War," 14 *A.J.I.L.* 73 (1920).

584. 3 *War Crimes Reports* 93; emphasis supplied.

585. 3 id. 83.

586. 15 id. 32.

587. 15 id. 203.

588. 11 id. 92.

589. 15 id. 33.

590. 15 id. 36.

principles on which states have based more or less expansive claims to penal jurisdiction: territoriality, nationality, protection of interests, passive personality, and universality.[591] These principles were invoked in varying combinations in the war crimes legislation enacted by the Allied Powers after the last war. The territoriality and passive personality principles, for instance, were invoked in the French Ordinance of August 28, 1944 which conferred jurisdiction on French military tribunals over war crimes committed,

> either in France or in territories under the authority of France, or against a French national, or a person under French protection, or a person serving or having served in the French armed forces, or a stateless person resident in French territory before 17th June 1940, or a refugee residing in French territory.[592]

The limits of the scope of jurisdiction thus granted are illustrated by the trial of *Robert Wagner*.[593] There a sentence of death imposed by a military tribunal on one Gruner was reversed by the Court of Cassation holding that because the criminal acts had been committed against an English soldier in Germany, the French military tribunal had no jurisdiction. The jurisdictional grant, on the other hand, contained in the Norwegian Law of December 12, 1946 was much wider, being based not only on the territoriality and passive personality principles but also on the more general "protective" theory. Under this Law, the Norwegian courts had jurisdiction so long as the acts charged "were committed in Norway or were directed against Norwegian citizens or Norwegian interests." Moreover, "Allied legal interests" and interests which, by royal proclamation, might be declared equivalent thereto were assimilated to Norwegian interests.[594] The same three principles were invoked in the Netherlands Extraordinary Penal Law Decree of December 22, 1943.[595] The Danish Law of July 12, 1946 on the Punishment of War Criminals

591. See Harvard Research in International Law, "Jurisdiction With Respect to Crime," 29 *A.J.I.L. Supp.* 455 (1935), and Arts. 3, 5, 7, 9, 10 of the Draft Convention.

592. 3 *War Crimes Reports* 93 (1946).

593. 3 id. 47–9.

594. 3 id. 83. See also the Chinese Law of Oct. 24, 1946, 14 id. 156–7.

595. 11 id. 97.

specified only the principles of territoriality and protection of interests and made punishable acts performed "in Denmark or to the detriment of Danish interests." [596] The Danish Law, however, probably achieved the same results as the Norwegian and Dutch statutes since presumably acts committed against Danes could be regarded as detrimental to Danish interests.

Substantial as was the jurisdiction thus conferred on continental European war crimes courts, the jurisdiction assumed and exercised by United States, British, and Commonwealth military tribunals, which were not burdened with a need to refer to municipal penal statutes, was even wider. The *locus* of the alleged offense was consistently disregarded.[597] So also was the nationality of the victims, so long, at least, as they were Allied nationals.[598] The qualification would seem unimportant so far as effectiveness of the law of war is concerned: The laws of warfare do not purport to govern the relations of an enemy belligerent with its own nationals; the murder and ill-treatment of a belligerent's own people are more appropriately categorized as crimes against humanity than war crimes. The nationality of the victim was disregarded in, for instance, the trial of *Sandrock,*[599] where a British military court convicted the

596. 15 id. 32.

597. See e.g., "Trial of Hisakasu," 5 *War Crimes Reports* 66 (1946); "Trial of Sawada," 5 id. 9 (1946); "Trial of Wipperman," 15 id. 47 (1947), and the cases cited in the text. In "The Trial of Umstatter," 15 id. 47 (1946), the place of the commission of the offense was not even specified by the prosecution; the American military government court convicted Umstatter anyway. See also *In re* Rohrig, Brunner, and Heinze, Special Criminal Court, Amsterdam, *Int. Law Rep. 1950,* Case No. 125.

598. In 1945, it was suggested at the U.N. War Crimes Commission that offenses against nationals of "technically enemy" countries like Hungary, Rumania, Bulgaria and Italy, and against stateless persons, should be regarded as war crimes. The Commission's Committee on Facts and Evidence in fact listed such offenses as war crimes. After the war, the mentioned ex-enemy countries set up their own tribunals to try war criminals and traitors. See *History of the United Nations War Crimes Commission and the Development of the Laws of War* 173, 474–5 (1948). Dept. of the Army, *Law of Land Warfare,* par. 507(a) (FM 27–10, July 1956) provides that "The jurisdiction of United States military tribunals in connection with war crimes is not limited to offenses committed against nationals of the United States but extends also to all offenses of this nature committed against nationals of allies and of cobelligerents and stateless persons."

599. 1 *War Crimes Reports* 35 (1945).

accused for killing a British prisoner of war and a Dutch civilian in Holland. In the Hadamar trial[600] a United States military commission assumed jurisdiction over a case involving the killing of over 400 Polish and Soviet nationals in a sanatorium in Germany. No American nationals were among the victims. Again, in the trial of Hashimoto,[601] an American military commission at Yokohama declared the defendant guilty of maltreating certain prisoners of war all of whom were Canadians. A British military court, in the trial of Schoengrath,[602] sentenced five of the accused to death for the killing in Holland of an *unknown* airman who had descended by parachute from a disabled bomber plane. The court assumed that the victim was an Allied airman. The prosecution had observed that to suppose the bomber to have been a neutral craft proceeding on a mission from Germany over Holland was too farfetched.

It may be observed that while the *situs* of the acts and the nationality of the victims were not regarded as restrictive of jurisdiction, in a few instances and "as a matter of international courtesy," the states assuming jurisdiction went through the process of obtaining the consent of the state which, under the territorial and passive personality theories, would have had concurrent jurisdiction.[603] For example, a United States military commission proceeded with the *Buchenwald Concentration Camp* case[604] only after the Russians, in whose zone of occupation the camp had stood, had declined to try it themselves and had declared their acquiescence to the commission's assumption of jurisdiction. Similarly, before the *Malmedy* case,[605] which involved the massacre of American prisoners of war

600. "Trial of Klein," 1 id. 46 (1945). A concise general account of this case may be had in Koessler, "Euthanasia in the Hadamar Sanatorium and International Law," 43 *J. Crim. Law. Criminology and Police Science* 735 (1953).

601. 15 *War Crimes Reports* 43.

602. 11 id. 83 (1946).

603. Koessler, supra note 567 at 40.

604. See *Conduct of Ilse Koch War Crimes Trial, Hearings before the Investigations Subcommittee of the Committee on Expenditures in the Executive Departments,* U. S. Senate, 80th Cong., 2d Sess. (1948) at 1197 et seq. See, generally, Koessler, "The Ilse Koch Senate Investigation and Its Legal Problems with Observations on Double Jeopardy and Res Judicata," 23 *Mo. L. Rev.* 1 (1958).

605. See *Malmedy Massacre Investigation, Hearings before the Subcommittee of the Committee on Armed Services,* U. S. Senate, 81st Cong., 1st Sess. at 1199 (1949).

and Belgian citizens in Belgium, was tried, the assent of the Belgian Government was secured by the American occupation authorities. These cases, however, did not appear to represent the regular practice of the other Allied Powers and even of the United States.

The time of the commission of the offense was also frequently disregarded by the American military government courts. They took jurisdiction over cases where the relevant acts had been committed prior to the formal entry of the United States into the war against Germany, upon the theory that the existence of a technical "state of war" at the time of the performance of the acts was not a jurisdictional requisite.[606] The same theory is discernible in the Chinese War Crimes Law of October 24, 1946 which provided for punishment of war crimes committed "during the war or a period of hostilities" against China.[607] This served to embrace the period, formally determined as commencing from the Japanese invasion of Manchuria in 1931, during which both China and Japan refused to recognize the existence of a "state of war" despite the *de facto* hostilities they waged.

The nationality of the accused in the war crimes trials was generally that of the enemy belligerent. It was not, however, always so. In many cases, the war crimes tribunals convicted nationals of neutral and even Allied Powers where such persons had in some way identified themselves with the enemy. In the trial of *Kramer,*[608] a British military court found five Polish citizens guilty of war crimes against Allied nationals. The Poles had accepted positions of responsibility in the administration of the Belsen concentration camp under the S.S. (*Schutzstaffeln der Nationalsozialistischen Deutschen Arbeiterpartei*) and had participated in the torture and ill-treatment of the inmates. The court adopted the prosecution's argument that they had thereby identified themselves with, and were as guilty as, the S.S. An example of a case involving neutral nationals is the trial and conviction of Espinosa, a Spaniard who as an inmate in the Gusen concentration camp had taken part in the maltreatment of

606. "Trial of Remmele," 15 *War Crimes Reports* 44 (1947).

607. 14 id. 155–6.

608. 2 id. 1 (1945). A French military tribunal condemned to death one Fromes, a Luxembourg national, who had joined the Gestapo; 15 id. 45. Similarly, in the Flossenberg trial, a Dutchman and a Yugoslav were among those convicted by an American military government court; id., 47.

the other prisoners.[609] It may be noted that while Allied and neutral citizens were sentenced by various tribunals, the legislation of several countries expressly excluded from the jurisdiction of their war crimes courts cases involving their own citizens. Thus, the aforementioned French Ordinance specified "enemy nationals or agents of other than French nationality who are serving enemy administration or interests." [610] From this limitation of jurisdiction, no necessary inference arises either that the Allied Powers did not, or that belligerents commonly do not, enforce the law of war against their own nationals. Acts of members of a belligerent's own armies which amount to war crimes against enemy forces or civilians are commonly punishable under the military law—that is, the law for the governance of the armed forces—of the belligerent and cognizable by courts-martial established under such law.[611]

The foregoing survey of decisions of war crimes tribunals after World War II suggests a tendency toward assertion and recognition of a very extensive jurisdiction, commonly described as universality of jurisdiction, over war crimes.[612] The import of "universality" may

609. 15 id. 46. In the Ravensbruck trial, a Swiss national was found guilty by a British military court; id.

610. 3 *War Crimes Reports* 93. Practically identical provisions were included, *inter alia,* in the Norwegian (3 id. 83), Danish (15 id. 32), Luxembourg (15 id. 33) and Chinese laws (14 id. 155).

611. This is made clear in Dept. of the Army, *Law of Land Warfare* par. 507(b) (FM 27–10, July 1956): "b. *Persons Charged With War Crimes.* The United States normally punishes war crimes as such only if they are committed by enemy nationals or by persons serving the interests of the enemy State. Violations of the law of war committed by persons subject to the military law of the United States will usually constitute violations of the Uniform Code of Military Justice and, if so, will be prosecuted under that Code. Violations of the law of war committed within the United States by other persons will usually constitute violations of federal or state criminal law and preferably will be prosecuted under such law (see pars. 505 and 506). Commanding officers of United States troops must insure that war crimes committed by members of their forces against enemy personnel are promptly and adequately punished." See also *British Manual of Military Law,* Pt. III, par. 637 note 3 (1958).

612. This tendency also finds expression in the 1949 Geneva Conventions for the protection of war victims. In a common article, the Conventions require all the Contracting Parties to enact municipal legislation providing "effective penal sanctions" against persons committing "grave breaches" of the Conventions. Each Party to the Conventions is further obligated "to search for persons alleged to have committed, or to have ordered to be committed, such

be succinctly summed up as the assertion, with promise of reciprocal tolerance, of jurisdiction by a state having possession of the accused to try and punish without regard to the geographic and time location of the physical events alleged to constitute a crime, and to the national identity of the accused or of the victim.

The assertion of Israeli jurisdiction in the recent Eichmann case would appear based upon this tendency toward the honoring of universality of jurisdiction in war crimes cases. Adolf Eichmann, who was alleged to have had charge of the "final solution" of the "Jewish problem" in Nazi Germany and German-occupied Europe during the last world war, was removed from Argentina by Israeli nationals, brought into Israel, and delivered to the Israeli Government.[613] The Israeli Government announced its intention to bring Eichmann to trial before an Israeli court under an Israeli statute for the murder of about 6,000,000 Jews during World War II. The removal of Eichmann from its territory was protested by Argentina, and was in substance held by the United Nations Security Council to have been in violation of Argentine sovereignty.[614] What is relevant for present purposes, however, is the assumption of jurisdiction to try and punish a nonnational for acts amounting to war crimes (whatever else they may amount to) committed at a time when the state asserting jurisdiction had not yet come into existence, in the territories of many different states, and against persons of many differing nationalities. Although an international tribunal may well be preferred as

---

grave breaches," and to "bring such persons, *regardless of their nationality,* before its own courts," unless it decides to extradite such persons. Art. 49, Wounded and Sick Convention; Art. 50, Wounded, Sick and Shipwrecked Convention; Art. 129, Prisoners of War Convention; Art. 146, Civilians Convention; italics supplied.

The implementing legislation enacted in the United Kingdom, The Geneva Conventions Act, 1957, provides in Art. 1(1) that "Any person, *whatever his nationality,* who, *whether in or outside the United Kingdom,* commits or aids, abets or procures the commission by any other person of any such grave breach . . . shall be guilty of felony . . ." Italics supplied; text in Draper, *The Red Cross Conventions* 119–24 (1958). Col. Draper, at 105–6 appropriately stresses that "*compulsory* universal penal jurisdiction," in respect of much of the law of war, has been established by the Conventions.

613. *N. Y. Times,* May 25, 1960, p. 1, cols. 5–6.

614. See the explanatory note that accompanied the Argentine complaint to the Security Council; *N. Y. Times,* June 16, 1960, p. 4, cols. 4–6. The Security Council resolution of June 23, 1960 is reported in id., June 24, 1960, p. 1, col. 1.

a forum over a municipal court, the competence of Israel to take jurisdiction over such acts does not seem vulnerable to serious question.[615]

This tendency toward universality of jurisdiction in respect of war crimes appropriately reflects the inclusive nature of the interests the law of war seeks to protect.[616] The Eichmann case affords unusually sharp illustration of the impact of war crimes upon a multitude of countries. Further, the interests sought to be secured by effective sanctions for the law of war are not exclusively the interests of the contending belligerents. In a world, like the contemporary one, caught in a vast network of interdependences for power and other values, the stakes of those who in a particular conflict may remain neutral are not limited to their interests as possible future belligerents. There appears, in particular, no cogent reason why, in the absence of any appropriate claim by a belligerent under extradition treaties, a neutral state into whose territory an alleged war criminal may have fled may not itself try and punish him; [617] a neutral state

615. See Robinson, "Eichmann and the Question of Jurisdiction," *Commentary* 1 (July 1960). In a letter to the *New York Times,* July 4, 1960, Mr. F. E. Oppenheimer, arguing that "the competence of Israeli courts [to try Eichmann] is not well established in international law," makes the singular statement that "the universality . . . principle [is] accepted merely as the basis of a subsidiary competence." Some observers are reported to have raised questions about the effect of the unusual manner in which Israeli custody over Eichmann was acquired upon the jurisdiction of Israeli courts to try him. *N. Y. Times,* May 26, 1960, p. 1, col. 8. The debates at the U.N. appear to include no reference to Israeli jurisdiction. Excerpts of the debates are found in id. June 23, 1960, p. 4, and id. June 24, 1960, p. 4. Some relevant issues relating to the jurisdictional implications of the manner in which custody is acquired are discussed in Garcia-Mora, "Criminal Jurisdiction of a State over Fugitives Brought from a Foreign Country by Force or Fraud: A Comparative Study," 32 *Ind. L.J.* 427 (1957); Morgenstern, "Jurisdiction in Seizures Effected in Violation of International Law," 29 *Brit. Y.B.I.L.* 265 (1952). See, in particular, Silving, "In Re Eichmann: A Dilemma of Law and Morality," 55 *A.J.I.L.* 307 (1961).

616. Cf. Cowles, "Universality of Jurisdiction Over War Crimes," 33 *Calif. L. Rev.* 217–18 (1945). See also "The Hostages Case," 8 *War Crimes Reports* at 54–5 (1948).

617. *The British Manual of Military Law,* Pt. III, par. 637 (1958) has explicitly taken the view that "the courts, whether military or civil, of neutral States may also exercise jurisdiction in respect of war crimes. This jurisdiction is independent of any agreement made between neutral and belligerent States. War crimes are crimes *ex jure gentium* and are thus triable by the courts of all States."

is indeed obliged to do so in cases of "grave breaches" of the 1949 Geneva Conventions.[618] Finally, the reduction of irrational and wanton destruction of human values forms part of the demands of the great majority of the peoples of the world, which demands have been given ample formal expression in the numerous international agreements and declarations concerning the treatment of war criminals made after World War I and during and after World War II.[619] It is no mere accident that the International Law Commission designated war crimes as one species of offenses "against the peace and security of mankind." [620]

If there is any policy limit to universality of jurisdiction, it is perhaps to be found in the necessity of ensuring a fair trial for the accused. Ordinarily, evidence may be expected to be most readily available at the place of the commission of the offense, and for that reason it might be desirable for another state having the body of the accused to refrain from taking jurisdiction and instead to bring the accused before a tribunal of the state of the *locus delicti*. On the other hand, while there may be added "poetic justice" in thus bringing the accused to the *situs* of the crime,[621] this recourse may make it more than ordinarily difficult to afford him a fair trial. Popular excitement may generate strong pressures upon the decision-maker for conviction regardless of personal guilt and for a merely pro forma trial. This possibility need not be academic. When, for instance, General Rendulic was acquitted by a United States military tribunal in Germany of the charge of devastating, without military necessity therefor, a Norwegian province, vehement popular indignation exploded in Norway.[622] Had Rendulic been brought to Norway and

618. See supra note 612.

619. Those agreements and declarations are collected in *History of the United Nations War Crimes Commission and the Development of the Laws of War* c. III, IV, V, and XII (1948), passim.

620. See Art. 2(11) of the "Draft Code of Offenses Against the Peace and Security of Mankind," in *Report of the International Law Commission (covering its third session, May 16–July 27, 1951)*, U.N. Gen. Ass., *Off. Rec.*, 6th Sess., Supp. No. 9, (A/1858) Pt. IV (1951). And see Pella, *Memorandum Concerning a Draft Code of Offenses Against the Peace and Security of Mankind* A/CN./4/39 (24 Nov. 1949), p. 50.

621. In the Moscow Declaration of Nov. 1, 1943, it was announced, rather melodramatically, that war criminals "will be brought back to the scene of their crimes and judged on the spot by the peoples they have outraged." Text in *History*, supra note 619 at 107.

622. See Taylor, supra note 577 at 325.

tried by a Norwegian tribunal, it need not be entirely fanciful to suppose that he might have been convicted, particularly since the standards of military necessity are necessarily fluid and general. The practical difficulties, it may be added, of securing evidence may be partly met by the creation of some international body authorized to investigate, and collate and assemble evidence on charges of alleged war crimes in various countries.[623]

Procedural Safeguards in War Crimes Prosecutions

Of supreme importance for the realization of community policy through war crimes prosecutions is the necessity of according to the accused a fair and impartial determination of their guilt. Without this requirement, the prosecutions may be indistinguishable from vengeance which, while it may occasionally discharge a useful cathartic function, would defeat community policy. Customary international law, however, lays down no detailed code of criminal procedure. Its principal thrust is that those charged with war crimes be given a fair trial in accordance with the "broad principles of justice and fair play which underlie all civilized concepts of law and procedure." [624] This standard of international due process is manifestly broad and imprecise. To attempt operational specification in full detail would necessitate prolonged inquiry into the procedural steps formally prescribed and actually followed by decision-makers, international and municipal, from the time of physical apprehension of a supposed criminal up to the execution of a final judgment. To isolate the common minimum elements of a fair trial, as that term is understood in the bulk of the countries of the world is, comprehensively conceived, a task of comparative constitutional law and criminal law administration.[625] All that is intended here, however, is to depict in brief the practice of the Allied war crimes tribunals in respect of this international standard and to indicate the more salient uniformities discernible.

An intelligent defense can scarcely be put up by an accused person unless he is informed, in one way or another, of the substance of the

623. Like the United Nations War Crimes Commission, established in 1943. See its *History*, supra note 619 at 2–3.

624. "The Justice Trial," 6 *War Crimes Reports* at 49 (1947). See Wright, "Due Process and International Law," 40 *A.J.I.L.* 402–3 (1946).

625. A useful beginning along this line is made in Tsai, "Judicial Administration of the Law of War: Procedure in War Crimes Trials" (Unpublished dissertation in the Yale Law Library, 1957).

charge made against him. The usual formal method of communicating this information is furnishing the accused a copy of a written indictment. The Charter of the Nuremberg Tribunal required that the indictment contain "full particulars specifying in detail the charges against the defendants," while the Tokyo Charter spoke of "a plain, concise and adequate statement of each offense charged." [626] In some of the trials, objections were raised to the indictments as being too vague and general, which objections were frequently overruled.[627] Clearly the precise form of indictment is of little moment, especially since bills of particular can always be requested, so long as the accused is actually enlightened as to the acts for which he is being held to answer.

Much more important is the matter of aid of counsel. That an accused was entitled to be represented by counsel of his own choice, or if he failed to designate one, by counsel appointed by the tribunal, was uniformly recognized in the Nuremberg and Tokyo Charters [628] and in the war crimes statutes and ordinances of, *inter alia,* the United States, Britain, France, Norway, Poland, the Netherlands, Canada, and Australia.[629] It should be mentioned that in the Nuremberg and in the "subsequent Nuremberg proceedings," the fact that the German lawyers chosen by the accused had themselves been mem-

626. Art. 16(a), Nuremberg Charter; Art. 9(a) Tokyo Charter. For equivalent provisions, see Art. 6 of the Rules of Procedure in American Military Government Courts (appended to the *Malmedy Massacre Investigations Hearings,* supra note 605 at 1205 et seq.); Art 4 of the Regulations on American Military Commissions (Annex I in Koessler, supra note 567 at 106 et seq.) and Art. IV(a) of Ordinance No. 7 on U. S. Military Tribunals (Appendix L in Taylor, supra note 568 at 286). Hereinafter cited as *Rules of Procedure AMG, Regulations AMC,* and *Ordinance No.* 7 respectively.

627. See cases cited in Appleman, *Military Tribunals and International Crimes* 320–1 (1954). The U. S. Supreme Court in *In re* Yamashita, 327 U.S. at 17 (1946), said that "charges of violations of the law of war triable before a military tribunal need not be stated with the precision of a common law indictment."

628. Art. 16(d) Nuremberg Charter; Art. 9(c) Tokyo Charter.

629. U.S.—Art. IV(c) of *Ordinance No. 7;* Art. 3(2) *Rules of Procedure AMG;* Britain—Regulation 7 of the Royal Warrant, 2 *War Crimes Reports* 128–9; France—Art. 179 of the *Code de Justice Militaire* 3 id. 98; Norway—3 id. 87–8; Poland—Art. 12(1) Decree of 1946, 7 id. 94; Netherlands—11 id. 104; Canada—Regulation 9, Act of Aug. 31, 1946, 4 id. 129; Australia—Regulation 10, War Crimes Act, 1945, 5 id. 100.

bers of the National Socialist Party and of organizations like the S.A. (*Sturmabteilungen der Nationalsozialistischen Deutschen Arbeiterpartei*) and the S.S. was not considered as disqualifying them as counsel before the tribunals. The assumption was that these counsel would be best acquainted with the structures of authority and command, and the political and social conditions, in the Third Reich, and could be expected to take especially to heart the interests of their clients.[630] The same attitude appeared to have been adopted by the Tokyo tribunal.[631] Allied counsel were commonly assigned to assist the German and Japanese lawyers. This practice was particularly desirable since the procedure utilized by the international military tribunals represented an eclectic amalgam of the Anglo-American and the Civil Law systems.[632] In general, it may be said that a right to assistance of counsel was regarded as of vital importance and was scrupulously respected.[633] This attitude seemed especially appropriate since the tribunals, in condemning as a war crime

630. Taylor, supra note 568 at 30, 46–8. Four defendants in the "subsequent Nuremberg proceedings" asked for non-German counsel. The requests of three of them were granted; two American and one Swiss lawyer were approved by the tribunals. As to the fourth, that by Alfred Krupp, see Taylor, "The Krupp Trial: Fact v. Fiction," 53 *Col. L. Rev.* 196 (1953).

631. See Keenan and Brown, *Crimes Against International Law* 146–7 (1950).

632. See Goodhart, "The Legality of the Nuremberg Trials," 58 *Jurid. Rev.* 4–5 (1946). Keenan and Brown, supra note 631 at 144–5; Carr, "The Judgment of the International Military Tribunal For the Far East," 34 *Tr. Grotius Soc.* 151 (1948). The same thing may be said of the "Dachau Trials" and the "subsequent Nuremberg proceedings"; see Taylor, supra note 568 at 86–90; Koessler, supra note 567 at 62 et seq.

Appleman, supra note 627 at 318–20 suggests that the greatest legitimate criticism that can be leveled against the American trials was that the same counsel were appointed to represent defendants or groups of defendants with conflicting interests arising from the inclination to shift responsibility to another or others. The point is a minor one and the difficulty easily removed by appointing more counsel or granting separate trials.

633. The extent to which deference was paid to this right in the American trials is suggested by the privileges granted to the defense counsel. They were paid substantial salaries by the Military Government, and housed and fed too, at nominal cost to themselves. They were further furnished office accommodations, as well as transportation facilities. It might be mentioned also that witnesses requested by the defense were procured, housed, fed, and compensated by the military authorities. See Ferencz, "Nuremberg Trial Procedure and the Rights of the Accused," 39 *J. of Crim. L. and Criminology* 147 (1948).

in itself the killing of Allied nationals without a fair trial, took the denial of aid of counsel as one of the indices of denial of a fair trial.[634]

Since the actors in a war crimes prosecution are frequently of diverse nationalities and tongues, there arises a problem of rendering the proceedings and the evidence intelligible to the defendant and his counsel. Obviously, language barriers may make impossible the presentation of any defense. The Nuremberg and Tokyo Charters required the examination and trial of any defendant to be conducted in or translated into a language understood by him.[635] Simultaneous translation systems were employed throughout the proceedings before the international tribunals. Ample provision was made in these trials, as well as in others, for the translation of all evidence, testimonial and documentary.

A right to be present at the trial if he so desired and to submit evidence on his behalf was guaranteed to the accused by the Charters of the Nuremberg and Tokyo tribunals and by the regulations governing procedure of, for example, the United States, British, Polish, French, and Dutch war crimes courts.[636] Recognition of this right, however, did not preclude some tribunals from trying and sentencing an accused *in absentia.* The Nuremberg Charter in Article 12 authorized the Tribunal to proceed against a person charged in his absence, "if he has not been found or if the Tribunal, for any reason, finds it necessary, in the interests of justice, to conduct the hearing in his absence." One of the defendants, Martin Bormann, had never been found and was absent throughout the proceedings. Nonetheless, the Tribunal found him guilty and sentenced him to death. The Tribunal acknowledged that Bormann's counsel, unable to refute the prosecution's evidence, had "labored under difficulties," but believed that the accused's physical presence would not have made

634. See e.g., "Trial of Sawada," 5 *War Crimes Reports* 1 at 12 (1946); "Trial of Hisakasu," 5 id. 66 at 74 (1946); "Trial of Shinohara," 5 id. 34–5 (1946) and "The Justice Trial," 6 id. 1 at 103 (1947).

635. Art. 16(c) Nuremberg Charter; Art. 9(b) Tokyo Charter. For similar provisions, see e.g., Art. 9, *Regulations, AMC;* Art. IV(b), *Ordinance No. 7.* See also "The Belsen Trial," 2 *War Crimes Reports* at 145 (1945), and "Trial of Killinger," 3 id. at 74–5 (1945).

636. Art. 16(e) Nuremberg Charter; Art. 9(d) Tokyo Charter. United States—Art. IV(d), *Ordinance No. 7;* Britain—Rule of Procedure 40A, 15 *War Crimes Reports* 191; Poland —7 id. 95; France—3 id. 98–9; Netherlands—11 id. 105.

any difference.[637] In the trial of *Wagner,*[638] a French Permanent Military Tribunal tried Richard Huber, President of the Special Court at Strasbourg established by German occupation forces, in his absence and condemned him to death. The decision of the tribunal was in accord with the *Code de Justice Militaire.* There seems room for doubt, however, as to whether the conviction of a person who has never been apprehended in the first place represents a sound policy. Prejudice may or may not result in such case and the course of moderation would seem to be to receive evidence but to refrain from passing sentence. Additionally, it should be noted that the war crimes trials were public trials. Those before the international military tribunals were of course at all times under the strong light of public scrutiny.

The character of the war crimes procedure developed after the last war is perhaps best indicated by a consideration of the rules of evidence employed by the tribunals. The Charter of the Nuremberg Tribunal declared:

> The Tribunal shall not be bound by technical rules of evidence. It shall adopt and apply to the greatest possible extent expeditious and nontechnical procedure, and shall admit any evidence which it deems to have probative value.[639]

The above provision set a general standard. Broadly speaking, it may be said that the rules of evidence followed by a great many of the tribunals were free and flexible, the theory apparently being to increase to a maximum the range of admissible evidence and to leave to the reasonable discretion of the decision-maker the determination of the relevancy of, and the allocation of probative force to, the various items offered and admitted.[640] The technical rules eschewed by the Charter consisted primarily of the exclusionary rules found in the Anglo-American law of evidence, rules which had evolved in a peculiar historical institutional context. Those rules are not part,

637. *Nazi Conspiracy and Aggression: Opinion and Judgment* 166 (1947).

638. 3 *War Crimes Reports* at 42 (1946).

639. Art. 19. Art. 13(a), Tokyo Charter, is couched in identical terms, with the added clause that "all purported admissions or statements of the accused are admissible."

640. See the cases cited in 15 *War Crimes Reports* 197–9. See also Keenan and Brown, supra note 631 at 148–53; Appleman, supra note 627 at 322 et seq.; Koessler, supra note 567 at 69 et seq.; Ferencz, supra note 633 at 148–9.

it appears, of continental civil law, and it would seem a reckless assumption that fair trial is a monopoly of the Anglo-American judicial system.

Perhaps the most conspicuous of the technical rules rejected was that on hearsay evidence. A substantial portion of the evidence submitted by both the prosecution and the defense in many of the trials consisted of affidavits, depositions, interrogations, and other written statements and documents. Where affidavits were offered instead of direct oral testimony, the precedent set at Nuremberg was that the defense counsel was entitled to secure and present cross-interrogatories or to require the production of the affiant for personal cross-examination where feasible.[641] In many cases, however, such recourse was not feasible for the defense. For instance, in the *Belsen* trial,[642] affidavits had been taken from a number of the ex-inmates of the Belsen concentration camp. By the time the trial took place, the liberated prisoners had disappeared; presumably they had gone back to their own countries or become part of the vast floating pool of "displaced persons." Similarly, many of the necessary witnesses were members of the Allied forces who had gone home overseas and had been demobilized. The movements of witnesses thus necessitated the use of affidavit evidence.

Certain other deviations from the Anglo-American rules on evidence by the American military commissions in occupied Germany may be noted. These commissions admitted confessions and admissions obtained from defendants during pre-trial interrogations without requiring a showing that they were completely voluntary in character.[643] Some of the confessions were secured, it appeared, through such debatable tactics and ruses as mock trials where the accused were led to believe that they were actually being tried and condemned. In several instances, the interrogators appeared to have used intimidation and violence.[644] Although conceivably confessions obtained by deceit or duress may be truthful, this occasional practice seemed most unfortunate, and certainly not easy to reconcile with

641. Ferencz, supra note 633 at 150; Appleman, supra note 627 at 323.

642. 2 *War Crimes Reports* at 131–2 (1945).

643. Koessler, supra note 567 at 72.

644. See the *Report of the Administration of Justice Review Board in the Malmedy Case, Malmedy Massacre Investigation Hearings,* supra note 605 at 1197 et seq.

common notions of a fair trial. Another rule sometimes dispensed with was the rule on *corpus delicti* requiring some corroboration before a confession may be taken as a basis for conviction. In some cases, it is reported, military commissions convicted the accused although their confessions were not corroborated by any other evidence.[645]

The liberality of the rules on evidence generally followed by the war crimes tribunals imparted added importance to the provisions for appeal and confirmation of sentences. The Nuremberg Charter, while declaring the judgment of the Tribunal as "final and not subject to revision," empowered the Allied Control Council to reduce or otherwise alter the sentences but not to heighten their severity.[646] Some of the defendants did appeal to the Council, which, however, did not see fit to exercise the authority granted by the Charter. The Charter of the Tokyo Tribunal likewise provided that sentence would be carried out "in accordance with the order of the Supreme Commander for the Allied Powers," who was at the same time authorized to modify, but not to increase, the sentences.[647] After the rendition of the judgment, the defendants were given ten days to appeal to the Supreme Commander. General MacArthur, after consultation with the representatives of the members of the Far Eastern Commission, confirmed all the sentences.[648] Several of the defendants then filed motions with the Supreme Court of the United States for leave to petition for a writ of *habeas corpus*. The Supreme Court rejected the motions, declaring that the International Military Tribunal for the Far East was not a tribunal of the United States, having been constituted by the Commander as agent of the Allied Powers.[649]

Convictions handed down by the United States military commissions and tribunals and military government courts were subject to an automatic *administrative* review.[650] Confirmation by the mili-

645. Koessler, supra note 567 at 74.

646. Arts. 26, 29.

647. Art. 17.

648. Horwitz, "The Tokyo Trial," *Int. Conciliation* No. 465, p. 573 (1950).

649. *Hirota v. MacArthur,* 338 U.S. 197 (1948).

650. In *Flick v. Johnson,* 174 F.2d 983 (D.C. Cir. 1949) cert. denied 338 U.S. 879 (1949), it was held that the decisions of the U.S. military tribunals at Nuremberg were not subject to review by the U.S. courts on the ground that those tribunals, established pursuant to Control Council Law No. 10, were "interna-

tary commander appointing the commission or court, and by the theater commander in cases of capital sentences, was required before sentences could be carried out. The confirming and reviewing authorities acted on the basis of recommendations formulated by the staff Judge Advocate after the latter had scrutinized the factual findings of the tribunal and their legal sufficiency. The reviewing authority was empowered to modify the sentence as well as to remit or suspend any part thereof.[651] Acquittals, it is worth noting, became final immediately and were not subject to review. In contrast, French law contemplated review by regular *judicial* agencies. Appeals from decisions of the French Permanent Military Tribunals could, during wartime, be taken to the Permanent Military Appeal Tribunals within twenty-four hours; in peacetime, the appeals went to the regular Court of Appeal.[652] Similarly, appeals from the Norwegian war crimes courts went to the Supreme Court of Norway,[653] while those from the Dutch tribunals were taken to the Court of Cassation.[654]

War Crimes Prosecutions and the Geneva Prisoners of War Convention of 1949

As was noted above, the Allied Powers after the last world war acted on the theory that there were, aside from the fundamental requirement of a "fair trial," no prescriptions of international law regulating the procedural aspects of war crimes trials. The 1929

---

tional courts." And see *In re* Yamashita, 327 U.S. 1 (1946), and *Johnson v. Eisentrager,* 339 U.S. 763 (1950) where the Supreme Court held that collateral attack, by means of habeas corpus proceedings, on sentences imposed by military commissions on enemy war criminals outside the U.S. was not available. See generally "Review of International Criminal Convictions," 59 *Yale L.J.* 997 (1950) and Fairman, "Some New Problems of the Constitution Following the Flag," 1 *Stan. L. Rev.* 587 (1949).

651. Art. 25, *Rules of Procedure AMG;* Art. 12, *Regulations, AMC;* Arts. XVII–XVIII, *Ordinance No. 7.* Very similar provisions are found in the British (2 *War Crimes Reports* 129), Canadian (4 id. 130), and Australian (5 id. 101) regulations.

652. 3 *War Crimes Reports* 99–100.

653. 2 id. 90–1.

654. 11 id. 105. The relevant Polish statute, on the other hand, provided that a war criminal convicted by the Supreme National Tribunal could only submit a petition for clemency to the President of the National Council. 7 id. 95–6.

Geneva Prisoners of War Convention contained certain provisions governing the conduct of trials of prisoners of war by the captor power. Article 63 of this Convention specified that a prisoner of war could be sentenced "only by the same courts and according to the same procedure as in the case of persons belonging to the armed forces of the detaining power." In the *Yamashita* case,[655] the United States Supreme Court, relying on the contextual location of those provisions, held that they were applicable to trials for acts committed by prisoners of war after the commencement of their captivity, that is to say, for offenses against the security enactments of the detaining power. They did not apply, in the opinion of the Court, where the acts charged had been performed prior to capture. Violations of the law of war are, of course, in the vast majority of cases, committed before capture and assumption of prisoner-of-war status. Justice Rutledge, in his dissent, pointed to the fact that these same provisions were verbally unqualified, and concluded therefrom that they were meant to cover all judicial proceedings, whether the supposed offenses occurred before or after capture.[656] Subsequent decision-makers, including the Tokyo Tribunal, chose to follow the majority opinion.[657] The contrary view would have compelled the United States, for instance, to proceed against accused enemy individuals before courts-martial and military commissions operating under the Articles of War which set forth more exacting rules of procedure and evidence than those actually applied by its war crimes tribunals.

Article 85 of the Geneva Prisoners of War Convention of 1949 declares that:

> Prisoners of war prosecuted under the laws of the Detaining Power for acts committed prior to capture shall retain, even if convicted, the benefits of the present Convention.

The purpose of this provision, it appears, was to make clear that the conventional safeguards guaranteed to prisoners of war are available

655. 327 U.S. 1 at 23–4 (1946); also *Johnson v. Eisentrager* 339 U.S. 763 at 790 (1950).

656. 327 U.S. at 76.

657. See e.g., *Judgment of the International Military Tribunal for the Far East* 27–8 (1948); "Trial of Dostler," 1 *War Crimes Reports* at 30 (1945); "High Command Trial," 12 id. at 63 (1948); "Trial of Rauter," 14 id. at 114–18 (1949).

though the judicial prosecution be for alleged war crimes done while the accused was still a combatant.[658] Thus the Conference in effect repudiated *Yamashita* and adopted Mr. Justice Rutledge's dissenting view. The first paragraph of Article 99 adds support to this conclusion, providing as it does that no prisoner of war may be tried or convicted for an act not forbidden "by the law of the Detaining Power or *by international law*" in force at the time of its commission. Furthermore Article 104 requires notification to the Protecting Power "in any case in which the Detaining Power has decided to institute judicial proceedings against a prisoner of war." [659] It is worth pointing out that Article 85 was sponsored by the United States delegation and accepted by all the members of the Conference, with the exception of Soviet Russia and her Eastern European bloc.[660]

Under the 1949 Convention, as a rule, the forum, general procedure, and penalties in war crimes trials of enemy prisoners of war must be that to which the armed forces of the captor are subject under its military law. The Convention, however, specifies certain basic conditions that must be satisfied in any case,[661] and lists what

658. See Draper, *The Red Cross Conventions* 64–5 (1958); Yingling and Ginnane, "The Geneva Conventions of 1949," 46 *A.J.I.L.* 409–11 (1952); Dillon, "The Genesis of the 1949 Convention Relative to the Treatment of Prisoners of War," 5 *Miami L.Q.* 58–9 (1950). Cf. Gutteridge, "The Geneva Conventions of 1949," 26 *Brit. Y.B.I.L.* 317–18 (1949).

Commission of Government Experts for the Study of Conventions for the Protection of War Victims, *Preliminary Documents Submitted by the International Committee of the Red Cross,* Vol. 2, p. 137–8 (1947); "The majority of breaches committed before capture with which POW are charged, constitute violations of the Hague and Geneva Conventions, usually described as 'war crimes.' . . . It may be asked whether this class of offense, committed before capture, should be provided for in the revised Convention. The International Committee, for their part, have upheld the view that the rules of procedure stipulated by the Convention in favor of POW should be applied to all offenses with which they are charged. The condition of POW is unfavorable; the principles of procedure set out in art. 60 and following represent a minimum. . . ." See also the *Summary Report of the Work of the Conference of Government Experts for the Study of the Conventions for the Protection of War Victims* 77–9 (1947).

659. See 2 Oppenheim-Lauterpacht 390 note 3.

660. See the reservations to Art. 85 by Soviet Russia in *Final Act of the Diplomatic Conference of Geneva, 1949,* 252 (U.S. Dept. of State Pub. 3938, General Foreign Policy Series 34, 1950).

661. Art. 102 of the 1949 Convention provides: "A prisoner of war can be

the Conference, doubtless aware of the variation in municipal practice, regarded as essential elements of fair trial. Thus, the accused must be tried by a military court, except where the captor expressly permits its civil courts to try members of its own forces for the same alleged offense. In all cases, the tribunal must be one which offers "the essential guarantees of independence and impartiality as generally recognized." [662] Some of these "essential guarantees" are specified and compiled in the Convention which thus projects a set of relatively detailed prescriptions on the judicial administration of the laws of war by municipal officials.[663] The Geneva Convention makes no saving mention of trials before international tribunals. Nonetheless, it is not lightly to be assumed that the Conference meant to preclude such proceedings, so long at least as the safeguards enumerated in the Convention are complied with.[664] Indeed, the Convention is ineffectual to prevent the future establishment of some international tribunal which, even if wholly composed of victorious belligerents, is certainly not likely to be any less independent and impartial than the regular military courts of the power which happened to capture the accused. To our minds, the ideal represented by a permanent international criminal court with jurisdiction over war crimes remains a valid goal of world public order.

---

validly sentenced only if the sentence has been pronounced by the same courts according to the same procedure as in the case of members of armed forces of the Detaining Power, *and if, furthermore, the provisions of the present Chapter have been observed*." Italics supplied.

662. Art. 84, id.

663. Arts. 86, 99, 105, id.

664. Draper, supra note 658 at 21 suggests that it is the "employment of *ad hoc national courts*" for war crimes trials which the Convention precludes.

7. BELLIGERENT OCCUPATION: THE MANAGEMENT OF CAPTURED ENEMY TERRITORY

For a clear and sharp focus upon the characteristic problems of belligerent occupation, it is necessary to distinguish a series of very different claims which contending belligerents and their nationals assert against each other about differing degrees of authority in situations marked by very different measures of effective control over each other's territory. The familiar technical terms, "invasion," "belligerent occupation," "military occupation," and "conquest," which have occasioned such learned disputation among the doctors, are employed in highly confused reference to these different claims, with their differing degrees of effective control and different applicable community policies.

In its factual reference, "invasion" is used to designate a sequence of combat situations, within an ongoing process of coercion, which comprises forcible entry into enemy territory, ensuing attack, and continuing military operations.[1] The land forces of one belligerent are introjected into the territorial domain of the opposing belligerent and come into violent contact with its armies. After a certain period of combat, at least a provisional decision in battle is reached and the military situation in a given area begins to be stabilized. "Belligerent occupation" is used to refer to stages or specific contexts in which, following successful invasion, assault, and beginning stabilization, the destruction of organized resistance is effected within a larger or lesser area, the resisting enemy troops expelled, and a considerable measure of effective control established. This degree

1. See, e.g., McNair, *Legal Effects of War* 319–20 (3rd ed., 1948); 2 Oppenheim, *International Law* 434 (7th ed., Lauterpacht, 1952) hereafter referred to as Oppenheim-Lauterpacht; Spaight, *War Rights on Land* 321 (1911); 3 Hyde, *International Law* 1877–8 (2nd rev. ed., 1945); Hall, *International Law*, s. 153 (8th ed., Pearce Higgins, 1924); Stone, *Legal Controls of International Conflict* 694 (rev. ed., 1959).

of control signified as "belligerent occupation" is commonly accompanied by and manifested in the constituting of structures of governmental administration within the occupied area.[2] Belligerent occupation is, of course, "military" occupation in the sense that it is established and principally maintained by means of armed force. "Military occupation," however, in contradistinction to belligerent occupation, is appropriately taken to refer to occupation that is established and maintained at the termination stages of a process of coercion, that is, after the general close of hostilities and the final surrender of one belligerent to the other. "Conquest" was, in traditional law, regarded as meaning the definitive and unambiguous appropriation of all or part of the territory of the defeated belligerent, which frequently had previously been under belligerent or military occupation.

The different degrees of effective control over enemy territory which characterize these various stages, and the differing expectations that attend such stages, may bear some elaboration. In the stage of invasion, the invading belligerent is engaged in acquiring effective control by assaulting the defending enemy forces. Success in establishing substantial control and firm possession distinguishes the stage of belligerent occupation from that of invasion.[3] It also

2. See "Trial of List," 8 *Law Reports of Trials of War Criminals* at 55–6 (1948); see also Conver, "The Development of Belligerent Occupation," 4 *Studies in the Social Sciences* 3 (Univ. of Iowa, 1912). Cf. Greenspan, *The Modern Law of Land Warfare* 214 (1959) who speaks of military occupation as being divided into two phases: the "combat or wake-of-battle" phase and the "occupational" phase. The latter occurs "when the tide of battle has receded well beyond the occupied territory, conditions there are fairly well settled, and administration becomes the main problem rather than battle."

3. Belligerent occupation of enemy territory may also be distinguished from occupation contexts where some element of consent on the part of the territorial sovereign may be present. See Robin, *Des Occupations Militaires en Dehors des Occupations de Guerre* 2, 9–15 (Extracts trans. by the Carnegie Endowment for International Peace, 1942) and Downey, "Revision of the Rules of Warfare," 43 *Proc. Am. Soc. I.L.* 103 (1949). Judge Advocate General's School, *Law of Belligerent Occupation* 14 (Text No. 11, 1944) cites as illustrations of "consensual occupation" those of Greenland, Iceland, and Dutch Guiana by United States forces in 1941. General accounts are offered in Briggs, "The Validity of the Greenland Agreement," 35 *A.J.I.L.* 506 (1941) and Zimmerman, "A Note on the Occupation of Iceland by American Forces," 62 *Pol. Sci. Q.* 103 (1947).

In respect of occupation pursuant to an armistice agreement, and more spe-

serves to crystallize the expectations of the inhabitants of the region involved that, for the immediate foreseeable future, the belligerent occupant, in lieu of the ousted sovereign, will in fact assert and exercise authority over such region. During the preceding stage of invasion, these expectations were as yet fluid and unsettled, reflecting the uncertainty of the outcome of the invading belligerent's efforts. It is of course rarely practicable to point to any particular degree of control as marking a precise dividing line between invasion and occupation. It is commonly more accurate to speak of a gradual acquisition and solidification of control by one belligerent and of the gradual settling of the corresponding expectations on the part of the inhabitants; the continuum ranges from initial attack to a fully functioning occupation government.

However effective the occupant's control may be within the occupied territory, such control may nonetheless remain precarious and tentative when viewed in relation to the over-all conduct of the war. Outside the captured territory, hostilities may continue to be waged by the forces of the legitimate government or by those of its allies, who may yet succeed, in the protracted course of the war, in

---

cifically on the Allied occupation of the Rhineland under the armistice of Nov. 11, 1918, see *American Military Government Occupied Germany, 1918–1920, Report of Officer in Charge of Civil Affairs,* Vol. 1 (1943); Fraenkel, *Military Occupation and the Rule of Law* (1944) and the Rhineland (German Decrees) Case, Reichgericht, Germany, *Annual Digest 1919–1922,* Case No. 315.

Neutral territory has also occasionally been subjected to belligerent occupation. U. S. War Department, *Military Government and Civil Affairs,* par. 7 (FM 27-5, 1940) refers to the establishment of military government, with or without the consent of the existing or prior government, in "(a) . . . neutral territory which has been dominated or occupied by the enemy; (b) technically neutral . . . [but] actually unfriendly or hostile [territory]; (c) . . . neutral territory the occupation of which is essential to a military operation."

Another special case is the belligerent occupation of the territory of a cobelligerent on which a technically hostile character had been impressed by a preceding occupation by the enemy; e.g., the reoccupation of France and the Low Countries by the Allied forces in 1944. In such case, though the ordinary law of belligerent occupation may be applicable (cf. *Tan Tuan et al. v. Lucena Food Control Board, Int. Law Rep. 1951,* Case No. 181, p. 590; contrast *Public Prosecutor v.* X [Eastern Java], *Annual Digest 1948,* Case No. 176) the occupant generally finds it expedient to enter into some agreement with the cobelligerent (represented by an exiled *de jure* government) for the regulation of their relationships upon expulsion of the enemy. See Coles, "Civil Affairs Agreements for Liberated Territories," 267 *Annals* 131 (1950).

reinvading and reoccupying the region presently held by the occupant.[4] In this sense, belligerent occupation represents a phase or incident of a continuing sequence of hostilities or combat. The expectations of the inhabitants as to whose authority will finally and permanently prevail in the occupied territory remain fluid and indeterminate. This condition of precariousness is resolved, and expectations about final and permanent authority become fixed, one way or the other, upon the general termination of hostilities. At hostilities' end, the ousted sovereign may have succeeded in recovering its territory and expelling the belligerent occupant; or the absent sovereign may have been finally defeated by the occupying belligerent. Where it is the belligerent occupant who proves eventually victorious, he may decide permanently to retain the territory previously occupied. This intent was, under the traditional law permitting "conquest," commonly formally manifested by a proclamation of annexation or a provision for cession in a peace treaty.[5] On the other hand, the successful belligerent may, as in the case of the Allied occupation of Germany after World War II, disclaim any intent to annex or incorporate the defeated belligerent's territory,[6] and may seek to hold such territory, in the future interest of basic order, only temporarily and pending reconstruction of indigenous structures of authority and control. Thus, while "military occupation"—or "post-surrender" occupation as it is sometimes called [7]—is no longer a precarious detention of territory, it is in a real sense a transitional stage.

The major claims made with respect to the stage of belligerent occupation are conveniently presented under three broad groups which generally refer to the bases of power—institutions, people,

4. See 3 Hyde, *International Law* 1878–9 (2nd rev. ed., 1945); and Spaight, *War Rights on Land* 309 (1911).

5. Anglo-American writers commonly regarded subjugation or conquest (*debellatio*) as involving the extinction of the political identity of the defeated state by annexation. E.g., 2 Oppenheim-Lauterpacht 600; 3 Hyde, supra note 4 at 2389–90; Fenwick, *International Law* 661 (3rd ed., 1948).

6. By the Declaration of Berlin of June 5, 1945, the Allied Powers assumed "supreme authority with respect to Germany" but explicitly stated that such assumption of authority did not effect the annexation of Germany. Text of the Declaration in 12 *Dept. of State Bull.* 1051 (1945) and 39 *A.J.I.L. Supp.* 171 (1945).

7. Von Glahn, *The Occupation of Enemy Territory* 276 (1957).

and resources—control of which the occupant has successfully wrested from its opponent.

The first group embraces claims relating to the constitution and management of processes of authoritative decision in the occupied area. Included here are, firstly, claims which belligerent occupants make to authority both to establish and operate new institutional structures, as well as to modify the pre-existing structures, for the prescribing and applying of policy within the territory occupied. Claims made in opposition have at times consisted of the comprehensive assertion that belligerent occupants are bereft of "legal status" and of any "legal power" to prescribe and apply policy for the occupied community. At other times, the more modest opposing claim is made that particular prescriptions or applications are in excess of the authority conceded to the occupant by the law of belligerent occupation. The same group of claims includes, secondly, claims of the restored sovereign to competence to review and rescind, modify or recognize, particular acts of the occupant done during the period of his possession. The contraposed assertion denies the competence of the restored sovereign to revise certain acts of the occupant or to recognize certain other acts.

The second broad group of claims relates to the control of the inhabitants of occupied territory. Authority is asserted by an occupant both to protect and enhance his military interests by policing the inhabitants and prohibiting and punishing hostile acts directed against him, and by harnessing their labor in various kinds of activities related in greater or lesser degree to such interests. Countering demands are made by the inhabitants for respect from the occupant for their lives, allegiance, and other values.

Claims in the third broad group relate to control of the material resources located, and wealth processes carried on, within the captured territory. The forthright taking and utilization of resources by a variety of procedures have been immemorial assertions of belligerents in occupation of their opponents' territory. More recent and sophisticated are the claims relating to management and manipulation of the financial and commercial processes—currency, banking, trade—of the occupied territory. The counterclaims raised are commonly that particular takings by the occupant are excessive or in disregard of prescribed procedure, and hence unlawful, and that particular financial and commercial regulations or transactions effected by the occupant are covert spoliation and hence, again, unlawful.

The above claims with respect to the stage of belligerent occupation are clearly different both from the claims characteristic of the preceding stage of invasion and from the claims distinctive to the succeeding stages of military occupation and conquest. Claims made with respect to invasion are claims about the conduct of hostilities. There are included here all the varying kinds of assertions, considered in the preceding chapter, about the permissible application of violence for depriving the enemy of its bases of power. With respect to military occupation, the major characteristic claims have been, in post-World War II experience, assertions of authority to establish comprehensive and continuing administration and to engage in reconstruction of the basic institutions of the defeated enemy regarded as posing future dangers to minimum public order. The traditional distinctive claim made in conquest was the claim finally to dispose of all or part of the defeated enemy's territory by permanent incorporation or distribution among the successful belligerents. Succinctly put, the conqueror's claim was to liquidate or to restructure the territorial domain of the vanquished belligerent. There are, of course, today much more subtle ways of keeping a defeated community in a permanent position of dependency than the heavy-handed acquisition of its territory.

The community-established decision-makers who pass upon the controversies with respect to belligerent occupation defined by the contraposed claims sketched above are, in general, the same decision-makers who deal with the other problems of the law of war. In the first instance, i.e., during the occupation and within the occupied area, the belligerent occupant in effect unilaterally determines the legitimacy of its own assertions of authority. The occupant's initial determinations are, however, subject to review both during the occupation period by the absent sovereign and its allies who may invoke reciprocities and retaliations, and after the end of the occupation by the restored sovereign who resumes effective decision-making within its recaptured territory. The restored sovereign has common occasion, for example, to pass upon the legitimacy of the occupant's acts whenever demands are presented by individual inhabitants for enforcement of a claim acquired under the occupant's legislation or for retention of the benefits of a transaction effected during the occupant's possession. Third states, belligerent or neutral, during and after the war, may also frequently be confronted with the need to assess the lawfulness of the occupant's acts. Such need arises, for instance, when claims based upon an act of a belligerent occupant are asserted and sought to be made effective with respect to property located within the third state, and their resolution requires reference, under the ordinary conflict of laws rules of the forum, to the law of the occupied territory.[8] Judges of international tribunals may, finally, have to make determinations of legitimacy in respect of acts of the occupant, most prominently in the context of war crimes trials.[9]

The policies the community projects for application by these authoritative decision-makers in belligerent occupation contexts include the general policies applicable to invasion and other combat situations: securing the legitimate military interests of the occupant and reducing to a minimum the destruction of values in coercion

8. *Amstelbank N.V. v. Guaranty Trust Co. of New York,* 177 Misc. 548, 31 N.Y.S. 2d. 194 (1941) and *Koninklije Lederfabriek "Oisterwijk" N.V. v. Chase National Bank,* 177 Misc. 186, 30 N.Y.S. 2d. 518 (1941) affirmed 32 N.Y.S. 2d. 131 (1941) illustrate one type of treatment meted out by a third state, non-participant but unfriendly to the occupant, to acts of such occupant sought to be given effect in the forum's territory during the war. In refusing to give effect to German decrees promulgated in occupied Holland, the New York court invoked doctrines relating to "recognition" of governments rather than the law of belligerent occupation. For critical comment, see McNair, *Legal Effects of War* 337 (3rd ed., 1948) and Shanker, "The Law of Belligerent Occupation in the American Courts," 50 *Mich. L. Rev.* 1066, 1071 (1952). Contrast *Bank of Ethiopia v. National Bank of Egypt and Liguori,* [1937] 1 Ch. 513; and see Wright, "The British Courts and Ethiopian Recognition," 31 *A.J.I.L.* 683 (1937).

Anglo-Czechoslovak and Prague Credit Bank v. Janssen, [1943] Victorian Law Reports 185; noted in 17 *Aust. L.J.* 329 (1944), involved the treatment by a belligerent third state of acts done by its opponent in occupation of territory of another country. Cases decided after termination of the war by third states—whether they were, during the war, neutrals or belligerents, enemies or allies of the occupant—exhibit a notable tendency. Third states have commonly applied the law of belligerent occupation, recognizing and giving effect only to occupation acts they regarded as legitimate under such law. E.g., *Aboitiz and Co. v. Price* 99 F. Supp. 602 (D.C., Utah, 1951); *Vitse v. Brasser and the Dutch State, Annual Digest 1948,* Case No. 200; *Rosenberg v. Fisher,* id., Case No. 150; *P. v. A.G.K. and P.,* id., Case No. 196.

9. See Brand, "The War Crimes Trials and the Laws of War," 26 *Brit. Y.B.I.L.* 414, 415–16 (1949); and Lauterpacht, "The Law of Nations and the Punishment of War Crimes," 21 id. 58, 77–9 (1945).

processes. In addition to these familiar contraposed policies, however, community authority about belligerent occupation may be observed to seek the maintenance of stability in the reasonable expectations of the inhabitants of the occupied territory and of others who have dealt with them, to which the occupant's acts have given rise. These policies relating to belligerent occupation are distinguishable from the policies applicable to military occupation. In military occupation, the policies of rehabilitation and replacement of damaged resources, and of reconstruction of institutional patterns regarded as likely to lead to recurrence of disruptions of basic order, become relevant. Traditional international law, that is, the law before its incorporation of the principle of minimum order and of the distinction between lawful and unlawful resort to coercion, recognized military conquest as a legitimate mode of changing a prevailing distribution of power and other values among nations. With the establishment of this principle and distinction, there appears cogent reason for urging [10] that conquest may no longer be regarded as a permissible mode of acquiring "title" or "sovereignty"—that is, the claim to comprehensive, continuing, and exclusive control that an independent body politic characteristically makes over its territorial base and that is customarily honored in community authority. Notwithstanding this change in community policy, however, problems remain with respect to the permanent disposition of territory brought under the belligerent or military occupation of the party or parties determined to have acted in lawful defense or enforcement action. The disposition of such territory is, it is believed, most appropriately effected by the collective determination of the organized community of states.

COMMUNITY POLICIES WITH RESPECT TO BELLIGERENT OCCUPATION CONTEXTS

The first set of policies embodied in community authority about belligerent occupation is composed, as noted, of the familiar complementary principles of military necessity and humanitarianism. That

10. As the late Judge Lauterpacht urged, in 1 Oppenheim, *International Law* 574–5 (8th ed., Lauterpacht, 1955). On nonrecognition of territorial conquests, see Ch. 4 supra.

belligerent occupation designates a phase of over-all hostilities in process finds reflection in the continued relevance of the general policies which, we observed in the preceding chapter, run through the whole of the combatant law of war. At the same time, both military necessity and humanitarianism, considered as determinants of the competence of the belligerent occupant, may be seen to differ somewhat in their specific requirements and manifestations from those appropriate in active combat situations. This variation is reflective of the fact that, while hostilities continue elsewhere, the stage of raging combat has passed and been terminated within the territory belligerently occupied.

The military necessity which community policy authorizes the occupant to promote and prosecute relates, in the first place, to the security of the occupation forces from hostile acts on the part of the inhabitants. Such security is of course not limited to the physical safety of the troops of the occupation garrison but extends also to safeguarding of their installations, armament, and equipment. Military necessity in occupation contexts relates, in the second place, to the maintenance of assured and adequate sources and procedures of procurement for the needs of the army of occupation.

Demand for humanitarianism or the minimization of destruction of values may be seen to infuse the great bulk of the detailed prescriptions relating to occupation contexts found in the Hague Regulations and the Geneva Civilians Convention. The manifestations of the humanitarian principle begin with the obligation imposed upon the occupant to restore order in the occupied territory and to maintain its economic and social life.[11] The occupant is required, in other words, to minimize the disruption of the internal value processes of the region occupied which is an inevitable result of the waging of combat in the preceding phase of invasion. The same principle of conservation runs through the various limitations imposed upon the competence of the occupant respecting the organization and administration of the territory, the policing of the inhabitants and utilization of their services, and the exploitation of the material resources of the region occupied. Thus, in quick anticipatory illustration, the occupant is required to respect the lives, wellbeing, property, religious conceptions and practices, and political

11. Art. 43, Hague Regulations. Cf. Schwarzenberger, "The Law of Belligerent Occupation: Basic Issues," 30 *Nordisk Tidss. for I.R.* 11 (1960).

allegiance [12] of the inhabitants. Restraint in the taking of resources by the occupant is sought by establishing a requirement of proportionality. These and other conservatory limitations do not, however, exhaust the specific requirements of the principle of humanitarianism. The principle has, in the Geneva Civilians Convention, assumed certain more positive forms. This Convention, for instance, seeks to impose an affirmative obligation upon the occupant to ensure the adequate feeding and medical care of the inhabitants by importation of supplies if necessary and by facilitating relief schemes for the benefit of the inhabitants.[13]

It is perhaps worthy of explicit mention that, despite our emphasis upon the character of belligerent occupation as a stage that follows successful combat operations in a continuing process of coercion, the relevancy of the above policies is not contingent upon resistance and combat being actually offered by the territorial sovereign. Thus, Article 2 of the Civilians Convention declares the Convention applicable "to all cases of total or partial occupation of the territory of a High Contracting Party, *even if the said occupation meets with no armed resistance*." The Convention would, in other words, apply to bloodless occupations exemplified in the last world war by the German occupation of Denmark.[14] The applicability of this Convention, furthermore, does not under its terms cease until "one year after the general close of military operations." Even after this period, however, certain provisions of the Convention continue to be applicable "for the duration of the occupation" and "to the extent that [the Occupying] Power exercises the functions of government in such territory." [15] Clearly, the general policies of military security and minimum destruction of values do not lose their relevancy in post-surrender occupation.

The second set of community policies, equally complementary, which are sought to be realized in belligerent occupation contexts, seem in measure comparable to the policies expressed in conflicts of law or private international law. Because the occupant and the re-

12. See e.g., Arts. 45–47, Hague Regulations; Arts. 27, 49–51, 58, Geneva Civilians Convention.

13. Arts. 55–56, 59–60, Civilians Convention.

14. See the general account provided in Ross, "Denmark's Legal Status During the Occupation," 1 *Jus Gentium* 1 (1949).

15. Art. 6, Civilians Convention.

stored sovereign (or, in the case of former colonial territories that achieved statehood soon after World War II, the newly established sovereign) each act in a different segment of time, the latter following the former in chronological sequence,[16] this set of belligerent occupation policies may also be insightfully analogized to the community policies embodied in the law of state and governmental succession. There is, on the one hand, the policy of promoting the security of reasonable expectations of the inhabitants, as of others outside the occupied territory, which may have been generated by acts of the occupant and by transactions effected among the inhabitants during the occupation. Maintaining stability in reasonable expectations among the inhabitants is an important aspect of the task, of pressing urgency for the restored sovereign, of facilitating orderly transition from war to peace. To thwart these expectations by a comprehensive refusal of the restored sovereign to accord any recognition or effect to occupation acts and transactions would, it has been aptly suggested, be "unjust to the individual inhabitants and impolitic as regards the community at large." [17] Beyond a direct and immediate interest in converting and readjusting its internal social economy to the conditions of peace, the restored sovereign shares with all other nations an inclusive interest in promoting free and peaceful intercourse among individuals across state boundaries.[18]

16. The relationship being successive, it is said to be governed by *a jus intertemporale* as distinguished from the *jus interlocale* regulating the relations of occupant and absent or exiled sovereign. See Feilchenfeld, *The International Economic Law of Belligerent Occupation* 130 (1942).

17. Spaight, *War Rights on Land* 366 (1911). See also Hall, *International Law* s. 163 (8th ed., Pearce Higgins, 1924) who speaks of the paralyzation of the whole social life of the community as a potential consequence.

18. Eloquent statement of these more general objectives as developed in private international law is offered in Yntema, "The Objectives of Private International Law," 35 *Can. B. Rev.* 721 (1957). Cf. Yntema, "The Historic Bases of Private International Law," 2 *A.J. Comp. L.* 297 (1953); Neuner, "Policy Considerations in the Conflict of Laws," 20 *Can. Bar Rev.* 479 (1942); Carlston, "The Grasp of Jurisdiction," 53 *Proc. Am. Soc. I.L.* 170 (1959).

Illustrative detail may be found in Jessup, *Transnational Law* (1956); Katz and Brewster, *International Transactions and Relations* 495 (1960); Lorenzen, *Selected Articles on the Conflict of Laws* (1947); Cheshire, *Private International Law* (5th ed., 1957); Carlston, *Nationalizations and the International System: An Approach to a Theory of Law and Organization in the World Society* c. VI (1961).

This more general interest may be seen to be at stake, both for the restored sovereign and third states in whose *fora* controversies may arise, in the protection and fulfillment of reasonable expectations of individuals outside the occupied territory. The kinds of factors that rationally may enter into determinations of reasonableness of differing particular expectations are sought to be explored below. One pervasive conditioning factor which may bear preliminary mention is the common awareness of the interactors in a specific situation that the occupant's possession is of a provisional and precarious nature.

On the other hand, the restored sovereign also shares a common interest of states in an exclusive competence to determine the specific forms and functioning of the authority and control institutions within its own territorial domain. Thus, the policy—prominent in conflicts of laws—of permitting a state substantially affected by events comprising the basis of a claim, to prescribe and apply its own policy to such events,[19] stands in relevant contraposition to the policy of safeguarding and fulfilling reasonable expectations of inhabitants and others. The projection of this policy for securing this shared interest is perhaps most clearly observable in the principle, basic in the law of belligerent occupation, which denies to the occupant the plenitude of competences designated as "sovereignty" and any general license to bind in perpetuity. The restored sovereign indeed may be regarded as having a special interest in such exclusive competence. For the events of belligerent occupancy not only transpired within its territory; they were also part of the process of coercion directed against the restored sovereign by an enemy belligerent.[20]

19. This point is well developed in Katzenbach, "Conflicts on an Unruly Horse: Reciprocal Claims and Tolerances in Interstate and International Law," 65 *Yale L.J.* 1087 (1956) and Falk, "International Jurisdiction: Horizontal and Vertical Conceptions of Legal Order," 32 *Temple L.Q.* 295 (1959). See also Falk, "The Relevance of Contending Systems of Public Order to the Delimitation of Legal Competence," 53 *Proc. Am. Soc. I.L.* 173 (1959); Cavers, "A Critique of the Choice-of-Law Problem," 47 *Harv. L. Rev.* 173 (1933).

20. This special interest and contraposed policy are deemphasized and possibly even overlooked in statements like that of 2 Oppenheim-Lauterpacht 618 that the restored sovereign "must recognize" acts of the prior occupant which the latter was competent under international law to perform and that the expelled occupant has "by international law a right to demand this." Cf. the statement in Lord McNair's *Legal Effects of War* 321 (3rd ed., 1948) that "it is customary" for the sovereign to accord recognition to an occupant's legitimate acts.

For this reason, the balance between maintaining stability in expectations by honoring acts of the occupant, and permitting the restored territorial sovereign to protect its legitimate exclusive interests which were substantially affected by such acts, tends in many contexts to shift toward the latter.

CLAIMS RELATING TO THE ESTABLISHMENT AND OPERATION OF GOVERNMENTAL PROCESSES IN OCCUPIED TERRITORY

Claims to Authority for the Governance of Occupied Territory: Military Necessity and the Maintenance of Vie Publique

THE SCOPE OF THE BELLIGERENT OCCUPANT'S AUTHORITY

The assertion of authority by a belligerent to constitute and operate processes and structures of governmental administration in territory captured from its opponent is made almost inevitable by the vacuum created by the expulsion of such opponent, i.e., the legitimate sovereign. Both the military interest of the occupant in the security of its armies and in the continuing success of its belligerent operations, and the interest of the inhabitants themselves in resuming their ordinary pursuits and mode of living disrupted by the preceding combat, join in requiring the filling of this vacuum by the re-establishment of order and the restoration or reconstitution of the mechanisms of government.[21] It is thus generally for the securing

---

See also 3 Hyde, *International Law* 1885 (2nd rev. ed., 1945) (making a preferential, rather than descriptive, statement); Ireland, "The Jus Postliminii and the Coming Peace," 18 *Tulane L. Rev.* 584, 591–2 (1944) and Morganstern, "Validity of the Acts of the Belligerent Occupant," 28 *Brit. Y.B.I.L.* 291, 299 (1951). On the other hand, there is some recognition, albeit imperfect and oblique, of the same special interest and contraposed policy observable in Feilchenfeld, supra note 16 at 134, 2 Wheaton, *International Law* 245 (7th ed., Keith, 1944), and in Stabell, "Enemy Legislation and Judgments in Norway," 31 *J. Comp. Leg. Int. L.* (Pts. III and IV) 3 (1949). This recognition has taken the form of an insistence that the treatment by the returned sovereign of the occupant's acts is governed by "municipal law" rather than by "international law."

21. This convergence of interests of occupant and inhabitants is made clear in the specification of the importance of military government to military com-

of this confluence of interests that international law accords the occupant competence for the governance of occupied territory.[22] The Hague Regulations, which together with the Geneva Civilians Convention set forth the conventional law of belligerent occupation, make clear the important humanitarian purpose underlying the concession of authority to the occupant:

> The authority of the legitimate power having in fact passed into the hands of the occupant, the latter shall take all measures in his power *to restore, and ensure, as far as possible, public order and safety, while respecting, unless absolutely prevented, the laws in force in the country.*[23]

The complementary military purpose for which the occupant may prescribe and apply policy has been rendered just as explicit in Article 64, second paragraph, of the Geneva Civilians Convention:

> The Occupying Power may, [however], subject the population of the occupied territory to provisions which are essential to enable the Occupying Power to fulfill its obligations under the

---

manders found in JAG's School, *Civil Affairs-Military Government: Selected Cases and Materials* 17 (1958):

> [A]n effective military government administration can [support military operations in the field] by:
>
> (a) Preserving law and order among the local populace with the result that behind-the-line casualties and losses of, or damage to, military supplies and property are minimized.
>
> (b) Controlling the movement of civilian personnel with the result that civilian interference with military movement, flow of supplies, reinforcements, etc., is reduced.
>
> (c) Establishing health and sanitation controls, with the result that the possibilities of military casualties from diseases and epidemics are minimized.
>
> (d) Re-establishing a friendly and cooperative local government with the result that some occupation troops can be released to field commanders and that a source of local supplies is obtained.

22. See Schwenk, "Legislative Power of the Military Occupant Under Article 43, Hague Regulations," 54 *Yale L.J.* 393, 395 (1945); JAG's School, *Law of Belligerent Occupation* 33, 36 (1944); 2 Oppenheim-Lauterpacht 343; Stone, *Legal Controls of International Conflict* 697 (2nd ed., 1959).

23. Art. 43, Hague Regulations.

present Convention, to maintain the orderly government of the territory, and *to ensure the security of the Occupying Power, of the members and property of the occupying forces or administration, and likewise of the establishments and lines of communication used by them.*

The broad scope of the authority conceded to the occupant is, curiously, most clearly indicated by its humanitarian or conservatory basis. The suggestion has been made that the word "safety" used in the English text of Article 43 of the Hague Regulations appears an inadequate rendition of the term *"vie publique"* employed in the authoritative French text. *"Vie publique"* is said to refer, not to physical safety which is embraced in the preceding *"l'ordre"* ("public order"), but to the "social functions and ordinary transactions which constitute daily life," in other words, to the entire social and economic life of the occupied region.[24] "The life of the occupied country," Professor Kohler wrote, "is not to cease or stand still, but is to find continued fulfillment even under the changed conditions resulting from occupation." [25] The range of authority indispensable for effective regulation clearly cannot be limited to the mere suppression of physical violence and anarchy, but must bear some reasonable correspondence to the comprehensiveness and complexity of the social and economic processes of a modern community. It is thus difficult to point with much confidence to any of the usual subjects of governmental action as being a priori excluded from the sphere of administrative authority conferred upon the occupant.[26]

24. Schwenk, supra note 22 at 398; 2 Wheaton, *International Law* 236 (7th ed., Keith, 1944).

25. Kohler, *The Administration of the Occupied Territories,* Vol. 1—*Belgium,* 6 (Dittmar trans., 1942).

26. Speaking only of the economic aspects, Brandt, "Problems of Invasion and Occupation," 21 *Foreign Aff.* 699 at 704 (1943) said: "A first task of the occupation command will be to establish the legal and administrative framework within which a system of economic reorganization can operate. The commanding general should seize complete economic control as soon as the first bridgehead is gained and delegate this power to his staff of military governors. . . . These are the central controls of the productive and distributive functioning of the national economy: (1) money and banking (2) transportation (3) communications—radio, telegraph, mails (4) public services—light, gas, water, sewage, sanitation (5) fuel and power (6) agriculture (7) industries and handicrafts (8) man power (9) distribution of goods, prices, rationing, policing of the market (10) medical services and public health."

This conclusion finds reflection in the practice of recent belligerent occupants. Occupants did in fact intervene in and subject to regulation practically every aspect of life in a modern state which legitimate sovereigns themselves are generally wont to regulate. These claims of occupants to broadened authority were matched, as is developed below, by claims to correspondingly wide competence on the part of restored sovereigns to terminate and undo the policies and institutional practices introduced by the occupant and to scrutinize occupation acts and transactions.

The particular institutional modalities through which the occupant's authority is to be exercised are not specified in international law. The occupant may be regarded as free, within certain general limitations, to establish such governmental structures as it deems necessary or convenient. It may, for example, set up a purely military administration completely staffed by officers and men of the occupation army.[27] However, because this recourse requires the commitment of large numbers of personnel that would otherwise be available for military operations, occupants frequently utilize pre-existing administrative structures, at least on local government levels. The extent to which these indigenous structures are in fact utilized and allowed to function—the boundaries, in other words, between the functions permitted to the local inhabitant officials and those retained and directly exercised by the occupant—have differed as circumstances and conditions, including the occupant's conceptions

27. The Special Criminal Courts set up in Holland after World War II declared in several cases that the establishment by the German occupant of a German *civil* administration "independent of the commander of the occupying army" and the vesting of "pseudoconstitutional and legislative powers" upon such administration, was unlawful under international law. See e.g., *In re* Vogt, *Annual Digest 1949,* Case No. 164; *In re* Arlt, id., Case No. 165; see also Note to Case No. 109, *Annual Digest 1947,* p. 241. Contrast *K.N.A.C. v. State of the Netherlands,* Holland, District Court of the Hague, *Annual Digest 1949,* Case No. 168. The generally accepted view is probably that formulated in the *British Manual of Military Law,* Pt. III, par. 158 (1958): "It is of little consequence whether the government imposed by the invader is called military government or civil government, for in either case, it is a government imposed by the necessities of war and, so far as it concerns the inhabitants and the rest of the world, the laws of war alone determine the legality of its acts." See further, in this connection, Vagts, "Military Command and Military Government," 59 *Pol. Sci. Q.* 248 (1944), and Akzin, "Introduction to a Study of Occupation Problems," *Int. Conciliation* No. 389, p. 263 (1943).

of the necessities of war, differ from occupied territory to occupied territory.[28] Occupants may also establish a complete civilian administration on a national scale, with native personnel topped by a superstructure of military administrators. This device, familiarly known as a "puppet government" and frequently resorted to in the last world war, has at times been made the subject of contemptuous deprecation. No occupant, however, can realistically be expected to relinquish control to a hostile indigenous administration. So far as concerns the ultimate location of both authority and effective control, all occupation administrations are "puppet" administrations. As colonial powers long ago discovered, creation of a native "puppet" government is probably the most economical method of controlling a hostile population.[29]

The authority of the belligerent occupant over an occupation administration begins with the authority to remove the public officials of the ousted legitimate sovereign and to replace them with other individuals less likely to be hostile to the occupant. Although it may not force them to serve in an occupation administration, the occupant may retain in office pre-occupation officials who freely choose to remain.[30] Retention of such officials serves, as noted above, the occupant's interest in effecting economies in military administrative personnel. The belligerent occupant may exact from occupation officials, whether retained or newly recruited, an oath not of allegiance but of obedience—of conscientious performance of duty and of abstention from acts prejudicial to the occupant.[31] These au-

28. The point is made and elaborated in Betts, "Military Government," 2 *Judge Advocate Journal,* No. 2, p. 23 (1945); see also Hula, "Control of the Conquered," 8 *Social Research* 136 (1941).

29. Watkins, "Military Occupation Policy of the Axis Powers," in Friedrich and Associates, *American Experiences in Military Government in World War II* 92 (1948).

30. Art. 54, Geneva Civilians Convention. See also *British Manual of Military Law,* Pt. III, pars. 516–17 (1958); JAG's School, *Law of Belligerent Occupation* 44 (1944); 2 Oppenheim-Lauterpacht 445; Colby, "Occupation Under the Laws of War," 25 *Col. L. Rev.* 904, 952 (1925).

31. *British Manual of Military Law,* Pt. III, par. 581 (1958). Greenspan, *The Modern Law of Land Warfare* 262 (1959) observes that "apart from any question of oaths, local officials owe strict obedience to the occupant and are accountable under the law of the territory for their actions. Acts to the disadvantage or damage of the occupying army may be punished under proclamation law . . ."

thorizations find ample reflection in the practice of recent occupants. For instance, in occupied Norway, it was decreed by Reich Commissioner Terboven that "Officials whose political attitude does not warrant the assumption that they will cooperate wholeheartedly in the establishment of a new political order may be dismissed from office." [32] In the Netherlands, Reich Commissioner Seyss-Inquart assumed the power to appoint and dismiss occupation officials in the higher executive and administrative levels, including judges of all courts, leaving the appointment and dismissal of lesser officials in the hands of the heads of ministries [33] subject, of course, to his approval. In the Philippines, the same procedure was adopted by the commander-in-chief of the Japanese occupation forces.[34] Seyss-Inquart also required from judges, other public officials, and teachers "a declaration in lieu of an oath that they will comply conscientiously with the general and other orders of the Reich Commissioner and the German authorities subordinate to him and that they will refrain from any action directed against the German Reich or the German armed forces." [35]

The peculiar status or lack of status of occupation or "puppet" governments requires some further consideration. In the Second World War, as is noted below, the Axis occupying powers set up in many of the occupied countries, in Asia as in Europe, occupation "puppet" governments upon which they sometimes purported to confer "independence." In *Co Kim Cham v. Valdez*,[36] the Supreme Court of the restored sovereign in the Philippines characterized the occupation governments which the Japanese occupant had estab-

32. Order concerning the Dismissal and Transfer of Officials, Oct. 7, 1940, in Lemkin, *Axis Rule in Occupied Europe* 499–500 (1944).

33. Fourth Order of the Reich Commissioner for the Occupied Netherlands Territories concerning Certain Administrative Measures, Aug. 20, 1940, id., 455–7.

34. Order No. 1, 1 *Official Journal of the Japanese Military Administration* 7 (1942).

35. Order of the Reich Commissioner for the Occupied Netherlands Territories concerning the Exercise of Governmental Authority in the Netherlands, May 29, 1940, sec. 7, in Lemkin, supra, note 32 at 449–50.

36. 75 Phil. 113 (1945). Compare *The King v. Maung Hmin and Three*, [1946] Rangoon Law Reports 1, 15 where the High Court of Judicature in Burma stated that "the so-called Independent Government of Burma [established by the Japanese occupation forces] had of course no legal status whatever and the statutes passed by that government are of no legal effect."

lished—i.e., the "Philippine Executive Commission" and the "independent" "Republic of the Philippines"—as *"de facto governments*—of paramount force." Neither characterizations of this type nor the transparent devices of occupants need obscure the basic consideration that an occupation government, whatever its precise composition in personnel, has neither authority nor effective power apart from the belligerent occupant. An occupation government rests upon the sufferance and military power of the occupant. What effective control such a government disposes can realistically be exercised only within the limits set by the military interests and political objectives of the occupant. It can claim no greater authority in the occupied area than the occupant itself. An occupation government is thus appropriately regarded as a mere organ or extension of the occupant and its actions as the actions of the occupant itself.[37] In particular, the lawfulness of its actions, and whatever potentiality they may have for binding the returning sovereign, must be measured by the same requirements of community authority that are applicable to actions of the occupant.[38] The belligerent occupant should not be permitted to escape responsibility for an unlawful act, or indirectly to secure the advantages of conquest, by the bootstrapping procedure of establishing a "puppet" government.[39] The contrary view will obviously reduce to futilities the limiting policies of belligerent occupation. Such is the rationale of the prohibition, in the Geneva Civilians Convention, against deprivation of protected persons in occupied territory of any of the benefits of the Convention

> by any change introduced . . . into the institutions or government of the said territory, nor by any agreement concluded between the authorities of the occupied territories and the Oc-

37. The most explicit judicial statement of this view is found in *In re* G. Criminal Court of Heraklion, Greece, *Annual Digest 1943–1945,* Case No. 151; see also *In re* Law 900 of 1943, Court of Cassation, Areopagus, Greece, id., Case No. 152. See, further, Zepos, "Enemy Legislation and Judgments in Liberated Greece," 30 *J. Comp. Leg. Int. L.* (Pts. III and IV) 27, 29 (1948) and Lemkin, supra, note 32 at 11.

38. See "Trial of List," 8 *War Crimes Reports* at 73–4 (1948); also Dept. of the Army, *Law of Land Warfare,* par. 366 (FM 27-10, 1956).

39. Cf. *State of the Netherlands v. Jessen,* Court of Appeal, the Hague, Holland, *Int. Law Rep. 1953,* 646–7.

cupying Power, nor by any annexation by the latter of the whole or part of the occupied territory.[40]

GENERAL LIMITATIONS UPON THE GOVERNMENTAL AUTHORITY OF THE OCCUPANT

The first requirement for, and the first limitation upon, the lawful assertion of authority by the occupant is, as indicated earlier, the successful acquisition and maintenance of a substantial degree of effective control. This requirement makes possible the delimitation of the geographical extension and the duration in time of the authority of the occupant. Only territory over which effective control has actually been established and maintained may be regarded as occupied and subjected to the occupant's authority.[41]

The particular instrumentalities and manner of asserting and procuring effective control are less important than the required aggregate effects, which are that the legitimate sovereign be effectively prevented from continued exercise of authority within the area involved, and that the occupant be able effectually to enforce its own policies.[42] Clearly, the determination of these effects is a function of

40. Art. 47, Civilians Convention.

41. Art. 42, Hague Regulations.

42. 2 Oppenheim-Lauterpacht 435; *British Manual of Military Law* (Pt. III), par. 503 (1958); see also Wickersham, "The Government of Occupied Territory," 37 *Proc. Am. Soc. I.L.* 27 (1943).

Downey, "Revision of the Rules of Warfare," 43 id. 103, 106 notes certain proposed additions to Art. 42 of the Hague Regulations:

> (1) A territory is no longer considered occupied after actual authority, previously established, ceases to be exercised.
>
> (2) All general and individual orders derived from an alleged occupation, but not backed by the exercise of actual authority . . . are void. Such orders become void when actual authority, previously established, ceases to be exercised.

These proposals appear to require a continuous and actual exercise of authority as distinguished from the capacity for its exercise. Taken literally, this exacting standard may exclude from the territorial domain of the occupant's authority areas where (as in the Philippines during World War II) the occupant's forces limit themselves to occasional incursions for purposes of effecting requisitions and taking punitive action against guerrilla bands. In North Burma during World War II, a singular situation presented itself: both Japanese and British forces periodically visited the same villages and towns. See Gledhill, "Some

differing factors. Thus, the presence of a fixed garrison of occupation troops in the city or town involved, or alternatively, the distance between such a garrison and such city or town, would seem obviously relevant considerations. It is said by commentators that the capability to dispatch, within a reasonable time, forces able to assume control in any particular area is a sufficient manifestation of control.[43] The presence of organized guerrilla movement, in or about the locality concerned, may be likewise relevant. Still other pertinent indices are perhaps the population density of the locality considered and the relative proximity or remoteness of such locality to the zone of active combat between the contending belligerents.[44] Proclamations, which have been customarily issued by occupying commanders, may provide helpful corroboration. Sometimes, however, proclamations have set forth extravagant claims.[45] They are most usefully regarded as a means of publicly registering and communicating to the inhabitants the new state of affairs.[46] By themselves, proclamations can rarely be regarded as conclusive evidence of effective occupation.

Fundamental in the law of belligerent occupation is the limitation that an occupant is not regarded as having acquired "sovereignty" over the territory brought under its effective control. Courts and publicists of many nations have long debated the "true nature" of

---

Aspects of the Operation of International and Military Law in Burma, 1941–1945," 12 *Modern L. Rev.* 191 (1949).

See also Birkhimer, *Military Government and Martial Law* 76–7 (3rd ed., 1914) where an interesting analogy is drawn between the requirement of effectiveness in belligerent occupation and the requirement of effectiveness in maritime blockade.

43. *British Manual of Military Law,* Pt. III, par. 502 (1958); Greenspan, *The Modern Law of Land Warfare* 214 (1959).

44. See Dept. of the Army, *Law of Land Warfare,* par. 356 (FM27–10, 1956).

45. For instance, on Jan. 3, 1942, one day after the Japanese forces entered the City of Manila, Philippines, the Japanese Commander-in-Chief issued a proclamation announcing that "the Japanese Army has occupied the Commonwealth of the Philippines . . ." 1 *Official Journal of the Japanese Military Administration* 2 (1942). At the time of the issuance of this proclamation, large areas of the Philippines were not under the effective control of the occupant. The proclamation brings to mind the so-called theory of "constructive" or "theoretical" occupation previously urged by some German writers. See Spaight, *War Rights on Land* 327–9 (1911).

46. Cf. Colby, "Occupation Under the Laws of War," 25 *Col. L. Rev.* 904, 908 (1925).

the occupant's authority, as well as the detailed competences that comprise such authority and their limitations. There is, however, an impressive consensus to the effect that occupation as a phase of a war in process is not to be considered as a permanent allocation or disposition of comprehensive and continuing exclusive authority.[47] While processes of armed contention continue, and even though in particular cases a very high probability may not realistically be ascribable to the prospect of the dispossessed belligerent or its allies expelling the occupant, an element of precariousness remains in the occupant's authority. Thus, only final victory at the termination of armed conflict was regarded in traditional law as authorizing the assertion of claims to assume or to dispose of sovereignty over the occupied territory, and even this authorization has, we noted above, been withdrawn in the contemporary law.

In its major aspects, this occupant-sovereign distinction may be seen to relate to the projected time dimension of the occupant's authority. The not unlimited purposes for which authority is conceded to the occupant—the protection of its military security and the restoration and maintenance of *vie publique* in the occupied area—may, as we observed above, indeed require a wide scope or domain of authority, understood in terms of the number of activities and interactions that may reasonably need regulation. What the occupant, "a bird of passage," so to speak, is denied by authoritative community policy, in contexts of uncertainty in common expectations about the final success of one or the other belligerent and about the final disposition of the territory involved, is time-binding competence. Authority to bind the indefinite future bears no neces-

47. Illustrative citations to the textwriters include: 2 Oppenheim-Lauterpacht 433–4; 3 Hyde, *International Law* 1878–9 (2nd rev. ed., 1945); Spaight, *War Rights on Land* 322 (1911); Fenwick, *International Law* 568 (3rd ed., 1948); McNair, *Legal Effects of War* 320 (3rd ed., 1948); Feilchenfeld, *The International Economic Law of Belligerent Occupation* 11, 87 (1942); Fiore, *International Law Codified* 571 (trans. Borchard, 5th Italian ed., 1918); Bustamante, *Manual de Derecho Internacional Publico* 531–2 (2nd ed., 1942); Lawrence, *The Principles of International Law* 413 (7th ed., Winfield, 1928); 2 Wheaton, *International Law* 233–4 (7th ed., Keith, 1944); Podesta Costa, *Manual de Derecho Internacional Publico* 382–3 (2nd ed., 1947); Greenspan, *The Modern Law of Land Warfare* 217–18 (1959). See also: Dept. of the Army, *Law of Land Warfare,* par. 358 (FM27–10, 1956); *British Manual of Military Law,* Pt. III, par. 510 (1958).

sary relation to the securing of the purposes of the law of belligerent occupation.

Illustration of the more specific manifestation of this general limitation may be drawn from practically every aspect of occupation law. Most familiar, perhaps, is the prohibition of annexation or incorporation of occupied territory into the territorial domain of the occupant. Recent breaches of this prohibition include the incorporation into the "Greater Reich" by Germany of portions of Poland, Luxembourg, France, Belgium, and Yugoslavia during the Second World War.[48] The converse claim to project the occupied territory as a new and distinct authorized participant in world authority and control processes is equally clearly *ultra vires* the occupant. This claim finds recent exemplification in the World War II actions of Japan which, purporting to act as sovereign of occupied territory, granted "independence" to the Philippines,[49] Burma,[50] and North China; [51] of Germany which established the "puppet state" of "Slovakia"; and of Italy which sired the "state" of "Croatia." [52]

Corollary to the prohibition of annexation are prohibitions of purported permanent acquisitions and dispositions of the bases of power of the occupied country. Thus, the inhabitants of the occupied territory may not be converted into nationals of the occupant and impressed into its armed forces. In the trial of Wagner,[53] a French

48. See Lemkin, *Axis Rule in Occupied Europe* 9 (1944). As to the peculiar treatment meted to Bohemia-Moravia (a province of dismembered Czechoslovakia), see *Civil Affairs Handbook* [Germany], *German Military Government Over Europe: The Protectorate of Bohemia-Moravia* (1944). In the Far East, it is reported that Japan formally annexed the Settlement of Singapore. See Murray-Aynsley, C. J., in *Sultan of Johore v. Tungku Abubakar,* 13 *Malayan L.J.* 3 (1950).

49. See 1 *Official Gazette, Republic of the Philippines,* 103–6 (1943); and *Civil Affairs Handbook* [Japan], *Japanese Administration of Occupied Areas: Philippine Islands* 52–5 (1944).

50. See Gledhill, supra note 42 at 198–9. See also *Chettiar v. Chettiar,* [1948] Burma Law Reports 278, *Int. Law Rep. 1956* 787.

51. See Wright, "The Legal Background in the Far East," in *Legal Problems in the Far Eastern Conflict* 37 (Institute of Pacific Relations, 1941). A journalistic account appears in Gayn, *The Fight For The Pacific* 211 et seq. (1941).

52. See Sereni, "The Status of Croatia under International Law," 35 *Am. Pol. Sci. Rev.* 1144 (1941). See also Sereni, "The Legal Status of Albania," id. 311; and "Trial of List," 8 *War Crimes Reports* at 72–4 (1948).

53. 3 *War Crimes Reports* 23 (1946). In this case, as in "Trial of Greifelt," 13 id. 1 (1948), the contention of the accused was that the incorporated territories having become part of Germany, the law of war—and, specifically, the law of

Permanent Military Tribunal held that the annexation of Alsace-Lorraine by Germany was an unlawful unilateral act that could not be regarded as having modified the Versailles Treaty under which the province had been ceded to France. The annexation being unlawful, the imposition of German nationality upon the people of Alsace and Lorraine and their compulsory recruitment into the *Wehrmacht* were also unlawful. A comparable ruling was laid down by the Belgian *Cour Militaire* at Liège in *Bindels v. Administration des Finances.*[54] Bindels, a native of the canton of Eupen, was tried and convicted on a charge of treasonous activity during the last world war. It was urged on appeal that, because of the annexation of the Belgian Cantons of Eupen, Malmédy, and Moresnet by Germany on May 18, 1940, he lost his Belgian nationality and acquired German nationality, and was hence not subject to Belgian law at the time of the offense charged. In convicting the accused and holding that the act of annexation by the German occupant was violative of the law of war and did not work a change in the nationality of the inhabitants, the Court said:

> [A]nnexation and the reintegration of territories in breach of a treaty are only possible in law when they are possible in fact. In other words, when the outcome of military operations is finally settled the incorporation of territories can also take place with finality. The nationality of the inhabitants of a region cannot be modified by every change in the fortunes of battle.[55]

---

belligerent occupation—became inapplicable therein. The same assertion was made in the trial before the International Military Tribunal at Nuremberg: see the Judgment of the Tribunal, 41 *A.J.I.L.* at 249 (1947); as well as in "The Trial of Altstotter," 6 *War Crimes Reports* 91–3 (1947). In each case, the argument was rejected by the tribunal. Art. 47 of the Geneva Civilians Convention was designed to meet and dispose of this argument.

One principal objection to authorizing the annexation of occupied territory in the course of a war is that such annexation usually involves, apart from the impressment of inhabitants, the treatment of the territory as loot. See Feilchenfeld, *The International Economic Law of Belligerent Occupation* 11 (1942); Baty, "The Legal Relations of Invaders to Insurgents," 36 *Yale L.J.* 966, 984 (1927). In the last war, the Axis occupants treated occupied countries, "puppet" or "independent," incorporated or otherwise, as loot with complete impartiality.

54. *Annual Digest 1947,* Case No. 17; see also *Deneffe v. Administration des Finances,* id., *1948,* Case No. 22.

55. *Annual Digest 1947* at 48.

It should be added that for certain purposes unrelated to the conduct of war, courts of restored sovereigns have in effect disregarded the illegality of annexations by a belligerent occupant. In *Bourseaux v. Krantz,*[56] for instance, the Belgian Court of Appeals refused to annul a marriage celebrated and registered by a German official in Eupen who acted under German legislation enacted for the illegally incorporated territories. Although the Court stated that such a marriage was an act "based on the modification of Belgian territory by the enemy" within the meaning of a Belgian law of May 5, 1944 which formally annulled all such acts, it held the "nullity" with respect to the marriage "unimportant" and a "mere irregularity of form."

The broad principle that denies the occupant competence to bind the future also finds expression in limitative requirements respecting the disposition of the material resources and the institutions of the occupied territory. With respect to resources, for instance, the competence of the occupant over immovable state property is limited to that of an "administrator" and "usufructuary" as distinguished from that of an "owner."[57] With respect to institutions, the belligerent occupant is required to refrain from altering and reconstructing the fundamental institutions of the territory occupied. The limited time-dimension of the occupant's authority is expressed finally—and perhaps even more clearly than in the above and other specific manifestations in respect of inhabitants, resources, and institutions—in a customary practice of restored sovereigns so taken for granted as frequently to escape explicit notice. This is the practice to the effect that policies prescribed by the occupant may no longer be invoked and applied from the moment the belligerent occupancy has terminated. We consider both the above specific manifestations and this customary practice in some detail below.[58]

The third general limitation upon the authority of the occupant is established in Article 43 of the Hague Regulations as a duty to

56. *Annual Digest 1948,* Case No. 171. To the same effect is *Krott v. Merkens,* id., *1946,* Case No. 148, where a Belgian court held that Eupen and Malmedy were "temporarily in fact under foreign sovereignty," and that a marriage concluded there "in German form" was valid under the maxim *locus regit actum.* The effort to secure stability of reasonable expectations is clearly visible here.

57. Article 55, Hague Regulations.

58. Infra, p. 771–90.

respect "unless absolutely prevented, the laws in force in the [occupied] country." The same conserving limitation is expressed in the first paragraph of Article 64 of the Geneva Civilians Convention with more particular reference to the criminal law and judicial system of the occupied region. This paragraph reads:

> The penal laws of the occupied territory shall remain in force, with the exception that they may be repealed or suspended by the Occupying Power in cases where they constitute a threat to its security or an obstacle to the application of the present Convention. Subject to the latter consideration and to the necessity for ensuring the effective administration of justice, the tribunals of the occupied territory shall continue to function in respect to all offences covered by said laws.

Under the saving clause of Article 43 of the Hague Regulations, the occupant is permitted to disregard and modify the existing laws of the territory occupied where it is "absolutely prevented" from respecting them. The obvious question is, "absolutely prevented" by what? The appropriate answer, it appears, requires reference once more to the purposes which underlie the concession of authority to the occupant: the protection of its military security and the restoration and maintenance of public order and *vie publique*.[59] These purposes define in broad strokes the permissible limits both for the prescribing of new laws and regulations and for the alteration of the old.

There are certain types of municipal law prescriptions whose con-

59. Schwenk, "Legislative Power of the Military Occupant Under Article 43, Hague Regulations," 54 *Yale L.J.* 393, 400–1 (1945). Some of the texts appear to imply that the phrase "absolutely prevented" has reference only to the military security of the occupant, i.e., that the occupant must respect existing laws unless absolutely prevented by military necessity. See 3 Hyde, *International Law* 1883 (2nd rev. ed., 1945); 2 Oppenheim-Lauterpacht 437; Fenwick, *International Law* 569 (3rd ed., 1948). Since the municipal laws of the occupied territory are presumably designed to secure the welfare and *vie publique* of the inhabitants, it is commonly the exception of military necessity that is invoked by the occupant in suspending the operation or enforcement of a particular law. It need not be inconceivable, however, that in the disorder and confusion, especially in the earlier phases of occupation, the interests of inhabitants themselves may demand improvisation and disregard of existing laws. Some illustration is afforded by *L.v.N.* (Bulgarian Occupation Case), Court of Appeal of Thrace, Greece, *Annual Digest 1947,* Case No. 110.

tinued operation is commonly regarded as inconsistent in varying degrees with the military security interests of the occupant and which, consequently, no one expects the occupant to respect and continue in effect. Perhaps the clearest illustration are the laws, constitutional and statutory, which define the civil and political rights and duties of the inhabitants vis-à-vis the legitimate sovereign, and which include laws relating to conscription in the armed services, suffrage and elections, the right to bear arms, the rights of assembly and petition, of freedom of speech and of the press, and the right to leave the country or to travel freely within it.[60] On the other hand, there are great masses of municipal laws whose application, generally speaking, bear so little significant relation to the security interests of the occupying belligerent as to give rise to a common expectation in the occupied community that the occupant will not suspend their operation and enforcement. The reference here is to the whole body of substantive private law, that is, those usually denominated as civil and commercial laws which define and regulate relationships of individual inhabitants in processes where the prin-

60. Stone, *Legal Controls of International Conflict* 699 (2nd ed., 1959); *British Manual of Military Law,* Pt. III, par. 519 (1958); Dept. of the Army, *Law of Land Warfare,* par. 371 (FM27–10, 1956); Spaight, *War Rights on Land* 355–6 (1911).

In the Philippines, Order No. 3 issued by the Japanese Commander-in-Chief on Feb. 20, 1942 and entitled "Concerning Basic Principle in Exercising Legislative, Executive, and Judicial Powers," suspended, among others, laws "especially provided with some political purpose, e.g., those prohibiting certain aliens, including the Japanese, from enjoying the right to exploit natural resources or to carry on or engage in certain businesses or professions." 1 *Official Journal of the Japanese Military Administration* 34 (1942). In a number of cases, the Supreme Court of the Philippines ruled that the Constitution of the Philippines was suspended in its operation during the period of the Japanese occupation; e.g., *de Cabauatan v. Uy Hoo,* G.R. No. L-2207, Jan. 23, 1951; *Ricamara v. Ngo Ki,* G.R. No. L-5836, April 29, 1953; *Talento v. Makiki,* 49 *Official Gazette* 4331 (1953); and *Bautista v. Uy Isabelo,* 49 id., 4336 (1953), *Int. Law Rep. 1953,* 643. These cases concerned sales of private agricultural land to aliens which the Constitution prohibited (Art. XIII[5]). The major premise adopted by the Philippine Supreme Court in these cases appears unnecessarily broad. Though the restored sovereign may well regard the occupant as authorized to suspend the operation of the Constitution in respect of the occupant's relationships with inhabitants, there seems little necessity to assume that even among the inhabitants *inter se,* the Constitution should in its entirety be held suspended in its applicability.

cipal value at stake is something other than power.[61] Similar expectations arise in respect of those provisions of the criminal law relating to offenses committed by one inhabitant against another. The occupant of course enacts penal legislation of his own, either defining new crimes and offenses incident to the state of belligerent occupancy and connected with the continued control of the occupied country and the protection of his forces,[62] or increasing the penalty for acts previously penalized by municipal criminal statutes as a crime against the legitimate sovereign but which are taken out of the territorial law and punished as new offenses against the occupant.[63] The Geneva Civilians Convention establishes certain requirements—prior publication and nonretroactivity,[64] conformity with the "general principles of law," and proportionality between offense and penalty [65]—for penal legislation enacted to secure the military interests of the occupant.

61. See Spaight, *War Rights on Land* 356 (1911); Stone, *Legal Controls of International Conflict* 699–700 (2nd ed., 1959); Podesta Costa, *Manual de Derecho Internacional Publico* 384 (2nd ed., 1947).

62. See Art. 64, Geneva Civilians Convention.

63. See *Alcantara v. Director of Prisons,* 75 Phil. 494, 497 (1945).

64. Art. 65, Geneva Civilians Convention. The prohibition of retroactivity in the occupant's penal legislation is a response to German practice in the last world war. The German occupant promulgated penal legislation retrospectively in Yugoslavia: "Order Concerning the Application of German Criminal Law and Criminal Statutes in the Occupied Yugoslav Territories," in Lemkin, *Axis Rule in Occupied Europe* 597–8 (1944); in Belgium: "Order Concerning Factory Trustees," April 29, 1941, id., 325–6; and in Luxembourg: "Order Concerning Insidious Attacks on the Party and the Movement," Jan. 15, 1941, id., 425–6. Art. 70 of the Civilians Convention prohibits imposition of punishment for acts committed prior to the occupation, either by protected persons or by refugee nationals of the occupant.

65. Art. 67 of the Civilians Convention. Again this is in response to recent practices. For example, the German Commander in Serbia issued an "Order concerning the Sheltering of Jews," Dec. 22, 1941 (see id., 601) providing that "any person who (a) shelters or hides Jews; (b) accepts for safekeeping objects of value of any description, including furniture and money, or acquires them by way of purchase, barter, or any other transaction, shall be punished by death." Again, the German Governor-General of the Occupied Polish Territories, in an "Order concerning Polish Jurisdiction in the Government General," Feb. 19, 1940 (see id., 529) forbade the Polish Courts from exercising mercy in any way.

However, in judging the severity of the penalties, certain considerations may be borne in mind. Gorman, "Military Courts in Occupied Areas," 17 *Ohio B.A.*

From the duty to respect the existing private law of the occupied territory, unless absolutely prevented, there would seem logically to follow a corollary obligation to refrain from importing wholesale into the occupied territory the occupant's own municipal law and legal system.[66] During World War II, in pursuance of its comprehensive objective of integrating Europe into a grandiose "New Order" under German hegemony, the German occupant wrought profound changes in the internal public orders of the occupied countries by transplanting therein large parts of German national law both public and private, including, for example, the German criminal and mercantile codes. Practically the entire corpus of German law was brought into the incorporated portions of Poland, Belgium, and France. German municipal law was also introduced into the non-incorporated occupied territories, though to a somewhat lesser degree, with emphasis upon laws relating to labor and economic organization.[67] Where the fundamental public order conceptions embodied in the occupant's national law are drastically different from those expressed in the law of the occupied country, and bear but minimal resemblance to perspectives of a public order of human dignity, the transplantation of the municipal law of the occupant into the country occupied may in practical consequence amount to much more than a technical usurpation of sovereignty. Thus, the imposition of German national law upon German-occupied territories assumed most tragic significance for the inhabitants of these territories. For German law included such aberrations as the principle

---

Rep. 479 at 484 (1944): "The purpose of a sentence of a military court is a deterrent one. Being temporarily in a country, there is no thought of reforming the accused. Certainly in the early stages, a sentence imposed should be sufficiently harsh to deter others from committing similar acts." See also Spaight, *War Rights on Land* 323–4 (1911).

66. Stone, supra note 61 at 700. As the Czech Supreme Administrative Court in "The War Services Law Case," *Annual Digest, 1927–1928,* Case No. 378, at 557–8 said: "The application of the laws of the occupying state do not by the fact of the occupation extend automatically to the occupied territory. Should the occupant consider it necessary from the viewpoint of his interests in maintaining and safeguarding his army or in the prosecution of the war to extend the application of a certain law in force in his own territory, he must do it expressly."

67. Lemkin, *Axis Rule in Occupied Europe* 25–6 (1944).

of analogy in criminal law,[68] presumption of future guilt,[69] and unrestrained official discretion to deviate from existing law.[70]

The general principle of respect for existing laws is commonly regarded as requiring the occupant largely to leave intact the municipal judicial system of the occupied country. Under this view, the pre-occupation courts are to continue exercising the jurisdiction conferred upon them by the old laws that survive the fact of occupation and by the new laws enacted by the occupant.[71] From such jurisdiction, however, certain types of cases are generally withdrawn by the occupant. These include cases involving offenses committed by members of the occupant's forces and violations by the inhabitants of security regulations promulgated by the occupant.[72] The first class

68. A German law of June 28, 1935 provided: "Any person who commits an act which the law declares to be punishable or which is deserving of penalty according to the fundamental conceptions of a penal law and sound popular feeling, shall be punished under the law of which the fundamental conception applies most nearly to the said act." See Loewenstein, "Law in the Third Reich," 45 *Yale L.J.* 812 and note 120 (1936). The Permanent Court of International Justice, in an advisory opinion for the Council of the League of Nations, held in effect that a decree of the Danzig Senate adopting the above German law verbatim was inconsistent with "Danzig's character as a State governed by the rule of law." Series A/B, No. 65, pp. 41–73; 3 Hudson, *World Court Reports* 516.

69. See e.g. Seyss-Inquart's decree of July 4, 1940, in Lemkin, supra note 67 at 478, providing that "The property of persons or associations which have furthered activities hostile to the German Reich or Germanism, or of whom it must be assumed that they will further such activities in the future, may be confiscated in whole or in part."

70. See e.g. the Fuhrer's decree of Aug. 20, 1942, id., 30 permitting the Reich Minister of Justice "to deviate from existing law," in the interests of a "vigorous administration of justice" for "the fulfillment of the tasks of the Greater German Reich." See Wolff, "Criminal Justice in Germany," 42 *Mich. L. Rev.* 1068–9 (1944); and Neumann, *Behemoth: The Structure and Practice of National Socialism* 440 et seq. (1942).

71. Art. 64, Geneva Civilians Convention; see also 2 Oppenheim-Lauterpacht 445–6.

72. See Art. 66, Geneva Civilians Convention; also: Dept. of the Army, *Law of Land Warfare,* par. 374 (FM27-10, 1956) (speaking of "military and civilian personnel of the occupying forces and occupation administration and persons accompanying them"); Nobleman, *Military Government Courts in Germany* 12–13 (Provost Marshal General's School, 1953); War Dept., *Manual of Military Government* par. 52d (FM27-5, 1940); 3 Hyde, *International Law* 1883 (2nd rev.

of cases are tried by a court-martial of the occupying army. The second class of offenses are prosecuted in military government courts or military tribunals established by the occupant. Courts-martial and military courts are not to be confused with each other. The first are, broadly speaking, concerned only with members of the occupant's army, the second only with inhabitants of the occupied territory.[73] Thus, the inhabitants are commonly subject to a dual court system: the ordinary pre-existing civil tribunals and the military courts newly established by the occupant—with a relatively distinct allocation of jurisdiction. However, the occupant may provide for the transfer of cases otherwise cognizable by the local courts to the military tribunals where it considers the local court an inappropriate forum for determining the controversy and where its exclusive interests are thought to be at stake.[74]

---

ed., 1945); Wolff, "Municipal Courts of Justice in Enemy Occupied Territory," 29 *Tr. Grotius Soc.* 99, 101–2 (1943); De Watteville, "The Military Administration of Occupied Territory in Time of War," 7 id., 133, 143 (1921). In the "German Military Courts in Greece" Case, *Annual Digest 1943–1945,* Case No. 149, the Court of Appeal of Athens of the restored sovereign recognized the occupant as authorized to establish military courts, with jurisdiction exclusive of the local courts.

73. Gorman, supra note 65 at 481. Note may also be taken of the agency known in U.S. military law as a "military commission" which in certain cases is given concurrent jurisdiction with the court-martial and, at the same time, jurisdiction over offenses by inhabitants of occupied territory against the occupant's security. Exposition is offered in Green, "The Military Commission," 42 *A.J.I.L.* 832 (1948).

The so-called "summary courts-martial" (*Standgerichte*) established by the German forces in the early stages of the occupation of Poland to deal, in more summary fashion than ordinary in military courts, with offenses against the occupant's security, were composed of a regimental commander and two soldiers. Trial and execution of death sentences took place on the spot. They seem rather a special variety of military tribunal than courts-martial as that term is used above. See *Civil Affairs Handbook* [Germany], *Military and Police Tribunals in Occupied Europe* 25 (1944). And see, generally, Nobleman, supra note 72 at c. 3.

74. Gorman, supra note 65 at 481 and War Dept., *Manual of Military Government,* par. 42d (FM27-5 1940). For instance, Art. II(3)(c) of Proclamation No. 4 on Allied Military Courts, issued by the Allied Military Government of Sicily and Adjacent Islands, giving to the Allied military courts jurisdiction over "any offense under the Italian Penal Code, or under the Ordinances of any commune, provided the Military Governor or an officer under his authority

Although the municipal courts are generally to be continued in operation, circumstances of reasonable necessity may arise which require their alteration, or even complete disregard, and the creation of new tribunals.[75] Disregard of the old, and the establishment of a new court may, for instance, be necessary where all the judges have fled before advancing forces of the occupying belligerent. The situation in Libya during the last world war provides recent illustration. There the British occupant, faced with a complete judicial and administrative vacuum caused by the evacuation of Italian judges and officials, proceeded to establish a system of "British Courts" with British officers as judges.[76] Alteration of the municipal judicial system may also occasionally be required by geographic and military circumstances.[77]

---

shall have ordered the trial of the case or class of cases by a military court." *Sicily Gazette* (July, 1943) No. 1, p. 13.

75. There is explicit recognition of this in the literature; see e.g., Spaight, *War Rights on Land* 358 (1911); 3 Hyde, *International Law* 1883 (2nd rev. ed., 1945); Betts, "The Law of Military Occupation," 4 *Fed. B.A.J.* 27, 28 (1940); Freeman, "War Crimes by Enemy Nationals Administering Justice in Occupied Territory," 41 *A.J.I.L.* 579, 585–7 (1947); and Nartatez, "The Right of the Military Occupant to Establish Courts in Occupied Territory," 24 *Phil. L.J.* 182 (1949).

76. Watts, "The British Military Occupation of Cyrenaica, 1942–1949," 37 *Tr. Grotius Soc.* 69 (1951) offers a brief account. Consult further Rennell, *British Military Administration of Occupied Territories in Africa* (1948).

A similar thing happened in Burma. Most of the Judges had fled with the retreating British forces. The Japanese occupant issued an ordinance creating a "Rangoon City court" giving it the civil and criminal jurisdiction previously possessed by the pre-occupation courts, i.e., the High Court, the Rangoon Small Causes Court, and the Magistrates Courts. The amalgamation was temporary until other courts could be established. See *Maung Hli Maung v. Ko Maung Maung* (1947) Rangoon Law Reports 1.

See also *in re* P. (Komotini Cases) *Annual Digest 1948,* Case No. 187, and *L.v.N.* id., *1947,* Case No. 110, and "Thrace (Notarial Services) Case," Court of Appeal of Thrace, id., *1949,* Case No. 167, for the situation in Thrace, Greece; *Endricci v. Eisenmayer,* id., *1946,* Case No. 152, respecting Italy; and "The Recognition of Divorce (Eastern Germany) Case," Federal Supreme Court, West Germany, *Int. Law Rep. 1956,* 795, with respect to Germany.

77. An example is furnished by the British occupation of Palestine in World War I. Communications with Constantinople had been cut so that recourse to the Ottoman Court of Cassation sitting in Constantinople, which under Turkish law was competent to hear appeals from the Palestine Moslem courts, was im-

Where the municipal judiciary has remained intact, the case for special tribunals with jurisdiction over special nonmilitary matters is much less clear.[78] In the last war, the Axis occupants did not hesitate to withdraw numerous matters from the jurisdiction of local courts and erect special courts to take charge of such matters. In the Philippines, for example, the occupation government established a "Court of Special and Exclusive Criminal Jurisdiction" principally to try violations of measures directed against "black market" operations.[79] In the German-occupied territories in Europe, special courts (*Sondergerichte*) were created by particular decrees issued for the protection of special interests, and were given jurisdiction over violations of those decrees. In Poland, for instance, special courts were created to try cases involving violations of the law on the use of the German salute, of the law requiring Jews to wear distinctive insignia, of the law establishing a Bank of Issue, and of the decrees relating to the sequestration of property.[80] In Norway, special tribunals were set up to try offenses against the decrees outlawing political parties and activities on behalf of the Royal House.[81] A Norwegian "Peoples Court," patterned after the German *Volksgerichtshof,* was also established and given jurisdiction over cases of "treason." [82] In Luxembourg, such offenses as conversation with prisoners of war, labor stoppages in disregard of German interests, and activities thought inimical to Germany and Germans were likewise tried before special courts.[83]

In addition to the ordinary military tribunals and the special

---

possible. The British occupant substituted in criminal cases the executive power of clemency exercised by the Chief Administrator, while in civil cases, the decisions of the Palestine Court of Appeal were made final. Bentwich, "The Legal Administration of Palestine under the British Military Occupation," 2 *Brit. Y.B.I.L.* 139, 142–3 (1921–1922).

78. Cf. 2 Garner, *International Law and the World War* 87 (1920).

79. See *Peralta v. Director of Prisons,* 75 Phil. 285 (1946).

80. The relevant decrees may be found in Lemkin, *Axis Rule in Occupied Europe* 33, 531, 537 (1944).

81. See id., 499, 500, and 503.

82. See *Civil Affairs Handbook* [Germany], *Military and Police Tribunals in Occupied Europe* (1944).

83. See Lemkin, supra, note 80 at 421. Note may also be taken of the summary penal jurisdiction exercised by German military commanders; they could impose penalties without any judicial procedure. See Lemkin, "German Administration of Justice under Military Occupation," 2 *Judge Advocate Journal* No. 2, p. 10, 12 (1945).

courts which it established, the German occupant brought, to a greater or lesser extent, into the occupied territories German courts exercising both criminal and civil jurisdiction and applying German national law and procedure.[84] Their criminal jurisdiction was not limited to crimes committed by German nationals and "racial Germans," but also extended to "political" crimes of non-German nationals, that is, to acts directed against the German Reich, Volk, or the National Socialist Party, rather than against the strictly military interests and security of the occupant. Their civil jurisdiction extended to actions where either of the parties was a German national or a "racial German." The cumulative effect of these practices was the maintenance of a sort of capitulatory regime for the German nationals and "racial Germans" in the occupied territories. It has been suggested in this connection that Article 66 of the Geneva Civilians Convention prohibits the subjection of inhabitants of occupied territory[85] to the jurisdiction of ex-territorial courts of the occupant. Article 66 provides that, in case of a breach of its security legislation, "The Occupying Power may hand over the accused to its properly constituted non-political military courts, on condition that the said courts sit in the occupational country. . . ." The history of this article indicates that it was designed to prevent, among other things, an occupant from extending its domestic court system into the occupied country.[86] Occupation courts, in other words, may not be set up as part of the occupant's national judicial system.

84. The extent to which German national courts were introduced into occupied territory varied according to the status—incorporated or nonincorporated—given to such territory by the occupant. See Lemkin, supra note 83 at 35; *Civil Affairs Handbook,* supra note 82 at 16, 18–20.

Detailed exposition of World War II German practice on this matter in, for example, Poland may be had from Segal, *The New Order in Poland* 28–33 (1942); *German Organization of Courts in the General Government of Poland* (Documents Relating to the Administration of Occupied Countries in Eastern Europe, No. 6, Polish Information Center, 1941); Ministry of Foreign Affairs, Poland, *German Occupation of Poland: Polish White Book* 90–102 (1942).

85. As distinguished from nationals of the occupying power. Freeman, supra note 75 at 600–1, explained: "However, it can hardly be said that adoption of the principle of extraterritoriality *per se* contravenes the limitations imposed by Article 43 [of the Hague Regulations]. Considerations of public order and the prestige and welfare of the occupying forces may justify a withdrawal of jurisdiction over the occupant's subjects from the local courts."

86. See Yingling and Ginnane, "The Geneva Conventions of 1949," 46 *A.J.I.L.* 393, 422–3 (1952).

The establishment by the occupant of a multitude of courts—military, special, and national—in the occupied territory will naturally result in the progressive restriction of the jurisdiction of the local courts and lead practically to their supersession. Technically, courts of restored sovereigns have sometimes held this supersession to be a violation of international law, at least where some reasonable necessity for such measures is not shown.[87] However, the matter of substance, with respect to both liability for war crimes and the returning sovereign's treatment of the judgments of such courts, would appear to be less the simple fact of their establishment than the character of their judgments and the procedure employed by them.[88] The Geneva Civilians Convention, as is noted below, sets

87. See *In re* Dr. J. H. Carp, *Annual Digest 1946,* Case No. 155, where the Dutch Special Court of Cassation held illegal the creation by the German occupant of the "Justices of the Peace" and the "Court of Appeal of the Peace" which had special jurisdiction, exclusive of the regular local courts, over Dutch nationals who collaborated with the occupant. The court said: "In setting up such exceptional tribunals, the occupant had respected neither the positive limits of his duties and powers, consisting in the maintenance of public life (i.e. *normal* public life) and public order (i.e. *normal* public order) in the occupied country, nor the negative limits set by the express injunction . . . to respect the laws in force in the occupied country except in cases of extreme emergency." Cf. *City of Antwerp v. Germany,* id., *1925–1926,* Case No. 361, where the German-Belgian Mixed Arbitration Tribunal held the creation of special tribunals, staffed by Germans, illegal since there is no occasion for such creation "either from the viewpoint of military necessity or of maintaining public order." These special courts had jurisdiction to assess damages caused by mob violence. See also *Re* Condarelli, Court of Cassation, Italy, *Int. Law Rep. 1952,* Case No. 133.

88. Support for the suggestion is offered in Freeman, "War Crimes by Enemy Nationals Administering Justice in Occupied Territory," 41 *A.J.I.L.* 579, 609 (1947), and in Brand, "The War Crimes Trials and the Laws of War," 26 *Brit. Y.B.I.L.* 414, 416, 424 (1949). Contrast Wolff, "Municipal Courts of Justice in Enemy Occupied Territory," 29 *Tr. Grotius Soc.* 99, 103–4, 112 (1943), where the argument is made that all the judgments of all courts established by the occupant in the regions prematurely annexed, or by "puppet" governments, and all judgments of the German courts in the nonincorporated territories, are null and void, on the theory that the establishment of such courts being illegal (either as a usurpation of sovereignty or as not justified by reasonable necessity), their judgments "have no legal basis." Wolff's view finds partial support in *In re* X, *Annual Digest 1919–1920,* Case No. 334, where a French Court of Appeal refused to consider a prior conviction by a court created by the occupant since said court was set up with the "very object" of suppressing the local

forth minimum procedural safeguards in the administration of criminal justice by occupational courts. It is common knowledge that in the last war the procedures used in courts established by belligerent occupants did not always conform to the minimal requirements of civilized justice and fair trial.

We turn to still another limitation that gives similarly clear expression to the policy of minimizing the disruption of internal value processes in occupied territory. The occupant's competence to establish and operate processes of governmental administration in the territory occupied does not extend to the reconstruction of the fundamental institutions of the occupied area.[89] This limitation is of course directly related to the requirement, noted above, of respect for existing laws; it may indeed be regarded as a special requirement of respect for more existing fundamental prescriptions. Most comprehensively considered, the fundamental prescriptions of a body politic formulate its basic public order goals and its major policies about appropriate allocations of power and other values. It is perhaps obvious that there are certain prescriptions which, though characterizable as fundamental, the occupant can rarely be expected to respect by continuing them in force. Occupants, for example, do not commonly govern in accordance with the division and allocation of competence established by the constitution of the occupied country.[90] One possible construction of the requirement of respect for fundamental prescription and institution is that, like the more general duty to respect existing law, it is subject to the legitimate security interests of the occupant and the reasonable demands of restoration and maintenance of *ordre public* and *vie publique*. The examples commonly given by textwriters—that an occupant may not convert a "democratic republic" into an "absolute monarchy," a

---

courts. The decision, however, intimated that if the prior conviction had not been for infanticide, but some other crime "reserved in principle by the law of war to the cognizance of the enemy as being likely to jeopardize the security of his army," the result might have been different.

89. See Greenspan, *The Modern Law of Land Warfare* 224 (1959).

90. See supra, note 60. *The British Manual of Military Law,* Pt. III, par. 519 (1958) observes that "[p]olitical laws and constitutional safeguards are as a matter of course suspended during occupation . . ." The same point is stressed in Dept. of the Army, *Law of Land Warfare,* par. 371 (FM27-10, 1956) which expressly includes among the laws which an occupant may alter, repeal, or suspend "[l]egislation dealing with political process[es] . . ."

federal into a unitary system or vice versa,[91] a "liberal" into a "fascist" or "communistic" economy[92]—suggest that the principal thrust of the prohibition is not the mere suspension of application of particular basic laws but the active transformation and remodeling of the power and other value processes of the occupied country.

Judicial constructions of this limitation are conspicuous, so far as we are aware, by their total absence. The best known case which brought about some controversy, at least among the commentators, about the applicability of this limitation is the denazification program of the Allied occupation forces in Germany. The process of denazification commenced as soon as the Allied armies entered German territory. In Proclamation No. 1, posted in occupied German territory on September 18, 1944, the Supreme Commander of the Allied forces stated among other things:

> The Allied Forces serving under my command have now entered Germany. We come as conquerors, but not as oppressors. In the area of Germany occupied by the forces under my command, we shall obliterate Nazi-ism and German Militarism. We shall overthrow the Nazi rule, dissolve the Nazi party and abolish the cruel, oppressive and discriminatory laws and institution which the Party has created. We shall eradicate that German Militarism which has so often disrupted the peace of the world . . .[93]

It has sometimes been suggested that the denazification program, which clearly contemplated the alteration and restructuring of fundamental institutions of National Socialist Germany, was inconsistent with the Hague Regulations, and more specifically with the rule forbidding changes in the basic institutions of the occupied country. This suggestion appears, for instance, in the most recent comprehensive digest of the law of belligerent occupation. Professor Von Glahn, in a passage making particular reference to the purge and reform measures adopted by the Allied occupants in respect of

91. Bustamante, *Manual de Derecho Internacional* 532 (1942); cf. Stone, *Legal Controls of International Conflict* 698 (2nd ed., 1959) and 2 Garner, *International Law and the World War* 78 et seq. (1920).

92. Feilchenfeld, *The International Economic Law of Belligerent Occupation* 89–90 (1942).

93. Office of Military Government for Germany [U.S.], *Military Government Gazette, Germany, United States Zone,* p. 1 (1946).

the educational system of Germany, stressed that these measures were "instituted or at least carried out subsequent to the time during which the Allied occupation authorities in Germany were still bound by the restrictions of the Hague Regulations, that is to say, after the beginning of the post-surrender administration of defeated Germany." [94] Without considering, for the moment, the question of applicability of the Hague Regulations, in whole or in part, to the situation of "military [post-surrender] occupation," [95] the partial sug-

94. Von Glahn, *The Occupation of Enemy Territory* 66 (1957).

95. Apart from the denazification program, there were other measures taken by the Allied occupants in Germany the conformity of which with the Hague Regulations was questioned: e.g., the abolition of the state of Prussia by fiat of the Allied Control Council, Control Council Law No. 46, Feb. 25, 1947, 6 Allied Control Authority-Germany, *Enactments and Approved Papers of the Control Council and Coordinating Committee,* 28 (1947); the compulsory surrender of all gold and silver, bullion and coin, and foreign exchange held by Germans in Germany, Control Council Proclamation No. 2, par. 15(a) and (b), 1 id., 86 (1945); and the decentralization and decartelization programs directed against German industry, Art. II(12), Protocol of Proceedings of the Berlin (Potsdam) Conference, Aug. 1, 1945, in *A Decade of American Foreign Policy, Basic Documents 1941–1949,* 81st Cong., First Sess., U. S. Senate, Doc. No. 123, p. 38 (1950); see also Stedman, "The German Decartelization Program," 17 *U. of Chi. L. Rev.* 441 (1950). See Mann, "The Present Legal Status of Germany," 33 *Tr. Grotius Soc.* 119, 127–9 (1948).

The question of applicability of the Hague Regulations to the post-surrender Allied occupation of Germany was a principal aspect of the debate concerning the "legal status" of Germany from the unconditional surrender in 1945 to the establishment in 1949 of the Federal (*Bundesrepublik Deutschland*) and Eastern (*Deutsche Demokratische Republik*) republics. This debate spawned an unusually voluminous literature. A comprehensive bibliographic survey of the polemics of both Continental and Anglo-American writers is offered in Kunz, "The Status of Occupied Germany Under International Law: A Legal Dilemma," 3 *Western Pol. Q.* 538 (1950). Feilchenfeld and Others, "Status of Germany," 1 *World Polity* 177 (1957) and Fritz (Pseud.), "Once Again: Germany's Legal Status," id. 229 have recently been made available. German writers of course stoutly maintained that the Allied Powers were mere belligerent occupants and that the Hague Regulations were applicable. See e.g., Laun, "The Legal Status of Germany," 45 *A.J.I.L.* 267 (1951). Non-German writers, however, have also held this conclusion, primarily, it appears, because of inability to break out of the belligerent occupation-annexation dichotomy. E.g., Brabner-Smith, "Concluding the War—The Peace Settlement and Congressional Powers," 34 *Va. L. Rev.* 553 (1948); and Bagge, "The Legal Position of the Allied Powers in Germany," 1 *Jus Gentium* 23 (1949).

Without seeking to revive protracted disputation nor to rehearse details, it may be observed that the constellation of events with which the Allied Powers

gestion may be made that the reconstruction measures initiated and executed while the Allied occupation was indisputably a belligerent occupation need not necessarily be regarded as inconsistent with the rule relating to fundamental institutions. The Allied belligerent occupants may fairly be said to have been "absolutely prevented" by their own security interests from respecting, for instance, the German laws with respect to the Nazi Party and other Nazi organizations and the "Nuremberg" racial laws. It is indeed difficult to envisage how the Allied occupants could be expected to protect their security interests if they were required to respect such laws.[96] From a some-

---

were confronted in 1945 was quite different from that with respect to which the law of belligerent occupation has traditionally been invoked and applied. The German forces in the field and the German Government had actually been destroyed; the German High Command had signed the "Act of Military Surrender"; text in *A Decade of American Foreign Policy,* supra 505. Armed hostilities had ceased in Europe and, at least from the date of the Japanese surrender (Instruments of Surrender, Sept. 2, 1945, id., 625–6), had come to a general close. There appeared no possibility however remote that the Allied Powers might yet be expelled by a reversal of military fortunes; *ultima victoria* had been achieved and Allied control could in no sense be characterized as precarious. There was no exiled German Government which could be regarded as the bearer of formal sovereignty. See, generally, Jennings, "Government in Commission," 23 *Brit. Y.B.I.L.* 112 (1946); 2 Oppenheim-Lauterpacht 602, and Fahy, "Legal Problems of German Occupation," 47 *Mich. L. Rev.* 11 (1948). See also *Dalldorf and others v. Director of Prosecutions,* British Zone of Germany, Control Commission Court of Appeal, *Annual Digest 1949,* Case No. 159.

96. Cf. Schwenk, "The Legislative Power of the Military Occupant Under Article 43, Hague Regulations," 54 *Yale L.J.* 393, 403 (1945). A somewhat different justification is submitted in Greenspan, *The Modern Law of Land Warfare* 224 (1959): "If a war is fought in proclaimed defense of democracy, for the freedom of humanity, and to protect the dignity of man, against states bent on crushing such ideals and whose own internal organization rejects such concepts, it surely cannot be claimed that, having occupied such a territory in the course of the war, the occupant should be bound to continue to enforce the very institutions against which he was fighting. Obviously the exigencies of the war will in that case demand that such institutions be eliminated, since, to put it on a purely military basis, the glaring contradictions apparent in such a course might well cause an alarming deterioration in the morale and fighting efficiency of the occupant's forces." Of course, in terms of impact upon authoritative community policy, the comprehensive nature of the occupant's belligerent objectives provides justification for fundamental alterations in the institutions of the occupied country only to the extent that such objectives are themselves characterizable as legitimate by general community perspectives.

what different perspective, the submission may be essayed that the rule enjoining respect for fundamental institutions is most appropriately interpreted as being limited in its protection to laws and institutions which comply with minimum, inclusively formulated, standards of human rights.[97] The submission is less revolutionary than might be supposed; it would seem but a reasonable implication from the general duty of a belligerent occupant, under both the Hague Regulations and the Geneva Civilians Convention, to maintain and safeguard fundamental human rights within the occupied territory.[98]

Claims of Restored Sovereigns to Review Prescriptions and Applications of Policy by the Belligerent Occupant

During the occupation and within the occupied area, to raise questions about the scope of the occupant's competence to prescribe and apply policy for the territory occupied is perforce a somewhat tenuous enterprise. As the decision-maker on the spot, the occupant itself determines in the first instance the limitations on his authority

97. 2 Oppenheim-Lauterpacht 447, 603 note 2. See also Fraenkel, *Military Occupation and the Rule of Law* 189 (1948). In the *British Manual of Military Law,* Pt. III, par. 510, note 1 (1958), Judge Lauterpacht, who was responsible for this revised edition, said: "Such an exceptional case arises where the law of the occupied State is such as to shock elementary conceptions of justice and of the rule of law. Thus, it is no part of the duty of the Occupant to give effect to a regime which is contemptuous of human rights and of modern notions of legality—as was the case of National-Socialist Germany. . . . There is room for the view that the Allied Powers were, in the terms of Hague Rule 43, 'absolutely prevented' from administering law and principles the application of which in occupied territory was utterly opposed to the modern conceptions of the rule of law."

98. Greenspan, supra note 96 at 226 stresses the fact that Art. 64 of the Geneva Civilians Convention authorizes the occupant to repeal or suspend the penal laws of the occupied territory "in cases where they constitute a threat to [the occupant's] security or *an obstacle to the application of the present Convention,*" as well as to enact laws *"which are essential to enable the Occupying Power to fulfill its obligations under the present Convention . . ."* Professor Greenspan states, at p. 227: "Since the aims and provisions of this convention are humanitarian, designed to protect the individual without discrimination both in his dignity and existence, it is obvious that Article 64 gives an occupant authority to do away with institutions, fundamental or not, in the occupied territory which conflict with the operation of such principles."

placed by the international law of belligerent occupation. Although the common expectation of the inhabitants may be of eventual review and rescission, the occupant simply enacts such legislative and regulatory measures as it regards within its competence (or at times, its naked power). Whatever courageous individual judges may say,[99] courts established by the occupant are rarely in a position to make controlling effective determinations of the concordance or conflict with international law of any particular policy prescribed by the occupant.[100] Militating against such independence there is, first, the inescapable fact that an occupant does enact a multitude of detailed prescriptions for the occupied territory; there are, further, the expectations of the inhabitants that these prescriptions will actually be enforced. Realistically, the limiting requirements of community authority, though regarded as continuously applicable during the period of occupation, can only be effectively invoked by the inhabitants after the successful recapture of the territory by the returning sovereign.

After termination of the occupation, the demands of individuals for enforcement, or for avoidance of enforcement, of claims grounded upon a prescription or application of policy by the occupant, commonly present the restored sovereign with both the opportunity and necessity for asserting authority to review acts of the occupant. Claims of restored sovereigns exhibit a large variation in the scope of

99. See e.g. *Public Prosecutor v. X, Annual Digest 1919–1922* (Supp. vol.), Case No. 160 and note, where the Norwegian Supreme Court asserted its competence to pass on the international legality of a German occupation measure; as could be expected, the justices were removed and replaced with less assertive ones. See also "Overlands Case," *Annual Digest 1943–1945*, Case No. 156, where another Norwegian court asserted the same competence. Contrast the decision of the Dutch Supreme Court in *In re* Jurisdiction of the Dutch Supreme Court for Economic Matters, *Annual Digest 1919–1922* (Supp. vol.), Case No. 161 and note, where it held it had no jurisdiction to review the occupant's measures; to the same effect is the decision of the French Conseil d'État in *In re* Lecoq and others, *Annual Digest 1943–1945*, Case No. 161.

100. Morganstern, "Validity of the Acts of the Belligerent Occupant," 28 *Brit. Y.B.I.L.* 291, 307 (1951). Note, however, that Art. 67 of the Geneva Civilians Convention requires courts in the occupied territory to "apply only those provisions of law which were applicable prior to the offense, and which are in accord with general principles of law . . ." See also 2 Oppenheim-Lauterpacht 454 note 1.

reviewing competence asserted with respect to such acts.[101] The large number of countries subjected to belligerent occupation during the last two world wars has resulted in a vast outpouring of cases decided and statutes enacted by organs of restored sovereigns in assertion of such competence. It is hence possible only to be illustrative and suggestive in outlining the more important claims that have been made.

One convenient itemization would appear to be as follows:

(a) Claims to authority to terminate from the time of reoccupation the applicability of policies promulgated by the occupant;

(b) Claims to authority to terminate from the time of reoccupation the continuing effects of certain acts or transactions executed during the occupation pursuant to policies prescribed by the occupant;

101. It has not escaped us that comparable claims are asserted by legitimate sovereigns even during their exile and before their return to their territorial domain. Thus: Schwelb, "Legislation for Enemy Occupied Territory in the British Empire," 30 *Tr. Grotius Soc.* 239 (1944); Schwelb, "Legislation in Exile: Czechoslovakia," 24 *J. Comp. Leg. Int. L.* 120 (1942); Lachs, "Polish Legislation in Exile," 24 id. 57; Anon., "Legislation in Exile: Norway," 24 id. 125; Cohn, "Legislation in Exile: Luxembourg," 25 id. 40 (1943); Fayat, "Legislation in Exile: Belgium," 25 id. 30; Drucker, "The Legislation of the Allied Powers in the United Kingdom," *Czechoslovak Y.B.I.L.* 45 (1942). The question of the authority of the absent sovereign to prescribe policy for inhabitants of the occupied territory is, realistically, a question respecting the effect *third states* may give, during and after the occupation, to such legislation in exile; the problems of policy raised are distinguishable from those involved in the above claims of the restored sovereign. So far as the inhabitants of the occupied territory are concerned, they can invoke legislation-in-exile only in the courts of the restored sovereign after the occupation; see *Public Prosecutor v. Reidar Hoaland,* Supreme Court of Norway, *Annual Digest 1943–1945,* Case No. 154.

Representative citations: *State of the Netherlands v. Federal Reserve Bank of New York* 201 F. 2d 455 (2nd Cir., 1953), noted in 52 *Mich. L. Rev.* 753 (1954) and 2 *Int. Comp. L.Q.* 647 (1953); *Auditeur Militaire v. G. Van Dieren, Annual Digest 1919–1922,* Case No. 310 and note; *De Nimal v. De Nimal,* id., Case No. 311 and note; Oppenheimer, "Governments and Authorities in Exile," 36 *A.J.I.L.* 568 (1942); Stein, "Application of the Law of the Absent Sovereign in Territory Under Belligerent Occupation: The Schio Massacre," 46 *Mich. L. Rev.* 341 (1948); Feilchenfeld, *The International Economic Law of Belligerent Occupation* 135–7 (1942); and Domke, "Dutch War-Time Legislation Before American Courts, 1953," 1 *Nederlands Tijdschrift voor Internationaal Recht* 365 (1953–1954).

(c) Claims to comprehensive and exclusive competence to abrogate retroactively, from the time of promulgation, prescriptions and applications of policy by the occupant;
(d) Claims to competence to abrogate retroactively, from the time of promulgation, occupation policies, acts, and transactions contrary to the international law of belligerent occupation;
(e) Claims to authority to review and revise or set aside judgments rendered by occupation courts and tribunals.

Restored sovereigns have asserted, in the first place, authority to terminate or to regard as terminated, from the time the occupant's effective control was dissolved by recapture of the territory and restoration of the sovereign, the applicability of the multitude of policies—the most general statutes as well as the most detailed ordinances or regulations—prescribed by an occupant during its possession. This assertion of authority to put an end to the prospective operation of laws, ordinances, and regulations enacted by the expelled occupant was, in World War II, frequently made in the initial proclamations of the returning sovereign. For instance, Proclamation No. 1 issued on August 1, 1945 by the Supreme Allied Commander, South East Asia, upon the reoccupation of Singapore, the Malay States, and adjacent territories, stated:

> 7. It is hereby declared that all Proclamations and legislative enactments of whatever kind issued by or under the authority of the Japanese Military Administration shall cease to have any effect.[102]

Similarly, in Proclamation No. 1 dated September 1, 1945, of the returning British forces in Hongkong, it was provided that

> Article 3. *Existing Law to be Respected*
> Subject to the provisions of any proclamations, enactments, or order of the British Military Administration and in so far as the military exigencies permit,
> (a) All laws existing immediately prior to the Japanese occupation will be respected and administered.
> . . .

102. Donnison, *British Military Administration in the Far East, 1943–46,* Appendix 3 at p. 451 (1956). An identical provision appears in the Proclamation issued by the British forces in British North Borneo on June 10, 1945, id., 453.

> Article 4. *Revocation of Enactments by Japanese Authorities* All proclamations, enactments, orders, and the like issued or made by or with the sanction of any Japanese authority during the period of Japanese occupation are hereby suspended unless and until expressly revived by the authority of the British Military Administration.[103]

Again, on October 23, 1944, the Commander of the United States forces reoccupying the Philippines issued a proclamation which said, *inter alia,*

> 3. That all laws, regulations, and processes of any other government in the Philippines than that of the said Commonwealth are null and void and without legal effect in areas of the Philippines free of enemy occupation and control.[104]

The case of *Baptista v. Castañeda*[105] decided by the Supreme Court of the Philippines affords more specific illustration of the prospective termination of policies promulgated by the occupant. During the Japanese occupation of the Philippines, the occupation government enacted, by the authority and with the approval of the commander-in-chief of the occupying forces, a "New Divorce Law" which repealed the pre-occupation divorce statute and specified many new grounds for divorce. The plaintiff had commenced, during the occupation, proceedings under this "New Divorce Law," invoking one of the newly specified grounds. After the expulsion of the Japanese occupant, the plaintiff sought to continue these proceedings. The case was dismissed, the court holding, without passing upon the competence of the occupation government to enact it, that the "New Divorce Law" was "no longer of any force and effect." [106] It should

103. Id., 454. Cf. Art. 1 of Proclamation No. 2 of 1944 issued by the Chief Civil Affairs Officer of the British armies in Burma; id.

104. 41 *Official Gazette* 784 (Commonwealth of the Philippines, 1945).

105. 76 Phil. 461 (1946).

106. 76 Phil. at 463. *Weiss v. Weiss,* Tribunal d'Arrondissement, Luxembourg, *Annual Digest 1949,* Case No. 173, provides similar illustration. The plaintiff asked the court to apply Luxembourg civil law to the administration of a decedent's estate, while the defendant invoked a rule of German civil law which was introduced by the occupation authorities and in force when the administration began. The court said (at p. 479): "the legal consequences of events which occurred during the occupation are governed by the ordinary law of this

be added that divorces granted under this law, and which had become final before the return of the sovereign, were not disturbed. The restored sovereign may, of course, decide to adopt and continue in operation a particular occupation enactment or regulation which it regards as desirable. In *Sosnowiec Iron Pipes Factory Ltd. v. Ministry of the Interior,*[107] for example, the Supreme Administrative Court of Poland gave effect to a decree of the German occupant declaring the village of Zawiercie to be a borough. A Polish law of 1919 on borough autonomy had listed Zawiercie as a borough. The Court said:

> [W]hile on the whole, it can be conceded that measures taken by occupying authorities should have as few consequences as possible beyond the period of the duration of the occupation, nevertheless this principle cannot be applied entirely without regard to the circumstances of such acts of the occupying authorities as were done in the exercise of ordinary administration; it [the principle] ceases altogether to apply in those cases in which the legitimate authorities do not refuse to accept such measures, but on the contrary consider them desirable and maintain them in force.[108]

More recent illustration is provided by the ordinance issued by the restored legitimate government in France, on October 9, 1945, expressly recognizing as having continuing effect a law enacted by the Vichy government relating to marriage and marital rights and duties.[109] Similarly, Constitutional Act No. 58 of 1945, passed by the restored sovereign in Greece, authorized the Greek cabinet to declare laws of the occupation period to have been promulgated in the interest of the Greek state. Where such a declaration was made, the law involved was to be enforceable even after liberation.[110] In *re G.,*[111] the Criminal Court of Heraklion (Crete) made clear that,

country. German laws then introduced and forcibly imposed lost all validity in this country as the immediate result of the liberation of Luxemburg."

107. *Annual Digest 1925–1926,* Case No. 363.

108. Id., at 476.

109. See Delaume, "Enemy Legislation and Judgments in France," 30 *J. Comp. Leg. Int. L.* 32, 33 (1948).

110. See Zepos, "Enemy Legislation and Judgments in Liberated Greece," 30 id. 27, 31 (1948).

111. *Annual Digest 1943–1945,* Case No. 151. The suggestion is made in a note

where no subsequent declaration of adoption or continuation was made in respect of a particular occupation law, that law was to be deemed to have terminated upon the end of the enemy occupation.

Restored sovereigns have also asserted authority prospectively to terminate certain types of acts or transactions done or entered into under and pursuant to laws and regulations prescribed by the occupant. The principal reference here intended is to transactions between private inhabitants and officials or organs of the occupation government, and which the restored sovereign regards as of a "continuing" nature. Legitimate governments have refused to give effect to claims for the continued enjoyment of benefits arising from such transactions without, however, seeking to undo the effects that had accrued during the occupation. Some illustration is offered by *Banaag v. Encarnacion,*[112] another Philippine case. A lease of public fisheries had been executed in 1943 in favor of the plaintiff by the proper official of the occupation government, acting under an executive order of such government, for a period of five years. In a petition for declaratory judgment brought after reoccupation by United

---

to this case that not all laws enacted by an occupation government automatically cease to have force and effect upon reoccupation: "It is perhaps necessary to distinguish between acts which are of a kind contemplated by Art. 43 of the Hague Regulations and acts which go beyond that category. The former (in so far as they tend to benefit the population and not merely to forward the military objects of the occupant) will, it is submitted, be applied by national courts even after the liberation of the territory. The state restored its full sovereignty will naturally be free to proceed to the modification or repeal of such laws. But meanwhile, the courts are bound to apply them." (at p. 440) None of the countries occupied and liberated during World War II appear to have accepted this view. On the contrary, as indicated above, special legislation by the restored sovereign was deemed necessary to continue in effect such legislative acts of occupation governments as were considered beneficial to the inhabitants.

112. 83 Phil. 325 (1949). The case of the 15,000 oak trees commonly given in the texts—2 Oppenheim-Lauterpacht 619 note 1; Hall, *International Law* s. 163 (8th ed., Pearce Higgins, 1924); Spaight, *War Rights on Land* 367 (1911)—does not seem a wholly satisfactory example since it is doubtful whether the contract for the felling of the trees was within the competence of the occupant in his capacity as usufructuary. On the general formulation essayed above, Spaight, *loc. cit.,* observed that were the restored sovereign obliged to recognize acts of administration executed during the occupation as having continuing prospective effects, a few weeks of occupation may result in the creation of obligations which may prejudice the sovereign for years.

States forces in 1945, the lessee prayed that the contract be declared valid for the entire period of five years, i.e., from 1943 to 1948. The Supreme Court of the Philippines, while holding that fisheries were "real estate" within the meaning of Article 55 of the Hague Regulations authorizing the occupant to act as "administrator and usufructuary" of "real estate" and other immovables belonging to the ousted sovereign, rejected this claim. In the view of the Court, the Japanese occupant, upon whose authority the lease had been executed, had ceased upon the return of the sovereign to be administrator and usufructuary of the fishing grounds involved. The lease was regarded as having expired at the date of the reoccupation of the province where the fisheries were located. Similarly, in *Woo Chan Shi and Pak Chuen Woo v. Brown,*[113] the Supreme Court of Hongkong held that although the appointment in 1943 of the plaintiffs as executors under a decedent's will by a court established under a Japanese occupation ordinance was lawful, this appointment became ineffective from the date of the British reoccupation of Hongkong in 1945. Plaintiffs were, according to the Court, no longer entitled to act as executors from that date forward. It may be observed that in both the Banaag and Woo Chan Shi cases, there was no question as to the competence of the occupant to perform the acts involved—granting a fisheries concession and appointing testamentary executors. Thus, it appears that recognition of the legitimacy, under the law of belligerent occupation, of the occupant's executive and administrative acts and transactions [114] may entail but a limited consequence: that the restored sovereign will not require the parties to retrogress from the value positions already respectively achieved as of the moment of reoccupation.

Both in the First and in the Second World War, restored sover-

113. *Annual Digest 1946,* Case No. 156. But cf. *Chop Sun Cheong Lung v. Lian Teck Trading Co.,* id., *1948,* Case No. 192, where the Supreme Court of the Malayan Union held that a tenancy lawfully created by the Japanese Enemy Property Custodian continued in effect until it was terminated by the original owner of the property after the occupation.

114. *In re* A., *Annual Digest 1943–1945,* Case No. 162, a Greek court suggested that not all acts or transactions lawful under the law of belligerent occupation need be secured from reversal or rescission, but only acts or transactions consummated under legislation of the occupant enacted for the welfare of the inhabitants as distinguished from legislation for the military security of occupation troops.

eigns sometimes ascribed even more severely limited consequences to policies prescribed by occupants and to their executive and administrative actions. Restored sovereigns claimed authority not only to terminate prospectively but also to abrogate retroactively prescriptions and applications of policy by the occupation government. The more comprehensive claims of this type comprised assertions of practically unlimited exclusive competence to concede or deny effect —recognizing or reversing in greater or lesser degree—to value changes that transpired in the occupied community during the period of occupation, under authority of occupation policies.

In Greece, for example, the restored sovereign enacted Constitutional Act No. 4 by which it assumed authority to declare any particular law or regulation promulgated by the occupation governments as amended or annulled even *ex tunc,* i.e., from the moment of their promulgation rather than from the moment of reoccupation. Where any such occupation law or regulation was annulled, the administrative acts and transactions executed thereunder were correspondingly invalidated *ex tunc.*[115] In France, similarly, the restored legitimate government appeared to assert competence to invalidate *ab initio* any specific law or regulation enacted either by the German administration in Alsace-Lorraine and Occupied France, or by the Vichy government. Which laws were to be subjected to retroactive annulment (i.e., from the time of enactment) and which laws to prospective termination (i.e., from the time of the sovereign's restoration) was determined by the legitimate government according to its own notions of public policy.[116] Again, in Luxembourg, the legitimate government undertook to nullify retroactively all legislative measures enacted during the period known as the *Zivilwervaltung* as well as decisions rendered under such measures and acts resulting from such decisions. The parties affected by the decisions annulled were to be reinstated to their status quo before such decisions were rendered.[117]

115. See Zepos, supra note 110 at 30–1.

116. Art. 4, Ordinance of Aug. 9, 1944, text in CCH, *War Law Service, Foreign Supp.,* par. 67,879.04 (1944). See also Delaume, supra note 109 at 33–6.

117. See the Grand Ducal Decree of April 22, 1941, "Determining the Effect of Measures Taken by the Occupier," as amended by the Grand Ducal Decrees of July 13, 1944 and Jan. 15, 1945; text in CCH, *War Law Service, Foreign Supp.* par. 65,430 (1945).

A similar range of competence was claimed by the sovereign in the Netherlands. On September 17, 1944, the Netherlands Government in London enacted a Decree on Occupation Measures (Decree No. 93). This Decree classified the laws and ordinances prescribed by the German occupant into four categories: (a) those to be regarded as never having had any validity whatsoever; (b) those to be regarded as becoming inoperative from the time of liberation or reoccupation; (c) those which, for reasons of expediency, were temporarily to be maintained in force; and (d) all others, the operation of which was provisionally to be suspended pending final decision.[118] The broadness of the competence asserted under this Ordinance is indicated by the fact that, under its terms, the restored sovereign could not only abrogate retroactively occupation policies that a third party observer might reasonably characterize as lawful under the international law of belligerent occupation, but could also attribute *post hoc* force and effect to occupation policies illegal under that law. Thus, in *Kloet v. Klok,*[119] the Supreme Court of the Netherlands ruled that class (b) and class (c) ordinances were to be treated *as if* they had been valid during the period of occupation without regard to their conformity or conflict with the Hague Regulations. It is worth noting that this comprehensive claim to authority was moved precisely by a general policy of stabilizing expectations and easing transition from war to postwar conditions. The report of the Court's decision states:

> Without an authoritative regulation of the chaotic situation it would have been uncertain which measures of the occupant must be deemed to have been legally in force. The unconditional annulment of occupation ordinances with reference to the period of occupation, even if they were invalid, might have led after the liberation to the disruption of economic life.[120]

118. *Bedrijfsgroep Bouw en Aardewerkambackten, The Hague v. Vonck, Annual Digest 1947,* Case No. 114. See also Jansma, "The Dutch Government's Treatment of the Decrees Made by the German Authorities during the Occupation of the Netherlands," 29 *J. Comp. Leg. Int. L.* (Pts. III and IV), 53–4 (1947).

119. *Annual Digest 1947,* p. 252. Compare the decision of the Special Court of Cassation of Holland in *In re* Policeman Balster, *Annual Digest 1946,* Case No. 115.

120. *Annual Digest 1947,* at 252.

In contrast with the above claims to authority for retroactive annulment limited chiefly if not solely by the restored sovereign's conceptions of public policy, claims to the more modest competence retroactively to annul—or to disregard as null and void *ab initio*—occupation policies, acts, and transactions upon the ground of inconsistency with general community authority about belligerent occupation have been made by restored sovereigns with an impressive consistency. With the exception of the Netherlands, as noted above, there appears no instance, to our knowledge, of a restored legitimate government undertaking to honor a legislative occupation measure or executive or administrative act or transaction that it regarded as violative of the law of war. Claims to invalidate unlawful acts of an occupant have been made so frequently as in fact to have given rise to the speculation whether a prescription of customary international law has crystallized that makes it unnecessary for states expressly to declare the invalidity of such acts.[121] In terms of impact upon expectations in the occupied community, policies and applications of policies patently contrary to the law of belligerent occupation can scarcely reasonably be regarded as giving rise to expectations that the restored government will honor them.

Competence to nullify unlawful acts of an occupant has been asserted both in unilateral legislation and judicial decision of returned sovereigns and in multilateral declarations as well as in peace treaties. The Inter-Allied Declaration of January 5, 1943 relating to acts of dispossession committed in Axis-occupied countries is perhaps the best known collective assertion of competence in this regard. The Declaration provided that the parties to it

> reserve all their rights to declare invalid any transfers of, or dealings with, property, rights and interests of any description whatsoever which are, or have been, situated in the territories which have come under the occupation or control, direct or indirect, of the governments with which they are at war or which belong or have belonged, to persons, including juridical persons, resident in such territories. This warning applies whether such transfers or dealings have taken the form of open looting or

121. See Morganstern, "Validity of the Acts of the Belligerent Occupant," 28 *Brit. Y.B.I.L.* 291 (1951).

plunder, or of transactions apparently legal in form, even when they purport to be voluntarily effected.[122]

The authority reserved in the Declaration was eventually exercised in the peace treaties with Italy, Romania, Bulgaria, and Hungary.[123] Each of these states was required to accept the "principles of the United Nations Declaration of January 5, 1943" and to make restitution of identifiable property located in their respective territories which had been "removed by force or duress" from any of the Allied countries.[124]

Annulment of unlawful occupation acts was effected by restored governments after both World War I and II in a vast indeterminate number of court decisions. It perhaps bears particular mention that even Belgian courts, while continuing to invoke the so-called "Belgian doctrine" of the "factual" nature of belligerent occupation, have frequently found it necessary or expedient to relate occupation acts to the law of war in refusing to honor such acts. The "Belgian doctrine," it may be recalled, purports to deny that a belligerent occupant has any "legal power" to enact measures for the occupied territory, or that the Hague Regulations, by establishing rules for the limitation of the naked power of the occupant, bestow any "legal status" upon it.[125] "Sovereignty" being "absolute and indivisible," a "mixed" regime conceding at least some "legal powers" to an occupant is—so an allegedly inexorable logic dictates—impossible. The orders of the occupying power are, Belgian courts have stated, not "laws" but merely "commands of the military authority of the occu-

122. U.S. *Dept. of State Bull.*, Jan. 9, 1943, p. 21.

123. Art. 75, Treaty of Peace with Italy, 49 *U.N. Treaty Series* 157; Art. 23, Treaty of Peace with Romania, 42 id. 50; Art. 24, Treaty of Peace with Hungary, 41 id., 186; Art. 22, Treaty of Peace with Bulgaria, 41 id. 64.

124. Similarly, by Art. 15(a) of the Treaty of Peace with Japan, Japan agreed to "return the property tangible and intangible and all rights or interests of any kind in Japan of each Allied Power and its nationals which was within Japan at any time between December 7, 1941, and September 2, 1945, unless the owner has freely disposed thereof without duress or fraud." Where such property could not be restored or had been damaged as a result of the war, compensation was required. Text in 46 *A.J.I.L. Supp.* 71 (1952).

125. See *Mathot v. Longue*, Court of Appeal of Liège, *Annual Digest 1919–1922*, Case No. 329; and *La Belgique Industrielle v. Masure*, Court of Cassation, *Int. Law Notes*, Sept.–Dec. 1917, p. 170.

pant," which are not "incorporated in the legislation or institutions of the country."[126] This "doctrine," realistically considered, has served as the technical if somewhat idiosyncratic expression of the demand for comprehensive and exclusive discretion in respect of the treatment of occupation acts and transactions. It has not, however, prevented Belgian courts from adducing other grounds—specifically, conflict with the Hague Regulations—to sustain an annulment of such an act or transaction, nor from honoring an act or transaction lawful under the Hague Regulations.

A case decided by the *Cour d'Appel de Liège* on March 21, 1951 provides some illustration.[127] The German occupant requisitioned a building from the plaintiffs and ordered the city of Liège to install a new heating system in the building. A German ordinance required the Belgian state to pay for requisitions made by the occupation army. After the occupation, the plaintiffs sued the city for payment of an indemnity for the house requisitioned. The *Cour d'Appel* reversed a lower court judgment for the plaintiff and held that the lower court, under the "Belgian doctrine," was not authorized to give any effect to the ordinances of the occupant nor to administrative measures implementing such ordinances. At the same time, however, the Court also considered the German ordinance invoked by the plaintiff as void upon the ground that it was inconsistent with Article 52 of the Hague Regulations which, in the view of the Court, required compensation for requisitions to be made by the occupant rather than the occupied country. Another case, *City of Malines v. Société Centrale Pour L'Exploitation du Gaz,*[128] illustrates how, notwithstanding the "Belgian doctrine," a Belgian court may concede effect to a lawful occupation act. The *Société Centrale* sought to recover from the city the cost of gas supplied to it during the German occupation in World War I. The German occupant had passed ordinances providing for an increase in the price of gas and it was this increased price that the *Société Centrale* sued for. The city resisted this demand, maintaining that the decrees of an occupant were invalid under Belgian law (i.e., the "Belgian doctrine"). The Brussels Court of Appeal, in affirming a judgment against the city, held that "circumstances of

126. *Cambier v. Lebrun,* Court of Cassation, *Annual Digest 1919–1922,* Case No. 325.

127. See 1 *A.J. Comp. L.* 119 (1952).

128. *Annual Digest 1925–1926,* Case No. 362.

war-time" including, in particular, the rise in the cost of raw materials and the necessity for providing for the needs of the inhabitants, warranted the occupation measures here in question. These measures were, according to the Court, "within the scope of the administrative acts permitted to the occupying Power by Hague Convention No. IV (Article 43 of the Annexed Regulations) with a view to the maintenance or re-establishment of order and safety," and hence regarded as applicable.[129]

We have, thus far, considered the retroactive annulment of executive and administrative acts of occupation governments taken under and in implementation of legislation enacted by such governments. We turn to claims to review judgments rendered during the occupation by courts established or continued by the occupant. There is observable in this connection a range of variations comparable to that noted with respect to executive and administrative acts, in the scope of competence asserted by differing restored sovereigns to recognize, revise, or repudiate occupation judgments.

Most notable, perhaps, is the treatment of occupation judgments by the restored government in Singapore after World War II. The British Military Administration issued a proclamation providing for the "setting aside of convictions by tribunals exercising jurisdiction during the Japanese occupation of the Settlement of Singapore." This Proclamation was preceded by an Order which quashed the convictions and sentences of persons convicted by *Japanese military tribunals* during the occupation. The combined effect of the Order and the Proclamation was, it appears, to set aside all convictions rendered in criminal cases by all courts functioning in Singapore during the period of occupation by the Japanese. This sweeping rescissive action was impelled by the restored sovereign's apprehensions about the nature of the changes introduced by the occupant in the criminal law procedure employed during the occupation, which changes included, for example, the use of torture by the Japanese military police during the process of interrogation and investigation. Apparently considering it impracticable to scrutinize judgments of conviction one by one and to test the fairness of the procedure followed in each case, the restored sovereign gave the convicted the benefit of

129. See also *Bochart v. Committee of Supplies of Corneaux,* Court of Appeal of Liège, id., 1919–1922, Case No. 327.

the doubt and simply annulled all convictions.[130] Judgments in civil cases obviously required a more discriminating approach. A Japanese Judgments and Civil Proceedings Ordinance enacted in 1946 authorized any person who regarded himself aggrieved by an occupation judgment or decree to apply to the courts, under certain conditions, for an order setting aside such decree or granting leave to appeal therefrom though it had long become final. The grounds specified in the Ordinance for setting aside an occupation judgment were cast in language of such generality as to vest in the Singapore courts very substantial discretion in recognizing or upsetting any particular judgment.[131] In practice, however, the statutory authority to annul seemed to have been used with considerable restraint, being, in general, utilized only where circumstances of unusual injustice or oppression were shown to have attended the rendition of the judgment complained of. Where the complainant had suffered from circumstances of injustice or oppression common to all members of the population, or to a considerable part of it, the loss was left to lie where it first fell. Where, however, a petitioner was able to show that he had sustained an injustice or oppression peculiar to him alone

130. See Note, "Powers and Duties of Enemy Occupant," 12 *Malayan L.J.* 1 (1946). See, further, *Camasura v. Provost Marshal,* 78 Phil. 131 (1947), where the Supreme Court of the Philippines set aside several convictions rendered during the enemy (Japanese) occupation upon the ground that such convictions had rested upon confessions extracted "through duress, intimidation and force" employed by military administration personnel. As will be noted below, however, the restored sovereign in the Philippines did not enact a comprehensive and consistent policy in respect of criminal sentences rendered during the occupation.

131. The grounds set forth in section 3(4) of the Ordinance are:

(a) That it was obtained as a result of such force, injury or detriment to any party to the proceedings or other person, or such threat thereof, as in the opinion of the appropriate court was sufficient to render the action of the party in relation to the proceedings involuntary;

(b) That any necessary party did not appear personally but was represented by any person appointed by any Japanese authority;

(c) That it was based on principles unknown to the existing law;

(d) On any other ground which the appropriate court considers to be sufficient.

As quoted in *Sultan of Johore v. Tungku Abubakar,* 16 *Malayan L.J.* 7 et seq. (1950).

and beyond the general lot of his fellows, he was granted relief.[132]

A similar range of authority to set aside or revise occupation judgments was claimed by the restored Greek Government. The Government could, under Constitutional Law No. 58 noted above, empower its courts to annul or amend, subject to certain conditions, and upon petition of the interested party, judgments handed down during the occupation.[133] In France, the Ordinance of the Provisional Government dated August 9, 1944 classified, it was noted earlier, occupation statutes and ordinances into those regarded as null *ab initio* and those regarded as nullified upon reoccupation. With respect to the first group, the Ordinance further prescribed the nullity of "the effects resulting from their application prior to the [reoccupation]"; with respect to the second, it provided that "[T]he nullity shall not avoid the effects resulting from [their] application prior to the [reoccupation]." [134] In Norway, the assumption of competence by the restored sovereign over occupation judgments was in measure more limited. Convictions in criminal cases were authorized by statute to be reopened upon certain grounds. The most significant of these grounds related to the character of the occupation enactment for the infraction of which the convictions had been rendered, the unlawfulness of such enactment under the international law of belligerent occupation, and its relation to the struggle between the belligerent occupant and the belligerent sovereign.[135]

132. See e.g. *In re* Sethuramaswany 16 *Malayan L.J.* 300, 304 (1950); *Chong Fong Shen v. Chang Phooi Hoong,* 13 id. 104 (1947); and *Cheang Sunny v. Ramanathan Chettiar* [1948] Singapore Law Reports 12.

133. See Zepos, "Enemy Legislation and Judgments in Liberated Greece," 30 *J. Comp. Leg. Int. L.* 27 (1948).

134. See supra note 116.

135. In Norway, the conditions enumerated by the statute for reopening of criminal convictions were:

> (a) If the decision was made directly pursuant to an unlawful (under the Hague Regulations) enactment issued during the occupation, or pursuant to enactments which had as their predominant object to serve the interests of the occupant, except cases where it is apparent that the decision was not affected thereby.
>
> (b) If a member of the Nasjonal Samling (Quisling's Party) or a person guilty of treason took part in the decision as a judge and there is reason to believe that the decision was affected thereby.
>
> (c) If the offense was committed as part of the opposition against the enemy and for that reason must be considered lawful.

The Singapore, Greek, French, and Norwegian statutes may be contrasted with the post-World War II practice in Burma, Indonesia, and the Philippines. The governments restored in the latter countries promulgated no comprehensive legislation on the treatment of occupation judgments. There the courts were left to establish general policies upon this matter. By a kind of common judicial logic, the initial emphasis of the courts of these three countries was upon the legitimacy or illegitimacy of the occupant's act of establishing or restructuring the occupation tribunal whose judgment was called into question. Where the act of establishment or reconstruction was characterized or conceded to be within the scope of authority permitted to the occupant under the law of war, the courts generally tended to ascribe presumptive validity to the judgments of the occupation tribunal and to refrain from rescinding them. It is thus relevant to observe that in these three countries the courts of the restored governments by and large acknowledged a wide competency in the occupant to alter, reorganize, amalgamate, and add to the indigenous court system of an occupied community. The Supreme Court of the Philippines, for instance, held the Japanese occupant competent to set up a "Court of Special and Exclusive Criminal Jurisdiction,"[136] to change the Court of Appeals from a single court with nation-wide territorial jurisdiction to five courts each with regional territorial jurisdiction, and to abolish a number of district courts of first instance.[137] The judgments promulgated during the occupation by these courts, as well as by the pre-occupation courts untouched by the occupant, were generally regarded as valid and not subject to reopening or annulment, save those judgments which were characterizable as being "of a political complexion." The cases where this exception was directly applied suggest that the reference prin-

(d) If the convicted person was prevented by reason of war from appearing or from producing evidence and there is reason to believe that the decision was affected thereby.

(e) If there is reason to believe that the decision was influenced by political considerations.

Stabell, "Enemy Legislation and Judgments in Norway," 31 *J. Comp. Leg. Int. L.* 3, 15 (1949). Civil judgments could also be reopened on the same grounds.

136. See *Peralta v. Director of Prisons,* 75 Phil. 285 (1946); and *People v. Benedicto Jose,* 75 Phil. 612 (1946).

137. *Co Kim Cham v. Valdez,* 75 Phil. 113 (1946); see also *Sameth v. Director of Prisons,* 76 Phil. 613 (1946).

cipally assigned to it was the relation of the law in question to the security and belligerent interests of the occupant. Thus, convictions for adultery,[138] or for illegal discharge of firearms at a fellow inhabitant,[139] for example, were held not to be "of a political complexion." Where a judgment was found to be "of a political complexion," its effect was deemed to have ceased upon termination of the occupation and the convicted person absolved from further service of sentence.

Similarly, the Court of Appeals of Batavia held the occupant authorized to alter the organization of local courts in occupied Netherlands East Indies. Among the changes made was the abolition of the *Raad von Justitie* which had jurisdiction over Europeans, Chinese, and other "foreign Easterners," and of the *Land Raad* with jurisdiction over native Indonesians. In their stead, the occupant created a *Tihoo Hooin* empowered to deal with persons of all nationalities except Japanese subjects. The judicial acts of the occupant were generally recognized as valid and effective "in so far as they had been performed in the interests of the continuity of legal order" and provided they were not "of a pronounced political character." The restructuring was disregarded as relating merely to "matters of judicial procedure," and the civil judgments of the *Tihoo Hooin* upheld as binding.[140]

In Burma, the High Court of Judicature ruled that the Japanese occupant did not exceed his power under the Hague Regulations in establishing the "Rangoon City Court." [141] The judgments of this

138. See *Herrero and Crisostomo v. Diaz,* 75 Phil. 489 (1946).

139. *Alcantara v. Director of Prisons,* 75 Phil. 494 (1946). Cf. *Indac v. Director of Prisons,* 77 Phil. 698 (1946) which concerned a petition for habeas corpus on behalf of a person convicted during the occupation for theft against the Japanese occupation forces. Respecting the assertion that the offense was "tinged with political color," the Supreme Court said: "The mere fact that the stolen goods belonged to the Japanese army does not, in the eyes of the law, excuse the deed, specially if the thief committed the act for his own personal benefit—not in pursuance of the resistance movement. . . . While it is true that the petition calls the prisoner's offense as 'sabotage,' however, it makes no assertion that it was performed in pursuance of guerrilla activities or in pursuance of the underground plans." 77 Phil. at 700.

140. *Mr. P. v. Mr. S.,* Netherlands East Indies, Court of Appeals, Batavia, *Annual Digest 1947,* Case No. 118. The editor, in a note on this case, doubts whether the alterations, which "in fact amounted to the overthrow of the entire judicial system of Indonesia," could stand the test of international legality.

141. See *Maung Hla Maung v. Ko Maung Maung* [1947] Rangoon Law Reports 1.

Court, both civil and criminal, were held enforceable after reoccupation by the Burmese court which would have been seized of the particular cases but for the creation of this new court.[142] In the same way, the Supreme Court established by the occupant in place of the original High Court of Judicature was held to have been duly constituted and its decisions binding after termination of the occupation. The High Court of Judicature re-established by the sovereign went so far as to say it was the "successor" of the occupation Supreme Court.[143] A simple, undifferentiated policy of recognition of occupation judgments was, it appeared, adopted. One finds no mention of the "acts-of-a-political-complexion" qualification.

Under this qualification, occupation judgments may be terminated in their effects, or reopened and revised, where the policies applied, although falling within the scope of authority conceded to the occupant, were so closely related to the belligerent effort of the occupant as to assume a "political complexion." This qualification could in all probability have served as a functional equivalent of the principal statutory grounds for nonrecognition and revision which were noted above.[144] Yet, clearly, the restored governments in Burma, Indonesia, and the Philippines paid in general more deference to judgments of occupation courts than did the legitimate sovereigns in France, Greece, Norway, and Singapore. It is a matter for speculation to what extent courts of the first three countries felt compelled to do so by what they may have conceived to be the dictates of juridical logic. Even so, the suggestion may be made that although an occupant is required by international law to maintain the local courts and is authorized in appropriate circumstances to change the local court system or to establish new tribunals, it does not necessarily follow that international law requires the restored sovereign indiscriminately to honor the judgments of these courts.[145] The

142. See *Abdul Aziz v. Sooratea Bara Bazaar Co., Ltd.* [1947] Rangoon Law Reports 18.

143. *U San Wa v. U Ba Thin* [1947] Rangoon Law Reports 80. See also Maung, "Enemy Legislation and Judgments in Burma," 30 *J. Comp. Leg. Int. L.* 11 (1948).

144. Supra, notes 131 and 135.

145. Contrast the view urged in Wolff, "Municipal Courts of Justice in Enemy Occupied Territory," 29 *Tr. Grotius Soc.* 99, 115 (1943), that the restored legitimate government may do anything it thinks fit with occupation judgments, e.g., void judgments though no violation of international law intervened, and confirm judgments which were attended by such a violation.

kinds of considerations that may reasonably be regarded as bearing upon sophisticated scrutiny of particular occupation judgments include, in addition to the factors of relation to the war effort of the expelled occupant and of concordance with the international law of war noted earlier, the degree of conformity to minimum international standards of procedural due process. The conditions which commonly attended enemy military occupation during the last world war were, notoriously, often unpropitious for the fair and impartial administration of justice.

CLAIMS RELATING TO THE CONTROL OF INHABITANTS: THE POLICING OF OCCUPIED TERRITORY

We turn to the second broad group of claims characteristically made in the stage of belligerent occupation. The occupant asserts authority to prescribe regulations for the protection of its forces and the military installations, supply and communication lines maintained and utilized by such forces. Integral with this assertion is the claim to subject the inhabitants to deprivations for breaching these security regulations and engaging in enterprises hostile to the occupant. A second kind of claim that occupants frequently make is to requisition the services of inhabitants for differing purposes that promote in varying degrees the interests of occupants. The inhabitants, for their part, demand restraint from the occupant in the policing of occupied territory and, in more particular, a reasonable respect for their lives, well-being, loyalties, familial and religious rights, and so on.

The contrapuntal nature of these assertions by occupant and inhabitants is stressed in common formulations about reciprocal duties of occupant and inhabitants. The Hague Regulations, from sheer necessity of preventing anarchy and chaos, impose—as we have noted—a duty upon the belligerent occupant to restore and ensure public order and civic life; the occupant, consequently, is generally regarded as possessing administrative authority over the occupied territory. Correspondingly, it is said, the inhabitants owe to the occupant a duty to comply with its commands, a duty of quiescence and of abstention from acts which might endanger the occupant's military security or prospects of victory.[146] Reciprocity has been a principal emphasis in these formulations. Thus, it has been said that where the occupant violates the duties imposed upon it by the law of war, the inhabitants are released from their obligation of obedience; [147] and that, conversely, inhabitants by disregard of that duty forfeit their claim to considerate treatment by the occupant.[148]

An impressive amount of learning has been expended in the effort to determine the "true nature" and the "juridical basis" of the inhabitant's duty of obedience. Some writers base this duty on international law,[149] upon the theory that if international law requires the occupant to maintain an orderly government, that same law must at the same time oblige the inhabitants to submit to the occupant's lawful ordinances. In the postulations of other commentators, this duty is grounded upon the municipal law of the occupied country into which the Hague Regulations have been transformed or incorporated, such incorporation being fictionalized as advance assent of the sovereign to occupation measures conforming to those Regulations.[150] The municipal law of the occupying state has also been put

146. See Spaight, *War Rights on Land* 323 (1911); 3 Hyde, *International Law* 1898–9 (2nd rev. ed., 1945); *British Manual of Military Law,* Pt. III, pars. 544 and 552 (1958); Dept. of the Army, *Law of Land Warfare* par. 432 (FM27-10, 1956); and Greenspan, *The Modern Law of Land Warfare* 264–6 (1959).

147. This suggestion is found in e.g., *In re* Heinemann, Special Criminal Court of Arnheim, Netherlands, *Annual Digest 1946,* Case No. 169; "Trial of Rauter," 14 *War Crimes Reports* at 129, 134–5 (1949) and Hammer and Salvin, "The Taking of Hostages in Theory and Practice," 38 *A.J.I.L.* 20, 27 (1944). Cf. Brand, "The War Crimes Trials and the Laws of War," 26 *Brit. Y.B.I.L.* 414, 427 (1949).

148. Spaight, supra note 146 at 323; see also note by Judge Lauterpacht in 2 Oppenheim-Lauterpacht 439.

149. See the citations collected supra note 146; see also Bordwell, *Law of War Between Belligerents* 299–302 (1908); and Oppenheim, "The Legal Relations between an Occupying Power and the Inhabitant," 33 *L.Q. Rev.* 363 (1917). Citations to continental writers of the same persuasion are offered in Baxter, "The Duty of Obedience to the Belligerent Occupant," 27 *Brit. Y.B.I.L.* 235, 240 (1950). Contrast Hall, *International Law* s. 159 (8th ed., Pearce Higgins, 1924) who wrote that the occupant's authority does not imply a correlative duty of obedience on the part of inhabitants any more than the right to attack and destroy an enemy obliges the latter to submit to such attack.

150. See the decision of the Belgian Court of Cassation of May 18, 1917, in 1 *Int. Law Notes* 136–8. Baxter, supra note 149 at 242 marshals the writers embracing this view.

forward as a possible basis, on a theory of delegation from the metropolitan legislative authorities of the occupying belligerent to its organ, the occupation administration.[151] It has even been suggested by Professor Stone, in ingenious *tour de force,* that the duty of obedience may be regarded as simultaneously rooted in a trinity of legal systems—international law, the municipal law of the occupant, and the municipal law of the occupied state.[152] The other extreme position consists of a forthright denial of the "legal" nature of that duty and an insistence that it rests simply on the occupant's naked military power and ability to coerce compliance.[153]

It is difficult to resist the impression that the disputations upon this matter have been more metaphysical than consequential in character. There appears room for the view that the controversy principally concerns varying technical verbalizations, cryptic in greater or lesser measure, of the same relevant policies, and that on the level of fact-situations, claims, community policies, and possible alternatives of decision, it is of but doubtful moment whether the "legal nature" of the duty of obedience be affirmed or denied, and if affirmed, what its "true juristic basis" is. With respect to the preliminary matter of terminology, all the modern writers speak of "obedience," not of "allegiance" or of "temporary allegiance," [154] a usage logically dictated by the occupant-sovereign distinction pervading the law on occupation. When considered as "autonomous" entities, however, these terms can of course afford only negligible criteria for determination of the specific measures to which the occupant may, conformably with community authority, compel submission.

151. Stone, *Legal Controls of International Conflict* 723 (2nd ed., 1959).

152. Id., 724.

153. Among the more recent assertions of this type are Baxter, supra note 149 at 243–4 and Von Glahn, *The Occupation of Enemy Territory* 45 (1957). See also 2 Cobbett, *Cases on International Law* 169 (5th ed., Walker, 1951) where the statement is made that since the occupant's "right of supreme control" rests on "avowed force," it does not carry with it any duty of obedience on the part of inhabitants "except such as may be dictated by prudence."

154. The doctrine of "temporary allegiance" was first formulated in *U.S. v. Hayward* 2 Gall. 485 (1815), reiterated in *U.S. v. Rice* 4 Wheat. 246 (1819), slightly qualified in *Shanks v. Dupont* 3 Pet. 242 (1830). It is not adhered to by any modern publicist today. The doctrine, together with its corollary, the suspension of allegiance to the sovereign, was resurrected by defense counsel in treason cases in the Philippines after the last war. The Supreme Court of the Philippines explicitly rejected them in *Laurel v. Misa* 77 Phil. 856 (1947).

The policies at stake in this confrontation of occupant and inhabitants relate, as indicated earlier, to the shared interest of belligerents in authority to protect their military security interests in territory captured by their arms, and to the equally inclusive interest of belligerents (which may on other occasions have to accept the role of ousted sovereign) in minimizing the destruction of values entailed by the enforcement of the occupant's security interests. The substantial monopoly of effective power which the occupant wields in the occupied territory creates, we also observed above, well-founded expectations on the part of the inhabitants that the security ordinances and regulations prescribed by the occupant will be enforced. Where, notwithstanding these expectations, the inhabitants singly or collectively commit open or surreptitious hostile acts, the occupant will of course visit punishment upon them. The fact that the inhabitants in engaging in such hostilities may have felt impelled by their identifications with and loyalties to the absent sovereign can make little difference so far as concerns deleterious impact upon the occupant's security. Indeed, ideological motivations may signal intensified danger for the occupant; such motivations may frequently be expected to weaken and perhaps nullify the deterrent value of threatened punishment. In inflicting such punishment, the occupant may find it difficult nicely to discriminate between the innocent and the guilty. Here, the countervailing policy of reducing the destruction of values acquires pointed relevancy. It may be well to observe that restraint and discrimination in the policing of occupied territory serve both military security and humanitarian purposes. Savage and ruthless repression may, instead of intimidating and paralyzing the inhabitants, generate a will to fight back with equal ferocity. Fair though firm treatment should, on the other hand, frequently permit economy in the amount of force that would otherwise be necessary to police the territory.

For an observer who recognizes these contrapuntal policies, inquiry would seem most meaningfully directed, not so much to an unusually occult "juridical basis" of a duty of obedience on the part of inhabitants, but rather to the appropriate accommodation in particular situations of the security interests of the occupant and the human rights of inhabitants. It is principally in the context of a war crimes trial that authoritative decision-makers have occasion to pass upon the claim of an occupant and the demands of inhabitants and to seek a viable equilibrium between their competing requirements. Considered in operational terms, the empirical question would seem to be: What deprivational measures imposed by occupation forces upon inhabitants, in deterrence and punishment of what hostile acts, have been declared by authoritative decision-makers to constitute war crimes? From such viewpoint, the conception of a reciprocal duty of obedience may be regarded as marking one traditional line of compromise between the policies at stake in the regulation of the control of people in occupied territory. To speak of a "legal duty of obedience" appears but a shorthand way of saying that reviewing decision-makers have refrained from imposing criminal responsibility upon members of occupation forces for responding to certain acts of inhabitants by inflicting certain deprivations upon such inhabitants.[155] Verbally to characterize this duty of obedience as purely "factual" neither provides relevant specification nor dissolves the policy problem involved. Moreover, to state that international law "permits an occupant to prohibit and punish but does not itself prohibit" hostile acts of inhabitants,[156] is to assert an exceedingly refined distinction that affords little operational criteria for decision-makers and no protection for the inhabitants. To distinguish between a prohibition of hostile acts by inhabitants and an authorization to the occupant to punish such acts may be expressive of patriotic assumptions; so far, however, as the scope of competence accorded the occupant is concerned, the distinction would seem largely beside the point.

The concepts of "war treason" and "war rebellion" appear in measure to be corollaries of the conception of a "legal duty of obedi-

155. It does not seem inappropriate to observe that even those who assert the merely "factual" character of the *duty* of obedience and a "right to resist" the occupant, do not deny that the occupant may legitimately respond to hostile acts with punitive action. In "The Trial of Rauter," 14 *War Crimes Reports* at 127–8 (1949) the Netherlands Special Court of Cassation, while declaring that the inhabitants are "neither ethically nor juridically obliged to obey" the occupant's regulations, acknowledged that "in general, countermeasures (against acts of resistance) *within the limits set by international law* may be taken (by the occupant) against them *with impunity*." (Italics supplied.) For the rulings of various war crimes tribunals to the effect an occupant is entitled to protect itself from guerrilla fighters and that punishment inflicted on guerrillas does not necessarily subject the occupant to liability for a war crime, see Ch. 6, supra p. 548–57.

156. As Baxter, supra note 149 at 266 and Stone, *Legal Controls of International Conflict* 726 (2nd ed., 1959) do.

ence." The term "war treason" was generally taken to cover the commission of all hostile acts, save hostilities in arms and espionage, by the civil population or persons not members of the regular armed forces of a belligerent.[157] "War rebellion" was used to refer to armed violence undertaken by inhabitants of the occupied territory as a group as distinguished from, on the one hand, a *levy en masse* in the face of an invading enemy, and on the other, from isolated and unorganized acts of hostility or sabotage.[158] Objection to the continued use of these terms has been made on the ground that they impart misleading municipal law connotations and may induce excessive harshness on the part of the occupant in punishing the acts involved.[159] Guerrilla warfare, resistance, and sabotage have been put forward as more modern substitutes.[160] Again, the matter seems largely one of legal aesthetics; it might be doubted whether the use of the latter rather than the former set of terms is likely to have substantial mitigating influence upon the behavior of occupants. Still, little objection can be urged against predilections in terminology so long as the important points are kept in mind: that belligerent occupants may punish hostile acts however they may be designated, and that to the extent occupants, in so doing, comply with the limitative requirements of general community authority, reviewing decision-makers have not condemned occupying troops as war criminals. The techniques of guerrilla warfare and sabotage have been developed, we noted before, into effective methods of combat, and the probabilities seem high that they will be utilized in future wars that involve land forces. In corresponding measure, however, occupants may be expected to be even more concerned with the protection of their security and perhaps more apt to resort to harsh deterrent

157. See e.g., Oppenheim, "On War Treason," 33 *L.Q. Rev.* 266, 283–4 (1917); Spaight, *War Rights on Land* 333–5 (1911); and Fenwick, *International Law* 573–4 (3rd ed., 1948).

158. 2 Oppenheim-Lauterpacht 258.

159. Baxter, "The Duty of Obedience to the Belligerent Occupant," 27 *Brit. Y.B.I.L.* 235, 261–2 (1950). Professor Baxter's efforts bore fruit when the old U.S. War Dept., *Rules of Land Warfare* (FM27-10, 1940) and the old *British Manual of Military Law* (1929) *Amendments No. 12* (1936) were revised. The references to "war treason" and "war rebellion" in the two manuals (pars. 349–50 of the U.S. manual and pars. 166–7, 444 of the British manual) no longer appear in the present revised manuals.

160. Baxter, supra note 159 at 264.

measures. If re-examination is required, it is re-examination of the location of points of equilibrium between the complementary policies outlined above. Changes in terminology alone do not seem likely to bring about great progress in such a re-examination.

The Geneva Civilians Convention, while it did not substantially alter the traditional position on guerrilla warfare and sabotage in occupied territory,[161] does project striking and severe limitations on the occupant's authority with respect to the policing of the area. Article 33 of this Convention provides:

> No protected person may be punished for an offense he or she has not personally committed. Collective penalties and likewise all measures of intimidation or of terrorism are prohibited.
>
> Pillage is prohibited.
>
> Reprisals against protected persons and their property are prohibited.

And Article 34:

> The taking of hostages is prohibited.

The prohibition of pillage in the second paragraph of Article 33 is of course a reiteration of the rule of Article 47 of the Hague Regulations. The first paragraph of Article 33, however, is a substantial departure from the Hague Regulations, Article 50 of which provided that:

> No general penalty, pecuniary or otherwise, shall be inflicted upon the population on account of the acts of individuals for which they cannot be regarded as jointly and severally responsible.

The inference drawn by belligerent occupants and commentators was that collective penalties were permissible for acts for which the community could be regarded as "jointly and severally" responsible.[162] This article, which provided no specification of the elements of communal responsibility, was in practice interpreted as conceding to the occupant very wide discretion in imposing collective punish-

161. Supra, p. 553.

162. Among others, 3 Hyde, *International Law* 1889 (2nd rev. ed., 1945); Spaight, *War Rights on Land* 408–9 (1911); and 2 Garner, *International Law and the World War* 156–7 (1920) drew the above inference.

ment. The Civilians Convention seeks to escape the problem of determining collective responsibility by establishing a blanket prohibition of vicarious penalties.

The immunity of inhabitants and their property from reprisals, contemplated in the third paragraph of Article 33 of the Civilians Convention, represents an innovation in previously accepted authority. In prior consensus,[163] Article 50 of the Hague Regulations, quoted above, was not regarded as precluding the legitimacy of claims to resort to reprisals against the general population for hostile acts of individual members thereof and for which no collective responsibility (however determined) could be ascribed to the general population. There is little reason to doubt that the removal of inhabitants of occupied territory from the category of permissible reprisal targets was in response to the surpassing excesses perpetrated by Germany in the last world war in ostensible invocation of reprisals.[164] The comprehensive prohibition of reprisals is obviously humanitarian in inspiration; the realism of the prohibition is less certain. The permissible area of self-help having thus been considerably restricted, even an occupant with a tradition of law-observance may at times find great difficulty in securing the protection of its forces. In any calculation of the realistic prospects of observance of this projected immunization from reprisals, account may appropriately be taken of the fact that respect for the human rights of inhabitants tends to vary directly with the ability of the occupant to maintain his security interests in the occupied area.[165]

The prohibition of the taking, and *a fortiori* the killing, of hostages is another important limitation upon the occupant's "police power." A distinction is sometimes drawn between hostages taken

163. The consensus is recorded in 2 Oppenheim-Lauterpacht 565 and JAG's School, *Law of Belligerent Occupation* 115–16 (1944).

164. A convenient summary is Hammer and Salvin, "The Taking of Hostages in Theory and Practice," 38 *A.J.I.L.* 20 (1944).

165. Apprehension that the Civilians Convention may have failed to consider this factor and thus fallen short of a realistic estimate of future practice has been voiced more than once: Albrecht, "War Reprisals in the War Crimes Trials and the Geneva Conventions of 1949," 47 *A.J.I.L.* 590, 613–14 (1953); Gutteridge, "The Rights and Obligations of an Occupying Power," 6 *Y.B. of World Affairs* 149, 169 (1952); Gutteridge, "The Protection of Civilians in Occupied Territory," 5 id. 290, 306–8 (1951); and Krafft, "The Present Position of the Red Cross Geneva Conventions," 37 *Tr. Grotius Soc.* 131, 146 (1951).

to guarantee the peaceable conduct of the inhabitants in the future, and individuals, so-called "reprisal prisoners," taken from the civil population to be killed in retaliation for hostile acts committed by unknown persons within the occupied area.[166] Reprisals, like hostage-taking, are designed to deter future acts of hostility; in practice, the difference relates merely to the time the individuals are taken, hostages being taken before, and "reprisal prisoners" after, the commission of a hostile act. Prior to the Geneva Conference in 1949, the taking of hostages was widely conceded to be a legitimate security measure under customary international law.[167] Their punishment or killing after the acts sought to be deterred were nevertheless committed was more doubtful,[168] although it is not easy to see what useful purpose could be served by permitting the taking of hostages if no deprivations may lawfully be imposed upon them in any case. Article 6(b) of the Charter of the International Military Tribunal at Nuremberg specified the killing of hostages as a war crime, as did also Allied Control Council Law No. 10 and the Australian, French, Dutch, and Chinese war crimes legislation.[169] The United States Military Tribunal in the Hostages case, however, held that under certain restrictive conditions and subject to extensive safeguards, hostages could lawfully be taken and, after a judicial determination that all preconditions had been strictly complied with, and as a remedy of the

166. See "Trial of List," 8 *War Crimes Reports* at 61, 63 (1948).

167. Such concession was by no means limited to German writers. Thus, e.g.: Hammer and Salvin, supra note 164 at 29; JAG's School, *Law of Belligerent Occupation* 121 (1944); War Dept., *Rules of Land Warfare,* pars. 358d and 359 (FM27-10, 1940); *British Manual of Military Law* (1929) *Amendments No. 12,* par. 464 (1936). Spaight, *War Rights on Land* 464–70 (1911) summarizes the relevant practice from the American Civil War up to just before World War I; 1 Garner, *International Law and the World War,* c. 15 (1920) describes German practice during World War I.

168. Lord Wright, "The Killing of Hostages as a War Crime," 25 *Brit. Y.B.I.L.* 296 (1948) and Kuhn, "The Execution of Hostages," 36 *A.J.I.L.* 271 (1942) vigorously denied that they could lawfully be executed. 3 Hyde, *International Law* 1902–3 (2nd rev. ed., 1945) took an inconclusive position.

169. Art. II, par. 1(b), Control Council Law No. 10, text in Taylor, *Final Report to the Secretary of the Army on the Nuremberg War Crimes Trials Under Control Council Law No. 10* 250 (1949). For the Australian Law, see 5 *War Crimes Reports* at 95; French, 3 id. 52; Netherlands, 11 id. 92–3; Chinese, 14 id. at 153.

very last resort, they could be sentenced to death.[170] The Civilians Convention now puts the matter of competence at rest, again as a response to the sanguinary practices of recent occupants too well known to need description.[171] In Article 28, the same Convention also forbids the use of inhabitants to immunize certain points and areas from enemy attack. The realism of the comprehensive new prescription has, however, yet to be demonstrated.

The Civilians Convention has thus diminished the police authority of the occupant by taking away previously acknowledged competences respecting vicarious penalties and hostages. To make up for this reduction of authority, however, the Convention empowers the occupant when it "considers it necessary, for imperative reasons of security, to take safety measures concerning [inhabitants]," to subject such inhabitants to "assigned residence or to internment." [172] Although the term is scrupulously avoided in the Convention, internment seems likely to evoke, in many minds, recollection of that terrible instrument of slavery and extermination—the concentration camp. The Convention seeks to prevent the re-creation of this infamous institution in two ways. Firstly, it requires subjection to internment—where internment is not a penalty for a security offense imposed by judicial sentence [173]—to be made according to a regular procedure that is conformable to the provisions of the Convention and that includes both a right to appeal and the automatic periodic review ["if possible every six months"] of decisions to intern. Secondly, the treatment of internees is regulated by the Convention with great specificity. Regulations, almost as numerous and minutely

170. "Trial of List," 8 *War Crimes Reports* 61–6 (1948). The requirements and conditions which the tribunal declared must be complied with are enumerated in id. 78–9.

171. For accounts of these practices, see Inter-Allied Information Committee, *The Axis System of Hostages* (Conditions in Occupied Territories, No. 1, 1941); Polish Ministry of Information, *The Black Book of Poland,* 92 et seq. (1942); Polish Ministry of Foreign Affairs, *German Occupation of Poland: Polish White Book,* 206 et seq. (1942).

172. Art. 78, Geneva Civilians Convention.

173. Under Art. 68, id., the penalty for a security offense "which does not constitute an attempt on the life or limb of members of the occupying forces or administration, nor a grave collective danger, nor seriously damage the property of occupying forces or administration or the installations used by them," may be either internment or simple imprisonment.

detailed as those governing the treatment of prisoners of war, are prescribed with respect to the place of internment, the feeding and clothing of internees, their hygienic and medical needs, their religious, intellectual and physical activities, their property and financial resources, the government of the internment camp, the internees' "relations with the exterior" [the Protecting Power and the state of their nationality], and, finally, their release and repatriation.[174] Future experience may prove that this authority to intern is ample and adequate for protecting the security interests of the occupant. It may, however, not be inappropriate to note that subjection to internment, like the imposition of collective penalties and the taking of hostages, is designed to be a preventive or prophylactic measure and as such addresses itself to innocent inhabitants. Neither the actual commission of a hostile act against the occupant nor the judicial determination of such commission is made a condition for internment.

Of potentially greater importance than the prohibitions of vicarious penalties, hostage-taking, and the authority to intern are the minimum international standards established by the Civilians Convention for the administration of criminal justice by tribunals of the occupant. Articles 65 to 77 constitute a rough and ready code of criminal law and procedure applicable in case of alleged violations of the security legislation of the occupant. Their substance is that protected persons are to be tried by the occupant's "properly constituted, non-political, military courts," and are entitled to a fair trial, with adequate procedural safeguards to ensure them full opportunity of defending themselves. The procedural rights of an accused inhabitant specified in Articles 71 to 75 include: written notice of charges, speedy trial, aid of counsel and interpreters, the right to present evidence and call witnesses, notification to the Protecting Power and the presence of its representatives at the trial, the rights of appeal where provided for in the law of the tribunal and of petition for pardon or reprieve in case of death sentences, and the suspension of death sentences until after notification to the Protecting Power and after opportunity for the latter to make representations to the occupant. Articles 67 to 69 regulate the penalties that may be imposed. Proportionality between the penalty and the offense is required. The occupant's courts are particularly enjoined to take

174. Arts. 79–135, id.

into consideration "the fact that the accused is not a national of the Occupying Power." [175] The permissible penalties are limited to internment, imprisonment, and death. Death may be imposed only in cases of conviction for espionage, serious acts of sabotage against military installations, and intentional offenses which caused the death of one or more persons, provided that "such offenses [were] punishable by death under the law of the occupied territory in force before the occupation began," and the accused was over 18 years of age at the time of the offense.[176] In the case of other offenses, the death penalty is outlawed and only imprisonment or internment may be lawfully imposed. In cases of imprisonment, the period of preventive detention prior to trial or punishment is to be deducted from the final sentence imposed. Article 76 prescribes with respect to the conditions of preventive detention of accused persons that these shall be "at least equal to those obtaining in prisons of the occupied country," and that special provision be made for women and minors.

These standards, which may seem commonplace in mature democratic polities, were, again, formulated in reaction to the summary and often primitively cruel procedures employed by German and Japanese occupation administrations in the last world war. They may, however, become difficult of application where the criminal law procedures prevailing in the occupant's own territorial domain do not themselves effectively embody these standards. Expectations that an occupant will respect demands of captured enemies which it denies to its own people at home are scarcely realistic.

Particular mention may also be made of Article 5, paragraph 2, which provides that in cases involving "absolute military security,"

175. Art. 67, id.

176. Art. 68, id. The quoted proviso met strong objection, and finally a reservation, on signature of the Convention, on the part of the United States and the United Kingdom, upon the grounds that it is absolutely necessary in occupied territory to be able to use the death penalty as deterrent against serious threats to the security of the occupant's forces and that a country in danger of occupation in any future war would be likely to abolish capital punishment solely to avoid its application during such occupation. It was the votes of countries which had suffered occupation by the Axis Powers in the last war, and those which had abolished death as a penalty, that kept this article. See Gutteridge, "The Geneva Conventions of 1949," 26 *Brit. Y.B.I.L.* 294, 324 (1949); Yingling and Ginnane, "The Geneva Conventions of 1949," 46 *A.J.I.L.* 393, 424 (1952).

a person "detained" as a spy or saboteur or one "under definite suspicion" of hostile activity may be regarded as having forfeited "rights of communication." The third paragraph of this same article is in need of clarification as its wording appears open to the interpretation that suspected persons may be legitimately denied trial; it provides that ". . . such persons shall nevertheless be treated with humanity, and *in case of trial,* shall not be deprived of the rights of fair and regular trial . . ."

A second type of claim occupants commonly make with respect to the control of inhabitants concerns the utilization of the manpower of the territory occupied. Occupants assert authority to harness the labor and services of inhabitants for a variety of enterprises that relate to the securing of the occupant's belligerent interests. The spectrum of possible degrees of relation to the belligerent interests of of an occupant is clearly a wide one. At one end of the spectrum lies active combatancy and participation in the armed services of the occupant. Article 51 of the Geneva Civilians Convention unequivocally forbids the impressment of inhabitants into the occupant's armed or auxiliary forces, as well as "pressure or propaganda" designed to secure the "voluntary enlistment" of inhabitants in such forces. This prohibition is but the most obvious expression of the broad principle requiring the occupant, a precarious possessor, to respect the loyalties of the inhabitants to the absent sovereign. Other component expressions include the prohibitions against compelling inhabitants to swear allegiance to the occupant [177] and against the coercive extraction from inhabitants of intelligence concerning the forces of the opposing belligerent, that is, the absent sovereign.[178] In the last world war, it may be recalled, the German laws on compulsory military service were extended to Alsace-Lorraine (after voluntary recruitment had failed) and to the Polish provinces unlawfully incorporated into the Reich.[179] In Yugoslavia the occupant,

177. Art. 45, Hague Regulations. This prohibition was violated when, for example, the German Governor-General of Poland issued a decree requiring from Polish citizens in the public service an oath which in part ran: "I do not consider myself bound by the oath of loyalty, nor any other service obligation I have contracted in relation to the former Polish State and its organs." *The Black Book of Poland,* supra note 171 at 534.

178. Art. 44, Hague Regulations.

179. See *In re* Wagner, Permanent Military Tribunal, France, *Annual Digest 1946,* Case No. 165; *The Black Book of Poland,* supra note 171 at 526–7.

acting through the "puppet" Croatian government, conscripted inhabitants for German-organized and German-officered Croat divisions which were made part of the *Wehrmacht*.[180]

At the other end of the spectrum are labor requisitions necessary for the maintenance and operation of the ordinary social and economic processes of the occupied country. Thus, Article 51 of the Civilians Convention just as explicitly authorizes the occupant to requisition the labor of inhabitants "for the public utility services, or for the feeding, sheltering, clothing, transportation or health of the population of the occupied country." [181] Realistically, of course, compulsory labor in these enterprises is not completely without relation to the belligerent interests of the occupant. By enabling the occupant to maintain an orderly administration in the occupied territory, and to prevent famine and epidemic and the disruption and paralysis of essential welfare services, such labor requisitions substantially assist the occupant in protecting its belligerent interests. Being indispensable, however, to the continuation of *vie publique* in the captured community, authority to make them is conceded to the occupant.

Between these two extremes may be located an indeterminate number of activities and enterprises related in many differing measures to the securing of the occupant's belligerent interests. The appraisal of any particular assertion of authority to requisition inhabitant labor for a particular activity or enterprise requires, once more, a balancing and accommodation of the complementary policies of military security and effectiveness and of minimum destruction of values (including, more specifically, the loyalties of inhabitants) in the detailed context in which the assertion is made. On the one hand, the cited Article 51 permits the occupant to exact from the inhabitants services which are necessary "for the needs of the army of occupation"; on the other hand, the same article forbids the coercing of inhabitants "to undertake any work which would involve them in the obligation of taking part in military operations." The needs of a modern army are clearly legion and embrace much more than the guns and ammunition the occupation troops may bear and the victuals they may consume. A latitudinarian interpretation of "needs,"

180. See "Trial of List," 8 *War Crimes Reports* at 73–4 (1948).

181. Dept. of the Army, *Law of Land Warfare,* par. 419 (FM27-10, 1956) offers an extended enumeration of permissible requisitions of services.

however, may reduce the contraposed policy of respect for inhabitants' loyalties to nonexistence. The distinction which commentators have put forward between "military preparations" and "military [combat] operations," [182] and between services which "directly and distinctly" promote war operations and services which amount merely to an "indirect participation" therein,[183] while constituting cryptic recognition of the necessity for compromising relevant policies, would seem to be difficult of application and to offer only illusory limitation upon the occupant's authority.

The line of compromise achieved in differing contexts has obviously been a moving one. Weighting heavily their own interests, belligerent occupants have not uncommonly engaged in the coercive harnessing of inhabitant labor to the construction of military roads, bridges, fortifications, and other defense works. In contrast, restored sovereigns have, in differing types of controversies, stated that the occupant is unauthorized to requisition services for the construction of coastal defenses,[184] of gun turrets, and of hangars at military airports.[185] The International Military Tribunal at Nuremberg appears

182. The distinction is made in, e.g., 2 Oppenheim-Lauterpacht 440, and Stone, *Legal Controls of International Conflict* 710 (2nd ed., 1959). The term "military operations" used by the Civilians Convention of 1949 had previously been used in the Hague Convention of 1899 (Art. 44), in the Oxford Code of 1880 (Art. 48) and in the Brussels Code of 1874 (Art. 36). It should perhaps be contrasted with the term employed in Article 52 of the Hague Regulations of 1907, which is "operations of the war"; see Graber, *The Development of the Law of Belligerent Occupation, 1863–1914* 93–109 (1949).

183. JAG's School, *Law of Belligerent Occupation* 155 (1944); Spaight, *War Rights on Land* 152 (1911); and Fenwick, *International Law* 570 (3rd ed., 1948) are among those who have put forward such a distinction. Dept. of the Army, *Law of Land Warfare* par. 420 (FM27-10, 1956) adopts partially this distinction: "The prohibition against forcing the inhabitants to take part in military operations against their own country precludes requisitioning their services upon *works directly promoting the ends of the war,* such as construction of fortifications, entrenchments, and military airfields or the transportation of supplies or ammunition in the zone of operations. There is no objection in law to their being employed voluntarily and for pay in such work."

184. See *Bouquet and Co. v. Slom, Annual Digest 1947,* Case No. 131. Cf. *In re* Shipbuilding Yard "Gusto," id. Case No. 132, relating to the construction of river dredges for the occupant.

185. *In re* Contractor Knols, id. *1946,* Case No. 144; *In re* Contractor Worp, id., Case No. 145. It might be added that English-speaking textwriters have tended to support this position: e.g., Graber, supra note 182 at 109; Spaight,

to have imposed stricter limitations upon labor requisitions by the occupant. In characterizing the policies of German occupation administrations as "in flagrant violation" of Article 52 of the Hague Regulations, the Tribunal referred not merely to "work on German fortifications and installations," but also to "work for the German war effort" including "German industry and agriculture." [186] From perspectives of preference, this comprehensive limitation is of course in line with demands for the maintenance of the lives and loyalties of the inhabitants. The inhabitants should not be exposed to the danger of assault and death at the hands of their legitimate government, nor compelled to perform acts or series of acts which, in the sovereign's eyes, must appear as treasonous aid and comfort to the enemy. However, the prospects of observance of such a limitation, in a war of substantial duration, seem at best uncertain.

The above ruling of the International Military Tribunal serves also to underscore the fact that the limitations projected in community authority about competence to utilize the labor resources of the occupied territory have reference not only to the nature of the enterprise in which inhabitant labor is utilized but also to the forces whose needs the occupant may legitimately seek to satisfy by requisitioning inhabitant labor. Under both the Hague Regulations [187] and the Geneva Civilians Convention,[188] compulsory labor may be lawfully exacted from inhabitants to fill the needs of "the army of occupation" as distinguished from the occupant's armies committed in theaters of war outside the occupied territory. In its chief practical aspect, the limitation is a quantitative rather than a qualitative one; for the satisfaction of the needs of garrison forces by procurement in the occupied region effects the release of the occupant's own resources, human and material, for the use of its forces engaged elsewhere.

This limitation was spectacularly honored in the breach by Germany in the last two world wars. German practice with respect to

---

War Rights on Land 152 (1911); 3 Hyde, *International Law* 1902 (2nd rev. ed., 1945); 2 Garner, *International Law and the World War* 137–9 (1920).

186. Judgment of the International Military Tribunal, 41 *A.J.I.L.* at 239 et seq. (1947).

187. Art. 52, Hague Regulations. See *In re* Zimmermann, Special Criminal Court, Leeuwarden, Holland, *Annual Digest 1949,* Case No. 196.

188. Art. 51, Geneva Civilians Convention.

the exploitation of the manpower of occupied territories extended to the deportation of whole populations into Germany for compulsory labor in its general war economy. The practice of deportation was initiated in the First World War when 160,000 Belgians were deported from the Belgian "Government General" and the *Zone d'étape* to Germany.[189] When this measure aroused vehement worldwide protest, the German occupant sought to justify it as a police regulation to prevent unemployment in the interests of public order and safety.[190] During the Second World War, the practice assumed staggering proportions. On June 30, 1943, the German Commissioner-General of Manpower declared that the number of foreign workers, including prisoners of war, engaged in the German war economy reached 12,100,000.[191] The conditions under which the deportations were effected, and under which the deportees were compelled to work inside Germany, failed to meet even the most rudimentary standards of humanity. The occupied countries were in fact treated as vast reservoirs of manpower held so cheaply by the occupant that not even subsistence costs were regarded as justified. Occasionally, the occupant felt it expedient to seek to disguise the coerced nature of the population movements. The veiling forms employed varied somewhat in their transparency: premature annexation of occupied territories; "treaties" entered into with "puppet" governments; individual labor "contracts"; and the unilateral alteration of the status of prisoners of war.[192]

The Hague Regulations make no specific mention of deportation for purposes of compulsory labor. Nonetheless, because the Hague Regulations forbid much less substantial encroachments upon the lives, allegiance, and other values of inhabitants, deportation as practiced by Germany would seem *a fortiori* to be unlawful. It may be observed in this connection that coerced population displacements from occupied territory for purposes other than compulsory

189. Relevant history may be obtained in Fried, "Transfer of Civilian Manpower from Occupied Territory," 40 *A.J.I.L.* 303 (1946).

190. Kohler, supra note 25 at 189–221; 2 Garner, supra note 78 at 178–185.

191. Int. Labour Office, *The Exploitation of Foreign Labour by Germany* 61 (1945). See for further descriptive studies, Kulisher, *The Displacement of Populations in Europe* (Int. Labour Office, 1943) and *Civil Affairs Handbook—Germany, Labor Controls in Occupied Europe* (1944).

192. Discussion of these veiling devices is offered in Fried, supra note 189 at 319–23 and in Int. Labour Office, *The Exploitation of Foreign Labour by Germany* 82–9 (1945).

labor may conceivably, in certain operational contexts, be held as permissible. It is true that Article 6(b) of the Nuremberg Charter defined as a war crime "the ill treatment or deportation to slave labor or *for any other purpose,* of civilian populations of or in occupied territory." [193] In the High Command case, where the accused generals removed the local population from areas lying on the path of advancing Allied armies and devastated such areas, the tribunal, while ruling that the devastation was justified by military necessity, did hold the deportation to be unlawful.[194] The defense had alleged that to have left the inhabitants in the devastated areas would have resulted in their own death through starvation. The prosecution suggested, and the tribunal probably agreed in effect, that the evacuation had been moved by other, less humanitarian, purposes—Germany desired to utilize the labor resources of the inhabitant population while denying such resources to the Allied forces. It is also true that the Geneva Civilians Convention prohibits, in Article 49, "individual or mass forcible transfers as well as deportation" of inhabitants to the occupant's home territory or to any other country "regardless of their motive." [195] The same article, however, permits the occupant to undertake the "total or partial evacuation" of any area, where "the security of the population or imperative military reasons" so require. Such evacuation may entail displacement outside the occupied territory "when for material reasons it is impossible to avoid such displacement." The civilians "evacuated" are to

193. Judge Phillips, in his concurring opinion in "The Trial of Milch," 7 *War Crimes Reports* at 45–6 (1947) considered the types of situations in which deportation of civilians during war becomes criminal: (1) if carried out "without a legal title," as where people are deported from a country occupied by an invader while the occupied enemy still has an army in the field and is still resisting; (2) when the purpose is illegal, such as "compelling the deportees to manufacture weapons for use against their homeland or to be assimilated in the working economy of the occupying country"; (3) when deportation procedures disregarded "generally recognized standards of decency and humanity." It will be noticed that the first ground is broad enough to cover all cases of deportation by a belligerent occupant.

194. 12 *War Crimes Reports* at 93 (1948).

195. The deportation of persons convicted of offenses against the occupant was regarded as permissible in U.S. War Dept., *Rules of Land Warfare,* par. 76g (FM27-10, 1940) and in U.S. War Dept., *Manual of Military Government,* par. 45d. This is perhaps now prohibited by Art. 76 of the Geneva Civilians Convention which requires that convicted protected persons serve their sentence in the occupied territory.

be returned to their homes as soon as hostilities in the area have ceased.

There remain to be noted certain other restrictions the Civilians Convention imposed upon the authority of the occupant to control and utilize the population of occupied territories. It is a profoundly disturbing commentary upon modern civilization that an explicit conventional prohibition of the extermination—the deliberate physical destruction—of inhabitants of occupied territory should have been found necessary. In reaction to the racial and *lebensraum* objectives prosecuted by National Socialist Germany in the unfortunate occupied countries, the Civilians Convention forbids extermination and all the cruder forms of violence against inhabitants whether as individuals or as members of a group.[196] With further respect to the goal of *lebensraum,* in implementation of which the German occupant sent German nationals to take over and settle the areas depopulated through extermination, the Convention prohibits the occupant from transferring parts of its own civilian population into the territory occupied.[197] Other conservatory provisions require the occupant to respect the individual honor, family rights, religious convictions and practices, and the manners and customs of the inhabitants, and to provide special protection for women against rape, enforced prostitution, and any form of indecent assault.[198] In specification of the occupant's duty to respect the religious rights of inhabitants, the Convention also requires the occupant to permit clergymen to minister to the religious needs of their constituencies, as well as to permit the distribution of articles dedicated to religious purposes.[199]

196. Art. 32, Civilians Convention.

197. Art. 49, last paragraph, id.

198. Art. 27, id.

199. Art. 58, id. Wartime accounts of practices of the Axis occupants in World War II include: Inter-Allied Information Committee, *Women Under Axis Rule* (Conditions in Occupied Territories No. 7, 1943); Id., *Religious Persecution* (Conditions in Occupied Territories No. 3, 1942); Polish Information Center, *Documents Relating to the Administration of Occupied Countries in Eastern Europe: German Persecution of Religious Life in Poland* (1942). Details of the German program to destroy indigenous Polish culture are provided in Polish Ministry of Information, *The Black Book of Poland* 443 et seq. (1942); Polish Ministry of Foreign Affairs, *German Occupation of Poland: Polish White Book,* 36 et seq. (1942); see also "Trial of Greiser," 13 *War Crimes Reports* 70 (1946).

CLAIMS RELATING TO THE CONTROL OF MATERIAL RESOURCES: THE EXPLOITATION OF OCCUPIED TERRITORY

We consider, finally, the third broad group of claims typically asserted in the stage of belligerent occupation. One type of specific claim embraced in this group is the common demand of belligerents to appropriate and utilize the material resources of territory captured from their enemies. That "war must support war" has been asserted by belligerents almost since men first learned to fight and kill efficiently in groups. The mitigation of the ruthlessness of this ancient and recurrent demand has been a major purpose of the law of belligerent occupation. Another and more recent type of specific claim subsumable in this group is the assertion of authority to manage the financial organization of occupied territory. The making of this claim, pregnant with vast possibilities of abuse, has been occasioned by the complexity of the economic structures and processes of most communities in the modern world. We deal briefly with each of these specific claims.

The Appropriation and Utilization of Property in Occupied Territory

The quantum of authority claimed and honored in traditional law with respect to the appropriation and utilization of property in occupied territory has varied depending upon two principal considerations: first, the public or private character of the resource involved; secondly, the utility or inutility of the resource for the waging of war. The significance of the distinctions between public and private property, and between *materiél de guerre* and innocuous property, lies in the value-conserving policy of the law of belligerent occupation in seeking to protect private property. Thus, as we have noted, Article 46 of the Hague Regulations declares that "Private property cannot be confiscated," while Article 47 states that "Pillage is formally forbidden." The principal thrusts of these protective prescriptions are that (a) there must be a legitimate necessity for the taking of private property, and (b) the occupant must pay compensation for the resource appropriated.[200] As might be expected,

200. See Jessup, "A Belligerent Occupant's Power over Property," 38 *A.J.I.L.* 457, 458 (1944).

however, the protection accorded to the private property of inhabitants is far from absolute. Thus, it is commonly stated that in case of doubt as to the appropriate characterization of particular property as "public" or "private," the property involved should be regarded as public until its private character is shown; [201] other qualifying propositions will be explored below. It may bear mention, further, that the substantiality of the protection provided for private property in terms of the requirement to make compensation may in a sense be contingent upon the sovereign's emerging victor in the war. The successful occupant is likely to impose upon the defeated sovereign, in the peace treaty, the burden of compensating its own nationals for property seized and requisitioned by the occupant.[202]

The characterization of property as public or private presents the initial problem of determining the kinds of factors that may appropriately be taken into account in making this characterization. Formal legal interest is commonly assumed to be one such factor. Clearly, however, the technical vestments of legal interest may frequently have to be pierced if both easy evasion of the occupant's demands and unduly harsh impact on the inhabitants are to be avoided. The first kind of contingency found illustration in the Second World War in the case of property of so-called "parastatal" corporations of the Italian Fascist state.[203] The most familiar examples of the second kind of contingency are deposits created by and trust funds set up for private individuals in government banks.[204]

201. *British Manual of Military Law,* Pt. III, par. 614 (1958); Dept. of the Army, *Law of Land Warfare* par. 394(c) (FM27-10, 1956); Greenspan, *The Modern Law of Land Warfare* 292 (1959).

202. As the Allied Powers did, after World War II, in the peace treaties with Italy—Art. 76(2); Bulgaria—Art. 28(2); Rumania—Art. 30(2); Hungary—Art. 32(2); and cf. Japan—Art. 19(a). For a general commentary, see Martin, "Private Property, Rights and Interests in the Paris Peace Treaties," 24 *Brit. Y.B.I.L.* 273 (1947).

203. See Greenspan, *The Modern Law of Land Warfare* 292 (1959). Professor Greenspan relates that among the factors considered by the British forces who were confronted with claims concerning "parastatal" property in North Africa, were: "The extent of the control by the state over the company which was the titular owner of the property, the financial interest of the state in the company, the manner in which the affairs of the company were conducted, and the purposes for which the enterprise existed."

204. Feilchenfeld, *The International Economic Law of Belligerent Occupation* 58–9 (1942); see also Dept. of the Army, *Law of Land Warfare* par. 394(a). (FM27-10, 1956).

In these and comparable cases, the location of economic enjoyment and of the risk of economic loss appears a factor of high relevance.[205] A third kind of factor is the extent of effective management and control exercised by governmental agencies for public objectives.[206] It has been noted in earlier chapters that in contexts of prolonged, generalized war, economic processes are commonly subjected in varying degrees to state direction, regulation, and control. In such contexts, it becomes difficult to point to enterprises—agricultural, industrial, distributive, or financial—which are *not* brought under some measure of governmental regulation and supervision in the total effort to secure belligerent success. Clearly, however, exclusive and indiscriminate significance cannot be assigned to the factor of

205. "[T]he most cogent evidence of public character," it is said in Dept. of the Army, supra note 204 at par. 394(b), "is such a complete or partial assumption by the State of the economic risk involved in the holding and management of the property in question that the State, rather than private individuals or corporation[s], would be subjected to a substantial portion of the loss were the property to be appropriated for the use of the occupant."

In more particular reference to property of mixed character, it is observed that the same kinds of factors indicated above appear relevant for determining what portion of the property should be considered public and what portion private. Two distinguishable "theories" have been put forward in this connection. The first, the so-called "predominant interest" theory, would regard the property as wholly public or wholly private depending upon whether the greater portion is ascertained, in multiple factor determination, to be public or private. The other, or "apportionment" theory, would simply treat each portion separately as public or private. See *Re:* Rental Payment Claims Involving Certain Real Property, 19 Office of U.S. High Commissioner for Germany [Office of the General Counsel], *Selected Opinions* 18 (1950).

The "apportionment" theory, while more respectful of claims of private individuals, may present the occupant with considerable difficulties in case of property that is neither fungible nor divisible. In mitigation of these difficulties, "predominant interest" might be invoked to pass upon the occupant's authority to take or use the property, while "apportionment" might be resorted to for purposes of fixing the extent of compensation to be made. The practice of the British Military Administration in Africa with respect to Italian property appears to have taken these lines. See Rennell, *British Military Administration of Occupied Territories in Africa* 423 et seq. (1948).

206. Thus, it is stated in Dept. of the Army, loc. cit., that subjection to "a large measure of governmental control and management" and performance of "functions essentially public," "indicate that the property should be regarded in practice as public." See further, Feilchenfeld, supra note 204 at 58, and JAG's School, *Law of Belligerent Occupation* 225–6 (1944); the latter offers specific indicia for each of the tests of "ownership, function, and direction."

governmental regulation and management without dissolving the distinction between public and private property and the mitigating policy it embodies.[207] Thus, the Soviet Union upon joining the war against Japan and rapidly overrunning the puppet state of Manchukuo, claimed that all enterprises in Manchuria "which had rendered service to the Japanese Army," without regard to any other circumstance, constituted "war booty."[208] For the purpose of avoiding such extravagant claims, the suggestion has been made that the relatively permanent or the exceptional emergency nature of the pattern of state direction and control should also be taken into account.[209] It should perhaps be observed that the degree of state management and control in fact exercised in respect of a particular enterprise in time of war is itself a function or aspect of the relation of such enterprise to the successful waging of war, and that this factor justifies taking and use by the occupant whether the enterprise be characterized as public or private.

With respect to the general class of public property, traditional law establishes certain subsidiary distinctions that express certain limitations upon the extent of authority conceded to the occupant. One distinction is between immovable and movable public property. With respect to immovable public property, the scope of authority the occupant may assert is summed up in Article 55 of the Hague Regulations in the terms "administrator" and "usufructuary." As one expression of the broad limiting principle that the occupant may not claim the exclusive and comprehensive competence designated as sovereignty, the occupant is not regarded as acquiring ownership over immovable state property. The limitation presses but lightly upon the military necessities of the occupant, since the utilization (*utendi, fruendi*) of such resources does not depend upon the recognition of legal interest in the occupant. As a practical matter, the applicable specific prohibitions are simply that the occupant may not wantonly dissipate or destroy the public resources and may not per-

207. Smith, "Booty of War," 23 *Brit. Y.B.I.L.* 227, 231 (1946) indicates the limits of the logic of this factor: "Since the only real test of ownership lies in the power of disposition and control, . . . this means that in time of war the distinction between public and private property ceases to have any real meaning."

208. See Lew, "Manchurian Booty and International Law," 40 *A.J.I.L.* 584 (1946).

209. The suggestion is Professor Feilchenfeld's; supra note 204 at 58, 61.

manently (i.e., for the indefinite future) alienate them (*salva rerum substantia*).[210]

With respect to public movable property, the authority of the occupant to take and utilize is made in customary law to depend upon the utility of the specific property for the conduct of war. Under Article 53 of the Hague Regulations, all public movables "which may be used for operations of the war" and "all kinds of ammunition of war" may be appropriated and utilized without any obligation of restoration or indemnification. It need not escape notice that the basic conception underlying this authority to seize public enemy property on land bears strong analogy with the conception of contraband or the seizing of goods flowing to the enemy by sea. The range of articles that may be useful for the carrying on of war operations, or, put a little differently, the degree of military utility of any particular category of movables, is, much as in contraband, dependent upon the character and dimensions of the particular conflict being waged. The categories specifically mentioned in Article 53—cash, funds, and realizable securities, depots of arms, means of transportation and communication, stores and supplies—are suggestive rather than exhaustive and refer to property which would be militarily useful in practically any conflict where land forces are committed. In the last two world wars, Article 53 was in practice interpreted to authorize the seizure of "everything and anything that [the occupant could] directly or indirectly make use of for military operations."[211] Thus, in the interesting case of *État*

210. Some illustration is provided by *État Français v. Lemarchand, Annual Digest 1948,* Case No. 198 where the Court of Appeal of Rouen held, in an action for restitution, that the dismantling of certain buildings owned by the French State and use of the materials in the construction of a German army training school was violative of the occupant's duty as usufructuary to preserve the capital. See also *Administration of Waters and Forests v. Falck,* Court of Cassation, France, id. *1927–1928,* Case No. 383.

211. 2 Oppenheim-Lauterpacht 399. Smith, supra note 207 at 228–9 speaks of the seizure of all movables for which a modern army can find any normal use. The old War Dept., *Rules of Land Warfare,* par. 321 (FM27-10, 1940) and *British Manual of Military Law* (1929) *Amendments No. 12,* par. 430 (1936) laid down a verbally more restrictive standard, distinguishing between movables which are "directly susceptible of military use" and those which are not. The more recent Dept. of the Army, *Law of Land Warfare* pars. 404, 408, 410 (FM27-10, 1956) has dropped the word "directly" in respect of public movables but retains it in respect of private movables. It seems a matter of much doubt

Français v. Établissements Monmousseau,[212] wine vats owned by the French Government and used in the making of wine for the French army were held by the Court of Appeals of Orléans to have been lawfully seized by the German occupant. Where the public movables involved exhibit but peripheral significance for the waging of war—where they are, in other words, innocuous property—customary law has required that they be held immune from seizure. Thus, under Article 56 of the Hague Regulations, the property of institutions devoted to religion, charity, and education as well as historic and artistic works are to be treated as private property.[213]

Authority on the part of the occupant to collect debts owed to the absent sovereign has been a matter of controversy among the commentators. On the one hand, the occupant-sovereign distinction is sometimes asserted to deny such authority: the occupant, a precarious possessor, is not regarded as a successor to, nor as the authorized agent

---

whether such retention will seriously influence future practice. Downey, "Captured Enemy Property: Booty of War and Seized Enemy Property," 44 *A.J.I.L.* 488 (1950) offers general comment and some distinctions of mixed value.

212. *Annual Digest 1948,* Case No. 197. Compare *P. v. A.G.K. and P.,* id., Case No. 196 where the Swiss Federal Tribunal held the seizure by the German occupant of a calculating machine owned by the Polish Government as unlawful upon the ground that such machine was not one which might be used for operations of war.

213. Art. 56 also refers to the "property of municipalities" along with "that of institutions dedicated to religion, charity etc." This is sometimes interpreted to mean that the property of local governments is assimilated to property devoted to religious, charitable, etc. purposes; see *British Manual of Military Law,* Pt. III, par. 611 (1958). This view, however, would seem to require the subsumption of disparate things under the same rubric; it is less than self-evident why *materiél de guerre* should be immune from seizure because it happens to be *biens des communes.* Thus, Franklin, "Municipal Property Under Belligerent Occupation," 38 *A.J.I.L.* 383, 391, 395 (1944), after inquiry into the history of Art. 56 of the Hague Regulations, concluded that municipal property should be regarded as immune only to the extent that it is in fact dedicated to religious, charitable, etc. purposes.

As to the special position of cultural property, see the 1954 Hague Convention for the Protection of Cultural Property in the Event of Armed Conflict, supra, p. 608. See also the useful historical monograph, De Visscher, "La Protection Internationale des Objets d'art et des Monuments Historiques," 16 *Revue de Droit International et de Legislation Comparée* 256 (1935); an English translation appears in 1 U.S. Dept. of State, *Documents and State Papers* 822 (1949).

of, the absent sovereign.[214] On the other hand, some of the textwriters appear to sustain authority in the occupant to collect matured debts, *dettes exigibles,* on the theory that such debts may be assimilated to "realizable securities," *valeurs exigibles,* at least when evidenced in writing.[215] The suggestion has also been made that the collection of outstanding debts is an aspect of the occupant's authorized function of maintaining public order and civil life. The question need not be merely an academic one, for once the debts are collected, the proceeds become state funds subject to seizure by the occupant.[216] If the occupant is conceded authority to appropriate public funds and realizable securities although denied the competence of a sovereign, it seems somewhat unreal to suppose he should be denied authority to take that which is functionally equivalent to funds and securities simply because of the occupant-sovereign dichotomy.

We turn to the category of private property. As we have indicated earlier, the characterization of property as private does not mean that such property becomes exempt from taking for the satisfaction of the belligerent occupant's needs. On the contrary, traditional law recognizes three procedures for the subjecting of private property to the military needs of the occupant. Put together, these three procedures permit the utilization of practically any resource the occupant may conceivably require. At the same time, the requirements of these three procedures reflect the countervailing policy of minimum destruction of values, principally by imposing some quantitative limits on the taking and utilization of resources and by permit-

214. E.g., Von Glahn, *The Occupation of Enemy Territory* 156–7 (1957). See, in this connection, *Tajtel v. Minister of Agriculture and State Lands, Annual Digest 1923–1924,* Case No. 246, where the Polish Supreme Court held that the release of a mortgage securing a debt to the Russian state (of which Poland had been a part), upon payment of the debt to the German occupant, was *ultra vires* the occupant.

215. E.g., 3 Hyde, *International Law* 1897 (2nd rev. ed., 1945); Latifi, *Effects of War on Property* 25–6 (1909); Bordwell, *The Law of War Between Belligerents* 324–5 (1908). For an interpretation of the term *"valeurs exigibles,"* see *In re* Van der Giessen, *Annual Digest 1948,* Case No. 599, where the Dutch Special Court of Cassation held that a contract for the delivery of things, here ships, did not constitute a *"valeur exigible"* which an occupant would be entitled to take.

216. Cf. Feilchenfeld, *The International Economic Law of Belligerent Occupation* 65 (1942); and Stone, *Legal Controls of International Conflict* 717 (2nd ed., 1959).

ting the spreading of the burdens of such taking throughout the occupied community.

The first procedure for effecting the transfer of resources from inhabitants to the occupant is that of seizure. Under Article 53, paragraph 2, of the Hague Regulations, private property obviously related to the conduct of military operations—such as means of transport and communication, arms and other war material (*munition de guerre*)—may be seized by the occupant. The concession made to the policy of minimizing destruction of values consists in requiring the restoration of the property and indemnification for its use at the termination of the war, or simply the payment of compensation if the articles shall have been consumed.[217] The issuance of a receipt by the seizing occupant may be regarded as impliedly required by Article 53, for the deprived owner would commonly find it difficult to substantiate a claim for restoration or indemnification without it.[218]

The much discussed case of *N. V. de Bataafsche Petroleum Maatschappij and others v. War Damage Commission*[219] offers recent illustration of one interpretation of the ambit of the term *"munitions de guerre."* When the returning British forces recaptured Singapore, they found, and seized as war booty, huge stocks of both refined petrol and crude oil stored therein by the Japanese occupant. These stocks represented oil which the Japanese occupant had extracted from the oil fields of the appellants in the Netherlands East Indies, refined at Palembang in the case of the petrol, and shipped to Singapore for storage and distribution. In claiming these stocks as their property, the appellant companies asserted that the seizure of crude oil "in the ground" from their oil fields by the Japanese occupation

217. *Pigeat et Hazard v. Cie de Traction,* Court of Appeals of Dijon, France, *Annual Digest 1943–1945,* Case No. 165, and *Austrian Treasury v. Auer,* Supreme Court of Austria, id. *1947,* Case No. 125, provide illustration of the application of this requirement.

218. See e.g., *Bilotte v. Groos and the State of the Netherlands, Annual Digest 1949,* Case No. 182, where the District Court of Arnhem held that the failure of German forces to issue a receipt upon seizing a car rendered the seizure invalid. See also *In re* Hinrichsen, id., Case No. 179, where the Hague Court of Cassation stated that seizure "may not be done without in some way being officially acknowledged, in order to ensure compliance with the rule that such goods must be returned and compensation fixed when peace is made."

219. *Int. Law Rep. 1956* 810; 22 *Malayan L.J.* 155 (1956); 51 *A.J.I.L.* 802 (1957); noted in 71 *Harv. L. Rev.* 568 (1958).

forces was unlawful, such oil being then a "raw material" and not *munitions de guerre*. In sustaining this contention, Whyatt, C.J., of the Singapore Court of Appeal, wrote:

> It may be that certain types of war material or semi-manufactured products, such as cloth for uniforms and leather for boots, which could possibly be made up into finished articles by army personnel without the assistance of civilian technicians and outside plant can, without stretching the meaning of "munitions-de-guerre" unduly, be regarded as having a sufficiently close connection with direct military use to bring them within Article 53. It is not, however, necessary to decide this point as the facts of this case show that there is no such close connexion in the present instance. According to the evidence, elaborate installations and civilian technicians were needed by the army to enable them to appropriate this oil and prepare it for use in their war machines. It had to be extracted from underground reservoirs, then transported to a refinery, and then subjected to a complicated refining process before it was of any use to any one. In these circumstances, it cannot be said, in my opinion, that at the moment of its seizure in the ground, the oil had a sufficiently close connexion with direct military use to bring it within the meaning of "munitions-de-guerre" in article 53.[220]

220. *Int. Law Rep. 1956* at 823. A learned brief for this conclusion is provided in E. Lauterpacht, "The Hague Regulations and the Seizure of Munitions de Guerre," 32 *Brit. Y.B.I.L.* 218 (1955–1956). It seems important to observe that Chief Justice Whyatt relied heavily upon—and indeed regarded the respondent Commission as bound by—the formulation contained in the old *British Manual of Military Law* (*Amendments No. 12* [1936]): " '*munitions de guerre*' are such 'things as are susceptible of direct military use.' " The revised *Manual,* Pt. III par. 613 (1958) has dropped the word "direct" in referring to "movable public property." In dealing with seizure of private movable property, Judge Lauterpacht, who was responsible for the revised manual, observed in a terse note on par. 597 that "The term 'war material' and the French equivalent '*munitions de guerre*' have eluded satisfactory definitions. Their use in the context of Hague Rules 53 would appear to give them a wide meaning and would cover all movable property which could serve as war material, see Oppenheim, vol. II, p. 404. *There is no justification for the view that 'war material' means material which could be used immediately and without being processed in any way for warlike purposes;* for example, crude oil could be included in the term 'war material.' " (Italics supplied.)

The tenuous nature of this ruling's contact with reality is perhaps best emphasized by noting that, taken seriously, the ruling would require the exclusion of uranium ore from the category of war material or *munitions de guerre*. Decisive significance should, we submit, be ascribed not so much to the length or complexity of the process by which particular material is made ready for the instant use of armed forces, but rather to the degree of military utility exhibited by the processed material. Support for this view is found in the opinion of Whitton, J. which, in this particular respect at least, displays much greater awareness of the exigencies of modern warfare:

> [C]hanges in the nature of warfare necessarily make it more difficult to determine whether crude oil is a "*munition de guerre.*" It seems to me, however, had the Japanese been fortunate enough in 1942 after capturing Singapore to find in the place this petrol ready for use, as the British Military Administration found it in 1945, it could not be correctly maintained it would have been a violation of Article 53 had they employed it for the purposes of their campaigns. If it is conceded a belligerent is entitled to seize petrol which is ready for immediate use it seems to me it cannot be logically maintained he is not entitled to seize the crude material out of which the finished products are created, since the protection accorded private property by the Regulations is obviously limited by the exclusion of what the signatories to the Convention presumably regarded as the legitimate necessaries of a belligerent occupier in the execution of his war effort, as the modern phrase has it, and once it is allowed that a certain kind of property is a necessary for the conduct of a war there scarcely seems reason to maintain that private interest can prevail in respect of the raw material out of which the property is made simply because in such circumstances extraction and processing have first to be carried out.[221]

All other kinds of private property less clearly related to the carrying on of military operations may be taken by an occupant by means of the process of requisitions. The principal conservatory requirements of this mode of taking relate, firstly, to the quantum of property that may be requisitioned; secondly, to compensation for property taken under this process; and thirdly, to the procedure of requisitions.

221. Id., at 846–7.

Assertions of occupants to authority to requisition private property are sought to be limited quantitatively both by limiting the purposes for which such authority may be asserted and by establishing a requirement of proportionality. As noted earlier, the legitimate purposes of requisition—establishing the burdens that may be imposed upon the material resources of the occupied territory—are defined to be the satisfaction of "the needs of the army of occupation" [222] and are commonly held to exclude the supplying of either the occupant's home territory or its forces operating outside the occupied territory. For instance, in *Gros Roman Cie. v. German State*,[223] the Franco-German Mixed Arbitral Tribunal ruled that the requisitioning of cloth in German-occupied Holland and the transporting of the cloth into Germany was violative of the Hague Regulations and did not result in the vesting of title to such property in the occupant. Similarly, the Italian Court of Cassation held in *Scotti v. Garbagnati and Marconi*,[224] that the requisition by German forces of the use of certain buildings for the benefit of an Italian firm engaged in exporting its products to Germany could not be sustained under the Hague Regulations. The possible implications appear to be that had occupancy of the buildings been taken for the German army in Italy, or even perhaps for an Italian firm supplying the needs of such army, the requisition might have been considered lawful. Again, requisitioning for purposes of selling the property taken at a profit, rather than for the direct use of the occupation forces, was declared unlawful by the Supreme Court of Poland in *Siuta v. Guzkowski*.[225]

The requirement of proportionality, designed to avoid the re-

222. Art. 52, Hague Regulations. Article 55 of the Civilians Convention speaks of "use by the occupation forces and administration personnel." See *Soubrouillard v. Kilbourg, Annual Digest 1948*, Case No. 180, where the French Court of Cassation held that lawful requisitions are limited to those effected by the army authorities, and that "civil authorities of the enemy" have no authority to requisition goods even for the "purpose of regulating economic life in general and agricultural production in particular." In this case, the *Kreisbanernschaft*, a "civil administrative organ" of the occupant, took a horse from the plaintiff and transferred it to the defendant at a price fixed by itself.

223. *Annual Digest 1923–1924*, Case No. 245. See also *In re* Fiebig, Special Criminal Court, the Hague, Holland, id. *1949*, Case No. 180.

224. Id. *1948*, Case No. 203.

225. Id. *1919–1922*, Case No. 342. See also, in this connection, *Kostoris v. Meinl*, Court of Appeal of Trieste, Italy, id. *1949*, Case No. 171, where the taking of the property of the plaintiff, a Jew, was held unlawful, having been carried

duction of the occupied territory to destitution, is said to protect the "resources of the [occupied] country" rather than the assets of a particular inhabitant. Thus, a farmer's last cow and loaf of bread may, Professor Feilchenfeld wrote,[226] be lawfully taken provided the occupant does not exhaust the bread and cattle supply of the occupied country as a whole. It may not be inapposite to observe that, so conceived, the protection of the requirement of proportionality is apt to be more shadowy than substantial. The more restricted conception taken by an Italian court in *Giovannini v. Renzi* [227] offers, to our mind, the possibility of more meaningful protection. There the court adopted the view that the term "country" in Article 52 of the Hague Regulations referred rather to the locality where the requisition is effected than to the entire occupied territory. This view should also in measure facilitate the determination of proportionality in a statistical sense; moreover, it permits account to be taken of the fact that normal distribution processes tend to be disrupted under the stress of war. The relevant provision of the Geneva Civilians Convention is worth noting:

> The Occupying Power may not requisition foodstuffs, articles or medical supplies available in the occupied territory, except for use of the occupation forces and administration personnel, and then *only if the requirements of the civilian population have been taken into account. . . .*[228]

There appears nothing to prevent an interpreter from reading this provision as referring to the civilian population of the locality where a particular requisition is levied.

The traditional requirement of proportionality projected in the Hague Regulations is a counsel of conservation and restraint. The Geneva Civilians Convention seeks a more affirmative protection against the stripping of the occupied territory by imposing upon the occupant a positive obligation to maintain certain minimum levels of food and medical supplies.

---

out in implementation of the occupant's anti-Semitic policy "which was started before the war and had nothing to do with the requirements of the war."

226. Feilchenfeld, *The International Economic Law of Belligerent Occupation* 37 (1942).

227. *Annual Digest 1948,* Case No. 209.

228. Art. 55, second par.

> To the fullest extent of the means available to it, the Occupying Power has the duty of ensuring the food and medical supplies of the population; *it should, in particular, bring in the necessary foodstuffs, medical stores and other articles if the resources of the occupied territory are inadequate.*[229]

The requirements in respect of compensation and requisitions procedure are conveniently considered together. A claim to requisition property may be asserted only by means of an order from the commanding officer in the locality.[230] The obvious purpose is to permit the fixing of responsibility for requisitions and to prevent looting by undisciplined individual soldiers; the requirement marks a shared interest of occupant and inhabitants. Payment in cash or, alternatively, the issuance of a receipt redeemable in cash at the earliest time possible, must accompany the taking of property. Failure to issue a receipt has been held by restored sovereigns to render the requisition unlawful and ineffective to transfer ownership to the occupant.[231] Even though a receipt was issued, courts have ruled that the requisition may still become unlawful where the receipt is not redeemed within a "reasonable" time.[232] Requisitions thus may be described as compulsory sales, the buyer-occupant determining, in the first instance, the price—the Geneva Civilians Convention specifies "fair value" [233]—of the goods requisitioned.

229. Art. 55, first par., Art. 56 establishes a similar obligation in respect of the maintenance of medical and hospital services and public health and hygiene in the occupied territory.

230. Art. 52, second par., Hague Regulations.

231. See the decision of the Belgian Court of Cassation in *Laurent v. Le Jeune, Annual Digest 1919–1922,* Case No. 343; and that of the Norwegian Court of Appeal in *Johansen v. Gross,* id. *1949,* Case No. 176. See, further, "Trial of Rust," 9 *War Crimes Reports* 71 (1948). The answer to whether or not the occupant acquired title through a lawful requisition has frequently been made determinative of claims of the opposing belligerent to seize the property involved as war booty. See Downey, "Captured Enemy Property: Booty of War and Seized Enemy Property," 44 *A.J.I.L.* 488, 489 (1950).

232. See e.g., decision of the Germano-Greek Mixed Arbitral Tribunal in *Karmatzucas v. Germany, Annual Digest 1925–1926,* Case No. 365, where a period of 9 years had elapsed without payment being made; also the decision of a Special Arbitral Tribunal in *Goldenberg and Sons v. Germany,* id., *1927–1928,* Case No. 369, where 7 years had passed before the occupant paid one-sixth of the price of the requisitioned articles.

233. Art. 55, Geneva Civilians Convention.

So far as the protection of inhabitants' property is concerned, the thrust of these requirements is largely felt after the termination of hostilities when indemnity for unpaid requisitions can be assessed against the defeated occupant and the return of property unlawfully taken demanded from the former occupant or its transferees. During the occupation, however, the occupant itself need not, in point of practical fact, pay for requisitioned goods. The occupant may shift the economic burden of payment to the inhabitants.[234] Article 49 of the Hague Regulations authorizes the occupant to levy upon inhabitants money contributions, in addition to taxes, for "the needs of the army or of the administration of the [occupied] territory." Authority to impose contributions, commonly called "occupation costs," is located by Article 51 in the "Commander-in-chief" of occupation forces, who must issue a written order. In contrast with taking by requisitions, contributions are demandable not from isolated particular individuals but from the community at large or in a particular locality.[235] A functional equivalent for the proportionality requirement in requisitions is found in the limitation that the incidence and assessment of contributions shall follow the rules in force with respect to taxation.[236] One underlying assumption appears to be that the pre-occupation patterns of taxation are familiar and acceptable to the inhabitants; adherence to such patterns both facilitates the collection of occupation costs and permits the mitigation of the economic shock by widening, so to speak, the area of impact. As in requisitions, funds raised by compulsory contributions may not be diverted to support the occupant's war effort outside the occupied territory.[237] Again, as in requisitions, a receipt is required

234. It might, however, be noted that courts of restored sovereigns have in effect held that the economic burden entailed by a requisition from a particular individual may not be shifted to another particular individual. Thus, in *Maltoni v. Companini, Annual Digest 1948,* Case No. 210, the Court of Appeal of Bologna, Italy, ruled that a requisition effected for the purpose of compensating another person from whom a previous requisition had been made, was unlawful as not being for the needs of the occupying army. See also *Secret v. Loizel,* Civil Tribunal of Peronne, France, id., *1943–1945,* Case No. 164.

235. This is stressed in Feilchenfeld, *The International Economic Law of Belligerent Occupation* 45 (1942) and in Spaight, *War Rights on Land* 387 (1911).

236. Contrast Stone, *Legal Controls of International Conflict* 714 (2nd ed., 1959) who asserts that the requirement of proportionality to local resources is limited to requisitions.

237. Art. 49, Hague Regulations. See 3 Hyde, *International Law* 1889 (2nd

to be given under the Hague Regulations.[238] Unlike in requisitions, however, traditional law has not required occupants to indemnify the inhabitants even with respect to that portion of the funds used for satisfying the needs of the occupation garrison. The practical significance of the required receipt is presumably contingent upon the possibility of exacting indemnity from the *defeated* occupant, or of compensation from the *defeated* sovereign to whom such burden is likely to be shifted.

These distinctions, requirements, and limitations mark the line of compromise that traditional law has sought to maintain between the military necessities of the occupant and the conservation of resources in occupied territory. It is easy to observe that this line has not been stationary, that in the practice of certain occupants in the last two world wars the line was pushed almost to the inhabitants' terminus. One explanatory factor may be seen to lie in the comprehensive nature of the belligerent objectives of these occupants. Enemy territory was overrun and occupied for the very purpose of drawing forth therefrom the sustenance and means for carrying on combat elsewhere. It does not seem extravagant to speak of the draining of the substance of occupied territory, of simmering the enemy, as it were, in its own juices. Public and private property was impartially given over to efficient and thorough-going plunder. In at least one instance, the occupant undertook to sell even immovable state property.[239] Agricultural products and all kinds of raw materials, industrial equipment, securities and holdings of foreign exchange were seized or requisitioned in massive quantities and exported to Germany, in utter disregard of the proportionality requirement, bringing famine, galloping inflation, and a vicious black market in the unfortunate territories.[240] The "occupation costs" exacted ran into astronomical figures, bereft of any relation to the

rev. ed., 1945), and Greenspan, *The Modern Law of Land Warfare* 304 (1959).

238. Art. 51, Hague Regulations.

239. See Order of the Reich Commissioner for the Occupied Netherlands Territories concerning the Alienation of Real Property Owned by the State and the Conclusion of Settlements of Disputes Involving Real Property Owned by the State, Oct. 4, 1940, in Lemkin, *Axis Rule in Occupied Europe* 478–9 (1944).

240. See Inter-Allied Information Committee, *Rationing Under Axis Rule* (Conditions in Occupied Territory No. 2, 1942) for tables showing the differences in food allowances for Germans and for inhabitants of the different occupied territories.

actual economic cost of maintaining the occupant's army and administering the occupied territory.[241] The choice contents of the libraries, galleries, and museums of occupied Europe were picked and sent to Germany; [242] in occupied Asia, even household goods were shipped to Japan. It would be tedious to recite once more the details of the "deliberate design and policy" of exploitation which have been adequately recounted in the decisions of the war crimes tribunals.[243]

THE MANAGEMENT OF FINANCIAL PROCESSES IN OCCUPIED TERRITORY: MONEY AND BANKING

We come now to claims to manage and control the financial organization of occupied territory. The assertion of these claims have in the last two general wars occasioned the employment of more subtle and less visible modes of taking and utilizing resources than seizures, requisitions, and contributions. With respect to these new techniques of exploitation, made possible by the very complexity of the economic and financial organization of modern states, conventional international law is completely silent. Specific prescriptions have yet to be refined from the broad principles relating to the scope of authority of occupants and the complementary policies of military necessity and conservation of resources.

Perhaps the most important of these financial measures is the issuance and control of currency in the occupied area. The occupant has generally been conceded competence to issue currency for circulation within the territory occupied, as one particular manifestation of its broad duty and authority to maintain law and *vie pu-*

241. A table of occupation costs assessed in the early part of the war is found in Reveille, *The Spoil of Europe* 104 (1941). Robinson, "Transfer of Property in Enemy Occupied Territory," 39 *A.J.I.L.* 219 (1945) mentions that of the 72.3 billion francs paid by the French people as occupation costs up to Dec. 31, 1940, 41.4 billions remained unused at that date deposited to the account of the occupant in the Bank of France; and that a year later, the unused credit balance rose to 62 billion francs. See also Klopstock, "Monetary Reform in Liberated Europe," 36 *Am. Econ. Rev.* 581 (1946).

242. Some of these—valuable works of art, for example—were disposed of in neutral territory, presumably for the raising of foreign exchange or for concealment purposes. See e.g., *Rosenberg v. Fischer,* Swiss Federal Tribunal, *Annual Digest 1948,* Case No. 150.

243. E.g., the Judgment of the International Military Tribunal at Nuremberg, *Misc. No. 12 (1946),* Cmd. 6964, pp. 54–6.

blique.[244] *Vie publique* clearly includes economic and financial processes; the maintenance of *vie publique* thus embraces the restoration and maintenance of a currency system that functions in the orderly way indispensable for a normal economic life. It is worthy of note that even in the one country, Burma, where the restored sovereign refused to recognize in the occupant a lawful power of issuance and to consider the military rupee issued by the Japanese occupant as "lawful currency," [245] such currency was acknowledged to have had some effective purchasing power during the occupation and to have been actually used as an exchange medium. Because the acceptance by inhabitants of military currency in the creation and discharge of debts is in fact enforced by the occupant, to withhold the characterization of "lawful currency" becomes unreal and irrelevant on the one hand, and, on the other, may work undue harshness on the inhabitants.

There are, it is said, principally three courses open to the occupant.[246] It may, firstly, leave in circulation the old currency issued by the ousted sovereign, providing new supplies and types of coverage should the coverage of such currency become inadequate. Secondly, the occupant may import its national currency into the occupied area. New issues of its own currency may, however, generate considerable strain on its coverage, and, should such issues flow back to the occupant's territorial domain, also considerable inflationary pressures.[247] The third alternative is the institution of new currency.

244. Relevant citations include: Feilchenfeld, *The International Economic Law of Belligerent Occupation* 70 (1942); Stone, *Legal Controls of International Conflict* 718 (2nd ed., 1959); "Opinion on the Legality of the Issuance of AMG Currency in Sicily," in *Occupation Currency Transactions, Hearings before the Committees on Appropriations, Armed Services, and Banking and Currency,* U. S. Senate, 80th Cong., 1st Sess., 73 et seq. (1947); Wilson, "The Laws of War in Occupied Territory," 18 *Tr. Grotius Soc.* 17, 22 (1932). For judicial recognition of the occupant's competence in this regard, see: *Haw Pia v. China Banking Corporation,* 80 Phil. 604 (1948), *Int. Law Rep. 1951,* 642; *Aboitiz and Co. v. Price,* 99 F. Supp. 602 (D.C., Utah, 1951); and *Eisner v. United States* 117 F. Supp. 197 (Ct. of Cl., 1954).

245. See *Ko Maung Tin v. U Gon Man* [1947] Rangoon Law Reports 149; and *Chan Taik v. Ariff Moosaje Dooply* [1948] Burma Law Reports 454, affmd *sub. nom. Dooply v. Chan Taik,* Supreme Court of Burma, *Int. Law Rep. 1951,* 641.

246. See Feilchenfeld, supra note 244 at 71, 76, 80.

247. See Bloch and Hoselitz, *Economics of Military Occupation* 8 (1944).

Conceivably, all three courses may be pursued simultaneously. The suggestion has been made that under the broad principle which enjoins respect for existing laws, the second and third courses should be regarded as authorized only when and in so far as the first is not practicable.[248] The occupant introducing its own or a new currency into the occupied region, it is said, should do so only to the extent necessary to satisfy military needs or to supplement the pre-occupation currency where it has become inadequate for the ordinary economic life of the region.

In practice, however, the third method has been heavily favored. Both the Axis and Allied occupants in the last war issued new military currency. The Allied armies issued Allied Military Currency in the old currency units of the occupied countries: *lira* in Italy, *reichsmarks* in Germany, and *schillings* in Austria.[249] In the Philippines, the Japanese occupant issued military *pesos,* or war-notes denominated in peso units, on a par valuation with the old peso currency, and forbade the circulation of any other kind of money.[250] In Hong Kong, military *yen* were issued; [251] in Singapore and Malaya, military dollars. The military *rupee* in Burma has already been mentioned. In the Netherlands East Indies, the occupant printed military *guilders*. These military currencies were prescribed exclusively for internal circulation within the respective occupied countries and could not be used in trade between the occupied countries nor imported into Japan. In occupied Europe, during the early stages of the occupation, German troops used special certificates (*Reichs kredit kassenscheine*) issued by the Reich Credit Institutes (*Reichs Kredit Kassen*) as money.[252] Like the Japanese fiat currency, the certificates

248. Mann, "Money in Public International Law," 26 *Brit. Y.B.I.L.* 259, 272 (1949).

249. For exposition, see Fairman, "Some Observations on Military Occupation," 32 *Minn. L. Rev.* 325–6 (1948); also Holborn, *American Military Government* 114, 135, 177 (1947). For the British practices in Africa, see *British Military Administration of Occupied Territories in Africa During the Years 1941–1943*, Cmd. 6589, p. 7 (1945).

250. See the proclamations issued by the Japanese Commander-in-Chief, dated Jan. 3, 1942, Jan. 10, 1942, Feb. 6, 1942, and May 7, 1942; 1 *Official Gazette* pp. 9–10, 43, 211 (1942).

251. Ward, *Asia for the Asiatics: The Techniques of Japanese Occupation* 124–7 (1945), offers an account of the currency and other financial practices of the Japanese occupation forces in Southeast Asia.

252. See Lemkin, *Axis Rule in Occupied Europe* 51 (1944) and Bloch and Hoselitz, supra note 247 at 17–20.

could be used only in the occupied countries and had no value in Germany. These certificates were later withdrawn by the occupant, and the central banks established in each of the occupied countries were required to absorb the issues and exchange them against local currencies. The burden of the exchange was charged off as "occupation costs." As to local currencies, a distinction was drawn by the German occupant between incorporated and nonincorporated areas. In the former, the old local currencies were abolished and the *Reichsmark* introduced as sole legal tender. In the latter, the old local currencies were generally continued in circulation, new rates of exchange with the *Reichsmark* laid down, and new issues thereof printed. In some cases, new local currency denominated in either the old or new monetary units were issued: thus, the *zloty* in Poland, the *dinar* in Serbia, the *carbovanet* in the Ukraine, and the *kuna* in Croatia. Cover for the new issue consisted of Reich credit notes, of clearing claims (accounting items in the books of the Reichsbank or the Clearing Office at Berlin) and, at least in Poland, of a first mortgage on the entire occupied territory.[253]

Whichever type of monetary organization is adopted, there arises an urgent problem of clarifying the occupant's duties with respect to the management and operation of the currency system in the occupied country. Where, for example, the occupant establishes rates of exchange between the military and local currency, the process of evaluation should, it is said, be carried out disinterestedly.[254] The charge has been made that, measured by the equilibrium rates prevailing before the outbreak of war, National Socialist Germany overvalued the Reichsmark in the conversion rates it prescribed vis-à-vis the currencies of occupied countries. The margin that accrued as profit for the occupant and an economic advantage in trade with the captured countries would seem difficult of justification.[255] It

253. Lemkin, supra note 252 at 53, 539.

254. Mann, supra note 248 at 276; Nussbaum, *Money in the Law, National and International* 497 note 31 (1950). Dept. of the Army, *Law of Land Warfare,* par. 430 (FM27-10, 1956): "Intentional debasement of currency by the establishment of fictitious valuation or exchange rates, or like devices, . . . are violative of international law." The same position is adopted by the *British Manual of Military Law,* Pt. III, par. 531 (1958).

255. See Schweitzer, "The Role of Foreign Trade in the Nazi War Economy," 51 *J. Pol. Economy* 322, 335 (1943). The exchange rates established by the German occupant, and the extent of overevaluation are set out in Reveille, *The Spoil of Europe* 93, 95 (1941).

should, however, be observed, with Professor Stone,[256] that states have at times resorted during peace to the fixing of fictitious rates of exchange (i.e., rates other than those established in the open exchange market) for the benefit of their public treasuries or to reduce costs of imported goods. It may thus be somewhat unreal always to expect a self-denying ordinance from an occupant who may be confronted with abnormal conditions.

Another problem that still awaits clarification is the scope and content of the occupant's duty with respect to inflation in the occupied territory. The occupant pays for heavy requisitions and purchases with the currency it has created. The volume of money in circulation of course increases while the quantity of goods and services available shrinks; the foreseeable consequences include the rise of price levels and the corresponding decline in the effective purchasing power of the circulating media. It has been urged that the general duty of the occupant to maintain and ensure public order should be interpreted to embrace a specific duty to cushion the impact of pressures toward inflation,[257] by price control measures, perhaps by self-restraint in requisitions and purchases as in the printing of new issues, and, paradoxically, by levying money contributions. The suggestion has been submitted, however, that such a specific duty may be too heavy a burden to impose upon an occupant.[258] The gist of this suggestion is that the behavior of money in occupation contexts is the function of many complex variables which make it difficult to ascertain with much confidence the role of failure to take this or that regulatory measure. Not all of these variables may lie within the effective control of the occupant. For instance, in the experience of the southeast Asian countries occupied by Japan in the last world war, the trend of the military fortunes of the occupant outside the occupied area was substantially reflected in the fluctuation in the level of real value of occupation currency. Continuing military success of the occupant's arms, reinforcing the expectations

256. Stone, *Legal Controls of International Conflict* 719 (2nd ed., 1959).

257. Feilchenfeld, supra note 244 at 82; Mann, supra note 248 at 276; Dept. of the Army, *Law of Land Warfare,* par. 430 (FM27-10, 1956); Kemmerer, "Allied Military Currency in Constitutional and International Law," *Proceedings of the Institute on Money and the Law* 88 (N.Y.U. School of Law, 1945). See, further, Hyde, "Concerning the Haw Pia Case," 24 *Phil. L.J.* 141, 144 (1949).

258. The suggestion is made in Fraleigh, "The Validity of Acts of Enemy Occupation Authorities Respecting Property Rights," 35 *Corn. L.Q.* 89, 114 (1949).

of inhabitants that the possession of the occupant will persist for some time, is registered in the stability of the currency's purchasing power. Serious military reverses, on the other hand, arousing hope in the inhabitants that the coming of the sovereign is nigh, quickly initiate and accelerate the depreciation of the currency. The deliberate induction or intensification of inflation or depreciation is rarely to the interest of the occupant.

With respect to responsibility for redemption of military currency, it seems pertinent to note that inscriptions on such currency ordinarily exhibit no promise to pay on the part of the issuer, nor any indication that the issuing occupant commits its own credit rather than that of the occupied country.[259] No prescription of the law of war specifically requires the occupant to maintain reserves against the notes issued.[260] The question is probably of limited practical moment. On the assumption that the sovereign will finally be defeated, the occupant leaves to the sovereign the redemption of the military currency, that is, the exchange of the occupation currency for regular national currency as part of an assessment of occupation costs.[261] Where the sovereign emerges victor, the burden of redemption may be expected to be imposed upon the occupant as a form of war indemnity.[262]

Closely related to the problems of occupation currency is the supervision and control of banks and other financial institutions. Belligerent occupants have commonly asserted authority to subject

259. This is stressed in Mann, supra note 248 at 275 and in Nussbaum, supra note 254 at 497.

260. Kemmerer, supra note 257 at 91 thoughtfully observed that the Allied Powers did not set up a fund to cover the military lira issued in Italy.

261. See *Occupation Currency Transactions,* supra note 244 at 31, 84, 95, 117; Fairman, supra note 249 at 326–7; Nussbaum, supra note 254 at 498. See also Fitzmaurice, "The Juridical Clauses of the Peace Treaties," 73 *Hague Recueil* 259 at 342–3 (1948).

262. Thus the Treaty of Peace with Italy, Art. 76(4) [49 *U.N. Treaty Series* 159] provided that "the Italian Government shall assume full responsibility for all Allied military currency issued in Italy by the Allied military authorities, including all such currency in circulation at the coming into force of the present Treaty." The Treaty with Hungary, Art. 32(4) [41 *U.N. Treaty Series* 204], and the Treaty with Romania, Art. 30(4) [42 *U.N. Treaty Series* 66] contain identical provisions. For an earlier example, see the Agreement Regarding the Marks, between Belgium and Germany (July 13, 1929) 104 *League of Nations Treaty Series* 202.

these institutions, whether state or privately owned, to detailed regulation, much as territorial sovereigns do in time of peace.[263] Authority to regulate and control banks, however, must be distinguished from authority to take and dispose of bank assets; the latter, as earlier noted, is generally regarded as extending only to assets in the nature of state funds and not to monies beneficially owned by private individuals.

Occupants commonly utilize existing banks, and sometimes establish new central banks, to effect the issuance and distribution of occupation currency.[264] Deposits of the old national currency are compulsorily converted into or exchanged for occupation currency. Presumably, such forced conversion or exchange may be considered as embraced in the general competence of the occupant to issue and require acceptance of military currency. It perhaps bears explicit notice, however, that the assertion of regulative authority over banks occasions wide opportunities for covert spoliation. The elaborate clearing system established by Germany in occupied Europe in the Second World War offers familiar illustration.[265] Banks in the occupied countries were compelled to finance "international trade" with the Reich—i.e., a one-way flow of goods into Germany—ostensible payment being made by setting up blocked accounting credits manipulatable at the will of the occupant. No capital was exported from Germany. It is reported that in some instances the occupant was not content with effective control over private banks and proceeded to convert them into German ownership. The methods used ranged from the forthright liquidation and transfer of assets to German banks, through coerced transfer of shares by private stockholders, to the more devious device of compelling the reduction and subsequently increasing the capitalization of the banks, the new stock

263. Such authority has generally been conceded, at least by the commentators; see Feilchenfeld, *The International Economic Law of Belligerent Occupation* 96–104 (1942); 3 Hyde, *International Law* 1898 (2nd rev. ed., 1945); Greenspan, *The Modern Law of Land Warfare* 230 (1959); Wilson, "The Laws of War in Occupied Territory," 18 *Tr. Grotius Soc.* 17 (1932).

264. Bloch and Hoselitz, *Economics of Military Occupation* 65–7 (1944) provides an account of such utilization of banks in occupied territory.

265. Details of the mechanics and operation of the German clearing system may be secured from Lemkin, *Axis Rule in Occupied Europe* 58–63 (1944); Reveille, *The Spoil of Europe* 286–92 (1941); and Schweitzer, supra note 255 at 336–7.

issues being absorbed by German banks.[266] It should be added that these acquisitions of bank stock were financed by the occupant with money assessed from the inhabitants as occupation costs. There were, so far as we are aware, no serious efforts made to relate these forced shifts of wealth to some reasonably conceived belligerent need.

There remains to be considered rather specialized problems relating to occupants' claims of authority to subject enemy banks and enterprises to sequestration and liquidation. In this context, the term "enemy" is commonly taken as referring to persons residing in territory outside the occupied region; inhabitants of the occupied region are appropriately excluded, for the occupant's control renders application to them of such control measures unnecessary. The permissible purpose of sequestration and liquidation of enemy banks and enterprises is prevention of enemy use of their assets to the prejudice of the occupant. The control measures, which are familiar strategies of economic warfare, are commonly resorted to by belligerent territorial sovereigns.[267] It would seem unreal and futile to refuse [268]—as Professor Hyde did refuse—to concede a similar competence to the belligerent occupant.[269] It is true that, in

266. These techniques are described in Inter-Allied Information Committee, *The Penetration of German Capital into Europe* (Conditions in Occupied Territories, No. 5, 1942). Those acquisitions were not limited to shares of stock of banking institutions; they extended also to stock in industrial enterprises. Cases are reported where local enterprises were compelled to join German cartels.

267. Some representative citations: Carroll, "Legislation on Treatment of Enemy Property," 37 *A.J.I.L.* 611 (1943); Dickinson, "Enemy Owned Property: Restitution or Confiscation?" 22 *Foreign Aff.* 126 (1943); Bullington, "The Treatment of Private Property of Aliens in Belligerent Territory," 37 *Proc. Am. Soc. I.L.* 59 (1943).

268. Hyde, "Concerning the Haw Pia Case," 24 *Phil. L.J.* 141 (1949).

269. Cf. Fraleigh, supra note 258 at 107. In *Haw Pia v. China Banking Corporation* 80 Phil. 604 (1948), *Int. Law Rep. 1951* 642, the Supreme Court of the Philippines recognized the Japanese occupant as authorized to sequestrate properties of Allied nationals. This ruling was followed in a number of cases including *Everett Steamship Corp. v. Bank of the Philippine Islands* 84 Phil. 202 (1949) and *Gibbs v. Rodriguez* 84 Phil. 230 (1949) *Int. Law Rep. 1951*, 661.

Other Allied courts have reached the same conclusion. Thus, in *Public Trustee v. Chartered Bank of India, Australia and China, Int. Law Rep. 1956*, 687, the Court of Original Civil Jurisdiction of Singapore held that the defendant's branch bank in Honkong was liquidated by the Japanese in "lawful exercise of their authority as a belligerent occupying power" (at 700). In *Cohendy v. Camilleri, Annual Digest 1946*, Case No. 159, the Court of Appeal of Pau,

the liquidation of enemy banks in occupied territory, a special complicating factor may intervene: the progressive depreciation of the occupation currency into which the enemy assets are liquefied.[270] Where such currency reaches worthlessness, the resulting impact upon the enemy bank and stockholders may indeed be severe. Nonetheless, at least in the absence of a showing that the occupant deliberately brought about the depreciation, harshness of impact need not be decisive of the unlawfulness of the sequestration and liquidation measures. Pragmatically conceived, the problem may be seen to be one of responsibility for the redemption of occupation currency, a matter which, as previously observed, is determined less by customary international law than by the outcome of the war as manifested in the peace treaty.

France, held that sequestration under an ordinance issued by the German occupant was of "a purely protective character," and was not to be regarded as an act of spoliation. See also *Scott v. Felice,* id., *1948.* Case No. 212, decided by the Tribunal Civil de la Seine, and *Martignone v. Societa Job,* id., *1948,* Case No. 201.

The practice was adopted by the Allied Occupying Powers as well as the Axis countries. See e.g. Proclamation No. 14 (April 8, 1943) of the British occupant in Eritrea, C.C.H., *War Law Service, Foreign Supp.* 65, 936.06; Proclamation No. 5 of the British occupant in North Africa (Dec. 15, 1942), id., 65, 952.30; and Proclamation No. 6 of the Allied Military Governor in Sicily (July 19, 1943), id., 65, 957.06.

270. The problems created by this factor with respect to payments of pre-occupation debts during the occupation, as well as post-occupation payments of debts incurred during the occupation, are explored in some of their aspects in Feliciano, "The Belligerent Occupant and the Returning Sovereign: Some Aspects of the Philippine Law of Belligerent Occupation," 28 *Phil. L.J.* 645 (1953).

TABLE OF CASES

NAME INDEX

SUBJECT INDEX